Seventeenth-Century Poetry

BLACKWELL ANNOTATED ANTHOLOGIES

Advisory Editors

Robert Cummings, University of Glasgow; David Fairer, University of Leeds; Christine Gerrard, University of Oxford; Andrew Hadfield, University of Wales, Aberystwyth; Angela Leighton, University of Hull; Michael O'Neill, University of Durham; Duncan Wu, University of Glasgow.

This new series of mid-length anthologies is devoted to poetry and the provision of key texts, canonical and post-canonical, with detailed annotation, sufficient to facilitate close reading, for use on specialist and appropriate survey courses. Headnotes and foot-of-page notes are designed to provide contexts for poets and poems alike, elucidating references and pointing to allusions. Selected variants may be given, where these provide vitally illuminating clues to a work's evolution and editorial history, and there are cross-references between poems.

Seventeenth-Century Poetry: An Annotated Anthology
Edited by Robert Cummings

Eighteenth-Century Poetry: An Annotated Anthology
Edited by David Fairer and Christine Gerrard

Romantic Poetry: An Annotated Anthology
Edited by Michael O'Neill

Victorian Poetry: An Annotated Anthology
Edited by Angela Leighton

Seventeenth-Century Poetry

An Annotated Anthology

Edited by

Robert Cummings

BLACKWELL *Publishers*

Copyright © Blackwell Publishers Ltd 2000
Editorial introduction, notes, selection and arrangement
copyright © Robert Cummings 2000

First published 2000

2 4 6 8 10 9 7 5 3 1

Blackwell Publishers Ltd
108 Cowley Road
Oxford OX4 1JF
UK

Blackwell Publishers Inc.
350 Main Street
Malden, Massachusetts 02148
USA

British Library Cataloguing in Publication Data

A CIP catalogue record for this book is available from the British Library.

Library of Congress Cataloging-in-Publication Data

Seventeenth-century poetry : an annotated anthology / edited by Robert
    Cummings.
        p.   cm. — (Blackwell annotated anthologies)
    Includes bibliographical references and index.
    ISBN 0-631-21065-2 (acid-free paper). — ISBN 0-631-21066-0 (pbk.
: acid-free paper)
    1. English poetry—Early modern, 1500–1700.   2. England—
Intellectual life—17th century Sources.   I. Cummings, R. M.
(Robert M.)   II. Series.
PR1209.S53   2000
821′.408—dc21   99-33568
                                                                              CIP

Typeset in 9½ on 11 pt Ehrhardt
by Ace Filmsetting Ltd, Frome, Somerset
Printed in Great Britain by T.J. International, Padstow, Cornwall

This book is printed on acid-free paper.

Contents

Index of Topics

Poems are listed here by short title under a limited number of thematic headings. The themes isolated, not always specifically and obviously dominant in the indexed poems, nonetheless reflect preoccupations in the poetry of the century. No attempt has been made at generic classification, though the themes sometimes have generic force: there is a brief technical account of genres in Lee Sonino, *A Handbook of Sixteenth-Century Rhetoric* (London: Routledge, 1970).

War and Peace

Pleasures of Town and Country

The Court

Houses, Gardens and Havens

Voyages

Death's Terrors and Consolations

God's Justice and Mercy

God's Recognition

Love's Enjoyments

Love's Pains

Friendship

Separation and Sorrow

Happiness and Misery

Beauty

Time's Stages

Alphabetical List of Authors

Acknowledgements

The headnotes list important previous editions, biographies and reference works, acknowledging, however inadequately, my debt to previous editors of the poets included in this anthology and to commentary by other writers. I have incurred further debts in many libraries, particularly Glasgow University Library, Edinburgh University Library, the National Library of Scotland, Aberdeen University Library, the Bodleian Library in Oxford, the British Library in London, the Folger Library and the Library of Congress in Washington. Members of the staff of these institutions have made my work as pleasant and easy as I could wish.

The version used of Ann Wharton's 'Paraphrase on the Last Speech of Dido' (Holkham Hall MS 691) is copyright the Earl of Leicester, and the version used of Martha Moulsworth's 'Memorandum' (Osborn MS fb 150) is copyright Yale University Library.

My personal debts are many. The most important is to Alistair Fowler, who in other circumstances first encouraged this collection, despaired of it and then brought it to life again. At Blackwell's, Andrew McNeillie's encouragement and Sandra Raphael's patience have been necessary supports. Advice has come from Lyndy Abraham, Richard Cronin, Elizabeth Hageman, Paul Hamilton, John Lepage, Jeremy Maule, David Norbrook, Claude Summers, Helen Wilcox, Michael Wilding: even if they do not recognize their influence, their admonitions have restrained my misjudgements. Donal Mackenzie, a walking concordance, has made me rethink many poems. Gillian Wright not only gave advice, but has always been ready to check a reference or a reading. I have been saved from many errors and follies by Stuart Gillespie, David Newell and John Ross.

Preface

Forty British poets are represented in this anthology from a century that opened with the reinvention of Britain and also contained a civil war, the execution of King Charles I, the period variously known as the Commonwealth or the Republic (with Oliver Cromwell as Lord Protector) and the eventual Restoration of the monarchy. Charles II returned from exile in France in 1660, but the remainder of the century was hardly tranquil, as his reign was followed by that of his brother, James II, who was sent into exile himself in 1688, to be succeeded by his daughter Mary and her husband, William of Orange.

In an anthology shaped by fairly conservative notions of the canon, there is little space for anything outside it. Even the inclusion of women writers until recently slighted or unknown is no longer unusual and confirms what is now a conventional view of the century. It is still safe to assume that 'the three major poets of the seventeenth century are Donne, Milton, and Dryden' (as R. C. Bald began his *Seventeenth-Century English Poetry* in 1959). The selection reflects that assumption. Donne and Dryden are represented by their later work; Cowley and Waller are allowed more space than usual, and more space is also given to translated verse. But no new territory is opened here, and no old territory is redefined.

In retrospect, the seventeenth century seems to us a time of great movements in the understanding of the material, mental and political worlds. Francis Bacon or Thomas Hobbes, Cromwell or Isaac Newton would not have been heroes or villains had this perception not been current at the time. But when Dryden wanted to characterize the past hundred years in his *Secular Masque* of 1700, he offered a weary allegory of innocence, war and love. Seventeenth-century anthologies made no attempt to sum up the age. The market was dominated in succession by collections of pastoral amatory lyrics, of 'drolleries', of topical satires. They may have a nostalgic side to them, fantasizing from the dark muddle of the English Republic about happier pre-war days. They may even serve as manuals of the Cavalier art of poetry, but the authors are almost never named, and they are almost always modern. They lack any historical view. The contents of one of them, *Wit's Interpreter* (1655), do not match the ambitious title-page with its inset icons of Sidney and Spenser, Shakespeare and Jonson. In the sixth edition of Dryden's *Miscellany Poems* (1716), when the publisher Jacob Tonson introduced earlier material (from Drayton or Donne or Milton) it was not with a view to constructing a history, but rather the contrary, because the popularity of those poets had survived the modernizing revolution of Dryden and his friends. The breadth and excellence of the publisher Humphrey Moseley's list in the mid-century (Milton, Waller and Crashaw together) suggest that he may have attempted to construct a modern English canon, but his motives were certainly more ambiguous. The purposes of the literary biographies by Edward Philips (*Theatrum Poetarum*, 1675) or William Winstanley (*Lives of the Most Famous English Poets*, 1687) were in fact hardly literary at all, but their views seem eccentric now. Had there been an approved canon in 1700, Donne would have been included in it, but not Marvell (even as a satirist) and perhaps not Milton, for he was already being dislodged ('his fame is gone like a candle in the wind,' said Winstanley). At the end of the century the heritage of Jonson was liveliest, the influence of Cowley widest and deepest, the reverence for Waller still sincere. Herbert was already considered faintly ridiculous as a literary figure.

Poetry cannot be entirely separated from the social and moral practices of its time, but its most distinctive character is an awareness of its own medium. Readers of this anthology will probably be more interested in how poems work than in what they are about, and the selection and annotation together give prominence to the special achievement of writing considered as something in itself. Waller's *Panegyric*, for example, is included not to illustrate Cromwell's fortunes, but because it shows both a classic form of English panegyric and the classic management of English couplets. It is scarcely credible, as Dr Johnson might have observed, that only a hundred years separate the *Faerie Queene* and Dryden's Virgil, though Dryden was consciously a disciple of Spenser. The difference follows a long debate on what English poetry should look like. More explicitly than any previous time in the English-speaking world, it was a critical century, and one in which a lot of critical energy was channelled into poetry.

This volume is led by concerns about how language is used – not the history of national troubles or private mentalities. Of course, in a century dominated in prospect and retrospect by war and revolution, there were pressures other than literary ones on the poets. Their lives as clergymen or academics or civil servants were liable to be interrupted. They were evicted from their livings (like Herrick), deprived of their university fellowships (like Crashaw or Cleveland or Cowley), disappointed in their promotions (like the least worldly of them, Herbert), banished like Waller or threatened with something worse, like Milton. Even in apparently private poems, public affairs weigh heavy; and retirement, a topic well represented in this selection, is a poetic preoccupation because its reality was elusive. But seventeenth-century poetry is often nervous of its material: Herrick confronts his minor subjects obliquely, as Milton did his great one. The most obvious pressures on the poems, from *Paradise Lost* to Herrick writing about Julia's legs, come not from politics or sex but from other poems. What this selection exposes is a search not for personal or ethnic or sexual or political identities, but for stylistic ones. The 'unlaboured' style of some women, or some writers for women, is free from this strain, as it is seen by us. But the history of seventeenth-century poetry is largely a sequence of poets' redefinitions of themselves against the shadows of other poets. The achievements they recognize most readily consist in ever closer approximations to an ideal of correctness; by something close to a paradox, this ideal is one we now identify as baroque.

Anthologies and their Stories

There are many other anthologies of seventeenth-century verse. Some are comprehensive within their limits, like the three volumes of George Saintsbury's *Minor Poets of the Caroline Period* (1905) or E. H. Fellowes's *English Madrigal Verse* (its latest revision in 1967) or H. E. Rollins's editions (beginning in 1923) of the Pepys and other ballad collections. Selective anthologies pose different problems, for some of these work frankly from the editors' 'individual reactions to the element of poetry which each piece contains'. So said Herbert Grierson and Geoffrey Bullough in the preface to *The Oxford Book of Seventeenth-Century Verse* (1934); it is the principle followed most thoroughly, with great success, in Norman Ault's *Seventeenth Century Lyrics* (1928). Most selections tell a story, typically about affiliations; the influence of Grierson's *Metaphysical Lyrics* (1921) or its reworking in Helen Gardner's *Metaphysical Poets* (1957, with later revisions) labelled a whole group of poets and invented a way of looking at the century which we all acknowledge, however we judge the view. Alastair Fowler's *New Oxford Book of Seventeenth-Century Verse* (1991), though it is confined to shorter poems and extracts from longer ones, tells a story about genre. Collections such as Hugh Kenner's *Seventeenth-Century Poetry* (1964) or Mario di Cesare's *George Herbert and the Seventeenth-Century Religious Poets* (1978) or Hugh MacLean's *Ben Jonson and the Cavalier Poets* (1974) or Thomas Clayton's *Cavalier Poetry* (1978) all claim poetic territory mapped, at least implicitly, by Grierson. Some, like Thomas Cain in *Jacobean and Caroline Poetry* (1981), have resisted Grierson's influence; and among the virtues of Germaine Greer's heroic *Kissing the Rod: An*

Anthology of Seventeenth-Century Women's Verse (1988) is its outright refusal of the map. But that refusal, like Noel Malcolm's in *The Origins of English Nonsense* (1997), was made possible by leaving familiar territory, and we still have no coherent stories about women's poetry, or indeed about nonsense. Perhaps there are none.

The most obvious alternative to the line created by Grierson is the organization of poems by the sometimes overlapping categories of genre and theme. The method is as old as the *Greek Anthology* and has been revived in the second volume of John Broadbent's Signet *Poets of the Seventeenth Century* (1974) and more ambitiously in the *Penguin Book of Renaissance Verse*, edited by David Norbrook and Henry Woudhuysen (1992), a partner to Harold Love's *Penguin Book of Restoration Verse* (revised edition, 1997). Peter Davidson's *Poetry and Revolution* (1999) adapts the principle to a more specialized view of the poetry of the middle of the century. Though the index of topics in this anthology reflects the shadows of both genre and theme, the chronological arrangement of the poems almost inevitably illustrates the evolution of a style. But it makes no argument about the evolution.

The Poets and Their Texts

The texts used here are based on those of early printed editions or, in a few cases, manuscript versions (or previous editors' transcriptions of manuscripts). The editions used, and editorial variations from them, have been indicated. Variants from the text as printed are sometimes given when no reliable decision between textual options can be made or, more often, when they suggest an interesting pattern of revision or indecision on the part of the poet. These variants are usually recorded without quotation marks and with brief and unspecific indications of their sources; they are modernized in the same way as the texts.

The *New Cambridge Bibliography of English Literature*, edited by George Watson (1969–77) lists both early and later editions of the poets. Information on the earliest ones is more clearly presented in the *Short Title Catalogue of English Books 1475–1640*, edited by A. W. Pollard and G. R. Redgrave, its three-volume revision completed by Katherine F. Panzer (London: Bibliographical Society, 1976–91), usually known as the *STC*, and the *Short Title Catalogue of English Books 1641–1700*, edited by D. G. Wing and revised in four volumes (New York: MLA, 1994), usually known as *Wing*. An electronic *English Short Title Catalogue 1475–1800* (London: British Library, 1998) brings these together with the *Eighteenth-Century Short Title Catalogue*. Collections of poetry are listed in Arthur E. Case's *Bibliography of English Poetical Miscellanies 1521–1750* (1935) and some of them have been reprinted in a series of *English Verse Miscellanies of the Seventeenth Century* under the general editorship of Peter Beal. For manuscript sources the major and indispensable guide is Peter Beal's *Index of English Literary Manuscripts 1450–1625* and *1625–1700* (London: Mansell, 1980–7).

The texts presented here are different in a number of respects from those the poets would have known. Some of the poets at least half-supposed, as most of us do, that writing was only a vehicle for the voice. But not all of them supposed it, and there is quite a large range of purely writerly effects in the poems. The importance of a book's format, then regularly emphasized, is lost. The publication in folio of Suckling's *Aglaura* (1638) or Cavendish's *Poems* (1653) or Marvell's *Miscellaneous Poems* (1681), or the appearance of *Paradise Lost* in quarto or Herbert's *Temple* in duodecimo are all statements made by the poets or on their behalf about their expectations of their readers – in general, the larger the format, the more imposing (and expensive) the book. Only facsimile editions can maintain these effects, and we are fortunate to have so many of seventeenth-century volumes, in particular, those issued by the Scolar Press.

The shape of the poems has usually been respected. The couplet arrangement of Waller's folio *Panegyric* makes it a different poem from the quatrains of the quarto version in more important ways than the change of format. Though the motives behind different patterns of indentation are mostly obscure, the difference between setting fourteeners as couplets (as in Chapman) and as quatrains (as in ballads) is clear even now. Some effects are subtler, but it is, for example, more than plausible to take it that unindented couplets represent Latin hexameters while couplets with the second line indented represent elegiac couplets, or the arrangement of tetrameter couplets as quatrains with the second line indented represents Horatian stanzas. These are effects confined to print and therefore able to be reproduced.

The use of strange types (italics or other semi-cursives) and sizes, the capitalization not just of initials but of whole words or lines, the setting of lines anywhere between off-horizontal and vertical are not followed here. Its importance lies in its being motivated by a mentality nervous of print, which would have preferred poems to be engraved on stone or written rather than printed on paper. At least at the beginning of the century, manuscript still had considerable prestige. Sylvester's manuscript *Colonies*, beautifully got up with gilt lettering, made a fit gift for King James in 1603, and some poets were aware of the satisfaction offered by the physical process of writing.

T. S. Eliot, writing as a child of print culture, said that the poet stands apart from his finished poem. Even those seventeenth-century writers who declared themselves for print (Drayton at the beginning of the century or Cavendish in the middle) were assiduous revisers of their own work, claiming for themselves the provisional character of the private manuscript. Some manuscript copies are so special that, like Traherne's poems, they have the particular privacy of drafts. The disgrace of any kind of publication, as it was commonly felt, was compounded by that of print, for to go into print was to lose control of the process by which the poem was produced and also to lose control of the audience. Alarmed to find her work in print, Katherine Philips complained that she 'Never writ any line in my life with an intention to have it printed, and who am of Lord Falkland's mind, that said, "He danger feared than censure less, / Nor could he dread a breach like to a press"' (*Letters to Poliarchus*, 45). On Falkland's part and presumably her own, this amounted less to aristocratic aloofness than to a terror of losing face. Oldham blamed his printer (*Upon a Bookseller*) for exposing him in his 'tender'st part of honour, wit', but in reality he was only blaming the misprints. Print was by this date the norm. Even earlier, others collaborated with the printer to make the best of it: Cowley in 1656 and Waller in 1664 justified the resort to authorized print by claiming that they were only establishing or rectifying their own canon. But for very few was print a proper vehicle for their verses.

Spelling

Modernization of the spelling has eliminated the vagaries of different printing houses over a period of a hundred years, but it has also eliminated the vagaries of individual writers. Spelling variants were part of the condition of the language, but at the same time it's not likely that unregulated spelling, however it was sometimes exploited for special effects, was anything other than an inconvenience. Some of the vagaries (beyond the general issue of period authenticity) are often regarded as precious in themselves ('murther', 'burthen', 'feebles' for 'foibles' and the like), but as long as they were normally available they had no special value. Spellings which reflect older pronunciation ('desart' for 'desert') have not been kept, for their retention would suggest merely eccentric deviation, whereas the whole cast of seventeenth-century speech was different. For some, like Milton's 'sovran' or 'soveran' for 'sovereign', it might be argued that they invoke a special association (in this case the Italian 'sovrano'). Even so, variants like this are kept only where the rhyme might be compromised if they were changed ('shew' may rhyme differently from 'show'). Aphetic forms (like 'scape or 'tice) are marked even when the unmarked form may have been almost standard. Unmodern stresses (Vaughan's 'liquid, loose retínue' or Milton's 'pérplexed paths of this drear wood') have been confirmed where wrong alternatives might suggest themselves too easily.

The general practice adopted here is not entirely consistent, but it has been adapted to what seems appropriate and useful in given contexts. Elisions in participles are not usually marked: 'warned' is given for the monosyllable, 'warnèd' for the disyllable, 'wandering' should be disyllabic or trisyllabic as the metre requires; but where a monosyllable is required, 'learned' is marked as 'learn'd' or 'naked' as 'nak'd'. Readers will naturally adjust the words to make the necessary number of syllables. Difficulties may occur where the elisions called for are not part of the ordinary language (everyone finds it normal to pronounce 'every' as 'ev'ry' or 'medicine' as 'med'cine' or even to imagine that 'heaven' is a monosyllable), but rather when they are required by an often rather specialized set of metrical licences. Donne's line 'Extreme, and scattering bright, can love inhere' is easily rendered as ten syllables (with 'scatt'ring'); so is his 'We're tapers too, and at our own cost die' (marked as 'We'are' in manuscripts); and so (a little less easily) is his 'And we in us find the eagle and the dove' ('the'eagle' as it's marked). Such lines are given in their bald form, but where unnatural elisions occur diacritical aids have occasionally been retained. In *Holy Sonnets* III we find 'But my' ever-waking part shall see that face', 'Then, as my soul, to' heaven her first seat, takes flight' and 'To where they' are bred, and would press me, to hell'. The improbable elision marks are retained in the first two cases because they would not be guessed at (and it's difficult to see how they would be realized in pronunciation); the mark is retained in the third case to suggest that the elision may be more difficult than would be suggested by 'they're'. Donne is especially awkward, and so, partly under Donne's influence, is Cowley, who wrote that his own verses 'are various and irregular, and sometimes . . . seem harsh and uncouth, if the just measures and cadences be not observed in the pronunciation. So that all their sweetness and numerosity . . . lies in a manner wholly at the mercy of the reader' (preface to *Poems*, 1656). If this is so, observed Samuel Johnson (in his *Life* of the poet), 'the art of reading them is at present lost.' Since it is not always possible to know what is normative in Cowley's verse, his elision marks have been kept more often than elsewhere. Though Dryden used these marks with some care (cancelling the metrical value of syllables with a slur), they have been abandoned on the grounds that his metrical intentions are clearer to modern readers, habituated to regularity as we are, than they would have been to his contemporaries.

Punctuation

The punctuation is based on that of the copy texts, silently adjusted where misprints seem to have occurred, with occasional interventions to clarify the sense. The order of punctuation marks is modern. Speech, rarely signalled at all in early texts, is marked with double inverted commas in the texts of poems. Double inverted commas are also used to mark maxims and proverbs. Italics for book titles and the like follow modern conventions; so does the use of capital letters, though some have been introduced to signal originally unmarked personifications.

Modern punctuation supposedly indicates how the parts of a sentence relate to each other grammatically or logically. Such a system was more or less in place by the end of the seventeenth century, but it won out in competition with an older prosodic or rhetorical system. This had an obvious advantage for poets in that by registering pauses it organized the music of the verse. In its most explicit form (as in Simon Daines's *Orthoepia Anglicana*, 1640) this system charts the length of pauses from the comma (a count of one) to the semicolon (a count of two) to the colon (a count of three) to the full stop (a count of six, or even longer). Some poets took care with punctuation. Donne's one surviving autograph poem, *A Letter to the Lady Carey*, is punctuated so as to control every rhythmic nuance, much more heavily than the version of the poem in the printed 1633 *Poems* (itself over-punctuated by modern standards). But most manuscript verse, even if not properly speaking in draft, represents a stage of preparation before publication and is minimally punctuated. The end of a sentence may be marked and little or nothing else. Often, as in Milton's early manuscripts, such marks are predominantly prosodic. Had the rhetorical system remained intact, or had it been reliably transmitted, there would be no argument against keeping it. But it was never uniformly applied and it was always at the mercy of copiers and printers who, as the century progressed, increasingly resorted to a grammatical system of punctuation which frequently contradicted it. Moreover, not all poets thought the question mattered. Cowley (or his publisher Moseley) advised the reader to correct substantive errors ('which are material, and corrupt the sense') with a pen; 'false pointings, false spellings, and such like venial faults . . . are recommended to his judgement and candour to mend as he reads them' (errata to *Poems*, 1656). Even poets who thought punctuation mattered evidently considered that errors in the printing of 'accidentals' mattered less than 'substantive' ones. Dryden's note on the 1667 edition of *Annus Mirabilis* lists errata, but only 'the grossest of them, not such as by false stops have confounded the sense, but such as by mistaken words have corrupted it'; the printers' 'false pointings' in the *Sylvae* (1685) and in the Virgil translation (1697) are also publicly reprehended, but the reader is left to correct them. No confidence can be placed in the printers' punctuation, and rarely is any authority intended for even the author's own manuscript punctuation. But the original punctuation of the printed texts has been only minimally adapted because the notions of syntax it represents are obsolete and untranslatable because – whatever mangling it suffered – it signals a way of breaking up texts for which there is no equivalent modern system.

Annotation

There are three levels of annotation. The author headnotes give biographical information, and sketch a literary context, with details of contemporary publication and a basic bibliography. More detailed bibliographies can be constructed easily from the material listed by the Modern Languages Association, made available through OCLC (Online Computer Library Center) Firstsearch. *Literary Resources on the Net* (http://andromeda.rutgers.edu/~jlynch/Lit/) and *Voice of the Shuttle* (http://humanitas.ucsb.edu/) give further guidance.

The headnotes to the poems, indicate occasions and contexts, and sometimes offer a statement of the poem's sense, not with a view to closing down argument about it but to serve as a kind of warning about the poem's territory. Elizabethan poems were usually advertised in this way, and it was a sort of novelty in the printing of seventeenth-century poetry to keep silent on a poem's drift (though manuscripts often add explanatory glosses).

The footnotes give variants, glosses and sources. They are mainly directed to explaining the obsolete senses of words or the obsolete construction of sentences. The difficulties are more often syntactic than lexical, so sentences are glossed rather than words. The indispensable guide to the difficulties of seventeenth-century vocabulary is the *Oxford English Dictionary* (second edition, 1989); its electronic version (1992 and regularly updated now) allows text and other searches. Earlier dictionaries are accessible through the *Early Modern English Dictionaries Database* (http://www.chass.utoronto.ca/english/emed/emedd/html); it includes such works as Henry Bullokar's *English Expositor* (1616) and Thomas Blount's *Glossographia* (1656). The glosses are restricted to those relevant senses likely to elude the modern reader.

The sense is, however, sometimes left to be inferred from quotation of a parallel use intended to make it clear and to elucidate implications which may not be seen at once. These quotations also suggest alternative poetic contexts for words, hinting at the possibilities commonly made available to seventeenth-century writers and readers in the poetical thesauruses used in schools and colleges to help in writing Latin verse. The most obvious case is the treatment of classical mythologies. I've avoided saying flatly that Venus is the goddess of love or Apollo the god of the sun, for there may be reason to imagine them in some of their other roles. Apollo presides over the opening of Homer's *Iliad* as the bringer of pestilence who (in Chapman's version) 'like the night ranged the host and roved . . . terribly', but at the beginning of Virgil's *Eclogue 4* he brings on the Golden Age; he bears names from his brightness (Phoebus), from his birthplace (the island Delos or the mountain Cynthus), from the sites of his worship (often including Clarus or Delphi); he is described from his unshorn hair, from his bow, from his lyre; he is also the god of poetry and music and medicine. Of the poets represented in this book, only Milton is likely to exploit such complications for more than decorative ends. In consequence the notes usually register only the relevant associations (probably only one), often by way of a parallel quotation. But mythological vocabulary was frequently debased. It was one of Donne's achievements, according to Carew, that he banished the 'train / Of gods and goddesses'; for most poets of the century they were only more or less learned metonymies, to be translated simply by 'love' (for Venus) or 'the sun' (for Apollo) or 'cup-bearer' (for Ganymede) or whatever. It is quite unimportant that the names belong to gods and goddesses, and in such cases the glosses reflect that fact. In the notes classical names are given in their Roman forms rather than the Greek ones: Juno not Hera, Jupiter not Zeus, and so on. Dictionaries of classical mythology are legion: the most generally useful for readers of earlier poetry remains John Lemprière's *Classical Dictionary*, first published in 1788 (still in the tradition of Renaissance mythographies) and now available in the revision by F. A. Wright (London: Routledge, 1949). A selection of earlier mythographies is included in Stephen Orgel's Garland series *The Renaissance and the Gods* (1977).

Another major aim of the annotation is to suggest the range of references which readers might be expected to bring to a poem. In this area there are limits to both what can be done and what ought to be done. Much that even ideal readers might bring to a poem is not able to be annotated. Much that was always private to a particular circle is beyond recovery. Indeed, much informing experience may have been private to the poet: 'I neglect God and his angels, for the noise of a fly,' said Donne in a sermon. In a poem such off-stage noises may well be promoted, but they cannot be annotated. But literary contexts would have been expected to survive, and they are systematically exploited in the poetry of the period. In consequence, they are highlighted. They are most often biblical, but also classical well beyond any decorative mythological apparatus. England was not yet monoglot, and Europe was still conscious of earlier times. The poetry is particularly ready to exploit the doubleness of vision following from an education almost entirely in Latin, which encouraged a view of the present as repeating a Trojan or Roman or Palestinian past or, indeed, anticipating a heavenly future.

The notes are characterized by subsidiary quotations. These have been introduced either to illustrate a word's use or to supply a relevant association. It is to be hoped that some at least may give pleasure in themselves, and that in accumulation they may help to create some sense of a literary context. Quotations from foreign writers, especially poets, are given where possible in such contemporary or nearly contemporary translations as preserve the point to be illustrated. An index sketches details of the more important authors cited.

In translated quotations, line references are to the original, and the translator's name is given after the reference: Ovid, *Metamorphoses* 1:296, Sandys, means that I am quoting Sandys's version of Ovid's Book 1, line 296. The index of frequently cited sources (in this case under Ovid) gives bibliographical explanations. Quotations from English poets are identified by poem and line number (or by Book or canto and stanza number); the edition is not identified. Quotations from English prose writers are identified by Book, chapter or whichever other division may have been used, but no page number is usually identified.

George Chapman (1559–1634)

When in 1598 Chapman dedicated his *Seven Books of the Iliads* (Books 1, 2, 7, 8, 9, 10, 11) to the Earl of Essex as the paramount living instance of 'Achilleian virtues', he was known on the one hand as a writer of comedy of humour, and on the other as the author of some ostentatiously obscure poems which associate him with the 'atheistic' intellectuals of the School of Night (the mathematician Matthew Roydon and the astronomer Thomas Harriot, as well as the poets Ralegh and Marlowe, whose *Hero and Leander* he completed that same year). He was born in Hitchin, Hertfordshire. Nothing is known of his education except that he took no degree. He served in the household of the old Privy Councillor Sir Ralph Sadler; he probably did military service during the English intervention against Spain in the Netherlands. He had returned to England when his first known poem, *The Shadow of Night* (1594), was published. The ambitions of Chapman's modern Achilles failed spectacularly when Essex lost his head in 1601. For the next decade the poet wrote mainly for the tragic theatre, often in trouble and at least once in prison on charges of libel. The support of Prince Henry (to whom he addresses his *Twelve Books of Homer's Iliads* around 1609, and the *Iliads* of 1616) sustained his sense of his own importance, and his public literary career never recovered from Henry's death (commemorated in an elegy partly adapted from Politian, 1612, and in the *Whole Works of Homer* of 1615). Chapman looked thereafter to the Earl of Somerset (as late as 1624 he dedicated to him *The Crown of all Homer's Works*), but Somerset's own fall in 1616 seems to have precipitated his retirement from London. The publishing history of the Homer does not suggest it was a runaway success. Neither does Chapman's response to his critics, like the 'envious windfucker' who accused him of translating out of Andreas Divus's Latin *ad verbum* translation in Spondanus's Homer (Basle, 1583), one of his regular aids. Many objected to his departures from Homer's manner and sense: Jonson, once a friend and one who had by heart parts of Chapman's *Iliad*, recorded in the margins of his copy of the 1615 *Works* his objections to Chapman's licences. The *Iliad*'s verse preface 'To the Reader' argues for the 'free grace' of the translator's 'natural dialect'. It is hardly true what Drayton (*To . . . Henry Reynolds*, 150) says, that it 'had been written in the English tongue', or what Coleridge says, that it has 'no air of a translation'. But there is a half-consensus over many generations that this is true. He is reckoned to have caught the 'slide and easiness' that Bacon thought typical of Homer (Bacon, *Essays*, 'Of Fortune'). he is 'plain-spoken, fresh, vigorous, and, to a certain degree, rapid', says Matthew Arnold. But Arnold goes on to say that he was not quite enough any of those things; and when Waller (of all people) professed himself unable to read him 'without rapture', or when Keats rewarded Cowden Clarke with one of his 'delighted stares' when he read out 'the sea had soaked his heart through' (*Ulysses in Phaeacia*, below), it was not because Chapman was any of those things. The eclipse of the various stars to which he hitched his wagon did nothing to improve an early disposition to rancorousness. He returned perhaps to his native Hitchin and his brother Thomas, where he occupied himself at a much reduced pace with translation from Hesiod (1618, and dedicated to Bacon) as well as of the *Homerica* (1624). He died in London and is buried in St Giles-in-the-Fields with a monument by Inigo Jones. The fullest account of his life is in Jean Jacquot, *George Chapman: sa vie, sa poésie, son théâtre, sa pensée* (Paris: 1951), where there is a listing of contemporary allusions; *Chapman's Homer: The Iliad, The Odyssey, the Lesser Homerica*, edited by Allardyce Nicoll, 2 vols (London: Routledge and Kegan Paul, 1957); *The Iliad* has been reprinted with a preface by Garry Wills (Princeton: Princeton University Press, 1998). The non-Homeric poems were not collected during Chapman's life. The standard modern edition is Phyllis Brooks Bartlett, *The Poems of George Chapman* (New York: MLA, 1941). This was by way of completing T. M. Parrott's projected *Plays and Poems* of which only *The Tragedies* (1910) and *The Comedies* (1914) actually appeared; these are superseded by *The Plays* under the general editorship of Allan Holaday: *The Comedies* (Urbana: University of Illinois Press, 1970) and *The Tragedies* (Cambridge: Brewer, 1987). The fullest listing of criticism is in T. P. Logan and D. S. Smith, *The New Intellectuals* (Lincoln: University of Nebraska Press, 1977).

[The Fight at the Wall]

The text is based on the *Whole Works* (1616). It covers Book 12:109–332 (translating Homer, *Iliad*, 12:105–328). Hector has accepted Polydamas' recommendation of a Trojan assault by foot rather than chariot on the great wall round the Greek camp. The Trojan allies duly advance. The margins mark two famous similes (at 166 of the bees, an 'apt comparison'; and at 289, of the snowstorm, one of the most famous in all Homer, recalled by Joyce at the end of *The Dead*). They also mark the set speeches which shape the episode: Polydamas' speech to Hector advising caution (220–40), Hector's to Polydamas recommending action (243–62) and Sarpedon's to Glaucus 'never equalled by any (in this kind) of all that have written' (311–32). Despite the broken syntax and the often affected diction, it survives as a lucid narration. The fourteeners are prevented from collapsing into ballad metre (8 + 6) by systematic but unpredictable variation of pause and by enjambment; this leaves the impression of the Greek taken phrase by phrase, and allowed its foreignness intact. For this reason the original difficult punctuation is very rarely adjusted.

Thus fitted with their well-wrought shields, down the steep dike they go;
And (thirsty of the wall's assault) believe in overthrow: 110
Not doubting but with headlong falls, to tumble down the Greeks,
From their black navy: in which trust, all on; and no man seeks
To cross Polydamas' advice, with any other course,
But Asius Hyrtacides, who (proud of his bay horse)
Would not forsake them; nor his man, that was their manager,   115
(Fool that he was) but all too fleet: and little knew how near
An ill death sat him, and a sure; and that he never more
Must look on lofty Ilion: but looks, and all, before,
Put on the all-covering mist of Fate; that then did hang upon
The lance of great Deucalides: he fatally rushed on   120
The left-hand way; by which the Greeks, with horse and chariot,
Came usually from field to fleet: close to the gates he got,
Which both unbarred and ope he found; that so the easier might
An entry be for any friend, that was behind in flight;
Yet not much easier for a foe: because there was a guard   125
Maintained upon it, past his thought; who still put for it hard,
Eagerly shouting: and with him, were five more friends of name
That would not leave him, though none else, would hunt that way for fame
(In their free choice) but he himself. Orestes, Iamenus,
And Adamas Asiades, Thoön, Oenomaus,   130
Were those that followed Asius: within the gates they found
Two eminently valorous, that from the race renowned
Of the right valiant Lapithës, derived their high descent.
Fierce Leonteüs was the one, like Mars in detriment;
The other mighty Polypoet', the great Pirithous' son.   135
These stood within the lofty gates, and nothing more did shun,
The charge of Asius and his friends, than two high hill-bred oaks,
Well-rooted in the binding earth, obey the airy strokes
Of wind and weather, standing firm, 'gainst every season's spite:
Yet they pour on continued shouts, and bear their shields upright: 140
When in the mean space Polypoet', and Leonteüs cheered
Their soldiers to the fleet's defence: but when the rest had heard
The Trojans in attempt to scale, clamour and flight did flow
Amongst the Grecians: and then (the rest dismayed) these two
Met Asius entering; thrust him back, and fought before their doors: 145

109   *dike* 'ditch'.
116   *Fool . . . fleet* referring to Asius, son of Hyrtacus; 'fleet' because swift (with his chariot), but also because he is about to 'slip away' in death.
119–20   'He is never to look on the high citadel of Troy again, for before then his eyes and all else will be covered by the mist of Death'; Deucalides, identified in the margin as the Cretan king Idomeneus, will kill Asius before nightfall.
126   He ignored the guard and pressed on.

131–5   The margin notes the analogy with Virgil's Pandarus and Bitias at the gates of their camp (*Aeneid* 9).
134   *like Mars in detriment* Not like the planet in its astrological 'detriment' (which would make its influence weak), but like the god in his destructiveness (he is 'bane of mortals').
141–5   Polypoetes and Leonteus fail to rouse the 'dismayed' Greeks quickly enough to defend the ships, and themselves fight in front of the gate.

Nor fared they then like oaks, that stood, but as a brace of boars
Couched in their own bred hill, that hear, a sort of hunters' shout
And hounds in hot trail coming on; then from their dens break out,
Traverse their force, and suffer not, in wildness of their way,
About them any plant to stand: but thickets, offering stay,   150
Break through, and rend up by the roots; whet gnashes into air,
Which tumult fills, with shouts, hounds, horns, and all the hot affair
Beats at their bosoms: so their arms, rung with assailing blows;
And so they stirred them in repulse, right well assured that those
Who were within, and on the wall, would add their parts; who knew   155
They now fought for their tents, fleet, lives, and fame; and therefore threw
Stones from the walls and towers, as thick, as when a drift wind shakes
Black-clouds in pieces, and plucks snow, in great and plumy flakes
From their soft bosoms, till the ground, be wholly clothed in white;
So earth was hid with stones and darts: darts from the Trojan fight,   160
Stones from the Greeks, that on the helms, and bossy Trojan shields
Kept such a rapping, it amazed, great Asius, who now yields
Sighs, beats his thighs: and in a rage, his fault to Jove applies.
"O Jove" (said he) "now clear thou show'st, thou art a friend to lies;
Pretending, in the flight of Greece, the making of it good,   165
To all their ruins: which I thought, could never be withstood,
Yet they, as yellow wasps, or bees (that having made their nest
The gasping cranny of a hill) when for a hunters' feast,
Hunters come hot and hungry in; and dig for honey combs:
They fly upon them, strike and sting: and from their hollow homes   170
Will not be beaten, but defend, their labours fruit, and brood:
No more will these be from their port, but either lose their blood
(Although but two, against all us) or be our prisoners made."
All this, to do his action grace, could not firm Jove persuade,
Who for the general counsel stood; and ('gainst his singular brave)   175
Bestowed on Hector that day's fame. Yet he, and these behave
Themselves thus nobly at this port: but how at other ports,
And all alongst the stony wall, sole force, 'gainst force and forts,
Raged in contention 'twixt both hosts: it were no easy thing,
(Had I the bosom of a God) to tune to life, and sing.   180
The Trojans fought not of themselves, a fire from heaven was thrown
That ran amongst them, through the wall, mar added to their own.
The Greeks held not their own: weak Grief, went with her withered hand,

147 *bred* 'where they were bred'.
151 *whet . . . air* 'noisily sharpen their gnashing teeth'.
154–6 'The two fought back the Trojans energetically, confident that those inside the wall would shortly add their force. Those indeed knew they were fighting for their lives and began to throw down rocks from the wall.'
160 *fight* 'troop'.
164–6 The margin notes that Asius is near death and 'blames Jove for it': Jupiter had seemed to promise that the Greeks would run and that their collapse would be irresistible.
172–3 'They will not budge from the gate without fighting to the end (only two though they be) or falling captive'; Chapman follows Spondanus: Homer says they will kill or be killed.
174–6 Jupiter could not be persuaded to reward Asius's individual courage, but standing by a larger purpose (for the

general Trojan good) determined that Hector should have the glory; the awkward gloss follows Spondanus.
178–80 'But it would be hard to describe how at other gates along the wall strength alone contended with strength and the stone defences together.'
182 *mar* 'damage' (modernizing 'meere').
183–8 'The Greeks (who had of necessity to drive out the Trojans in order to save their ships and their camp) were demoralized by their inability to keep their troops in the fight; their spirits were more lowered by this than they were lifted by having to fight. Even the gods pitied their condition and all that were their friends (though they could not remove their troubles) helped them by supporting the best of them.' Chapman has attempted an explanatory expansion of the Greek.

And dipped it deeply in their spirits; since they could not command
Their forces to abide the field, whom harsh Necessity   185
(To save those ships should bring them home and their good fort's supply)
Drove to the expulsive fight they made; and this might stoop them more
Than Need itself could elevate: for even gods did deplore
Their dire estates, and all the gods, that were their aids in war:
Who (though they could not clear their plights) yet were their friends thus far,   190
Still to uphold the better sort: for then did Polypoet' pass
A lance at Damasus, whose helm, was made with cheeks of brass,
Yet had not proof enough; the pile, drove through it, and his skull;
His brain in blood drowned; and the man, so late so spiritful,
Fell now quite spiritless to earth. So emptied he the veins   195
Of Pylon, and Ormenus' lives: and then Leonteus gains
The life's end of Hippomachus, Antimachus's son;
His lance fell at his girdle stead, and with his end, begun
Another end: Leonteus, left him, and through the press
(His keen sword drawn) ran desperately, upon Antiphates;   200
And lifeless tumbled him to earth. Nor could all these lives quench
His fiery spirit, that his flame, in Menon's blood did drench,
And raged up, even to Iamen's, and young Orestes' life;
All heaped together, made their peace, in that red field of strife.
Whose fair arms while the victors spoiled; the youth of Ilion   205
(Of which there served the most and best) still boldly built upon
The wisdom of Polydamas, and Hector's matchless strength;
And followed, filled with wondrous spirit; with wish, and hope at length
(The Greeks' wall won) to fire their fleet. But (having past the dike,
And willing now, to pass the wall) this prodigy did strike   210
Their hearts with some deliberate stay: a high-flown eagle soared
On their troop's left hand, and sustained, a dragon all engored,
In her strong seres, of wondrous size, and yet had no such check
In life and spirit, but still she fought; and turning back her neck
So stung the eagle's gorge, that down, she cast her fervent prey,   215
Amongst the multitude; and took, upon the winds, her way;
Crying with anguish. When they saw, a branded serpent sprawl
So full amongst them; from above, and from Jove's fowl let fall:
They took it an ostent from him; stood frighted; and their cause
Polydamas thought just, and spake: "Hector, you know, applause   220
Of humour hath been far from me; nor fits it, or in war,
Or in affairs of court, a man, employed in public care,
To blanch things further than their truth, or flatter any power:
And therefore, for that simple course, your strength hath oft been sour
To me in counsels: yet again, what shows in my thoughts best,   225
I must discover: let us cease, and make their flight our rest
For this day's honour; and not now, attempt the Grecian fleet;
For this (I fear) will be the event; the prodigy doth meet
So full with our affair in hand. As this high flying fowl,

198 'The lance fell where his girdle was, and with his death another life was taken in revenge.'
205 'While the victors stripped them of their armour.'
210–11 *this . . . with some deliberate stay* 'this omen curbed their rashness.'
212–13 'and held a bloody snake in her strong talons'.

215 *fervent* 'fierce'.
217–19 When they saw a speckled ('branded') serpent fall from the eagle ('Jove's bird') they took it for a sign ('ostent').
220–1 *applause . . . me* 'I have never approved mere whims.'
223 'To smooth over things to the extent of falsifying them'.

Upon the left wing of our host (implying our control) 230
Hovered above us; and did truss, within her golden seres
A serpent so imbrued, and big, which yet (in all her fears)
Kept life, and fervent spirit to fight, and wrought her own release;
Nor did the eagle's eyrie, feed: so though we thus far press
Upon the Grecians; and perhaps, may overrun their wall, 235
Our high minds aiming at their fleet; and that we much appal
Their trussèd spirits; yet are they, so serpent-like disposed
That they will fight, though in our seres; and will at length be lost
With all our outcries; and the life, of many a Trojan breast,
Shall with the eagle fly, before, we carry to our nest 240
Them, or their navy": thus expounds the augur this ostent;
Whose depth he knows; and these should fear. Hector, with countenance bent
Thus answered him: "Polydamas, your depth in augury
I like not; and know passing well, thou dost not satisfy
Thyself in this opinion: or if thou think'st it true, 245
Thy thoughts, the gods blind; to advise, and urge that as our due,
That breaks our duties; and to Jove, whose vow and sign to me
Is passed directly for our speed: yet light-winged birds must be
(By thy advice) our oracles, whose feathers little stay
My serious actions. What care I, if this, or the other way 250
Their wild wings sway them: if the right, on which the sun doth rise,
Or, to the left hand, where he sets? 'Tis Jove's high counsel flies
With those wings, that shall bear up us: Jove's, that both earth and heaven,
Both men and gods sustains and rules: one augury is given
To order all men, best of all; fight for thy country's right. 255
But why fear'st thou our further charge? for though the dangerous fight
Strew all men here about the fleet, yet thou need'st never fear
To bear their fates; thy wary heart, will never trust thee, where
An enemy's look is; and yet fight: for, if thou dar'st abstain,
Or whisper into any ear, an abstinence so vain 260
As thou advisest: never fear, that any foe shall take
Thy life from thee, for 'tis this lance." This said, all forwards make,
Himself the first: yet before him, exulting Clamour flew;
And thunder-loving Jupiter, from lofty Ida blew
A storm that ushered their assault, and made them charge like him: 265
It drove directly on the fleet, a dust so fierce and dim,
That it amazed the Grecians: but was a grace divine,
To Hector and his following troops, who wholly did incline
To him, being now in grace with Jove: and so put boldly on
To raze the rampire: in whose height, they fiercely set upon 270
The parapets, and pulled them down, razed every foremost fight;
And all the buttresses of stone, that held their towers upright;
They tore away, with crows of iron; and hoped to ruin all.

230 *implying our control* 'signifying our being overpowered' making explicit the ominous force of the eagle's appearance on the left; for 'left wing' *1609* reads 'left hand'.

231–2 *and . . . imbrued* 'and seized ("did truss") in its claws a blood-red ("imbrued") snake'.

237 *trussèd* 'captive'.

246–8 'If you do believe what you are saying, the gods have blinded you: to urge our abandoning the fight now is a betrayal of what we must do, and do for Jupiter's sake, whose promise to me was that we should have the advantage ("speed").'

258–9 *thy . . . is* 'Your caution will never put you in danger's way.'

270 *rampire* 'rampart'.

271 *foremost fight* 'bulwark'; the phrase is unique in Chapman, who uses also 'forefight' (274 and elsewhere), modelled on the Latin 'propugnaculum'. The character of the fortifications is anyway obscure.

273 *crows* 'crowbars'.

The Greeks yet stood, and still repaired, the forefights of their wall
With hides of oxen, and from thence, they poured down stones in showers   275
Upon the underminers' heads. Within the foremost towers,
Both the Ajaces had command; who answered every part,
The assaulters, and their soldiers; repressed, and put in heart:
Repairing valour as their wall: spake some fair, some reproved,
Whoever made not good his place: and thus they all sorts moved;   280
   "O countrymen, now need in aid, would have excess be spent:
The excellent must be admired; the meanest excellent;
The worst, do well: in changing war, all should not be alike,
Nor any idle: which to know, fits all, lest Hector strike
Your minds with frights, as ears with threats, forward be all your hands,   285
Urge one another: this doubt down, that now betwixt us stands,
Jove will go with us to their walls." To this effect, aloud
Spake both the princes: and as high (with this) the expulsion flowed.
And as in winter time, when Jove, his cold-sharp javelins throws
Amongst us mortals; and is moved, to white earth with his snows: 290
(The winds asleep) he freely pours, till highest prominents,
Hill-tops, low meadows, and the fields, that crown with most contents
The toils of men: sea-ports, and shores, are hid, and every place,
But floods (that snow's fair tender flakes, as their own brood, embrace:)
So both sides covered earth with stones, so both for life contend,   295
To show their sharpness: through the wall, Uproar stood up on end.
Nor had great Hector and his friends, the rampire overrun,
If Heaven's great counsellor, high Jove, had not enflamed his son
Sarpedon (like the forest's king, when he on oxen flies)
Against the Grecians: his round targe, he to his arm applies   300
Brass-leaved without: and all within, thick ox-hides quilted hard:
The verge nailed round with rods of gold, and with two darts prepared
He leads his people: as ye see, a mountain lion fare,
Long kept from prey: in forcing which, his high mind makes him dare,
Assault upon the whole full fold: though guarded never so   305
With well-armed men, and eager dogs; away he will not go,
But venture on, and either snatch, a prey, or be a prey:
So fared divine Sarpedon's mind, resolved to force his way
Through all the forefights, and the wall: yet since he did not see
Others as great as he, in name, as great in mind as he: 310
He spake to Glaucus: "Glaucus, say, why are we honoured more
Than other men of Lycia, in place? with greater store
Of meats and cups? with goodlier roofs? delightsome gardens? walks?
More lands, and better? so much wealth, that court and country talks
Of us, and our possessions; and every way we go,   315
Gaze on us as we were their gods? this where we dwell, is so:
The shores of Xanthus ring of this; and shall not we exceed,
As much in merit, as in noise? Come, be we great in deed
As well as look; shine not in gold, but in the flames of fight;

---

277 'Ajax son of Telamon (the hero), and Ajax the Locrian
were in control and took on all parts, checking the attackers
and encouraging their own troops.'
281–2 'The surplus of your help is now required: those
who excel are wonderful, but even the least of them, even
the worst have a task before them.'

288 *expulsion* of projectiles.
294 *as their own brood* Chapman's addition.
299 *forest's king* 'lion' (as Homer has it). Sarpedon was
Jupiter's son (hence 'divine', 308) by Europa.
317 Xanthus is the divine name of the river Scamander in
Lycia.

That so our neat-armed Lycians, may say, 'See, these are right   320
Our kings, our rulers; these deserve, to eat, and drink the best;
These govern not ingloriously: these, thus exceed the rest,
Do more than they command to do.' O friend, if keeping back
Would keep back age from us, and death; and that we might not wrack
In this life's human sea at all: but that deferring now   325
We shunned death ever; nor would I, half this vain valour show,
Nor glorify a folly so, to wish thee to advance:
But since we must go, though not here; and that, besides the chance
Proposed now, there are infinite fates, of other sort in death,
Which (neither to be fled nor 'scaped) a man must sink beneath: 330
Come, try we, if this sort be ours: and either render thus,
Glory to others, or make them, resign the like to us."

331 'Come let us see if it is our fate to die now.'

[Ulysses in Phaeacia]

The extracts below are based on the *Whole Works* (1616). They cover Books 5·608–70 (translating Homer, *Odyssey*, 5:453–93), 6:71–213 (translating 6:48–144), 7:111–80 (translating 7:81–132). The shift from fourteeners to pentameter couplets (and these freely treated), motivated by the less 'heroic' character of the *Odyssey*, necessitates a freer treatment of the original. Sailing from the island of the nymph Calypso, who has long detained him, Ulysses is shipwrecked by the angry sea-god Neptune. He comes ashore on the island of Phaeacia (Corfu), where he is found by the princess Nausicaa who invites him to the palace of her father Alcinous, 'those gardens feigned . . . of renowned / Alcinous, host of old Laertes' son' (*Paradise Lost*, 4:438–41). The names Nausicaa and Alcinous may have either three or four syllables.

Then forth he came, his both knees faltering; both
His strong hands hanging down; and all with froth
His cheeks and nostrils flowing. Voice and breath   610
Spent to all use; and down he sunk to death.
The sea had soaked his heart through: all his veins,
His toils had racked, to a labouring woman's pains.
Dead weary was he. But when breath did find
A pass reciprocal; and in his mind,   615
His spirit was recollected: up he rose,
And from his neck did the amulet unloose
That Ino gave him; which he hurled from him
To sea. It sounding fell; and back did swim
With the ebbing waters; till it straight arrived,   620
Where Ino's fair hand, it again received.
Then kissed he the humble earth; and on he goes,
Till bulrushes showed place for his repose;
Where laid, he sighed, and thus said to his soul:
"O me, what strange perplexities control   625
The whole skill of thy powers, in this event?
What feel I? if till care-nurse night be spent,

613 Homer says his flesh 'swelled', but Chapman confuses the verb for 'swell' with the verb for 'labour'.
615 *A pass reciprocal* 'an answering path'.
617–18 The sea-nymph Ino or Leocothoa had equipped the threatened Ulysses with a veil or scarf ('this tablet, with this ribbon strung' says Chapman) which she promised would preserve his life at sea and which she had asked to return to the sea when he reached land (5:346–50).
625–6 'What unpredictabilities hinder the exercise of your powers in this situation?'

I watch amidst the flood; the sea's chill breath,
And vegetant dews, I fear will be my death:
So low brought with my labours. Towards day,   630
A passing sharp air ever breathes at sea.
If I the pitch of this next mountain scale,
And shady wood; and in some thicket fall
Into the hands of sleep: though there the cold
May well be checked; and healthful slumber hold   635
Her sweet hand on my powers; all care allayed,
Yet there will beasts devour me. Best apaid
Doth that course make me yet; for there, some strife,
Strength, and my spirit, may make me make for life.
Which, though impaired, may yet be fresh applied,   640
Where peril, possible of escape is tried.
But he that fights with Heaven, or with the sea,
To indiscretion, adds impiety."
     Thus to the woods he hasted; which he found
Not far from sea; but on far-seeing ground;   645
Where two twin underwoods, he entered on;
With olive trees, and oil-trees overgrown:
Through which, the moist force of the loud-voiced wind,
Did never beat; nor ever Phoebus shined;
Nor shower beat through; they grew so one in one;   650
And had, by turns, their power to exclude the sun.
Here entered our Ulysses; and a bed
Of leaves huge, and of huge abundance spread
With all his speed. Large he made it; for there,
For two or three men, ample coverings were;   655
Such as might shield them from the winter's worst;
Though steel it breathed; and blew as it would burst.
     Patient Ulysses joyed, that ever day
Showed such a shelter. In the midst he lay,
Store of leaves heaping high on every side.   660
And as in some out-field, a man doth hide
A kindled brand, to keep the seed of fire;
No neighbour dwelling near; and his desire
Served with self-store; he else would ask of none;
But of his fore-spent sparks, rakes the ashes on: 665
So this out-place, Ulysses thus receives;
And thus nak'd virtue's seed, lies hid in leaves.
Yet Pallas made him sleep, as soon as men
Whom delicacies, all their flatteries deign;
And all that all his labours could comprise,   670
Quickly concluded, in his closèd eyes.

---

629   *vegetant* 'in the grass'.
637   *best apaid* 'more profitable'. The following rationalization is Chapman's own.
674   *oil-trees* Homer's tree is not identified.
657   Chapman's marginal note commends the 'metaphorical hyperbole': it is not Homer's.

658   *Patient* 'long-suffering'.
661   The margin points to the simile. The moralization (667) is Chapman's own.
669   'Yet the goddess Pallas Athene (his protector) made him sleep like men to whom delights grant all their blandishments': he sleeps as well as if he had been comfortably abed.

*[Pallas Athene has encouraged Nausicaa in a dream to wash her clothes in readiness for her suitors.
She rises.]*

Straight rose the lovely morn, that up did raise
Fair-veiled Nausicaa; whose dream, her praise
To admiration took. Who no time spent
To give the rapture of her vision vent,
To her loved parents: whom she found within.   75
Her mother set at fire, who had to spin
A rock, whose tincture with sea-purple shined;
Her maids about her. But she chanced to find
Her father going abroad: to Council called
By his grave Senate. And to him, exhaled   80
Her smothered bosom was. "Loved Sire" (said she)
"Will you not now command a coach for me?
Stately and complete? fit for me to bear
To wash at flood, the weeds I cannot wear
Before repurified? Yourself it fits   85
To wear fair weeds; as every man that sits
In place of Council. And five sons you have;
Two wed; three bachelors; that must be brave
In every day's shift, that they may go dance;
For these three last, with these things must advance   90
Their states in marriage: and who else but I
Their sister, should their dancing rites supply."
    This general cause she showed; and would not name
Her mind of nuptials to her sire, for shame.
He understood her yet; and thus replied: 95
"Daughter! nor these, nor any grace beside,
I either will deny thee, or defer,
Mules, nor a coach, of state and circular,
Fitting at all parts. Go; my servants shall
Serve thy desires, and thy command in all."   100
    The servants then (commanded) soon obeyed;
Fetched coach, and mules joined in it. Then the maid
Brought from the chamber her rich weeds, and laid
All up in coach: in which, her mother placed
A maund of victuals, varied well in taste,   105
And other junkets. Wine she likewise filled
Within a goat-skin bottle, and distilled
Sweet and moist oil into a golden cruse,
Both for her daughter's, and her handmaids' use;

---

71 'Up roos the sunne and up roos Emelye' (Chaucer, *Knight's Tale*, A 2273).

72–3 Homer says simply she marvelled at her dream.

76–7 Her mother sits spinning wool (from the rock or distaff), coloured crimson with the expensive dye ('Tyrian purple') obtained from the *murex* shellfish.

80–1 *exhaled . . . bosom* 'she breathed out her pent-up feelings'. Chapman has a long note applauding Nausicaa's mixture of restraint and near-wantonness, and her father's loving indulgence of it.

84 *weeds* 'clothes' (also in 86, 103, 159).

89–92 Her bachelor brothers have to look fine in fresh changes of clothing each day, and she has to supply these party clothes (for their 'dancing rites').

98 *of state and circular* 'imposing and well made'; but Homer means it had fine wheels.

105 *maund* 'basket'.

108 *cruse* 'jug'.

To soften their bright bodies, when they rose   110
Cleansed from their cold baths. Up to coach then goes
The observèd maid: takes both the scourge and reins;
And to her side, her handmaid straight attains.
Nor these alone, but other virgins graced
The nuptial chariot. The whole bevy placed;   115
Nausicaa scourged to make the coach mules run;
That neighed, and paced their usual speed; and soon,
Both maids and weeds, brought to the river side;
Where baths for all the year, their use supplied.
Whose waters were so pure, they would not stain;   120
But still ran fair forth; and did more remain
Apt to purge stains; for that purged stain within,
Which, by the water's pure store, was not seen.
　　These (here arrived) the mules uncoached, and drave
Up to the gulfy river's shore, that gave   125
Sweet grass to them. The maids from coach then took
Their clothes, and steeped them in the sable brook.
Then put them into springs, and trod them clean,
With cleanly feet; advent'ring wagers then,
Who should have soonest, and most cleanly done.   130
When having throughly cleansed, they spread them on
The floods shore, all in order. And then, where
The waves the pebbles washed, and ground was clear,
They bathed themselves; and all with glittering oil,
Smoothed their white skins: refreshing then their toil   135
With pleasant dinner, by the river's side.
Yet still watched when the sun, their clothes had dried.
Till which time (having dined) Nausicaa
With other virgins, did at stool-ball play;
Their shoulder-reaching head-tires laying by.   140
Nausicaa (with the wrists of ivory)
The liking stroke struck; singing first a song;
(As custom ordered) and amidst the throng,
Made such a show; and so past all was seen;
As when the chaste-born, arrow-loving Queen,   145
Along the mountains gliding; either over
Spartan Taygetus, whose tops far discover;
Or Erymanthus; in the wild boar's chase;
Or swift-hoofed hart; and with her, Jove's fair race
(The field nymphs) sporting. Amongst whom, to see   150
How far Diana had priority
(Though all were fair) for fairness; yet of all,

---

112 *observèd* 'notable'; but presumably translating Hom-
er's 'bright', applied to the reins.
113 'And her handmaid goes along at her side'.
121–3 *did more remain . . . seen* 'was the fitter to cleanse
stains, for the deep stains were cleansed and made invisible
by the abundance of clean water'.
127 *sable* Homer's water (like wine, blood and earth) is
often 'black'.
139 *stool-ball* Homer's women play ball, Chapman's play
this female version of cricket (a stool is the wicket).

140 *shoulder-reaching* The head-dresses are equipped with
veils.
142 *liking stroke* 'winning shot'; Homer says she led the
singing.
145 The margin marks the simile. Homer straightaway
names the goddess as Artemis (Diana), who bathed in the
Eurotas in sight of the mountain Taygetus and hunted on
the mountain Erymanthus in Arcadia.
147 *far discover* 'are visible from afar'.

(As both by head and forehead being more tall)
Latona triumphed; since the dullest sight,
Might easily judge, whom her pains brought to light;   155
Nausicaa so (whom never husband tamed),
Above them all, in all the beauties flamed.
But when they now made homewards, and arrayed;
Ordering their weeds, disordered as they played;
Mules and coach ready; then Minerva thought,   160
What means to wake Ulysses, might be wrought,
That he might see this lovely-sighted maid,
Whom she intended, should become his aid:
Bring him to town; and his return advance.
Her mean was this, (though thought a stool-ball chance)   165
The Queen now (for the upstroke) struck the ball
Quite wide off the other maids; and made it fall
Amidst the whirlpools. At which, out shrieked all;
And with the shriek, did wise Ulysses wake:
Who, sitting up, was doubtful who should make   170
That sudden outcry; and in mind, thus strived:
"On what a people am I now arrived?
At civil hospitable men, that fear
The gods? or dwell injurious mortals here?
Unjust, and churlish? Like the female cry   175
Of youth it sounds. What are they? Nymphs bred high,
On tops of hills? or in the founts of floods?
In herby marshes? or in leafy woods?
Or are they high-spoke men, I now am near?
I'll prove, and see." With this, the wary peer   180
Crept forth the thicket; and an olive bough
Broke with his broad hand; which he did bestow
In covert of his nakedness; and then,
Put hasty head out: look how from his den,
A mountain lion looks, that, all imbrued   185
With drops of trees; and weather-beaten-hued;
(Bold of his strength) goes on; and in his eye,
A burning furnace glows; all bent to prey
On sheep, or oxen; or the upland hart;
His belly charging him; and he must part   190
Stakes with the herdsman, in his beasts' attempt,
Even where from rape, their strengths are most exempt:
So wet, so weather-beat, so stung with need,
Even to the home-fields of the country's breed,

153–5 Latona is the mother of Diana ('whom her pains brought to light'), proud that her daughter (though Chapman muddles the syntax) is tallest.
158–9 'When they got ready to go home, setting in order the clothing they had messed up as they played'; Homer says they folded their laundry.
160 Chapman's marginal note unfolds the point of the sudden association of the girls' game and the shipwrecked Ulysses, that not even the least of things is made to come to pass without God's providence.
171 *strived* 'debated (with himself)'.

179 *high-spoke* 'shrill-voiced'; Homer's distinction is between human speech and that of nymphs.
180 *prove* 'try'. *peer* 'lord'.
183 *in covert of* 'to cover'.
185 *imbrued* 'soaked'.
190–2 'His belly enjoining him to go shares with the herdsman when he attacks his animals – even where they are least vulnerable to depredation' (in the fold).
194–5 'Ulysses was to intrude even on the privacy of the women of the place.'

Ulysses was to force forth his access,   195
Though merely naked; and his sight did press
The eyes of soft-haired virgins. Horrid was
His rough appearance to them: the hard pass
He had at sea, stuck by him. All in flight
The virgins scattered, frighted with this sight,   200
About the prominent windings of the flood.
All but Nausicaa fled; but she fast stood:
Pallas had put a boldness in her breast;
And in her fair limbs, tender fear compressed.
And still she stood him, as resolved to know   205
What man he was; or out of what should grow
His strange repair to them. And here was he
Put to his wisdom; if her virgin knee,
He should be bold, but kneeling, to embrace;
Or keep aloof, and try with words of grace,   210
In humblest suppliance, if he might obtain
Some cover for his nakedness; and gain
Her grace to show and guide him to the town.

196   *merely* 'completely'. *press* 'oppress'.
201   'About the jutting banks of the inlet'.

204   *compressed* 'repressed'.
207   *repair to them* 'coming to them'.

[Nausicaa invites Ulysses to follow her to her father's palace.]

Ulysses, to the lofty-builded court
Of King Alcinous, made bold resort;
Yet in his heart cast many a thought, before
The brazen pavement of the rich court, bore
His entered person. Like heaven's two main lights,   115
The rooms illústrated, both days and nights.
On every side stood firm a wall of brass,
Even from the threshold to the inmost pass;
Which bore a roof up, that all sapphire was;
The brazen thresholds both sides, did enfold   120
Silver pilasters, hung with gates of gold;
Whose portal was of silver; over which
A golden cornice did the front enrich.
On each side, dogs of gold and silver framed,
The houses guard stood; which the deity (lamed)   125
With knowing inwards had inspired; and made,
That Death nor Age, should their estates invade.
   Along the wall, stood every way a throne;
From the entry to the lobby: every one,
Cast over with a rich-wrought cloth of state.   130
Beneath which, the Phaeacian princes sat
At wine and food; and feasted all the year.

114–15   *before . . . person* 'before he set foot on the rich pavement of the palace'. The affected syntax is Chapman's own.
116   *illustrated* 'were illuminated'.
125–7   *which . . . inspired* 'into which the lame artificer-god Vulcan had breathed consciousness and made immortal and

ageless'; Chapman borrows the conceit from Virgil: 'Some forcing metals fine shall brazen shapes with breath indue' (*Aeneid*, 6:847, Phaer).
130–2   Chapman's formal canopies replace Homer's soft throws.

Youths forged of gold, at every table there,
Stood holding flaming torches; that, in night
Gave through the house, each honoured guest, his light.   135
    And (to encounter feast with housewifery)
In one room fifty women did apply
Their several tasks. Some, apple-coloured corn
Ground in fair querns; and some did spindles turn.
Some work in looms: no hand, least rest receives;   140
But all had motion, apt, as aspen leaves.
And from the weeds they wove (so fast they laid,
And so thick thrust together, thread by thread),
That the oil (of which the wool had drunk his fill)
Did with his moisture, in light dews distil.   145
    As much as the Phaeacian men excelled
All other countrymen, in art to build
A swift-sailed ship: so much the women there,
For work of webs, past other women were.
Past mean, by Pallas' means, they understood   150
The grace of good works; and had wits as good.
    Without the hall, and close upon the gate,
A goodly orchard ground was situate,
Of near ten acres; about which, was led
A lofty quickset. In it flourishèd   155
High and broad fruit trees, that pomegranates bore;
Sweet figs, pears, olives, and a number more
Most useful plants, did there produce their store.
Whose fruits, the hardest winter could not kill;
Nor hottest summer wither. There was still   160
Fruit in his proper season, all the year.
Sweet Zephyr breathed upon them, blasts that were
Of varied tempers: these, he made to bear
Ripe fruits: these blossoms: pear grew after pear;
Apple succeeded apple; grape, the grape;   165
Fig after fig came; Time made never rape,
Of any dainty there. A spritely vine
Spread here his root; whose fruit, a hot sun-shine
Made ripe betimes. Here grew another, green.
Here, some were gathering; here, some pressing seen.   170
A large-allotted several, each fruit had;
And all the adorned grounds, their appearance made,
In flower and fruit, at which the King did aim,
To the precisest order he could claim.
    Two fountains graced the garden; of which, one   175
Poured out a winding stream, that overrun
The grounds for their use chiefly: the other went
Close by the lofty palace gate; and lent
The city his sweet benefit: and thus
The gods the court decked of Alcinous.   180

---

136 *encounter* 'match'.
138 *apple-coloured* 'ripe-yellow'.
142–5 Chapman supposes a kind of waterproofing process.
150–1 Pallas Athene was goddess of both wisdom and weaving.

155 *quickset* 'hedge', and 'led' rather than 'laid' following the Greek literally.
162 *Zephyr* 'the divinity in the west wind'.
166–7 'Time never gathered the dainties there' (Chapman's addition).
171 *several* 'enclosure'.

Michael Drayton (1563–1631)

Drayton gives a version of his own life in the epistle *To . . . Henry Reynolds*. An elementary school education (perhaps under Leonard Cox) was succeeded by an education in manners in the household of Sir Henry Goodyer of Polesworth (a partisan of Mary Queen of Scots, also the uncle of Donne's friend and the father of Anne, supposedly the inspiration of *Idea* in 1593). Here his poetic ambitions were sympathetically viewed and he evidently had access to a considerable library; and though counted among the the earliest of 'professional' writers, Drayton needed the patronage derived from his association with the Goodyers. From Polesworth he eventually went on to London, 'bequeathed' to Lucy, Countess of Bedford. He may have acted as tutor to her; and to her he dedicated in 1594 his *Matilda*, not his first published work (he had experimented with biblical paraphrase, love sonnets and pastoral) but his first venture into the public and historical poetry to which he was increasingly committed. Among the new poets, he attracted the notice of Spenser as one 'Whose Muse full of high thoughts invention, / Doth like himself [in his pastoral guise as Roland] heroically sound' (*Colin Clout's Come Home Again*, 446–7). It is as Spenser's heir that Drayton is usually seen, but his literary friendships were various: historians and antiquarians (William Camden and John Selden) as well as the poets he names in the epistle to Reynolds (Daniel and Jonson, Chapman, Sylvester and Sandys, Sir William Alexander and Drummond, the Beaumonts and Browne). The patronage of Sir Walter Aston saved him from the necessity of working in the theatre, which he hated. He often wrote in dying forms, even when his versions of them seem mod-ern: 'odes' (which are really like ballads), sonnets, pastorals, Spenserian satires, Bartasian biblical epics, historical 'legends' or quasi-epics (one of which got into the 1610 and last edition of the *Mirror for Magistrates*). When he writes in new 'documentary' kinds, it is as if he misses the point: epistles which miss out on the letter-like qualities of the new Donnean verse epistle (Jonson remarks the lack between them of 'ambling visits' made in verse). Drayton's major experiment, the eccentric *Poly-Olbion*, which might be promoted as georgic, is instead a ramshackle *Canterbury Tales* of a history-cum-geography poem. For a market whose existence seems doubtful, Drayton constantly refashioned his work. He lived sparely on his patrons' charity, and when he died 'honest Mr Michael Drayton had about some five pounds lying by him' (Henry Peacham, *The Truth of our Times*). The standard biography is B. H. Newdigate, *Michael Drayton and his Circle* (Oxford: Blackwell, 1941). Drayton himself prepared collected editions of his own work. The first is *Poems* (1605); of this there is an augmented revision in 1619 (with a facsimile, Menston: Scolar Press, 1969). Two more collections follow: the major one is *The Battle of Agincourt* (1627, with a facsimile, Menston: Scolar Press, 1972) and the other *The Muses' Elysium* (1630). The standard edition is *The Works*, ed. J. W. Hebel, K. Tillotson and B. H. Newdigate, 5 vols (Oxford: Blackwell, 1931–41). Criticism is listed in S. A. and D. R. Tannenbaum, *Elizabethan Bibliographies* 2 (1941) with Supplement 7 (1967) by G. R. Guffey. Earlier criticism is described by R. Noyes, *Drayton's Literary Vogue since 1631* (Bloomington: Indiana University Studies, 1935).

From *Poly-Olbion*

Poly-Olbion. Or a Chorographical Description of Tracts, Rivers, Mountains, Forests and other Parts of this Renowned Isle . . . with Intermixture of the most Remarkable Stories, Antiquities, Wonders, Rarities, Pleasures and Commodities of the Same. The First Part (Songs 1–18), dedicated to Prince Henry, was printed in 1612 and reissued in 1613. The publishers, reluctant to undertake the Second Part, delayed publication till 1622 of a work finished by 1619. 'I have met with barbarous ignorance and base detraction; such a cloud hath the devil drawn over the world's judgement, whose opinion is in a few years fallen below all balladry, that the lethargy is incurable' ('To any what will read it', 1622). The First Part comes with encyclopaedic notes by John Selden, who pretends at the conclusion of his introductory epistle that there is something in the poem for everyone: 'To gentlewomen and their loves is consecrated all the wooing language, allusions to love passions, and sweet embracements feigned by the Muse amongst hills and rivers. Whatsoever tastes of description, battle, story, abstruse antiquity, and . . . law of the kingdom, to the more severe reader' ('From the Author of the illustrations'). Drayton knew otherwise: 'there is this great disadvantage against me; that [the poem] cometh out at this time, when verses are wholly deduced to chambers, and nothing esteemed in this lunatic age, but what is kept in cabinets and must only pass by transcription' ('To the General Reader', 1612). Drayton set his face against the fashionable tide: 'What poet recks the praise upon such antics heaped, / Or envies that their lines, in cabinets are kept? / Though some fantastic fool promove their ragged rhymes, / And do transcribe them o'er a hundred several times, / And some fond women wins, to think them wondrous rare, / When they lewd beggary trash, nay very gibb'rish are' (*Poly-Olbion*, 19:179–84). The poet is not sure of his own purposes; Jonson's judgement

was that 'Drayton's *Poly-Olbion*, if [he] had performed what he promised to write, the deeds of all the worthies, had been excellent. His long verses pleased him not' (*Conversations with Drummond*, who thought it [*Character of Several Authors*] 'one of the smoothest poems I have seen in English'). It is too much a virtuoso poem and too ostentatiously extraordinary to have won many friends.

[Wildlife in the Fens]

1622. (Poly-Olbion, 25:31–191). Drayton's Holland, who speaks here, is the fenland of Lincolnshire (now drained): 'this Holland . . . is divided into two parts. the Lower and the Higher: the Lower hath in it foul and slabby quavemires, yea and most troublesome fens, which the very inhabitants themselves for all their stilts cannot stalk through. And considering that it is very low and flat, fenced it is on the one side against the ocean, on the other from those waters which overwhelm the up-

per part of the Isle of Ely, with mighty piles and huge banks opposed against the same' (Camden, *Britain*, 'Lincolnshire'); and later Camden writes: 'All this tract over at certain seasons, good God, what store of fowls is here to be found. I mean not those vulgar birds which in other places are highly esteemed and bear a great price . . . but such as we have no Latin names for . . . greatly sought for by those that love the tooth so well, I mean, pewits, godwits, knots'.

> Ye Acherusian fens, to mine resign your glory,
> Both that which lies within the goodly territory
> Of Naples, as that fen Thesprotia's earth upon,
> Whence that infernal flood, the smutted Acheron
> Shoves forth her sullen head, as thou most fatal fen,   35
> Of which Etruria tells, the watery Trasimene,
> In history although thou highly seemst to boast,
> That Hannibal by thee o'erthrew the Roman host.
> I scorn the Egyptian fen, which Alexandria shows,
> Proud Mareotis, should my mightiness oppose,   40
> Or Scythia, on whose face the sun doth hardly shine,
> Should her Maeotis think to match with this of mine,
> That covered all with snow continually doth stand.
> I stinking Lerna hate, and the poor Libyan sand.
>   Marica that wise nymph, to whom great Neptune gave   45
> The charge of all his shores, from drowning them to save,
> Abideth with me still upon my service pressed,
> And leaves the looser nymphs to wait upon the rest:
> In summer giving earth, from which I square my peat,

31–5 The Acherusian marshlands (now dry) near Naples (Pliny, *Natural History*, 3.5.60) were part of a coast noted for its fish; Acherusia was also a lake in Epirus (in modern Albania), the source of the filthy ('smutted' is a coinage) River Acheron (*Natural History*, 4.1), not the underworld river. Both have underworld associations, the one close to Avernus, the other to Aornos, both etymologically suggesting 'birdless': 'O'er which no fowl unstruck with hasty death / Can stretch her strengthless wings; so dire a breath / Mounts high heaven from black jaws' (Virgil, *Aeneid*, 6:239–40, Sandys in *Relation*, of the Italian Avernus, Aeneas's route to the underworld).
33 *Thesprotia* Thesposia (1622); but Pliny (4.1) gives the correct form.
35–8 The marshy Lake Trasimene in Tuscany ('Etruria')

is the site of Hannibal's victory over the Romans (217 BC).
39–40 'On the south side of [Alexandria] is the Lake Mareotis, in time past resembling a sea . . . made by the labour of man . . . which naturally produces no water, having a dry and sandy bottom, but replenished yearly by the inundations of Nile' (Sandys, *Relation*).
41–2 Lake Maeotis, now the Sea of Azov (an inlet from the Black Sea), was in Pliny's time rich in fowl and fish (10.8.23).
44 Lerna was the marsh where Hercules defeated the hydra; Libya is desert.
45 *Marica* The margin gives: 'A nymph suposed to have charge of the shore'; the nymph of the river Liris, understood here (by a false etymology) as a marsh-nymph, absorbing floods.
49 The margin glosses peat: 'fuel cut out of the marsh'.

And faster feedings by, for deer, for horse, and neat.   50
My various fleets for fowl, O who is he can tell,
The species that in me for multitudes excel!
The duck, and mallard first, the falconers' only sport,
(Of river-flights the chief, so that all other sort,
They only green-fowl term) in every mere abound,   55
That you would think they sat upon the very ground,
Their numbers be so great, the waters covering quite,
That raised, the spacious air is darkened with their flight;
Yet still the dangerous dikes, from shot do them secure,
Where they from flash to flash, like the full Epicure   60
Waft, as they loved to change their diet every meal;
And near to them ye see the lesser dibbling teal
In bunches, with the first that fly from mere to mere,
As they above the rest were lords of earth and air.
The goosander with them, my goodly fens do show   65
His head as ebon-black, the rest as white as snow,
With whom the widgeon goes, the golden-eye, the smeath;
And in odd scattered pits, the flags, and reeds beneath,
The coot, bald, else clean black; that whiteness it doth bear
Upon the forehead starred, the water-hen doth wear   70
Upon her little tail, in one small feather set.
The water-ouzel next, all over black as jet,
With various colours, black, green, blue, red, russet, white,
Do yield the gazing eye as variable delight,
As do those sundry fowls, whose several plumes they be.   75
The diving dabchick, here among the rest you see,
Now up, now down again, that hard it is to prove,
Whether under water most it liveth, or above:
With which last little fowl (that water may not lack;
More than the dabchick doth, and more doth love the brack)   80
The puffin we compare, which coming to the dish,
Nice palates hardly judge, if it be flesh or fish.
   But wherefore should I stand upon such toys as these,
That have so goodly fowls, the wandering eye to please.
Here in my vaster pools, as white as snow or milk,   85
(In water black as Styx) swims the wild swan, the elk,
Of Hollanders so termed, no niggard of his breath,
(As poets say of swans, which only sing in death)
But oft as other birds, is heard his tunes to rote,
Which like a trumpet comes, from his long archèd throat;   90
And towards this watery kind, about the flash's brim,
Some cloven-footed are, by nature not to swim.

---

50 'And firmer grassland exhausted, supply food for deer, horse and cattle'.
51 'Who can tell how my tidal pools ['fleets' glossed as 'brooks and pools worn by the water, into which the rising floods have recourse'] excel in number and variety of fowl.'
54–5 'The best of river quarry, so they consider the rest unready for game'.
60–1 'Where they fly from pool to pool like right connoisseurs of the table'.
62–3 'And next the smaller paddling teal in flocks'.
73–5 'Along with what the eye sees only as patches of various colour, affording as much delight as the birds whose feathers are so coloured'.
79–81 'Along with the dabchick we mention the puffin which needing a greater expanse of water loves the salt water ['brack' so glossed in the margin] more than the dabchick'.
86 The river of the underworld being black.
86–8 'The elk, as my local people call it, a noisy bird'; swans were sacred to Apollo and imagined to sing in rapture before their deaths (Plato, *Phaedo*, 84e).
89 *rote* 'repeat' (Drayton's coinage).
92 'Some are not web-footed, not adapted for swimming.'

There stalks the stately crane, as though he marched in war,
By him that hath the heron, which (by the fishy carr)
Can fetch with their long necks, out of the rush and reed,   95
Snigs, fry, and yellow frogs, whereon they often feed:
And under them again, (that water never take,
But by some ditch's side, or little shallow lake
Lie dabbling night and day) the palate-pleasing snite,
The bidcock, and like them the redshank, that delight   100
Together still to be, in some small reedy bed,
In which these little fowls in summer's time were bred.
The buzzing bittern sits, which through his hollow bill,
A sudden bellowing sends, which many times doth fill
The neighbouring marsh with noise, as though a bull did roar;   105
But scarcely have I yet recited half my store:
And with my wondrous flocks of wild-geese come I then,
Which look as though alone they peopled all the fen,
Which here in winter time, when all is overflowed,
And want of solid sward enforceth them abroad,   110
The abundance then is seen, that my full fens do yield,
That almost through the isle, do pester every field.
The barnacles with them, which wheresoe'er they breed,
On trees, or rotten ships, yet to my fens for feed
Continually they come, and chief abode do make,   115
And very hardly forced my plenty to forsake:
Who almost all this kind do challenge as mine own,
Whose like I dare aver, is elsewhere hardly known.
For sure unless in me, no one yet ever saw
The multitudes of fowl, in moulting time they draw: 120
From which to many a one, much profit doth accrue.
    Now such as flying feed, next these I must pursue;
The sea-mew, sea-pie, gull, and curlew here do keep,
As searching every shoal, and watching every deep,
To find the floating fry, with their sharp-piercing sight,   125
Which suddenly they take, by stooping from their height.
The cormorant then comes (by his devouring kind)
Which flying o'er the fen, immediately doth find
The fleet best stored of fish, when from his wings at full,
As though he shot himself into the thickened scull,   130
He underwater goes, and so the shoal pursues,
Which into creeks do fly, when quickly he doth choose,
The fin that likes him best, and rising, flying feeds.
The osprey oft here seen, though seldom here it breeds,
Which over them the fish no sooner do espy,   135
But (betwixt him and them, by an antipathy)
Turning their bellies up, as though their death they saw,

94 *carr* 'bog'.
96 *Snigs* 'eels'.
99 *snite* 'snipe' (a standard variant).
109–11 'Of which is seen in times of winter flood the plenty that my fens yield, when the geese gather to migrate in search of dry land'.
113–14 Barnacle geese (which breed in the Arctic) were supposed to be generated miraculously: 'So, rotten sides of broken ships do change / To barnacles; O transformation strange! / 'Twas first a green tree, then a gallant hull, / Lately a mushroom, now a flying gull' (Sylvester, *Divine Weeks*, 1.6:1127–30).
130 'Propelling himself into the crowded fish-basket'.
136 *antipathy* 'responsive instinct'.

They at his pleasure lie, to stuff his gluttonous maw.
   The toiling fisher here is towing of his net:
The fowler is employed his limèd twigs to set.   140
One underneath his horse, to get a shoot doth stalk;
Another over dikes upon his stilts doth walk:
There other with their spades, the peats are squaring out,
And others from their carrs, are busily about,
To draw out sedge and reed, for thatch and stover fit,   145
That whosoever would a landscape rightly hit,
Beholding but my fens, shall with more shapes be stored,
Than Germany, or France, or Tuscan can afford:
And for that part of me, which men High Holland call,
Where Boston seated is, by plenteous Wytham's fall,   150
I peremptory am, large Neptune's liquid field,
Doth to no other tract the like abundance yield.
For that of all the seas environing this isle,
Our Irish, Spanish, French, howe'er we them enstyle,
The German is the great'st, and it is only I,   155
That do upon the same with most advantage lie.
What fish can any shore, or British sea-town show,
That's eatable to us, that it doth not bestow
Abundantly thereon? the herring king of sea,
The faster feeding cod, the mackerel brought by May,   160
The dainty sole, and plaice, the dab, as of their blood;
The conger finely soused, hot summers' coolest food;
The whiting known to all, a general wholesome dish;
The gurnet, rochet, maid, and mullet, dainty fish;
The haddock, turbot, birt, fish nourishing and strong;   165
The thornback, and the skate, provocative among:
The weever, which although his prickles venom be,
By fishers cut away, which buyers seldom see:
Yet for the fish he bears, 'tis not accounted bad;
The sea-flounder is here as common as the shad;   170
The sturgeon cut to kegs (too big to handle whole)
Gives many a dainty bit out of his lusty jowl.
Yet of rich Neptune's store, whilst thus I idly chat,
Think not that all betwixt the whirlpool, and the sprat,
I go about to name, that were to take in hand,   175
The atomy to tell, or to cast up the sand;
But on the English coast, those most that usual are,
Wherewith the stalls from thence do furnish us for fare;
Amongst whose sundry sorts, since thus far I am in,
I'll of our shell-fish speak, with these of scale and fin: 180

139–48   The margin marks these labours as 'The pleasures of the fens'.
141   *horse* 'stalking horse'.
145   *stover* 'animal fodder'.
148   Though the georgic landscape suggested is predominantly Netherlandish.
150–2   'Where the River Wytham debouches into the North Sea at Boston: I am absolutely confident ('peremptory') that no part of the ocean ('Neptune's liquid field') is as rich in fish.'

155   The 'German Ocean' is the North Sea.
162   *conger . . . soused* 'pickled eel'.
166   *provocative among* 'occasionally aphrodisiac'.
171   *kegs* 'portions to fit a ten-gallon barrel'.
174   *whirlpool* 'whale'; the 'sprat' is proverbially small.
175–6   Recalling Spenser, 'O what an endless work have I in hand, / To count the sea's abundant progeny' (*Faerie Queene*, 4:12.1); *atomy* 'anatomy': recalling Donne, 'So the world's carcass would not last, if I / Were punctual in this Anatomy' (*First Anniversary*, 339–40); *cast up* 'count up'.

The sperm-increasing crab, much cooking that doth ask,
The big-legged lobster, fit for wanton Venus' task,
Voluptuaries oft take rather than for food,
And that the same effect which worketh in the blood
The rough long oyster is, much like the lobster limbed: 185
The oyster hot as they, the mussel often trimmed
With orient pearl within, as thereby nature showed,
That she some secret good had on that shell bestowed:
The scallop cordial judged, the dainty whelk and limp',
The periwinkle, prawn, the cockle, and the shrimp,   190
For wanton women's tastes, or for weak stomachs bought.

181–91 ' "A likerous mouth most han a likerous tayl". Es
pecially if they shall further it by choice diet . . . and by
their good will eat nothing else but lascivious meats' (Burton,
Anatomy, 3.2.2.1); salty food (from 'salt' comes 'salacity') is
especially aphrodisiac.

185 *long oyster* 'langouste'.
186 *trimmed* 'decked'.

To My Most Dearly Loved Friend Henry Reynolds Esquire, Of Poets and Poesy

1627 (*Elegies upon Sundry Occasions*); the reference
to Sandys's translation of Ovid indicates composi-
tion some time after 1621. Henry Reynolds is usu-
ally identified with the author of a version of Tasso's
Aminta (1628), the essay on poetry *Mythomystes*,
versions of the fables of Ariadne and Narcissus, and
a few lesser pieces: see Mary Hobbs, 'Drayton's
"Most Dearly-Loved Friend Henry Reynolds Esq",
Review of English Studies, 24 (1973) 414–28. The
verse epistle on poetry on this public scale is not
anticipated in English, though Sir John Beaumont's
are roughly contemporary. Horace's *Ars Poetica* is
the most celebrated example of the kind from an-
tiquity, but more is owed here to his *Epistles* 2.1,
which includes a historical discussion of the drama:
Drayton's pretended informalities are absorbed into
a roll-call of English poets. Though he writes as if
from a tradition that has superseded the Drab, his
own manner (with its frank use of exclamations and
inversions) owes a lot to it. Its survey of contempo-
rary poetry is so obviously partial as to require the
graceless apology that concludes it.

My dearly lovèd friend how oft have we,
In winter evenings (meaning to be free),
To some well chosen place used to retire;
And there with moderate meat, and wine, and fire,
Have passed the hours contentedly with chat,   5
Now talked of this, and then discoursed of that,
Spoke our own verses 'twixt ourselves, if not
Other men's lines, which we by chance had got,
Or some stage-pieces famous long before,
Of which your happy memory had store;   10
And I remember you much pleasèd were,
Of those who livèd long ago to hear,
As well as of those, of these latter times,
Who have enriched our language with their rhymes,
And in succession, how still up they grew,   15
Which is the subject, that I now pursue;

15–46 Horace's programme was more ambitious: 'Rome
was my nurse, and schoolmistress, and in her was I taught /
What damagement the Trojan rout by dire Achilles caught.
/ Athens she me instructed so that sciences I knew, / And
that wisely I could discern the false thing from the true'
(*Epistles*, 2.2:41–5, Drant).

For from my cradle (you must know that) I,
Was still inclined to noble poesy,
And when that once *Pueriles* I had read,
And newly had my *Cato* construèd,   20
In my small self I greatly marvelled then,
Amongst all other, what strange kind of men
These poets were; and pleasèd with the name,
To my mild tutor merrily I came,
(For I was then a proper goodly page,   25
Much like a pygmy, scarce ten years of age)
Clasping my slender arms about his thigh.
"O my dear master! cannot you" (quoth I)
"Make me a poet, do it; if you can,
And you shall see, I'll quickly be a man,"   30
Who thus me answered smiling, "Boy, quoth he,
If you'll not play the wag, but I may see
You ply your learning, I will shortly read
Some poets to you"; Phoebus be my speed,
To it hard went I, when shortly he began,   35
And first read to me honest Mantuan,
Then Virgil's *Eglogues*, being entered thus,
Methought I straight had mounted Pegasus,
And in his full career could make him stop,
And bound upon Parnassus bi-cleft top.   40
I scorned your ballad then though it were done
And had for Finis, William Elderton.
But soft, in sporting with this childish jest,
I from my subject have too long digressed,
Then to the matter that we took in hand,   45
Jove and Apollo for the Muses stand.
      That noble Chaucer, in those former times,
The first enriched our English with his rhymes,
And was the first of ours, that ever brake,
Into the Muses' treasure, and first spake   50
In weighty numbers, delving in the mine
Of perfect knowledge, which he could refine,
And coin for current, and as much as then
The English language could express to men,
He made it do; and by his wondrous skill,   55

19–20 Leonard Culmann's *Sententiae Pueriles*, and the *Disticha Catonis* (generally in Erasmus's edition) were beginners' textbooks in Latin.
24 The tutor is sometimes identified with Leonard Cox (very old by then), author of the *Art and Craft of Rhetoric* (1532).
25 Drayton served as a page with Sir Henry Goodyer (hence 'goodly') of Polesworth, a friend of Sidney, and uncle of Donne's friend of the same name; to Goodyer he confessed himself 'beholding for the most part of my education' (pages of this class were trained as gentlemen).
34 *Phoebus be my speed* 'the god of poetry be my help' ('me Phoebus iuvat').
36 *honest Mantuan* the 'good old Mantuan' of Shakespeare's

Holofernes (*Love's Labours Lost*, IV.ii.95); his *Eclogues* (translated by George Turberville, 1567) were the most common introduction to Latin poetry.
38–40 The winged horse Pegasus struck Mount Helicon with its hoof and produced the Muses' fountain Hippocrene (Ovid, *Metamorphoses*, 5.262); here it is brought to a halt (in a piece of virtuoso dressage) on twin-peaked Parnassus, also sacred to the Muses.
41–2 Elderton's ballads were published mainly in the 1570s and 1580s; 'Finis quod X' is a common signature of authorship.
46 'Let the gods support the Muses'.
48–52 'Thou hast redeemed, and opened us a mine / Of rich and pregnant fancy' (Carew's *Elegy on Donne*, 37–8).

Gave us much light from his abundant quill.
And honest Gower, who in respect of him,
Had only sipped at Aganippe's brim,
And though in years this last was him before,
Yet fell he far short of the other's store.   60
When after those, four ages very near,
They with the Muses which conversèd, were
That princely Surrey, early in the time
Of the Eighth Henry, who was then the prime
Of England's noble youth; with him there came   65
Wyatt; with reverence whom we still do name
Amongst our poets, Bryan had a share
With the two former, which accounted are
That time's best makers, and the authors were
Of those small poems, which the title bear,   70
Of *Songs and Sonnets*, wherein oft they hit
On many dainty passages of wit.
Gascoigne and Churchyard after them again
In the beginning of Eliza's reign,
Accounted were great meterers many a day,   75
But not inspirèd with brave fire, had they
Lived but a little longer, they had seen,
Their works before them to have buried been.
Grave moral Spenser after these came on
Than whom I am persuaded there was none   80
Since the blind bard his *Iliads* up did make,
Fitter a task like that to undertake,
To set down boldly, bravely to invent,
In all high knowledge, surely excellent.
The noble Sidney, with this last arose,   85
That heroë for numbers, and for prose.
That throughly paced our language as to show,
The plenteous English hand in hand might go
With Greek and Latin, and did first reduce
Our tongue from Lyly's writing then in use;   90
Talking of stones, stars, plants, of fishes, flies,
Playing with words, and idle similes,

56 But Cartwright praises the 1635 translation of Chaucer's *Troilus* by Kynaston 'Whose faithful quill such constant light affords, / That we now read [Chaucer's] thoughts, who read his words' (*Upon the Translation*, 7–8).
57–8 Where Chaucer drank deep of the Muses' well, Gower only sipped.
61 'Then nearly four generations after Chaucer and Gower': Lydgate, Skelton and the Scots are notable omissions.
63–72 Poems by Thomas Howard, Earl of Surrey, Sir Thomas Wyatt, Sir Francis Bryan and others are collected in Tottel's miscellany *Songs and Sonnets* (1557). In Drayton's imaginary epistle, Surrey's mistress Geraldine is promised immortality 'If ever Surrey truly were inspired. / And famous Wyatt ... To whom Phoebus (the poets' god) did drink / A bowl of nectar, filled up to the brink; / And sweet-tongued Bryan (whom the Muses kept, / And in his cradle rocked him whilst he slept)' sing her praises too (*England's Heroical Epistles*, 2.148–54).

73 Puttenham commends Gascoigne (died 1577) 'for a good metre and for a plentiful vein' (*Art*, 1.31); but Gabriel Harvey classes Churchyard (died 1604) with Elderton among 'notorious ballad-makers and Christmas carollers' (*Letter Book*).
79–84 To take Spenser as Homer's successor is to take him at his word in the Letter to Ralegh, prefixed to the *Faerie Queene*, but also to claim him as an 'original'.
86–90 Sidney is a 'heroë' (the trisyllable was still standard) as a reformer of English verse ('numbers'; and in *Astrophil* his own hero), as the inventor of English heroic romance, and as one who 'brought back' ('reduced') English prose from Lyly's 'Euphuism' (well described, 91–2), explicitly disowned by Sidney: 'Now for similitudes ... I think all herbarists, all stories of beasts, fowls and fishes are rifled up, that they may come in multitudes to wait upon any of our conceits, which certainly is as absurd a surfeit to the ears as is possible' (*Apology*).

As the English, apes and very zanies be
Of everything, that they do hear and see,
So imitating his ridiculous tricks, 95
They spake and writ, all like mere lunatics.
   Then Warner though his lines were not so trimmed,
Nor yet his poem so exactly limed
And neatly jointed, but the critic may
Easily reprove him, yet thus let me say; 100
For my old friend, some passages there be
In him, which I protest have taken me,
With almost wonder, so fine, clear, and new
As yet they have been equallèd by few.
   Neat Marlowe bathèd in the Thespian springs 105
Had in him those brave translunary things,
That the first poets had, his raptures were,
All air, and fire, which made his verses clear,
For that fine madness still he did retain,
Which rightly should possess a poet's brain. 110
   And surely Nashe, though he a proser were
A branch of laurel yet deserves to bear,
Sharply satiric was he, and that way
He went, since that his being, to this day
Few have attempted, and I surely think 115
Those words shall hardly be set down with ink,
Shall scorch and blast, so as his could, where he,
Would inflict vengeance; and be it said of thee,
Shakespeare, thou hadst as smooth a comic vein,
Fitting the sock, and in thy natural brain, 120
As strong conception, and as clear a rage,
As anyone that trafficked with the stage.
   Amongst these Samuel Daniel, whom if I
May spake of, but to censure do deny,
Only have heard some wise-men him rehearse, 125
To be too much historian in verse;
His rhymes were smooth, his metres well did close,
But yet his manner better fitted prose:
Next these, learn'd Jonson, in this list I bring,
Who had drunk deep of the Pierian spring, 130

---

97 Jonson thought that William Warner, 'since the king's coming to England, had marred all his *Albion's England*' (*Conversations with Drummond*); first published in four Books (1586), successively expanded to sixteen (1606), this 'historical map' in badly managed fourteeners ('untrimmed' and 'unlimed' ['unfiled']) was plundered by Drayton for *England's Heroical Epistles* and *Poly-Olbion*.
105 *Thespian springs* Aganippe or Hippocrene on Mount Helicon, near the town of Thespiae; but the sense is contaminated by Thespis, the founder of Greek drama.
106–10 Poets 'are so beloved of the gods, that whatsoever they write, proceeds of a divine fury' (Sidney, *Apology*); 'translunary' ('beyond the moon' and so unchanging, but also lunatic) is a coinage; the verses are rendered 'clear' ('brilliant') by rising (like fire and air) above base earthiness.

111–18 Nashe's output is reduced to his exchanges with Harvey: *Strange News* (1592), and *Have with you to Saffron Walden* (1596).
121 'As strong an imagination, and as brilliant an inspiration'.
125–8 'Samuel Daniel was . . . no poet' (Jonson, *Conversations with Drummond*); Reynolds echoes the judgement in *Mythomystes*: 'many good judgements have wished [Daniel's *Civil Wars*] were somewhat more than a true chronicle history in rhyme'; he praises Daniel for writing 'smoothly and clearly'.
130 As Chaucer implicitly had done of the synonymous Aganippe (58).

Whose knowledge did him worthily prefer,
And long was lord here of the theatre,
Who in opinion made our learn'st to stick,
Whether in poems rightly dramatic,
Strong Seneca or Plautus, he or they,   135
Should bear the buskin, or the sock away.
Others again here livèd in my days,
That have of us deservèd no less praise
For their translations, than the daintiest wit
That on Parnassus thinks, he high'st doth sit,   140
And for a chair may 'mongst the Muses call,
As the most curious maker of them all;
As reverent Chapman, who hath brought to us,
Musaeus, Homer, and Hesiodus
Out of the Greek; and by his skill hath reared   145
Them to that height, and to our tongue endeared,
That were those poets at this day alive,
To see their books thus with us to survive,
They would think, having neglected them so long,
They had been written in the English tongue.   150
   And Sylvester who from the French more weak,
Made Bartas of his *Six Days' Labour* speak
In natural English, who, had he there stayed,
He had done well, and never had bewrayed,
His own invention, to have been so poor   155
Who still wrote less, in striving to write more.
   Then dainty Sandys that hath to English done,
Smooth-sliding Ovid, and hath made him run
With so much sweetness and unusual grace,
As though the neatness of the English pace,   160
Should tell the jetting Latin that it came
But slowly after, as though stiff and lame.
   So Scotland sent us hither, for our own
That man, whose name I ever would have known,
To stand by mine, that most ingenious knight,   165
My Alexander, to whom in his right,
I want extremely, yet in speaking thus
I do but show the love, that was 'twixt us,
And not his numbers which were brave and high,

133–6 'Jonson rendered our most learned men unable to answer ['stick'] whether on a strict account of what made drama he was superior both to Seneca in tragedy ['buskin'] and Plautus in comedy ['sock']'; Jonson himself promotes Shakespeare above them (*To the Memory of . . . Shakespeare*, 35–52).

143–50 Drayton commends Chapman (Reynolds in *Mythomystes* calls him 'my good old friend') as a translator of the Greek poets: 'Of their full words the true interpreter: / And by thy travail, strongly hast expressed / The large dimensions of the English tongue' (*To . . . Chapman, and his . . . Hesiod*, 4–6).

151–6 *Moses in a Map of his Miracles* (1604) is directed to 'thou translator of that faithful Muse / This All's creation that divinely sung / From courtly French . . .To make him master of thy genuine tongue, / Sallust to thee and Sylvester thy friend' (1:29–33). Sylvester welcomed Drayton of the *Heroical Epistles* as 'our new Naso that so passionates / The heroic sighs of love-sick potentates' (*Divine Weeks*, 2.1.1:49–50).

157–62 The second of his *Elegies* is addressed to Sandys in Virginia: 'Go on with Ovid, as you have begun, / With the first five Books; let your numbers run / Glib as the former, so shall it live long, / And do much honour to the English tongue' (39–42); *The First Five Books of Ovid's Metamorphoses* came out in 1621, and the complete *Ovid's Metamorphoses Englished* in 1626; 'jetting' ('strutting') is oddly applied to Ovid's Latin.

163–74 Drayton corresponded with Drummond of Hawthornden (they never met) from 1618 onwards; Sir William Alexander of Menstry is their friend in common.

So like his mind, was his clear poesy,   170
And my dear Drummond to whom much I owe
For his much love, and proud I was to know,
His poesy, for which two worthy men,
I Menstry still shall love, and Hawthornden.
Then the two Beaumonts and my Browne arose,   175
My dear companions whom I freely chose
My bosom friends; and in their several ways,
Rightly born poets, and in these last days,
Men of much note, and no less nobler parts,
Such as have freely told to me their hearts,   180
As I have mine to them; but if you shall
Say in your knowledge, that these be not all
Have writ in numbers, be informed that I
Only myself, to these few men do tie,
Whose works oft printed, set on every post,   185
To public censure subject have been most;
For such whose poems, be they ne'er so rare,
In private chambers, that encloistered are,
And by transcription daintily must go;
As though the world unworthy were to know,   190
Their rich composures, let those men that keep
These wondrous relics in their judgement deep,
And cry them up so, let such pieces be
Spoke of by those that shall come after me,
I pass not for them: nor do mean to run,   195
In quest of these, that them applause have won,
Upon our stages in these latter days,
That are so many, let them have their bays
That do deserve it; let those wits that haunt
Those public circuits, let them freely chant   200
Their fine composures, and their praise pursue,
And so my dear friend, for this time adieu.

175–81 Francis Beaumont the dramatist and Sir John the poet, his brother (who addresses the *Metamorphosis of Tobacco* to Drayton, 1602, and contributes verses to others of his works); Drayton supplied complimentary verses to William Browne's *Britannia's Pastorals* (1613).

185–6 Horace (*Ars Poetica*, 373) says that gods nor men nor 'columnae' ('posts', as the sign of a bookseller's shop) forgive mediocrity in a poet.

187–95 Repeating the complaint against 'closet poetry' in the Epistle to the general reader in *Poly-Olbion* (1613) and later in *Poly-Olbion*, 21 (1622); Donne is the obvious target.

195 *pass* 'care'.

195–201 Marlowe, Jonson and Francis Beaumont are the dramatists mentioned; Drayton had earlier rejected his own theatrical experience when 'With those the throngèd theatres that press, / I in the circuit for the laurel strove' (*Idea* [1619], 47:5–6); 'others vaunt it with the frolic swain, / And strut the stage with reperfumèd words' (*The Shepherd's Garland*, 8:3–4).

Thomas Campion (1567–1620)

When Camden wanted to describe the contemporary English achievement in poetry in his *Remains* (1605), he listed Sidney and Spenser, Daniel, Hugh Holland, Campion, Drayton, Chapman, Marston and Shakespeare. At this date Campion's only published English verse was (perhaps) five songs attached to the 1591 edition of Sidney's *Astrophil and Stella*, a song for the *Gesta Grayorum* (1594) and, with Philip Rosseter, *A Book of Airs* (1601). Unless Camden was wrong, he is thinking of Campion's Latin *Poemata* (1595, revised and enlarged 1619). In the view of one friendly epigrammatist these had already raised him to the rank of Sir Thomas More. As it was finally worked out in English, the success was intimately related to his achievement in Latin. 'The vulgar and unartificial custom of rhyming hath . . . deterred many excellent wits from the exercise of English poesy,' writes Campion in *Observations in the Art of English Poesy* (1602), a work which capitalizes on what Sidney had in practice managed. Campion wants an English poetry which, beyond the facts of stress or not stress, is attentive to the length and quality of syllables, and can manage 'by art' rather than luck the difference between the 'pure' iambic, 'The more secure, the more the stroke we feel,' and the 'licenciate' iambic, 'Hark how these winds do murmur at thy flight.' He claims the possibility is already half realized; he would not have been worried that Daniel's *Defence of Rhyme* (1603) objected that his supposedly new metres were nothing but variations on traditional English ones. But he brings the science of music (his 1610 collection of treatises under the title *A New Way of Making Four Parts in Counterpoint* survived influentially in John Playford's reprints to the end of the century)

as well as a musician's ear to his practice. *A Book of Airs* is prefaced by a letter 'To the Reader' explaining that only one of its poems is written on the model of the Graeco-Roman lyric poets, who tied themselves 'strictly to the number, and value of their syllables', the rest being 'after the fashion of the time, ear-pleasing rhymes without art'. The selection here is entirely of rhymed poems. But always he brings to his practice his experience of Latin quantitative verse, and, along with that, ambitions to replicate the modes of Latin poetry in English: his songs, he asserts, are epigrams. Campion's poetic career seems oddly stretched out, though the circulation of his work in MS would have mitigated the effect. He was in his mid-thirties before the twenty-one songs of *A Book of Airs* were published; twelve years passed before his next collection (*Two Books of Airs*, 1613) and another four before his next (*The Third and Fourth Books of Airs*, 1617). He wrote his first contribution to a masque in 1594 as a former student of Gray's Inn, another in 1607 and three in 1613. His life has an unplanned aspect to it. He took no degree from Cambridge (where he studied in the relaxed atmosphere of 1580s Peterhouse), he studied law unwillingly at Gray's Inn (his Latin epigrams register distaste for it), he was almost forty before he took a degree in medicine from Caen in Normandy (1605). The standard edition is *Works*, edited by Percival Vivian (Oxford: Clarendon Press, 1909), which supplies the most detailed biography; incomplete but generally more useful is *Works*, edited by Walter R. Davis (1969), which includes translations from a selection of the Latin verse. Margaret B. Bryan, *English Literary Renaissance* 4 (1974), 404–11, describes recent criticism.

My sweetest Lesbia, let us live and love

Philip Rosseter, *A Book of Airs* (1601), 1.1. It offers variations on Catullus 5:1–6, closely translated in the first stanza and using versions of its 'nox est perpetua una dormienda' as a refrain. The many versions of Catullus's poem include Jonson's 'Come, my Celia',

and Crashaw's 'Come let us live my dear'; another, 'My dearest mistress, let us live and love' (William Corkine's *Second Book of Airs*, 1612) is sometimes attributed to Campion. The recollections of Propertius are distinctive.

> My sweetest Lesbia, let us live and love,
> And, though the sager sort our deeds reprove,
> Let us not weigh them: heaven's great lamps do dive
> Into their west, and straight again revive,

But, soon as once set is our little light,   5
Then must we sleep one ever-during night.

If all would lead their lives in love like me,
Then bloody swords and armour should not be,
No drum nor trumpet peaceful sleeps should move,
Unless alarm came from the camp of Love: 10
But fools do live, and waste their little light,
And seek with pain their ever-during night.

When timely death my life and fortune ends,
Let not my hearse be vexed with mourning friends,
But let all lovers, rich in triumph, come,   15
And with sweet pastimes grace my happy tomb;
And, Lesbia, close up thou my little light,
And crown with love my ever-during night.

6   *ever-during* favoured by the Rheims–Douai translation of
the Bible for 'everlasting'.
7–8   'If all would lead such a life . . . there would be no
cruel steel nor ship of war' (Propertius, 2.15:41–3).
11–12   'While it is light, waste not life's fruit' (Propertius

2.15:49).
13–18   'Let not my funeral procession go with an array of
masks, nor a trumpet wail my death . . . three little books
suffice . . . and you following' (Propertius 2.13:19–27).

When thou must home to shades of under ground

Philip Rosseter, *A book of Airs* (1601), 1.20. The singer
anticipates his death at the hands of a cruel mistress.

When thou must home to shades of underground,
And there arrived, a new admirèd guest,
The beauteous spirits do engirt thee round,
White Iope, blithe Helen, and the rest,
To hear the stories of thy finished love,   5
From that smooth tongue whose music Hell can move;

Then wilt thou speak of banqueting delights,
Of masques and revels which sweet youth did make,
Of tourneys and great challenges of knights,
And all these triumphs for thy beauty's sake: 10
When thou hast told these honours done to thee,
Then tell, O tell, how thou didst murder me.

1–4   Virgil's Mourning Fields are peopled by disappointed
lovers: Phaedra, Procris and so on (*Aeneid*, 6: 440–9); the
rare name Iope (more commonly Cassiopea) suggests a source
in Propertius: 'There are thousands of beauties in the un-
derworld . . . Iope is with you, and bright Tyro' (Propertius,
2.28.49–53). Campion imagines a congregation of murder-
ous mistresses.

5–6   'To listen to you, who can move Hell with your sweet
words, telling of the love now over'.
12   'A cruel lady was the end of this wretch' (Propertius,
2.1.78).

Never weather-beaten sail more willing bent to shore

Two Books of Airs (1613), 1.11. Petrarch, *Rime*, 151
('Non d'atra e tempestosa onda marina'), a love son-
net, supplies material for this hymn.

> Never weather-beaten sail more willing bent to shore,
> Never tired pilgrim's limbs affected slumber more,
> Than my weary sprite now longs to fly out of my troubled breast.
> O come quickly, sweetest Lord, and take my soul to rest.
>
> Ever-blooming are the joys of Heaven's high paradise,   5
> Cold Age deafs not there our ears, nor vapour dims our eyes;
> Glory there the sun outshines, whose beams the blessèd only see:
> O come quickly, glorious Lord, and raise my sprite to thee.

1 'Never weary pilot fled to port from the cruel storm of the ocean as I flee [my own despair]' (*Rime*, 151:1–2).
2 *affected* 'desired'.

6–7 'Never heaven's light overwhelmed mortal vision [as that haughty look did mine]' (151:5–6); 'vapour' is cataract of the eye.

Now winter nights enlarge

The Third and Fourth Books of Airs (1617), 3.12. Horace, *Odes*, 1.9, is the model for the invitation to a winter's evening drinking: 'Thou seest the hills candied with snow / Which groaning woods can scarce undergo ... Dissolve the frost with logs piled up / to the mantle-tree; let the great cup / Out of a larger sluice / Pour the reviving juice' (1–8, Fanshawe); its themes are here depersonalized.

> Now winter nights enlarge
>   The number of their hours,
> And clouds their storms discharge
>   Upon the airy towers;
> Let now the chimneys blaze   5
>   And cups o'erflow with wine,
> Let well-tuned words amaze
>   With harmony divine.
> Now yellow waxen lights
>   Shall wait on honey Love,   10
> While youthful revels, masques, and courtly sights,
>   Sleep's leaden spells remove.
>
>   This time doth well dispense
>   With lovers' long discourse;
>   Much speech hath some defence,   15
>   Though beauty no remorse.
>   All do not all things well:
>   Some measures comely tread,
>   Some knotted riddles tell,
>   Some poems smoothly read.   20

4 *airy* 'lofty'.
13–14 'This season allows for [though 'dispense with' can mean the opposite] the lengthy talk of lovers.'

17 Translating 'non omnia possumus omnes' (Virgil, *Eclogues*, 8:63).

> The summer hath his joys,
>   And winter his delights;
> Though Love and all his pleasures are but toys,
>   They shorten tedious nights.

Thrice toss these oaken ashes in the air

The Third and Fourth Book of Airs (1617), 3.18. There are three MS versions, two with music, one in sonnet form, most likely a 'literary' imitation. The singer vacillates between desire for love reciprocated and desire for its ending. Virgil's 'pharmaceutical' *Eclogue 8* (64–109), itself modelled on Theocritus, *Idylls*, 2, is the major source: 'Around his waxen image first I wind / Three woollen fillets, of three colours joined; / Thrice bind about his thrice-devoted head, Which round the sacred altar thrice is led . . . Restore my Daphnis to my longing arms' (Dryden).

> Thrice toss these oaken ashes in the air,
> Thrice sit thou mute in this enchanted chair;
> Then thrice three times tie up this true love's knot,
> And murmur soft, She will, or she will not.
>
> Go burn these pois'nous weeds in yon blue fire,   5
> These screech-owl's feathers, and this prickling briar,
> This cypress gathered at a dead man's grave:
> That all thy fears and cares an end may have.
>
> Then come, you fairies, dance with me a round,
> Melt her hard heart with your melodious sound.   10
> In vain are all the charms I can devise:
> She hath an art to break them with her eyes.

1 'Bear out these ashes; cast them in the brook; / Cast backwards o'er your head; nor turn your look' (*Eclogues*, 8:101–2, Dryden); 'thrice' because 'Unequal numbers please the gods' (75).
2 Apollodorus's underworld 'chair of forgetfulness' (*Epitome*, 1.24) suggests the function.
3 'Knit with three knots the fillets; knit them straight; / Then say, 'These knots to love I consecrate' (*Eclogues*, 8:77–8).
5 'These poisonous plants, for magic use designed, / (The noblest and the best of all the baneful kind' (*Eclogues*, 8:95–6).
6 'A screech-owl's feathers found on low-lying tombs' (Propertius, 3.6:29).

Aemilia Lanyer (1569–1645)

The sentimental course, and some circumstantial details, of Aemilia Lanyer's earlier life may be inferred from the notebooks of the astrologer Simon Forman, whom she consulted in her late twenties, in 1597, because she was in debt and anxious about her husband's prospects for preferment (like Donne, he was serving with the Earl of Essex in the Azores expedition). Four years earlier she had married the soldier and court musician (Forman calls him a 'minstrel') Alfonso Lanyer (cousin of the more successful Nicholas Lanier), apparently to secure a father for the child she was carrying. The true father was Lord Hunsdon, the Lord Chamberlain, who had been her lover from the late eighties, and whose favours as well as those of his friends at court (including even Queen Elizabeth) she remembered fondly. She had been born Aemilia Bassano, the daughter of a Venetian court musician and his common-law wife, and after her father's death she was brought up or farmed out by her mother. She remembered her upbringing on the Kent coast, probably with the Countess Dowager of Kent, 'the nobler guide of my ungoverned days' (*To the Lady Susan*, 2). A talent for music and languages was presumably the foundation of her precarious existence among the great or nearly great; in the poem below she writes of Anne Clifford as if she had been a pupil. How she commended herself to the Countess of Cumberland is not known. The numerous and variously adjusted dedications of *Salve Rex Judaeorum* (1611) may represent a bid to confirm or win favour from the range of the dedicatees and beyond: one gift copy to Prince Henry survives, and another (from Alfonso) to the Lord Chancellor of Ireland, Thomas Jones. Alfonso Lanyer died in 1613, leaving in dispute the ownership of a patent granted him by King James. Lanyer lived on, briefly as a schoolmistress in a London suburb, and then as grandmother to the children of her son Henry, another court musician. She died in 1645, seemingly well enough off. The standard edition is edited by Susanne Woods, *The Poems of Aemilia Lanyer: Salve Deus Rex Judaeorum* (Oxford: Oxford University Press, 1993). Karen L. Nelson has prepared an 'Annotated Bibliography: Texts and Criticism of Aemilia Bassano Lanyer', in *Aemilia Lanyer: Gender, Genre, and the Canon*, ed. Marshall Grossman (Lexington: University Press of Kentucky, 1998), pp. 235–54.

The Description of Cookham

From *Salve Deus Rex Judaeorum* (1611). *The Description of Cookham* is an appendix to the long meditation on Christ's Passion which forms the title poem. It is less a description of a place than of a mother (the unhappily married Margaret, née Russell, Countess of Cumberland) and daughter (Anne née Clifford, from February 1609 Countess of Dorset), both of whom figure among the dedicatees of a volume written partly 'in commendation of some particular persons of our own sex, such as for the most part, are so well known to myself, and others, that I dare undertake Fame dares not to call any better. And this have I done, to make known to the world, that all women deserve not to be blamed' ('To the Virtuous Reader').

Their tombs are side by side in the parish church at Appleby in Cumbria. The royal manor at Cookham in Berkshire, leased by Lady Margaret's brother and occasionally occupied by her (11), flourishes in her presence (17–92) and languishes in her absence (127–204); it is remembered as the garden of Lady Anne's now lost childhood (93–126), and as the growing place of a single tree (53–66, 157–78) which for Lady Margaret herself defines the pleasures which for reasons never explained she must leave behind. Wordsworth's sonnet *Countess' Pillar* celebrates Lady Anne's 'memorial of her last parting with her pious mother' (her death in 1616) and her institution of a charitable trust for the poor of the parish of Brougham.

Farewell (sweet Cookham) where I first obtained
Grace from that Grace where perfect grace remained;
And where the Muses gave their full consent,
I should have power the virtuous to content:

1–4 'Where I was favoured by that noble lady who is the embodiment of gracefulness, and where I wrote verses freely ('the Muses gave their full consent') which pleased good women'.

Where princely palate willed me to indite,   5
The sacred story of the soul's delight,
Farewell (sweet place) where Virtue then did rest,
And all delights did harbour in her breast:
Never shall my sad eyes again behold
Those pleasures which my thoughts did then enfold: 10
Yet you (great Lady) mistress of that place,
From whose desires did spring this work of grace;
Vouchsafe to think upon those pleasures past
As fleeting worldly joys that could not last:
Or, as dim shadows of celestial pleasures,   15
Which are desired above all earthly treasures.
O how (methought) against you thither came,
Each part did seem some new delight to frame!
The house received all ornaments to grace it,
And would endure no foulness to deface it.   20
The walks put on their summer liveries,
And all things else did hold like similies:
The trees with leaves, with fruits, with flowers clad,
Embraced each other, seeming to be glad,
Turning themselves to beauteous canopies,   25
To shade the bright sun from your brighter eyes:
The crystal streams with silver spangles graced,
While by the glorious sun they were embraced:
The little birds in chirping notes did sing,
To entertain both you and that sweet spring.   30
And Philomela with her sundry lays,
Both you and that delightful place did praise.
Oh how methought each plant, each flower, each tree
Set forth their beauties then to welcome thee!
The very hills right humbly did descend,   35
When you to tread upon them did intend,
And as you set your feet, they still did rise,
Glad that they could receive so rich a prize.
The gentle winds did take delight to be
Among those woods that were so graced by thee.   40
And in sad murmur uttered pleasing sound,
That pleasure in that place might more abound:
The swelling banks delivered all their pride,
When such a phoenix once they had espied.
Each arbour, bank, each seat, each stately tree,   45
Thought themselves honoured in supporting thee.
The pretty birds would oft come to attend thee,
Yet fly away for fear they should offend thee:

---

5 *princely palate* 'royal taste' (*1611*'s 'palace' for 'palate' is a mild archaism); the dedicatory poem to the young Princess Elizabeth (shortly to be the Princess Palatine) invites her to the feast of poetry contained in *Salve Deus Rex Judaeorum* (*To the Lady Elizabeth's Grace*, 9); Sylvester designs his *Paranetus* for 'princes' dainty taste' (*To Sir Robert Carie*, 21).
10 *enfold* unfold (1611).
11–12 Lady Margaret.
17–18 'How everywhere created some new pleasure in preparation for your coming.'
21–2 'The walks put on the badges of summer; other things assumed like appearances.'
31 *Philomela* 'the nightingale'.
44–5 'The rising (or 'pregnant') banks gave birth to their best when once they had seen such a rarity'; the dedicatory poems to Princess Elizabeth and Lady Arabella Stuart carelessly allow them both to be phoenixes, though only one of these mythical birds could live at any time.

The little creatures in the burrow by
Would come abroad to sport them in your eye;   50
Yet fearful of the bow in your fair hand
Would run away when you did make a stand.
Now let me come unto that stately tree,
Wherein such goodly prospects you did see;
That oak that did in height his fellows pass,   55
As much as lofty trees, low growing grass:
Much like a comely cedar straight and tall,
Whose beauteous stature far exceeded all:
How often did you visit this fair tree,
Which seeming joyful in receiving thee,   60
Would like a palm tree spread his arms abroad,
Desirous that you there should make abode:
Whose fair green leaves much like a comely veil,
Defended Phoebus when he would assail:
Whose pleasing boughs did yield a cool fresh air,   65
Joying his happiness when you were there.
Where being seated, you might plainly see,
Hills, vales, and woods, as if on bended knee
They had appeared, your honour to salute,
Or to prefer some strange unlooked for suit: 70
All interlaced with brooks and crystal springs,
A prospect fit to please the eyes of kings:
And thirteen shires appeared all in your sight,
Europe could not afford much more delight.
What was there then but gave you all content,   75
While you the time in meditation spent,
Of their Creator's power, which there you saw,
In all his creatures held a perfect law;
And in their beauties did you plain descry,
His beauty, wisdom, grace, love, majesty.   80
In these sweet woods how often did you walk,
With Christ and his Apostles there to talk;
Placing his holy writ in some fair tree,
To meditate what you therein did see:
With Moses you did mount His holy hill,   85
To know His pleasure, and perform His will.
With lovely David did you often sing,

---

51 The Countess is hunting; and she takes on the role of Diana.
54 'From where you enjoyed such fine views'.
57–62 'Deborah, a prophetess . . . judged Israel at that time. And she dwelt under the palm tree of Deborah' (Judges 4: 4–5).
64 'Warded off the sun when it was dangerously hot'.
70 'Or offering a service you had not asked for'; but 'to prefer a suit' is properly the reverse, to 'make entreaty'.
73 Loosely: 'As two broad beacons, set in open fields, / Send forth their flames far off to every shire' (*Faerie Queene*, 1.11.14).
76–80 'To thee, to thee, all royal pomps belong, / Clothèd art thou in state and glory bright: / For what is else this eye-delighting light / But unto thee a garment wide and long?' (Psalms 104: 1–2, Mary Herbert). The dedicatory letter to the pious Countess ends with a prayer that 'God send your Honour long to continue, that your light may so shine before men, that they may glorify your Father which is in Heaven: and that I and many others may follow you in the same track.' A portrait at Appleby shows her with a psalm-book.
81–92 The Countess walks with Bible in hand, contemplating her obligations to recognition, obedience, devotion, charity: 'While [the two disciples] communed together and reasoned, Jesus himself drew near, and went with them' (Luke 24: 15); 'The Lord came down upon mount Sinai . . . and the Lord called Moses up to the top of the mount; and Moses went up' (Exodus 19: 20); King David sang 'Evening and morning, and at noon will I pray' (Psalms 5: 17), 'Joseph nourished his father and brethren, and all his father's household, with bread' (Genesis 47: 12); 'pinèd' is 'starved'.

His holy hymns to Heaven's eternal King.
And in sweet music did your soul delight,
To sound his praises, morning, noon, and night.   90
With blessèd Joseph you did often feed
Your pinèd brethren, when they stood in need.
And that sweet Lady sprung from Clifford's race,
Of noble Bedford's blood, fair stem of grace;
To honourable Dorset now espoused,   95
In whose fair breast true virtue then was housed:
O what delight did my weak spirits find,
In those pure parts of her well-framèd mind:
And yet it grieves me that I cannot be
Near unto her, whose virtues did agree   100
With those fair ornaments of outward beauty,
Which did enforce from all both love and duty.
Unconstant Fortune, thou art most to blame,
Who casts us down into so low a frame:
Where our great friends we cannot daily see,   105
So great a difference is there in degree.
Many are placèd in those orbs of state,
Parters in honour, so ordained by Fate;
Nearer in show, yet farther off in love,
In which, the lowest always are above.   110
But whither am I carried in conceit?
My wit too weak to conster of the great.
Why not? although we are but born of earth,
We may behold the Heavens, despising death;
And loving Heaven that is so far above,   115
May in the end vouchsafe us entire love.
Therefore sweet Memory do thou retain
Those pleasures past, which will not turn again:
Remember beauteous Dorset's former sports,
So far from being touched by ill reports;   120
Wherein myself did always bear a part,
While reverend Love presented my true heart:
Those recreations let me bear in mind,
Which her sweet youth and noble thoughts did find:
Whereof deprived, I evermore must grieve,   125
Hating blind Fortune, careless to relieve.
And you sweet Cookham, whom these Ladies leave,
I now must tell the grief you did conceive
At their departure; when they went away,
How everything retained a sad dismay: 130
Nay long before, when once an inkling came,

93–6 Lady Anne was a Clifford on her father's side, a Bedford on her mother's (the Russells were Earls of Bedford); she had just married Richard Sackville, the (dishonourable) Earl of Dorset, who gave a house to true virtue in marrying her.
104–6 'Who throws us so far down in the scheme of things ('frame'), that differences of rank ('degree') prevent our seeing our friends'.
108–10 'Many are removed to far-off centres of power; they leave us to take up honours allotted them; they affect closeness but their heart is not in it; love is the province of the afflicted.'
111–12 'Where is my argument taking me? It is not my place to question and explain ('conster') the great.'
119–21 The sports the young Lady Anne and the poet enjoyed together were beyond rumour and reproach.
126 *careless to relieve* 'indifferent whether I rise again'.
127 The address to Cookham is not sustained: at 135 'you' is the Countess. It is briefly resumed at the conclusion (206).
131 *inkling* 'rumour'.

Methought each thing did unto sorrow frame:
The trees that were so glorious in our view,
Forsook both flowers and fruit, when once they knew,
Of your depart, their very leaves did wither,   135
Changing their colours as they grew together.
But when they saw this had no power to stay you,
They often wept, though speechless, could not pray you;
Letting their tears in your fair bosoms fall,
As if they said, "Why will ye leave us all?"   140
This being vain, they cast their leaves away,
Hoping that pity would have made you stay:
Their frozen tops, like Age's hoary hairs,
Shows their disaster, languishing in fears:
A swarthy rivelled rind all overspread,   145
Their dying bodies half-alive, half-dead.
But your occasions called you so away,
That nothing there had power to make you stay:
Yet did I see a noble grateful mind,
Requiting each according to their kind,   150
Forgetting not to turn and take your leave
Of these sad creatures, powerless to receive
Your favour, when with grief you did depart,
Placing their former pleasures in your heart;
Giving great charge to noble Memory,   155
There to preserve their love continually:
But specially the love of that fair tree,
That first and last you did vouchsafe to see:
In which it pleased you oft to take the air,
With noble Dorset, then a virgin fair: 160
Where many a learnèd book was read and scanned
To this fair tree; taking me by the hand,
You did repeat the pleasures which had past,
Seeming to grieve they could no longer last.
And with a chaste, yet loving kiss took leave,   165
Of which sweet kiss I did it soon bereave:
Scorning a senseless creature should possess
So rare a favour, so great happiness.
No other kiss it could receive from me,
For fear to give back what it took of thee: 170
So I ingrateful creature did deceive it,
Of that which you vouchsafed in love to leave it.
And though it oft had given me much content,
Yet this great wrong I never could repent:
But of the happiest made it most forlorn,   175
To show that nothing's free from Fortune's scorn,
While all the rest with this most beauteous tree,
Made their sad consort Sorrow's harmony.

---

132 'Everything seemed to fit itself for mourning.'
143 'Instead of flowers, chill shivering winter dresses / With icicles her (self-bald) borrowed tresses: / About her brows a periwig of snow' (Sylvester, *Divine Weeks*, 1.4:701–3).
145 Cause and effect are compressed: 'A dismal ('swarthy') frost ('rind'), a dark ('swarthy') wrinkled bark ('rind'), spread over their dying trunks.'
167 *senseless creature* 'tree': trees lack a sensitive soul.
178 'Made Sorrow's harmony their sad company'; or made it their 'sad music'.

The flowers that on the banks and walks did grow,
Crept in the ground, the grass did weep for woe.   180
The winds and waters seemed to chide together,
Because you went away they knew not whither:
And those sweet brooks that ran so fair and clear,
With grief and trouble wrinkled did appear.
Those pretty birds that wonted were to sing,   185
Now neither sing, nor chirp, nor use their wing;
But with their tender feet on some bare spray,
Warble forth sorrow, and their own dismay.
Fair Philomela leaves her mournful ditty,
Drowned in dead sleep, yet can procure no pity: 190
Each arbour, bank, each seat, each stately tree,
Looks bare and desolate now for want of thee;
Turning green tresses into frosty gray,
While in cold grief they wither all away.
The sun grew weak, his beams no comfort gave,   195
While all green things did make the earth their grave:
Each briar, each bramble, when you went away,
Caught fast your clothes, thinking to make you stay:
Delightful Echo wonted to reply
To our last words, did now for sorrow die: 200
The house cast off each garment that might grace it,
Putting on dust and cobwebs to deface it.
All desolation then there did appear,
When you were going whom they held so dear.
This last farewell to Cookham here I give,   205
When I am dead thy name in this may live
Wherein I have performed her noble hest,
Whose virtues lodge in my unworthy breast,
And ever shall, so long as life remains,
Tying my heart to her by those rich chains.   210

189–90 'The nightingale abandons her sad song for sleep
and silence; but even the silence achieves nothing.'

John Donne (1572–1631)

In 1614, in his early forties, Donne proposed publication of a collection of his poems, explaining to his friend Sir Henry Goodyer that it was to be 'not for much public view, but at mine own cost, a few copies', and as 'a valediction to the world, before I take orders'. This farewell to the world would have been predominantly worldly (the love poems are well represented), predominantly serious (many of the early epistles are omitted), and ended with the *Obsequies to the Lord Harington*, whose conclusion promises poetic silence. Donne took pains to bring the poems together, borrowing back copies from friends in a process he says 'cost me more diligence . . . than it did to make them'. But the collection remained an embarrassment; Jonson reported that once he was in orders Donne 'repenteth highly and seeketh to destroy all his poems' (*Conversations with Drummond*), and Thomas Browne, contributing memorial verses to the still miscellaneous *Poems* of 1633, worried about the reception of its 'loose raptures' among those that 'sing not, but in sanctified prose'. The volume never appeared: Donne is the type of the 'cabinet' poet, of whom Drayton complains in the preface to *Poly-Olbion*. Strangely for a poet who more than any other determined what poetry would look like for the rest of the century, Donne affected to consider his poems unfit for sale.

He was born in London, the son of a prosperous ironmonger, but from the age of four the stepson of a prominent Catholic physician (trained in Oxford and Bologna). His mother's family was Catholic and literary: her father was John Heywood, the writer of interludes (and married to Sir Thomas More's niece), her brothers were the Jesuits Jasper and Ellis, the first of them the translator of Seneca. Donne's early education, though not Jesuit, was private and Catholic. With his brother Henry he went up to Hart Hall, Oxford, in 1584, from where as Catholics they went on without degrees to Cambridge and the continent; both entered Thavies Inn in 1591, from where John went on to Lincoln's Inn in 1592, and Henry, found with a Catholic priest in his chambers, to arrest and death (from the plague) in Newgate. Donne is remembered by Sir Richard Baker from this period as 'very neat; a great visitor of ladies, a great frequenter of plays, a great writer of conceited verses' – the ones mainly unrepresented in the 1614 collection. To this period belong the earliest versions of the *Satires* (later approved and improved) and the often risky verse epistles addressed to male friends. On the eve of his entry to Thavies Inn Donne had himself painted (perhaps by Nicholas Hilliard) fashionably dressed, long-haired, wearing earings, his hand on the hilt of a sword with the motto 'Antes muerto que mudado' ('How much shall I be changed / Before I am changed!'); a few years later he was painted again, no longer a son of the Roman Church, as a melancholy lover in the shade of a Spanish hat with the blasphemous motto 'Illumina tenebras nostras domina' ('Enlighten our darkness O lady'). In 1596–7 he joined the Earl of Essex's naval expeditions to Cadiz and to the Azores: two famous verse epistles *The Storm* and *The Calm* (not included here) belong to this adventure. In 1597 a promising political career began in the service of Sir Thomas Egerton, the Lord Keeper; and in the Parliament of 1601 he sat as MP for Brackley in Northamptonshire.

The following year his career was cut short by the revelation of his marriage to Egerton's kinswoman Ann More. From then until 1615 he lived, at Mitcham and in London, a fond husband and father, both financially and spiritually insecure. From the financial insecurity the kindness of well-disposed patrons, notably Mrs Magdalen Herbert and Lucy, Countess of Bedford, afforded only temporary relief: a tract on suicide, *Biathanatos* (not published till 1646), is an early product of this period. The controversial anti-Jesuit tracts *Pseudo-Martyr* (1610) and *Ignatius his Conclave* (in Latin and English 1611) signal his re-entry into the establishment (he was already being encouraged to take orders). He delayed any decision (the *Holy Sonnets* belong to this period). Persuaded to write a consolatory poem for the parents of the prematurely dead Elizabeth Drury, *The First Anniversary* (1611), he won the patronage of Sir Robert, whom he accompanied the next year on a tour of France and the Low Countries. In 1614 he sat as MP for Taunton in the 'Addled' Parliament (so called from its failure to enact any legislation at all); and on the dissolution of that Parliament made through the Earl of Somerset an appeal to the King for secular preferment. Izaak Walton's *Life* records the King's reply: 'I know Mr Donne is a learned man, has the abilities of a learned divine; and will prove a powerful preacher, and my desire is to prefer him that way.' In 1615 Donne took orders in the Church of England. He was appointed a royal chaplain and by royal command made DD of Cambridge University; in 1616 he was made Divinity Reader at Lincoln's Inn.

For the remainder of his life he enjoyed great celebrity as a preacher. In 1619 he served as chaplain to Viscount Doncaster's embassy to Germany. He was elected Dean of St Paul's in 1621. Personal griefs (the death of Ann Donne in 1617, the death of children, the death of friends) and personal illness (that of 1623 produced his single most frequently published work, the *Devotions*, in three editions between 1624 and 1627) hardly interrupted the equanimity of his last years: 'His great and most blessed change was from a temporal to a spiritual employment, in which he was so happy, that he accounted the former part of his life to be lost' (Walton). Walton's quoted account of his preparation for death is famous: 'Several charcoal fires being first made in his large study, he brought with him into that place his winding-sheet in his hand, and having put off all his clothes, had this sheet put on him, and so tied with knots at his head and feet, and his hands so placed as dead bodies are usually fitted, to be shrouded and put into their coffin, or grave. Upon this urn he thus stood, with his eyes shut, and with so much of the sheet turned aside as might show his lean, pale and death-like face, which was purposely turned towards the East, from whence he expected the second coming of his and our Saviour Jesus.' He died on 31 March 1631, survived by six of his twelve children.

The poetry published in Donne's lifetime conforms to the image of the godly man he prepared for himself. *An Anatomy of the World* (1611), reprinted as *The First Anniversary* along with *The Second Anniversary: Of the Progress of the Soul* (1612), was reprinted again in the year of his election as Dean of St Paul's (1621) and again in 1625. The obscure *Elegy on Prince Henry* was printed in the third edition of Sylvester's *Lachrymae Lachrymarum* (1613), the quasi-official memorial volume. Selections of sermons were published every year between 1622 and 1627, the *Devotions* in 1624 (two different editions, and a third in 1627). His son John Donne edited the first major collection, *LXXX Sermons* (1640). The *Poems* of 1633 (facsimile, Menston: Scolar Press, 1969), organized as the accidents of the MSS it worked from dictated, carries an appendix of encomia led by Henry King's but most famously including Thomas Carew's, which remains among the best accounts of the poet. The edition of 1635, besides slightly enlarging the canon, organizes the poems generically, as do the succeeding five editions up to 1669. Poetry once exclusive to the manuscript-reading cabinet came to control the taste of two generations. Early editions are described in G.L. Keynes *A Bibliography of Donne*, fourth edition (Oxford: Clarendon Press, 1973). Of the *Variorum Edition of the Poetry of John Donne*, under the editorship of Gary A. Stringer, volume 6 (*The Anniversaries and the Epicedes*) has so far appeared (Bloomington: Indiana University Press, 1995). The classic modern edition remains *The Poems*, edited by H. J. C. Grierson (Oxford: Clarendon Press, 1912; last reprinted in 1968), but it is superseded by the standard multi-volume Oxford Clarendon edition comprising Helen Gardner, *The Divine Poems* (1952, revised 1978) and *Elegies, Songs and Sonnets* (1965), W. Milgate, *Satires, Epigrams, and Verse Letters* (1967) and *The Epithalamions, Anniversaries and Epicedes* (1978). There are at least three fine single-volume popular editions of the *Poems*: by John Shawcross (New York: Anchor, 1967); A. J. Smith (Harmondsworth: Penguin, 1971); C. A. Patrides (London: Everyman's Library, 1991). Theodore Redpath's edition of *The Songs and Sonnets* (London: Methuen, 1956, revised edition, 1983) has useful commentary. The *Sermons* are edited by George R. Potter and Evelyn M. Simpson, 10 vols (Berkeley and Los Angeles: University of California Press, 1953–62). Evelyn Simpson has edited *Essays in Divinity* (Oxford: Clarendon Press, 1952); T. J. Healy has edited *Ignatius his Conclave* (Oxford: Clarendon Press, 1969). There is an edition by Michael Rudick and M. Pabst Battin of *Biathanatos* (New York: Garland, 1982). Anthony Raspa has edited *Devotions upon Emergent Occasions* (New York and London: Oxford University Press,1987, reprinting the edition from McGill-Queen's University Press, 1975) and *Pseudo-Martyr* (Montreal: McGill-Queen's University Press, 1993). The classic life is Izaak Walton, *The Life of Dr John Donne* (1640), revised in *Lives* (1675); the standard modern biography is R. C. Bald, *John Donne: A Life* (Oxford: Clarendon Press, corrected edition 1986). There is a facsimile of the 1651 *Letters to Several Persons of Honour* (Hildesheim and New York: Georg Olms, 1974); Edmund Gosse's *The Life and Letters of John Donne*, 2 vols (1899) remains the main source. H. C. Combs and H. R. Sullens's *Concordance to the English Poems of Donne* (Chicago: Packard, 1940) is the only concordance. Recent criticism is described in John R. Roberts, *An Annotated Bibliography of Modern Criticism 1912–1967* (Columbia, MO, 1973), and *1968–1978* (Columbia, MO, 1982). Early criticism is anthologized in A. J. Smith, *Donne: The Critical Heritage* (1975). Unless otherwise indicated, texts of the poems are taken from the 1633 *Poems*. References to Donne's *Sermons* are to the volumes and numbers of the Potter–Simpson edition.

Air and Angels

The poem explores an anti-Platonic argument about how love is embodied, not by attaching itself to the body but to a reciprocal love.

> Twice or thrice had I loved thee,
> Before I knew thy face or name;
> So in a voice, so in a shapeless flame,
> Angels affect us oft, and worshipped be,
>   Still when, to where thou wert, I came   5
> Some lovely glorious nothing I did see,
>   But since my soul, whose child love is,
> Takes limbs of flesh, and else could nothing do,
>   More subtle than the parent is,
> Love must not be, but take a body too,   10
>   And therefore what thou wert, and who
>   I bid Love ask, and now
> That it assume thy body, I allow,
> And fix itself in thy lip, eye, and brow.
>
> Whilst thus to ballast love, I thought,   15
> And so more steadily to have gone,
> With wares which would sink admiration,
> I saw, I had love's pinnace overfraught,
>   Every thy hair for love to work upon
> Is much too much, some fitter must be sought;   20
>   For, nor in nothing, nor in things
> Extreme, and scattering bright, can love inhere;
>   Then as an angel, face, and wings
> Of air, not pure as it, yet pure doth wear,
>   So thy love may be my love's sphere;   25
>   Just such disparity
> As is 'twixt air and angel's purity,
> 'Twixt women's love, and men's will ever be.

1–4 'The lover does not desire this or that body but the splendour of the divine presence ... this is why lovers are ignorant of what they desire' (Ficino, *De Amore*, 2.6), a notion repeated in *The Good-Morrow*, 6–7.
3–4 God 'maketh his angels spirits; his ministers a flaming fire' (Psalms, 104: 4).
7–10 The soul is moved to love of earthly things, and 'weighted down (as they say) with this desire, it descends into the body where it concerns itself with begetting and moving and feeling' (Ficino, *De Amore*, 4.4). Falling in love (as in *The Good-Morrow*) is like being born. *1633*'s comma after 'since' is removed.
13–14 'Nor will the lover's vision of the beautiful take the form of a face, or of hands, or of anything that is the flesh' (Plato, *Symposium*, 211a, and taken up in *Negative Love*, 1–2: 'I never stooped so low as they / Which on an eye, cheek, lip, can prey'); but Shakespeare, *Sonnets*, 106, has 'Then in the blazon of sweet beauty's best, / Of hand, of foot, of lip, of eye, of brow, / I see [the poets'] antique pen would have expressed / Even such a beauty as you master now'.
15–18 Petrarch's unsteady 'galley [is] chargèd with forgetfulness' (*Rime*, 189, Wyatt); Donne's is overloaded with a cargo that would confound ('sink') admirers.

19 Though by God 'the very hairs of your head are all numbered' (Matthew 10: 30).
21–2 'Love can attach itself ('inhere') neither to the immaterial ('nothing') nor to the distracting multiplicity of the material.' Ficino recommends detachment from the beauty that is 'exterior, wanting, scattered' (*De Amore*, 6.18); Donne's exterior beauty is vivid and intense.
23–4 'Angels assume bodies of air, condensing it by a divine power' (Thomas Aquinas, *Summa Theologica*, 1.51.2: 'Whether angels assume bodies') and they do so 'not for themselves, but on our account; that by conversing familiarly with men they may give evidence of that intellectual companionship which men expect to have with them in the life to come.'
25–8 'The beloved is said to be in the lover, inasmuch as the beloved abides in the apprehension of the lover, according to Philip 1: 7, "because I have you in my heart": while the lover is said to be in the beloved ... inasmuch as the lover is not satisfied with a superficial apprehension of the beloved, but strives to gain an intimate knowledge of everything pertaining to the beloved, so as to penetrate into his very soul' (Aquinas, *Summa Theologica*, 2.1.28.2: 'Whether mutual indwelling is an effect of love'). He adds: 'nothing hinders a thing from being both container and contents in different ways.'

The Canonization

The general debt is to Ovid, *Elegies*, 1.15, addressed to those envious of poets' fame ('Envy why carpest thou my time is spent so ill', Marlowe), where the poet recommends himself to lovers ('And in sad lovers heads let me be found', 38).

For God's sake hold your tongue, and let me love,
    Or chide my palsy, or my gout,
My five gray hairs, or ruined fortune flout,
      With wealth your state, your mind with arts improve,
        Take you a course, get you a place,   5
        Observe his Honour, or his Grace,
Or the King's real, or his stampèd face
    Contèmplate, what you will, approve,
    So you will let me love.

Alas, alas, who's injured by my love?   10
    What merchants' ships have my sighs drowned?
Who says my tears have overflowed his ground?
      When did my colds a forward spring remove?
        When did the heats which my veins fill
        Add one more, to the Plaguy Bill?   15
Soldiers find wars, and lawyers find out still
    Litigious men, which quarrels move,
    Though she and I do love.

Call us what you will, we are made such by love;
    Call her one, me another fly,   20
We're tapers too, and at our own cost die,
      And we in us find the eagle and the dove,
        The phoenix' riddle hath more wit
        By us, we two being one, are it.
So, to one neutral thing both sexes fit.   25
    We die and rise the same, and prove
    Mysterious by this love.

2–3   The details (variable in different MSS) belong to satiric caricature: Martial's Vetustilla has 'three hairs and four teeth' (3.93).
6   'Flatter the powerful'.
7–8   'Or gaze on the King's real [some MSS have 'royal'] face or, if you please, try his face in coin.'
10–15   'Love subverts kingdoms, overthrows cities, tombs, families' (Burton, *Anatomy*, 3.2.1.1); but Donne varies Ovid's declaration that poems survive 'While bondmen cheat, fathers be hard, bawds whorish, / And strumpets flatter' (*Elegies*, 15: 17–18): his poems do not 'postpone an early spring' or add to the list of those dead from plague.
19–20   'And there are other beasts that in a fit of mad desire, hoping to enjoy the flame because it's bright, find in the end it burns as well. Alas my place is with this kind' (Petrarch, *Rime*, 19). Jonson imagines dust (*The Hourglass*, 7–8) as the remains of a lover who 'in his mistress' flame, playing like a fly, / Was turned to cinders by her eye'.

21   The lovers' 'mystery' (dying and rising the same) is suggested by a sequence of apparent self-contradictions: candles that fulfil their function by expending themselves ('Pauvre chandelle que je suis; je me consume, je me detruis', Corrozet, *Hecatomgraphie*, 1.6); the pairing of the strong eagle and the mild dove ('Nor doth the bird of Jove / Get a degenerous dove', Horace, *Odes*, 4.4: 31–2, Fanshawe); the phoenix that renews itself in destructive fire.
23–7   Comparing himself with strange things in nature, Petrarch begins with the phoenix, which 'burns and dies, yet renews its strength' (*Rime*, 135: 14). The 'neutrality' (double sex) of the lovers makes sense of the puzzle (adds 'wit' to it) that the phoenix can be at once father and mother to its progeny; their sexual 'death' makes sense of its resurrection ('rising it dies, and dying rises', Camerarius, *Emblemata*, 3.100). Sixteenth-century editions of Petrarch sometimes represent a phoenix rising from an urn he shares with Laura.

We can die by it, if not live by love,
    And if unfit for tombs and hearse
Our legend be, it will be fit for verse;
      And if no piece of chronicle we prove,   30
      We'll build in sonnets pretty rooms;
      As well a well wrought urn becomes
The greatest ashes, as half-acre tombs,
    And by these hymns, all shall approve   35
Us canonized for Love.

And thus invoke us; "You whom reverend love
    Made one another's hermitage;
You, to whom love was peace, that now is rage,   40
      Who did the whole world's soul contract, and drove
      Into the glasses of your eyes
      So made such mirrors, and such spies,
That they did all to you epitomise,
    Countries, towns, courts: Beg from above
A pattern of our love."   45

28–34 Of a fly in amber Herrick writes 'The urn was little, but the room / More rich than Cleopatra's tomb' (*The Amber Bead*, following Martial's famous 4.59). The lines turn on oppositions of large and small: 'piece' may mean 'fortress', 'chronicles' are typically long, tombs (which may be 'tomes') are public (like the 'hearses' on which funerary verses or 'legends' [*1633* gives a plural] were hung), but sonnets are single rooms or *stanze*, and urns are private. But in *Valediction: Of the Book* 'annals' are to be written out of the lovers' letters.

37–45 Would-be lovers are to pray to the canonized lovers to intercede on their behalf. The specification of the saints' titles is liturgically conventional.

39 *rage* 'rapture'.

41 They compressed the world's soul into the shiny convexes of their eyes (as the world in *The Sun Rising*, 26, is contracted to a room); thus they were able to reflect (as mirrors) and look into (as spies) all that was in the world. *1633* alone has 'contract'; MSS agree on the alchemical 'extract'.

44–5 The sainted lovers are to ask God for a model of the love the would-be lovers might live by. Many MSS read 'your love'.

The Ecstasy

The poem is ostensibly an 'ode on a question moved' whether love should require sexual consummation, but it is centrally concerned with whether and how the 'mystery' of love should be made manifest. It pretends allegiance to a tradition of poetical treatments of love problems, including Sidney's 'In a grove most rich of shade' (*Astrophil and Stella*, Song 8), Greville's 'In the time when herbs and flowers' (*Caelica*, 75), Lord Herbert's *Ode on a Question Moved*, Wither's 'When Philomela with her strains' (*Fair Virtue*, Sonnet 3), or even such slight dramatized persuasions to love as Morley's 'Besides a fountain of sweet briar and roses' (*Madrigals*, 14). But the issues invoked reach back to the extended debate on the motives of love that takes up the first half of Plato's *Phaedrus*, and are rehearsed through the sixteenth century in (mainly Italian) manuals of love theory. Extensive debts to Leone Ebreo are indicated in Gardner. The literary-critical issue is whether Donne's way of going about the question should be taken seriously. A central mystical passage (29–48) is symmetrically flanked on the one side by an account of the lovers' situation (1–28), on the other by the pleas of one lover or both together for the propriety of sex (49–76); both these put in doubt the gravity of the Platonic argument at the centre, and the reader's confidence is further disturbed by the irregularity of the relation of the 'ecstatic' lover (who may be simply 'out of his mind') to a hypothetical spectator (addressed directly at 21–8, and involved again in the poem's conclusion) with whom identification is invited.

Where, like a pillow on a bed,
   A pregnant bank swelled up, to rest
The violet's reclining head,
   Sat we two, one another's best;
Our hands were firmly cémented   5
   With a fast balm, which thence did spring,
Our eyebeams twisted, and did thread
   Our eyes, upon one double string,
So to intergraft our hands, as yet
   Was all the means to make us one,   10
And pictures in our eyes to get
   Was all our propagation.
As 'twixt two equal armies, Fate
   Suspends uncertain victory,
Our souls (which to advance their state,   15
   Were gone out) hung 'twixt her, and me.
And whilst our souls negotiate there,
   We like sepulchral statues lay,
All day, the same our postures were,
   And we said nothing, all the day.   20
If any, so by love refined,
   That he soul's language understood,
And by good love were grown all mind,
   Within convenient distance stood,
He (though he knows not which soul spake,   25
   Because both meant, both spake the same)
Might thence a new concoction take,
   And part far purer than he came.
This ecstasy doth unperplex
   (We said) and tell us what we love,   30
We see by this, it was not sex,
   We see, we saw not what did move:
But as all several souls contain

2 *pregnant* 'swelling'; but fertile of modest violets.

5–6 'With this she seizeth on his sweating palm, / The precedent of pith, and livelihood, / And trembling in her passion, calls it balm, / Earth's sovereign salve' (Shakespeare, *Venus and Adonis*, 25–8). Adonis's moist palm betokens sensuousness; Donne also uses it (in a letter to Henry Goodyer of 1607) in the Paracelsian sense of 'natural inborn preservative' – it is what keeps the lovers steadfast; and there is an alchemical 'cementation' ('high-temperature interpenetration') of the hands (as 9–10).

7–8 The lovers gaze on each other, the beams they emit (as it was supposed to be how sight operated) threading their eyes. Carew mollifies the image for his lovers, who twine 'a pure wreath of eye-beams' (*To a Lady*, 5–6).

11–12 A lyric in *England's Helicon* warns against men: 'They will look babies in your eyes, / And speak so fair as fair may be' (*The Shepherd's Sun*, 29–30), gazing at their own reflections in the beloved's eyes.

13–14 'Then Jupiter in heaven above in equal balance weighs / Their destinies both' (Virgil, *Aeneid*, 12:725–7, Phaer).

15 'Our souls (which had left our bodies to promote their own advantage) conferred in the air.'

18–20 'Princes' images on their tombs do not lie as they were wont [in more pious days], seeming to pray up to Heaven, but with their hands under their cheeks, as if they died of the toothache' (*Duchess of Malfi*, IV. ii. 156); married couples can be imagined in this way together.

21–8 The already pure observer is to be heated ('concocted') to a greater purity by a revelation of the lovers' spiritual love as 'they who have had God's continual sunshine upon them . . . should have received the best concoction, the best digestion of the testimonies of his love, and consequently be the purer' (*Sermons*, 1.1).

29–32 'This rapture, unentangling body and soul, makes clear what it is we love, and (something we did not understand before) that it was not the fact that we are man and woman ('sex') that affected us.'

33–6 'We can understand all things by her [the soul], but what she is we cannot apprehend' (Burton, *Anatomy*, 1.1.2.5). Separate souls, while not composite, can be thought of as containing experience: 'Memory and sensation, together with the feelings consequent upon memory and sensation, may be said to write words in our souls' (Plato, *Philebus*, 39a); but 'the regulating principle of love brings together . . . hot and cold, wet and dry . . . and compounds them in an ordered harmony' (*Symposium*, 188b).

Mixture of things, they know not what,
  Love, these mixed souls, doth mix again,   35
    And makes both one, each this and that.
A single violet transplant,
  The strength, the colour, and the size
(All which before was poor, and scant)
    Redoubles still, and multiplies.   40
When love, with one another so
  Interinanimates two souls,
That abler soul, which thence doth flow,
  Defects of loneliness controls.
We then, who are this new soul, know,   45
  Of what we are composed, and made,
For, the atomies of which we grow,
  Are souls, whom no change can invade.
But O alas, so long, so far
  Our bodies why do we forbear?   50
They are ours, though not we, we are
  The intelligences, they the sphere.
We owe them thanks, because they thus,
  Did us, to us, at first convey,
Yielded their senses' force to us,   55
  Nor are dross to us, but allay.
On man Heaven's influence works not so,
  But that it first imprints the air,
So soul into the soul may flow,
  Though it to body first repair.   60
As our blood labours to beget
  Spirits, as like souls as it can,
Because such fingers need to knit
  That subtle knot, which makes us man:
So must pure lovers' souls descend   65
  To affections, and to faculties,
Which sense may reach and apprehend,

37–40 As violets (which are to hand) are improved by transplantation, so are souls: 'each one being transformed into the other becomes two, at once lover and beloved; and two multiplied by two makes four, so that each of them is twin and both together are one and four' (Leone Ebreo, *Dialoghi d'Amore*).

42 *interinanimates* interanimates (*1633* and a few MSS); Love moves the souls to breathe into ('inanimate') one another; so it is said in Donne's coinage to 'interinanimate' them.

44 'Checks the deficiencies which result from being single'.

45–8 The new soul is 'abler' in being more conscious of itself, knowing that its indivisible components ('atomies') are themselves immutable souls whose components are unknowable.

51–2 'Intelligences' are the controlling influences of the planets, here made their vehicles.

55–6 'Gave over to us the power of their senses' partly because the higher souls are in communion only when the motor and perceptual powers of the sensible soul are at rest, partly because their resting bodies are the necessary additive which makes the refined gold of their souls workable (as an 'alloy'). The preferred reading of the MSS is 'forces, sense'.

57–8 'Air is as the common link of things . . . because it seems to have a middle and indifferent nature. For its is a body which receives and conveys light, opacity, the tints of all colours . . . in which the radiations of the heavenly bodies . . . communicate and dispute' (Bacon, *De principiis atque originibus*, following Aristotle, *De Anima*, 419c). So in *Air and Angels* the immaterial assumes material existence in order to have effect. *1633* misreads 'For' for 'So' at 59.

61–4 'Spirit is a most subtle vapour, which is expressed from the blood, and the instrument of the soul, to perform all his actions; a common tie or medium between the body and the soul' (Burton, *Anatomy*, 1.1.2.2).

65–7 An exchange is proposed: if the blood labours to meet the soul halfway as 'spirit', the higher soul should respond by making itself open to the operations of the 'sensible soul' by which the body 'lives, hath sense, appetite, judgement, breath, and motion' (Burton, *Anatomy*, 1.1.2.6).

> Else a great prince in prison lies,
>   To our bodies turn we then, that so
>   Weak men on love revealed may look;   70
>   Love's mysteries in souls do grow,
>   But yet the body is his book.
>   And if some lover, such as we,
>   Have heard this dialogue of one,
>   Let him still mark us, he shall see   75
>   Small change, when we're to bodies gone.

68 'Love that doth reign and live within my thought' abashed by the cruel mistress 'to the heart apace / Taketh his flight where he doth lurk and plain' (Petrarch, *Rime*, 140, Surrey); but were the lover welcome, love would move freely in the world.

73–6 The lover 'such as we' recognizes already that the two are already one, and their love is already an object of his admiration and hence sees 'small change' if the lovers do turn to their bodies.

The Funeral

The poet here imagines not dying (as his late hymns do) but being dead (as in *The Will*, *The Relic* and *The Damp*). Propertius, 2.23A, gives instructions to his mistress for the order of his funeral, but the appeal here is to a stranger, and the imagination of it probably triggered by a remote case: Giraldus Cambrensis reports (most fully in *Speculum Ecclesiae*, 2.8) the exhumation of Arthur, and the discovery of the tresses of a woman's hair round the bones. Tebaldeo's sonnet on a bracelet of hair ('O chiome, parte della treccia d'oro') is translated three times by Drummond ('O hair, sweet hair').

> Who ever comes to shroud me, do not harm
>   Nor question much
> That subtle wreath of hair, which crowns my arm;
> The mystery, the sign you must not touch,
>   For 'tis my outward soul   5
> Viceroy to that, which unto Heaven being gone,
>   Will leave this to control,
> And keep these limbs, her provinces, from dissolution.
>
> For if the sinewy thread my brain lets fall
>   Through every part,   10
> Can tie those parts, and make me one of all;
> Those hairs which upward grew, and strength and art
>   Have from a better brain,
> Can better do it; except she meant that I
>   By this should know my pain,   15
> As prisoners then are manacled, when they're condemned to die.

3   *subtle* because both fine (Catullus, 64:63, talks of Ariadne's losing the 'subtle crown from her golden hair') and mysterious.

5–9   As a sacrament is an 'outward and visible sign of an inward and spiritual grace' (as the Catechism defines it), so is the mistress's tress a sign of the soul; and a vicegerent too, for it holds together the dead limbs as the soul commanded the live ones.

9–11   'Nerves, or sinews . . . proceed from the brain, and carry the animal spirits' (Burton, *Anatomy*, 1.2.2.3); 'the animal spirits . . . brought up to the brain, and diffused by the nerves, to the subordinate members, give sense and motion to them all' (1.1.2.2).

12–15   'I shall be better held together by those hairs which were hers and grew upward towards heaven; unless she meant (with the gift of the tress) that I should know my punishment.'

Whate'er she meant by it, bury it by me,
    For since I am
Love's martyr, it might breed idolatry,
If into others' hands these relics came;   20
    As 'twas humility
To afford to it all that a soul can do,
    So, 'tis some bravery,
That since you would have none of me, I bury some of you.

22   'It was submissive in me to afford it every devotion, but now I defy your reluctance by burying it.'

The Good-Morrow

Though the notion of specifically sexual awakening is commonplace, the Christian connotations of sleeping and waking (as in Romans 13: 11) are latent in the informing conceit. Former loves are dreamy anticipations of true love. Shakespeare's 'What is your substance, whereof are you made, / That millions of strange shadows on you tend?' (*Sonnets*, 53) makes of the beloved something impersonally anticipated; Petrarch's 'in other forms I seek to trace . . . a faint resemblance of thy matchless grace' (*Rime*, 16:12–14) makes it something remembered. Distinctive here is the unembarrassed prominence of the lover as object of the beloved's love.

I wonder by my troth, what thou, and I
Did, till we loved, were we not weaned till then?
But sucked on country pleasures, childishly?
Or snorted we in the seven sleepers' den?
'Twas so; but this, all pleasures fancies be.   5
If ever any beauty I did see,
Which I desired, and got, 'twas but a dream of thee.

And now good-morrow to our waking souls,
Which watch not one another out of fear;
For love, all love of other sights controls,   10
And makes one little room, an everywhere.
Let sea-discoverers to new worlds have gone,
Let maps to others, worlds on worlds have shown,
Let us possess one world, each hath one, and is one.

My face in thine eye, thine in mine appears,   15
And true plain hearts do in the faces rest,

2–3 'For everyone that useth milk is unskilful . . . But strong meat belongeth to them that are of full age' (Hebrews 5: 12–14); 'country pleasures' (some MSS read 'childish pleasures, sillily') are rustic and unsophisticated, but also sexual.
4 Seven Christian youths of Ephesus took refuge in a cave from the Diocletian persecution, to emerge 200 years later into a Christianized world.
5–7 'Barring this all pleasures are imaginary, all beautiful women I possessed prefigured you'; Petrarch tries to reconstruct from others the remembered 'true beauty I desired in you' (*Rime*, 16).
9–10 'Which do not watch each other out of jealousy, for love checks all love for anything else we look at'.

12–14 Spenser asks the 'tradeful merchants' why they sail the world: 'For lo my love doth in herself contain / All this world's riches that may far be found' (Spenser, *Amoretti*, 15); distinctive (if the maps are star-maps) is the suggestion of plurality of worlds. *1633* reads 'other' for most MSS 'others'.
14 *one world* The plurality of other worlds is contrasted with the sufficient oneness of the lovers'; some MSS read 'our world' , contrasting the otherness of worlds beyond the lovers with the sense that they possess each other.
15–18 Together making one world, each lover is a hemisphere. The 'plain hearts' evident in their faces are transmogrified into 'cordiform' hemispheric maps (using

> Where can we find two better hemispheres
> Without sharp north, without declining west?
> What ever dies, was not mixed equally;
> If our two loves be one, or, thou and I   20
> Love so alike, that none do slacken, none can die.

heart-shaped projections) which together make a globe; but since they make a private world, the contingencies of the world outside (cold and dark) do not operate on them.
19 'It is not easy . . . for a thing to be immortal that is composed of many elements not put together in the best way' (Plato, *Republic*, 611b).

21 Love just alike in all; none of these loves can die (some MSS). *1633*'s reading is firmer; but 'slacken' suggests a shift (by way of the notion of 'tempering') from a medical to a musical metaphor.

Love's Deity

'How terrible is Love! . . . but he delights in my reproaches, and thrives on my curses. What a miracle that Venus, born from the green sea, should bring forth fire from water' (*Greek Anthology*, 5.176). The distinction is between the gratification of passion and passion itself (as in Dryden's version of Lucretius, *Concerning the Nature of Love*, 42). Here the possibil- ity of mutual love is abjured, and the experience ex- ecrated: 'the lover who is not loved in return is en- tirely dead, and he will never live again unless indignation revive him' (Ficino, *De Amore*, 2.8). The poem is imitated less indignantly by Suckling in the song 'O for some honest lover's ghost'.

> I long to talk with some old lover's ghost,
>   Who died before the God of Love was born:
> I cannot think that he, who then loved most,
>   Sunk so low, as to love one which did scorn.
> But since this god produced a destiny,   5
> And that vice-nature, custom, lets it be;
>   I must love her, that loves not me.
>
> Sure, they which made him god, meant not so much:
>   Nor he, in his young godhead practised it.
> But when an even flame two hearts did touch,   10
>   His office was indulgently to fit
> Actives to passives. Correspondency
> Only his subject was; it cannot be
>   Love, till I love her, that loves me.
>
> But every modern god will now extend   15
>   His vast prerogative, as far as Jove.
> To rage, to lust, to write to, to commend,
>   All is the purlieu of the God of Love.
> O were we wakened by this tyranny
> To ungod this child again, it could not be   20
>   I should love her, who loves not me.

5–6 'Since love has assigned us our lot, and habit makes it seem natural'; '[Custom] little by little and as it were by stealth, establishes the foot of her authority in us . . . Use is the most effectual master of all things' (Montaigne, *Essays*, 1.22, 'Of Custom').
11–13 'His task was kindly to fit lover to beloved; his study was to effect just agreement.'
15–16 Spenser's modern goddess Mutability complains to

Nature that Jupiter and his fellows 'challenge to themselves the whole world's reign / Of which the greatest part is due to me' (*Faerie Queene*, 7.7.15); but here Love's (tyrannical) privilege impinges on old and sacred liberties.
17–18 'Then pours he forth in patchèd sonnettings / His love, his lust, and loathsome flatterings' (Joseph Hall, *Virgidemiarum*, 1.7: 11–12); Love has taken every place for somewhere he has special rights ('purlieu').

Rebel and atheist too, why murmur I,
　As though I felt the worst that love could do?
Love may make me leave loving, or might try
　A deeper plague, to make her love me too,   25
Which since she loves before, I'm loath to see;
Falsehood is worse than hate; and that must be,
　If she whom I love, should love me.

24–5 *Twickenham Garden*, 26–7, varies the couplet.

A Nocturnal upon St Lucy's Day, Being the Shortest Day

A meditation for the vigil of St Lucy's Eve (12–13 December, for the English working with the Julian calendar then the longest night). The associations of night are commonly less elegiac than erotic (even if the lover is in distress) as in Petrarch's 'Le stelle e il cielo e gli elementi a prova' (*Rime*, 164), or Sidney's 'With how sad steps O Moon thou climb'st the skies' (*Astrophil*, 31); and while the associations of 'nocturnal' are complicated (most obviously liturgical) the few pieces advertising themselves as 'night pieces', from the genre of painting (Herrick's *The Night-Piece, to Julia*, Waller's *The Night-Piece*) are unambiguously love poems. The name Lucy suggests light, but St Lucy was blinded and her festival celebrated in winter darkness: on this pseudo-paradox the poem is built. Its subject is undetermined: some readers take it as a farewell to the Countess of Bedford (seriously ill in 1611–12), others to his wife (whom Donne believed dead in 1612, while he was in Paris). Its focus is on the poet's own deprivation and a witty fascination with nothingness: he puts himself with that sect of friars who 'went beyond all, beyond the Ignorants, and the Minorites, and the Minims, and all, and called themselves, *Nullanos*, Nothings' (*Sermons*, 2.14). Its leading vocabulary is alchemical. Quotations from Paracelsus are taken from W. A. Murray, 'Donne and Paracelsus', *Review of English Studies*, 25 (1949).

'Tis the year's midnight, and it is the day's,
Lucy's, who scarce seven hours herself unmasks,
　The sun is spent, and now his flasks
　Send forth light squibs, no constant rays;
　　The world's whole sap is sunk: 5
The general balm the hydropic earth hath drunk,
Whither, as to the bed's feet life is shrunk,
Dead and interred; yet all these seem to laugh,
Compared with me, who am their epitaph.

Study me then, you who shall lovers be   10
At the next world, that is, at the next spring:
　For I am every dead thing,
　In whom love wrought new alchemy.
　　For his art did express
A quintessence even from nothingness,   15

3–4 'The sun is exhausted, and his powder flasks supply only short-lived fireworks.'
5–6 'There is hope of a tree . . . though the root thereof wax old in the earth . . . yet through the scent of water it will bud . . . But man dieth and wasteth away . . . As the waters fail from the sea, and the flood decayeth and drieth up: So man lieth down and riseth not' (Job 14: 7–12); here the thirsty ('hydropic', regularly misspelled 'hydroptic') earth has drunk the Paracelsian 'balsam' which preserves all living things.

7–9 'A sick bed is a grave, and all that the patient says there is but a varying of his own epitaph. Every night's bed is a type of the grave' (*Devotions*, 3: Meditation); the foot of the bed is as low as life can sink.
9 *epitaph* which speaks what they were.
13–15 'In whom love worked a rival chemistry and pressed out a fifth and spiritual essence from nothingness'; whereas in the 'old' alchemy 'Man is a quintessence, the microcosm, the child of the whole universe' (Paracelsus).

From dull privations, and lean emptiness
He ruined me, and I am re-begot
Of absence, darkness, death; things which are not.

All others, from all things, draw all that's good,
Life, soul, form, spirit, whence they being have,   20
   I, by Love's limbeck, am the grave
   Of all, that's nothing. Oft a flood
     Have we two wept, and so
Drowned the whole world, us two; oft did we grow
To be two chaoses, when we did show   25
Care to aught else; and often absences
Withdrew our souls, and made us carcasses.

But I am by her death, (which word wrongs her)
Of the first nothing, the elixir grown;
   Were I a man, that I were one,   30
   I needs must know, I should prefer,
     If I were any beast,
Some ends, some means; yea plants, yea stones detest,
And love, all, all some properties invest,
If I an ordinary nothing were,   35
As shadow, a light, and body must be here.

But I am none; nor will my Sun renew.
You lovers, for whose sake, the lesser sun
   At this time to the Goat is run
   To fetch new lust, and give it you,   40
     Enjoy your summer all;
Since she enjoys her long night's festival,
Let me prepare towards her, and let me call
This hour her Vigil, and her Eve, since this
Both the year's, and the day's deep midnight is.   45

16–18 'Love unbuilt ('ruined') me from what was not there ('privations', 'emptiness') . . . things which have no being' ('not' functions as an adjective).

21–2 'Distilled over love's fire, I am where everything that is nothing ends up.'

22–4 As in *Valediction of Weeping*, 14–20.

24–7 Since each was the other's informing principle, their coherence was forfeit when either was distracted; and since each was the other's soul their absences from each other were fatal.

29 Her death has made him yet less than a chaos or a carcass. He returns to his condition as the quintessence or elixir of nothingness, a 'first nothing' since it is less than the necessarily secondary nothingness of privation.

30–4 Understanding in man has a 'reflecting action, by which it judgeth of its own doings' (Burton, *Anatomy*, 1.1.2.10); by appetite, beasts are 'inclined to follow that good which the senses shall approve, or avoid that which they hold evil' (1.1.2.8); 'attraction . . . as a lodestone draws iron, draws meat into the stomach [and] is very necessary in plants' (1.1.2.5), and again 'Natural love or hatred is that sympathy or antipathy which is seen in animate and inanimate creatures . . . metals, stones, heavy things go downward' (3.1.1.2).

36 'Wherever the whole human being goes, there as his comrade goes his shadow' (Paracelsus). A shadow is an 'ordinary nothing', but since the poet has lost his light, he has no shadow.

38–40 The sun ('lesser' because wintry and because not Lucy) enters Capricorn ('the Goat', typically lustful) at the solstice.

The Sun Rising

An execration of the sun (so the title in some MSS, 'To the Sun') as in Ovid, *Amores* 1.13 ('To the Dawn that she hold back' since she forces lovers to leave their beds), turns into a welcome as Petrarch, *Rime*, 188 (inviting the sun to stop in its course so that the laurel will always be in light).

Busy old fool, unruly sun,
Why dost thou thus,
Through windows, and through curtains call on us?
Must to thy motions lovers' seasons run?
Saucy pedantic wretch, go chide 5
Late schoolboys, and sour prentices,
Go tell court-huntsmen, that the King will ride,
Call country ants to harvest offices.
Love, all alike, no season knows, nor clime,
Nor hours, days, months, which are the rags of time. 10

Thy beams, so reverend, and strong
Why shouldst thou think?
I could eclipse and cloud them with a wink,
But that I would not lose her sight so long:
If her eyes have not blinded thine, 15
Look, and tomorrow late, tell me,
Whether both the Indias of spice and mine
Be where thou left'st them, or lie here with me.
Ask for those kings whom thou saw'st yesterday,
And thou shalt hear, all here in one bed lay. 20

She's all States, and all Princes, I,
Nothing else is.
Princes do but play us, compared to this,
All honour's mimic; all wealth alchemy;
Thou sun art half as happy as we, 25
In that the world's contracted thus.
Thine age asks ease, and since thy duties be
To warm the world, that's done in warming us.
Shine here to us, and thou art everywhere;
This bed thy centre is, these walls, thy sphere. 30

1–3 'Then coming up early at the windows . . . the moon, busy ['sedula'] with light that stayed too long, opened my mistress's sleeping eyes' (Propertius, 1.3:31–3).

5–6 'Thou cozen'st boys of sleep, and dost betray them / To pedants that with cruel lashes pay them' (*Amores*, 1.13.17–18, Marlowe).

7 James I was a passionate hunter.

8 'The painful hind by thee to field is sent, / Slow oxen early in the yoke are pent' (*Amores*, 1.13.15–16); the ant, unlike the grasshopper (or love, which is at all times the same), is an observer of seasons.

9–10 'Only our love hath no decay; / This no tomorrow hath, nor yesterday' (*The Anniversary*, 7–8); here instead of the standard 'rage of Time' he varies 'Feathers and dust, today and yesterday' (*The Calm*, 18)

17 The East Indies for spice, the West for gold.

24 *alchemy* 'trash and illusion'.

25 *half as happy* happier than he was because his workload is reduced, but not reaching to the doubled happiness of the two lovers.

27 After the death of Phaeton Apollo is found 'denying to the world his duty to perform. / My lot (quoth he) hath had enough of this unquiet state / From first beginning of the world' (Ovid, *Metamorphoses*, 2:385–7, Golding).

30 The miracle is confirmed in the squaring of the circle.

Twickenham Garden

Twickenham Park was the home of Lucy, Countess of Bedford, from 1607 to 1618. The classic statement of the contrast between the beauty of the spring and the misery of the lover is Petrarch, *Rime*, 310 ('The west wind returns and brings back sunny weather . . . but for me sighs return'). But here the hopelessness of the lover's (only pretended) suit lays waste the beauties of the season and the garden.

> Blasted with sighs, and súrrounded with tears,
>   Hither I come to seek the spring,
>   And at mine eyes, and at mine ears,
> Receive such balms, as else cure everything,
>   But O, self-traitor, I do bring   5
> The spider love, which transubstantiates all,
>   And can convert manna to gall,
> And that this place may thoroughly be thought
> True Paradise, I have the serpent brought.
>
> 'Twere wholesomer for me, that winter did   10
>   Benight the glory of this place,
>   And that a grave frost did forbid
> These trees to laugh and mock me to my face;
>   But that I may not this disgrace
> Endure, nor yet leave loving, Love let me   15
>   Some senseless piece of this place be;
> Make me a mandrake, so I may groan here,
> Or a stone fountain weeping out my year.
>
> Hither with crystal vials, lovers come,
>   And take my tears, which are Love's wine,   20
>   And try your mistress' tears at home,
> For all are false, that taste not just like mine;
>   Alas, hearts do not in eyes shine,
> Nor can you more judge women's thoughts by tears,
>   Than by her shadow, what she wears.   25
> O perverse sex, where none is true but she,
> Who's therefore true, because her truth kills me.

1 'Bitter tears rain from my face with a tormented wind of sighs, when I turn my eyes on you' (*Rime*, 17); *surrounded* 'drowned' (with the etymological sense of Latin *superundatus*).
5–9 In parody of gifts which lovers offer their mistresses (as Polyphemus to Galatea, Theocritus, 11; or Marlowe's Passionate Shepherd). Proverbially, 'where the bee sucks honey, the spider sucks poison': the poet's 'spider-love' sucks only poison, performing a 'counter-miracle' by turning manna 'like wafers made with honey' (Exodus 16: 31, and a figure of Christ, John 6: 31–3) to gall; and he brings the serpent that he might lose Eden.
12 *grave* 'heavy' (though some MSS read 'gray'); and opposed to the gaiety of the trees.
14–16 'But that I may not have to feel this disfavour, but still go on being in love, let me survive here deprived of sense.' In *Love's Deity*, 24, that 'Love may make me leave loving' is supposed a worse fate than unreciprocated loving; some MSS are defective at this point and others substitute 'nor leave this garden' at 15; but *1633* is supported by Huyghens's Dutch translation (1630), and at least one good early MS.
17–18 Deprived of sense, he can still love: 'Boughs live for love, and every flourishing tree in turn feels the passion' (Burton, *Anatomy*, 3.2.1.1); see *Nocturnal*, 33–4. The fork-rooted (and so humanoid) mandrake (mandragora) was supposed to shriek when uprooted; here it is only to groan (though *1633* and some MSS read 'grow'), much as Henry's wretched mourners live on 'so many mandrakes on his grave' (*Elegy on Prince Henry*, 54); Ovid writes of Niobe: 'But yet she wept . . . There upon a mountain's top / She weepeth still in stone' (*Metamorphoses*, 6:310–12, Golding).
19–22 Mourners, not lovers, were supposed to have stored their grief in tear-bottles (Psalms 56: 8 as well as in pagan antiquity); but 'The lover's tears are sweet, their mover makes them so' (Campion, *So tired are all my thoughts*, 9), and so a mistress's bitter tears would be testable as false.
25–6 *Love's Deity*, 24–5, varies the couplet.

A Valediction Forbidding Mourning

Izaak Walton quotes a corrupt version, describing it as a copy of verses Donne gave to his wife when he left for France with the Drury family in 1611. *1633* prints four poems titled as 'valedictions'; others share the occasion of parting. The subjects vary: here it is the expected reunion (hence the title), which overtakes the standard Platonic rationalizations of the inconsequence of parting.

As virtuous men pass mildly away,
    And whisper to their souls, to go,
Whilst some of their sad friends do say,
    The breath goes now, and some say, "No."

So let us melt, and make no noise,
    No tear-floods, nor sigh-tempests move,   5
'Twere profanation of our joys
    To tell the laity our love.

Moving of the earth brings harms and fears,
    Men reckon what it did and meant,   10
But trepidation of the spheres,
    Though greater far, is innocent.

Dull sublunary lovers' love
    (Whose soul is sense) cannot admit
Absence, because it doth remove   15
    Those things which elemented it.

But we by' a love, so much refined,
    That ourselves know not what it is,
Inter-assurèd of the mind,
    Care less, eyes, lips, hands to miss.   20

Our two souls therefore, which are one,
    Though I must go, endure not yet
A breach, but an expansion,
    Like gold to airy thinness beat.

If they be two, they are two so   25
    As stiff twin compasses are two,

1–4 'Cicero saith that to philosophise is no other thing than for a man to prepare himself to death . . . I verily believe, these fearful looks, and astonishing countenances wherewith we encompass it, are those that more amaze and terrify us, than death' (Montaigne, *Essays*, 1.19: 'That to philosophise is to learn how to die', Florio).
9–12 'Moved sometimes / With wicked people's execrable crimes . . . [God's] right hand doth make, / Not all the Earth, but part of it to quake' (Sylvester, *Divine Weeks*, 1.3:471–4); but the apparent oscillation of the stars (in fact owing to the movement of the earth's axis but explained by assuming a north–south motion of the 8th (starry) or 9th (crystalline) spheres) was part of the regular order of things.
13–16 'Terrestrial ('sublunary') lovers, animated by physical desire ('sense') cannot suffer to be apart, because absence removes the things ('eyes, lips, hands', 20) that make up their love.'
17–20 The love is refined and not the lovers. 'But we, made mutually confident about our spiritual affinity, by a love refined beyond our own comprehension, care less about missing our bodies': 'I never stooped so low, as they / Which on an eye, cheek, lip, can prey' (*Negative Love*, 1–2). MSS regularize the syllable count with 'and hands'; some early printings have 'Careless'.
24 The airiness of gold may suggest only lightness and flexibility (as in Herrick, *Julia's Petticoat*); but it may suggest cancelling the earthly (as when Shakespeare's Cleopatra becomes 'fire and air' and gives her 'other elements' to 'baser life' (*Antony*, V. ii. 288–9). The alchemical symbol for gold is a circle with its centre marked.

Thy soul the fixed foot, makes no show
　　To move, but doth, if the other do.

And though it in the centre sit,
　　Yet when the other far doth roam,   30
It leans, and harkens after it,
　　And grows erect, as that comes home.

Such wilt thou be to me, who must
　　Like the other foot, obliquely run.
Thy firmness makes my circle just,   35
　　And makes me end, where I begun.

25–36 'I am like the compass, keeping one foot in you as my centre; the other suffers the turns of fortune, but cannot do otherwise than return to you' (Guarini, *Madrigals*, 96). Whitney counts it among a wife's virtues to let her husband 'go where he please [and] at home to spend her days' (*Em-* *blems*, 93). The image of the compasses is common in Donne and elsewhere: the device of Donne's patron Doncaster was a pair of compasses with the motto 'It ended where it began' (*rediit unde fuit*); but how the analogy might work (or not) here is much debated.

A Valediction of Weeping

The occasion of parting yields a hyperbolical account of tears: 'As drops from a still . . . doth Cupid's fire provoke tears from a true lover's eyes' (Burton, *Anatomy*, 3.2.3). The central stanza is quoted in Samuel Johnson's *Life of Cowley* as exemplifying the metaphysical poets' tendency to abstruse conceit.

Let me pour forth
My tears before thy face, whilst I stay here,
For thy face coins them, and thy stamp they bear,
And by this mintage they are something worth,
　　For thus they be   5
　　Pregnant of thee,
Fruits of much grief they are, emblems of more,
When a tear falls, that *thou* falls which it bore,
So thou and I are nothing then, when on a divers shore.

On a round ball   10
A workman that hath copies by, can lay
An Europe, Afric, and an Asia,
And quickly make that, which was nothing, All,
　　So doth each tear,
　　Which thee doth wear,   15
A globe, yea world by that impression grow,
Till thy tears mixed with mine do overflow
This world, by waters sent from thee, my heaven dissolvèd so.

3–4 Stamped with the mistress's image the poet's tears acquire value; most current coinage would still carry Queen Elizabeth's image.
6 *pregnant* 'impressive' (Latin *premens*, repeating 'something worth'); but punningly 'with child' (Latin *praegnans*), carrying the image of the mistress).
7 *emblems of more* they carry the image of Ann More (who may reappear at 19), and their fragility figures the fragility of the lovers' union.
11 *copies* flat maps (gores) to be pasted on to the blank ball to make a geographical globe.
16 As in *The sun rising*, 21, 'She's all states.'
17–18 The tears of the reflected weeping mistress (the speaker's 'heaven') increase the tears he weeps and flood the world reflected in them.

O more than Moon,
Draw not up seas to drown me in thy sphere,   20
Weep me not dead, in thine arms, but forbear
To teach the sea, what it may do too soon,
    Let not the wind
    Example find,
To do me more harm, than it purposeth,   25
Since thou and I sigh one another's breath,
Whoe'er sighs most, is cruellest, and hastes the other's death.

19–20 'O, train me not, sweet mermaid, with thy note, / To drown me in thy sister's flood of tears' (Shakespeare, *Comedy of Errors*, III. ii. 45–6). Were she to weep, his reflection would drown in the sphere of her eye, and himself would die in her arms; but this 'possibility' is shadowed by the hyperbole that as 'more than Moon' (with whom Queen Elizabeth was poetically identified) she may draw tides so strong they reach the moon's sphere.
26–7 Like the 'last lamenting kiss, / Which sucks two souls, and vapours both away' (*The Expiration*, 1–2).

Holy Sonnets

Nineteen poems are given here, consisting of what were in the course of their history two independent sequences of twelve poems with eight poems in common, together with a remainder of three poems unconnected with either sequence. The two sequences were most probably written in 1609–10, though an early date in the 1590s has been suggested. The three others are later. The first twelve poems below appear under the capital roman numbers I–XII, in the order and under the general title *Holy Sonnets*, in the 1633 printing and in the MS collections deriving from papers probably prepared by Donne himself in 1614 and again in 1619. The next four, appearing under small Roman numbers i–iv, come from the alternative and probably earlier MS collection (where they stand instead of the set VII–X of the later authorized sequence) sometimes titled *Divine Meditations* and first printed in 1635. As it appears in the MSS, the form of this collection is: i, I, ii, XII, II, III, iii, IV, V, iv, VI, XI. The 1635 printing conflates the two sequences; and its order, adopted by Grierson and other editors, is: i, I, ii, II, iii, III, IV, iv, V, VI, VII, VIII, IX, X, XI, XII. The remaining three sonnets, given under the arabic numbers 1–3, come from the Westmoreland MS, now in the New York Public Library, prepared around 1620 by Donne's friend Rowland Woodward from a set of *Divine Meditations* expanded to sixteen by the addition of the alternative *Holy Sonnets* VII–X, and given in the order i, I, ii, XII, II, III, iii, IV, V, iv, VI, XI, VII, VIII, IX, X (as happens elsewhere in the MS tradition), and expanded further to nineteen by this small group. These were first printed by Gosse in 1894 and 1899. The nineteen sonnets are given here in the order proposed by Gardner (and followed by others), except that her inversion of ii and iii is ignored.

Some readers have taken individual sonnets as separate poems; and indeed some sonnets were early copied independently of the sequences to which they are reckoned to belong. But Gardner has interpreted the *1633* sequence I–XII to represent, first a sequence of six poems on Last Things (death and judgement and therefore dominated by fear), followed by a less obvious sequence of six expanded from an original two (XI and XII) on atoning love (three on God's love for man, three on man's reciprocal love for God). The putatively earlier sequence given in some MSS contained, instead of the sequence on atoning love, one on penitential themes. In either case the whole becomes a sustained meditation on contrition. Either organization is produced by editorial second thoughts, even if they are Donne's own; even if conceived separately, the poems are readily organized sequentially. Important among influences that might favour thematic grouping is the inescapable one of Jesuit meditation (carried into organized collections such as Jean de Sponde's *Sonnets sur la mort* and Jean de La Ceppède's *Douze méditations sur le sacre mystère de notre rédemption*). Donne's poems share their worked-up emotionalism with his own erotic lyrics (though at the service of more intensely scrutinized preoccupations), their inward focus on mental processes with secular traditions of sonnet writing, and their spiritual pathos with medieval Franciscan hymnody.

Earlier collections of holy sonnets include Henry Constable's *Spiritual Sonnets* (published only in the nineteenth century, but written in the 1590s), Henry Lok's *Sundry Christian Passions* (1593, 1597), Barnabe Barnes's *Divine Century of Spiritual Sonnets* (1595), William Alabaster's *Divine Meditations* (1597–8). Donne's are predominantly Italian in kind: the octets are densely rhymed, and turn dramatically on the opening of the sestet; the couplet endings are unemphatic. The scheme abbaabbacdcdee is common in Sidney; the scheme abbaabbacddcee (used in I, V, VI, VII, VIII, IX, XI and 3) is exceedingly rare in English.

I As due by many titles I resign

Body and soul belong to God, but control of the
divine territory is usurped by an alien wickedness.

> As due by many titles I resign
> Myself to thee, O God, first I was made
> By thee, and for thee, and when I was decayed
> Thy blood bought that, the which before was thine,
> I am thy son, made with thyself to shine,   5
> Thy servant, whose pains thou hast still repaid,
> Thy sheep, thine image, and till I betrayed
> Myself, a temple of thy Spirit divine;
> Why doth the devil then usurp on me?
> Why doth he steal nay ravish that's thy right?   10
> Except thou rise and for thine own work fight,
> O I shall soon despair, when I do see
> That thou lov'st mankind well, yet wilt'not choose me.
> And Satan hates me, yet is loath to lose me.

1–6 Echoing the Catechism: 'First, I learn to believe in
God the Father, who hath made me . . . Secondly, in God
the Son, who hath redeemed me . . . Thirdly, in God the
Holy Ghost, who sanctifieth me'; *many titles* the sense is
legal; the Jesuit Luis de la Puente's *Meditations* (translated
1619) uses a similar conveyancing metaphor.
3 *decayed* 'Then if thy brother be . . . fallen in decay with
thee; then thou shalt relieve him' (Leviticus 25: 35: on the
redemption of land).
5 'Then shall the righteous shine forth as the sun in the
kingdom of their father' (Matthew 13: 43), with a character-
istic pun on son/sun.

6 Matthew 20: 1–16 (the parable of the labourers in the
vineyard).
7 *sheep* Matthew 18: 12–13 (the parable of the lost sheep);
image 'And God said, let us make man in our image' (Gen-
esis 1: 26).
8 'Know ye not that your body is the temple of the Holy
Ghost . . . and ye are not your own?' (1 Corinthians 6: 19).
13 Matthew 20: 16: 'for many be called but few chosen'.
1633's contraction mark on 'wilt'not' may force the accent
on to 'me' and skew the rhyme with 'lose me'.

II O my black soul! now thou art summoned

The fear of damnation is relieved by the possibility of
repentance. But repentance is difficult and its efficacy
controversial; the movement from black through red
to white may be only a symbolical (alchemically based)
convenience. The note is surer in the late *An Hymn to
the Saints*, 33–6: 'And, who shall dare to ask then
when I am / Dyed scarlet in the blood of that pure
Lamb, / Whether that colour which is scarlet then, /
Were black or white before in eyes of men?' Burton,
Anatomy, 3.4.2.6 brings together some of the same
conceits: 'He looks down from Heaven upon Earth,
that he may hear the mourning of prisoners, and de-
liver the children of death. And though our sins be
red as scarlet, he can make them white as snow.'

> O my black soul! now thou art summonèd
> By sickness, Death's herald, and champion;
> Thou art like a pilgrim, which abroad hath done
> Treason, and durst not turn to whence he's fled,
> Or like a thief, which till death's doom be read,   5
> Wisheth himself deliverèd from prison;

2 *herald, and champion* The near-dead metaphor in 'herald'
('precursor') is quickened by the collocation with 'cham-
pion' (defender of the royal title, here Death's).
3 *pilgrim* 'stranger'.
4 *turn to whence he's fled* 'return to the place from which
he's fled' ('home').

5–8 The condemned prisoner appears also in *Obsequies to
the Lord Harington*, 21–3.
5 *doom* 'judgement'.

But damned and haled to execution,
Wisheth that still he might be imprisonèd;
Yet grace, if thou repent, thou canst not lack;
But who shall give thee that grace to begin?   10
O make thyself with holy mourning black,
And red with blushing, as thou art with sin;
Or wash thee in Christ's blood, which hath this might
That being red, it dyes red souls to white.

7   *damned and haled* 'condemned and hauled'.
9   *if thou repent* The parenthesis is already ominous, raising the question explicit in the next line.
10–14   'Though your sins be as scarlet, they shall be as white as snow' (Isaiah 1: 18); 'The blood of Jesus . . . cleanseth

us from all sin' (1 John 1: 7); the great multitude of white-robed saints standing before the throne of God had 'washed their robes and made them white in the blood of the Lamb' (Revelation 7: 14).

III This is my play's last scene, here heavens appoint

The fear of damnation is relieved by wishing away the sins belonging to the body and offering the self for judgement as if spiritually purified.

This is my play's last scene, here heavens appoint
My pilgrimage's last mile; and my race
Idly, yet quickly run, hath this last pace,
My span's last inch, my minute's latest point,
And gluttonous death, will instantly unjoint   5
My body, and soul, and I shall sleep a space,
But my' ever-waking part shall see that face,
Whose fear already shakes my every joint:
Then, as my soul, to' heaven her first seat, takes flight,
And earth-born body, in the earth shall dwell,   10
So, fall my sins, that all may have their right,
To where they' are bred, and would press me, to hell.
Impute me righteous, thus purged of evil,
For thus I leave the world, the flesh, the devil.

1–4   The conceit of life as a play goes back at least as far as Plato (it is not biblical); as a pilgrimage famously to Hebrews 11: 13; as a race to Hebrews 12: 1; as a span to the Prayer Book version of Psalms 39: 5: 'thou hast made my days as it were a span long.'
3   *Idly, yet quickly* The paradox is spurious: his race is run in the one way because empty and ineffective, the other because it is short; *pace* step, or a measure of distance.
4   *latest* Some MSS read 'last', which is unmetrical, but sustains the accumulated instances of the one word; the 'minute' is the first strictly temporal measure. *point* is a full rhyme with 'appoint'; so 'unjoint'/ 'joint' following.
5   *gluttonous* 'death shall feed on them' (Psalms 49: 14, 'gnaweth upon them' in the Prayer Book); *unjoint* 'sever'; but hinting at the primary sense of 'disjoint' as if dying were like being butchered.
6–7   *I shall sleep . . . face* 'I sleep, but my heart waketh' (Song of Solomon 5: 2); 'For now we see through a glass, darkly; but then face to face' (1 Corinthians 13: 12), 'I will behold thy face in righteousness: I shall be satisfied, when I

awake, with thy likeness' (Psalms 17: 15), echoes which weigh against the terrifying face being Satan's.
7   Some MSS read 'Or presently, I know not, see that face', which seems to offer a choice between the soul's resting an intermediate time before judgement and its immediate ascension to heaven at death. The revision promotes Donne's later view that the virtuous soul immediately enjoys bliss.
9–10   'Earth is the centre of my body, heaven is the centre of my soul; these two are the natural places of these two' (*Devotions*, 2 'Meditation').
11–12   Southwell (*Sin's Heavy Load*) imagines the human soul taking flight, discharged of the weight of sin which now presses on Christ.
13   *Impute me righteous* 'God imputeth righteousness without works' (Romans 4: 6); but Donne imagines the possibility that he is already sinless.
14   'From fornication, and all other deadly sin, and from all the deceits of the world, the flesh, and the devil: Good Lord, deliver us' (Litany of the *Book of Common Prayer*).

IV   At the round earth's imagined corners, blow

A plea for time to repent as the summons to judgement is imagined. Hooker writes on the difficult relationship, confronted at the sonnet's climax, between Christ's sacrifice and the sinner's repentance: 'It is therefore true, that our Lord Jesus Christ by one most precious and propitiatory sacrifice . . . hath thereby once reconciled us to God, purchased his general free pardon, and turned away divine indignation from mankind. But we are not for that cause to think any office of penitence either needless or fruitless on our own behalf' (*Laws of Ecclesiastical Polity*, 6.5.3).

At the round earth's imagined corners, blow
Your trumpets, angels, and arise, arise
From death, you numberless infinities
Of souls, and to your scattered bodies go,
All whom the flood did, and fire shall o'erthrow,   5
All whom war, dearth, age, agues, tyrannies,
Despair, law, chance, hath slain, and you whose eyes,
Shall behold God, and never taste death's woe,
But let them sleep, Lord, and me mourn a space,
For, if above all these, my sins abound,   10
'Tis late to ask abundance of thy grace,
When we are there; here on this lowly ground,
Teach me how to repent; for that's as good
As if thou' hadst sealed my pardon, with thy blood.

1–2 'I saw four angels standing on the four corners of the earth, holding the four winds of the earth' (Revelation 7: 1: though not these, but the seven angels of Revelation 8: 2 blow trumpets); *imagined* not so much 'fancied' as 'pictorially figured'; this meditation proceeds from an exceptionally well-realized 'composition of place'.
2–4 As in the earlier version of *Holy Sonnets*, 3:7, Donne supposes that the soul sleeps before the Judgement.
5–7 'The flood that did, and dreadful fire that shall, / Drown, and burn up the malice of the earth' (Greville, *Caelica*, 88.7–8); the final chorus of Buchanan's *Baptistes* offers a similar rhetorically random litany of disasters: 'Whom fire spares, sea doth drown; whom sea, / Pestilent air doth send to clay; / Who war scapes, sickness takes away' (Burton's translation, *Anatomy*, 1.1.1.1). God's four judgements on Jerusalem (Ezekiel 14: 21) are 'the sword, and the famine, and the noisome beast, and the pestilence'; Death on his pale horse (Revelation 6: 8) has power 'to kill with the sword, and with hunger, and with death, and with the beasts of the earth.'
6 *dearth 1633* and all MSS but one read 'death', but this is in itself awkward, and the quotations from Ezekiel and Revelation both suggest the move from war to famine.
8 'We shall not all sleep, but we shall be changed, in a moment, in the twinkling of an eye, at the last trump . . . we shall be changed' (1 Corinthians 15: 51–2).
12 *there* i.e. at the Last Judgement.
13–14 'For godly sorrow worketh repentance to salvation not to be repented of' (2 Corinthians 7: 10).
14 *my* The personal sense of the possessive is specific, but the formulation is still strong. Hooker writes: 'There is not anything that we could do that could pacify God . . . if the goodness and mercy of our Lord Jesus Christ were not' (*Ecclesiastical Polity*, 6.5.3); but at 6.5.5 he calls repentance 'a grinding of the old Adam even into dust and powder, a deliverance out of the prisons of Hell'.

V   If poisonous minerals, and if that tree

His humanity opens the poet to damnation; but acknowledging his sinfulness, he prays for mercy.

> If poisonous minerals, and if that tree,
> Whose fruit threw death on else immortal us,
> If lecherous goats, if serpents envious
> Cannot be damned; alas; why should I be?
> Why should intent or reason, born in me,   5
> Make sins, else equal, in me, more heinous?
> And mercy being easy, and glorious
> To God, in his stern wrath, why threatens he?
> But who am I, that dare dispute with thee?
> O God, O! of thine only worthy blood,   10
> And my tears, make a heavenly Lethean flood,
> And drown in it my sins' black memory,
> That thou remember them, some claim as debt,
> I think it mercy, if thou wilt forget.

1–4   Despite such texts as Romans 8: 22 ('the whole creation groaneth and travaileth in pain together') it is usually supposed that irrational entities lack immortal souls and, though there are popular and philosophical currents of thought that would allow beasts salvation, cannot be damned. 'Only perchance beasts sin not; wretched we / Are beasts in all, but white integrity' (*To Sir Henry Wotton* ('Sir, more than kisses'), 40–1). The list of malign entities comprises none the less a portrayal of Hell. Goats are proverbially lecherous (as in Spenser, *Faerie Queene*, 1.4.24); and serpents envious (*Faerie Queene* 1.4.31); *that tree . . . threw death* 'of the tree of the knowledge of good and evil, thou shalt not eat of it: for in the day that thou eatest thereof thou shalt surely die'

(Genesis 2: 17). Shakespeare uses 'throw' similarly: the adder's tongue 'may with a mortal touch / Throw death' (*Richard II*, III. ii. 21–2).

11   *heavenly Lethean flood* Lethe being an underworld river, there is an oxymoron hinted.

12   *black memory* The epithet is transferred from 'sins', but suggests the obscurity of forgetting.

13–14   On Psalms 19: 12 ('Cleanse thou me from secret faults') Donne writes that David must entreat God to remember his sins: 'Remember them, O Lord, for else they will not fall into my pardon' (*Sermons*, 5.16). But David also asks God to forget: 'Remember not the sins of my youth' (Psalms 25: 7).

VI   Death be not proud, though some have called thee

The fear of death becomes a mere puzzle, and the poet is reassured of eternal life. The first line is alluded to in the opening of the *Elegy on Mrs Bulstrode* (died 4 August, 1609): 'Death I recant, and say, unsaid by me / What'er hath slipped, that might diminish thee.' Donne's recantation is itself rebuked in another *Elegy on Mrs Bulstrode*, probably by the Countess of Bedford, beginning 'Death be not proud, thy hand gave not this blow'.

> Death be not proud, though some have called thee
> Mighty and dreadful, for, thou art not so,
> For, those, whom thou think'st, thou dost overthrow,
> Die not, poor death, nor yet canst thou kill me;
> From rest and sleep, which but thy pictures be,   5
> Much pleasure, then from thee, much more must flow,
> And soonest our best men with thee do go,

2   *mighty and dreadful* properly epithets of God (Psalms 24: 8, Daniel 9: 4).

3–4   Because 'this mortal shall have put on immortality' (1 Corinthians 15: 54).

5   *pictures* Sleep is proverbially the 'image' of death; 'picture' is imaginatively stronger.

7   Proverbially 'The good die young.'

Rest of their bones, and souls' delivery.
Thou art slave to fate, chance, kings, and desperate men,
And dost with poison, war, and sickness dwell.   10
And poppy, or charms can make us sleep as well,
And better than thy stroke; why swell'st thou then?
One short sleep past, we wake eternally,
And death shall be no more, Death thou shalt die.

8   The revision to 'bones' from an earlier 'bodies' is grimmer; but Death's service becomes Christlike: 'the creature itself also shall be delivered from the bondage of corruption into the glorious liberty of the children of God' (Romans 8: 21); 'There shall come out of Sion the Deliverer' (Romans 11: 26).

12   *swell'st* with pride.
12–13   *better . . . wake* 'Now is it high time to awake out of sleep: for now is our salvation nearer' (Romans 13: 11). As in *Holy Sonnets* 3 and 4 the soul must wait to enjoy bliss.
14   'Death, I will be thy death' (Hosea 13: 14, Geneva).

VII   *Spit in my face you Jews, and pierce my side*

More culpable than Christ's killers, the poet offers to submit to his humiliations. The Douai Bible's annotation on Romans 8: 17 ('Yet so, if we suffer with him, that we may be also glorified with him') reads: 'Christ's pains or passions have not so satisfied for all, that Christian men may be discharged of their particular suffering or satisfying for each man's own part: neither be our pains nothing worth to the attainment of Heaven, because Christ hath done enough. But quite contrary: he was by his passion exalted to the glory of Heaven: therefore we by compassion or partaking with him in the like passions, shall attain to be followers with him in his kingdom.'

Spit in my face you Jews, and pierce my side,
Buffet, and scoff, scourge, and crucify me,
For I have sinned, and sinned, and only he,
Who could do no iniquity, hath died:
But by my death cannot be satisfied   5
My sins, which pass the Jews' impiety:
They killed once an inglorious man, but I
Crucify him daily, being now glorified;
Oh let me then, his strange love still admire:
Kings pardon, but he bore our punishment.   10
And Jacob came clothed in vile harsh attire
But to supplant, and with gainful intent.
God clothed himself in vile man's flesh, that so
He might be weak enough to suffer woe.

3–4   'He hath made him to be sin for us, that knew no sin' (2 Corinthians 5: 21)
4–5   *by my death cannot be satisfied / My sins* Because it is Christ alone 'Whom God hath set forth to be a propitiation through faith in his blood, to declare his righteousness for the remission of sins' (Romans 3: 25).
7–8   *I crucify him daily* 'they crucify to themselves the Son of God afresh' (Hebrews 6: 6); *glorified* Despite the awkwardness, qualifying 'him' (Christ).

9   *strange* 'extreme'; but also 'incomprehensible' in ways restated in the 'greater wonder' of the following sonnet.
11–12   *Jacob . . . supplant* Jacob wore goatskins to simulate the hairiness of his elder twin Esau (Genesis 27: 16) and usurp his rights as firstborn. Esau complained (punning on the Hebrew root), 'Is he not rightly named Jacob? for he hath supplanted me' (Genesis 27: 36).

VIII   Why are we by all creatures waited on?

The poet asks why created nature is subject to man;
and why the Creator put himself to man's service.

> Why are we by all creatures waited on?
> Why do the prodigal elements supply
> Life and food to me, being more pure than I,
> Simple, and further from corruption?
> Why brook'st thou, ignorant horse, subjection?   5
> Why dost thou bull, and boar, so sillily
> Dissemble weakness, and by' one man's stroke die,
> Whose whole kind, you might swallow and feed upon?
> Weaker I am, woe is me, and worse than you,
> You have not sinned, nor need be timorous,   10
> But wonder at a greater wonder, for to us
> Created nature doth these things subdue,
> But their Creator, whom sin, nor nature tied,
> For us, his creatures, and his foes, hath died.

1   *are we* am I (onc MS).

2–4   The elements (generally earth, air, fire, water) are by definition simple; compounded, they are unstable and corruptible; *prodigal* 'lavish', for the reason given.

5–8   God gave man dominion over the beasts before the Fall (Genesis 1: 28) and again after the Flood (Genesis 9: 2–3).

6–7   *sillily / Dissemble* 'simulate without motive (and therefore pitifully)'.

11   *1635* cuts the second 'wonder' to regularize the line. The 'wonder' is the 'strange love' of the previous sonnet.

12   *Created nature . . . Creator* Created nature is the world of creatures. The antithesis is witty: Augustine (*De Trinitate*, 15.1) calls God 'Nature not created but creating'.

13   *whom sin, nor nature tied* God acts for us 'according to the good pleasure of his will' (Ephesians 1: 5).

14   *foes* 'the friendship of the world is enmity with God' (James 4: 4).

IX   What if this present were the world's last night?

Thinking on doomsday, the poet turns to a picture not of Christ the Judge, but Christ Crucified, and deflects his terror of the end by reflecting on Christ's pity for men. What roused compassion in *Holy Sonnet* VII here offers reassurance.

> What if this present were the world's last night?
> Mark in my heart, O soul, where thou dost dwell,
> The picture of Christ crucified, and tell
> Whether his countenance can thee affright,
> Tears in his eyes quench the amazing light,   5
> Blood fills his frowns, which from his pierced head fell.
> And can that tongue adjudge thee unto hell,
> Which prayed forgiveness for his foes' fierce spite?
> No, no: but as in my idolatry
> I said to all my profane mistresses,   10

5–6   *Sermons*, 4.13 on John 11: 35 ('Jesus wept') plays more luridly with blood and tears: 'here all the body was eye; every pore of his body made an eye by tears of blood'; *amazing light* 'dreadful light'; in Revelation 19: 12 'His eyes were as a flame of fire.' Sight was sometimes reckoned to involve emission of beams from the eye.

8   *prayed forgiveness* 'Father, forgive them' spoken from the cross (Luke 23: 34); *foes' fierce spite* 'They were the more fierce' of the chief priests and the people rejecting Pilate's appeasement (Luke 23: 5); one MS reads 'rank' for 'fierce'.

9–12   Donne avoids this Platonic conceit in his erotic persuasions (though *Valediction of the Book*, 35–6, has 'For, though mind be the heaven, where love doth sit, / Beauty's convenient type may be to figure it.'

Beauty, of pity, foulness only is
A sign of rigour: so I say to thee,
To wicked spirits are horrid shapes assigned,
This beauteous form assumes a piteous mind.

14 'In his compassion he takes on this parody of beauty.' All MSS read 'assures'. The octet makes plain that the image of Christ crucified is ugly. Notions of the ugly and the beautiful are reversed by the recognition that Christ is piteous ('the Lord is very pitiful,' James 5: 11) and has taken on deformity; the inverted syntax throws the shocking oddity of the reversal into relief: '*this* beauteous form' is an affront to expectations. A similar shocking irony informs La Ceppède, *Les Théorèmes*, 1.3.20, addressing the Church: 'Belle pour qui ce beau meurt en vous bien-aimant . . . Voyez s'il fut jamais un si parfait amant.'

X   *Batter my heart, three-personed God; for, you*

The poet prays that God renew him or, occupied as he is by an enemy, that God repossess him. A confusion of possible metaphors complicates the poem, or at least the commentary on it. The primary conceit is military, complicated by a parenthetical allusion to tinkering in the first quatrain, and by the casting of the defecting city or state as an adulterous female: Hosea's sustained analogy between his wife and Gomer's infidelity to him and Israel's to Jehovah supplies a biblical precedent. The standard Petrarchist military analogies of erotic endeavour (as in Sidney's *Astrophil and Stella*, 36: 'Stella, whence doth these new assaults arise, / A conquered, yielding, ransacked heart to win?') compromise the clarity of the primary analogy, the more so since Donne's concern is personal.

Batter my heart, three-personed God; for, you
As yet but knock, breath, shine, and seek to mend;
That I may rise, and stand, o'erthrow me, 'and bend
Your force, to break, blow, burn and make me new.
I, like an usurped town, to' another due,   5
Labour to' admit you, but O, to no end,
Reason your viceroy in me, me should defend,
But is captíved, and proves weak or untrue,
Yet dearly' I love you,' and would be lov'd fain,
But am betrothed unto your enemy,   10
Divorce me, 'untie, or break that knot again,
Take me to you, imprison me, for I
Except you 'enthral me, never shall be free,
Nor ever chaste, except you ravish me.

1   *Batter* as in battering against walls or gates.
2   *knock, breathe, shine* The first verb mitigates the 'batter' ('Behold I stand at the door and knock', Revelation 3: 20); the others modulate to a sense appropriate to improving a defective metal vessel. But to suggest that mending would suffice would suggest that man was naturally good: the demand is therefore for complete renewal.
5   *to another due* rightfully belonging to another, the 'you' of the next line.
7   *Reason, your viceroy* Sylvester (*Weeks and Works*, 1.6:528–37) uses a similar allegory: God plants 'intellectual Power' in the head that 'it might (as from a citadel) / Command the members that too-oft rebell / Against his Rule' and 'Reason, there / Keeping continual garrison' might subdue the vices.

8   *captíved* standard for 'captured'.
9   A line difficult in the mouth: some editors remove the contraction mark before 'and'.
10   *your enemy* 'the world', because as in *Holy Sonnet* VIII, 'the friendship of the world is enmity with God' (James 4: 4).
11   *knot* of marriage.
12–13   Paul calls himself 'the prisoner of the Jesus Christ' (Ephesians 3: 1); and at Romans 6: 18 says 'Being then made free from sin, ye became the servants of righteousness.'
14   In *Holy Sonnet* I, Satan 'ravishes' God's rights in the poet; here God is to 'ravish' them back. The normally secondary sense of 'sexually forcing' is thrown into prominence by the antithesis with 'chaste'.

XI   Wilt thou love God, as he thee! then digest

The poet reflects that God loves us as adopted chil-
dren to be recovered at any price when lost.

> Wilt thou love God, as he thee! then digest,
> My soul, this wholesome meditation,
> How God the Spirit, by angels waited on
> In heaven, doth make his temple in thy breast,
> The Father having begot a Son most blest,　　　　　　5
> And still begetting (for he ne'er begun)
> Hath deigned to choose thee by adoption,
> Co-heir to' his glory', and Sabbath's endless rest;
> And as a robbed man, which by search doth find
> His stol'n stuff sold, must lose or buy' it again:　　　10
> The Son of glory came down, and was slain,
> Us whom he' had made, and Satan stoln, to unbind.
> 'Twas much, that man was made like God before,
> But, that God should be made like man, much more.

3 *by angels waited on* 'thousand thousands ministered unto him, and ten thousand times ten thousand stood before him' (Daniel 7: 10).

4 *temple* 'Know ye not that your body is the temple of the Holy Ghost?' (1 Corinthians 6: 19).

6 *he ne'er begun* he is the 'son most blest', who never began because 'The same was in the beginning with God' (John 1: 2). God meanwhile continues to 'beget' adoptive children (John 1: 12–13).

7 'But ye have received the Spirit of adoption . . . The Spirit itself beareth witness . . . that we are the children of God . . . heirs of God, and joint-heirs [Douai has 'co-heirs' from the Vulgate 'coheredes'] with Christ' (Romans 8: 15–17).

9–10 *unbind* Victims of robbery could obtain release of stolen property at a price.

13–14 'So God created man in his own image' (Genesis 1: 27); 'Great is the mystery of godliness: God was manifest in the flesh, justified in the Spirit, seen of angels, preached unto the Gentiles, believed on in the world, received up into glory' (1 Timothy 3: 16).

XII   Father, part of his double interest

Christ has a double entitlement to the Kingdom, as the son of the King and as a man. The latter entitle-ment is doubly invested in humankind: by the legal dispensation of the Old Testament, and by the quick-ening dispensation of the New. The difficulties of the conceit are reflected in some copyists' confusion over pronouns in the sestet.

> Father, part of his double interest
> Unto thy kingdom, thy Son gives to me,
> His jointure in the knotty Trinity,
> He keeps, and gives to me his death's conquest.
> This Lamb, whose death, with life the world hath blest,　　　5
> Was from the world's beginning slain, and he
> Hath made two wills, which with the legacy
> Of his and thy kingdom, do thy sons invest,
> Yet such are these laws, that men argue yet
> Whether a man those statutes can fulfil;　　　　　　10

6 *from the world's beginning slain* According to the 'eternal purpose which he purposed in Christ Jesus' (Ephesians 3: 11), the Lamb was 'slain from the foundation of the world' (Revelation 13: 8).

7–8 *wills, which . . . do* Some MSS begin a new sentence after 'wills', with 'he' taking the verb 'doth'. Other MSS retain 'doth' despite emending 'he' to 'which'; *two wills* the two Testaments.

9 *these* Some MSS read 'thy'; others 'those'.

None doth, but thy all-healing grace and Spirit,
Revive again what law and letter kill,
Thy law's abridgement, and thy last command
Is all but love; O let this last Will stand!

11 'His mercy is above all his works, able to satisfy for all men's sins, a ransom for all. His mercy is a panacea, a balsam for an afflicted soul, a sovereign medicine' (Burton, *Anatomy*, 3.4.2.6).

12 *Revive again* Revive and quicken (some MSS); 'the letter killeth, but the spirit giveth life' (2 Corinthians 3: 6).
13 *last command* 'Love one another' (John 13: 34).

Sonnets from 1635

i   *Thou hast made me, and shall thy work decay*

Faced with death, the poet prays in a heavy rewriting of Psalm 6 (the first of the so-called Penitential Psalms) that he may be able to turn to God. Placed first in 1635 and the MS tradition on which it relies, it brings together the themes of death and guilt and reconciliation which run through the *Divine Meditations*.

Thou hast made me, and shall thy work decay?
Repair me now, for now mine end doth haste,
I run to death, and death meets me as fast,
And all my pleasures are like yesterday,
I dare not move my dim eyes any way,   5
Despair behind, and death before doth cast
Such terror, and my feebled flesh doth waste
By sin in it, which it t'wards hell doth weigh;
Only thou art above, and when towards thee
By thy leave I can look, I rise again;   10
But our old subtle foe so tempteth me,
That not one hour myself I can sustain,
Thy grace may wing me to prevent his art
And thou like adamant draw mine iron heart.

1 'Shall the thing formed say to him that formed it, Why hast thou made me thus?' (Romans 9: 20).
2 *Repair me* 'He healeth the broken in heart' (Psalms 147: 3).
4 *like yesterday* Calvin writes on Psalms 90: 4 ('as yesterday when it is past') 'whatever is still before our eyes has a hold upon our minds, but we are less affected by the recollection of what is past.'
7 *feebled* a standard form at the time, supplied from the MSS; 1635 has 'feeble'.
10 *By thy leave* God's compassion 'is not of him that willeth, nor of him that runneth, but of God that showeth mercy' (Romans 9: 16).

12 *myself I can* Some MSS have the less awkward 'I can myself'.
13 *wing* 'hasten', but also, since the soul ascends, 'supply with wings'; *prevent* 'frustrate', but the word is chosen because the grace is 'prevenient'.
14 *like adamant* 'Repentance is . . . an attractive lodestone to draw God's mercy and graces unto us' (Burton, *Anatomy*, 3.4.52). Georgette de Montenay's *Emblemes* (1571, etc.) 'Non tuis viribus' ('Not by thy own powers') shows a heart drawn upward by a suspended 'adamant', identified with the magnet by way of a false etymology ('adamare', 'to love').

ii *O might those sighs and tears return again*

The poet grieves for sins past, themselves sins of misplaced grieving. 'For godly sorrow worketh repentance to salvation not to be repented of: but the sorrow of the world worketh death' (2 Corinthians 7: 10).

O might those sighs and tears return again
Into my breast and eyes, which I have spent,
That I might in this holy discontent
Mourn with some fruit, as I have mourned in vain;
In mine idolatry what showers of rain   5
Mine eyes did waste? what griefs my heart did rent?
That sufferance was my sin I now repent,
'Cause I did suffer I must suffer pain.
Th'hydropic drunkard, and night-scouting thief,
The itchy lecher, and self-tickling proud   10
Have the remembrance of past joys, for relief
Of coming ills: to (poor) me is allowed
No ease; for, long, yet vehement grief hath been
Th'effect and cause, the punishment and sin.

4   *Mourn with some fruit* 'He that goeth forth and weepeth, bearing precious seed, shall doubtless come again with rejoicing, bringing his sheaves with him' (Psalms 126: 6).
5   *mine idolatry* Lovers conventionally idolize their mistresses: 'but as in my idolatry / I said to all my profane mistresses' (*Holy Sonnets,* IX); here the word takes a more serious inflexion from Colossians, 3: 5: 'Mortify therefore your members which are upon the earth; fornication, uncleanness, inordinate affection, evil concupiscence, and covetousness, which is idolatry.'
6   *rent* 'rend' (standard).
7   *sufferance* combining the senses of 'grief' and 'license' (as

by 'suffering our thoughts to look back with pleasure on the sins which we have committed', *Sermons,* 1.5) to suggest the fraudulent indulgence of grief.
9   Horace advises the hydropical (swollen with excess liquid) man to adopt the regimen of the nocturnal thief: 'Thieves rise at all times of the night to murder . . . take heed, for dropsies breed of sloth ['curres hydropicus']' (*Epistles,* 1.2.32–4, Drant); Donne's 'hydropic' means rather 'unquenchably thirsty'; his 'night-scouting' is modelled on Latin *noctivagus.*
10   *itchy* 'lecherous'; but also 'poxed'; *self-tickling* self-flattering.
12   *(poor)* the brackets contain the irruption of self-pity.

iii   *I am a little world made cunningly*

In fear of death the poet prays, first that he may repent of his sins, then that he may earnestly love God.

I am a little world made cunningly
Of elements, and an angelic sprite,
But black sin hath betrayed to endless night
My world's both parts, and (O) both parts must die.
You which beyond that heaven which was most high   5

1   *cunningly* 'with skill': God is represented as a craftsman, as in *Holy Sonnets* I. The body is composed of elements (earth, air, fire and water); the spirit is called 'angelic' because it is pure.
3–4   'For we know that the law is spiritual: but I am carnal, sold under sin' and 'O wretched man that I am! who shall deliver me from the body of this death?' (Romans 7: 14, 24). The death of the soul is entertained in Jewish scripture: 'the soul that sinneth, it shall die' (Ezekiel 18: 4) and 'in death there is no remembrance of thee' (Psalms 6: 5). But though

'the wages of sin is death' (Romans 6: 23), the soul may or must be born again 'of water and of the spirit' (John 3: 5).
4–8   Donne writes To the Countess of Bedford ('T'have written then'), 67–8: 'We'have added to the world Virginia, 'and sent / Two new stars lately to the firmament' – referring to the *novae* of 1572 and 1604. Galileo's *Starry Messenger* (1610) added four of Jupiter's moons. Donne here proposes new astronomical and geographical discoveries as a fresh source of tears. Other hyperbolically ample floods of tears are refused in *A Valediction of Weeping* and *The Canonization.*

Have found new spheres, and of new land can write,
Pour new seas in mine eyes, that so I might
Drown my world with my weeping earnestly,
Or wash it if it must be drowned no more:
But O it must be burnt, alas the fire   10
Of lust and envy burnt it heretofore,
And made it fouler. Let their flames retire,
And burn me O Lord, with a fiery zeal
Of thee and thy house, which doth in eating heal.

9   God promises Noah, 'neither shall all flesh be cut off any more by the waters of a flood; neither shall there any more be a flood to destroy the earth' (Genesis 9: 11). Baptism replaces the flood, when in the ark 'eight souls were saved by water. The like figure whereunto even baptism doth also now save us' (1 Peter 3: 20–1).

10   'The heavens shall pass away with a great noise, and the elements shall melt with fervent heat, the earth also and the works that are therein shall be burned up' (2 Peter 3: 10).

13–14   'For the zeal of thine house hath eaten me up' (Psalms 69: 9).

iv   *If faithful souls be alike glorified*

Confident of the sincerity of his repentance, the poet decides it is unknowable by any but God. 'Then hear thou in heaven thy dwelling place, and forgive, and do, and give to every man according to his ways, whose heart thou knowest; (for thou, even thou only, knowest the hearts of the children of men)' (1 Kings 8: 39). As in *Holy Sonnet* ii, the thoughts are sorrowful 'for godly sorrow worketh repentance' (2 Corinthians 7: 10).

If faithful souls be alike glorified
As angels, then my father's soul doth see,
And adds this even to full felicity,
That valiantly I Hell's wide mouth o'erstride:
But if our minds to these souls be descried   5
By circumstances, and by signs that be
Apparent in us, not immediately,
How shall my mind's white truth by them be tried?
They see idolatrous lovers weep and mourn,
And vile blasphemous conjurers to call   10
On Jesus' name, and pharisaical
Dissemblers feign devotion. Then turn
O pensive soul, to God, for he knows best
Thy grief, for he put it into my breast.

1–8   Aquinas, *Summa Theologica*, Supplement, 72.1 summarizes some of the possibilities of what the saints in Heaven may know. The confusion of the saintly dead and angels is allowed in Hooker, *Ecclesiastical Government*, 1.6.1 and blamed in Calvin, *Institutes*, 3.20.23. Bacon is clear on the distinction of human and angelic intelligence: 'To God . . . and it may be to the angels and higher intelligences it belongs to have an affirmative knowledge of forms immediately, and from the first contemplation. But this assuredly is more than man can do' (*Novum Organum*, 2.15); men proceed inductively. Donne's father died when he was four.

3   *adds . . . to full felicity* The paradox is playful; but in *Obsequies to the Lord Harington*, 5–10, Donne also imagines gladdening the heart of the dead.

4   *o'erstride* leap over.

10   *vile blasphemous conjurers* In Acts 19: 13 'vagabond Jews' attempt an exorcism by calling on Jesus' name.

11–12   *pharisaical / Dissemblers* 'Woe unto you, scribes and Pharisees, hypocrites' (Matthew 23: 13); 'And when thou prayest, thou shalt not be as the hypocrites are . . . pray to thy Father which is in secret; and thy Father which seeth in secret shall reward thee openly' (Matthew 6: 5–6).

12–14   Donne turns from his earthly father to his heavenly one: 'Look down from heaven . . . Doubtless thou art our father, though Abraham be ignorant of us, and Israel acknowledge us not : thou, O Lord art our father' (Isaiah 63: 15–16); *pensive* sad; but (with an etymological twist) hung between possibilities.

14   One MS gives the more fluent 'Thy true grief, for he put it in my breast'.

Sonnets from the Westmoreland MS

1 Since she whom I loved hath paid her last debt

Donne's wife Ann died on 15 August 1617, aged 33, seven days after delivering her twelfth child, a daughter who survived only briefly. Donne's epitaph for the wife, whose monument no longer survives, was printed first in the 1633 edition of Stow's *Survey*. Donne was left, says Walton, 'a man of a narrow, unsettled estate . . . burying with his tears all his earthly joys in his most dear and deserving wife's grave; and betook himself to a most retired and solitary life. In this retiredness, which was often from the sight of his dearest friends, he became *crucified to the world*, and all those vanities, those imaginary pleasures, that are daily acted on that restless stage, and they were as perfectly crucified to him.'

> Since she whom I loved, hath paid her last debt
> To Nature, and to hers, and my good is dead
> And her soul early into heaven ravishèd,
> Wholly in heavenly things my mind is set.
> Here the admiring her my mind did whet 5
> To seek thee God; so streams do show the head,
> But though I have found thee, and thou my thirst hast fed,
> A holy thirsty dropsy melts me yet.
> But why should I beg more love, whenas thou
> Dost woo my soul, for hers offering all thine: 10
> And dost not only fear lest I allow
> My love to saints and angels (things divine)
> But in thy tender jealousy dost doubt
> Lest the World, Flesh, yea Devil, put thee out?

1–2 *paid her last debt / To Nature, and to hers* The awkwardness of the standard periphrasis for dying is aggravated by the following ellipsis, presumably 'to the things of nature', including mortality.
5–6 'Beloved, let us love one another . . . He that loveth not knoweth not God; for God is love' (1 John 4: 7–8). The image of the stream is paralleled in Castiglione's *Courtier*, 4.62: 'the body, where that beauty shineth, is not the fountain from whence beauty springeth' (Hoby).
7–8 'As the hart panteth after the water brooks . . . My soul thirsteth for God' (Psalms 42: 1–2); *dropsy* 'pathological thirst'.
9–10 *when . . . thine* 'seeing that you already offer all your love to win my soul's love'.
11–12 'And I fell at his feet to worship him [the angel]. And he said to me, See thou do it not . . . worship God' (Revelation 19: 10). As for the saints, 'not they, but their God, is our God' (Augustine, *City of God*, 8.27). The parenthesis of '(things divine)' is editorial.
13–14 'From fornication, and all other deadly sin, and from all the deceits of the world, the flesh and the devil: Good Lord deliver us' (the Litany of the *Book of Common Prayer*). God is jealous (Exodus 20: 5 and frequently) and his mercies are tender (frequently in the Psalms), but the collocation is unusual.

2 Show me, dear Christ, thy spouse so bright and clear

The visible Church is to be revealed as Christ's bride, not in the distorted guises supplied in recent history. The ecumenism is evident also in a sermon preached before the Earl of Carlisle (Viscount Doncaster, with whom he had travelled in Germany in 1619) at Sion House in 1622: 'the Church is such a hill, as may be seen everywhere . . . trouble not thyself to know the forms and fashions of foreign particular Churches; neither of a Church in the lake, nor a Church upon seven hills; but since God hath planted in thee a Church, where all things necessary for salvation are administered to thee, and where no erroneous doctrine is affirmed and held, that is the hill, and that is the Catholic Church' (*Sermons*, 5.13).

Show me, dear Christ, thy spouse, so bright and clear.
What is it is she, who on the other shore
Goes richly painted? or which robbed and tore
Laments and mourns in Germany and here?
Sleeps she a thousand, then peeps up one year?   5
Is she self-truth and errs? now new, now' outwore?
Doth she', and did she and shall she evermore
On one, on seven, or on no hill appear?
Dwells she with us, or like adventuring knights
First travel we to seek and then make love?   10
Betray kind husband thy spouse to our sights,
And let mine amorous soul court thy mild dove,
Who is most true, and pleasing to thee, then
When she's embraced and open to most men.

1   *spouse so bright and clear* 'The marriage of the lamb is come, and his wife hath made herself ready. And to her was granted that she should be arrayed in fine linen, clean and white' (Revelation 19: 7–8; Vulgate: 'splendenti et candido', Douai: 'glittering and white').
2–4   The Roman Church (personified as the 'great whore that sitteth upon many waters . . . arrayed in purple and scarlet colour, and decked with gold', Revelation 17: 1–4) is contrasted with the Calvinist Church (personified as the ruined Sion 'Thus solitary,'and like a widow thus . . . Still in the night she weeps' (Lamentations 1: 1–2, Donne's version).
4–6   It is improbable that the true Church should wake only once in a thousand years, or should err, or should be alternately innovatory and *passé*.

6   *self-truth* 'truth to herself' (on the analogy of 'self-confidence'); but perhaps 'truth itself'.
8   The Temple Mount in Jerusalem, the seven hills of Rome, the lake of Geneva.
9–10   In the spirit of Daniel's 'Let others sing of knights and paladins . . . But I must sing of thee, and those fair eyes, / Authentic shall my verse in time to come' (*Delia*, 46).
11–14   *Betray . . . thy wife* The literal aspect of the metaphor is forgotten: 'Christ and his Church are all one, as man and wife are all one, yet the wife is . . . easilier found at home, than the husband; we can come to Christ's Church, but we cannot come to him' (*Sermons*, 5.13).

3 *O, to vex me, contraries meet in one*

Augustine anticipates the poet's fear of the instability of his own conversion: 'my heart was driven to and fro with every wind, time still slipped away, and I was slow in being converted to my Lord; from day to day, I deferred to live in thee, but I deferred not to die daily in myself. While I thus desired a happy life, I yet feared to seek it in its true abode, and I fled from it while yet I sought it . . . Woe be to my audacious soul, which hoped that, had it forsaken thee, it might find something else which was better. Though it turn and toss upon the back and side and breast it hath found all things hard: and that thou alone art Rest . . . Yet I could not stand still to enjoy my God, for, though I was drawn to thee by thy beauty, by and by I was plucked from thee again by my own weight . . . Thus came I to understand, by proper experience, that which I have read; *how the flesh lusteth against the spirit, and the spirit against the flesh* [Galatians 5: 17]. I had, I say, experience in them both, but now there was more of me in that which I approved, than in that which I misliked in myself' (*Confessions*, 6.11, 16, 7.17, 8.5, Toby Matthew).

O, to vex me, contraries meet in one:
Inconstancy unnaturally hath begot
A constant habit; that, when I would not,
I change in vows and in devotion.
As humorous is my contrition   5
As my profane love, and as soon forgot:
As riddlingly distempered, cold and hot,

3   *habit* 'settled disposition'.
5   *humorous* 'capricious', but with the suggestion that the speaker is at the mercy of his body chemistry; Donne reinvents the intruding 'fondling motley humorist' of *Satire* 1.
7   *distempered* specifically because the balance of humours is awry.

As praying, as mute; as infinite, as none.
I durst not view Heaven yesterday; and, to-day,
In prayers and flattering speeches, I court God:
Tomorrow, I quake with true fear of His rod.
So my devout fits come and go away
Like a fantastic ague, save that here
Those are my best days, when I shake with fear.

    10

10 'They did flatter him with their mouth . . . For their heart was not right with him, neither were they steadfast in his covenant' (Psalms 78: 36–7).
11 'Then will I visit their transgression with the rod' (Psalms 89: 32). Calvin, *Institutes*, 1.4.4, distinguishes 'the voluntary fear that arises out of reverence' and the 'slavish, forced, fear, which God's judgment extorts'. The sonnet's conclu-
sion might throw in doubt which the 'true fear' is.
13 *fantastic ague* a feverish trembling caused by delusive imagination. Augustine distinguished real and fantastic experience more firmly and 'marvelled that now I was come to love thee, and not any fantastical imagination in thy stead' (*Confessions*, 7.17).

To the Countess of Bedford

Donne wrote four verse epistles (among other verses) for Lucy, Countess of Bedford, a favourite of Queen Anne, and the most glamorous of the literary ladies of the Jacobean court. She enjoyed the literary suits of Florio, Jonson (who sent her a copy of Donne's *Satires*, with an epigram commending her as a 'rare reader'), Daniel, Sir John Davies of Hereford, Drayton,
Chapman and Dowland. She was herself a poet. This strenuously baroque poem proposes to treat only the Countess's beauty, the poet offering himself as pilgrim or historian of it before surrendering to its mystery. Its difficulty would have flattered the Countess, but it is a poem which lends itself to paraphrase: letters are not vehicles for wholly private reflexions.

Madam,
You have refined me, and to worthiest things
(Virtue, Art, Beauty, Fortune) now I see
Rareness, or Use, not Nature value brings;
And such, as they are circumstanced, they be.
    Two ills can ne'er perplex us, sin to excuse;
    But of two good things, we may leave and choose.

    5

Therefore at court, which is not virtue's clime,
(Where a transcendent height (as, lowness me)
Makes her not be, or not show): all my rhyme
Your virtues challenge, which there rarest bee;
    For, as dark texts need notes: there some must be
    To usher virtue, and say, *This is she*.

    10

1–4 'You have cleared my mind so that I see that the value of things is not intrinsic (from Nature) but comes either from the want ('rareness') of them or how they are customarily thought of ('use'). Their value is conditional ('circumstanced').' Against Troilus's 'What's aught, but as 'tis valued?' (*Troilus and Cressida*, II. ii. 53), Hector argues that 'value dwells not in particular will; / It holds his estimate and dignity / As well wherein 'tis precious of itself / As in the prizer.'
5–6 'But while there are no situations in which we have to choose the lesser of two evils, of two good things we may favour one and leave the other.'
7–12 'So at court virtue is a stranger (her height making her as invisible as my lowliness makes me) and my poetic powers are challenged by those virtues which you alone have. For as difficult texts need explanation, virtue needs virtuous company to identify her.'

So in the country's beauty; to this place
You are the season (Madam) you the day,
'Tis but a grave of spices, till your face   15
Exhale them, and a thick close bud display.
 Widowed and réclused else, her sweets she enshrines
 As China, when the sun at Brázil dines.

Out from your chariot, morning breaks at night,
And falsifies both computations so;   20
Since a new world doth rise here from your light,
We your new creatures, by new reckonings go.
 This shows that you from nature loathly stray,
 That suffer not an artificial day.

In this you've made the court the Antipodes,   25
And willed your delegate, the vulgar sun,
To do profane autumnal offices,
Whilst here to you, we sacrificers run;
 And whether priests, or organs, you we 'obey,
 We sound your influence, and your dictates say.   30

Yet to that deity which dwells in you,
Your virtuous soul, I now not sacrifice;
These are petitions, and not hymns; they sue
But that I may survey the edifice.
 In all religions as much care hath been   35
 Of temples' frames, and beauty, 'as rites within.

As all which go to Rome, do not thereby
Esteem religions, and hold fast the best,
But serve discourse, and curiosity,
With that which doth religion but invest,   40
 And shun the entangling labyrinths of schools,
 And make it wit, to think the wiser fools.

13–16 'So beauty in the country is a stranger: you are the time of this place's flourishing, and its daylight (and also its seasoning). It is where sweet smells die, till you draw them up and open the bud shut fast.'

17–18 'As China shuts up her treasures in the dark when it is noon ('dinner'-time) in Brazil'. Donne's sun visits India and America in *The Sun Rising*, 17. The sun 'glassed her locks in Ganges' streams' while Drummond tried to sleep (*Song 2*: 'It Autumn was', 9).

19–24 Even the night-time arrival of her carriage ('chariot' because it has solar associations) brings morning; being a new sun she makes nonsense of both ways of computing the length of days (the 'solar or natural day' of sunrise to sunrise, or the 'artificial day' of sunrise to sunset); but she shockingly ('loathly') departs from nature in allowing no sunset.

25–30 By shining in the country she has plunged the court into darkness (as if it were on the other side of the Earth); she commissions the common sun to occupy itself in such secular duties as ripening fruits, while she is the focus of holy ceremonies. As organs her worshippers sound out what she pours in ('influence'), as priests they speak out her commands: 'Let every thing that hath breath, praise the Lord' (Psalms 150: 6).

33–4 Hymns of praise are fit for the virtuous soul, this poem is only a petition to view the body ('edifice'): 'your body is the temple of the Holy Ghost' (1 Corinthians 6: 19).

35–6 'The country parson hath a special care of his church, that all things be decent, and befitting his name by which it is called' (Herbert, *The Country Parson*, 13).

37–42 'Not all who visit Rome take occasion to assess religious persuasions and commit themselves to the best, but rather for the sake of something to talk about or curiosity about the mere trappings of religion; they avoid the perplexities of theology and think it clever to despise deeper men.'

So in this pilgrimage I would behold
You as you're virtues temple, not as she,
What walls of tender crystal her enfold,   45
What eyes, hands, bosom, her pure altars be;
    And after this survey, oppose to all
    Babblers of chapels, you the Escorial.

Yet not as consecrate, but merely 'as faire;
On these I cast a lay and country eye.   50
Of past and future stories, which are rare,
I find you all record, and prophecy.
    Purge but the book of Fate, that it admit
    No sad nor guilty legends, you are it.

If Good and Lovely were not one, of both   55
You were the transcript, and original,
The elements, the parent, and the growth
And every piece of you, is both their All,
    So 'entire are all your deeds, and You, that you
    Must do the same thing still: you cannot two.   60

But these (as nice thin School divinity
Serves heresy to further or repress)
Taste of poetic rage, or flattery,
And need not, where all hearts one truth profess;
    Oft from new proofs, and new phrase, new doubts grow,   65
    As strange attire aliens the men we know.

Leaving then busy praise, and all appeal,
To higher courts, senses' decree is true,
The mine, the magazine, the commonweal,
The story of beauty, 'in Twick'nam is, and you.   70
    Who hath seen one, would both; as, who had been
    In Paradise, would seek the cherubin.

43–6 'I would admire you as the temple of Virtue not as Virtue herself, the alabaster skin that contains her, the features where we come to worship.' The 'tender crystal' is identical with the 'specular stone' described by Pliny (*Natural History*, 36.45) and modern authorities ('a shining kind of substance. . . transparent like the air', says Guido Panciroli). 'You teach . . . the use of specular stone, / through which all things within without were shown. / Of such were temples; so, and of such you are' (To the Countess of Bedford, 'Honour is so sublime perfection', 28–31).

45–6 'To all who prattle of lesser sanctuaries oppose the pomp of the Escorial [Philip II's massive monastery outside Madrid, a wonder of the modern world]'.

49–52 So Shakespeare: 'whereof are you made / that millions of strange shadows on you tend?' (*Sonnets*, 53) or Constable: 'all those beauties [of former poets] were but figures of thy praise, / And all those poets did of thee but prophesy' (*To his Mistress upon . . . a Petrarch he gave her*).

53–4 'Purge the sum of things of whatever is sad or guilty, and you will be left.'

55–60 'If the Good and the Beautiful were two, you would be at once the ideal and the copy of both; what constitutes them, what generates them, or is generated by them, and what constitutes you, is at once *their* whole being (so entirely good and beautiful is everything you do) and *your* own whole being (so entirely good and beautiful is everything you are).' It is a starting point for Plato that 'the good is also beautiful' (*Symposium*, 201c). Shakespeare's Florizel tells Perdita to do nothing but what she is at that moment doing 'And own no other function' (*Winter's Tale*, IV. iii. 140–3).

61–6 'But (as mincing and oversubtle theology only serves either to promote untruths or to repress them) these discriminations smack either of poetical excess or of calculation. They are unnecessary in cases where we all feel the one truth in our hearts. New ways of demonstrating or saying things breed new uncertainties, as new clothes make old friends unrecognizable.'

67–8 'Leaving aside elaborate encomium and resort to metaphysical judgements, what the senses tell us is true.'

69 *magazine* 'storehouse'.

72 But the cherubim bar the way: God 'placed at the east of the garden of Eden Cherubims, and a flaming sword which turned every way, to keep the way of the tree of life' (Genesis 3: 24).

Obsequies to the Lord Harington, Brother to the Countess of Bedford

Sir John Harington (born 1592), second Baron Harington of Exton, died of smallpox at Twickenham Park, in February 1614. A close friend of Prince Henry, himself already dead, he had been widely expected to be influential in Henry's new Protestant court; he remained widely admired for his looks and his learning. Donne submitted the *Obsequies* to Lord Harington's sister Lucy, Countess of Bedford, under a letter (printed in *1633*) protesting he expected no reward; he later confessed to Goodyer that the reward he got was disappointing. Though written some months after the event (as he seems to admit in the last line), Donne creates a fiction of immediacy. 'The lamenting of deaths was chiefly at the very burials of the dead, also at month's minds [commemorations] and longer times, by custom continued yearly, when as they used many offices of service and love towards the dead, and thereupon are called *Obsequies* in our vulgar' (Puttenham, *Art*, 1.24). Donne's Elegy on Prince Henry was written to rival Edward Herbert in obscureness (Jonson, *Conversations with Drummond*);

this rivals it again. It never seems quite to find its subject, partly because Harington was young, untried and had no history, partly because in so far as he had one it was uncongenial. Built on a serious of questions – 'Where can I affirm ... my thoughts' (41), 'Why should then these men ... be dead?' (101), 'why so quickly be / Thy ends ... closed up?' (105), 'Why didst thou not ... tell us what to do?' (129), 'Why wouldst thou not ... stay here' (149), 'why wouldst thou be any instrument to this unnatural course' (155) – it never finds an answer to any of them. Always on the edge of imagining alternatives for itself which are not taken up, it moves only reluctantly to the triumph at the end. And this, apparently the poem's climax, is itself qualified by considerations that it may be undeserved. The true climax is the acknowledgement of the rightness if not the 'justice' of God's dispositions. But the poem's virtues consist in its recollection of such sentimentally rich preoccupations as those with ecstasy, centredness or flux.

> Fair soul, which wast, not only, as all souls be,
> Then when thou wast infusèd, harmony,
> But didst continue so; and now dost bear
> A part in God's great organ, this whole sphere:
> If looking up to God; or down to us,   5
> Thou find that any way is pervious,
> 'Twixt Heaven and Earth, and that man's actions do
> Come to your knowledge, and affections too,
> See, and with joy, me to that good degree
> Of goodness grown, that I can study thee,   10
> And, by these meditations refined,
> Can unapparel and enlarge my mind,
> And so can make by this soft ecstasy,
> This place a map of Heaven, myself of thee.
> Thou seest me here at midnight, now all rest;   15

1–2 'It is not easy ... for a thing to be immortal that is composed of many elements not put together in the best way' (Plato, *Republic*, 611b): 'whatever dies was not mixed equally' (*Good-Morrow*, 19); each soul is here considered a fresh creation 'infused' by God but whose care is the individual's responsibility; temperate men, as Harington was (3), 'attune the harmonies of the body for the sake of the concord of the soul' (*Republic*, 591d). Aristotle, *De Anima*, 407b, rejects the notion that the soul is a harmony.

4 The supraterrestrial spheres ('this whole sphere') are imagined as making a musical harmony to which Harington's departed soul contributes.

5–6 Dryden borrows the couplet in *Eleonora*, 342–3; but 'No man cometh unto the Father, but by me' (John 14: 6):

'How far has devilish insolence spread when we unhesitatingly transfer to the dead what properly belongs to God and Christ' (Calvin, *Institutes*, 3.20.22).

7–8 The saints 'do not abandon their own repose so as to be drawn into earthly cares' (*Institutes*, 3.20.24).

9–14 'Some men draw some reasons, out of some stories of some credit, to imprint a belief of ecstasy and raptures; that the body remaining upon the floor, or in the bed, the soul may be gone out to the contemplation of heavenly things' (Donne, *Sermons*, 6.4).

15–28 'No difference / Night makes between the peasant and the prince, / The poor and rich, the prisoner and the judge, / He that, condemned for some notorious vice, / Seeks in the mines the baits of avarice; / Or, swelting at the

Time's dead low-water; when all minds devest
Tomorrow's business, when the labourers have
Such rest in bed, that their last churchyard grave,
Subject to change, will scarce be a type of this,
Now when the client, whose last hearing is   20
Tomorrow, sleeps, when the condemnèd man,
(Who when he opes his eyes, must shut them then
Again by death) although sad watch he keep,
Doth practise dying by a little sleep,
Thou at this midnight seest me, and as soon   25
As that sun rises to me, midnight's noon,
All the world grows transparent, and I see
Through all, both Church and State, in seeing thee;
And I discern by favour of this light,
Myself, the hardest object of the sight.   30
God is the glass; as thou when thou dost see
Him who sees all, seest all concerning thee,
So, yet unglorified, I comprehend
All, in these mirrors of thy ways, and end;
Though God be our true glass, through which we see   35
All, since the being of all things is He,
Yet are the trunks which do to us derive
Things, in proportion fit by perspective,
Deeds of good men, for by their living here,
Virtues, indeed remote, seem to be near;   40
But where can I affirm, or where arrest
My thoughts on his deeds? which shall I call best?
For fluid virtue cannot be looked on,
Nor can endure a contemplation;
As bodies change, and as I do not wear   45
Those spirits, humours, blood I did last year,
And, as if on a stream I fix mine eye,
That drop, which I looked on, is presently
Pushed with more waters from my sight, and gone,
So in this sea of virtues, can no one   50

furnace, fineth bright / Our soul's dire sulphur; resteth yet at night. / He that, still stooping, tows against the tide / His laden barge alongst a river's side . . . upon his pallet resteth yet at night . . . Even now I listened for the clock to chime / Day's latest hour; that for a little time, / The night might ease my labours . . . [but] now before mine eyes / Heaven's glorious host in nimble squadrons flies' (Sylvester, *Divine Weeks*, 1.1:562–99). Time has a 'low-water' because the tide does; the rest of the grave is 'subject to change' because 'the dead shall be raised incorruptible, and we shall be changed' (1 Corinthians 15: 52) and so cannot be an adequate figure ('type') of the timeless midnight.

26 Crashaw calls Christ's Nativity 'Love's noon in Nature's night' (*Hymn of the Nativity*, 2).

27–8 'And when this power of reason within me . . . raised itself up . . . and withdrew its thoughts from experience, abstracting itself from the contradictory throng of phantasms in order to seek for that light in which it was bathed . . . And I saw thy invisible things understood by means of things created' (Augustine, *Confessions*, 7.17.23).

30 Self-knowledge is hard because 'man never achieves a clear knowledge of himself unless he has first looked upon God's face' (Calvin, *Institutes*, 1.1.2) and because 'the more deeply a man examines himself, the more dejected he becomes' (*Institutes*, 2.1.3).

31 Harington sees God 'face to face' the poet 'through a glass, darkly' (1 Corinthians, 13: 12).

36 'The things that are beneath thee [God] . . . are real in so far as they come from thee' (Augustine, *Confessions*, 7.11.17).

37–9 'It is good men's deeds that are the telescopes ('trunks') which convey ('derive') things to us proportioned to our understanding ('in proportion fit') as if by geometric rule ('by perspective').'

41 *affirm* 'make firm'.

43–4 'For that is truly real which remains immutable' (Augustine, *Confessions*, 7.11.17); virtue, as it is lived, is adapted to circumstances.

45–52 'Our bodies also aye / Do alter still from time to time, and never stand at stay. / We shall not be the same we were today or yesterday' (Ovid, *Metamorphoses*, 15:214–16,

Be' insisted on, virtues, as rivers, pass,
Yet still remains that virtuous man there was;
And as if man feeds on man's flesh, and so
Part of his body to another owe,
Yet at the last two perfect bodies rise,   55
Because God knows where every atom lies;
So, if one knowledge were made of all those,
Who knew his minutes well, he might dispose
His virtues into names, and ranks; but I
Should injure nature, virtue, and destiny,   60
Should I divide and discontinue so,
Virtue, which did in one entireness grow.
For as, he that would say, spirits are framed
Of all the purest parts that can be named,
Honours not spirits half so much, as he   65
Which says, they have no parts, but simple be;
So is't of virtue; for a point and one
Are much entirer than a million.
And had Fate meant to have his virtues told,
It would have let him live to have been old,   70
So then, that virtue in season, and then this,
We might have seen, and said, that now he is
Witty, now wise, now temperate, now just:
In good short lives, virtues are fain to thrust,
And to be sure betimes to get a place,   75
When they would exercise, lack time, and space.
So was it in this person, forced to bee
For lack of time, his own epitome.
So to exhibit in few years as much,
As all the long-breathed chronicles can touch;   80
As when an angel down from Heaven doth fly,
Our quick thought cannot keep him company,
We cannot think, now he is at the sun,
Now through the moon, now he through the air doth run,
Yet when he's come, we know he did repair   85

Golding); 'Things ebb and flow: and every shape is made to pass away. / The time itself continually is fleeting like a brook. / For neither brook nor lightsome time can tarry still. But look / As every wave drives other forth, and that that comes behind / Both thrusteth and is thrust itself' (15:178–81). Virtuousness has an identity even if virtues do not.

53–6 Donne (*Sermons*, 3.3) quotes Justin Martyr's raising the worry that a man who eats a fish that has eaten a man 'eats, and becomes the other man'; but man and fish are resolved into their several elements. At the Resurrection God knows 'in what corner of the world every atom, every grain of every man's dust sleeps' and 'shall recollect that dust, and then recompact that body, and then re-animate that man' (*Sermons*, 7.3).

57–62 'So if one could sum up everything known by those who knew his particulars ('minutes'), one might catalogue his various virtues. But I should misrepresent nature, virtue and what God appoints ('destiny') were I to divide and split up a virtue which grew whole and simple.'

63–6 'Spirit is a most subtle vapour, which is expressed from the blood. . . a common tie or medium between the body and the soul, as some will have it; or as Paracelsus, a fourth soul of itself' (Burton, *Anatomy*, 1.1.2.3): he adds a simple spiritual soul (not a refinement of corporeal blood) to the vegetal, animal and rational souls.

67–8 The indivisible geometrical point and arithmetical unit are 'more whole' than divisible multiplicities.

74–8 'In the short lives of good men, virtues crowd together so as not to be distinguishable: they have no opportunity of securing a place early enough ('betimes') to exercise themselves. This man was obliged for lack of time to be an abridgement of his own possibilities.'

81–91 We only infer the stations in an angel's progress (but in *Devotions*, Prayer 19, Donne supposes that only God is 'able to do all at once'); we infer succession in angelic intuition (wrongly according to 91–2): for 'if from the knowledge of a known principle they were straightway to perceive as known all its consequent conclusions, then there would be no discursive process at all. Such is the condition of the

To all 'twixt Heaven and Earth, sun, moon, and air.
And as this angel in an instant, knows,
And yet we know, this sudden knowledge grows
By quick amassing several forms of things,
Which he successively to order brings;   90
When they, whose slow-paced lame thoughts cannot go
So fast as he, think that he doth not so;
Just as a perfect reader doth not dwell,
On every syllable, nor stay to spell,
Yet without doubt, he doth distinctly see   95
And lay together every A, and B;
So, in short-lived good men, is not understood
Each several virtue, but the compound good.
For, they all virtue's paths in that pace tread,
As angels go, and know, and as men read.   100
O why should then these men, these lumps of balm
Sent hither, the world's tempest to becalm,
Before by deeds they are diffused and spread,
And so make us alive, themselves be dead?
O soul, O circle, why so quickly be   105
Thy ends, thy birth and death closed up in thee?
Since one foot of thy compass still was placed
In Heaven, the other might securely 've paced
In the most large extent, through every path,
Which the whole world, or man the abridgement hath.   110
Thou know'st, that though the tropic circles have
(Yea and those small ones which the poles engrave)
All the same roundness, evenness, and all
The endlessness of the equinoctial;
Yet, when we come to measure distances,   115
How here, how there, the sun affected is,
When he doth faintly work, and when prevail,
Only great circles, then, can be our scale:
So, though thy circle to thyself express
All, tending to thy endless happiness,   120
And we, by our good use of it may try,
Both how to live well young, and how to die,
Yet, since we must be old, and age endures
His torrid zone at court, and calentures
Of hot ambitions, irreligion's ice,   125
Zeal's agues; and hydropic avarice,

---

angels' (Aquinas, *Summa Theologica*, 1.58.3).
99 *in that pace* 'at that speed'.
101–2 Sylvester calls Christ 'The balm from Heaven which hoped health hath wrought us' (*Divine Weeks*, 1.1.8).
105–10 Harington's life, with its centre in Heaven, could have formed a circle containing the possibilities of the whole world or of the little world of man. Joseph Hall writes, like Donne, of one foot of the compass as Faith 'pitched in the centre unmovable', and of the other as Charity making 'a perfect circle of beneficence' *(Epistles,* 1608). Jonson congratulates Morison on leaving a 'summed circle' for our ad-

miration (*To the Immortal Memory . . . of that Noble Pair*, 9); Donne laments the small scale of Harington's circle.
111–18 The tropics and the circles which mark ('engrave') the poles are as round, even, and endless as the equator ('equinoctial'). But the 'great circle' of the ecliptic, marking the sun's orbit, is invoked to measure what affects us all.
123–30 Harington exemplifies how to cope with the infirmities of only one season (128); he never lived through the feverish sunstrokes ('calentures') of courtly ambition, the alternating cold and heat of atheism and zealotry, the swellings and thirsts ('hydropsy') of acquisitiveness.

Infirmities which need the scale of truth,
As well, as lust and ignorance of youth;
Why didst thou not for these give medicines too,
And by thy doing tell us what to do?   130
Though as small pocket-clocks, whose every wheel
Doth each mismotion and distemper feel,
Whose hands get shaking palsies, and whose string
(His sinews) slackens, and whose soul, the spring,
Expires, or languishes, whose pulse, the fly,   135
Either beats not, or beats unevenly,
Whose voice, the bell, doth rattle, or grow dumb,
Or idle, 'as men, which to their last hours come,
If these clocks be not wound, or be wound still,
Or be not set, or set at every will;   140
So, youth is easiest to destruction,
If then we follow all, or follow none;
Yet, as in great clocks, which in steeples chime,
Placed to inform whole towns, to employ their time,
An error doth more harm, being general,   145
When, small clocks' faults, only 'on the wearer fall.
So work the faults of age, on which the eye
Of children, servants, or the state rely.
Why wouldst not thou then, which hadst such a soul,
A clock so true, as might the sun control,   150
And daily hadst from Him, who gave it thee,
Instructions, such as it could never be
Disordered, stay here, as a general
And great sun-dial, to have set us all?
O why wouldst thou be any instrument   155
To this unnatural course, or why consent
To this, not miracle, but prodigy,
That when the ebbs, longer than flowings be,
Virtue, whose flood did with thy youth begin,
Should so much faster ebb out, than flow in?   160
Though her flood was blown in, by thy first breath,
All is at once sunk in the whirlpool death.
Which word I would not name, but that I see

131–54 Though relying on short lives for moral guidance might seem like relying on unreliable pocket-clocks, your short life could have been trusted entirely. 'Now hath time made me his numbering clock' (*Richard II*, V. v. 50).

132–40 The deficiencies of small clocks are listed (with the human analogies marked from 134): susceptibility to shock ('mismotion') and temperature change ('distemper'), unstable hand movement, faulty regulation (in clockwork, 'the string . . . conserves the regularity of the motion', *Sermons*, 7.17), the spring loses its elasticity, the striking mechanism (controlled by the 'fly') speeds up, the bell decays, the owners set them wrongly or neglect to set them at all.

141–2 Young men are led astray either by adjusting to every model of life ('If I should set my watch as some girls do / By every clock in th' town, 'twould ne'er go true', Middleton, *Women beware Women*, IV. i. 11–15) or by refusing them all.

143–54 But as faulty town or church clocks do general harm, so do the faulty lives of our elders in the public eye. 'The lives of princes should like dials move / Whose regular example is so strong, / They make the times by them go right or wrong' (Webster, *White Devil*, I. ii. 287–9). Harington's 'clock' was so set as to be a check ('control') on the sun itself, and was daily regulated by God himself. Why did he not stay as a 'sun-dial' by which our 'clocks' might be set?

155–62 'Why would you allow yourself to be used counter to nature and agree to this monstrous (far from divinely miraculous) crime against it ('prodigy'): in nature tides are slower to go out than to come in, but the tide of virtue that began with you has gone out faster than it came in. Though virtue came in with the favouring wind of your breath behind it, the whirlpool of death has sucked it back out.'

Death, else a desert, grown a court by thee.
Now I grow sure, that if a man would have 165
Good company, his entry is a grave.
Methinks all cities, now, but ant-hills be,
Where, when the several labourers I see,
For children, house, provision, taking pain,
They're all but ants, carrying eggs, straw, and grain; 170
And churchyards are our cities, unto which
The most repair, that are in goodness rich.
There is the best concourse, and confluence,
There are the holy suburbs, and from thence
Begins God's city, New Jerusalem, 175
Which doth extend her utmost gates to them;
At that gate then triumphant soul, dost thou
Begin thy triumph; but since laws allow
That at the triumph day, the people may,
All that they will, 'gainst the triumpher say, 180
Let me here use that freedom, and express
My grief, though not to make thy triumph less.
By law, to triumphs none admitted be,
Till they as magistrates get victory,
Though then to thy force, all youth's foes did yield, 185
Yet till fit time had brought thee to that field,
To which thy rank in this state destined thee,
That there thy counsels might get victory,
And so in that capacity remove,
All jealousies, 'twixt Prince and subjects' love, 190
Thou couldst no title, to this triumph have,
Thou didst intrude on death, usurp'st a grave.
Then (though victoriously) thou hadst fought as yet
But with thine own affections, with the heat
Of youth's desires, and colds of ignorance, 195
But till thou shouldst successfully advance
Thine arms 'gainst foreign enemies, which are
Both envy, and acclamation popular
(For, both these engines equally defeat,
Though by a divers mine, those which are great) 200
Till then thy war was but a civil war,
For which to triumph, none admitted are;
No more are they, who though with good success,
In a defensive war, their power express,
Before men triumph, the dominion 205
Must be *enlarged*, and not *preserved* alone;

164–76 Death is turned from wasteland into a court of good company. The cities of the living are mere ant-hills; graveyards are where virtuous men have resorted, the suburbs of Heaven, the site of its outer gates.

177–82 The Christian soldier Harington is granted a triumph. But were it the triumphal entrance into the city granted by the Senate to victorious Roman commanders, he would have only an imperfect claim to it. The poet proposes to use the license the tribunes of the people had to list their objections (Livy, 38.47.1).

183–92 Only generals holding defined magisterial office were eligible for triumphs (Livy, 28.38.4). Harington was of the class to hold equivalent office, so as to have swayed affairs and guaranteed the harmony of king and people. But, dying prematurely, he lost his entitlement.

194–5 Restates lines 128 and 185.

196–206 Valerius Maximus, *Facta et Dicta Memorabilia*, 2.8.4, specifies that triumphs might be decreed only for the enlargement of Roman rule. Harington never moved into the world, and never faced either odium or vulgar applause, both metaphorically instruments of war ('engines') which in their different ways undermine ('by a divers mine . . . defeat') the great.

Why shouldst thou then, whose battles were to win
Thyself, from those straits Nature put thee in,
And to deliver up to God that state,
Of which He gave thee the vicariate   210
(Which is thy soul and body) as entire
As He, who takes endeavours, doth require,
But didst not stay, to enlarge His kingdom too,
By making others; what thou didst, to do;
Why shouldst thou triumph now, when Heaven no more   215
Hath got, by getting thee, than 't had before?
For, Heaven and thou, even when thou lived'st here,
Of one another in possession were;
But this from triumph most disables thee,
That, that place which is conquered, must be   220
Left safe from present war, and likely doubt
Of imminent commotions to break out.
And hath he left us so? or can it be
His territory was no more than he?
No, we were all his charge, the diocese   225
Of every 'exemplar man, the whole world is,
And he was joinèd in commission
With tutelar angels, sent to everyone.
But though this freedom to upbraid, and chide
Him who triumphed, were lawful, it was tied   230
With this, that it might never reference have
Unto the Senate, who this triumph gave;
Men might at Pompey jest, but they might not
At that authority, by which he got
Leave to triumph, before, by age, he might;   235
So, though triumphant soul, I dare to write,
Moved with a reverential anger, thus,
That thou so early wouldst abandon us;
Yet I am far from daring to dispute
With that great Sovereignty, whose absolute   240
Prerogative hath thus dispensed with thee,
'Gainst Nature's laws, which just impugners be
Of early triumphs; and I (though with pain)

207–12 'It is proper to say that man is naturally depraved and faulty . . . wherever God's grace is absent' (Calvin, *Institutes*, 2.1.11); but 'Know ye not that your body is the temple of the Holy Ghost . . . which ye have of God, and ye are not your own? . . . glorify God in your body, and in your spirit, which are God's' (1 Corinthians 6: 19–20). Harington returned his body and soul over which he had only a deputed authority ('vicariate'), as a harmonious whole, as is required by God who accepts our efforts.
213–16 The 'civil war' (201) is occasioned by a rebellion of body against soul. But 'every man is also a soldier in that great and general war, between Christ and Belial . . . and is bound . . . to shut himself up against all overtures of peace' (*Sermons*, 4.7) to secure God's general victory.
217–18 'Of such is the kingdom of heaven' (Matthew 19: 14) is spoken of little children.
220–2 Livy (39.29.5) makes it a condition of the triumph that conquered territory be passed on 'pacified'.

225–6 'It was his duty to care for us all; such patterns of virtue should look after the whole world.'
227–8 'God has innumerable guardians whom he has bidden to look after our safety . . . [so that] we have been placed beyond all chance of evil' (Calvin, *Institutes*, 1.14.11). The living Harington was among these; the dead Harington has left us.
229–35 The license to complain did not extend to the senate who granted the triumph, as when it allowed one to the scarcely bearded Pompey, not of an age even to be a senator (Plutarch, *Life of Pompey*, 14).
239–43 Arguments from merit, based on Nature's laws, are redundant: 'None excel by their own effort or diligence . . . Christ does not allow any of those whom he has once for all engrafted into his body to perish: for in preserving their salvation he will perform what he has promised – namely, he will show forth God's power, which is "greater than all" [John 10: 29]' (Calvin, *Institutes*, 3.22.7).

Lessen our loss, to magnify thy gain
Of triumph, when I say, it was more fit, 245
That all men should lack thee, than thou lack it.
Though then in our time, be not suffered
That testimony of love, unto the dead,
To die with them, and in their graves be hid,
As Saxon wives, and French *soldurii* did; 250
And though in no degree I can express,
Grief in great Alexander's great excess,
Who at his friend's death, made whole towns devest
Their walls and bulwarks which became them best:
Do not, fair soul, this sacrifice refuse, 255
That in thy grave I do inter my Muse,
Who, by my grief, great as thy worth, being cast
Behindhand, yet hath spoke, and spoke her last.

250 'Caesar says [*De Bello Gallico*, 3.22] there were some, whom he calls *devotos*, and *clientes* (the latter laws call them *soldurios*) which . . . always when the lord died, celebrated his funeral with their own' (*Biathanatos*). There is no evidence for suttee among Saxon wives, virtuous as they were (Tacitus, *Germania*, 18).
251–4 The poet is incapable of expressing grief on the excessive scale of Alexander's, who at his friend Hephaestion's

funeral 'commanded . . . that all the battlements of the walls of cities should also be overthrown' (Plutarch, *Life of Alexander*, 72).
255–9 Obsequy verses might properly be buried with the lamented corpse. Donne's poem was written some months after the funeral (hence 'cast / Behindhand'), which makes proper the larger promise to abandon poetry altogether; but he was already thinking of ordination.

A Hymn to Christ, at the Author's Last Going into Germany

Donne served as chaplain to the Earl of Doncaster's peace-making mission to Germany in the early stages of the Thirty Years War. After many delays, it left England in May 1619. The poem's central comparison occurs also in Donne's valedictory Sermon on 18 April 1619: 'Remember me thus . . . as I shall remember you . . . and Christ Jesus remember us all in his kingdom, to which, though we must sail through a sea, it is the sea of his blood, where no soul suffers shipwreck' (*Sermons*, 2.11). Donne may have seen

Montenay's *Emblems*, 11: ' Like as this ship, which is but low, / Thus through all danger go, / No care it takes, that the winds with might / Do rage and blow all day and night, / But directly his course takes to the star, / Which shineth so bright over all; / So should a man to God and truth always / Run, and not to Satan or worldly lies,' suggestive despite the indifferent English. In the MSS the last two lines of each stanza are written as one, a style preferred by some editors and commentators.

In what torn ship soever I embark,
That ship shall be my emblem of thy ark;
What sea soever swallow me, that flood
Shall be to me an emblem of thy blood;
Though thou with clouds of anger do disguise 5
Thy face; yet through that mask I know those eyes,
    Which, though they turn away sometimes,
        They never will despise.

I sacrifice this island unto thee,
And all whom I loved there, and who loved me; 10

1–2 'Torn are thy sails, thy guardian gods are lost' (Horace, *Odes*, 1.14:9–10); but the appeal here is to the promise of salvation figured in Noah's ark: 'the like figure . . . doth also now save us . . . by the resurrection of Jesus Christ' (1 Peter 3: 21).
5–6 'Wherefore hidest thou thy face, and holdest me for

thine enemy?' (Job 13: 24).
8 'A broken and a contrite heart, O God, thou wilt not despise (Psalms 51: 17).
9–10 'For your sake I give up the place where I have loved and been loved.'

When I have put our seas 'twixt them and me,
Put thou thy seas betwixt my sins and thee.
As the tree's sap doth seek the root below
In winter, in my winter now I go,
    Where none but thee, the eternal root   15
       Of true love I may know.

Nor thou nor thy religion dost control,
The amorousness of an harmonious soul,
But thou wouldst have that love thyself: as thou
Art jealous, Lord, so I am jealous now,   20
Thou lov'st not, till from loving more, thou free
My soul: whoever gives, takes liberty:
    O, if thou car'st not whom I love
       Alas, thou lov'st not me.

Seal then this bill of my divorce to all,   25
On whom those fainter beams of love did fall;
Marry those loves, which in youth scattered be
On fame, wit, hopes (false mistresses) to thee.
Churches are best for prayer, that have least light:
To see God only, I go out of sight: 30
    And to 'scape stormy days, I choose
       An everlasting night.

15 'For you are dead . . . just as trees during the winter . . . What have we if we are dead? The root is deep within: where our root is, there is our life also' (Augustine, *Enarrationes in Psalmos*, on Psalms 37: 2); 'The root of all is God' (*Sermons*, 9.1).
17–18 'Neither you nor your religion (from Latin *religare*, 'bind') check ('control') the lovingness of a temperate soul.'
19–20 'God very commonly takes on the character of a husband to us . . . the union by which he binds us to himself must rest upon mutual faithfulness' (Calvin, *Institutes*, 2.8.18 on Exodus 20: 5); 'love doth belong to God

principally, that is, rather than to any thing else' (*Sermons*, 1.5).
21–4 'He loves you less who loves something as well as you, which he does not love on account of you' (Augustine, *Confessions*, 10.29); *more* 'others'; but remembering his dead wife Ann More.
25 'Before thou go to the house of thine age, and the mourners go about in the streets, prepare thyself by casting off thy sins, and all that is gotten by thy sins' (*Sermons*, 2.12); 'I have suffered the loss of all things, and do count them but dung, that I may win Christ' (Philippians 3: 8).

A Hymn to God the Father

Walton dates the poem to 1623 in the sickness which produced the *Devotions* and probably the *Hymn to God my God*: 'He caused it to be set to a most grave and solemn tune, and to be often sung to the organ by the choristers of St Paul's Church. . . especially at the evening service . . . The words of this hymn [he said] have restored to me the same thoughts of joy that possessed my soul in my sickness when I composed it' (Walton, *Life of Donne*). It is a meditation on guilt and human weakness: 'the motions of sins, which were by the law, did work in our members, to bring forth fruit unto death . . . But sin, taking occasion by the commandment, wrought in me all manner of concupiscence . . . For that which I do, I allow

not: for what I would, that do I not; but what I hate, that do I. . . . Now if I do that I would not, it is no more I that do it, but sin that dwelleth in me' (Romans 7: 5–20). But it is dominated by wordplay both with his own name (Donne) and his wife's (More): 'Can sick men play so nicely with their names?' (*Richard II*, II. i. 84). Trivial taken singly, the MSS variants suggest a poem differently conceived, as even the titles *To Christ* and *Christo Salvatori* may indicate. They may be more proper: 'For the Father judgeth no man, but hath committed all judgement unto the Son' (John 5: 22). The famous musical setting by Pelham Humfrey is later (1688).

1

Wilt thou forgive that sin where I begun,
   Which was my sin, though it were done before?
Wilt thou forgive that sin; through which I run,
   And do run still: though still I do deplore?
      When thou hast done, thou hast not done,   5
        For, I have more.

2

Wilt thou forgive that sin which I have won
   Others to sin? and, made my sin their door?
Wilt thou forgive that sin which I did shun
   A year, or two: but wallowed in, a score?   10
      When thou hast done, thou hast not done,
        For I have more.

3

I have a sin of fear, that when I have spun
   My last thread, I shall perish on the shore;
But swear by thyself, that at my death thy Son   15
   Shall shine as he shines now, and heretofore;
      And, having done that, thou hast done,
        I fear no more.

1–4 'Behold I was shapen in iniquity: and in sin did my mother conceive me' (Psalms 51: 5); the sin is original sin and so a disposition to sinfulness (which justifies the singular 'that sin . . . do run' of *1633* against MSS 'those sins . . . do them').
4 *deplore* 'lament': the content of the lament follows in 5–6.
5 *done* 'acted', 'completed' and 'Donne'.
7–8 'Our example may make weaker persons than we are, worse' (*Sermons*, 3.6). Some MSS read 'by which I've won'.
13–18 'My heavy life hangs on so weak a thread that . . . it shall soon be at the shore' (Petrarch, *Rime*, 37:1–4); but Christ promises (God 'swears by himself' at Genesis 22: 16 [recalled at Hebrews 3: 13–14] and blesses Abraham for the offered sacrifice of Isaac 'because thou hast done this thing, and hast not withheld thy son'), 'Let not your heart be troubled, neither let it be afraid. Ye have heard how I said unto you, I go away, and come again unto you' (John 14: 27–8), and 'then shall the righteous shine forth as the sun in the kingdom of their Father' (Matthew 13: 43). For *1633*'s 'Son', some MSS spell 'sun' and follow with 'it'.

Hymn to God my God, in my sickness

First printed in 1635. Walton assigns the poem to Donne's deathbed, specifically to 23 March 1631, eight days before death. But Sir Julius Caesar (d.1636) writes that these are verses written 'in his great sickness December 1623' (to which Walton dated *Hymn to God the Father*). Walton puts the poem in a tradition of deathbed meditations defined by Prudentius, David and Hezekiah, 'who upon the renovation of his years paid his thankful vows to almighty God in a royal hymn, which he concludes in these words, the Lord was ready to save, therefore I will sing my songs to the stringed instruments all the days of my life in the temple of my God' (*Life of Donne*, quoting Isaiah 38: 20). Hezekiah was responsible for the restoration of the Temple (2 Chronicles 29: 5–36), whose 'holy room' Donne transplants to Heaven.

Since I am coming to that holy room,
   Where, with thy choir of saints for evermore,
   I shall be made thy music; as I come

3–5 The *Prayer Book*'s Orders for the Visitation of the Sick give a version of Psalms 71: 20–2: 'Yet didst thou turn and refresh me: yea, and broughtest me from the deep of the earth again . . . Therefore will I praise thee . . . playing upon an instrument of music'; in *Upon the Translation of the Psalms*, 51–5, Donne writes: 'And, till we come the extemporal song

I tune the instrument here at the door,
And what I must do then, think here before.   5

Whilst my physicians by their love are grown
Cosmographers, and I their map, who lie
Flat on this bed, that by them may be shown
That this is my South-west discovery
Per fretum febris, by these straits to die,   10

I joy, that in these straits, I see my West;
For, though those currents yield return to none,
What shall my west hurt me? As West and East
In all flat maps (and I am one) are one,
So death doth touch the resurrection.   15

Is the Pacific Sea my home? Or are
The eastern riches? Is Jerusalem?
Anian, and Magellan, and Gibraltar,
All straits, and none but straits are ways to them,
Whether where Japheth dwelled, or Ham, or Shem.   20

We think that Paradise and Calvary,
Christ's cross, and Adam's tree, stood in one place;
Look Lord, and find both Adams met in me;
As the first Adam's sweat surrounds my face,
May the last Adam's blood my soul embrace.   25

So, in his purple wrapped receive me Lord,
By these his thorns give me his other crown;
And as to others' souls I preached thy Word,
Be this my text, my sermon to mine own,
Therefore that he may raise the Lord throws down.   30

to sing . . . may / These their sweet learnèd labours [the Sidneys' Psalms] . . . Be as our tuning.' Here the 'instrument' is the poet himself.

7 *map* As the world's epitome man is its 'map'; Donne elsewhere fantasizes on a reversal: 'If all the veins in our bodies were extended to rivers, and all the sinews to veins of mines, and all the muscles that lie upon one another, to hills . . .' (*Devotions*, 4: Meditation), then the world would be man's 'map'; and he thinks of the physicians examining his fluids as sea-discoverers 'patiently attending when they should see any land in this sea, any earth, any cloud' (*Devotions*, 19: Meditation).

9–10 The fever is imagined as a channel (*fretum* means 'heat' as well as 'channel') leading to final rest; on the analogy of the cold and undiscovered north-west passage, it is the known torrid passage to the Pacific by way of the straits of Magellan, supposedly navigable only westward.

13–15 'In a flat map, there goes no more to make West East, though they be distant in an extremity, but to paste the flat map upon a round body, and then West and East are all one' (*Sermons*, 6.1).

18 A standard list: '*Fretum* or a strait is a narrow passage between two lands, as the Strait of Magellan, Anian, Gibral-

tar etc.' (Peacham, *The Complete Gentleman*, ch. 7). Anian is the Bering strait, here thought of as a north-west passage to the 'eastern riches'.

20 The sons of Noah inherited the continents: Japheth Europe, Ham Africa, and Seth Asia.

21–5 'That cross, our joy, and grief . . . Stood in the self-same room in Calvary, / Where first grew the forbidden learned tree' (*Progress of the Soul*, 73–8). The identity of the locations is a metaphorical convenience, not seriously entertained.

24–5 Adam and Christ are parallel: 'The first Adam was made a living soul; the last Adam was made a quickening spirit' (1 Corinthians 15: 45). Adam's sweat 'drenches' ('surrounds' with the sense of Latin *superundare*) the poet, Christ's blood redeems him.

27 The crown of thorns ('thorns of a sharp sickness', *Devotions*, 2: Prayer) is to be exchanged for a 'crown of glory that fadeth not away' (1 Peter 5: 4).

30 'The Lord upholdeth all that fall, and raiseth up all those that be bowed down' (Psalms 145: 14); 'When men are cast down, then thou shalt say, there is lifting up' (Job 22: 29).

Ben Jonson (1572–1637)

'His grandfather came from Carlisle, and he thought from Annandale to it; he served Henry II, and was a gentleman. His father lost all his estate under Queen Mary; having been cast in prison and forfeited, at last turned minister. So he was a minister's son. He himself was posthumous born a month after his father's decease; brought up poorly, put to school by a friend (his master Camden), after taken from it, and put to another craft (I think it was to be a wright or brick-layer), which he could not endure. Then went he to the Low Countries, but resuming soon he betook himself to his wonted studies. In his service in the Low Countries he had, in the face of both the camps, killed an enemy and taken *opima spolia* ['spoils of honour'] from him; and since his coming to England, being appealed to the fields, he had killed his adversary, which had hurt him in the arm, and whose sword was ten inches longer than his; for the which he was imprisoned, and almost at the gallows. Then took he his religion by trust of a priest who visited him in prison. Thereafter he was twelve years a papist. He was Master of Arts in both the universities, by their favour, not his study' (*Conversations with Drummond*). Not substantiated in detail, this is the version of his own life which Jonson gave William Drummond when he visited Scotland in 1618–19. As well as the gratuitous boastfulness of a powerfully built man (he weighed nearly 280 pounds), there is anxiety about his origins, his class and his religion, and there is also assurance about his own talents (he was befriended by the great historian William Camden, he was honoured by Oxford and Cambridge). When he met Drummond Jonson had already (in 1616) published his folio *Works*, a bid for classic status, which secured him from that date the virtual laureateship (and a pension of 100 marks a year, increased by Charles I in 1629). Drayton might have been the more obvious choice, but as Jonson told Drummond, 'Drayton feared him, and he esteemed not of him.' He is first heard of as an actor-playwright in 1597, the date of his first spell in prison (for his part in the *Isle of Dogs*). Theatrical writing, first for the public theatre and then court masques, occupied Jonson, not always happily, for the rest of his life. But even while writing for the public stage he counted among his patrons Lucy, Countess of Bedford, Elizabeth, Countess of Rutland and Lady Mary Wroth – the Queen's friends (Jonson was among the few poets not to join the public mourning of Prince Henry in 1612). His quarrelsomeness could have cancelled his influence entirely ('Daniel was at jealousies with him', 'He beat Marston, and took his pistol from him', 'Sir William Alexander was not half kind unto him, and

neglected him, because a friend to Drayton', 'Markham was not of the number of the faithful, i.e. poets, and but a base fellow'); but from early in the reign of James his articulate firmness on points of literary principle made him an intellectual patron of his own contemporaries, and later of younger writers. He perhaps served as Professor of Rhetoric at Gresham's College in London. His most comprehensive statement (compiled rather than authored) of literary principles, *Timber*, belongs to the 1630s. An attempt to return to writing for the public stage, with *The New Inn* (1629), proved finally disastrous; and his defeat in the quarrel with Inigo Jones effectively closed his career as a writer of masques. But for the last decade of his life, and despite concluding what Aubrey calls his 'long retirement' in squalor, Jonson remained easily the greatest and most influential poet in English. On his death a collection of over thirty elegies was published as *Jonsonus Virbius* (1638); the most eloquent tribute, on his tomb, was brief: 'on a pavement square of blue marble, about 14 inches square, O RARE BEN JONSON which was done at the charge of Jack Young, afterwards knighted, who, walking there when the grave was covering, gave the fellow eighteen pence to cut it' (Aubrey). Documents for the life and reputation are given in Herford and Simpson's edition of the *Works*, vol. 1; the *Conversations with Drummond* are also printed there. David Riggs, *Ben Jonson: A Life* (Cambridge, MA: Harvard University Press, 1989) is a good recent biography.

The collections known as *Epigrams* and *The Forest* appear in the folio *Works* (1616). John Benson pirated a supplement of what poems he could get hold of in 1640, first as *Ben Jonson's Execration upon Vulcan. With Divers Epigrams* and then as *Q. Horatius Flaccus, his Art of Poetry. Englished by Ben Jonson. With Other Works.* The quasi-authoritative edition of Sir Kenelm Digby added *The Underwood* to the non-dramatic texts in the second folio *Works*, 2 vols (1640–1). The standard is still *The Works of Ben Jonson*, ed. C. H. Herford and Evelyn Simpson, 11 vols (Oxford: Clarendon Press, 1925–52); the *Poems* appear in vol. 8 (with commentary in vol. 11). Ian Donaldson's Oxford Authors *Ben Jonson* (Oxford: Oxford University Press, 1985) revises and supplements the 1975 Oxford Standard Authors annotation to the *Poems*; George Parfitt's edition of *The Complete Poems* (London: Penguin, 1988) is revised from the 1975 Penguin edition. Both these include *Conversations with Drummond*. Mario A. di Cesare and Ephim Fogel have prepared *A Concordance to the Poems of Ben Jonson* (Ithaca, NY: Cornell University Press, 1978); and there is one by Steven L.

Bates and Sidney D. Orr (Columbus: University of Ohio Press, 1978). David C. Judkins surveys work on Jonson's poetry in *Ben Jonson: A Reference Guide* (Boston: G. K. Hall, 1982); earlier criticism is anthologized in *Ben Jonson: The Critical Heritage 1599–1798*, ed. D. H. Craig (London: Routledge, 1990).

On my First Daughter

1616 (*Epigrams*, 22). The father takes two consolations, that the child was owed to Heaven and that her innocence is safe, the mother a third, that she enjoys Heaven. The affecting concern for the fleshly birth is borrowed from Martial's epitaph for the slave girl Erotion (5.34). The closing formula is standard with Jonson there and elsewhere. The *Planudean Anthology* (3.ch. 31) collects elegies on sons and daughters.

> Here lies to each her parent's ruth,
> Mary, the daughter of their youth:
> Yet, all Heaven's gifts, being Heaven's due,
> It makes the father, less, to rue.
> At six months' end, she parted hence   5
> With safety of her innocence;
> Whose soul Heaven's Queen (whose name she bears)
> In comfort of her mother's tears,
> Hath placed amongst her virgin-train:
> Where, while that severed doth remain,   10
> This grave partakes the fleshly birth.
> Which cover lightly, gentle earth.

7–9 'These follow the Lamb whithersoever he shall go. These were bought from among men, the first fruits to God and the Lamb . . . they are without spot before the throne of God' (Revelation 14: 4–5, Rheims–Douai translation); Mary stands in for the Lamb by a sentimental piety.

10 'Until the reunion of separated soul and body (at the resurrection) the grave possesses that part of her which is mortal.'

On My First Son

1616 (*Epigrams*, 45). The boy Benjamin died in 1603 while Jonson was in Paris with Camden (*Conversations with Drummond*): 'he saw in a vision his eldest son (then a child and in London) appear unto him with the mark of a bloody cross on his forehead as if it had been cutted with a sword [but] of a manly shape and of that growth that he thinks he shall be at the resurrection'; Camden dismissed the vision as 'an apprehension of his fantasy', but letters from the boy's mother confirmed the fact. Seneca, *De Consolatione ad Marciam*, 14.3, relates the parallel case of news coming to Caesar of his daughter's death while he was in Britain. Jonson appropriates Seneca's consolations: 'The only happiness is happiness which comes to us over a long time ['lenta felicitas']: the gods did not mean to go on giving when they gave you an already perfect son' (12.4); 'you should not be pained that something has been taken away, but be grateful to have had it' (12.2). These and other passages (on the same opening) are marked in Jonson's copy of the folio *Scripta quae supersunt* (Paris, 1599).

> Farewell, thou child of my right hand, and joy;
>   My sin was too much hope of thee, loved boy,
> Seven years thou wert lent to me, and I thee pay,
>   Exacted by thy fate on the just day.
> O, could I lose all father, now. For why,   5

1   *child of my right hand* Benjamin: in Hebrew 'son of the right hand' (the gloss on Genesis 35: 18).
2–3   Jonson recommends Wroth to 'think life a thing but lent' (To Sir Robert Wroth, 3:106), and commonly does so himself. The jubilee (falling every seven times seven years) is the time of restoration (Leviticus 25: 8).
5   *lose* loose (*1616*); 'Could I forget I was ever a father.'

Will man lament the state he should envy?
To have so soon 'scaped world's, and flesh's rage,
And, if no other misery yet age?
Rest in soft peace, and ask, say here doth lie
Ben Jonson his best piece of poetry. 10
For whose sake, henceforth, all his vows be such,
As what he loves may never like too much.

10 *his best piece of poetry* 'the best thing he made'.
12 'That whatever he loves he may never hold too dear':
the difficult distinction (playing with a common opposition)

is clearer in the Martial that Jonson translates (6.29.8:
'Quidquid amas, cupias non placuisse nimis').

On Lucy Countess Of Bedford

1616 (*Epigrams*, 76). Lucy Harington, Countess of
Bedford, the most glamorous of the Jacobean patrons
of poetry, is also addressed in *Epigrams* 84 (thanking
her for a gift of venison) and 94 (sending her a copy
of Donne's *Satires*); a version of the *Ode enthousiastike*
is inscribed to her, and a gift copy of *Cynthia's Revels*
(1601). She danced in several masques, including
Jonson's *Masque of Blackness* (1605); as it was there, a
role is invented for her here. The distinctively

Jonsonian lines 13–16 do not alter the poems's affini-
ties with the literary sonnets of Sidney, obviously
with *Astrophil* 1 ('Loving in truth, and fain my love
in verse to show') on superfluous busyness about in-
vention, or 99 ('When far-spent night persuades each
mortal eye'), on the anxieties of invention, where the
beloved is only fantasized 'With windows ope then
most my heart doth lie / Viewing the shape of dark-
ness and delight').

This morning, timely rapt with holy fire,
I thought to form unto my zealous Muse,
What kind of creature I could most desire,
To honour, serve, and love; as poets use.
I meant to make her fair, and free, and wise, 5
Of greatest blood, and yet more good than great,
I meant the day-star should not brighter rise,
Nor lend like influence from his lucent seat.
I meant she should be courteous, facile, sweet,
Hating that solemn vice of greatness, pride; 10
I meant each softest virtue, there should meet,
Fit in that softer bosom to reside.
Only a learnèd, and a manly soul
I purposed her; that should, with even powers,
The rock, the spindle, and the shears control 15
Of destiny, and spin her own free hours.
Such when I meant to feign, and wished to see,
My Muse bade, *Bedford* write, and that was she.

5 'Fair' and 'free' (including 'noble' and 'liberal') are com-
monly combined; 'wise' is novel.
7–9 As in *Epigrams*, 94, she is 'Life of the Muses' day,
their morning star'; here 'lucent' by way of compliment to
Lucy.
9 *facile* 'affable'.
10 Pride is 'a solemn vice when things go well' (Claudian,
De Consolatu Stilichonis, 2:161).

15–16 To control the instruments of the three Fates
(Clotho's rock or distaff, Lachesis's spindle, and the shears
of Atropos) is to be master of one's destiny.
18 'In Stella's face I read, / What love and beauty be, then
all my deed / But copying is, what in her nature writes'
(*Astrophil*, 3:12–14).

Inviting a Friend to Supper

1616 (*Epigrams*, 101). One of the two MSS may represent a draft. The occasion is unknown, but the invitation is more than just generically conventional. Similar pieces are found in Martial 5.78, 10.48 (perhaps the germ of this poem) and 11.52; other poetic invitations (Catullus 13; Horace *Epistles*, 1.5) foreshadow Jonson's treatment. The etiquette of the ideal supper is laid out in *Leges Conviviales* (themselves made up of scraps of Horace and Martial) designed for the Apollo Room at the Devil Tavern; here the etiquette defines the limits of frankness and friendly security: the invited friend is plausibly often taken to be Jonson's old teacher, the historian William Camden. The epigrammatic conceit consists in building up a largely fantastic supper of wildfowl and refusing admission to two undesirables with bird names.

> Tonight, grave sir, both my poor house, and I
>   Do equally desire your company:
> Not that we think us worthy such a guest,
>   But that your worth will dignify our feast,
> With those that come; whose grace may make that seem   5
>   Something, which, else, could hope for no esteem.
> It is the fair acceptance, Sir, creates
>   The entertainment perfect: not the cates.
> Yet shall you have, to rectify your palate,
>   An olive, capers, or some better salad   10
> Ushering the mutton; with a short-legged hen,
>   If we can get her, full of eggs, and then,
> Lemons, and wine for sauce: to these, a coney
>   Is not to be despaired of, for our money;
> And, though fowl, now, be scarce, yet there are clerks,   15
>   The sky not falling, think we may have larks.
> I'll tell you of more, and lie, so you will come:
>   Of partridge, pheasant, woodcock, of which some
> May yet be there; and godwit, if we can:
>   Knot, rail, and ruff too. Howsoe'er, my man   20
> Shall read a piece of Virgil, Tacitus,
>   Livy, or of some better book to us,
> Of which we'll speak our minds, amidst our meat;
>   And I'll profess no verses to repeat:
> To this, if aught appear, which I know not of,   25
>   That will the pastry, not my paper, show of.
> Digestive cheese, and fruit there sure will be;
>   But that, which most doth take my Muse, and me,
> Is a pure cup of rich Canary wine,

7–8 'The wine your drinking will commend' (Martial, 5.78:16, anonymous British Library MS Egerton 2982); *cates* 'provisions'.

9 *rectify* 'set up' (as an appetizer).

11 Shallow's dinner for Falstaff includes 'a couple of short-legged hens, a joint of mutton, and any . . . kickshaws' (*2 Henry IV*, V. i. 25).

16 Correcting the proverb 'When the sky falls, we shall have larks.'

17 'If you ask, what more? / I'll lie, to make you come' (Martial, 11.52:13, Killigrew).

19–20 Sir Epicure Mammon extravagantly considers knot and godwit (like the rail, expensive marsh birds) good enough only for his footboy (*The Alchemist*, II. ii. 81).

21 'Yet with your taste your hearing shall be fed, / And Homer's sacred lines, and Virgil's read' (Juvenal, 11.180–1, Congreve); Tacitus and Livy make the bias to history, the 'better book' may be the guest's own.

24 'I'll promise no more verses to recite' (Martial, 11.52:16, Killigrew).

25–6 The MS flaunts an ugly feminine rhyme 'know of' / 'show of'; the pastry-cook will supply the surprises, not the poet-host.

Which is the Mermaid's, now, but shall be mine: 30
  Of which had Horace, or Anacreon tasted,
    Their lives, as do their lines, till now had lasted.
Tobacco, nectar, or the Thespian spring,
    Are all but Luther's beer, to this I sing.
Of this we will sup free, but moderately,   35
    And we will have no Poley, or Parrot by;
Nor shall our cups make any guilty men:
    But, at our parting, we will be, as when
We innocently met. No simple word,
    That shall be uttered at our mirthful board,   40
Shall make us sad next morning: or affright
  The liberty, that we'll enjoy to night.

30 The sweet wine has been ordered from the Cheapside tavern frequented by Jonson.
33–4 Tobacco (often elevated this way), the nectar of the gods and water from the Muses' spring are inferior agents of inspiration; German beer was weaker than English.
36 *Poley, or Parrot* may be the 'two damned villains' (*agents provocateurs*) who set on Jonson during one of his times in prison (*Conversations with Drummond*). Poley (variously spelled, here suggesting Polly) was the betrayer of the Catholic Babington Plot in 1586, and present at the death of Marlowe; Parrot cannot be certainly identified.
37–42 'No dangerous secret, no ill-natured jest, / No freedoms, which next day will break your rest' (Martial, 10.48.21–2, Hay).

An Epitaph On S. P. A Child Of Queen Elizabeth's Chapel

1616 (*Epigrams*, 120). One MS, possibly copied from a draft, has a fuller title: 'Upon Sal. Pavy a boy of 13 years of age and one of the Company of the Revels to Queen Elizabeth'. The boy actor Salamon Pavy died in 1602: he had parts in *The Poetaster* and in *Cynthia's Revels*. This is a classic epigram on premature death, distinguished for its fastidious management of the leading conceit (borrowed from Martial); the cadence is fixed by the carefully managed feminine rhymes.

Weep with me all you that read
    This little story:
And know, for whom a tear you shed,
    Death's self is sorry.
'Twas a child, that so did thrive   5
    In grace, and feature,
As Heaven and Nature seemed to strive
    Which owned the creature.
Years he numbered scarce thirteen
    When Fates turned cruel,   10
Yet three filled zodiacs had he been
    The stage's jewel;
And did act (what now we moan)
    Old men so duly,
As, sooth, the Parcae thought him one,   15
    He played so truly.
So, by error to his fate

1–2 The 'story' is imagined inscribed: 'If, passenger, thou canst but read: / Stay, drop a tear for him that's dead' (*An Epitaph on Henry Lord La Warr*, 1–2).
11–12 The periphrasis suggests three years crammed with variety.
15–18 In Martial, 10.53, the life of Scorpus the charioteer is cut short by the Fates ('Parcae') because he had won so many races they thought him old.

They all consented;
But viewing him since (alas, too late)
They have repented;   20
And have sought (to give new birth)
In baths to steep him;
But, being so much too good for earth,
Heaven vows to keep him.

21–2   The child Pelops, murdered by his father Tantalus and served as a meal to the gods to test their omniscience, was restored to life by Mercury at Jupiter's command, in some versions using the cooking cauldron.

23–4   Proverbially (since Menander) 'Whom the gods love, dies young.'

Why I Write not of Love

1616 (*Forest* 1). Aubrey records 'an ingenious remark' of Lady Hoskins that Jonson 'never writes of love, or if he does, does it not naturally'. There are parallels to his own disclaimer here: 'I ne'er attempted Vulcan 'gainst thy life; / Nor made least line of love to thy loose wife' (*An Execration upon Vulcan*, 5–6) or *An*

Elegy, 1–2. Randolph complains to Cupid that he has never been in love: 'I am neglected. Let the cause be known; / Art thou a niggard of thy arrows grown, / That were so prodigal' (*A Complaint against Cupid*, 21–2). Jonson's poem avoids any personal explanation.

Some act of Love's bound to rehearse,
I thought to bind him, in my verse:
Which when he felt, "Away" (quoth he)
"Can poets hope to fetter me?
It is enough, they once did get   5
Mars, and my mother, in their net:
I wear not these my wings in vain."
With which he fled me: and again,
Into my rhymes could ne'er be got
By any art. Then wonder not,   10
That since, my numbers are so cold,
When Love is fled, and I grow old.

5–6   The jealous husband, the smith-god Vulcan, trapped Venus and Mars in a net: 'Down they went; and straight / About them clinged, the artificial sleight / Of most wise Vulcan' (*Odyssey*, 8:296–7, Chapman); Vulcan's artifice is identified with the poet's.

7   'Light art thou, and more windy than thy wings / Joy with uncertain faith thou tak'st and brings' (Ovid, *Amores*, 2.9: 49–50, Marlowe).

To Penshurst

1616 (*Forest* 2). Probably written in the summer of 1612: the King's 'brave son' (77) died in November that year. Penshurst, near Tonbridge in Kent, was built in the fourteenth century, passed later to the Sidneys, and then belonged to Robert Sidney, Lord Lisle (and from 1618 Earl of Leicester); brother to Sir Philip Sidney (born at Penshurst), father of Lady Mary Wroth (to whose husband *Forest* 3 is dedicated); Sir Robert was himself a poet (edited by P. J. Croft, Oxford: Clarendon Press, 1984), patron of

Dowland, of Chapman, of Jonson himself. Jonson's birthday ode (*Forest* 14) for his son, Sir William Sidney, was written in 1611. Jonson's (sometimes interlocking) couplets lead us from outside the estate (1–6), through its periphery (7–30) to its gardens (31–46), and by way of the tenants and the estate workers (47–58) to its hall (59–75), to its chambers (76–89), to its lady and its lord (90–102). Familiarity allows a particular modulation of the estate poem, a kind already authenticated in such epigrams as Martial, 3.58

(the praise of Faustinus' Baian farm and the dispraise of Bassus' suburban mansion) or idylls in praise of sumptuousness such as Statius, *Silvae*, 1.3 (on the villa of Manilius Vopiscus at Tivoli) and 2.2 (on the villa of Pollius Felix at Sorrento). His concern is not with the promotion of country simplicity or of luxurious *otium* but (conveniently falling in with the tenor of a succession of royal proclamations requiring the gentry to resort to their country estates) with rural community, the obligations of hospitality and the working economy. The energies of sixteenth-century anti-court satire are influentially redirected to the praise of country life; so that Jonson, with his reinvigoration of classical complaints about 'modern' excess, has claims to have invented a new genre, represented in the country-house or estate poetry of Fanshawe, Carew, Waller, Herrick, Marvell and others (how-

ever little they may share of his moral programme). Remarkably for a work reckoned to be responsible for 'the country-house poem' the house itself is invisible in it. The description of Kalendar's house in the *Arcadia*, probably based on Penshurst, indicates why: 'The house itself was built of fair and strong stone, not affecting so much any extraordinary kind of fineness, as an honourable representing of a firm stateliness. The lights, doors and stairs, rather directed to the use of the guest, than to the eye of the artificer: and yet as the one chiefly heeded, so the other not neglected; each place handsome without curiosity, and homely without loathsomeness: not so dainty as not to be trod on, nor yet slubbered up with good fellowship: all more lasting than beautiful, but that the consideration of the exceeding lastingness made the eye believe it was exceeding beautiful' (1.2.6).

> Thou art not, Penshurst, built to envious show,
> Of touch, or marble; nor canst boast a row
> Of polished pillars, or a roof of gold:
> Thou hast no lantern, whereof tales are told;
> Or stair, or courts; but stand'st an ancient pile, 5
> And these grudged at, art reverenced the while.
> Thou joy'st in better marks, of soil, of air,
> Of wood, of water: therein thou art fair.
> Thou hast thy walks for health, as well as sport:
> Thy Mount, to which the dryads do resort, 10
> Where Pan, and Bacchus their high feasts have made,
> Beneath the broad beech, and the chestnut shade;
> That taller tree, which of a nut was set,
> At his great birth, where all the Muses met.
> There, in the writhèd bark, are cut the names 15
> Of many a sylvan, taken with his flames;
> And thence the ruddy satyrs oft provoke
> The lighter fauns, to reach thy Lady's Oak.
> Thy copse, too, named of Gamage, thou hast there,
> That never fails to serve thee seasoned deer, 20

1–6 'No ivory ceiling, nor roof adornèd / With light-out-streaming gold, in my house shineth: / No beams from Hymet' press pillars formèd / Where the sky-touching hill Afric confineth' (Horace, *Odes* 2.18:1–4, Ashmore). Lord Sackville's newly built Knole is the local model of the prodigy house, but Lord Salisbury's Theobalds is a more famous case.

2 *touch and marble* 'black and white marble'.

7–8 The 'better marks' ('distinctions') of Penshurst reside not in the building but in the estate. Statius commends the natural beauty of a villa at Tivoli 'how kindly the temper of the soil! how beautiful beyond human art the enchanted scene! Nowhere has Nature more lavishly spent her skill' (*Silvae*, 1.3:15–17); but the emphasis on how a house is situated is usually functional (Bacon's essay *Of Building*, dismissive of architectural fabric, gives a short account). The four elements ('wood' for fire) suggests cosmic completeness.

10–12 'Under that shade the rustic Dryades / And wanton fauns themselves with sporting please; / And oft, as she by night from Pan doth fly, / This silent house doth Syrinx terrify. / There oft hath Bacchus kept his revelling / When wine has made the tree more richly spring' (Martial, 9.61:11–16, May). 'Mounts' (the Penshurst Mount survives) were a feature of contemporary gardens: Bacon (*Of Gardens*) recommends they be thirty feet high and placed centrally.

13–14 The taller tree is that planted on Sir Philip Sidney's birthday, 30 November 1554; Martial's 9.61 celebrates a commemorative tree planted by Julius Caesar.

15–16 'On the gnarled bark ('writhèd' as if it had winced) are cut the names of country boys (cast as woodland gods) who love like the poet himself implicitly does.'

17–18 'From there the satyrs flushed with excitement challenge the speedier ('lighter') fauns to run to the Lady's Oak (so named when Lady Barbara went into labour under it).'

When thou wouldst feast, or exercise thy friends.
  The lower land, that to the river bends,
Thy sheep, thy bullocks, kine, and calves do feed:
  The middle grounds thy mares, and horses breed.
Each bank, doth yield thee conies; and the tops   25
  Fertile of wood, Ashour, and Sydney's copse,
To crown thy open table, doth provide
  The purpled pheasant, with the speckled side:
The painted partridge lies in every field,
  And, for thy mess, is willing to be killed.   30
And if the high-swoln Medway fail thy dish,
  Thou hast thy ponds, that pay thee tribute fish,
Fat, agèd carps, that run into thy net.
  And pikes, now weary their own kind to eat,
As loath, the second draught, or cast to stay,   35
  Officiously, at first, themselves betray.
Bright eels, that emulate them, and leap on land;
  Before the fisher, or into his hand.
Then hath thy orchard fruit, thy garden flowers,
  Fresh as the air, and new as are the Hours.   40
The early cherry, with the later plum,
  Fig, grape, and quince, each in his time doth come:
The blushing apricot, and woolly peach
  Hang on thy walls, that every child may reach.
And though thy walls be of the country stone,   45
  They're reared with no man's ruin, no man's groan;
There's none, that dwell about them, wish them down;
  But all come in, the farmer and the clown:
And no one empty-handed, to salute
  Thy Lord, and Lady, though they have no suit.   50
Some bring a capon, some a rural cake,
  Some nuts, some apples; some that think they make
The better cheeses, bring 'em; or else send
  By their ripe daughters, whom they would commend
This way to husbands; and whose baskets bear   55
  An emblem of themselves, in plum, or pear.
But what can this (more than express their love)
  Add to thy free provisions, far above

---

21   Lady Barbara (née Gamage) fed the deer in a nearby copse. The deer supply the Sidney table with 'spiced' venison and the hunt with 'mature' quarry.

25–30   Ashour and Sidney's Copse are wooded hillocks: Martial's 'painted partridge' (3.58:15) is kept in a poultry yard, but wild nature here sacrifices itself for the Sidneys.

30–8   'Fishponds the stranger trout and mullet feed, / The homebred pike, which called does come with speed. / Fat carps here know their names, and to you make, / And all a pastime is, no pains to take' (Martial, 10.30:21–4, Killigrew). Fishing the Medway was difficult.

35–6   'Unwilling to wait for the fisher to throw his line or his net a second time, dutifully give themselves up the first time'.

39–44   Statius praises 'the twice-bearing apple trees of Alcinous and the boughs that never stretched unladen to the air' (*Silvae*, 1.3:81–2); Dryden's farmer 'feeds on fruits, which, of their own accord, / The willing ground and laden trees afford' (*Georgics*, 2:501–3, Dryden).

40   Reused in Jonson's *Song of Welcome to King Charles* (*c.*1630); the Hours ('seasons') are 'new' because they are never old.

47–51   'No farmer there doth empty-handed go / To visit you. One honey in the comb, / Another curds and cream from his own home / By the next wood's side; some sleepy dormice give, / A kid, or capons forcèd chaste to live; / And with their baskets the plump girls are sent / Their mothers' gifts and service to present' (Martial, 3.58:33–40, British Library Egerton MS 2982). The estate workers are spontaneously generous, expecting nothing ('they have no suit'); the fruits the girls bring are 'emblems of themselves' because they are ripe and blushing.

The need of such? whose liberal board doth flow,
    With all, that hospitality doth know!   60
Where comes no guest, but is allowed to eat,
    Without his fear, and of thy Lord's own meat:
Where the same beer, and bread, and selfsame wine,
    That is his Lordship's, shall be also mine.
And I not fain to sit (as some, this day,   65
    At great men's tables) and yet dine away.
Here no man tells my cups; nor, standing by,
    A waiter, doth my gluttony envy:
But gives me what I call, and lets me eat;
    He knows, below, he shall find plenty of meat;   70
Thy tables hoard not up for the next day,
    Nor, when I take my lodging, need I pray
For fire, or lights, or livery: all is there;
    As if thou, then, wert mine, or I reigned here:
There's nothing I can wish, for which I stay.   75
    That found King James, when hunting late, this way,
With his brave son, the Prince, they saw thy fires
    Shine bright on every hearth as the desires
Of thy Penates had been set on flame,
    To entertain them; or the country came,   80
With all their zeal, to warm their welcome here.
    What (great, I will not say, but) sudden cheer
Didst thou, then, make 'em! and what praise was heaped
    On thy good lady, then! who therein, reaped
The just reward of her high housewifery;   85
    To have her linen, plate, and all things nigh,
When she was far; and not a room, but dressed,
    As if it had expected such a guest!
These, Penshurst, are thy praise, and yet not all.
    Thy Lady's noble, fruitful, chaste withal.   90
His children thy great Lord may call his own:
    A fortune, in this age, but rarely known.
They are, and have been taught religion: thence
    Their gentler spirits have sucked innocence.
Each morn, and even, they are taught to pray,   95
    With the whole household, and may, every day,
Read, in their virtuous parents' noble parts,
    The mysteries of manners, arms, and arts.

61–6 The guests eat the same food Sir Robert eats without fearing he will take it amiss ('without his fear'). Jonson told Drummond he had complained to Lord Salisbury that 'You promised I should dine with you, but I do not – for he had none of his meat' (*Conversations*); he remembered Martial, 3.60.

67–72 'Harvest being done, neighbours invited, there / No dish reserved is for the next day's fare; / All eat their fill; nor does the waiter curse / The full fed, well-drenched guest, 'cause he has worse' (Martial, 3.58:41–4, British Library Egerton MS 2982). The envious waiter appears in Joseph Hall's *Virgedemiarum*, 'What though the scornful waiter looks askile ['askance']' (5.2:135, a poem on the decay of

hospitality).

73 *livery* 'provision for his horse'.

76–7 Prince Henry died in November 1612.

77–81 The fires of the hearth become a metaphor of the warmth of the household ('Penates') and the zeal of the nation.

83–92 Statius's eulogy of Pollius Felix's villa at Sorrento ends with praise of Pollius's wife Polla for her generous hospitality and her chastity, a model for those 'whose hallowed love keeps fast the laws of chaste affection' (*Silvae*, 2.2:143–end). The 'fruitful' Lady Barbara had ten children.

98 *mysteries* 'professions'.

> Now, Penshurst, they that will proportion thee
>   With other edifices, when they see   100
> Those proud, ambitious heaps, and nothing else,
>   May say, their lords have built, but thy Lord dwells.

99–102 'Houses are built to live in, and not to look on' (Bacon, *Of Building*). If they compare ('proportion') this house with the prodigy houses they will see this is truly a house for living in. Martial ends a satirical address to a grand villa owner: 'Apartments grand: no place to eat or sleep! / What a most noble house you do not keep' (Martial, 12.50:8, Hay).

Song. To Celia ('Come my Celia')

1616 (Forest 5); the earlier printed versions given in *Volpone* (1607) and in Alfonso Ferrabosco's *Book of Airs* (1609) vary slightly. There are many MSS. Volpone seduces Corvino's wife (III. vii. 165–83) with arguments drawn from Catullus 5 ('Vivamus mea Lesbia, atque amemus'). But he underpins these with notions drawn from his own morality of discretion and deception. Other versions of Catullus 5 include Campion's 'My sweetest Lesbia' and Crashaw's 'Come let us live and love my dear'.

> Come my Celia, let us prove,
> While we may, the sports of love;
> Time will not be ours, forever:
> He, at length, our good will sever.
> Spend not then his gifts in vain.   5
> Suns, that set, may rise again:
> But, if once we lose this light,
> 'Tis, with us, perpetual night.
> Why should we defer our joys?
> Fame, and rumour are but toys.   10
> Cannot we delude the eyes
> Of a few poor household spies?
> Or his easier ears beguile,
> So removèd by our wile?
> 'Tis no sin, love's fruit to steal,   15
> But the sweet theft to reveal:
> To be taken, to be seen,
> These have crimes accounted been.

1 *prove* 'try out'.
4 *sever* Personified Time has a scythe.
6–8 Closely translating Catullus 5:4–6 (and quoted by Burton, *Anatomy*, 3.2.5.5); Ralegh's version in *The History of the World* (1.2.5) runs, 'The sun may set and rise; / But we, contrariwise, / Sleep after our short light / One everlasting night.'
10 'Let's not give a penny for the muttering ['rumores'] of old men' (Catullus 5:2–3).

11–14 'Rude man, 'tis vain, thy damsel to commend, / To keepers' trust' (Ovid, *Amores*, 3.1:1, Marlowe); the lovers can outwit the husband's spies or distract ('remove') the husband.
17–18 Translating Horace's 'deprendi miserum est' in a declaration of his own immunity from discovery by an angry husband (*Satires*, 1.2:134).

Songs To Celia ('Kiss me, sweet')

1616 (Forest 6); an earlier printed version of 19–22 is given in Volpone (1607), III. vii. 236–9. There are many fewer MSS than for the companion poem with which it shares its subject, discretion in adultery.

Counting kisses, widely done in Renaissance poetry, goes back to Catullus 5; counting mistresses (like Leporello in *The Marriage of Figaro*) goes back to Anacreon 14 (Cowley, *Anacreontics*, 6).

Kiss me, sweet: the wary lover
Can your favours keep, and cover,
When the common courting jay
All your bounties will betray.
Kiss again: no creature comes.   5
Kiss, and score up wealthy sums
On my lips, thus hardly sundered,
While you breathe. First give a hundred,
Then a thousand, then another
Hundred, then unto the tother   10
Add a thousand, and so more:
Till you equal with the store,
All the grass that Romney yields,
Or the sands in Chelsea fields,
Or the drops in silver Thames,   15
Or the stars, that gild his streams,
In the silent summer-nights,
When youths ply their stoln delights.
That the curious may not know
How to tell 'em as they flow,   20
And the envious, when they find
What their number is, be pined.

8–11 Closely translating Catullus, 5.7–9 (and quoted by Burton, *Anatomy*, 3.2.3).
12–22 Based on Catullus 7, imitated closely by Stanley: 'Number the sands that do restrain / And fetter the rebellious main: / Count those pale fires that do dispense / To us both light and influence: / The drops of the vast sea divide, / These in themselves be multiplied, / That all when added

into one, / May by our kisses be outgone, / By which when number they surmount, / We'll teach arithmetic to count' (*Imitatio Catulliana*). For Catullus's exotic place-names (cancelled by Stanley) Jonson substitutes local ones: Romney Marsh in Kent (famous for its pasture), the sands of Chelsea (still with a sand and pebble shoreline) and the Thames.
22 *pined* 'pained'.

Song. To Celia ('Drink to me, only, with thine eyes')

1616 (Forest 9); readings from a more primitive version circulated in MS. The subject is often treated in epigrams deriving from one by Agathias Scholasticus (much translated and imitated twice by Ronsard, in the sonnets 'Ma dame but' and 'J'avais en regardant'): 'I care not for wine, but if you would make me drunk, taste the cup first and I will receive it when you offer it. For, once you touch it with your lips, it is no longer easy to abstain or to fly from the sweet cup-bearer. The cup ferries your kiss to me, and tells me what joy it tasted' (Greek Anthology, 5.261). But Jonson 'reconstructs' a poem from Philostratus's homoerotic Epistles (a debt long recognized) 33, 32, 60, 2, 46 as follows: 'So set the

cups down, and leave them alone, especially for fear of their fragility; and drink to me with your eyes: it was such a draught that Zeus too drank . . . do not squander the wine, but pour in water only, and bringing it to your lips, fill the cup with kisses and so pass it to the thirsty' (33), 'Your eyes are clearer than wine glasses, so one can see the soul through them . . . When I see you I am immediately thirsty and stand still, reluctant, and hold the cup away; and I do not put it to my lips but know I am drinking you' (32), 'And if you ever sip from the cup, all that is left becomes warmer with your breath and sweeter than nectar' (60), 'I have sent you a garland of roses, not to honour you (though I would fain do that as well), but to favour the roses so that they may not wither' (2), 'If you wish to favour a lover, send back what is left of them, since they now breathe a fragrance, not of roses only, but of you' (46). The famous musical setting is by Colonel Mellish, though the air is probably traditional.

> Drink to me, only, with thine eyes,
>   And I will pledge with mine;
> Or leave a kiss but in the cup,
>   And I'll not look for wine.
> The thirst, that from the soul doth rise,   5
>   Doth ask a drink divine:
> But might I of Jove's nectar sup,
>   I would not change for thine.
> I sent thee, late, a rosy wreath,
>   Not so much honouring thee,   10
> As giving it a hope, that there
>   It could not withered be.
> But thou thereon didst only breathe,
>   And sent'st it back to me:
> Since when it grows, and smells, I swear,   15
>   Not of itself, but thee.

1–2   An invitation to exchange love-glances as drinkers ritually drink each other's health ('pledge').
5   Playfully glancing at Psalms 42: 1: 'As the hart panteth after the water brooks, so panteth my soul after thee, O God.'
7–8   'Only if I might drink of Jove's nectar, would I refuse thine'; but this seems grudging, as he had meant to say 'Even if I might sup Jove's, I would not change your nectar for it.' Catullus, 70, says his mistress says she prefers the poet to any suitor 'even if Jupiter himself wooed her'; but he does not believe her.

Epode

1616 (*Forest* 11); but first printed (along with *And must I sing* (*Forest* 10), and the brief *Phoenix Analysed* and *Ode enthousiastike*) as a contribution to *The Phoenix and the Turtle* appended to *Love's Martyr* in Robert Chester *Love's Martyr* (1601), notably distinct in that at lines 67–91 all first person plurals are singular. One of several MSS may represent a draft. The poems of the printed appendix, by Shakespeare, Marston and Chapman, among others, relate imperfectly or not at all to the topical scheme apparently intended, concerning the marriage of Sir John Salusbury to Ursula Stanley and the birth of their daughter Jane. The poem proposes a definition of virtue, opposed to which is desire as distinguished from 'true love' (43). It is the characterization of love which occupies the bulk of the centre. It concludes by offering in 'a person like our Dove' (91) an exemplification of the coincidence of love and virtue. The *Epode* is named either for its long lines being answered by short ones, or because it follows on a preliminary ode (*Forest*, 10), the 'epode', or as Jonson calls it 'stand', being the final part of a Greek choric triad, or because it is the hymn song before the altar of the deity. The posture is grave and the manner difficult, remote from that of erotic elegy or indeed of epithalamion, promised in the preliminary *Forest*, 10:30 as a poem sung 'to deep ears' (like Pindar's Second Olympian Ode). This gravity exploits the specifically moral connotation of the form; but perhaps, like Horace's in his two most celebrated epodes (2 and 16), the pose is ironic.

Not to know vice at all, and keep true state,
    Is virtue, and not fate:
Next, to that virtue, is to know Vice well,
    And her black spite expel.
Which to effect (since no breast is so sure,   5
    Or safe, but she'll procure
Some way of entrance) we must plant a guard
    Of thoughts to watch, and ward
At the eye and ear (the ports unto the mind)
    That no strange, or unkind   10
Object arrive there, but the heart (our spy)
    Give knowledge instantly,
To wakeful Reason, our affections' king:
    Who (in the examining)
Will quickly taste the treason, and commit   15
    Close, the close cause of it.
'Tis the securest policy we have,
    To make our sense our slave.
But this true course is not embraced by many:
    By many? scarce by any.   20
For either our affections do rebel,
    Or else the sentinel
(That should ring 'larum to the heart) doth sleep,
    Or some great thought doth keep
Back the intelligence, and falsely swears,   25
    They're base, and idle fears
Whereof the loyal conscience so complains.
    Thus by these subtle trains,
Do several passions invade the mind,
    And strike our reason blind.   30
Of which usurping rank, some have thought Love
    The first; as prone to move
Most frequent tumults, horrors, and unrests,
    In our inflamèd breasts:
But this doth from the cloud of error grow,   35
    Which thus we overblow.
The thing, they here call Love, is blind Desire,
    Armèd with bow, shafts, and fire;
Inconstant, like the sea, of whence 'tis born,

1–4 'The first redress is to withstand, not willingly to slide, / The second is to have the fault by mean and measure tried' (Seneca, *Hippolytus*, 14.1, Studley): the distinction is between temperance which is unmoved by temptation, and continence which contains it (as in Aristotle, *Nicomachean Ethics*, 1152a). Calling ignorance of vice ('temperance') a virtue makes it a moral choice; but the tendency to vice ('incontinence') seems to follow from 'black spite' (constitutional 'melancholy').
13–30 The earlier version of *Every Man in his Humour*, II. ii. 12–33, builds a simpler allegory (similar to that in Plato, *Republic*, 441–2) of reasons and the affections: Nature 'placed Reason (as a king) . . . to have the marshalling of our affections'. The roles here given the heart (spy at 11, master of the watch at 23–4) may follow Wright's *Passions of the Mind*

(1601): 'humours affecting the heart, cause pain or pleasure, thereby inviting Nature to prosecute the good that pleaseth, and to fly the evil that annoyeth' (ch. 9). Reason acts prudentially (ch. 16) to detect ('taste') unnatural ('unkind') inclinations from the senses, and confine ('commit close') their immediate ('close') motive. But the will is often either overcome or persuaded by some sophistry ('great thought', 'subtle trains') that the warning ('intelligence') it has of rebellion is ill-founded (ch. 13).
31 'Divines and philosophers commonly affirm that all other passions acknowledge love to be their fountain, root, and mother' (Wright, ch. 20).
35–55 But this opinion comes from a confusion we can readily blow away by distinguishing between love and desire: 'the

Rough, swelling, like a storm: 40
With whom who sails, rides on the surge of fear,
  And boils, as if he were
In a continual tempest. Now, true Love
  No such effects doth prove;
That is an essence far more gentle, fine,   45
  Pure, perfect, nay divine;
It is a golden chain let down from Heaven,
  Whose links are bright, and even.
That falls like sleep on lovers, and combines
  The soft, and sweetest minds   50
In equal knots: this bears no brands, nor darts,
  To murder different hearts,
But, in a calm, and god-like unity,
  Preserves community.
O, who is he, that (in this peace) enjoys   55
  The elixir of all joys?
A form more fresh, than are the Eden bowers,
  And lasting, as her flowers:
Richer than Time, and as Time's virtue, rare:
  Sober, as saddest care: 60
A fixèd thought, an eye untaught to glance;
  Who (blessed with such high chance)
Would, at suggestion of a steep desire,
  Cast himself from the spire
Of all his happiness? But soft: I hear   65
  Some vicious fool draw near,
That cries, we dream, and swears there's no such thing,
  As this chaste love we sing.
Peace, Luxury, thou art like one of those
  Who, being at sea, suppose,   70
Because they move, the continent doth so.
  No, Vice, we let thee know,
Though thy wild thoughts with sparrows' wings do fly,
  Turtles can chastely die;
And yet (in this to express ourselves more clear)   75
  We do not number here,
Such spirits as are only continent,
  Because lust's means are spent:
Or those, who doubt the common mouth of fame,
  And for their place and name,   80
Cannot so safely sin. Their chastity

one ... a love like the sea, frenzied, savage and raging like stormy waves in the soul, a veritable sea of earthly Aphrodite surging with the fevered passions of youth; the other the pull of a heavenly cord of gold that does bring fiery shafts afflicting wounds hard to cure, but impels men to the pure and unsullied form of absolute beauty, inspiring with a chaste madness' (Lucian, *Demosthenis Encomium*, 13). Jonson's note on *Hymenaei*, 320, acknowledges Homer, *Iliad*, 8:19–24, for the golden chain, and commentary by Plato and Macrobius identifying it as the great chain of being 'to which strength and evenness of connexion, I have not absurdly likened this uniting of humours and affections by the sacred power of marriage'.

59   *Time's virtue* 'truth'.
63   Remembering Seneca's 'tickle top of court delight' (*Thyestes*, 392, Heywood); desire is precipitate and so liable to be hurled headlong ('steep').
70–1   'To seas we flee, and as we flee, both towns and hills do fall' (Virgil, *Aeneid*, 3:72, Phaer). Lust ('Luxury') projects its own motions and motives on the world.
73–4   Sparrows are proverbially lecherous and turtle-doves chaste.
79–82   'Who, without fear, is chaste: is chaste in sooth: / Who, because means want, doeth not, she doth ... her mind is stained' (Ovid, *Amores*, 3.4.3–5, Marlowe); *doubt* 'fear'.

Is mere necessity.
    Nor mean we those, whom vows and conscience
        Have filled with abstinence:
Though we acknowledge, who can so abstain,   85
        Makes a most blessèd gain.
He that for love of goodness hateth ill,
        Is more crown-worthy still,
Than he, which for sin's penalty forbears;
        His heart sins, though he fears.   90
But we propose a person like our Dove,
        Graced with a Phoenix' love;
A beauty of that clear, and sparkling light,
        Would make a day of night,
And turn the blackest sorrows to bright joys: 95
        Whose odorous breath destroys
All taste of bitterness, and makes the air
        As sweet as she is fair.
A body so harmoniously composed,
        As if Nature disclosed   100
All her best symmetry in that one feature!
        O, so divine a creature,
Who could be false to? chiefly when he knows
        How only she bestows
The wealthy treasure of her love on him;   105
        Making his fortunes swim
In the full flood of her admired perfection?
        What savage, brute affection,
Would not be fearful to offend a dame
        Of this excelling frame?   110
Much more a noble, and right generous mind
        (To virtuous moods inclined)
That knows the weight of guilt: he will refrain
        From thoughts of such a strain.
And to his sense object this sentence ever,   115
    Man may securely sin, but safely never.

87–90 'The good hate vice for that they love virtue with all their heart. / The wicked they hate wickedness, for fear of further smart' (Horace, *Epistles*, 1.16:52–3, Drant); 'crown-worthy' is 'praiseworthy' in the MSS: the crown is the 'crown of life' (Revelation 2: 10).
100–2 'As if Nature revealed her finest proportion in that one form'.
110–14 'Brute feelings would be intimidated by the excellence of the body; a noble mind given to virtuous thoughts . . . would harbour no such feelings.'

115–16 'He will always confront his appetite with the reflection that while we may sin carelessly ('securely') we cannot sin with impunity ('safely')'; the distinction is frail, and confused in some MSS. The reflection rewrites Seneca's 'Some have commit offence full safe from any bitter blame, / But none without the stinging pricks of conscience did the same' (*Hippolytus*, 164, Studley).

Her Triumph from *A Celebration of Charis*

1640 (*Underwood* 2); the final stanza is printed earlier in *The Devil is an Ass* (1616), appears independently or adapted in many MSS, and is much imitated by Suckling, Carew, Ford, Cavendish and others. This is the fourth of ten pieces in *Underwood* 2 (none distributed so widely in MSS). The sequence, mainly in tumbling seven-syllable lines, ironically records the progress of a late affair (like Horace's in *Odes*, 4.1); the hyperboles here escape the irony. Jonson draws on Ovid's triumph of Cupid, 'Lo I confess, I am thy captive I, / And hold my conquered hands for thee to tie . . . Yoke Venus' doves, put myrtle on thy hair, / Vulcan will give thee chariots rich and fair. / The people thee applauding, thou shalt stand / Guiding the harmless pigeons with thy hand' (*Amores*, 2.1:19–25, Marlowe); but he forsakes the triumph for a blazon.

> See the chariot at hand here of Love
>   Wherein my Lady rideth!
> Each that draws, is a swan, or a dove
>   And well the car Love guideth.
> As she goes, all hearts do duty   5
>   Unto her beauty;
> And enamoured, do wish, so they might
>   But enjoy such a sight,
> That they still were, to run by her side,
> Thorough swords, thorough seas, whither she would ride.   10
>
> Do but look on her eyes, they do light
>   All that Love's world compriseth!
> Do but look on her hair, it is bright
>   As Love's star when it riseth!
> Do but mark her forehead's smoother   15
>   Than words that soothe her!
> And from her archèd brows, such a grace
>   Sheds itself through the face,
>   As alone there triumphs to the life.
> All the gain, all the good, of the elements' strife.   20
>
> Have you seen but a bright lily grow,
>   Before rude hands have touched it?
> Have you marked but the fall o' the snow
>   Before the soil hath smutched it?
> Have you felt the wool of beaver?   25
>   Or swan's down ever?
> Or have smelled o' the bud o' the briar?
>   Or the nard in the fire?
>   Or have tasted the bag o' the bee?
> O so white! O so soft! O so sweet is she!   30

3–4 Jonson's own note to *Haddington Masque*, 44: 'Both doves and swans were sacred to this goddess [Venus], and as well with one as the other her chariot is induced by Ovid, *Metamorphoses*, 10.[708–9]'; Horace protests to Venus 'More fitting you should revel on the wings of your bright swans to the house of Paulus Maximus' (*Odes*, 4.1:9–11).

10 'Through seas, through flames, through thousand swords and spears' (Spenser, *Hymn in Honour of Love*, 288); 'thorough' (required by the metre for *1640*'s 'through') was archaic, 'whither' is for 'whithersoever'.

11–12 'Everything that I as her lover look on is made bright by her eyes.'

13–14 Spenser compares Florimell's hair to a comet, 'All as a blazing star doth far outcast / His hairy beams' (*Faerie Queene*, 3.1.16), and Britomart's hair to sunbeams that 'through the persant air shoot forth their azure streams' (*Faerie Queene*, 3.9.20).

21–30 Imitated from Martial (of a dead child): 'She who than down of agèd swans more fair, / More soft was than Galaesian lambkins are . . . Whiter than lilies in their virgin growth, / Or snow new fallen . . . Whose breath the Paestan rosaries excelled, / The honey in Hymettian hives distilled, / Or chafèd ambers scent' (5.37:4–6, Sherburn).

My Picture left in Scotland

1640 (Underwood 9); printed earlier in Benson's edition of the *Poems*. The most important of the MSS is Drummond's own which gives the date as 19 January 1619. Jonson sent this poem along with *The Hourglass (Underwood 8)*, an imitation of Amaltei, after his return to London from Hawthornden. Presumably a piece of gallantry addressed to Drummond's wife, it can be associated retrospectively with the gift of a portrait. The counterpointing of contradictory patterns of rhyme and line-length reflects Drummond's experiments with Italian madrigal schemes.

> I now think, Love is rather deaf, than blind,
> For else it could not be,
>   That she,
> Whom I adore so much, should so slight me,
> And cast my love behind: 5
> I'm sure my language to her, was as sweet,
> And every close did meet
> In sentence, of as subtle feet,
>   As hath the youngest he,
> That sits in shadow of Apollo's tree. 10
> O, but my conscious fears,
> That fly my thoughts between,
> Tell me that she hath seen
>   My hundreds of gray hairs,
>   Told seven and forty years. 15
> Read so much waste, as she cannot embrace
> My mountain belly, and my rocky face,
> And all these through her eyes, have stopped her ears.

1 Cupid is traditionally blind or blindfold, and the mistress deaf to the pleas of her lover.

7–10 'And all my closes meet / In numbers of a subtle feet' (Drummond MS). The sense here is harder: 'And the cadences, as rhythmically delicate ('of subtle feet') as are managed by the youngest poet sitting in the laurel's shade, fell together with my meaning ('sentence').' We make ourselves understood by contriving a coincidence of breath-units and sense-units (Jonson, *English Grammar*, 2.9).

16–17 The 'waste' ('desert') is also a 'waist': the *Answer* to Sir William Burlase (*Underwood*, 52) likewise admits to a 'prodigious waist', the *Epistle to my Lady Covell (Underwood*, 56) admits to 'twenty stone, within two pound'. Dekker in *Satiro-Mastix* (1602) says Jonson's face is 'full of pocky-holes and pimples'.

An Ode. To Himself

1640 (Underwood 23); at line 6 'oft' is supplied. Like the ode *On The New Inn* ('Come leave the loathèd stage') it is associated with the failure of that play in 1629. As there ('Leave things so prostitute, / And take the Alcaic lute, / Or thine own Horace, or Anacreon's lyre; / Warm thee by Pindar's fire', 41– 4), Jonson proposes abandoning the courtship of popular taste. The aloof presentation of the poet's vocation is Horatian: 'Me ivy (meed of learned heads) / Ranks with the gods', 'I hate lay-vulgar: make no noise / Room for a priest of Helicon' (*Odes*, 1.1:29– 30, 3.1:1–2, Fanshawe).

Where dost thou careless lie,
   Buried in ease and sloth?
Knowledge, that sleeps, doth die;
   And this security,
     It is the common moth,   5
That eats on wits, and arts, and oft destroys them both.

   Are all the Aonian springs
     Dried up? lies Thespia waste?
Doth Clarius' harp want strings,
   That not a nymph now sings!   10
     Or droop they as disgraced,
To see their seats and bowers by chattering pies defaced?

   If hence thy silence be,
     As 'tis too just a cause;
Let this thought quicken thee,   15
   Minds that are great and free,
     Should not on fortune pause,
'Tis crown enough to virtue still, her own applause.

   What though the greedy fry
     Be taken with false baits   20
Of worded balladry,
   And think it poesy?
     They die with their conceits,
And only piteous scorn, upon their folly waits.

   Then take in hand thy lyre,   25
     Strike in thy proper strain,
With Japhet's line, aspire
   Sol's chariot for new fire,
     To give the world again:
Who aided him, will thee, the issue of Jove's brain.   30

   And since our dainty age,
     Cannot endure reproof,
   Make not thyself a page,

1–6 'Shake off your heavy trance, / And leap into a dance, / Such as no mortals use to tread, Fit only for Apollo / To play to' (Francis Beaumont, *Masque of the Inner Temple*, 322–5).

3 'Virtue that's buried, and dead sloth, / Differ not much' (Horace, *Odes*, 4.9.29–30, Fanshawe).

4–5 As Horace imagines his book being eaten by moths (*Satires*, 20:12), the mind is imagined here eaten by carelessness ('security').

7–9 'Are the fountains of the Muses (in Aonia) dry? Has Thespia (at the foot of Helicon) been devastated? Is Apollo's lyre broken?'

12 Pindar attacks Simonides and Bacchylides as chattering in vain like crows against himself, an eagle (*Olympian*, 2:87–8).

18 'He has reached the heights who knows wherein he rejoices and has not placed his felicity in another's power' (Seneca, *Epistles*, 23.2); 'You should not be asking me what I want from virtue, for it is its own reward' (Seneca, *De Vita Beata*, 9.4).

19 *fry* could still be applied to human young.

21 *balladry* 'a poet should detest a ballad maker' (*Conversations with Drummond*).

23 'The greedy fry die with what they take in' (punning on the etymology).

27 'With Prometheus climb as high as the sun': 'Iapetus' bold son stole down / The elemental fire' (Horace, *Odes*, 1.3:27–8, Fanshawe).

30 Minerva or Wisdom, who helped Prometheus steal the fire of the sun (Servius on Virgil, *Eclogues*, 6:42), issued from Jupiter's head (Hesiod, *Theogony*, 924).

> To that strumpet the stage,
> But sing high and aloof, 35
> Safe from the wolf's black jaw, and the dull ass's hoof.

35–6 Recalled from the Apologetical Dialogue in *Poetaster*, 226–7. Ronsard writes of the glory won by those who 'with courage high, disdain the envious dogs that snap behind' (*Odes*, 2.20:27–8); Midas, misjudging the music of Apollo and Pan, earned ass's ears (Ovid, *Metamorphoses*, 11:178–9), but did not kick.

To the Immortal Memory, and Friendship of that Noble Pair, Sir Lucius Cary, and Sir H. Morison

1640 (*Underwood* 70). Sir Henry Morison, nephew of the traveller Fynes Morison, died of smallpox at Carmarthen in August 1629. Sir Lucius Cary, Lord Falkland (who died in 1643 at Newbury), was the son of Sir Henry (addressed in *Epigrams*, 66) and Elizabeth (author of the *Tragedy of Mariam*). Falkland was himself a considerable poet (and author of an elegy on his friend), celebrated for his 'prodigious parts of learning and knowledge' (Clarendon, *History*, 7:217), and his house at Great Tew in Oxfordshire was 'a university in a less volume'. He contributed an eclogue to Jonson's memorial volume (called *Jonsonus Virbius* at his suggestion). This is the first declared attempt at Pindaric writing in English, for some tastes over-literary; but it is largely Italian in inspiration. The Puttenham-like vernacularization of the terminology for the division of the triads (of strophe, antistrophe, epode) which constitute the poem is owed to Minturno, and the manner owes less to Pindar than to Lampridio's neo-Latin imitations or Chiabrera's Italian ones. The extent of the borrowings from Seneca (mostly from a single short epistle arguing for quality against length of life) contributes to the poem's soberly literary character.

The Turn

> Brave infant of Saguntum, clear
> Thy coming forth in that great year,
> When the prodigious Hannibal did crown
> His rage, with razing your immortal town.
> Thou, looking then about, 5
> Ere thou wert half got out,
> Wise child, didst hastily return,
> And mad'st thy mother's womb thine urn.
> How summed a circle didst thou leave mankind
> Of deepest lore, could we the centre find! 10

The Counterturn

> Did wiser Nature draw thee back,
> From out the horror of that sack,
> Where shame, faith, honour, and regard of right
> Lay trampled on; the deeds of death, and night,
> Urged, hurried forth, and hurled 15
> Upon the affrighted world:

1–4 Pliny cites among prodigious births the case of the infant of Saguntum in Spain who returned to the womb in the year Hannibal razed the town (Pliny, *Natural History*, 7.3.2). Here Hannibal is 'prodigious' (perhaps translating Horace's *dirus*, *Odes*. 3.6.36 and 2.12.2) and not the illustrious ('clear') birth.
8–10 'I should have been as though I had not been; I should have been carried from the womb to the grave' (Job 10: 19); but the complaint is turned to celebration of the perfection emblematized in the circle.
12–18 Lucan promises 'outrage strangling law, and people strong . . . whose conquering swords their own breasts launched . . . the kingdom's league uprooted / the affrighted world's force bent on public spoil, / trumpets, and drums like deadly threatening other' (*Pharsalia*, 1:2–7, Marlowe).

Sword, fire, and famine, with fell fury met;
And all on utmost ruin set;
As, could they but life's miseries foresee,
No doubt all infants would return like thee?   20

The Stand

For, what is life, if measured by the space,
Not by the act?
Or maskèd man, if valued by his face,
Above his fact?
Here's one out-lived his peers,   25
And told forth fourscore years;
He vexèd time, and busied the whole state;
Troubled both foes, and friends;
But ever to no ends:
What did this stirrer, but die late?   30
How well at twenty had he fall'n, or stood!
For three of his fourscore, he did no good.

The Turn

He entered well, by virtuous parts,
Got up and thrived with honest arts:
He purchased friends, and fame, and honours then,   35
And had his noble name advanced with men:
But weary of that flight,
He stooped in all men's sight
To sordid flatteries, acts of strife,
And sunk in that Dead Sea of life   40
So deep, as he did then death's waters sup;
But that the cork of title buoyed him up.

The Counter-turn

Alas, but Morison fell young:
He never fell, thou fall'st my tongue.
He stood, a soldier to the last right end,   45
A perfect patriot, and a noble friend,
But most a virtuous son.
All offices were done
By him, so ample, full, and round,
In weight, in measure, number, sound,   50

---

19   As the boy escapes 'the world's and flesh's rage' in *On my First Son.*

21–4   'By its actions we measure life, not by its length' (Seneca, *Epistles*, 93.4); Jonson's Cicero says he will 'shine, for ever glorious in my facts. / The vicious count their years, virtuous their acts' (*Catiline*, 3.1.82–3). The hypocrite ('maskèd man') will be judged by what he does ('fact').

25–31   'Life is long if full . . . what benefit does this older man derive from the eighty years he has spent in idleness? a person like him has not lived, he has merely tarried a while in life; he has simply been a long time dying' (Seneca, *Epistles*, 93.2,3).

40   'He sank into life's Dead Sea (from Seneca *Epistles*, 67.4 of an existence not tranquil but merely undisturbed and sluggish) so deep it was as if he drank from Lethe (and so lost memory)'.

45–9   'Your other friend [as against the man in lines 25–31] departed in the bloom of his manhood. But he fulfilled all the duties of a good citizen, a good friend, a good son; in no respect had he fallen short. His age may have been incomplete, but his life was complete' (Seneca, *Epistles*, 93.4).

44   *fall'st* 'errest' (like Latin *fallor*); MS 'trip'st' fails to pick up on 'fell . . . fell'.

50   'But by number, weight, and measure, thou didst order all things' (Wisdom 11: 21).

As though his age imperfect might appear,
His life was of humanity the sphere.

The Stand

Go now, and tell out days summed up with fears,
And make them years;
Produce thy mass of miseries on the stage,   55
To swell thine age;
Repeat of things a throng,
To show thou hast been long,
Not lived; for life doth her great actions spell,
By what was done and wrought   60
In season, and so brought
To light: her measures are, how well
Each syllabe answered, and was formed, how fair;
These make the lines of life, and that's her air.

The Turn

It is not growing like a tree   65
In bulk, doth make man better be;
Or standing long an oak, three hundred year,
To fall a log, at last, dry, bold, and sere:
A lily of a day,
Is fairer far, in May,   70
Although it fall, and die that night;
It was the plant, and flower of light.
In small proportions, we just beauties see:
And in short measures, life may perfect be.

The Counterturn

Call, noble Lucius, then for wine,   75
And let thy looks with gladness shine:
Accept this garland, plant it on thy head,
And think, nay know, thy Morison's not dead.
He leaped the present age,
Possessed with holy rage,   80

52 'His life was the perfection ('sphere') of human nature'.
58–9 'After seventy years, all is sorrow . . . they do not
live, but linger' (Burton, *Anatomy*, 1.2.3.10).
62–4 'The standards by which life is judged are how well
each smallest component ('syllabe', Jonson's usual form for
'syllable') fits, and how beautifully shaped it is. It is these
that make up life's continuum ('lines'), and its music ('air')';
the 'measure' of life is like the metre of a poem.
65–9 Seneca's man of 80 years 'has lived only in the
sense that a tree lives' (*Epistles*, 93.4); 'O grief of griefs . . .
To see that virtue should despisèd be / Of him, that first
was raised to virtuous parts, / And now broad spreading
like an aged tree / Lets none shoot up that nigh him
planted be' (Spenser, *Ruins of Time*, 449–54, marked in
Jonson's copy).

69–72 The lily ('flower of light') is short-lived, 'which to-
day is, and tomorrow is cast into the oven' (Matthew 6: 30),
but 'even Solomon in all his glory was not arrayed like one
of these' (6: 29).
73–4 'Just as one of small stature can be a perfect man, so
in a small compass of time can life be perfect' (Seneca, *Epis-
tles*, 93.7).
75–84 'We should therefore praise and number in the com-
pany of the blest that man who has invested well the portion
of time, however little, that has been allotted to him . . .
Why do you ask "How long did he live?" He still lives. At
one bound he has passed over into posterity and consigned
himself to the guardianship of memory' (Seneca, *Epistles*,
93.5). The apparatus of the celebration (wine, oil, flowers) is
as pagan as the sentiment.

To see that bright Eternal Day:
Of which we priests, and poets say
Such truths, as we expect for happy men,
And there he lives with memory; and Ben

The Stand

Jonson, who sung this of him, ere he went   85
Himself to rest,
Or taste a part of that full joy he meant
To have expressed,
In this bright asterism:
Where it were friendships schism,   90
(Were not his Lucius long with us to tarry)
To separate these twi-
Lights, the Dioscuri;
And keep the one half from his Harry.
But fate doth so alternate the design,   95
Whilst that in heaven, this light on earth must shine.

The Turn

And shine as you exalted are;
Two names of friendship, but one star:
Of hearts the union. And those not by chance
Made, or indenture, or leased out to advance   100
The profits for a time.
No pleasures vain did chime,
Of rhymes, or riots, at your feasts,
Orgies of drink, or fained protests:
But simple love of greatness, and of good;   105
That knits brave minds, and manners, more than blood.

The Counterturn

This made you first to know the why
You liked, then after, to apply
That liking; and approach so one the tother,
Till either grew a portion of the other: 110
Each stylèd by his end,
The copy of his friend.

81 'The glory of God did lighten it . . . and the nations of them which are saved shall walk in the light of it . . . there shall be no night there' (Revelation 21: 23–5, of the heavenly Jerusalem).
84–5 Horace names himself at the end of *Odes*, 4.6. The division of the name is a form of 'jointing syllabes' (as Jonson calls it in *A Fit of Rhyme against Rhyme*, 10), demonstrated at 92–3.
89 *asterism* 'constellation'; Chapman addresses Lady Mary Wroth as a new star in the 'Sidneian asterism' (dedicatory poems prefixed to the *Iliad*).
92–3 The break or tmesis mimics the separation of the twins ('Dioscuri') of the constellation Gemini, Castor and Pollux who, as stars, never appear together: Jupiter half acceded to the immortal Pollux's request that the dead Castor

might be restored to life by allowing them to share immortality, alternately living and dying every day (Ovid, *Fasti*, 5:715–20). Martial (1.36 and 9.51) invokes the myth to express the love of the brothers Lucanus and Tullus.
98 'Sure on our birth some friendly planet shone; / And, as our souls, our horoscope was one' (Persius 5:45–6, Dryden).
99–106 Jonson would not value his 'friend and son' if 'show, / Profit, or chance had made us' (*Epigram to a Friend and Son*, 2–3); 'those who love each other for their utility do not love each other for themselves . . . the friendship of young people seems to aim only at pleasure . . . Perfect friendship is the friendship of men who are good and alike in virtue, for these wish well alike to each other as good' (*Nicomachean Ethics*, 1156a–b).

You lived to be the great surnames,
And titles, by which all made claims
Unto the virtue. Nothing perfect done, 115
But as a Cary, or a Morison.

The Stand

And such a force the fair example had,
As they that saw
The good, and durst not practise it, were glad
That such a law 120
Was left yet to mankind;
Where they might read, and find
Friendship, indeed, was written, not in words:
And with the heart, not pen,
Of two so early men, 125
Whose lines her rolls were, and records.
Who, ere the first down bloomed on the chin,
Had sowed these fruits, and got the harvest in.

126 'The whole history (legal and other records being kept
as 'rolls') of friendship was in the affinity (in the 'lines' of their
hearts) of the two friends, young ('early') though they were.'

Horace Epode 2: The Praises of a Country Life

1640 (*Underwood* 85). The ironical inflexion of the con-
clusion (lines 67–70) aside, Horace's 'Beatus ille' is
the most influential of the classical types of the re-
tirement poem. Traces of the Golden Age are over-
laid by observation of contemporary country life. This
is the most literal of the three versions in this volume
(the others are Cowley's and Dryden's) and it was
printed facing the Latin and translated couplet by
couplet, Horace's alternating trimeters and dimeters
represented by alternating decasyllabics and
octosyllabics. Drummond reports that Jonson rated
his version highly; he also had by heart Henry Wotton's
The Character of a Happy Life. Following some Latin
texts, the couplet at lines 13–14 is displaced from its
usual position after 10 (which it occupies in Jonson's
MSS).

"Happy is he, that from all business clear,
    As the old race of mankind were,
With his own oxen tills his sires' left lands,
    And is not in the usurer's bands:
Nor soldier-like started with rough alarms, 5
    Nor dreads the sea's enragèd harms:
But flees the Bar and courts, with the proud boards,
    And waiting-chambers of great lords.
The poplar tall, he then doth marrying twine
    With the grown issue of the vine; 10
And with his hook lops off the fruitless race,
    And sets more happy in the place:

3 *sires' left lands* 'lands inherited from his fathers' (*paterna
rura*); matching the 'unbought viands' at line 48.
4 *bands* 'bonds', but playing on 'shackles'.
7 *boards* 'tables' (Jonson's addition: remembering his
complaint to Lord Salisbury, 'You promised I should
dine with you, but I do not – for he had none of his meat'

(*Conversations with Drummond*).
9–10 Mature vines were typically propped on elms or pop-
lars. MSS show a naturalizing attempt, 'There, or the tall
witch-hazel he doth twine / With sprouting tendrils.'
11–12 'He grafts more fruitful shoots in the place of sterile
ones.'

Or in the bending vale beholds afar
   The lowing herds there grazing are:
Or the pressed honey in pure pots doth keep   15
   Of earth, and shears the tender sheep:
Or when that Autumn, through the fields lifts round
   His head, with mellow apples crowned,
How plucking pears, his own hand grafted had,
   And purple-matching grapes, he's glad!   20
With which, Priapus, he may thank thy hands,
   And, Sylvan, thine that kept'st his lands!
Then now beneath some ancient oak he may
   Now in the rooted grass him lay,
Whilst from the higher banks do slide the floods?   25
   The soft birds quarrel in the woods,
The fountains murmur as the streams doe creep,
   And all invite to easy sleep.
Then when the thundering Jove, his snow and showers
   Are gathering by the wintry hours;   30
Or hence, or thence, he drives with many a hound
   Wild boars into his toils pitched round:
Or strains on his small fork his subtle nets
   For the eating thrush, or pitfalls sets:
And snares the fearful hare, and new-come crane,   35
   And counts them sweet rewards so ta'en.
Who (amongst these delights) would not forget
   Love's cares so evil, and so great?
But if, to boot with these, a chaste wife meet
   For household aid, and children sweet;   40
Such as the Sabine's, or a sunburned blowze,
   Some lusty quick Apulian's spouse,
To deck the hallowed hearth with old wood fired
   Against the husband comes home tired;
That penning the glad flock in hurdles by   45
   Their swelling udders doth draw dry:
And from the sweet tub wine of this year takes,
   And unbought viands ready makes:
Not Lucrine oysters I could then more prize,
   Nor turbot, nor bright golden-eyes;   50
If with east floods, the winter troubled much,
   Into our seas send any such:
The Ionian godwit, nor the Guinea hen

---

13 *bending* 'curving' (and so sheltered); the Latin *reducta* ('led back') suggests 'secluded' (Dryden gives 'afar').

15 *pressed* 'expressed from the comb'.

20 *purple-matching* 'competing with crimson dye'.

21–2 *Priapus . . . Sylvan* gods of the garden and of garden boundaries.

24 *rooted* translating *tenax*.

26 *quarrel* translating *queror* ('complain'), but echoing 'carol'.

32 *toils pitched* 'strong nets planted'.

33 Horace's *rara* means the nets are wide-meshed; Jonson means they are finer (hence some read 'subtler') than the toils.

34 *eating* 'greedy'.

39 *to boot with* 'in addition to'.

41–2 The Sabines and the Apulians here represent sturdy peasant stock.

44 *against* 'before'.

49–50 These luxury fish (like the luxury fowl of 53–4) were exotic for Horace too. The *Oxford English Dictionary* cites Richard Turnbull (1591): 'the fish *scarus*, which some take to be the gilt-head or golden-eye'.

51 *bright* east (MSS), which is the sense: floods in the east drive these fish into western waters.

53 Godwits were expensive birds (and Ionia long vanished); Guinea hens (fortuitously relatively common now) were a recent import from Guinea (Latin, *Afra avis*).

> Could not go down my belly then
> 　More sweet than olives, that new gathered be　55
> 　　From fattest branches of the tree:
> Or the herb sorrel, that loves meadows still,
> 　Or mallows loosing body's ill:
> Or at the Feast of Bounds, the lamb then slain,
> 　Or kid forced from the wolf again.　60
> Among these cates how glad the sight doth come
> 　Of the fed flocks approaching home!
> To view the weary oxen draw, with bare
> 　And fainting necks, the turnèd share!
> The wealthy household swarm of bondmen met,　65
> 　And 'bout the steaming chimney set!"
> These thoughts when usurer Alfius, now about
> 　To turn mere farmer, had spoke out
> 'Gainst the Ides, his moneys he gets in with pain,
> 　At the Kalends, puts all out again.　70

57–8　The sorrel which ever loves meadows is wild (not from the kitchen garden); marsh mallow is mildly laxative.
59　*Feast of Bounds* domesticating the Roman *Terminalia*, though the sacrificial lamb and the goat rescued from the wolf are Roman paraphernalia.
64　*turnèd share* 'upturned plough' (its work done).

66　*steaming* shining (MSS), which translated Horace's sense: Jonson has a boiling pot on his fire.
69–70　*'Gainst the Ides . . . At the Kalends* 'Before mid-month . . . At the new month': within at most a fortnight (and as soon as the next day) he resumed his money-lending. Fanshawe domesticates the festivals: 'At *Michaelmas* calls all his moneys in: / But at *Our Lady* puts them out again'.

To the Memory of my Beloved the Author, Mr William Shakespeare

Shakespeare *Works* (1623). Jonson is awkwardly over-explicit about his own ingenuousness, but suspicions of frigidity or irony derive from wrong expectations of the manners of compliment. 'I loved the man and do honour his memory (on this side idolatry) as much as any' (*Timber*). The poem, cast as a triumph (hence the apostrophe to Britain at its centre), celebrates the achievements of English, and almost incidentally of Shakespearean English, in relation to those of Greece and Rome.

> To draw no envy, Shakespeare, on thy name,
> 　Am I thus ample to thy book and fame;
> While I confess thy writings to be such
> 　As neither man nor Muse can praise too much;
> 'Tis true, and all men's suffrage. But these ways　5
> 　Were not the paths I meant unto thy praise;
> For silliest ignorance on these may light,
> 　Which, when it sounds at best, but echoes right;
> Or blind affection, which doth ne'er advance
> 　The truth, but gropes, and urgeth all by chance;　10
> Or crafty malice might pretend this praise,
> 　And think to ruin, where it seem'd to raise.

1–2　'It is not to make you an object of envy that I write so fulsomely of you.'
4–10　'It being the common opinion ('suffrage') that you are beyond praise, I chose a different way to praise you. Simple ('silliest') ignorance can parrot what's usual, a friend might guess in the dark and hit on it.'

11–12　'It is as great a spite to be praised in the wrong place, and by a wrong person, as can be done to a noble nature' (*Timber*). Jonson's verses for Browne's *Britannia's Pastorals* begin likewise: 'Some men, of books or friends not right, / May hurt them more with praise, than foes with spite.'

These are, as some infamous bawd or whore
  Should praise a matron; what could hurt her more?
But thou art proof against them, and indeed,   15
  Above the ill fortune of them, or the need.
I therefore will begin. Soul of the age!
  The applause, delight, the wonder of our stage!
My Shakespeare, rise! I will not lodge thee by
  Chaucer, or Spenser, or bid Beaumont lie   20
A little further, to make thee a room:
  Thou art a monument without a tomb,
And art alive still while thy book doth live
  And we have wits to read and praise to give.
That I not mix thee so, my brain excuses,   25
  I mean with great, but disproportioned Muses,
For if I thought my judgment were of years,
  I should commit thee surely with thy peers,
And tell how far thou didst our Lyly outshine,
  Or sporting Kyd, or Marlowe's mighty line.   30
And though thou hadst small Latin and less Greek,
  From thence to honour thee, I would not seek
For names; but call forth thund'ring Aeschylus,
  Euripides and Sophocles to us;
Pacuvius, Accius, him of Cordova dead,   35
  To life again, to hear thy buskin tread,
And shake a stage; or, when thy socks were on,
  Leave thee alone for the comparison
Of all that insolent Greece or haughty Rome
  Sent forth, or since did from their ashes come.   40
Triumph, my Britain, thou hast one to show
  To whom all scenes of Europe homage owe.
He was not of an age but for all time!
  And all the Muses still were in their prime,
When, like Apollo, he came forth to warm   45
  Our ears, or like a Mercury to charm!
Nature herself was proud of his designs

18 'The charming grace, the glory of the stage, / The applause the darling pastime of the age' (Martial on the actor Latinus, 9.28:1–2, Killigrew).

19–20 Like Basse's *Elegy on Shakespeare*: 'Renownèd Spenser, lie a thought more nigh / To learned Chaucer; and rare Beaumont lie / A little nearer Spenser to make room / For Shakespeare in your threefold, fourfold tomb.'

22 The burden, much echoed, of a number of epigrams on Euripides: 'This is not thy monument, Euripides, but thou art the memorial of it' (*Greek Anthology*, 7.46).

25–8 'I can explain to myself not taking you along with these poets, great but unlike you.'

27–30 'If I thought my judgement were of merely temporary glory, I should compare you with poets with whom you have more in common': Lyly is outshone (though the lily is 'flower of light'), Kyd is 'sporting' because the kid capers, Marlowe he reportedly thought 'fitter for admiration than for parallel'.

31–3 'And though you had little of the classics [the phrasing from Minturno's *Arte Poetica*], I shouldn't have to search far for names.'

35 'If it be asked who was the best: Pacuvius doth bear / The bell for lore, and Accius doth sound his thumping gear' (Horace, *Epistles*, 2.1:56, Drant). They fill out the triad of Latin tragedians with Seneca ('him of Cordova') to match the English and Greek ones.

36–7 *buskin . . . socks* for 'tragedy' (literalized so that Shakespeare's 'boot' punningly shakes what it treads on) and 'comedy'.

39 Bacon, says Jonson, adapting the elder Seneca on Roman eloquence, has 'performed that in our tongue, which may be compared, or preferred, either to insolent Greece, or haughty Rome' (*Timber*).

41 Some would prefer lines 51–4 at this point; but the later naming of the comic ancients relates to their status as 'natural' writers; and the poem's midpoint is properly occupied by the modern victor.

45–6 *Apollo . . . Mercury* for 'poetry' and 'eloquence'.

47–9 Shakespeare's is the 'language of nature'.

And joyed to wear the dressing of his lines,
Which were so richly spun, and woven so fit,
As, since, she will vouchsafe no other wit.   50
The merry Greek, tart Aristophanes,
Neat Terence, witty Plautus, now not please,
But antiquated and deserted lie,
As they were not of Nature's family.
Yet must I not give Nature all: thy art,   55
My gentle Shakespeare, must enjoy a part.
For though the poet's matter nature be,
His art doth give the fashion; and, that he
Who casts to write a living line, must sweat,
(Such as thine are) and strike the second heat   60
Upon the Muses' anvil; turn the same
(And himself with it) that he thinks to frame,
Or, for the laurel, he may gain a scorn;
For a good poet's made, as well as born;
And such wert thou. Look how the father's face   65
Lives in his issue, even so the race
Of Shakespeare's mind and manners brightly shines
In his well-turnèd, and true-filèd lines;
In each of which he seems to shake a lance,
As brandished at the eyes of ignorance.   70
Sweet Swan of Avon! what a sight it were
To see thee in our waters yet appear,
And make those flights upon the banks of Thames,
That so did take Eliza and our James!
But stay, I see thee in the hemisphere   75
Advanced, and made a constellation there!
Shine forth, thou star of poets, and with rage
Or influence, chide or cheer the drooping stage;
Which, since thy flight from hence, hath mourned like night,
And despairs day, but for thy volume's light.   80

51–4 His comedy supersedes that of one Greek ('merry Greek' was colloquially 'merry fellow') and two Romans: Horace (*Epistles*, 2.1:58–9) praises Plautus for his 'swift delivered style' ('wit'), and Terence for 'art' ('neatness').

55–6 Jonson asserted 'that Shakespeare wanted art' (*Conversations with Drummond*).

59–62 'He who plans ('casts') to write such living lines as you do must return his work to be hammered out a second time'; he must 'lay his rude ill turned stuff again into the frame' (Horace, *Ars Poetica*, 441, Drant); he must 'bring all to the forge, and file again, turn it anew' (*Timber*); and 'himself with it' because he 'is in travail with expression of another' (*Timber*).

64 Proverbially 'the poet is born not made.'

65–6 'Shakespeare's literary children are characteristically his' (as wine shows its 'race' or characteristic flavour); but 'race' implies also 'he flowed with that facility, that sometime it was necessary he should be stopped' (*Timber*).

69–70 Punning on Shakespeare's name (as at 37).

71 *Swan* 'poet' (because swans are sacred to Apollo and were imagined to sing in rapture before their deaths, Plato, *Phaedo*, 84e).

75–6 Shakespeare is stellified as the constellation Cygnus.

77–8 'Rebuke or encourage with adverse or benign astrological effects'.

80 'This time / Had been enough, to have scattered all the stars . . . and made the world / Despair of day, or any light, but ours' (*Catiline*, 4:758–61).

Pleasure reconciled to Virtue. A Masque. As it was presented at court before King James. 1618

Works, 1640–1; there is an earlier MS transcription by Ralph Crane, which was sent to Sir Dudley Carleton (the basis of Herford and Simpson's text), this despite his having been advised that Jonson was 'grown so dull that his device is not worth the relating much less the copying out'. The printed text ends with a note 'This pleased the King so well, as he would see it again'; it was indeed presented again with alterations and additions but for the sake of the Queen, who had missed the first performance. The long description of the first staging which Orazio Busino sent to Venice on 24 January suggests it was a near disaster, rescued only by some spectacular dancing by the Duke of Buckingham. The fault may have been with the performance. But while this masque does not carry the freight of arcane learning that Jonson's masques sometimes do, it aims rather obviously at edification. Jonson told Drummond that 'next himself only Fletcher and Chapman could make a masque', but he had firm notions of what a masque was. The preface to *Hymenaei* (1606, long before the famous quarrel with the architect of his 'devices', Inigo Jones) is the clearest statement of his prejudices, arguing that what is offered the 'understanding' is 'impressing, and lasting', while what is offered to 'sense' is 'but momentary, and merely taking'. Masques in performance may well have prospered or failed by virtue of their machinery or their sets or their dancing but 'though bodies oft-times have the ill luck to be sensually preferred, they find afterwards, the good fortune (when souls live) to be utterly forgotten.' But recognition of the poet's superior contribution explains the preference of kings for 'the most high, and hearty inventions, to furnish the inward parts: (and those grounded upon antiquity, and solid learnings) which, though their voice be taught to sound to present occasions, their sense, or doth, or should always lay hold on more removed mysteries'. It is only fools that cry out against 'all endeavour of learning, and sharpness in these transitory devices . . . It is not my fault, if I fill them out nectar, and they run to metheglin.' The anti-masque consists of a dramatization of Philostratus's descriptions of a couple of lost or imaginary works of art: the image of Comus (*Imagines*, 1.2, but elaborated from Rabelais's Gaster in the *Quart Livre*) and the assault on Hercules by the Pigmies (*Imagines*, 2.22). So much is learned comedy. But the articulating argument, which brings these together and connects them with the masque proper, rewrites Xenophon's allegory of Hercules' confrontation at the crossroads with Pleasure and Virtue (*Memorabilia*, 2.1) to make both antagonists of dissolute and pigmy vice (1618 is the year of the *Declaration of Sports*). Mercury's speech prepares their reconciliation, represented in the dance.

As well as Herford and Simpson, there are three important modern editions: R. A. Foakes's in *A Book of Masques in Honour of Allardyce Nicoll* (Cambridge: Cambridge University Press, 1967); Stephen Orgel's in *The Complete Masques of Ben Jonson* (New Haven and London: Yale University Press, 1969); David Lindley's in *Court Masques: Jacobean and Caroline Entertainments, 1605–1640* (Oxford: Oxford University Press, 1995). Inigo Jones's sketches, including those for Comus's entry, are reproduced in *Inigo Jones: The Theatre of the Stuart Court*, by Stephen Orgel and Roy Strong, 2 vols (London: Sotheby Parke Bernet, 1973).

The scene was the mountain Atlas. Who had his top ending in the figure of an old man, his head and beard all hoary, and frost, as if his shoulders were covered with snow; the rest wood, and rock. A grove of ivy at his feet; out of which, to a wild music of cymbals, flutes, and tabors is brought forth Comus the god of cheer, or the belly, riding in triumph, his head crowned with roses, and other flowers, his hair curled: they that wait upon him crowned with ivy, their javelins done about with it; one of them going with Hercules's bowl borne before him, while the rest presented him with this hymn.

The anthropomorphic Mount Atlas (in performance its eyes rolled) is from Virgil: 'His shoulders hid with snow, and from his hoary beard adown, / The streams of waters fall, with ice and frost his face doth frown' (*Aeneid*, 4:250–1, Phaer). It was here that Hercules wrestled with another giant, Antaeus (mimed before the action starts). The description of Comus abandons Philostratus's description for a hybrid of the wine-god Bacchus (Busino calls him a 'chubby Bacchus') and his foster-father Silenus, who follows Bacchus's chariot in Ovid, 'big-bellied, reeling, and old' (Sandys's note on *Metamorphoses*, 4:26), with hints from Rabelais's Gaster in the *Fourth Book*. Hercules' bowl is a metaphor of excess: Seneca says that 'intemperance in drink and Hercules' bowl destroyed Alexander' (*Epistles*, 83.23), but (following Servius on Virgil, *Aeneid*, 8:278) it can be imagined as a great wooden bowl.

Room, room, make room for the bouncing belly,
First father of sauce, and deviser of jelly;
Prime Master of Arts, and the giver of wit,
That found out the excellent engine, the spit;
The plough, and the flail, the mill, and the hopper,   5
The hutch and the bolter, the furnace and copper,
The oven, the bavin, the mawkin, the peel,
The hearth and the range, the dog and the wheel.
He, he first invented both hogshead and tun,
The gimlet and vice too, and taught 'em to run;   10
And since with the funnel, an hippocras bag
He's made of himself, that now he cries swag;
Which shows though the pleasure be but of four inches,
Yet he is a weezle, the gullet that pinches
Of any delight, and not spares from this back,   15
Whatever to make of the belly a sack!
Hail, hail plump paunch, O the founder of taste,
For fresh-meats, or powdered, or pickle, or paste,
Devourer of broiled, baked, roasted, or sod;
And emptier of cups, be they even or odd;   20
All which have now made thee so wide in the waist,
As scarce with no pudding thou art to be laced,
But eating and drinking until thou dost nod,
Thou break'st all thy girdles, and break'st forth a god.

To this the Bowl-bearer. Do you hear my friends? to whom did you sing all this now? pardon me only that I ask you, for I do not look for an answer; I'll answer myself, I know it is now such a time as the Saturnals for all the world, that every man stands under the eaves of his own hat, and sings what please him; that's the right, and the liberty of it. Now you sing of god Comus here the belly-god; I say it is well, and I say it is not well: it is well as it is a ballad, and the Belly worthy of it; I must needs say, and 'twere forty yards of ballad more, as much ballad as tripe. But when the belly is not edified by it, it is not well; for where did you ever read or hear, that the belly had any ears? Come never pump for an answer, for you are defeated; our fellow Hunger there that was as ancient a retainer to the belly as any of us, was turned away for being unseasonable, not unreasonable,

1–9 The 'hymn' is partially developed from Rabelais, *Fourth Book*, 57–61, whose Master Gaster ('Belly') is 'the first master of arts in this world' (57). He embodies the proverb 'Hunger is a great Teacher' (Erasmus, *Adagia*, 4.2.48) or that 'From Poverty comes Wisdom' (*Adagia*, 1.5.22): 'from the beginning he invented the smith's art, and husbandry to manure the ground, that it might yield him corn' (*Fourth Book*, 61). His inventions here are a jumble of the machinery of food and drink production, preparation, consumption: less familiar items are the 'hopper' ('grain-funnel'), 'hutch' and 'bolter' ('container' which takes flour from the 'sieve'), 'bavin' ('kindling'), 'mawkin' ('oven mop'), 'peel' ('oven shovel'), 'the dog and the wheel' ('turnspit'); the 'gimlet' breaches the hogshead or tun, the 'vice' ('tap') stops the aperture.

10–15 The text is disputed and the sense doubtful. 'He has swallowed wine enough from his cup ('funnel') to have made a straining bag ('hippocras bag') of himself so that now he cries for relief ('swag' for 'assuage'); which shows that short as the pleasure of drinking is (measured by the throat), he is himself like a throat ('weezle') that stints ('pinches')

the gullet of delight and itself retains ('spares . . . back') nothing from it that might make a great bag of the belly.' Spenser's Gluttony (though big-bellied) has a neck like a crane the better to savour what goes down his throat, or up it again (*Faerie Queene*, 1.4.21).

17–18 The meat comes 'fresh, cured ('powdered'), pickled, or in pasties, grilled . . . stewed'. The foodstuffs described in Rabelais's *Fourth Book*, 59–60, number hundreds of items.

19 *be . . . odd* 'be they however many'.

21 'So that even without proceeding to the dumpling you can scarcely be corseted'; 'pudding' is also a cushioning coil of rope used aboard ship: 'you can hardly be laced up with ship's rope.'

The Bowl-bearer's speech. The Roman Saturnalia (Saturnals), like Twelfth Night, was a time of licence, when men need not doff their caps to their superiors. The speech again relies on Rabelais. It is good that a ballad is sung (though 'a poet should detest a ballad-maker', *Conversations with Drummond*), for this personified belly deserves as much, and

but unseasonable; and now is he poor thin-gut, fain to get his living with teaching of starlings, magpies, parrots, and jackdaws, those things he would have taught the belly. Beware of dealing with the belly, the belly will not be talked to, especially when he is full; then there is no venturing upon Venter, he will blow you all up, he will thunder indeed la: some in derision call him the Father of Farts; but I say he was the first inventor of great ordnance, and taught us to discharge them on festival days; would we had a fit feast for him i'faith, to show his activity; I would have something now fetched in to please his five senses, the throat, or the two senses the eyes: pardon me for my two senses, for I that carry Hercules' bowl in the service, may see double by my place; for I have drunk like a frog today: I would have a tun now brought into dance, and so many bottles about him. Ha! you look as if you would make a problem of this, do you see? do you see? a problem: why bottles? and why a tun? and why a tun? and why bottles to dance? I say that men that drink hard, and serve the belly in any place of quality (as the jovial tinkers, or the lusty kindred) are living measures of drink, and can transform themselves, and do every day to bottles, or tuns when they please: and when they ha' done all they can, they are as I say again (for I think I said somewhat like it afore) but moving measures of drink, and there is a piece in the cellar can hold more than all they. This will I make good, if it please our new god but to give a nod, for the belly does all by signs; and I am all for the belly, the truest clock in the world to go by.

Here the first anti-masque [of dancing bottles], *after which*

> *Hercules.* What rites are these? breeds earth more monsters yet?   25
> Antaeus scarce is cold: what can beget
> This store? (and stay) such contraries upon her,
> Is earth so fruitful of her own dishonour?
> Or 'cause his vice was inhumanity,
> Hopes she by vicious hospitality   30
> To work an expiation first? and then
> (Help virtue!) these are sponges, and not men:
> Bottles? mere vessels? half a tun of paunch?
> How? and the other half thrust forth in haunch?
> Whose feast? the Belly's? Comus? and my cup   35
> Brought in to fill the drunken orgies up?
> And here abused? that was the crowned reward,
> Of thirsty heroes, after labour hard?
> Burdens, and shames of nature, perish, die;
> (For yet you never lived) but in the sty   40
> Of vice have wallowed, and in that swine's strife
> Been buried under the offence of life:

---

were it longer it would match the belly's guts ('tripe'). But it is not good for proverbially 'The belly has no ears' (as 'Gaster was created without ears, even like the image of Jupiter in Candia. He only speaks by signs,' *Fourth Book*, 57, following Erasmus, *Adagia*, 2.8.84). Hunger ('Poverty, the mother of the sixty-nine Muses' is an old resident on Gaster's island, *Fourth Book*, 57) is 'unseasonable' in times of plenty: hence poets starve, and hunger teaches birds to sing 'against their nature, making poets of ravens, jackdaws, chattering jays, parrots, and starlings, and poetesses of magpies' (57), for scraps of food. Gaster 'invented arms and the art of war to defend corn . . . cannons, field-pieces, culverins, bombards, basiliskos, murdering instruments that dart iron' (61). As Comus has transformed himself to a 'hippocras bag' so his retinue consists in bottles (wicker flasks, says Busino) to gratify the belly's servants, a mix of proverbially jolly tinkers and dashing young blades ('lusty kindred'). Hourglasses and sundials are redundant 'there being no clock more regular than the belly' (*Fourth Book*, 64). The anti-masque of dancing bottles anticipates the dancing *olla podrida* in *Neptune's Triumph* (1624).

25–9   Antaeus's body would be on stage. His mother Earth should have shown more respect than contrarily to generate the monstrous dancing bottles.
40–2   'The ignoble never lived, they were awhile / Like swine, or other cattle here on earth: / Their names are not recorded on the file / Of life' (*Epithalamion [for] Jerome Weston*, 153–6).

Go reel and fall under the load you make,
Till your swoln bowels burst with what you take.
Can this be pleasure, to extinguish man? 45
Or so quite change him in his figure? can
The belly love his pain? and be content
With no delight but what's a punishment?
These monsters plague themselves, and fitly too,
For they do suffer what, and all they do, 50
But here must be no shelter, nor no shroud
For such: sink grove, or vanish into cloud.

At this the whole grove vanished, and the whole Music was discovered, sitting at the foot of the mountain, with Pleasure, and Virtue seated above them. The choir invited Hercules to rest with this song.

Great friend and servant of the good,
Let cool a while thy heated blood,
And from thy mighty labour cease. 55
    Lie down, lie down,
And give thy troubled spirits peace,
    Whilst virtue, for whose sake
Thou dost this god-like travail take,
May of the choicest herbage make 60
    (Here on this mountain bred)
      A crown, a crown
For thy immortal head.

Here Hercules being laid down at their feet, the second anti masque which was of pygmies, appeared.

1st Pygmy. Antaeus dead! and Hercules yet live!
Where is this Hercules? what would I give 65
To meet him now? meet him? nay, three such other,
If they had hand in murder of our brother?
With three? with four? with ten? nay with as many
As the name yields? pray anger there be any
Whereon to feed my just revenge, and soon: 70
How shall I kill him? hurl him 'gainst the moon,
And break him in small portions? give to Greece
His brain? and every tract of earth a piece.
2. He is yonder. *1.* Where? *3.* At the hill-foot, asleep.
1. Let one go steal his club. *2.* My charge, I'll creep. 75
4. He's ours. *1.* Yes, peace. *3.* Triumph, we have him boy.
4. Sure, sure, he is sure. *1.* Come, let us dance for joy.

---

53 The opposition of Pleasure and Virtue is drawn from Xenophon, *Memorabilia*, 2.1.21–34, and again at 159–60.
53–63 Recalling the promises of Browne's 'Steer hither, steer, your wingèd pines / All beaten mariners' in the *Inner Temple Masque*.
60 Ivy is the available 'herbage' (the scene description): 'Me ivy (meed of learned heads) / Ranks with the gods' (Horace, *Odes*, 1.1.29, Fanshawe); Hercules is identified with learned eloquence.

63 'While Hercules is asleep in Libya after conquering Antaeus, the Pygmies set upon him meaning to avenge Antaeus, for they claim to be his brothers . . . earthborn, and quite strong . . . but Hercules stands erect and laughs at the danger' (Philostratus, *Imagines*, 2.22); Busino describes them dressed as frogs.
72–3 Since the Greeks were intellectuals (Cicero, *De Oratore*, 3.15.56–7).

At the end of their dance they thought to surprise him, when suddenly being awaked by the music, he roused himself, they all run into holes. Song.

<blockquote>

Wake Hercules, awake; but heave up thy black eye,
'Tis only asked from thee to look, and these will die,
      Or fly: 80
    Already they are fled,
Whom scorn had else left dead.

</blockquote>

At which Mercury descended from the hill, with a garland of poplar to crown him.

<blockquote>

Mercury. Rest still thou active friend of Virtue; These
Should not disturb the peace of Hercules.
Earth's worms, and Honour's dwarfs (at too great odds)   85
Prove, or provoke the issue of the gods.
See, here a crown the aged hill hath sent thee,
My grandsire Atlas, he that did present thee
With the best sheep that in his fold were found,
Or golden fruit in the Hesperian ground,   90
For rescuing his fair daughters, then the prey
Of a rude pirate, as thou cam'st this way;
And taught thee all the learning of the Sphere,
And how like him thou might'st the heavens upbear;
As that thy labour's virtuous recompense   95
He, though a mountain now, hath yet the sense
Of thanking thee for more, thou being still
Constant to goodness, guardian of the hill;
Antaeus by thee suffocated here,
And the voluptuous Comus god of cheer   100
Beat from his grove, and that defaced, but now
The time's arrived that Atlas told thee of, how
By unaltered law, and working of the stars,
There should be a cessation of all jars,
'Twixt Virtue and her noted opposite   105
Pleasure; that both should meet here in the sight
Of Hesperus, the glory of the West,
The brightest star that from his burning crest
Lights all on this side the Atlantic seas,
As far as to thy pillars, Hercules.   110
See where he shines, Justice, and Wisdom placed

</blockquote>

83   Mercury crowns Hercules in Philostratus, *Imagines*, 2.21 (after the fight with Antaeus). When Evander finishes the story of Hercules and Cacus, 'the poplar with its Herculean shade' covers his hair (*Aeneid*, 8:276). Sometimes Hercules is identified with the sun or Time: 'The green and white poplar decks Hercules's head / Time's changes bring in night and day by turn' (Alciati, *Emblems*, 212).

85–6   'The dishonourable pygmies (born of the Earth) take on too much when they try or challenge the children of the gods' (Hercules was the bastard son of Jupiter).

87–94   Mount Atlas presents Hercules with the garland. When human (here confused with Mercury's grandfather), he possessed along with his brother Hesperus flocks of golden-coloured sheep, in Diodorus Siculus's account (*Bibliotheke*, 4.26.2–3) identified with the golden Apples of the Hesperides, gathered by Hercules as the last of his labours; he rewarded Hercules' rescue of his abducted daughters by teaching him 'all the learning of the sphere' or astronomy (4.27.5), used to gloss Hercules' temporarily taking on Atlas's burden of the heavens.

102–10   Hercules' education in star lore has advised him of a time when Virtue and Pleasure should be reconciled in front of a new western star (King James) that from his bright elevation ('burning crest') illuminates the Atlantic shore down to the straits of Gibraltar (the 'Pillars of Hercules', dealt with by Diodorus, 4.18.4–5).

About his throne, and those with Honour graced
Beauty, and Love: it is not with his brother
Bearing the world, but ruling such another
Is his renown. Pleasure, for his delight   115
Is reconciled to Virtue, and this night
Virtue brings forth, twelve princes have been bred
In this rough mountain, and near Atlas' head
The hill of knowledge; one, and chief of whom
Of the bright race of Hesperus is come,   120
Who shall in time, the same that he is be,
And now is only a less light than he;
These now she trusts with Pleasure, and to these
She gives an entrance to the Hesperides,
Fair Beauty's garden; neither can she fear   125
They should grow soft, or wax effeminate here;
Since in her sight, and by her charge all's done,
Pleasure the servant, Virtue looking on.

Here the whole choir of music called the twelve masquers forth from the top of the mountain, which then opened with this Song.

Ope agèd Atlas, open then thy lap,
And from thy beamy bosom strike a light,   130
That men may read in the mysterious map
      All lines
      And signs
Of royal education, and the right.
   See how they come and show,   135
   That are but born to know.
         Descend
         Descend
Though Pleasure lead,
   Fear not to follow: 140
They who are bred
   Within the hill
   Of Skill,
May safely tread
   What path they will,   145
No ground of good is hollow.

In their descent from the hill, Daedalus came down before them, of whom Hercules questioned Mercury.

Hercules. But Hermes stay, a little let me pause,
Who's this that leads? *Mercury.* A guide that gives them laws
To all their motions, Daedalus the wise.

113–14 'He is famed not for carrying a world on his shoulders like his brother Atlas, but for ruling a world.'
117–28 The 'twelve princes' (the number of the male masquers), chief among them Prince Charles, are to be admitted to the earthly paradise of the Hesperides, to enjoy its pleasures under the eye of Virtue.
129–46 'I, that the Good know, will uncloud the beam, / In whose light lies the reason; with much ease, / To Vice, and her love, men may make access . . . But before Virtue, do the gods rain sweat . . . You must wade to her; her path long and steep' (Hesiod, *Works and Days*, 286–91, Chapman); the song encourages the otherwise dangerously easy descent for those already tried on the heights of the 'hill of Skill' (of 'True Education').

Hercules. And doth in sacred harmony comprise 150
His precepts? *Mercury.* Yes. *Hercules.* They may securely prove
Then any labyrinth, though it be of Love.

Here while they put themselves in form, Daedalus had his first Song.

Come on, come on; and where you go,
    So interweave the curious knot,
As e'en the observer scarce may know 155
    Which lines are Pleasure's, and which not:
First figure out the doubtful way,
At which a while all youth should stay,
Where she and Virtue did contend,
Which should have Hercules to friend. 160
Then as all actions of mankind,
    Are but a labyrinth, or maze:
So let your dances be entwined,
    Yet not perplex men unto gaze;
But measured, and so numerous too, 165
As men may read each act you do;
And when they see the graces meet,
Admire the wisdom of your feet:
For dancing is an exercise,
    Not only shows the mover's wit, 170
But maketh the beholder wise,
    As he hath power to rise to it.

The first dance. After which Daedalus again. Song 2.

O more, and more, this was so well,
As praise wants half his voice to tell,
    Again yourselves compose, 175
And now put all the aptness on,
Of figure, that proportion,
    Or colour can disclose.
That if those silent arts were lost,
Design, and Picture, they might boast 180
    From you a newer ground,
Instructed to the heightening sense
Of dignity and reverence,
    In your true motions found.
Begin, begin; for look, the fair 185
Do longing listen to what air

153–72 The dancing floor represented by Vulcan on the shield of Achilles was 'All full of turnings; that was like the admirable maze / For fair-haired Ariadne made, by cunning Daedalus; / And in it, youths, and virgins danced; all young and beauteous, / And glued in another's palms' (Homer, *Iliad*, 18:591–4, Chapman).
164–6 'Yet not confuse men into bewilderment; but be harmonious and rhythmical so that your various motions can be made out.'
167–72 'Socrates . . . was not ashamed to account dancing among the serious disciplines . . . [since it had] a concinnity

of moving the foot and the body, expressing some pleasant or profitable affects or motions of the mind' (Sir Thomas Elyot, *The Governor*, 1.20).
175–84 'Take up your positions, assuming readiness for whatever patterns best reveal harmony and colour, so that if the arts of drawing and painting were lost they might possess a new foundation in your movements, taught by them the elevated notions of worth and worship.'
185–7 'Your ladies listen longingly to the tune to which you will dance your second turn ('touch').'

You form your second touch;
That they may vent their murmuring hymns,
Just to the tune you move your limbs,
    And wish their own were such. 190
Make haste, make haste, for this
The labyrinth of Beauty is.

The second dance. That ended. Daedalus. Song 3.

It follows now you are to prove
The subtlest maze of all, that's Love.
    And if you stay too long, 195
    The fair will think you do 'em wrong:
Go choose among, but with a mind
As gentle as the stroking wind
    Runs o'er the gentler flowers.
And so let all your actions smile, 200
As if they meant not to beguile,
    The ladies but the hours.
Grace, laughter, and discourse may meet,
    And yet the beauty not go less:
For what is noble should be sweet, 205
    But not dissolved in wantonness.
    Will you that I give the law
      To all your sport and sum it,
It should be such should envy draw,
    But ever overcome it. 210

Here they danced with the Ladies, and the whole revels followed; which ended, Mercury called to him in this following speech: which was after repeated in song by two trebles, two tenors, a bass, and the whole chorus. Song 4.

An eye of looking back were well,
Or any murmur that would tell
    Your thoughts, how you were sent,
      And went
To walk with Pleasure, not to dwell. 215
These, these are hours by Virtue spared
Herself, she being her own reward:
    But she will have you know,
      That though
Her sports be soft, her life is hard: 220
You must return unto the hill
    And there advance
With labour, and inhabit still
    That height and crown,
From whence you ever may look down 225
    Upon triumphèd Chance.

209–10 The admiration it excites should overwhelm the envy it attracts.
211–36 'He has reached the heights who knows wherein he rejoices and has not placed his felicity in another's power . . . this joy is a solid thing, yet which opens up as it is entered into it . . . look to the true good and rejoice in what is your own' (Seneca, *Epistles*, 23.2, 5–6).

She, she it is in darkness shines,
'Tis she that still herself refines,
By her own light to every eye
More seen, more known when Vice stands by;   230
And though a stranger here on earth,
In Heaven she hath her right of birth:
    There, there is Virtue's seat,
  Strive to keep her your own,
      'Tis only she can make you great,   235
  Though place here make you known.

After which, they danced their last dance, returned into the scene, which closed, was a mountain again as before.

Martha Moulsworth (1578–1646)

Martha Moulsworth was a daughter of Robert Dorset, a Canon of Christ Church, Oxford, from the 1570s, who died in 1580 as Dean of Chester and a DD of Oxford. Letters survive to his former pupil Philip Sidney; and he is commemorated in a MS collection of Latin poems. Moulsworth was two and a half when he died, so the account of his fatherly attentions given in the poem has to be understood as fiction. She first married Nicholas Prynne, a London goldsmith, by whom she had two children (baptized in 1602 and 1604); both died young. Then in 1605 she married the widower Thomas Thorowgood, a draper, with whom she lived in Hoddesdon along with his daughter Elizabeth. On Thorowgood's death she married another goldsmith, resident in Hoddesdon, the 65-year-old Bevill Moulsworth, twice a widower and father of another Elizabeth. She bore him a son Bevill, who died early. She herself survived into a comfortable old age in Hoddesdon. Her funeral sermon, by Thomas Hassall, is printed in Evans and Little. The poem, possibly autograph, is in a commonplace book containing mainly political material in another hand (Yale University Library, Osborn MS fb 150). It was first published as *'My Name Was Martha': A Renaissance Woman's Autobiographical Poem by Martha Moulsworth* in an edition by Robert C. Evans and Barbara Wiedemann (West Cornwall, CT: Locust Hill, 1993) and then in a greatly expanded edition by Robert C. Evans and Anne C. Little as *'The Muses Females Are': Martha Moulsworth and Other Woman Writers of the English Renaissance* (West Cornwall, CT: Locust Hill, 1995). The expanded edition includes essays by many hands filling in the detail and the background of Moulsworth's life, dealing with the status of women as writers or as widows, with the rhetoric of autobiography, and with details of the poem's own rhetoric. Its appendices are a rich resource.

November the 10th 1632 : The Memorandum of Martha Moulsworth, Widow

The poem (a birthday poem to herself) is a 'record of events', but with the fuller sense of 'things to be borne in mind'. Its sense of record is enforced at every turn, but the account of her education at her father's hands is certainly a fiction, her account of her children perfunctory, the omission of her stepchildren in such a context puzzling (particularly of the first Elizabeth, to whom she seems to have been attached). The poem is an organized fiction, with too much a sense of its own shape (even the shape of its own couplets) for it to be a one-off piece. But nothing else survives, except perhaps the epitaph in Broxbourne parish church of her husband Bevill and her son of the same name. Notes marked '(Moulsworth)' are marginal entries in the MS. Mainly they record dates and register biblical allusions; those on lines 7–10 and 37–8 are witty. The punctuation is editorial.

> The tenth day of the winter month November,
> A day which I must duly still remember,
> Did open first these eyes, and showed this light.
> Now on that day, upon that day, I write:
> This season fitly, willingly, combines   5
> The birthday of myself, and of these lines.
> The time the clock (the yearly stroke is one),
> That clock by fifty-five returns hath gone.
> How few, how many warnings it will give,
> He only knows in whom we are, and live.   10

---

4 'November 10th 1632' (Moulsworth).

7–10 'My Muse is tell-clock, and echoeth every stroke with a coupled rhyme so many times viz. 55 Acts 17.28 etc.' (Moulsworth). Her poem is a chiming clock (Cleveland calls the cock a 'tell-clock'), sounding one couplet for every year. She remembers 'In him we live, and move, and have our being' (Acts 17: 28); and 'Of that day and hour knoweth no man ... but my Father only' (Matthew 24: 36).

In carnal state of sin original
I did not stay one whole day natural:
The seal of grace in sacramental water
So soon had I, so soon become the daughter
Of earthly parents, and of Heavenly Father.   15
Some christen late for state, the wiser rather.
My name was Martha: Martha took much pain
Our Saviour Christ her guest to entertain.
God give me grace my inward house to dight
That he with me may sup, and stay all night.   20
My father was a man of spotless fame,
Of gentle birth, and Dorset was his name.
He had, and left lands of his own possession.
He was of Levi's tribe by his profession
His mother Oxford knowing well his worth   25
Arrayed in scarlet robe did send him forth.
By him I was brought up in godly piety,
In modest cheerfulness, and sad sobriety.
Nor only so: beyond my sex and kind
He did with learning Latin deck my mind,   30
And why not so? The Muses females are
And therefore of us females take some care.
Two universities we have of men:
O that we had but one of women then!
O then, that would in wit and tongues surpass   35
All art of men that is, or ever was.
But I of Latin have no cause to boast:
For want of use I long ago it lost.
Had I no other portion to my dower,
I might have stood a virgin to this hour.   40
But, though the virgin Muses I love well,
I have long since bid virgin life farewell.
Thrice this right hand did holy wedlock plight,
And thrice this hand with pledged ring was dight,
Three husbands me, and I have them enjoyed,   45
Nor I by them, nor they by me annoyed;
All lovely, loving all, some more, some less:
Though gone, their love, and memory I bless.

11–15 Calvin defines a sacrament as the 'outward sign by which the lord seals on our consciences the promises of his good will' (*Institutes*, 4.14.1) and as 'the sign of the initiation by which we may be reckoned God's children' (4.15.1); he argues that 'through baptism we are released and made exempt from original sin' (4.15.9), but that it would be much better 'to omit from baptism all theatrical pomp' (4.15.19). Unlike Luther, Calvin does not believe that baptism is necessary to salvation, though it is commonly believed he did (4.15.20).

16 'Some delay the baptism of their children to prepare showy celebrations of it; others more wisely (for they always may die) have their children baptized early ('rathe').'

17–18 'Luke 10: 41' (Moulsworth): 'And Jesus answered and said unto her, Martha, Martha, thou art careful and troubled about many things.'

20 'Revelation 3: 20', 'Luke 24: 29' (Moulsworth): 'if any man hear my voice, and open the door, I will come into him, and will sup with him, and he with me', 'And he went in to tarry with them.'

24 *of Levi's tribe* 'a clergyman' (Deuteronomy 10: 8).

26 *scarlet robe* since the Oxford Master's and Doctor's robes include scarlet.

28 *sad* 'constant', 'demure'.

30 *my* dropped in MS.

33 *Two universities* Oxford and Cambridge.

38 'Latin is not the most marketable marriage metal' (Moulsworth); 'latten' is a brass-like metal. Erasmus's colloquy 'Of the learned woman and the Abbot' is a robust apology for female Latinity.

Until my one and twentieth year of age,
I did not bind myself in marriage: 50
My Spring was late, some think that sooner love;
But backward Springs do oft the kindest prove.
My first knot held five years, and eight months more;
Then was a year set on my mourning score.
My second bond ten years nine months did last; 55
Three years eight months I kept a widow's fast.
The third I took a lovely man, and kind.
Such comeliness in age we seldom find:
From Mortimers he drew his pedigree,
Their arms he bore, not bought with herald's fee; 60
Third wife I was to him, as he to me
Third husband was: in number we agree.
Eleven years, and eight months his autumn lasted:
A second Spring too soon away it hasted.
Was never man so buxom to his wife: 65
With him I led an easy darling's life.
I had my will in house, in purse, in store:
What would a woman old or young have more?
Two years almost outwearing since he died,
And yet, and yet, my tears for him not dried. 70
I by the first, and last some issue had,
But root, and fruit is dead, which makes me sad.
My husbands all on holy days did die:
Such day, such way, they to the saints did hie.
This life is workday even at the best, 75
But Christian death, and holy day of rest.
The first, the first of martyrs did befall,
St Stephen's feast to him was funeral:
The morrow after Christ our flesh did take,
This husband did his mortal flesh forsake. 80
The second on a double-sainted day
To Jude, and Simon took his happy way.
This Simon, as an ancient story saith,
Did first in England plant the Christian faith;
Most sure it is that Jude in holy writ 85
Doth warn us to maintain, and fight for it;
In which all those that live, and die, may well
Hope with the saints eternally to dwell.

49 'First husband, Mr Nicolas Prynne, April 18, 1598' (Moulsworth).
52 *backward* 'behindhand'.
54 *score* 'record', usually of food and drink consumed.
55 'Second Mr Thomas Thorowgood, February 3, 1604' (Moulsworth): '1604' represents any date before 25 March in 1605.
57 'Third Mr Bevill Moulsworth, June 15, 1619' (Moulsworth).
60 *herald's fee* University graduates and the like were properly entitled to buy the status of gentleman; Moulsworth was a gentleman born.
65 *buxom* 'indulgent' or 'good-tempered' (and not yet specialized to apply to women).

73 *root, and fruit* Three children are known. She calls children part 'root' (as Jesus is 'a root of Jesse' in Isaiah 11: 10) and part 'fruit' (as Jesus is the 'fruit' of Mary's womb in Luke 1: 42).
77–9 The feast-day of St Stephen, the first martyr (Acts 7: 54–60), is 26 December, the day after Christmas; Prynne died in 1603.
81–4 Sts Simon and Jude share a feast-day on 28 October. Thorowgood died in 1615. For Simon's preaching in England see 'Nicephorus's History' (Moulsworth, a presumably second-hand reference to the *Ecclesiastica Historia* of the Byzantine historian).
85 'Jude verse 3' (Moulsworth): 'ye should earnestly contend for the faith which was once delivered unto the saints.'

The last on St Mathias' day did wend
Unto his home, and pilgrimage's end.   90
This feast comes in that season which doth bring
Upon dead winter's cold, as lively spring.
His body wintering in the lodge of death
Shall feel a Spring, with bud of life, and breath;
And rise in incorruption, glory, power   95
Like to the body of our Saviour.
In vain it were, profane it were for me,
With sadness to ask, which of these three
I shall call husband in the resurrection,
For then shall all in glorious perfection,   100
Like to the immortal heavenly angels live,
Who wedlock's bonds do neither take nor give;
But in the mean time, this must be my care,
Of knitting here a fourth knot to beware.
A threefold cord though hardly yet is broken,   105
Another ancient story doth betoken
That seldom comes a better; why should I
Then put my widowhood in jeopardy?
The virgin's life is gold, as clerks us tell
The widow's silver, I love silver well.   110

89 St Mathias's day is 24 February. Bevill Moulsworth died in 1631.

95 '1 Corinthians 15: 42' (Moulsworth): 'It is sown in corruption; it is raised in incorruption.'

96 'Philippians 3: 21' (Moulsworth): '[Christ] shall change our vile body, that it may be fashioned like unto his glorious body.'

98–102 'Matthew 22: 28, 30' (Moulsworth): the Sadducees ask of a woman who had married seven brothers in succession: 'in the resurrection whose wife shall she be of the seven?' and Jesus answers, 'in the resurrection they neither marry, nor are given in marriage.'

103–4 But the proverb has it, 'Keep yourself from a widow that has been thrice married.'

105 'Ecclesiastes 4: 12' (Moulsworth): 'a threefold cord is not quickly broken.'

106–7 The proverb 'Seldom comes a better' is explained by the story of monks who fare successively worse under three successive abbots, and decide against praying for a fourth.

109–10 Sir John Davies, *A Contention betwixt a Wife, a Widow, and a Maid* rehearses the virtues of each state: maids are 'The purest gold, that suffers no allay' (214). Silver (not a point made by Davies) is already synonymous with ready money.

Edward, Lord Herbert of Cherbury (1583–1648)

Edward Herbert was the eldest son of the family that included the poet George Herbert. He was knighted in 1603 and created Baron Cherbury in 1629. Educated privately and then at University College, Oxford, his public career was military and diplomatic (he was the French ambassador in the early 1620s). *The Autobiography* (edited by J. M. Shuttleworth, Oxford, 1976), written late in life, covers only the years up to 1624 (when his public life effectively ended), but is summary and for the most part exterior. His later life was complicated by the Civil War (and the strenuously Platonic triplets of *The Idea* are noted as 'made at Alnwick, in his expedition to Scotland with the army, 1639'). His major literary achievement was the *De Veritate* (1624, translated by Meyrick H. Carré, Bristol, 1937) which, as the full title has it, purports to distinguish truth from 'revelation, from the probable, from the possible, and from the false', but which became famous for its scheme of natural religion, which derives from the common experience of mankind the principles that God exists and must be worshipped, that obedience to notions of piety and virtue is peremptory, and that we are rewarded or punished in

the hereafter: Herbert is known, on the strength of this work and later developments of it, as 'the father of Deism'. His poems, having circulated in MSS, were posthumously edited as *Occasional Verses* (1665), perhaps by his younger brother Henry, and inscribed to his grandson. 'Composed in various and perplexed times', as the editor has it in an inflated preface, they are hardly touched by their circumstances; but they were always notorious for obscurity: Jonson (*Conversations with Drummond*) reports that Donne wrote his *Elegy on Prince Henry* to 'match Edward Herbert in obscureness'; his own *Elegy for Dr Donne* is one of the more distinguished assertions of the impossibility of matching Donne. The standard account of Cherbury and his work is M. M. Rossi, *La Vita, le Opere, i Poemi di Edoardo Herbert* (Florence, 1947); the standard modern edition of the *Poems* is by G. C. Moore Smith (Oxford, 1923); there is a Scolar Press facsimile of 1657 (Menston, 1969). A checklist of works by and about Cherbury has been compiled by J. M. Shuttleworth in the *National Library of Wales Journal*, 20 (1977), 151–68.

An Ode upon a Question moved, Whether Love should continue for ever?

Printed first in *1665*; this text is based on *An Ode* (British Library Additional MS 37157, with corrections in Cherbury's hand). The MS is dated 1630; but the poem, like Donne's *The Ecstasy*, is a difficult reworking of Sidney's song 'In a grove most rich of shade', suggesting a version of the rivalry in 'obscureness' that provoked Donne to his *Elegy on Prince Henry*. The clearest anticipation of the subject of love's immortality (clearer than in the overtly Platonizing *Platonic Love* poems, 'Madam, believe it' and 'Madam, your beauty', 'Disconsolate and Sad') is in the madrigal *I must depart* (dated May 1608). The elaborated argument assumes that 'a Common Notion when it is

mingled with inner apprehension must be trusted, even though the other faculties may resist it' (*De Veritate*, chapter 8) and that since 'every Common Notion, and indeed every lawful natural impulse, is directed towards Eternal Blessedness' (chapter 4) then it must exist. The simple-looking but rare stanza (famous from Tennyson's *In Memoriam*) is used again in Cherbury's *I am the first that ever loved* and by Jonson in an *Elegy* ('Though beauty be the mark of praise'). The passages from Pico's *Discourse* (translated by Stanley) should not be supposed to align Cherbury with an academic tradition of Platonism.

> Having interred her infant-birth,
> The watery ground that late did mourn,
> Was strewed with flowers for the return
> Of the wished bridegroom of the earth.

1–2 Philemon Holland (translating Ammanius Marcellinus, 1609) has the ground 'besobbed and drenched with the mid-Winter frosts that now thawed'.

4 *bridegroom* 'the sun, which is as a bridegroom coming out of his chamber' (Psalms 19: 4–5).

The well accorded birds did sing   5
    Their hymns unto the pleasant time,
    And in a sweet consorted chime
Did welcome in the cheerful Spring.

To which, soft whistles of the wind,
    And warbling murmurs of a brook,   10
    And varied notes of leaves that shook,
An harmony of parts did bind.

While doubling joy unto each other,
    All in so rare consent was shown,
    No happiness that came alone,   15
Nor pleasure that was not another.

When filled with joys none can express,
    That loving and belovèd pair,
    Melander and Celinda fair,
The season with their loves did bless.   20

And in such desires as dwell
    In those to love's perfection got,
    Were most assurèd they could not
Love too much that love so well.

Walking thus towards a pleasant grove,   25
    Which did, it seemed, in new delight
    The pleasures of the time unite,
To give a triumph to their love,

They stayed at last, and on the grass
    Reposèd so, as o'er his breast   30
    She bowed her gracious head to rest,
Such a weight as no burden was.

While over either's compassed waist
    Their folded arms were so composed,
    As if in straitest bonds enclosed,   35
They suffered for joys they did taste.

Long their fixed eyes to heaven bent,
    Unchanged, they did never move,
    As if so great and pure a love
No glass but it could represent.   40

5–12 Developed from Sidney's 'In a grove most rich of shade, / Where birds wanton music made, / May then young his pied weeds showing, / New perfumes with flowers fresh growing.'

14 *consent* 'harmony' (relying on the etymology of 'concent', 'singing together').

17 *filled with joys* with a love (1665).

18 *loving and beloved* mutually happy (1665).

21–4 Omitted in 1665.

28 *triumph* 'pageant': the personified beauties of spring are enlisted to celebrate love's victory.

34–6 Pressing the common conceit of lovers as each other's prisoners: 'now like slave-born Muscovite: / I call it praise to suffer tyranny' (*Astrophil*, 2:1–11).

39–40 In Pico's *Platonic Discourse*, the lover 'in the sun's glass reads / Her [the beloved's] face' (*The Sonnet*, 78–9).

When with a sweet, though troubled look.
   She first brake silence, saying, "Dear friend,
   O that our love might take no end,
Or never had beginning took!

I speak not this with a false heart,   45
   (Wherewith his hand she gently strained)
   Or that would change a love maintained
With so much faith on either part.

Nay, I protest, though Death with his
   Worst counsel should divide us here,   50
   His terrors could not make me fear,
To come where your loved presence is.

Only if love's fire with the breath
   Of life be kindlèd, I doubt,
   With our last air 'twill be breathed out,   55
And quenchèd with the cold of death.

That if affection be a line,
   Which is closed up in our last hour;
   O here 'twould grieve me, any power
Could force so dear a love as mine!"   60

She scarce had done, when his shut eyes
   An inward joy did represent,
   To hear Celinda thus resent
A love which he so much did prize.

Then with a look, it seemed, denied   65
   All beauty's power but hers, yet so,
   As if to her breath he did owe
This borrowed life, he thus replied;

"O you, wherein, they say, souls rest
   Till they descend, pure heavenly fires,   70
   Shall lustful and corrupt desires
With your immortal seed be blest?

---

46 *strained* 'squeezed'.
49–53 'Though death with the worst intentions ('counsel')
should separate us, I should follow you beyond the grave.'
The phrasing echoes Psalms 23: 4: 'though I walk through
the valley of the shadow of death, I will fear no evil: for thou
art with me.'
53–5 'But if love begins with the breath of our kisses, I
fear ('doubt') it will not survive our breathing.'
57–8 Pico's *Discourse* argues that material things have a
beginning to which they cannot return (2.11); but lines may
be circular, and Cherbury wrote to Sir George More: '*circu-
lus* you know is *capacissima figura*, to which the mind ought
to be like, that can most worthily love you.'

59 *here* how (1665).
60 *force* 'overpower'.
63–4 *resent /A love which* intent / To a love (1665); *resent*
'feel'.
66 *beauty's* earthly (1665).
67–8 Lovers exchange breath in kissing, but recalling Gen-
esis 2: 7: 'God . . . breathed into his nostrils the breath of
life; and man became a living soul.'
69–76 *You* the stars ('pure heavenly fires'). Pico's *Platonic
Discourse*: 'Formed by the eternal look of God . . . The soul
descends into man's heart, / Imprinting there with wondrous
art / What worth she borrowed from her star' (Sonnet, 85–9).
72 *seed* 'the soul'.

And shall our love, so far beyond
    That low and dying appetite,
    And which so chaste desires unite,   75
Not hold in an eternal bond?

Is it perchance we should remove
    Ourselves from these vile objects here,
    As if on earth that nothing were
Made for our knowledge or our love?   80

No sure, for if none can ascend
    Even to the visible degree
    Of things created, how should we
The invisible comprehend?

Or rather since that Power expressed   85
    His greatness in His works alone,
    Being here best in's creatures known,
Why is He not loved in them best?

But is't not true, which you pretend,
    That since our love and knowledge here,   90
    Only as parts of life appear,
So they with it should take their end?

O no, beloved, I am most sure,
    Those virtuous habits we acquire,
    As being in the soul entire,   95
Shall with it evermore endure.

For if where sins and vice reside
    They lasting characters infuse
    It by strong consequence ensues
The better parts must still abide.   100

Else should our souls in vain elect,
    And vainer yet were Heaven's laws,
    When to an everlasting cause
They gave a perishing effect.

---

74 *dying appetite* 'passing lust'.

77–80 Is it, because we should decline [= refuse], / And wholly from our thoughts exclude / Objects that may the sense delude, / And study only the divine? (1665). Pico's *Discourse* (2.6) asks: 'If love can be only of visible things, how can it be applied to ideas, invisible natures?' Melander's gambit is to invert the question.

89–92 Setting up Celinda's point of lines 52–6.

95 *in the soul entire* with the soul entire (1665, and so originally in MS, but corrected in Herbert's hand). The difficult suggestion that acquired virtuous habits might be integral with the soul is cancelled in the corrected MS reading. They must be identical with the worth the soul borrows from her star (69–76).

96 *Shall* Must (1665).

97–100 For if where sins and vice reside, / We find so foul a guilt remain, / As never dying in his stain, / Still punished in the soul doth bide, /Much more that true and real joy, / Which in a virtuous love is found, / Must be more solid in its ground, / Than fate or death can e'er destroy (1665). The case rests on the assumption of God's benevolent justice.

101–4 'That eternal causes should bring forth chanceable effects is as sensible as that the sun should be the author of darkness' (Sidney, *Arcadia*, 3.10.5). The 'everlasting cause' is the soul, the 'perishing effect' the joy of love.

Nor here on earth then, nor above,   105
   Our good affection can impair,
   For where God doth admit the fair,
Think you that he excludeth love?

These eyes again then, eyes shall see,
   And hands again these hands enfold,   110
   And all chaste pleasures can be told
Shall with us everlasting be.

For if no use of sense remain
   When bodies once this life forsake,
   Or they could no delight partake,   115
Why should they ever rise again?

And if every imperfect mind
   Make love the end of knowledge here,
   How perfect will our love be, where
All imperfection is refined?   120

And as when man did first obtain
   The forbid knowing good and ill,
   The act was punishèd, yet still
The knowledge did in him remain,

So though our love never impure   125
   Some outward frailty may retain,
   It shall be cleansèd from its stain
But in itself shall still endure;

Or else our love never forbid
   Lay subject to a greater curse,   130
   And frailty should be punished worse
Than what man in perfection did.

Let then no doubt, Celinda, touch,
   Much less your fairest mind invade,
   Were not our souls immortal made,   135
Our loves alone might make them such.

So when one wing can make no way,
   Two joinèd can themselves dilate,
   So can two persons propagate,
When singly either would decay.   140

106 *impair* 'decay'.

113–16 In the *De Veritate* ch. 5, Herbert seems to deny the resurrection of the body; its use here is witty.

117–20 *Discourse* 2.20: 'others . . . remembering that more perfect beauty which the soul (before immersed in the body) beheld, are inflamed with an incredible desire of reviewing it, in pursuit whereof they separate themselves as much as possible from the body.'

121–32 Omitted in *1665*.

136 *loves alone might* equal loves can (*1665*).

137–40 Because proverbially 'The bird must flutter that flies with one wing'; and 'One is no number: have they not perished that there was not two left to make a number?' (Lyly, *Midas*, 3.1.22); *dilate* 'carry abroad'.

So when from hence we shall be gone,
    And be no more, nor you, nor I,
    As one another's mystery,
Each shall be both, yet both but one."

Thus said, in her up-lifted face,   145
    Her eyes which did that beauty crown,
    Were like two stars, that having fall'n down,
Looked up again to find their place:

While such a moveless silent peace
    Did seize on their becalmèd sense,   150
    One would have thought some influence
Their ravished spirits did possess.

147–8   *Looked* Look (1665); eyes, commonly identified with stars, here belong in heaven.
149–52   Spenser's holy lovers are rewarded with such 'sweet contentment, that it doth bereave / Their soul of sense, through infinite delight, / And them transport from flesh into the spright. / In which they see such admirable things, / As carries them into an ecstasy' (*Hymn of Heavenly Beauty*, 257–61); 'influence' is understood literally as an influx from the stars.

William Drummond of Hawthornden (1585–1649)

'His censure of my verses was that they were all good, especially my epitaph of the prince, save that they smelled too much of the schools, and were not after the fancy of the time': so wrote Drummond in the notes that are generally printed among Jonson's works as *Conversations with Drummond*. A poetic disciple most obviously of Sidney, he pursued the Italianization of English poetry more thoroughly than any poet of his generation. He committed himself to a view of poetry free of fashionable 'scholastical quiddities', standing out against the metropolitan assault on 'those ornaments with which [poetry] has amused the world some thousand years. Poesy is not a thing that is yet in the finding out and search' (letter to Arthur Johnson). Hence Ben Jonson's observations on his datedness or provinciality. Born at Hawthornden, Drummond was educated at the Edinburgh High School and Edinburgh University, where he graduated in 1605 (and whose library is the most important beneficiary of Drummond's own). He spent the next five years in London and in France, where among other things he studied law. The formation of his literary taste, inclined in a remarkable degree to modern literatures (and more 'continental' than English), belongs to this period. He is the first Scottish poet to write in London English, and uses it in some respects like a foreign language (sometimes imperfectly: the rhymes not always true, and the grammar sometimes treated as dispensable) with an ear for imagined musical effects. In 1610 he succeeded to his father's estates at Hawthornden, where he lived the rest of his life as a gentleman scholar, poet and essayist. His first published poem was an elegy on Prince Henry. His major poetical efforts were over by 1630. Collections of the poems during Drummond's life are *Poems* (1614 and 1616) and *Flowers of Sion* (1623 and 1630). He corresponded with Drayton; and he was visited by Jonson (whom 'Drayton feared'), an 'event' celebrated in the so-called *Conversations*. He married in 1630 and had nine children. Drawn into political controversy towards the end of his life, the main achievement of his later years was *The History of Scotland*, published posthumously in 1655. *Poems* (1656 and 1659) was edited by Milton's nephew Edward Phillips. The important *Works* (Edinburgh, 1711) brings together the historical and poetical work, letters, poems and short essays, and reprints the extended meditation on mutability and death first published as *A Midnight's Trance* (1619, revised as *A Cypress Grove*, for the 1623 *Flowers of Sion*). The standard edition is L. E. Kastner's *The Poetical Works of William Drummond of Hawthornden* (Edinburgh: Scottish Text Society, N.S. 3–4, 1913). David Masson's *Drummond of Hawthornden* (London, 1873) remains the standard biography. R. H. MacDonald, *The Library of Drummond of Hawthornden* (Edinburgh: Edinburgh University Press, 1971), describes his reading.

Tears, on the Death of Moeliades

The text is from *Poems* (1616). Published first by Andrew Hart of Edinburgh in 1613, it was minimally revised for a so-called third edition in 1614, and in that form incorporated in the *Poems* of 1614. The readings of 1614 are normally transmitted through Edward Phillips's edition of 1656 to the *Works* of 1711. Variants from the substantially revised *1616* are very selectively recorded. Prince Henry died of smallpox on 6 November 1612. Burton says it was 'as if our dearest friends' lives perished with his' (*Anatomy*, 1.2.4.7). Europe mourned the hoped-for champion of the Protestant cause. Very few English poets (Shakespeare, Jonson, Drayton, Daniel) failed to join in the general mourning. Most did, and among them Browne, Campion, Chapman, Donne (though only to 'rival Edward Herbert in obscureness', Jonson told Drummond), Drummond's friend William Alexander, Edward's brother George Herbert (in Latin in a Cambridge collection), Henry King, Ralegh, Sylvester, Tourneur, Webster, Wither. Dennis Kay's *Melodious Tears* (Oxford: Clarendon Press, 1990) gives the fullest account of its scale and character.

This is Drummond's first published poem, an ambitious, self-consciously a virtuoso public poem. Its closest analogue is Sidney's lament for Amphialus ('Since to that death is gone the shepherd high', *Arcadia*, 3), but the couplet refrains are perhaps on the model of Donne's *Anniversaries*. Drummond supplies a note: 'The name which in these verses is given Prince Henry, is that which he himself in the challenges of his martial sports and masquerades was wont to use, *Moeliades, Prince of the Isles*, which in anagram maketh *Miles a Deo* ['God's soldier'].'

O Heavens! then is it true that thou art gone,
And left this woeful isle her loss to moan,
Moeliades? bright day-star of the West,
A comet, blazing terror to the East:
And neither that thy sprite so heavenly wise,   5
Nor body (though of earth) more pure than skies,
Nor royal stem, nor thy sweet tender age,
Of adamantine Fates could quench the rage?
O fading hopes! O short-while-lasting joy!
Of earth-born man, which one hour can destroy!   10
Then even of Virtue's spoils Death trophies rears,
As if he gloried most in many tears.
Forced by grim Destinies, heavens neglect our cries,
Stars seem set only to act tragedies:
And let them do their worst, since thou art gone,   15
Raise whom they list to thrones, enthroned dethrone,
Stain princely bowers with blood, and even to Gange,
In cypress sad, glad Hymen's torches change.
Ah! thou hast left to live, and in the time,
When scarce thou blossomed in thy pleasant prime,   20
So falls by northern blast a virgin rose,
At half that doth her bashful bosom close:
So a sweet flourish languishing decays,
That late did blush when kissed by Phoebus' rays:
So Phoebus mounting the meridian's height,   25
Choked by pale Phoebe, faints unto our sight,
Astonished Nature sullen stands to see
The life of all this All, so changed to bee,
In gloomy gowns the stars about deplore,
The sea with murmuring mountains beats the shore,   30
Black darkness reels o'er all, in thousand showers
The weeping air, on Earth her sorrow pours,
That (in a palsy) quakes to find so soon
Her lover set, and night burst forth ere noon.
　　If Heaven (alas) ordained thee young to die,   35
Why was it not where thou thy might didst try?
And to the hopeful world at least set forth

2–4   Henry was a sun to Britain in the West, a fateful comet to the Ottomans in the East: European rulers still harboured crusading ambitions.

8   *adamantine Fates* cruel Destinies (1614), which is the sense; *rage* 'ardour'.

11   'Death raises as tokens of its victory what had been won by Virtue'; 'Did Wisdom this our wretched time espy / In one true chest to rob all virtue's treasure?' (Sidney, 'Since to that death', 46–7).

14   *act* 'activate' (a standard sense).

17   'Kill princes in their palaces; and as far as India ('Gange' for 'Ganges') turn wedding celebrations ('glad Hymen's torches') to funeral mourning': just over a month before Henry's death the Elector Palatine had arrived in England to marry Henry's sister Princess Elizabeth.

19   *left* 'ceased'.

21–4   Drummond reuses these lines in a proposed epitaph

for William Ramsay. Chapman's *Epicede* (314) speaks of Henry as a rose 'blasted in the bud'; Drummond's detail of the rose closing her petals with the wind at half-strength is an overelaboration.

23   *flourish* Phillips substitutes 'flower', which gives the sense.

25   'So the sun at noon, eclipsed by the moon, disappears from view.'

29   *about* 'round about', but an awkwardly placed adverb: Phillips substitutes 'this loss'; *deplore* 'weep' (a standard use).

31   'Night like a drunkard reels / Beyond the hills' (Drummond, *Song 2* ['Phoebus arise'], 42–3).

33–4   The sun 'is as a bridegroom coming out of his chamber' (as in Psalms 19: 5); Phineas Fletcher has 'the palsies of the trembling earth' (*Sicelides*, 2.8.107).

36   Why was't not where thou might'st thy valour try (1614); 'Why was it not in war?'

37   *hopeful* wondering (1614).

Some little spark of thine expected worth?
Moeliades, O that by Hister's streams,
Amongst shrill-sounding trumpets, flaming gleams 40
Of warm encrimsoned swords, and cannons' roar,
Balls thick as rain poured by the Caspian shore,
Amongst crushed lances, ringing helms, and shields,
Dismembered bodies ravishing the fields,
In Turkish blood made red like Mars's star, 45
Thou ended hadst thy life, and Christian war!
Or as brave Bourbon thou hadst made old Rome,
Queen of the world, thy triumph's place, and tomb!
So heaven's fair face to the unborn which reads
A book had been of thine illustrious deeds: 50
So to their nephews agèd sires had told
The high exploits performed by thee of old,
Towns razed, and raised, victorious, vanquished bands,
Fierce tyrants flying, foiled, killed, by thy hands.
And in dear arras, virgins fair had wrought 55
The bays and trophies to thy country brought:
While some new Homer imping pens to Fame,
Deaf Nilus' dwellers had made hear thy name.
That thou didst not attain those honours' spheres,
It was not want of worth, O no, but years 60
A youth more brave, pale Troy with trembling walls
Did never see, nor she whose name appals
Both Titan's golden bowers, for bloody fights
Mustering on Mars's field such Mars-like knights.
The heavens had brought thee to the highest height, 65
Of wit, and courage, showing all their might
When they thee framed: ay me! that what is brave
On Earth, they as their own so soon should crave.
Moeliades sweet courtly nymphs deplore,
From Thulë to Hydaspes' pearly shore. 70
　　When Forth thy nurse, forth where thou first didst pass
Thy tender days (who smiled oft on her glass
To see thee gaze) meandering with her streams,
Heard thou hadst left this Round, from Phoebus' beams
She sought to fly, but forcèd to return 75

39 *Hister* 'the lower Danube' (against the Turk).

41 *encrimsoned* vermilion (1614).

44 Huge heaps of slaughtered bodies long the fields (1614); the revision's *ravishing* is owed to Shakespeare's 'rotten damps ravish the morning air' (*Lucrece*, 778).

47 Charles Bourbon's troops were active in the Sack of Rome (1527), usually taken as an outrage.

49 *the unborn* coming worlds (1613).

51 *nephews* 'grandchildren' (commonly so in the period).

55 *dear* Phillips's substituted 'rich' gives the sense; *arras* 'tapestry'.

56 *bays* 'conqueror's laurels'.

57 *pens* wings (1614). The revision manages the conceit more precisely: 'pens' or 'feathers' are 'imped' or 'engrafted' on falcons' wings to improve their flight. Fame is conceived here as winged.

58 The fame should be heard above the sound of the Nile cataracts.

60 *those honours' spheres* 'ranks of those honours'.

61–4 'Troy's walls never faced a braver enemy, nor Rome whose name terrifies the east where the sun rises and the west where it sets, and which could gather on the Campus Martius such warlike knights.'

70 From ruddy Hesperus' rising to Aurore (1613), and so at 96, 120, 142, 196; 'From the northenmost known place (Thulë) to shores of the furthest east [Hydaspes was a tributary of the Indus]'.

71 Prince Henry was born in 1594 in Edinburgh (on the Forth).

74–7 'At thy rebuke the waters fled; at the voice of thy thunder they hasted away' (Psalms 104: 7); the 'Cyclades' are Aegean islands, here standing for islands in general.

74 *this Round* 'the earthly globe'.

By neighbour brooks, she gave herself to mourn:
And as she rushed her Cyclades among,
She seemed to plain, that Heaven had done her wrong.
With a hoarse plaint, Clyde down her steepy rocks,
And Tweed through her green mountains clad with flocks,   80
Did wound the ocean, murmuring thy death,
The ocean that roared about the Earth,
And it to Mauritanian Atlas told,
Who shrunk through grief, and down his white hairs rolled
Huge streams of tears, that changèd were in floods,   85
With which he drowned the neighbour plains and woods.
The lesser brooks as they did bubbling go,
Did keep a consort unto public woe:
The shepherds left their flocks with downcast eyes,
Disdaining to look up to angry skies: 90
Some broke their pipes, and some in sweet-sad lays,
Made senseless things amazèd at thy praise.
His reed Alexis hung upon a tree,
And with his tears made Doven great to be.
Moeliades sweet courtly nymphs deplore,   95
From Thulë to Hydaspes' pearly shore.
    Chaste Maids which haunt fair Aganippe Well,
And you in Tempe's sacred shade who dwell,
Let fall your harps, cease tunes of joy to sing,
Dishevellèd make all Parnassus ring   100
With anthems sad, thy music Phoebus turn
In doleful plaints, whilst Joy itself doth mourn:
Dead is thy darling, who decored thy bays,
Who oft was wont to cherish thy sweet lays,
And to a trumpet raise thine amorous style,   105
That floating Delos envy might this isle.
You Acidalian archers break your bows,
Your brandons quench, with tears blot beauty's snows,
And bid your weeping mother yet again
A second Adon's death, nay, Mars's plain: 110
His eyes once were your darts, nay, even his name
Wherever heard, did every heart inflame:
Tagus did court his love, with golden streams,
Rhine with his towns, fair Seine, with all she claims.
But ah (poor lovers) Death did them betray,   115

---

78   *plain* 'complain'.

79–86   The news carries from the Scottish rivers to the sea and thence to Africa. The treatment of Atlas is from Virgil: 'His shoulders hid with snow, and from his hoary beard adown, / The streams of waters fall, with ice and frost his face doth frown' (*Aeneid*, 4:250–1, Phaer).

88   *consort* 'accompaniment'.

89–94   The breaking of musical pipes, which can move even things without feeling ('senseless') is, like suspending them on trees, a standard elegiac move. Alexis is Drummond's friend Sir William Alexander, whose *Elegy on the Death of Prince Henry* came out in 1612; the Doven is a local river.

97–102   The Muses dance round Aganippe; Tempe is cel-ebrated by the poets, whose hair is 'dishevellèd' in grief and who sing on Parnassus; Phoebus Apollo is here as god of poetry.

103   *decored* Phillips's substituted 'adorned' gives the sense for what was still a standard word.

106   The floating island Delos was the birthplace of Apollo, and so of poetry.

107–10   The cupids ('Acidalian' from Venus's sacred fountain) are to destroy the instruments of their power (Phillips's substituted 'torches' for 'brandons' gives the sense), and bid Venus weep as she did for the death of Adonis or might for the death of her husband Mars.

113–14   The rivers of Spain, Germany and France join the Scottish ones.

And (not suspected) made their hopes his prey!
Tagus bewails his loss, with golden streams,
Rhine with his towns, fair Seine with all she claims.
Moeliades sweet courtly nymphs deplore,
From Thulë to Hydaspes' pearly shore.   120
   Delicious meads, whose chequered plain forth brings,
White, golden, azure flowers, which once were kings,
In mourning black, their shining colours dye,
Bow down their heads, whilst sighing zephyrs fly.
Queen of the fields, whose blush makes blush the morn,   125
Sweet rose, a Prince's death in purple mourn.
O Hyacinths, for ay your AI keep still,
Nay, with moe marks of woe your leaves now fill:
And you, O flower of Helen's tears first born,
Into those liquid pearls again you turn.   130
Your green locks, forests, cut, in weeping myrrhs,
The deadly cypress, and ink-dropping firs,
Your palms and myrtles change; from shadows dark
Winged sirens wail, and you sad echoes mark
The lamentable accents of their moan,   135
And plain that brave Moeliades is gone.
Stay sky thy turning course, and now become
A stately arch, unto the Earth his tomb:
Over which ay the watery Iris keep,
And sad Electra's sisters which still weep.   140
Moeliades sweet courtly nymphs deplore,
From Thulë to Hydaspes' pearly shore.
   Dear ghost, forgive these our untimely tears,
By which our loving mind, though weak, appears,
Our loss not thine (when we complain) we weep,   145
For thee the glistering walls of Heaven do keep,
Beyond the planets' wheels, above that source
Of spheres, that turns the lower in its course,
Where sun doth never set, nor ugly night
Ever appears in mourning garments dight: 150
Where Boreas' stormy trumpet doth not sound,
Nor clouds in lightnings bursting, minds astound.
From Care's cold climates far, and hot Desire,
Where Time is banished, ages ne'er expire:

---

121 Fair meads amidst whose grassy velvet springs (1613); Eye-pleasing meads whose painted plain forth brings (1614).
122 'Those flowers are spread which names of princes bear' (*Poems*, Part 1, Sonnet 17:7): 'sad flowers, by names of boys / And kings once known .. Self-loved Narcissus, Hyacinth, together / With Crocus golden haired, Adonis dressed / In purple' (Ausonius, *Cupid Crucified*, 9–11, Stanley).
125 *whose blush makes blush the morn* whose blushes stain the morn (1613).
127 'O hyacinth let AI be on thee still' (Sidney 'Since to that death', 29); Ovid, *Metamorphoses*, 10:215–16, tells how Apollo inscribed the leaves of the metamorphosed Hyacinthus with the letters AI AI ('Alas, alas').
128 *moe* 'more' (and so 1711); but the assonance with 'woe' is required.

129 *Helen's tears* 'Elecampane ['horse-heal'] sprang first (as men say) from the tears of Lady Helena' (*Pliny*, 21.10.33).
132 Cypress is deadly because funereal.
137–8 'And well (methinks) becomes this vaulty sky / A stately tomb to cover him deceased' (Sidney, 'Since to that death', 58–9).
139 *watery Iris* 'the rainbow'.
140 And soft-eyed Pleiades which still do weep (1613). Electra was one of seven sisters, daughters of Atlas, commemorated in the constellation Pleiades, conventionally associated with rain.
147–8 'Above the revolutions of the planets, above the *primum mobile* (in the empyrean)'.
150 *Boreas' stormy trumpet* 'the loud north wind'.
154 'Where there is no time, there is no end to the duration of life.'

Amongst pure sprites environèd with beams,   155
Thou think'st all things below to be but dreams,
And joy'st to look down to the azured bars
Of Heaven, indented all with streaming stars;
And in their turning temples to behold,
In silver robe the moon, the sun in gold,   160
Like young eye-speaking lovers in a dance,
With majesty by turns retire, advance,
Thou wond'rest Earth to see hang like a ball,
Closed in the ghastly cloister of this All:
And that poor men should prove so madly fond,   165
To toss themselves for a small foot of ground.
Nay, that they even dare brave the powers above,
From this base stage of change, that cannot move.
All worldly pomp and pride thou seest arise
Like smoke, that scatt'reth in the empty skies.   170
Other hills and forests, other sumptuous towers,
Amazed thou find'st, excelling our poor bowers,
Courts void of flattery, of malice minds,
Pleasure which lasts, not such as Reason blinds:
Far sweeter songs thou hear'st and carollings,   175
Whilst Heavens do dance, and choir of angels sings,
Than mouldy minds could feign, even our annoy
(If it approach that place) is changed in joy.
    Rest blessed sprite, rest satiate with the sight
Of him, whose beams both dazzle and delight,   180
Life of all lives, cause of each other cause,
The sphere, and centre, where the mind doth pause:
Narcissus of himself, himself the well,
Lover, and beauty, that doth all excel.
Rest happy ghost, and wonder in that glass,   185
Where seen is all that shall be, is, or was,
While *shall be*, *is*, or *was* do pass away,
And nought remain but an eternal day.
Forever rest, thy praise Fame may enrol
In golden annals, whilst about the Pole   190

157–8   *bars . . . indented* 'girdles . . . inlaid': we are to imagine a decorated armillary sphere.
158   'Heaven, inlaid with beaming stars', replacing 1614's 'powdered with troops of stars'.
164   *ghastly* the enclosed space (cloister) of the universe is terrifying (because of its scale); Phillips substitutes 'mighty'.
165–6   'And that men should prove so foolish as to busy themselves for the advantage of occupying so little of it', 'fight for a plot / Whereon the numbers cannot try the cause, / Which is not tomb enough and continent / To hide the slain' (*Hamlet*, IV. iv. 62–5).
169–70   'My days are consumed like smoke' (Psalms 102: 3).
175–6   Spenser's worthy souls 'hear such heavenly notes, and carollings / Of God's high praise, that fills the brazen sky, / And feel such joy and pleasure inwardly, / That maketh them all worldly cares forget' (Spenser, *Hymn of Heavenly Beauty*, 262–5).

177   *mouldy* 'earthly'; Phillips substitutes 'muddy'.
181–8   'Before all time, all matter, form, and place, / God all in all, and all in God it was: / Immutable, immortal, infinite . . . Himself alone, self's palace, host, and guest' (Sylvester, *Divine Weeks*, 1.1.54–61); but the Prince enjoys the reflections of God's self-existence in paradise ('the stately heavens . . . Are mirrors of God's admirable might', Sir William Alexander, *Doomsday*, 1.7) until ('while') the coming of 'a new heaven and a new earth' with 'no need of the sun, neither of the moon, to shine in it' (Revelation 21: 1, 23), and time yields to eternity. God may properly love himself ('borne . . . to the inmost of Himself in love of that pure radiance which He is, He himself being that which he loves' [Plotinus, *Enneads*, 6.8.16, McKenna]); but the comparison with Narcissus is shocking.
188–94   Meanwhile his fame will survive on earth as long as the constellation of the Wagoner 'Boötes' circles the Pole Star, and the sun rises in the mornings.

The slow Boötes turns, or sun doth rise
With scarlet scarf, to cheer the mourning skies:
The virgins to thy tomb may garlands bear
Of flowers, and on each flower let fall a tear.
Moeliades sweet courtly nymphs deplore,   195
From Thulë to Hydaspes' pearly shore.

Song ('Phoebus arise')

Printed first in *Poems* (1614) and given here in the slightly revised version of 1616. This 'free canzone' consists of three madrigals (1–12, 13–30, 31–43) and a farewell stanza (44–6), on principles represented in the madrigals of Sidney's Basileus ('Why dost thou haste away' and 'When two suns do appear', *Arcadia*, 3, in 'Last Part'): lines of six and ten syllables are mixed and rhymed at will. The lush vocabulary covers a pattern so stretched out it threatens to fall into prose.

Phoebus arise,
And paint the sable skies
With azure, white, and red:
Rouse Memnon's mother from her Tithon's bed,
That she thy carrier may with roses spread,   5
The nightingales thy coming each where sing,
Make an eternal Spring,
Give life to this dark world which lieth dead.
Spread forth thy golden hair
In larger locks than thou wast wont before,   10
And emperor-like decore
With diadem of pearl thy temples faire:
Chase hence the ugly night
Which serves but to make dear thy glorious light.
This is that happy morn,   15
That day long wishèd day,
Of all my life so dark,
(If cruel stars have not my ruin sworn,
And Fates not hope betray?)
Which (only white) deserves   20
A diamond for ever should it mark:
This is the morn should bring unto this grove
My love, to hear, and recompense my love.
Fair king who all preserves,
But show thy blushing beams,   25

1–5 The sun ('Phoebus') is invited to wake the dawn (Aurora is the mother of the Ethiopian prince Memnon, whose statue sang when struck by the rays of the rising sun, and wife to the immortal but infirm Tithonus) and she is to fling roses on his chariot ('carrier').

10 *larger* 'dispersed more at large'.

11 *decore* 'adorn' (standard).

19 And fate my hopes betray (*1614*); the awkward revision is grammatically more accurate.

20–1 'Let this auspicious morning be expressed / With a white stone, distinguished from the rest' (Persius, 2:1–2, Dryden, whose note explains that the Romans 'used to mark their fortunate days, or anything that luckily befell them, with a white stone').

24–8 If the all-preserving sun shines he will see eyes sweeter than Daphne's (the river Peneus was the father of the nymph who was Apollo's first love): 'He sees her eyes as bright as fire the stars to represent' (*Metamorphoses*, 1:499, Golding).

And thou two sweeter eyes
Shalt see than those which by Peneus' streams
Did once thy heart surprise:
Nay, suns, which shine as clear
As thou when two thou did to Rome appear.   30
Now Flora deck thyself in fairest guise,
If that ye, winds, would hear
A voice surpassing far Amphion's lyre,
Your stormy chiding stay,
Let Zephyr only breathe,   35
And with her tresses play,
Kissing sometimes these purple ports of death.
The winds all silent are,
And Phoebus in his chair
Ensaffroning sea and air,   40
Makes vanish every star:
Night like a drunkard reels
Beyond the hills to shun his flaming wheels.
The fields with flowers are decked in every hue,
The clouds bespangle with bright gold their blue:
Here is the pleasant place
And everything, save her, who all should grace.

30 'As you appeared when two suns appeared to the Ro-
mans' (Cicero, *Republic*, 1.10.15).
31–7 Let flowers bloom and the winds relax if they would
hear a voice sweeter than Amphion's lyre: 'Deaf stones by
the ears Amphion drew' (Horace, *Odes*, 3.11:1–2, Fanshawe)
to build Thebes. Let western breezes play with her hair and
kiss her lips: 'of death' because their song 'kills' the listener.

39–41 The sun in his chariot yellows the sea and sky.
42–3 'And flecked darkness like a drunkard reels / Forth
from day's path and Titan's fiery wheels' (*Romeo and Juliet*,
II. iii. 3–4).

Craton's Death

Printed first in *Poems*, 1614, and given here from the
1616 version. Adapted from Ronsard's 'Berteau le
pêcheur s'est noyé', itself advertised as a version from

Greek (probably *Greek Anthology*, 7.585 by Julian of
Egypt; but there are a few similar epigrams). *1614*
calls the fisherman by the Sidneian name 'Lalus'.

Amidst the waves profound,
Far far from all relief,
The honest fisher Craton, ah! is drowned
Into his little skiff:
The boards of which did serve him for a bier,   5
So that to the black world when he came near,
Of him no waftage greedy Charon got,
For he in his own boat
Did pass that flood, by which the gods do swear.

4   *1656* normalizes to 'Shut in this little skiff'; 'Into' is for
the metre's sake.

7   *waftage* 'fare': the ferryman Charon is regularly paid to
carry the dead across the Styx (the river by which the Gods
take oaths); *1614* has 'silver'.

The Statue of Venus Sleeping

First printed in *Poems* (1616): *Madrigals and Epigrams*, 42. Another epigram on the subject is 'Passenger vex not thy mind / To make mine eyes unfold, / For when thou them doest behold, / Thine perhaps thy will make blind' (printed in *1614* and suppressed), translated literally from an epigram by Etienne Tabourot, itself inspired by something like the *Greek Anthology*, 16.211.

Break not my sweet repose
Thou, whom free will, or chance, brings to this place,
Let lids these comets close,
O do not seek to see their shining grace:
For when mine eyes thou seest, they thine will blind,   5
And thou shalt part, but leave thy heart behind.

To Sir William Alexander
('Though I have twice been at the doors of Death')

This reply to Alexander's *On the Report of the Death of the Author* is first printed with Alexander's quatrains as an appendix to *The Cypress Grove* (1623); Drummond had been seriously ill in 1620 (he gives details in a letter to Alexander). The pastoral typenames are part of the apparatus of literary friendship. A version in the Hawthornden MSS reads: 'Though I have twice been at the gates of Death / And twice escaped those ports that ever mourn, / This but a respite is, a pause of breath, / For I by signs find I shall soon return. / Amidst thy heaven-born cares and courtly toils / Alexis when thou shalt hear wandering Fame / Tell Death hath triumphed o'er my mortal spoils / And that I am on earth but a sad name; / If thou e'er held'st me dear! by all our love, / By every soft discourse soul-charming verse, / I conjure thee, and by the maids of Jove, / To write this sad remembrance on my hearse, / Here Damon lies whose song did sometime grace / The murmuring Esk, may roses deck this place.'

Though I have twice been at the doors of Death,
And twice found shut those gates which ever mourn,
This but a lightening is, truce ta'en to breathe,
For late-borne sorrows augur fleet return.
   Amidst thy sacred cares, and courtly toils,   5
Alexis, when thou shalt hear wandering Fame
Tell, Death hath triumphed o'er my mortal spoils,
And that on Earth I am but a sad name;
   If thou e'er held me dear, by all our love,
By all that bliss, those joys Heaven here us gave,   10
I conjure thee, and by the maids of Jove,
To grave this short remembrance on my grave.
   Here Damon lies, whose songs did sometime grace
   The murmuring Esk, may roses shade the place.

5 Alexander collaborated on the version of the Psalms, undertaken by King James (Oxford, 1631), cares or toils both sacred and courtly.

11 *maids of Jove* the Muses were daughters of Jupiter.
14 The Esk flows north into the Forth.

To an Owl

Printed first in *1656*, from a MS supplied by Drummond's brother-in-law, Sir John Scott of Scotstarvet, a madrigal whose scheme is modelled exactly on Basileus's 'Why dost thou haste away' (Sidney, *Arcadia*, 3, in 'Last Part').

Ascalaphus tell me,
So may night's curtain long time cover thee,
So ivy ever may
From irksome light keep chamber thine and bed,
And in moon's livery clad   5
So mayst thou scorn the choristers of day:
When plaining thou dost stay
Near to the sacred window of my dear,
Dost ever thou her hear
To wake, and steal swift hours from drowsy sleep?   10
And when she wakes, doth e'er a stolen sigh creep
Into thy listening ear?
If that deaf god doth yet her careless keep,
In louder notes my grief with thine express,
Till by thy shrieks she think on my distress.   15

1–10 The syntax is convoluted: 'Tell me if you hear my beloved wake . . . and night will continue to protect you, and ivy to protect you from the light.' Ascaphalus, son of a nymph of the underworld, blabbed to Pluto of Proserpina's having eaten seven pomegranate seeds, and so prevented her return to the upper world. She turned him to an owl: 'and by and by his head / Was nothing else but beak and down, and mighty glaring eyes. / Quite altered from himself between two yellow wings he flies' (Ovid, *Metamorphoses*, 5: 545–6, Golding).
4 From irksome light keep thy chamber and bed (*1656*); the normalization of the MS reading (given here) throws the metre.
13 *that deaf god* 'Sleep'.

On a lamp

Printed first in Kastner from the Hawthornden MSS. Translated closely from Maurizio Moro's madrigal, 'Lume fido e amato'. The lamp is 'love's confidant' in a number of Greek epigrams (e.g. *Greek Anthology*, 5.4, 5, 7)

Faithful and lovèd light
That silent sees our thefts,
Be glad at the sweet sound of kisses sweet.
O! do not die! but if thou lov'st to die,
Die amidst our delight   5
When languish both our breasts.
So, thou mayst die at ease;
For lamps to me, no stars, are her fair eyes.

Lady Mary Wroth (1587–c.1653)

'Daughter to the right noble Robert Earl of Leicester, and niece to the ever famous and renowned Sir Philip Sidney knight, and to the most excellent Lady Mary Countess of Pembroke late deceased': so Lady Mary Wroth advertised herself on the title-page of *The Countess of Montgomery's Urania* (1621). Lady Mary was born on 18 October, probably in 1587, at Penshurst – the house whose modest strengths Ben Jonson famously celebrated. Daughter of Barbara Gammage (Sir Walter Ralegh's cousin) and Sir Robert Sidney (Earl of Leicester only after 1618), she grew up profoundly conscious of her Sidneian heritage. She is one from the 'twilight of whose sprite' she might be known to be a Sidney, says Jonson (*Epigrams*, 103). Her husband was a sportsman: 'How blest art thou can love the country, Wroth,' says Jonson (*To Sir Robert Wroth*), who enjoyed his hospitality there; but in 'exscribing' the wife's sonnets, Jonson says he became 'a better lover, and much better poet' (*A Sonnet. To the noble Lady, the Lady Mary Wroth*). Perhaps mischievously, Jonson told William Drummond that Lady Mary's cousin, the Countess of Rutland, 'was nothing inferior to her father, Sir Philip Sidney, in poesy' (*Conversations with Drummond*); but it is as a beauty he celebrates her (*Epigrams*, 79; *Underwood*, 50), or as a virtuous widow. Though Frederick Fleay surmised a hundred years ago that Jonson was her lover, it is as a poet that Jonson celebrates Lady Mary. But she was not a virtuous widow and perhaps not a virtuous wife.

Sir Robert Wroth died in 1614. Lady Mary was left with a son a month old and with serious debts, aggravated by the loss of the bulk of her inheritance with the untimely death of the son. Her position at court was compromised, partly by the distractions of relative poverty, partly by her association with her cousin William, Earl of Pembroke. Pembroke, a favoured candidate for the young man of Shakespeare's *Sonnets*, was the most glamorous of the courtly intellectuals or intellectual courtiers whose society she cultivated. He was 'the greatest Maecenas to learned men of any Peer of his time, or since' (says Aubrey), patron of Massinger and Chapman, giver of an annual book allowance to Ben Jonson, dedicatee of Shakespeare's First Folio, himself a poet; but he was 'immoderately given up to women' (says Clarendon, *History*, 1.123). The affair probably produced two children, but seems otherwise to have been damaging. Its vicissitudes and frustrations are perhaps recorded in the details of the *Urania*, a long and calculatedly incomplete romance to whose echoes of contemporary events Lady Mary's informed contemporaries seem to have been especially alert. Ladies such as the Countess of Montgomery, whose title the book carries in its own, those whose company she kept at Penshurst and elsewhere, made up its primary audience. The publication of the first part may have been ill-advised; the second part remained in manuscript till very recently, as did *Love's Victory*, a pastoral drama which might have been privately performed. *Urania* survives its scandalous allusions. Drummond, less well informed than those who took exception to them, but whose own verse shares with hers a belated Sidneian legacy, singles out only Lady Mary's talent for displaying 'passion's power, affection's several strains' (*To my Lady Mary Wroth*).

The records for Lady Mary's life after the 1620s are few; even the date of her death, some time in the early 1650s, is not exactly known. Josephine A. Roberts's revised *The Poems of Lady Mary Wroth* (Baton Rouge and London: Louisiana State University Press, 1992, first edition 1983) is standard; there is a modernized edition by R. E. Pritchard (Keele: Keele University Press, 1996). Josephine A. Roberts's *The First Part of The Countess of Montgomery's Urania* (Binghamton, NY: Center for Medieval and Early Renaissance Studies, 1995) does not give the appended *Pamphilia to Amphilanthus* (given in *The Poems*); the poems from the Newberry Library MS *Second Part* (published in Roberts's edition, 1999) are also given in *The Poems*. *Love's Victory* has been edited from the Penshurst MS by Michael Brennan (London: Roxburghe Club, 1988), and in a modernized edition in *Renaissance Drama by Women*, ed. S. P. Cerasano and Marion Wynne-Davies (London and New York: Routledge, 1996). The fullest account of the life is in Gary Waller, *The Sidney Family Romance: Mary Wroth, William Herbert, and the Early Modern Construction of Gender* (Detroit: Wayne State University Press, 1993). The editing work post-dates the still useful contextualizing bibliography by Elizabeth H. Hageman, 'Recent Studies in Women Writers of the English Seventeenth Century, 1604–1674', reprinted from *English Literary Renaissance* in *Women in the Renaissance*, ed. with Kirby Farrell and Arthur Kinney (Amherst: University of Massachusetts Press, 1988).

From *The Countess of Montgomery's Urania*

The *Urania* in its various manifestations supplies the selections below. Most are taken from *Pamphilia to Amphilanthus*, in its later published form an appendix to the *Urania*, which is made up of related sequences (variously accounted for by modern critics) of twenty-five songs and eighty-three sonnets. An earlier version of the material (including some later discarded) survives in manuscript in the Folger Library in Washington: the more important variants are recorded. Pamphilia, whose passion for Amphilanthus is re-quited only in the startling closing pages of the romance (strictly unconcluded), writes everywhere (in bed or on trees) with wonderful fluency: the collection has no definable connections with her story. Others of the poems are dispersed through the narrative like arias in opera: their situation is briefly indicated. The poem numbers are from Josephine Roberts's edition: U represents *The Countess of Montgomery's Urania* (1621); P represents *Pamphilia to Amphilanthus* (1621).

'Why do you so much wish for rain, when I'

U36 (Book 3) When Musalina, parted from Amphilanthus, arrived home in Romania, 'sad rhymes came often into her thoughts . . . contenting herself, or rather forcing content to be showed, when no rem-edy was, her love being gone . . . which gave form to these lines following a great drought being in that country, and everyone wishing for rain.'

> Why do you so much wish for rain, when I,
> Whose eyes still showering are, stand you so nigh?
> Think you that my poor eyes now cannot lend
> You store enough? alas, but rightly bend
> Your looks on me, and you shall see a store   5
> Able to moisten earth, and ten earths more:
> Sighs to make heaven as soft as tender wool,
> And grief sufficient to make up the full
> Of all despairs; then wish not, since in me
> Contained are tears, grief, and misery.   10

7   *soft* 'pitiful', and so ready to rain. The extraordinary simile, encouraged by the rhyme, recalls 'He giveth snow like wool' (Psalms 147: 16).

8   *full* 'entirety'.

Lindamira's complaint

U37–43 (Book 3). Pamphilia, resisting her old friend Dorilena's urgings to repeat her own poems, tells her instead the story of Lindamira 'feigning it to be written in a French story'. Lindamira's history – ending in the loss of royal favour 'after fourteen years' unchanged affection', in 'miserable crosses from her husband possessed with . . . more furious madness in jealousy', and in 'her honour . . . cast down, and laid open to all men's tongues and ears' – occasions a complaint which, says Pamphilia, 'because I liked it, or rather found her estate so near agree with mine, I put into sonnets.' Wroth writes her own life in Lindamira's, rather as Sidney in the *Old Arcadia* did his in Philisides's. The many obscurities in the sequence follow principally from the privacy of its concerns. This is a less ambitious but more accomplished sequence than the 'Crown of Sonnets dedicated to Love' in *Pamphilia to Amphilanthus*.

1

Dear eyes farewell, my sun once, now my end,
   While your kind willing grace I felt, all joy
   In soul I knew withdrawn, you now destroy
   The house that being gave to love's best friend.
You now alas to other objects bend   5
   That warmth of bliss which best delights enjoy,
   Striving to win an oft won idle toy,
   By falsehood nursed, such creatures seldom mend.
Try your new loves, affect the choice of store,
   And be assured they likewise will choose more,   10
   Which I yet grieve; for though the loss I bear
I would have none with you to challenge right;
   But bear you must for making choice so light:
   Yet still your beams I'll love, shine you elsewhere.

2–3 'For a time I felt your grace, [and then] I knew in my heart that joy was gone, since now you are wrecking the place [my heart] that gave birth to what was friendliest to your love.'
8 *mend* improve.
9 *affect . . . store* 'aim to choose from among plenty'.
12 *with you . . . right* 'lay claim to you by right'.
13 'But I must suffer your frivolity.'

2

O deadly rancour to a constant heart,
   Frowns, and neglect, my only favours be:
   Sometimes a cold respect is granted me;
   But hot flames to those eyes joy in my smart.
Once yet for justice' sake weigh my hard part,   5
   In gratefulness I should kind usage see;
   For being tied alone to you else free,
   Till by your wrongs now joined with heart-broke smart.
A glorious triumph you no doubt shall have,
   To crown your victory on murder's grave,   10
   While falsehood bears the arms my life hath won.
I only for twice seven years' love shall gain
   Change, worse than absence, or death's cruel'st pain:
   The last yet got, you have your labour done.

4 'But warm beams [as with Stella's 'flamy glistering lights' in Sidney's *Astrophil and Stella*, 76] to those whose eyes delight in my pain.'
5 *my hard part* 'my cruel lot'.
10 *murder's grave* 'the grave of her whom you have murdered.'
11 'While others treacherous to me (and perhaps to you) carry off those tokens of your love that were my destruction.'
12 *twice seven years' love* The duration of Lindamira's service to the Queen who dismisses her.
13 *change* 'inconstancy'.

3

A surgeon I would ask, but 'tis too late,
   To stay the bleeding wound of my hurt heart:
   The root is touched, and the last drops depart
   As weeping for succeeding others' fate.
Alas that my killed heart should wail my state,   5

3 *root* a standard term for 'bottom [of the heart]'.

Or leisure have to think on aught but smart,
  Nor doth it, but with pity bear a part,
  With her embraced yours like a loving mate.
But now unmarried by a new disdain
  Cold death must take the body from her love   10
  And thou poor heart must end for my unworth.
Conscience is lost, and outward fairness gains
  The place where worth did, or else seemed to move,
  Thus worldlike change new trial still brings forth.

7–8 'Nor can it but sympathetically participate with her whom you now embrace, who is yours like a loving mate.'
9–10 'Already separated from her by her new disdain, death must take my very person from her love.'

11–13 *unworth . . . worth* alluding to the poet's name.
12 'Fidelity is lost and fine looks win over virtue.'
14 'Thus the world's mutability brings new afflictions.'

4

O memory, could I but lose thee now,
  At least learn to forget as I did move
  My best, and only thoughts to wait on love,
  And be as registers of my mad vow.
Could I but let my mind to reason bow,   5
  Or see plain wrongs, neglects, and slightings prove
  In that dear sphere, which as the heavens above
  I prized, and homage to it did allow.
Canst thou not turn as well a traitor too
  Since heaven-like powers teach thee what to do?   10
  Canst not thou quite forget thy pleasures past;
Those blessèd hours, the only time of bliss,
  When we feared nothing but we time might miss
  Long enough to enjoy what's now offcast.

2–4 'At least learn to forget how I persuaded my best and only thoughts to attend on love, and be the recorders of the insane promise I made.'
7 *sphere* Amphilanthus is for Pamphilia 'That blessèd sphere, which gazing souls hold dear' (2:2).

9–10 'Instructed by the lover thought heavenly, can I not be treacherous too?'
13–14 'We feared nothing but not having time enough to enjoy the intimacy that's now discarded.'

5

Leave me vain Hope, too long thou hast possessed
  My mind, made subject to thy flattering skill,
  While April mornings did my pleasures fill,
  But cloudy days soon changed me from that rest;
And weeping afternoons to me addressed   5
  My utter ruin framed by Fortune's will,
  When Knowledge said Hope did but breed, and kill,
  Producing only shadows at the best.
Yet Hope 'tis true, thy faults did fair appear
  And therefore loth to think thou counselled'st me   10

5 *to me addressed* 'prepared for me'.
7 'While I knew well enough that Hope destroyed its own': Hope is proverbially deceptive.

10 'And therefore I was reluctant to think I relied on hope, or wilfully I would shut my eyes to hope's deceits, but catch instead at glittering nothings.'

Or wilfully thy errors would not see
But catch at sun-motes which I held most dear;
Till now alas with true-felt loss I know,
Thyself a bubble each fair face can blow.

14 Beauty inspires only fragile hopes.

6

Though you forsake me, yet alas permit
  I may have sorrow, for my poisoned cross;
  Think not, though dead to joy I cannot hit
  Upon a torture, for my soul-pierced loss.
Or if by chance I smile, I hopes engross,   5
  Nor for I die not, I do bliss admit,
  Most grief will oft give leave for show to toss
  Upon the waves, where shipwrecked comfort split.
Think then your will, and left, leave me yet more;
  Vex not my loathèd life, to ruin bent;   10
  Be satisfied with glut of your bad change:
Lay me unthought on, in the love-killed store,
  My grief's my own, or since for you 'tis sent,
  Let me have that part from you while you range.

2 *cross* 'affliction'.
5–6 '(Do not imagine) if I should smile that I am piling up my hopes, nor because I am still alive that I entertain some happiness.'
7 *show* 'pretence [of happiness]'.
11 *with glut . . . change* 'with indulgence of the passion you have now wickedly taken up'.

12 *in the love-killed store* 'among those who have died for love of you'.
14 *that part from you* 'my grief' (since it is yours by virtue of your having occasioned it).

7

Some do, perhaps, both wrong my love, and care,
  Taxing me with mistrust, and jealousy,
  From both which sins in love-like freedom, free
  I live – these slanders but new-raisèd are.
What though from grief, my soul I do not spare,   5
  When I perceive neglect's slight face on me?
  While unto some the loving smiles I see,
  I am not jealous, they so well do fare.
But doubt myself lest I less worthy am,
  Or that it was but flashes, no true flame,   10
  Dazzled my eyes, and so my humour fed.
If this be jealousy, then do I yield,
  And do confess I thus go armed to field,
  For by such jealousy my love is led.

3 *love-like* 'loving'.
4 *new-raisèd* as troops enlisted in emergency, inferior and untried.
6 *slight* 'slighting'.

9 *worthy* alluding to the poet's name.
11 *humour* 'mood'.
14 *such jealousy* the fear of her own unworthiness.

'If a clear fountain still keeping a sad course'

U 49. The Duke of Brunswick (Cauterino) sings 'in manner or imitation of sapphics'. This example, like some others including Sir Philip Sidney's 'Get hence foul grief' (*Old Arcadia* 59), is remote from classical precedent in being rhymed. Its anxiety to avoid the iambic pattern into which English adaptations often fall may make it seem rhythmically uncertain.

If a clear fountain still keeping a sad course,
   Weep out her sorrows in drops, which like tears fall;
   Marvel not if I lament my misfortune,
      brought to the same call.

Who thought such fair eyes could shine, and dissemble?   5
   Who thought such sweet breath could poison love's shame?
   Who thought those chaste ears could so be defilèd?
      hers be the sole blame.

While love deserved love, of mine still she failed not,
   Fool I to love still where mine was neglected,   10
   Yet faith, and honour, both of me claimèd it,
      although rejected.

Oft have I heard her vow, never sweet quiet
   Could once possess her while that I was elsewhere,
   But words were breath then, and as breath they wasted   15
      into a lost air.

So soon is love lost, not in heart imprinted,
   Silly I, knew not the false power of changing,
   Love I expected, yet (ah) was deceivèd,
      more her fond ranging.   20

Infant Love tied me not to mistrust change,
   Vows kept me fearless, yet all those were broken:
   Love, faith, and friendship by her are dissolvèd,
      suffered unspoken.

21   'My innocent love obliged me not to fear inconstancy.'

'Love leave to urge, thou knowest thou hast the hand'

P8. Pamphilia submits to Love's charms but deplores her own weakness in succumbing to a blind master. The manuscript carries the forms 'you', 'your', etc. for the more familiar and contemptuous 'thou', 'thy', etc. of the printed version.

Love leave to urge, thou knowest thou hast the hand;
   'Tis cowardice to strive where none resist:
   Pray thee leave off, I yield unto thy band,
   Do not thus, still, in thine own power persist.

1   *thou hast the hand* as the rider has 'the upper hand' with the horse.   3   *band* restraint.

Behold, I yield; let forces be dismissed,   5
    I am thy subject, conquered, bound to stand,
    Never thy foe, but did thy claim assist,
    Seeking thy due of those who did withstand.
But now it seems thou wouldst I should thee love,
    I do confess, 'twas thy will made me choose,   10
    And thy fair shows made me a lover prove,
    When I my freedom did, for pain refuse.
Yet this Sir God, your boyship I despise,
    Your charms I obey, but love not want of eyes.

6 *stand* stand still (as a stabled horse might); but used for the contrast with 'withstand'.
12 'When I rejected my freedom and chose pain'.

13 *Sir God . . . boyship* in mock deference. Sidney has 'sir fool' in *Astrophil and Stella*; Randolph's *Complaint against Cupid* uses 'boyship' for Cupid.

'Come darkest Night, becoming sorrow best'

P22, a MS note in Wroth's own hand in a copy of 1621 gives a title: 'For Absence'. Pamphilia welcomes the night as proper to grief at her lover's absence (as in Sidney's *Astrophil and Stella*, 89, 'Now that of absence the most irksome night'); the autumnal colouring is Shakespearean (as in Sonnet 89).

Come darkest Night, becoming sorrow best,
    Light leave thy light, fit for a lightsome soul:
    Darkness doth truly suit with me oppressed,
    Whom absence' power doth from mirth control.
The very trees with hanging heads condole   5
    Sweet summer's parting, and of leaves distressed,
    In dying colours make a griefful roll;
    So much (alas) to sorrow are they pressed.
Thus of dead leaves, her farewell carpet's made,
    Their fall, their branches, all their mournings prove,   10
    With leafless naked bodies, whose hues vade
    From hopeful green, to wither in their love.
If trees, and leaves for absence mourners be,
    No marvel that I grieve, who like want see.

4 'Whom the power of his absence prevents from being happy'.
6 *distressed* 'afflicted'; punning on the etymological sense 'stripped'.
7 *griefful roll* 'wreath full of grief'; pronounced more as contemporary spellings like 'greeful' would suggest.

9 *her farewell carpet* 'the carpet laid out at summer's parting'.
10–12 The pronouns seem out of control: 'the fall of the leaves and the leafless nakedness of the branches testify to the grief of both; the leaves' colours pass away'; 'vade' may be a variant of 'fade', but some writers use both, in distinct senses.
14 *like want see* 'feel a similar lack'.

'When last I saw thee, I did not thee see'

P24. Sidney in *Astrophil and Stella* 38 ('This night while sleep begins with heavy wings') and Shakespeare, Sonnet 43 ('When most I wink, then do mine eyes best see') similarly bend to the service of sentiment the kind of Platonizing vision where the lover can behold beauty 'in itself simple and pure, and frame it within his imagination sundered from all matter . . . and have it with him day and night . . . without mistrust ever to lose it' (Castiglione, *Courtier*, 4.66, Hoby).

When last I saw thee, I did not thee see,
    It was thine image which in my thoughts lay
    So lively figured, as no time's delay
    Could suffer me in heart to parted be;
And sleep so favourable is to me,   5
    As not to let thy loved remembrance stray:
    Lest that I waking might have cause to say,
    There was one minute found to forget thee.
Then since my faith is such, so kind my sleep
    That gladly thee presents into my thought,   10
    And still true-lover-like thy face doth keep,
    So as some pleasure shadow-like is wrought.
Pity my loving, nay of conscience give
Reward to me in whom thyself doth live.

3–4 'Time could allow no gap to separate my heart from you'; 'delay' is 'the rack of unrefrained desire' (Sidney, *Arcadia*, 3: 'O stealing time the subject of delay').
5 *favourable* 'well-disposed'.

12 'The beauties which we daily see with these our dim eyes ... be nothing else but dreams and most thin shadows of beauty' (Castiglione, *Courtier*, 4.69, Hoby); Wroth reverses the point.
14 *thyself* Corrected from 'my self' in the draft MS.

'When everyone to pleasing pastime hies'

P26. Pamphilia favours her own thoughts over other pastimes, as lovers do (Sidney, *Astrophil and Stella*, 27, 'Because I oft in dark abstracted guise').

When everyone to pleasing pastime hies,
    Some hunt, some hawk, some play, while some delight
    In sweet discourse, and music shows joy's might:
    Yet I my thoughts do far above these prize.
The joy which I take is, that free from eyes   5
    I sit and wonder at this day-like night,
    So to dispose themselves as void of right,
    And leave true pleasure for poor vanities.
When others hunt, my thoughts I have in chase;
    If hawk, my mind at wishèd end doth fly: 10
    Discourse, I with my spirit talk and cry;
    While others music choose as greatest grace.
O God say I, can these fond pleasures move,
Or music be but in sweet thoughts of love?

4 *do* Corrected from 'did' in the draft MS.
7 *void of right* 'rightly at leisure'.
9 *my thoughts I have in chase* 'I am pursuing my thoughts';

'This roving humour ... I have ever had, and like a ranging spaniel ... I have followed all' (Burton, *Anatomy*, 'Democritus to the Reader').

Song: 'The springing time of my first loving'

P73, except as noted. Donne's *Love's Growth* (or in some MSS *Spring*) argues first that the growth of love makes it natural in a bad sense 'like the grass', and then supernatural since 'No winter shall abate the spring's increase'; Wroth is merely amazed by the continuing summer-time of love. Though the means are minimal and seem obvious, the verse pattern is not common: Mary Sidney's version of Psalm 118 ('The Lord is good, you see and know') uses a similar scheme, but with the feminine rhymes in the refrain couplet.

The springing time of my first loving,
Finds yet no winter of removing;
Nor frosts to make my hopes decrease:
But with the summer still increase.

The trees may teach us love's remaining,   5
Who suffer change with little paining,
Though winter make their leaves decrease,
Yet with the summer they increase.

As birds by silence show their mourning
In cold, yet sing at spring's returning: 10
So may love nipped awhile decrease,
But as the summer soon increase.

Those that do love but for a season,
Do falsify both love and reason:
For reason wills, if love decrease,   15
It like the summer should increase.

Though love sometimes may be mistaken,
The truth yet ought not to be shaken:
Or though the heat awhile decrease,
It with the summer may increase   20

(And since the spring-time of my loving
Found never winter of removing:
Nor frosts to make my hopes decrease),
Shall as the summer still increase.

1 *springing* spring (*1621*); but corrected in the draft MS.
2 *removing* parting; 'My trust on his true love / Truly attending / Shall never thence remove' (Psalms 52: 8, Mary Herbert).
4 *increase* a noun here: all the other occurrences are verbs.

15–16 Love should rationally follow the natural order of decay and restoration.
20–4 The parenthesis is editorial; 'may increase' and 'shall increase' are in apposition.

'Juno still jealous of her husband Jove'

P97. The mythological conceit (not common in the English sonnet) is developed to an unusual degree; Pamphilia identifies herself not with the jealous Juno ('She looked about her for her Jove . . . Whom when she found not in the heaven, "Unless I guess amiss, / Some wrong against me" (quoth she) "now my husband working is"' (Ovid, *Metamorphoses*, 1:605–8, Golding)) but with the sexually driven Jupiter.

Juno still jealous of her husband Jove,
        Descended from above, on earth to try,
        Whether she there could find his chosen love,
        Which made him from the heavens so often fly.
Close by the place where I for shade did lie,   5
        She chasing came, but when she saw me move,
        "Have you not seen this way" (said she) "to hie
        One, in whom virtue never ground did prove?

8 *never ground did prove* 'never tried the soil' (to grow in).

He, in whom love doth breed, to stir more hate,
    Courting a wanton nymph for his delight;   10
    His name is Jupiter, my Lord, by fate,
    Who for her, leaves me, heaven, his throne, and light."
"I saw him not" (said I) "although here are
Many, in whose hearts, Love hath made like war."

'No time, no room, no thought, nor writing can'

P101; except as noted. Pamphilia reconciles herself to the absence of her lover. The sonnet's obvious char- acter of a letter evokes the love-lorn heroines of Ovid's *Heroides.*

No time, no room, no thought, nor writing can
    Give rest, or quiet to my loving heart,
    Nor can my memory or fancy scan,
    The measure of my still renewing smart.
Yet would I not (dear love) thou shouldst depart;   5
    But let thy passions as they first began,
    Rule, wound, and please; it is thy choicest art,
    To give disquiet, which seems ease to man.
When all alone, I think upon thy pain,
    How thou dost travail our best selves to gain,   10
    Then hoürly thy lessons I do learn;
    Think on thy glory, which shall still ascend,
Until the world come to a final end,
And then shall we thy lasting power discern.

1–3   *nor ... Nor* or ... Or *(1621).*
2–3   'Neither memory nor imagination can measure the extent of my always fresh pain'; but the prosodic sense is latent: strong feeling is not to be 'metred'.

6   *thy* my *(1621).*
7–8   'It is your most exquisite torture to leave me in a position which I feel as painful and you imagine is easy.'
10   'How you struggle to improve our situation.'

Robert Herrick (1591–1674)

Herrick was born in Cheapside, London. A year later his father died (perhaps by suicide), and Herrick was brought up by his uncle, like his father a goldsmith and a banker. To this uncle he was apprenticed in 1607, but failed to complete his training, going on instead to Cambridge, first to St John's College and then to Trinity Hall. In 1623 he was ordained, served as chaplain to Buckingham in the expedition to the Isle de Rhé in 1627, and in 1629 was presented to the living of Dean Prior. Writing a grossly effusive elegy on King James in 1625, and wondering why no truly great voice had spoken out for the King while he was alive, Richard James specifies that 'Some Jonson, Drayton or some Herrick would / Before this time have charactered the mould / Of his perfections' (*The Muses' Dirge*). This is a remarkable tribute, first for putting the youngish Herrick in company with Jonson and Drayton, and secondly for imagining for him the role of a public panegyrist. Among the MSS of Herrick's poems the most frequently copied are the short epigram *The Curse*, and a longer *Welcome to Sack*. Some ten pieces made it into print before 1648.

When *Hesperides* (based on a collection originally projected for 1640) came out in 1648, dedicated to the future Charles II, it promised poems 'of brooks, of blossoms, birds, and bowers: / Of April, May, of June, and July-Flowers . . . Maypoles, hock-carts, wassails, wakes'. There are ominous things in the list, and even the innocent-looking things are less truly innocent in a culture set on the abolition of maypoles and Christ-mas: something a little sharper than nostalgia informs this volume in 1648, and the Devonshire summer idyll advertised with such seeming ingenuousness (but Herrick hated Devon) revolves round poems which the war has touched ('Fortune is now your captive; other kings / Hold but her hands; you hold both hands and wings', *To the King upon his Taking Leicester*; 'Lift up thy sword then suffer it to fall', *To the Lord Hopton, on his Fight in Cornwall*). A catholic selection of about sixty pieces was reprinted in *Wit's Recreations* (1650); but the collection as a whole was promptly neglected: twenty years later the edition was still unsold. An expurgated Herrick was rescued in the nineteenth century as a poet of careless country life; now he is more likely to be taken as a typically anxious poet of contingent things. He was ejected from his living in 1647, and lived in London on the charity of well-to-do friends till the Restoration, after which he returned to Devon. The only authoritative collection is *Hesperides: Or the Works both Humane and Divine* (1648); there is a facsimile edition (Menston: Scolar Press, 1969). The standard modern edition is L. C. Martin's *The Poetical Works of Robert Herrick* (Oxford: Clarendon Press, 1956). There is a *Concordance to the Poems of Robert Herrick* by Malcolm L. Macleod (New York: Oxford University Press, 1936; Folcroft: Folcroft Press, 1970). Elizabeth H. Hageman has prepared *Robert Herrick: A Reference Guide* (Boston: G. K. Hall, 1983); it is supplemented (up to 1997) by Maryclaire Moroney, *English Literary Renaissance*, 29 (1999).

To Perilla

Hesperides, 14. A close analogue is Tibullus 3.2 (Lygdamus, dying of grief over his estrangement from his wife, enjoins his wife and mother together to mourn over his ashes). The name 'Perilla' is borrowed from Ovid's stepdaughter, herself a poet; Herrick's Perilla is coupled with Corinna for 'her wit, / And for the graceful use of it' (*On the Loss of his Mistresses*, 9–10). The funeral customs alluded to, modest as they are, are coloured by classical pagan reminiscence and, where they survived, were the subject of Puritan reproach.

> Ah my Perilla! dost thou grieve to see
> Me, day by day, to steal away from thee?
> Age calls me hence, and my gray hairs bid come,
> And haste away to mine eternal home;
> 'Twill not be long (Perilla) after this,   5
> That I must give thee the supremest kiss;
> Dead when I am, first cast in salt, and bring

6 *supremest kiss* 'last kiss' (as to the already dead: Niobe gives her dead sons *oscula suprema* (Ovid, *Metamorphoses*, 6:278). 7–8 Salt is a preservative for corpses, and so stands for incorruption; it was sometimes superstitiously set by corpses. The body is to be anointed with consecrated oil or chrism ('cream') drawn from the weeping eyes (the 'religious spring'). Lygdamus's bones are washed in wine and milk.

Part of the cream from that religious spring;
With which (Perilla) wash my hands and feet;
That done, then wind me in that very sheet   10
Which wrapped thy smooth limbs (when thou didst implore
The gods' protection, but the night before)
Follow me weeping to my turf, and there
Let fall a primrose, and with it a tear:
Then lastly, let some weekly-strewings be   15
Devoted to the memory of me:
Then shall my ghost not walk about, but keep
Still in the cool, and silent shades of sleep.

10–12   The shroud is to be prepared from the wedding-sheet.
13–16   'Let me with funeral flowers his body strow . . .
This unavailing gift, at least, I may bestow!' (Virgil, *Aeneid*,
6:884–6, Dryden); but at his funeral oration for Valentinian
St Ambrose says, 'I will not sprinkle his grave with flowers,
but pour on his spirit the odour of Christ.'
17–18   The unburied dead had no resting-place. 'Redeem
from this reproach my wandering ghost,' says Virgil's
Palinurus to Aeneas, 'And in a peaceful grave my corpse
compose' (*Aeneid*, 6.371, Dryden).

A Song to the Masquers

Hesperides 15, written for an entertainment or in imitation of such masque summonses as Jonson's 'Come on, come on; and where you go' (*Pleasure Reconciled to Virtue*, 153) or 'Come, noble nymphs' in *Neptune's Triumph* (473–503, repeated in *The Fortunate Isles*).

1

Come down, and dance ye in the toil
    Of pleasures, to a heat;
But if to moisture, let the oil
    Of roses be your sweat.

2

Not only to yourselves assume   5
    These sweets, but let them fly;
From this, to that, and so perfume
    E'en all the standers-by.

3

As Goddess Isis (when she went,
    Or glided through the street)
Made all that touched her with her scent,   10
    And whom she touched, turn sweet.

1–2   *toil of pleasures* The opposition of labour and pleasure
is cancelled by invoking the sense of 'weaving', as in Jonson's
song 'Why do you wear the silkworm's toils?' (*Neptune's
Triumph*, 484), or Shakespeare's Cleopatra's 'strong toil of
grace' (*Antony*, V. iii. 342).
3–4   'Why do you smell of ambergris, / Of which was
formèd Neptune's niece, / The Queen of Love' (Jonson,
Neptune's Triumph, 494–6).
9–12   'Amongst these pleasures . . . you might see the pomp
of the goddess [Isis] triumphantly march forward . . . the
women . . . bespread the ways with herbs . . . others dropped
in the ways as they went balm and other precious ointments'
(Apuleius, *The Golden Ass*, 11.8–9, Adlington).

Delight in Disorder

Hesperides, 83; based on Jonson's praise of careless-ness in *Epicoene* ('Still to be neat, still to be dressed'), itself adapted from an anonymous Latin epigram first printed in Scaliger's edition of the Virgilian *Appen-dix, Semper munditias, semper Basilissa, decoras* (com-plaining of a mistress who is too precise in her dress). This poem loses touch with exclusively sexual mo-tives.

> A sweet disorder in the dress
> Kindles in clothes a wantonness:
> A lawn about the shoulders thrown
> Into a fine distraction:
> An erring lace, which here and there   5
> Enthrals the crimson stomacher:
> A cuff neglectful, and thereby
> Ribbons to flow confusedly:
> A winning wave (deserving note)
> In the tempestuous petticoat: 10
> A careless shoe-string, in whose tie
> I see a wild civility:
> Do more bewitch me, then when art
> Is too precise in every part.

1–2 'Numbers ne'er tickle, or but lightly please, / Unless they have some wanton carriages' (*A Request to the Graces*, 9–10); only the final couplet offers a perfect rhyme.
4 *distraction* The 'disorder' of the fine shawl makes for 'perturbation' in the poet.
5 'A wandering lace which only here and there binds in ('enthrals') the stomacher' (the rich stomacher should be held securely under the bodice), so as to charm ('enthral') it;

Julia's 'azure robe' has feelings of its own: 'erring here, and wandering there, / Pleased with digression everywhere' (*Julia's Petticoat*, 3–4).
12 *wild civility* So 'lawny films I see / Play with a wild civility' (*Art above Nature, to Julia*, 13–14); or reversed, 'Be she showing in her dress / Like a civil wilderness' (*What kind of Mistress he would Have*, 5–6). The random distribution of houses in Sidney's *Arcadia* shows 'civil wildness' (1.2.2).

The Definition of Beauty

Hesperides, 102; one of a number of definition poems, often exploiting variations of the ancient formula (fre-quent in Plato), 'X is no other thing than Y.' The 'golden section' is described, whereby a line is di-vided 'by an extreme and mean proportion' (the for-mulation of Billingsley's *Euclid*) so that the ratio of the whole to the larger part is the same as the ratio of the larger part to the smaller.

> Beauty, no other thing is, than a beam
> Flashed out between the middle and extreme.

To Anthea Lying in Bed

Hesperides, 104. So Julia appears 'Half with a lawn of water hid' (*Upon Julia Washing herself in the River*, 6, based on Martial, 8.68:5–8). Apuleius's description of a *tableau vivant* of Venus 'all naked save that her fine and comely middle was lightly covered with a thin silken smock, and this the wanton wind blew hither and thither, sometime lifting it . . . sometime making it to cling close to her' (*Golden Ass*, 10.31, Adlington) is influential on writing about half-cov-ered bodies. Spenser's Acrasia 'was arrayed, or rather disarrayed, / All in a veil of silk and silver thin' (*Faerie Queene*, 2.12.77).

So looks Anthea, when in bed she lies,
O'ercome, or half betrayed by tiffanies:
Like to a twilight, or that simpering dawn,
That roses show, when misted o'er with lawn.
Twilight is yet, till that her lawns give way;   5
Which done, that dawn, turns then to perfect day.

3 *simpering* 'shimmering' (Herbert's stars 'simper and shine', *The Search*, 14).

4 The pallor of Shakespeare's Venus at the thought of Adonis's death is 'Like lawn being spread upon the blushing rose' (*Venus and Adonis*, 590).

Corinna's Going a-Maying

Hesperides, 178. King James's *Declaration of Sports*, issued in 1618, formally permitted 'May games, Whitsun ales and morris dances, and the setting up of May-poles and other sports therewith used . . . women shall have leave to carry rushes to church for the decorating of it.' Puritan opposition forced the *Declaration*'s retraction; but in 1633 Charles I ordered its republication. This makes the poem edgier than might be supposed from its preoccupation with rural pursuits, or from its unfussy treatment of literary commonplaces. Corinna, one of Herrick's fantasy mistresses, is celebrated as Ovid's 'real' mistress; the name echoes the pastoral 'Corin' (as in Shakespeare's *As You Like It*).

Get up, get up for shame, the blooming morn
Upon her wings presents the god unshorn.
　　　See how Aurora throws her fair
　　　Fresh-quilted colours through the air:
　　　Get up, sweet-slug-a-bed, and see   5
　　　The dew-bespangling herb and tree.
Each flower has wept, and bowed toward the east,
Above an hoür since; yet you not dressed,
　　　Nay! not so much as out of bed?
　　　When all the birds have matins said,   10
　　　And sung their thankful hymns: 'tis sin,
　　　Nay, profanation to keep in,
When as a thousand virgins on this day,
Spring, sooner than the lark, to fetch in may.

Rise; and put on your foliage, and be seen   15
To come forth, like the spring-time, fresh and green;
　　　And sweet as Flora. Take no care
　　　For jewels for your gown, or hair:
　　　Fear not; the leaves will strew
　　　Gems in abundance upon you: 20
Besides, the childhood of the day has kept,
Against you come, some orient pearls unwept:
　　　Come, and receive them while the light
　　　Hangs on the dew-locks of the night:

1–2 The 'wings of the morning' (Psalms 139: 9) show the sunlight: Apollo is 'unshorn' (Horace, *Odes*, 1.21.2) because sunbeams scatter like hair.
3–4 'But let the sun in triumph ride, / Scattering his beamy light' (Carew, *An Hymeneall Song*, 2–3); but there the light is not largesse, but bedclothes.
7 'Each bedewed flower turns to the rising sun.'
12 Inverting the notion that keeping the May festival is profane.

14 *may* 'hawthorn blossom'; but they bring the month too.
15–16 Ovid invokes Flora herself: 'Come, mother of flowers, that we may honour thee with merry games' (*Fasti*, 5:183).
21–2 'The morning has reserved some dew in preparation for your coming.'
24–7 In the Song of Solomon, the bride welcomes the groom whose 'head is filled with dew, and [whose] locks with the drops of the night' (5:2); the bridegroom sun ('Titan') awaits his welcome.

And Titan on the eastern hill   25
Retires himself, or else stands still
Till you come forth. Wash, dress, be brief in praying:
Few beads are best, when once we go a-maying.

Come, my Corinna, come; and coming, mark
How each field turns a street; each street a park   30
    Made green, and trimmed with trees: see how
    Devotion gives each house a bough,
    Or branch: each porch, each door, ere this,
    An Ark, a Tabernacle, is
Made up of whitethorn neatly interwove;   35
As if here were those cooler shades of love.
    Can such delights be in the street,
    And open fields, and we not see't?
    Come, we'll abroad; and let's obey
    The proclamation made for May: 40
And sin no more, as we have done, by staying;
But my Corinna, come, let's go a-maying.

There's not a budding boy, or girl, this day,
But is got up, and gone to bring in may.
    A deal of youth, ere this, is come   45
    Back, and with whitethorn laden home.
    Some have dispatched their cakes and cream,
    Before that we have left to dream:
And some have wept, and wooed, and plighted troth,
And chose their priest, ere we can cast off sloth: 50
    Many a green-gown has been given;
    Many a kiss, both odd and even:
    Many a glance too has been sent
    From out the eye, Love's firmament:
Many a jest told of the keys' betraying   55
This night, and locks picked, yet we're not a-maying.

Come, let us go, while we are in our prime;
And take the harmless folly of the time.
    We shall grow old apace, and die
    Before we know our liberty.   60
    Our life is short; and our days run

---

28 *beads* 'prayers'.

30–5 The fields are crowded thoroughfares, the streets are decorated with greenery, the houses converted to tabernacles. 'And ye shall take you . . . the boughs of goodly trees . . . and willows of the brook; and ye shall rejoice . . . ye shall dwell in booths seven days' (Leviticus 23: 40, for the Feast of Tabernacles); Ovid gives a pagan version for the feast of Anna Perenna: 'Scattered on the green grass the common people drink, boys and girls together . . . some make a leafy house of boughs' (*Fasti*, 3:525–8); 'whitethorn' is hawthorn.

36 *cooler* white and green rather than red.

40 The *Declaration of Sports*, but also the summons that the sun makes.

47–8 'Some have eaten their festive treats before we have even waked.'

51 'Many a girl has been tumbled in the grass and many a kiss given, returned or not.'

54 Love inhabits the eye as stars their spheres.

55–6 'Were beauty under twenty locks kept fast, / Yet love breaks through and picks them all at last' (*Venus and Adonis*, 575–6).

57–70 'Let us enjoy the pleasures that are present, let us cheerfully use the creatures as in youth . . . "Let us live my Lesbia, and love" [Catullus, 5:1] . . . "Come let us take our fill of love, and pleasure and dalliance, for this is our portion, this is our lot" [Proverbs 7: 18]' (Burton, *Anatomy*, 3.4.2.1). Catullus 5:5–6 is invoked at 67–8, and at 58 the conclusion of Horace's welcome to spring 'Short folly mix with counsels best: / 'Tis sweet sometimes to be in jest' (*Odes*, 4.12:27–8, Hawkins).

As fast away as does the sun:
And as a vapour, or a drop of rain
Once lost, can ne'er be found again:
    So when or you or I are made   65
    A fable, song, or fleeting shade;
    All love, all liking, all delight
    Lies drowned with us in endless night.
Then while time serves, and we are but decaying;
Come, my Corinna, come, let's go a-maying.   70

To the Virgins, to make much of Time

Hesperides, 208; but this, the classic English *carpe diem* poem, was current in MSS and first printed in the *Academy of Compliments* (1646), possibly in an earlier (rather than simply corrupt) version. Playford's *Select Musical Airs* (1652) includes what may be an intermediate version with the setting by William Lawes. Burton makes a collection of like sentiments from the poets: 'Such above the rest as have daughters to bestow, should be very careful and provident to marry them in due time . . . For if they tarry longer, to say truth, they are past date, and nobody will respect them . . . A virgin, as the poet holds, a desirous and sportive girl, is like a flower, a rose withered on a sudden . . . "She that was erst a maid as fresh as may, / Is now an old crone, time so steals away" [Ausonius] Let them take time then while they may, make advantage of youth, and as he prescribes, "Fair maids, go gather roses in the prime, / And think that as a flower so goes on time" [Ausonius] Let's all love, while we are in the flower of years, fit for love matters, and while time serves: for "Suns that set may rise again, /but if once we lose this light, /'Tis with us perpetual night" [Catullus, Jonson's version] Time past cannot be recalled' (*Anatomy*, 3.2.5.5).

1

Gather ye rose-buds while ye may,
    Old Time is still a-flying:
And this same flower that smiles today,
    To morrow will be dying.

2

The glorious lamp of heaven, the sun,   5
    The higher he's a getting;
The sooner will his race be run,
    And nearer he's to setting.

3

That age is best, which is the first,
    When youth and blood are warmer;   10
But being spent, the worse, and worst
    Times, still succeed the former.

4

Then be not coy, but use your time;
    And while ye may, go marry:
For having lost but once your prime,   15
    You may for ever tarry.

1 An immediate echo of Spenser: 'Gather therefore the rose, whilst yet is time' (*Faerie Queene*, 2.12.75).
9–12 'Think not, hereafter will the loss repay; / For every morrow will the taste decay, / And leave less relish than the former day' (Ovid, *Ars Amatoria*, 3:65–6, Congreve); at 11–12 *1646* reads 'Expect not then the last and worst / Which still succeeds the former.'

15–16 Invoking Posidippus's famous epigram on Opportunity: 'none whom I have once raced by on my winged feet will now, however much he wants, take hold of me from behind' (*Greek Anthology*, 16.275).

The Hock-Cart, or Harvest Home: To the Right Honourable, Mildmay, Earl of Westmorland

Hesperides, 250. Mildmay Fane succeeded to the Westmorland title in 1628; his estates were temporarily sequestered in 1642. Two shorter pieces are addressed to Mildmay Fane, one urging the publication of his poems (some were printed as *Otia Sacra*, 1648). A harvest companion to *Corinna's Going a-Maying*; but directed (offensively for some readers) more to the interests of work than play. Tibullus's celebration of a summer festival (2.1), the poem's model, is more frankly festive, but also more frankly a poem for the landlord. Herrick's wrily ambiguous reminder at the poem's conclusion that life is not a party follows an energetic celebration of revelry.

> Come sons of summer, by whose toil,
> We are the lords of wine and oil:
> By whose tough labours, and rough hands,
> We rip up first, then reap our lands.
> Crowned with the ears of corn, now come, 5
> And, to the pipe, sing Harvest-Home.
> Come forth, my Lord, and see the cart
> Dressed up with all the country art.
> See, here a malkin, there a sheet,
> As spotless pure, as it is sweet: 10
> The horses, mares, and frisking fillies
> (Clad, all, in linen, white as lilies.)
> The harvest swains, and wenches bound
> For joy, to see the hock-cart crowned.
> About the cart, hear, how the rout 15
> Of rural younglings raise the shout;
> Pressing before, some coming after,
> Those with a shout, and these with laughter.
> Some bless the cart; some kiss the sheaves;
> Some prank them up with oaken leaves: 20
> Some cross the fill-horse; some with great
> Devotion, stroke the home-borne wheat:
> While other rustics, less attent
> To prayers, than to merriment,
> Run after with their breeches rent. 25
> Well, on, brave boys, to your Lord's hearth,
> Glittering with fire; where, for your mirth,
> Ye shall see first the large and chief
> Foundation of your feast, fat beef:
> With upper stories, mutton, veal 30
> And bacon, (which makes full the meal)
> With several dishes standing by,
> As here a custard, there a pie,

1–14 Tibullus is half Anglicized: 'Be silent all, O vintage, power divine! / Hither, with clusters from the purple vine: / Hither, O Ceres, to our rites repair; / And bind with wreaths of corn thy radiant hair. / On this religious Day, and solemn feast, / Rest let the ground, and let the peasant rest; / No toilsome plough, nor tiresome labour mind, / The oxen from their weighty yokes unbind, / And let them at the heaped up rack be fed, / With each a flowery garland on his head' (2.1:1–8, Dart).

4 *rip* 'plough'.

9 *malkin* 'rag-doll' (made from cleaning cloths); in John Taylor's *Jack-a-Lent* (1630) Tim Tatters makes an ensign out of a baker's malkin for the Shrove Tuesday festivities.

21–2 'Some bless the shaft-horse, some pay their devotions to the sheaves.'

And here all tempting frumenty.
And for to make the merry cheer,   35
If smirking wine be wanting here,
There's that, which drowns all care, stout beer;
Which freely drink to your Lord's health,
Then to the plough (the common-wealth)
Next to your flails, your vanes, your vats;   40
Then to the maids with wheaten hats:
To the rough sickle, and crooked scythe,
Drink frolic boys, till all be blithe.
Feed, and grow fat; and as ye eat,
Be mindful, that the lab'ring neat   45
(As you) may have their fill of meat.
And know, besides, ye must revoke
The patient ox unto the yoke,
And all go back unto the plough
And harrow (though they're hanged up now).   50
And, you must know, your Lord's word's true,
Feed him ye must, whose food fills you.
And that this pleasure is like rain,
Not sent ye for to drown your pain,
But for to make it spring again.   55

34 Matthew Stevenson's *The Twelve Months* (1661): 'The frumenty [a seasoned malt and milk drink] pot welcomes home the harvest cart, and the garland of flowers crowns the captain of the reapers . . . the pipe and the tabor are now busily set a-work; was the seasoned malt and milk drink to welcome home the harvest cart' (quoted Brand).
36 'If there is no sparkling wine, there is strong beer.'
38 'But let each man Messalla's Health commend, / And name to every glass my absent friend' (Tibullus, 2.1:31–2).
39 *plough . . . common-wealth* it being held in common.
40 *vanes . . . vats 1648*'s 'fanes . . . fats' may pun on Fane's

name.
47 *revoke* 'call back'.
50 The ploughshare is hung up in Tibullus, 2.1:6 (but not in Dart's translation); Herrick borrows this foreign custom again: 'And all go back unto the plough / And harrow (though they're hanged up now)' (*A New-year's Gift sent to Sir Simeon Steward*, 45–6).
53–4 Virgil's husbandman enjoys the restless cycle of labour and return: 'Each fertile month does some new gifts present, / And with new work his industry content' (*Georgics*, 2.516–18, Cowley).

To Meadows

Hesperides, 274. The meadows, despoiled of their flowers by country girls, are left bare. A wider point about prodigality and bankruptcy is made by way of the identification of the girls with the vanished fairies of old England: 'Witness those rings and roundelays / Of theirs which yet remain, / Were footed in Queen Mary's days / On many a grassy plain / But since of late Elizabeth / And later James came in, / They never danced on any heath / As when the time had been' (Corbett, *The Fairies' Farewell*, 25–32).

1
Ye have been fresh and green,
    Ye have been filled with flowers:
And ye the walks have been
    Where maids have spent their hours.

2
You have beheld, how they   5
    With wicker arks did come

6 *arks* 'baskets'.

To kiss, and bear away
The richer cowslips home.

3

You've heard them sweetly sing,
And seen them in a round: 10
Each virgin, like a spring,
With honeysuckles crowned.

4

But now, we see, none here,
Whose silvery feet did tread,
And with dishevelled hair,   15
Adorned this smoother mead.

5

Like unthrifts, having spent,
Your stock, and needy grown,
You're left here to lament
Your poor estates, alone.   20

8   The cowslips ('cows' lips') are richer for the kiss.
11–12   'On Holy Thursday ... wells ... were decorated with boughs of trees, garlands of tulips, and other floral devices' (Brand).

20   *estates* 'conditions' but also 'legal possessions'.

A Nuptial Song, or Epithalamy, on Sir Clipsby Crewe and his Lady

Hesperides, 283; a truncated version is printed in Poole's *English Parnassus* (1657). Five MS versions represent copies from an earlier stage of composition: the number and order of the stanzas varies (though stanza 14 appears regularly before stanza 8). Two MSS give seven extra stanzas. Sir Clipsby Crewe (1599–1648) married Jane Pultney (1609–39) on 7 July 1625 at St Margaret's, Westminster. Herrick later wrote a consolatory epistle *To the Lady Crewe, upon the Death of her Child* and an epitaph *Upon the Lady Crewe*. Epithalamia are historically tied to a sequence of events on a wedding day: in Puttenham's account 'at the first part of the night, when the spouse and the husband are brought to bed', then 'about midnight or one ... to refresh the faint and wearied bodies and spirits' and then 'in the morning ... with new applausions, for that either of them had so well behaved themselves that night' (*Art*, 1.26). This poem describes a different sequence (from the couple's leaving the church through to the bedding of the bride); but along with other modern examples it so far mixes likely English customs with the apparatus of paganism (derived most obviously from Catullus's epithalamion for Manlius Torquatus, No. 61) as to obscure any real succession of events. This may explain the divergent order of stanzas in the MS versions.

1

What's that we see from far? the spring of day
Bloomed from the east, or fair enjewelled May
Blown out of April; or some new-

1–10   'What more than usual light (throughout the place extended) / Makes Juno's fame so bright? / Is there some greater deity descended?' (Jonson, *Hymenaei*, 83–6).
3   *blown* 'brought by the wind' (but as 'blossom').
3–6   Donne, with Kepler's recent discovery of two new stars in mind, invites the bejewelled Princess Elizabeth to 'make / Thyself a constellation ... Be thou a new star, that to us portends / Ends of much wonder' (*Epithalamion for the Lady Elizabeth*, 35–40). The bride, like a *nova*, is brighter than the seven known planets (which include the sun and moon).

5

      star filled with glory to our view,
          Reaching at heaven,
To add a nobler planet to the seven?
    Say, or do we not descry
Some goddess, in a cloud of tiffany
       To move, or rather the
      Emergent Venus from the sea?

                                   10

2

'Tis she! 'tis she! or else some more divine
Enlightened substance; mark how from the shrine
      Of holy saints she paces on,
      Treading upon vermilion
           And amber; spice-
ing the chafed air with fumes of Paradise.
      Then come on, come on, and yield
A savour like unto a blessèd field,
        When the bedabbled morn
      Washes the golden ears of corn.

                                   15

                                   20

3

See where she comes; and smell how all the street
Breathes vineyards and pom'granates: O how sweet!
      As a fired altar, is each stone,
      Perspiring pounded cinnamon.
           The phoenix' nest,
Built up of odours, burneth in her breast.
      Who therein would not consume
His soul to ash-heaps in that rich perfume?
        Bestroking Fate the while
      He burns to embers on the pile.

                                   25

                                   30

4

Hymen, O Hymen! Tread the sacred ground;
Show thy white feet, and head with marjoram crowned:
      Mount up thy flames, and let thy torch
      Display the bridegroom in the porch,
          In his desires
More towering, more disparkling than thy fires:

                                   35

---

8 *tiffany* silk gauze (but etymologically 'theophany', and it reveals a goddess).

9–10 'As that fair star, the messenger of morn, / His dewy face out of the sea doth rear: / Or as the Cyprian goddess, newly born / Of the Ocean's fruitful froth, did first appear' (Spenser, *Faerie Queene*, 2.12.65). Venus is the morning star; she was also born from the sea.

14–15 *vermilion . . . amber* carpets dyed vermilion, perfumed with ambergris.

15–16 *spice- / ing* This break or tmesis (Jonson calls it 'jointing syllabes', *A Fit of Rhyme against Rhyme*, 10) is imported from Greek; as at 3–4, and again at 59–60.

16–20 Martial compares kisses to 'the odour of myrtle, of the Arabian spice-gatherer, of rubbed amber; of fire pale with frankincense, of the earth when sprinkled with summer rain' (3.65:5–7); 'The smell of my son is the smell of a field which the Lord hath blessed' (Genesis 27: 27, Isaac of Jacob); *chafed* 'warmed', but figuratively 'inflamed'.

24 *Perspiring* 'exhaling'.

25–8 The funeral pyre of the phoenix is built of spices.

29–30 'Blessing his fortune while he burns on the pyre'.

31–3 Jonson's Hymen (god of marriage) enters 'his head crowned with roses and marjoram, in his right hand a torch' (*Hymenaei*, 50–2); Catullus's Hymen has 'snowy feet' (61:9–10).

34 'It was the custom for the man to stand [in the porch] expecting the approach of his bride' (Jonson's note on *Hymenaei*, 361–2: 'The longing bridegroom in the porch, / Shows you again the bated torch').

36 'Reaching higher and flying further'; but the association with a spark suggests 'scattering flame'.

Show her how his eyes do turn
And roll about, and in their motions burn
      Their balls to cinders: haste,
      Or else to ashes he will waste.   40

5

Glide by the banks of virgins then, and pass
The showers of roses, lucky-four-leaved grass:
      The while the cloud of younglings sing,
      And drown ye with a flowery Spring:
         While some repeat   45
Your praise, and bless you, sprinkling you with wheat:
      While that others do divine;
Blest is the bride, on whom the sun doth shine;
         And thousands gladly wish
      You multiply, as doth a fish.   50

6

And beauteous bride we do confess you're wise,
In dealing forth these bashful jealousies:
      In Love's name do so; and a price
      Set on yourself, by being nice:
         But yet take heed;   55
What now you seem, be not the same indeed,
      And turn apostate: Love will
Part of the way be met; or sit stone-still.
         On then, and though you slow-
ly go, yet, howsoever, go.   60

7

And now you're entered; see the coddled cook
Runs from his torrid zone, to pry, and look,
      And bless his dainty mistress: see,
      The agèd point out, This is she,
         Who now must sway   65
The house (Love shield her) with her yea and nay:
      And the smirk butler thinks it
Sin, in's nap'ry, not to express his wit;
         Each striving to devise
      Some gin, wherewith to catch your eyes.   70

37–40 Eyes may literally turn and figuratively burn; here like wheels they get hotter as they turn.

41–4 Flowers (here roses and clover) are strewn on the way from the betrothed couple's houses to the church.

46 'The English, when the bride comes from the church, are wont to cast wheat upon her head' (Thomas Moffet, *Health's Improvement* (1655), quoted by Brand).

47–8 What others divine is a proverb, knowingly italicized.

50 'Bless the children . . . that they may grow as fish into a multitude in the midst of the earth' (Genesis 48: 16, Geneva Bible, and King James marginal note).

54–8 The bride is to be reluctant ('nice'); but only to seem so, not to be so truly, deserting her proper allegiance: the lover will not move if he gets no encouragement.

59–60 The break mimics slowness, but enforces union.

61 *coddled* 'stewed' (because the kitchen is hot; but also 'drunk').

62 *torrid zone* from classical times properly applied to the equatorial regions.

64 When Helen is viewed by the old men of Troy 'Those wise, and almost withered men; found this heat in their years; / That they were forced (though whispering) to say . . . In her sweet countenance shine / Looks like the goddesses' (Homer, *Iliad*, 3:154–8).

67 'The ready ('smirk') butler makes a show of his ingenuity with the table linen, each item worked into some device ('gin') to catch your eye.'

8

To bed, to bed, kind turtles, now, and write
This the short'st day, and this the longest night;
      But yet too short for you: 'tis we,
      Who count this night as long as three,
            Lying alone,   75
Telling the clock strike ten, eleven, twelve, one.
      Quickly, quickly then prepare;
And let the young-men and the bride-maids share
            Your garters; and their joints
            Encircle with the bride-groom's points.   80

9

By the brides eyes, and by the teeming life
Of her green hopes, we charge ye, that no strife,
      (Farther than gentleness tends) gets place
      Among ye, striving for her lace:
            O do not fall   85
Foul in these noble pastimes, lest ye call
            Discord in, and so divide
The youthful bride-groom, and the fragrant bride:
            Which Love forfend; but spoken
            Be't to your praise, no peace was broken.   90

10

Strip her of Spring-time, tender-whimpering-maids,
Now Autumn's come, when all those flowery aids
      Of her delays must end; dispose
      That lady-smock, that pansy, and that rose
            Neatly apart;   95
But for prick-madam, and for gentle-heart;
      And soft-maiden's-blush, the bride
Makes holy these, all others lay aside:
            Then strip her, or unto her
            Let him come, who dares undo her.   100

11

And to enchant ye more, see everywhere
About the roof a siren in a sphere;
      (As we think) singing to the din
      Of many a warbling cherubin:
            O mark ye how   105

---

71   *kind turtles* 'fond doves'.
72–5   'O nyght, allas! why nyltow over us hove / As longe
as whan Almena lay by Jove?' (Chaucer, *Troilus and Criseyde*,
3:1427–8); but here the 'three nights in one' that Jupiter
spent with Alcmena will pass briefly for the couple, and will
drag for the bachelor poet.
77–100   François Misson's *Memoirs* (quoted in Brand) have:
'When bed-time is come, the bride-men pull off the bride's
garters . . . This done, and the garters being fastened to the
hats of the gallants, the bride-maids carry the bride to the

bride chamber, where they undress her and lay her in bed.'
The 'points' (80) are laces for attaching hose to doublet; the
'laces' (84) are ties for the sprigs of rosemary handed out as
favours.
94–6   The flowers in the nosegays are chosen for their names,
supplying an alternative account of the bride's defloration.
102–6   The roof-beams are painted with birds or angels;
their music ('numbers') is imagined.
104   *cherubin* cherubim (*1648*, which is the correct plural),
but the rhyme fails.

The soul of Nature melts in numbers: now
　　　　See, a thousand Cupids fly,
　To light their tapers at the bride's bright eye.
　　　　　　To bed; or her they'll tire,
　　　Were she an element of fire.　　　　　　　　　　110

12

And to your more bewitching, see, the proud
Plump bed bear up, and swelling like a cloud,
　　　　Tempting the two too modest; can
　　　　Ye see it brustle like a swan,
　　　　　　　And you be cold　　　　　　　　115
To meet it, when it woos and seems to fold
　　The arms to hug you? throw, throw
Yourselves into the mighty overflow
　　　　　　Of that white pride, and drown
　　　The night, with you, in floods of down.　　　120

13

The bed is ready, and the maze of Love
Looks for the treaders; everywhere is wove
　　　　Wit and new mystery; read, and
　　　　Put in practice, to understand
　　　　　　　And know each wile,　　　　　125
Each hieroglyphic of a kiss or smile;
　　And do it to the full; reach
High in your own conceit, and some way teach
　　　　　　Nature and art, one more
　　　Play than they ever knew before.　　　　　130

14

If needs we must for ceremony's sake,
Bless a sack-posset; luck go with it; take
　　　　The night-charm quickly; you have spells,
　　　　And magics for to end, and hells,
　　　　　　　To pass; but such　　　　　　135
And of such torture as no one would grutch
　　To live therein for ever: fry
And consume, and grow again to die,
　　　　　　And live, and in that case,
　　　Love the confusion of the place.　　　　　140

106–7 When Spenser's bride stands at the altar 'the angels which continually, / About the sacred altar doe remain, / Forget their service and about her fly' (*Epithalamion*, 229–31).
108 'Marriage Love's object is; at whose bright eyes / He lights his torches' (Jonson, *Hymenaei*, 737–8).
113–14 'Whiles the proud bird ruffing his feathers wide, / And brushing his fair breast, did her invade' (Spenser, *Faerie Queene*, 3.11.32, on Jupiter's rape of Leda).
117 *you* it (*1648*).
121–2 'It follows now you are to prove / The subtlest maze of all, that's Love' (Jonson, *Pleasure Reconciled to Virtue*, 123–4); 'treaders' of a maze are dancers of a winding dance.
126 *hieroglyphic* 'hint'.

132 *sack-posset* a sort of sillabub taken 'immediately before the retirement of the company . . . the bride and bridegroom invariably tasting it first; and to this was given the name of "benediction-posset"' (Brand).
133–4 'You have spells and charms ('magics') at the finish of the day, and pains to go through.'
137–8 Like the death and rebirth of the phoenix in fire: 'Two Phoenixes, whose joinèd breasts / Are unto one another mutual nests, / Where motion kindles such fires, as shall give / Young phoenixes, and yet the old shall live / Whose love and courage never shall decline' (Donne, *Epithalamion for the Lady Elizabeth*, 23–7).
140 *confusion* damnation (in MSS, which is the sense).

15

But since it must be done, dispatch, and sew
Up in a sheet your bride, and what if so
　　　It be with rock, or walls of brass,
　　　Ye tower her up, as Danaë was;
　　　　　　Think you that this,　　　　　　　　　　145
Or hell itself a powerful bulwark is?
　　　I tell ye no; but like a
Bold bolt of thunder he will make his way,
　　　　　And rend the cloud, and throw
　　　The sheet about, like flakes of snow.　　　　150

16

All now is hushed in silence; midwife-moon,
With all her owl-eyed issue begs a boon
　　　Which you must grant; that's entrance; with
　　　Which extract, all we can call pith
　　　　　　And quintessence　　　　　　　　　155
Of planetary bodies; so commence
　　　All fair constellations
Looking upon ye, that that nation's
　　　　　Springing from two such fires,
　　　May blaze the virtue of their sires.　　　　160

141–2 The bride's friends sew her in a sheet to prevent the groom's too easy access. But stone walls, or 'Danae in brazen tower immured / From night adulterers' (Horace, *Odes*, 3.16:1–2, Fanshawe), or Hell would be no defence.
151 Spenser addresses the moon: 'And sith of women's labours thou hast charge, / And generation goodly dost enlarge, / Incline thy will to effect our wishfull vow, / And the chaste womb inform with timely seed' (*Epithalamion*, 383–6).
153–60 'And with the boon granted, draw out the benign influences of the planets; may the stars looking down on you grant that the issue of such fires as you are, blaze out their parents' virtue.'

Upon a Child that Died

Printed first as *Hesperides*, 310; and in *Wits' Recreations* (1650) as *On a Child*. One of twenty-five epitaphs, but the identity of the child is unknown.

　　　Here she lies, a pretty bud,
　　　Lately made of flesh and blood:
　　　Who, as soon, fell fast asleep,
　　　As her little eyes did peep.
　　　Give her strewings; but not stir　　　　　5
　　　The earth, that lightly covers her.

6 'This grave partakes the fleshly birth, / Which cover lightly, gentle earth' (Jonson, *On my First Daughter*, 11–12); following Martial, 5.34:9–10.

The Mad Maid's Song

Hesperides, 412; and then printed from a different text in *The Academy of Compliments* (1650). There is an inferior version in MS. Herrick brings a combination of ballad motifs to the edge of nonsense: 'the English have more songs and ballads on the subject of madness than any of their neighbours' (Percy, *Reliques*, 2.3.17–22, who includes six so-called mad songs). The maid and her dead lover appear to be fairies.

1

Good morrow to the day so fair;
   Good morning Sir to you:
Good morrow to mine own torn hair
   Bedabbled with the dew.

2

Good morning to this primrose too;   5
   Good morrow to each maid;
That will with flowers the tomb bestrew,
   Wherein my love is laid.

3

Ah woe is me, woe, woe is me,
   Alack and welladay!   10
For pity, Sir, find out that bee,
   Which bore my love away.

4

I'll seek him in your bonnet brave;
   I'll seek him in your eyes;
Nay, now I think they've made his grave   15
   In th'bed of strawberries.

5

I'll seek him there; I know, ere this,
   The cold, cold earth doth shake him;
But I will go, or send a kiss
   By you, Sir, to awake him.   20

6

Pray hurt him not; though he be dead,
   He knows well who do love him,
And who with green-turfs rear his head,
   And who do rudely move him.

7

He's soft and tender (pray take heed)   25
   With bands of cowslips bind him;
And bring him home, but 'tis decreed,
   That I shall never find him.

To Sycamores

Hesperides, 420, and later *The New Academy of Compliments* (1671). Two MSS give inferior versions. Sycamore (Greek, 'fig-mulberry') suggests 'sick-amour' or 'sigh-amour', as already in Desdemona's song 'A poor soul sat sighing, by a sycamore tree' (*Othello*, IV. iii. 38); here the trees are themselves lovers: 'palms nod mutual vows, poplar sighs to poplar, plane to plane, and alder murmurs to alder' (Burton, *Anatomy*, 3.2.1.1).

> I'm sick of love; O let me lie
> Under your shades, to sleep or die!
> Either is welcome; so I have
> Or here my bed, or here my grave.
> Why do you sigh, and sob, and keep   5
> Time with the tears, that I do weep?
> Say, have ye sense, or do you prove
> What crucifixions are in love?
> I know ye do; and that's the why,
> You sigh for love, as well as I.   10

1 'If ye find my beloved . . . tell him, I am sick of love' (Song of Solomon 5: 8).

8 *crucifixions* 'torments' (perhaps remembering Catullus, 85:1–2: 'I hate and love . . . I am in torment [*excrucior*]'.

To Daisies, Not to Shut so Soon

Hesperides, 441. The title exploits the etymological resonance of 'daisies' ('days' eyes').

1

> Shut not so soon; the dull-eyed night
>   Has not as yet begun
> To make a seizure on the light,
>   Or to seal up the sun.

2

> No marigolds yet closèd are;   5
>   No shadows great appear;
> Nor doth the early shepherd's star
>   Shine like a spangle here.

3

> Stay but till my Julia close
>   Her life-begetting eye;   10
> And let the whole world then dispose
>   Itself to live or die.

3–4 'To take possession of the light or to lock away the sun'.
5 *marigolds* open and shut with the sun.

7 *shepherd's star* the Evening Star: 'The star that bids the shepherd fold' (Milton, *Comus*, 93).

Lovers how they Come and Part

Hesperides, 737.

A Gyges-ring they bear about them still,
To be, and not seen when and where they will.
They tread on clouds, and though they sometimes fall,
They fall like dew, but make no noise at all.
So silently they one to th'other come,   5
As colours steal into the pear or plum,
And air-like, leave no pression to be seen
Where'er they met, or parting place has been.

1   Gyges' ring rendered its wearer invisible; the most fa-   4   *but* as if to suggest that the dew were comparatively noisy.
mous account of it Plato, *Republic*, 359d–360b.   5–6   'If you can see the colour come / Into the blushing
2   'To be where they want and when, but still invisible'.   peach or plum' (*Impossibilities to his Friend*, 3–4)

Upon Julia's Clothes

Hesperides, 779. Herrick can celebrate nakedness, 'Away with silks, away with lawn' (*Clothes do but cheat and cozen us*). Here he celebrates an ambiguous effect of dress. The clothes may melt ('liquefy') to suggest Julia naked; they may on the other hand condense to liquidity against her: Petronius calls a thin garment 'woven air' (*Satyricon*, 55), and Spenser imagines Acrasia's veil made of 'scorchèd dew' (*Faerie Queene*, 2.12.77). The 'vibration' or swinging of the skirts is meanwhile refined to an effect of light: Lord Herbert writes how a foil allows the diamond better to 'vibrate its native lustre' (*Autobiography*), Vaughan of the 'quick vibrations' of starlight (*Midnight*, 12).

Whenas in silks my Julia goes,
Then, then (methinks) how sweetly flows
That liquefaction of her clothes.

Next, when I cast mine eyes and see
That brave vibration each way free;   5
O how that glittering taketh me!

4   *cast* as if he were angling.

The White Island: or Place of the Blest

Noble Numbers, 128. 'The snow-white cliffs of fertile Albion' (Browne, *Britannia's Pastorals*, 1.1:488) mark the island as Britain, distressed and looking for re- covery to a New Jerusalem. The stanza (available from Jonson, *Gypsies Metamorphosed*, 496–9) varies that of *His Litany, to the Holy Spirit*.

In this world (the Isle of Dreams)
While we sit by sorrow's streams,
Tears and terrors are our themes
Reciting:

1–4   'By the rivers of Babylon, there we sat down, yea we
wept, when we remembered Zion' (Psalms 137: 1).

But when once from hence we fly,   5
More and more approaching nigh
Unto young Eternity
        Uniting:

In that whiter island, where
Things are evermore sincere;   10
Candour here, and lustre there
        Delighting:

There no monstrous fancies shall
Out of hell an horror call,
To create (or cause at all)   15
        Affrighting.

There in calm and cooling sleep
We our eyes shall never steep;
But eternal watch shall keep,
        Attending   20

Pleasures, such as shall pursue
Me immortalised, and you;
And fresh joys, as never to
        Have ending.

7 'To an Eternity new to us'.
10 *sincere* 'pure' (of colour).
11 'Here shining white and there reflected light'.

18 'And God shall wipe away all tears from their eyes' (Revelation 21: 4).
19–20 'One short sleep past we wake eternally' (Donne, *Holy Sonnets*, VI:13).

Good Friday: Rex Tragicus, or Christ going to his Cross

Noble Numbers, 263. George Sandys's *Christ's Passion*, a tragedy translated from the Latin of Hugo Grotius, was published in 1640 with complimentary verses by Lucius Cary, Lord Falkland.

Put off thy robe of purple, then go on
To the sad place of execution:
Thine hour is come; and the tormentor stands
Ready, to pierce thy tender feet, and hands.
Long before this, the base, the dull, the rude,   5
The inconstant, and unpurgèd multitude
Yawn for thy coming; some ere this time cry,
How he defers, how loth he is to die!
Amongst this scum, the soldier, with his spear,
And that sour fellow, with his vinegar,   10
His sponge, and stick, do ask "Why thou dost stay?"

1 'And when thy had mocked him, they took off the purple from him . . . and led him out to crucify him' (Mark 15: 20).
3 'Jesus knew that his hour was come that he should depart out of this world' (John 13: 1).

5–6 'The contrary and unwashed rabble gape eagerly ('yawn') for the event.'
10–11 'And one ran and filled a sponge full of vinegar, and put it on a reed, and gave him to drink' (Mark 15: 36).

So do the scurf and bran too: go thy way,
Thy way, thou guiltless man, and satisfy
By thine approach, each their beholding eye.
Not as a thief, shalt thou ascend the mount, 15
But like a person of some high account:
The cross shall be thy stage; and thou shalt there
The spacious field have for thy theatre.
Thou art that Roscius, and that marked-out man,
That must this day act the tragedian, 20
To wonder and affrightment: thou art he,
Whom all the flux of nations comes to see;
Not those poor thieves that act their parts with thee:
Those act without regard, when once a King,
And God, as thou art, comes to suffering. 25
No, no, this scene from thee takes life and sense,
And soul and spirit plot, and excellence.
Why then begin, great King! ascend thy throne,
And thence proceed, to act thy passion
To such an height, to such a period raised, 30
As Hell, and Earth, and Heaven may stand amazed.
God, and good angels guide thee; and so bless
Thee in thy several parts of bitterness;
That those, who see thee nailed unto the tree,
May (though they scorn thee) praise and pity thee. 35
And we (thy lovers) while we see thee keep
The laws of action, will both sigh, and weep;
And bring our spices, to embalm thee dead;
That done, we'll see thee sweetly burièd.

12 *scurf and bran* 'Asses, fools, dolts, chaff and bran, chaff and bran' (Shakespeare, *Troilus*, I. ii. 245).
17 Only the grossest murderers 'This stage of death deserved' (*Christ's Passion*, 4:47).
19 'He is the actor (Roscius, Cicero's friend, is the type), the man "set as a mark for the arrow" (Lamentations 3: 12), that must today play the victim's part.'
24 The thieves' parts go unregarded.

37 *laws of action* 'rules of the plot': 'The fable [plot] is called the imitation of one entire, and perfect action; whose parts are so joined, and knit together, as nothing in the structure can be changed or taken away, without impairing, or troubling the whole' (Jonson, *Timber*).
38–9 'And there came also Nicodemus .. and brought a mixture of myrrh and aloes . . . Then took they the body of Jesus, and wound it in linen clothes with the spices' (John 19: 39–40).

A Carol presented to Dr Williams Bishop of Lincoln as a New-Year's Gift

Printed first in Martin, edition from Bodleian MS Ashmole 36, 37 fol. 298; the punctuation is editorial. John Williams (1582–1650), Bishop of Lincoln from 1621, was committed to the Tower on 11 July 1637 for 'perjury and subornation of perjury'. 'This bishop had been for some years in the Tower . . . when the lords who were the most active and powerful presently resolved to have him at liberty. Some had much kindness for him, not only as a known enemy to the Archbishop of Canterbury, but as a supporter of those opinions and those persons which were against the Church itself' (Clarendon, *History*, 4.134). His imprisonment is ambiguously regretted earlier in the *Hesperides*: 'So you, my Lord, though you have now your stay, / Your night, your prison, and your ebb; you may / Spring up afresh; when all these mists are spent, / And star-like, once more, gild our firmament' (*Upon the Bishop of Lincoln's Imprisonment*, 9–12). He was released on 16 November 1640. Cowley wrote a couplet epistle *Upon his Enlargement out of the Tower*. 'Poetical rejoicings . . . that were to honour the persons of great princes . . . were called *encomia*; we may call them carols of honour' (Puttenham, *Art*, 1.23); Williams's ambiguous reputation is not quite comfortably honoured here.

Fly hence pale Care, no more remember
Past sorrows with the fled December;
But let each present cheek appear
Smooth as the childhood of the year
   And sing a carol here.   5
'Twas brave, 'twas brave could we command the hand
Of Youth's swift watch to stand,
As you have done your day:
Then should we not decay;
But all we wither, and our light   10
Is spilt in everlasting night,
Whenas your sight
Shows like the heavens above the moon,
Like an eternal noon
That sees no setting sun.   15

Keep up those flames, and though you shroud
Awhile your forehead in a cloud,
Do it like the sun to write
In th' air, a greater text of light.
Welcome to all our vows,   20
And since you pay
To us the day
So long desired,
See we have fired
Our holy spikenard, and there's none   25
But brings his stick of cinnamon,
His eager eye, or smoother smile,
And lays it gently on the pile,
Which, thus enkindled, we invoke
Your name amidst the sacred smoke.   30

   Chorus
Come then great Lord
And see our altar burn
With love of your return;
And not a man here but consumes
His soul to glad you in perfumes.   35

---

2   The sorrows of the old year have fled with its last month.
6–9   'If we could make time ('Man is a watch, wound up at first, but never / Wound up again', *The Watch*, 1–2) stop for youth as you have extended your time of power, then we should never die.'
10–11   'Suns that set may rise again, / But if once we lose this light, / 'Tis with us perpetual night' / (Catullus, 5:5–6, Jonson).
13–14   'A wise man's mind, as Seneca holds, is like the state of the world above the moon, ever serene' (Burton, *Anatomy*, 2.3.3).

19   'So look the mornings when the sun / Paints them with fresh vermilion' (*The Maiden-blush*, 1–2); sunlight is 'woven' through cloud to produce the 'greater text'.
20   'Receive our prayers.'
25–6   Complementary spices to be burned on the altar built for Williams: 'Thus the rare cinnamons with the spikenard join' (Martial, 5.13:3, Robert Fletcher).

Henry King (1592–1669)

Henry King was born the eldest son of Dr John King, a friend of Hooker and of Donne, Dean of Christ Church, Oxford, from 1604, and from 1611 Bishop of London; he himself died as Bishop of Chichester in 1669. Along with his brother John (who was three years younger) he went to Westminster School, where George Herbert was an exact contemporary; the two brothers proceeded together to Christ Church. King's advancement in the Church was (almost scandalously) rapid: 'one of the principal prebends of St Paul's ... is bestowed on the Bishop of London's eldest son, a youth of two and twenty years old [in fact 24], who is well provided already of spiritual livings, besides a young wife [Anne Berkeley] worth four or five thousand pound at least' (Chamberlain, *Letters*, 21 December 1616). As 'dearest friend and executor' of Donne, whose love for the father was 'doubled upon his heir', he was responsible for causing Donne 'to be carved in one entire piece of white marble, as it now stands' in St Paul's (Walton, *Life of Donne*). His later career was less sure: made Bishop of Chichester in 1642, this fierce Royalist was ejected in 1643 and lived privately until the Restoration, when he returned to his bishopric. *Poems, Elegies, Paradoxes and Sonnets*, a collection of predominantly early work, came out in 1657 anonymously at the instigation of 'friends who honour you', anxious to stem the circulation of inauthentic versions (current in MSS, of which there are seven major collections, and in printed miscellanies). During his retirement he had prepared a version of the Psalms (1651, reissued in 1654 and again in 1671). There is a Scolar facsimile of *1657* (Menston, 1973). The standard edition of the *Poems* is by Margaret Crum (Oxford: Clarendon Press, 1965). The sermons (funerary, congratulatory, expository) remain uncollected. There is a *Bibliography* by Geoffrey Keynes (London: St Paul's Bibliographies, 1977).

The Exequy

1657; the poem is frequent in MSS, where the title may appear as *An Exequy to his Matchless never to be forgotten Friend*. King married Anne Berkeley in 1617; she bore five children (two died in infancy) and herself died early in 1624 (she was buried on 5 January at St Gregory by St Paul's); *The Exequy* 'follows her out' to the grave. The sentiments are worked out in patterns of poetic thinking on the edge of triteness, but which come across as mellowed by previous use: 'the fled star' (35) like the 'falling star' of *Sic Vita*, the narrowness of the 'longest date' (48) like that which 'Can never yield a hope of our relief' (in *The Surrender*, 26), the 'right and interest' in his dead wife like the 'borrowed light ... straight called in and paid to night' (*Sic Vita*). The informing metaphor is that of the sea-voyage, which makes of the elegy a farewell poem, which can still (unlike that in *To his Unconstant Friend*, 65–6) reserve the certainty of reunion; or even a love poem, which comes close (at 79–88) to embracing epithalamic motifs. The eleven (elegiac) paragraphs are built up from fluid couplets (typically run on by a half line) to give the effect of what Howell (*Epistolae Ho-elianae*, 2.16, a letter which reflects on Anne King herself as a poet) calls 'exact concinnity and evenness of fancy'. *The Anniverse* recalls the death six years later, about which time King may have remarried, but is still insistent on the urgency of his grief: 'only he / Is Nature's true born child, who sums his years / (Like me) with no arithmetic but tears.'

> Accept thou shrine of my dead saint,
> Instead of dirges this complaint;
> And for sweet flowers to crown thy hearse,
> Receive a strew of weeping verse
> From thy grieved friend, whom thou mightst see   5
> Quite melted into tears for thee.
>   Dear loss! since thy untimely fate
> My task hath been to meditate
> On thee, on thee: thou art the book,

2 *complaint* From a complaint a rectification of hurt might be expected (here, reunion with the beloved).

4 *strew* 'strewing' (a rare word).

The library whereon I look   10
Though almost blind. For thee (loved clay)
I languish out not live the day,
Using no other exercise
But what I practise with mine eyes:
By which wet glasses I find out   15
How lazily time creeps about
To one that mourns: this, only this
My exercise and business is:
So I compute the weary hours
With sighs dissolvèd into showers.   20
    Nor wonder if my time go thus
Backward and most preposterous;
Thou hast benighted me, thy set
This eve of blackness did beget,
Who wast my day (though overcast   25
Before thou hadst thy noon-tide passed)
And I remember must in tears,
Thou scarce hadst seen so many years
As day tells hours. By thy clear sun
My love and fortune first did run;   30
But thou wilt never more appear
Folded within my hemisphere,
Since both thy light and motion
Like a fled star is fall'n and gone,
And twixt me and my soul's dear wish   35
The earth now interposèd is,
Which such a strange eclipse doth make
As ne'er was read in almanac.
    I could allow thee for a time
To darken me and my sad clime,   40
Were it a month, a year, or ten,
I would thy exile live till then;
And all that space my mirth adjourn,
So thou wouldst promise to return;
And putting off thy ashy shroud   45
At length disperse this sorrow's cloud.
    But woe is me! the longest date
Too narrow is to calculate
These empty hopes: never shall I
Be so much blest as to descry   50
A glimpse of thee, till that day come
Which shall the earth to cinders doom,
And a fierce fever must calcine
The body of this world like thine,

---

11 *clay* the earthly part of the beloved.

15 *glasses* 'eyes'; but alluding to hour-glasses.

22 *preposterous* 'backward' (the literal sense); the extended sense 'perverse' is secondarily invoked.

23 *set* literalizing the benighting.

29 Anne King was about 24.

32 *my hemisphere* 'the half-circle of my arms'; but also 'the world I inhabit'.

36 *earth* because it covers her; but also the planet, which eclipses his metaphorical sun.

42 *thy exile live* 'live the durations of thy exile'.

45 *ashy* 'pale'; but here also literally 'of ashes'.

51–60 'The heavens and the earth ... are kept in store, reserved unto fire against the day of judgement' (2 Peter 3: 7).

53 *calcine* 'reduce to ashes', but with the connotation 'purify'.

(My little world!) that fit of fire   55
Once off, our bodies shall aspire
To our souls' bliss: then we shall rise,
And view ourselves with clearer eyes
In that calm region, where no night
Can hide us from each other's sight.   60
    Mean time, thou hast her earth: much good
May my harm do thee. Since it stood
With Heaven's will I might not call
Her longer mine, I give thee all
My short-lived right and interest   65
In her, whom living I loved best:
With a most free and bounteous grief,
I give thee what I could not keep.
Be kind to her, and prithee look
Thou write into thy Doomsday Book   70
Each parcel of this rarity
Which in thy casket shrined doth lie:
See that thou make thy reckoning straight,
And yield her back again by weight;
For thou must audit on thy trust   75
Each grain and atom of this dust,
As thou wilt answer Him that lent,
Not gave thee my dear monument.
    So close the ground, and 'bout her shade
Black curtains draw, my bride is laid.   80
    Sleep on my love in thy cold bed
Never to be disquieted!
My last good night! Thou wilt not wake
Till I thy fate shall overtake:
Till age, or grief, or sickness must   85
Marry my body to that dust
It so much loves; and fill the room
My heart keeps empty in thy tomb.
Stay for me there; I will not fail
To meet thee in that hollow vale.   90
And think not much of my delay;
I am already on the way,
And follow thee with all the speed
Desire can make, or sorrows breed.
Each minute is a short degree,   95
And every hour a step towards thee.
At night when I betake to rest,
Next morn I rise nearer my west

67–8 The rhyme may be broken to signal grief. Two MSS give: 'Most freely though thou see me weep, / I gave thee what I could not keep.'

70 *Doomsday Book* Revelation 20: 12: 'the dead were judged out of those things which were written in the books, according to their works'; but alluding to the historical *Doomsday Book* as a record of 'parcels' of land.

77–8 So Jonson: 'thou wert lent to me' (*On my First Son*).

78 *monument* the body of the beloved, it being a token of her having lived; because 'His goodly corps . . . Was quite dismembered, and his members chaste / Scattered on every mountain . . . That of Hippolytus was left no moniment' (Spenser, *Faerie Queene*, 1.5.38).

82 But King goes on to make clear that there is to be a waking.

90 *hollow vale* 'Let the heathen be wakened and come up to the valley of Jehoshaphat: for there will I sit to judge' (Joel 3: 12); *1657* reads 'hallow'.

Of life, almost by eight hours' sail,
Than when sleep breathed his drowsy gale.   100
    Thus from the sun my bottom steers,
And my days' compass downward bears:
Nor labour I to stem the tide
Through which to thee I swiftly glide.
    'Tis true, with shame and grief I yield,   105
Thou like the van first tookst the field,
And gotten hast the victory
In thus adventuring to die
Before me, whose more years might crave
A just precedence in the grave.   110
But hark! My pulse like a soft drum
Beats my approach, tells thee I come;
And slow howe'er my marches be,
I shall at last sit down by thee.
    The thought of this bids me go on,   115
And wait my dissolution
With hope and comfort. Dear (forgive
The crime) I am content to live
Divided, with but half a heart,
Till we shall meet and never part.   120

101   *bottom* 'hull', and so commonly by synecdoche for 'ship'.
102   *compass* 'limit'; but it is the needle of the mariner's compass that must 'bear downward'.
106–7   Relying on 'Take unto you the whole armour of God, that ye may be able to withstand in the evil day' (Ephesians 6: 13).
109   *crave* 'demand'.
111   *pulse* 'heartbeat'.

To my Noble and Judicious Friend Sir Henry Blount upon his *Voyage*

1657; MSS (one of which carries King's corrections) differ slightly. *A Voyage into the Levant. A Brief Relation of a Journey, lately Performed by Master H.B. Gentleman, from England by the way of Venice, into Dalmatia, Slavonia, Bosnia, Hungary, Macedonia, Thessaly, Thrace, Rhodes and Egypt, unto Grand Cairo: with Particular Observations concerning the Modern Condition of the Turks, and other People under that Empire* by Henry Blount (1602–82, knighted 1640) was first published in 1636 and much reprinted. It is praised here as a corrective to the fantasies that maps and travel-books normally encourage, but the energies of the poem (as in Herrick's *Country Life*) are with the fantasy. Blount gives a more generous account of the Ottoman Turks than King suggests.

Sir, I must ever own myself to be
Possessed with human curiosity
Of seeing all that might the sense invite
By those two baits of profit and delight:
And since I had the wit to understand   5
The terms of native or of foreign land;
I have had strong and oft desires to tread
Some of those voyages which I have read.
Yet still so fruitless have my wishes proved,
That from my country's smoke I never moved: 10

4   Recalling Faustus's 'world of profit and delight'.
10   *smoke* Proverbially, 'the smoke of a man's own country is better than the fire of another's.'

Nor ever had the fortune (though designed)
To satisfy the wanderings of my mind.
Therefore at last I did with some content,
Beguile myself in time, which others spent;
Whose art to provinces small lines allots,   15
And represents large kingdoms but in spots.
Thus by Ortelius' and Mercator's aid
Through most of the discovered world I strayed.
I could with ease double the Southern Cape,
And in my passage Afric's wonders take: 20
Then with a speed proportioned to the scale
Northward again, as high as Zembla sail.
Oft hath the travel of my eye outrun
(Though I sat still) the journey of the sun:
Yet made an end, ere his declining beams   25
Did nightly quench themselves in Thetis' streams.
Oft have I gone through Egypt in a day,
Not hindered by the droughts of Libya;
In which, for lack of water, tides of sand
By a dry deluge overflow the land.   30
There I the Pyramids and Cairo see,
Still famous for the wars of Tuman Bey,
And its own greatness; whose immurèd fence
Takes forty miles in the circumference.
Then without guide, or stronger caravan   35
Which might secure the wild Arabian,
Back through the scorchèd deserts pass, to seek
Once the world's lord, now the beslavèd Greek,
Made by a Turkish yoke and Fortune's hate
In language as in mind, degenerate.   40
    And here all rapt in pity and amaze
I stand, whilst I upon the Sultan gaze;
To think how he with pride and rapine fired
So vast a territory hath acquired;
And by what daring steps he did become   45
The Asian fear, and scourge of Christendom:
How he achieved, and kept; and by what arts
He did concentre those divided parts;
And how he holds that monstrous bulk in awe,
By settled rules of tyranny, not law: 50
So rivers large and rapid streams began,
Swelling from drops into an ocean.
    Sure whoe'er shall the just extraction bring

13–76 The historical meditation is stimulated by the maps: Vida recommends that the schoolboy 'to maps repair, / And see imagined cities rising there; / Range with his eyes the earth's fictitious ball, / And pass o'er figured worlds that hang the wall' (Vida, *Art of Poetry*, 1:391–4, Pitt). Maps were so used at Westminster School.

17 Ortelius (1527–98) and Mercator (1512–94) were the great map-makers of early modern times.

22 Nova Zembla is in the Arctic: 'So Zembla's rocks (the beauteous work of frost) / Rise white in air, and glitter o'er the coast' (Pope, *Temple of Fame*, 53–4).

26 'I have finished my journeying before the sun has set in the sea'; Thetis was a minor sea goddess, invoked here (by a common confusion) for Tethys the wife of Oceanus.

32 *Tuman Bey* The last of the Mameluke sultans of Egypt before the Ottoman conquest in 1517.

33 *immured fence* 'defensive wall', its size derived from Blount.

35 *stronger* Security was the motive for travelling together in caravans.

38–9 The Byzantine Empire finally fell to the Ottomans in 1453.

Of this gigantic power from the spring,
Must there confess a Higher Ordinance   55
Did it for terror to the Earth advance.
For mark how 'mongst a lawless straggling crew
Made up of Arab, Saracen, and Jew,
The world's disturber, faithless Mahomet
Did by impostures an opinion get: 60
O'er whom he first usurps as Prince, and then
As Prophet does obtrude his Alcoran.
Next, how fierce Ottoman his claim made good
From that unblessed religion, by blood;
Whilst he the eastern kingdoms did deface,   65
To make their ruin his proud Empire's base.
Then like a comet blazing in the skies,
How death-portending Amurath did rise,
When he his hornèd crescents did display
Upon the fatal plains of Serbia;   70
And farther still his sanguine tresses spread,
Till Kroja life and conquests limited.
Lastly, how Mahomet thence styled the Great,
Made Constantine's his own Imperial Seat;
After that he in one victorious bond   75
Two Empires grasped, of Greece and Trebizond.
   This, and much more than this, I gladly read,
Where my relators it had storièd;
Besides that people's manners and their rites,
Their warlike discipline and ordered fights;   80
Their desp'rate valour, hardened by the sense
Of unavoided Fate and Providence:
Their habit, and their houses, who confer
Less cost on them than on their sepulchre:
Their frequent washings, and the several bath   85
Each mesquit to itself annexèd hath:
What honour they unto the Mufti give,
What to the sovereign under whom they live:
What quarter Christians have; how just and free
To inoffensive travellers they be: 90
Though I confess, like stomachs fed with news,
I took them in for wonder, not for use,
Till your experienced and authentic pen
Taught me to know the places and the men;
And made all those suspected truths become   95

---

55   *Higher Ordinance* God's, as against the order of Nature that turns water-drops into oceans.
60   *opinion* as Macbeth buys 'golden opinions'.
63–76   The account is misleading. Osman I (1281–1326) was the first Ottoman emperor, but his achievement was local. Murad II (1421–51) suffered major defeats in Serbia, and died not at Kroja in Serbia but at Adrianople (Edirne). Constantinople fell to Mohammed II ('The Conqueror') in 1453, Trebizond in 1462: both were Greek.
69   *hornèd crescents* The Ottoman emblem was the crescent moon, but diabolical associations are encouraged.

71   *sanguine tresses* casting him as a Fury: Virgil's Alecto has 'black bloody locks' (*Aeneid* 7:346).
78   *relators* 'historians', glancing at George Sandys's *Relation of a Journey ... Containing a Description of the Turkish Empire* (1615) and similar titles.
86   *mesquit* 'mosque' (often the centre of a complex of public amenities).
87–8   'What honour they render their religion (the 'Mufti' occupying a position like an archbishop) and what the state.'
91   *fed with news* 'satisfied with novelties'.
93   *authentic* 'reliable'.

Undoubted now, and clear as axiom.
   Sir, for this work more than my thanks is due;
I am at once informed and cured by you.
So that, were I assured I should live o'er
My periods of time run out before; 100
Ne'er needed my erratic wish transport
Me from my native lists to that resort,
Where many at outlandish marts unlade
Ingenuous manners, and do only trade
For vices and the language. By your eyes 105
I here have made my full discoveries;
And all your countries so exactly seen,
As in the voyage I had sharer been.
By this you make me so; and the whole land
Your debtor: which can only understand 110
How much she owes you, when her sons shall try
The solid depths of your rare *History*,
Which looks above our gadders' trivial reach,
The commonplace of travellers, who teach
But table-talk; and seldomly aspire 115
Beyond the country's diet or attire;
Whereas your piercing judgement does relate
The policy and manage of each state.
And since she must here without envy grant
That you have further journeyed the Levant 120
Than any noble spirit by her bred
Hath in your way as yet adventurèd;
I cannot less in justice from her look,
Than that she henceforth canonise your book
A rule to all her travellers, and you 125
The brave example; from whose equal view
Each knowing reader may himself direct,
How he may go abroad to some effect,
And not for form: what distance and what trust
In those remoter parts observe he must: 130
How he with jealous people may converse,
Yet take no hurt himself by that commerce.
So when he shall embarked in dangers be,
Which wit and wary caution not foresee;
If he partake your valour and your brain, 135
He may perhaps come safely off again,
As you have done; though not so richly fraught
As this return hath to our staple brought.
   I know your modesty shuns vulgar praise,
And I have none to bring: but only raise 140
This monument of honour and of love,
Which your long-known deserts so far improve,
They leave me doubtful in what style to end,
Whether more your admirer or your friend.

---

96   *clear as axiom* 'self-evident'.
102 *lists* 'territory' or 'pleasures'.
103–4 *unlade ingenuous manners* 'discard their natural ways'.
114 *commonplace* 'theme'.

123–5 'I cannot look for less from England than that she approve your book as the authoritative rule.'
138 *staple* 'Exchange'.

Francis Quarles (1592–1644)

Quarles was born in 1592 near Romford in Essex, the son of a minor civil servant; he died, a fierce Royalist, in 1644, but rendering 'thanks to God for his special love to him, in taking him into his own hands to chastise, while others were exposed to the fury of their enemies, the power of pistols, and the trampling of horses.' He entered Christ's College, Cambridge, in 1608 and proceeded from there to Lincoln's Inn. In 1613 he accompanied the newly married Princess Elizabeth, now Electress Palatine, to Germany, as 'cup-bearer'. By 1618, the year when Germany's miseries began, he had returned to England and married Ursula Woodgate (they had eighteen children); in the 1620s he served as secretary to Archbishop Ussher in Dublin, from where he signed his Sidneian *Argalus and Partheneia* ('this book differs from my former, as a courtier from a churchman'). His 'former' book had been *A Feast for Worms* (1620), a history of Jonah inflated by 'meditations' which, like others of Quarles's biblical paraphrases (of the Book of Esther in 1621, of Job in 1624, of Lamentations in 1624), collected in the *Divine Poems* of 1630, proved immensely popular. The multiple editions of 'the darling of our plebeian judgements' (Edward Phillips, *Theatrum Poeticum*) excited the contempt of poets of less missionary persuasion: 'For if any man design to compose a sacred poem, by only turning a story of the scripture, like Mr Quarles . . . into rhyme; he is so far from elating of poesy, that he only abases divinity' (Cowley, Preface to *Poems*, 1656). These narratives, like his prose meditations in the 1640s, are obliquely informed by the experience of continental Europe, and Germany in particular, in the course of the Thirty Years' War. In 1632 the immensely popular *Divine Fancies* (a collection of epigrams, meditations and observations, edited by William T. Liston (New York: Garland, 1992)) bear more obviously on the poetic manner of the *Emblems* (1635), written from retirement in Essex. These are based on the collaborative Jesuit miscellany the *Typus Mundi* (Antwerp, 1627), and the *Pia Desideria* of the Jesuit Hermann Hugo (Antwerp, 1624), translated later in the century by Edmund Arwaker as *Divine Addresses* (1686). That these handbooks of continental Catholic devotion should have been absorbed so easily into the work of a Protestant devotional poet (and this without the extensive alterations he is sometimes credited with) is unsurprising in a mode whose appeal is almost entirely sentimental (the love affair between Love and the soul) and whose inspiration is so firmly biblical or patristic. The *Hieroglyphics of the Life of Man* (1638), printed along with the *Emblems* after 1643, are based on the single metaphor of life as a burning candle. His ideal is implicit in his commendation of Phineas Fletcher as one whose 'each room was beautified / With new invention, carved on every side, / To please the common and the curious-eyed' (*To my Dear Friend, the Spenser of this Age*, 11–13).

Early editions are described by John Horden in *Francis Quarles: A Bibliography of his Works to the Year 1800*, Oxford Bibliographical Society Publications, N.S. 2 (1953). *The Complete Works in Prose and Verse* was edited by A. B. Grosart, Chertsey Worthies Library (1880–1); the additional *Hosanna; or, Divine poems on the Passion of Christ* and *Threnodes* are edited by John Horden (Liverpool: Liverpool University Press, 1960), whose text of the *Emblems* is available on the Chadwyck-Healey English Poetry Database. There are facsimile editions of the *Emblems* (Menston: Scolar Press, 1970, and, edited by A. D. Cousins, Delmar: Scholars' Facsimiles and Reprints, 1991), and the *Hieroglyphics* (Menston: Scolar Press, 1970). An outline of his life is given by his widow in a 'Short Relation' attached to *Solomon's Recantation* (1645). The standard life is K. J. Höltgen, *Francis Quarles (1592–1644) meditativer Dichter, Emblematiker, Royalist: eine biographische und kritische Studie* (Tübingen, 1978).

Wherefore hidest thou thy face, and holdest me for thy enemy? (Job 13: 24) ('Why dost thou shade thy lovely face? O why')

1635 (*Emblems*, 3.7). The illustration, showing the soul pleading with an Amor shading its face, is from Hugo, *Pia Desideria*, 1.7; the poem is independent of Hugo. Rochester or a poet of his circle supplies a secular 'parody' of the poem, *The Mistress*, which by scrupulously minimal adjustments converts it to a love poem (but lines 22–4 are omitted and a final stanza substituted, based on the final stanza of *Emblems*, 3.12). The quotation from Augustine is found in *Patrologia Latina*, 40:865. Following Hugo, Quarles misplaces the quotation from Anselm, *Prayers*, chapter 10 (*Patrologia Latina*, 158:884).

Why dost thou shade thy lovely face? O why
Does that eclipsing hand, so long, deny
The sunshine of thy soul-enlivening eye?

Without that light, what light remains in me?
Thou art my Life, my Way, my Light; in thee   5
I live, I move, and by thy beams I see:

Thou art my Life: if thou but turn away,
My life's a thousand deaths: thou art my Way;
Without thee, Lord, I travel not, but stray.

My Light thou art; without thy glorious sight,   10
Mine eyes are darkened with perpetual night:
My God, thou art my Way, my Life, my Light.

Thou art my Way; I wander, if thou fly:
Thou art my Light; if hid, how blind am I?
Thou art my Life; if thou withdraw, I die: 15

Mine eyes are blind and dark; I cannot see;
To whom, or whither should my darkness flee,
But to the Light? And who's that Light but thee?

My path is lost; my wandering steps do stray;
I cannot safely go, nor safely stray;   20
Whom should I seek but thee, my Path, my Way?

O, I am dead: to whom shall I, poor I
Repair? to whom shall my sad ashes fly
But Life? and where is Life but in thine eye?

And yet thou turn'st away thy face, and fliest me;   25
And yet I sue for grace, and thou d'niest me;
Speak, art thou angry, Lord, or only triest me?

Unscreen those heavenly lamps, or tell me why
Thou shad'st thy face; perhaps, thou think'st, no eye
Can view those flames, and not drop down and die: 30

1–3 'Make thy face to shine upon thy servant' (Psalms 119: 135).

4 'I am come a light into the world, that whosoever believeth on me should not abide in darkness' (John 12: 46).

5 'I am the way, the truth, and the life' (John 14: 6); 'For in him we live, and move, and have our being' (Acts 17: 28).

6–7 'For ye are dead, and your life is hid with Christ in God' (Colossians 3: 3).

9 'He taketh away the heart of the chief of the people of the earth, and causeth them to wander in a wilderness where there is no way' (Job 12: 24).

16–18 'Thy word is a lamp unto my feet and a light unto my path' (Psalms 119: 105); 'I am the light of the world: he that followeth me shall not walk in darkness' (John 8: 12).

23 'I have taken upon me to speak unto the Lord, which am but dust and ashes' (Genesis 18: 27).

27 'Hide not thy face far from me; put not thy servant away in anger' (Psalms 27: 9) as against 'Try my . . . heart. For thy lovingkindness is before mine eyes' (Psalms 26: 2–3).

28–30 Moses asks God, 'show me now thy way, that I may know thee'; and God replies, 'thou shalt see my back parts: but my face shall not be seen' (Exodus 33: 13–23).

If that be all; shine forth, and draw thee nigher;
Let me behold and die; for my desire
Is phoenix-like to perish in that fire.

Death-conquered Laz'rus was redeemed by thee;
If I am dead, Lord set death's prisoner free;   35
Am I more spent, or stink I worse than he?

If my puffed light be out, give me leave to tine
My flameless snuff at that bright lamp of thine;
O what's thy light the less for lighting mine?

If I have lost my path, great shepherd, say,   40
Shall I still wander in a doubtful way?
Lord, shall a lamb of Israel's sheepfold stray?

Thou art the pilgrim's path; the blind man's eye;
The dead man's life; on thee my hopes rely;
If thou remove, I err; I grope; I die: 45

Disclose thy sunbeams; close thy wings, and stay;
See see, how I am blind, and dead, and stray,
O thou, that art my Light my Life, my Way.

Why dost thou hide thy face? Happily thou wilt say, none can see thy
face and live: Ah Lord, let me die, that I may see thee; let me see thee,
that I may die: I would not live, but die; that I may see Christ. I desire
death, that I may live with Christ, I despise life. (St Augustine,
Soliloquies, Chapter 1)

O excellent hiding, which is become my perfection! My God, thou hidest
thy treasure, to kindle my desire; thou hidest thy pearl, to inflame the
seeker; thou delay'st to give, that thou may'st teach me to importune:
seem'st not to hear, to make me persevere. (Anselm, *Meditations*, Chapter
10)

Epigram

If Heaven's all-quickening eyes vouchsafe to shine
Upon our souls, we slight; if not, we whine;
Our equinoctial hearts can never lie
Secure, beneath the tropics of that eye.

31–6   'His eyes were as a flame of fire . . . and his counten-
ance was as the sun shineth in his strength. And when I saw
him, I fell at his feet as dead. And he laid his right hand
upon me, saying unto me, Fear not . . . I am he that liveth,
and was dead: and behold, I am alive for evermore' (Revela-
tion 1: 14–18). The story of Lazarus, revived when he 'had
lain in the grave four days already', is at John 11: 1–46.
37   'If a man walk in the night, he stumbleth, because there
is no light in him' (John 11: 10);

38–9   'For thou wilt light ['tine'] my candle: the Lord my
God will enlighten my darkness' (Psalms 18: 28).
40–2   'I am not sent but unto the lost sheep of the house of
Israel' (Matthew 15: 24).

Epigram 1–2   'If Heaven shines on us, we disdain it; if
not, we complain.'

O that thou wouldst hide me in the grave, and thou wouldst keep me secret until thy wrath be past (Job 14: 13) ('O whither shall I flee? what path untrod')

1635 (*Emblems*, 3.12). The illustration, from Hugo *Pia Desideria* 1.12, shows the soul taking refuge in a cave from an Amor armed with thunderbolts; the poem, a meditation on the charitable uses of punishment, is largely independent of Hugo's. The biblical quotations are used in a sometimes perverse half-classicized way, against the grain. The quotation from Augustine can be found in *Patrologia Latina* 36:235.

O whither shall I flee? what path untrod
Shall I seek out, to 'scape the flaming rod
Of my offended, of my angry God?

Where shall I sojourn? What kind sea will hide
My head from thunder? where shall I abide,   5
Until his flames be quenched, or laid aside!

What if my feet should take their hasty flight,
And seek protection in the shades of night?
Alas, no shades can blind the God of Light:

What, if my soul should take the wings of day,   10
And find some desert; if she spring away,
The wings of vengeance clip as fast as they:

What if some solid rock should entertain
My frighted soul? Can solid rocks restrain
The stroke of justice, and not cleave in twain?   15

Nor sea, nor shade, nor shield, nor rock, nor cave,
Nor silent deserts, nor the sullen grave,
Where flame-eyed Fury means to smite, can save.

The seas will part; graves open; rocks will split;
The shield will cleave; the frighted shadows flit;   20
Where Justice aims, her fiery darts must hit.

No, no, if stern-browed Vengeance means to thunder,
There is no, place, beneath, nor under,
So close, but will unlock, nor rive in sunder.

2 'Let him take his rod away from me' (Job 9: 34), 'flaming' from the 'flaming sword which turned every way' (Genesis 3: 24) to guard Eden.
4–6 The sea itself thunders (as at Jeremiah 6: 23); and while God's anger may be laid aside, it 'shall burn, and shall not be quenched' (Jeremiah 7: 20).
10–12 The Psalmist takes comfort from God's being everywhere: 'If I take the wings of the morning , and dwell in the uttermost parts of the sea, even there shall thy hand lead me' (Psalms 139: 9–10); but here winged Nemesis flies ('clips') in pursuit.
13–14 'It shall come to pass, while my glory passeth by, that I will put thee in a clift of the rock, and will cover thee

with my hand' (Exodus 33: 22); but 'is not my word like as fire? saith the Lord; and like a hammer that breaketh the rock in pieces?' (Jeremiah 23: 29).
18 'His eyes were as a flame of fire, and . . . he was clothed with a vesture dipped in blood, and his name is called The Word of God' (Revelation 19: 12–13).
19–20 'The earth did quake, and the rocks rent; and the graves were opened; and many bodies of the saints which slept arose' (Matthew 27: 51–2); 'there brake he . . . the shield, and the sword, and the battle' (Psalms 76: 3); 'God shall shoot at them with an arrow; suddenly shall they be wounded' (Psalms 64: 7).

'Tis vain to flee; 'tis neither here nor there   25
Can 'scape that hand until that hand forbear;
Ah me! where is he not, that's everywhere?

'Tis vain to flee; till gentle Mercy show
Her better eye, the farther off we go,
The swing of Justice deals the mightier blow: 30

The ingenious child, corrected, does not fly
His angry mother's hand, but clings more nigh,
And quenches, with his tears, her flaming eye.

Shadows are faithless, and the rocks are false;
No trust in brass; no trust in marble walls;   35
Poor cots are even as safe as princes' halls:

Great God, there is no safety here below;
Thou art my fortress, though thou seem'st my foe,
'Tis thou, that strik'st the stroke, must guard the blow:

Thou art my God; by thee I fall or stand;   40
Thy grace hath given me courage to withstand
All tortures, but my conscience, and thy hand.

I know thy justice is thyself; I know,
Just God, thy very self is mercy too;
If not to thee, where? whither should I go?   45

Then work thy will; if passion bid me flee,
My reason shall obey; my wings shall be
Stretched out no further than from thee to thee.

Whither fly I? To what place can I safely fly? To what mountain? To
what den? To what strong house? What castle shall I hold? What walls
shall hold me? Whithersoever I go, myself follows me: For whatsoever
thou fliest, O man, thou may'st, but thy own conscience: wheresoever O
Lord I go, I find thee, if angry, a revenger; if appeased, a redeemer: what
way have I, but to flee from thee, to thee: that thou may'st avoid thy
God, address thee to thy Lord. (St Augustine on Psalm 31, Vulgate 30)

Epigram

Hath vengeance found thee? Can thy fears command
No rocks to shield thee from her thundering hand?
Know'st thou not where to 'scape? I'll tell thee where;
My soul make clean thy conscience; hide thee there.

27 'He looketh to the ends of the earth, and seeth under
the whole heaven' (Job 28: 24).
30 'Beware lest he take thee away with his stroke' (Job 36:
18).
31–3 'God dealeth with you as with sons; for what son is
he whom the father chasteneth not?' (Hebrews 12: 7); but
here the innocent ('ingenious' misused for 'ingenuous') child
appeals to the mother.

35–6 'Alas, alas, that great city Babylon ... for in one
hour is thy judgement come ... all maner vessels of most
precious wood, and of brass, and iron, and marble ... are
departed from thee' (Revelation 18: 10–14); '[God] accepteth
not the persons of princes nor regardeth the rich more than
the poor ... In a moment shall they die' (Job 34: 19–20).
38–9 'Thou art my rock and my fortress' (Psalms 31: 3);
'he woundeth, and his hands make whole' (Job 5: 18).

George Herbert (1593–1633)

'Being nobly born, and as eminently endowed with gifts of the mind, and having by industry and happy education perfected them to that great height of excellency whereof his fellowship of Trinity College in Cambridge, and his Oratorship in the University, together with that knowledge which the King's court had taken of him, could make relation far above ordinary. Quitting both his deserts and all the opportunities he had for worldly preferment, he betook himself to the sanctuary and temple of God, choosing rather to serve at God's altar, than to seek the honour of state-employments.' So the Cambridge University printers addressed the reader of the first edition of *The Temple* in 1633; the volume comes with Herbert's renunciation of the world explicit in it. He was born in Montgomery Castle (or at Black Hall near it); he died in 1633 in a parsonage at Bemerton, near Salisbury. Brought up by his remarkable mother Mrs Magdalen Herbert (the subject of Herbert's sequence of nineteen epigrams in Latin and Greek, *Memoriae Matris Sacrum*, published with Donne's memorial sermon for her in 1627, *Sermons*, 8.2), he entered Westminster School probably in 1604. From there he went on to Trinity College, Cambridge, in 1609, the year of his mother's remarriage to Sir John Danvers, the regicide. His immersion in the world was never as complete as his brother Edward's (Lord Herbert of Cherbury's). The sonnets given in Walton as sent to his mother in the New Year of 1610 ('My God, where is that ancient heat towards thee' and 'Sure, Lord, there is ink enough in thee to dry / Oceans of ink') already argue a vocation to the Church and to poetry; the Latin elegy on Prince Henry (in *Epicedium Cantabrigiense*, 1612) is, inappropriately for a public collection of funeral verses, a sustained interrogation of Providence. From 1614 he held Fellowships at Trinity, on course for a career in the Church. Even so, he was pulled to the world: the Lectureship in Rhetoric he held in 1618 was remembered for an ingratiating analysis of a speech by King James, and his service as Public Orator 1620–7 (a sleeping orator towards the end of the period), was an opportunity for political networking. But in 1624, the year he sat as MP for the Borough of Montgomery, he was ordained as deacon. In 1626 he was installed as a Canon of Lincoln Cathedral and Prebendary of Leighton, where he undertook restoration of the church; and from this date he seems to have strengthened his association with Nicholas Ferrar and the religious community of Little Gidding in Huntingdonshire. His brother Edward described his later life as 'little less than sainted', the reputation that carried his life and his poems together as the century's most influential models of Anglican piety. Before the offer of a living at Bemerton in Wiltshire and his ordination as a priest in 1630, he had probably completed *The Temple*. He married his stepfather's cousin Jane Danvers, in 1629. Barnabas Oley's 'Prefatory View of the Life' in *Remains* (1652) is the first biography; Walton's *Life* (1670) is classic (and gives the only text of some poems). The standard modern biography is Amy M. Charles, *A Life of George Herbert* (Ithaca, NY: Cornell University Press, 1977).

A draft of the collection (almost half the poems of the published *Temple* and six later discarded) is preserved in the so-called Williams MS (in Dr Williams' Library, London) with autograph corrections; it dates probably from before Herbert's ordination as deacon in 1624. The first and only published collection of Herbert's English poems is the posthumously printed duodecimo, *The Temple. Sacred Poems and Private Ejaculations* (Cambridge, 1633); there were eleven editions before the end of the century. There is a facsimile of the 1633 edition (Menston: Scolar Press, 1968). *The Remains*, including *A Priest to the Temple* and proverbs collected under the title *Jacula Prudentum*, was published in 1652, prefaced by Barnabas Oley's biography; there is a facsimile edition (Menston: Scolar Press, 1970). The standard edition is F. E. Hutchinson, *The Works* (Oxford: Clarendon Press, 1941) which also includes miscellaneous prose. A. B. Grosart's edition of the *Complete Works* (1874) has the best version of the Latin verse; the *English Works*, edited by G. H. Palmer (1905), is eccentric but often valuable. There are many popular editions, of which the most useful is *The Complete English Works*, ed. Ann Pasternak Slater (London: Everyman's Library, 1995). There are facsimile editions by Amy M. Charles of the *Williams Manuscript of George Herbert's Poems* (Delmar: Scholars' Facsimiles and Reprints, 1977) and of the *Bodleian Manuscript of George Herbert's Poems* (Delmar: Scholars' Facsimiles and Reprints, 1984); Mario A. Di Cesare has prepared *The Temple: A Diplomatic Edition of the Bodleian Manuscript* (Binghamton, NY: Medieval and Renaissance Texts and Studies, 1995) promoting its independent importance. Mario A. Di Cesare and Rigo Mignani have published *A Concordance to the Complete Writings* (Ithaca, NY: Cornell University Press, 1977). Earlier criticism is described in C. A. Patrides, *George Herbert: The Critical Heritage* (London: Routledge, 1983). Maureen Boyd and Cedric C. Brown have edited from a Bodleian MS George Ryley's *Mr. Herbert's Temple and Church Militant Explained and Improved* (New York: Garland, 1987), a commentary (completed in 1715) important for its re-implication of *The Temple* in biblical contexts. John R. Roberts's revised *George Herbert: An Annotated Bibliography of Modern Criticism 1905–1984* (Columbia: University of Missouri Press, 1978) describes criticism of this century.

The Agony

The images of man's sin and Christ's love are identical: 'it is a great motive [to contrition] to know the malice and turpitude that a sin containeth in itself, the which no way is known better, than by seeing what Christ suffered to destroy the said sin' (Antonio de Molina, *A Treatise of Mental Prayer*, St Omer, 1617, John Sweetnam).

Philosophers have measured mountains,
Fathomed the depths of seas, of states, and kings,
Walked with a staff to Heaven, and traced fountains:
But there are two vast, spacious things,
The which to measure it doth more behove: 5
Yet few there are that sound them; Sin and Love.

Who would know Sin, let him repair
Unto mount Olivet; there shall he see
A man so wrung with pains, that all his hair,
His skin, his garments bloody be.   10
Sin is that press and vice, which forceth pain
To hunt his cruel food through every vein.

Who knows not Love, let him assay
And taste that juice, which on the cross a pike
Did set again abroach; then let him say   15
If ever he did taste the like.
Love is that liquor sweet and most divine,
Which my God feels as blood; but I, as wine.

1–6 'Philosophy should be your substantial food, poetry your banqueting stuff; philosophy hath more of reality in it than any knowledge, the philosopher can fathom the deep, measure mountains, reach the stars with a staff, and bless heaven with a girdle' (Howell, *Epistolae Ho-elianae*, 1.5.9, dated 25 Oct. 1627); but he goes on: 'on Sundays and holidays, let Divinity be the sole object of your speculation, in comparison whereof all other knowledge is but cob-web learning.' A 'staff' is a measuring rod.
8–12 Mount Olivet is the scene of the agony in the garden (Luke 22: 39–46). The picture is developed from Isaiah, 'Wherefore art thou red in thine apparel, and thy garments like him that treadeth in the winefat? I have trodden the winepress alone; and of the people there was none with me:

for I will tread them in mine anger . . . and their blood shall be sprinkled upon my garments' (63: 2–3); but divine rage is translated to divine suffering, necessitated by sinful man: 'Christ the true vine, grape, cluster, on the cross / Trod the winepress alone, unto the loss / Of blood, and life' (Christopher Harvey, *School of the Heart*, Epigram 47:1–3).
13–18 Harvey's epigram continues: 'Draw, thankful heart, and spare not: / Here's wine enough for all, save those that care not.' The pike broaches Christ's side ('one of the soldiers with a spear pierced his side, and forthwith there came out blood and water', John 19: 34) to release what the contrite receive as wine: 'But he doth bid us take his blood for wine' (*Divinity*, 21). Christ rather bids us take wine for his blood (Mark, 14: 24).

Affliction 1

Some first thoughts from the Williams MS are given in the notes. This is the first of five poems of the same title and, since Walton, who quotes lines 37–66 as 'a pious reflection on God's providence, and some passages of his life', taken as autobiographical. The occasion remains undefined: the bereavements of lines 31–6 are sometimes identified with the deaths of Herbert's brothers Charles and William in 1617, sometimes with the deaths in 1624–5 of Ludovick Stuart, James Hamilton, and King James, on whom (says Walton) Herbert's 'court-hopes' depended; Francis Bacon and Lancelot Andrewes (on whom other hopes depended) both died in 1626, and Herbert's mother in 1627. But the poem is less concerned with affliction, or even patience in the face of affliction, than with a resolution to acknowledge a commitment to God hitherto misunderstood and irregularly embraced. Archbishop John Sharp of York died with the final couplet on his lips.

When first thou didst entice to thee my heart,
    I thought the service brave:
So many joys I writ down for my part,
    Besides what I might have
Out of my stock of natural delights,   5
Augmented with thy gracious benefits.

I lookèd on thy furniture so fine,
    And made it fine to me:
Thy glorious household-stuff did me entwine,
    And 'tice me unto thee.   10
Such stars I counted mine: both heaven and earth
Paid me my wages in a world of mirth.

What pleasures could I want, whose King I served,
    Where joys my fellows were?
Thus argued into hopes, my thoughts reserved   15
    No place for grief or fear.
Therefore my sudden soul caught at the place,
And made her youth and fierceness seek thy face.

At first thou gav'st me milk and sweetnesses;
    I had my wish and way: 20
My days were strawed with flowers and happiness;
    There was no month but May.
But with my years sorrow did twist and grow,
And made a party unawares for woe.

My flesh began unto my soul in pain,   25
    "Sicknesses cleave my bones;
Consuming agues dwell in every vein,
    And tune my breath to groans."
Sorrow was all my soul; I scarce believed,
Till grief did tell me roundly, that I lived.   30

When I got health, thou took'st away my life,
    And more; for my friends die:
My mirth and edge was lost; a blunted knife
    Was of more use than I.

---

2 'I was happy with the employment you offered.'

6 *gracious benefits* grace's perquisites (MS); 'gracious' (defining the order of Christ's spiritual covenant) and 'natural' (defining the order of the world) are opposed, but an arch courtliness obtrudes.

7–10 Creation is 'like a spacious and splendid house, provided and filled with the most exquisite and abundant furnishings' (Calvin, *Institutes*, 1.14.20); for 'fine' the MS has 'rich', and the stuff 'did me bewitch / Into thy family'.

11–12 'I thought of these incorruptible beauties as my own: heaven and earth supplied me with every happiness': 'Take stars for money' (*The Church-Porch*, 171).

15–16 *my thoughts . . . fear* I was preserved / Before that I could fear (MS).

17 'Therefore my rash ('eager, hot, and undertaking', he

says in *The Answer*, 6) soul snatched at the summit' ('place' in falconry is the high point of the hawk's flight).

21 *strawed* strowed (MS), 'strewed'.

23–4 'As I got older, sorrows (plural as in MS, but cancelled for euphony) wove themselves into something bigger, and without my noticing combined to work my grief': in *Providence* the 'twist chequered with night and day' is spun for our good (57–8).

26 'My bones are pierced in me . . . and my sinews take no rest' (Job 30: 17).

29–30 *I scarce . . . lived* I did not know / That I did live, but by a pang of woe (MS); 'I will not swear these are my hands: let's see; / I feel this pin prick. Would I were assured / Of my condition' (*King Lear*, IV. vii. 55–7).

Thus thin and lean without a fence or friend,   35
I was blown through with every storm and wind.

Whereas my birth and spirit rather took
    The way that takes the town;
Thou didst betray me to a lingering book,
    And wrap me in a gown.   40
I was entangled in the world of strife,
Before I had the power to change my life.

Yet, for I threatened oft the siege to raise,
    Not simpering all mine age,
Thou often didst with Academic praise   45
    Melt and dissolve my rage.
I took thy sweetened pill, till I came where
I could not go away, nor persevere.

Yet lest perchance I should too happy be
    In my unhappiness,   50
Turning my purge to food, thou throwest me
    Into more sicknesses.
Thus doth thy power cross-bias me, not making
Thine own gift good, yet me from my ways taking.

Now I am here, what thou wilt do with me   55
    None of my books will show
I read, and sigh, and wish I were a tree;
    For sure then I should grow
To fruit or shade: at least some bird would trust
Her household to me, and I should be just.   60

Yet, though thou troublest me, I must be meek;
    In weakness must be stout.
Well, I will change the service, and go seek
    Some other master out.
Ah my dear God! though I am clean forgot,   65
Let me not love thee, if I love thee not.

39–42 'You surrendered me to study (with a book 'holding me back') and a life in the university ('a gown'); Oley's *Life of Herbert* says 'his birth and spirit prompted him to martial achievements . . .and not to sit simpering over a book'.

43 'And then because I threatened to end my confinement'.

45–8 'I took the academic honours you gave me to make me forget my political ambitions, until I found myself in a position where I could neither abandon the academic life nor commit myself to it'; 'where' is supplied from MSS for *1633*'s 'near'.

51–4 'You make me rely on the "pill" of academe (the 'purge' of worldly ambitions), and so increase my sicknesses. My natural bent is thwarted by your contrary inclination: I cannot follow the one, nor welcome the other.' Quarles prays that God start a new game: 'New sole [throw] my bowls, and make their bias true: / I'll cease to game, till fairer ground be given, / Nor wish to win until the mark be Heaven' (*Emblems*, 1.10:52–4).

57–60 'O that I were an orange-tree, / That busy plant!' (*Employment*, 21–2); 'Blest is the man that . . . in God's Law sets his delight . . . He shall be like an happy tree, / Which, planted by the waters, shall / With timely fruit still laden stand' (Psalms 1: 1–3, doubtfully Herbert's version).

61–2 'You require, impossibly, that I meekly submit to your vexations, and yet bravely persevere in my submission.'

64 'No man can serve two masters: for either he will hate the one, and love the other; or else he will hold to the one and despise the other. Ye cannot serve God and Mammon' (Matthew 6: 24).

65–6 'Dear God ('King' in MS), though I should make no show in the world, let me not love you at all if not entirely.' The resolution (but the sense of these quibbling lines is famously disputed) is to forsake the world and love God: 'If any man love not the Lord Jesus Christ, let him be Anathema [outcast] Maranatha [Come O Lord]' (1 Corinthians 16: 22).

Prayer 1

Remarkably for a sonnet, the poem is almost aggressively unstructured, the various half-riddling periphrases for prayer isolated one from another, or in doubtful relation. Something of this separateness is found in the Psalms, which typically multiply short sense-units; but two alphabetical (and otherwise random) litanies of epithets are found in two *Greek Anthology* hymns, one to Bacchus, another to Apollo (9.524, 525), and Herbert's Latin hymn to Bacon uses this licence. A problem of definition seems posed, but the solution is (typically) withheld.

> Prayer the Church's banquet, angels' age,
>   God's breath in man returning to his birth,
>   The soul in paraphrase, heart in pilgrimage,
> The Christian plummet sounding heaven and earth;
> Engine against the Almighty, sinner's tower,   5
>   Reversèd thunder, Christ-side-piercing spear,
>   The six-days-world transposing in an hour,
> A kind of tune, which all things hear and fear;
> Softness, and peace, and joy, and love, and bliss,
>   Exalted manna, gladness of the best,   10
>   Heaven in ordinary, man well dressed,
> The Milky Way, the bird of paradise,
>   Church-bells beyond the stars heard, the soul's blood,
>   The land of spices; something understood.

1   With a contrast between eucharistic feasting at set times and by divine invitation, and the aeon-long occupation of the angels.
2   Man gives back what animates him: 'And the Lord God breathed into his nostrils the breath of life' (Genesis 2: 7).
3   'So the soul makes itself intelligible, and the heart reaches out in devotion.'
4   Prayer measures the temple building in devout hearts, recalling 'the plummet in the hand of Zerubbabel with . . . the eyes of the Lord, which run to and fro through the whole earth' (Zechariah 4: 10); miraculously, this falls upwards.
5–6   'Prayer hath the nature of violence; in the public prayers of the congregation, we besiege God, says Tertullian, and we take God prisoner, and bring God to our conditions' (Donne, *Sermons*, 5.18); the 'engine' is a ram: Donne punningly addresses the Lamb of God as a 'strong ram, which has battered heaven for me' (*La Corona*, 7:9); the 'sinners' tower' not a refuge ('thou hast been . . . a strong tower from the enemy', Psalms 61: 3), but a timber-tower used in siege attack; 'reversèd thunder' a return (as fear) of God's wrath ('thou shalt be visited of the Lord of hosts with thunder', Isaiah 29: 6); the 'Christ-side-piercing spear' the provoker of redeeming blood ('one of the soldiers with a spear pierced his side, and forthwith there came out blood and water', John 19: 34). *Artillery*, 17–20, employs similar violence.
7   'Resetting the work-a-day world for an hour to a tune we hear with devotion': 'Serve the Lord with fear, and rejoice with trembling' (Psalms 2: 11).
10   'This is the bread which the Lord hath given you to eat' (Exodus 16: 15, of manna); it is a benefit lifted up and returned: 'Thou shalt take the breast of the ram of Aaron's consecration, and wave it for a wave offering before the Lord' (Exodus 29: 26).
11   'Heaven in homespun, man in his best'.
12   'There is a way, well seen when skies be clear, / The Milky named: by this, the gods resort / Unto the Almighty Thunderer's high Court' (Ovid, *Metamorphoses*, 1:168–70, Sandys); birds of paradise never touch earth and 'Foodless they live; for the air always feeds them' (Sylvester, *Divine Weeks*, 1.5:802).
13   'Think when the bells do chime, / 'Tis angels' music' (*The Church-Porch*, 387–8).
14   Like incense, prayer concentrates the riches of far-off places: 'And the smoke of the incense, which came with the prayers of the saints, ascended up before God' (Revelation 8: 4); 'And the Lord said unto Moses, Take unto thee sweet spices, stacte, and onycha, and galbanum . . . And thou shalt make it a perfume . . . tempered together, pure and holy . . . and put of it before the testimony in the tabernacle of the congregation, where I will meet with thee' (Exodus 30: 34–6).

The Temper 1

In the Williams MS, *The Christian Temper* is the first of two poems so titled. It is the poet's essay, says Ryley, 'towards the discovery of his ordinary temper'. The steel is to be 'tempered' in which his love is engraved (2), the breast is to be 'tempered' like a musical instrument (23).

How should I praise thee, Lord! how should my rhymes
　　Gladly engrave thy love in steel,
　　If what my soul doth feel sometimes,
　　　　My soul might ever feel!

Although there were some forty heavens, or more,　　　　　　5
　　Sometimes I peer above them all;
　　Sometimes I hardly reach a score,
　　　　Sometimes to Hell I fall.

O rack me not to such a vast extent;
　　Those distances belong to thee:　　　　　　　　　　　　10
　　The world's too little for thy tent,
　　　　A grave too big for me.

Wilt thou mete arms with man, that thou dost stretch
　　A crumb of dust from Heaven to Hell?
　　Will great God measure with a wretch?　　　　　　　　15
　　　　Shall he thy stature spell?

O let me, when thy roof my soul hath hid,
　　O let me roost and nestle there:
　　Then of a sinner thou art rid,
　　　　And I of hope and fear.　　　　　　　　　　　　　　20

Yet take thy way; for sure thy way is best:
　　Stretch or contract me thy poor debtor:
　　This is but tuning of my breast,
　　　　To make the music better.

1 The Psalmist says 'I will praise thee, O Lord, with my whole heart' (9: 1), 'My mouth shall speak the praise of the Lord' (145: 21). Herbert's apparent question turns into a declaration only at lines 3–4.
5 *some forty heavens* a hundred (MS); 'forty' commonly means 'many' (though the constellations are numbered at forty-eight); and like Paul, the poet is 'such an one, caught up to the third heaven ['the highest heaven: for we need not to dispute subtly upon the word' says the Geneva gloss] . . . caught up into Paradise, and heard unspeakable words' (2 Corinthians 12: 2–4).
9 *rack* 'stretch'.
11 'It is he that sitteth upon the circle of the earth . . . that stretcheth out the heavens . . . as a tent to dwell in' (Isaiah 40: 22); 'He that descended is the same also that ascended up far above all heavens, that he might fill all things'

(Ephesians 4: 10); 'But will God indeed dwell on the earth? behold, the heaven . . . cannot contain thee; how much less this house that I have builded?' (1 Kings 8: 27).
13–16 Man is to be perfected 'Till we all come in the unity of the faith . . . unto a perfect man, unto the measure of the stature of the fulness of Christ' (Ephesians 4: 13); 'now by faith all arms are of a length' (*Faith*, 27); swords are 'met' ('measured') before duelling.
16 'Will he trouble to consider your puny measure?'
16–20 'Yea the sparrow hath found an house, and the swallow a nest for herself, where she may lay her young, even thine altars . . . Blessed are they that dwell in thy house' (Psalms 84: 3–4).
23–4 'I shall be made thy music, as I come / I tune the instrument here at the door' (Donne, *Hymn to God my God, in my Sickness*, 3–4).

Whether I fly with angels, fall with dust, 25
Thy hands made both, and I am there:
Thy power and love, my love and trust
Make one place everywhere.

25 Whether I angel it, or fall to dust (MS).

Jordan 1

The first of two poems of the same title. The order for baptism in the Book of Common Prayer establishes Jordan as the type of purifying water since 'by the baptism of thy well-beloved son Jesus Christ, thou didst sanctify the flood Jordan, and all other waters, to this mystical washing away of sin.' The leprosy-stricken Syrian general Naaman on Elisha's advice bathes seven times in Jordan 'and his flesh came again like unto the flesh of a little child, and he was clean. And he returned to the man of God, he and all his company, and came, and stood before him. and he said, Behold, now I know that there is no God in all the earth, but in Israel' (2 Kings 5: 14–15). Jordan is a Hebraized 'true Helicon'. With *Jordan 2*, *The Forerunners* and two sonnets given in Walton's *Life* ('My God, where is that ancient heat' and 'Sure, Lord, there is enough'), the poem is a manifesto for literary plainness; but it implies further the purifying virtue of plain speaking.

Who says that fictions only and false hair
Become a verse? Is there in truth no beauty?
Is all good structure in a winding stair?
May no lines pass, except they do their duty
  Not to a true, but painted chair? 5

Is it no verse, except enchanted groves
And sudden arbours shadow coarse-spun lines?
Must purling streams refresh a lovers loves?
Must all be veiled, while he that reads, divines,
  Catching the sense at two removes? 10

Shepherds are honest people; let them sing:
Riddle who list, for me, and pull for prime:
I envy no man's nightingale or spring;
Nor let them punish me with loss of rhyme,
  Who plainly say, "My God, my King". 15

1–2 'Who can paint her face and curl her hair, and change it into an unnatural colour, but therein doth work reproof to her maker, who made her?' (Homily against excess of Apparel); Ryley is so uncomfortable with 'hair' that he emends it to 'air'.

3 'A good builder to a high tower will not make his stair upright, but winding almost the full compass about, that the steepness be the more unsensible' (Sidney, *Arcadia*, 4.4.1); Bacon's punning 'All rising to great place is by a winding stair' ('Of great place') suggests the phrase was quasi-proverbial.

5 Whitaker quotes Augustine, 'He who teaches hearts [God] hath his chair in Heaven' and goes on ironically, 'What is this chair in Heaven? . . . knowest thou not that this chair is found on earth? Wast thou never at Rome, or sawest thou never the chair of Peter?' (*A Disputation on Holy Scripture*, 5.8).

6–8 Parodying the clichés of romance: groves are enchanted, arbours in the middle of nowhere ('sudden'), streams 'purling'.

12 'I care nothing if it please them to play their games, and draw for the winning hand'; 'pulling for prime' belongs in the fashionable card game of primero. Sir John Harington (*Epigrams*, 2.99) writes of one Marcus's life ruined by gambling at primero.

14–15 Rhyme is restored at the end of *Denial*, and lost at the end of *Home* and of *Grief*; there is no disturbance of the scheme here. The plain saying (celebrated in *Antiphon 1*) derives from 'I will extol thee, my God, O King' (Psalms 145: 1).

Denial

Full rhyme is established only in the last stanza; and the poem as a whole exploits so-called 'rhyme counterpoint', whereby rhyming lines are mismatched in length (as in *Longing*, another poem of critical dis-tress). The devotions are damaged by the poet's self-preoccupation: 'If I regard iniquity in my heart, the Lord will not hear me' (Psalms 66: 18).

When my devotions could not pierce
　　Thy silent ears;
Then was my heart broken, as was my verse:
　　My breast was full of fears
　　　　And disorder:　　　　　　　　　　　　5

My bent thoughts, like a brittle bow,
　　Did fly asunder:
Each took his way; some would to pleasures go,
　　Some to the wars and thunder
　　　　Of alarms.　　　　　　　　　　　　10

As good go any where, they say,
　　As to benumb
Both knees and heart, in crying night and day,
　　"Come, come, my God, O come,"
　　　　But no hearing.　　　　　　　　　15

O that thou shouldst give dust a tongue
　　To cry to thee,
And then not hear it crying! all day long
　　My heart was in my knee,
　　　　But no hearing.　　　　　　　　　20

Therefore my soul lay out of sight,
　　Untuned, unstrung:
My feeble spirit, unable to look right,
　　Like a nipped blossom, hung
　　　　Discontented.　　　　　　　　　25

O cheer and tune my heartless breast,
　　Defer no time;
That so thy favours granting my request,
　　They and my mind may chime,
　　　　And mend my rhyme.　　　　　　30

2 *silent ears* 'Vouchsafe your silent ears to plaining music, / Which to my woes gives still an early morning' (Sidney, *Arcadia*, First Eclogues, 'Ye goat-herd gods').
6 *bent* 'wayward'; but 'pulled back' asserts itself in the simile.
8–10 The careers closed off in *Affliction 1*, 37–8.
14 'O when wilt thou come unto me?' (Psalms 101: 2).
16–18 'Shall the dust praise thee?' (Psalms 30: 9); 'He that planted the ear, shall he not hear?' (Psalms 94: 9).

19 'Now therefore I bow the knee of mine heart, beseeching thee of grace: I have sinned, O Lord, I have sinned, and I acknowledge mine iniquities' (Prayer of Manasses).
21–2 'We hanged our harps upon the willows' (Psalms 137: 2); the tuned instrument of *The Temper 1*, 21–4 is now useless.
26 'Make me to hear joy and gladness; that the bones which thou hast broken may rejoice' (Psalms 51: 8).
29 *mind* heart (MS corrected to 'soul').

Christmas

The Williams MS includes the preliminary sonnet as *Christmas Day*. The sonnet is not so inconclusive as to suggest the necessity for a new ending; the second part, an epode, allows surreal effects to supervene on a drab allegory.

All after pleasures as I rid one day,
    My horse and I, both tired, body and mind,
    With full cry of affections, quite astray;
I took up in the next inn I could find.
'There when I came, whom found I but my dear,   5
    My dearest Lord, expecting till the grief
    Of pleasures brought me to him, ready there
To be all passengers' most sweet relief?
Thou, whose glorious, yet contracted light,
    Wrapped in night's mantle, stole into a manger;   10
    Since my dark soul and brutish is thy right,
To man of all beasts be not thou a stranger:
    Furnish and deck my soul, that thou mayst have
    A better lodging, than a rack, or grave.

The shepherds sing; and shall I silent be?   15
    My God, no hymn for thee?
My soul's a shepherd too; a flock it feeds
    Of thoughts, and words, and deeds,
The pasture is thy word: the streams, thy grace
    Enriching all the place.   20
Shepherd and flock shall sing, and all my powers
    Outsing the daylight hours.
Then we will chide the sun for letting night
    Take up his place and right:
We sing one common Lord; wherefore he should   25
    Himself the candle hold.
I will go searching, till I find a sun
    Shall stay, till we have done;
A willing shiner, that shall shine as gladly,
    As frost-nipped suns look sadly.   30
Then we will sing, and shine all our own day,
    And one another pay:
His beams shall cheer my breast, and both so twine,
Till even his beams sing, and my music shine.

1–3 The passions ('affections') of the gentlemanly hunter after pleasures are identified with yelping hounds; 'rid' is a standard variant of 'rode'.

6–7 As weariness tosses the sinner to God's breast in *The Pulley*, 18–20; 'grief' (grief *from* pleasures) operates like a collective noun.

9 *contracted* because incarnated in a child, but also concentrated in him.

13–14 Furnish my soul to thee, that being dressed / Of better lodging thou may'st be possessed (MS); the substituted 'rack' means both 'manger' and 'instrument of torture'.

15 'And the shepherds returned, glorifying and praising God' (Luke 2: 20).

18 'We acknowledge and bewail our manifold sins . . . by thought, word and deed, against thy Divine Majesty' (the Prayer Book's Order for Communion); but here the flock is shepherded.

19–20 'He leads me to the tender grass, / Where I both feed and rest; / Then to the streams that gently pass; / In both I have the best' (*The 23rd Psalm*, 5–8, Herbert's version).

26 'Supply his own light'.

27 'How neatly do we give one only name / To parents' issue and the sun's bright star!' (*The Son*, 5–6).

31–2 'While he is mine, and I am his, / What can I want or need?' (*The 23rd Psalm*, 3–4).

Vanity 1

The first of two poems so titled. The poet's complaint is not against the fragility of wordly goods and achievement (as in Ecclesiastes), but against the soul's diversion from its 'dear God'. The fundamental complaints of the Preacher are rendered specific. 'For what matter is it for us to know how high the Pleiades are, how far distant Perseus and Cassiopeia from us ... We are neither wiser ... nor modester, nor better, nor richer, nor stronger, for the knowledge of it ... An alchemist spends his fortunes to find out the Philosopher's Stone forsooth, cure all diseases, make men long-lived ... and beggars himself' (Burton, *Anatomy*, 1.2.4.7); 'To avoid [poverty], we will take any pains, – hasten to India's furthest bounds, we will leave no haven, no coast, no creek of the world unsearched, though it be to the hazard of our lives; we will dive to the bottom of the sea' (1.2.4.6).

> The fleet astronomer can bore,
> And thread the spheres with his quick-piercing mind:
> He views their stations, walks from door to door,
> Surveys, as if he had designed
> To make a purchase there: he sees their dances,   5
> And knoweth long before,
> Both their full-eyed aspècts, and secret glances.
>
> The nimble diver with his side
> Cuts through the working waves, that he may fetch
> His dearly-earnèd pearl, which God did hide   10
> On purpose from the vent'rous wretch;
> That he might save his life, and also hers,
> Who with excessive pride
> Her own destruction and his danger wears.
>
> The subtle chemic can devest   15
> And strip the creature naked, till he find
> The callow principles within their nest:
> There he imparts to them his mind,
> Admitted to their bed-chamber, before
> They appear trim and dressed   20
> To ordinary suitors at the door.

1–2   The astronomer must literally be swift ('fleet') to keep up with the motion of the spheres; in fact he traces celestial movements in the thread-like lines of his star-maps. The threading conceit prepares for the the pearl-diver.

3–5   From the planets' 'stations' (their apparent arrest when they are farthest from Earth or closest to it) the astronomer adopts the role of door-to-door surveyor (who takes his measurements from a 'station') of their 'houses' (associated zodiacal signs).

5   'Vain would be the attempt to tell all the figures [of the stars and planets] circling as in a dance, and their juxtapositions and their revolutions' (Plato, *Timaeus*, 40c). From the stars' 'dances' the astronomer adopts the role of a lover, enjoying their 'aspects' (their observed positions relative to each other, 'full-eyed' when facing, 'glancing' when oblique).

8–14   'Alas! who was it that first found / Gold hid of purpose under ground, / That sought out pearls, and dived to find / Such precious perils for mankind!' (Boethius, *De Consolatione*, 2, metrum 5: 27–30, Vaughan); the lady's vanity is a surer destruction than the diver's.

15–21   Bacon observes among chemists a tendency to 'go on struggling with nature, not courting her' (*Wisdom of the Ancients*, 20: 'Ericthonius, or Imposture'); he himself is described, in phrasing nearly identical with Herbert's, as 'Nature's midwife, stripping her callow brood, and clothing them in new attire' (Arthur Wilson, *History of Britain*, 120). But this 'subtle' chemist is a violent mechanic, imposing his will on the unclothed ('devested') productions of nature: 'he that knoweth well the natures ... of volatile and fixed in respect of the fire ... may superinduce upon some metal the nature and form of gold' (Bacon, *Of the Advancement of Learning*, 2.8.3).

What hath not man sought out and found,
But his dear God? who yet his glorious law
Embosoms in us, mellowing the ground
    With showers and frosts, with love and awe,   25
So that we need not say, "Where's this command?"
    Poor man, thou searchest round
To find out death, but missest life at hand.

22–8   The conclusion takes Pauline counsel: 'Say not in thine heart, Who shall ascend into heaven? . . . Or, Who shall descend into the deep? . . . But [the righteousness which is of faith says] the word is nigh thee, even in thy mouth, and in thy heart: that is, the word of faith, which we preach' (Romans 10: 6–8). True love and and true awe have the same mellowing effect on the heart as rain and frost on the soil.

Virtue

Izaak Walton gives a version in *The Compleat Angler*: 'Come let me tell you what holy Mr. Herbert says of such days and flowers as these, and then we will thank God that we enjoy them.' But the point is not to trust their enjoyments: 'Beauty in her own course is overtaken . . . The fragrant rose once plucked the briery thorn, / Shows rough and naked, on which the rose was born . . . Instruct thy soul, thy thoughts have perfect made, / These beauties last till death, all others fade' (Ovid, *Art of Love*, 2: 113–20, Heywood); Ovid's Latin says 'endure to the last pyres', but Herbert's 'virtue' endures beyond them. The poem was famously adapted by John Wesley.

Sweet day, so cool, so calm, so bright,
The bridal of the earth and sky:
The dew shall weep thy fall to night;
    For thou must die.

Sweet rose, whose hue angry and brave   5
Bids the rash gazer wipe his eye:
Thy root is ever in its grave,
    And thou must die.

Sweet spring, full of sweet days and roses,
A box where sweets compacted lie;   10
My music shows ye have your closes,
    And all must die.

Only a sweet and virtuous soul,
Like seasoned timber, never gives;
But though the whole world turn to coal,   15
    Then chiefly lives.

2   The sun is 'as a bridegroom coming out of his chamber' (Psalms 19: 5).
5   'Sweet rose, so fragrant and so brave' (Wesley).
6   'Drayton's sweet muse is like a sanguine dye, / Able to ravish the rash gazer's eye' (*Return of Parnassus*, 1.2); Bacon was supposed to be driven to rage by the sight of a rose. Belphoebe's eyes are 'So passing persant, and so wondrous bright, / That quite bereaved the rash beholder's sight' (Spenser, *Faerie Queene*, 2.3.23).

10   A scent-box (or a herb-scented drawer as the 'chest of sweets' in *Mortification*, 2); or (from the musical reference at 11) a chest of viols. Wesley rewrote the line as 'Storehouse where sweets unnumbered lie'.
15   'The elements shall melt with fervent heat, the earth also and the works that are therein shall be burned up' (2 Peter 3: 10); seasoned timber will not survive the Last Day, but the seasoned soul will.

The Pearl. Matthew 13

'Again, the kingdom of heaven is like unto a merchant man, seeking goodly pearls: Who, when he had found one pearl of great price, went and sold all that he had, and bought it' (Matthew 13: 45–6). The language of the parable is sustained only in the mercantile colouring given the rehearsal of what is 'sold', the ways of learning, honour and pleasure (motivated by curiosity, pride and lust). Isaiah reprehends human achievement, summed up in Babylon, as destructive of piety: 'Thy wisdom and thy knowledge, it hath perverted thee, and thou has said in thy heart, I am and none else beside me' (47: 10), but here the love of God survives the distractions of learning, honour and pleasure. The account of the 'ways' of vanity reflects Agrippa: 'Arithmeticians and geometricians number and measure all things, but neglect the measures and numbers of their lives and souls. The musicians are all for sounds and songs, not minding the diseases of corrupt manners . . . Cosmographers describe the situations of countries, the forms of mountains . . . but they make a man never the wiser or better . . . he knoweth nothing, unless he know the will of God's Word' (*Vanity of Sciences*, chapter 100).

I know the ways of learning; both the head
And pipes that feed the press, and make it run;
What Reason hath from Nature borrowèd,
Or of itself, like a good housewife, spun
In laws and policy; what the stars conspire,   5
What willing nature speaks, what forced by fire;
Both the old discoveries, and the new-found seas,
The stock and surplus, cause and history:
All these stand open, or I have the keys:
        Yet I love thee.   10

I know the ways of honour, what maintains
The quick returns of courtesy and wit:
In vies of favours whether party gains,
When glory swells the heart, and mouldeth it
To all expressions both of hand and eye,   15
Which on the world a true-love-knot may tie,
And bear the bundle, wheresoe'er it goes:
How many drams of spirit there must be
To sell my life unto my friends or foes:
        Yet I love thee.   20

I know the ways of pleasure, the sweet strains,
The lullings and the relishes of it;

1–2 'For others, both ancients and moderns, have in the sciences drunk a crude liquor like water, either flowing of itself from the understanding or drawn up by logic as the wheel draws up the bucket. But we drink and pledge others with a liquor made of many well-ripened grapes, collected and plucked from particular branches, squeezed in the press, and at last clarified and fermented in a vessel' (Bacon, *Novum Organum*, 1.123); and (on the scholastic method of reading scripture), 'divinity has been reduced into an art, as into a cistern [Herbert's 'head'], and the streams of doctrines and positions have been derived and arranged from thence to water every part' (*De Augmentis*, 9.1).
3–5 'The men of experiment are like the ant; they only collect and use; the reasoners resemble spiders, who make cobwebs [for Herbert, of theory] out of their own substance' (*Novum Organum*, 1.95); the ant's borrowings (the Williams MS has 'purchased') make a debt, the thrifty ('like a good housewife') spider spends only its own.
5–7 The theorized disciplines are astrology ('what the stars conspire'), physics, alchemy ('what forced by fire'), geography.
8 'What was known and what we have added to what is known, what is now and what was once the case'.
13–17 'Which party gains in competitions for favour, when ambition reshapes the heart to all those gestures which charm the world to love it, and which everywhere take the prize.'
18–19 'How much I must drink to lose myself with my friends, or what courage I need to die at my enemy's hand.'
21–4 'Strains', 'lullings' ('gustos' in Williams MS), 'relishings' ('embellishments'), and 'propositions' ('what is offered for embellishment'), come together to suggest that pleasure ('mirth') is like music.

The propositions of hot blood and brains;
What mirth and music mean; what love and wit
Have done these twenty hundred years, and more: 25
I know the projects of unbridled store:
My stuff is flesh, not brass; my senses live,
And grumble oft, that they have more in me
Than he that curbs them, being but one to five:
    Yet I love thee.   30

I know all these, and have them in my hand:
Therefore not seeled, but with open eyes
I fly to thee, and fully understand
Both the main sale, and the commodities;
And at what rate and price I have thy love;   35
With all the circumstances that may move:
Yet through these labyrinths, not my grovelling wit,
But thy silk twist let down from Heaven to me,
Did both conduct and teach me, how by it
    To climb to thee.   40

26–9 Where both [of mirth and music] their baskets are with all their store, / The smacks of dainties and their exaltation: / What both the stops and pegs of pleasure be: / The joys of company or contemplation (Williams MS; the first three lines are cancelled). Tanner MS reads as *1633*, but with 'unbundled' for 'unbridled' suggests 'scattered abundance'. *1633*'s sense is, 'I know the outpourings of unrestrained tumult ('store' = 'stour').
28 'My five senses grumble that they outnumber the one rational check on them (and so have more rights).'
32 *seeled* sealed (*1633*). Falcons' eyes were 'seeled' or sewn up during training, but the poet is already an expert hunter after God, not liable to distraction.

33–4 'I understand both what I am buying ('the pearl') and the goods I must sell to secure it ('commodities').'
37–40 'The universe to the eye of human understanding is framed like a labyrinth . . . No excellence of wit, no repetition of chance experiments, can overcome difficulties such as these. Our steps must be guided by a clue' (Bacon, preface to *The Great Instauration*). We must take the offered clue. 'Joseph who is in the well, and Jeremy who is in the dungeon, do as much as they can for the typing and fitting of that rope which is offered and let down to them, to them to draw them. God saves us by a calling, and he saves us by drawing' (Donne, *Sermons*, 1.9). *1633*'s 'the labyrinths' is corrected from MSS.

Man

Succeeding stanzas, varying a basic scheme, enumerate instances of man's superior place in creation. It is then a poem about the dignity of man (and so much it has in common with Sylvester's praise of man in the *Divine Weeks*), or a sacred version of Bacon's projected 'Inventory of the Possessions of Man, wherein should be set down and briefly enumerated all the goods and possessions . . . which men now hold and enjoy' (*De Augmentis*, 3.5), but while man, as flesh and mind, occupies a central place in the cosmic hierarchy (lines 31–6), his virtue is that he is worthy to receive and serve God.

    My God, I heard this day,
That none doth build a stately habitation,
    But he that means to dwell therein.
    What house more stately hath there been,

1–3 So Cardinal Bellarmine: 'The end of a palace is the dweller therein . . . the end of man is only his Lord God' (*A . . . Treatise framing a Ladder*, translated by T.B.). 'A witty mason, doth not (with rare art) / Into a palace, Paros rocks convert . . . To the end the screech-owl, and night-raven should / In those fair walls their habitations hold: / But rather, for some wise and wealthy prince' (Sylvester, *Divine Weeks*, 1.6:438–47); but here both architect and inhabitant are God: 'Know ye not that your body is the temple of the Holy Ghost' (1 Corinthians 6: 19).

Or can be, than is man? to whose creation   5
    All things are in decay.

    For Man is everything,
And more: he is a tree, yet bears more fruit;
    A beast, yet is, or should be more:
    Reason and speech we only bring.   10
Parrots may thank us, if they are not mute,
    They go upon the score.

    Man is all symmetry,
Full of proportions, one limb to another,
    And all to all the world besides: 15
    Each part may call the farthest, brother:
For head with foot hath private amity,
    And both with moons and tides.

    Nothing hath got so far,
But man hath caught and kept it, as his prey.   20
    His eyes dismount the highest star:
    He is in little all the sphere.
Herbs gladly cure our flesh; because that they
    Find their acquaintance there.

    For us the winds do blow,   25
The earth doth rest, heaven move, and fountains flow.
    Nothing we see, but means our good,
    As our *delight*, or as our *treasure*:
The whole is, either our cupboard of *food*,
    Or cabinet of *pleasure*.   30

    The stars have us to bed;
Night draws the curtain, which the sun withdraws;
    Music and light attend our head.

---

5 'All the admirable creatures made beforn . . . Are but essays, compared in every part, / To this divinest masterpiece of art' (*Divine Weeks*, 1.6:474–8); or here 'deficient' ('in decay').

7–12 'The common division of the soul is into . . . vegetal, sensitive, rational, which make . . . vegetal plants, sensible beasts, rational men . . . The inferior may be alone, but the superior cannot subsist without the other; so sensible includes vegetal, rational both' (Burton, *Anatomy*, 1.1.2.5). Williams MS's 'more fruit' (adopted here against *1633*'s 'no fruit') may argue unusual confidence in a poet whose fruits are always credited to God. Speech in parrots is credited to man (it goes 'on the score' as a debt).

13–15 Spenser's man embodies a universal mathematics: 'The frame thereof [man's body] seemed partly circular, / And part triangular, O work divine; / Those two the first and last proportions are' (*Faerie Queene*, 2.9.22).

17–18 'The eye cannot say unto the hand, I have no need of thee: nor again the head to the feet' (1 Corinthians 12:

21). As the head is to the feet so is the moon to the tides: it is very likely, says Bacon, that 'there is a magnetic power which operates by consent between . . . the globe of the moon and the waters of the sea' (*Novum Organum*, 2.45). The plurality of moons is post-Galilean (though Galileo disputed the lunar control of tides).

21 Sylvester's man goes 'not his face down to the earthward bending . . . but toward the azure skies' / Bright golden lamps lifting his lovely eyes' (*Divine Weeks*, 1.6:522–5).

23–4 'How many things are related of a man's skull . . . and that which is more to be admired, that such and such plants should have a peculiar virtue to such particular parts' (Burton, *Anatomy*, 2.4.1.3).

25–6 The totality of elements (air, earth, fire and water) is enumerated.

33 'Look how the floor of heaven / Is thick inlaid with patens of bright gold: / There's not the smallest orb which thou behold'st / But in his motion like an angel sings' (*Merchant of Venice*, V. i. 58–61).

All things unto our *flesh* are kind
In their *descent* and *being*; to our *mind*   35
In their *ascent* and *cause*.

Each thing is full of duty:
Waters united are our navigation;
Distinguished, our habitation;
Below, our drink; above, our meat;   40
Both are our cleanliness. Hath one such beauty?
Then how are all things neat?

More servants wait on man,
Than he'll take notice of: in every path
He treads down that which doth befriend him,   45
When sickness makes him pale and wan.
Oh mighty love! Man is one world, and hath
Another to attend him.

Since then, my God, thou hast
So brave a palace built; O dwell in it,   50
That it may dwell with thee at last!
Till then, afford us so much wit;
That, as the world serves us, we may serve thee,
And both thy servants be.

34–6 'The world is fairest of creations and [God] is the best of causes' (*Timaeus*, 29b); the body enjoys the created world ('descended' from a creative principle), the soul enjoys the Creator (inferred from an 'ascending' chain of causes); 'the soul makes the double progress of ascent and descent corresponding to the double concern it has for itself and for matter' (Giordano Bruno, *Heroic Frenzies*, 1.4).

38–41 'Let there be a firmament . . . and let it divide the waters from the waters . . . Let the waters under the heaven be gathered together unto one place, and let the dry land appear' (Genesis 1: 6–9). We sail on the sea ('waters united') and live on the dry land; we drink the waters under the firmament; the waters above the firmament supply our meat ('the rain cometh down, and . . . watereth the earth . . . that it may give seed to the sower, and bread to the eater', Isaiah 55: 10); we wash indifferently in rivers and rain .

43–6 Burton quotes Pliny: 'We are careless of that which is near us, and follow that which is afar off . . . wholly neglecting that which is under our eyes' (*Anatomy*, 2.4.1.2).

47–8 'Thy hands both made us, and also made us lords of all thy creatures; giving us one world in our selves, and another to serve us' (*Priest to the Temple*; 'The author's prayer before the sermon').

Life

Vaughan writes: 'Hark how like a busy bee he hymns it to the flowers, while in a handful of blossoms gathered by himself, he foresees his own dissolution', and quotes the poem (*Mount of Olives*). The Psalmist complains, 'As for man his days are as grass: as a flower of the field, so he flourisheth' (103: 15); but here there is virtue in living and dying like a flower: 'Our actions are like roses which are more graceful when fresh, yet more fragrant when dry' (St François de Sales, *Introduction to the Devout Life*, 4.14).

I made a posy, while the day ran by:
Here will I smell my remnant out, and tie
My life within this band.
But time did beckon to the flowers, and they

1–3 The 'posy' ('bouquet' and 'poem'), the 'remnant' (of the poet's days) and 'life' are in turn identified with the passing day.

> By noon most cunningly did steal away,   5
>   And withered in my hand.
>
> My hand was next to them, and then my heart:
> I took, without more thinking, in good part
>   Time's gentle admonition:
> Who did so sweetly death's sad taste convey,   10
> Making my mind to smell my fatal day;
>   Yet sug'ring the suspicion.
>
> Farewell dear flowers, sweetly your time ye spent,
> Fit, while ye lived, for smell or ornament,
>   And after death for cures.   15
> I follow straight without complaints or grief,
> Since if my scent be good, I care not, if
>   It be as short as yours.

15   'Herbs, and roots, by dying lose not all, / But they, yea ashes too, are med'cinal' (Donne, *First Anniversary*, 403–4). 17–18   'You fragrant flowers then teach me that my breath / Like yours may sweeten and perfume my death' (King, *A Contemplation upon Flowers*, 17–18).

Jordan 2

In the Williams MS the title is *Invention*; though second in the sequence, it is the earlier of the two poems riddlingly called *Jordan*. Where *Jordan I* is about obliqueness, this is about complication. The debt to Sidney is marked in its preoccupations with the distinction between 'inventions fine' and 'invention, Nature's child' (*Astrophil*, 1:6, 10), and its concluding abandonment of effort: 'Fool said my Muse to me, look in thy heart and write' (1:14), as again in 'all my deed / But copying is, what in her Nature writes' (*Astrophil*, 3:13–14). But here God supplies the place of Nature.

> When first my lines of heavenly joys made mention,
> Such was their lustre, they did so excel,
> That I sought out quaint words, and trim invention;
> My thoughts began to burnish, sprout, and swell,
> Curling with metaphors a plain intention,   5
> Decking the sense, as if it were to sell.
>
> Thousands of notions in my brain did run,
> Offering their service, if I were not sped:
> I often blotted what I had begun;
> This was not quick enough, and that was dead.   10
> Nothing could seem too rich to clothe the sun,
> Much less those joys which trample on his head.

2   'Such was the lustre and excellence of the heavenly joys'.
4   The ' lustre' suggests 'burnish' ('shine'), which suggests 'spread' (MS reading). 'Burnish' is 'also a term among hunters, when harts spread their horns' (John Bullokar, *An English Expositor*).
5   The wanton lover can 'with quaint metaphors her [the beloved's] curled hair / Curl o'er again' (*Dullness*, 7–8).
6   'I will not praise, that purpose not to sell' (Shakespeare, *Sonnets*, 21:6); MS reads 'praising' for 'decking'.

8   'If I were in difficulty'.
10   *quick* 'lively'.
12   'If I beheld the sun when it shined . . . And my heart hath been secretly enticed . . . this also were an iniquity . . . for I should have denied the God that is above' (Job 31: 26–8); 'heavenly joys' excel the appearances of nature. In *Memoriae Matris Sacrum*, 3: 3, Herbert's sainted mother tramples ('superat') the sun's head.

As flames do work and wind, when they ascend,
So did I weave myself into the sense.
But while I bustled, I might hear a friend   15
Whisper, "How wide is all this long pretence!
There is in love a sweetness ready penned:
Copy out only that, and save expense."

14   So I bespoke me much insinuation (MS).   18   Copy out only that: there needs no alteration (MS).
16   'How wide of the mark is all this prolonged display'
('preparation' in MS).

Providence

Bacon, usually distrustful of explanations by way of final causes (*De Augmentis*, 3.4, 5), allegorizes the fable of Prometheus (a name which 'clearly and expressly signifies Providence') as follows: 'Man, if we look to final causes, may be regarded as the centre of the world . . . For the whole world works together in the service of man; and there is nothing from which he does not derive use and fruit. The revolutions and courses of the stars serve him both for the distinction of the seasons and distribution of the quarters of the world. The appearances of the middle sky afford him prognostications of weather. The winds sail his ships and work his mills and engines. Plants and animals of all kinds are made to furnish him either with dwelling and shelter or food or medicine, or to lighten his labour, or to give him pleasure and comfort; insomuch that all things seem to be going about man's business and not their own' (*De Sapientia Veterum*, 26). The poem challenges comparison with Psalm 104, which 'by presenting a lively image of God's wisdom, power and goodness in the creation of the world, and in the order of nature, encourages us to praise him for the manifestation he has made of himself in this frail and perishable life' (Calvin). Its riddling (rather in Sylvester's manner) threatens the shape of the argument: the praise of the fulness of God's creation (29–92) and its orderliness (93–140) is framed on the one hand by the poet's confident arrogation to himself of priestly privileges (1–28) and on the other by a confession of his inadequacy (141–52).

O sacred Providence, who from end to end
Strongly and sweetly movest! shall I write,
And not of thee, through whom my fingers bend
To hold my quill? shall they not do thee right?

Of all the creatures both in sea and land   5
Only to man thou hast made known thy ways,
And put the pen alone into his hand,
And made him secretary of thy praise.

Beasts fain would sing; birds ditty to their notes;
Trees would be tuning on their native lute   10
To thy renown: but all their hands and throats
Are brought to man, while they are lame and mute.

1–2   'Wisdom reacheth from one end to the other mightily; and sweetly doth she order all things' (Wisdom 8: 1); the margin offers 'profitably' for 'sweetly'.
3–4   That fingers are adapted to hold a pen signals their proper use. Sylvester has an analogous praise of the mouth: 'By thee, we calm the Almighty's indignation . . . By thee, we warble to the King of Kings' (*Divine Weeks*, 1.6:617–20); the hands are 'Mind's ministers, the clerks of quick conceits' (1.6:662).
5–8   'And [man's] mature and settled sapience / Hath some alliance with [God's] Providence' (*Divine Weeks*, 1.6:986–7); Walton calls Bacon 'the great Secretary of Nature' (*Life of Herbert*).
9   'Beasts long to sing; birds long for words to sing to.'

Man is the world's high-priest: he doth present
The sacrifice for all; while they below
Unto the service mutter an assent,   15
Such as springs use that fall, and winds that blow.

He that to praise and laud thee doth refrain,
Doth not refrain unto himself alone,
But robs a thousand who would praise thee fain,
And doth commit a world of sin in one.   20

The beasts say, "Eat me": but, if beasts must teach,
The tongue is yours to eat, but mine to praise.
The trees say, "Pull me": but the hand you stretch,
Is mine to write, as it is yours to raise.

Wherefore, most sacred Spirit, I here present   25
For me and all my fellows praise to thee:
And just it is that I should pay the rent,
Because the benefit accrues to me.

We all acknowledge both thy power and love
To be exact, transcendent, and divine;   30
Who dost so strongly and so sweetly move,
While all things have their will, yet none but thine.

For either thy command, or thy permission
Lay hands on all: they are thy right and left.
The first puts on with speed and expedition;   35
The other curbs sin's stealing pace and theft.

Nothing escapes them both; all must appear,
And be disposed, and dressed, and tuned by thee,
Who sweetly temper'st all. If we could hear
Thy skill and art, what music would it be!   40

Thou art in small things great, not small in any:
Thy even praise can neither rise, nor fall.
Thou art in all things one, in each thing many:
For thou art infinite in one and all.

Tempests are calm to thee; they know thy hand,   45
And hold it fast, as children do their father's,
Which cry and follow. Thou hast made poor sand
Check the proud sea, e'en when it swells and gathers.

13–14 'All Christians are called a royal priesthood [1 Peter
2: 9] because through Christ we offer that sacrifice of praise
to God of which the apostle speaks: "the fruit of our lips
giving thanks to his name" [Hebrews 13: 15]' (Calvin, *Institutes*, 4.18.17).
21–4 'Why do the prodigal elements supply / Life and
food to me' (Donne, *Holy Sonnets*, VIII, 2–3).
33–6 'Either you put us under an obligation to do good, or
you allow less than perfection: the one is peremptory, the
other checks the worst in us'; Paul permits married couples
to deviate from a life of prayer 'that Satan tempt you not' (1
Corinthians 7: 5), but adds 'I speak this by permission, and
not of commandment' (7: 6). The 'stealth' of sin's steps is
played with in his 'theft' of our happiness.
48 'He maketh the storm a calm: so that the waves thereof
are still' (Psalms 107: 29); God says, 'Here shall thy proud
waves be stayed' (Job 38: 11), and has 'placed the sand for
the bound of the sea' (Jeremiah 5: 22).

Thy cupboard serves the world: the meat is set,
Where all may reach: no beast but knows his feed.   50
Birds teach us hawking; fishes have their net:
The great prey on the less, they on some weed.

Nothing engendered doth prevent his meat:
Flies have their table spread, ere they appear.
Some creatures have in winter what to eat;   55
Others do sleep, and envy not their cheer.

How finely dost thou times and seasons spin,
And make a twist chequered with night and day!
Which as it lengthens winds, and winds us in,
As bowls go on, but turning all the way.   60

Each creature hath a wisdom for his good.
The pigeons feed their tender offspring, crying,
When they are callow; but withdraw their food
When they are fledge, that need may teach them flying.

Bees work for man; and yet they never bruise   65
Their master's flower, but leave it, having done,
As fair as ever, and as fit to use;
So both the flower doth stay, and honey run.

Sheep eat the grass, and dung the ground for more:
Trees after bearing drop their leaves for soil: 70
Springs vent their streams, and by expense get store:
Clouds cool by heat, and baths by cooling boil.

Who hath the virtue to express the rare
And curious virtues both of herbs and stones?
Is there an herb for that? O that thy care   75
Would show a root, that gives expressions!

And if an herb hath power, what have the stars?
A rose, besides his beauty, is a cure.

51   Fowl teach us to hunt fowl, fish teach us to hunt fish.
53   'Nothing is born into a world which cannot already sustain it.'
56   'Hibernating creatures do not envy their winter fare.'
57–60   We grow old with the winding of the seasons' threads into a cord ('twist'), not in a straight line but like a bowl following its bias to the jack. 'Turning' has a positive value here: for the stars in their motions 'winding is their fashion / Of adoration' (*The Star*, 27–8).
62–4   'The pigeons feed their wailing offspring when they are featherless, but refuse them food when they are feathered.'
70   *bearing* 'fruiting'.
71–2   The circulation of water between springs discharging their flow to the sea, whence it returns, makes loss and gain identical; as (by an analogous process), 'The ample sea doth take / The liquid homage of each other lake ... the heavens exhale, from [the sea], / Abundant vapours ... And yet it

swells not for those tribute streams, / Nor yet it shrinks not for those boiling beams' (*Divine Weeks*, 1.7:72–5). Cooling clouds are an effect of heat-induced evaporation; boiling water ('baths' being 'hot springs') is an effect of a heat-source's losing heat to it: heat and cold (as Bacon, *Novum Organum*, 2.18.14, argues) are effects rather than principles.
73–6   'Who can describe ('express', also 'squeeze out') the healing powers ('virtues') of herbs and stones? There is no herb for that – unless in your love you gave us a herb ('root', also 'word') that would allow us to speak ('expressions', also 'juices')'.
78   'In the knowledge of simples, wherein the manifold wisdom of God is wonderfully to be seen [the parson] is to know what herbs may be used instead of drugs ... So where the apothecary useth for loosing rhubarb [unfamiliar as a garden plant] ... the parson useth damask or white roses' (*Priest to the Temple*, ch. 23).

Doubtless our plagues and plenty, peace and wars
Are there much surer than our art is sure.   80

Thou hast hid metals: man may take them thence;
But at his peril: when he digs the place,
He makes a grave; as if the thing had sense,
And threatened man, that he should fill the space.

E'en poisons praise thee. Should a thing be lost?   85
Should creatures want for want of heed their due?
Since where are poisons, antidotes are most:
The help stands close, and keeps the fear in view.

The sea, which seems to stop the traveller,
Is by a ship the speedier passage made.   90
The winds, who think they rule the mariner,
Are ruled by him, and taught to serve his trade.

And as thy house is full, so I adore
Thy curious art in marshalling thy goods.
The hills with health abound; the vales with store;   95
The south with marble; north with furs and woods.

Hard things are glorious; easy things good cheap.
The common all men have; that which is rare,
Men therefore seek to have, and care to keep.
The healthy frosts with summer-fruits compare.   100

Light without wind is glass: warm without weight
Is wool and furs: cool without closeness, shade:
Speed without pains, a horse: tall without height,
A servile hawk: low without loss, a spade.

All countries have enough to serve their need: 105
If they seek fine things, thou dost make them run
For their offence; and then dost turn their speed
To be commerce and trade from sun to sun.

Nothing wears clothes, but man; nothing doth need
But he to wear them. Nothing useth fire,   110

79–80 'Our destinies are doubtless more certainly determined in the stars than astrologers can know': 'Astrology is true, but the astrologers cannot find it' (*Outlandish Proverbs*, 64).

81 It is 'more valiant to despise hid gold / (Which wisely Nature did withhold) /Than force it to man's use' (Horace, *Odes*, 3.3:49–50, Fanshawe).

85–8 'What ranker poison? what more deadly bane / Than aconite, can there be touched or ta'en? / And yet his juice best cures the burning bite / Of stinging serpents' (*Divine Weeks*, 1.3:791–4); the word 'poison' was still available for 'drug'.

87–8 As nettle and dock grow together: 'every clime . . . every private place, hath his proper remedies growing in it,

peculiar almost to the domineering and most frequent maladies of it' (Burton, *Anatomy*, 2.4.1.2).

89–92 'One country doth not bear all things, that there may be a commerce' (*Priest to the Temple*, ch. 4).

93–6 Creation is 'like a spacious and splendid house, provided and filled with the most exquisite and abundant furnishings' (Calvin, *Institutes*, 1.14.20).

100 'The bracing effects of winter are as necessary to health as the fruits of summer.'

104 *spade* as in cards, where the ace scores high.

110–12 Sylvester gives a hard account of primitive man's invention of fire (*Divine Weeks*, 2.1.4:226–40); here fire is turned to signal man's singular affection to God, with distinctively human hopes or imaginations as its fuel.

But man alone, to show his heavenly breed:
And only he hath fuel in desire.

When the earth was dry, thou mad'st a sea of wet:
When that lay gathered, thou didst broach the mountains:
When yet some places could no moisture get,   115
The winds grew gardeners, and the clouds good fountains.

Rain, do not hurt my flowers; but gently spend
Your honey drops: press not to smell them here:
When they are ripe, their odour will ascend,
And at your lodging with their thanks appear.   120

How harsh are thorns to pears! and yet they make
A better hedge, and need less reparation.
How smooth are silks compared with a stake,
Or with a stone! yet make no good foundation.

Sometimes thou dost divide thy gifts to man,   125
Sometimes unite. The Indian nut alone
Is clothing, meat and trencher, drink and can,
Boat, cable, sail and needle, all in one.

Most herbs that grow in brooks, are hot and dry.
Cold fruits' warm kernels help against the wind.   130
The lemon's juice and rind cure mutually.
The whey of milk doth loose, the milk doth bind.

Thy creatures leap not, but express a feast,
Where all the guests sit close, and nothing wants.
Frogs marry fish and flesh; bats, bird and beast;   135
Sponges, non-sense and sense; mines, the earth and plants.

To show thou art not bound, as if thy lot
Were worse than ours; sometimes thou shiftest hands.
Most things move the under-jaw; the crocodile not.
Most things sleep lying; the elephant leans or stands.   140

114–16 'He sendeth the spring into the valleys, which run among the hills . . . He watereth the hills from his chambers' (Psalms 104: 10–13); the winds 'become' gardeners.
121 'Hawthorn is rougher than the pear tree.'
126–8 The coconut: Thomas Herbert's *Relation of some Years' Travel* (1634) lists among its uses 'timber for canoes, masts, anchors: the leaves for tents or thatching: the rinds for sails, mattresses, cables and linen: the shells for furniture: the meat for victualling . . . The shell [contains] sweet and excellent liquor, like new white-wine'; he omits the plates and cups ('trenchers' and 'cans'). Sylvester ends his long panegyric "Tis what you will: or will be what you would' (*Divine Weeks*, 1.3: 868).
129–32 'The Lord hath created medicines out of the earth' (Ecclesiasticus 38: 4), here presented as a set of pharmacological paradoxes: cold wet conditions produce hot dry herbs (anti-phlegmatics), warm nuts (anti-flatulents) grow in cold fruits (flatulents), lemon juice (astringent) is countered by the rind, whey is laxative while milk is binding.
133–6 'Nature proceeds little by little . . . in such a way that it is impossible to establish any line of demarcation . . . In regard to sense . . . the sponge is in every respect like a vegetable' (Aristotle, *History of Animals*, 588b); frogs are intermediate between land and water animals (*History of Animals*, 589a), bats are intermediate between land animals and fliers (*Parts of Animals*, 697b); coal is mineralized wood. Drummond allows for 'Things numberless which [God could] make, / That actually shall never being take' (Drummond, *Hymn of the Fairest Fair*, 63–4).
140 Thomas Browne thinks the notion that the elephant 'being unable to lie down . . . sleepeth against a tree' is an absurdity (*Pseudodoxia*, 3.1); Pliny (*Natural History*, 8.37.1) claims only the upper jaw of the crocodile is mobile.

But who hath praise enough? nay who hath any?
None can express thy works, but he that knows them:
And none can know thy works, which are so many,
And so complete, but only he that owes them.

All things that are, though they have several ways,   145
Yet in their being join with one advice
To honour thee: and so I give thee praise
In all my other hymns, but in this twice.

Each thing that is, although in use and name
It go for one, hath many ways in store   150
To honour thee; and so each hymn thy fame
Extolleth many ways, yet this one more.

141 'Who can utter the mighty acts of the Lord? Who can show forth all his praise?' (Psalms 106: 2).
144 *only he that owes them* God himself owns them: 'Such knowledge is too wonderful for me; it is high, I cannot attain unto it' (Psalms 139: 6); 'For as the heavens are higher than the earth, so are my ways higher than your ways, and my thoughts than your thoughts' (Isaiah 55: 9).
145–8 'By the fact of their existence all creatures join with one resolve ('advice'), though in their different ways, to honour you: I praise you in all my hymns, but here (acknowledging myself part of your creation) I praise you again.'
149–52 Sometimes seen as an alternative to the previous stanza: 'Everything declares your praise in one obvious way, but might always potentially in more: each hymn praises you in many obvious ways, but this in another secret way.'

Artillery

'What god lords it in my bowels, what hurricane of fire blows down the meditations of my secret heart. Had I, sitting in my porch, swallowed a star flying in the evening air?' (*In Sacras Scripturas*, 4–5). Herbert's experience of finding stars lodged with him (repeated in *The Star*) recalls Isaiah's: 'Then flew one of the Seraphims unto me, having a live coal in his hand, which he had taken with the tongs from off the altar: And he laid it upon my mouth, and said, Lo, this hath touched thy lips; and thine iniquity is taken away, and thy sin purged' (6: 6–7). But it is militarized: the vocabulary of God's wrath ('He hath bent his bow, and set me as a mark for the arrow,' Lamentations 3: 12) is identical with that of God's love: 'A thousand of thy strongest shafts, my light, / Draw up against this heart with all thy might, / And strike it through' (Christopher Harvey, *School of the Heart*, Epigram 33).

As I one evening sat before my cell,
Methoughts a star did shoot into my lap.
I rose, and shook my clothes, as knowing well,
That from small fires comes oft no small mishap.
    When suddenly I heard one say,   5
    "Do as thou usest, disobey,
    Expel good motions from thy breast,
Which have the face of fire, but end in rest."

I, who had heard of music in the spheres,
But not of speech in stars, began to muse: 10

4–5 'Behold, how great a matter a little fire kindleth' (James, 3: 5).
6–7 'Rejoice, O young man, in thy youth . . . but know thou, that for all these things God will bring thee into judgement . . . Therefore remove sorrow from thy heart, and put away evil from thy flesh' (Ecclesiastes 11: 9–10); the star ironically counsels the expulsion of 'good motions'.
8 'His eyes were as a flame of fire . . . And he laid his right hand upon me, saying unto me, Fear not' (Revelation 1: 14–17).
9 'There's not the smallest orb which thou behold'st / But in his motion like an angel sings' (*Merchant of Venice*, V. i. 60–1); 'the morning stars sang together, and all the sons of God shouted for joy' (Job 38: 7).

But turning to my God, whose ministers
The stars and all things are; "If I refuse,
    Dread Lord," said I, "so oft my good;
    Then I refuse not even with blood
    To wash away my stubborn thought: 15
For I will do, or suffer what I ought.

But I have also stars and shooters too,
Born where thy servants both artilleries use.
My tears and prayers night and day do woo,
And work up to thee; yet thou dost refuse.   20
    Nor, but I am (I must say still)
    Much more obliged to do thy will,
    Than thou to grant mine: but because
Thy promise now hath even set thee thy laws.

Then we are shooters both, and thou dost deign   25
To enter combat with us, and contest
With thine own clay. But I would parley fain:
Shun not my arrows, and behold my breast.
    Yet if thou shunnest, I am thine:
    I must be so, if I am mine.   30
    There is no articling with thee:
I am but finite, yet thine infinitely."

11–12 'Who maketh his angels spirits; his ministers a flaming fire' (Psalms 104: 4).
12–16 Ryley glosses: 'if I have so oft refused compliance with the offers of thy grace; I will refuse them no more: but resign myself into thy hands, and yield to do or suffer what thou wilt, even to the loss of this natural life so I may have the guilt of my past stubbornness pardoned', and quotes 2 Corinthians 10: 5: 'bringing into captivity every thought to the obedience of Christ'.
17–18 'I have tears and prayers born in the heart where the faithful use such artillery.'

24 'But before faith came we were kept under the law . . . wherefore the law was our schoolmaster to bring us unto Christ. . . . But after that faith is come, we are no longer under a schoolmaster' (Galatians 3: 23–5).
27–8 'I would treat for peace,' but the peace is secured by their mutual exposure to each other's weaponry.
29–30 'Lord, thou art mine, and I am thine, / If mine I am' (*Clasping of Hands*, 1–2).
31 'I have considered it, and find / There is no dealing with thy mighty passion' (*The Reprisal*, 1–2).

The Collar

The preceding poem (*The Jews*) ends with a prayer that the 'sweet sap' of true religion be restored to the Jews, whose legalism has dried it up. Here the poet mounts a choleric rebellion against the constraints of his misundertood calling, refusing the 'yoke . . . which neither our fathers nor we were able to bear' (Acts 15: 10). The poem poses a choice between deadly Pharisaical legalism and the new Christian liberty. The inhibiting 'collar' recalls the noose of Georgette de Montenay's emblem *Rectum iudicium* ('Right judgement', *Monumenta Emblematum Christianorum* [Frankfurt, 1619] 4), and may be informed by it: a Christian soldier, threatened with strangulation in Death's noose, is offered an alternative mild yoke from Heaven ('Take my yoke upon you . . . for my yoke is easy, and my burden is light,' Matthew 11: 29–30). The terms of this opposition are from Paul: 'But now we are deliv-

ered from the law, that being dead wherein we were held; that we should serve in newness of the spirit, and not in the oldness of the letter' (Romans 7: 6), 'Stand fast therefore in the liberty wherewith Christ hath made us free, and be not entangled again with the yoke of bondage' (Galatians 5: 1). Calvin summarizes the issues: 'He therefore teaches that we must be released from the bonds of the law, unless we wish to perish miserably under them. From what bonds? The bonds of harsh and dangerous requirements, which remit nothing of the extreme penalty of the law and suffer no transgression to go unpunished . . . we should not be borne down by an unending bondage, which would agonise our consciences with the fear of death' (*Institutes*, 2.7.15). The poem is more purely ejaculatory than any other in *The Temple*; it moves none the less in the trajectory of many poems in the sequence, from derangement (in lines 1–16 created by misconstrued obligation, in 17–32 by misconstrued liberty) to order. It complicates but does not depart from the pattern of Psalm 102, which begins with 'I have eaten ashes like bread and mingled my drink with weeping . . . I am withered like grass'

(9–11) and ends with 'he hath looked down . . . to hear the groaning of the prisoner; to loose those that are appointed to death' (19–20). The eccentric delays of rhyme and variations of line-length, never truly out of control, are scrupulously resolved in the final quatrain.

> I struck the board, and cried, "No more,
> I will abroad.
> What? shall I ever sigh and pine?
> My lines and life are free; free as the road,
> Loose as the wind, as large as store. 5
> Shall I be still in suit?
> Have I no harvest but a thorn
> To let me blood, and not restore
> What I have lost with cordial fruit?
> Sure there was wine 10
> Before my sighs did dry it: there was corn
> Before my tears did drown it.
> Is the year only lost to me?
> Have I no bays to crown it?
> No flowers, no garlands gay? all blasted? 15
> All wasted?
> Not so, my heart: but there is fruit,
> And thou hast hands.
> Recover all thy sigh-blown age
> On double pleasures: leave thy cold dispute 20
> Of what is fit, and not. Forsake thy cage,
> Thy rope of sands,
> Which petty thoughts have made, and made to thee
> Good cable, to enforce and draw,
> And be thy law, 25
> While thou didst wink and wouldst not see.

1   The 'board' is the communion table: 'whenever at his board / I do but taste [my Saviour's blood], straight it cleanseth me' (*Conscience*, 14).

4   *lines* 'directions', 'free' as against the 'straight' line in which he grows in *The Flower*; the verse lines are free too.

5   *store* 'plenty'.

6   'Am I always (or unprotestingly) to be brought to book?'; but the sense is complicated by the readier 'Am I always to be petitioning you?'

7–9   'Am I to have no reward but to have the blood drained from me by guilt; is my loss not to be restored by the wine-yielding restorative ('cordial') grape?' He is like those who would (impossibly) 'gather grapes of thorns' (Matthew 7: 16).

10–12   'And it shall come to pass, if ye shall hearken diligently unto my commandments . . . that I will give you the rain of your land in his due season . . . that thou mayest gather in thy corn, and thy wine, and thine oil . . . Take heed to yourselves, that your heart be not deceived . . . and then the Lord's wrath be kindled against you . . . that there be no rain, and that the land yield not her fruit' (Deuteronomy 11: 13–7; a threat repeated in Isaiah 5: 5–6); in idolatrous Jerusalem the children ask 'Where is the corn and

wine?' (Lamentations 2: 12); the neglectful and unreceptive 'shall lament . . . for the fruitful vine. Upon the land of my people shall come thorns and briars' (Isaiah 32: 12–3).

13–14   'Thou crownest the year with thy goodness; and thy paths drop fatness' (Psalms 65: 11); evergreen and imperishable 'bays' make crowns for poets.

19   *sigh-blown* modelled on 'fly-blown'.

20   *double* Jerusalem receives 'of the Lord's hand double for all her sins' (Isaiah 40: 2); the unused pleasures are doubled by the accumulation of interest; but they are also deceitful.

21   The stop is editorial (a colon in MS).

22–6   'Abandon the prison you have built for yourself, abandon the impossible attempt to reconcile the petty contradictions you have got yourself into, the system of restraints, compulsions and regulations you have contrived for yourself, while you were wilfully blind.' Erasmus (*Adages*, 1.4.78) describes the Greek proverb 'To weave ropes or nets of sand' ('to attempt the impossible') as suited to describe the reconciling of contradictions. In *Misery*, man is carried away by selfish impulses when his knowledge of God 'winks'; here a contrary error of over-scrupulousness has operated.

Away; take heed:
I will abroad.
Call in thy death's head there: tie up thy fears.
He that forbears   30
To suit and serve his need,
Deserves his load."
But as I raved and grew more fierce and wild
At every word,
Methoughts I heard one calling, "Child":   35
And I replied, "My Lord."

29 'The law of the spirit . . . hath made me free from the
law of sin and death' (Romans 8: 2).
30–2 'He that neglects to follow and satisfy his wants, de-
serves his burden'; but Herbert writes in a letter to his mother:
'What an admirable thing it is, that God puts his shoulder to
our burden' (Walton).
33–6 'Then when I am all grimly set to murmur and men-
ace, some friend takes me by the sleeve and whispers, "This
cup was once your Lord's." I taste the vintage, it is good'
(*In Memoriae Matris Sacrum*, 8: 6–10).
35–6 'For ye have not received the spirit of bondage again
to fear; but ye have received the Spirit of adoption, whereby
we cry, Abba, Father' (Romans 8: 15).

Joseph's Coat

'Now Israel loved Joseph more than all his children,
because he was the son of his old age: and he made
him a coat of many colours' (Genesis 37: 3); the coat
is naturally symbolic of a father's favour. The dress
of the poet's grief and the occasion of more, it is still
for him a manifestation of God's love and power: 'I
will greatly rejoice in the Lord . . . for he hath clothed
me with the garments of salvation . . . as a bride-
groom decketh himself with ornaments' (Isaiah 61:
10). The poem is also a celebration of poetry's trans-
forming power: 'Happy is he, whose heart / Hath
found the art / To turn his double pains to double
praise' (*Man's Medley*, 34–6).

Wounded I sing, tormented I indite,
Thrown down I fall into a bed, and rest:
Sorrow hath changed its note: such is his will,
Who changeth all things, as him pleaseth best.
For well he knows, if but one grief and smart   5
Among my many had his full career,
Sure it would carry with it even my heart,
And both would run until they found a bier
To fetch the body; both being due to grief.
But he hath spoiled the race; and given to Anguish   10
One of Joy's coats, 'ticing it with relief
To linger in me, and together languish.
I live to show his power, who once did bring
My joys to weep, and now my griefs to sing.

1 Echoing 'Wherefore I sing' from the final stanza of *Praise
3*: 'I sing because I am wounded.'
3 *will* The rhyme is broken (Palmer would repair it by
emending to 'right').
8–9 'And both grief and my heart would be off together to
prepare my funeral: I belong body and heart to grief.'
10 'But God has frustrated this escape of grief with my
heart; favouring grief with a gift of seeming joy, enticing it
to stay behind in me.'

The Pulley

The poem develops a theme most famously expressed by Augustine, 'our heart is restless until it finds rest in thee' (*Confessions*, 1.1). But the restlessness is a condition of the rest: 'Let us therefore fear, lest, a promise being left us of entering into his rest, any of you should seem to come short of it' (Hebrews 4: 1): we may lose true bliss by imagining we already have it. Nicol Burne's anti-Calvinist *Disputation* (Paris, 1581) attributes to Calvinists the notion that, magically and effortlessly, we 'by certain pulleys, or engines are lifted up to heaven'; but Herbert's 'pulley' is less a lifting engine than a rack. The story of Pandora's box, which is designed to show why man is cursed but hopeful is rewritten to show why he is blessed but discontent.

When God at first made man,
Having a glass of blessings standing by;
Let us (said he) pour on him all we can:
Let the world's riches, which dispersed lie,
    Contract into a span.   5

So strength first made a way;
Then beauty flowed, then wisdom, honour, pleasure:
When almost all was out, God made a stay,
Perceiving that alone of all his treasure
    Rest in the bottom lay.   10

For if I should (said he)
Bestow this jewel also on my creature,
He would adore my gifts instead of me,
And rest in Nature, not the God of Nature.
    So both should losers be.   15

Yet let him keep the rest,
But keep them with repining restlessness:
Let him be rich and weary, that at least,
If goodness lead him not, yet weariness
    May toss him to my breast.   20

2 'My head with oil, my cup with wine / Runs over day and night. / Surely thy sweet and wondrous love / Shall measure all my days' (Psalms 23: 5–6, Herbert).
5 *span* a man's size (by understatement) or the length of his days.
11–15 'Charge them that are rich in this world, that they be not highminded, nor trust in uncertain riches, but in the living God, who giveth us richly all things to enjoy' (1 Timothy 6: 17).
14–15 Man would rest content with his 'stock of natural delights' and forgo God's 'gracious benefits' (*Affliction 1*, 5–6); God would lose man's worship.
19 'The goodness of God leadeth thee to repentance' (Romans 2: 4); but not human goodness.

The Flower

Lord Herbert of Cherbury writes, 'Consider the rose in winter. It does not continue to thrive in virtue of its root, not of its stems, nor even of its seed, but, hidden within the bosom of nature, in virtue of its own power of fertility' (*De Veritate*, chapter 6); but his brother here disputes this principle of natural self-sufficiency, arguing that the revival of a flower after winter or of the spirit after desolation (this poem answers a sequence beginning with *The Search*, 'Whither, O whither art thou fled') is a miracle. 'Thou visitest the earth and waterest it . . . thou makest it soft with showers: thou blessest the springing thereof. Thou crownest the year with thy goodness; and thy paths drop fatness . . . the valleys also are covered over with corn; they shout for joy, they also sing' (Psalms 65: 9–13); but the poem is as much an admonition as a praise.

How fresh, O Lord, how sweet and clean
Are thy returns! even as the flowers in spring;
To which, besides their own demesne,
The late-past frosts tributes of pleasure bring.
        Grief melts away   5
        Like snow in May,
As if there were no such cold thing.

Who would have thought my shrivelled heart
Could have recovered greenness? It was gone
    Quite underground; as flowers depart   10
To see their mother-root, when they have blown;
        Where they together
        All the hard weather,
Dead to the world, keep house unknown.

These are thy wonders, Lord of power,   15
Killing and quickening, bringing down to Hell
    And up to Heaven in an hour;
Making a chiming of a passing-bell,
        We say amiss,
        This or that is: 20
Thy Word is all, if we could spell.

O that I once past changing were,
Fast in thy Paradise, where no flower can wither!
    Many a spring I shoot up fair,
Off'ring at heaven, growing and groaning thither: 25
        Nor doth my flower
        Want a spring-shower,
My sins and I joining together:

But while I grow in a straight line,
Still upwards bent, as if heaven were mine own,   30
    Thy anger comes, and I decline:
What frost to that? what pole is not the zone,
        Where all things burn,
        When thou dost turn,
And the least frown of thine is shown?   35

3–4 'To which, to add to what means they of themselves possess, the passing of the cold has brought pleasant relief.'
9 'Can the rush grow up without mire? can the flag grow without water? Whilst it is yet in his greenness, and not cut down, it withereth before any other herb. So are the paths of all that forget God' (Job 8: 11–13).
9–11 Herbert invites his mother's garden to share his grief: 'Let all the buds and flowers go back to find their roots and their ancestral graves' (*Memoriae Matris Sacrum*, 5:13); Donne's 'sap' hibernates 'As the tree's sap doth seek the root below / In winter' (*Hymn to Christ*, 13–14).
15–17 'For thou hast power of life and death: thou leadest to the gates of hell, and bringest up again' (Wisdom 16: 13).
18 'Turning a funeral toll to a bridal peal'.
19–21 'In our ignorance we imagine fixed distinctions be-

tween things (destroying and reviving, Hell and Heaven, grief and joy); if we studied to good effect we should understand your Word was paramount': 'For the word of the Lord is right; and all his works are done in truth . . . For he spake, and it was done; he commanded, and it stood fast' (Psalms 33: 4–9).
25 *Offering* 'aiming'.
28 'For the fields of Heshbon languish . . . I will water thee with my tears, O Heshbon' (Isaiah 16: 8–9).
29–30 'The righteous shall flourish like the palm tree; he shall grow like a cedar in Lebanon' (Psalms 92: 12).
32–5 'Compared to the cold of your least frown, the polar regions are like the tropics': 'He casteth forth his ice like morsels: who can stand before his cold?' (Psalms 147: 17).

And now in age I bud again,
After so many deaths I live and write;
I once more smell the dew and rain,
And relish versing: O my only light,
            It cannot be   40
            That I am he
On whom thy tempests fell all night.

These are thy wonders, Lord of love,
To make us see we are but flowers that glide:
Which when we once can find and prove,   45
Thou hast a garden for us, where to bide.
            Who would be more,
            Swelling through store,
Forfeit their Paradise by their pride.

36–9 'For there is hope of a tree, if it be cut down, that it will sprout again . . . Though the root thereof wax old in the earth, and the stock thereof die in the ground; Yet through the scent of water it will bud, and bring forth boughs like a plant' (Job 14: 7–9).
44 'To make us see that we whose days slip away are but flowers; and if we can act out ('prove') this discovery'.

47–9 'If we imagine ourselves more than flowers, puffed up with imagination of our own sufficiency ('store'), our pride loses us the garden': 'For whosoever exalteth himself shall be abased' (Luke 14: 11).

Aaron

Selected emblems (the means of the whole poem are minimal) of the old priesthood are spiritualized: 'thou shalt make a plate of pure gold, and grave upon it . . . HOLINESS TO THE LORD. And thou shalt put it on a blue lace, that it may be upon the mitre; upon the forefront of the mitre it shall be' (Exodus 28: 36–7); 'thou shalt put in the breastplate of judgement, the Urim and the Thummim ['Lights and Perfections'], and they shall be upon Aaron's heart, when he goeth in before the Lord: and Aaron shall bear the judgement of the children of Israel upon his heart, before the Lord continually' (30); and 'beneath upon the hem of [the robe] thou shalt make pomegranates of blue, and of purple, and of scarlet, round about the hem thereof, and bells of gold between them round

about . . . And it shall be upon Aaron, to minister: and his sound shall be heard when he goeth in unto the holy place before the Lord, and when he cometh out, that he die not' (33–5). But the Levitical priesthood is abolished in the Christian dispensation: 'If therefore perfection were by the Levitical priesthood . . . what further need was there, that another priest should rise after the order of Melchisedec, and not be called after the order of Aaron?' (Hebrews 7: 11). 'Happy it is for us, though we write no new emblems of our own, if we can have this holy imprese of God written not on our foreheads, but in our hearts, *Holiness to the Lord*' (Joseph Hall, *The Imprese of God*: Sermon on Zechariah, 14: 20).

            Holiness on the head,
            Light and perfections on the breast,
Harmonious bells below, raising the dead
            To lead them unto life and rest.
                  Thus are true Aarons dressed.   5

            Profaneness in my head,
            Defects and darkness in my breast,
A noise of passions ringing me for dead
            Unto a place where is no rest.
                  Poor priest thus am I dressed.   10

8   My jangling passions signal the 'body of this death' (Romans 7: 24).

Only another head
I have, another heart and breast,
Another music, making live not dead,
Without whom I could have no rest:
In him I am well dressed.   15

Christ is my only head,
My alone only heart and breast,
My only music, striking me e'en dead;
That to the old man I may rest,
And be in him new dressed.   20

So holy in my head,
Perfect and light in my dear breast,
My doctrine tuned by Christ (who is not dead,
But lives in me while I do rest)
Come people; Aaron's dressed.   25

15 'For as many of you as have been baptized into Christ have put on Christ' (Galatians 3: 27).
16 Perfected, we 'may grow up into him in all things, which is the head, even Christ' (Ephesians 4: 15).
18–19 'Ye have not so learned Christ; if so be that ye have heard him . . . That ye put off . . . the old man, which is corrupt according to the deceitful lusts' (Ephesians 4: 20–2).
23–4 'I live, yet not I, but Christ liveth in me' (Galatians 2: 20).

The Forerunners

'It was said by the Borgia of the expedition of the French into Italy, that they came with chalk in their hands to mark out their lodgings, not with arms to force their way in. I in like manner would have my doctrine enter quietly into the minds that are fit and capable of receiving it' (Bacon, *Novum Organum* 1.35). 'Forerunners' or 'harbingers' are sent in advance of a royal progress to secure lodgings by chalking doors; these chalkings stand at once for the ageing poet's white hair (though he died before he was 40) and (though beautiful language is abjured not as in itself reprehensible but only as liable to abuse) the bleaching of his poetic language to make it fit for God.

The harbingers are come. See, see their mark;
White is their colour, and behold my head.
But must they have my brain? must they dispark
Those sparkling notions, which therein were bred?
    Must dullness turn me to a clod?   5
Yet have they left me, *Thou art still my God.*

Good men ye be, to leave me my best room,
E'en all my heart, and what is lodgèd there:
I pass not, I, what of the rest become,
So *Thou art still my God*, be out of fear.   10

1–2 'These hairs of age are messengers, / Which bid me fast, repent, and pray; / They be of death the harbingers, / That doth prepare and dress the way' (Willam Hunnis, *Gray Hairs*, in *A Handful of Honeysuckles*).
3–4 'Must the whiteness advance into the brain, evicting the brilliance it bred': the pagan world enjoyed glory and pleasure till 'our Saviour did destroy the game, / Disparking oracles, and all their treasure' (*The Church Militant*, 146–7).
6 'I trusted in thee, O Lord: I said, Thou art my God' (Psalms 31: 14).
9–10 'I care nothing if I can safely keep my motto of reassurance': 'He loseth nothing that loseth not God' (*Outlandish Proverbs*, 35).

He will be pleasèd with that ditty;
And if I please him, I write fine and witty.

Farewell sweet phrases, lovely metaphors.
But will ye leave me thus? when ye before
Of stews and brothels only knew the doors,   15
Then did I wash you with my tears, and more,
    Brought you to church well dressed and clad;
My God must have my best, e'en all I had.

Lovely enchanting language, sugar-cane,
Honey of roses, whither wilt thou fly?   20
Hath some fond lover 'ticed thee to thy bane?
And wilt thou leave the church, and love a sty?
    Fie, thou wilt soil thy broidered coat,
And hurt thyself, and him that sings the note.

Let foolish lovers, if they will love dung,   25
With canvas, not with arras clothe their shame:
Let folly speak in her own native tongue.
True beauty dwells on high: ours is a flame
    But borrowed thence to light us thither.
Beauty and beauteous words should go together.   30

Yet if you go, I pass not; take your way:
For, *Thou art still my God*, is all that ye
Perhaps with more embellishment can say.
Go birds of spring: let winter have his fee,
    Let a bleak paleness chalk the door,   35
So all within be livelier than before.

11   *ditty* 'theme'.
12   'Nothing that's plain, / But may be witty, if thou hast the vein' (*Church-Porch*, 239–40).
13–24   'And when I passed by thee, and saw thee polluted in thine own blood . . . Then . . . I throughly washed away thy blood from thee, and I anointed thee with oil. I clothed thee also with broidered work . . . Thus wast thou decked with gold and silver, and thy raiment was of fine linen, and silk . . . But thou didst trust in thine own beauty, and playedst the harlot' (Ezekiel 16: 6–15, of God and Jerusalem).
14–15   'When I found you fit only for the brothel, I washed you with penitent tears': 'Doth poetry / Wear Venus' livery, only serve her turn?' (*My God, where is that ancient heat*).

25–7   To exchange tapestry ('arras') for plain canvas mitigates the punishment of Jerusalem: 'I will also give thee into [thy enemies'] hand, and . . . they shall strip thee also of thy clothes . . . and leave thee naked and bare' (Ezekiel 16: 39).
27–30   'Ah then my hungry soul, which long hast fed / On idle fancies . . . And with false beauties' flattering bait misled, / Hast after vain deceitful shadows sought, / Which all are fled . . . Ah cease to gaze on matter of thy grief. / And look at last up to that sovereign light' (Spenser, *Hymn of Heavenly Beauty*, 288–95).
34   'Let winter take what is owed him (summer's spoils); the chalk marks my door as fit to receive the royal party.'

Love 3

The final poem in the Church and the third of the three *Love* poems. It celebrates a paradisal communion, but resolves its own difficulties in ways determined by the order of service for the earthly one. 'We do not presume to come to this thy table (O merciful Lord) trusting in our own righteousness, but in thy manifold and great mercies: we be not worthy, so much as to gather up the crumbs under thy table: but thou art the same Lord whose property is always to have mercy: grant us therefore (gracious Lord) so to eat the flesh of thy dear son Jesus Christ, and to drink his blood, that our sinful bodies may be made clean by his body, and our souls washed through his most precious blood, and that we may evermore dwell in him, and he in us' (*Book of Common Prayer*: Order for Communion). The quick exchanges of the love-dialogue (found in the song-books) are already imitated in Southwell's *St Peter's Complaint*: 'At Sorrow's door I knocked. They craved my name. / I answered, "One, unworthy to be known." / "What one?" say they. "One worthiest of blame." / "But who?" "A wretch, not God's, nor yet his own" (118–21).

Love bade me welcome: yet my soul drew back,
    Guilty of dust and sin.
But quick-eyed Love, observing me grow slack
    From my first entrance in,
Drew nearer to me, sweetly questioning,   5
    If I lacked any thing.

"A guest," I answered, worthy to be here:
    Love said, "You shall be he."
"I the unkind, ungrateful? Ah my dear,
    I cannot look on thee."   10
Love took my hand, and smiling did reply,
    "Who made the eyes but I?"

"Truth Lord, but I have marred them: let my shame
    Go where it doth deserve."
"And know you not," says Love, "who bore the blame?"   15
    "My dear, then I will serve."
"You must sit down," says Love, "and taste my meat":
    So I did sit and eat.

2 The soul is conscious of mortality ('guilty of dust') and sinfulness, but it has also abused Love: 'How hath man parcelled out thy glorious name, / And thrown it on that dust which thou hast made' (*Love 1*, 3–4).
3 'What wonders shall we feel, when we shall see / Thy full-eyed love! / When thou shalt look us out of pain' (*The Glance*, 20); Love is not only not blind, its eyes 'quicken' (or 'revive') the soul, grown slow ('slack').
6 'If there be any of you which cannot quiet his own conscience, but requireth further comfort or counsel . . . then let him come to me' (Order for Communion).
7–10 'We be not worthy, so much as to gather up the crumbs under thy table' (Order for Communion).
9 As Judas was: 'As they did eat, he said . . . one of you shall betray me' (Matthew 26: 21); *Unkindness* (its refrain varying 'I would not use a friend as I do thee') and *Ungratefulness* are earlier poems on the theme.
10 'There shall no man see me, and live' (Exodus 33: 20).
12 'He that formed the eye, shall he not see' (Psalms 94: 9); 'And praise him who did make and mend our eyes' (*Love 2*, 14).
15 'Christ hath redeemed us from the curse of the law' (Galatians 3: 13).
16–18 Love refuses the soul's offer. 'Blessed are those servants whom the lord when he cometh shall find watching: verily I say unto you, that he shall gird himself, and make them to sit down to meat, and will come forth and serve them' (Luke 12: 37); 'I am among you as he that serveth' (Luke 22: 27). Love is himself the meal: 'Take, eat; this is my body' (Matthew 26: 26).

Thomas Carew (1595–1640)

'Thomas Carew was a younger brother of a good family, and of excellent parts, and had spent many years of his youth in France and Italy; and returning from travel, followed the court; which the modesty of that time disposed men to do some time before they pretended to be of it; and he was very much esteemed by the most eminent persons in the court, and well looked upon by the King himself, some years before he could obtain to be Sewer to the King ... He was a person of a pleasant and facetious wit, and made many poems (especially in the amorous way) which for the sharpness of the fancy and the elegancy of the language, in which that fancy was spread, were at least equal, if not superior to any of that time' (Clarendon, *Life*). Son of a Master in Chancery, a graduate of Merton College, Oxford, former student of the Middle Temple (where he studied law 'very little') he had served (dishonourably) with Sir Dudley Carleton's embassies in Venice and The Hague, and (apparently well enough) with Sir Edward Herbert's (later Cherbury's) embassy in Paris. Then, for a decade he modestly 'followed the court' before in 1630 being made Gentleman of the Privy Chamber and Sewer (waiter or usher) in Ordinary to the King. His single most ambitious poem is a courtly masque, *Coelum Britannicum* (1634), ostensibly a celebration of the virtues of the Caroline court: truth, religion, justice and the rest gathered under the aegis of eternity. But as Clarendon indicates, it was his amorous verse that made him famous. In a poem addressed to him, Davenant imagined the assembled love poets of the city rejoicing over the death of the poet who had outbid them: 'For every lover that can verses read, / Hath been so injured by thy Muse and thee, / Ten thousand, thousand times, he wished thee dead' (*To Thomas Carew*, 6–8). This squib does less than justice to his moral or indeed to his poetic intelligence. Despite the scandalousness of his early reputation, it is not courtly indulgence that he celebrates (or Townshend would not have troubled to invite the *Answer*) and, though Pope puts him in the 'mob of gentlemen who wrote with ease', his immediate reputation (borne out by MS evidence) was for poetic costiveness. In 1639 he accompanied the army north on the first Bishops' War; on his return south he died, but where is not known. He was buried at St Dunstan's Church in Westminster.

The poems were first collected, perhaps by Aurelian Townshend, in *Poems* (1640), still authoritative for most of the canon. The editions in 1642 and 1651 were enlarged. Carew's poetry was very frequently copied in MS collections, before and after the publication of the 1640 volume. Almost forty miscellanies carry ten or more poems, and at least three of these represent major collections, one with more than eighty poems. There is a facsimile edition of the 1640 *Poems*; it includes poems from Bodleian MS Don. b. 9 (Menston: Scolar Press, 1969). The standard edition is Rhodes Dunlap's *The Poems of Thomas Carew* (Oxford: Clarendon Press, 1949, revised 1957). There is a survey of criticism by David C. Judkins in *English Literary History*, 7 (1977), 245–8.

An Elegy upon the Death of Doctor Donne, Dean of Paul's

1640; lines 91–2 are taken from the version in Donne's *Poems* (1633), preferred by some editors. Donne died on 31 March 1631; this appeared first as one of the twelve 'Elegies upon the Author' printed in the posthumous *Poems*. 'Witty Carew's' elegy is referred to in Edward Herbert's *Elegy for Dr Donne*, 47–51, which mimics some of its phrasing. It may have been influential on other contributions to the volume (Herbert's was not), but a common subject and a commonly felt obligation to honour Donne in a Donnean mode may explain the similarities. 'When Donne and Beaumont died, an epitaph / Some men (I well remember) thought unsafe, / And said they did presume to write, unless / They could their tears in their expression dress' (R. Gostelow, *On the Death of Mr Randolph*). Even in this most Donnean of his poems, Carew pretends not to be able to take advantage of the possibilities that should have been enabled by Donne's achievement.

> Can we not force from widowed poetry
> Now thou art dead (great Donne) one elegy,

1–3 Henry King writes, 'Widowed invention justly doth forbear / To come abroad knowing thou art not here' (*Upon the Death of Dr Donne*, 13–14).

To crown thy hearse? Why yet did we not trust,
Though with unkneaded dough-baked prose, thy dust,
Such as the unscissored Lecturer from the flower   5
Of fading rhetoric, short-lived as his hour,
Dry as the sand that measures it, might lay
Upon the ashes, on the funeral day?
Have we nor tune, nor voice? didst thou dispense
Through all our language both the words and sense?   10
'Tis a sad truth. The pulpit may her plain,
And sober Christian precepts still retain,
Doctrines it may, and wholesome uses, frame,
Grave homilies, and lectures, but the flame
Of thy brave soul, that shot such heat, and light,   15
As burnt our earth, and made our darkness bright,
Committed holy rapes upon the will,
Did through the eye the melting heart distil,
And the deep knowledge, of dark truths, so teach
As sense might judge what fancy could not reach,   20
Must be desired forever. So the fire
That fills with spirit and heat the Delphic choir,
Which kindled first by thy Promethean breath
Glowed here awhile, lies quenched now in thy death.
The Muses' garden, with pedantic weeds   25
O'er-spread, was purged by thee, the lazy seeds
Of servile imitation thrown away,
And fresh invention planted; thou didst pay
The debts of our penurious bankrupt age:
Licentious thefts, that make poetic rage   30
A mimic fury, when our souls must be
Possessed, or with Anacreon's ecstasy,
Or Pindar's, not their own, the subtle cheat
Of sly exchanges, and the juggling feat
Of two-edged words, or whatsoever wrong   35
By ours was done the Greek or Latin tongue,

3–4 Prose might be truer (as with *In Answer of an Elegiacal
Letter*, 15–16); but 'dough-baked' ('unfinished') is Donne's
expression for what is tasteless and flat in men incapable of
being moved (*A Letter to Lady Carey*, 20).
5–8 'Such as the long-haired young preacher (*1633* reads
'churchman': lecturers were unbeneficed clergy) might read
over your remains ('ashes' only metaphorically), stuff picked
('flower') from dated manuals and destined to last no longer
than the sand in the glass that measures the time allotted for
his oration.'
9–10 'Was it given to you alone among those who use
English to deal out words and sense?'
15–20 *that . . . reach* The details of the parenthesis identify
Donne with Apollo (the sun, the rapist, the oracle); his last
success is to have brought to the eyes and ears ('sense') what
before could not have been imagined.
22–3 'The flame that fires the poets (the 'Delphic choir'
from Apollo's shrine at Delphi) . . . kindled by your fiery
(Prometheus was the thief of fire) breath'.
25–8 Unable to write, Donne wrote that his Muse affected

'a chast fallownesse; / Since she . . . to too many hath shown
/ How love-song weeds, and satiric thorns are grown /
Where seeds of better arts, were early sown' (*To Mr Rowland
Woodward*, 3–6).
27 Drummond praises Mary Wroth's 'choice inventions
free' (*To my Lady Mary Wroth*, 5). The opposition of imita-
tion and invention is picked up in that of 'poetic rage' and
'mimic fury' (30–1).
28–9 Henry King reborrows from the 'bankrupt mine' of
wit 'that ore to bury thee' (*To the Memory of Dr Donne*, 43–
6). Donne repays the original loan and compensates for any
collateral disadvantage (35–6).
32–3 Sidney lets 'Pindar's apes flaunt in their phrases fine'
(*Astrophil*, 3:3); Pindar and Anacreon write very different
kinds of odes.
33–4 'The cunning deceptions worked by the substitution
of one form for another ('sly exchanges' or enallage) and the
illusory deftness of ambiguities ('two-edged words' as if
'swords'): Quintilian derides 'double or rather duplicitous
phrases' (*Institutes*, 9.2.69–70).

Thou hast redeemed, and opened us a mine
Of rich and pregnant fancy, drawn a line
Of masculine expression, which had good
Old Orpheus seen, or all the ancient brood   40
Our superstitious fools admire, and hold
Their lead more precious than thy burnished gold,
Thou hadst been their Exchequer, and no more,
They each in other's dung had searched for ore.
Thou shalt yield no precedence, but of time,   45
And the blind fate of language, whose tuned chime
More charms the outward sense; yet thou may'st claim
From so great disadvantage, greater fame,
Since to the awe of thy imperious wit
Our troublesome language bends, made only fit   50
With her tough thick-ribbed hoops, to gird about
Thy giant fancy, which had proved too stout
For their soft melting phrases. As in time
They had the start, so did they cull the prime
Buds of invention many a hundred year,   55
And left the rifled fields, besides the fear
To touch their harvest, yet from those bare lands
Of what was only thine, thy only hands
(And that their smallest work) have gleanèd more
Than all those times, and tongues, could reap before.   60
    But thou art gone, and thy strict laws will be
Too hard for Libertines in poetry,
They will recall the goodly exiled train:
Of gods, and goddesses, which in thy just reign
Was banished nobler poems; now, with these,   65
The silenced tales in th' *Metamorphoses*

37–8   Bacon writes, 'If it be true that Democritus said, "that the truth of nature lieth hid in certain deep mines and caves" . . . it were good to divide natural philosophy into the mine and the furnace, and to make two professions or occupations of natural philosophers, some to be pioneers and some smiths; some to dig, and some to refine and hammer' (*Advancement*, 2.7.1). Jonson asks 'Whose work could this be, Chapman, to refine / Old Hesiod's Ore' (*To George Chapman*); but Drayton's Chaucer (like Carew's Donne) both delves first in the mine and refines the ore (*Epistle to Henry Reynolds*, 49–53).

38–9   *drawn . . . expression* 'tapped a vein of masculine expression' to continue the mining metaphor; but 'strong lines' are suggested. Jonson writes of masculine writers that they prefer 'what is rough, and broken . . . And if it would come gently, they trouble it of purpose. They would not have it run without rubs, as if that style were more strong and manly, that struck the ear with a kind of unevenesse. These men err not by chance, but knowingly' (*Timber*).

39–44   'Which if it had been seen by Orpheus (the 'father of song') or any of the ancients so admired by our superstitious fools today, who think antique lead finer than your bright gold, then you would have been a treasury ('Exchequer') for the ancients; and the moderns would not be searching in their rubbish for ore'; *1633* has 'dust' for 'dung', and 'raked' for 'searched'.

45–7   'We must concede they came before you historically, and that as chance would have it our verse depends on the merely superficial charms of rhyme.'

49–52   The poem's centre: 'Our difficult (*1633* reads 'stubborn') language bows in reverence ('bends') before your commanding intelligence.' But it bends in another sense: something otherwise uncontainable is baled in the tough hoops of English, which the typically softer ancient Southern languages could not have coped with. Jonson, in *Timber*, congratulates himself on not being hooped in: 'too much pickedness is not manly.'

53–60   'They came first historically and for centuries drew on unused resources, in the end not only to leave the fields depleted but an intimidating legacy which the moderns have been reluctant to appropriate; yet from your own unworked ('bare') field you have gleaned more of worth (even while engaged on the greater work of your vocation as a priest) than all previous generations from the common land.'

62–6   Poetic 'freethinkers' (reluctant to submit to Donne's 'just reign') will reintroduce Ovidian fictions; Carew later proposes Sandys (translator of the Psalms as well as Ovid) as a model for Christian poetry: 'tear those idols from my heart . . . I no more shall court the verdant Bay, / But the dry leafless trunk on Golgotha' (*To George Sandys*, 31–4). The Epicurean and neo-Ovidian French *libertin* poets refused the authority of Malherbe and his literary Puritanism.

Shall stuff their lines, and swell the windy page
Till verse refined by thee, in this last age
Turn ballad-rhyme, or those old idols be
Adored again with new apostasy.   70
     O! pardon me that break with untuned verse
The reverend silence, that attends thy hearse,
Whose solemn, awful murmurs, were to thee
More than these rude lines, a loud elegy,
That did proclaim in a dumb eloquence   75
The death of all the arts, whose influence
Grown feeble, in these panting numbers lies
Gasping short-winded accents, and so dies.
So doth the swiftly-turning wheel, not stand
In the instant we withdraw the moving hand,   80
But some short time retain a faint weak course,
By virtue of the first impulsive force;
And so, whilst I cast on thy funeral pile,
Thy crown of bays, O let it crack awhile
And spit disdain, till the devouring flashes   85
Suck all the moisture up, then turn to ashes,
     I will not draw thee envy, to engross
All thy perfections, or weep all the loss,
Those are too numerous for one elegy,
And this too great to be expressed by me.   90
Though every pen should share a distinct part,
Yet art thou theme enough to tire all art;
Let others carve the rest; it shall suffice,
I on thy grave this epitaph incise.
Here lies a King, that ruled as he thought fit   95
The universal monarchy of wit,
Here lies two flamens, and both those the best,
Apollo's first, at last the true God's priest.

69   Peacham complains to Drayton that 'only almanac and ballad rhymes / Are in request now' (*Thalia's Banquet*, 93:2–3).
70   *apostasy* 'reversion to idolatry'.
77–8   Echoing Shakespeare's *1 Henry IV*, I. i. 2–3: 'Find we a time for frighted peace to pant, / And breathe short-winded accents of new broils.'
79–82   Donne maintains that the force of inertia sustains the universe after Elizabeth Drury's death: 'But as a ship which hath struck sail, doth run / By force of that force which before, it won' (*Second Anniversary*, 7–8).

84   *crack* 'crackle'.
87–8   'I will not make you (but *1633* has 'the envy') the object of envy by writing your virtues large'; Jonson writes, 'To draw no envy, Shakespeare, on thy name, / Am I thus ample' (*To the Memory of . . . Shakespeare*, 1–2).
94   *grave 1633*'s 'tomb' loses the pun on 'engrave' / 'incise'.
97–8   *flamens* 'priests'; Sir Lucius Cary calls him 'a twofold priest; in youth / Apollo's; afterwards the voice of truth' (*An Elegy*, 7–8).

To Saxham

1640; in some MSS the title is *A Winter's Entertainment*. Like *To the King at his Entrance into Saxham*, it was probably written in the winter of early 1620. Carew's friend John Crofts returned at this time from Edward Herbert's Paris embassy, presumably to visit his father's manor at Little Saxham near Bury in Suffolk. The house was built in the early sixteenth century and demolished in the late eighteenth; the estate included an extensive game reserve (made much of in lines 21–30). Clearly indebted to *To Penshurst*, the energies of Jonson's poem are much diluted; and the praise of hospitality is moved to the fore, perhaps in reponse to the more measured hospitality of households thought of as 'Puritan'.

Though frost, and snow, locked from mine eyes,
That beauty which without door lies;
Thy gardens, orchards, walks, that so
I might not all thy pleasures know;
Yet (Saxham) thou within thy gate,   5
Art of thyself so delicate;
So full of native sweets, that bless
Thy roof with inward happiness;
As neither from, nor to thy store
Winter takes aught, or Spring adds more.   10
The cold and frozen air had starved
Much poor, if not by thee preserved;
Whose prayers have made thy table blest
With plenty, far above the rest.
The season hardly did afford   15
Course cates unto thy neighbours' board,
Yet thou hadst dainties, as the sky
Had only been thy volary;
Or else the birds, fearing the snow
Might to another deluge grow: 20
The pheasant, partridge, and the lark,
Flew to thy house, as to the ark.
The willing ox, of himself came
Home to the slaughter, with the lamb,
And every beast did thither bring   25
Himself, to be an offering.
The scaly herd, more pleasure took,
Bathed in thy dish, than in the brook,
Water, earth, air, did all conspire,
To pay their tributes to thy fire,   30
Whose cherishing flames themselves divide
Through every room, where they deride
The night, and cold abroad; whilst they
Like suns within, keep endless day.
Those cheerful beams send forth their light,   35
To all that wander in the night,
And seem to beckon from aloof,
The weary pilgrim to thy roof;
Where if refreshed, he will away,
He's fairly welcome, or if stay   40
Far more, which he shall hearty find,
Both from the master, and the hind.
The strangers' welcome, each man there
Stamped on his cheerful brow, doth wear;

6 *delicate* 'delightful'.
8 *roof* 'house' (a common synecdoche, as at line 38).
11 *starved* 'killed with cold'.
18 *volary* 'aviary'; Jonson calls Drayton 'an Orpheus, that wouldst try / To make the air one volary' (*The Vision*, 35–6).
24 Lambs are proverbially (after Isaiah 53: 7) brought to the slaughter.
27 *scaly herd* 'fish'; Drayton has 'finny herd' (*Poly-Olbion*, 2:439).

29–30 At the poem's centre three elements combine to honour the remaining fourth ('fire' here standing for 'hearth').
37 *aloof* 'afar'.
41 'If the refreshed traveller should choose to leave, he is permitted ('welcome') to; if to stay, he is warmly invited ('welcome') to, and he shall find the 'welcome' (now a noun) hearty'; in *To Penshurst*, Lord Lisle entertains 'the farmer and the clown' (48): Carew's 'hind' includes tenants and labourers.

Nor doth this welcome, or his cheer 45
Grow less, 'cause he stays longer here.
There's none observes (much less repines)
How often this man sups or dines.
Thou hast no porter at the door
To examine, or keep back the poor; 50
Nor locks, nor bolts; thy gates have been
Made only to let strangers in;
Untaught to shut, they do not fear
To stand wide open all the year;
Careless who enters, for they know, 55
Thou never didst deserve a foe;
And as for thieves, thy bounty's such;
They cannot steal, thou giv'st so much.

To Ben Jonson. Upon Occasion of his Ode of Defiance annexed to his Play of the New Inn

1640; there a is version (in a few details slightly more primitive) in Carew's own hand, *To Ben Jonson upon Occasion of his Ode to Himself*, in the Public Record Office. *The New Inn*, first performed in 1629, was published in 1631 along with an ode inspired by 'the just indignation the author took at the vulgar censure of his play'. This nicely turned rebuke to Jonson's pretensions by a near 'son of Ben' is one of many replies. James Howell records a supper in 1636 with

Ben Jonson: 'one thing intervened which almost spoiled the relish of the rest, that Ben began to engross all the discourse, to vapour extremely of himself, and, by vilifying others, to magnify his own Muse. Tom Carew buzzed me in the ear, that though Ben had barrelled up a great deal of knowledge, yet it seems he had not read the *Ethics*, which, among precepts of morality, forbid self commendation' (*Epistolae Ho-Elianae*, 2.13).

'Tis true (dear Ben) thy just chastising hand
Hath fixed upon the sotted age a brand
To their swoln pride, and empty scribbling due,
It can nor judge, nor write, and yet 'tis true
Thy comic Muse from the exalted line 5
Touched by thy *Alchemist*, doth since decline
From that her zenith, and foretells a red
And blushing evening, when she goes to bed,
Yet such, as shall outshine the glimmering light
With which all stars shall gild the following night. 10
Nor think it much (since all thy eaglets may
Endure the sunny trial) if we say
This hath the stronger wing, or that doth shine
Tricked up in fairer plumes, since all are thine;
Who hath his flock of cackling geese compared 15
With thy tuned choir of swans? or else who dared
To call thy births deformed? but if thou bind

5–10 Jasper Mayne's Elegy in *Jonsonus Virbius* isolates *The Alchemist* (1610) for praise; Jonson was often reckoned to have a long decline. 'Homer in the *Odyssey* may be compared to the setting sun: the size remains without the force' (Longinus, 9.13); but Carew rallies a compliment in 9–10.
11–12 Eagles bring up only the young that can stare at the sun (Pliny, *Natural History*, 10.3.5): 'if thou be that princely eagle's bird, / Show thy descent by gazing 'gainst the sun' (Shakespeare, *3 Henry VI*, II. i. 91–2).

15–16 All Jonson's geese are swans: the geese belong to the poetasters; swans are poetically tuneful from their singing at death (a notion even Pliny, 10.32.1, discounts).
17–20 'Even if you favour all your progeny equally, we may be allowed to discriminate.' By 'city-custom' (understanding 'borough-kind') the youngest inherited all property; by 'gavelkind' 'the male children equally to inherit . . . or females for want of males' (Harrison, *Description of England*, 2.9).

By city–custom, or by gavelkind,
In equal shares thy love on all thy race,
We may distinguish of their sex, and place;   20
Though one hand form them, and though one brain strike
Souls into all, they are not all alike.
Why should the follies then of this dull age
Draw from thy pen such an immodest rage
As seems to blast thy (else–immortal) bays,   25
When thine own tongue proclaims thy itch of praise?
Such thirst will argue drouth. No, let be hurled
Upon thy *Works*, by the detracting world,
What malice can suggest; let the rout say,
The running sands, that (ere thou make a play)   30
Count the slow minutes, might a Goodwin frame
To swallow when thou hast done thy shipwrecked name.
Let them the dear expense of oil upbraid
Sucked by thy watchful lamp, that hath betrayed
To theft the blood of martyred authors, spilt   35
Into thy ink, whilst thou growest pale with guilt;
Repine not at the taper's thrifty waste,
That sleeks thy terser poems, nor is haste
Praise, but excuse; and if thou overcome
A knotty writer, bring the booty home;   40
Nor think it theft, if the rich spoils so torn
From conquered authors, be as trophies worn.
Let others glut on the extorted praise
Of vulgar breath, trust thou to afterdays:
Thy laboured works shall live, when Time devours   45
The abortive offspring of their hasty hours.
Thou art not of their rank, the quarrel lies
Within thine own verge, then let this suffice,
The wiser world doth greater thee confess
Than all men else, than thyself only less.   50

21–2 'Though shaped by one hand and animated by one mind'; 'striking souls' is like 'striking fire' with a fllint (though touched by a memory of striking 'Upon the Muses' anvil' in Jonson's verses on Shakespeare, 59–61).
25 The rage is worse than lightning, which does not strike the laurel (Pliny, *Natural History*, 2.56).
28 *Works* alluding to Jonson's ambitious titling of the 1616 folio.
29–32 'Let the mob say that the sand that runs through the hourglass while you write would make a sandbank (the Goodwin Sands are off Ramsgate) big enough to swallow your wrecked pretensions.' Jonson commends his own un-Shakespearean slowness: 'No matter how slow the style be at first, so it be laboured, and accurate' (*Timber*).
33–6 The oil feeds the lamp that exposes the poets 'mar-

tyred' to Jonson's plagiarism, their blood mixed with his ink (for Jonson, to 'imitate' is for the poet to 'convert the substance, or riches of another poet, to his own use', *Timber*). The author in the 'Apologetical Dialogue' added to *Poetaster* has to 'spend half my nights, and all my days / Here in a cell, to get a dark, pale face' (221).
37–8 'You have no cause to complain of wasted oil: your thrift ensures it puts a shine on your poems, and makes them more polished ('terser')'.
43–6 'The common rhymers pour forth verses, such as they are, extempore, but there never came from them one sense, worth the life of a day' (*Timber*).
47–8 'You are above them, the complaint we make concerns what is under your own control.'

A Song

1640; widely distributed in MSS (where the number and order of the stanzas may vary) and much imitated. Settings include those by Henry Lawes and John Wilson. Carew turns the 'Tell me' formula, commonly used in the English songbooks (and repeated outside them, as in King's 'Tell me no more how fair she is', or Cartwright's 'Tell me no more of minds embracing minds'). The playful literalization of blazon metaphors is famously anticipated in Shakespeare's Sonnet 99 ('The forward violet thus did I chide').

Ask me no more

where Jove bestows,
When June is past the fading rose:
For in your beauty's orient deep,
These flowers as in their causes, sleep.

Ask me no more whither doth stray,   5
The golden atoms of the day:
For in pure love Heaven did prepare,
Those powders to enrich your hair.

Ask me no more whither doth haste,
The nightingale when May is past: 10
For in your sweet dividing throat,
She winters and keeps warm her note.

Ask me no more where those stars light,
That downwards fall in dead of night:
For in your eyes they sit and there,   15
Fixèd become as in their sphere.

Ask me no more if East or West,
The phoenix builds her spicy nest:
For unto you at last she flies,
And in your fragrant bosom dies.   20

3–4 For on your cheeks and lips they be / Fresher than on any tree (MS). But 'causes' gives a spurious Aristotelian colouring: the lady might be the 'cause' of roses in that they are made of her (she is their 'material cause'), or that she generates them ('efficient cause') or that it is for her sake they exist ('final cause'), or simply that she is like them ('formal cause'). Arthur Johnson's Latin version of the poem says that 'all the roses come to you who suffice for a thousand rose-gardens and cradle a thousand beginnings ['semina'] for their flowers.' She is the repository of floral possibilities; they rise from her as daylight over the eastern sea (her beau-

ty's 'orient deep'). Some MSS represent the roses as 'damask' or 'flaming'.
5–6 Supposing with the Epicureans that light consists of atoms emitted by the sun (Lucretius, 2:144–57).
11 *dividing* 'descanting'.
13–16 Varying Herbert of Cherbury's 'two stars, that having fall'n down, / Looked up again to find their place' (*Ode on a Question Moved*, 147–8).
17–18 The phoenix builds its pyre of spices, always in the East.

In Answer of an Elegiacal Letter upon the Death of the King of Sweden from Aurelian Townshend, inviting me to write on that subject

1640. The great Protestant hero of the Thirty Years War, Gustavus II Adolphus, was killed in battle at Lützen in November 1632, a loss comparable for some Englishmen with Prince Henry's in November 1612. British aloofness from the Thirty Years War did not prevent public grief. *The Swedish Intelligencer*, Third Part (1633), published ten elegies, including a fine one by Henry King; and Dudley North's *Forest of Varieties* (1645) belatedly includes *An Incentive to our*

Poets upon the Death of the Victorious King of Swedeland; Quarles's *Shepherds' Oracles* (1646) revives the lament: 'Sweden, the glory of the world, is dead: / Our strength is broke, and all our hopes are vain (Eclogue 10, 210–11). Townshend's *Elegiacal Letter* is more a praise of Carew, than an elegy on Gustavus. Carew's refusal to elegize or eulogize Gustavus (*a recusatio* like Horace's 'What lake, what river's ignorant / Of the sad war? What seas with paint / Of Latin slaughters is not red? . . . But let us in Dioneian [of love] cell / Seek matter for a lighter quill', *Odes* 2.1: 33–40, Fanshawe), overbalances into praise of Townshend's minor gifts. He declines the invitation to heroic elegy not only as above his own 'faint flagging rhyme' (93), but recommends that Townshend divert the 'loftier pitch' (91) of his *Elegiacal Letter* to indulging the preferences of a court and country at peace: 'Of all the princes of Europe, the king of England alone seemed to be seated upon that pleasant promontory, that might safely view the tragic suffering of his neighbours about him, without any other concernment than what arose from his own princely heart and Christian compassion' (Clarendon, *Life*, of the situation in 1639); King Charles discouraged the cult of Gustavus.

Why dost thou sound, my dear Aurelian,
In so shrill accents, from thy Barbican,
A loud alarum to my drowsy eyes,
Bidding them wake in *Tears* and *Elegies*
For mighty Sweden's fall? Alas! how may   5
My lyric feet, that of the smooth soft way
Of Love, and Beauty, only know the tread,
In dancing paces celebrate the dead
Victorious King, or his majestic hearse
Profane with th'humble touch of their low verse?   10
Virgil, nor Lucan, no, nor Tasso more
Than both, not Donne, worth all that went before,
With the united labour of their wit
Could a just poem to this subject fit,
His actions were too mighty to be raised   15
Higher by verse, let him in prose be praised,
In modest faithful story, which his deeds
Shall turn to poems: when the next age reads
Of Frankfort, Leipzig, Wurzburg; of the Rhein,
The Lech, the Danube; Tilly, Wallenstein,   20
Bavaria, Papenheim; Lützen-field, where he
Gained after death a posthume victory,
They'll think his acts things rather feigned than done
Like our Romances of the Knight o'th' Sun.
Leave we him then to the grave chronicler,   25
Who though to *Annals* he can not refer
His too-brief story, yet his *Journals* may
Stand by the Caesars' years, and every day
Cut into minutes, each, shall more contain
Of great designment than an Emperor's reign;   30

2 *Barbican* 'watchtower'; but Townshend lived in the area of London so called.
6–7 Remembering Townshend's *Elegiacal Letter*: 'thy wit . . . in lyric feet / Steals to thy mistress' (7–9).
8 *dancing paces* 'choric feet', like Jonson's in the Cary-Morison *Ode*.
11–12 Virgil and Lucan serve as examples of heroic or historical poets, Tasso and Donne as examples of Christian poets, and the latter Protestant. Townshend's poem refers to Carew's *Elegy* on Donne.
15–8 Inverting Bacon's point that 'because the acts or events of true history have not that magnitude which satisfieth the mind of man, poesy feigneth acts and events greater and more heroical' (*Advancement*, 2.4.2).

19–21 Frankfurt, Leipzig and Würzburg are all sites of Swedish victories. The Rhein, Lech and Danube are all rivers. Tilly, Wallenstein, Bavaria and Pappenheim were Imperial generals. Despite Gustavus's death, Lützen was a victory over Wallenstein.
24 The Knight of the Sun was the hero of Calahorra's *Mirror of Princely Deeds*, the favoured reading of Cervantes's Master Nicholas the Barber.
26–30 Jonson's argument in the Cary-Morison *Ode*: 'Repeat of things a throng, / To show thou hast been long, / Not lived' (57–9). Records of years ('annals') are inappropriate to a life lived in days ('journals'); Tacitus's *Annals* cover the more than fifty years between Tiberius and Nero.

And (since 'twas but his churchyard) let him have
For his own ashes now no narrower grave
Than the whole German continent's vast womb,
Whilst all her cities do but make his tomb:
Let us to supreme Providence commit   35
The fate of monarchs, which first thought it fit
To rend the Empire from the Austrian grasp,
And next from Sweden's, even when he did clasp
Within his dying arms the sovereignty
Of all those provinces, that men might see   40
The Divine Wisdom would not leave that land
Subject to any one king's sole command.
Then let the Germans fear if Caesar shall,
Or the united Princes, rise, and fall,
But let us that in myrtle bowers sit   45
Under secure shades, use the benefit
Of peace and plenty, which the blessed hand
Of our good King gives this obdurate land,
Let us of revels sing, and let thy breath
(Which filled Fame's trumpet with Gustavus' death,   50
Blowing his name to heaven) gently inspire
Thy past'ral pipe, till all our swains admire
Thy song and subject, whilst they both comprise
The beauties of the *Shepherds' Paradise*;
For who like thee (whose loose discourse is far   55
More neat and polished than our poems are,
Whose very gait's more graceful than our dance)
In sweetly-flowing numbers may advance
The glorious night? When, not to act foul rapes,
Like birds, or beasts, but in their angel-shapes   60
A troop of deities came down to guide
Our steerless barks in passion's swelling tide
By Virtue's card, and brought us from above
A pattern of their own celestial love.
Nor lay it in dark sullen precepts drowned   65
But with rich fancy, and clear action crowned

31–4 Others of Gustavus's elegists use similar conceits, derived from Lucan, 'And he that lies unburied, / With heavens high cope is coverèd' (*Pharsalia*, 7:819, Gorges). Germany is a 'churchyard' first in allusion to the (enforced) pieties of Gustavus's troops, and then as a burial ground.

36–7 Frederick V of the Palatinate, by accepting Bohemia's offer of the crown, sought to take the Empire from Ferdinand II.

38–9 Gustavus's hopes of the Empire were disappointed at Lützen.

43–4 Leave to the Germans fears about the rise and fall of the Emperor Ferdinand (regularly titled 'Caesar') or the alliance of Protestant Princes.

45–6 'Let us that sit as lovers (myrtle is Venus's plant) carefree ('secure') in the shade'.

48 *obdurate* as represented in Parliament: Charles dissolved his Third Parliament in March 1629.

53–4 The reference to *The Shepherd's Paradise* has caused difficulty; Townshend may have written a brief masquing accompaniment ('comprising' its beauties) to Walter Montagu's notoriously long comedy; or the allusion may be to his *Tempe Restored*.

59–82 Townshend's *Tempe Restored* is an allegory of desire turned to heroic virtue and divine beauty (the King and Queen); but it is so general a pattern for masque (given e.g. by Mercury's speech in Carew's own *Coelum Britannicum*, 37–93) that no specific reference may be intended.

59–63 Spenser describes how Jupiter 'leaving heaven's kingdom, here did rove / In strange disguise, to slake his scalding smart; / Now like a ram, fair Helle to pervert, / Now like a bull, Europa to withdraw' (*Faerie Queene*, 3.11.30); but the divinities of Townshend's masque descend as stars by which with virtue as a compass ('card') we might steer our rudderless ('steerless') lives in the sea of passion.

64 'Beg from above / A pattern of our love' (Donne, *The Canonization*, 44–5).

65–70 The veil of allegory is turned to masque costume, something like Spenser's 'veil of silk and silver thin / that his no whit her alabaster skin' (*Faerie Queene*, 2.12.77).

Through a mysterious fable (that was drawn
Like a transparent veil of purest lawn
Before their dazzling beauties) the divine
Venus, did with her heavenly Cupid shine.   70
The story's curious web, the masculine style,
The subtle sense, did Time and Sleep beguile;
Pinioned and charmed they stood to gaze upon
The angelic forms, gestures, and motion.
To hear those ravishing sounds that did dispense   75
Knowledge and pleasure, to the soul, and sense.
It filled us with amazement to behold
Love made all spirit, his corporeal mould
Dissected into atoms melt away
To empty air, and from the gross allay   80
Of mixtures, and compounding accidents
Refined to immaterial elements;
But when the Queene of Beauty did inspire
The air with perfumes, and our hearts with fire,
Breathing from her celestial organ sweet   85
Harmonious notes, our souls fell at her feet,
And did with humble reverend duty, more
Her rare perfections, than high state adore.
        These harmless pastimes let my Townshend sing
To rural tunes; not that thy Muse wants wing   90
To soar a loftier pitch, for she hath made
A noble flight, and placed th'heroic shade
Above the reach of our faint flagging rhyme;
But these are subjects proper to our clime.
Tourneys, masques, theatres, better become   95
Our halcyon days; what though the German drum
Bellow for freedom and revenge, the noise
Concerns not us, nor should divert our joys;
Nor ought the thunder of their carabins
Drown the sweet airs of our tuned violins;   100
Believe me friend, if their prevailing powers
Gain them a calm security like ours,
They'll hang their arms up on the olive bough,
And dance, and revel then, as we do now.

71–2 'The strange knottiness of the story, its energetic style, its difficult sense, abridged the time it took and kept us awake'; not a likely description of *Tempe Restored*.
73 'Time stopped and Sleep stayed back, magically frozen, their wings clipped.'
75–6 Varying the commendation of Donne, who did 'dispense / Through all our language both the words and sense' (*Elegy*, 9–20); the soul acquires knowledge, the sense pleasure.
78–82 By a process of alchemical rarefaction a quintessence is extracted from the mixture of elements in ordinary matter.

83–8 'I have been in Heaven, I think, / For I heard an angel sing, / Notes my thirsty ears did drink' (*On his Hearing her Majesty Sing*, 1–3); though Henrietta Maria did not use her 'celestial organ' ('heavenly throat') in *Tempe Restored*.
90 *rural* 'pastoral'.
99 *carabins* 'cavalry muskets'.
103 'His warlike arms, the idle instruments / Of sleeping praise, were hung upon a tree' (*Faerie Queene*, 2.12.80).

Owen Felltham (1602?–1668)

Felltham was born in Suffolk, in what year is not known (between 1602 and 1604). He visited the Low Countries before 1627, and consorted with London poets in the twenties and thirties (he contributed an elegy to Randolph's *Poems* in 1638). His royalism, mitigated in the poem on Buckingham given below, runs to the notoriously excessive conclusion to the *Epitaph* on the dead King: 'Here CHARLES the First, and CHRIST the Second lies.' He died at Great Billinglsey in Northamptonshire in the service of the Earls of Thomond. The first hundred brief essays of *Resolves Divine, Moral, Political* (1623) was published when Felltham was about 21 and written earlier; a further hundred were added for the second edition (1628). The number, order and content of the essays vary in the many subsequent editions (twelve by 1709);

the eighth edition (1661) also contains *A Brief Character of the Low Countries under the States* (first published 1652) along with some forty-one poems (some previously published in miscellanies, some previously circulated in MS) under the title *Lusoria*, some letters and other pieces. Randolph describes Felltham's prose style as 'pure, and strong, and round . . . Well-settled, full of nerves . . . That in a little hath comprisèd much'; these Senecan virtues survive in the verse. The only modern edition is by Ted-Larry Pebworth and Claude J. Summers: *The Poems of Owen Felltham 1604? 1668* (University Park, PA: SCN Editions and Studies, 1973); Pebworth also compiled 'An Annotated Bibliography of Owen Felltham', *Bulletin of the New York Public Library*, 79 (1976), 209–24.

On the Duke of Buckingham slain by Felton, the 23rd August 1628

1661, but current in MSS. George Villiers, Duke of Buckingham, was the last of James I's favourites and the first of Charles's: 'his ascent was so quick that it seemed rather a flight than a growth; and he was such a darling of fortune that he was at the top before he was seen at the bottom' (Clarendon, *History*, 1.70). Preparing for the relief of the besieged Huguenot fortress of La Rochelle, he was assassinated by John

Felton, a disappointed former army lieutenant: 'He spoke very frankly of what he had done, and bore the reproaches of those who spake to him with the temper of a man who thought he had not done amiss' (*History*, 1.61). F. W. Fairholt collected 'Poems and Songs Relating to George Villiers Duke of Buckingham' in *Early English Poetry* (Percy Society), 29 (1850).

> Sooner I may some fixèd statue be,
> Than prove forgetful of thy death or thee!
> Canst thou be gone so quickly? Can a knife
> Let out so many titles and a life?
> Now I'll mourn thee! O that so huge a pile   5
> Of state should pash thus in so small a while!
> Let the rude genius of the giddy train,
> Brag in a fury that they have stabbed Spain,
> Austria, and the skipping French: yea, all
> Those home-bred papists that would sell our fall: 10
> The eclipse of two wise Princes' judgements: more,
> The waste, whereby our land was still kept poor.
> I'll pity yet, at least thy fatal end,

3–4 'He chose no other instrument to do it with than an ordinary knife, which he bought of a common cutler for a shilling' (*History*, 1.53).

6 *pash* 'be dashed'.

7–10 'Let the popular voice proclaim this was in blow against Spain, Austria, France and the treacherous Catholics at home'; but Clarendon isolates 'two particulars, which lie heaviest

upon his memory': the war with Spain (*History*, 1.73–4) and the war with France (1.81).

11–12 Both James and Charles misjudged Buckingham, who misspent the Crown's revenues and encouraged court expenses 'so vast . . . that they had a sad prospect of that poverty and necessity which afterwards befell the Crown, almost to the ruin of it' (*History*, 1.18).

Shot like a lightning from a violent hand,
Taking thee hence unsummed. Thou art to me   15
The great example of mortality.
And when the times to come shall want a name
To startle greatness, here is Buckingham
Fall'n like a meteor: and 'tis hard to say
Whether it was that went the stranger way,   20
Thou or the hand that slew thee: thy estate
Was high, and he was resolute above that.
Yet since I hold of none engaged to thee,
Death and that liberty shall make me free.
Thy mists I knew not: if thou hadst a fault,   25
My charity shall leave it in the vault,
There for thine own accounting: 'tis undue
To speak ill of the dead though it be true.
And this even those that envied thee confess,
Thou hadst a mind, a flowing nobleness,   30
A fortune, friends, and such proportion,
As call for sorrow, to be thus undone.
 Yet should I speak the vulgar, I should boast
Thy bold assassinate, and wish almost
He were no Christian, that I up might stand,   35
To praise the intent of his misguided hand.
And sure when all the patriots in the shade
Shall rank, and their full musters there be made,
He shall sit next to Brutus, and receive
Such bays as heathenish ignorance can give.   40
But then the Christian (poising that) shall say,
Though he did good, he did it the wrong way.
They oft decline into the worst of ill,
That act the People's wish without Law's will.

15   *unsummed* 'half-fledged'.
23   'Since I am attached to nobody obliged to you'.
25   'I did not know you beyond what you seemed; if you
had faults, I leave them buried.'
27–8   A grudging admission, the proverbial 'Speak well of
the dead'.
33–4   'Were I to voice the common opinion, I should praise
your bold assassin.'

37–40   'Man may . . . Be both a Patriot and a Royalist' (*On
Thomas Lord Coventry*, 25–6); but it is not easy, and a place
next to Caesar's assassin in the underworld is a doubtful
honour.
44   That act the people's wish without their wills (some
MSS).

Upon a Rare Voice

1661. 'So did she sing / Like the harmonious spheres
that bring / Unto their Rounds their music's aid
(Lovelace, *Gratiana Singing and Dancing*, 19–21).

When I but hear her sing, I fare
Like one that raisèd holds his ear
To some bright star in the supremest round;
  Through which, besides the light that's seen,
  There may be heard, from Heaven within,   5
The rests of anthems, that the angels sound.

3   *supremest round* 'highest sphere' (of the fixed stars).   6   'The pauses in the hymns the angels sing': 'silence'.

To Phryne

1661. An execration, like Donne's *The Apparition*, but without second thoughts. In *Epodes*, 14, Horace laments his hopeless love for a promiscuous freed-woman Phryne; the name suggests 'harlot'.

When thou thy youth shalt view
Fumed out, and hate thy glass for telling true,
  When thy face shall be seen
Like to an Easter apple gathered green:
  When thy whole body shall   5
Be one foul wrinkle, lame and shrivelled all,
  So deep that men therein
May find a grave to bury shame and sin:
  When no clasped youth shall be
Pouring his bones into thy lap and thee: 10
  When thy own wanton fires
Shall leave to bubble up thy loose desires:
  Then wilt thou sighing lie,
Repent and smart, and so by two deaths die.

2 *fumed out* 'evaporated'.

4 Cowley describes a face looking 'like a winter apple / When 'tis shrunk up together and half-rotten' (*Love's Riddle*, 1.1); Phryne's face reverts to the sour unripeness of the crabapple.

10 *his bones* thy bones (*1661*); proleptically, as if she were literally a grave.

12 'Shall cease to heat the cauldron of your lust'.

14 *two deaths* of your beauty and your desire.

Thomas Randolph (1605–1635)

Thomas Randolph was born in 1605; he died in 1635 at Blatherwyke in Northamptonshire, where he was tutor to the children of William Stafford, the uncle of the Anthony to whom he addresses the poem below. He was reckoned precociously gifted: Aubrey says he wrote a poem on the Incarnation when he was 9, treasured by Thomas's brother. His career at Trinity College, Cambridge, with the gloss put on it by his life in London, was glamorous. The connection with Jonson, encouraged by his own verses addressed to Jonson (*An Answer* to his *Ode* on the failure of *The New Inn*, 'to persuade him not to leave the stage', an abjuration of poetry on his own account in *An Eclogue*, and a *Gratulatory* 'for adopting him to be his son') made for a view of him as Jonson's heir, which made the more poignant his precocious death, supposedly from alcoholic excess. His brother Robert's long commemorative poem celebrates the easiness of the verse: 'Though I can tell, a rugged sect there is, / Of some fly-wits will judge asquint on this; / And from the easy flux of language guesse / The fancy's weak, because the noise is less; / As if that channel which doth smoothly glide / With even streams, flowed with a shallow tide' (82–6). Oddly in view of his celebrity, there is no MS collection which attempted to bring Randolph's work together; and the profile in the MSS (which at most carry a score or so of poems) is of an author of short pieces and topical squibs. His earliest printed work in English (following a number of pieces in Latin) is the academic comedy *Aristippus* (1630); his literary bent was predominantly theatrical, and *The Muses' Looking Glass* (performed 1630) its fullest expression. The poems (both English and Latin) were first printed as a collection along with two plays: *Poems, with The Muses' Looking glass and Amyntas* edited by Randolph's brother Robert (1638, reprinted in 1640, 1643, 1652, 1662, and twice in 1668). *1640*, though in general less carefully printed than *1638*, carries corrections as well as additions. The only complete modern edition is by W. Carew Hazlitt, *Poetical and Dramatic Works* (1875). For the *Poems* there are editions by J. S. Parry (1917) and G. Thorn-Drury (1929). A few poems have subsequently been added to the canon. There is a *Bibliography* by S. A. and D. R. Tannenbaum, *Elizabethan Bibliographies* 6, with Supplement 3 by G. R. Guffey.

An Ode to Mr Anthony Stafford to hasten him into the Country

1640; *1638* differs slightly. Anthony Stafford (1587–1645), best known as a devotional writer, is addressed as a valued critic in the complimentary verses prefacing Randolph's *Jealous Lovers*; and it was in the house of his uncle William that Randolph died. The friendship was well enough known to supply a conceit in Robert Wild's allegorical comedy *The Benefice* (performed at Cambridge in 1641): 'Tom's dead and every Muse hath vowed to be, / For Stafford's sake, a *Stafford's Niobe*' (Stafford wrote *Stafford's Niobe*, 1611). The poem is as much an encouragement to himself as to Stafford, and as much a praise of poetry as of the country; but the themes of rural contentment from Horace's *Epode 2* (which, along with Claudian's *Old Man of Verona*, is quoted in Randolph's translation) are recast as Pindaric and enthused. Revett's homage in *Ode: Hastening his Friend into the Country* is frankly Anacreontic.

Come spur away,
I have no patience for a longer stay;
But must go down,
And leave the chargeable noise of this great town.
I will the country see,
Where old simplicity.
Though hid in gray,
Doth look more gay
Than foppery in plush and scarlet clad.

5

4 *chargeable* 'burdensome'.
7 'Where folk have always hidden their simple virtues under homespun (grey being its regular colour), and make a finer show than the fools dressed in velvet ('plush' was courtly, but also the typical livery of the stage clown) and scarlet (the cloth of judges)'.

Farewell you city wits that are   10
   Almost at civil war;
'Tis time that I grow wise, when all the world grows mad.

    More of my days
I will not spend to gain an idiot's praise;
   Or to make sport   15
For some slight puisne of the Inns of Court.
   Then worthy Stafford say
   How shall we spend the day,
    With what delights,
    Shorten the nights?   20
When from this tumult we are got secure;
   Where Mirth with all her freedom goes,
   Yet shall no finger lose;
Where every word is thought, and every thought is pure.

    There from the tree   25
We'll cherries pluck, and pick the strawberry;
   And every day
Go see the wholesome country girls make hay,
   Whose brown hath lovelier grace,
   Then any painted face,   30
    That I do know
    Hyde Park can show.
Where I had rather gain a kiss than meet
   (Though some of them in greater state
   Might court my love with plate)   35
The beauties of the Cheap, and wives of Lombard Street.

    But think upon
Some other pleasures, these to me are none;
   Why do I prate
Of women, that are things against my fate?   40
   I never mean to wed
   That torture to my bed;
    My Muse is she
    My love shall be.
Let clowns get wealth, and heirs; when I am gone,   45
   And the great bugbear, grisly death

10–11 'Men wise in the ways of the city (typically lawyers) are at each other's throats': 'He feared no merchants' storms, nor drums of war, / Nor ever knew the strifes of the hoarse bar' (Claudian, *Old Man of Verona*, 7–8); the resonance of 'civil war' is still dominantly Roman.
15–16 'Or to write for Law School freshmen ('puisnes')' – for the stage (whose patrons were often students).
21–3 'When we are safely out of this tumult to where we can merrily enjoy every licence and yet suffer no loss'; 'finger' by a standard metaphor signifies what is small and inconsiderable, but Randolph writes two epigrams on the loss of one of his own fingers.
29–32 So the duped Northerner in the ballad returns home swearing no more 'To deal with the plumes of a Hyde Park peacock, / But find out a russet coat wench, and a haycock' (*News from Hyde Park*, 94–5).
36 Hinting a confusion of bankers' wives (rich in disposable silver or 'plate') and whores in these two fashionable commercial areas of the City.
45–8 'Why out of ignorant love counsel you me / To leave the Muses and my poetry? / Which should I leave and never follow more, / I might perchance get riches and be poor' (*On the inestimable Content he enjoys in the Muses; to those of his Friends that dehort him from Poetry*, 179–82). Wealth and begetting sons to inherit it are signals of boorishness; the poet's best pieces of poetry (countering Jonson, *On my First Son*) are his poems.

Shall take this idle breath,
If I a poem leave, that poem is my son.

Of this no more;
We'll rather taste the bright Pomona's store.   50
No fruit shall 'scape
Our palates, from the damson, to the grape;
Then full we'll seek a shade,
And hear what music's made:
How Philomel   55
Her tale doth tell:
And how the other birds do fill the choir;
The thrush and blackbird lend their throats
Warbling melodious notes;
We will all sports enjoy, which others but desire.   60

Ours is the sky.
Whereat what fowl we please our hawk shall fly;
Nor will we spare
To hunt the crafty fox, or timorous hare,
But let our hounds run loose   65
In any ground they'll choose;
The buck shall fall,
The stag and all:
Our pleasures must from their own warrants be,
For to my Muse, if not to me,   70
I'm sure all game is free;
Heaven, Earth, are all but parts of her great royalty.

And when we mean
To taste of Bacchus' blessings now and then,
And drink by stealth   75
A cup or two to noble Berkeley's health,
I'll take my pipe and try
The Phrygian melody;
Which he that hears
Lets through his ears   80
A madness to distemper all the brain.
Then I another pipe will take
And Doric music make,
To civilize with graver notes our wits again.

50–2 'And when his fruits with Autumn ripened be, / Gathers his apples from the tree. / And joys to taste the pears himself did plant, / And grapes that naught of purple want' (Horace, *Epodes*, 2:17–20); 'Ruddy-cheeked Pomona' (Carew, *To his Friend G.N. from Wrest*, 94) is goddess of all fruits.

55–9 'And birds do chaunt with warbling throat' (*Epodes*, 2:26); *queruntur* is Horace's word, but Philomel ('the nightingale') 'tells her tale' (of rape by Tereus) only for the rhyme's sake.

61–4 'Or lays his nets . . . To catch the black-bird, or the thrush. / Sometimes the hare he courses' (*Epodes*, 2:33–6).

67–8 Horace's 'tusked swine' (*Epodes*, 2:31–2) are domesticated; 'buck' and 'stag' are distinguished as the males of the fallow and red deer.

69 'Our pleasures must of themselves be their justifications.'

72 *royalty* 'authority'.

74 *Bacchus' blessings* 'wine'.

76 *Berkeley* Stafford dedicated his *Guide of Honour* to George, Lord Berkeley (1601–58) in 1634; he is also the dedicatee of Burton's *Anatomy*.

78–84 The Phrygian mode in Greek music is vehement, the Doric grave.

William Habington (1605–1654)

William Habington was born on the eve of the Gunpowder Plot, for supposed involvement in which his father Thomas, a prominent Catholic, was sentenced to death but reprieved; he died in 1654. The poet's education was among English Catholics in France, first in the Jesuit School at St Omer and then probably at Clermont College in Paris; it was completed privately by his father, a well-known antiquary and historian of Worcestershire. By 1629 Habington had settled in London, involved with courtly poets, such as Davenant and Shirley, and with the court where, under the influence of Henrietta Maria, Catholicism was no embarrassment. In 1633 he married Lucy Herbert, daughter of Lord Powys, perhaps clandestinely. The wooing and marriage are celebrated in *Castara*: the First and Second Parts in 1634 (with a new and augmented edition in 1635), the Third Part in a third and again augmented edition in 1640. The three parts are prefaced by prose essays 'A Mistress',

'A Wife' (with a supplement of elegies on 'my best friend and kinsman' George Talbot, prefaced by 'A Friend'), 'A Holy Man'. The emphasis throughout is on an unfashionable (not merely 'Platonic') species of chastity: as Araphil, the poet worships at an altar of purity. The refinement of his diction and versification seems to have attracted Herrick. But after the three editions of the 1630s, Habington sinks from view, 'almost forgotten' says Edward Phillips in 1675. Only a few poems are found in MS collections. His tragi-comic *Queen of Arragon* (1640) was successfully revived in the 1660s and then forgotten again; he followed his father as a historian, but his historical works, *The History of Edward IV* and the collection of *Observations upon History* (both 1641), are likewise neglected. The obscurity of the rest of his life was little disturbed by the War. The standard edition is *The Poems*, edited by Kenneth Allott (Liverpool, 1948).

To Roses in the Bosom of Castara

1640 (Part 1). The theme at its simplest is represented in anonymous Greek epigram: 'Which is it? is the garland the rose of Dionysius, or is he the garland's rose? I think the garland is less lovely' (*Greek Anthology*, 5.142). But the poem turns on the notion of the heart as a refuge. Daniel's heart is slain by the rigour of the sanctuary he sought in the 'sacred refuge' of Delia's breast (*Delia*, 31); here the 'nunnery' of the breast (a conceit briefly imitated, as by Lovelace in *To Lucasta, Going to the Wars*, by Herrick in *Upon Roses*), turns into a tomb.

> Ye blushing virgins happy are
> In the chaste nunnery of her breasts,
> For he'd profane so chaste a fair,
> Whoe'er should call them Cupid's nests.
>
> Transplanted thus how bright ye grow,   5
> How rich a perfume do ye yield!
> In some close garden, cowslips so
> Are sweeter than in the open field.
>
> In those white cloisters live secure
> From the rude blasts of wanton breath,   10
> Each hour more innocent and pure,
> Till you shall wither into death.

---

4 'The lovely clusters of her breasts, / Of Venus' babe the wanton nests' (Sidney, *Arcadia*, 2.11, Pyrochles's Song, 53–4.

5–6 'Let scent and looks be sweet and bless that hand, /

That did transplant thee to that sacred land' (Carew, *On a Damask Rose sticking upon a Lady's Breast*, 3–4).

7 *close* 'enclosed' (a walled garden).

10 *breath* for 'wind', but also his own.

Then that which living gave you room,
Your glorious sepulchre shall be.
There wants no marble for a tomb,   15
Whose breast hath marble been to me.

15–16 Herrick addresses roses under a lawn scarf: 'Die when you will, your sepulchre is known, / Your grave her bosom is, the lawn the stone' (*Upon the Roses in Julia's Bosom*, 1–2); here, by a turn less ornamental, Castara's bosom is white while her heart is hard.

Upon Castara's Departure

1640 (Part 1). Nature mourns the absence of the beloved. Browne exhibits the mechanism of the allegory: 'So shuts the marigold her leaves / At the departure of the sun; / And from the honeysuckle sheaves / The bee goes when the day is done . . . So is all woe; as I, now she is gone' (*Celia is Gone*, 7–12).

Vows are vain. No suppliant breath
Stays the speed of swift-heeled death.
Life with her is gone and I
Learn but a new way to die.
See the flowers condole, and all   5
Wither in my funeral.
The bright lily, as if day
Parted with her, fades away.
Violets hang their heads, and lose
All their beauty. That the rose   10
A sad part in sorrow bears,
Witness all those dewy tears,
Which as pearl, or diamond-like,
Swell upon her blushing cheek.
All things mourn, but O behold   15
How the withered marigold
Closeth up now she is gone,
Judging her the setting sun.

2 *swift-heeled* an echo of Greek.   **6** *funeral* 'death'.

To my worthy Cousin Mr. E. C. In Praise of the City Life, in the Long Vacation

1640 (Part 2). The addressee may be Edward Cranfield, who married Habington's cousin Catherine Parker. The poem promotes those advantages of city life (with an amount of playfully gratuitous detail) identical with those of country life. The epistle *To my noblest Friend, I.C. Esquire* states the terms: 'I hate the country's dirt and manners, yet / I love its silence; I embrace the wit / And courtship, flowing here in a full tide. / But loathe the expense, the vanity and pride' (1–4). François Boisrobert's *L'hiver de Paris* outlines similar benefits.

I like the green plush which your meadows wear,
I praise your pregnant fields, which duly bear
Their wealthy burden to the industrious boor.

1 *plush* is specified because the most citified of fabrics; Quarles's summer meadows also wear 'green plush' (*Emblems* 3.13:21).

3 'Their golden harvest to the industrious farmer'.

Nor do I disallow that who are poor
In mind and fortune, thither should retire: 5
But hate that he who's warm with holy fire
Of any knowledge, and 'mong us may feast
On nectared wit, should turn himself to a beast,
And graze in th' country. Why did nature wrong
So much her pains, as to give you a tongue 10
And fluent language; if converse you hold
With oxen in the stall, and sheep in th' fold?
But now it's long vacation you will say
The town is empty, and who ever may
To th' pleasure of his country home repair, 15
Flies from the infection of our London air.
In this your error. Now's the time alone
To live here; when the city-dame is gone,
T' her house at Brentford; for beyond that she
Imagines there's no land, but Barbary, 20
Where lies her husband's factor. When from hence
Rid is the country Justice whose nonsense
Corrupted had the language of the inn,
Where he and his horse littered: we begin
To live in silence, when the noise of th' Bench 25
Not deafens Westminster, nor corrupt French
Walks Fleet Street in her gown. Ruffs of the Bar,
By the vacation's power translated are,
To cut-work bands. And who were busy here,
Are gone to sow sedition in the shire. 30
The air by this is purged, and the term's strife,
Thus fled the city: we the civil life
Lead happily. When in the gentle way,
Of noble mirth, I have the long-lived day,
Contracted to a moment: I retire 35
To my Castara, and meet such a fire
Of mutual love: that if the city were
Infected, that would purify the air.

18–21 The geography of this good *bourgeoise* is limited to a summer house up the Thames, and the Barbary Coast in North Africa where her merchant husband has an agent.
23 *inn* 'lodging'; but an Inns of Court reference is assumed until it emerges the judge bedded there ('littered', jocularly).
25–7 Trials of the Courts of Chancery, Common Pleas and the King's Bench were held in Westminster Hall; Fleet Street, near the Inns of Court and criminal courts of the Old Bailey, filled in term-time with gowned lawyers mouthing Norman-French jargon.
27–9 Overbury's 'mere common lawyer' wears a distinctive collar: 'His laundress is shrewdly troubled in fitting him a ruff: his perpetual badge' (*Characters*); but the pleated ruff gives way in the vacation to fashionable 'cut-work' bands:

'He is not a gentleman, nor in the fashion, whose band of Italian cut-work now standeth him not at the least in three or four pounds. Yea, a seamster in Holborn told me that there are of threescore pound price apiece' (Peacham, *Truth of our Times*).
30 'I cannot but with grief and wonder remember the virulency and animosity expressed on all occasions from many of good knowledge in the excellent and wise profession of the common law, towards the Church and churchmen' (Clarendon, *History*, 4.38); increasing anti-Church agitation in the country at large was often blamed on clerical 'lecturers' (Clarendon, *History*, 6.39).
38 *infected* with plague: minor outbreaks occurred regularly.

Against them who lay Unchastity to the Sex of Women

1640 (Part 2). A reply to Donne's *Go, and catch a falling star* ('Ride ten thousand days and nights, / Till age snow white hairs on thee, / Thou, when thou return'st, wilt tell me / All strange wonders that befell thee, / And swear / Nowhere / Lives a woman true, and fair'); but Donne's impossible things are turned into improbabilities, rarities and delusions.

They meet but with unwholesome springs,
And summers which infectious are:
They hear but when the mermaid sings,
And only see the falling star:
    Who ever dare,   5
Affirm no woman chaste and fair.

Go cure your fevers: and you'll say
The dog-days scorch not all the year:
In copper-mines no longer stay,
But travel to the west, and there   10
    The right ones see:
And grant all gold's not alchemy.

What madman 'cause the glow-worm's flame
Is cold, swears there's no warmth in fire?
'Cause some make forfeit of their name,
And slave themselves to man's desire;   15
    Shall the sex free
From guilt, damned to the bondage be?

Nor grieve Castara, though 'twere frail,
Thy virtue then would brighter shine,
When thy example should prevail,   20
And every woman's faith be thine,
    And were there none;
'Tis majesty to rule alone.

2 *infectious* summer being the time of plague.

3–4 'Go, and catch a falling star ... Teach me to hear mermaids singing' (1–5).

8 'Cure what is amiss with yourself and you'll admit it is not summer heat (the 'dog-days' of July and August) that brings on your fever; leave the mines of baser metal and travel west to where true gold is found'; America is the land of gold, Lucy Herbert belongs to Worcestershire.

12 Compared to Donne and his mistress in bed, 'All honour's mimic; all wealth alchemy' (*The Sun Rising*, 12).

17–18 'Shall innocent women be constrained by the reputation of those who prostitute themselves to male desire?'

Edmund Waller (1606–1687)

'When he was a brisk young spark, and first studied poetry; methought, said he, I never saw a good copy of English verses; they want smoothness; then I began to essay' (Aubrey). 'Our language owes more to him than the French does to Cardinal Richelieu and the whole academy . . . Suckling and Carew . . . wrote some few things smoothly enough: but . . . he undoubtedly stands first in the list of refiners . . . He sought out, in this flowing tongue of ours, what parts would stand, and be of lasting use, and ornament: and he did this so successfully, that his language is now as fresh as it was at first setting out. Were we to judge barely by the wording, we could not know what was wrote at twenty, and what at fourscore . . . Before his time, men rhymed indeed, and that was all: as for the harmony of measure, and that dance of words, which good ears are so much pleased with, they knew nothing of it. Their poetry then was made up almost entirely of monosyllables; which when they come together in any cluster, are certainly the most harsh untunable things in the world. If any man doubts of this, let him read ten lines of Donne . . . There was no distinction of parts, no regular stops, nothing for the ear to rest upon . . . Mr Waller removed all these faults; brought in more polysyllables, and smoother measures; bound up his thoughts better; and in a cadence more agreeable to the nature of the verse he wrote in: so that wherever the natural stops of that were, he contrived the little breakings of his sense so as to fall in with them. And for that reason, since the stress of our verse lies commonly upon the last syllable, you'll hardly ever find him using a word of no force there . . . He commonly closes with verbs; in which we know the life of language consists' (preface to the *Second Part of Mr Waller's Poems*, 1690). So Francis Atterbury reminded readers late in the century what the reformation of English poetry had been about. Johnson notes that his excellence has 'some abatements', that 'he uses the expletive *do* very frequently', that 'his rhymes are sometimes weak words: so is found to make the rhyme twice in ten lines', that Kathleen Philips had already censured his use of double rhymes, that he 'uses the obsolete termination of verbs, as waxeth, affecteth; and sometimes retains the final syllable of the preterite, as *amazèd, supposèd*'.

Waller's first printed poem is a pair of Latin couplets *To the King on his Return*, one of a University collection welcoming King Charles back from Scotland (*Rex Redux*, Cambridge, 1633). By this time he had long left King's College (where he had gone from Eton) without a degree, had served in four Parliaments (he was 'nursed in Parliaments, where he sat in his infancy', Clarendon, *Life*), and eloped with a wealthy heiress (she died in 1634). Then, 'at an age when other men used to give over writing verses . . . he surprised the town with two or three pieces of that kind; as if a tenth Muse had been newly born, to cherish drooping poetry' (Clarendon). This should not suggest fluency: MS evidence suggests he worked by piecing together trial efforts. Apparently charming and certainly very wealthy, he was welcome in the company of Lord Falkland's Great Tew, and the Sidneys' Penshurst (but he never knew Ben Jonson). His political reputation (though he served regularly in Parliaments after the Restoration) never recovered from his part in 'Waller's Plot', a failed attempt to secure London for the King, in which he betrayed his fellow-conspirators. He lived in exile with his second wife until 1652, when his mother persuaded Cromwell to grant a pardon. 'When King Charles returned, he received Mr Waller very kindly, and no man's conversation is more esteemed now at court than his' (Aubrey). He was from 1661 a member of the Royal Society. From 1667, when his second wife died, he lived increasingly in retirement. A general biography is in Thorn-Drury's edition; Wallace L. Chernaik, *The Poetry of Limitation: A Study of Edmund Waller* (New Haven: Yale University Press, 1968) supplies detail on Waller's politics.

Atterbury's justification for publishing the 1690 edition was the abundance of manuscripts abroad of Waller's poetry and his fear of corruption of the text. A number of MS collections had been current from the beginning: the first printed edition of 1645, by Thomas Walleeley, is pirated ('an adulterate copy, surreptitiously and illegally imprinted, to the derogation of the author, and the abuse of the buyer'). The three subsequent editions that same year (all by Humphrey Moseley) attempted to stabilize the text. So the edition of 1664 in which, despite Waller's misgivings, it is disingenuously claimed that 'the poems which have been so long, and so ill, set forth under his name, are here to be found as he first writ them'. By 1694 there were seven editions of this basic collection. *Divine Poems* belongs to1685; the *Second Part of Mr Waller's Poems* to 1690. Elijah Fenton's *Works in Verse and Prose* (1729) attempts a canonical collection, and includes his *Observations on Some of Mr Waller's Poems*. There is a facsimile edition of a composite second and third edition of the *Poems* and three *Parliamentary Speeches with Poems from a Bodleian MS* (Menston: Scolar Press, 1971). Though the canon is larger than he allowed, the best available edition is *The Poems*, by G. Thorn-Drury for the Muses' Library (1893). Work on Waller is described by David Judkins in *English Literary Renaissance*, 7 (1977), 252–5.

Upon his Majesty's Repairing of Paul's

1645 (Moseley). The volume opens with a sequence of royalist compliments. Later editions add to this poem a postscript from Horace (*Ars Poetica*: 404–5), 'The grace of kings / Attempted by the Muses' tunes and strings' (Jonson), ruefully added if it were ever a bid for patronage. It quickly achieved classic status, a poem 'whose flight / Has bravely reached and soared' above even Denham's height (*Cooper's Hill*, 19–20). St Paul's Cathedral was critically ruinous in King James's time, but restoration was not begun until 1632; here the repair becomes an emblem of the successes of Charles's personal rule. Wenzel Hollar's engraving shows Inigo Jones's reconstructed St Paul's, baroque scrolls and obelisks and a Corinthian portico covering over the Gothic fabric. Wren's St Paul's was built after the Great Fire of 1666 had destroyed the 'improved' original.

> That shipwrecked vessel which the Apostle bore
> Scarce suffered more upon Melita's shore,
> Than did his temple in the sea of time
> (Our nation's glory, and our nation's crime).
> When the first monarch of this happy isle   5
> Moved with the ruin of so brave a pile,
> This work of cost and piety begun
> To be accomplished by his glorious son;
> Who all that came within the ample thought
> Of his wise sire has to perfection brought.   10
> He, like Amphion, makes those quarries leap
> Into fair figures from a confused heap:
> For in his art of regiments is found
> A power like that of harmony in sound.
>   Those antique minstrels sure were Charles-like kings, 15
> Cities their lutes, and subjects' hearts their strings;
> On which with so divine a hand they struck,
> Consent of motion from their breath they took.
> So all our minds with his conspire to grace
> The Gentiles' great Apostle, and deface   20
> Those state-obscuring sheds, that like a chain
> Seemed to confine and fetter him again;
> Which the glad Saint shakes off at his command,
> As once the viper from his sacred hand:
> So joys the agèd oak when we divide   25
> The creeping ivy from his injured side.
>   Ambition rather would affect the fame
> Of some new structure, to have borne her name.
> Two distant virtues in one act we find,
> The modesty and greatness of his mind;   30

1–2 Paul's voyage to Rome and shipwreck on Malta are described in Acts 27.
5 King James initiated repair of the damaged church in the 1620s, and Charles ('his glorious son') completed it.
11 Being taught by Mercury (being eloquent), 'Deaf stones by the ears Amphion drew' (Horace, *Odes*, 3.11:1–2) to build Thebes.
13–18 'Just as in the music of harps and flutes or singers, harmony of the different notes must be preserved . . . so is a community harmonized by agreement among different elements, brought about by harmonizing the interests of those of high and low and middle station' (Cicero, *On the Republic*,

2.42.69); *regiment* 'government'.
20 Paul 'is a chosen vessel unto me, to bear my name before the Gentiles' (Acts 9: 15).
21–2 The houses built against the cathedral wall were removed in 1632.
23–4 'And when Paul had gathered a bundle of sticks, and laid them on the fire, there came a viper out of the heat, and fastened on his hand . . . And he shook off the beast into the fire, and felt no harm' (Acts 28: 3–5).
25–6 Ivy and oak are usually mutually supportive; but Ovid parallels them with the eagle and the snake (*Metamorphoses*, 4:365).

Which not content to be above the rage
And injury of all-impairing age,
In its own worth secure, doth higher climb,
And things half swallowed from the jaws of Time
Reduce, an earnest of his grand design,   35
To frame no new church, but the old refine:
Which, spouse-like may with comely grace command
More than by force of argument or hand.
For doubtful reason few can apprehend,
And war brings ruin, where it should amend: 40
But beauty with a bloodless conquest finds
A welcome sovereignty in rudest minds.
    Not aught which Sheba's wondering queen beheld
Amongst the works of Solomon, excelled
His ships and building, emblems of a heart   45
Large both in magnanimity and art:
While the propitious Heavens this work attend,
Long-wanted showers they forget to send;
As if they meant to make it understood
Of more importance than our vital food.   50
    The sun, which riseth to salute the choir
Already finished, setting shall admire
How private bounty could so far extend;
The King built all, but Charles the western end:
So proud a fabric to devotion given,   55
At once it threatens and obliges Heaven.
    Laomedon that had the gods in pay,
Neptune, with him that rules the sacred day,
Could no such structure raise, Troy walled so high,
The Atrides might as well have forced the sky.   60
    Glad, though amazèd, are our neighbour kings
To see such power employed in peaceful things.
They list not urge it to the dreadful field,
The task is easier to destroy, than build.

35   *reduce* 'bring back' (still standard).

42–4   'And when the queen of Sheba had seen all Solomon's wisdom, and the house that he had built . . . and his ascent by which he went up unto the house . . . there was no more spirit in her' (1 Kings 10: 4–5); his fame seems to have come to her from his 'navy of ships' (9: 26).

51   The sun, rising over the choir at the east end of the church, marvels as it sets in the west at Inigo Jones's portico, financed by Charles (but from ecclesiastical fines); it threatens heaven with obelisks set on either side of the western gable, it obliges Heaven because built as an act of piety.

57–60   Apollo (the sun 'that rules the sacred day') 'saw the King [Laomedon] begin to rear / New Troy's scarce founded walls; with what ado, / And with how great a charge they slowly grew. / Who, with the father of the swelling main [Neptune], / Indues a mortal shape: both entertain / Themselves for unregarded gold to build / The Phrygian tyrant's walls' (Ovid, *Metamorphoses*, 11:199–204, Sandys). Had Troy equalled St Paul's, the Greek brothers Agamemnon and Menelaus ('the Atrides') could not have taken it.

63   'They dare not provoke such power to war.'

At Penshurst

1645 (Moseley). Dorothy Sidney (eldest of Robert Sidney's children, the granddaughter of Jonson's patron, married in 1639 aged 21) is celebrated in later versions of Waller's erotic poems as Sacharissa. The Penshurst estate is an echo-chamber for her attractions: the 'pastoral hyperbole' (whereby things flourish in the beloved's presence) goes back to Theocritus, but enjoyed an energetic revival in the seventeenth century.

Had Dorothea lived when mortals made
Choice of their deities, this sacred shade
Had held an altar to her power that gave
The peace and glory, which these alleys have
Embroidered so with flowers where she stood,   5
That it became a garden of the wood:
Her presence has such more than human grace
That it can civilize the rudest place,
And beauty too, and order can impart
Where nature ne'er intended it, nor art.   10
The plants acknowledge this, and her admire
No less than those of old did Orpheus' lyre:
If she sit down, with tops all towards her bowed,
They round about her into arbours crowd:
Or if she walk, in even ranks they stand   15
Like some well-marshalled and obsequious band.
Amphion so made stones and timber leap
Into fair figures from a cónfused heap:
And in the symmetry of her parts is found
A power like that of harmony in sound: 20
   Ye lofty beeches, tell this matchless dame
That if together ye fed all one flame,
It could not equalize the hundredth part
Of what her eyes have kindled in my heart.
Go boy and carve this passion on the bark   25
Of yonder tree, which stands the sacred mark
Of noble Sidney's birth; when such benign,
Such more than mortal-making stars did shine;
That there they cannot but for ever prove
The monument and pledge of humble love: 30
His humble love whose hope shall ne'er rise higher,
Than for a pardon that he dares admire.

12–20 'A Hill there was ... Which in a flowery mantle flourished still:/ Yet wanted shade. Which, when the gods' descent [Orpheus] / Sat down, and touched his well-tuned instrument, / A shade received. Nor ... poplar, various oaks ... Soft linden, smooth-rind beech ... were absent' (Ovid, *Metamorphoses*, 10:86–92, Sandys). Being taught by Mercury (being eloquent), 'Deaf stones by the ears Amphion drew' (Horace, *Odes*, 3.11:1–2) to build Thebes. Line 20 is repeated from *Upon his Majesty's Repairing of Paul's*, 14. 21–8 The beeches, the inscribed trees and the commemorative oak for Sidney are from Jonson, *To Penhurst*, 12–16. 31–2 'The humble love of him who hopes for no more than that he be forgiven for admiring you'.

To my Young Lady Lucy Sidney

1645 (Moseley). One in a run of poems about Penshurst and the Sidneys: Lucy, sister of Dorothy (Sacharissa), was born in 1615 and at the time of the poem's writing a budding beauty (like Marvell's little T. C., and many others). Horace *Odes*, 2.5 combines the promise of mature sexuality with that of the season's fulfilment. Later editions title the poem *To a very Young Lady*, conceding the irrelevance of the immediate subject suggested in its quasi-allegorical vocabulary.

Why came I so untimely forth
Into a world which wanting thee
Could entertain us with no worth

Or shadow of felicity?
    That time should me so far remove   5
    From that which I was born to love?

Yet fairest blossom do not slight
That age which you may know so soon;
The rosy morn resigns her light,
And milder glory to the noon: 10
    And then what wonders shall you do,
    Whose dawning beauty warms us so?

Hope waits upon the flowery prime,
And summer, though it be less gay,
Yet is not looked on as a time   15
Of declination or decay.
    For with a full hand that does bring
    All that was promised by the spring.

4 Carew says that 'fortune, honour . . . long life, / Children, or friends . . . a good wife . . . he / But shadows of felicity'; and that true happiness is 'a wench about thirteen, / Already voted to the Queen / Of lust and lovers' (*Second Rapture*, 3–9).
5 'Why is it that time should have moved me back so far?'
9–12 'My eyes dare gladly play / With such a rosy morn: whose beams both fresh and gay / Scorch not . . . But lo, while I do speak it groweth noon with me, / Her flamy

glittering lights increase with time and place . . . No wind, no shade, no cool: what help then in my case?' (Sidney, *Astrophil*, 76.6–12). Waller's 14-year-old Henrietta Maria is 'Like bright Aurora, whose refulgent ray / Foretells the fervour of ensuing day' (*Of the Danger his Majesty Escaped*, 121–2). *1645* misprints 'Moon' for 'moon'.
13–18 'Spring is the growing time promising the harvest to be, the other seasons are for cropping and gathering in the fruits' (Cicero, *De Senectute*, 19.70).

The Self-banished

1645 (Moseley); a transcription of Atterbury's notes from Waller's MS in a British Library copy of *Poems* (1686) gives the variants recorded. 'Travelling is an antidote of love. For this purpose, saith Propertius (3.21), my parents sent me to Athens; time and ab-

sence wear away pain and grief, as fire goes out without fuel: "As far as eye can see, so far the soul can love"' (Burton, *Anatomy*, 3.2.5.2). The lover ('servant') threatens to banish himself; but he gambles in the last stanza on the lady's concern that he love her.

It is not that I love you less,
Than when before your feet I lay:
But to prevent the sad increase
Of hopeless love, I keep away.

In vain (alas) for everything   5
Which I have known belong to you,
Your form does to my fancy bring,
And makes my old wounds bleed anew.

3–4 Since I must without redress / Love on, I choose to keep away (MS).
5–7 In vain! your heavenly form I find / Where're I am, whate'er I do, / Is present to my love-sick mind (MS); 'your form' is 'the idea (or even the memory) of you'.

8 The MS gives an additional stanza: Anew they bleed, and rage the more, / The more I strive their smart to cure. / Double to what I felt before, / From love and absence I endure.

Who in the spring, from the new sun,
Already has a fever got: 10
Too late begins those shafts to shun,
Which Phoebus through his veins has shot.

Too late he would the pain assuage,
And to thick shadows does retire;
About with him he bears the rage,   15
And in his tainted blood the fire.

But vowed I have, and never must
Your banished servant trouble you;
For if I break, you may mistrust
The vow I made to love you too.   20

9   *Who in* Whom (*1645*).
14   And does to streams and shades retire (MS).
17–19   But the vow's made and never must / Your ban-
ished servant trouble you: / Since if I break it you'll mis-
trust (MS).

Song

1645 (Moseley); a transcription of Atterbury's notes from Waller's MS in a British Library copy of *Poems* (1686) gives the variants recorded. Rufinus's epigram on fading beauty is behind it: 'I send you this garland ... woven from flowers with my own hands, lilies and roses and dewy anemones, and tender narcissus and purple-gleaming violets. Wear it and give over vanity: you and the garland both flower and fade' (*Greek Anthology*, 5.74).

Go lovely rose,
Tell her that wastes her time and me,
That now she knows
When I resemble her to thee
How sweet and fair she seems to be.   5

Tell her that's young,
And shuns to have her graces spied,
That hadst thou sprung
In deserts, where no men abide,
Thou must have uncommended died.   10

Small is the worth
Of beauty from the light retired;
Bid her come forth,
Suffer herself to be desired,

2–5   Tell her, who looks and breathes like thee, / That nothing blows, / On earth, so sweet and fair as she / Though wondrous sweet and fair thou be (MS). She wastes her time by not seizing the day; she wastes the poet by leaving him unfulfilled.
6–10   Tell her that's young / And spurns to have her graces shown / That hadst thou sprung / In deserts there thou still hadst grown / Unseen and unobserved alone [the final couplet corrected to] In lonely deserts all thy pride / Unsung and unobserved had died (MS).
9   'In wastelands where no men remain': what was once fertile is now waste.

11–12   Tell her the worth / Of beauty lessens when retired (MS).
11–16   'But beauty's waste [expense] hath in the world an end, / And kept unused the user so destroys it' (Shakespeare, *Sonnets*, 9.11–12); 'What greater torment could have been / Than to enforce the fair to live retired? / For what is beauty if it be not seen?' (Daniel, *Complaint of Rosamond*, 513–15); but Propertius claims (in an argument against artifice) 'lovelier the arbutus growing in desert caverns' (1.2.11).

And not blush so to be admired.

15

Then die that she,
The common fate of all things rare,
   May read in thee
How small a part of time they share,
   That are so wondrous sweet and fair.

20

On a Girdle

1645 (Moseley); not in Walkeley. A transcription of Atterbury's notes from Waller's MS in a British Library copy of *Poems* (1686) gives the MS variant recorded. The poet crowns himself with an emblem of his conquest; Browne's epigram on a girdle, 'This during light I give to clip your waist, / Fair, grant mine arms that place when day is past' (*Britannia's Pastorals*, 1.3:481–2), offers it as a signal of his hope.

That which her slender waist confined,
Shall now my joyful temples bind;
No monarch but would give his crown
His arms might do what this has done.

It was my Heaven's extremest sphere,   5
The pale which held that lovely deer,
My joy, my grief, my hope, my love,
Did all within this circle move.

A narrow compass, and yet there
Dwells all that's good, and all that's fair;   10
Give me but what this ribbon tied,
Take all the sun goes round beside.

4 'If he might conquer (by 'arms') such territory'; 'If he might embrace (with his 'arms') her waist'.
5 'She was my empyrean' ('my source of bliss').
6–7 My joy, my grief, my hope, my fear, / The stars that guide the course of love (MS).
6 Shakespeare *Venus and Adonis*, 230–1, where Venus speaks of holding Adonis in her arms: 'Within the circuit of this ivory pale, / I'll be a park, and thou shalt be my deer'.
10–12 Dwelt all that's good, and all that fair; / Give me but what this ribbon bound, / Take all the rest the sun goes round (editions from *1664*).

A Panegyric to my Lord Protector

1655 Folio; in the same year appeared a probably pirated Quarto, *A panegyric to my Lord Protector of the Present Greatness, and Joint Interest, of His Highness and this Nation*, a title that presses the poem's point. Except as part of Richard Watson's *The panegyric and The storm . . . answered*, it was not reprinted (according to Aubrey, at Waller's own insistence) until 1690, then as *A panegyric upon Oliver Cromwell* in Bennet's edition, as *Poem upon the Death of Oliver Cromwell* in Tonson's (with minor and probably unauthorized stylistic corrections). The poem may have circulated in MS soon after the Protectorate was established in December 1653. There is no specific occasion; Waller addresses Cromwell's 'monarchical' solution to the problem of 'settling' the state, but its views are difficult to read. Like Claudian, who supplies the epigraph to the 1655 Folio (*De Consolatu Stilichonis*, 3, Pref. 5–6: 'Virtue rejoices to call verse to witness; heroes love song for they achieve what is worthy of song'), Waller fell under suspicion of moral duplicity: Charles Cotton called the poem 'vicious', a monument to malice and duplicity (*To Poet E. W.*). At least two extended 'answers' to it survive. The Royalist Richard Watson in *The Panegyric. . . Answered* (Bruges, 1659) sets six lines against each quatrain of the Quarto version; the Republican Lucy Hutchinson's forty-seven quatrains 'whilst with a smooth and yet a servile tongue' are published in David Norbrook, 'Lucy Hutchinson versus Edmund Waller: An Unpublished Reply to Waller's *A Panegyrick to my Lord Protector*', *The Seventeenth Century*, 11 (1996), 61–86. Its heroic commonplaces (sometimes shared with those of Denham's *Cooper's Hill*) are elsewhere appropriated or parodied. The appropriations included Waller's own in *Upon his Majesty's Happy Return*, offered to Charles II at the Restoration, and for whose generally acknowledged inferiority he famously apologized to the King by saying, 'Poets, Sir, succeed better in

fiction than in truth.' 'Such a series of verses had rarely appeared before in the English Language,' wrote Dr Johnson, 'its great fault is the choice of its hero.' The Quarto and most later editions print the poem in quatrains; Waller's couplets have a tendency to pair off as stanzas.

> While with a strong, and yet a gentle hand,
> You bridle faction, and our hearts command,
> Protect us from ourselves, and from the foe;
> Make us unite, and make us conquer too;
> Let partial spirits still aloud complain,   5
> Think themselves injured that they cannot reign,
> And own no liberty but where they may
> Without control upon their fellows prey.
> Above the waves as Neptune showed his face,
> To chide the winds, and save the Trojan race;   10
> So has your Highness raised above the rest,
> Storms of ambition tossing us repressed:
>   Your drooping country torn with civil hate,
> Restored by you, is made a glorious state;
> The seat of empire, where the Irish come,   15
> And the unwilling Scotch, to fetch their doom.
> The sea's our own; and now all nations greet,
> With bending sails each vessel of our fleet;
> Your power extends as far as winds can blow,
> Or swelling sails upon the globe may go.   20
>   Heaven, that has placed this island to give law,
> To balance Europe, and her states to awe,
> In this conjunction does on Britain smile,
> The greatest leader, and the greatest isle;
> Whether this portion of the world were rent,   25
> By the rude ocean, from the continent,
> Or thus created, it was sure designed
> To be the sacred refuge of mankind.
> Hither the oppressèd shall henceforth resort,
> Justice to crave, and succour at your court;   30
> And then your Highness, not for ours alone,
> But for the world's Protector shall be known:
> Fame, swifter than your wingèd navy, flies

1–12 'The . . . design of men . . . in the introduction of that restraint upon themselves, in which we see them live in Commonwealths, is the foresight of their own preservation . . . of getting themselves out from that miserable condition of war which is necessarily consequent . . . to the natural passions of men when there is no visible power to keep them in awe' (Hobbes, *Leviathan*, 2.17.1). The Long Parliament, here represented as a centre of discontent, was dissolved in April 1653; the Instrument of Government (December 1653) which established the Protectorate allowed Cromwell quasi-imperial powers. The first Anglo-Dutch War was concluded to British advantage in April 1654.

9–12 Neptune intervened to save Aeneas and the Trojans threatened by storm, 'smoothed the sea, / Dispelled the darkness, and restored the day . . . As, when in tumults rise

the ignoble crowd . . . If then some grave and pious man appear, / They hush their noise' (Virgil, *Aeneid*, 1:142–3, Dryden).

16 *fetch their doom* 'obtain their law'. In April 1654 Ireland and Scotland were united with England.

22 *balance* The 'Balance of Power', long a feature of English foreign policy, here concerns France and Spain (an Anglo-French treaty was concluded in late 1655).

23 *conjunction* of Cromwell and Britain: 'where the public and private interest are most closely united [in monarchy], there is the public most advanced' (Hobbes, *Leviathan*, 2.19.4); but there is an astrological resonance.

25–6 The British are 'A race of men from all the world disjoined' (Virgil, *Eclogues*, 1:66, Dryden).

28 Jews were readmitted to Britain in late 1655.

Through every land that near the ocean lies,
Sounding your name, and telling dreadful news   35
To all that piracy and rapine use.
With such a chief the meanest nation blessed,
Might hope to lift her head above the rest;
What may be thought impossible to do
For us embracèd by the sea and you?   40
    Lords of the world's great waste, the ocean, we
Whole forests send to reign upon the sea,
And every coast may trouble, or relieve,
But none can visit us without your leave;
Angels and we have this prerogative,   45
That none can at our happy seat arrive,
While we descend at pleasure to invade
The bad with vengeance, and the good to aid:
Our little world, the image of the great,
Like that amidst the boundless ocean set,   50
Of her own growth has all that Nature craves,
And all that's rare, as tribute from the waves;
As Egypt does not on the clouds rely,
But to her Nile owes more than to the sky,
So what our earth, and what our heaven denies,   55
Our ever constant friend, the sea, supplies;
The taste of hot Arabia's spice we know,
Free from the scorching sun that makes it grow;
Without the worm in Persian silks we shine,
And without planting drink of every vine;   60
    To dig for wealth we weary not our limbs;
Gold, though the heaviest metal, hither swims;
Ours is the harvest where the Indians mow;
We plough the deep, and reap what others sow.
Things of the noblest kind our own soil breeds,   65
Stout are our men, and warlike are our steeds;
Rome, though her eagle through the world had flown,
Could never make this island all her own;
Here the Third Edward, and the Black Prince too,
France-conquering Henry flourished, and now you   70
For whom we stayed, as did the Grecian state,

---

36   The Barbary pirates were defeated in April 1655.

39–40   'Those [the navy's] towers of oak o'er fertile plains might go, / And visit mountains where they once did grow' (*To the King, on his Navy*, 25–6); though in Ovid's Golden Age 'no wounded pine / Did yet from hills to faithless seas decline' (Ovid, *Metamorphoses*, 1:94–5, Sandys).

45–6   Heaven planted our 'dear and happy isle', but 'to exclude the world, did guard / With watery if not flaming sword' (Marvell, *Appleton House*, 321–6).

53–4   So that we view the proverbially and spontaneously fertile Nile in a country dry 'even under the showery Pleiades' (Lucan, *Pharsalia*, 8:852).

56–64   'And the Gentiles shall walk in thy light, and kings at the brightness of thy rising up ... the multitude of the sea shall be converted unto thee, and the riches of the Gentiles shall come unto thee ... they shall bring gold and incense ... All the sheep of Kedar shall be gathered unto thee ... and the ships of Tarshish ... and their silver, and their gold' (Isaiah 60: 3–9); with some debt to Virgil, *Eclogues*, 4:21–30, but Denham's eulogy of London as an emporium (*Cooper's Hill*, 181–90) is an immediate model.

63–4   There is no *colonial* point. The harvest is not of corn but gold (and Watson's Anti-*Panegyric* asks: 'Would you / Not have the Spaniard carry it for you too'); the 'ploughs' are ships' keels.

69–70   The conjunction of Edward III and the Black Prince (as in Denham, *Cooper's Hill*, 77–8) with Henry V covers up a dynastic discontinuity.

Till Alexander came to urge their fate:
  When for more worlds the Macedonian cried,
He wist not Thetis in her lap did hide
Another yet, a world reserved for you   75
To make more great, than that he did subdue:
He safely might old troops to battle lead
Against the unwarlike-Persian, and the Mede,
Whose hasty flight did, from a bloodless field,
More spoil than honour to the victor yield;   80
  A race unconquered, by their clime made bold,
The Caledonians armed with want and cold,
Have, by a fate indulgent to your fame,
Been from all ages kept for you to tame;
Whom the old Roman wall so ill confined,   85
With a new chain of garrisons you bind,
Here foreign gold no more shall make them come,
Our English iron holds them fast at home;
They, that henceforth must be content to know,
No warmer region than their hills of snow,   90
May blame the sun, but must extol your grace,
Which in our senate has allowed them place;
Preferred by conquest, happily o'erthrown,
Falling they rise, to be with us made one;
So kind dictators made, when they came home,   95
Their vanquished foes free citizens of Rome.
  Like favour find the Irish, with like fate
Advanced to be a portion of our state;
While by your valour and your courteous mind
Nations divided by the sea are joined.   100
  Holland, to gain your friendship, is content
To be our outguard on the continent;
She from her fellow-provinces would go,
Rather than hazard to have you her foe:
In our late fight, when cannons did diffuse,   105
Preventing posts, the terror and the news,
Our neighbour princes trembled at their roar,
But our conjunction makes them tremble more.
  Your never-failing sword made war to cease;

---

72 'For whom we waited as the Greeks did till Alexander the Great pushed them to their destiny'; Dryden, *Heroic Stanzas*, 49–50, makes the same connection.
73–5 'One world suffixed not Alexander's mind; / Cooped up, he seemed in earth and seas confined' (Juvenal 10:168–9, Dryden); not knowing that the sea ('Thetis') had kept back another world (Britain) which you would make greater than his world.
77–80 After his defeat of the Persian and Median armies of Darius at the Battle of Issus, Alexander 'beheld the bathing vessels, the water-pots, the pans, and the ointment boxes, all of gold, curiously wrought, and smelt the fragrant odours with which the whole place was exquisitely perfumed . . . and said, "This, it seems, is royalty"' (*Life*, 20–1, Dryden).
85 The Scots, scarcely held back by Hadrian's Wall, were to be contained by a chain of five great forts.
87–8 'All the treasure in the world would not have suf-
ficed had the Romans wanted to wage war with gold rather than iron . . . not gold but good soldiers are the sinews of war' (Machiavelli, *Discourses*, 2.10).
95–6 'There was nothing did more advance the greatness of Rome, than that she did always unite and incorporate those whom she conquered into herself' (Plutarch, *Life of Romulus*, Dryden). The 1654 Act of Union gave the Scots representation in Parliament (and the Irish, 98).
99 *your courteous* your bounteous (Quarto); and obliging (*1690*).
101 Even during the Anglo–Dutch war, Cromwell favoured Anglo–Dutch union. The Dutch of Watson's Anti-*Panegyric* are meretricious: 'But for her trade's advance she may style friend / The Pagan, Turk, him, or infernal fiend.'
105–6 'In the late war (concluded in April 1654), when the sound of cannon brought the terrible news of battle before the messengers could'.

And now you heal us with the arts of peace;   110
Our minds with bounty and with awe engage,
Invite affection, and restrain our rage.
Less pleasure take brave minds in battles won,
Than in restoring such as are undone;
Tigers have courage, and the rugged bear,   115
But man alone can, whom he conquers, spare.
To pardon willing, and to punish loath,
You strike with one hand, but you heal with both;
Lifting up all that prostrate lie, you grieve
You cannot make the dead again to live: 120
When fate, or error had our age misled,
And o'er these nations such confusion spread,
The only cure, which could from Heaven come down,
Was so much power and clemency in one!
    One, whose extraction from an ancient line,   125
Gives hope again that well-born men may shine,
The meanest in your nature mild and good,
The noble rest secured in your blood.
Oft have we wondered how you hid in peace
A mind proportioned to such things as these!   130
How such a ruling spirit you could restrain!
And practise first over yourself to reign!
Your private life did a just pattern give,
How fathers, husbands, pious sons should live,
Born to command, your princely virtues slept   135
Like humble David's, while the flock he kept;
But when your troubled country called you forth,
Your flaming courage, and your matchless worth
Dazzling the eyes of all that did pretend
To fierce contention, gave a prosperous end: 140
Still as you rise, the state exalted too,
Finds no distemper while 'tis changed by you.
Changed like the world's great scene, when without noise,
The rising sun night's vulgar lights destroys.
    Had you, some ages past, this race of glory   145
Run, with amazement, we should read your story;
But living virtue, all achievements past,
Meets envy still, to grapple with at last.
This Caesar found, and that ungrateful age,
With losing him fell back to blood and rage: 150

---

116 Adapting Virgil's statement of Rome's mission 'to spare the conquered' (*Aeneid*, 6:853).

117 Like Shakespeare's Duke of York: 'Whose smile and frown, like to Achilles' spear, / Is able with the change to kill and cure' (*2 Henry VI*, V. i. 99–100).

124 *clemency* piety (Quarto); for King Charles Waller had written, 'To thee his chosen more indulgent, he [God] / Dares trust such power with so much piety' (*To the King on his Navy*, 31–2).

129–30 'And when Saul saw David go forth against the Philistine, he said . . . whose son is this youth?' (1 Samuel 17: 55).

144 'Even as you rise Britain rises, but suffers no disorders

. . . no more than the world does when the rising sun in silence chases the many and undistinguished ('vulgar') stars'; at 153 they return.

145–8 'Were it history we should read you story with amazement, but envy attaches to the living': Milton's sonnet sets 'Cromwell, our chief of men' in 'a cloud, not of war only but detractions rude'.

149–52 The well-intended assassination of Caesar precipitated civil war: 'there are very many that think themselves wiser and abler to govern the public better than the rest . . . and thereby bring it into distraction and civil war' (Hobbes, *Leviathan*, 2.17.9).

Mistaken Brutus thought to break their yoke,
But cut the bond of union with that stroke.
That sun once set, a thousand meaner stars
Gave a dim light to violence and wars,
To such a tempest, as now threatens all,   155
Did not your mighty arm prevent the fall.
    If Rome's great senate could not wield that sword,
Which of the conquered world had made them lord,
What hope had ours, while yet their power was new,
To rule victorious armies but by you?   160
You that had taught them to subdue their foes,
Could order teach, and their high spirits compose,
To every duty could their minds engage,
Provoke their courage, and command their rage.
So when a lion shakes his dreadful mane,   165
And angry grows, if he that first took pain
To tame his youth, approach the haughty beast,
He bends to him, but frights away the rest.
As the vexed world, to find repose, at last
Itself into Augustus' arms did cast;   170
So England now does, with like toil oppressed,
Her weary head upon your bosom rest.
    Then let the Muses, with such notes as these
Instruct us what belongs unto our peace;
Your battles they hereafter shall indite,   175
And draw the image of our Mars in fight:
Tell of towns stormed, of armies overrun,
And mighty kingdoms by your conduct won;
How, while you thundered, clouds of dust did choke
Contending troops, and seas lay hid in smoke: 180
Illustrious acts high raptures do infuse,
And every conqueror creates a Muse.
    Here in low strains your milder deeds we sing,
But there (my Lord) we'll bays and olive bring
To crown your head, while you in triumph ride   185
O'er vanquished nations, and the sea beside;
While all your neighbour-princes unto you,
Like Joseph's sheaves pay reverence and bow.

165–8 'So, when a lion shakes his dreadful mane, / And beats his tail, with courage proud, and wrath, / If his commander came, who first took pain / To tame his youth, his lofty crest down goeth' (Tasso, *Jerusalem Delivered*, 8.83, Fairfax).
173–4 Watson points ironically to Jesus weeping over Jerusalem: 'If thou hadst known . . . the things which belong unto thy peace! but now they are hid from thine eyes' (Luke 19: 42).
181–2 Translating the epigraph from Claudian.
188 As Joseph dreams: 'we were binding sheaves in the field, and, lo, my sheaf arose . . . and, behold, your sheaves stood round about, and made obeisance to my sheaf' (Genesis 37: 7).

On St James's Park, as lately Improved by his Majesty

1664; but first published with Waller's approval (superseding a pirated edition) as a broadside, 1661. Inadequately maintained during the Commonwealth, St James's Park was re-created by the new King as a combination of formal gardens, orchards, tree-lined walks, pools, aviaries, fishponds. This royal park was also public, affording amusements: sight-seeing, music-making, winter skating, summer bathing. Gardens are not created in a season (Pepys remarks, 27 July 1662, that the park 'is now every day more pleasant, by the new works upon it'): Waller's poem considers the improvements in prospect. More important, he considers in the manner of *Cooper's Hill* (implicitly repaying Denham's compliment to him in that poem) those sites of historical interest which can be surveyed from the park: Whitehall (87), Westminster Abbey (91), Parliament House (99), Westminster Hall (105), St James's Palace (125). The eye or the fancy contains English history; and in the reconstructed 'sacred groves' the King walks in (67–74), it goes behind it (rather as Virgil takes us behind the monuments of imperial Rome, the Capitol 'Now roofed with gold, then [in Evander's time] thatched with homely reeds' (Virgil, *Aeneid*, 8:347–8, Dryden). King Charles's Amphion-like reconstruction of the park and his Noah-like repopulation of it, amounts to a reconstruction of the kingdom's (still fragile) history.

Of the first Paradise there's nothing found;
Plants set by Heaven are vanished, and the ground;
Yet the description lasts; who knows the fate
Of lines that shall this Paradise relate?
   Instead of rivers rolling by the side   5
Of Eden's garden, here flows in the tide;
The sea, which always served his empire, now
Pays tribute to our Prince's pleasure too.
Of famous cities we the founders know;
But rivers, old as seas, to which they go,   10
Are Nature's bounty; 'tis of more renown
To make a river, than to build a town.
   For future shade, young trees upon the banks
Of the new stream appear in even ranks;
The voice of Orpheus, or Amphion's hand,   15
In better order could not make them stand;
May they increase as fast, and spread their boughs,
As the high fame of their great owner grows!
May he live long enough to see them all
Dark shadows cast, and as his palace tall!   20
Methinks I see the love that shall be made,
The lovers walking in that amorous shade;
The gallants dancing by the river's side;
They bathe in summer, and in winter slide.
Methinks I hear the music in the boats,   25
And the loud echo which returns the notes;
While overhead a flock of new-sprung fowl
Hangs in the air, and does the sun control,
Darkening the sky; they hover o'er, and shroud
The wanton sailors with a feathered cloud.   30

1–4 That Paradise is easily lost: 'What luckless apple did we taste, / To make us mortal, and thee waste' (Marvell, *Appleton House*, 327–8).
5–6 'And a river went out of Eden to water the garden; and from thence it was parted and became four heads' (Genesis 2: 10); the Park pool (not in fact fed tidally) is about half a mile long.
9–10 London itself was supposed founded by the Trojan Brutus (Spenser, *Faerie Queene*, 3.9.46); but rivers, fed by precipitation of water evaporated from the sea, are of an age with it.
15 'A Hill there was ... Which in a flowery mantle flourished still: / Yet wanted shade. Which, when the gods' descent [Orpheus] / Sat down, and touched his well-tuned instrument, / A shade received. Nor ... poplar, various

oaks ... Soft linden, smooth-rind beech ... were absent' (Ovid, *Metamorphoses*, 10:86–92, Sandys). Being taught by Mercury (being eloquent), 'Deaf stones by the ears Amphion drew' (Horace, *Odes*, 3.11:1–2, Fanshawe) to build Thebes.
25–6 Informed by a literary memory: 'The music was of cornets, whereof one answering the other, with a sweet emulation, striving for the glory of music, and striking upon the smooth face of the quiet lake, was then delivered up to the castle walls, which with a proud reverberation, spreading it into the air; it seemed before the harmony came to the ear, that it had enriched itself in travail' (Sidney, *Arcadia* 3.15.3).
27–30 The Park is so well supplied with bird-life that it can block ('control') the sun, shading the merry-making boaters not with what might have been a metaphorically feathery cloud, but literally a cloud of feathers.

Beneath, a shoal of silver fishes glides,
And plays about the gilded barges' sides;
The ladies, angling in the crystal lake,
Feast on the waters with the prey they take;
At once victorious with their lines, and eyes,   35
They make the fishes, and the men, their prize.
A thousand Cupids on the billows ride,
And sea-nymphs enter with the swelling tide;
From Thetis sent as spies, to make report,
And tell the wonders of her sovereign's court.   40
All that can, living, feed the greedy eye,
Or dead, the palate, here you may descry;
The choicest things that furnished Noah's ark,
Or Peter's sheet, inhabiting this Park;
All with a border of rich fruit-trees crowned,   45
Whose loaded branches hide the lofty mound.
Such various ways the spacious alleys lead,
My doubtful Muse knows not what path to tread.
Yonder, the harvest of cold months laid up,
Gives a fresh coolness to the royal cup;   50
There ice, like crystal firm, and never lost,
Tempers hot July with December's frost;
Winter's dark prison, whence he cannot fly,
Though the warm spring, his enemy, draws nigh.
Strange! that extremes should thus preserve the snow,   55
High on the Alps, or in deep caves below.
   Here, a well-polished mall gives us the joy
To see our Prince his matchless force employ;
His manly posture, and his graceful mien,
Vigour and youth, in all his motions seen;   60
His shape so lovely, and his limbs so strong,
Confirm our hopes we shall obey him long.
No sooner has he touched the flying ball,
But 'tis already more than half the Mall;
And such a fury from his arm has got,   65
As from a smoking culverin 'twere shot.
   Near this my Muse, what most delights her, sees
A living gallery of agèd trees;
Bold sons of Earth, that thrust their arms so high,
As if once more they would invade the sky.   70

35–6 'For thou thyself art thine own bait, / That fish, that is not catched thereby, / Alas, is wiser far than I' (Donne, *The Bait*, 26–8).

37–40 An erotic conceit transferred: 'And a thousand Cupids born, / And playing in each eye' (William Browne, *On a Fair Lady's Yellow Hair* (19–20); these are putti in the retinue of the sea-goddess Thetis.

43–4 Noah's ark was stocked by 'every beast after his kind . . . and every creeping thing . . . and every fowl' (Genesis 7: 14); Peter dreamed 'a great sheet knit at the four corners, and let down to the earth: Wherein were all manner of fourfooted beasts of the earth, and creeping things, and fowls of the air' (Acts 10: 11–12).

49–50 Britain's first ice-house was built by the winter of 1660. The novelty of the idea provokes ingenuity: 'Straw ripens fruits with kindly heat (we know) / Yet serves in hot Spain to conserve the snow, / That cools their wines' (Bancroft, *Epigrams*, 2.126).

57 The 'mall' is the alley in which 'pall-mall' ('croquet') was played. It was re-imported from France; Pepys first saw it here in April 1661, but Blount's *Glossographia* (1656) calls it a game 'heretofore used at the Alley near St James'.

68 *living gallery* A 'colonnade of trees' is at the poem's centre, the king having subdued the arboreal 'bold sons of earth' ('Titans'); Marvell retires to a 'yet green, yet growing Ark' (*Upon Appleton House*, 484).

In such green palaces the first kings reigned,
Slept in their shades, and angels entertained;
With such old counsellors they did advise,
And, by frequenting sacred groves, grew wise.
Free from the impediments of light and noise, 75
Man, thus retired, his nobler thoughts employs.
Here Charles contrives the ordering of his states,
Here he resolves his neighbouring Princes' fates;
What nation shall have peace, where war be made,
Determined is in this oraculous shade; 80
The world, from India to the frozen North,
Concerned in what this solitude brings forth.
His fancy, objects from his view receives;
The prospect, thought and contemplation gives.
That seat of Empire here salutes his eye, 85
To which three kingdoms do themselves apply;
The structure by a prelate raised, Whitehall,
Built with the fortune of Rome's Capitol;
Both, disproportioned to the present state
Of their proud founders, were approved by Fate. 90
From hence he does that antique pile behold,
Where royal heads receive the sacred gold;
It gives them crowns, and does their ashes keep;
There made like gods, like mortals there they sleep;
Making the circle of their reign complete, 95
Those suns of Empire! where they rise, they set.
When others fell, this, standing, did presage
The crown should triumph over popular rage;
Hard by that House, where all our ills were shaped,
The auspicious temple stood, and yet escaped. 100
So snow on Etna does unmelted lie,
Whence rolling flames and scattered cinders fly;
The distant country in the ruin shares;

71–2 Thomas Browne writes of 'ranks of Trees standing like pillars in . . . the courts of famous buildings, and the porticos of the *templa subdialia* ['open-air temples'] of old; somewhat imitating . . . cloister buildings, and the *exedrae* ['patios'] of the ancients, wherein men discoursed, walked and exercised; for that they derived the rule of columns from trees . . . is illustrated by Vitruvius' (*Garden of Cyrus*, 4). Virgil's Evander entertains Aeneas in a grove: 'Some god, they knew – what god, they could not tell – / Did there amidst the sacred horror dwell' (*Aeneid*, 8:351–2, Dryden); 'And as [Elijah] lay and slept under a juniper-tree, behold, then an angel touched him' (1 Kings 19: 4–5).
74 The second Roman king Numa had nocturnal meetings with the nymph (his 'wife') Egeria who instructed him in statecraft (Livy, 1.19.5, Ovid, *Metamorphoses*, 15:479–84).
81 From India in the east (Bombay came to Charles in 1661 as part of his marriage settlement) to the Canadian North-west (like Donne's 'frozen North discoveries', *Satires*, 3:22; the Hudson Bay Company was incorporated at the end of the decade): the commercial world is implied.
83 'More boundless in my fancy than my eye' (*Cooper's Hill*, 14).

85–90 Whitehall is the centre of royal administration: the emphatic 'three kingdoms' (England, Ireland, Scotland) turns from Republican vocabulary. Cardinal Wolsey (a 'prelate') refurbished the mansion (which belonged to the see of York), before it was acquired by the crown: the historical transfer from Church to King makes the 'disproportion'. Rome's 'disproportion' is the reverse: once the centre of a secular Empire, it passed to the Papacy.
91–6 English kings are crowned in Westminster Abbey (the 'antique pile'), and (notionally) buried there.
97–100 The Abbey's survival of the Civil Wars and the Commonwealth (when many churches, notably St Paul's, were vandalized) promised the survival of the monarchy; but the passage reflects Denham's on King Henry's destruction of the monasteries: 'What crime could any Christian king incense / To such a rage?' (*Cooper's Hill*, 118–19). The nearby Parliament House in the Palace of Westminster is reprehended for the war.
101–2 Cowley's note on his ode *To Mr Hobbes*, 86, acknowledges Claudian's description of Etna: 'In midst of boiling heat, the snow doth fall upon the top, and never melts at all' (*De Raptu Proserpinae*, 1:164–8, Digges).

What falls from heaven the burning mountain spares.
Next, that capacious Hall he sees, the room   105
Where the whole nation does for justice come;
Under whose large roof flourishes the gown,
And judges grave, on high tribunals, frown.
Here, like the people's pastor he does go,
His flock subjected to his view below;   110
On which reflecting in his mighty mind,
No private passion does indulgence find;
The pleasures of his youth suspended are,
And made a sacrifice to public care.
Here, free from court compliances, he walks,   115
And with himself, his best adviser, talks;
How peaceful olive may his temples shade,
For mending laws, and for restoring trade;
Or, how his brows may be with laurel charged,
For nations conquered, and our bounds enlarged.   120
Of ancient prudence here he ruminates,
Of rising kingdoms, and of falling states;
What ruling arts gave great Augustus fame,
And how Alcides purchased such a name.
His eyes, upon his native palace bent,   125
Close by, suggest a greater argument.
His thoughts rise higher, when he does reflect
On what the world may from that star expect
Which at his birth appeared, to let us see
Day, for his sake, could with the night agree;   130
A prince, on whom such different lights did smile,
Born the divided world to reconcile!
Whatever Heaven, or high extracted blood
Could promise, or foretell, he will make good;
Reform these nations, and improve them more,   135
Than this fair Park, from what it was before.

105–6 Westminster Hall was the centre of the English judiciary.

109 *people's pastor* Like King David (an analogy pressed most famously by Dryden) Charles is shepherd and king together.

124 *Alcides* Alexander Ross's *Mystagogus Poeticus* explains Hercules as 'the type of a good king, who ought to subdue all monsters, cruelty, disorder and oppression'.

125 *native palace* Charles was born in St James's Palace.

127–30 'And that his birth should be more singular, / At noon of day, was seen a silver star' (Herrick, *A Pastorall upon the Birth of Prince Charles*, 19–20).

Of English Verse

1668. The poem inverts conventional promises of immortality for the beloved, and diverts attention to the fragility of the poetic medium, so that the closing assertion of the fragility of love is actually unsettling. The chemist Robert Boyle apparently refused to study English poems because 'they could not be certain of lasting applause, the changes of our language being so great and sudden that the rarest poems within few years will pass as obsolete.' Waller's own were regarded by contemporaries as offering a permanent standard of purity.

Poets may boast (as safely vain)
Their works shall with the world remain;
Both, bound together, live, or die,
The verses and the prophecy.
But who can hope his lines should long   5
Last in a daily changing tongue?
While they are new, envy prevails,
And as that dies, our language fails;
When architects have done their part,
The matter may betray their art;   10
Time, if we use ill-chosen stone,
Soon brings a well-built palace down.
Poets that lasting marble seek
Must carve in Latin or in Greek;
We write in sand, our language grows,   15
And, like the tide our work o'erflows.
Chaucer his sense can only boast;
The glory of his numbers lost;
Years have defaced his matchless strain,
And yet he did not sing in vain.   20
The beauties which adorned that age,
The shining subjects of his rage,
Hoping they should immortal prove,
Rewarded with success his love.
This was the generous poet's scope   25
And all an English pen can hope,
To make the fair approve his flame,
That can so far extend their fame.
Verse, thus designed, has no ill fate
If it arrive but at the date   30
Of fading beauty, if it prove
But as long-lived as present love.

1–4 As Ovid did: 'The living, not the dead can Envy bite, / For after death all men receive their right. / Then though Death rakes my bones in funeral fire, / I'll live, and as he pulls me down mount higher' (*Amores*, 1.15:39–42, Marlowe).
13–14 But 'Lines not composed, as heretofore, in haste / Polished like marble, shall like marble last' (*To the Duchess*, 11–12).
15–16 'One day I wrote her name upon the strand, / But came the waves and washèd it away' (Spenser, *Amoretti*, 75).
17–19 Cartwright commends Kynaston's 1635 Latin trans-

lation of Chaucer's *Troilus*: ''Tis to your happy cares we owe, that we / Read Chaucer now without a dictionary.'
21–4 This denies Apollo's disappointment at failing to secure Daphne: 'Like Phoebus thus, acquiring unsought praise, / He catched at love, and filled his arm with bays' (*The Fable of Phoebus and Daphne applied*, 10–20).
22 'The brilliant subjects of his inspiration (ladies)'.
30–2 'If it last as long as the fading beauty of one who will reward me with her love and as long as that love'.

Of the Last Verses in the Book

1686; printed first in *Divine Poems* (1685). Waller's son records them as 'the last verses my dear father wrote'; Aubrey says he wrote them a fortnight before he died (21 October 1687). Many of Waller's last verses celebrate a new fluency enabled by the body's decay: 'The soul contending to that light to flee / From her dark cell, we practise how to die; / Employing thus the poet's winged art, / To reach this love, and grave it in our heart' (*Divine Love*, 6:31–4). There is a half-line postscript from Virgil, *Eclogues*, 5.56: 'he marvels at Heaven's threshold' (of the dead Daphnis soaring above the world).

When we for age could neither read nor write,
The subject made us able to indite.
The soul, with nobler resolutions decked,
The body stooping, does herself erect:
No mortal parts are requisite to raise   5
Her, that unbodied can her Maker praise.

The seas are quiet, when the winds give o'er;
So calm are we, when passions are no more:
For then we know how vain it was to boast
Of fleeting things, so certain to be lost.   10
Clouds of affection from our younger eyes
Conceal that emptiness, which age descries.

The soul's dark cottage, battered and decayed,
Lets in new light through chinks that time has made.
Stronger by weakness, wiser men become   15
As they draw near to their eternal home:
Leaving the old, both worlds at once they view,
That stand upon the threshold of the new.

13–18 'The body is the soul's poor house, or home, / Whose ribs the lathes are, and whose flesh the loam' (Herrick, *The Body*). William Lathum's *Prosopopeia Corporis Animae* is a very elaborate development of the stock conceit.

Sir Richard Fanshawe (1608–1666)

Born the son of Sir Henry Fanshawe of Ware Park in Hertfordshire, brought up in the Cripplegate school of the distinguished classical scholar Thomas Farnaby, he went on in 1623 to Jesus College, Cambridge, which he left three years later without a degree to enter the Inner Temple. But the law too he abandoned. In the 1630s he travelled in France and Spain, latterly serving as secretary to the English Embassy at Madrid; in the 1640s he occupied various diplomatic posts, and travelled in Ireland, in the western counties, and on the continent, after 1644 with his wife Anne. His translation of Guarini's *Il pastor fido* was published in 1647, and reissued in 1648 with additional poems. It is as a translator, at least the finest of his generation, that Fanshawe is most distinguished; Denham's lines on his version of Guarini are famous: 'A new and nobler way thou dost pursue . . . True to his sense, but truer to his fame. / Fording his current, where thou find'st it low / Let'st in thine own to make it rise and flow; / Wisely restoring whatsoever grace / It lost by change of times, or tongues, or place' (*To Sir Richard Fanshawe*, 21–8).

Fanshawe was captured at the Battle of Worcester in 1651, but he made his peace with the victorious Parliament and spent the rest of the 1650s in retirement. To this period belongs the greater part of his work: *Selected Parts of Horace* (1652), *The Lusiads* (1655), and a Latin version of Fletcher's *Faithful Shepherdess* (1658), and translations from Hurtado de Mendoza, not published until after his death (1670). After the Restoration Fanshawe was again engaged in diplomatic business, from 1664 as ambassador to Spain, where he died of a fever. Among materials for the life are *Original Letters of his Excellency Sir Richard Fanshawe* (1701) and the *Memoirs of Lady Fanshawe*, edited by H. C. Fanshawe (1907). The only contemporary collection with original verse is *Il Pastor Fido . . . with an Addition of divers other Poems* (1648). Now the standard edition is *The Poems and Translations of Sir Richard Fanshawe*, edited by Peter Davidson, 2 vols (Oxford: Clarendon Press, 1997–9); but *Shorter Poems and Translations*, edited by N. W. Bawcutt (Liverpool: Liverpool University Press, 1964) remains useful.

An Ode upon Occasion of his Majesty's Proclamation in the year 1630. Commanding the Gentry to Reside upon their Estates in the Country

1648. Earlier versions appear in two MSS: British Library Additional MS 15228 (a copy from the mid-1630s with corrections in Fanshawe's hand) and Bodleian Library MS Firth c.1 (a later scribal copy). More important variants are given in the notes. A number of proclamations were issued during the reigns of James I and Charles I urging country gentlemen to return from London to their estates. James I had indeed written an *Elegy* 'concerning his counsel for ladies and gentlemen to depart the city of London'. The occasion of Fanshawe's poem is the Proclamation of 9 September 1630; and while its themes derive from a tradition of praises of country life out of Horace or in Virgil's *Georgics*, its contrast of the happy condition of England's countryside with the unhappy condition of continental Europe (rather than simply like Horace's *Epode 2* or Randolph's *Ode*, the unhappy circumstance of the city) locates it in its historical moment. Clarendon writes eloquently of 'the two crowns of France and Spain worrying each other, by their mutual incursions and invasions of each other, whilst they had both a civil war in their own bowels . . . all Germany weltering in its own blood, and con-

tributing to each other's destruction, that the poor crown of Sweden might grow great out of their ruins . . . Denmark and Poland being adventurers in the same destructive enterprises. Holland and the United Provinces wearied and tired with their long and chargeable war . . . beginning to be more afraid of France their ally than of Spain their enemy . . . Of all the princes of Europe, the king of England alone seemed to be seated upon that pleasant promontory, that might safely view the tragic suffering of his neighbours about him, without any other concernment than what arose from his own princely heart and Christian compassion (Clarendon, *Life*, of the situation in 1639). The poem refuses an occasion to write heroic verse, as Carew does with *In Answer of an Elegiacal Letter upon the Death of the King of Sweden*; but the refusal is silently doubled, for at the poem's centre (69–72), having prepared for a panegyric of the Caroline peace, he declines that option in favour of the pleasures of the flower garden and the kitchen. The metre represents an Englishing of sapphics. Quotations from Horace are in Fanshawe's version.

Now war is all the world about,
And everywhere Erinys reigns,
Or else the torch so late put out
    The stench remains.

Holland for many years hath been   5
Of Christian tragedies the stage,
Yet seldom hath she played a scene
    Of bloodier rage.

And France that was not long composed
With civil drums again resounds,   10
And ere the old are fully closed
    Receives new wounds.

The great Gustavus in the west
Plucks the Imperial Eagle's wing,
Than whom the earth did ne'er invest   15
    A fiercer King:

Revenging lost Bohemia,
And the proud wrongs which Tilly did,
And tempereth the German clay
    With Spanish blood.   20

What should I tell of Polish bands,
And the bloods boiling in the north?
'Gainst whom the furied Russians
    Their troops bring forth.

Both confident: this in his purse,   25
And needy valour set on work;
He in his axe; which oft did worse
    The invading Turk.

Who now sustains a Persian storm:
There Hell (that made it) suffers schism.   30
This war (forsooth) was to reform
    Mahometism.

1–4   Virgil's Alecto (like Erinys a Fury) inflames Turnus against the Trojans: "'Behold the Fates' infernal minister! "War, death, destruction, in my hand I bear." / Thus having said, her smouldering torch, impressed / With her full force, she plunged into his breast' (*Aeneid*, 7:454–7, Dryden). The wars are listed 5–32.

5–8   Holland resumed war with Spain in 1621; but Holland was famous for its sacred drama (Grotius in Latin, Vondel in Dutch).

9–12   Marie de Medici attempted a coup against Richelieu in September 1630, raising the spectre of the civil wars of the previous century.

13–14   *Gustavus* Germanicus (MSS). The Protestant Gustavus Adolphus of Sweden invaded Germany (the Empire) in July 1630.

17–18   The Imperial General Tilly defeated Protestant Bo-hemia at the Battle of the White Mountain in 1620; 'did' is given as 'dud' for the rhyme in early texts.

19–20   'And mixes (or slakes) the German spoil with Spanish blood'; the Imperial troops were often Spanish.

21–4   Polish claims to the Russian throne provoked resistance early in the century. The MSS have 'furred' for 'furied'.

25–8   Poland relied on mercenary armies; Russia conquered Kazan and Astrakhan; 'Turk' is used loosely for Tatar.

29–32   Who now with Persians hath a bout, / Their swords with mutual blood made wet; And Mohamet is fallen out / With Mohamet (British Library MS); Who 'gainst the Persian now unsheathes /His crooked scimitar sharp-set; / And Mohamet dire fury breathes / 'Gainst Mohamet (Bodleian MS). Sunni Turkey was long at war (1602–27) with Shi'ite Persia.

Only the island which we sow,
(A world without the world) so far
From present wounds, it cannot show   35
    An ancient scar.

White peace (the beautiful'st of things)
Seems here her everlasting rest
To fix, and spreads her downy wings
    Over the nest.   40

As when great Jove, usurping reign,
From the plagued world did her exile
And tied her with a golden chain
    To one blest isle:

Which in a sea of plenty swam   45
And turtles sang on every bough,
A safe retreat to all that came
    As ours is now.

Yet we, as if some foe were here,
Leave the despisèd fields to clowns,   50
And come to save ourselves as 'twere
    In wallèd towns.

Hither we bring wives, babes, rich clothes
And gems; till now my sovereign
The growing evil doth oppose: 55
    Counting in vain

His care preserves us from annoy
Of enemies his realms to invade,
Unless he force us to enjoy
    The peace he made.   60

To roll themselves in envied leisure
He therefore sends the landed heirs,

---

33 *sow* 'cultivate'.

34 Echoing Virgil on the British 'A race of men from all the world disjoined' (*Eclogues*, 1:66, Dryden).

37–48 Peace is identified with the divine dove: 'He shall cover thee with his feathers, and under his wings shalt thou trust (Psalms 91: 4); but the latent allusion to the winged Astraea is made explicit in 41–4. Astraea, who fled from the earth when the Olympians defeated the Titans ('great Jove, usurping reign'), re-embodies herself in just governments: in Jonson's *Golden Age Restored*, Astraea is invoked along with the personified Golden Age: 'Descend you long long wished, and wanted pair, / And as your softer times divide the air, / So shake all clouds off, with your golden hair' (75–7).

43 Homer's Jupiter uses this chain as an image of his own fixed purpose: 'Let down our golden chain; / And, at it, let all deities, their utmost strengths constrain, / To draw me to the earth from heaven' (*Iliad*, 8.18–19, Chapman).

46 *turtles* 'doves'.

49–52 'We abandon the countryside to the peasantry ('clowns') and take refuge from imaginary enemies in walled towns'; recalling Juvenal's picture of life while Astraea was still on earth, 'while yet the bounteous year / Her common fruits in open plains exposed; / Ere thieves were feared, or gardens were enclosed' (6:17–18, Dryden).

56–60 'Thinking it meaningless for himself solicitously to protect us from the annoyance of enemy invasion, if we do not take advantage of the peace'.

61–4 Therefore the happy lords of land / Sends to their vine and figtree home. / (I would not stay the king's command / If I were one.) (British Library MS but cancelled).

Whilst he proclaims not his own pleasure
So much as theirs.

The sap and blood o'th'land, which fled   65
Into the root, and choked the heart,
Are bid their quickening power to spread
    Through ev'ry part.

O, 'twas an act, not for my Muse
To celebrate, nor the dull age,   70
Until the country air infuse
    A purer rage!

And if the fields as thankful prove
For benefits received, as seed,
They will, to quite so great a love,   75
    A Virgil breed;

A Tityrus, that shall not cease
The Augustus of our world to praise
In equal verse, author of peace
    And halcyon days.   80

Nor let the gentry grudge to go
Into those places whence they grew,
But think them blest they may do so:
    Who would pursue

The smoky glory of the town,   85
That may go till his native earth,
And by the shining fire sit down
    Of his own hearth,

Free from the griping scrivener's bands,
And the more biting mercer's books;   90
Free from the bait of oilèd hands
    And painted looks?

The country too e'en chops for rain:
You that exhale it by your power

<hr>

65–6 Hervey's *De Motu Cordis* (on the circulation of the blood) was published in 1628.

72 *rage* 'inspiration'.

75–6 'They will requite the benefits they receive from the sower by breeding a poet who will celebrate them and give us pleasure.'

77–80 The Tityrus of *Eclogue* 1 was Virgil himself, the panegyrist of Augustus: 'When great Augustus made war's tempests cease, / His halcyon days brought forth the arts of peace' (Denham, *Progress of Learning*, 73–4); the 'equal verse' will match its subject.

85 *smoky* insubstantial as well as dirty: 'the love of smoke and noise, / And all that wealthy Rome enjoys' (Horace, *Odes* 3.29:11–12).

86–8 The pleasures of the domestic hearth are Horatian

(as *Epodes*, 2:43–4: 'Built of old logs . . . a fire as high as half a room').

89 *griping scrivener* 'grasping debt-broker'; Dryden renders Horace's *solutus omni faenore* (*Epodes*, 2:4) as 'from the griping scrivener free'.

90–2 Peacham's essay on following the fashion in *The Truth of our Times* (1638) considers fopperies of dress in detail: 'mercer's books' were proverbially where young men of fashion might find their debts listed; the perfumed ('oilèd') hands and made-up faces belong to whores.

93 *chops* chaps or cracks open (a standard sense); but the additional 'for rain' suggests a more jawing movement.

94–6 The sun, which draws up ('exhales') water from the surface of the earth, is asked to send down the fertile ('fat') rain.

Let the fat drops fall down again 95
    In a full shower.

And you bright beauties of the time,
That waste yourselves here in a blaze,
Fix to your orb and proper clime
    Your wandering rays. 100

Let no dark corner of the land
Be unembellished with one gem,
And those which here too thick do stand
    Sprinkle on them.

Believe me ladies you will find 105
In that sweet life, more solid joys,
More true contentment to the mind,
    Than all town-toys.

Nor Cupid there less blood doth spill,
But heads his shafts with chaster love, 110
Not feathered with a sparrow's quill
    But of a dove.

There shall you hear the nightingale
(The harmless siren of the wood)
How prettily she tells a tale 115
    Of rape and blood.

The lyric lark, with all beside
Of Nature's feathered choir: and all
The commonwealth of flowers in'ts pride
    Behold you shall. 120

The lily (Queen), the (royal) rose,
The gillyflower (prince of the blood),
The (courtier) tulip (gay in clothes),
    The (regal) bud,

The violet (purple senator), 125
How they doe mock the pomp of state,
And all that at the surly door
    Of great ones wait.

97–100 'The country is your orb and proper sphere' (James I, *Elegy*); but Fanshawe addresses the ladies.
100 The British Library MS has a cancelled additional stanza: Like those bright stars that never peep / Into the other hemisphere, / Nor water in the western deep / Their thirsty Bear.
103–4 'Scatter the gems that lie too thick in London on the dark corners.'
111 *sparrow's quill* The sparrow is proverbially lustful.
114–16 'The sweet songstress of the wood ('harmless' because she lures no one to destruction), how prettily (because in this English wood the story is longer her own) she tells

the story of Philomela's rape by her brother-in-law Tereus and her murder of his son Itys.'
117–28 Not in MSS.
117 *lyric* songful.
118–28 'And why take ye thought for raiment? Consider the lilies of the field, they toil not, neither do they spin: And yet . . . Solomon in all his glory was not arrayed like one of these' (Matthew 6: 28–9).
127–8 'The great man, home conducted, shuts his door. / Old clients, wearied out with fruitless care, / Dismiss their hopes of eating, and despair' (Juvenal, *Satires*, 1: 132–4, Dryden).

Plant trees you may, and see them shoot
Up with your children, to be served   130
To your clean boards, and the fair'st fruit
    To be preserved:

And learn to use their several gums,
"'Tis innocence in the sweet blood
Of cherry, apricocks and plums   135
    To be imbrued."

129–32 'You may plant trees, watch them grow . . . and see their fruits served on your scrubbed tables or made into preserves.'

134 'It is no sin (the cancelled reading of British Library MS) for apricots and plums to be preserved in cherry (most editors prefer MSS 'cherries') cordial' (whereas it is a sin for men to be steeped in one another's blood): the whole is marked as a 'sentence' or maxim.

John Milton (1608–1674)

The publisher Humphrey Moseley, apparently gratified by the reception of Waller's *Poems* earlier in 1645, advertised Milton's *Poems . . . Both English and Latin composed at several Times* with something like trepidation. He offered poems commended by 'the applause of the learnedst academics, both domestic and foreign': the Latin poems carry testimonials in Latin and Italian, registering astonishment at the new Englishman's achievement, Sir Henry Wotton contributes a prefatory letter to *Comus*. 'Perhaps trivial airs may please thee better', says Moseley, and though he claims that 'the author's more peculiar excellency in these studies, was too well known to conceal his papers,' Milton was certainly by now more famous as the author of a succession of pamphlets on Church government and on divorce. A glance would in any case reveal that the poet whom Moseley promoted as having 'sweetly excelled' Spenser was aiming rather to be as 'sage and serious' (as Milton himself called Spenser in the *Areopagitica*, published a year before). Milton's ambitions for a 'fit audience' already assumed it would be few; when the Bodleian Library lost its copy of *Poems* in 1647 he was pleased to send a new one to where it would be safe from the 'low mob of readers' (*Ad Joannem Rousium*, 80). For a century, *Paradise Lost* attracted what praise and blame attached to Milton. In the middle of the eighteenth century Joseph Warton could say of *L'Allegro* and *Il Penseroso*, that 'by a strange fatality' they 'lay in a sort of obscurity, the private enjoyment of a few curious readers, till they were set to admirable music by Mr Handel' (*An Essay on the Genius and Writings of Pope*, 1756). The 1645 volume parades difficulty and excess of manner (it is reticent about the poet's feelings, and indeed about his moral and political preoccupations) over a remarkable range of minor genres, as if its author's originality consisted in going over what had already been done. Familiarity has rendered charming what was once only nearly so. Johnson (though often an intemperately hostile witness) was just in observing that 'Milton never learned the art of doing little things with grace.' This fault has perhaps encouraged an accommodation of the concerns of the shorter poems with those of the later and epic Milton. The connection is indeed explicit in the final poem of the volume, the *Epitaphium Damonis*: 'I meditating sat some statelier theme, / The reeds no sooner touched my lip, though new, / And unessayed before, than wide they flew, / Bursting their waxen bands, nor could sustain / The deep-toned music of the solemn strain' (155–9, Cowper); it is implicit in many places elsewhere. The 'British' subject Milton was meditating never found an answering epic style,

but its theme, if it can be inferred from the *History of Britain* (1670, but written in the 1640s), would have been the abuse of choice and the refusal of true liberty.

Milton was born in Cheapside, in 1608, the son of a well-to-do and musically talented scrivener; he died in London in late 1674. Privately educated at first, he proceeded in 1620 to St Paul's School (where the grammarian Alexander Gill was master) and in 1625 to Christ's College, Cambridge (where Cleveland was a younger contemporary). He graduated BA in 1629, MA in 1632. His first (anonymously) published poem *On Shakespeare* (in the second Shakespeare Folio of 1632) sets him in undistinguished company; but the commissions for *Arcades* and *Comus* argue that his superior talent was already known (perhaps through Henry Lawes). After leaving Cambridge he studied privately, perhaps intending to enter the Church, living first with his family at Hammersmith and then at Horton in Buckinghamshire. The years 1638–9 he spent abroad, chiefly in Italy. On his return he settled in London, having abandoned his notions of the Church. A moment of sudden eloquence in *The Reason of Church Government* (1642) reveals that he had already conceived as his life's project 'a work not to be raised from the heat of youth, or the vapours of wine, like that which flows at waste from the pen of some vulgar amorist, or the trencher fury of a rhyming parasite . . . but by devout prayer to that eternal Spirit who can enrich all utterance and knowledge, and sends out his seraphim with the hallowed fire of his altar, to touch and purify the lips of whom he pleases'. The poems here are taken mainly from the 1645 volume (which includes a few pieces published earlier, notably *Comus* and *Lycidas*); the remainder come from a second edition, *Poems . . . upon Several Occasions*, a revision which, by including earlier suppressed work as well as poems written since 1645, aims at establishing the canon of the shorter poems. Despite Moseley's claim that Milton's papers were circulating freely, new poems by Milton have not come to light; and the canon is small. Thomas Warton (Joseph's brother), whose edition of 1785 attempted the recovery of Milton's earlier poems, lamented that 'their number is so inconsiderable'. The few additional poems include sonnets and translations from the Psalms, all probably done in the 1650s. The tragic *Samson Agonistes*, the epic *Paradise Lost* and the georgic *Paradise Regained* absorbed Milton's poetic energies for the next two decades. But from 1649, despite rapidly failing eyesight, his appointment as Secretary for foreign languages to the Council of State also required his taking on the polemical *Defensio pro Populo*

Anglicano (1651) and its sequel, the *Defensio Secunda* (1654), major apologies for the English Republic. At the Restoration, the mediation of Marvell or Davenant and others led to his pardon after his (illegal) arrest and imprisonment on charges of treason. Milton married three times: in 1642 Mary Powell who, after briefly deserting him, bore him four children (she died in 1652, three days after bearing the third daughter); in 1656 he married Katherine Woodcock, who died in 1658; the child she bore him also died; in 1663 he married Elizabeth Minshull, who long survived him. Helen Darbishire has collected *Early Lives of Milton* (London: Constable, 1932). The standard biography is William Riley Parker, *Milton: A Biography*, revised by Gordon Campbell (Oxford: Clarendon Press, 1997); Gordon Campbell has also prepared *A Milton Chronology* (Basingstoke: Macmillan, 1997).

The standard edition of the *Works* is edited by F. A. Patterson and others (New York: Columbia University Press, 1931–40) with two volumes of index. *Complete Poetical Works*, ed. H. F. Fletcher, 4 vols (Urbana: University of Illinois Press, 1943–8) gives facsimiles of the early editions; there are facsimiles of the 1645 *Poems . . . both English and Latin* (Menston: Scolar Press, 1968) and of the partly autograph MS of many of the poems surviving at Trinity College, Cambridge (Menston: Scolar Press, 1970). The *Complete Shorter Poems*, ed. John Carey (London and New York: Longman, 1997), a companion to *Paradise Lost*, ed. Alastair Fowler (London and New York: Longman, 1998), gives the richest and most up-to-date commentary. Carey gives prose translations of the Latin poems; the classic version is William Cowper's (published

posthumously, 1808). The most comprehensive collection of criticism is in *A Variorum Commentary on the Poems of John Milton* under the general editorship of M. Y. Hughes (London: Routledge, 1970–); the shorter poems are treated in volume 2 (three parts), ed. A. S. P Woodhouse (1972), and the third part contains a valuable account of Milton's prosody by Edward Weismiller. William Ingram and Kathleen Swaim have prepared *A Concordance to Milton's English Poetry* (Oxford: Clarendon Press, 1972). Early criticism is gathered in John T. Shawcross, *Milton: The Critical Heritage*, 2 vols (London: Routledge, 1970–2). More recent criticism is described in D. H. Stevens, *A Reference Guide to Milton* (Chicago: University of Chicago Press, 1930), H. F. Fletcher, *Contributions to a Milton Bibliography 1800–1930*, University of Illinois Studies in Language and Literature, 16 (1931), and Calvin Huckabay, *John Milton: An Annotated Bibliography 1929–68* (Pittsburgh: Dusquesne University Press, 1969); Calvin Huckabay and Paul J. Klemp, *John Milton: An Annotated Bibliography 1968–88* (Pittsburgh: Dusquesne University Press, 1997); P. J. Klemp *The Essential Milton: An Annotated Bibliography of Major Modern Studies* (Boston: G. K. Hall, 1989); and E. Jones, *Milton's Sonnets: An Annotated Bibliography 1900–1992* (Binghamton, NY: Medieval and Renaissance Texts and Studies, 1994). An abundance of guides and dictionaries is available. The most comprehensive is *A Milton Encyclopaedia*, ed. W. B. Hunter and others, 8 vols (Lewisburg, PA: Bucknell University Press, 1978–80); with *Selections*, ed. W. B. Hunter and John Shawcross (Lewisburg, PA: Bucknell University Press, 1986).

On the Morning of Christ's Nativity. Composed 1629

Milton summarizes the poem in a Latin epistle to Charles Diodati: 'The promised King of peace employs my pen, / The eternal covenant made for guilty men, / The new-born Deity with infant cries / Filling the sordid hovel, where he lies: / The hymning angels, and the herald star, / That led the wise, who sought him from afar, / And idols on their own unhallowed shore / Dashed, at his birth, to be revered no more!' (*Elegiae*, 6:87–8, Cowper); the Christmas dawn suggested the theme, and the poem is a birthday gift for Christ. It is informed by traditions rather than sources. Virgil, *Eclogues* 4, is the classic panegyric model, especially as Christianized; but there are debts to Christian hymnody from Prudentius onward. Tasso (*Sopra la Capella del Presepio* and *Nel Giorno della Natività*) is a major influence, the latter bringing together and informing the contrast of the bright regions of heaven with the dark world of incarnation, the awe of nature, the cessation of the oracles, the defeat of the pagan gods. The poem is an attempt in the sublime Pindaric manner, modernized in its use of the stanza, derived from the Italian canzone

and madrigal, possibly by way of Spenser (certainly inviting comparison with him) and Drummond; but, at least before the sonorous and difficult final couplets, thoroughly Anglicized. The stanza of the introduction is one used also by Phineas Fletcher. Thomas Warton's famous complaint (in 1791), that the poem is a 'string of affected conceits' is no longer accepted; the poem is self-consciously hung 'on well-balanced hinges' (122), and most readers acknowledge a more or less sophisticated articulation of three movements (stanzas 1–8, 9–17, 18–26), each preserving contrasts (however shifting) between light and harmony on the one hand, gloom and discord on the other; its often stagey accessories encourage the sense of an affinity with scene changes in masques. Large organized abstractions supervene on the detail and on what conventionally would be a modest (or, as in Crashaw, less than modest) presentation of the incarnation. This is not a Christmas poem, but one that confronts the possibility of a new and inhuman transfiguration of the world.

1

This is the month, and this the happy morn
Wherein the Son of Heaven's eternal King,
Of wedded maid, and virgin mother born,
Our great redemption from above did bring;
For so the holy sages once did sing,   5
    That he our deadly forfeit should release,
And with his Father work us a perpetual peace.

2

That glorious form, that light unsufferable,
And that far-beaming blaze of majesty,
Wherewith he wont at Heaven's high council-table,   10
To sit the midst of trinal unity,
He laid aside; and here with us to be,
    Forsook the courts of everlasting day,
And chose with us a darksome house of mortal clay.

3

Say heavenly Muse, shall not thy sacred vein   15
Afford a present to the infant God?
Hast thou no verse, no hymn, or solemn strain,
To welcome him to this his new abode,
Now while the Heaven by the sun's team untrod,
    Hath took no print of the approaching light,   20
And all the spangled host keep watch in squadrons bright?

4

See how from far upon the eastern road
The star-led wizards haste with odours sweet:
O run, prevent them with thy humble ode,
And lay it lowly at his blessed feet;   25
Have thou the honour first, thy Lord to greet,

1 *This . . . this* mimics Virgil's repetition of 'now' in *Eclogues*, 4:4–8.

3–7 The Hebrew prophets ('holy sages') announced the birth: 'Behold a virgin shall conceive and bear a son' (Isaiah 7: 14); 'Of the increase of his government and peace there shall be no end' (9: 7); and the 'deadly forfeit' laid at Genesis 2: 17 ('in the day that thou eatest thereof [the apple] thou shalt surely die'), is repaid: 'as in Adam all die, even so in Christ shall all be made alive' (1 Corinthians 15: 22).

8 *light unsufferable* The tropics are uninhabitable in Sandys by reason of the sun's 'unsufferable beams' (Ovid, *Metamorphoses*, 1: 49).

10–11 The 'council-table' domesticates God's throne: 'And round about the throne were four and twenty seats . . . And out of the throne proceeded lightnings . . . And before the throne was a sea of glass' (Revelation 4: 4–6); the 'trinal unity' of Father, Son and Holy Ghost act like a cabinet committee.

13 'There shall be no night' in the heavenly Jerusalem (Revelation 21: 25).

14 *darksome . . . clay* Marston describes the body as a 'smoky house of mortal clay' (*Scourge of Villainy*, 3.8:194).

15–16 'Urania' (as in *Paradise Lost*, 7:1) is no longer the Muse of astronomy, but one whose genius ('vein') is for heavenly poetry, giving not presents 'unto him that ought to be feared' (Psalms 76: 11) but birthday gifts for the new-born Jesus (Milton's *Elegiae*, 6:87).

19 Ovid describes the four horses of the sun (*Metamorphoses*, 2.153–5).

21 *spangled host . . . squadrons bright* The stars (Shakespeare's 'spangled starlight sheen', *Midsummer Night's Dream*, II. i. 29) metamorphose to angels (Spenser's 'bright squadrons', *Faerie Queene*, 2.8.2).

22–3 Wise men might still inoffensively be called 'wizards'. 'The star which they saw in the east, went before them . . . and when they were come into the house . . . they presented unto him gifts; gold, and frankincense, and myrrh' (Matthew 2: 9–11).

24 'anticipate their treasures with this lowly song' (though the 'ode' is not typically lowly).

And join thy voice unto the angel choir,
From out his secret altar touched with hallowed fire.

The Hymn.

1

It was the winter wild,
While the Heaven-born-child,   30
    All meanly wrapped in the rude manger lies;
Nature in awe to him
Had doffed her gaudy trim,
    With her great Master so to sympathise:
It was no season then for her   35
To wanton with the sun her lusty paramour.

2

Only with speeches fair
She woos the gentle air
    To hide her guilty front with innocent snow,
And on her naked shame,   40
Pollute with sinful blame,
    The saintly veil of maiden white to throw,
Confounded, that her maker's eyes
Should look so near upon her foul deformities.

3

But he her fears to cease,   45
Sent down the meek-eyed Peace,
    She crowned with olive green, came softly sliding
Down through the turning sphere
His ready harbinger,
    With turtle wing the amorous clouds dividing,   50
And waving wide her myrtle wand,
She strikes a universal peace through sea and land.

27–8 Urania is to join with the 'multitude of the heavenly host, praising God' (Luke 2: 13) which appears as the angel directs the shepherds to Bethlehem; like Isaiah, whose lips are 'touched' by 'a live coal' taken by a seraph 'from off the altar', she is to speak a purified dialect: in *The Reason of Church Government* Milton alludes to the passage (Isaiah 6: 6–7) and advises the poet to pray to the 'eternal spirit' who sends his seraphim on such work.

29–36 In Milton's Latin Elegy on Spring (55–60) the earth casts off her rags and exposes herself to the embraces of the sun; so Sylvester's 'Nature . . . seems with smiles to woo the gaudy spring' (*Divine Weeks*, 2.1.4.163–5). But in Petrarch, the rays of the sun are darkened at Easter 'for pity of their Maker' (*Rime*, 3).

38 *woos* 'entreats'.

41 *pollute . . . blame* 'polluted by the disgrace of the Fall' ('Earth felt the wound', *Paradise Lost*, 9:782).

42 'Harlots and their mates, by . . . doing of open penance in sheets . . . are often put to rebuke' (Harrison, *Description of England*, 2.11).

46–50 In Drummond's *Hymn of the Ascension*, 'Heaven's axle seems to bend, / Above each turning sphere / That robed in glory Heaven's King may ascend'. Here, Christ's messenger the dove ('turtle') of peace, crowned with olive (as returning to the ark, Genesis 8: 11), but carrying Venus's myrtle (the plant of love), descends through the single sphere made by the sum of the spheres, to break though the clouds that cling to her as if in love (in William Browne's *On a Fair Lady's Yellow Hair*, 'the amorous air' plays with the lady's locks).

4

No war, or battle's sound
Was heard the world around:
   The idle spear and shield were high up hung;   55
The hookèd chariot stood
Unstained with hostile blood,
   The trumpet spake not to the armèd throng,
And kings sat still with awful eye,
As if they surely knew their sovran Lord was by.   60

5

But peaceful was the night
Wherein the Prince of light
   His reign of peace upon the earth began:
The winds with wonder whist,
Smoothly the waters kissed,   65
   Whispering new joys to the mild ocean,
Who now hath quite forgot to rave,
While birds of calm sit brooding on the charmèd wave.

6

The stars with deep amaze
Stand fixed in steadfast gaze,   70
   Bending one way their precious influence,
And will not take their flight,
For all the morning light,
   Or Lucifer that often warned them thence;
But in their glimmering orbs did glow,   75
Until their Lord himself bespake, and bid them go.

7

And though the shady gloom
Had given day her room,
   The sun himself withheld his wonted speed,
And hid his head for shame,   80
As his inferior flame,
   The new enlightened world no more should need;

53–60 'He shall be a judge among the nations. . . and they shall beat their swords into ploughshares, and their spears into pruning hooks: nation shall not lift sword against nation, neither shall they learn war any more' (Isaiah 2: 4); 'For while all things were in quiet silence, and that night was in the midst of her course, thine almighty Word leapt down from heaven' (Wisdom 18: 14–15). In Spenser's account of the first age of man, 'No war was known, no dreadful trumpet's sound' (*Faerie Queene*, 5 proem 9). More than a century before Christ, Antiochus Eupator had invaded Judea with 'three hundred chariots armed with hooks' (2 Maccabees 13: 2). The awfulness of the kings, once their terribleness, is now their reverence.

64 *whist* 'hushed'.

68 *birds of calm* 'the halcyon, whom the sea obeys, / When she her nest upon the water lays' (Drayton, *Noah's Flood*, 425–6).

69–76 The wonder-struck stars, their streaming light and power focused on the child, glowing with love behind their visible glimmer, will not leave the sky even after the rising of the morning star ('Lucifer' – 'light-bearer'); Prudentius, *Apotheosis*, 626, calls Christ 'the new Lucifer'.

77–8 Spenser's Arthur prays for night to 'yield her room to day' (*Faerie Queene*, 3.4.60).

78–84 Spenser's Phoebus hesitates to look on Eliza: 'He blushed to see another sun below, / Ne durst again his fiery face outshow' (*April*, 77–8). The identification of Christ and the sun is from Malachi 4: 2: 'unto you that fear my name shall the Sun of righteousness arise with healing in his wings.' The sun is reduced to his throne (as in Ovid, *Metamorphoses*, 2:24) and his fiery chariot (the synecdoche 'burning axletree' following *Metamorphoses*, 2:297).

He saw a greater sun appear
Then his bright throne, or burning axle-tree could bear.

8

The shepherds on the lawn,   85
Or ere the point of dawn,
    Sat simply chatting in a rustic row;
Full little thought they then,
That the mighty Pan
    Was kindly come to live with them below;   90
Perhaps their loves, or else their sheep,
Was all that did their silly thoughts so busy keep.

9

When such music sweet
Their hearts and ears did greet,
    As never was by mortal finger strook,   95
Divinely-warbled voice
Answering the stringèd noise,
    As all their souls in blissful rapture took:
The air such pleasure loth to lose,
With thousand echoes still prolongs each heavenly close.   100

10

Nature that heard such sound
Beneath the hollow round
    Of Cynthia's seat, the airy region thrilling,
Now was almost won
To think her part was done,   105
    And that her reign had here its last fulfilling;
She knew such harmony alone
Could hold all Heaven and Earth in happier union.

11

At last surrounds their sight
A globe of circular light,   110
    That with long beams the shame-faced night arrayed,
The helmèd cherubim

89–90 E. K. writes on Spenser, *May*, 54: 'Great Pan is Christ, the very god of all shepherds, which calleth himself the great and good shepherd. The name is most rightly (methinks) applied to him, for Pan signifieth all or omnipotent, which is only the Lord Jesus.' He comes 'kindly' because he 'naturalizes' or 'humanizes' himself.
92 *silly* 'simple'; but aptly of thoughts of sheep, conventionally 'silly'.
93–100 'And suddenly there was with the angel a multitude of the heavenly host praising God, and saying, Glory to God in the highest, and on earth peace, good will toward men' (Luke 2: 13–14). *The Shepherd's Song . . . for Christmas* in *England's Helicon* lets the shepherd speak: 'Sweet music heavenly rare, / Mine ears doth greet.'
99–100 Echo is cast as in love with what it repeats: 'Love still possessed / Her soul' (Ovid, *Metamorphoses*, 2:395, Sandys). The lines are taken over in Oldham's version of

Moschus, *Lament for Bion*, 42–3: 'While the glad hills loth the sweet sounds to lose, / Lengthened in echoes every heavenly close'.
102–3 Spenser's Mutability passes through 'the region of the air' climbing 'to the circle of the moon . . . where Cynthia reigns' (*Faerie Queene*, 7.6.7–8).
104–8 Nature conceives her own demise, as if 'the first heaven and the first earth were passed away' (Revelation 21: 1), and new order founded on the marriage of the Lamb (19.7) sustained by the angelic music.
109–14 'The angel of the Lord came upon them and the glory of the Lord shone round about them' (Luke 2: 9). A circular body of light (Milton's gloss on 'glory') clothes (but invoking a fanciful connection of 'arrays' with 'rays') the darkness, before defining itself as lines of armed angels (the Geneva version calls the 'host' at 2: 13 'soldiers') with extended ('displayed') wings.

And sworded seraphim,
   Are seen in glittering ranks with wings displayed,
Harping in loud and solemn choir,   115
With unexpressive notes to Heaven's new-born heir.

12

Such music (as 'tis said)
Before was never made,
   But when of old the sons of morning sung,
While the creator great   120
His constellations set,
   And the well-balanced world on hinges hung,
And cast the dark foundations deep,
And bid the weltering waves their oozy channel keep.

13

Ring out yea crystal spheres,   125
Once bless our human ears,
   (If ye have power to touch our senses so)
And let your silver chime
Move in melodious time;
   And let the bass of Heaven's deep organ blow,   130
And with your ninefold harmony
Make up full consort to the angelic symphony.

14

For if such holy song
Enwrap our fancy long,
   Time will run back, and fetch the age of gold,   135
And speckled vanity
Will sicken soon and die,
   And leprous sin will melt from earthly mould,
And Hell itself will pass away,
And leave her dolorous mansions to the peering day.   140

116 *unexpressive* 'for who, though with the tongue / Of angels can relate, or to what things / Liken' this mystery (*Paradise Lost*, 7:298–301).
117–19 'when all the morning stars sang together, and all the sons of God shouted for joy' (Job 38: 7).
122 *hinges* God 'hangeth the earth upon nothing' (Job 26: 7); and in Sylvester's *Little Bartas* the earth is 'propless . . . Self-counterpoised, 'mid the soft air suspending' (265–6). But Mary Sidney Herbert's version of Psalms 89: 11 calls the axis of the Earth the 'unseen hinge of North and South'. The 'hinges' mark the turning-point of the 224-line poem.
123–4 'He so did earth's foundations cast, / It might remain for ever fast . . . These [waters] in the Ocean met, and joined, / Thou hast within a bank confined' (Psalms 104: 5, 9, Henry King).
125–35 The music of the eight spheres (from the moon to the fixed stars, 'crystal' only with reference to their supraterrestrial character, not to the crystalline sphere) is to be joined by the 'bass' of the earth. Plutarch (*On the Generation of the Soul*, 1029C–D) adjusts the number of the spheres (eight) to equal the number of the Muses (nine) by counting the Earth as the ninth and lowest sphere, so permitting a harmony of celestial and terrestrial. In his Prolusion *On the Music of the Spheres*, Milton takes our inability to hear the music ('If ye have power . . .') to follow from human corruption; Earth's rejoining the 'symphony' would be an effect of Christ's restoration of us to incorruption, or a cause: 'If our hearts were pure . . . our ears would be filled with the beautiful music of the circling stars, and then all things would return to the Age of Gold'.
136 *speckled* 'spotted with disease' (as leprosy, 138).
139–40 Remembering Hercules's exposure of Cacus's underground kingdom: 'The ghosts repine at violated night, / And curse the invading sun, and sicken at the sight' (Virgil, *Aeneid*, 8:243, Dryden).

15

Yea Truth, and Justice then
Will down return to men,
   The enamelled arras of the rainbow wearing,
And Mercy set between,
Throned in celestial sheen,   145
   With radiant feet the tissued clouds down steering,
And Heaven as at some festival,
Will open wide the gates of her high palace hall.

16

But wisest Fate says no,
This must not yet be so,   150
   The babe lies yet in smiling infancy,
That on the bitter cross
Must redeem our loss;
   So both himself and us to glorify:
Yet first to those ychained in sleep,   155
The wakeful trump of doom must thunder through the deep.

17

With such a horrid clang
As on mount Sinai rang
   While the red fire, and smouldering clouds outbrake:
The agèd Earth aghast   160
With terror of that blast,
   Shall from the surface to the centre shake;
When at the world's last session,
The dreadful judge in middle air shall spread his throne.

18

And then at last our bliss   165
Full and perfect is,
   But now begins; for from this happy day
The old dragon under ground
In straiter limits bound,

141–4 'Mercy and truth are met together; righteousness and peace have kissed each other' (Psalms 85: 10). Mercy dominates, modelled on the angel who comes 'down from Heaven, clothed with a cloud, and a rainbow was upon his head, and his face was as it were the Sun, and his feet as pillars of fire' (Revelation 10: 1), and here the coloured rainbow tapestry stands in for peace (Genesis 9: 13, 'a token of a covenant'). At 143–4, *1673* has 'Orbed in a rainbow; and like glories wearing, / Mercy will sit between.'
146 'Guiding the silver-gold clouds downwards with her fiery feet'; the clouds are 'tissued' because coloured by the dawn light, like the throne of Spenser's Mercilla: 'All over her a cloth of state was spread, / Not of rich tissue, nor of cloth of gold . . . But like a cloud' (*Faerie Queene*, 5.9.28).
154 'Now is the Son of man glorified, and God is glorified in him' (John 13: 31).
155–6 'For the Lord himself shall descend from heaven with a shout, with the voice of the archangel, and with the

trump of God: and the dead in Christ shall rise first' (1 Thessalonians 4: 16).
157–64 Invoking the descent of God on Sinai: 'there were thunders and lightnings, and a thick cloud . . . and the voice of the trumpet [Vulgate 'clangor'] . . . And Mount Sinai was altogether on a smoke, because the Lord descended on it in fire . . . and the whole mount quaked greatly' (Exodus 19: 16–18). Milton's Paraphrase of Psalms 114: 7 amplifies the command to tremble: 'Shake earth . . . be aghast.' The throne (the 'great white throne' of Revelation 20: 11) is 'spread' because Hebrew royal thrones were spread with canopies (hence derivatives of the same Hebrew root may signify 'throne' and 'covering' and the 'full moon').
168–9 'I saw an angel come down . . . and he laid hold on the dragon, that old serpent, which is the Devil, and Satan . . . and cast him into the bottomless pit, and set a seal upon him that he should deceive the nations no more' (Revelation 20: 1–3).

Not half so far casts his usurpèd sway,   170
And wroth to see his kingdom fail,
Swinges the scaly horror of his folded tail.

19

The oracles are dumb,
No voice or hideous hum
     Runs through the archèd roof in words deceiving.   175
Apollo from his shrine
Can no more divine,
     With hollow shriek the steep of Delphos leaving.
No nightly trance, or breathèd spell,
Inspires the pale-eyed priest from the prophetic cell.   180

20

The lonely mountains o'er,
And the resounding shore,
     A voice of weeping heard, and loud lament;
From haunted spring, and dale
Edgèd with poplar pale,   185
     The parting genius is with sighing sent,
With flower-inwoven tresses torn
The nymphs in twilight shade of tangled thickets mourn.

21

In consecrated earth,
And on the holy hearth,   190
     The lars, and lemurs moan with midnight plaint,
In urns, and altars round,
A drear and dying sound
     Affrights the flamens at their service quaint;
And the chill marble seems to sweat,   195
While each peculiar power forgoes his wonted seat.

22

Peor, and Baalim,
Forsake their temples dim,
     With that twice-battered god of Palestine,
And moonèd Ashtaroth,   200

173–80 'At that time all oracles surceased, and enchanted spirits, that were wont to delude the people, thenceforth held their peace' (E. K. on Spenser's *May*, 54). E. K. dates the event to the time of Christ's passion; but Prudentius, *Apotheosis*, 438–43, to the time of the incarnation.
180 *pale-eyed* 'of pale aspect'.
185 *pale* 'The poplar white here overhangs the cave' (Virgil, *Eclogues*, 9:41, Fleming).
186 *genius* 'The ancients supposed that every country and particular place had their tutelar Genius; which they accustomed to worship at their entrance and departure' (Sandys on Ovid, *Metamorphoses*, 3:24–5).
187–9 'The troubled nymphs alike in doleful strains / Proclaim his death through all the fields and plains' (Bion's *Lamentation*, 35–6, Oldham).

190–1 *lars and lemurs* The benign gods of the hearth and the spirits of the evil dead are equally stricken.
192–5 'Ivory statues weep. / The sacred groves resound with yelling cries / And fearful menaces' (Ovid, *Metamorphoses*, 15:792–3, Sandys: before Caesar's death). Cicero (*De Divinatione*, 2.27.58) talks of idols sweating.
194 'Affrights the priests at their outlandish rites'.
196 'The passive gods . . . abandon to the spoil / Their own abodes' (Virgil, *Aeneid*, 2:351–2, Dryden).
197–228 'Behold, the Lord rideth upon a swift cloud, and shall come into Egypt: and the idols of Egypt shall be moved at his presence, and the heart of Egypt shall melt in the midst of it' (Isaiah 19: 1). Milton's infant Christ appears finally as the infant Hercules strangling the serpents sent by the jealous Juno (Theocritus, 24). But the defeat of the old

Heaven's queen and mother both,
　Now sits not girt with tapers' holy shine,
The Libyc Hammon shrinks his horn,
In vain the Tyrian maids their wounded Thammuz mourn.

23

And sullen Moloch fled,   205
Hath left in shadows dread,
　His burning idol all of blackest hue;
In vain with cymbals' ring,
They call the grisly king,
　In dismal dance about the furnace blue;   210
The brutish gods of Nile as fast,
Isis and Horus, and the dog Anubis haste.

24

Nor is Osiris seen
In Memphian grove, or green,
　Trampling the unshowered grass with lowings loud: 215
Nor can he be at rest
Within his sacred chest,
　Naught but profoundest Hell can be his shroud,
In vain with timbrelled anthems dark
The sable-stolèd sorcerers bear his worshipped ark.   220

25

He feels from Judah's land
The dreaded infant's hand,
　The rays of Bethlehem blind his dusky eyen;
Nor all the gods beside,
Longer dare abide,   225
　Not Typhon huge ending in snaky twine:

gods, ranked by accidents of association, is presented as largely magical. A more sustained attempt at a conspectus of Near-Eastern paganism is given in the pageant of fallen angels in *Paradise Lost*, 1:392–522. Israelite whoring after false gods is frequent: 'And they forsook the Lord and served Baal and Ashtaroth' (Judges 2: 13); 'Israel joined himself unto Baal-Peor [sometimes simply Peor]: and the anger of the Lord was kindled against Israel' (Numbers 25: 3); defections to other 'Baalim' include Baal-Berith at Judges 8: 33, Baal-Zebub at 2 Kings 1: 2. Dagon's idol was 'twice-battered' when it fell to the ground after the Philistines took the captured ark into his temple (1 Samuel 5: 2–4). Solomon 'went after Ashtoreth' (1 Kings 11: 5), a bull-headed (hence 'moonèd' by way of 'horned') Semitic version of Venus; she was worshipped as queen of Heaven on the eve of the Exile (Jeremiah 44: 25); Milton's plural 'Ashtaroth' (from singular 'Ashtoreth' as often in Hebrew) concedes her composite character. Her crescent-moon horns connect her with Ammon: under threat from Typhoeus, Jupiter disguised himself as a ram ('whence the horns of Libyan Ammon came', *Metamorphoses*, 5:328, Sandys) and in that guise was worshipped in Libya: he now shrinks his horns like a snail. Thammuz was the lover of Ashtoreth (a pair like Venus and Adonis), killed by a boar and mourned yearly by Phoenician ('Tyrian') maids. Solomon worshipped (1 Kings 11: 7) the bull-headed Ammonite god Moloch (its root shared with the word for 'king'): his brazen idols contained furnaces (where brimstone might burn 'blue') for the sacrifice of children, whose cries (Sandys reports) were drowned by the noise of 'trumpets and timbrels'. The gods of Egypt ('Nile') are likewise literally brutish (to the Romans ridiculously so): the cow-horned mother goddess Isis, her falcon son Horus, her jackal son Anubis, and her husband Osiris, sometimes worshipped as the bull Apis ('with lowings loud') kept at Memphis in Egypt (where proverbially it never rains). Osiris is often represented in an ark or coffin, his power locked up by the power of his brother Typhon (Plutarch, *De Iside*, 366D–F), and recalling Isis's recovery of his dispersed corpse, an act commemorated in the rites of Osiris-Apis; as god of the underworld he finds shelter ('shroud') in Hell, but even here the power of the infant Christ penetrates; it defeats even the Egyptian Typhon (or Seth), the dismemberer of Osiris, here represented as the snake-tailed Greek Typhon (with whom he was sometimes identified). Details are available in Selden's learned *De Diis Syris* (1617) and Sandys's illustrated *Relation of a Journey [in] Egypt etc.* (1615).

Our babe to shew his godhead true,
Can in his swaddling bands control the damnèd crew.

26

So when the sun in bed,
Curtained with cloudy red,   230
   Pillows his chin upon an orient wave,
The flocking shadows pale,
Troop to the infernal jail,
   Each fettered ghost slips to his several grave,
And the yellow-skirted fays,   235
Fly after the night-steeds, leaving their moon-loved maze.

27

But see the virgin blest,
Hath laid her babe to rest.
   Time is our tedious song should here have ending:
Heaven's youngest teemèd star,   240
Hath fixed her polished car,
   Her sleeping Lord with handmaid lamp attending:
And all about the courtly stable,
Bright-harnessed angels sit in order serviceable.

229–31 Resumes the identification of Christ and the sun (83–4). Its elaboration is like Drummond's on the Passion: 'in the East ye do behold / Forth from his crystal bed the sun to rise, / With rosy robes' (*Hymn*, 1–3). But it sustains its point by jailing or binding the unredeemed dead ('flocking shadows', 'fettered' because refusing delivery from 'the body of this death', Romans 7: 24), or routing the unredeemable fairy world, made 'yellow-skirted' by the rising sun (as at *Paradise Lost*, 5:187, the sun paints the morning mist's 'fleecy skirts with gold'), and leaving their dance ('maze') to follow the horses of night's metaphorical chariot ('night-steeds' suggesting by a false etymology 'nightmares').
239 Fletcher, *Purple Island*, 8.58, closes his 'tedious song' at sunset.
240 *youngest teemèd* 'last born': that of Bethlehem.
244 'Angels in bright armour sit ready to do service.'

L'Allegro and Il Penseroso

The association of poems and apparent answers to them is common in the seventeenth century (Strode's reply to John Fletcher's song in praise of melancholy in *The Nice Valour* is a relevant example). Milton's elaboration of the double scheme may have been encouraged by the practice of academic debate on factitious topics (the first of Milton's *Prolusions* concerns 'Whether day is more excellent than night'); the location of arguments in the biases of a personality (and the near indifference to the actualities of countryside or town) may derive from Theophrastan character-writing, which appears in Nicholas Breton's *Fantastics* or less systematically in Burton's *Anatomy*. An important guide to how the poems might have been opposed is Burton's 'Abstract' of melancholy (printed in the 1628 edition of the *Anatomy*), which distinguishes pleasant from painful melancholy and describes activities appropriate to each. Milton's opposition is not so bald. The poet summons Mirth (the Grace Euphrosyne) and Melancholy (the Grace Aglaia) and then fantasizes their wooing of him with pleasures appropriate in both cases to a young seventeenth-century gentleman. The thematic texture of the poems is dominated by the sort of 'rural lyricism' or prettified georgic poetry fashionable in French poetry of the period: hence the poems' importance to the descriptive tradition of the next century. The shift from the madrigal verse in the preludes to couplets in the continuations is a feature common in masques (as after *Comus*, 866). The treatment of the couplets is very free and may owe something to John Fletcher's variations of octo- and heptasyllables; the syntax is likewise fluid (even, as in *L'Allegro* lines 100–14, moving in and out of direct speech) so as to encourage indifference to its logic.

Hence loathèd Melancholy
Of Cerberus, and blackest Midnight born,
In Stygian cave forlorn
    'Mongst horrid shapes, and shrieks, and sights unholy,
Find out some uncouth cell,   5
    Where brooding darkness spreads his jealous wings,
And the night-raven sings;
    There under ebon shades, and low-browed rocks,
As ragged as thy locks,
    In dark Cimmerian desert ever dwell.   10
But come thou goddess fair and free,
In Heaven yclept Euphrosyne,
And by men, heart-easing Mirth,
Whom lovely Venus at a birth
With two sister Graces more   15
To ivy-crowned Bacchus bore;
Or whether (as some sager sing)
The frolic wind that breathes the spring,
Zephyr with Aurora playing,
As he met her once a-maying,   20
There on beds of violets blue,
And fresh-blown roses washed in dew,
Filled her with thee a daughter fair,
So buxom, blithe, and debonair.
Haste thee nymph, and bring with thee   25
Jest and youthful Jollity,
Quips and cranks, and wanton wiles,
Nods, and becks, and wreathèd smiles,
Such as hang on Hebe's cheek,
And love to live in dimple sleek;   30
Sport that wrinkled Care derides,
And Laughter holding both his sides.

1–32 'Dull-sprited Melancholy, leave my brain; / To Hell, Cimmerian Night . . . come sporting Merriment, / Cheek-dimpling Laughter . . . I shall break my sides' (Marston, *Scourge of Villainy*, 3.11).

1–10 The allegorical genealogy parodies those in Hesiod's *Theogony* (122–5 gives the Sky and Day as her children by Erebus). The dark heart-gnawing dog Cerberus (living by the underworld River Styx) punningly replaces Erebus, and may encourage another punning allusion, but an apt one, to Homer's Cimmerians: 'Night holds fixed wings, feathered all with banes, / Above those most unblessed Cimmerians' (*Odyssey*, 11:14, Chapman).

5 *uncouth cell* 'remote hermitage' (as in Browne, *Shepherd's Pipe*, 7:17).

7 *night-raven* 'by such hateful birds he meaneth all misfortunes' (E. K. on Spenser, *June*, 23).

9 *ragged* 'rugged' (a commonly favoured form).

11 'Myrthe, that is so faire and fre' (Chaucer, *Romaunt*, 633).

12–16 'Whom the gods call X, men Y' is a Homeric formula. Hesiod names the Graces as Euphrosyne (Mirth), Aglaia (Splendour) and Thalia (Youth); Ficino (*De amore*, 5.2) identifies Mirth with the pleasure afforded by music. This par-entage is given in Servius on *Aeneid*, 1:720: it suggests sex ('Venus') and wine ('Bacchus', to whom ivy was sacred).

17–24 Milton prefers mirth derived from the experience of the breeze ('Zephyr') among flowers at dawn ('Aurora'). In Jonson's *Entertainment at Highgate*, Aurora, Zephyr and Flora share a song.

22 Varying 'morning roses newly washed with dew' (Shakespeare, *The Taming of the Shrew*, II. i. 174).

24 'So joyful, happy, gay': Randolph's *Aristippus*, 498, so defines the effect of wine.

25 Horace's invocation of Venus (*Odes*, 1.30) expands to include Cupid, the Graces, Youth and so on.

27 *Quips and cranks* 'Repartees and sleights': they are disingenuous.

28 Burton has Musaeus's Hero answering Leander 'with becks and nods and smiles' (*Anatomy*, 3.2.2.4).

29 *Hebe* 'Youth'; but, since she was cup-bearer to the gods, with associations of revelry.

30 *dimple* for 'dimpled cheek' whose 'sleekness' a dimple would interrupt.

31–2 Fletcher, *Purple Island*, 4.13: 'Here [in the midriff] sportful laughter dwells, here ever sitting, / Defies all lumpish griefs, and wrinkled care.'

Come, and trip it as ye go
On the light fantastic toe,
And in thy right hand lead with thee,   35
The mountain nymph, sweet Liberty;
And if I give thee honour due,
Mirth, admit me of thy crew
To live with her, and live with thee,
In unreprovèd pleasures free;   40
To hear the lark begin his flight,
And singing startle the dull night,
From his watch-tower in the skies,
Till the dappled dawn doth rise;
Then to come in spite of sorrow,   45
And at my window bid good morrow,
Through the sweet-briar, or the vine,
Or the twisted eglantine.
While the cock with lively din,
Scatters the rear of darkness thin,   50
And to the stack, or the barn door,
Stoutly struts his dames before,
Oft listening how the hounds and horn
Cheerly rouse the slumbering morn,
From the side of some hoar hill,   55
Through the high wood echoing shrill.
Sometime walking not unseen
By hedge-row elms, on hillocks green,
Right against the eastern gate,
Where the great sun begins his state,   60
Robed in flames, and amber light,
The clouds in thousand liveries dight,
While the ploughman near at hand,
Whistles o'er the furrowed land,
And the milkmaid singeth blithe,   65
And the mower whets his scythe,
And every shepherd tells his tale
Under the hawthorn in the dale.
Straight mine eye hath caught new pleasures
Whilst the landscape round it measures,   70

---

34 'Dancing to fashionably capricious "fantastic" music'.
36 Liberty is not conceived merely as licence, though it is Liberty that allows the poet to live 'free' (40) with Mirth. Liberty is also 'free / As mountain winds' (Shakespeare, *Tempest*, I. ii. 501–2), and Bodin's *Republic*, with the Swiss example to hand, remarks how mountain people 'love popular liberty'.
45–6 Drayton's 'whistling lark ymounted on her wings, / To the gray morrow, her good morrow sings' (*Eclogues*, 9:89–90); 'in spite of sorrow' because she 'grows mute, and sad, to think she must descend to the dull earth' (Walton, *Compleat Angler*, Day 1). Some think the poet, or the dawn, comes to the window.
47–8 Sweet-briar and eglantine are normally the same plant, wild rose; 'eglantine' may be for 'woodbine' or wild honey-suckle.
49–65 William Browne's unhappy Fida wakes to a morn-

ing of cocks, ploughmen, milkmaids, hounds and the rising sun (*Britannia's Pastorals* 1.4:482–96). Milton's own *Prolusion* 1 contains an extended description of dawn.
50 'Chases the dispersed rear of darkness's army': as the lark has kept watch (43), so the cock is a bugler.
55 *hoar* Virgil's shepherd takes his flock to pasture early 'while the grass is still white' (*Georgics*, 3:325).
57 'Sometimes I can be seen walking'; in *Penseroso*, 65, he walks 'unseen' at night.
59–62 Spenser's Phoebus dances from 'the golden oriental gate / Of greatest heauen' (*Faerie Queene*, 1.5.2). In Ovid 'The wakeful morning from the East displays / Her purple doors', *Metamorphoses*, 2:112–13, Sandys), where the sun begins his progress ('state').
67–8 *tells his tale* 'counts the number of his sheep'; but resting shepherds conventionally tell stories.
70 *landscape* 'picture'.

Russet lawns, and fallows gray,
Where the nibbling flocks do stray,
Mountains on whose barren breast
The labouring clouds do often rest:
Meadows trim with daisies pied,   75
Shallow brooks, and rivers wide.
Towers, and battlements it sees
Bosomed high in tufted trees,
Where perhaps some beauty lies,
The cynosure of neighbouring eyes.   80
Hard by, a cottage chimney smokes,
From betwixt two agèd oaks,
Where Corydon and Thyrsis met,
Are at their savoury dinner set
Of herbs, and other country messes,   85
Which the neat-handed Phyllis dresses;
And then in haste her bower she leaves,
With Thestylis to bind the sheaves;
Or if the earlier season lead
To the tanned haycock in the mead,   90
Sometimes with secure delight
The upland hamlets will invite,
When the merry bells ring round,
And the jocund rebecks sound
To many a youth, and many a maid,   95
Dancing in the chequered shade;
And young and old come forth to play
On a sunshine holiday,
Till the livelong daylight fail,
Then to the spicy nut-brown ale,   100
With stories told of many a feat,
How Faery Mab the junkets ate,
She was pinched, and pulled she said,
And he by Friar's-lantern led
Tells how the drudging goblin sweat,   105
To earn his cream-bowl duly set,
When in one night, ere glimpse of morn,
His shadowy flail hath threshed the corn,
That ten day-labourers could not end,

71   The adjectives are transferred from the shepherds (who wear coarse russet or grey homespun); but the red in grass is plausibly explained as an effect of burning in the summer drought, the grey in the fallows as an effect of the plough's exposing the chalky subsoil.

74   *labouring* Horace, *Odes*, 1.7:16, talks of the south wind giving birth to rain.

75   'Meadows richly arrayed with red and white daises'; with a memory of Shakespeare's 'proud pied April (dressed in all his trim)' (*Sonnets*, 98).

77–8   'Carried close in the clustered trees'.

80   *cynosure* The pole-star ('cynosure') draws all eyes; this only neighbouring eyes.

83–98   The rustic names are drawn from Virgilian pastoral; and the diction ('neat-handed', 'bower' to mean 'cottage',

'secure' to mean 'carefree', 'rebecks' for 'fiddles', the 'chequered shade' based on Shakespeare's *Titus Andronicus*, II. iii. 15, the 'sunshine holiday' on Spenser's *January*, 3) literary or exotic.

102–3   'This is Mab the mistress-fairy, / That doth nightly rob the dairy . . . she that pinches country wenches' (Jonson, *Entertainment at Althorp*).

104   *And he by friar's lantern led* 'And he deluded by the will o' the wisp'; *1673* has 'And by the friar's lantern led', still referable to 'she'.

105–6   Hobgoblins 'grind corn for a mess of milk, cut wood, or do any manner of drudgery work' (Burton, *Anatomy*, 1.2.1.2); *sweat* 'sweated'.

108   *shadowy* 'ghostly'; but alluding to the Homeric 'far-shadowing' (for spears).

Then lies him down the lubber fiend. 110
And stretched out all the chimney's length,
Basks at the fire his hairy strength;
And crop-full out of doors he flings,
Ere the first cock his matin rings.
Thus done the tales, to bed they creep, 115
By whispering winds soon lulled asleep.
Towered cities please us then,
And the busy hum of men,
Where throngs of knights and barons bold,
In weeds of peace high triumphs hold, 120
With store of ladies, whose bright eyes
Rain Influence, and judge the prize,
Of wit, or arms, while both contend
To win her grace, whom all commend.
There let Hymen oft appear 125
In saffron robe, with taper clear,
And pomp, and feast, and revelry,
With masque, and antic pageantry,
Such sights as youthful poets dream
On summer eves by haunted stream. 130
Then to the well-trod stage anon,
If Jonson's learned sock be on,
Or sweetest Shakespeare Fancy's child,
Warble his native wood-notes wild,
And ever against eating cares, 135
Lap me in soft Lydian airs,
Married to immortal verse
Such as the meeting soul may pierce
In notes, with many a winding bout
Of linkèd sweetness long drawn out, 140
With wanton heed, and giddy cunning,
The melting voice through mazes running;
Untwisting all the chains that tie
The hidden soul of harmony.

---

110 *lubber fiend* 'drudging devil'.
111 *chimney* 'fireplace'.
113 *crop full* 'belly-full'.
114 'Before the first cock announces daybreak'; alluding to the office of matins, but with an unfocused sexual innuendo, as in Spenser (*Faerie Queene*, 3.10.48).
118 Sylvester's peasant displaced to London wonders at the 'busy-buzzing swarms ... Ebbing and flowing over all the streets' (*Divine Weeks*, 2.1.1.364–5).
120 The 'weeds of peace' include armour for show: 'For jousts, and tournies, and barriers; the glories of them are chiefly in ... the bravery of their liveries; or in the goodly furniture of their horses and armour' (Bacon, *Of Masques and Triumphs*).
122 *rain influence* their eyes, like stars, control the outcome.
125–7 Jonson's Hymen (god of marriage) enters 'in a saffron-coloured robe ... in his right hand a torch of pine tree' (*Hymenaei*); the clarity of the taper contrasts with the 'sputtering' torch at the marriage of Orpheus and Eurydice (Ovid,

Metamorphoses, 10:6–7, Sandys); Shakespeare's Theseus promises to wed Hippolyta 'With pomp, with triumph, and with revelling' (*Midsummer Night's Dream*, I. i. 19).
130 *haunted* The older Milton still wanders 'where the Muses haunt / Clear spring' (*Paradise Lost*, 3:27–8).
131–4 In *Elegy* 1:27–8, Milton tells Diodati that the 'circular theatre's show' makes a rest from study. Jonson's comedy ('sock' from the footwear of Roman comic actors) is learned, Shakespeare's the product of natural fancy: in Tasso, Erminia's weeping is interrupted by the 'artless woodland piping' of a shepherd (*Jerusalem Delivered*, 7.6).
135 *eating cares* Horace's are dispelled by wine (*Odes* 2.11:18).
136 *Lydian airs* 'Fie on these Lydian tunes which blunt our sprites / And turn our gallants to hermaphrodites' (Guilpin, *Skialethia, Satirae Preludium*, 1–2).
138 *meeting* 'responsive' (as Latin *obvius*).
139 *bout* 'circuit'.
142 *melting* 'liquid'; but with an additional active sense.

That Orpheus' self may heave his head   145
From golden slumber on a bed
Of heaped Elysian flowers, and hear
Such strains as would have won the ear
Of Pluto, to have quite set free
His half-regained Eurydice.   150
These delights, if thou canst give,
Mirth with thee, I mean to live.

145–50 Orpheus secured Eurydice's release from Pluto only on condition he did not look back as he led her out of the underworld; he lost her by so doing (Ovid, *Metamorphoses*, 10:1–77).
146 *golden slumber* conventional; but the Elysian flowers (asphodel) would be golden.

151–2 Reversing the contract of Marlowe's *Come Live with Me*: 'If these delights thy mind may move, / Then live with me, and be my love.'

Il Penseroso

Hence vain deluding joys,
    The brood of Folly without father bred,
How little you bestead,
    Or fill the fixèd mind with all your toys;
Dwell in some idle brain,   5
    And fancies fond with gaudy shapes possess,
As thick and numberless
    As the gay motes that people the sunbeams,
Or likest hovering dreams
    The fickle pensioners of Morpheus' train.   10
But hail thou goddess, sage and holy,
Hail divinest Melancholy,
Whose saintly visage is too bright
To hit the sense of human sight;
And therefore to our weaker view,   15
O'erlaid with black, staid Wisdom's hue.
Black, but such as in esteem,
Prince Memnon's sister might beseem,
Or that starred Ethiop queen that strove
To set her beauties' praise above   20
The sea-nymphs, and their powers offended.

1–10 Sylvester turns Matthieu's celebratory history of Henri IV into an elegy with: 'Hence, hence false pleasures, momentary joys; / Mock us no more with your illuding toys' (*Henry the Great*, 331–2).
3–4 'How little use you are to the steadfast mind, how little you occupy it with your trivialities.'
6–10 'Confusedly about the silent bed / Fantastic swarms of dreams there hoverèd . . . they resemble may / The unnumbered motes which in the sun do play' (Sylvester, *Divine Weeks*, 2.3.1:564–71). Morpheus is the most gifted of the shape-shifting ('fickle') children of Sleep (Ovid, *Metamorphoses*, 11:633–45); his brothers are 'pensioners' as dependent on him (as Horace, *Epistolae*, 2.2:78, calls poets 'clients' of Bacchus).
12–16 'There is no great genius without a touch of madness', Burton, *Anatomy*, 'Democritus to the Reader', paraphrases Aristotle's *Problemata*, 30; so the disease is transformed into a goddess: Burton, 3.4.1.2, calls 'ecstasy' a 'divine melancholy, a spiritual wing . . . to lift us up to Heaven'. Boethius's Philosophy has 'a countenance full of majesty, and eyes shining as with fire . . . when she raised her head higher, it pierced the sky and baffled the onlookers' (*De Consolatione*, Prose 1).
17–21 Memnon of Ethiopia, son of Tithonus and the Dawn, killed by Achilles, is celebrated as a type of blasted youthful promise (black, but 'the shining son of the morning', *Odyssey*, 4:186). His sister, not known in classical sources, stands here as a type of female black beauty. Cassiopeia of Ethiopia, punished for boasting herself more beautiful than the Nereids, was eventually 'starred' as the constellation of that name.

Yet thou art higher far descended,
Thee bright-haired Vesta long of yore,
To solitary Saturn bore;
His daughter she (in Saturn's reign,   25
Such mixture was not held a stain)
Oft in glimmering bowers, and glades
He met her, and in secret shades
Of woody Ida's inmost grove,
While yet there was no fear of Jove.   30
Come pensive nun, devout and pure,
Sober, steadfast, and demure,
All in a robe of darkest grain,
Flowing with majestic train,
And sable stole of cypress lawn,   35
Over thy decent shoulders drawn.
Come, but keep thy wonted state,
With even step, and musing gait,
And looks commercing with the skies,
Thy rapt soul sitting in thine eyes: 40
There held in holy passion still,
Forget thyself to marble, till
With a sad leaden downward cast,
Thou fix them on the earth as fast.
And join with thee calm Peace, and Quiet,   45
Spare Fast, that oft with gods doth diet,
And hears the Muses in a ring,
Aye round about Jove's altar sing.
And add to these retirèd Leisure,
That in trim gardens takes his pleasure;   50
But first, and chiefest, with thee bring,
Him that yon soars on golden wing,
Guiding the fiery-wheelèd throne,
The cherub Contemplation,
And the mute Silence hist along,   55
'Less Philomel will deign a song,

22–30 Vesta ('bright-haired' because she was the goddess of the hearth-fire) was the eldest daughter of Saturn ('solitary' because his power was still unchallenged by Jupiter, 30). But the virgin Vesta bore no children (Homer, *Hymn to Venus*, 22–32), and the Golden Age incest on the Cretan Mount Ida (where Jupiter was reared) is Milton's invention.
31 *nun* 'priestess' (a vestal virgin).
33–5 A long dark-dyed ('of darkest grain') robe flows behind; the shoulders are modestly ('decent' is transferred) covered with a shawl of black crape ('cypress', originally 'Cyprus', is linked with the funereal cypress tree in a new etymology). Spenser's Una is similarly veiled, 'And over all a black stole she did throw' (*Faerie Queene*, 1.1.4).
39–40 So Spenser's Speranza: 'And ever up to Heaven, as she did pray, / Her steadfast eyes were bent, ne swerved other way' (*Faerie Queene*, 1.9.14).
42 'Surrender your passion to stony semblance of yourself'; punningly (on 'marvel') 'faint with wonder'. Milton repeats the pun in *On Shakespeare*: 'make us marble with too much conceiving.' Melancholy is thought of (Niobe-like) as

a statue, as in Pope's adaptation when Eloisa addresses the statues of the saints: 'Though cold like you, unmoved and silent grown, / I have not yet forgot myself to stone' (*Eloisa to Abelard*, 23–4).
45–55 The Muses 'who . . . dance on soft feet . . .about the altar of almighty Jupiter' (Hesiod, *Theogony*, 3–4), here heard by Fast, are replaced by personifications of meditative virtues. 'Contemplation' is a cherub because cherubim contemplate; he guides the 'fiery-wheelèd throne' because as they manifest themselves to Ezekiel (1: 4–28, 10: 1–22) the cherubim move on fiery wheels.
43 'Thrown downward steadily as if lead-weighted': Vaenius's lover 'absorbed in gazing on his beloved' is represented by Cupid with a plumb-line (*Emblemata Amatoria*, 'Ad amussim').
55 *hist* 'summon'.
56–64 Milton's Sonnet 1 ('O nightingale that on yon bloomy spray') advertises the bird as the 'mate' of the Muse and Love, and Milton as serving both. The sadness of Philomela's condition ('plight') is her rape by her brother-in-law Tereus

In her sweetest, saddest plight,
Smoothing the rugged brow of night,
While Cynthia checks her dragon yoke,
Gently o'er the accustomed oak;   60
Sweet bird that shunn'st the noise of folly,
Most musical, most melancholy!
Thee chantress oft the woods among,
I woo to hear thy evensong;
And missing thee, I walk unseen   65
On the dry smooth-shaven green,
To behold the wandering moon,
Riding near her highest noon,
Like one that had been led astray
Through the heaven's wide pathless way;   70
And oft, as if her head she bowed,
Stooping through a fleecy cloud.
Oft on a plat of rising ground,
I hear the far-off curfew sound,
Over some wide-watered shore,   75
Swinging slow with sullen roar;
Or if the air will not permit,
Some still removèd place will fit,
Where glowing embers through the room
Teach light to counterfeit a gloom,   80
Far from all resort of mirth,
Save the cricket on the hearth,
Or the bellman's drowsy charm,
To bless the doors from nightly harm:
Or let my lamp at midnight hour,   85
Be seen in some high lonely tower,
Where I may oft outwatch the Bear,
With thrice great Hermes, or unsphere
The spirit of Plato to unfold
What worlds, or what vast regions hold   90
The immortal mind that hath forsook
Her mansion in this fleshly nook:

(Ovid, *Metamorphoses*, 6:412–674), its sweetness the song of the nightingale to which she is transformed . The poeticization of the landscape is encouraged by specific memories: in Sylvester (*Divine Weeks*, 2.4.1.942–51) the Muse descends on King David (already visited by the nightingale and the bee) like a falling star on 'new-shaven fields'; Virgil's Iopas sings of 'the wandering moon' (*Aeneid*, 1:742).
59–60 'While the moon pulls in her dragon team over the familiar oak': so Marlowe describes the apparent slowing of moon's movement: 'that night-wandering, pale and watery star, / When yawning dragons draw her thirling car' (*Hero and Leander*, 1:107–8). The dragon-drawn chariot of Night comes from Ovid, *Metamorphoses*, 7:218–19.
73 *plat* 'patch'.
76 The water 'swings' tidally against the shore: Marina's attempted suicide in Browne's *Britannia's Pastorals* 'did make the stream so roar, / That sullen murmurings fillèd all the shore' (1.1:203–4).

77–8 'Or if the weather will not allow walking, some quiet place away from company will suffice.'
80 Recalling Spenser's 'A little glooming light, much like a shade' (*Faerie Queene*, 1.1.14).
83 The bellman keeps the night-watch, counting the hours, as in e.g. Herrick's *The Bellman*.
87–8 Hermes Trismigestus ('thrice great'), in the *Hermetica* 2 (*To Asclepius*), invites contemplation of the Great and Little Bears circling the Pole to show that moving things move in relation to things that stand fast: Milton stays up to watch the constellation fade in the morning light.
88–92 *unsphere . . . nook* 'or draw down Plato's soul from the star assigned it (*Timaeus*, 41e) to explain what regions are inhabited by the undying soul once it has left its dwelling place in this body' (as in the myth of Er, *Republic*, 614–21).

And of those demons that are found
In fire, air, flood, or underground,
Whose power hath a true consent 95
With planet, or with element.
Sometime let gorgeous Tragedy
In sceptered pall come sweeping by,
Presenting Thebes, or Pelops' line,
Or the tale of Troy divine. 100
Or what (though rare) of later age,
Ennobled hath the buskined stage.
But, O sad Virgin, that thy power
Might raise Musæus from his bower,
Or bid the soul of Orpheus sing 105
Such notes as warbled to the string,
Drew iron tears down Pluto's cheek,
And made Hell grant what love did seek.
Or call up him that left half told
The story of Cambuscan bold, 110
Of Camball, and of Algarsyf,
And who had Canacee to wife,
That owned the virtuous ring and glass,
And of the wondrous horse of brass,
On which the Tartar king did ride; 115
And if aught else, great bards beside,
In sage and solemn tunes have sung,
Of tourneys and of trophies hung;
Of forests, and enchantments drear,
Where more is meant than meets the ear, 120
Thus Night oft see me in thy pale career,
Till civil-suited Morn appear,
Not tricked and frounced as she was wont,
With the Attic boy to hunt,
But kerchiefed in a comely cloud, 125
While rocking winds are piping loud,
Or ushered with a shower still,
When the gust hath blown his fill,

93–6 Burton gives accounts of the 'seven kinds of etherial spirits or angels, according to the number of the seven planets' and of the 'fiery' and 'aerial spirits or devils', 'water-devils' and 'terrestrial devils' (*Anatomy*, 1.2.1.2).

97–102 Ovid (*Amores*, 3.1:12–14) represents Tragedy as violent but stately: 'her cloak ['palla'] on ground did lie. / Her left hand held abroad a regal sceptre, / The Lydian buskin in fit paces kept her' (Marlowe version). The 'buskin' is the platform boot worn by tragic actors. The 'sceptre' signifies royalty, the main source for the matter of tragedy, Thebes being the city of Oedipus, the matter of Sophocles, Pelops' line being Agamemnon and his children, the matter of Aeschylus; the 'tale of Troy divine' (because built by the gods) is the matter of Euripides (as in *Hecuba* and the *Troades*).

103–8 The arch-poets Musaeus and his master Orpheus both inhabit 'shady groves' in the underworld (*Aeneid*, 6:645, 667–70). The expansion restates *L'Allegro*, 145–50, but allows iron Pluto to melt.

110–15 Chaucer's *Squire's Tale* was left unfinished.

Cambuscan (the form in early printings of Chaucer) was a Tartar knight and father of Camball (the form in John Lane's continuation of 1615), Algarsyf and Canacee. Chaucer does not say who had Canacee to wife, but in Spenser's pseudo-continuation (*Faerie Queene*, 4.3.52) it is Triamond. The magic ('virtuous') mirror and the ring are gifts to Canacee, the brass horse a gift to her father.

116–20 Spenser, and the Italian romance poets, but it is of laconical styles that Seneca wrote (*Epistolae Morales*, 114) that 'there is more to be understood than heard.'

122–4 The preferred day is like Shakespeare's 'civil night . . . sober-suited matron' (*Romeo and Juliet*, III. ii. 10–11), not decked out and curled as the rosy Aurora was when she seduced the Attic hunter Cephalus (Ovid, *Metamorphoses*, 7:700–7).

126 *rocking winds* Sandys (Ovid, *Metamorphoses*, 7:585) has this of tree-shaking wind; Milton's is more a lullaby, to prepare the 'stillness' of the following shower.

Ending on the rustling leaves,
With minute drops from off the eaves.　130
And when the sun begins to fling
His flaring beams, me goddess bring
To archèd walks of twilight groves,
And shadows brown that Sylvan loves
Of pine, or monumental oak,　135
Where the rude axe with heavèd stroke,
Was never heard the nymphs to daunt,
Or fright them from their hallowed haunt.
There in close covert by some brook,
Where no prophaner eye may look,　140
Hide me from Day's garish eye,
While the bee with honeyed thigh,
That at her flowery work doth sing,
And the waters murmuring
With such consort as they keep,　145
Entice the dewy-feathered Sleep;
And let some strange mysterious dream,
Wave at his wings in airy stream,
Of lively portraiture displayed,
Softly on my eyelids laid.　150
And as I wake, sweet music breathe
Above, about, or underneath,
Sent by some spirit to mortals' good,
Or the unseen Genius of the Wood.
But let my due feet never fail,　155
To walk the studious cloister's pale,
And love the high embowèd roof,
With antic pillars' massy proof,
And storied windows richly dight,
Casting a dim religious light.　160
There let the pealing organ blow,
To the full-voiced choir below,
In service high, and anthems clear,
As may with sweetness, through mine ear,

130　*minute* 'falling by the minute'.

132–4　Marlowe's morning star has 'flaring beams' (*Hero and Leander*, 2:332), Browne's Pan walks through 'archèd groves' (*Britannia's Pastorals*, 2.4:747), Milton's wood-god ('Sylvan') enjoys the 'shadows brown' that are an unauthorized variant in Fairfax's Tasso (in particular *Jerusalem Delivered*, 14:37).

136–7　Numa in search of wisdom visits an ancient grove, sacred to Pan and for ages violated by no axe, in Ovid, *Fasti*, 4:649–50; Milton's oak is 'monumental' because a witness of the past.

141–4　Shakespeare's 'garish sun' (*Romeo and Juliet*, III. ii. 25) is rendered bizarre in the translation to 'eye'. Drayton combines brooks and bees to mock the song of the Sylvans: 'the small brooks . . . With each cadence of their murmuring. / Each bee with honey on her laden thigh' (*The Owl*, 117–21). Spenser creates a harmony ('consort') of a 'trickling stream', a 'murmuring wind' and 'swarming bees' (*Faerie Queene*, 1.1.41).

146–51　The wings belong to 'dewy-feathered Sleep' ('dewy' because dew evaporates in the sun): Milton may recall (but confusedly) *Faerie Queene*, 1.1.44: 'on his little wings the dream he bore'. Lines 149–50 are parallel and qualify 'dream'; 'displayed' qualifies 'portraiture'. Jonson's *Vision of Delight* includes an invocation of Fancy, 'Break Fancy from thy cave of cloud, / And spread thy purple wings . . . Create of airy forms, a stream . . . let it like an odour rise . . . And fall like sleep upon their eyes, / Or music in their ear' (45–54).

151–4　'Where should this music be? In the air or the earth?' (Shakespeare, *Tempest*, I. ii. 390, of Ariel's music). Local divinities ('genii') are part of the apparatus of ordinary masques.

157　*embowèd* vaulted.

158　'And love the high vaulted roof secure from ruin ('proof') on massive gothic ('antic' being 'old' and 'grosteque') pillars'.

159　*storied* 'illustrated' (Italian 'istoriato').

160　'Darkness in churches congregates the sight' (Howell, *Epistolae*, 1.5.22).

Dissolve me into ecstasies,   165
And bring all Heaven before mine eyes.
And may at last my weary age
Find out the peaceful hermitage,
The hairy gown and mossy cell,
Where I may sit and rightly spell   170
Of every star that heaven doth shew,
And every herb that sips the dew;
Till old experience do attain
To something like prophetic strain.
These pleasures Melancholy give,   175
And I with thee will choose to live.

165 'Untie body and soul and carry me out of myself'. *sic's Duel*, 102–4) is 'so poured / Into loose ecstasies, that
Those admitted to the presence of Sapience in Spenser's she is placed / Above herself'.
Hymn of Heavenly Beauty, 260–5 'see such admirable things, 170 *spell / Of* investigate.
/ As carries them into an ecstasy, / And hear such heavenly 173–4 As Virgil does contemplating the child who will bring
notes, and carollings . . . . And feel such joy . . . That maketh back the Golden Age (*Eclogues*, 4:53–9, in Dryden's version,
them all worldly cares forget'. Crashaw's nightingale (*Mu-* 64–71).

A Masque presented at Ludlow Castle, 1634 [Comus]

Printed here on the basis of *1645*. Milton's own work-ing text, the Trinity MS in Cambridge, gives evi-dence of first thoughts, only some of which are recorded here. Other texts authorized by Milton prob-ably derive from it rather than *1645*: the early fair-copy transcript in the Bridgewater MS in the British Library, and the earlier and later printings (*1637*, under the composer Henry Lawes's name rather than Milton's, but by some considered to give Milton's preferences in accidentals, and *1673*). Two British Library MSS (one in Henry Lawes's hand) give the songs. The masque was performed on 29 September 1631 (Michaelmas, the feast of St Michael and all angels, who 'succour and defend us on earth'), part of the celebrations for the installation of the Earl of Bridgewater as Lord President of the Council of Wales and Lord Lieutenant of Wales and the Welsh Marches. It represents the reunion in the border castle at Ludlow in Shropshire of the parents and the three children from whom they are supposed to have been sepa-rated. The boys (aged only 11 and 9) had already acted at Whitehall in Carew's demanding *Coelum Britannicum* (*The British Heaven*) in February of the same year: the god of pleasantry Momus is the anti-masque protagonist. Lady Alice was 15. As they par-ticipate in the represented occasion of the reunion, Alice and her Brothers are resolutely unallegorical and play themselves; their music tutor Henry Lawes both wrote the music (as he probably had for Carew's masque and certainly had for an earlier collaboration with Milton, *Arcades*) and played the Attendant Spirit. But the antimasque (inflated to 957 lines, exceeding the total length of even *Coelum Britannicum*'s seven anti-masques) is allegorical. Milton engages here in a

typically paradoxical way with a genre he distrusts ('*Comus* is the death of the masque,' says T. S. Eliot). The inconsistencies of plot and of styling may be an accident of the masque's assembly from separately written sections, but the investment of interest in the disorderly side of the entertainment is an affront to its point. Like that in Jonson's *Pleasure Reconciled* Milton's anti-masque sets itself to enliven a tableau out of Philostratus, his sickly god of revelry (*Ima-gines*, 1.2). Though the family history could have sup-plied them (the children's uncle had three years before been convicted of a grotesque series of rapes), the forces of disorder which threaten the reunion do not belong to the reality of family life. The disorderly sexuality, loaded with literary reminiscence and noisy with mainly unspecific Christian and Platonic resonances, is a metaphor. The un-Jonsonian refusal of reconciliations between virtue and pleasure may reflect a pointed refusal of accommodation with courtly practice; it certainly encourages an enlargement of the masque's scope. *Comus* is a poem much allegor-ized, and (in consequence of its stronger than usual dramatic interest), much psychoanalysed. Its burden is simple enough: 'Let us walk honestly, as in the day, not in rioting [*kōmois*] and drunkenness, not in chambering and wantonness, not in strife and envy-ing' (Romans 13: 13). Donne's old friend Sir Henry Wotton supplied Milton with a letter (printed at the poem's head) commending the unprecedented sweet-ness (there is 'nothing yet parallel in our language') and 'Doric delicacy of the songs', by which he must mean they are simple and like madrigals; the non-lyric part he calls 'tragical', drawing attention to its English-on-buskins manner, its ambitious syntax and rearranged word-order. The distinction between song and speech is not firmly maintained, particularly from line 859; but earlier too, lyric passages may be irregularly measured (as 93–144), or passages of speech rhymed (as 494–511).

The 'persons' are given as: the Attendant Spirit afterwards [from line 489] in the habit of Thyrsis, Comus with his crew, the Lady, the Elder Brother, the Second Brother, Sabrina the Nymph. The 'chief persons which presented' are: the Lord Brackley (John, the Elder Brother), Mr Thomas Egerton, the Lady Alice Egerton.

The first scene discovers a wild wood.
The Attendant Spirit descends or enters.

Before the starry threshold of Jove's court
My mansion is, where those immortal shapes
Of bright aerial spirits live ensphered
In regions mild of calm and serene air,
Above the smoke and stir of this dim spot,   5
Which men call Earth, and with low-thoughted care
Confined, and pestered in this pinfold here,
Strive to keep up a frail, and feverish being
Unmindful of the crown that virtue gives
After this mortal change, to her true servants   10
Amongst the énthroned gods on sainted seats.
Yet some there be that by due steps aspire
To lay their just hands on that golden key
That opes the Palace of Eternity:
To such my errand is, and but for such,   15
I would not soil these pure ambrosial weeds,
With the rank vapours of this sin-worn mould.
            But to my task. Neptune besides the sway
Of every salt flood, and each ebbing stream,
Took in by lot 'twixt high, and nether Jove,   20

The Attendant Spirit is described in both the Trinity and Bridgewater MSS as a 'guardian spirit or daemon'. Plutarch describes the human soul entering the dwelling-place ('mansion') of the *daemones*: 'it rose joyfully into clear, bright air . . . it felt . . . like a sail being unfurled' (*Socrates's Daimonion*, 590); these *daemones* aid earthly souls aspiring to virtue (593–4).

1–5   The spheres of the planets and stars, seen from the sphere of air which encloses the earth, are foreshortened to a sill before the gates of Heaven. Between lines 4 and 5 the Trinity MS has, after much correction: 'Amidst the Hesperian Gardens, on whose banks / Bedewed with nectar and celestial songs / Eternal roses grow, and hyacinth / And fruits of golden rind, on whose fair tree / The scaly-harnessed dragon ever keeps / His unenchanted eye, and round the verge / And sacred limits of this blissful isle / The jealous Ocean that old river winds / His far-extended arms till with steep fall / Half his waste flood the wide Atlantic fills / And half the slow unfathomed Stygian pool. / But soft I was not sent to court your wonder / With distant worlds, and strange removèd clime / Yet thence I come and from thence behold / The smoke . . .' But these lines, which classicize details from Dante's Eden, also in the sphere of the air (*Purgatorio*, 28–9), are crossed through.

7   *pestered . . . pinfold* 'crowded into this pen'; Odysseus's companions 'all are shut in well-armed sties' by Circe (*Odyssey*, 10:283, Chapman).

7–8   Originally in reverse order and interrupted by 'Beyond the written date of mortal change' (Trinity).

9–11   'And round about the throne were four and twenty seats: and upon the seats I saw four and twenty elders sitting . . . and they had on their heads crowns of gold' (Revelation 4: 4).

13   'And I will give unto thee the keys of the kingdom of heaven' (Matthew 16: 19), glossed in the Geneva Bible as 'the ministry of the Gospel'; with a memory of virtuous Aeneas, chosen to pluck the 'golden bough' (*Aeneid*, 6:129–46).

14   *Palace of Eternity* the Heavenly Jerusalem; but recalling Spenser's 'pillars of eternity' (*Faerie Queene*, 7.8.2).

16   *ambrosial weeds* 'Heavenly vesture'.

17   *sin-worn mould* 'soil wasted by sin' (Latin uses *effetus* for exhausted soil, which may suggest the fetid 'rank vapours').

18–29   'When the three divine sons of Saturn – Neptune, Jupiter and Pluto ['high, and nether Jove' – divided the world by lot (as in Homer, *Iliad*, 15:187–93] Neptune – besides control of the seas and the rivers, assumed rule ['imperial' – Milton's second thought in Trinity – because supra-national] of all islands ['sea-girt' is used by Chapman for the Homeric 'flowed-round'] . . . and commits their differ-

Imperial rule of all the sea-girt isles
That like to rich, and various gems inlay
The unadornèd bosom of the deep,
Which he to grace his tributary gods
By course commits to several government,   25
And gives them leave to wear their sapphire crowns,
And wield their little tridents, but this isle
The greatest, and the best of all the main
He quarters to his blue-haired deities,
And all this tract that fronts the falling sun   30
A noble peer of mickle trust, and power
Has in his charge, with tempered awe to guide
An old, and haughty nation proud in arms:
Where his fair offspring nursed in princely lore,
Are coming to attend their father's state,   35
And new-entrusted sceptre, but their way
Lies through the perplexed paths of this drear wood,
The nodding horror of whose shady brows
Threats the forlorn and wandering passenger.
And here their tender age might suffer peril,   40
But that by quick command from sovran Jove
I was dispatched for their defence, and guard;
And listen why, for I will tell ye now
What never yet was heard in tale or song
From old, or modern bard in hall, or bower.   45
      Bacchus that first from out the purple grape,
Crushed the sweet poison of misusèd wine
After the Tuscan mariners transformed
Coasting the Tyrrhene shore, as the winds listed,
On Circe's island fell (who knows not Circe   50
The daughter of the Sun? Whose charmèd cup
Whoever tasted, lost his upright shape,
And downward fell into a grovelling swine)
This nymph that gazed upon his clustering locks,

ent administrations to lesser gods ['tributary' because kings pay tribute to emperors, and because lesser rivers are tributary to greater], but Britain he divides among his favoured tritons ['blue-haired' rather than sapphire-crowned because they dispense with merely secular signs of power].' The British were fathered by Neptune's son Albion (Spenser, *Faerie Queene*, 4.11.15–16), and Britain was 'The happiest isle that Neptune's arms embrace' (Drummond's 1627 *Paraineticon*) and the focus of trading routes: 'The tritons, herdsmen of the glassy field, / Shall give thee what far-distant shores can yield' (Drummond, *Forth Feasting*, 373–4).

30–4 'A lord (the Earl of Bridgewater) of great ('mickle' is a Spenserism) trustworthiness has charge of all the western part, to restrain the ancient and warlike Welsh with moderation.'

37 Remembering Virgil: 'Through that deceitful wood unwinding ways perplexed he sought' (Aeneid, 9: 391–2, Phaer).

43–5 'I will no less Orlando's acts declare, / (A tale in prose ne verse yet sung or said)' (Ariosto, *Orlando Furioso*,

1.2, Harington). The allusion is varied in *Paradise Lost*, 1:16: 'Things unattempted yet in prose or rhyme'.

46–77 'Noah was he who immediately after the flood first planted a vineyard, and showed the use of wine unto men. Therefore some write that of Noachus he was called Boachus, and after Bacchus, by the ethnics [gentiles]' (Sandys on Ovid, *Metamorphoses*, 3:528–691, the story of the transformation into dolphins of the Tuscan or Tyrrhene pirates who refused to carry Bacchus home). Ovid's description of Bacchus's epiphany ('Ivy gave their oars a forced restraint; / Whose creeping bands the sails with berries paint. / He, head-bound with a wreath of clustered vines') supplies the seducer of Circe (54–6) and his effect on the pirates' imagination ('Stern tigers, lynxes . . . spotted panthers, round about him lie') supplies the effect of Comus's 'potion' (71–2). The genealogy of Comus (etymologically 'revelry') is invented, but Nonnos (*Dionysiaca*, 37:11–13) gives Circe as the mother of Faunus, another abductor of virgins.

50–3 A rhetorical return opens a parenthesis introducing the beautiful witch Circe, resisted by Odysseus, but who converted his men to beasts (Homer, *Odyssey*, 10:135–574).

With ivy berries wreathed, and his blithe youth,   55
Had by him, ere he parted thence, a son
Much like his father, but his mother more,
Whom therefore she brought up and Comus named,
Who ripe, and frolic of his full grown age,
Roving the Celtic, and Iberian fields,   60
At last betakes him to this ominous wood,
And in thick shelter of black shades imbowered,
Excels his mother at her mighty art,
Offering to every weary traveller,
His orient liquor in a crystal glass,   65
To quench the drouth of Phoebus, which as they taste
(For most do taste through fond intemperate thirst)
Soon as the potion works, their human countenance,
The express resemblance of the gods, is changed
Into some brutish form of wolf, or bear,   70
Or ounce, or tiger, hog, or bearded goat,
All other parts remaining as they were,
And they, so perfect is their misery,
Not once perceive their foul disfigurement,
But boast themselves more comely than before   75
And all their friends, and native home forget
To roll with pleasure in a sensual sty.
Therefore when any favoured of high Jove,
Chances to pass through this adventurous glade,
Swift as the sparkle of a glancing star,   80
I shoot from heaven to give him safe convoy,
As now I do: but first I must put off
These my skyrobes spun out of Iris' woof,
And take the weeds and likeness of a swain,
That to the service of this house belongs,   85
Who with his soft pipe, and smooth-dittied song,
Well knows to still the wild winds when they roar,
And hush the waving woods, nor of less faith,
And in this office of his mountain watch,
Likeliest, and nearest to the present aid   90
Of this occasion. But I hear the tread
Of hateful steps, I must be viewless now.

---

60 Jonson's masque *Neptune's Triumph* (1624) welcomes Albion (Prince Charles) back to England from Celtiberia (Spain) and the breakdown of a projected Spanish alliance.
65 *orient* 'ruby-red'.
67–77 Like the beasts in Browne's *Inner Temple Masque* or like Ariosto's 'masquing matachinas' (*Orlando Furioso*, 6.61, Harington) they lose only their 'countenance' and not their bodily shape (but with it the 'similitude' and 'image of God / express', *Paradise Lost*, 7:521, 528–9), so reversing the character of Homer's sailors: 'Swine's snouts, swine's bodies, took they, bristles, grunts; / But still retained the souls they had before' (Odyssey, 10: 239–40, Chapman).
76 *friends . . . forget* 'disregard those they left behind'.
80 *glancing* 'shooting'.
81 *convoy* 'escort'.

82–91 The Spirit next appears (488–99) as a shepherd, greeted as a musician (Lawes assumes a role closer to his own identity) and guessed to be about the rescue of lost sheep (hence the 'mountain watch').
83 'My robes like the sky woven from the threads of the rainbow'. In Daniel's *Vision of the Twelve Goddesses* (1604) Juno wears a 'sky-colour robe' (presumably blue); in Francis Beaumont's *Masque of the Inner Temple and Gray's Inn* (1613) Iris comes 'apparelled in a robe of discoloured taffeta figured in variable colours, like the rainbow'. The confusion in the vocabulary (robes are not 'spun') is evident from the Bridgewater MS's 'webs' for 'robes'.

Comus enters with a charming-rod in one hand, his glass in the other, with him a rout of monsters, headed like sundry sorts of wild beasts, but otherwise like men and women, their apparel glistering, they come in making a riotous and unruly noise, with torches in their hands.

Comus. The star that bids the shepherd fold,
Now the top of heaven doth hold,
And the gilded car of day,   95
His glowing axle doth allay
In the steep Atlantic stream,
And the slope sun his upward beam
Shoots against the dusky pole,
Pacing toward the other goal   100
Of his chamber in the east.
Meanwhile welcome Joy, and Feast,
Midnight-Shout, and Revelry,
Tipsy Dance, and Jollity.
Braid your locks with rosy twine   105
Dropping odours, dropping wine.
Rigour now is gone to bed,
And Advice with scrupulous head,
Strict Age, and sour Severity,
With their grave saws in slumber lie.   110
We that are of purer fire
Imitate the starry choir,
Who in their nightly watchful spheres,
Lead in swift round the months and years.
The sounds, and seas with all their finny drove   115
Now to the moon in wavering morris move,
And on the tawny sands and shelves,
Trip the pert fairies and the dapper elves;
By dimpled brook, and fountain brim,
The wood-nymphs decked with daisies trim,   120
Their merry wakes and pastimes keep:
What hath night to do with sleep?
Night hath better sweets to prove,

Stage Direction. Like the entry in Browne's *Ulysses and Circe.* Trinity explains the glass as a 'glass of liquor' (as 65).

93 Recalling 'the evening star bade them drive the sheep to the pens' (Virgil, *Eclogues*, 6:85–6).

94–101 Ovid represents the sun as a 'bright chariot . . . The beam and axletree of massy gold' (*Metamorphoses*, 2:106–7, Sandys, whose endnote explains 'They attribute a chariot to the sun in regard of the swiftness of his motion . . . they make it of gold and reflecting stones, in regard of his splendour', and who in a marginal note explains that the setting sun 'was feigned to descend into the sea . . . in that it so appeared to the eye'); but at 2:297 the whole sky is described as a 'glowing axeltree'. The 'steepness' of the Atlantic is transferred from the downward ('slope') motion of the sun, or the upward motion of its last rays shot into the darkening sky ('dusky pole', originally 'northern') as it hastens to 'wavy bowers' of Tethys (2:68–9) whence in the east it will rise again as 'a bridegroom coming out of his chamber' (Psalms 19: 5). 'Tartessian' (Spanish or Western) originally stood for

'Atlantic', recalling another Ovidian sunset: 'Phoebus now entering the Tartessian Main' (14.416).

111–14 Parodying the Second Song in *Coelum Britannicum*, which precedes the masquers' main dance: 'Jove is tempering purer fire, / And will with brighter flames attire / These glorious lights' (923–5). These surpass the 'rapid orbs, that bear / The changing seasons of the year' (1016–17), and finally 'With wreathes of stars circled about, / Gild all the spacious firmament' (1048–9).

115–22 The 'starry choir' is brought to the level of earthly festivals ('wakes') and morrises, and earthly fairy pastimes ('learned shepherds', says William Browne, called fairy rings the 'zodiac', *Britannia's Pastorals*, 1.2:394); and the diction is appropriately Spenserian or sub-Spenserian: Spenser's Proteus 'Along the foamy waves driving his finny drove' (*Faerie Queene*, 3.8.29); Shakespeare's 'yellow sands' (*Tempest*, I. ii. 376); Browne's 'dimpled waters' (*An Epistle*, 50) or his daisy-ruff 'neatly trim' (*Britannia's Pastorals*, 3.1.819). E. K. glosses Spenser's 'dapper' (*October*, 13) as 'pretty'.

Venus now wakes, and wakens Love.
Come let us our rites begin,   125
'Tis only daylight that makes sin
Which these dun shades will ne'er report,
Hail goddess of nocturnal sport
Dark-veiled Cotytto, t' whom the secret flame
Of midnight torches burns; mysterious Dame   130
That ne'er art called, but when the dragon-womb
Of Stygian darkness spits her thickest gloom,
And makes one blot of all the air,
Stay thy cloudy ebon chair,
Wherein thou rid'st with Hecat', and befriend   135
Us thy vowed priests, till utmost end
Of all thy dues be done, and none left out,
Ere the blabbing eastern scout,
The nice morn on the Indian steep
From her cabined loophole peep,   140
And to the tell-tale sun descry
Our concealed solemnity.
Come, knit hands, and beat the ground,
In a light fantastic round.

The Measure.

Break off, break off, I feel the different pace,   145
Of some chaste footing near about this ground.
Run to your shrouds, within these brakes and trees,
Our number may affright: some virgin sure
(For so I can distinguish by mine art)
Benighted in these woods. Now to my charms,   150
And to my wily trains, I shall ere long
Be well stocked with as fair a herd as grazed
About my mother Circe. Thus I hurl
My dazzling spells into the spongy air,
Of power to cheat the eye with blear illusion,   155
And give it false presentments, lest the place

---

124   *Venus* the evening star of line 93 as well as, clinching
the symmetry, the goddess of love.
126–7   'To be taken, to be seen, / These have crimes ac-
counted been' (Jonson, *To Celia*).
128–42   'Involved in thickest gloom, / Cotytto's priests her
secret torch illume' (Juvenal, *Satires*, 2:91–2, Gifford). Ad-
dressed as 'Dame' because 'among our vulgar witches, the
honour of Dame is given with a kind of pre-eminence to
some special one at their meetings (Jonson, *Masque of Queens*,
note 2), she is cast here as companion of the better-known
Hecate, worshipped by witches and imagined as the moon.
Medea's invocation of Hecate in Ovid (*Metamorphoses*, 7:207–
19) supplies the chariot ('chair', black rather than the usual
silver because the moon, as in *Samson Agonistes*, 89, is 'si-
lent'), the dragon-womb (since the chariot is drawn by drag-
ons), and the hatred of the morning ('nice' because she is
'blushing'). Browne (*Britannia's Pastorals*, 1.5:541) uses 'ebon
chair' to mean 'dark throne' (for Death). The vocabulary for
the dawn and the sun is borrowed from Phineas Fletcher:

'The thick-locked boughs shut out the tell-tale sun, (For
Venus hated his all blabbing light)' (*Britain's Ida*, 2:22). The
morning's 'peephole' ('cabined' transferred from the sun it-
self who 'in his moist cabin dives', Sylvester, *Bethulia's Res-
cue*, 3:87; his 'chamber' of 101) in the eastern hills is taken
from John Gerard's *Herball* (1597) account of the banyan 'in
which [the Indians] cut certain loopholes or windows . . . to
receive thereby the fresh cool air'. Lines 133–7 are much
corrected in the Trinity MS.
147   *shrouds* 'shelters'.
147–51   Altered from Trinity: Some virgin sure benighted
in these woods / For so I can distinguish by mine art / Run
to your shrouds, within these brakes and trees, / Our number
may affright; now to my trains / And to my mother's charms.
151   *trains* 'deceits'.
154–5   'blear' is transferred from 'eye', misted by the the
dazzling (originally 'powdered', presumably literally so) spells
into false imaginations ('presentments'); *spongy* 'thick and
moist' (as against transparently 'liquid').

And my quaint habits breed astonishment,
And put the damsel to suspicious flight,
Which must not be, for that's against my course;
I under fair pretence of friendly ends,   160
And well-placed words of glozing courtesy
Baited with reasons not unplausible
Wind me into the easy-hearted man,
And hug him into snares. When once her eye
Hath met the virtue of this magic dust,   165
I shall appear some harmless villager
Whom thrift keeps up about his country gear,
But here she comes, I fairly step aside
And hearken, if I may, her business here.

The Lady enters.

Lady. This way the noise was, if mine ear be true,   170
My best guide now, methought it was the sound
Of riot, and ill-managed merriment,
Such as the jocund flute, or gamesome pipe
Stirs up among the loose unlettered hinds,
When for their teaming flocks, and granges full   175
In wanton dance they praise the bounteous Pan,
And thank the gods amiss. I should be loath
To meet the rudeness, and swilled insolence
Of such late wassailers; yet O where else
Shall I inform my unacquainted feet   180
In the blind mazes of this tangled wood?
My brothers when they saw me wearied out
With this long way, resolving here to lodge
Under the spreading favour of these pines
Stepped as they said to the next thicket-side   185
To bring me berries, or such cooling fruit
As the kind hospitable woods provide.
They left me then, when the gray-hooded even
Like a sad votarist in palmer's weed
Rose from the hindmost wheels of Phoebus' wain.   190
But where they are, and why they came not back,
Is now the labour of my thoughts, 'tis likeliest
They had engaged their wandering steps too far,
And envious darkness, e'er they could return,
Had stoln them from me, else O thievish Night   195
Why shouldst thou, but for some felonious end,

---

157 *quaint habits* 'strange clothes'.
161 *glozing* 'smooth'.
167–9 *1637* and *1673* omit 167 and reverse 168 and 169; the *Errata* to *1673* (only perhaps on Milton's authority) give 169 as 'And hearken, if I may her business hear'.
167 *thrift* 'hard work'.
168 *fairly* 'respectfully'.
174–7 So the shepherds sing in Jonson's *Pan's Anniversary*: 'Pan is our All, by him we breathe, we live, / We move, we are; 'tis he our lambs doth rear.' The peasants are 'unlettered' because ignorant of the biblical Word.

178 *swilled* 'drunken'.
180 Uncompressed: 'Shall I a stranger and on foot find out the way?'
184 *spreading favour* 'agreeable cover'.
188–90 Evening dark takes over as sunlight fades ('Phoebus' wain' being 'the gilded car of day', 95: originally 'chair' as at 134). The simile unfolds 'gray-hooded' into an image of prayerfulness (the 'sad votarist') and pilgrimage (the 'palmer's weeds').
195 *thievish Night* used by Phineas Fletcher (*Piscatory Eclogues*, 5:176), vitalized here by the theft of the brothers.

In thy dark lantern thus close up the stars,
That Nature hung in heaven, and filled their lamps
With everlasting oil, to give due light
To the misled and lonely traveller?   200
This is the place, as well as I may guess,
Whence even now the tumult of loud mirth
Was rife, and perfect in my listening ear,
Yet nought but single darkness do I find.
What might this be? A thousand fantasies   205
Begin to throng into my memory
Of calling shapes, and beckoning shadows dire,
And airy tongues, that syllable men's names
On sands, and shores, and desert wildernesses.
These thoughts may startle well, but not astound   210
The virtuous mind, that ever walks attended
By a strong siding champion Conscience . . .
O welcome pure-eyed Faith, white-handed Hope,
Thou hovering angel girt with golden wings,
And thou unblemished form of Chastity,   215
I see ye visibly, and now believe
That he, the Supreme Good, t' whom all things ill
Are but as slavish officers of vengeance,
Would send a glistering guardian if need were
To keep my life and honour unassailed.   220
Was I deceived, or did a sable cloud
Turn forth her silver lining on the night?
I did not err, there does a sable cloud
Turn forth her silver lining on the night,
And casts a gleam over this tufted grove.   225
I cannot halloo to my brothers, but
Such noise as I can make to be heard farthest
I'll venture, for my new enlivened spirits
Prompt me; and they perhaps are not far off.

SONG

Sweet Echo, sweetest nymph that liv'st unseen   230
Within thy airy shell

197 *dark lantern* Quarles specifies the use: 'like dark lan-
terns, to accomplish treason / With greater closeness' (*Em-
blems*, 5.12:12–13). The light is shuttered in.
203 *Was rife, and perfect* 'Flowed out to the exclusion of all
else'.
204 *single* 'unbroken'.
208 'And airy tongues that lure night travellers' (Trinity).
Shakespeare, *Romeo and Juliet*, II. ii. 162 gives Echo an 'airy
tongue'.
210–20 A Christian development of the commonplaces rep-
resented in e.g. Ashmore's argument to his version of Horace,
Odes, 3.22: 'If thou, within, do feel no sin, / That tortureth
thy mind, / Thou may'st from thence a sure defence /
Against all dangers find.' Conscience take the part of the
virtuous. The Pauline triad (1 Corinthians 13: 13) of 'clear-
sighted' Faith, 'guiltless' Hope (a 'flittering angel' originally

in the Trinity MS and in *1637*), and Charity is adapted to
promote Chastity (originally 'unspotted' in Trinity).
217–20 God (designated the highest good by Augustine,
De Trinitate, 2) 'to whom vengeance belongeth' (Psalms 94:
1) 'shall reward evil' (Psalms 54: 5) on the enemies of the
good; and 'the angel of the Lord encampeth round about
them that fear Him, and delivereth them' (Psalms 34: 7).
230–43 The licence of the madrigal form makes teasingly
present the echo effects (of 'parley' or reciprocated speech)
more apparent in the music. Mere sound, personified Echo
inhabits an 'airy shell' (because conches are echoic; but the
Trinity MS registers an alternative 'cell'), and is 'daughter
of the sphere' ('heavenly', as in *At a Solemn Music*, voice
and verse and 'sphere-born harmonious sisters'): celestial
harmony resounds in the final alexandrine (which originally
began 'And hold in counterpoint').

By slow Meander's margent green,
And in the violet-embroidered vale
Where the love-lorn nightingale
Nightly to thee her sad song mourneth well.   235
Canst thou not tell me of a gentle pair
That likest thy Narcissus are?
O if thou have
Hid them in some flowery cave,
Tell me but where   240
Sweet queen of parley, daughter of the sphere.
So mayst thou be translated to the skies,
And give resounding grace to all Heaven's harmonies.

Comus. Can any mortal mixture of Earth's mould
Breath such divine enchanting ravishment?   245
Sure something holy lodges in that breast,
And with these raptures moves the vocal air
To testify his hidden residence;
How sweetly did they float upon the wings
Of silence, through the empty-vaulted night   250
At every fall smoothing the raven down
Of darkness till it smiled: I have oft heard
My mother Circe with the Sirens three,
Amidst the flowery-kirtled Naiades
Culling their potent herbs, and baleful drugs,   255
Who as they sung, would take the prisoned soul,
And lap it in Elysium, Scylla wept,
And chid her barking waves into attention,
And fell Charybdis murmured soft applause:
Yet they in pleasing slumber lulled the sense,   260
And in sweet madness robbed it of itself,
But such a sacred, and homefelt delight,
Such sober certainty of waking bliss
I never heard till now. I'll speak to her
And she shall be my queen. Hail foreign wonder   265
Whom certain these rough shades did never breed
Unless the goddess that in rural shrine
Dwell'st here with Pan, or Sylvan, by blest song
Forbidding every bleak unkindly fog

232 *Meander's margent* where the swan's song echoes: 'Then like Meander Swans, before my death, in fatal notes, / I'll sigh my latest breath' (Thomas Bateson, *Second Set of Madrigals*, 20).
237 *likest thy Narcissus* only because, like Echo's beloved, they are beautiful.
249–51 *float . . . darkness* silence and night together are imagined as a dark bird.
250 *empty-vaulted* 'starless'.
253–5 In Browne's *Inner Temple Masque* the Sirens (three in some Homeric commentary, and so illustrated in Alciati, *Emblems*, 116) are Circe's attendants; in Aurelian Townsend's *Tempe Restored*, she enters with the Naiades (freshwater nymphs, whose skirts recall the 'kirtle / Embroidered all with leaves of myrtle' the passionate shepherd promises in Marlowe's poem).

255 *potent herbs* The Trinity MS reveals much indecision about this phrase (with 'powerful', 'mighty' as cancelled alternatives, but taken straight from Virgil, *Eclogues*, 7:19 (*potentibus herbis*).
256–61 The rock Scylla (once a monster with barking dogs at the waist: hence the 'barking waves', a phrase from Virgil, *Aeneid*, 7:588) and the whirlpool Charybdis made a twin peril for Odysseus. The praise of music ('homefelt' because it 'strikes home') rewrites *L'Allegro*, 135–44, and *Il Penseroso*, 161–6.
265 Imitating Braggadocchio's confronting Belphoebe (*Faerie Queene*, 2.3.39), itself in a line of imitations of Odysseus confronting Nausicaa in *Odyssey* 6. He takes her for the presiding deity (like the 'rural queen' of *Arcades*).

To touch the prosperous growth of this tall wood.   270
Lady. Nay gentle shepherd ill is lost that praise
That is addressed to unattending ears,
Not any boast of skill, but extreme shift
How to regain my severed company
Compelled me to awake the courteous echo   275
To give me answer from her mossy couch.
Comus. What chance good lady hath bereft you thus?
Lady. Dim darkness, and this leafy labyrinth.
Comus. Could that divide you from near-ushering guides?
Lady. They left me weary on a grassy turf.   280
Comus. By falsehood, or discourtesy, or why?
Lady. To seek in th' valley some cool friendly spring.
Comus. And left your fair side all unguarded lady?
Lady. They were but twain, and purposed quick return.
Comus. Perhaps forestalling night prevented them.   285
Lady. How easy my misfortune is to hit!
Comus. Imports their loss, beside the present need?
Lady. No less than if I should my brothers lose.
Comus. Were they of manly prime, or youthful bloom?
Lady. As smooth as Hebe's their unrazored lips.   290
Comus. Two such I saw, what time the laboured ox
In his loose traces from the furrow came,
And the swinked hedger at his supper sat;
I saw them under a green mantling vine
That crawls along the side of yon small hill,   295
Plucking ripe clusters from the tender shoots,
Their port was more than human, as they stood;
I took it for a fairy vision
Of some gay creatures of the element
That in the colours of the rainbow live   300
And play in th' pleated clouds. I was awe-struck,
And as I passed, I worshipped; if those you seek
It were a journey like the path to Heaven,
To help you find them. *Lady.* Gentle villager
What readiest way would bring me to that place?   305
Comus. Due west it rises from this shrubby point.
Lady. To find out that, good shepherd, I suppose,
In such a scant allowance of starlight,
Would overtask the best land-pilot's art,
Without the sure guess of well-practised feet.   310
Comus. I know each lane, and every alley green
Dingle, or bushy dell of this wild wood,

---

273   *shift* 'necessity'.
277–90   Strict line-for-line dialogue, often with forced antitheses, is typical of Euripides.
286   *hit* 'reach'.
287   'Is their loss of more than immediate importance?'
290   *Hebe* 'Youth itself'.
292   *traces* 'harness'.
293   *swinked* 'hard-worked' (a bolder use than 'laboured' in 291).
294   *mantling* the vine 'clothes' the hill.

296   In Euripides' *Iphigenia in Tauris* a peasant takes Pylades and Orestes for gods.
299   *element* 'sky'.
301   *pleated* The association of clouds and cloth, already suggested in the 'silver lining' of 221, is Spenserian: Mercilla's cloth of state is 'like a cloud' bordered by sunbeams 'amongst the plights enrolled' (*Faerie Queene*, 5.9.28).
310   *sure guess* The etymology of 'pilot' ('steersman') is picked up in the cancelled Trinity MS 'steerage'.

And every bosky burn from side to side
My daily walks and ancient neighbourhood,
And if your stray attendance be yet lodged, 315
Or shroud within these limits, I shall know
Ere morrow wake, or the low-roosted lark
From her thatched pallet rouse, if otherwise
I can conduct you lady to a low
But loyal cottage, where you may be safe 320
Till further quest. *Lady*. Shepherd I take thy word,
And trust thy honest-offered courtesy,
Which oft is sooner found in lowly sheds
With smoky rafters, than in tap'stry halls
And courts of princes, where it first was named, 325
And yet is most pretended: in a place
Less warranted than this, or less secure
I cannot be, that I should fear to change it,
Eye me blest Providence, and square my trial
To my proportioned strength. Shepherd lead on ... 330

The two Brothers.

Elder Brother. Unmuffle ye faint stars, and thou fair moon
That wont'st to love the traveller's benison,
Stoop thy pale visage through an amber cloud,
And disinherit Chaos, that reigns here
In double night of darkness, and of shades; 335
Or if your influence be quite dammed up
With black usurping mists, some gentle taper
Though a rush-candle from the wicker hole
Of some clay habitation visit us
With thy long-levelled rule of streaming light, 340
And thou shalt be our Star of Arcady,
Or Tyrian Cynosure. *Second Brother*. Or if our eyes
Be barred that happiness, might we but hear
The folded flocks penned in their wattled cotes,
Or sound of pastoral reed with oaten stops, 345
Or whistle from the lodge, or village cock
Count the night watches to his feathery dames,
'Twould be some solace yet, some little cheering

313 *bosky* 'bushy' (on the model of Italian *boscoso*).
315–16 'Should your lost friends still be lodged and sheltered here': 'shroud' is a participle (Spenser's Cupid is 'shrouded' in an ivy-tod, *March*, 68); but the Trinity MS reveals indecision about its propriety.
317–18 *the low-roosted ... rouse* 'the lark wake from her straw bed on the ground'.
323–5 Baucis and Philemon in their 'humble shed' offer bacon from their 'smoky chimney' (Ovid, *Metamorphoses*, 8, Sandys). Spenser values humble courtesies, though 'Of court it seems, men courtesy do call' (*Faerie Queene*, 6.1.1).
326–8 'It cannot be that I should fear to change my situation from one which could hardly be less protected ('warranted') or less safe.'
329–30 *square ... strength* 'do not test me beyond my capacity.'

331–5 Sylvester writes of cloudy skies as 'muffled' (*Divine Weeks*, 1.3.33, and frequently). Quarles has 'muffled in silent shade ... afraid / To let one star gaze out ... There was a double night' (*Born in the Night*, 5–9).
332 'That art friendly to the traveller's good'.
333 *Stoop ... visage* Chapman has stars begin 'to stoop' (*Odyssey*, 12:444); Spenser has Artegall 'stoop' his head (*Faerie Queene*, 5.12.19).
334 Light first succeeded to Chaos (Genesis 1: 3).
340 *long-levelled* 'aimed from a distance'.
341–2 *Star ... Cynosure* Arcturus (in the Great Bear, by which the Greeks navigated, and so called from the stellified Arcas of Arcadia), and the Pole Star (in the Lesser Bear, by which the Phoenician Tyrians navigated).
345 Shepherd's pipes were (following Virgil) of oat-stems, punctured at intervals with 'stops'.

In this close dungeon of innumerous boughs.
But O that hapless virgin our lost sister   350
Where may she wander now, whither betake her
From the chill dew, amongst rude burrs and thistles?
Perhaps some cold bank is her bolster now
Or 'gainst the rugged bark of some broad elm
Leans her unpillowed head fraught with sad fears.   355
What if in wild amazement, and affright,
Or while we speak within the direful grasp
Of savage hunger, or of savage heat?
Elder Brother. Peace brother, be not over-éxquisite
To cast the fashion of uncertain evils;   360
For grant they be so, while they rest unknown,
What need a man forestall his date of grief,
And run to meet what he would most avoid?
Or if they be but false alarms of fear,
How bitter is such self-delusion?   365
I do not think my sister so to seek,
Or so unprincipled in virtues' book,
And the sweet peace that goodness bosoms ever,
As that the single want of light and noise
(Not being in danger, as I trust she is not)   370
Could stir the constant mood of her calm thoughts,
And put them into misbecoming plight.
Virtue could see to do what Virtue would
By her own radiant light, though sun and moon
Were in the flat sea sunk. And Wisdom's self   375
Oft seeks to sweet retirèd solitude,
Where with her best nurse Contemplation
She plumes her feathers, and lets grow her wings
That in the various bustle of resort
Were all too ruffled, and sometimes impaired.   380
He that has light within his own clear breast
May sit in th' centre, and enjoy bright day,
But he that hides a dark soul, and foul thoughts
Benighted walks under the midday sun;
Himself is his own dungeon. *Second Brother.* 'Tis most true   385
That musing Meditation most affects
The pensive secrecy of desert cell,
Far from the cheerful haunt of men, and herds,
And sits as safe as in a senate-house,

351–7   Much rewritten in the Trinity MS. The lines from 355 stood originally as 'She leans her thoughtful head musing at our unkindness / Or else in wild amazement and affright / So fares as did forsaken Proserpine / When the big rolling [replacing 'wallowing'] flakes of pitchy clouds / And darkness wound her in. *Elder Brother.* Peace brother peace.' A marginal note refers to a redraft now lost, presumably surviving in 357–65, lacking in both MSS.
358   The hunger of beasts, the sexual rage of men.
360–1   *be . . . evils* 'avoid precise reckonings of unpredictable misfortunes'.
366   *so to seek* 'to be imagined in that way' (353–8).

367   *unprincipled* 'uninstructed'.
368   *bosoms* 'embraces'.
373–5   Spenser has: 'Virtue gives herself light through darkness for to wade' (*Faerie Queene*, 1.1.12); though sun and moon fell flat in the sea (with 'flat' transferred).
375–80   Rewritten in Marvell's *Garden*, 53–4.
379   *resort* 'crowds'.
384–5   Walks in black vapours, though the noontide brand / Blaze in the summer solstice (deleted in the Trinity MS to admit the lines printed).
386   *affects* 'loves'.

For who would rob a hermit of his weeds,   390
His few books, or his beads, or maple dish,
Or do his gray hairs any violence?
But beauty like the fair Hesperian tree
Laden with blooming gold, had need the guard
Of dragon-watch with unenchanted eye,   395
To save her blossoms, and defend her fruit
From the rash hand of bold Incontinence.
You may as well spread out the unsunned heaps
Of miser's treasure by an outlaw's den,
And tell me it is safe, as bid me hope   400
Danger will wink on opportunity,
And let a single helpless maiden pass
Uninjured in this wild surrounding waste.
Of night, or loneliness it recks me not,
I fear the dread events that dog them both,   405
Lest some ill-greeting touch attempt the person
Of our unownèd sister. *Elder Brother.* I do not, brother,
Infer, as if I thought my sister's state
Secure without all doubt, or controversy:
Yet where an equal poise of hope and fear   410
Does arbitrate the event, my nature is
That I incline to hope, rather than fear,
And gladly banish squint suspicion.
My sister is not so defenceless left
As you imagine, she has a hidden strength   415
Which you remember not. *Second Brother.* What hidden strength,
Unless the strength of Heaven, if you mean that?
Elder Brother. I mean that too, but yet a hidden strength
Which if Heaven gave it, may be termed her own:
'Tis chastity, my brother, chastity: 420
She that has that, is clad in complete steel,
And like a quivered nymph with arrows keen
May trace huge forests, and unharboured heaths,
Infamous hills, and sandy perilous wilds,
Where through the sacred rays of chastity,   425
No savage fierce, bandit, or mountaineer
Will dare to soil her virgin purity,

390–1 The Trinity MS shows indecision about the order, and the 'weeds' start as a 'hairy gown'.

393–400 Alciati, *Emblems*, 22 (*Custodiendas Virgines* – 'Put a Guard on your Girls'), confirms the role of dragons in the protection of virgins. The tree in the Garden of the Hesperides bore golden apples and was protected by a dragon, 'sleepless' (hence the 'unenchanted eye') according to Ovid, *Metamorphoses*, 9:190. Jonson anticipates the set of associations: 'Who will not judge him worthy to be robbed / That sets his doors wide open to a thief / And shows the felon where his treasure lies. / Again, what earthy spirit but will attempt / To taste the fruit of Beauty's golden tree, / When leaden sleep seals up the Dragon's eyes?' (*Every Man in his Humour*, III. ii. 15–20).

409 MSS preserve in addition: ' I could be willing though now in th' dark to try / A tough encounter with the shaggi-

est ruffian / That lurks by hedge or lane of this dead circuit / To have her by my side, though I were sure / She might be free from peril where she is.'

410–11 *where . . . event* 'where an equal balance of hope and fear weighs the outcome'.

413 Quarles has 'squint-eyed Suspicion' (*A Feast for Worms*, 11.90).

421 *complete steel* 'full armour'.

422–30 Remembering Spenser's chaste Belphoebe who ranges the wild forest (*Faerie Queene*, 2.3.39), wearing a 'quiver gay, / Stuffed with steel-headed darts' (2.3.29). Horace's upright man (*Odes*, 3.22) survives deserts and mountains, wild beasts and bandits; the 'infamous cliffs' ('ill-famed') are from Horace, *Odes*, 1.3.20.

423 *unharboured* 'without shelter'.

Yea there, where very desolation dwells
By grots, and caverns shagged with horrid shades,
She may pass on with unblenched majesty,   430
Be it not done in pride, or in presumption.
Some say no evil thing that walks by night
In fog, or fire, by lake, or moorish fen,
Blue meagre hag, or stubborn unlaid ghost,
That breaks his magic chains at curfew time,   435
No goblin, or swart fairy of the mine,
Hath hurtful power o'er true virginity.
Do ye believe me yet, or shall I call
Antiquity from the old Schools of Greece
To testify the arms of chastity?   440
Hence had the huntress Dian her dread bow
Fair silver-shaftèd queen for ever chaste,
Wherewith she tamed the brinded lioness
And spotted mountain pard, but set at nought
The frivolous bolt of Cupid, gods and men   445
Feared her stern frown, and she was queen o'th' woods.
What was that snaky-headed-Gorgon shield
That wise Minerva wore, unconquered Virgin,
Wherewith she freezed her foes to cóngealed stone?
But rigid looks of chaste austerity,   450
And noble grace that dashed brute violence
With sudden adoration, and blank awe.
So dear to Heaven is saintly chastity,
That when a soul is found sincerely so,
A thousand liveried angels lackey her,   455
Driving far off each thing of sin and guilt,
And in clear dream, and solemn vision
Tell her of things that no gross ear can hear,
Till oft converse with heavenly habitants
Begin to cast a beam on the outward shape,   460
The unpolluted temple of the mind,
And turns it by degrees to the soul's essence,
Till all be made immortal: but when lust
By unchaste looks, loose gestures, and foul talk,

429 *shagged* 'hairy' (commonly used of rough vegetation).
430 *unblenched* 'unblemished'.
432–7 Varying the reassurances of Fletcher's Clorin: 'if I keep / My virgin flower uncropped, pure, chaste, and fair, / No goblin, wood-god, fairy, elf, or fiend, / Satyr or other power that haunts the groves, / Shall hurt my body, or by vain illusion / Draw me to wander after idle fires; / Or voices calling me in dead of night, / To make me follow, and so tole me on / Through mire and standing pools, to find my ruin' (*The Faithful Shepherdess*, 1.1.115–23). Burton, *Anatomy*, 1.2.1.2, describes the species of 'fiery, aerial, terrestrial, watery, and subterranean devils, besides those fairies, satyrs, nymphs'.
434 'Bloodless and fleshless night-spirits, ghosts that refuse to be conjured down'; 'wrinkled' stood originally for 'meagre'.
441–4 The huntress-goddess Diana is conventionally (in the 'old Schools of Greece') allegorized as Chastity (hence the opposition of her arrows and Cupid's); Vincenzo Cartari, *Imagini* (1560) illustrates from Pausanias an image of Diana bearing in one hand a leopard and in the other a lion, which he cannot explain.
447–9 Minerva's shield carries an image of the petrifying Gorgon's head (Homer, *Iliad*, 5:741). Petrarch equips Laura with a Gorgon shield in *The Triumph of Chastity*, 119.
455 'A thousand of God's angels attend on her.'
458 As in *Arcades*, 73–4, the music of the spheres is heard by 'none . . . with gross unpurgèd ear'.
459–63 'He who has apprehended the beauty of the Good . . . forgets all bodily sensation and all bodily movements . . . the beauty of the Good bathes his mind in light, and takes all his soul up into itself, and draws it forth from the body, and changes the whole man into eternal substance' (*Hermetica*, 10.6).
463–75 Plato, *Phaedo*, 81: the pure soul 'lives in bliss and is released from the error and folly of men, their fears and wild

But most by lewd and lavish act of sin,   465
Lets in defilement to the inward parts,
The soul grows clotted by contagion,
Imbodies, and imbrutes, till she quite lose
The divine property of her first being.
Such are those thick and gloomy shadows damp   470
Oft seen in charnel vaults, and sepulchres
Lingering, and sitting by a new made grave,
As loath to leave the body that it loved,
And linked itself by carnal sensuality
To a degenerate and degraded state.   475
Second Brother. How charming is divine philosophy!
Not harsh, and crabbed as dull fools suppose,
But musical as is Apollo's lute,
And a perpetual feast of nectared sweets,
Where no crude surfeit reigns. *Elder Brother.* List, list, I hear   480
Some far-off halloo break the silent air.
Second Brother. Methought so too; what should it be?
Elder Brother. For certain
Either some one like us night-foundered here,
Or else some neighbour woodman, or at worst,
Some roving robber calling to his fellows.   485
Second Brother. Heaven keep my sister, again, again, and near,
Best draw, and stand upon our guard. *Elder Brother.* I'll halloo,
If he be friendly he comes well, if not,
Defence is a good cause, and Heaven be for us.

The Attendant Spirit habited like a shepherd.

That halloo I should know, what are you? speak;   490
Come not too near, you fall on iron stakes else.
Spirit. What voice is that, my young Lord? speak again.
Second Brother. O brother, 'tis my father's Shepherd sure.
Elder Brother. Thyrsis? Whose artful strains have oft delayed
The huddling brook to hear his madrigal,   495
And sweetened every muskrose of the dale,
How cam'st thou here good swain? hath any ram
Slipped from the fold, or young kid lost his dam,
Or straggling wether the pent flock forsook?
How couldst thou find this dark sequestered nook?   500
Spirit. O my loved master's heir, and his next joy,

---

passions and all other human ills ... But the soul which has
been polluted ... is engrossed by the corporeal, which the
continual association and constant care of the body have made
natural to her ... such a soul is depressed and dragged down
again into the visible world, because she is afraid of the invis-
ible ... prowling about tombs and sepulchres, in the neigh-
bourhood of which, as they tell us, are seen certain ghostly
apparitions of souls which have not departed pure, but are
cloyed with sight and therefore visible'. Virgil, *Aeneid*, 6:730–
8 gives another rendering. Satan transformed to a serpent
laments the obligation 'This essence to incarnate and imbrute,
/ That to the height of deity aspired' (*Paradise Lost*, 9:166–7).
472 *Lingering* hovering (MSS and *1637*).

478 'Sweet and musical / As bright Apollo's lute' (Shake-
speare, *Love's Labours Lost*, IV. iii. 339–40).
480 *crude surfeit* 'sour nausea'.
483 *night-foundered* 'brought to grief by night's onset'.
489 *Defence is a good cause* 'Self-defence is a legally ad-
equate ground of action'.
491 *iron stakes* 'swords' (originally 'pointed').
493 The genitive is editorial.
494–6 The music of Theocritus's Thyrsis falls like echo-
ing water hurrying down ('huddling') from the rock (1:7–8);
Orpheus charms the course of rivers (Apollonius, *Argonautica*,
1:27).
501 *next* 'nearest'.

I came not here on such a trivial toy
As a strayed ewe, or to pursue the stealth
Of pilfering wolf, not all the fleecy wealth
That doth enrich these downs, is worth a thought   505
To this my errand, and the care it brought.
But O my virgin lady, where is she?
How chance she is not in your company?
Elder Brother. To tell thee sadly shepherd, without blame,
Or our neglect, we lost her as we came.   510
Spirit. Ay me unhappy then my fears are true.
Elder Brother. What fears good Thyrsis? Prithee briefly show.
Spirit. I'll tell ye, 'tis not vain, or fabulous,
(Though so esteemed by shallow ignorance)
What the sage poets taught by the heavenly Muse,   515
Storied of old in high immortal verse
Of dire Chimeras and enchanted isles,
And rifted rocks whose entrance leads to Hell,
For such there be, but unbelief is blind.
          Within the navel of this hideous wood,   520
Immured in cypress shades a sorcerer dwells
Of Bacchus, and of Circe born, great Comus,
Deep skilled in all his mother's witcheries,
And here to every thirsty wanderer,
By sly enticement gives his baneful cup,   525
With many murmurs mixed, whose pleasing poison
The visage quite transforms of him that drinks,
And the inglorious likeness of a beast
Fixes instead, unmoulding reason's mintage
Charactered in the face; this have I learned   530
Tending my flocks hard by in the hilly crofts,
That brow this bottom glade, whence night by night
He and his monstrous rout are heard to howl
Like stabled wolves, or tigers at their prey,
Doing abhorrèd rites to Hecate   535
In their obscurèd haunts of inmost bowers,
Yet have they many baits, and guileful spells
To inveigle and invite the unwary sense
Of them that pass unweeting by the way.
This evening late by then the chewing flocks   540
Had ta'en their supper on the savoury herb
Of knotgrass dew-besprent, and were in fold,

---

503   *stealth* 'plunder'.

513–18   But in *Paradise Lost*, 2: 626–8, the fallen angels find 'worse / Than fables yet have feigned, or fear conceived, / Gorgons and Hydras, and Chimeras dire'.

519   An afterthought in the Trinity MS.

526   *with . . . murmurs mixed* 'prepared with spells' (but 'mixed murmurs' is a poetic cliché).

530   *charactered* 'imprinted' (drawing on the minting metaphor).

531–2   *hilly . . . glade* 'fields on the hills that rise above the clearing down here'.

532–4   Recalling the noise heard from 'the sounding savage woods' of Circe's island by Aeneas's crew: 'From thence were wailings heard, and lions' wrathful loud did groan, / Resisting in their bands . . . bristled groaning bores, and bears at mangers yelling yawl, / And figures foul of wolves they hear for woe to fret and wail' (*Aeneid*, 7:15–18, Phaer); the wolves are 'stabled' as if at their business in the sheepfolds.

535–6   Euripides' Medea, planning murder, invokes Hecate 'who inhabits her innermost chambers' (*Medea*, 394).

540–2   'when by then the cattle ('chewing flocks') had eaten the knotgrass moist with dew' (or 'cowgrass' from their predilection for it).

I sat me down to watch upon a bank
With ivy canopied, and interwove
With flaunting honeysuckle, and began 545
Wrapped in a pleasing fit of melancholy
To meditate upon my rural minstrelsy,
Till fancy had her fill, but ere a close
The wonted roar was up amidst the woods,
And filled the air with barbarous dissonance 550
At which I ceased, and listened them a while,
Till an unusual stop of sudden silence
Gave respite to the drowsy frighted steeds
That draw the litter of close-curtained sleep.
At last a soft and solemn-breathing sound 555
Rose like a stream of rich distilled perfumes,
And stole upon the air, that even Silence
Was took e'er she was ware, and wished she might
Deny her nature, and be never more
Still to be so displaced. I was all ear, 560
And took in strains that might create a soul
Under the ribs of Death, but O ere long
Too well I did perceive it was the voice
Of my most honoured lady, your dear sister.
Amazed I stood, harrowed with grief and fear, 565
And O poor hapless nightingale thought I,
How sweet thou sing'st, how near the deadly snare!
Then down the lawns I ran with headlong haste
Through paths, and turnings often trod by day,
Till guided by mine ear I found the place 570
Where that damned wizard hid in sly disguise
(For so by certain signs I knew) had met
Already, ere my best speed could prevent,
The aidless innocent lady his wished prey,
Who gently asked if he had seen such two, 575
Supposing him some neighbour villager;
Longer I durst not stay, but soon I guessed
Ye were the two she meant, with that I sprung
Into swift flight, till I had found you here,
But further know I not. *Second Brother.* O Night and Shades, 580
How are ye joined with Hell in triple knot
Against the unarmèd weakness of one virgin

543–5 'I know a bank whereon the wild thyme blows . . . Quite overcanopied with lush woodbine' (*Midsummer Night's Dream*, II. i. 249–51).

547 *meditate . . . minstrelsy* 'play my country music' (based on the Virgilian 'meditate the Muse').

550 *barbarous dissonance* as 'the barbarous dissonance / Of Bacchus and his revellers' that dismember Orpheus (*Paradise Lost*, 7:32–5).

553–4 At the end of Tibullus 2.1, Sleep follows the horse-drawn carriage of night. Spenser *Faerie Queene*, 5.5.1, gives Night a 'humid curtain'.

555–7 Chapman remarks (*Ovid's Banquet of Sense*, 328) a similar 'allusion drawn from the effects of sounds and odours', and glosses it to mean that 'the virtues of good men live in them, because they stir up pure inclinations to the like, as if infused in perfumes and sounds.'

557–64 So Florizel tells Perdita: 'When you do dance, I wish you / A wave o' th' sea, that you might ever do / Nothing but that: move still, still so: / And own no other function' (*Winter's Tale*, IV. iii. 140–3); and so in Drummond's sonnet ('Dear chorister') the nightingale sends 'Such sad lamenting strains, that Night attends; / Become all ear, stars stay to hear thy plight'.

581 *triple knot* Suggests an unholy alliance: the Catholic powers responded to the 1605 Oath of Allegiance with a 'triple knot', to which King James had in 1607 taken a triple wedge (in the *Triplici Nodo Triplex Cuneus*).

Alone, and helpless! is this the confidence
You gave me brother? *Elder Brother*. Yes, and keep it still,
Lean on it safely, not a period   585
Shall be unsaid for me: against the threats
Of malice or of sorcery, or that power
Which erring men call Chance, this I hold firm,
Virtue may be assailed, but never hurt,
Surprised by unjust force, but not enthralled,   590
Yea even that which mischief meant most harm,
Shall in the happy trial prove most glory.
But evil on itself shall back recoil,
And mix no more with goodness, when at last
Gathered like scum, and settled to itself   595
It shall be in eternal restless change
Self-fed, and self-consumed. If this fail,
The pillared firmament is rottenness,
And earth's base built on stubble. But come let's on.
Against the opposing will and arm of Heaven   600
May never this just sword be lifted up,
But for that damned magician, let him be girt
With all the grisly legions that troop
Under the sooty flag of Acheron,
Harpies and Hydras, or all the monstrous forms   605
'Twixt Africa and Ind, I'll find him out,
And force him to restore his purchase back,
Or drag him by the curls, to a foul death,
Cursed as his life. *Spirit*. Alas good venturous youth,
I love thy courage yet, and bold emprise,   610
But here thy sword can do thee little stead,
Far other arms, and other weapons must
Be those that quell the might of hellish charms,
He with his bare wand can unthread thy joints,
And crumble all thy sinews. *Elder Brother*. Why prithee shepherd   615
How durst thou then thyself approach so near
As to make this relation? *Spirit*. Care and utmost shifts
How to secure the lady from surprisal,
Brought to my mind a certain shepherd lad
Of small regard to see to, yet well skilled   620
In every virtuous plant and healing herb
That spreads her verdant leaf to the morning ray,

584   *period* 'sentence'.
586–92   So Jonson, *To Sir Thomas Roe*: 'Fortune upon him breaks herself, if ill, / And what would hurt his virtue, makes it still' (*Epigrams*, 98).
593–7   Like the unpurified waste of an alchemical operation.
597–9   As against Spenser's 'steadfast rest of all things firmly stayed / Upon the pillars of Eternity' (*Faerie Queene*, 7.8.2), and resigned to the work of time's 'consuming sickle'.
602–6   Remembering Phineas Fletcher's anti-Jesuit *Locustae*, 2.39: 'All hell run out, and sooty flags display.' Dante's harpies (human-faced and bird-bodied) build their nests among the blackened foliage in the wood of suicides (*Inferno*, 13:10); his Furies (*Inferno*, 9:40) are girt (*cinte*) with

green hydras. Africa was classically a source of monsters, India of wealth; Sylvester has monsters 'New brought from Afric, or from Ind' (*Bethulia's Rescue*, 4:351–2).
605   *forms* bugs (MSS and *1637*); the sense is 'bugbears'.
608–9   *to . . . life* and cleave his scalp / down to the hips (MSS and *1637*): a minced version of Dante, *Inferno*, 28:24.
610   *emprise* 'purpose'.
611   *little stead* cancelled in the Trinity MS in favour of 'small avail' (the sense), then restored.
614   *unthread* replacing MS 'unquilt'.
619–28   There is no agreement on the identity of the physician 'shepherd', expert in the magical ('virtuous') pharmacopoeia, who paid for Milton's verses with herbs from his satchel ('scrip').

He loved me well, and oft would beg me sing,
Which when I did, he on the tender grass
Would sit, and hearken even to ecstasy,   625
And in requital ope his leathern scrip,
And show me simples of a thousand names
Telling their strange and vigorous faculties;
Amongst the rest a small unsightly root,
But of divine effect, he culled me out;   630
The leaf was darkish, and had prickles on it,
But in another country, as he said,
Bore a bright golden flower, but not in this soil:
Unknown, and like esteemed, and the dull swain
Treads on it daily with his clouted shoon,   635
And yet more med'cinal is it than that moly
That Hermes once to wise Ulysses gave;
He called it haemony, and gave it me,
And bad me keep it as of sovran use
'Gainst all enchantments, mildew blast, or damp   640
Or ghastly Furies' apparition;
I pursed it up, but little reckoning made,
Till now that this extremity compelled,
But now I find it true; for by this means
I knew the foul enchanter though disguised,   645
Entered the very lime-twigs of his spells,
And yet came off: if you have this about you
(As I will give you when we go) you may
Boldly assault the necromancer's hall;
Where if he be, with dauntless hardihood,   650
And brandished blade rush on him, break his glass,
And shed the luscious liquor on the ground,
But seize his wand, though he and his cursed crew
Fierce sign of battle make, and menace high,
Or like the sons of Vulcan vomit smoke,   655
Yet will they soon retire, if he but shrink.
Elder Brother. Thyrsis lead on apace, I'll follow thee,
And some good angel bear a shield before us.

629–41 An afterthought in the Trinity MS (636–7 are an insert) connected the herb with that which Mercury gives Ulysses to withstand Circe's enchantments (*Odyssey*, 10:305). Sandys (on Ovid, *Metamorphoses*, 14:292), who credits its existence, allegorizes it: Circe 'deforms our souls with all bestial vices ... which are not to be resisted but by the divine assistance, Moly, the gift of Mercury, which signifies temperance.' Moly is frequently invoked by the poets as a panacea. Sylvester (*Divine Weeks*, 2.1.1:228–59) apostrophizes the Tree of Life as 'Strong counter-bane ... sacred plant divine' and asks whether it might have been Moly; but a marginal note records 'we cannot say what tree it was.' No more easily identified is Milton's 'haemony', whose name evokes magic (Haemonia or Thessaly was a land of witches),

but could be given a Christianizing etymology: 'blood-wine'.
631 Marvell's Conscience is a 'heaven-nursed plant' with a 'prickling leaf' (*Upon Appleton House*, 355–7).
634–5 *dull ... shoon* Demetrius, *On Style*, 106 (on the use of enlivening detail), quotes a fragment of Sappho about 'the hyacinth on the hills trod underfoot by the shepherd' sharpened by 'on the ground the purple flower'. The 'clouted shoon' ('hobnail boots', but available as a metonym of 'peasant') perform the same function.
646 *lime-twigs* 'entrapments'.
655 Vulcan's son Cacus vomits smoke on Hercules in Virgil, *Aeneid*, 8:252–3.

The scene changes to a stately palace, set out with all manner of deliciousness: soft music, tables spread with all dainties. Comus appears with his rabble, and the lady set in an enchanted chair, to whom he offers his glass, which she puts by, and goes about to rise.

Comus. Nay lady sit; if I but wave this wand,　　　　　　　　　
Your nerves are all chained up in alabaster,　　　　　　　　660
And you a statue, or as Daphne was
Root-bound, that fled Apollo. *Lady.* Fool do not boast,
Thou canst not touch the freedom of my mind
With all thy charms, although this corporal rind
Thou hast immanacled, while Heaven sees good.　　　　　665
Comus. Why are you vexed Lady? why do you frown?
Here dwell no frowns, nor anger, from these gates
Sorrow flies far: see here be all the pleasures
That Fancy can beget on youthful thoughts,
When the fresh blood grows lively, and returns　　　　　　670
Brisk as the April buds in primrose-season.
And first behold this cordial julep here
That flames, and dances in his crystal bounds
With spirits of balm, and fragrant syrups mixed.
Not that nepenthes which the wife of Thon,　　　　　　　675
In Egypt gave to Jove-born Helena
Is of such power to stir up joy as this,
To life so friendly, or so cool to thirst.
Why should you be so cruel to yourself,
And to those dainty limbs which nature lent　　　　　　　680
For gentle usage, and soft delicacy?
But you invert the covenants of her trust,
And harshly deal like an ill borrower
With that which you received on other terms,
Scorning the unexempt condition　　　　　　　　　　　685
By which all mortal frailty must subsist,
Refreshment after toil, ease after pain,
That have been tired all day without repast,
And timely rest have wanted, but fair Virgin
This will restore all soon. *Lady.* 'Twill not false traitor,　　690
'Twill not restore the truth and honesty
That thou hast banished from thy tongue with lies,
Was this the cottage, and the safe abode
Thou told'st me of? What grim aspects are these,
These ugly-headed monsters? Mercy guard me!　　　　　695
Hence with thy brewed enchantments, foul deceiver,
Hast thou betrayed my credulous innocence

660　*alabaster* because her skin is white and because the stone is used in funeral sculpture.
661–2　*root-bound* Daphne, fleeing Apollo, metamorphosed to laurel: 'And late swift feet, now roots, are less than slow' (Ovid, *Metamorphoses*, 1:551, Sandys).
662–6　*Fool . . . Lady?* An afterthought in the Trinity MS, developed from a passage originally at 756.
671　*Brisk* originally qualifying 'blood'.
672–705　An afterthought in the Trinity MS, like 662–6, developed from a passage originally at 756.

674　*spirits* 'distillation'.
675–8　*nepenthes* 'uncare'; Thon's wife gave Helen of Troy (daughter of Jupiter by Leda) a drug 'that (drowning cares and angers) did decline / All thought of ill' (Homer, *Odyssey*, 4:221, Chapman).
687　Echoing Despair's 'Sleep after toil, port after stormy seas, / Ease after war, death after life does greatly please' (Spenser, *Faerie Queene*, 1.9.40); but Comus makes rest a condition of our contract with life.

With visored falsehood, and base forgery,
And would'st thou seek again to trap me here
With lickerish baits fit to ensnare a brute?   700
Were it a draught for Juno when she banquets,
I would not taste thy treasonous offer; none
But such as are good men can give good things,
And that which is not good, is not delicious
To a well-governed and wise appetite.   705
Comus. O foolishness of men! that lend their ears
To those budge doctors of the Stoic fur,
And fetch their precepts from the Cynic tub,
Praising the lean and sallow abstinence.
Wherefore did Nature pour her bounties forth,   710
With such a full and unwithdrawing hand,
Covering the earth with odours, fruits, and flocks,
Thronging the seas with spawn innumerable,
But all to please, and sate the curious taste?
And set to work millions of spinning worms,   715
That in their green shops weave the smooth-haired silk
To deck her sons, and that no corner might
Be vacant of her plenty, in her own loins
She hutched the all-worshipped ore, and precious gems
To store her children with; if all the world   720
Should in a pet of temperance feed on pulse,
Drink the clear stream, and nothing wear but frieze,
The All-giver would be unthanked, would be unpraised,
Not half his riches known, and yet despised,
And we should serve him as a grudging master,   725
As a penurious niggard of his wealth,
And live like Nature's bastards, not her sons,
Who would be quite surcharged with her own weight,
And strangled with her waste fertility;
The earth cumbered, and the winged air darked with plumes,   730
The herds would over-multitude their lords,

---

698   *visored* 'vizarded' (as Comus's rout 'headed like sundry sorts of wild beasts' literally are).

700   *lickerish* 'tempting'.

701   *draught* 'nectar': 'White-wristed Juno. . . took the cup of him and smiled. / The sweet-peace-making draught went round' (Homer, *Iliad*, 1:595–8, Chapman).

707–8   *budge . . . fur* the preachers of abstinence are got up in the budge (woolly lambskin) used in academic or civic robes ('Stoic fur' began as 'Stoic gown'). Comus elides the difference between the serene austerity of the Stoics and the currish incivility of the Cynics whose most famous professor, Diogenes, lived in a tub.

710–55   A persuasion to enjoyment fed from a long tradition, but remarkable for its play with the tradition of thanksgiving (as to Venus in Lucretius 1, or Ovid, *Fasti* 4, or to God in Psalm 104 or Sylvester's *Little Bartas*) which allows the threat of surfeit (728–36) to dominate over the threat of sterility (common since Seneca's *Hippolytus*, famous in Shakespeare's *Venus and Adonis*, 163–74).

713   *thronging* cramming (the Trinity MS; which cancels 'the fields with cattle and air with fowl' in favour of the present 714); 'For [man], the sea doth many millions nurse' (*Little Bartas*, 491).

715–17   'For him, the . . . forests, breed . . . silly Worms, his silken robes to spin' (483–6); 'shops' are factories.

718–20   The earth encloses ('hutches') mineral wealth; but there is contamination from 'hatch' since the sun was supposed to act on the 'womb' of the earth to bring its raw material to metallic fruition.

721–2   'Prove thy servants, I beseech thee, ten days, and let them give us pulse to eat, and water to drink' (Daniel 1: 12, where Daniel and his captive friends insist on fasting); 'Not that it was a thing abominable to eat dainty meats, and to drink wine,' explains the Geneva Bible gloss, 'but if they should have hereby been won to the King [Nebuchadnezzar] and have refused their own religion'.

722   *frieze* 'homespun.'

725–7   Our refusals would be misinterpreted as God's grudgingness, as if we were children (though of Nature, not God) without rights; and 'against him that is a niggard of his meat, the whole city shall murmur' (Ecclesiasticus 31: 24). Line 726 is an afterthought in the Trinity MS.

The sea o'erfraught would swell, and the unsought diamonds
Would so emblaze the forehead of the deep,
And so bestud with stars, that they below
Would grow inured to light, and come at last   735
To gaze upon the sun with shameless brows.
List lady be not coy, and be not cozened
With that same vaunted name virginity,
Beauty is Nature's coin, must not be hoarded,
But must be current, and the good thereof   740
Consists in mutual and partaken bliss,
Unsavoury in the enjoyment of itself
If you let slip time, like a neglected rose
It withers on the stalk with languished head.
Beauty is Nature's brag; and must be shown   745
In courts, at feasts, and high solemnities
Where most may wonder at the workmanship;
It is for homely features to keep home,
They had their name thence; coarse complexions
And cheeks of sorry grain will serve to ply   750
The sampler, and to tease the housewife's wool.
What need a vermeil-tinctured lip for that,
Love-darting eyes, or tresses like the morn?
There was another meaning in these gifts,
Think what, and be advised, you are but young yet.   755
Lady. I had not thought to have unlocked my lips
In this unhallowed air, but that this juggler
Would think to charm my judgement, as mine eyes
Obtruding false rules pranked in reason's garb.
I hate when Vice can bolt her arguments,   760
And Virtue has no tongue to check her pride:
Impostor do not charge most innocent Nature,
As if she would her children should be riotous
With her abundance, she good cateress
Means her provision only to the good   765
That live according to her sober laws,
And holy dictate of spare temperance:
If every just man that now pines with want
Had but a moderate and beseeming share

732–6 The unharvested gems born (Pliny, *Natural History*, 36.29) in the depths of ocean would multiply so as to emblazon and stud the roof of undersea caves, in a parody of heaven. Chapman has 'all those stars, with which the brows [not in Homer] of ample heaven are crowned' (*Iliad*, 18:485). Drummond's *Song* ('It Autumn was') imagines 'one whom some abysm / Of the deep ocean kept had' brought to the surface and surprised into 'uncouth rapture' by the brightness of the sun and stars (145–67).

737–55 So Spenser's Braggadocchio advises Belphoebe to exchange her forest life for the 'joyous court' (*Faerie Queene*, 2.3.39).

739 With the implication of Carew's 'Jupiter . . . will never refuse to stamp Beauty, and make it current with his own impression' (*Coelum Britannicum*, 292–4).

743 *neglected* 'unpicked' (like Virgil's white privet, *Eclogues* 2:18).

745 *Nature's brag* 'what Nature is proud of'.

749–51 Ugly girls can work at embroidery or get ready the wool for spinning.

753 *like the morn* 'like sunshine': 'Who is she that looketh forth as the morning?' (Song of Solomon 6: 8).

756 See notes to 662, 672.

760 *bolt* 'refine': as Shakespeare's Coriolanus is 'ill-schooled in bolted language' (III. i. 317).

762–79 Lucan, *Pharsalia*, 4:373–81: 'O Luxury! thou prodig' vain, / That never canst the mean retain; / And thou insatiate Gluttony, / Pampered with superfluity, / That rak'st and robb'st both land and seas, / Thy wanton appetite to please. / O learn, and better do advise, / How small relief will life suffice, / For Nature doth excess despise' (Gorges).

Of that which lewdly-pampered luxury 770
Now heaps upon some few with vast excess,
Nature's full blessings would be well dispensed
In unsuperfluous even proportion,
And she no whit encumbered with her store,
And then the Giver would be better thanked, 775
His praise due paid, for swinish gluttony
Ne'er looks to Heaven amidst his gorgeous feast,
But with besotted base ingratitude
Crams, and blasphemes his Feeder. Shall I go on?
Or have I said enough? To him that dares 780
Arm his profane tongue with contemptuous words
Against the sun-clad power of Chastity;
Fain would I something say, yet to what end?
Thou hast nor ear, nor soul to apprehend
The sublime notion, and high mystery 785
That must be uttered to unfold the sage
And serious doctrine of Virginity,
And thou art worthy that thou shouldst not know
More happiness than this thy present lot.
Enjoy your dear wit, and gay rhetoric 790
That hath so well been taught her dazzling fence,
Thou art not fit to hear thyself convinced;
Yet should I try, the uncontrollèd worth
Of this pure cause would kindle my rapt spirits
To such a flame of sacred vehemence, 795
That dumb things would be moved to sympathise,
And the brute Earth would lend her nerves, and shake,
Till all thy magic structures reared so high,
Were shattered into heaps o'er thy false head.
Comus. She fables not, I feel that I do fear 800
Her words set off by some superior power;
And though not mortal, yet a cold shuddering dew
Dips me all o'er, as when the wrath of Jove
Speaks thunder, and the chains of Erebus
To some of Saturn's crew. I must dissemble, 805
And try her yet more strongly. Come, no more,
This is mere moral babble, and direct
Against the canon laws of our foundation;

776–9 'Men by their voluntary falling from God, having spoiled themselves of the benefits which they received of him, cast themselves headlong into infinite calamities' (Geneva Bible note on Luke 15: 11 – the prodigal son); but this glutton is untamed by calamity.

779–806 Added after the completion of the Trinity MS.

782 *sun-clad* The 'woman clothed with the sun' (Revelation 12: 1) is identified with the Church, sometimes with the Virgin Mary.

785 *mystery* 'truth'.

786–7 *sage and serious* applied to Spenser in Milton's *Areopagitica*.

791 'They that follow the blind blindly . . . are like him that, trusting to the false rules of a master of fence ['fencing'], ventures presumptuously' (Hobbes, *Leviathan*, 1.5.21).

797 Horace (*Odes*, 1.34) describes how thunder on a clear day, as the 'insensible [*bruta*] earth' shook, persuaded him of God's power. The ribs of a vault may be called 'nerves'.

798 When Spenser's chaste Britomart 'reverses' Busirane's spells, his magic house self-destructs: 'those goodly rooms . . . Now vanished utterly and quite subversed' (*Faerie Queene*, 3.12.42).

800 *fables not* 'tells no lies'.

803–5 Recalling Horace, *Odes*, 1.34 (note to 797), and bringing in thundering Jupiter's violent deposition of his father Saturn and the other giants, consigned to the underworld Erebus (as Horace, *Odes*, 3.1, Fanshawe: 'Jove / Whose arm the giants did confound').

808 *canon … foundation* implying his foundation's identity with the Papacy.

I must not suffer this, yet 'tis but the lees
And settlings of a melancholy blood;   810
But this will cure all straight, one sip of this
Will bathe the drooping spirits in delight
Beyond the bliss of dreams. Be wise, and taste . . .

*The Brothers rush in with swords drawn, wrest his glass out of his hand, and break it against the
ground; his rout make sign of resistance but are all driven in; the Attendant Spirit comes in.*

Spirit. What, have you let the false enchanter scape?
O ye mistook, ye should have snatched his wand   815
And bound him fast; without his rod reversed,
And backward mutters of dissevering power,
We cannot free the lady that sits here
In stony fetters fixed, and motionless;
Yet stay, be not disturbed, now I bethink me,   820
Some other means I have which may be used,
Which once of Meliboeus old I learned
The soothest shepherd that e'er piped on plains.
          There is a gentle nymph not far from hence,
That with moist curb sways the smooth Severn stream,   825
Sabrina is her name, a virgin pure,
Whilom she was the daughter of Locrine,
That had the sceptre from his father Brute.
The guiltless damsel flying the mad pursuit
Of her enragèd stepdame Guendolen,   830
Commended her fair innocence to the flood
That stayed her flight with his cross-flowing course,
The water nymphs that in the bottom played,
Held up their pearlèd wrists and took her in,
Bearing her straight to aged Nereus' hall,   835
Who piteous of her woes, reared her lank head,
And gave her to his daughters to imbathe
In nectared lavers strewed with asphodel,
And through the porch and inlet of each sense
Dropped in ambrosial oils till she revived,   840
And underwent a quick immortal change
Made Goddess of the River; still she retains

809–10   *lees … blood* 'amid the mass of blood … the clotted
mud, / Sunk down in lees, earth's melancholy shows'
(Sylvester, *Divine Weeks*, 1.1:77–9).
816   *his rod reversed* Ovid, *Metamorphoses*, 14:300 has the
same elliptical phrasing for the reverse motion of the wand,
employed to undo Circe's turning of Ulysses' men to beasts;
see note to 798.
817   *of dissevering power* 'power to dissolve the spell'.
822–42   Meliboeus is Spenser's name (borrowed from Virgil)
for Chaucer, and so Milton's for Spenser, who tells (*Faerie
Queene*, 2.10.17–19) the story of Sabrina, daughter of the
pseudo-historical Locrine, son of the Trojan Brutus. He
betrayed his proud first wife Guendolen, who revenged her-
self on husband, mistress and daughter; the last (in Spenser's
version, as in Milton's, only the last) by drowning her in the
river that bears her name (as Severn). On a cue from Drayton,
who also tells the story (*Poly-Olbion*, 6:13–78), Milton elabor-

ates a metamorphosis of the daughter into the river or its
'goddess' (841). Spenser's revival of Marinell in the bower
of his sea-nymph mother Cymoent (*Faerie Queene*, 3.4.40–3,
4.11.6–7) informs the treatment; and Virgil's account of
Aristaeus underwater (*Georgics*, 4: 333–424).
834   Much revised in the Trinity MS before 'pearlèd' (for
its marine associations) is put for 'white' and 'took' for 're-
ceive', 'carry', 'take' (following *Faerie Queene*, 3.4.41).
835   *Nereus* 'th' eldest, and the best' of the sons of Ocean
and Tethys (*Faerie Queene*, 4.11.18), father of the sea-nymphs.
836–47   Cyrene prepares her son to confront Proteus by
bathing him in ambrosia (*Georgics*, 4:415–17); Venus bathes
the dead Aeneas with ambrosia and nectar, and so makes
him a god (Ovid, *Metamorphoses*, 14:605–8).
836   *lank* 'drooping'.
838   'In ponds sweetened with herbs from Elysium'.

Her maiden gentleness, and oft at eve
Visits the herds along the twilight meadows,
Helping all urchin-blasts, and ill-luck signs 845
That the shrewd meddling elf delights to make,
Which she with precious vialled liquors heals.
For which the shepherds at their festivals
Carol her goodness loud in rustic lays,
And throw sweet garland-wreaths into her stream 850
Of pansies, pinks, and gaudy daffodils.
And, as the old swain said, she can unlock
The clasping charm, and thaw the numbing spell,
If she be right invoked in warbled song,
For maidenhood she loves, and will be swift 855
To aid a virgin such as was herself
In hard besetting need, this will I try
And add the power of some adjuring verse.

SONG

Sabrina fair
Listen where thou art sitting 860
Under the glassy, cool, translucent wave,
In twisted braids of lilies knitting
The loose train of thy amber-dropping hair,
Listen for dear honour's sake,
Goddess of the silver lake, 865
Listen and save.

Listen and appear to us
In name of great Oceanus,
By the earth-shaking Neptune's mace,
And Tethys' grave majestic pace, 870
By hoary Nereus' wrinkled look,
And the Carpathian wizard's hook,
By scaly Triton's winding shell,

845 'Remedying all goblin-blights and evidences of misfortune'. After 846 the Trinity MS specifies 'And often takes our cattle with strange pinches [pangs]'.

852 *swain* Meliboeus (822). The supposedly quoted following line is revised from an original 'Each clasping charm and secret holding spell'.

863 *amber-dropping* 'golden': Wither's *Epithalamion* for Princess Elizabeth, 315–18, gives Sabrina and her daughters 'locks of amber'.

868–80 Cataloguing exotic names, as Dryden indicates when translating *Georgics*, 4:336–47, challenges the language. The lists of water-nymphs there, and more ambitiously at *Faerie Queene*, 4.11.48–51, are models. Lines 869–74 are an afterthought in the Trinity MS, and Bridgewater gives 871–82 distributed antiphonally between the brothers. Lines 879–82 are crossed through in Trinity, as to be replaced by 883–4. Neptune with his trident ('mace') controls earthquakes ('earth-shaking' his standard epithet) as well as waters, Tethys is the 'Dame' of Oceanus (*Faerie Queene*, 4.11.18); the 'Carpathian wizard' is the shape-changing Proteus, who in-

habits 'Neptune's Carpathian flood' (*Georgics*, 4:387) carries a hook as 'shepherd of the seas' (*Faerie Queene*, 3.8.30); Triton blows 'his trumpet shrill' before the sea gods (*Faerie Queene*, 3.8.30), 'winding' as both 'sounding' and 'whorled'; Glaucus 'that wise soothsays understood' (*Faerie Queene*, 4.11.13) was magically changed from man to sea-beast and, after due purification, to god; Leucothea, the 'white goddess', saved Ulysses from drowning (Homer, *Odyssey*, 5:333–462; at 462 her hands are lovely): called Ino when mortal, she drowned herself and her son Melicertes, who on deification was called Palemon or Portunus, and presided over harbours; Homer calls the nereid Thetis 'silver-footed' (as at *Iliad*, 1:538); the 'sirens three' (253) are reduced to two (as in Homer) but, instead of being monstrous and murderous like Homer's (*Odyssey*, 12:39–52), are rendered beneficent like Xenophon's (*Memorabilia*, 2.6.11: 'singing to those who were desirous of virtue'); Parthenope's tomb was supposed to survive at Naples, Ligea's comb and rock (of diamond for steadfastness, *Faerie Queene*, 1.6.4) belong to the native mythology of mermaids.

And old sooth-saying Glaucus' spell,
By Leucothea's lovely hands,   875
And her son that rules the strands,
By Thetis' tinsel-slippered feet,
And the songs of Sirens sweet,
By dead Parthenope's dear tomb,
And fair Ligea's golden comb,   880
Wherewith she sits on diamond rocks
Sleeking her soft alluring locks,
By all the nymphs that nightly dance
Upon thy streams with wily glance,
Rise, rise, and heave thy rosy head   885
From thy coral-paven bed,
And bridle in thy headlong wave,
Till thou our summons answered have.
                                Listen and save.

Sabrina rises, attended by water-nymphs, and sings.

By the rushy-fringèd bank,   890
Where grows the willow and the osier dank,
My sliding chariot stays.
Thick set with agate, and the azurn sheen
Of turquoise blue, and emerald green
That in the channel strays,   895
Whilst from off the waters fleet
Thus I set my printless feet
O'er the cowslip's velvet head,
That bends not as I tread,
Gentle swain at thy request   900
I am here.

Spirit. Goddess dear
We implore thy powerful hand
To undo the charmèd band
Of true virgin here distressed,   905
Through the force, and through the wile
Of unblessed enchanter vile.
Sabrina. Shepherd 'tis my office best
To help ensnarèd chastity;
Brightest lady look on me,   910
Thus I sprinkle on thy breast
Drops that from my fountain pure,
I have kept of precious cure,
Thrice upon thy fingers tip,

---

884 *wily glance* as the fish sport 'with quick glance' in *Paradise Lost*, 7:405.
892 'My current comes to a stop.'
893–5 A collection of colour effects like Sylvester's 'green emerald, / The agate by a thousand titles called, / The sky-like turkis' (*Divine Weeks*, 1.3:909–11). In Davenant's *Temple of Love* (1635) the masquers enter in a 'maritime chariot made of a spongy rockstuff mixed with shells, sea-weeds, coral, and pearl'.

897–9 *printless . . . tread* because only water: but the effect is borrowed from Virgil's Camilla who 'Flew o'er the field, nor hurt the bearded grain' (*Aeneid*, 7:808–11, Dryden). The phrasing echoes Shakespeare's 'printless foot' (*Tempest*, J. i. 34) of the sea deities.
914–15 *thrice . . . thrice* 'Three woollen fillets, of three colours joined; / Thrice bind about his thrice-devoted head . . . Unequal numbers please the gods' (Virgil, *Eclogues*, 8:73–5).

Thrice upon thy rubied lip, 915
Next this marble venomed seat
Smeared with gums of glutinous heat
I touch with chaste palms moist and cold,
Now the spell hath lost his hold;
And I must haste ere morning hour 920
To wait in Amphitrite's bower.

Sabrina descends, and the lady rises out of her seat.

Spirit. Virgin, daughter of Locrine
Sprung of old Anchises' line,
May thy brimmèd waves for this
Their full tribute never miss 925
From a thousand petty rills,
That tumble down the snowy hills:
Summer drouth, or singèd air
Never scorch thy tresses fair,
Nor wet October's torrent flood 930
Thy molten crystal fill with mud,
May thy billows roll ashore
The beryl, and the golden ore,
May thy lofty head be crowned
With many a tower and terrace round, 935
And here and there thy banks upon
With groves of myrrh, and cinnamon.
Come lady while Heaven lends us grace,
Let us fly this cursed place,
Lest the sorcerer us entice 940
With some other new device.
Not a waste, or needless sound
Till we come to holier ground,
I shall be your faithful guide
Through this gloomy covert wide, 945
And not many furlongs thence
Is your father's residence,
Where this night are met in state
Many a friend to gratulate
His wished presence, and beside 950
All the swains that there abide,
With jigs, and rural dance resort,
We shall catch them at their sport,
And our sudden coming there

---

917 *glutinous heat* 'hot glue' (by a suggestive exchange of noun and adjective), since glue is heated for use. Compare Psalms 44: 25–6 'our belly cleaveth unto the earth. Arise for our help, and redeem us for thy mercy's sake'; in the Rheims-Douai Bible, following the Vulgate *conglutinatus*, 'is glued in the earth' (43: 25).
921 *Amphitrite's bower* 'the sea' since she is Neptune's wife. Sabrina is to attend her morning toilet; she appears in *Faerie Queene*, 4.11.11 'decked with pearls, which th' Indian seas for her prepare'.

924 *Anchises's line* the 'Trojan kings' of Britain descended from Aeneas's father: Locrine was his great-great-great-grandson.
935 Like Spenser's Thames, ' Wearing a diadem embattled wide / With hundred turrets' (*Faerie Queene*, 4.11.28). Bristol on the Severn estuary was already important in intercontinental trade.
937 The Trinity MS marks 'Song ends'.
949–50 *gratulate . . . presence* 'to welcome his desired appearance here'.

Will double all their mirth and cheer;   955
Come let us haste, the stars grow high,
But night sits monarch yet in the mid sky.

The scene changes, presenting Ludlow Town and the President's Castle, then come in country-dancers, after them the Attendant Spirit, with the two brothers and the lady.

SONG

Spirit. *Back Shepherds, back, enough your play,*
Till next sunshine holiday,
Here be without duck or nod   960
Other trippings to be trod
Of lighter toes, and such court guise
As Mercury did first devise
With the mincing dryades
On the lawns, and on the leas.   965

This second song presents them to their father and mother.

Noble Lord, and Lady bright,
I have brought ye new delight,
Here behold so goodly grown
Three fair branches of your own,
Heaven hath timely tried their youth,   970
Their faith, their patience, and their truth.
And sent them here through hard assays
With a crown of deathless praise,
To triumph in victorious dance
O'er sensual folly, and intemperance.   975

The dances ended, the Spirit epiloguises.

Spirit. To the Ocean now I fly,
And those happy climes that lie
Where day never shuts his eye,
Up in the broad fields of the sky:

---

959 *sunshine holiday* already in *L'Allegro*, 98; based on Spenser's 'sunshine day' (*January*, 3).

962–5 Mercury, sometimes represented as leader of the Graces (Cartari, *Imagini dei Dei Antichi*), stage-manages the finale of *Coelum Britannicum*, though not with wood-nymphs ('dryades'). In Jonson's *Pan's Anniversary* (176–8), the 'best of leaders' Pan leads naiads and dryads 'and to their dances more than Hermes [Mercury] can'. Drayton has holidaying shepherds 'mincen on the plain' (*Eglogues*, 7:13), but the word was already mainly negative.

970–1 Heaven has tested them early. 'Being justified by faith . . . we glory in tribulations also: knowing that tribulation worketh patience; and patience, experience [*dokimē*: 'testedness']' (Romans 5: 1–4).

973 'Ye shall receive a crown of glory that fadeth not away' (1 Peter 5: 4).

976–1023 The Trinity MS has two versions, the first shorter (missing 1000–11) and crossed through. Lines 976–1011 are omitted in Bridgewater except for a version of 976–99 given as a prologue.

976 To the Ocean 'westward'; because 'Half [Ocean's] waste flood the wide Atlantic fills' (Trinity MS: see note to 1–5).

977–88 The 'clear-voiced' Hesperides (to be contrasted with the 'Sirens three', 253) guarded the golden apples in gardens placed westward beyond the ocean (Hesiod, *Theogony*, 215–16). Virgil's underworld Elysium consists of 'large feildis of hailsum air' (*Aeneid*, 6:887, Douglas); in the New Jerusalem 'there shall be no night' (Revelation 22: 5). The Hours (Order (sometimes 'rosy-bosomed'), Justice, Peace) are daughters of Jupiter by Themis, and the Graces, his daughters by Ocean's daughter Euronyme, supply other threesomes (*Theogony*, 901–11).

There I suck the liquid air 980
All amidst the Gardens fair
Of Hesperus, and his daughters three
That sing about the golden tree:
Along the crispèd shades and bowers
Revels the spruce and jocund Spring, 985
The Graces, and the rosy-bosomed Hours,
Thither all their bounties bring,
There eternal Summer dwells,
And West winds, with musky wing
About the cedarn alleys fling 990
Nard, and Cassia's balmy smells.
Iris there with humid bow,
Waters the odorous banks that blow
Flowers of more mingled hue
Than her purfled scarf can shew, 995
And drenches with Elysian dew
(List mortals if your ears be true)
Beds of hyacinth, and roses
Where young Adonis oft reposes,
Waxing well of his deep wound 1000
In slumber soft, and on the ground
Sadly sits the Assyrian Queen;
But far above in spangled sheen
Celestial Cupid her famed son advanced,
Holds his dear Pysche sweet entranced 1005
After her wandering labours long,
Till free consent the gods among
Make her his eternal bride,
And from her fair unspotted side
Two blissful twins are to be born, 1010
Youth and Joy; so Jove hath sworn.
      But now my task is smoothly done,
I can fly, or I can run
Quickly to the green Earth's end,
Where the bowed welkin slow doth bend, 1015
And from thence can soar as soon
To the corners of the Moon.
      Mortals that would follow me,

989 *musky* 'perfumed' (as musk-plants are).

991 *Nard . . . cassia* Perfumes brought together again in Milton's Eden: 'groves of myrrh, / And flowering odours, cassia, nard, and balm' (*Paradise Lost*, 5:292–3). Nard anoints Jesus's feet (Mark 14: 3); the king's garments 'smell of myrrh, and aloes, and cassia' (Psalms 45: 8).

995 *purfled* 'embroidered'; the Trinity MS has 'watchet' ('sky-blue') corrected to 'Yellow, watchet, green and blue', as apter to the rainbow, then cancelled.

996 *Elysian* Originally 'manna', corrected to 'Sabaean' ('Arabian'); the biblical context is sustained in the first Trinity draft where 'young Adonis oft' (999) stood as 'many a cherub soft'.

997 Inserted in the Trinity MS.

999–1011 Venus (the 'Assyrian Queen' Astarte or Ashtoreth, likewise a goddess of love) and the wounded Adonis, still sad among paradisal blisses, are contrasted with Venus's son Cupid ('Desire') promoted to the stars (invoking Shakespeare's 'spangled starlight sheen', *Midsummer Night's Dream*, II. i. 29) and his beloved Psyche ('Soul') rescued (like the Lady) from the suffering the world had imposed on her. The contrast is already available in Spenser (*Faerie Queene*, 3.6.46–50). Spenser, following Apuleius, makes Pleasure the child of the second union; Milton's Youth and Joy represent two of the three Graces (Ficino, *De Amore*, 5.2); Splendour is less aptly invoked here, but perhaps emerges as Virtue (1019).

1017 *corners* 'horns'.

> Love Virtue, she alone is free,
> She can teach ye how to climb　　　　　　　　1020
> Higher than the sphery chime;
> Or if Virtue feeble were,
> Heaven itself would stoop to her.

1019–21 As few may return from Virgil's underworld 'To few great Jupiter imparts this grace, / And those of shining worth, and heavenly race' (*Aeneid*, 6:129–30, Dryden).
1021 *the sphery chime* 'the music-making spheres', but the exchange of noun and adjective refines the planets and stars to mere sound.
1022–3 More than an answer to 'Bow down thine ear to me; deliver me speedily' (Psalms 31: 2). So Wither praises all those angels who 'Have pleasèd been, from Heaven to stoop . . . From evil spirits, us to guard' (*Haleluiah*, Part 2: Hymn 56: 'For the Day of St Michael, and all Angels'). Milton inscribed Camillo Cardoyn's *album amicorum* with this couplet, at Geneva on 10 June 1639.

Lycidas

1645; first printed in a 1638 commemorative volume by his Cambridge acquaintances, *Justa Eduardo King Naufrago ab Amicis Moerentibus Amoris et mneias charin* ('Rites done by his grieving friends for the shipwrecked Edward King, in love and remembrance') containing twenty-three pieces in Greek or Latin, along with *Obsequies to the Memory of Mr Edward King* containing thirteen English pieces, including one by Cleveland. There is a facsimile edition, with notes and translations, by Edward Le Comte (Norwood, PA, 1978). Milton's is the longest and most ambitious poem in the volume; its place at the end suggests late submission, perhaps with the design of summarizing its themes. Edward King was at the time of his death on 10 August 1637 a Fellow of Christ's College, Cambridge (where with Milton he had been a commoner): he would have progressed to a career in the Church (his piety is marked in the preface, which describes King kneeling in prayer as the ship went down in the Irish Sea), and he wrote verses (given in Norman Postlethwaite and Gordon Campbell, 'Edward King, Milton's *Lycidas*: Poems and Documents', *Milton Quarterly*, 18 (1994), 77–111). Milton's nephew Edward Phillips reports, not reliably, that he and Milton were close friends. The poem is not (like Cowley's on Harvey, or even Milton's own *Epitaphium Damonis* on Diodati) a personal elegy. The allegorical account of the studies pursued together (lines 23–36, based on a similar passage in Castiglione's *Alcon*) attracted notoriously unfavourable comment from Dr Johnson. The poem's exhibitionism is not of grief; and its imagination of death by drowning draws on Spenser's ostentatious fiction of the death and regeneration of Marinell (*Faerie Queene*, 3.4.19–43), taken up also for Sabrina's drowning and regeneration in *Comus*. The poem is distracted from its occasion in a death, in a moment of striking lucidity, by its attack on the corrupt Church, by questions of the poet's mission (Ben Jonson died in the same week as King) and by preoccupation with its own devices as a pastoral elegy. Larger features of Milton's chosen mode (consciously at odds with other contributions to the *Justa* collection) include pastoral impersonation (from Theocritus), obtruding the poet's concerns about his own fate (from Bion), the turn from mourning to rejoicing in triumph over mortality (Virgil), satirical reflection on the imperfections of the real world (Sannazaro). These features are precariously mixed in the elegiac tradition, and there is no clear sense of how they are balanced in Milton's distinctly mannerist treatment of them. The poem's specifically Spenserian allegiance is marked by its reproduction of the emotional dynamic of Spenser's *November*, and of its virtuosity. As the poem's shifts of direction may, its metrical vagaries suggest excitement. But the management of the excitement comes from practice with exotic and difficult Italian *canzone* patterns (*At a Solemn Music* exactly mimics the stanza of Petrarch's final ode, *Rime* 366, 'Vergine bella'). The random-looking mixing of long and short lines, the association of remote lines by way of rhyme, the disappointments of rhyme, the occasional resolutions (the 'broken sonnet' of 1–14, the *ottave* of 124–31, or the end) are all worked at. Something of Milton's care with it is evident from the drafts in the Trinity MS (sketches of 1–14, 58–63, and 142–50, as well as a partially corrected draft of the whole, still primitive at 58–63 and 142–50). *1645* prefaces the poem with a statement of double purpose:

In this monody the Author bewails a learned friend, unfortunately drowned in his passage from Chester on the Irish Seas, 1637. And by occasion foretells the ruin of our corrupted clergy then in their height.

Yet once more, O ye laurels, and once more
Ye myrtles brown, with ivy never sere,
I come to pluck your berries harsh and crude,
And with forced fingers rude,
Shatter your leaves before the mellowing year. 5
Bitter constraint, and sad occasion dear,
Compels me to disturb your season due:
For Lycidas is dead, dead ere his prime,
Young Lycidas, and hath not left his peer:
Who would not sing for Lycidas? He knew 10
Himself to sing, and build the lofty rhyme.
He must not float upon his watery bier
Unwept, and welter to the parching wind,
Without the meed of some melodious tear.
   Begin then, sisters of the sacred well, 15
That from beneath the seat of Jove doth spring,
Begin, and somewhat loudly sweep the string.
Hence with denial vain, and coy excuse,
So may some gentle Muse
With lucky words favour my destined urn, 20
And as he passes turn,
And bid fair peace be to my sable shroud.
For we were nursed upon the self-same hill,
Fed the same flock; by fountain, shade, and rill.
   Together both, ere the high lawns appeared 25
Under the opening eyelids of the morn,
We drove afield, and both together heard
What time the grey fly winds her sultry horn,

'Lycidas' appears in Theocritus, Bion and Virgil. It is the name of a horribly drowned Greek sailor in Lucan, *Pharsalia*, 3:635–46; and of the speakers in Sannazaro's *Piscatoriae*, 1 (on the drowned Phyllis), and in Giles Fletcher's *Adonis* (on the drowned Clere Haddon). In Bathurst's Latin translation of Spenser's *Shepherds' Calendar* it is the name of the Protestant pastor Piers.

1–5 Laurel, dark ('brown') myrtles and evergreen ('never sere') ivy (associated variously with victory, love and learning) are emblematic of various poetic achievement, intimating ambitions to variety. The harvest is premature (Milton writes to Diodati, September 1637, of nursing his talent in silence); but so is the death: 'The farmer does not rudely pluck apples that are unripe, but cruel death plunged you in dark Avernus before your time' (Castiglione, *Alcon*, 31–2). 'Yet once more' signals Wotton's reluctance to write (*On the King's Birthday*, 1633) because he is old; the reverse is true here: Milton scatters the leaves (in Virgil, *Eclogues*, 5:40, Mopsus invites the shepherds to 'scatter the ground with leaves' for the dead Daphnis) 'before the year has mellowed'. There is a grim memory of enforced observation of Roman rites from 2 Maccabees 6: 7: 'And in the day of the king's birth every month they were brought by bitter constraint to eat of the sacrifices; and when the feast of Bacchus was kept, the Jews were compelled to go in procession to Bacchus, carrying ivy.'
6 *dear* Spenser uses 'dear constraint' to mean 'dire distress' (*Faerie Queene* 1.1.53).

10 'Who would deny songs for Gallus?' (Virgil, *Eclogues*, 10:3).
10–11 *he knew ... rhyme* 'He could well ['well' is present in the Trinity MS] sing and write verses'; the architectural metaphor (from Latin *condere carmen*) is in Spenser, *Ruins of Rome*, 349: 'To build with level of my lofty rhyme'.
12 In Fletcher, *Purple Island*, 1.30, the dying swan 'tides on her watery hearse'.
13 *welter ... wind* 'wither in the desiccating wind'.
14 'Without the recompense of a poetical lament'.
15–16 Theocritus (1:64) invites the 'country Muses' to 'begin', Moschus's refrain in the *Lament for Bion* invites the 'Sicilian Muses' to 'begin'; Milton goes behind these to the Muses of the Pierian spring ('the sacred well') 'not far from the highest peak of Olympus' (Hesiod, *Theogony*, 62) from where Jupiter rules.
17 *somewhat loudly* echoing Virgil's *paulo maiora* (*Eclogues*, 4:1) and advertising an unaccustomed sublimity.
19 *Muse* for 'poet', whose 'lucky words' are 'happily phrased' before being recognized at 22 as 'well-wishing'.
20 *destined urn* 'the grave destined for me' (the urn is pagan apparatus, as the 'sable shroud' (22) is only metaphorically dyed with grief).
25 *high lawns* 'hill-pastures'.
26 Job 41: 18: 'the eyelids of the morning'.
28 *grey fly* an unspecific attempt to localize Latin *cicada*: the sultriness of its drone is transferred from 'time'.

Battening our flocks with the fresh dews of night,
Oft till the star that rose, at evening, bright,   30
Toward heaven's descent had sloped his westering wheel.
Meanwhile the rural ditties were not mute,
Tempered to the oaten flute,
Rough satyrs danced, and fauns with cloven heel,
From the glad sound would not be absent long,   35
And old Damaetas loved to hear our song.
          But O the heavy change, now thou art gone,
Now thou art gone, and never must return!
Thee shepherd, thee the woods, and desert caves,
With wild thyme and the gadding vine o'ergrown,   40
And all their echoes mourn.
The willows, and the hazel copses green,
Shall now no more be seen,
Fanning their joyous leaves to thy soft lays.
As killing as the canker to the rose,   45
Or taint-worm to the weanling herds that graze,
Or frost to flowers, that their gay wardrobe wear,
When first the whitethorn blows;
Such, Lycidas, thy loss to shepherd's ear.
          Where were ye Nymphs when the remorseless deep   50
Closed o'er the head of your loved Lycidas?
For neither were ye playing on the steep,
Where your old bards, the famous Druids lie,
Nor on the shaggy top of Mona high,
Nor yet where Deva spreads her wizard stream: 55
Ay me, I fondly dream!
Had ye been there – for what could that have done?
What could the Muse herself that Orpheus bore,

29 *battening* fattening; Virgil, *Georgics*, 3:324–6, feeds flocks on grass wet with morning dew.
30–1 Hesperus (Venus) is visible in the western evening sky only in descent.
33 *Tempered . . . flute* 'attuned to the shepherd's pipe' (following Spenser's naturalization of the Latin *avena*, as in *January*, 72, 'oaten pipe'.
34–5 'A numerous throng / Of tripping satyrs crowded to the song; / And sylvan fauns' (Virgil, *Eclogues*, 6:27–8).
36 *Damaetas* Damaetas appears in Virgil as Corydon's poetical master (*Eclogues*, 2: 37–8).
37–49 Bion's *Lament for Adonis* (see Oldham's version, 62–7) and Moschus's *Lament for Bion* fix the generic propriety of nature's mourning the dead beloved. Milton's lines 45–9 moderate it.
39–40 'The cooler cave . . . Whose mouth the curling vines have overspread' (Virgil, *Eclogues*, 5:6–7, Dryden).
41 Echo mourns in the *Lament for Bion* (in Oldham's version, 71).
45–6 'The greatest ox a little taint-worm killeth, / And many a man a little canker spilleth' (Breton, *Solemn Passion of the Soul's Love*, 107–8). The 'canker' is a larval infection of plants, typically the rose: the young man's 'shame', says Shakespeare, is 'like a canker in the fragrant rose' (Sonnet 95).
50 Virgil, himself imitating Theocritus (1.66–9), addresses

the Muses: 'What lawns or woods withheld you from his aid, / Ye nymphs, when Gallus was to love betrayed, / Not steepy Pindus could retard your course, / Nor cleft Parnassus, nor the Aonian source' (*Eclogues*, 10:9–10, Dryden).
52–5 The geographical sweep takes in the Anglo-Welsh coastline on the Irish Sea. Bardsey ('bards' island') is where the Druids are supposed to be buried. Anglesey (Mona) had 'shaggy' slopes (Sylvester's God liberally adorns 'the shaggy Earth . . . with Woods', *Divine Weeks*, 1.1:407–8): Drayton recalls its one-time forests, 'To dwell in my black shades the wood-gods did delight' (*Poly-Olbion*, 9:430). The Dee ('which Britons long ygone / Did call divine', Spenser, *Faerie Queene*, 4.11.39) is called 'wizard' for the reasons that Drayton called it 'an ominous Flood, / That changing of his fords, the future ill, or good, / Of either country [Wales or England] told' (*Poly-Olbion*, 10:206–8).
58–63 The Trinity MS draft has: 'What could the golden-haired Calliope / For her enchanting son / When she beheld (the gods far-sighted be) / His gory scalp roll down the Thracian lea.' The last two lines are cancelled for 'Whom universal nature might lament / And heaven and hell deplore / When his divine head down the stream was sent / Down the swift Hebrus to the Lesbian shore'. This is unhappy, and something closer to the present version is rewritten on another leaf. The death of Orpheus (son of the Muse Calliope, 'enchanting' because he could sing all nature

The Muse herself for her enchanting son
Whom universal nature did lament, 60
When by the rout that made the hideous roar,
His gory visage down the stream was sent,
Down the swift Hebrus to the Lesbian shore.
        Alas! What boots it with uncessant care
To tend the homely slighted shepherd's trade, 65
And strictly meditate the thankless Muse,
Were it not better done as others use,
To sport with Amaryllis in the shade,
Or with the tangles of Neaera's hair?
Fame is the spur that the clear spirit doth raise 70
(That last infirmity of noble mind)
To scorn delights, and live laborious days;
But the fair guerdon when we hope to find,
And think to burst out into sudden blaze,
Comes the blind Fury with the abhorrèd shears, 75
And slits the thin spun life. But not the praise,
Phoebus replied, and touched my trembling ears;
Fame is no plant that grows on mortal soil,
Nor in the glistering foil
Set off to the world, nor in broad rumour lies, 80
But lives and spreads aloft by those pure eyes,
And perfect witness of all-judging Jove;
As he pronounces lastly on each deed,
Of so much fame in Heaven expect thy meed.

into dance, dismembered by Thracian Bacchantes and his head cast into the River Hebrus, mourned by guilty nature) is treated notably by Ovid *Metamorphoses*, 11:1–66 (Golding's version of which may colour this) and Virgil, *Georgics*, 4:517–27. The impotence of his mother to save him is remarked in an epigram of Antipater: 'For dead thou art; and the daughters of Memory bewailed you much, above all your mother Calliope. Why sigh we for our dead sons, when not even the gods have power to protect their children from death?' (*Greek Anthology*, 7.8), and by Ovid 'To Thracian Orpheus what did parents good, / Or songs amazing wild beasts of the wood' (*Amores*, 3.8:21, on the death of the poet Tibullus). The epithet 'swift' for Hebrus is from Virgil (*Aeneid*, 1:317).
64–84 Not only a rejection of fleshly delights, but of the poetry inspired by them (with something of the contrast drawn between erotic-cum-convivial verse and epic-cum-sacred verse in *Elegia 6*, addressed to Diodati). Milton joins Drummond's worldly achievers in their final regret: 'Alas (say they) what boots our toils and pains, / Of care on earth is this the furthest gains?' (*In the Shadow of the Judgment*, 341–2). The praise 'not of men, but of God' (Romans 2: 29) is granted to those whose circumcision is of the heart.
65–6 The phrasing and the Muses' thanklessness comes from Spenser's *June*, 66–7, where these 'daughters of the highest Jove . . . holden scorn of homely shepherd's quill'. To 'meditate the muse' is, following Virgil, *Eclogues*, 1:2, to make verses.
67–9 'How much more easy was it to sustain / Proud Amaryllis' (Virgil, *Eclogues*, 2:14–15, Dryden). Neaera is Virgilian too (with Amaryllis in *Eclogues*, 3), and with tangled hair reappears in Horace and Tibullus.

70–3 Spenser asks who would strive for excellence unless rewarded with 'Due praise, that is the spur of doing well' (*Tears of the Muses*, 454). Even for noble ('clear') minds the thirst for glory is a customary infirmity, says Grillo (cited by Warton); even with wise men, says Tacitus, 'the desire for glory is the last to be abandoned' (*Historiae*, 4.6). Spenser's Contemplation advises those ambitious for earthly fame to cultivate the power 'That glory does to them for guerdon grant' (*Faerie Queene*, 1.10.59); but Redcross is recommended to a 'painful pilgrimage' (61) which will take him to Heaven.
75 *blind Fury* Spenser's 'blind Fury' Erynnis (*Ruins of Rome*, 323) may suggest the phrasing; but Milton means the Fate Atropos, who cuts the thread of life.
77 Virgil's Phoebus 'plucked my ear and warned me' not to pursue too ambitious a poetic programme (*Eclogues*, 6:3–4).
78–84 'Not to value glory when you have done well, that is beyond glory. The great dead and departed can take no pleasure from the praise which cannot reach them and which they cannot hear. But we can look forward to life eternal, which will never obliterate the memory of what we have done well on earth' (*Prolusion 7: Learning Makes Men Happier than Ignorance*). True fame is not in earthly plants (like the green victory laurel), nor in gilt like the 'golden foil . . . displayed' over the masonry of Spenser's House of Pride (*Faerie Queene*, 1.4.4) or the 'glistering glory' of his Philotime or Ambition (2.7.46), but the approval of the Almighty. Spenser's Braggadocchio (though disingenuously) says: 'Fame is my meed, and glory virtue's pray' (3.10.31); Milton's reward is 'so much' less obvious.

O Fountain Arethuse, and thou honoured flood,   85
Smooth-sliding Mincius, crowned with vocal reeds,
That strain I heard was of a higher mood:
But now my oat proceeds,
And listens to the Herald of the Sea
That came in Neptune's plea,   90
He asked the waves, and asked the felon winds,
What hard mishap hath doomed this gentle swain?
And questioned every gust of rugged wings
That blows from off each beaked promontory,
They knew not of his story,   95
And sage Hippotades their answer brings,
That not a blast was from his dungeon strayed,
The air was calm, and on the level brine,
Sleek Panope with all her sisters played.
It was that fatal and perfidious bark   100
Built in the eclipse, and rigged with curses dark,
That sunk so low that sacred head of thine.
     Next Camus, reverend Sire, went footing slow,
His mantle hairy, and his bonnet sedge,
Inwrought with figures dim, and on the edge   105
Like to that sanguine flower inscribed with woe.
Ah! Who hath reft (quoth he) my dearest pledge?
Last came, and last did go,
The pilot of the Galilean lake,
Two massy keys he bore of metals twain,   110
(The golden opes, the iron shuts amain)
He shook his mitred locks, and stern bespake,

85–8 'Thy sacred succour, Arethusa, bring, / To crown my labour' (Virgil *Eclogues*, 10:1); or here to resume a lower pastoral mode, the 'oat' of 88. Arethusa is a Sicilian spring specially honoured by Theocritus, whereas Mincius (that 'winds along the meads, / And shades his happy banks with bending reeds', *Georgics*, 3:14–15) is the river of Virgil's birthplace Mantua, 'crowned' as in Ovid, *Metamorphoses*, 5:388 'woods crown the lake' (Sandys), but also because Virgil's 'pipes' celebrated it. 'Smooth-sliding' (originally 'soft-sliding') derives from Sylvester (*Divine Weeks*, 2.1:116) on the waters of Eden.

89–97 Triton, bearing a conch trumpet (hence 'Herald'), comes in defence of his father the sea-god Neptune, charged with King's death, and interrogates other suspects. The 'felon' winds are 'savage' but also 'criminal'. Hippotades, the patronymic of Aeolus the wind god, is 'sage' because he 'soothes the spirit and checks the rage of the winds' endungeoned by Jupiter (Virgil, *Aeneid*, 1:57).

99 Spenser lists the fifty nereids at *Faerie Queene*, 4.11.48–51, supplying almost all, but not Panope, with descriptive epithets; 'sleek' is applied poetically to calm water.

103–6 In Moschus's *Lament for Bion*, 70–5, the river Meles weeps for Homer and Bion. The briefly suggestive personification of the river Cam recalls Virgil's Tiber rising 'through the shadows of the poplar wood ... An azure robe was o'er his body spread, / A wreath of shady reeds adorned his head' (*Aeneid*, 8:31–4, Dryden). In Spenser's marriage of Thames and Medway, Isis's 'footing' (her 'course') is directed by her 'small grooms' (*Faerie Queene*, 4.11.25), the

'hair' (the river weed) of the Medway is crowned with flowers (46); in *Elegiae*, 1:11, Milton calls the Cam 'sedge-bearing'. The flag-like plants bordering rivers are comparable to the 'lettered hyacinth' of Theocritus (10:28) 'that sweet flower that bears, / In sanguine spots the tenor of our woes' (Drummond's Epitaph to *Tears on the Death of Moeliades*): Ovid *Metamorphoses*, 10:174–219 tells the story of Apollo and Hyacinthus, with at 215–16 how Apollo inscribed the leaves of the metamorphosed boy with the letters AI AI ('Alas, alas').

107 *pledge* 'child' (as Latin *pignus*).

109–12 Christ chooses Peter as his pilot on Galilee (Luke 5: 3–11), and gives him 'the keys of the kingdom of heaven: and whatsoever thou shalt bind on earth shall be bound in heaven: and whatsoever thou shalt loose on earth shall be loosed in heaven' (Matthew 16: 19), which the Geneva Bible gloss explains as 'They are bound whose sins are retained, heaven is shut against them ... how happy are they, to whom heaven is open, which embrace Christ'; the finality of 'amain' ('forcefully') is new unless from Isaiah 22: 22 'he shall shut, and none shall open' (spoken prophetically of Christ). Peter denounces false teachers, 'there shall be false teachers among you, who privily shall bring in damnable heresies ... And through covetousness shall they with fained words make merchandise of you' (2 Peter 2: 1–3); he fierily denounces papal corruptions in Dante's *Paradiso*, 27:10–66 (and picked up by Beatrice, 29:70–126). His 'locks' (with a distracting pun) are 'mitred' because he is a bishop (not as a primate but an overseer).

How well could I have spared for thee, young swain,
Enow of such as for their bellies sake,
Creep and intrude, and climb into the fold? 115
Of other care they little reckoning make,
Than how to scramble at the shearers' feast,
And shove away the worthy bidden guest,
Blind mouths! that scarce themselves know how to hold
A sheep-hook, or have learned aught else the least 120
That to the faithful herdman's art belongs!
What recks it them? What need they? They are sped;
And when they list, their lean and flashy songs
Grate on their scrannel pipes of wretched straw,
The hungry sheep look up, and are not fed, 125
But swoln with wind, and the rank mist they draw,
Rot inwardly, and foul contagion spread:
Besides what the grim wolf with privy paw
Daily devours apace, and nothing said,
But that two-handed engine at the door, 130
Stands ready to smite once, and smite no more.

113–31 The complaint picks up on features of Christ's extended pastoral analogy (John 10: 1–28): 'He that entereth not by the door into the sheepfold, but climbeth up some other way, the same is a thief and a robber . . . [who] cometh not, but for to steal, and kill, and destroy . . . he that is an hireling, and not the shepherd . . . seeth the wolf coming, and leaveth the sheep, and fleeth', itself relying on the pastoral metaphor of Ezekiel 34: 'Woe be to the shepherds of Israel that do feed themselves.'

113–15 'Rather than lose you I would have dispensed with the superfluity ('enow' is plural 'enough', here by understatement) of those whose God is their belly [Philippians 3: 4], and creep . . .'

117–18 Christ is prophetically cast as 'a lamb to the slaughter, and as a sheep before her shearers is dumb, so he openeth not his mouth' (Isaiah 53: 7). Shepherds and shearers (who have no 'care') have opposed vocations: 'There shall arise within thee, by degrees, / A clergy, that shall more desire to fleece, / Than feed the flock' (Wither, *Britain's Remembrancer*, 8:1467–9). The riot of shearing feasts is contrasted with the exclusiveness of being both 'worthy' and 'bidden' at the marriage feast of the King: 'they which were bidden are not worthy' (Matthew 22: 8).

119–20 'Ye blind guides, which strain at a gnat and swallow a camel' (Matthew 23: 24, of the Pharisees). Etymologically, 'bishops' are overseers; but these are blind. Etymologically 'pastors' are feeders (of their sheep); but these are eaters. The 'sheep-hook' becomes the episcopal crozier, irrelevant to true shepherds' needs.

122 'What does it matter to them? . . . They are satisfied.'

123–4 'And when they please, they grind out their insubstantial and fantastic songs on beggarly pipes of wretched straw.' Adapting (to emphasize the meagreness of the diet) Virgil's: 'mangle a miserable tune on a strident straw' (*Eclogues*, 3:27). Milton (*Of Reformation*) complains of the bishops' 'fantastic and declamatory flashes'.

125–7 An attack like Dante's on frivolous teaching: 'the ignorant sheep return from the pasture fed with wind' (*Paradiso*, 29:106–7), or like Joseph Hall's on the Mass: 'Beating their empty maws that would be fed, / With the scant morsels of the sacrist's bread' (*Virgidemiae*, 4.7.61–2); ignorance, unlike hunger, is contagious.

128–9 So at the end of the sonnet 'Cromwell, our chief of men': 'Help us to save free conscience from the paw / Of hireling wolves, whose gospel is their maw': Dante's wolf represents the avarice of the Papacy (*Inferno*, 1:49–57). Corrected Trinity MS and *1638* read 'little' for 'nothing'; *1645* restores Trinity's original 'nothing'. Archbishop Laud himself complained of Romanist intriguers at court, and an anti-Roman proclamation was issued in December 1637. By 1645 (the year of Laud's execution), 'nothing' would again seem apposite.

130–1 The 'engine' is an 'instrument' of retribution and reform, contrasted with the 'abhorrèd shears' of Atropos (75) or the implied shears of the shearers (117). It recalls (with a slippage from two-edgedness to two-handedness repeated in Benlowes's preface to *Theophila* where Christ's 'two-handed sword' signifies 'the Word and the Spirit, which wounds and heals') St John's vision in Revelation: 'out of [Christ's] mouth went a sharp two-edged sword' (1: 16), 'out of his mouth goeth a sharp sword, that with it he should smite the nations' (19: 15). Milton may remember Knox's acceptance of the 'twa-handed sweard' of Reformation from the martyr Wishart, and wish for a violent end to the corrupt clergy. But there is a two-handedness to God's justice: 'As many as I love, I rebuke and chasten . . . Behold I stand at the door and knock' (Revelation 3: 19–20); the 'engine', like the 'word', discriminates: 'The word of God is quick, and powerful, and sharper than any two-edged sword . . . and is a discerner of the thoughts and intents of the heart' (Hebrews 4: 12). Like Mercury's 'golden wand' in *Epitaphium Damonis*, 23, the sword divides the damned from the saved, and what destroys the corrupted clergy assures Lycidas's salvation.

> Return Alpheus, the dread voice is past,
> That shrunk thy streams; return Sicilian Muse,
> And call the vales, and bid them hither cast
> Their bells, and flowrets of a thousand hues. 135
> Ye valleys low where the mild whispers use,
> Of shades and wanton winds, and gushing brooks,
> On whose fresh lap the swart star sparely looks,
> Throw hither all your quaint enamelled eyes,
> That on the green turf suck the honeyed showers, 140
> And purple all the ground with vernal flowers.
> Bring the rathe primrose that forsaken dies,
> The tufted crow-toe, and pale jessamine,
> The white pink, and the pansy freaked with jet,
> The glowing violet, 145
> The musk-rose, and the well attired woodbine,
> With cowslips wan that hang the pensive head,
> And every flower that sad embroidery wears:
> Bid amaranthus all his beauty shed,
> And daffadillies fill their cups with tears, 150
> To strew the laureate hearse where Lycid lies.
> For so to interpose a little ease,
> Let our frail thoughts dally with false surmise.
> Ay me! Whilst thee the shores, and sounding seas
> Wash far away, where'er thy bones are hurled, 155
> Whether beyond the stormy Hebrides
> Where thou perhaps under the whelming tide
> Visit'st the bottom of the monstrous world;
> Or whether thou to our moist vows denied,

132–3 'At thy rebuke the waters fled; at the voice of thy thunder they hasted away' (Psalms 104: 7); but the pastoral mode is recalled with the invocation to Alpheus (a river reckoned to go underground in Arcadia and emerge with 'fountain Arethusa', as in 85, in Sicily).

134–41 Moschus's *Lament for Bion* opens with a summons to the flowers to mourn Bion.

136–8 *use* 'resort'.

138 *swart star* 'star that turns things black': Horace's Bandusian fountain is immune from 'the fierce season of the flaming dog-star' (August) offering 'lovely coolness' to tired oxen (*Odes*, 3.13:9–12).

139–40 'In that enamelled pansy by, / There thou shalt have her curious eye' (Herrick, *Mrs Elizabeth Wheeler, under the Name of the Lost Shepherdess*, 9–10).

142–50 The elaboration is an afterthought in the Trinity MS, and in two versions, of which the earlier reads: 'Bring the rathe primrose that unwedded dies / Colouring the pale cheek of unenjoyed love / And that sad flower that strove / To write his own woes on the vermeil grain / Next add Narcissus that still weeps in vain / The woodbine and the pansy freaked with jet / The glowing violet / The cowslip wan that hangs his pensive head / And every bud that sorrow's livery wears / Let daffadillies fill their cups with tears / Bid amaranthus all his beauty shed / To strew the laureate hearse.' The corrected second version differs from the final one only in reading 'beauties' for 'beauty' at 149. But it reveals a few rejected readings: at line 146 Milton first had

'garish columbine' for 'well-attired woodbine'; and in 148 he wrote 'escutcheon bears' for 'embroidery wears', and experimented with their permutations. Lines 149–50 were inverted. There is a funereal appropriateness in naming eleven flowers rather than the coronal twelve of Spenser, *April*, 136–44 with which Milton is in competition. Jonson's virtuoso list in *Pan's Anniversary*, 11–38, names over thirty (and may give Milton his form 'daffadillies'); Shakespeare in *Winter's Tale*, IV. iv. 118–27 names fewer but with its 'pale primroses / That die unmarried' gives Milton his 'rathe ['prematurely ripe'] primrose that unwedded dies / Colouring the pale cheek' (as the Trinity MS originally had it). 'Crow-toe' is the wild hyacinth, 'jessamine' jasmine. The pansy is 'flecked with black' ('freak' a portmanteau of 'streak' and 'fleck', but the sense 'caprice' jars in the funereal context, as 'white pink' jars). The violet, musk-rose and woodbine come together on Shakespeare's bank where the wild thyme grows (*Midsummer Night's Dream*, II. i. 249–52). 'Sad amaranthus, made a flower but late' (Spenser, *Faerie Queene*, 3.6.45) is an only imaginary crimson flower, etymologically 'fadeless' and here bidden to fade.

153–62 In *1638* the stop is a semi-colon, making the clauses 'Whilst … hold' (154–62) dependent on 153: the reality contradicts the imagination of any hearse. The grammatical dependence survives the merely rhetorical strengthening of the punctuation. The geographical conspectus takes in the eastern shoreline ('shores' is a potent substitution for Trinity's 'floods') of the Atlantic, from the Hebrides in the north

Sleep'st by the fable of Bellerus old,   160
Where the great vision of the guarded Mount
Looks toward Nemancos and Bayona's hold;
Look homeward angel now, and melt with ruth.
And, O ye dolphins , waft the hapless youth.
          Weep no more, woeful shepherds weep no more,   165
For Lycidas your sorrow is not dead,
Sunk though he be beneath the watery floor,
So sinks the day-star in the ocean bed,
And yet anon repairs his drooping head,
And tricks his beams and with new spangled ore,   170
Flames in the forehead of the morning sky:
So Lycidas sunk low, but mounted high,
Through the dear might of him that walked the waves:
Where other groves, and other streams along,
With nectar pure his oozy locks he laves,   175
And hears the unexpressive nuptial song,
In the blest kingdoms meek of joy and love.
There entertain him all the saints above,
In solemn troops, and sweet societies
That sing, and singing in their glory move,   180
And wipe the tears for ever from his eyes.
Now Lycidas the shepherds weep no more;
Henceforth thou art the Genius of the Shore,
In thy large recompense, and shalt be good

(with its 'whelming' originally only 'humming' tides, 'monstrous' because 'full of monsters': 'more deformèd monsters thousandfold . . . came rushing in the foamy waves', Spenser, *Faerie Queene*, 2.12.25), through Land's End where 'in spite of our tearful prayers' Lycidas may 'lie dead near where they say Bellerus lived' (a hero or giant invented from the peninsula's Latin name 'Bellerium', in the Trinity MS originally the giant-slayer Corineus, as in *Faerie Queene*, 2.10.10). An early vision of the archangel Michael gave its name to St Michael's Mount, where King Arthur slew a Spanish giant (Geoffrey of Monmouth, *History of the Kings of Britain*, 10.3), and later the site of a priory and a castle (hence 'guarded'). From Cornwall we look south beyond Cape Finisterre in north-west Spain to the province once called Nemancos and Bayona with its recent Castillo de Montereal.
163 Michael is to look back to bereft England and away from Spain, and weep.
164 Sylvester reflects on the dolphin: 'Lover of ships, of men, of melody, / Thou up and down through the moist world dost ply' (*Divine Weeks*, 5.1:461–2), before digressing to the story of Arion. Dolphins carry ('waft') Spenser's Marinell to his mother's undersea home: 'a team of dolphins rangèd in array, / Drew the smooth charret of sad Cymoent . . . As swift as swallows, on the waves they went, / That their broad flaggy fins no foam did rear' (*Faerie Queene*, 3.4.33).
165 Shakespeare's Balthasar sings 'Sigh no more, ladies, sigh no more / Men were deceivers ever, / One foot on sea and one on shore' (*Much Ado about Nothing*, III. ii. 57–9).
168–71 'So the sun which sets into the sea soon puts his head in order again and rearranges his beams and with fresh gold spangles comes bright into the dawn sky', repairing

locks which like Lycidas's (175) would be muddy from the sea. In Browne's *Britannia's Pastorals*, an oak grew from the body of Pan's dead beloved, whose leaves 'bore / Written thereon in rich and purest ore / The name of Pan' and whose lustre exceeded the 'bright spangles which . . . Shine in the hair' of the sea-goddess Thetis's followers (2.4:843–8).
170 'And adorns his beams, and with freshly glittering gold'.
173 'But the ship was now in the midst of the sea, tossed with waves . . . And in the fourth watch of the night, Jesus went unto them, walking on the sea' (Matthew 14: 24–5).
175 In Dante's earthly Paradise 'the nectar of which men fable' comes true (*Purgatorio*, 28:144) and in Milton's Eden 'crispèd brooks . . . Ran nectar' (*Paradise Lost*, 4:237–40); in Ovid's Golden Age 'With milk and nectar were the rivers filled' (*Metamorphoses*, 1:111).
176 'I heard a great voice of much people in heaven, saying, Alleluia . . . And again they said, Alleluia . . . And the four and twenty Elders, and the four beasts fell down, and worshipped God that sat on the throne, saying, Amen, Alleluia . . . And I heard as it were the voice of a great multitude, and as the voice of many waters, and as the voice of mighty thunderings, saying, Alleluia . . . for the marriage of the Lamb is come' (Revelation 19: 1–7). The 'unexpressive' retention of the Hebrew 'Amen' and 'Alleluia' was a matter of debate with biblical translators.
181 'God shall wipe away all tears from their eyes' (Revelation 7: 17, 21: 4).
183–4 God recompenses Lycidas by making him tutelary deity of the seas. Sannazaro's Lycidas grants as much to the drowned Phyllis 'you shall be goddess [*numen*] of the waters, a happy sign for fishers always' (*Piscatoriae*, 1:97–8).

To all that wander in that perilous flood.   185
Thus sang the uncouth swain to the oaks and rills,
While the still morn went out with sandals gray,
He touched the tender stops of various quills,
With eager thought warbling his Doric lay:
And now the sun had stretched out all the hills,   190
And now was dropped into the western bay;
At last he rose, and twitched his mantle blue:
Tomorrow to fresh woods, and pastures new.

186   *uncouth* Harvey begins the prefatory Epistle to the *Shepherds' Calendar* with the proverb 'Uncouth, unkissed': the new poet Spenser 'unknown to most men, is regarded but of few', but is soon to be 'wondered at of the best'.
188–9   'And fingered the holes of his various (not just the 'homely shepherd's quill' of Spenser's *June*, 66) pipes, singing his rustic (but Doric is the dialect of Greek *literary* pastoral) song'.
190   So Virgil closes *Eclogues*, 1: 'For see yon sunny hill the shade extends' (Dryden).

191   Like Lycidas himself.
192   'And shepherds wonted solace is extinct. / The blue in black, the green in gray is tinct' (Spenser, *November*, 107–8); but Milton's shepherd retains the hope that blue symbolizes.
193   'Tomorrow shall ye feast in pastures new' (Phineas Fletcher, *Purple Island*, 6.77).

Sonnets

1645 includes ten sonnets, six of them neo-Petrarchan love sonnets of which five are in Italian (and interrupted by a brief canzone); two are private, one ('How soon hath Time the subtle thief of youth') reflecting on his own laxness, the other ('Captain or colonél, or knight in arms') deflecting a threat to his person; the other two (*To the Lady Margaret Ley* and 'Lady that in the prime of earliest youth') are complimentary. *1673* adds fourteen sonnets, three of them to public figures (Fairfax, Cromwell, Vane), three to friends (Edward Lawrence and Cyriak Skinner), three satirical (two on his own divorce tracts, one on the 'new forcers of conscience'); one is complimentary (to Lawes), one elegiac (on Mrs Thomason), one is occa-

sional (on the Piedmont massacre) and two are personal (one on his blindness, one on a dream of his dead wife). The English sonnets are regularly written to Italian schemes (octets invariably of the rhyme scheme *abbaabba*, and the sestets mainly avoiding end couplets). More important, his manner indicates that he has set himself to school with humanist Latinizers of the Petrarchan tradition, notably Giovanni della Casa (on whose *Rime e Prose* of 1563 his marginalia survive) who disassembled the ideal Petrarchan 'monotony' and invented a new contorted Italian out of the fragments. Milton's syntax reflects that example, and is further conditioned by the example of the lyric Horace.

Captain or colonél, or knight in arms

The scribal fair copy in the Trinity MS is titled 'On his door when the city expected an assault', corrected by Milton to 'When the assault was intended to the city, 1642', the date then deleted, the title in *1673*. After the Parliamentary defeat at Edgehill in October 1642, the Royalist army moved towards London, de-

feating another Parliamentary force at Brentford on 12 November. The poem may belong here. The style is stiffened, and the tone complicated, by Horatian echoes, which extend beyond the quotation at lines 7–8 to the whole manner. The text followed here is *1645*'s.

Captain or colonél, or knight in arms,
Whose chance on these defenceless doors may seize,
If ever deed of honour did thee please,
Guard them, and him within protect from harms,

1   *colonél* pronounced as if French (the modern pronunciation was already current).

2   *defenceless doors* Milton's Aldersgate Street house was outside the city wall.

He can requite thee, for he knows the charms   5
    That call fame on such gentle acts as these,
    And he can spread thy name o'er lands and seas,
    What ever clime the sun's bright circle warms.
Lift not thy spear against the Muses' bower,
    The great Emathian Conqueror bid spare   10
    The house of Pindarus, when temple and tower
Went to the ground: and the repeated air
    Of sad Electra's Poet had the power
    To save the Athenian walls from ruin bare.

5–8 'The poets being indeed the trumpeters of all praise ... were in conscience and credit bound ... to yield ... honour to all such amongst men, as ... by more than human and ordinary virtues showed in their actions here upon earth' (Puttenham, *Art*, 1.16).
5–6 *charms* 'songs': as the 'charm of earliest birds' (*Paradise Lost*, 4:642) or as Latin *carmina*; but they also have magical power to bring fame to noble ('gentle') deeds.
7–8 'What care ... shall eternise your virtues ... wherever the sun shines on habitable shores' (Horace, *Odes* 4.14:1–6).
10–12 'Alexander [Emathia is a district of his native Macedonia] destroying Thebes, when he was informed that the

famous lyric poet Pindar was born in that city ... commanded ... that no man should upon pain of death do any violence to that house by fire or otherwise' (E. K. on Spenser's *October*, quoting Pliny, *Natural History*, 7.29.109).
12–14 After a defeat of Athens, it was proposed to 'turn the country into sheep-pasture; yet afterwards ... a man of Phocis, singing the first chorus in Euripides's *Electra*, which begins, "Electra, Agamemnon's child, I come / Unto thy desert home", they were all melted with compassion, and it seemed to be a cruel deed to destroy and pull down a city which had been so famous, and produced such men' (Plutarch, *Lysander*, 15, Dryden).

To Mr Henry Lawes, on his Airs

First published in *Choice Psalms* (1648) by Henry Lawes and his brother William as *To my Friend Mr Henry Lawes*, distinguished from the present text (from *1673*) only in punctuation. The title's reference to Lawes's *Airs* (anticipated in added titles to two of the three drafts in the Trinity MS) must post-date 1653 when they were first printed. The first Trinity MS draft gives the date 9 February 1645 (for 1646), pre-

sumably for a projected earlier printing of *Choice Psalms*. Henry Lawes (1596–1662) was from 1630 a member of the King's Music, and *Choice Psalms* is dedicated to the King. Lawes set most of the major lyricists of his time (and collaborated with Milton on *Arcades* and *Comus*); he is the subject of many tributes, among them an earlier one by Waller (1635).

Harry whose tuneful and well measured song
    First taught our English music how to span
    Words with just note and accent, not to scan
    With Midas' ears, committing short and long;
Thy worth and skill exempts thee from the throng,   5
    With praise enough for Envy to look wan;
    To after age thou shalt be writ the man,
    That with smooth air couldst humour best our tongue.
Thou honour'st verse, and verse must lend her wing
    To honour thee, the priest of Phoebus' choir   10

3–4 Ovid relates how Midas judged Pan's music superior to Apollo's and ended 'Punished in that offending part: who bears / Upon his skull a slow-paced ass's ears' (*Metamorphoses*, 11:178–9). The fault avoided by Lawes is joining ('committing'; the first Trinity draft has 'misjoining') short notes and long syllables and mismatching patterns of stress ('accent'): 'In joining of words to harmony there is nothing more offensive to the ear than to place a long syllable with a short note, or a short syllable with a long note' (Campion, *Observations*). Waller also commends the Lawes's attention to verbal textures: 'others with division hide / The light of

sense ... But you alone may truly boast / That not a syllable is lost' (*To Mr Henry Lawes*, 19–22).
5 'Me ivy, meed of learned heads, / Ranks with the gods ... Away out of the common road' (Horace, *Odes*, 1.1:29–32, Fanshawe).
7–8 'You will be titled ('writ') the man who could best fit ('humour') our language with music.'
9 'Verse must lend her pen' (pretending that the synonymy of 'pen' and 'wing' is symmetrical).
10 'To honour you as leader ('priest' suggesting 'elder') of the singers who prefer Apollo to Pan' (unlike Midas).

That tun'st their happiest lines in hymn, or story.
Dante shall give Fame leave to set thee higher
Than his Casella, whom he wooed to sing
Met in the milder shades of Purgatory.

11   *1648* has a marginal note: 'the story of Ariadne set by him in music' (Cartwright's *Ariadne Deserted*).
12–14   Met in the morning by a lakeside in Purgatory, the smiling musician Casella sings for Dante the poet's own canzone *Amor che nella mente mi ragiona* (*Purgatorio*, 2:76–117).

On the late Massacre in Piedmont

First printed in 1673, and occasioned by the massacre in April 1655 of the Protestant Vaudois on the orders of the Duke of Savoy. As Latin secretary to Cromwell, Milton was involved in Cromwell's attempt to organize a Protestant European response. Peter Gilles's *History of the Waldenses in Piedmont* (Geneva, 1654), apparently given credit by Milton, supposes that the Vaudois (or Valdenses) went back to Apostolic times; hence the violence of the reaction. The limited diction, sanctioned by Italian theorists of heroic diction, derives partly from its strictly biblical rhetoric, but partly from its infection by biblically coloured newsletter coverage of the events (the scattered limbs, the hurling from precipices, the echoing screams). The poem gives no hint of how vengeance might be secured against the Piedmontese atrocity, but Cromwell considered invading Piedmont from Nice; a likely model in Horace (*Odes*, 1.2, an appeal to Augustus to avenge Persian atrocities) proposed an end to civil strife and war in the East.

Avenge O Lord thy slaughtered saints, whose bones
Lie scattered on the Alpine mountains cold,
Even them who kept thy truth so pure of old
When all our fathers worshipped stocks and stones,
Forget not: in thy book record their groans   5
Who were thy sheep and in their ancient fold
Slain by the bloody Piedmontese that rolled
Mother with infant down the rocks. Their moans
The vales redoubled to the hills, and they
To Heaven. Their martyred blood and ashes sow   10
O'er all the Italian fields where still doth sway
The triple Tyrant: that from these may grow
A hundredfold, who having learned thy way
Early may fly the Babylonian woe.

1–2   'The souls of them that were slain for the word of God . . . cried . . . avenge our blood' (Revelation 6: 9–10); 'Our bones are scattered at the grave's mouth' (Psalms 141: 7). the 'Alpine mountains cold' may derive from Fairfax (*Jerusalem Delivered*, 13.60, a phrase not in Tasso).
4   Idolatrous Judah turns from the true God and commits 'adultery with stones and with stocks' (Jeremiah 3: 9).
5   'The dead were judged out of those things which were written in the books, according to their works' (Revelation 20: 12).
6–9   'For thy sake we are killed all the day long; we are counted as sheep for the slaughter' (Psalms 44: 22);.

10–13   'In the blood of the martyrs is the seed of the Church' (Tertullian, *Apologeticus*, 50).
11   *sway* punning on 'rule' and 'stagger'.
12   *triple Tyrant* the Pope, on account of his tiara; but alluding to the triple-bodied tyrant Geryon overcome by Hercules (*Aeneid*, 8:202).
14   'Flee out of the midst of Babylon . . . be not cut off in her iniquity, for this is the time of the Lord's vengeance' (Jeremiah 51: 6); Babylon is customarily identified with Rome.

When I consider how my light is spent

First printed in 1673, the sonnet cannot be dated. None of the suggested dates between 1642 and 1655 is supported by external evidence for the condition of the poet's sight, even less for his anxieties about failing inspiration (sometimes offered as a gloss on 'blindness'). It is a meditation, couched in almost exclusively scriptural language, on God's ways with those who love him, and the fragility of human notions of justice. Petrarch's movement from dismay to reassurance in the sonnet beginning 'My eyes, our sun is darkened' and ending, 'Praise Him, who binds and loosens, who in an instant locks and opens, who makes us happy after grief' (*Rime*, 275: 'Occhi miei') is analogous.

When I consider how my light is spent,
  Ere half my days, in this dark world and wide,
  And that one talent which is death to hide,
  Lodged with me useless, though my soul more bent
To serve therewith my Maker, and present   5
  My true account, least he returning chide,
  "Doth God exact day-labour, light denied,"
  I fondly ask; but Patience to prevent
That murmur, soon replies, "God doth not need
  Either man's work or his own gifts, who best   10
  Bear his mild yoke, they serve him best, his state
Is kingly. Thousands at his bidding speed
And post o'er land and ocean without rest:
They also serve who only stand and wait."

1 'When I consider, how I have offended ... I much admire / He casts me not into eternal fire: / But he in mercy makes me kiss his rod' (Quarles, *Divine Meditations*, 33). Light is 'spent' as a candle might be.
3–4 Like the 'unprofitable servant' who 'was afraid, and went and hid [the Lord's] talent in the earth ... and his lord ... said unto him, Thou wicked and slothful servant ... I should have received mine own with usury'; and the lord commanded he be cast 'into outer darkness' (Matthew 25: 25–30); 'useless' puns on 'use' as 'interest'.
6 The affront to ordinary justice 'murmured' of by the day-labourers who worked all day for the same penny wage as those who worked for an hour is compounded by the injustice of expecting the poet to work in the dark (Matthew 20: 1–16).
8–9 *prevent ... murmur* 'frustrate that complaint', rather than forestall it. But Patience enters before the expected 'turn' of the sonnet on line 9.
10 *gifts* 'the return of his own gifts'.
11 'My yoke is easy' (Matthew 11: 30).
11–12 'The chariots of God are twenty thousand, even thousands of angels' (Psalms 67: 17); 'kingly' (though it excludes 'tyrannical') is a daringly unstable word.
12–14 'Wait on the Lord, undaunted stand; / His heavenly will attend, / Who timely aid will send' (Psalms 27: 14, Sandys).

Methought I saw my late espousèd saint

First printed in 1673, the poem's actual occasion is obscured by ostentatious literary reminiscence, starting with Euripides' *Alcestis*. Dreaming of the beloved is a commonplace of sonnets (as in Sidney's poem cited below), and the turn to dreaming the dead beloved's return already well worked, famously by Giovanni Pontano in his *Tumuli* and elsewhere, less famously by William Fowler in *A Dream* where 'Sche quhome I loued, quhase death is all my woe' visits the poet to reassure him with a kiss. Milton lost two wives, Mary three days after giving birth to a daughter, Katherine four months after giving birth to a daughter (on the day after the Feast of the Purification of the Virgin).

Methought I saw my late espousèd saint
  Brought to me like Alcestis from the grave,
  Whom Jove's great son to her glad husband gave,
  Rescued from death by force though pale and faint.
Mine as whom washed from spot of child-bed taint,   5

1 The vision is introduced by a formula famously used in Ralegh's complimentary sonnet for the *Faerie Queene* 'Methought I saw the grave where Laura lay'; the 'saint' (standardly used of the blessed dead in Heaven) is one to whom the poet was 'recently married'.
2–4 Alcestis died in her husband's place, a sacrificed ac-counted so great 'that in recognition of her magnanimity it was granted ... that her soul should rise from the Stygian depths' (Plato, *Symposium*, 179c). In Euripides's *Alcestis*, Hercules ('the noble son of mighty Zeus', 1136) returns her to her husbnd Admetus, veiled (1005) and still spectral-seeming (1125–7) but real.

Purification in the Old Law did save,
And such, as yet once more I trust to have
Full sight of her in Heaven without restraint,
Came vested all in white, pure as her mind:
Her face was veiled, yet to my fancied sight,   10
Love, sweetness, goodness, in her person shined
So clear, as in no face with more delight.
But O as to embrace me she inclined
I waked, she fled, and day brought back my night.

6–7 'Now when the days of her purifying are out (whether it be for a son or for a daughter) she shall bring to the priest a lamb of one year old ... and a young pigeon or a turtle dove ... Who shall offer it before the Lord, and make an atonement for her: so she shall be purged of the issue of her blood. This is the law for her that hath borne a male or female' (Leviticus 12: 6–7); Milton's formula echoes Luke 2: 22 'when the days of [Mary's] purification according to the law of Moses were accomplished'. The purified mother is imagined in white, like the saints of Heaven 'which came out of tribulation, and have washed their robes, and made them white in the blood of the Lamb' (Revelation 7: 14). 10–14 Sidney dreams of Stella who 'not only shines but sings, / I start, look, hark, but what in closed up sense / Was held, in opened sense it flies away' (*Astrophil*, 38:9–10); the particular turn may be owing to Pontano, 'the night is day to me and light ... the day is dark to me and night' (*Tumuli*, 2.60, one of several poems about his wife's haunting his dreams).

The Fifth Ode of Horace, Liber I

First printed in 1673, with a Latin text appended, and a gloss on the subject: 'Horace, who had swum like a shipwrecked man from Pyrrha's allurements, declares the wretchedness of those still ensnared by her love.' No date can be attached to it. No attempt has been made (despite Milton's claim) to follow Horace's scheme (fourth Asclepiadean), nor (despite some attempts to show otherwise) to write quantitative verse at all. It is made something that Horace might have recognized by its addiction to some of his phrases ('liquid odours', 'credulous, all gold', 'always vacant, always amiable'), and by its tracking the original line by line in defiance of English syntax.

Quis multa gracilis te puer in rosa

Rendered almost word for word without rhyme according to the Latin measure, as near as the language will permit.

What slender youth bedewed with liquid odours
Courts thee on roses in some pleasant cave,
    Pyrrha for whom bind'st thou
    In wreaths thy golden hair,
Plain in thy neatness; O how oft shall he   5
On faith and changèd gods complain: and seas
    Rough with black winds and storms
    Unwonted shall admire:
Who now enjoys thee credulous, all gold,
Who always vacant always amiable   10
    Hopes thee; of flattering gales
    Unmindful. Hapless they
To whom thou untried seem'st fair. Me in my vowed
Picture the sacred wall declares t' have hung
    My dank and dropping weeds   15
    To the stern God of Sea.

Sir John Suckling (1609–1642)

'Natural, easy Suckling', says Congreve's Millamant (*The Way of the World*, IV. i). Having left Trinity College, Cambridge, without a degree, he fell heir to great wealth on the death of his father (Comptroller of James I's Household). He played the knight in arms for some years, joining Buckingham's expedition to the Île de Rhé in 1627, and serving with Lord Wimbledon in the Low Countries. He was knighted before joining Sir Henry Vane's embassy to Gustavus Adolphus in Germany. 'He returned to England an extraordinary accomplished gent, grew famous at court for his ready sparkling wit . . . he was incomparably ready at reparteeing . . . he was the greatest gallant of his time, and the greatest gamester, both for bowling and cards' (Aubrey). To write his very brief Socinian *Account of Religion by Reason* he went on an expedition to Bath 'like a young prince for all manner of equipage and convenience', with 'a cartload of books' and two friends – Davenant and the Jack Young who had paid for Ben Jonson's epitaph in Westminster Abbey. *Aglaura* was lavishly produced at his own expense in 1637 ('no tinsel', says Aubrey, 'all the lace pure gold and silver, which cost him . . . I have forgot'). In 1639 he led a troop to Scotland in the first Bishops' War, an expedition, extravagantly mounted like his play, which was the subject of a satirical ballad. He sat as MP in the Parliament of 1640. In 1641 he was involved, like Davenant, in a plot to rescue Strafford. After its failure, he fled to die in exile, taking his own life by poison in Paris.

It came easy to Suckling to cut a glamorous figure while he lived. Whatever his ready gifts, his literary reputation was less natural. While he lived, his only publication was the tragicomedy of *Aglaura*, got up absurdly as a folio (1638). His posthumous reputation was carefully nurtured. *Fragmenta Aurea* consisted of all his 'incomparable pieces . . . published by a friend to perpetuate his memory' (1646, reprinted with corrections 1648); *The Last Remains* were made up 'of all his poems and letters, which have been so long expected, and never till now published' (1659). The two collections were reprinted as *Works* three times before the end of the century. Suckling's is a Restoration reputation, and this because he amazed his readers not with excess, but by disembarrassing his poetry of all the difficulties that attended the heritage of Donne and Jonson. The standard modern edition is *The Works*, 2 vols (Oxford: Clarendon Press, 1971): Thomas Clayton edits *The Non-Dramatic Works* and L. A. Beaurline *The Plays*. There is a facsimile edition of *Aglaura* (Menston: Scolar Press, 1970). Work on Suckling is described by David Judkins in *English Literary Renaissance*, 7 (1977), 252–5.

Song

Printed in *Aglaura* (at 4.2:14) 1638, but widely current (including a Latin version by Henry Bold): settings include those by William Lawes and Thomas Arne. Sung by Orsames, 'a young lord antiplatonic'. A Folger Library MS gives the title (adapted from the play) 'A gentleman having repulse from a gentlewoman, a friend gives him counsel'; it counters Ovid's advice to the still anxious lover: 'Let him that loves look pale, for I protest, / That colour in a lover still shows best' (*Art of Love*, 1:729, Thomas Heywood).

> Why so pale and wan fond lover?
>   Prithee why so pale?
> Will, when looking well can't move her
>   Looking ill prevail?
>   Prithee why so pale?   5
>
> Why so dull and mute young sinner?
>   Prithee why so mute?
> Will, when speaking well can't win her,
>   Saying nothing do 't?
>   Prithee why so mute?   10

6 *sinner* signor (Folger MS); which may be the sense.

Quit, quit for shame, this will not move,
        This cannot take her;
If of herself she will not love,
        Nothing can make her:
        The devil take her.   15

Sonnet 3

1646. One of three self-consciously Donnean pieces,
titled as a group to recall *Songs and Sonnets*; this
recalls *Love's Deity*.

O for some honest lover's ghost,
        Some kind unbodied post
        Sent from the shades below.
        I strangely long to know
Whether the nobler chaplets wear,   5
Those that their mistress' scorn did bear,
        Or those that were used kindly.

For whatsoe'er they tell us here
        To make those sufferings dear,
        'Twill there I fear be found,
        That to the being crowned,   10
To have loved alone will not suffice,
Unless we also have been wise,
        And have our loves enjoyed.

What posture can we think him in,   15
        That here unloved again
        Departs, and 's thither gone
        Where each sits by his own?
Or how can that Elizium be
Where I my mistress still must see   20
        Circled in others' arms?

For there the judges all are just,
        And Sophonisba must
        Be his whom she held dear;
        Not his who loved her here: 25
The sweet Philoclea since she died

2 *post* 'ambassador'.
4–7 'I long to know whether those happy in love or un-
happy wear the finer garlands.' Virgil's soldiers and poets
wear 'snowy fillets' (*Aeneid*, 6:665), but not his lovers.
13–14 But 'To love and be wise is not given even to Jupi-
ter' (Burton, *Anatomy*, 'Democritus to the Reader').
15–18 'What shall we think of his situation whose love is
not returned on earth and who joins the lovers of the under-
world who sit contented by their beloveds?'; Virgil's disap-
pointed lovers 'In secret solitude and myrtle shades / Make
endless moans, and, pining with desire, / Lament too late
their unextinguished fire' (*Aeneid*, 6: 442–4, Dryden).

22 'Beyond the reach of our false justice, we shall meet
true judges . . . Minos and Rhadamanthus . . . and all those
half-divinities who were upright on earth' (Plato, *Apology*,
41a); but here they decide for the lovers, not for those who
unavailingly desire love.
23–8 Sophonisba is 'Of female faith, the long-lived story'
(Marston, *Sophonisba*, 5.3:139), faithful to Massinissa though
obliged to marry Syphax, who loved her. Philoclea loves
Pyrochles but is wooed (unsuccessfully) by Amphialus: the
story is a major strand in Sidney's *Arcadia*.

Lies by her Pyrocles's side,
Not by Amphialus.

Some bays (perchance) or myrtle bough
For difference crowns the brow   30
Of those kind souls that were
The noble martyrs here;
And if that be the only odds
(As who can tell) ye kinder gods,
Give me the woman here.   35

29–30 The bays are for poetry: Waller's unhappy poet-lover 'catched at love, and filled his arm with bays' (*The Story of Phoebus and Daphne Applied*, 20); the myrtle is for love (which may be disappointed).

A Ballad. Upon a Wedding

1646; but in addition to a few minor adjustments, its stanza 16 is repositioned (following Clayton) to prepare for the summons of the cook (85) and that stanza's two halves have been transposed (to make sense of 'running on' about the bride). *1646* includes all the stanzas printed here: their order (because contingent on the pattern of a wedding day reported by outsiders) is easily confused; the obliqueness of the style (one MS gives the title 'A ballad, or parley, between two west-country men on sight of a wedding'; *Wit's Recreations Refined* (1650) gives 'A Discourse between two Country-men') makes for a high frequency of minor variation between the textual witnesses. The poem was already itself parodied before 1640. The marriage may be Lord Lovelace's to Lady Anne Wentworth, 11 July 1638; and allowed such a context, the addressee 'Dick' may be Richard Lovelace. Carew's *Hymeneal Song* on the Lovelace–Wentworth match uses a courtly slowed version of the same tailed rhyme ballad stanza, and the two may be companion pieces. 'I tell thee Dick' was current as the name of a ballad tune, testimony to the popularity of this ballad.

I tell thee Dick where I have been,
Where I the rarest things have seen;
O things without compare!
Such sights again cannot be found
In any place on English ground,   5
Be it at wake, or fair.

At Charing Cross, hard by the way
Where we (thou know'st) do sell our hay,
There is a house with stairs;
And there did I see coming down   10
Such folk as are not in our town,
Vorty at least, in pairs.

Amongst the rest, one pest'lent fine,
(His beard no bigger though than thine)
Walked on before the rest: 15
Our landlord looks like nothing to him:

4–6 'The very rustics . . . instead of tilts, tournaments . . . have their wakes, whitsun-ales, shepherds' feasts' (Burton, *Anatomy*, 3.2.4.1); the *Declaration of Sports*, republished in 1633, promoted such festivals, condescended to here.
7–8 Charing Cross is close to Haymarket: nearby Spring Gardens was fashionable.

12 *vorty* 'forty' (a dialect marker; some MSS give 'volk' at 11).
13 *pest'lent* 'confoundedly'.

The King (God bless him) 'twould undo him,
    Should he go still so dressed.

At course-a-park, without all doubt,
He should have first been taken out   20
    By all the maids in th'town:
Though lusty Roger there had been,
Or little George upon the green,
    Or Vincent of the Crown.

But wot you what? the youth was going   25
To make an end of all his wooing;
    The parson for him stayed:
Yet by his leave (for all his haste)
He did not so much wish all past,
    (Perchance) as did the maid.   30

The maid (and thereby hangs a tale)
For such a maid no Whitsun ale
    Could ever yet produce:
No grape that's kindly ripe, could be
So round, so plump, so soft as she,   35
    Nor half so full of juice.

Her finger was so small, the ring
Would not stay on which they did bring,
    It was too wide a peck:
And to say truth (for out it must)   40
It looked like the great collar (just)
    About our young colt's neck.

Her feet beneath her petticoat,
Like little mice stole in and out,
    As if they feared the light: 45
But O, she dances such a way!
No sun upon an Easter day
    Is half so fine a sight.

He would have kissed her once or twice,
But she would not, she was so nice,   50
    She would not do't in sight,
And then she looked as who should say,
I will do what I list today;
    And you shall do't at night.

17–18 'It would bankrupt the King ... to dress like this.'
19–21 At 'course-a-park' a girl calls out a boy to chase her, 'Which would not run except they might be caught' (*Britannia's Pastorals*, 1.3.20).
22–4 *Roger ... George ... Vincent* village names. Herrick's drunken beggar would be thought 'So good as George-a-Green' (*Hymn to Bacchus*, 22); the 'Crown' is presumably a tavern.
32 At Whitsun festivals 'two persons are chosen .. to be lord and lady of the ale, who dress as suitably as they can to the characters they assume' (Francis Douce, quoted in Brand, *Observations*).
39 'It was too wide by the circumference of a peck' (a two-gallon measure).
43–5 'Her pretty feet / Like snails did creep / A little out, and then, / As if they played at bo-peep, / Did soon draw in again' (Herrick, *Upon her Feet*).
40–2 'It was formerly a popular custom to rise early on Easter day and walk into the fields to see the sun dance' (Brand, *Observations*).

Her cheeks so rare a white was on, 55
No daisy makes comparison,
　　(Who sees them is undone),
For streaks of red were mingled there,
Such as are on a Catherine pear,
　　(The side that's next the sun). 60

Her lips were red, and one was thin,
Compared to that was next her chin;
　　(Some bee had stung it newly).
But (Dick) her eyes so guard her face;
I durst no more upon them gaze, 65
　　Than on the sun in July.

Her mouth so small when she does speak,
Thou'dst swear her teeth her words did break,
　　That they might passage get,
But she so handled still the matter, 70
They came as good as ours, or better,
　　And are not spent a whit.

If wishing should be any sin,
The parson himself had guilty been
　　(She looked that day so purely), 75
And did the youth so oft the feat
At night, as some did in conceit,
　　It would have spoiled him, surely.

Passion O me! how I run on!
There's that that would be thought upon, 80
　　(I trow) besides the bride.
The bus'ness of the kitchen's great,
For it is fit that men should eat;
　　Nor was it there denied:

Just in the nick the cook knocked thrice, 85
And all the waiters in a trice
　　His summons did obey,
Each serving man with dish in hand,
Marched boldly up, like our trained band,
　　Presented, and away. 90

When all the meat was on the table.
What man of knife, or teeth, was able
　　To stay to be entreated?
And this the very reason was,
Before the parson could say grace, 95
　　The company was seated.

---

59 'So cherries blush, and Catherine pears, / And apricocks, in youthful years' (Herrick, *The Maiden Blush*, 3–4).
67–9 The bride literally minces her words.
72 *spent* spoiled (some MSS); which is the sense.
74 *parson himself* syncopated to three syllables.

89 *trained band* or 'train-band', a division of citizen militia.
90 *Presented* as if they 'presented arms'.
93 'To be entreated to delay'.

Now hats fly off, and youths carouse;
Healths first go round, and then the house,
    The bride's came thick and thick:
And when 'twas named another's health,   100
Perhaps he made it hers by stealth.
    (And who could help it, Dick?)

O'th' sudden up they rise and dance;
Then sit again and sigh, and glance:
    Then dance again and kiss: 105
Thus several ways the time did pass,
Till every woman wished her place,
    And every man wished his.

By this time all were stoln aside
To counsel and undress the bride;   110
    But that he must not know:
But yet 'twas thought he guessed her mind,
And did not mean to stay behind
    Above an hour or so.

When in he came (Dick) there she lay   115
Like new-fall'n snow melting away
    ('Twas time I trow to part);
Kisses were now the only stay,
Which soon she gave, as who would say,
    Good-bye, with all my heart.   120

But just as heavens would have to cross it,
In came the bridemaids with the posset:
    The bridegroom ate in spite;
For had he left the women to't
It would have cost two hours to do't,   125
    Which were too much that night.

At length the candles out and out,
All that they had not done, they do't:
    What that is, who can tell?
But I believe it was no more   130
Than thou and I have done before
    With Bridget, and with Nell.

---

99 Jocularly for 'thick and fast'.
116 Because she is white and submissive: Herrick's groom throws the sheets around 'like flakes of snow' (*A Nuptial Song,* 150).
122–6 The groom finishes off the sillabub ('posset') nor-mally eaten 'immediately before the retirement of the company . . . the bride and bridegroom invariably tasting it first' (Brand).
132 *Bridget . . . Nell* type names.

Out upon it, I have loved

1659; much reproduced in MS and print (an earlier printed version is in *Wit and Drollery*, 1656). *Windsor Drollery* (1656) and *Academy of Compliments* (1684) carry a five-line version. There is a musical setting by Henry Lawes. The pretended sentiments correspond with Donne's: fairground novelties are 'not less cared for after three days / By children, than the thing which lovers so / Blindly admire, and with such worship woo' (*Farewell to Love*, 13–15), but are complicated by gallant raillery. There is an answer, possibly by Sir Toby Matthews (so *Last Remains*), possibly by Suckling himself (so *Wit and Drollery*, accepted by Clayton).

1
Out upon it, I have loved
   Three whole days together;
And am like to love three more,
   If it prove fair weather.

2
Time shall moult away his wings   5
   Ere he shall discover
In the whole wide world again
   Such a constant lover.

3
But the spite on't is, no praise
   Is due at all to me: 10
Love with me had made no stay,
   Had it any been but she.

4
Had it any been but she
   And that very face,
There had been at least ere this   15
   A dozen dozen in her place.

11 *stay* stays (*1659*): 'Love had not stopped over with me.'

Richard Crashaw (1612–1649)

In 1634, the year of Crashaw's graduation from Pembroke College, Cambridge University Press published his *Epigrammatum Sacrorum Liber,* a collection of Greek and Latin exercises on the Sundays and holy days of the Church year. Their stylistic models are in similar Jesuit exercises where conceits are multiplied from a few basic paradoxes, and so are their thematic preoccupations. Herbert's *Temple* had been published the previous year by the same Press, but Crashaw, admiring as he was of Herbert, had already determined on a different path. He is acknowledged as the un-English poet in the English tradition, formed by Spanish or Italian sympathies and tastes. Crashaw was orphaned at 14: his mother died before he was 7, his stepmother died when he was 8, his father, a Puritan clergyman and controversialist, died in 1626. Schooled at Charterhouse, he went on to Pembroke College and exposure to an anti-Puritan tendency which he evidently found congenial. In 1635 he was elected to a Fellowship at Peterhouse, then under John Cosin the obvious centre of High Church opinion and liturgical ceremoniousness; Lucy Hutchinson complains of their 'stretching superstition to idolatry'. He also visited Nicholas Ferrar's community at Little Gidding (and tutored Ferrar's nephew). In 1638 he was ordained. Crashaw left Cambridge in 1643, though not till the following year was he officially ejected from his Fellowship. He visited Leiden and spent some time in Oxford. But in 1645 he joined other Royalists in exile, including his friend Cowley, at Paris. By now he was Catholic, and in the following year he went on to Rome. There he eventually secured the patronage of Cardinal Pallotto and a post in the Cathedral of Loreto. When he sends to an unnamed gentlewoman a copy of the *Temple*, he claims an affinity with its author: 'And though Herbert's name do owe / These devotions, fairest, know / That while I lay them on the shrine / Of your white hand, they are mine' (*On Mr George Herbert's Book,* 15–18). But the declaration of a Herbertian inspiration in the title of *Steps to the Temple*, published after Crashaw had left England, is a gesture of literary and not devotional piety. Though Cowley claims that 'even in error sure no danger is / When joined with so much piety as his' (*On the Death of Mr. Crashaw,* 5–51), his work had no vigorous afterlife until this century.

The Latin poems were reprinted in 1670 and 1674; a selection of the *Epigrammata Sacra* was translated by Clement Barksdale (1682); George Walton Williams's edition of *The Complete Poetry* (New York: New York University Press, 1970) includes literal translations. *Steps to the Temple. Sacred poems with other Delights of the Muses* appeared first in 1646 (with an intended separation of sacred and secular pieces), then in a revised and enlarged edition in 1648. There is a facsimile edition of 1646 along with selections from Bodleian MS Tanner 465 (Menston: Scolar Press, 1970). *Carmen Deo nostro,* posthumously published in Paris in 1652, contains further revisions of poems already published as well as new poems; the eccentric typography and the engravings may derive from Crashaw himself. Other editions followed in 1670 and 1690. The standard one is L. C. Martin, *The Poems English, Latin and Greek,* revised edition (Oxford: Clarendon Press, 1957). Robert M. Cooper has prepared a *Concordance to the English Poetry of Richard Crashaw* (Troy: Whitston, 1980). There is a survey of criticism by A. R. Cirillo, *English Literary Renaissance,* 10 (1980), 183–93, updated by John R. Roberts, *English Literary Renaissance,* 21 (1991), 425–45, and a more ambitious survey by John R. Roberts, *Richard Crashaw: An Annotated Bibliography of Criticism, 1632–1980* (Columbia: University of Missouri Press, 1985).

A Hymn to the Name and Honour of the Admirable Saint Teresa

This text is based on *1652*, with corrections supplied from *1648*. *1646* and *1648* are titled *In memory of the virtuous and learned lady Madre de Teresa that sought an early martyrdom.* The fuller versions of the title carry a sense of the subject's range: *1652* sets it out as an inscription: *A hymn to the name and honour of the admirable St Teresa, foundress of the Reformation of the Discalced Carmelites, both men and women; a woman of angelical height of speculation, for masculine courage of performance, more than a woman. Who yet a child, outran maturity, and durst plot a martyrdom*; another, again set out as an inscription, is given in an important Pierpont Morgan Library MS which goes on: *but was reserved by god to die the living death of the life of his love. Of whose great impressions as her noble heart had most heroically expressed them, in her spiritual posterity most fruitfully propagated them, and in these her heavenly writings most sublimely, most sweetly taught them to the world.* This is the first of three poems on the Spanish mystic Teresa of Avila. The second, *An Apology,* 'having been writ when the author was yet among Protestants', excuses the choice of a Spanish subject in the *Hymn*; the third, *The Flaming Heart*, develops the *Hymn* lines 79–96 (the piercing of the heart by the angelic dart). The poem is based on Teresa's autobiography *La Vida de la Santa Madre Teresa de Jesus* (1588), perhaps in Sir Toby Matthew's translation *The Flaming Heart or the Life of the Glorious St Teresa* (1623, and Antwerp, 1642). The Pierpont

Morgan MS has references to Teresa's autobiography (the *Life*) at 47, 94 and 98 (given below); and at 173 to the biography by her Jesuit confessor Ribera. Bernini's famous sculpture in the Cornaro Chapel of Santa Maria della Vittoria in Rome was not begun until 1645.

> Love, thou art absolute sole Lord
> Of life and death. To prove the word,
> We'll now appeal to none of all
> Those thy old soldiers, great and tall,
> Ripe men of martyrdom, that could reach down   5
> With strong arms, their triumphant crown;
> Such as could with lusty breath
> Speak loud into the face of death
> Their great Lord's glorious name; to none
> Of those whose spacious bosoms spread a throne   10
> For Love at large to fill. Spare blood and sweat;
> And see him take a private seat,
> Making his mansion in the mild
> And milky soul of a soft child.
>   Scarce has she learnt to lisp the name   15
> Of martyr; yet she thinks it shame
> Life should so long play with that breath
> Which spent can buy so brave a death.
> She never undertook to know
> What death with love should have to do;   20
> Nor has she e'er yet understood
> Why to show love, she should shed blood.
> Yet though she cannot tell you why,
> She can love, and she can die.
>   Scarce has she blood enough to make   25
> A guilty sword blush for her sake;
> Yet has she' a heart dares hope to prove
> How much less strong is Death than Love.
>   Be Love but there; let poor six years
> Be posed with the maturest fears   30
> Man trembles at, you straight shall find

1–14 The poem offers to test the proposition ('prove the word') that life and death are only and unconditionally determined by love. A Christian turn is given to Virgil's 'All-powerful Love! what changes canst thou cause / In human hearts, subjected to thy laws!' (*Aeneid*, 4:412, Dryden). More is allowed the early Christian martyrs than Paul allows the 'fathers of old time': 'Who through faith subdued kingdoms, wrought righteousness, obtained promises, stopped the mouths of lions . . . They were stoned, they were sawn asunder, were tempted, were slain with the sword . . . [but they] received not the promise: God having provided some better thing for us' (Hebrews 11: 33–40). But the pattern is similar: Teresa's projected martyrdom is a 'better thing' than that of those who by 'blood and sweat' earn the 'crown of glory that fadeth not away' (1 Peter 5: 4). Love fills the throne in their

bosoms (in *1646* 'built', but 'spread' because Hebrew royal thrones were spread with canopies); they 'know the love of Christ' and 'are filled with all the fulness of God' (Ephesians 3: 19); but Love's retirement (altered from a less staccato *1646* original at 11: 'For Love their lord, glorious and great') to Teresa's unheroic ('milky') soul redefines its mission.

19–20 Jonson's Karolin sings: 'Though I am young, and cannot tell, / Either what death, or love is well' (*Sad Shepherd*, 1.5).

21–2 'God commendeth his love toward us, in that . . . Christ died for us' (Romans 5: 8).

32 'Surviving long is not living long: short lives may last an age' (Crashaw's Latin epigram *On the Blessed Martyrs*, 19–20).

Love knows no nonage, nor the mind.
'Tis Love, not years or limbs that can
Make the martyr, or the man.
    Love touched her heart, and lo it beats   35
High, and burns with such brave heats;
Such thirsts to die, as dares drink up,
A thousand cold deaths in one cup.
Good reason. For she breathes all fire.
Her weak breast heaves with strong desire   40
Of what she may with fruitless wishes
Seek for amongst her mother's kisses.
    Since 'tis not to be had at home
She'll travel to a martyrdom.
No home for hers confesses she   45
But where she may a martyr be.
    She'll to the Moors; and trade with them,
For this unvalued diadem.
She'll offer them her dearest breath,
With Christ's name in't, in change for death.   50
She'll bargain with them; and will give
Them God; teach them how to live
In him: or, if they this deny,
For him she'll teach them how to die.
So shall she leave amongst them sown   55
Her Lord's blood; or at least her own.
    Farewell then, all the world! Adieu.
Teresa is no more for you.
Farewell, all pleasures, sports, and joys
(Never till now esteemèd toys),   60
Farewell whatever dear may be,
Mother's arms or father's knee.
Farewell house, and farewell home!
She's for the Moors, and martyrdom.
    Sweet, not so fast! lo thy fair spouse   65
Whom thou seek'st with so swift vows,
Calls thee back, and bids thee come
To embrace a milder martyrdom.
    Blest powers forbid, thy tender life
Should bleed upon a barbarous knife;   70
Or some base hand have power to rase
Thy breast's chaste cabinet, and uncase
A soul kept there so sweet, O no;

37–8 The *Golden Legend* gives it that St John the Evangelist's faith was tested by drinking from a poisoned chalice.
47 'When I read of the martyrdoms suffered by saintly women for God's sake, I used to think they had purchased the fruition of God very cheaply; and I had a keen desire to die as they had done, not out of any love for God of which I was conscious, but in order to attain as quickly as possible to the fruition of the great blessings which, as I read, were laid up in Heaven. I used to discuss with my brother how we could become martyrs. We agreed to go off to the country of the Moors, begging our bread for the love of God, so that they might behead us there; and, even at so tender an age, I believe the Lord had given us sufficient courage for this, if we could have found a way to do it' (*Life*, 1).
48 *unvalued diadem* 'priceless crown' (of martyrdom).
55–6 'The blood of the martyrs is the seed of the Church' (Tertullian, *Apologeticus*, 50).
65 'My beloved spake, and said unto me, Rise up, my love, my fair one, and come away' (Song of Solomon 2: 10).
71 *rase . . . cabinet* 'force the pure treasure-store of thy breast': 'Here lies the ruined cabinet / Of a rich soul more highly set' (Richard Fletcher, *An Epitaph*).

Wise Heaven will never have it so.
Thou art Love's victim; and must die   75
A death more mystical and high.
Into Love's arms thou shalt let fall
A still-surviving funeral.
His is the dart must make the death
Whose stroke shall taste thy hallowed breath;   80
A dart thrice dipped in that rich flame
Which writes thy spouse's radiant name
Upon the roof of Heaven; where aye
It shines, and with a sovereign ray
Beats bright upon the burning faces   85
Of souls which in that name's sweet graces
Find everlasting smiles. So rare,
So spiritual, pure, and fair
Must be the immortal instrument
Upon whose choice point shall be sent   90
A life so loved; and that there be
Fit executioners for thee,
The fair'st and first-born sons of fire
Blest seraphim, shall leave their choir
And turn Love's soldiers, upon thee   95
To exercise their archery.
      O how oft shalt thou complain
Of a sweet and subtle pain.
Of intolerable joys;
Of a death, in which who dies   100
Loves his death, and dies again.
And would for ever so be slain.
And lives, and dies; and knows not why
To live, but that he thus may never leave to die.
      How kindly will thy gentle heart   105
Kiss the sweetly-killing dart!
And close in his embraces keep
Those delicious wounds, that weep
Balsam to heal themselves with. Thus
When these thy deaths, so numerous,   110
Shall all at last die into one,
And melt thy soul's sweet mansion;
Like a soft lump of incense, hasted

75–8 'Thou art a sacrifice ('victim') to Love, and must die a death more sublime and spiritual ('mystical'); thou shalt drop into Love's arms as a dead body ('funeral'), but not dead.'

79–96 'I saw an angel very near me, towards my left side, and he appeared to me in a corporeal form . . . He was not great; but rather little; yet withal, he was of very much beauty. His face was so inflamed, that he appeared to be of those most superior angels, who seem to be, all in a fire . . . I saw, that he had a long dart of gold in his hand; and at the end of the iron below, methought, there was a little fire; and I conceived, that he thrust it, some several times, through my very heart, after such a manner, as that it passed the very inwards, of my bowels; and when he drew back, methought, it carried away, as much, as it had touched within

me; and left all that, which remained, wholly inflamed with a great love of Almighty god. The pain of it, was so excessive, that it forced me to utter those groans; and the suavity, which that extremity of pain gave, was also so very excessive, that there was no desiring at all, to be rid of it' (*Life*, 29).

80 'Whose stroke your holy breath shall taste'.

82–3 'The heavens declare the glory of God' (Psalms 19: 1).

90 *sent* 'dispatched' (replacing *1646*'s 'spent').

94–5 The fiery seraphim would leave off singing around God's throne and descend to the spiritual wounding of Teresa.

100–1 'For, the soul . . .would always be very glad, if she might ever be dying, of this disease' (*Life*, 20).

By too hot a fire, and wasted
Into perfuming clouds, so fast   115
Shalt thou exhale to Heaven at last
In a resolving sigh, and then
O what? Ask not the tongues of men.
Angels cannot tell. Suffice,
Thyself shall feel thine own full joys   120
And hold them fast for ever. There
So soon as thou shalt first appear,
The moon of maiden stars, thy white
Mistress, attended by such bright
Souls as thy shining self, shall come   125
And in her first ranks make thee room;
Where 'mongst her snowy family
Immortal welcomes wait for thee.
    O what delight, when révealed Life shall stand
And teach thy lips Heaven with his hand;   130
On which thou now may'st to thy wishes
Heap up thy consecrated kisses.
What joys shall seize thy soul, when she
Bending her blessèd eyes on thee
(Those second smiles of Heaven) shall dart   135
Her mild rays through thy melting heart!
    Angels, thy old friends, there shall greet thee
Glad at their own home now to meet thee.
    All thy good works which went before
And waited for thee, at the door,   140
Shall own thee there; and all in one
Weave a constellation
Of crowns, with which the king thy spouse
Shall build up thy triumphant brows.
    All thy old woes shall now smile on thee   145
And thy pains sit bright upon thee
All thy sorrows here shall shine,
And thy sufferings be divine.
Tears shall take comfort, and turn gems
And wrongs repent to diadems.   150
Even thy deaths shall live; and new
Dress the soul that erst they slew.
Thy wounds shall blush to such bright scars
As keep account of the Lamb's wars.
    Those rare works where thou shalt leave writ   155
Love's noble history, with wit
Taught thee by none but him, while here

118–19 'Though I speak with the tongues of men and of angels' (1 Corinthians 13: 1).

123–4 The Church, outshining other saints as the moon outshines the stars (mitigating the 'woman clothed with the sun, and the moon under her feet, and upon her head a crown of twelve stars', Revelation 12: 1) welcomes Teresa to her 'snowy family' (who 'walk with me in white: for they are worthy', Revelation 3: 4).

129 'He [Christ] showed me a pure river of water of life' (Revelation 22: 1); but *1646*'s 'she shall stand' suggests the Church.

145–54 'God shall wipe away all tears from their eyes; and there shall be no more death, neither sorrow, nor crying, neither shall there be any more pain: for the former things are passed away . . . Behold, I make all things new' (Revelation 21: 4–5). The vividness of the wounds signals the Lamb's victory over the servants of the Beast (17: 14).

They feed our souls, shall clothe thine there.
Each heavenly word by whose hid flame
Our hard hearts shall strike fire, the same 160
Shall flourish on thy brows, and be
Both fire to us and flame to thee;
Whose light shall live bright in thy face
By glory, in our hearts by grace.
    Thou shalt look round about, and see 165
Thousands of crowned souls throng to be
Themselves thy crown. Sons of thy vows
The virgin-births with which thy sovereign spouse
Made fruitful thy fair soul, go now
And with them all about thee bow 170
To Him, "Put on" (he'll say) "put on
(My rosy love) that thy rich zone
Sparkling with the sacred flames
Of thousand souls, whose happy names
Heaven keep upon thy score". (Thy bright 175
Life brought them first to kiss the light
That kindled them to stars) and so
Thou with the Lamb, thy Lord, shalt go;
And wheresoe'er he sets his white
Steps, walk with Him those ways of light 180
Which who in death would live to see,
Must learn in life to die like thee.

159–62 Our flinty hearts yield sparks when struck by Teresa's words: 'Did not our heart burn within us, while he talked with us by the way' (Luke 24: 32); she meanwhile is clothed in the fire of her words (a version of the 'woman clothed with the sun', Revelation 12: 1).

165–82 'They are virgins. These are they which follow the Lamb whithersoever he goeth: These were redeemed from among men, being the firstfruits unto God and to the Lamb' (Revelation 14: 4).

In the Holy Nativity of our Lord God A Hymn Sung as by the Shepherds

The revision of *1652*, on which the text below is based, differs from *1646* and *1648* (in some respects intermediate) in its exploitation of choric repetition and its pruning of more extravagantly sensuous elements; a selection of earlier readings is given below. Like its companion poem, the *Hymn in the Glorious Epiphany* (first published in 1648), it is a great exercise in antiphonal hymnody. Both, along with the shorter and simpler *New Year's Day* are closely focused meditations on biblical texts. Here the text is Luke 2: 8–20: 'And there were in the same country shepherds . . . keeping the night watches over their flock. And behold, an angel of our Lord stood beside them, and the brightness of God did shine round about them . . . And the Angel said to them, Fear not: for behold I evangelise to you great joy, that shall be to all the people: because this day is born to you a Saviour which is Christ our Lord, in the city of David. And this shall be a sign to you, You shall find the infant swaddled in clothes: and laid in a manger . . . And . . . the shepherds spake one to another: Let us go over to Bethlehem, and let us see this word that is done, which our Lord hath showed to us. And they came with speed: and they found Mary and Joseph, and the infant laid in the manger. And seeing it, they understood of the word that had been spoken to them concerning this child . . . And the shepherds returned, glorifying and praising God in all things that they had heard, and seen, as it was said to them' (Rheims-Douai Bible). Crashaw's epigram on Luke 2: 8–14 (*Epigrammata Sacra*, 100) is witty with its pastoralism (Christ is at once shepherd and lamb), but the pastoralism is developed in this later poem at the expense of wit (though comedy may be admitted) so that its most obvious affinities are with Virgil, *Eclogues*, 4.

Chorus. Come we shepherds whose blessed sight
    Hath met Love's noon in Nature's night;
Come lift we up our loftier song
    And wake the sun that lies too long.

To all our world of well-stoln joy   5
    He slept; and dreamt of no such thing.
While we found out Heaven's fairer eye
    And kissed the cradle of our King.
Tell him he rises now, too late
    To show us aught worth looking at.   10

Tell him we now can show him more
    Than he e'er showed to mortal sight;
Than he himself e'er saw before;
    Which to be seen needs not his light.
Tell him, Tityrus, where thou hast been   15
Tell him, Thyrsis, what thou hast seen.

Tityrus. Gloomy night embraced the place
Where the noble infant lay.
The babe looked up and showed his face;
In spite of darkness, it was day.   20
It was thy day, sweet! and did rise
Not from the east, but from thine eyes.

Chorus. It was thy day, sweet! and did rise
Not from the east, but from thine eyes.

Thyrsis. Winter chid aloud; and sent   25
The angry north to wage his wars.
The north forgot his fierce intent;
And left perfumes instead of scars.
By those sweet eyes' persuasive powers
Where he meant frost, he scattered flowers.   30

Chorus. By those sweet eyes' persuasive powers
Where he meant frost, he scattered flowers

1–2 Come we shepherds who have seen / Day's King deposèd by Night's Queen (*1646*).
3 *loftier song* lofty (*1646*); echoing Virgil's *paulo maiora* (*Eclogues*, 4:1), advertising an unshepherdly sublimity.
4 To wake the sun that sleeps too long (*1646*).
5–6 He in this our general joy, / Slept (*1646*); the joys are stolen because the sleeping sun is not witness to them.
7 *Heaven's fairer eye* the fair-eyed boy (*1646*); 'Unto you shall the Sun of righteousness arise with healing in his wings' (Malachi 4: 2).
15–16 *Tityrus . . . Thyrsis* pastoral type-names.
19–22 'Begin, auspicious boy! to cast about / Thy infant eyes, and with a smile, thy mother single out' (Virgil, *Ec-*logues, 4:60, Dryden). The conceit of day breaking from the eyes is commonly erotic, as Habington's 'Expecting from thy eyes the break of day' (*To Castara complaining her Absence in the Country*).
25 *aloud* the world (*1646*).
30 'Unbidden earth shall wreathing ivy bring, / And fragrant herbs (the promises of spring), / As her first offerings to her infant king' (Virgil, *Eclogues*, 4:18–20). 'For as the earth bringeth forth her bud, and as the garden causeth the things that are sown in it to spring forth; so the Lord God will cause righteousness and praise to spring forth before all the nations' (Isaiah 61: 11).

Both. We saw thee in thy balmy nest,
Young dawn of our eternal day!
We saw thine eyes break from their east   35
And chase the trembling shades away.
We saw thee; and we blessed the sight,
We saw thee by thine own sweet light.

Tityrus. Poor World (said I) what wilt thou doe
To entertain this starry stranger?   40
Is this the best thou canst bestow?
A cold, and not too cleanly, manger?
Contend, ye powers of Heaven and earth,
To fit a bed for this huge birth.

Chorus. Contend, ye powers of Heaven and earth.   45
To fit a bed for this huge birth.

Thyrsis. Proud world, said I; cease your contést
And let the mighty babe alone.
The phoenix builds the phoenix' nest.
Love's architecture is his own.   50
The babe whose birth embraves this morn,
Made his own bed ere he was born.

Chorus. The babe whose birth embraves this morn,
Made his own bed ere he was born.

Tityrus. I saw the curled drops, soft and slow,   55
Come hovering o'er the place's head;
Offering their whitest sheets of snow
To furnish the fair infant's bed:
Forbear, said I; be not too bold.
Your fleece is white but 'tis too cold.   60

Chorus. Forbear, said I; be not too bold.
Your fleece is white but 'tis too cold.

Thyrsis. I saw the obsequious seraphims
Their rosy fleece of fire bestow.
For well they now can spare their wings,   65
Since Heaven itself lies here below.
Well done, said I: but are you sure
Your down so warm, will pass for pure?

---

33 *balmy nest* to anticipate 'the phoenix' nest' (46).
34 *Young* Bright (*1646*).
39–54 Not in *1646*.
40 *starry* 'bright' (but also descended from heaven).
44 'To make fit a bed for this immense event'.
49–52 Southwell has 'Behold the father in his daughter's son, / The bird that build the nest is hatched therein' (*The Nativity of Christ*, 1–2); 'embraves' for 'beautifies' is a Spenserism.
55–60 The snow belongs with Sylvester's notorious 'peri-

wig of snow' (*Divine Weeks*, 1.4:693) or Browne's 'fleece of silent waters' (*On one Drowned in the Snow*).
63 I saw the officious angels bring, / The down that their soft breasts did stow (*1646*); *obsequious seraphims* 'fiery angels prompt to serve'.
67–8 Fair youth (said I) be not too rough, / Thy down though soft 's not soft enough (*1646*). The revision points up the rosy fieriness of the fleece: it is not conventionally 'pure as snow'.

Chorus. Well done, said I: but are you sure
Your down so warm, will pass for pure?   70

Tityrus. No no, your King's not yet to seek
Where to repose his royal head
See see, how soon his new-bloomed cheek
'Twixt 's mother's breasts is gone to bed.
Sweet choice, said we! no way but so   75
Not to lie cold, yet sleep in snow.

Chorus. Sweet choice, said we! no way but so
Not to lie cold, yet sleep in snow.

Both. We saw thee in thy balmy nest,
Bright dawn of our eternal day!   80
We saw thine eyes break from their east
And chase the trembling shades away.
We saw thee: and we blessed the sight.
We saw thee, by thine own sweet light.

Chorus. We saw thee: and we blessed the sight.   85
We saw thee, by thine own sweet light.

Full Chorus. Welcome, all wonders in one sight!
   Eternity shut in a span.
Summer in winter, Day in night.
   Heaven in earth, and God in man.   90
Great little one! whose all-embracing birth
Lifts earth to Heaven, stoops Heaven to earth.

Welcome. Though nor to gold nor silk.
   To more than Caesar's birthright is;
Two sister-seas of virgin-milk,   95
   With many a rarely-tempered kiss
That breathes at once both maid and mother,
Warms in the one, cools in the other.

Welcome, though not to those gay flies
   Gilded in th' beams of earthly kings;   100
Slippery souls in smiling eyes;
   But to poor shepherds, home-spun things:
Whose wealth's their flock; whose wit, to be
Well read in their simplicity.

71–4   The babe no sooner 'gan to seek, / Where to lay his lovely head, / But straight his eyes advised his cheek, / 'Twixt mother's breasts to go to bed (*1646*).

76   Because breasts, though conventionally 'snow', are warm.

79–86   Not in *1646*.

87   Welcome to our wondering sight (*1646*).

88   'Immensity cloistered in thy dear womb' (Donne, *La Corona*, 2:14).

91–2   'O of celestial seed . . . The nodding frame of heaven, and earth, and main! / See to their base restored' Virgil, *Eclogues*, 4:49–51.

93   *1652* cancels: 'She sings thy tears asleep, and dips / Her kisses in thy weeping eye, / She spreads the red leaves of thy lips, / That in their buds yet blushing lie. / She 'gainst those mother-diamonds tries / The points of her young eagle's eyes.'

99   *flies* 'parasites'.

102   *home-spun* simple (*1646*).

Yet when young April's husband showers 105
   Shall bless the fruitful Maia's bed
We'll bring the first-born of her flowers
   To kiss thy feet and crown thy head.
To thee, dread lamb! whose love must keep
The shepherds, more than they the sheep. 110

To thee, meek majesty! soft King
   Of simple graces and sweet loves.
Each of us his lamb will bring
   Each his pair of silver doves;
Till burned at last in fire of thy fair eyes, 115
Ourselves become our own best sacrifice.

105–6 As *The Weeper*, 79–84. The Roman month (*Maius*) is masculine.
110 The shepherds, while they feed their sheep (*1646*).
113–16 'And if he be poor he shall take one lamb . . . to make an atonement for him . . . and two turtledoves' (Leviticus 14: 21–2); but 'present your bodies a living sacrifice, holy, acceptable unto God' (Romans 12: 1).

Saint Mary Magdalene or the Weeper

The poem exists in two versions, the first represented in the printing of 1646 and some MSS, the second in the printings of 1648 and 1652; this text is based on the revision of *1652*, with misreadings corrected from *1648*. The revision cancels three (8, 11, 17) of the original twenty-three stanzas, but adds another ten (15–22, 27, 31) and borrows another from the *1646* poem *The Tear*; some of the local adjustments are recorded in the notes. Crashaw writes on the Magdalene in about a dozen poems; she is the subject of many hundreds in the period, for her tears make her a rich subject for poets, one indeed recommended by Emmanuele Tesauro's great manual of baroque poetics, the *Cannonocchiale Aristotelico*. She is a compound figure: the Mary Magdalene first mentioned in Luke 8: 2, and who meets the resurrected Christ in the garden (John 20: 11–8) is accommodated to the sister of Lazarus (John 11: 33) and to the sinner who anoints Christ's feet (Luke 7: 38). But she is presented here only as the sum of her motiveless tears. Unsurprisingly for a poem written over many years, there is no obvious informing argument and no single informing influence. The conceits on which the stanzas are built, indifferently biblical or classical in origin, are developed by reminiscence of patristic sermon rhetoric or overwrought neo-Latin epigram (François Remond, John Owen, even Herbert); but Crashaw can go beyond even a model like the type of the Baroque poet, Giambattista Marino. Crashaw uses a common lyric measure, notionally a mix of six- and eight-syllable lines, but treats it with great licence (only slightly less than in *1646*).

Lo where a wounded heart with bleeding eyes conspire.
Is she a flaming fountain, or a weeping fire!

1

   Hail, sister springs!
   Parents of silver-footed rills!
   Ever bubbling things!
   Thawing crystal! snowy hills,
Still spending, never spent! I mean 5
Thy fair eyes, sweet Magdalene!

2

   Heavens thy fair eyes be;
   Heavens of ever-falling stars.

1–6 'O that my head were waters, and mine eyes a fountain of tears' (Jeremiah 9: 1); and conflating the conventional 'silveriness' of water with its more exotic 'footing', as of Milton's Camus (*Lycidas*, 103); *1646* has 'silver-forded'.
3–5 'As floods, which frosts in icy fetters bind, / Thaw with the approaching sun . . . Byblis, spent in tears, / Becomes a living fountain' (Ovid, *Metamorphoses*, 9:661–4, Sandys).

'Tis seed-time still with thee
And stars thou sow'st, whose harvest dares   10
Promise the earth to countershine
Whatever makes heaven's forehead fine.

3
But we're deceivèd all.
Stars indeed they are too true;
For they but seem to fall,   15
As heaven's other spangles do.
It is not for our earth and us
To shine in things so precious.

4
Upwards thou dost weep.
Heaven's bosom drinks the gentle stream.   20
Where th' milky rivers creep,
Thine floats above; and is the cream.
Waters above the heavens, what they be
We're taught best by thy tears and thee.

5
Every morn from hence   25
A brisk cherub something sips
Whose sacred influence
Adds sweetness to his sweetest lips.
Then to his music. And his song
Tastes of this breakfast all day long.   30

6
Not in the evening's eyes
When they red with weeping are
For the sun that dies,
Sits Sorrow with a face so fair,
Nowhere but here did ever meet   35
Sweetness so sad, sadness so sweet.

7
When Sorrow would be seen
In her brightest majesty
(For she is a Queen)
Then is she dressed by none but thee.   40

9–12 So Crashaw elsewhere, varying the commoner conceit of eyes as fallen stars: 'O 'tis not a tear, / 'Tis a star about to drop / From thine eye' (*The Tear*, 2–4); 'They that sow in tears shall reap in joy' (Psalms 126: 5).
19–20 'Do not the tears run down the widow's cheek . . . The prayer of the humble pierceth the clouds' (Ecclesiasticus 35: 15–17). But the weeper 'upsets the order of nature, for while heaven customarily rains down on earth, earth now waters heaven: showers of tears leap forth even above the heavens, to God himself . . . the Psalmist indeed sings of these waters of lamentation "Praise him . . . ye waters that be above the heavens" [Psalms 148: 4] ' (St Peter Chrysologus

in an admired sermon on Mary Magdalene). The character of 'the waters above the firmament' (Genesis 1: 6–7) was a vexed question. The Milky Way is a heavenly transfer of the land 'flowing with milk and honey' (Exodus 3: 8).
25–30 Crashaw's own 'Sweet-lipped angel-imps, that swill their throats / In cream of morning Helicon' (*Music's Duel*, 76–7).
26 *brisk* Dryden calls the swallow 'brisk' (*Hind and the Panther*, 3:429).
34–6 Dowland sets 'Sorrow was there made fair . . . She made her sighs to sing, / And all things with so sweet a sadness move' (*Second Book of Airs*, 1:7–11).

Then, and only then, she wears
Her proudest pearls; I mean, thy tears.

8

    The dew no more will weep
    The primrose's pale cheek to deck,
    The dew no more will sleep   45
    Nuzzled in the lily's neck;
Much rather would it be thy tear,
And leave them both to tremble here.

9

    There's no need at all
    That the balsam-sweating bough   50
    So coyly should let fall
    His med'cinable tears; for now
Nature hath learned to extract a dew
More sovereign and sweet from you.

10

    Yet let the poor drops weep   55
    (Weeping is the ease of woe)
    Softly let them creep,
    Sad that they are vanquished so.
They, though to others no relief,
Balsam may be, for their own grief.   60

11

    Such the maiden gem
    By the purpling vine put on,
    Peeps from her parent stem
    And blushes at the bridegroom sun.
This watery blossom of thy eyen,   65
Ripe, will make the richer wine.

12

    When some new bright guest
    Takes up among the stars a room,
    And Heaven will make a feast,
    Angels with crystal vials come   70
And draw from these full eyes of thine
Their master's water: their own wine.

---

42 *proudest* richest (*1646*); which is the sense.

43–8 'The pearly dew falling on soft roses . . . would wish itself your tear' (François Remond, *De Lacrimis*, 3–4).

47–8 'Be thy tear' and 'tremble here' are reversed from *1646*.

50–2 Elaborating 'Drop tears as fast as the Arabian trees / Their medicinal gum' (*Othello*, V. ii. 346–7). Balsam or myrrh or amber (*1646*'s cancelled stanza 8 has an 'amber-weeping tree') might all be medicinally efficacious ('sovereign').

61–6 Taken from the *The Tear*, which reads 'wanton spring' for 'purpling vine', and 'manly' for 'bridegroom'; Milton

(*On the Morning of Christ's Nativity*, 35–44) also stresses nature's modesty with the sexually aggressive sun.

67–72 Byrd sets 'If that a sinner's sighs be angels' food, / Or that repentant tears be angels' wine, / Accept, O Lord . . . these hearty sighs' (*Psalms, Sonnets, Songs*, 30:1–4).

70–2 'Put thou my tears into thy bottle' (Psalms 56: 8; *1646* reads 'bottles' for 'vials'); but recalling Donne's 'Hither with crystal vials, lovers come / And take my tears, which are Love's wine' (*Twickenham Garden*, 19). The transformation of water to wine echoes the miracle at Cana (John 2: 1–11).

13

     Golden though he be,
     Golden Tagus murmurs tho;
     Were his way by thee,
     Content and quiet he would go.   75
So much more rich would he esteem
Thy silver, than his golden stream.

14

     Well does the May that lies
     Smiling in thy cheeks, confess   80
     The April in thine eyes.
     Mutual sweetness they express.
No April e'er lent kinder showers,
Nor May returned more faithful flowers.

15

     O cheeks! Beds of chaste loves   85
     By your own showers seasonably dashed.
     Eyes! nests of milky doves
     In your own wells decéntly washed.
O wit of love! that thus could place
Fountain and garden in one face.   90

16

     O sweet contést; of woes
     With loves, of tears with smiles disputing!
     O fair, and friendly foes,
     Each other kissing and confuting!
While rain and sunshine, cheeks and eyes   95
Close in kind contrarieties.

17

     But can these fair floods be
     Friends with the bosom fires that fill thee?
     Can so great flames agree
     Eternal tears should thus distil thee?   100
O floods, O fires! O suns O showers!
Mixed and made friends by love's sweet powers.

73–8 Remond, *De Lacrimis*, 5–6, says that Pactolus would flow richer from the Magdalene's eyes. The Spanish Tagus, like the Lydian Pactolus, was celebrated for its golden sands.
74 *tho* 'then' (corrected from *1646*'s 'though').
79–84 'Clear or cloudy, sweet as April showering . . . so is her face to me . . . like mild May all flowering' (Dowland, *Second Book of Airs*, 21:1–3); the English April is proverbially showery. *In the Holy Nativity*, 97–100, Crashaw reuses the conceit. *1646* has 'softer showers' and 'fairer flowers'.
85–90 'His eyes are as the eyes of doves by the rivers of water, washed with milk, and fitly set. His cheeks are as a bed of spices, as sweet flowers: his lips like lilies, dropping sweet smelling myrrh' (Song of Solomon 5: 12–13).
91–6 This central stanza is unnumbered in *1652*. The 'contrarieties' are usually treated more easily, as in Cowley's 'Ne'er yet did I behold so glorious weather, / As this sunshine and rain together' (*Weeping*, 13–14).
97–102 'Rivers of tears, quench not my ardent heat: / Nor my love's fire, dries up my brain's salt sweat. / Water and fire, in temper disagree; / Yet will accord, so they may torture me' (Owen, *Epigrammata*, 1.74:2–6, Thomas Pecke).

18

> 'Twas his well-pointed dart
> That digged these wells, and dressed this vine;
> And taught the wounded heart 105
> The way into these weeping eyen.
> Vain loves avaunt! bold hands forbear!
> The lamb hath dipped his white foot here.

19

> And now where'er he strays,
> Among the Galilean mountains, 110
> Or more unwelcome ways,
> He's followed by two faithful fountains;
> Two walking baths; two weeping motions;
> Portable, and compendious oceans.

20

> O thou, thy Lord's fair store! 115
> In thy so rich and rare expenses,
> Even when he showed most poor,
> He might provoke the wealth of princes.
> What prince's wanton'st pride e'er could
> Wash with silver, wipe with gold. 120

21

> Who is that king, but he
> Who calls 't his crown to be called thine,
> That thus can boast to be
> Waited on by a wandering mine,
> A voluntary mint, that strews 125
> Warm silver showers where'er he goes!

22

> O precious prodigal!
> Fair spendthrift of thyself! thy measure
> (Merciless love!) is all.
> Even to the last pearl in thy treasure. 130
> All places, times, and objects be
> Thy tears' sweet opportunity.

103–4 Christ (as Love with his 'dart') is at once gardener (as at John 20: 15, where Mary Magdalene mistakes him), well (as at John 4: 14: 'whosoever drinketh of the water that I shall give him shall never thirst') and vine (as at John 15: 1: 'I am the true vine').

108 The Apocalyptic Lamb of God (Revelation 5: 6) is matched with Pegasus, the eyes of the Magdalen with the fountain Hippocrene created when Pegasus struck Helicon with his hoof.

112–14 The 'fountains' are from Jeremiah 9: 1; for 'baths', Southwell calls St Peter's eyes 'pools of Hesebon, baths of grace' (*St Peter's Complaint*, 283). Lancelot Andrewes, *XCVI Sermons* (Crashaw contributed verses to the 1631 edition), has: 'Mary Magdalene wept enough to have made a bath';

the point is not the amount of water in a bath, but that bath-water washes clean (as in Hugo, *Pia Desideria*, 1.8, adapted in Quarles 3.8.

117–20 'You laying out so much, a treasury fit for our Lord: even when he was at his lowest, he could command ['provoke'] royal riches'. Marino translates 'A woman in the city . . . stood at his feet behind him weeping, and began to wash his feet with tears, and did wipe them with the hairs of her head' (Luke 7: 37–8) into 'O wealth! O treasure! Two showers of silver, one of gold' (*La Maddalena ai piedi di Cristo*, 6).

121–2 'Who is the king that would not call it his signal honour to be called yours.'

23

Does the day-star rise?
Still thy stars doe fall and fall.
Does day close his eyes?   135
Still the fountain weeps for all.
Let night or day do what they will,
Thou hast thy task; thou weepest still.

24

Does thy song lull the air?
Thy falling tears keep faithful time.   140
Does thy sweet-breathèd prayer
Up in clouds of incense climb?
Still at each sigh, that is, each stop,
A bead, that is, a tear, does drop.

25

At these thy weeping gates,   145
(Watching their watery motion)
Each wingèd moment waits,
Takes his tear, and gets him gone.
By thine eye's tinct ennobled thus
Time lays him up; he's precious.   150

26

Not, so long she lived,
Shall thy tomb report of thee;
But, so long she grieved,
Thus must we date thy memory.
Others by moments, months, and years   155
Measure their ages; thou, by tears.

27

So do perfumes expire.
So sigh-tormented sweets, oppressed
With proud unpitying fire.
Such tears the suffering rose that's vexed   160
With ungentle flames does shed,
Sweating in a too warm bed.

28

Say, ye bright brothers,
The fugitive sons of those fair eyes
Your fruitful mothers!   165

133–5 *1646* has 'Does the night arise? / Still thy tears fall
and fall. / Does night loose her eyes?'
139–44 'Distress likes dumps ['dirges'] when time is kept
with tears' (Shakespeare, *Lucrece*, 1127). *1646* has: 'Thy tears'
just cadence still keeps time.' The notes ('stops') of the song
are sighs, the prayers ('beads') it offers are tears.
145–7 Thus dost thou melt the year / Into a weeping
motion, / Each minute waiteth here (*1646*).
149–50 'Time lays up each moment ennobled by the elixir
of your tears.'

155–6 'Your weeping is a water-clock whose each drop
measures a death' (Herbert, *Lucus*, 23: 9–10).
157–62 Marino compares Christ's blood with 'the liquid
perfumes sweetly distilled from a pot of lovely flowers by
the warming fire that crackles beneath it' (*Sudore del Sangue*).
163–8 Say watery brothers / Ye simpering ['glimmering']
sons of those fair eyes, / Your fertile mothers. / What hath
our world that can entice / You to be born? What is 't can
borrow / You from her eyes swoln wombs of sorrow (*1646*).

What make you here? what hopes can 'tice
You to be born? what cause can borrow
You from those nests of noble sorrow?

29

    Whither away so fast?
For sure the sordid earth   170
Your sweetness cannot taste
Nor does the dust deserve your birth.
Sweet, whither haste you then? O say
Why you trip so fast away?

30

    "We go not to seek,   175
The darlings of Aurora's bed,
The rose's modest cheek
Nor the violet's humble head.
Though the field's eyes too weepers be
Because they want such tears as we.   180

31

    Much less mean we to trace
The fortune of inferior gems,
Preferred to some proud face
Or perched upon feared diadems.
Crowned heads are toys. We go to meet   185
A worthy object, our Lord's feet."

169–72 'For what place do you leave the eyes?' A lyric formula is adapted: 'Whither so fast? See how the kindly flowers / Perfumes the air, and all to make thee stay' (Pilkington, *First Book of Songs*, 5).

170 *sordid* sluttish (*1646*).

176–8 The rose and violet (being of her colour) are the dawn's darlings.

179–80 Added with 181–4 in *1648*. Herrick (*To Primroses Filled with Morning Dew*, 12–14) finds 'it strange to see, / Such pretty flowers . . . To speak by tears'.

181–6 'The proud Egyptian Queen [Cleopatra], her Roman guest [Antony] . . . With pearl dissolved in gold, did feast . . . And now (dear Lord!) thy lover, on the fair / And silver tables of thy feet, behold! / Pearl in her tears, and in her hair, / Offers thee gold' (Sherburne, *And she washed his feet with her tears*).

183 *preferred* 'elevated'.

Samuel Butler (1613–1680)

When *Hudibras* first appeared in 1662, Butler was already almost 50. Though Pepys could not read it and sold on his copy at a loss (*Diary*, 26 December, 1662), this was Butler's moment of fame: nine editions were published within a year. The Second Part was published in 1664, the Third in 1678. He enjoyed no other fame. What Johnson in his *Life* described as a 'mist of obscurity' covering most of what passed between his birth at Strensham in Worcestershire and his death in London is little dispelled even now. He probably attended the King's School at Worcester, and possibly went to Oxford; he seems to have done secretarial work for local and other families, including (says Aubrey) that of the Duchess of Kent. It is not known when he started living in London, familiar with Gray's Inn lawyers, but if Aubrey is right in saying he 'had a club' every night with them and with Cleveland (with whom he has obvious imaginative affinities), it must have been in the fifties. A number of loyalist pamphlets attributable to him appeared at this time. Only in 1670, despite the King's enthusiasm for his poem, did he secure belated promotion to public service, joining the Duke of Buckingham's embassy to Versailles in 1670, and perhaps his embassy to The Hague in 1672. He worked as Buckingham's secretary probably until 1674. Wood says that he had a hand in *The Rehearsal* (1671), the year *To the Memory of the Most Renowned Duval* was published, apart from *Hudibras* the only poem published with Butler's authority. 'Satirical wits disoblige whom they converse with; and consequently make to themselves many enemies and few friends; and this was his manner and case' (Aubrey). Two years before his death a Plymouth doctor, James Yonge, observed him at the Wits' Coffee House in Covent Garden: 'an old paralytic claret drinker, a morose surly man, except elevated with claret, when he becomes very brisk and incomparable company'. He died of a consumption and was buried with his feet against the north wall of Inigo Jones's Covent Garden church of St Paul's. His papers, left to his friend William Longueville, form the basis of Robert Thyer's *Genuine Remains in Verse and Prose*, 2 vols (1759), which superseded the largely spurious non-Hudibrastic writings collected in *Posthumous Works in Prose and Verse* (1715–17). The most complete edition of Butler's work includes *Hudibras*, and *Characters and Passages from Notebooks*, edited by A. R. Waller (Cambridge: Cambridge University Press, 1905 and 1908), and *Satires and Miscellaneous Poetry and Prose*, edited by René Lamar (Cambridge: Cambridge University Press, 1928), the only modern edition available. Standard editions are *Hudibras*, edited by John Wilders (Oxford: Clarendon Press, 1967) and *Prose Observations*, edited by Hugh de Quehen (Oxford: Clarendon Press, 1979); Charles W. Daves has edited *Characters* (Cleveland and London: Press of Case Western Reserve University, 1970). G. R. Wasserman's *Samuel 'Hudibras' Butler*, revised edition (Boston: Twayne, 1989) is the most up-to-date overview incorporating material from his *Samuel Butler and the Earl of Rochester: A Reference Guide* (Boston: G. K. Hall, 1986).

Satyr upon the Weakness and Misery of Man

Genuine Remains, 1759; but lines 169–83 are added from Thyer's note on 168: 'on a vacancy on the sheet opposite this line, I find the following verses, which probably were intended to be added.' A draft version (given in Lamar) is in British Library MS Additional 32625. Burton begins his chapter on 'Discontents, Miseries, etc.' as causes of melancholy (*Anatomy*, 1.2.3.10) by repeating from Hyginus (*Fables*, 220) the story of Dame Cura who made an image of 'dirty slime', which Jupiter put life into. Saturn decided the disagreement between them as to who should own him by giving his earthly and mortal part to Care (hence he is called *homo* from *humus*), and to Jupiter his soul when he dies: 'A general cause, a continuate cause, an inseparable accident to all men, is discontent, care, misery; were there no other particular affliction . . . to molest man in this life, the very cogitation of that common misery were enough to macerate, and make him weary of his life.' In this satire, untypically thinks Thyer, Butler has exchanged banter for bitterness.

> Who would believe, that wicked earth,
> Where Nature only brings us forth,
> To be found guilty, and forgiven,

1–18 'As we have been by nature created, oil will sooner be pressed from a stone than any good work from us . . . he saved us, not because of deeds done by us in righteousness, but on account of his own mercy' (Calvin, *Institutes*, 3.14.5);

Should be a nursery for Heaven;
When all, we can expect to do,   5
Will not pay half the debt we owe,
And yet more desperately dare,
As if that wretched trifle were
Too much for the eternal powers,
Our great and mighty creditors,   10
Not only slight what they enjoin,
But pay it in adulterate coin?
We only in their mercy trust,
To be more wicked and unjust:
All our devotions, vows, and prayers   15
Are our own interest, not theirs:
Our offerings, when we come to adore,
But begging presents, to get more:
The purest business of our zeal
Is but to err, by meaning well,   20
And make that meaning do more harm,
Than our worst deeds, that are less warm:
For the most wretched and perverse
Does not believe himself, he errs.
    Our holi'est actions have been   25
The effects of wickedness and sin;
Religious houses made compounders
For th' horrid actions of the founders;
Steeples, that tottered in the air,
By lechers sinned into repair;   30
As if we had retained no sign,
Nor character of the divine
And heavenly part of human nature,
But only the coarse earthy matter.
Our universal inclination   35
Tends to the worst of our creation,
As if the stars conspired to imprint
In our whole species, by instinct,
A fatal brand, and signature
Of nothing else, but the impure.   40
The best of all our actions tend
To the preposterousest end,
And, like to mongrels, we're inclined

'He calls sins debts because we owe penalty for them and we could in no way satisfy it unless we released by [God's] forgiveness . . . those who trust that God is satisfied with their own or others' merits, and that by satisfaction forgiveness of sins is paid for . . . share not at all in this free gift' (3.20.45, on the Lord's Prayer). But the idea of a nursery ('a training ground') contradicts this. Spenser's 'sacred nursery / Of virtue . . . hidden . . . From view of men, and wicked world's disdain' (*Faerie Queene*, 6 Proem 3) is a garden; Butler's is an arena for exercise of failing virtue. Antinomian beliefs, whereby men felt themselves justified in sin, were common in the 1640s and later.
19–22 Rochester makes age and experience lead man to an understanding 'That all his life he has been in the wrong'

(*Satyr*, 24–6); but here the 'justified sinner' complacently credits his own good intentions. Thyer specifies a political application: 'the mistaken zeal of a set of mad enthusiasts did more mischief . . . than the vices of all our kings put together.'
27 Men do not willingly fund good works, but fear or vanity will persuade them: if thou canst thunder upon him, as papists do, with satisfactory and meritorious works, or persuade him by this means he shall save his soul out of Hell . . . then he will listen' (*Anatomy*, 3.1.3); 'compounders' make settlements in discharge of a liability.
41–2 'Our best efforts effect the reverse of our good intentions'; the sense of monstrosity is picked up in the pessimism of 43–6.

To take most to the ignobler kind;
Or monsters, that have always least   45
Of th' human parent, not the beast.
Hence 'tis we've no regard at all
Of our best half original;
But, when they differ, still assert
The interest of the ignobler part;   50
Spend all the time we have upon
The vain capriches of the one,
But grudge to spare one hour, to know
What to the better part we owe.
As in all compound substances   55
The greater still devours the less;
So, being born and bred up near
Our earthy gross relations here,
Far from the ancient nobler place
Of all our high paternal race,   60
We now degenerate, and grow
As barbarous, and mean, and low,
As modern Grecians are, and worse,
To their brave nobler ancestors.
Yet, as no barbarousness beside   65
Is half so barbarous as pride,
Nor any prouder insolence
Than that, which has the least pretence,
We are so wretched, to profess
A glory in our wretchedness;   70
To vapour sillily, and rant
Of our own misery, and want,
And grow vain-glorious on a score,
We ought much rather to deplore,
Who, the first moment of our lives,   75
Are but condemned, and given reprieves;
And our great'st grace is not to know,
When we shall pay 'em back, nor how,
Begotten with a vain caprich,
And live as vainly to that pitch.   80
  Our pains are real things, and all
Our pleasures but fantastical;
Diseases of their own accord,
But cures come difficult and hard;
Our noblest piles, and stateliest rooms   85
Are but out-houses to our tombs;
Cities, though e'er so great and brave,

52   *caprich* 'caprice' (the earlier pre-French form).
59–60   Heaven or (as in Hyginus's fable) Jupiter.
63–4   Abuse of the modern Greeks was a commonplace: 'Admirable in arts, and glorious in arms, famous for government, affecters of freedom . . . now they delight in ease, and no further for the most part endeavour their profit, than their bellies compel them' (Sandys, *Relation of a Journey*, 1:77).
65   *barbarousness* 'forgetfulness of culture'.
70–4   'Many men are of such a perverse nature, they are

well pleased with nothing . . . neither with riches nor poverty, they complain when they are well and when they are sick, grumble at all fortunes, prosperity and adversity' (*Anatomy*, 1.2.3.10).
75–8   Extending Pliny's observation that man 'is born naked, and falls a-whining at the very first' (quoted by Burton, *Anatomy*, 1.2.3.10); but it is given Calvinist colouring here.
85–8   Inverting Donne's calling graveyards 'the holy suburbs' of the New Jerusalem (*Obsequies*, 174–5).

But mere ware-houses to the grave;
Our bravery's but a vain disguise,
To hide us from the world's dull eyes,   90
The remedy of a defect,
With which our nakedness is decked;
Yet makes us swell with pride, and boast,
As if we'd gained by being lost.
  All this is nothing to the evils,   95
Which men, and their confed'rate devils
Inflict, to aggravate the curse
On their own hated kind, much worse;
As if by Nature they'd been served
More gently, than their fate deserved,   100
Take pains (in justice) to invent,
And study their own punishment;
That, as their crimes should greater grow,
So might their own inflictions too.
Hence bloody wars at first began,   105
The artificial plague of man,
That from his own invention rise,
To scourge his own iniquities;
That if the Heavens should chance to spare
Supplies of constant poisoned air,   110
They might not, with unfit delay,
For lingering destruction stay;
Nor seek recruits of Death so far,
But plague themselves with blood and war.
  And if these fail, there is no good,   115
Kind Nature ere on man bestowed,
But he can easily divert
To his own misery and hurt;
Make that, which Heaven meant to bless
The ungrateful world with, gentle peace   120
With luxury and excess, as fast
As war and desolation, waste;
Promote mortality, and kill,
As fast as arms, by sitting still;
Like earthquakes slay without a blow,   125
And only moving overthrow;
Make law and equity as dear,
As plunder and free-quarter were,

---

89 *bravery* 'finery and show'.

91 Life itself is the defect which dresses non-existence: 'Blindness seizes on us in the beginning, labour in the middle, grief in the end, labour in all' (Burton, *Anatomy*, 1.2.3.10, quoting Petrarch).

95–104 'We are thus bad by nature . . . but far worse by art, every man the greatest enemy unto himself' (*Anatomy*, 1.1.1.2).

105–14 The blame for the late Civil Wars is with the Puritans: 'When Gospel-trumpeter surrounded, / With long-eared rout to battle sounded' (*Hudibras*, 1.1:9–10); and it is treated as a correlative of their obsession with guilt.

109–10 'One cause of the sickness, is the corruption and

infection of the air' (W. Kemp, *A Brief Treatise of the Pestilence* [1665], p. 35).

115–26 'We study many times to undo ourselves abusing those good gifts which God hath bestowed upon us . . . Our intemperance it is that pulls so many incurable diseases upon our heads . . . that which crucifies us most, is our own folly, madness . . . weakness, want of government, our facility and proneness in yielding to several lusts . . . by which means we metamorphose ourselves and degenerate into beasts' (*Anatomy*, 1.1.1.2).

127–30 'Where such kind of men [lawyers and physicians] swarm, they will make more work for themselves, and that body politic diseased, which was otherwise sound' (*Anatomy*,

And fierce encounters at the Bar
Undo as fast, as those in war;   130
Enrich bawds, whores, and usurers,
Pimps, scriveners, silenced ministers,
That get estates by being undone
For tender conscience, and have none;
Like those, that with their credit drive   135
A trade without a stock, and thrive;
Advance men in the Church and State
For being of the meanest rate,
Raised for their double-gilt deserts,
Before integrity and parts;   140
Produce more grievous complaints
For plenty, than before for wants,
And make a rich and fruitful year
A greater grievance, than a dear;
Make jests of greater dangers far,   145
Than those they trembled at in war;
Till, unawares, they've laid a train
To blow the public up again;
Rally with horror, and in sport
Rebellion and destruction court,   150
And make fanatics, in despite
Of all their madness, reason right,
And vouch to all they have foreshown,
As other monsters oft have done.
Although from truth and sense as far,   155
As all their other maggots are:
For things said false, and never meant,
Do oft prove true by accident.
  That wealth, that bounteous Fortune sends
As presents to her dearest friends,   160
Is oft laid out upon a purchase
Of two yards long in parish churches;
And those too happy men that bought it,
Had lived, and happier too, without it.

'Democritus to the Reader'); the tribunals of common and
statute law were distinct in Butler's day from those of
equity: appeal to equity (which is supposed to supersede
'law' by appeal to natural justice) amounted to a cripplingly
expensive new process; *free-quarter* the citizen's obligation
to billet soldiery.

131–40 'Ill government proceeds from unskilful, slothful,
griping, covetous, unjust, rash, or tyrannising magistrates,
when they are fools, idiots, children, proud, wilful, partial,
indiscreet, oppressors' (*Anatomy*, 'Democritus to the Reader').

131–2 A promiscuous bundle of those advantaged by
maladministration: scriveners are 'notaries' or 'brokers'; the
'ministers' are Nonconformists silenced by the 1662 Act of
Uniformity and subsequent regulation.

135–6 'Who prosper in their business by deferring payments,
though they have no security ('stock')'.

139–40 'Raised by virtue of their bribes ('double-gilt' [*1759*
reads 'double-guil'd', a pun Thyer thinks 'rather low'] for

'gold paid twice over') rather than their integrity and talents
('parts')'.

141–4 Lawyers 'take upon themselves to make the peace,
but are indeed the very disturbers of our peace, a company
of irreligious harpies, scraping, griping catchpoles . . . that
do more harm . . . than sickness, wars, hunger, diseases'
(*Anatomy*, 'Democritus to the Reader').

145–58 'So, ere the storm of war broke out, / Religion
spawned a various rout, / Of petulant capricious sects, /
The maggots of corrupted texts' (*Hudibras*, 3.2.7–10); 'mag-
gots' (as here at 156) are 'whimsies'.

147–9 'Till without our knowledge they have set things up
('laid a train') to inflame the people again (as in the forties),
they make merry ('rally') with horror'.

153–4 'Give reality to their (raving) prophecies, as other
enormities have before'.

159–64 'Our money buys the graves that our wealth drives
us to.'

For what does vast wealth bring, but cheat,   165
Law, luxury, disease, and debt,
Pain, pleasure, discontent, and sport
An easy-troubled life, and short?
  For men ne'er digged so deep into
The bowels of earth below,   170
For metals that are found to dwell
Near neighbour to the pit of Hell,
And have the magic power to sway
The greedy souls of men that way;
But with their bodies have been fain   175
To fill those trenches up again;
When bloody battles have been fought
For sharing that which they took out.
For wealth is all things that conduce
To man's destruction, or his use;   180
A standard both to buy and sell
All things from Heaven down to Hell.
  But all these plagues are nothing near
Those far more cruel and severe,
Unhappy man takes pains to find,   185
T' inflict himself upon his mind;
And out of his own bowels spins
A rack and torture for his sins:
Torments himself, in vain, to know
That most, which he can never do;   190
And the more strictly 'tis denied,
The more he is unsatisfied;
Is busy in finding scruples out,
To languish in eternal doubt,
Sees spectres in the dark, and ghosts,   195
And starts, as horses do at posts;
And, when his eyes assist him least,
Discerns such subtle objects best:
On hypothetic dreams and visions
Grounds everlasting disquisitions,   200
And raises endless controversies
On vulgar theorems and hearsays:
Grows positive and confident
In things so far beyond the extent
Of human sense, he does not know,   205

165–8 'He is rich, wealthy, fat; what gets he by it? pride, insolency, lust, ambition, cares, fears, suspicion, trouble, anger, emulation, and many filthy diseases of body and mind' (*Anatomy*, 2.5.3); 'luxury', 'pleasure' and 'sport' are temporary (or even malign) reliefs in Butler's list.

169–82 'For treasure they [earth's] secret entrails rent; / The powerful evil, which all power invades, / By her well hid, and wrapped in Stygian shades. / Cursed steel, more cursèd gold she now forth brought: / And bloody-handed war, who with both fought' (Ovid, *Metamorphoses*, 1:138–42, Sandys).

187–8 'Though public pun'shment we escape, the sin / Will rack and torture us within' (Cowley, *Dialogue*, 37–8).

195–208 'Even they that be perfectly awake, if they be timorous and superstitious, possessed with fearful tales, and alone in the dark, are subject to the like fancies, and believe they see spirits and dead men's ghosts walking in church-yards; whereas it is . . . their fancy only' (Hobbes, *Leviathan*, 1.2.7).

199–228 It is one of the excellencies of man that 'he can by words reduce the consequences he finds to general rules . . . But this privilege is allayed by another; and that is by the privilege of absurdity, to which no living creature is subject, but men only. And of men, those are of all most subject to it that profess philosophy' (Hobbes, *Leviathan*, 1.5.6–7).

Whether they be at all, or no;
And doubts as much in things, that are
As plainly evident, and clear:
Disdains all useful sense, and plain,
To apply to the intricate and vain;   210
And cracks his brains in plodding on
That, which is never to be known;
To pose himself with subtleties,
And hold no other knowledge wise;
Although, the subtler all things are,   215
They're but to nothing the more near:
And the less weight they can sustain,
The more he still lays on in vain;
And hangs his soul upon as nice
And subtle curiosities,   220
As one of that vast multitude,
That on a needle's point have stood:
Weighs right and wrong, and true and false
Upon as nice and subtle scales,
As those that turn upon a plane   225
With th' hundredth part of half a grain;
And still the subtiler they move,
The sooner false and useless prove.
So man, that thinks to force and strain
Beyond its natural sphere his brain,   230
In vain torments it on the rack,
And, for improving, sets it back;
Is ign'rant of his own extent,
And that to which his aims are bent,
Is lost in both, and breaks his blade   235
Upon the anvil, where 'twas made:
For as abortions cost more pain
Than vig'rous births; so all the vain
And weak productions of man's wit,
That aim at purposes unfit,   240
Require more drudgery, and worse
Than those of strong and lively force.

215–16 'The more rarefied things are, the nearer they are to non-existence'; in his note on *Hudibras*, 1.1:143–4, Butler attributes this notion to Seneca (*Epistolae Morales*, 82.24). 221–32 What 'Schools use to tell, / Ten thousand angels in one point can dwell' (Crashaw, *On a Prayer-Book*, 13–14). 225–6 'With balances as precise as those that shift from the level with a fraction of the smallest known unit of weight'.

229–42 'For the thoughts are to the desires as scouts and spies to range abroad and find the way to the things desired . . . to have passions indifferently for everything, [is called] giddiness and distraction; and to have stronger and more vehement passions for anything than is ordinarily seen in others is that which men call madness' (Hobbes, *Leviathan*, 1.8.16).

John Cleveland (1613–1658)

The reader of Cleveland 'carouses essences', raw material distilled in the superheated imagination (Thomas Shipman, *The Poet: Upon that Incomparable Enthusiast Mr John Cleveland*). So said a fellow enthusiast. But Cleveland's name enters critical vocabulary as the label of a pernicious syndrome in style. Hobbes does not name Cleveland but was thinking of him when he wrote of 'the ambitious obscurity of expressing more than is perfectly conceived, or perfect conception in fewer words than it requires. Which expressions, though they have had the honour to be called strong lines, are indeed no better than riddles' (*Answer to Davenant*). Riddles are at least soluble. To 'clevelandise', according to Fuller's *Worthies* (1662) is to endeavour 'to imitate the masculine style', which consists in using epithets 'pregnant with metaphors, carrying in them a difficult plainness, difficult at the hearing, plain at the considering thereof'. For Dryden in the *Essay of Dramatic Poesy* (1668) 'Clevelandism' is synonymous with catachresis, 'wresting and torturing a word into another meaning'. It may reduce itself to mere exoticism: Evelyn in a letter of 1665 to Sir Peter Wyche notes that 'such as have lived long in the Universities do greatly affect words and expressions nowhere in use besides, as may be observed in Cleveland's poems for Cambridge.' Cleveland was a University man. In 1631 he took his degree from Christ's College Cambridge, where he was a younger contemporary of Milton; in 1634 he

was elected to a Fellowship at St John's College, and (like Herbert) served the University as Praelector in Rhetoric. In 1643 (like Cowley anticipating ejection) he joined the King at Oxford. His journalism in the Royalist cause got him posted as Judge Advocate to Newark; he sat out the six-month siege by the Scots before (according to a late and unreliable story) being dismissed by the victorious General Leslie to 'go about his business and sell his ballads'. His movements until 1655 are unknown. In that year he was arrested at Norwich. A petition to Cromwell (whose election as MP for Cambridge he had opposed in 1640) secured his release. His remaining few years were spent in London, where friends at Gray's Inn looked after him, including (says Aubrey) Samuel Butler.

Brian Morris, *John Cleveland (1613–1658): A Bibliography of his Poems* (Oxford: Clarendon Press, 1967), lists the editions of Cleveland's poems up to 1699. The first collection is as an appendix to *The Character of a London Diurnal* (started in 1644), published in 1647. *The Poems* first appeared, so titled, in 1651; and by the year of Cleveland's death eighteen editions had been published. There is a facsimile of the eleventh edition of 1653 (Menston: Scolar Press, 1971). An attempt to stabilize the text and canon was made by two of Cleveland's old Cambridge students, John Lake and Samuel Drake: *Clevelandi Vindiciae* (1677). The standard edition is *The Poems* (Oxford: Clarendon Press, 1967), ed. Brian Morris and Eleanor Withington.

Upon the Death of Mr King

Obsequies to the Memory of Mr Edward King (1638); printed with minor variations in *1651*. The headnote to Milton's *Lycidas* gives details of the occasion.

> I like not tears in tune, nor will I prize
> His artificial grief, that scans his eyes,
> Mine weep down pious beads: but why should I
> Confine them to the Muses' rosary?
> I am no poet here; my pen's the spout   5
> Where the rainwater of my eyes runs out
> In pity of that name, whose fate we see
> Thus copied out his grief's hydrography.

1–2 'Elegies ('tears') which are musical and tears ('eyes') which can be measured ('scanned') are worthless; 'artificial' is sometimes applied to quantitative verse and so to all the Latin verses in the memorial volume.
4 'Why should my tears be ordered?'

5–6 The quasi-standard 'eye-conduits' facilitates the link between tear-ducts and gargoyles.
8 *hydrography* 'the delineation of the sea . . . a description of the water' (Blount, *Glossographia*); the metaphor requires the word's application to the sea itself.

The Muses are not mermaids, though upon
His death the ocean might turn Helicon.   10
The sea's too rough for verse; who rhymes upon't,
With Xerxes strives to fetter th' Hellespont.
My tears will keep no channel, know no laws
To guide the streams; but like the waves, their cause,
Run with disturbance, till they swallow me   15
As a description of his misery.
But can his spacious virtue find a grave
Within the impostumed bubble of a wave?
Whose learning if we sound, we must confess
The sea but shallow, and him bottomless,   20
Could not the winds to countermand thy death,
With their whole card of lungs redeem thy breath?
Or some new island in thy rescue peep,
To heave thy resurrection from the deep?
That so the world might see thy safety wrought,   25
With no less miracle than thyself was thought.
The famous Stagirite, who in his life
Had Nature as familiar as his wife,
Bequeathed his widow to survive with thee,
Queen Dowager of all Philosophy: 30
An ominous legacy that did portend
Thy fate, and predecessor's second end:
Some have affirmed, that what on earth we find
The sea can parallel for shape and kind:
Books, arts, and tongues were wanting; but in thee   35
Neptune hath got an university.
    We'll dive no more for pearls. The hope to see
Thy sacred relics of mortality
Shall welcome storms, and make the seamen prize
His shipwreck now more than his merchandise.   40
He shall embrace the waves and to the tomb

10 *Helicon* where the Muses are worshipped, properly a mountain but here standing for Aganippe or Hippocrene, the fountains of inspiration.

11–12 'Grief brought to numbers cannot be so fierce, / For, he tames it, that fetters it in verse' (Donne, *The Triple Fool*, 10–11); 'fetter' alludes to metrical feet. The Persian Xerxes built bridges across the Hellespont (the Dardanelles) to cross into Europe and invade Greece; when the first effort was destroyed by a storm the enraged Xerxes 'ordered his men to give the Hellespont three hundred lashes and to sink a pair of shackles into the sea' (Herodotus, 7.34–5).

13–16 'As a proud stream that swoln with rain / Comes pouring down the hills amain / So Pindar flows' (Horace, *Odes*, 4.2.5–8); to imitate him is to meet the fate of Icarus who fell to a 'watery grave'. The verses run like the waves (the 'cause' of his grief by taking King) and swallow the poet, who repeats his subject's fate (and so becomes its 'description') by drowning.

18 *impostumed* 'swollen'; 'From the swoln fluxure of the clouds, [Heaven] doth shake / A rank impostume upon every lake' (Drayton, *Barons' Wars*, 2.16).

21–2 'Could not all the winds from all the quarters of the globe supply breath to revive you?'; winds were named by compass points, and shown on the sea-card or chart: 'All the quarters that they [the winds] know / In th' shipman's card' (Shakespeare, *Macbeth*, I. iii. 16–17).

23–4 With the memory of how whales might be taken for islands and give false hope of rescue as in Milton, *Paradise Lost*, 1.200–8.

26 *than ... thought* since you yourself were thought a miracle (*1651* reads 'wonder', which is theologically less loaded).

27 *Stagirite* Aristotle, from his birthplace Stagira.

30 *Queen Dowager* Nature, widow of Aristotle, king of philosophers; but playing on King's name.

31–2 'That Aristotle drowned himself in Euripus as despairing to resolve the cause of its ... ebb and flow seven times a day, with this determination, "If I do not have you, you shall have me" ... is generally believed amongst us' (Browne, *Pseudodoxia Epidemica*, 7.13); as Aristotle drowned, so should King.

33–4 'Whatsoever is engendered and bred in any part of the world beside is found in the sea' (Pliny, *Natural History*, 9.1.2).

As to a Royaller Exchange shall come.
What can we now expect? Water and fire.
Both elements our ruin do conspire;
And that dissolves us which doth us compound,   45
One Vatican was burnt, another drowned.
We of the gown our libraries must toss
To understand the greatness of our loss,
By pupils to our grief, and so much grow
In learning as our sorrows overflow.   50
When we have filled the roundlets of our eyes,
We'll issue it forth, and vent such elegies,
As that our tears shall seem the Irish Seas,
We floating islands, living Hebrides.

42 The Royal Exchange, founded in 1566, was the centre of English commercial activity; it served as an emporium of rare commodities.
45 'We are dissolved in that element of water that constitutes us.'
46 *Vatican* 'library'; 'Learning would rather choose / Her Bodley, or her Vatican to lose [than you]' (Cowley, *To the Lord Falkland*, 3–4). The burned library is that at Alexandria; King is the drowned library.
47 'We in the universities must turn our books over and over.'

49 'Learn from our grief and turn ourselves into weeping eyes.'
54 Spenser's 'wandering islands' are 'But straggling plots, which to and fro do run / In the wide waters' (*Faerie Queene* 2.12.11–13), insecure ground for deluded sailors; but these recall the new island that might have rescued the drowning King (23 4). Sylvester calls the floating islands of Loch Lomond 'The trembling Cyclads in great Lomond lake' (*Divine Weeks*, 2.4.1:1046).

Epitaph on the Earl of Strafford

1647; the authorship is open to question. Thomas Wentworth, Earl of Strafford, was executed for treason (as an agent of the King's personal rule) on 12 May 1641 on Tower Hill, 'where with a composed undaunted courage, he told the people "he was come thither to satisfy them with his head; but that he much feared the reformation which was begun in blood would not prove so fortunate to the kingdom as they expected and he wished"' (Clarendon, *History*, 3.203);

King Charles's assent to the Act of Attainder on him (by some regarded as a betrayal) was secured finally by a letter from Strafford himself (3.200). Hollar's engravings of both the trial and the execution are reproduced in Graham Parry, *Hollar's England* (London: Michael Russell, 1980). The many poets who took up the subject include Stanley, Fanshawe, Denham. Strafford is buried at Wentworth Woodhouse (the family estate) in Yorkshire.

Here lies wise and valiant dust,
Huddled up 'twixt fit and just:
Strafford, who was hurried hence
'Twixt treason and convenience.
He spent his time here in a mist;   5
A Papist, yet a Calvinist.
His Prince's nearest joy, and grief.
He had, yet wanted all relief.
The prop and ruin of the state;
The people's violent love, and hate: 10

4 *treason and convenience* the one on the Parliament's part, the other on the King's.
6 On the scaffold he made 'great expressions to his devotion to the Church of England, and the Protestant religion established by law and professed in that Church' (Clarendon, *History*, 3.203); rumour called him Catholic.

8 The King might have been his relief, but was not.
9–10 'The enemy and martyr of the state, / Our nation's glory and our nation's hate' (Denham's draft of *On the Earl of Strafford's Trial and Death*, 17–18).

One in extremes loved and abhorred.
Riddles lie here; or in a word,
Here lies blood; and let it lie
Speechless still, and never cry.

13–14   Proverbially 'Murder will out'; but this will not.

Sir John Denham (1615–1669)

'I am sure there are few who make verses, have observed the sweetness of these two lines in *Cooper's Hill*: "Though deep, yet clear, though gentle, yet not dull, / Strong without rage, without o'erflowing full". And there are yet fewer who can find the reason of that sweetness' (Dryden, Preface to the *Aeneis*). Nearer the beginning of his career, in the preface to *The Rival Ladies* (1664), Dryden indicates that *Cooper's Hill* is 'a poem, which . . . for the majesty of its style is, and ever will be, the exact standard of good writing'. Denham did more than invent a strong form of the heroic couplet, and *Cooper's Hill*, even if we discount his minor squibs, is not even typical of what he did write: *The Sophy* (1642, acted the year before to great acclaim) is an orientalist blank-verse tragedy, his Virgilian translation *The Destruction of Troy* (1656, but written twenty years before, and part of a larger and still unpublished enterprise) is in the 'concatenated' couplets to which he afterwards refined the alternative. When *Cooper's Hill* appeared in 1642, some doubted his authorship of it. But he is more than most a poet of one poem. His poem *On Abraham Cowley's Death* praises its subject for his energy and originality in the face of the traditions he exploited; his verses *To Sir Richard Fanshawe* praise him for the 'new and nobler way' he took as a trans-

lator. But only in this one serious poem did Denham make himself, as Johnson put it, 'an original', and even that begins with a bow to Waller.

His life was disorganized. Born in Dublin, son of the Chief Justice, he lost his mother when he was 4. At Oxford he was the 'dreamingst young fellow' and 'not suspected to be a wit' (Aubrey). He was a gambler and, until he inherited his father's estates in 1639, had trouble maintaining his habit. In the 1640s he served the Royalist cause, eventually with the court in exile in Paris. At the Restoration he was knighted, made Surveyor General (Christopher Wren was his assistant), sat in Parliament, was a member of the Royal Society and famously (it was the subject of a lampoon by Butler) went mad. *Poems and Translations* was published in 1668, the year before his death, and was reprinted many times over the next century and a half. Brendan O' Hehir's *Harmony from Discords: A Life of Sir John Denham* (Berkeley and Los Angeles: University of California Press, 1968) is the standard biography. T. H. Banks's *The Poetical Works*, second edition (Hamden: Archon Books, 1969) is the standard edition. But to the textual complications of *Cooper's Hill* Brendan O' Hehir's *Expans'd Hieroglyphicks* (Berkeley and Los Angeles: University of California Press, 1969) is the indispensable guide.

Cooper's Hill

1668; with at 188 the six-line addition from the MS insertion in the Osborn copy in Yale University Library. The history of the texts is complicated. A first version of the poem is represented in MS drafts, in an edition of 1642 by Walkeley (reprinted by Moseley in 1650) and in Hall's 1643 Oxford edition, perhaps printed from a copy of 1642 corrected by Denham. A second version is represented by J. B.'s 1655 printing, and by the version, superior in accuracy and slightly altered, followed here (and reprinted in 1671). The complication is more than bibliographical: revision of the poem proceeded through the events it alludes to. A historically rich landscape provokes reflections on a political crisis, or is used to illustrate it. Cooper's Hill rises above Runnymede outside Egham in Surrey (where Denham lived); the poet takes long views north-east to London and St Pauls (13–38), westward to Windsor (39–110), south-east to the ruins of Chertsey Abbey (111–56) and immediately downwards to the River Thames (157–240) and Runnymede, the scene of a hunt (241–328) and once the scene of the signing of Magna Carta (329–64). The poem ends with a meditation, provoked by the

memory of Magna Carta, on the balance of royal and popular power; but the whole poem offers meditations on English history as a succession of swings between monarchical tyranny (exemplified by King John's abuse of political liberties and Henry VIII's abuse of ecclesiastical liberties), and popular tyranny (which is only threatened), both destructive of commerce, agriculture and, most urgently, of religion. Its pessimism is almost untempered. The first version, conceived before the Civil War, is a plea for moderation on the part of both King and Parliament. The occasion of the first version had long dissolved before the appearance of the second. Now what was already recognized as a classic of English verse ("Tis dignity in others, if they be / Crowned Poets; yet live princes under thee', Herrick, *To Mr Denham, on his Prospective Poem*, 15–16) is rescued from a too insistent topicality. It is drastically adapted, most noticeably by the expansion of the stag-hunt, in the condensation of the lines on Charles and Windsor and also in the conclusion. It stands apart from its own origins (and is regularly treated as stating a universal principle of *discordia concors*) and above the various encomia of

Cromwell (which already plundered its commonplaces) published round the same date.

The poem is of a mixed kind often described as 'georgic'. The consequent emphasis on the descriptive elements is misleading, but everywhere attested. Johnson confirms Denham as the father of topographical poetry, admitting only as 'embellishments' what may be supplied by 'historical retrospection or incidental meditation'; phrasing based on Pope's in his note to the *Iliad*, 16:466, the description of a flood, 'tending to some hint, or leading to some reflection upon moral life or political institutions'. In some traditions of local poetry the descriptive elements are almost wholly mute; Denham's exaggeration of them owes something to recent traditions of retirement poetry (with a specific debt to Casimir, *Epodes*, 1), or to recent topographical poetry (he acknowledges Waller). The immediate early acclaim was sustained for a century and a half: important early criticism includes treatments by John Dennis, by Dr Johnson and by John Scott (*Critical Essays*, 1785).

Sure there are poets which did never dream
Upon Parnassus, nor did taste the stream
Of Helicon; we therefore may suppose
Those made not poets, but the poets those,
And as courts make not kings, but kings the court,   5
So where the Muses and their train resort,
Parnassus stands; if I can be to thee
A poet, thou Parnassus art to me.
Nor wonder, if (advantaged in my flight,
By taking wing from thy auspicious height)   10
Through untraced ways, and airy paths I fly,
More boundless in my fancy than my eye:
My eye, which swift as thought, contracts the space
That lies between, and first salutes the place
Crowned with that sacred pile, so vast, so high,   15
That whether 'tis a part of earth, or sky,
Uncertain seems, and may be thought a proud
Aspiring mountain, or descending cloud,
Paul's, the late theme of such a Muse whose flight
Has bravely reached and soared above thy height: 20
Now shalt thou stand though sword, or time, or fire,
Or zeal more fierce than they, thy fall conspire,
Secure, whilst thee the best of poets sings,
Preserved from ruin by the best of kings.
Under his proud survey the city lies,   25
And like a mist beneath a hill doth rise;

1–3 'I never did on cleft Parnassus dream, / Nor taste the sacred Heliconian stream; / Nor can remember when my brain, inspired, / Was by the Muses into madness fired' (Persius, Prologue to *Satires*, 1–3, Dryden).
5 The court is 'where the king lieth' (Harrison, *Description*, 2.15).
8 'Highway since you my chief Parnassus be' (Sidney, *Astrophil*, 84:1).
9–11 Denham borrows his own version of Virgil's account of Daedalus: 'Boldly presuming with auspicious wings / Through untraced airy ways to take his flight' (*Aeneid*, 6:15); *auspicious* 'well-omened'.
13–15 'They climb the next ascent, and, looking down, / Now at a nearer distance view the town. / The prince with wonder sees the stately towers ... The gates and streets; and hears, from every part, / The noise and busy concourse of the mart' (*Aeneid*, 1:419–22, Dryden, the prospect over Carthage); 'saluting' inanimate places is bold (but Virgil's sailors salute Italy, *Aeneid*, 3:524).
16–18 'These things seem small and undistinguishable / Like far-off mountains turned into clouds' (Shakespeare, *Midsummer Night's Dream*, IV. i. 186–7).
19–24 The margin notes Waller's *Upon his Majesty's repairing of Paul's*.
21–2 'Immortalized in Waller's verse you will survive the accident of war or time or Puritan malice'; the anti-prelatical Lord Brooke hoped to 'see no one stone left upon another' of the renovated cathedral.
23–4 'How, best of kings, dost thou a sceptre bear! / How, best of poets, dost thou laurel wear!' (Jonson, *To King James*, 1–2).
26–8 Dugdale's *History of St Paul's Cathedral* (1658) complains of the effects of coal-smoke on the fabric of the cathedral.

Whose state and wealth the business and the crowd,
Seems at this distance but a darker cloud:
And is to him who rightly things esteems,
No other in effect than what it seems: 30
Where, with like haste, though several ways, they run
Some to undo, and some to be undone;
While luxury, and wealth, like war and peace,
Are each the other's ruin, and increase;
As rivers lost in seas some secret vein   35
Thence reconveys, there to be lost again.
O happiness of sweet retired content!
To be at once secure, and innocent.
Windsor the next (where Mars with Venus dwells,
Beauty with strength) above the valley swells   40
Into my eye, and doth itself present
With such an easy and unforced ascent,
That no stupendious precipice denies
Access, no horror turns away our eyes:
But such a rise, as doth at once invite   45
A pleasure, and a reverence from the sight.
Thy mighty master's emblem, in whose face
Sat meekness, heightened with majestic grace.
Such seems thy gentle height, made only proud
To be the basis of that pompous load,   50
Than which, a nobler weight no mountain bears,
But Atlas only that supports the spheres.
When Nature's hand this ground did thus advance,
'Twas guided by a wiser power than Chance;
Marked out for such an use, as if 'twere meant   55
To invite the builder, and his choice prevent.
Nor can we call it choice, when what we choose,
Folly, or blindness only could refuse.
A crown of such majestic towers doth grace
The gods' great mother, when her heavenly race   60
Do homage to her, yet she cannot boast
Among that numerous, and celestial host,

33–4 'From ruin life, from life doth ruin spring, / Peace war ensues, war peace, then strife again' (William Harbert, *Lamentation of Britain*, 667–8).

35–6 A cycle of waters is imagined from the sea to 'a secret source of subterranean floods' to the earth's rivers to the sea again (Virgil, *Georgics*, 4:366).

39–40 'In the fables of the Greeks, Harmony was born from the union of Mars and Venus, of whom the latter is fierce and contentious and the former generous and pleasing' (Plutarch, *Isis and Osiris*, 370d); 'the universe is now one and at peace through the power of love, and now many and at war with itself owing to some sort of strife' (Plato, *Sophist*, 242e).

43–4 'No amazing ('stupendious' was the normal form until 1700) steepness prevents our climbing the hill; no rugged growth discourages our viewing it.'

47 The harmonies of Windsor are metaphors of Charles I.

50–2 In Carew's *Coelum Britannicum* a scene dominated by a 'sphere, with stars placed in their several images; borne up by a huge naked figure kneeling and bowing forwards' (170) yields to one showing a hill whose lower part 'was wild and craggy, and above somewhat more pleasant and flourishing: about the middle part of this mountain were seated the three kingdoms of England, Scotland, and Ireland' (835); *pompous* 'magnificent'.

56 *prevent* 'anticipate'; the architect would otherwise have had to raise ('advance') the ground artificially.

59–60 Spenser's Thames wears a 'coronet . . . In which were many towers and castles set . . . Like as the mother of the gods . . . When to Jove's palace she doth take her way; / Old Cybele, arrayed with pompous pride, / Wearing a diadem embattled wide / With hundred turrets' (*Faerie Queene*, 4.11.27–8).

More heroes than can Windsor, nor doth Fame's
Immortal book record more noble names.
Not to look back so far, to whom this isle   65
Owes the first glory of so brave a pile,
Whether to Caesar, Albanact, or Brute,
The British Arthur, or the Danish Knute,
(Though this of old no less contest did move,
Than when for Homer's birth seven cities strove;   70
Like him in birth, thou shouldst be like in fame,
As thine his fate, if mine had been his flame)
But whosoe'er it was, Nature designed
First a brave place, and then as brave a mind.
Not to recount those several kings, to whom   75
It gave a cradle, or to whom a tomb,
But thee (great Edward) and thy greater son,
(The lilies which his father wore, he won)
And thy Bellona, who the consort came
Not only to thy bed, but to thy fame,   80
She to thy triumph led one captive king,
And brought that son, which did the second bring.
Then didst thou found that Order (whether love
Or victory thy royal thoughts did move)
Each was a noble cause, and nothing less,   85
Than the design, has been the great success:
Which foreign kings, and emperors esteem
The second honour to their diadem.
Had thy great destiny but given thee skill,
To know as well, as power to act her will,   90
That from those kings, who then thy captives were,
In after-times should spring a royal pair
Who should possess all that thy mighty power,
Or thy desires more mighty, did devour;
To whom their better fate reserves whate'er   95
The victor hopes for, or the vanquished fear;
That blood, which thou and thy great grandsire shed,

---

63 *Coelum Britannicum* ends with a vision of British heroes emerging from a descended cloud, 'and in the lower part was seen afar off the prospect of Windsor Castle, the famous seat of the most honourable order of the Garter' (1010).

65–6 Adapting Waller's couplet on King James 'When the first monarch of this happy isle, / Moved with the ruin of so brave a pile' (*Upon his Majesty's repairing of St Paul's*, 5–6).

67–8 William the Conqueror built the castle on the site of an Anglo-Saxon fort; Denham mystically (or politically) rehearses claims of greater (pre-Norman) antiquity. Albanact is a son of Brutus (*Faerie Queene* 2.10.14); the historical 'Danish Knute' is distinguished from the legendary giant-slaying 'bold Canutus' (*Faerie Queene*, 2.10.11–12).

70 'Seven cities strive for the learned root of Homer: Smyrna, Chios, Colophon, Ithaca, Pylos, Argos, Athens' (*Greek Anthology*, 16.298, the most famous epigram of a group).

71–2 'Your origins are obscure like Homer's, and had I his genius, you would be as famous as he is.'

77–8 The margin identifies Edward III (who carried the French fleur-de-lis on his arms) and the Black Prince (who

secured Aquitaine for the English).

79–81 The margin identifies Queen Philippa (Bellona is the goddess of war, a surname of Minerva). David II of Scotland (identified in the margin) was captured at the battle of Neville's Cross, traditionally by Philippa herself; the defeated Jean II of France (le Bon) was brought to London by the Black Prince.

83–4 Peter Heylyn's *History of St George* (1631) rehearses various legends surrounding the foundation of the Order of the Garter, rejecting the story of Edward's transforming a gallant gesture in picking up the Countess of Salisbury's fallen garter: he thinks it commemorates the victory at Calais.

91–2 Charles I was descended from David II; Henrietta Maria from Jean le Bon.

95–6 'Who will live to enjoy what victors might hope to enjoy and what their defeated enemies fear they might'.

97 'Which you [Edward III] shed in the French wars and your grandfather Edward I shed in the Scottish wars'.

And all that since these sister nations bled,
Had been unspilt, had happy Edward known
That all the blood he spilt, had been his own.   100
When he that patron chose, in whom are joined
Soldier and martyr, and his arms confined
Within the azure circle, he did seem
But to foretell, and prophesy of him,
Who to his realms that azure round hath joined,   105
Which Nature for their bound at first designed.
That bound, which to the world's extremest ends,
Endless itself, its liquid arms extends;
Nor doth he need those emblems which we paint,
But is himself the soldier and the saint.   110
Here should my wonder dwell, and here my praise,
But my fixed thoughts my wandering eye betrays,
Viewing a neighbouring hill, whose top of late
A chapel crowned, till in the common fate,
The adjoining abbey fell: (may no such storm   115
Fall on our times, when ruin must reform).
Tell me (my Muse) what monstrous dire offence,
What crime could any Christian king incense
To such a rage? Was't luxury, or lust?
Was he so temperate, so chaste, so just?   120
Were these their crimes? They were his own much more:
But wealth is crime enough to him that's poor,
Who having spent the treasures of his crown,
Condemns their luxury to feed his own.
And yet this act, to varnish o'er the shame   125
Of sacrilege, must bear devotion's name.
No crime so bold, but would be understood
A real, or at least a seeming good.
Who fears not to do ill, yet fears the name,
And free from conscience, is a slave to fame.   130
Thus he the church at once protects, and spoils:
But princes' swords are sharper than their styles.
And thus to the ages past he makes amends,
Their charity destroys, their faith defends.

102–6 The red cross of St George within the blue garter emblematizes the sea-girt kingdoms; one MS has it that the prophecy is of King James, but King Charles inherits the union, however fragile.

110 Rubens painted King Charles as St George (now at Buckingham Palace).

113–15 St Anne's Hill (identified in the margin) in Chertsey (not visible from the supposed vantage-point) was the site of Chertsey Abbey, despoiled at the Dissolution of the Monasteries (1542).

117–19 'O Muse! the causes and the crimes relate . . . Can heavenly minds such high resentment show, / Or exercise their spite in human woe?' (Virgil, *Aeneid*, 1:8–11, Dryden); and Venus's attempted pacification of Aeneas: 'My son! from whence this madness . . . Why this unmanly rage? (*Aeneid*, 2:594–5).

118 Henry VIII coveted the papally bestowed French title 'Most Christian King'.

119 The opposition of 'luxury' and 'lust' is deliberately weak; but Henry's motives for appropriating Church property are reduced to greed.

127–30 'The prince should act to get a hold on government and keep it; his methods will be judged honourable and praiseworthy; the common people are always deceived by appearances and impressed by results' (Machiavelli, *The Prince*, ch. 19); but concern with reputation is a worse master than conscience.

131–4 Henry's authorship of a tract against Luther earned him the title 'Defender of the Faith'; but his violent Dissolution of the monasteries and the charitable works associated with them is a more lasting legacy; 'styles' puns on 'pens' and 'titles'.

Then did Religion in a lazy cell,   135
In empty, airy contemplations dwell;
And like the block, unmoved lay: but ours,
As much too active, like the stork devours.
Is there no temperate region can be known,
Betwixt their frigid, and our torrid zone?   140
Could we not wake from that lethargic dream,
But to be restless in a worse extreme?
And for that lethargy was there no cure,
But to be cast into a calenture?
Can knowledge have no bound, but must advance   145
So far, to make us wish for ignorance?
And rather in the dark to grope our way,
Than led by a false guide to err by day?
Who sees these dismal heaps, but would demand
What barbarous invader sacked the land?   150
But when he hears, no Goth, no Turk did bring
This desolation, but a Christian king;
When nothing, but the name of zeal, appears
'Twixt our best actions and the worst of theirs,
What does he think our sacrilege would spare,   155
When such the effects of our devotions are?
Parting from thence 'twixt anger, shame, and fear,
Those for what's past, and this for what's too near:
My eye descending from the hill, surveys
Where Thames among the wanton valleys strays.   160
Thames, the most loved of all the Ocean's sons,
By his old sire to his embraces runs,
Hasting to pay his tribute to the sea,
Like mortal life to meet eternity.
Though with those streams he no resemblance hold,   165
Whose foam is amber, and their gravel gold;
His genuine, and less guilty wealth to explore,
Search not his bottom, but survey his shore;
O'er which he kindly spreads his spacious wing,
And hatches plenty for the ensuing spring.   170

135–8   Recalling the Aesopic fable of King Log and King
Stork: 'the frogs . . . to Jove cried / To have a King. He
heard their prayers 'tis said / And flung them down a beam
['block'] to be their head. / But they disliked with peace,
again did call, / On which he sent a stork that ate them all'
(Robert Fletcher, *Dialogue between two water Nymphs Thamesis
and Sabrina*, 62–6).
143   'Was there no cure for pathological torpor but fever
and frenzy?'
145–6   Burton cites from Joseph Scaliger: 'It is wise ignor-
ance not to wish to know / What the Great Master hath not
deigned to show, / Though ignorance is learning quite enow'
(*Anatomy*, 1.2.4.7).
149   Recalling Virgil's 'disordered heap of ruin [*disiectas
moles*] . . . Stones rent from stones' (*Aeneid*, 2:608, Dryden).
151–2   'Not Helen's face, nor Paris, was in fault; / But by
the gods was this destruction brought' (*Aeneid*, 2:600–2).
153   King complains to the 'over-active zealots' of the 1640s
'That neither tomb nor temple could escape, / Nor dead

nor living your licentious rape' (*Elegy upon King Charles*,
168–70).
158   'Anger and shame for our history, fear for our future'.
160–4   Thames's 'old sire' is the Tame (Spenser, *Faerie
Queene*, 4.11.24–5); both return their waters to the sea;
Spenser's minor rivers 'tribute pay' to the Thames (4.11.29).
165–88   Virgil claims superiority for Italy's unfabulous wealth:
'neither Median woods . . . Fair Ganges, Hermus rolling golden
sand . . . Nor any foreign earth of greater name, / Can with
sweet Italy contend in fame' (*Georgics*, 2:136–9).
165–6   *1642* names Tagus (in Spain and Portugal) and
Pactolus (in Lydia), both celebrated for their gold-bearing
sands.
167–8   The genuine wealth of the shore is less 'guilty' be-
cause 'ungilt' and because it is men of the degenerate Iron
Age who, not 'with rich Earth's just nourishments content,
/ For treasure they her secret entrails rent; / The powerful
evil, which all power invades' (Ovid, *Metamorphoses*, 1:137–
40).

Nor then destroys it with too fond a stay,
Like mothers which their infants overlay.
Nor with a sudden and impetuous wave,
Like profuse kings, resumes the wealth he gave.
No unexpected inundations spoil 175
The mower's hopes, nor mock the ploughman's toil:
But God-like his unwearied bounty flows;
First loves to do, then loves the good he does.
Nor are his blessings to his banks confined,
But free, and common, as the sea or wind; 180
When he to boast, or to disperse his stores
Full of the tributes of his grateful shores,
Visits the world, and in his flying towers
Brings home to us, and makes both Indies ours;
Finds wealth where 'tis, bestows it where it wants 185
Cities in deserts, woods in cities plants.
So that to us no thing, no place is strange,
While his fair bosom is the world's Exchange.
Rome only conquered half the world, but trade
One commonwealth of that and her hath made; 190
And though the sun his beam extends to all
Yet to his neighbour sheds most liberal,
Lest God and Nature partial should appear
Commerce makes everything grow everywhere.
O could I flow like thee, and make thy stream 195
My great example, as it is my theme!
Though deep, yet clear, though gentle, yet not dull,
Strong without rage, without o'erflowing full.
Heaven her Eridanus no more shall boast,
Whose fame in thine, like lesser current's lost; 200

171–2 Waller blames the sea for the beaching of whales ('her own brood') 'as careless dames whom wine and sleep betray / To frantic dreams, their infants overlay' (*The Battle of the Summer Islands*, 2:305–7).

174 'Like kings who pour out gifts, takes back the crops he watered'.

175–6 'The lofty skies at once come pouring down, / The promised crop and golden labours drown' (Virgil, *Georgics*, 1:325–6, Dryden); Virgil illustrates the burning of Troy with the burning of crops: 'As flames rolled by the winds conspiring force, / O'er full-eared corn, or torrents raging course / Bears down the opposing oaks, the fields destroys / And mocks the ploughman's toil' (*Aeneid*, 2:305–7, Denham).

178 'And God saw . . . that it was good' (Genesis 1: 4 etc.).

179–94 'I will extend peace to her like a river, and the glory of the Gentiles like a flowing stream: then shall ye suck, ye shall be borne upon her sides, and be dandled upon her knees' (Isaiah 66: 12); but Ovid's Golden Age is ignorant of trade: 'To visit other worlds, no wounded pine / Did yet from hills to faithless seas decline. / Then, unambitious mortals knew no more, / But their own country's nature-bounded shore' (*Metamorphoses*, 1:94–6, Sandys). 'All men know there is nothing imports this island more than trade; it is that wheel of industry which sets all others a-going; it is that which preserves the chiefest castles and walls of this kingdom, I mean the ships' (James Howell, *Letters*, 1.6.52, dated May 1644 and lamenting the decay of shipping).

183 *flying towers* 'high-built ships' (like Virgil's *turritae puppes*, *Aeneid*, 8:693); but some understand 'tours'.

184 *both Indies* West and East.

188 'London, in the bosom of the Thames, is the commercial centre of the world'; the buoyant six lines which follow on the superiority of commerce to conquest (or even the sun) are added to *1668* in Denham's hand.

195–8 Horace's ideal poet will enrich Rome with language 'pithy, and plain withal . . . let his words like flowing water fall' (*Epistles*, 2.2:120, Drant: for *vemens et liquidus, puroque simillimus amni*). Burton is unfastidious: 'So that as a river runs, sometimes precipitate and swift, then dull and slow; now direct, then winding; now deep, then shallow; now muddy, then clear; now broad, then narrow; doth my style flow' (*Anatomy*, 'Democritus to the Reader'). Denham's couplets are commended for their accurate movement, based on Cartwright, 'Low without creeping, high without loss of wings; / Smooth, yet not weak, and by a thorough care, / Big without swelling, without painting fair' (*To the Memory of Ben Jonson*, 122–4); or Randolph: 'Not long and empty; lofty but not proud; / Subtle but sweet, high but without a cloud' (*To Mr Felltham on his Book of Resolves*, 93–4).

199 *Eridanus* the River Po imagined as the Milky Way.

Thy nobler streams shall visit Jove's abodes,
To shine among the stars, and bathe the gods.
Here Nature, whether more intent to please
Us or herself, with strange varieties
(For things of wonder give no less delight   205
To the wise maker's, than beholder's sight.
Though these delights from several causes move
For so our children, thus our friends we love),
Wisely she knew, the harmony of things,
As well as that of sounds, from discord springs.   210
Such was the discord, which did first disperse
Form, order, beauty through the universe;
While dryness moisture, coldness heat resists,
All that we have, and that we are, subsists.
While the steep horrid roughness of the wood   215
Strives with the gentle calmness of the flood.
Such huge extremes when Nature doth unite,
Wonder from thence results, from thence delight.
The stream is so transparent, pure, and clear,
That had the self-enamoured youth gazed here,   220
So fatally deceived he had not been,
While he the bottom, not his face had seen.
But his proud head the airy mountain hides
Among the clouds; his shoulders and his sides
A shady mantle clothes; his curled brows   225
Frown on the gentle stream, which calmly flows,
While winds and storms his lofty forehead beat:
The common fate of all that's high or great.
Low at his foot a spacious plain is placed,
Between the mountain and the stream embraced: 230
Which shade and shelter from the hill derives,
While the kind river wealth and beauty gives;
And in the mixture of all these appears
Variety, which all the rest endears.
This scene had some bold Greek, or British bard   235
Beheld of old, what stories had we heard,
Of fairies, satyrs, and the nymphs their dames,
Their feasts, their revels, and their amorous flames!

205–6 'For wonders delight their creators (as our children delight us) as much as their viewers (as our friends delight us)'.

209–14 'The Earth, and every other thing in the world [is] tempered and conserved by things of dislike and contrary quality. It is not then without cause that Nature is so desirous of contraries, making of them all decency, and beauty ... This kind of tempering is the cause, that such things as before were diverse and different, do accord and agree together ... the contrariety becoming unity; and the discord concord' (Louis Leroy, *Of the Interchangeable Course or Variety of Things*, Robert Astley).

215–18 Gerard Langbaine's Latin version of Longinus *On the Sublime* appeared at Oxford in 1636; 'but one shouldn't always aim at the high-flown and the sublime; in a picture nothing sets off light so well as shade' (Pliny, *Letters*, 3.13).

219–22 Yet Narcissus saw himself reflected in 'a spring ... whose silver waters were as smooth as any mirror, nor less clear' (Ovid, *Metamorphoses*, 3:407, Sandys).

223–8 *1642*'s image of 'our surly supercilious lords' is cancelled. Cooper's Hill is 220 feet high.

229 *plain* Runnymede.

234 'They say variety is what gives pleasure' (Cicero, *De Finibus*, 2.3.10).

235–40 'Whilome, when Ireland flourishèd in fame ... The gods then used (for pleasure and for rest) / Oft to resort thereto ... But none therein more pleasure found / Than Cynthia ... With all her nymphs ... With whom the woody gods did oft resort' (Spenser, *Faerie Queene*, 7.6.38–9); British fairies left at the Reformation: 'But now alas they all are dead / Or gone beyond the seas, / Or further from religion fled / Or else they take their ease' (Corbett, *The Fairies' Farewell*, 37–40). Jonson admits them to Penshurst.

'Tis still the same, although their airy shape
All but a quick poetic sight escape.   240
There Faunus and Sylvanus keep their courts
And thither all the horned host resorts,
To graze the ranker mead, that noble herd
On whose sublime and shady fronts is reared
Nature's great masterpiece; to show how soon   245
Great things are made, but sooner are undone.
Here have I seen the King, when great affairs
Gave leave to slacken, and unbend his cares,
Attended to the chase by all the flower
Of youth, whose hopes a nobler prey devour: 250
Pleasure with praise, and danger, they would buy,
And wish a foe that would not only fly.
The stag now conscious of his fatal growth,
At once indulgent to his fear and sloth,
To some dark covert his retreat had made,   255
Where nor man's eye, nor heaven's should invade
His soft repose; when the unexpected sound
Of dogs, and men, his wakeful ear doth wound.
Roused with the noise, he scarce believes his ear,
Willing to think the illusions of his fear   260
Had given this false alarm, but straight his view
Confirms, that more than all he fears is true.
Betrayed in all his strengths, the wood beset,
All instruments, all arts of ruin met;
He calls to mind his strength, and then his speed,   265
His wingèd heels, and then his armèd head;
With these to avoid, with that his fate to meet:
But fear prevails, and bids him trust his feet.
So fast he flies, that his reviewing eye
Has lost the chasers, and his ear the cry;   270
Exulting, till he finds, their nobler sense
Their disproportioned speed does recompense.
Then curses his conspiring feet, whose scent
Betrays that safety which their swiftness lent.
Then tries his friends, among the baser herd,   275
Where he so lately was obeyed and feared,

239–40 'The poet's eye . . . Doth glance from heaven to earth, from earth to heaven; / And as imagination bodies forth / The forms of things unknown, the poet's pen / Turns them to shapes and gives to airy nothing / A local habitation and a name' (Shakespeare, *Midsummer Night's Dream*, V. i. 12–17). But the imagination of the mythical Faunus and Sylvanus is interrupted by a real hunt.
244–5 'On whose uplifted brows are raised their shadowing antlers'.
247–328 The hunt is much expanded from *1642* and firmer for the new possibility of identifying the King and the hunted stag: 'The mountain partridge or the chasèd roe / Might now for emblems of his fortune go' (King, *An Elegy upon King Charles*, 149–50).
248 *Gave* Give (1688).
250–2 'Impatiently he views the feeble prey . . . And rather

would the tusky boar attend, / Or see the tawny lion downward bend' (Virgil, *Aeneid*, 4:156–9, Dryden).
253–5 'Aware that his antlers have made him the object of men's deadly attentions, and yielding to his fear and his weariness, the stag has taken cover where neither men nor sun might disturb him.'
265–74 'Ere long the stag thought it better to trust the nimbleness of his feet, than to the slender fortification of his lodging: but even his feet betrayed him; for howsoever they went, they themselves uttered themselves to the scent of their enemies' (Sidney, *Arcadia*, 1.10:1).
269–73 'Looking back, he finds he has lost the hounds . . . happy till he finds that their superior sense of smell compensates for their relative slowness; then curses the feet which have treacherously colluded with them.'

His safety seeks: the herd, unkindly wise,
Or chases him from thence, or from him flies.
Like a declining statesman, left forlorn
To his friends' pity, and pursuers' scorn,   280
With shame remembers, while himself was one
Of the same herd, himself the same had done.
Thence to the coverts, and the conscious groves,
The scenes of his past triumphs, and his loves;
Sadly surveying where he ranged alone   285
Prince of the soil, and all the herd his own;
And like a bold knight-errant did proclaim
Combat to all, and bore away the dame;
And taught the woods to echo to the stream
His dreadful challenge, and his clashing beam.   290
Yet faintly now declines the fatal strife;
So much his love was dearer than his life.
Now every leaf, and every moving breath
Presents a foe, and every foe a death.
Wearied, forsaken, and pursued, at last   295
All safety in despair of safety placed,
Courage he thence resumes, resolved to bear
All their assaults, since 'tis in vain to fear.
And now too late he wishes for the fight
That strength he wasted in ignoble flight: 300
But when he sees the eager chase renewed,
Himself by dogs, the dogs by men pursued:
He straight revokes his bold resolve, and more
Repents his courage, than his fear before;
Finds that uncertain ways unsafest are,   305
And doubt a greater mischief than despair.
Then to the stream, when neither friends, nor force,
Nor speed, nor art avail, he shapes his course;
Thinks not their rage so desperate to assay
An element more merciless than they.   310
But fearless they pursue, nor can the flood
Quench their dire thirst; alas, they thirst for blood.
So towards a ship the oar-finned galleys ply,
Which wanting sea to ride, or wind to fly,
Stands but to fall revenged on those that dare   315

277–82 So the stag observed by Shakespeare's Jacques is
deserted by the unnaturally prudent herd: 'Left and aban-
doned of his velvet friends . . . thus misery doth part / The
flux of company' (*As You Like It*, II. i. 49–52). When the
mob cried out for Strafford's head 'the privy council was
called together to advise what course was to be taken . . .
Instead of considering how to rescue [the King's] honour
and his conscience from this infamous violence and con-
straint, they press the King to pass the Bill of Attainder,
saying "there was no other way to preserve himself and his
posterity . . . that he ought to be more tender of the safety of
the kingdom, than of any one person how innocent soever"'
(Clarendon, *History*, 3.197).
283 'Thence . . . to the groves that witnessed his triumphs
and loves' (Ovid has 'conscious fields', *Metamorphoses*, 7:385).
The stag shot by Ascanius returns home 'Possessed with

fear, and seeks his known abodes, / His old familiar hearth,
and household gods' (Aeneid, 7:500–1, Dryden). King Charles
was executed outside the Banqueting Hall in Whitehall.
289 Virgil's Tityrus teaches the woods to echo to Amaryl-
lis's name (*Eclogues*, 1:5).
290 *beam* the trunk of the antlers.
295–8 'But the stag was in the end so hotly pursued, that
(leaving his flight) he was driven to make courage of despair;
and so turning his head, made the hounds (with change of
speech) to testify that he was at a bay' (Sidney, *Arcadia*,
1.10.1).
313–14 'Whoever saw a well-manned galley fight with a
tall ship, might make unto himself some kind of comparison
of the difference of these two knights' (Sidney, *Arcadia*,
3.18.9): a contest between strength and nimbleness.

Tempt the last fury of extreme despair.
So fares the stag among the enragèd hounds,
Repels their force, and wounds returns for wounds.
And as a hero, whom his baser foes
In troops surround, now these assails, now those,   320
Though prodigal of life, disdains to die
By common hands; but if he can descry
Some nobler foe approach, to him he calls,
And begs his fate, and then contented falls.
So when the King a mortal shaft lets fly   325
From his unerring hand, then glad to die,
Proud of the wounds, to it resigns his blood,
And stains the crystal with a purple flood.
This a more innocent, and happy chase,
Than when of old, but in the selfsame place,   330
Fair Liberty pursued, and meant a prey
To lawless power, here turned, and stood at bay.
When in that remedy all hope was placed
Which was, or should have been at least, the last.
Here was that charter sealed, wherein the crown   335
All marks of arbitrary power lays down:
Tyrant and slave, those names of hate and fear,
The happier style of king and subject bear:
Happy, when both to the same centre move,
When kings give liberty, and subjects love.   340
Therefore not long in force this charter stood;
Wanting that seal, it must be sealed in blood.
The subjects armed, the more their princes gave,
The advantage only took the more to crave:
Till kings by giving, give themselves away,   345
And even that power, that should deny, betray.
"Who gives constrained, but his own fear reviles,
Not thanked, but scorned; nor are they gifts, but spoils."
Thus kings, by grasping more than they could hold,
First made their subjects by oppression bold: 350
And popular sway, by forcing kings to give
More than was fit for subjects to receive,

319–24 As Turnus seeks out Aeneas: 'Death is my choice; but suffer me to try / My force, and vent my rage before I die' (*Aeneid*, 12.676–80, Dryden); Denham inverts Virgil's simile for Turnus: 'Thus, when a fearful stag is closed around / With crimson toils, or in a river found, / High on the bank the deep-mouthed hound appears . . . The persecuted creature, to and fro, / Turns here and there . . . and, if he gains the land, / The purple death is pitched along the strand' (Aeneid, 12:749–55).

321–4 'Kalendar . . . was amongst the first that came in to the besieged deer; whom when some of the younger sort would have killed with their swords, he would not suffer, but with a cross-bow sent a death to the poor beast' (Sidney, *Arcadia*, 1.10.1).

329–54 The place of the hunt is Runnymede, where King John was obliged in 1215 to agree to a statement of his subjects' legal liberties. The 'Liberty' that stood at bay was represented by the Barons. Sir Edward Coke's *Second Insti-*

tute (1642) contains a commentary on Magna Carta biased so as to advance the claims of 'liberty' against 'prerogative'.

339 'Happy when both move from the extremes they otherwise occupy'.

342 'Since it was not confirmed by the movement of king and people to a common centre, the charter's principles had to be imposed by war.'

347–8 The couplet is marked as a 'sentence': 'His own fear cheapens the man who gives under pressure, he is owed not gratitude but contempt: what he gives are not gifts but booty.' Proverbially, 'A gift expected is paid, not given.'

351–4 King contrives a more specific point, that Parliament's insistence liberated anarchy and the army: 'Still you pressed on, till you too late descried, / 'Twas now less safe to stay than be denied. / For like a flood broke loose the armèd rout, / Then shut him closer up, and shut you out' (*Elegy on King Charles*, 427–30).

Ran to the same extremes; and one excess
Made both, by striving to be greater, less.
When a calm river raised with sudden rains,   355
Or snows dissolved, o'erflows the adjoining plains,
The husbandmen with high-raised banks secure
Their greedy hopes, and this he can endure.
But if with bays and dams they strive to force
His channel to a new, or narrow course;   360
No longer then within his banks he dwells,
First to a torrent, then a deluge swells:
Stronger, and fiercer by restraint he roars,
And knows no bound, but makes his power his shores.

355–64   The distinction between 'high-raised banks' (357), 'bays and dams' (359) and 'shores' (364) is suitably hazy. The flood comes from Virgil's description of the year of Caesar's assassination: 'Then, rising in his might, the king of floods [the Po] / Rushed through the forests, tore the lofty woods, / And, rolling onward, with a sweepy sway, / Bore houses, herds, and labouring hinds away' (Virgil, *Georgics*, 1: 479–80).

Richard Lovelace (1618–1658)

'Our times are much degenerate from those / Which your sweet Muse, which your fair Fortune chose' (Marvell, *To his Noble Friend Mr Richard Lovelace*). Marvell is not the only voice in 1649 to suggest that history has overtaken the idyll that Lovelace is supposed to represent. The selection here suggests a poet who lives with the war. An heir to estates in Kent, he was educated first at Charterhouse and then at Oxford, 'the most amiable and beautiful person that ever eye beheld, a person also of innate modesty, virtue, and courtly deportment, which made him then, but especially after when he retired to the great city, much admired and adored by the female sex' (Anthony à Wood). The idyll, such as it was, was brief. For two years he lived an adored and glamorous courtier in the 'great city'. In 1639 he served, like Suckling, in the Bishops' Wars. On his return he retired to his Kentish estates; but in 1642, delegated to present a Royalist manifesto to Parliament, he was imprisoned briefly in the Gatehouse. On his release he followed General Goring to the Low Countries and to France. On his return to England in 1647, he was again imprisoned, now for his supposed involvement with Royalist disturbances in Kent, and while in prison, he prepared the poems of *Lucasta* for publication (more carefully than his merely 'cavalier' reputation might suggest). His reputation as a lyrist too easily overwhelms his subtler and more serious talent. In his last years he was 'very melancholy (which brought him at length to a consumption) became very poor in body and person, was the object of charity, went in ragged clothes (whereas when he was in his glory he wore cloth of gold and silver) and mostly lodged in obscure and dirty places, more befitting the worst of beggars and poorest of servants' (Anthony à Wood). According to Aubrey he died in a cellar in Long Acre. The charity came from Sir John Mennes and from Charles Cotton, who contributed the first of the *Elegies Sacred to the Memory of the Author* attached to *Lucasta. Postume Poems* (1659–60). *Lucasta: Epodes, Odes, Sonnets, Songs* (1649) is the authority for half the poems; the enlarged *Lucasta: Posthume Poems* (1659), prepared by his brother Dudley, is the authority for the remainder. *The Poems*, ed. C. H. Wilkinson, revised edition (Oxford: Clarendon Press, 1953) is the standard edition. There is a facsimile of *1649* (Menston: Scolar Press, 1972). Criticism is described by David Judkins, *English Literary Renaissance*, 7 (1977), 248–52.

Song. Set by Mr Henry Lawes. To Lucasta, Going Beyond the Seas

1649. A valediction, insisting on the indifference of separation or even death. The vocabulary of sighs and winds (though it seems borrowed from Donne's *Valediction of Weeping*) serves no argument beyond Horace's comfort in thinking about the beloved: 'In th' dull fields set me . . . That ne'er from clouds, and mists is free, / But still doth angry tempests bear . . . I Lalage will love the whiles' (*Odes*, 1.22:16–23, Ashmore); the Platonic conclusion is a surprise. The setting by Lawes survives; the stanza (a simple rhyme scheme complicated by shifts in line-lengths) varies that of *To Lucasta* ('I laugh and sing').

1

If to be absent were to be
    Away from thee;
    Or that when I am gone,
    You or I were alone;
Then my Lucasta might I crave   5
Pity from blustering wind, or swallowing wave.

2

But I'll not sigh one blast or gale
    To swell my sail,

5–6 'Then I should be reduced to begging not to die at sea'.

Or pay a tear to 'suage
The foaming blue-god's rage;   10
For whether he will let me pass
Or no, I'm still as happy as I was.

3

Though seas and land betwixt us both,
Our faith and troth,
Like separated souls,   15
All time and space controls:
Above the highest sphere we meet
Unseen, unknown, and greet as angels greet.

4

So then we do anticipate
Our after-fate,   20
And are alive in th' skies,
If thus our lips and eyes
Can speak like spirits unconfined
In Heaven, their earthy bodies left behind.

10 *blue-god* 'sea'; Neptune is represented with blue hair or flesh.
15 'Like souls released from their bodies, overmaster space and time'.
17 'We meet above the limits of the universe (in heaven) and converse as angels, so that the rest of the world neither sees nor knows what we do.'

19–24 The souls of men 'are deprived of contemplation, borrowing science from sense . . . Their only means of release from this bondage is the amatory life; which by sensible beauties, exciting in the soul a remembrance of the intellectual, raiseth her from this terrene life to the eternal; by the flame of love refined into an angel' (Pico, *Platonic Discourse*, 1.12, Stanley).

Song. Set by Mr John Lanier. To Lucasta, Going to the Wars

1649. The setting by Lanier does not survive. The poem hinges on the surprising admission of the identity of love's interests and war's (as against Tibullus 1.10:65–6: 'Let the man with slaughter in his hands carry shield and sword, and keep far from gentle Venus'. Sidney's Argalus fails to reassure Parthenia in a like situation; 'but he discoursing unto her, how much it imported his honour (which since it was dear to him, he knew it would be dear unto her) her reason overclouded with sorrow, suffered her not presently to reply, but left the charge thereof to tears, and sighs' (*Arcadia*, 3.12.5).

1

Tell me not (sweet) I am unkind,
That from the nunnery
Of thy chaste breast, and quiet mind,
To war and arms I flee.

2

True; a new mistress now I chase,   5
The first foe in the field;
And with a stronger faith embrace
A sword, a horse, a shield.

2 Roses are happy 'In the chaste nunnery' of Castara's breasts (Habington, *To Roses in the Bosom of Castara*, 1–2); but a rose's life or a nun's is not for a gentleman.

5–8 The new mistress is 'honour'.

3

Yet this inconstancy is such,
As you too shall adore;
I could not love thee (dear) so much,
Loved I not honour more.

10

---

10 *you* the shift from 'thou' is for the sake of euphony.
11–12 In Sedley's *The Mulberry Garden* (1688) Eugenio

(based on Lovelace) says: 'Though love possess, honour must
rule my heart.'

The Grasshopper. To My Noble Friend, Mr Charles Cotton. Ode

1649. The addressee, celebrated also by Clarendon and Herrick, is the father of the poet (who contributed an elegy to *1659*). It is partly an invitation poem (like Campion's *Now winter nights enlarge*), partly an account of happiness such as men can sustain and the Anacreontic grasshopper (as in Cowley's *Grasshop-* *per*) cannot. But the sense is strong (as in Jonson's *Inviting a Friend to Supper*) of happiness under threat; and the poem's gravity comes from its response to the collapse of the long Caroline summer. Its spoken and unlyric character admits metrical irregularities.

1

O thou that swing'st upon the waving hair
Of some well-fillèd oaten beard,
Drunk every night with a delicious tear
Dropped thee from Heaven, where now thou art reared.

2

The joys of earth and air are thine entire,
That with thy feet and wings dost hop and fly;
And when thy poppy works thou dost retire
To thy carved acorn-bed to lie.

5

3

Up with the day, the sun thou welcom'st then,
Sport'st in the gilt-plaits of his beams,
And all these merry days mak'st merry men,
Thyself, and melancholy streams.

10

4

But ah the sickle! Golden ears are cropped;
Ceres and Bacchus bid good-night;
Sharp frosty fingers all your flowers have topped,
And what scythes spared, winds shave off quite.

15

---

3 'Noisy grasshopper, drunk with dew drops, singing your country song, filling the wilderness with your voice' (Meleager, *Greek Anthology*, 7.196); grasshoppers are supposed to suck dew from the grass (Pliny, *Natural History*, 1.3.25).
9–10 'And Phoebus fresh as bridegroom to his mate, / Came dancing forth, shaking his dewy hair' (Spenser, *Faerie Queene*, 1.5.2).

11–12 'And all that happy time gladden us mortals and yourself and the riversides that sadness haunts' ('tumbling streames, / (Places which sad Fancy loves)', (Fanshawe, *My quenched and discontinued Muse*, 6–7); Lucasta herself weeps 'sad streams' (*Lucasta Weeping*, 8).
14 *Ceres and Bacchus* 'corn and grapes', 'bread and wine'.

5

Poor verdant fool! and now green ice, thy joys
    Large and as lasting, as thy perch of grass,
Bid us lay in 'gainst winter, rain, and poise
    Their floods, with an o'erflowing glass.   20

6

Thou best of men and friends! we will create
    A genuine summer in each other's breast;
And spite of this cold time and frozen fate
    Thaw us a warm seat to our rest.

7

Our sacred hearths shall burn eternally   25
    As vestal Flames, the North-wind, he
Shall strike his frost-stretched wings, dissolve and fly
    This Etna in epitome.

8

Dropping December shall come weeping in,
    Bewail the usurping of his reign;   30
But when in showers of old Greek we begin,
    Shall cry, he hath his crown again!

9

Night as clear Hesper shall our tapers whip
    From the light casements where we play,
And the dark hag from her black mantle strip,   35
    And stick there everlasting day.

10

Thus richer then untempted kings are we,
    That asking nothing, nothing need:
Though lord of all what seas embrace; yet he
    That wants himself, is poor indeed.   40

17 'You were a foolish green thing, and are now a frozen green thing'; the elliptical 'green ice' is a perverse rendering of Virgil's north and south poles set in *caerulea glacie* (*Georgics*, 1:236).

21 'The sun is gone. But yet Castara stays, / And will add stature to [winter's] pigmy days' (Habington, *To the Winter*, 5–6).

26 'All fires are vestal now, and we as they, / Do in our chimneys keep a lasting day; / Boasting within doors this domestic sun' (Cartwright, *On the Great Frost. 1634*, 47–9); but in keeping the hearth aflame, they keep the King alive: Ovid's Vesta protests against the assassination of Caesar: 'he was my priest, it was at me those sacrilegious hands struck with the steel' (*Fasti*, 3:699–700).

28 'So contraries on Etna's top conspire, / Here hoary frosts, and by them breaks out fire' (Cowley, *To Mr Hobbes*, 86–7); but here the fire wins.

30 'Rainy December shall enter weeping to complain his reign (or rain) is superseded; but our showers of Greek will restore him'; like Crashaw's 'Sidneian showers / Of sweet discourse, whose powers / Can crown old winter's head with flowers' (*Wishes to his (supposed) Mistress*, 88–90), or the 'shower of Heliconian melody' the Greek poet asks to refresh him (*Greek Anthology*, 9.364).

33–6 'As the bright evening star shines out, our lamps shall chase night from the lit windows where we talk'; Phosphor or Lucifer (the morning star, but likewise Venus) may be intended: 'Night chased away / Lucifer, herald of the day' (Seneca, *Hippolytus*, 751–2, Sherburne). Night is less a goddess than a witch: 'dark hag' plays with 'night-hag'.

37–8 Like Virgil's farmer: 'late returning home, he supped at ease, / And wisely deemed the wealth of monarchs less' (Virgil, *Georgics*, 4.132, Dryden); 'untempted', as kings are not.

39–40 'The great dominion is self-dominion' (Seneca, *Epistulae*, 113.30).

Lucasta Weeping. Song. Set by Mr John Lanier

The meteorological cycle of evaporation and precipitation is used for frivolous compliment: there is no coherence to the conceit.

1

Lucasta wept, and still the bright
  Enamoured god of day,
With his soft handkerchief of light,
  Kissed the wet pearls away.

2

But when her tears his heat o'ercame,   5
  In clouds he quenched his beams,
And grieved, wept out his eye of flame
  So drownèd her sad streams.

3

At this she smiled, when straight the sun
  Cleared, with her kind desires;   10
And by her eyes' reflection,
  Kindled again his fires.

To Althea, From Prison. Song. Set by Dr John Wilson

1649. John Wilson's setting is first printed in Playford's *Select Airs* (1659 edition); it was also set by Lawes. Wilkinson prints four MS versions in full and gives details of two others; it is printed as a broadside and much imitated. Sometimes associated with Lovelace's confinement in the Gatehouse in 1642, it lacks any particularity beyond its Royalist sentiments. Its play with senses of 'liberty' (from wantoning and tippling through the winds' enlargement to transcendent love) is distinctive.

1

When Love with unconfinèd wings
  Hovers within my gates;
And my divine Althea brings
  To whisper at the grates:
When I lie tangled in her hair,   5
  And fettered to her eye;
The gods that wanton in the air,
  Know no such liberty.

2

When flowing cups run swiftly round
  With no allaying Thames,   10

1–4 *unconfined* 'unimprisoned'; 'unconstrained' like the spirits in *To Lucasta, Going Beyond the Seas*, 23, but only because the visit is imagined. 'Nor canst thou in thy prison be / Without some loving signs from me: / When thou dost spy / A sunbeam peep into thy room, 'tis I' (Shirley, *To his Mistress Confined*, 9–12).

5–6 Real imprisonment is re-imagined as a metaphorical one.
7–8 Most MSS read 'birds' for 'gods'; birds' freedom is proverbial; the wantoning gods must be Cupids.
10 *allaying Thames* 'diluting water', like Shakespeare's 'allaying Tiber' (*Coriolanus*, I. ii. 47–8).

Our careless heads with roses bound,
  Our hearts with loyal flames;
When thirsty grief in wine we steep,
  When healths and draughts go free,
Fishes that tipple in the deep,   15
  Know no such liberty.

3
When (like committed linnets) I
  With shriller throat shall sing
The sweetness, mercy, majesty,
  And glories of my King;   20
When I shall voice aloud, how good
  He is, how great should be;
Enlargèd winds that curl the flood,
  Know no such liberty.
4
Stone walls do not a prison make,   25
  Nor iron bars a cage;
Minds innocent and quiet take
  That for an hermitage;
If I have freedom in my love,
  And in my soul am free;   30
Angels alone that soar above,
  Enjoy such liberty.

11–12 'But if that golden age would come again, / And Charles here rule, as he before did reign . . . I should delight to have my curls half drowned / In Tyrian dews, and head with roses crowned' (Herrick, *The Bad Season makes the Poet Sad*, 6–12).
31–2 *To Lucasta, Going Beyond the Seas*, 23–4.

The Snail

1659. One of two poems on the snail (the other is 'The centaur, siren, I forgo'), both focused on the paradoxes inherent in its description. Its tone may be owed to French Anacreontic models, but its manner is owed to the riddle, beginning with Symphosius's *Aenigmata* (No. 28 is on a snail) through to Nicolas Reusner's collected *Aenigmatographia*); and to the emblem, particularly Camerarius's *Symbolorum et Emblamatum Centuriae* (especially 4.97–100 on snails). Wither's 'When thou a dangerous way doest go, / Walk surely, though thy pace be slow' (*Emblems*, 1.19: *Lente sed attente*) presents only an unflamboyant recommendation of perseverance and caution. Lovelace's 'emblem' is remarkable for the variety and concentration of its allegories. The poem is an 'analysis' (37) of paradoxical possibilities: mathematical (5–12), temporal (13–20), biological (21–36), economical (37–50) and spiritual (51–66).

Wise emblem of our politic world,
Sage snail, within thine own self curled;
Instruct me softly to make haste,
Whilst these my feet go slowly fast.
  Compendious snail! thou seem'st to me,   5
Large Euclid's strict epitome;

1–4 'It is the exemplary wisdom of the snail to isolate itself from a scheming world'; the snail's self-containedness is Camerarius's point (in 4.100).
3–4 'The verses ('feet') are to mimic the snail's cautious speed.'

5–12 The snail briefly and profitably summarizes the whole of geometry, illustrating all the figures from the centre to the circumference (completely). And so it epitomizes all creation: just as molten lead 'In many fashions mazeth to and fro; / Runs here direct, there crookedly doth go . . . Almost

And in each diagram, dost fling
Thee from the point unto the ring.
A figure now triangular,
An oval now, and now a square;   10
And then a serpentine dost crawl
Now a straight line, now crook'd, now all.
 Preventing rival of the day,
Thou art up and openest thy ray,
And ere the morn cradles the moon,   15
Thou art broke into a beauteous noon.
Then when the sun sups in the deep,
Thy silver horns ere Cynthia's peep;
And thou from thine own liquid bed
New Phoebus heav'st thy pleasant head.   20
 Who shall a name for thee create,
Deep riddle of mysterious state?
Bold Nature that gives common birth
To all prodúcts of seas and earth,
Of thee, as earthquakes, is afraid,   25
Nor will thy dire deliv'ry aid.
 Thou thine own daughter then, and sire,
That son and mother art entire,
That big still with thyself dost go,
And liv'st an aged embryo;   30
That like the cubs of India,
Thou from thyself a while dost play:
But frighted with a dog or gun,
In thine own belly thou dost run,
And as thy house was thine own womb,   35
So thine own womb, concludes thy tomb.
 But now I must (analysed King)
Thy economic virtues sing;
Thou great staid husband still within,
Thou, thee, that's thine dost discipline;   40
And when thou art to progress bent,
Thou mov'st thy self and tenement,
As warlike Scythians travelled, you
Remove your men and city too;
Then after a sad dearth and rain,   45
Thou scatt'rest thy silver train;
And when the trees grow nak'd and old,

(in the instant) every form doth form', so the waters God pours onto the newly created earth fall 'In sundry figures; some in fashion round, / Some square, some crosse, some long, some lozenge-wise, / Some triangles, some large, some lesser size' (Sylvester, *Divine Weeks*, 1.3:85–95).

13–20 'You are up before the sun and outdo him: at your noon before the morning puts the moon to bed; as the sun sets in the sea, your silver horns are out before the moon's; from your bed of mucus you supply the sun's place.'

21–36 The snail's namelessness is tied to its horrific and unnatural mode of generation. Being hermaphroditic, it plays all family roles at once, confusing the order of generations and even the sites of birth and death.

31–4 'Most admirable is that foreign [Patagonian] creature called by the name of *sue* .. which ... shuts up her cubs in a depending scrip [the pseudo-womb made by her tail], and so protects them from the huntsman' (John Stephens, *Satirical Essays*, 90).

37–8 'Now I must continue my breakdown of your marvellous powers by celebrating your talents as a household manager.'

39 *staid* 'constant'.

43 The Scythians were the type of nomadism: 'No house, no home, no mansion good or bad, / But ever (as the Scythian hordas stray) / From place to place their wandering cities gad' (*Jerusalem Delivered*, 17.21, Fairfax).

Thou cloathest them with cloth of gold,
Which from thy bowels thou dost spin,
And draw from the rich mines within.   50
     Now hast thou changed thee saint; and made
Thyself a fane that's cupolaed;
And in thy wreathèd cloister thou
Walkest thine own Grey-Friar too;
Strict, and locked up, thou art hood all o'er   55
And ne'er eliminat'st thy door.
On salads thou dost feed severe,
And 'stead of beads thou drop'st a tear,
And when to rest, each calls the bell,
Thou sleep'st within thy marble cell;   60
Where in dark contemplation placed;
The sweets of Nature thou dost taste;
Who now with time thy days resolve,
And in a jelly thee dissolve.
Like a shot star, which doth repair   65
Upward, and rarefy the air.

51–2 'Now you have made yourself holy, and built a domed chapel for yourself.'

55–6 'Like a monk in a closed order you wear your cowl low and never cross the threshold, you feed austerely on herbs and by way of counting your rosary you weep.'

63–6 The jelly-like algae appearing after rain were supposed the remains of fallen stars: 'As he whose quicker eye doth trace / A false star shot to a marked place, / Does run apace, / And thinking it to catch, / A jelly up does snatch' (Suckling, *Farewell to Love*, 11–15); here the star's (or the snail's) fiery soul is dispersed in the thicker air.

Abraham Cowley (1618–1667)

'Of his works that are published it is hard to give one general character, because of the difference of their subjects and the various forms and distant times of their writing. Yet this is true of them all, that in all the several shapes of his style there is still very much of the likeness and impression of the same mind; the same unaffected modesty, and natural freedom, and easy vigour, and cheerful passions, and innocent mirth' (Sprat, *Account of the Life and Writings*). Though he was less than 50 when he died, the length of his poetic career, its variety (lyrics, odes, epics, comedies, essays), the consistency of the applause for his achievement and the definitive character of his influence combine to create the sense of the grand old man: when he left London Katherine Philips announced that 'the man whom all mankind admired, / (By every grace adorned, and every Muse inspired) / Is now triumphantly retired' (*Upon Mr. Abraham Cowley's Retirement*, 73–5). It was in the end a fragile reputation. Already by Johnson's time Cowley's life and work were the occasion for a digression on poetry which lies the wrong side of good sense. He was still at Westminster School when *Poetical Blossoms* appeared in 1633. He proceeded to Trinity College, Cambridge, from where he graduated BA in 1639 and where the following year he obtained a fellowship. In 1643, anticipating ejection, he gave up the fellowship and joined the King at Oxford. After the Royalist defeat at Marston Moor in 1644 he worked for Henrietta Maria's court in exile at Paris. When he returned to England in the mid-1650s, he organized the publication of his poems and in 1657, made an MD of Oxford, was restored to his Cambridge fellowship. His ambitious Latin poem, the *Plantarum Libri*, follows from his medical interests; though never a Fellow of the Royal Society, he was active in founding and promoting it. In 1663 he abandoned both Cambridge and London for his 'triumphant' retirement in Barn Elms: 'I never had any other desire so strong . . . as . . . that I might be master at last of a small house and a large garden . . . and there dedicate the remainder of my life only to the culture of them and study of Nature' (*The Garden*). His death was widely mourned and his funeral unprecedentedly splendid for a poet's.

Johnson's *Life* has promoted a view of him as somehow of the School of Donne. It was rather Spenser, on Sprat's account, who inspired his earliest efforts in poetry; and his later efforts (besides creating an unhappy fashion for Pindarics) made possible a poetry that could argue naturally, that never abandoned 'the language of the city and court', and that by deforming traditional metres brought verse closer to prose and made it 'fit for all manner of subjects'. Jean Loiseau, *Abraham Cowley: sa vie, son oeuvre* (Paris: Didier, 1931) is the standard biography. Most of Cowley's mature English verse is collected in *Poems* (1656), divided into sections with separate title-pages: *Miscellanies*, *The Mistress* (published without permission in 1647), *Pindaric Odes*, and *Davideis*; there is a facsimile edition (Menston: Scolar Press, 1971). Additional *Verses lately written upon Several Occasions* were published in 1663. Thomas Sprat's edition of the *Works* (1668), reprinted eleven times by the end of the century, includes those two volumes (with some additional poems), miscellaneous prose works including *A Proposition for the Advancement of Experimental Philosophy*, and *A Vision, concerning . . . Cromwell the Wicked*, and from MS the mixed verse and prose *Essays*. It also includes *An Account of the Life and Writings of Abraham Cowley*. Succeeding editions add some juvenilia, plays previously published in English and Latin and English versions (by Aphra Behn among others) of the Latin *Plantarum Libri*. The *Poemata Latina* were published separately in 1668. A. B. Grosart's *The Complete Works in Verse and Prose* (Edinburgh: Chertsey Worthies' Library, 1881) is nearest to a complete edition; of *The Collected Works of Abraham Cowley*, edited by Thomas O. Calhoun, Laurence Heyworth and Allan Pritchard, only the first volume has appeared (Newark: University of Delaware Press, 1989). The standard edition of the *English Writings* is A. R. Waller's, 2 vols (Cambridge, 1905–6). Allan Pritchard has edited *The Civil War* (Toronto: University of Toronto Press, 1973, published as a fragment in 1679); there is *A Critical Edition of Abraham Cowley's Davideis*, ed. Gayle Shadduck (New York: Garland, 1987). There are accounts of early criticism in Jean Loiseau, *Abraham Cowley's Reputation in England* (Paris: Didier, 1931) and A. H. Nethercot, *The Reputation of Abraham Cowley 1660–1800* (New York: Haskell House, 1960, reprinted from 1923). M. R. Perkin has prepared *Abraham Cowley: A Bibliography* (Folkestone: Dawson, 1977); there is a survey by Dennis G. Donovan, *English Literary Renaissance*, 6 (1976), 466–75.

Ode. Of Wit

1656 (*Miscellanies*). Longinus's influence is evident: a Greek-Latin version of Longinus was published at Oxford in 1636 with notes by Gerard Langbaine, and John Hall's English version appeared in 1652. The poem's addressee (sometimes identified with William Hervey) is unknown; but the opening turn to this master of 'wit'and the climax in personal compliment establishes the poem's proper tone, and the impossibility of its subject. 'Sublimity is the echo of a noble mind,' says Longinus (9.2), but its description proceeds mainly negatively, by enumerating the faults of the failed sublime; so with 'wit' here.

1

Tell me, O tell, what kind of thing is wit,
    Thou who master art of it.
For the first matter loves variety less;
Less women love 't, either in love or dress.
    A thousand different shapes it bears,   5
    Comely in thousand shapes appears.
Yonder we saw it plain; and here 'tis now,
Like spirits in a place, we know not how.

2

London that vents of false ware so much store,
    In no ware deceives us more.   10
For men led by the colour, and the shape,
Like Zeuxis' birds fly to the painted grape;
      Some things do through our judgement pass
      As through a multiplying glass.
And sometimes, if the object be too far,   15
We take a falling meteor for a star.

3

Hence 'tis a "wit" that greatest word of fame
    Grows such a common name.
And wits by our creation they become,
Just so, as tit'lar Bishops made at Rome.   20
    'Tis not a tale, 'tis not a jest
    Admired with laughter at a feast,
Nor florid talk which can that title gain;
The proofs of wit forever must remain.

4

'Tis not to force some lifeless verses meet   25
    With their five gouty feet.

3   'The substance or matter that hath neither form nor any colour, which they call Materia prima, is a subject capable of all forms' (Plutarch, *Moralia*, 16.290, Holland); matter before differentiation is in love with variety.

8   'Like ghosts and other fabrications of the fancy, whose appearance is inexplicable'.

9   'London that sells ('vents') such abundance of faked goods'.

9–20   Longinus, *On the Sublime* (7.1), contrasts true sublimity with the mere show of it which when looked into proves vain and hollow; the itch for novelty is responsible (5.1).

12   Zeuxis painted grapes so convincingly that birds flew to them (Pliny, *Natural History*, 35.365).

13–16   We are given to overrate things: we see them through a magnifying ('multiplying') glass, or mistake a transitory bright exhalation (as meteors were taken to be) for a steady star: Longinus says of Callisthenes that he is 'not so much risen to the heights as carried from the ground' (3.2).

17   'Author' and 'wit' are becoming interchangeable, and (in view of 21–3) with those skilled in 'raillery'.

20   'Like bishops attached to merely nominal sees'.

26   'With their lame pentameters'.

All everywhere, like man's, must be the soul,
And reason the inferior powers control.
      Such were the numbers which could call
      The stones into the Theban wall.   30
Such miracles are ceased; and now we see
No towns or houses raised by poetry.

5

Yet 'tis not to adorn, and gild each part;
      That shows more cost, than art.
Jewels at nose and lips but ill appear;   35
Rather than all things wit, let none be there.
      Several lights will not be seen,
      If there be nothing else between.
Men doubt, because they stand so thick in th' sky,
If those be stars which paint the galaxy.   40

6

'Tis not when two like words make up one noise;
      Jests for Dutch men, and English boys.
In which who finds out wit, the same may see
In an'grams and acrostics poetry.
      Much less can that have any place   45
      At which a virgin hides her face,
Such dross the fire must purge away; 'tis just
The author blush, there where the reader must.

7

'Tis not such lines as almost crack the stage
      When Bajazet begins to rage.   50
Nor a tall metaphor in the Oxford way,
Nor the dry chips of short-lunged Seneca.
      Nor upon all things to obtrude,
      And force some odd similitude.
What is it then, which like the Power Divine   55
We only can by negatives define?

---

27 The soul is the essential 'whatness' of a body (Aristotle, *De Anima*, 412b), what gives a thing its character.
29–30 When Horace (*Odes*, 3.11) prays to Mercury for eloquence he invokes Amphion ('taught by you / Deaf stones by the ears Amphion drew'), who charmed stones into building Thebes.
33–40 'Only a sophist has bells on his harness wherever he goes' (Longinus, 23.4).
36 *several* 'distinct'.
39–40 'This question seems on the point of being settled, if we believe the report of Galileo [in *Sidereus Nuntius*, 1610], who has resolved this confused appearance of light into stars numbered and placed' (Bacon, *Descriptio Globi Intellectualis*, 1653, but written in 1612); Cowley always holds to the modern view.
41–8 Longinus defines puerility as 'a pedantic thought, so overworked that it ends in frigidity' (3.4): punning is in this category, affected by schoolboys and the Dutch (the poet Huyghens was addicted to wordplay). Jonson complains of the 'insolent, and obscene speeches' in Aristophanes and Plautus: 'scurrility came forth in the place of wit' (*Timber*); but the fire of inspired true wit cleanses such impurities.
49–50 Longinus complains of turgid parody of the tragic manner in Aeschylus (3.1); Cowley refers to Marlowe (in whose *Tamburlaine* Bajazeth figures), and the breathless and choppy style of Seneca.
51 Nor a tall met'phor in the bombast way (*1668*); *1656*'s 'Oxford way' may be a swipe at William Cartwright 'in whom hallowed fancies and reason grew visions' (David Lloyd, *Memoirs*).
55–6 Aquinas introduces his account of God's simplicity with 'because we cannot know what God is, but rather what He is not, we have no means for considering how God is, but rather how He is not' (*Summa Theologica*, 1.3).

8
In a true piece of wit all things must be,
  Yet all things there agree.
As in the ark, joined without force or strife,
All creatures dwelt; all creatures that had life.   60
  Or as the primitive forms of all
  (If we compare great things with small)
Which without discord or confusion lie,
In that strange mirror of the Deity.

9
But Love that moulds one man up out of two, 65
  Makes me forget and injure you.
I took you for myself sure when I thought
That you in anything were to be taught.
  Correct my error with thy pen;
  And if any ask me then,   70
What thing right wit, and height of genius is,
I'll only show your lines, and say, " 'Tis This."

59 'Man is a lump, where all beasts kneaded be, / Wisdom makes him an ark where all agree' (Donne, *To Sir Edward Herbert at Julyers*, 1–2).
61–4 'The deity, intending to make this world like the fairest and most perfect of intelligible beings, framed one visible animal comprehending within itself all other animals of a kindred nature' (Plato, *Timaeus*, 30d); it is a mirror because 'he desired that all things should be as like himself as they could be' (30a).

65–8 'How would you like to be rolled into one, so that you could always be together . . . and never parted? . . . No lover on earth would dream of refusing such an offer' (Plato, *Symposium*, 192e). Love in this account is a longing of partial creatures for an original wholeness; the friend is proverbially the *alter ego*.

On the Death of Mr William Hervey

1656 (*Miscellanies*). William Hervey (1619–42) was contemporary with Cowley at Cambridge. Johnson, while holding that the poem contains 'much praise but little passion', notoriously contrasts its naturalness with the frigidities of Milton's *Lycidas*; and the prominence of the catalogue praises may render the loss of their object more poignant. Its simple overall movement (from images of dark to images of light) leaves its concern with the dead Hervey uninterfered with. The epigraph (from Martial, 6.29.7) means: 'To those of rare worth life is short and old age rare.'

Immodicis brevis est aetas, et rara senectus. Martial

1
It was a dismal, and a fearful night,
Scarce could the morn drive on the unwilling light,
When Sleep, Death's image, left my troubled breast,
  By something liker Death possessed.
My eyes with tears did uncommanded flow, 5
  And on my soul hung the dull weight
  Of some intolerable fate.
What bell was that? Ah me! Too much I know.

2 Morning is a herdsman: 'Come, Lucifer [the Morning Star], drive on the lagging day' (Virgil, *Eclogues*, 8:17, Dryden).

3 Sleep is proverbially death's image, or ape or brother.
8 A clock bell is taken for the passing bell, announcing a death.

2

My sweet companion, and my gentle peer,
Why hast thou left me thus unkindly here,   10
Thy end forever, and my life to moan;
    O thou hast left me all alone!
Thy soul and body when death's agony
    Besieged around thy noble heart,
    Did not with more reluctance part   15
Than I, my dearest friend, do part from thee.

3

My dearest friend, would I had died for thee!
Life and this world henceforth will tedious bee.
Nor shall I know hereafter what to do
    If once my griefs prove tedious too.   20
Silent and sad I walk about all day,
    As sullen ghosts stalk speechless by
    Where their hid treasures lie;
Alas, my treasure's gone, why do I stay?

4

He was my friend, the truest friend on earth;   25
A strong and mighty influence joined our birth.
Nor did we envy the most sounding name
    By friendship given of old to Fame.
None but his brethren he, and sisters knew,
    Whom the kind youth preferred to me;   30
    And even in that we did agree,
For much above myself I loved them too.

5

Say, for you saw us, ye immortal lights,
How oft unwearied have we spent the nights?
Till the Ledacan Stars so famed for love,   35
    Wondered at us from above.
We spent them not in toys, in lusts, or wine;
    But search of deep philosophy,
    Wit, eloquence, and poetry,
Arts which I loved, for they, my friend, were thine.   40

6

Ye fields of Cambridge, our dear Cambridge, say,
Have ye not seen us walking every day?
Was there a tree about which did not know

---

17 'And the king was much moved . . . and wept, and as he went, thus he said, O my son Absalom . . . would I had died for thee' (2 Samuel 18: 33).
22–3 Cowley combines two motives of burial to suggest that ghosts guard their treasure: 'Sad troubled ghosts about their graves do stray' (*The Separation*, 12); 'As some from men their buried gold commit / To ghosts that have no use of it!' (*Bathing in the River*, 10–11).
25–8 'Sure on our birth some friendly planet shone; / And,

as our souls, our horoscope was one' (Persius, 5:45–6, Dryden); 'But where shall I in all antiquity / So fair a pattern find . . . As in yourself' (Spenser, *Faerie Queene*, 6, Proem 6).
35 So Jonson makes it 'friendships schism . . . To separate these twi- / Lights, the Dioscuri' (*Ode to the Immortal Memory of Cary and Morison*, 90–3). Castor and Pollux (Leda's sons) are the loving twins of the constellation Gemini.
43–4 Because like Socrates and Phaedrus they might have sat in the shade of 'a tall plane tree' (*Phaedrus*, 229b).

The love betwixt us two?
Henceforth, ye gentle trees, for ever fade;   45
        Or your sad branches thicker join,
        And into darksome shades combine,
Dark as the grave wherein my friend is laid.

7

Henceforth no learnèd youths beneath you sing,
Till all the tuneful birds to' your boughs they bring;   50
No tuneful birds play with their wonted cheer,
        And call the learnèd youths to hear,
No whistling winds through the glad branches fly,
        But all with sad solemnity,
        Mute and unmovèd be,   55
Mute as the grave wherein my friend does lie.

8

To him my Muse made haste with every strain
Whilst it was new, and warm yet from the brain.
He loved my worthless rhymes, and like a friend
        Would find out something to commend.   60
Hence now, my Muse, thou canst not me delight;
        Be this my latest verse
        With which I now adorn his hearse,
And this my grief, without thy help shall write.

9

Had I a wreath of bays about my brow,   65
I should contemn that flourishing honour now,
Condemn it to the fire, and joy to hear
        It rage and crackle there.
Instead of bays, crown with sad cypress me;
        Cypress which tombs does beautify;   70
        Not Phoebus grieved so much as I
For him, who first was made that mournful tree.

10

Large was his soul; as large a soul as e'er
Submitted to inform a body here.
High as the place 'twas shortly in Heaven to have,   75
        But low, and humble as his grave.
So high that all the virtues there did come

---

58   Jonson prays to Apollo to 'heat my brain / With Delphic fire' (*An Ode to James Earl of Desmond*, 11–12).
59–60   Kinder than Horace's critics: 'A wise and honest man will cry out shame / On artless verse' (*Ars Poetica*, 445, Jonson), but friendlier than the flatterers who leave the poet not knowing 'Whether his soothing friend speak truth or no' (425).
62–4   'Let this I leave at your coffin be my last poem (as in Donne's *Obsequies*, 257–8), inspired not by the Muse but by grief' (Sidney's *Astrophil*, 94: 'Grief find the words').
65–70   'If I had won laurels for poetry, I should disdain them now … Crown me with funereal cypress, not poetic laurels.'
71–2   Cyparissus accidentally killed a stag favoured by Apollo; resolved to mourn forever, he was turned to a cypress tree by the god: 'I for thee will mourn: / Mourn thou for others: hearses still adorn' (Ovid, *Metamorphoses*, 10:141–2, Sandys).
74   'Lowered itself to give form to a body' ('For of the soul the body form doth take', Spenser, *Hymn in Honour of Beauty*, 132).

As to their chiefest seat
Conspicuous, and great;
So low that for me too it made a room.   80

11

He scorned this busy world below, and all
That we, mistaken mortals, pleasure call;
Was filled with inn'cent gallantry and truth,
          Triumphant ore the sins of youth.
He like the stars, to which he now is gone,   85
          That shine with beams like flame,
          Yet burn not with the same,
Had all the light of youth, of the fire none.

12

Knowledge he only sought, and so soon caught,
As if for him knowledge had rather sought.   90
Nor did more learning ever crowded lie
          In such a short mortality.
When ere the skilful youth discoursed or writ,
          Still did the notions throng
          About his eloquent tongue,   95
Nor could his ink flow faster then his wit.

13

So strong a wit did Nature to him frame,
As all things but his judgement overcame;
His judgement like the heavenly moon did show,
          Tempering that mighty sea below.   100
O had he lived in learning's world, what bound
          Would have been able to control
          His over-powering soul?
We've lost in him arts that not yet are found.

14

His mirth was the pure spirits of various wit,   105
Yet never did his God or friends forget.
And when deep talk and wisdom came in view,
          Retired and gave to them their due.
For the rich help of books he always took,
          Though his own searching mind before   110
          Was so with notions written o'er
As if wise Nature had made that her book.

78–9 'As to their great and illustrious capital'.
83 Innocence and truth qualify mere courtliness.
85–8 Stars were thought to be composed of ether, a rarefied superlunary element.
92 'In so brief an earthly existence'.
97–100 'Fancy [or wit], without the help of judgement, is not commended as a virtue; but the latter which is judgement, and discretion, is commended for itself' (Hobbes, *Le-*

viathan, 1.8.3); his passions were regulated by his judgement as tidal motion is by the moon.
105 *pure spirits* 'distillation'.
110–12 'It seems to me that the soul is like a book . . . the conjunction of memory with sensations, together with the feelings consequent on them, may be said to write words in our souls' (Plato, *Philebus*, 38–9).

15

So many virtues joined in him, as we
Can scarce pick here and there in history.
More than old writers' practice e'er could reach,   115
      As much as they could ever teach.
These did Religion, Queen of Virtues sway,
      And all their sacred motions steer,
      Just like the first and highest sphere
Which wheels about, and turns all Heaven one way.   120

16

With as much zeal, devotion, piety,
He always lived, as other saints do die.
Still with his soul severe account he kept,
      Weeping all debts out ere he slept.
Then down in peace and innocence he lay,   125
      Like the sun's laborious light,
      Which still in water sets at night,
Unsullied with his journey of the day.

17

Wondrous young man, why wert thou made so good,
To be snatched hence ere better understood?   130
Snatched before half of thee enough was seen!
      Thou ripe, and yet thy life but green!
Nor could thy friends take their last sad farewell,
      But Danger and infectious Death
      Maliciously seized on that breath   135
Where life, spirit, pleasure always used to dwell.

18

But happy thou, ta'en from this frantic age,
Where Ign'rance and Hypocrisy does rage!
A fitter time for Heaven no soul e'er chose,
      The place now only free from those.   140
There 'mong the blest thou dost forever shine,
      And wheresoe'er thou casts thy view
      Upon that white and radiant crew,
See'st not a soul clothed with more light than thine.

19

And if the glorious saints cease not to know   145
Their wretched friends who fight with life below;
Thy flame to me does still the same abide,
      Only more pure and rarified.

113–14 'His virtues outnumbered those of all virtuous men described in history.'
119–20 'The tenth heaven or first mover . . . maketh his revolution . . . carrying . . . the other heavens violently from east to west, from their proper revolutions, which is from west to east' (Peacham, *The Complete Gentleman*, ch. 7).
124 Proverbially 'Repentance is the laundress of the soul'.

137–8 Jonson congratulates his son that he has 'so soon scaped world's, and flesh's rage, / And, if no other misery, yet age' (*On his First Son*).
143–4 'They shall walk with me in white: for they are worthy' (Revelation 3: 4).

There whilst immortal hymns thou dost rehearse,
    Thou dost with holy pity see   150
    Our dull and earthly poesy,
Where grief and mis'ry can be joined with verse.

149 'They sing . . . the song of the Lamb, saying, Great and marvellous are thy works, Lord God Almighty' (Revelation 15: 3); 'rehearse' is 'repeat'.

To Mr Hobbes

1656 (*Pindaric Odes*). Thomas Hobbes (1588–1679, and already 68 when this poem was published) was the intellectual hero of the century. Aubrey reports that Waller 'said to me, when I desired him to write some verses in praise of him that he was afraid of the churchmen. He quoted Horace – ['I'd write a work of hazard great: / And walk on embers in deceit – / Full ashes raked', *Odes*, 2.1:7–8, Fanshawe] – that what was chiefly to be taken notice of in his elegy was that he . . . pulled down all the churches, dispelled the mists of ignorance, and laid open their priestcraft.' Sheffield supplied an elegy which said as much: 'While in dark ignorance we lay afraid / Of fancies, ghosts, and every empty shade; / Great Hobbes appeared, and by plain Reason's light / Put such fantastic forms to shameful flight' (*On Mr Hobbes, and his Writing*, 19–22). Cowley's poem appears in the decade of the publication of the English translation of the *De Cive* (his materialist politics), and of *Leviathan*, both later publicly burned in Oxford. This poem, drawing on the resources of the Pindaric victory ode (a hugely influential gambit), offers a history of enlightenment implicitly making Hobbes's achievement continuous with Bacon's and disregarding the scandal of his impiety.

1

    Vast bodies of philosophy
    I oft have seen, and read,
    But all are bodies dead,
  Or bodies by art fashionèd;
I never yet the living soul could see,   5
    But in thy books and thee.
  'Tis only God can know
Whether the fair idea thou dost show
Agree entirely with his own or no.
    This I dare boldly tell,   10
'Tis so like truth 'twill serve our turn as well.
Just, as in Nature thy proportions be,
As full of concord their variety,
As firm the parts upon their centre rest,
And all so solid are that they at least   15
As much as Nature, emptiness detest.

2

Long did the mighty Stagirite retain
The universal intellectual reign,
Saw his own country's short-lived leopard slain;

11–16 The perfection of the universe (its proportion, concord, centredness, plenitude) is reflected in Hobbes's work. 'Such was God's poem . . . The ungoverned parts no correspondence knew . . . Till they to number and fixed rules were brought / By the Eternal Mind's poetic thought' (*Davideis*, 1:451–6, and note 34).

17 *Stagirite* Aristotle, from his birthplace in Macedonia. 19–21 Cowley's note glosses the leopard of Daniel's vision of world empires (Daniel, 7: 6) as the Grecian Empire (Alexander the Great was Aristotle's pupil); the eagle is the Roman military ensign. Aristotle survives both empires.

The stronger Roman eagle did outfly,   20
Oftener renewed his age, and saw that die.
Mecca itself, in spite of Mohamet possessed,
And chased by a wild deluge from the east,
His monarchy new planted in the west.
But as in time each great imperial race   25
Degenerates, and gives some new one place:
    So did this noble empire waste,
    Sunk by degrees from glories past,
And in the schoolmen's hands it perished quite at last.
    Then nought but words it grew,   30
    And those all barb'rous too.
  It perished, and it vanished there,
The life and soul breathed out, became but empty air.

3

The fields which answered well the ancients' plough,
Spent and outworn return no harvest now,   35
In barren age wild and unglorious lie,
    And boast of past fertility,
The poor relief of present poverty.
  Food and fruit we now must want
  Unless new lands we plant.   40
We break up tombs with sacrilegious hands;
    Old rubbish we remove;
To walk in ruins, like vain ghosts, we love,
    And with fond divining-wands
  We search among the dead   45
  For treasures burièd,
  Whilst still the liberal earth does hold
So many virgin mines of undiscovered gold.

4

The Baltic, Euxine, and the Caspian,
And slender-limbed Mediterranean,   50
Seem narrow creeks to thee, and only fit
For the poor wretched fisher-boats of wit.
Thy nobler vessel the vast ocean tries,
    And nothing sees but seas and skies,
    Till unknown regions it descries,   55

22–4 'Aristotle conquered even Mecca despite the advent of Islam, and when the Turks inundated the Arab lands, planted his kingdom in the medieval west.' Bacon several times invokes Daniel's prophecy of 12: 4, 'many shall run to and fro, and knowledge shall be increased' (*Advancement*, 2.14), but regularly identifies only three stages in the history of learning: the Greek, Roman and Modern ('neither the Arabians nor the Schoolmen need be mentioned,' *Novum Organum*, 78). Cowley counts the Schoolmen (the medieval Scholastics) as doomed Aristotelians, but his note is more generous to the Arabs.

30–3 Combines Bacon's complaints of the Scholastics who did 'out of no great quantity of matter and infinite agitation of wit spin out to us those laborious webs of learning' (Bacon, *Advancement*, 4.5), and of the Humanist *literati* who 'began to hunt more after words than matter' (4.2).

34–40 Carew writes that Donne's antecedents were able to 'cull the prime / Buds of invention many a hundred year, / And left the rifled fields' (*Elegy on Donne*, 53–6), but that Donne planted 'fresh invention' (28).

41–6 Varying 'Why seek ye the living among the dead?' (Luke 24: 5), Cowley's note explains the divining-wands as rods of hazel 'used for the finding out either of veins, or hidden treasures of gold and silver'.

47–8 Carew writes that Donne 'opened us a mine / Of rich and pregnant fancy' (37–8).

49–56 'Learning, like a Caspian Sea, / Hath hitherto received all little brooks . . . Let her turn Ocean now' (Greville, *Treaty of Human Learning*, 72). Cowley's note explains that 'all the navigation of the ancients' was in the seas mentioned.

Thou great Columbus of the golden lands of new philosophies.
　　　Thy task was harder much than his,
　　　　For thy learn'd America is
　　　Not only found out first by thee,
And rudely left to future industry,　　　　　　　　　　　　　　60
　　　　But thy eloquence and thy wit,
Has planted, peopled, built, and civilized it.

5

　　　　I little thought before,
　　　　(Nor being my own self so poor
　　　　Could comprehend so vast a store)　　　　　　　　65
　　　That all the wardrobe of rich eloquence,
　　　　　Could have afforded half enough,
　　　　　Of bright, of new, and lasting stuff,
To clothe the mighty limbs of thy gigantic sense.
Thy solid reason like the shield from heaven　　　　　　70
　　　　To the Trojan hero given,
Too strong to take a mark from any mortal dart,
Yet shines with gold and gems in every part,
And wonders on it graved by the learn'd hand of art,
　　　　A shield that gives delight　　　　　　　　　　75
　　　　Even to the enemies' sight,
Then when they're sure to lose the combat by 't.

6

Nor can the snow which now cold age does shed
　　　　Upon thy reverend head,
Quench or allay the noble fires within,　　　　　　　　80
　　　　But all which thou hast been,
　　　　And all that youth can be thou'rt yet,
　　　　So fully still dost thou
Enjoy the manhood, and the bloom of wit,
And all the natural heat, but not the fever too.　　　　85
So contraries on Etna's top conspire,
Here hoary frosts, and by them breaks out fire.
A secure peace the faithful neighbors keep,
The emboldened snow next to the flame does sleep.
　　　　And if we weigh, like thee,　　　　　　　　　90
　　　　Nature, and causes, we shall see

---

56 Columbus is the type of the explorer (St Paul is the 'Columbus' of rapture, *The Ecstasy*, 46).

58–62 Hobbes not only discovers new philosophical territory but tames it; America was still synonymous with barbarism.

63–9 Milton instructs the English Language that she 'from thy wardrobe bring thy chiefest treasure . . . cull those richest Robes . . . Which deepest spirits, and choicest wits desire' (*At a Vacation Exercise*, 18–22); Carew writes that only the toughest English can 'gird about / [Donne's] giant fancy' (*Elegy on Donne*, 51–2). Cowley's note explains that 'no wardrobe can furnish clothes to fit a body taller and bigger than ever any was before.'

70–7 Cowley's note cites Virgil's description of the shield

prepared by Vulcan for Aeneas, portraying the future history of Rome (*Aeneid*, 8:625–728); and how hostile swords were ineffectual against it (12:728–41), 'which is just the case of men's arguing against solid, and that is, divine reason'.

86 Cowley's note acknowledges Claudian's description of Etna: 'In midst of boiling heat, the snow doth fall upon the top, and never melts at all . . . The snow [the heat] ne'er offends, whose inward cold / Condenseth it, and if dissolve some should . . . Yet most upon the top congealed is / Or never lower falls' (*De Raptu Proserpinae*, 1:164–8, Digges), 'where methinks is somewhat of that which Seneca objects to Ovid, that he never knew when to stop'.

That thus it needs must be,
To things immortal Time can do no wrong,
And that which never is to die, for ever must be young.

Brutus

1656 (Pindaric Odes). The ode apparently displeased the Royalists but, despite the central position it occupies among the odes, it is a panegyric muted by qualification and doubtfulness of direction. The tyrannicide Cromwell is never named, and could only have been made uncomfortable by the association with Brutus, especially a Brutus so ambiguously identified with the public good. 'The very enemies of Brutus would say that he had no other end or aim, from first to last, save only to restore to the Roman people their ancient government' (Plutarch, *Life*: 'Comparison with Dion'); but the inefficacy of good intentions is acknowledged in the final stanza (and again in the essay *On the Government of Oliver Cromwell*). The *Ode on Brutus* of Sheffield (who also adapted Shakespeare's *Julius Caesar* in *The Tragedy of Marcus Brutus*) isolates in Cowley's poem an argument about the claims of public good in order to be able to set against it the claims of friendship; he brings to his reply a quarrel not only with Cowley's implicit version of English history, but also with his version of Roman history.

1
Excellent Brutus, of all human race,
The best till Nature was improved by Grace,
Till men above themselves Faith raisèd more
        Than Reason above beasts before.
Virtue was thy life's centre, and from thence   5
Did silently and constantly dispense
        The gentle vigorous influence
To all the wide and fair circumference:
And all the parts upon it leant so easily,
Obeyed the mighty force so willingly   10
That none could discord or disorder see
        In all their contrariety.
Each had his motion natural and free,
And the whole no more moved than the whole world could be.

2
From thy strict rule some think that thou didst swerve   15
(Mistaken honest men) in Caesar's blood;
What mercy could the tyrant's life deserve,
From him who killed himself rather than serve?
The heroic exaltations of Good

1–2 The division between the orders of Nature and Grace is historical: Brutus is the best man before the Christian era and so lived without 'grace'.
5–14 Two centres are available: one for the orbit of Faith (unknown to Brutus), the other for the orbit of Reason: 'into our reason flow, and there do end / All, that this natural world doth comprehend: / Quotidian things, and equidistant hence, / Shut in, for man, in one circumference' (Donne, *Elegy on Prince Henry*, 5–8). In Brutus, Virtue stands at the centre of Reason's circle (or concentric series) as the sun does in the centre of the solar system ('the whole world').
15–18 'Some honest men reprehend your murder of Caesar, but wrongly. An man who was prepared to die for liberty was entitled to kill a tyrant'; Sheffield thinks suicide the better option in those circumstances than rebellion: 'Happy for Rome had been that noble pride; / The world had then remained in peace, and only Brutus died' (*Ode*, 41–2).
19–21 'Good heroically manifested is so far above us as to be unintelligible and so mistaken for Evil.' Hobbes argues that in times of war 'notions of right and wrong, justice and injustice have no place' (*Leviathan*, 1.8.13); and further, of subjects fractious under sovereign power, that 'all men are by nature provided of notable multiplying glasses (that is their passions and self-love), through which every little payment [made to the sovereign power] appeareth a great grievance' (2.18.20).

Are so far from understood,   20
We count them vice: alas our sight's so ill,
That things which swiftest move seem to stand still.
We look not upon virtue in her height,
On her supreme idea, brave and bright,
In the original light: 25
But as her beams reflected pass
Through our own nature or ill-custom's glass.
And 'tis no wonder so,
If with dejected eye
In standing pools we seek the sky,   30
That stars so high above should seem to us below.

3

Can we stand by and see
Our mother robbed, and bound, and ravished be,
Yet not to her assistance stir,
Pleased with the strength and beauty of the ravisher?   35
Or shall we fear to kill him, if before
The cancelled name of friend he bore?
Ingrateful Brutus do they call?
Ingrateful Caesar who could Rome enthral!
An act more barbarous and unnatural   40
(In the exact balance of true virtue tried)
Then his successor Nero's parricide!
There's none but Brutus could deserve
That all men else should wish to serve,
And Caesar's usurped place to him should proffer;   45
None can deserve't but he who would refuse the offer.

4

Ill Fate assumed a body thee to affright,
And wrapped itself in th' terrors of the night,
"I'll meet thee at Philippi," said the sprite;
"I'll meet thee there," said'st thou,   50
With such a voice, and such a brow,
As put the trembling ghost to sudden flight,
It vanished as a taper's light
Goes out when spirits appear in sight.
One would have thought t' had heard the morning crow,   55

26–7 'We see notions of virtue only as filtered by our own prejudices or as reflected in corrupt practice.'
30–1 In Carew's Song *To a Lady that Desired I would Love her*, 'Grief is a puddle, and reflects not clear / Your beauty's rays' (16–17).
32–5 Rome is an allegorical mother to her citizens; Marcus Brutus's motives are identified with those of his ancestor Lucius Junius Brutus, who led the rising against the Tarquins after the rape of Lucretia; Sheffield argues that Rome was not raped by Caesar since they were already married or, more crudely, that she enjoyed the rape: 'Often she cast a kind admiring glance / On the bold struggler for delight' (*Ode*, 95–6).
36–7 'Caesar had a belief that [Brutus] was his own child' (Plutarch, *Life of Marcus Brutus*, Dryden).

42 Nero murdered his mother Agrippina, Caesar (metaphorically) raped his mother Rome.
47–50 At Philippi was fought and lost the last battle in the Roman Republican cause. Brutus's dream or vision of Caesar is described at the end of Plutarch's *Life of Caesar*; Hobbes uses it to illustrate the power of fantasy in guilty men (*Leviathan*, 1.2.6).
53–4 Thomas Browne says, 'That candles and lights burn dim and blue at the apparition of spirits, may be true, if the ambient air be full of sulphurious spirits' (*Pseudodoxia*, 23.4).
55–7 'As if it had heard the cock crowing or seen the sun rising' ('well-appointed', because splendidly robed, whereas Shakespeare's dawn comes in 'russet mantle clad' over the 'high eastward hill', *Hamlet*, I. i. 171–2).

Or seen her well-appointed star
Come marching up the eastern hill afar.
Nor durst it in Philippi's field appear,
    But unseen attacked thee there.
Had it presumed in any shape thee to oppose,   60
Thou wouldst have forced it back upon thy foes:
    Or slain 't like Caesar, though it be
A conqueror and a monarch mightier far than he.

5
What joy can human things to us afford,
When we see perish thus by odd events,   65
    Ill men, and wretched accidents,
The best cause and best man that ever drew a sword?
    When we see
The false Octavius, and wild Antony,
    God-like Brutus, conquer thee?   70
What can we say but thine own tragic word,
That Virtue, which had worshipped been by thee
As the most solid Good, and greatest deity,
    By this fatal proof became
    An idol only, and a name,   75
    Hold noble Brutus and restrain
The bold voice of thy generous disdain:
    These mighty gulfs are yet
Too deep for all thy judgement and thy wit.
The Time's set forth already which shall quell   80
Stiff Reason, when it offers to rebel.
    Which these great secrets shall unseal,
    And new philosophies reveal.
A few years more, so soon hadst thou not died,
Would have confounded human virtue's pride,   85
    And showed thee a God crucified.

69 Octavius (later Augustus) was false to the ideal of the Republic and to Antony; Antony was wild not only in Egypt. 'Not all the wisdom and power of the Roman Senate, nor the wit and eloquence of Cicero, nor the courage and virtue of Brutus, was able to defend their country, or themselves, against the unexperienced rashness of a beardless boy, and the loose rage of a voluptuous madman' (Cowley, *On the Government of Oliver Cromwell*).

71–5 Brutus took his last farewells saying that he 'was leaving behind him such a reputation of his virtue as none of his conquerors . . . should ever be able to acquire' (Plutarch, *Life of Marcus Brutus*, Dryden).
75 *idol* 'phantom'.

The Grasshopper

1656; Cowley translated eleven Anacreontic pieces 'paraphrastically' as an appendix to the *Miscellanies*; these were reprinted in *Anacreon done into English out of the original Greek* (Oxford, 1683) with others by Francis Willis, Thomas Wood and John Oldham. Edited first and published with a Latin translation by Stephanus (Paris, 1554) the *Anacreontea*, Hellenistic

'odes' in imitation of Anacreon (whose work survives mainly in fragments) enjoyed immediate success under the earlier poet's name. Thomas Stanley's roughly contemporary English version preserves the simplicity of the Greek, overwritten by Cowley's ornamental (or humanizing) periphrases. The poem is *Anacreontea*, 34.

Happy insect, what can be
In happiness compared to thee?
Fed with nourishment divine,
The dewy morning's gentle wine!
Nature waits upon thee still,   5
And thy verdant cup does fill,
'Tis filled wherever thou dost tread,
Nature self's thy Ganymede.
Thou dost drink, and dance, and sing;
Happier then the happiest king!   10
All the fields which thou dost see,
All the plants belong to thee,
All that summer hours produce,
Fertile made with early juice.
Man for thee does sow and plough;   15
Farmer he, and landlord thou!
Thou does innocently joy;
Nor does thy luxury destroy;
The shepherd gladly heareth thee,
More harmonious than he.   20
Thee country hinds with gladness hear,
Prophet of the ripened year!
Thee Phoebus loves, and does inspire;
Phoebus is himself thy sire.
To thee of all things upon earth,   25
Life is no longer than thy mirth.
Happy insect, happy thou,
Dost neither age, nor winter know.
But when thou'st drunk, and danced, and sung,
Thy fill, the flowery leaves among   30
(Voluptuous, and wise withal,
Epicurean animal!)
Sated with thy summer feast,
Thou retir'st to endless rest.

6 'Wherever you go, Nature herself is your cup-bearer ('Ganymede'), filling the leaves with dew.'
13 Cowley's text read 'hours' where the text now received reads 'woods'.
18 *luxury* 'feasting'.
19–22 'The shepherds gladly hear a creature who sings even more than they do; the farm-workers gladly hear the song that signals the advent of harvest.'
23–4 Phoebus is at once the sun and the god of poetry.
31–2 The beastly epicure (in the bad sense) is turned to a philosophical connoisseur of the world's pleasures, who wisely believes them the only ones.

The College at Ramah

1656 (*Davideis*, 1:661–880). 'So David fled, and escaped, and came to Samuel to Ramah . . . And he and Samuel went and dwelt in Naioth' (1 Samuel 19: 18). Naioth ('habitations') was a resort of the prophets. 'The description of the Prophets' College at Naioth looks at first sight as if I had taken the pattern of it from ours at the Universities; but the truth is ours were formed after the pattern of the Jews,' says Cowley (note 47). He explains that 'prophets' were 'religious persons, who separate themselves from the business of the world, to employ their time in the contemplation and praise of God'. They sang and played on instruments (1 Samuel 10: 5); they preached (1 Samuel 19: 20). 'They are the first religious orders heard of in antiquity, for whom David afterwards composed psalms. They are called . . . scribes, because they laboured in reading, writing, learning and teaching the scriptures; and they are called Sons of the Prophets.' From there being communities of them at Bethel and Jericho (2 Kings 2: 3, 5) it can be inferred that 'colleges of them were founded in several towns.' But the motive of the digression is the promotion of a Baconian 'great instauration' of learning. Cowley's *Proposition for the Advancement of Experimental Philosophy* (1661) includes an account of a college whose architecture is soberly modelled on the continental Charterhouses, and whose syllabus is firmly biased to 'natural philosophy' ('physics'), so that even literary study is directed to poets who treat of scientific subjects (like his own *De Plantis*), and the study of Divinity is forbidden. Here on the contrary the syllabus is biased to Divinity: the architecture is based on the arrangement of the old Oxford schools round the Bodleian Library (he calls Heaven 'the beatific Bodley of the Deity' in *Ode: Mr. Cowley's Book Presenting Itself*, 24); the organization (with Fellows, etc.) is like that of an Oxford or Cambridge college, just as that of More's Utopia is like that of the London Inns of Court. Fanshawe's *The Escorial* gives a similar extended account of a 'college'. Cowley's encyclopaedic notes are not reproduced, but cited selectively.

Midst a large wood that joins fair Ramah's town
(The neighbourhood fair Ramah's chief renown)
A college stands, where at great prophets' feet
The prophets' sons with silent dil'gence meet,
By Samuel built, and mod'rately endowed,   665
Yet more to's lib'ral tongue than hands they owed:
There himself taught, and his blest voice to hear,
Teachers themselves lay proud beneath him there.
The House was a large square; but plain and low;
Wise Nature's use art strove not to outgo.   670
An inward square by well-ranged trees was made;
And midst the friendly cover of their shade,
A pure, well-tasted, wholesome fountain rose;
Which no vain cost of marble did enclose;
Nor through carved shapes did the forced waters pass,   675
Shapes gazing on themselves in th' liquid glass.
Yet the chaste stream that 'mong loose pebbles fell
For cleanness, thirst, religion served as well.
The Scholars, Doctors and Companions here,
Lodged all apart in neat small chambers were: 680
Well-furnished chambers, for in each there stood,
A narrow couch, table and chair of wood;
More is but clog where use does bound delight;
And those are rich whose wealth 's proportioned right
To their life's form; more goods would but become   685
A burden to them, and contract their room.
A second court more sacred stood behind,
Built fairer, and to nobler use designed:
The Hall and Schools one side of it possessed;
The Library and Synagogue the rest.   690
Tables of plain-cut fir adorned the Hall;

670–5   In Spenser's Bower of Bliss, 'One would have thought . . . That Nature had for wantonness ensued Art / And that Art at Nature did repine; / So striving each the other to undermine' (*Faerie Queene*, 2.12.59), and the central fountain 'with curious imagery / Was overwrought, and shapes of naked boys' (60).
678   'When they go into the tabernacle of the congregation, they shall wash with water, that they die not' (Exodus 30: 20, noted by Cowley).
679   'I have learned much of my Masters, or Rabbis, more

of my Companions, most of my Scholars, was the speech of an ancient Rabbi,' whence Cowley's note derives this distinction (with Doctors for Rabbis); 'After the Scholars had made good progress, they were elected . . . Companions to the Rabbis, like our Fellows of Colleges to the Masters.'
682   The Shunammite couple prepare for the prophet Elisha 'a little chamber [and] set for him there a bed, and a table, and a stool' (2 Kings 4: 10, note by Cowley).
683   'Where considerations of usefulness rule over pleasure, more would only be an impediment.'

And with beasts' skins the beds were covered all.
The reverend Doctors take their seats on high,
The elect Companions in their bosoms lie.
The Scholars far below upon the ground,   695
On fresh-strewed rushes place themselves around.
With more respect the wise and ancient lay;
But ate not choicer herbs or bread than they,
Nor purer waters drank, their constant feast;
But by great days, and sacrifice increased.   700
The Schools built round and higher, at the end
With their fair circle did this side extend;
To which their Synagogue on the other side,
And to the Hall their Library replied.
The midst towards their large gardens open lay,   705
To admit the joys of spring and early day.
In th' Library a few choice authors stood;
Yet 'twas well stored, for that small store was good;
Writing, man's spir'tual physic was not then
Itself, as now, grown a disease of men.   710
Learning (young virgin) but few suitors knew;
The common prostitute she lately grew,
And with her spurious brood loads now the press;
Laborious effects of idleness!
Here all the various forms one might behold   715
How letters saved themselves from death of old;
Some painfully engraved in thin wrought plates,
Some cut in wood, some lightlier traced on slates;
Some drawn on fair palm leaves, with short-lived toil,
Had not their friend the cedar lent his oil.   720
Some wrought in silks, some writ in tender barks;
Some the sharp style in waxen tables marks;
Some in beasts' skins, and some in biblus reed;
Both new rude arts, which age and growth did need.
The Schools were painted well with useful skill;   725
Stars, maps, and stories the learn'd wall did fill.
Wise wholesome proverbs mixed around the room,
Some writ, and in Egyptian figures some.
Here all the noblest wits of men inspired,
From earth's slight joys, and worthless toils retired,   730
Whom Samuel's fame and bounty thither lead,
Each day by turns their solid knowledge read.
The course and power of stars great Nathan thought,
And home to man those distant wonders brought,

---

692 Cowley quotes Homer, *Odyssey*, 14:50 for the custom.
693–4 Cowley's note explains the odd phrasing: the Doctors are supposed to lie down on the prepared beds with the Companions next to them ('as John is said to lean on Jesus's bosom, John 13: 23').
710 Juvenal's 'incurable itch to scribble' (7:50–1) was not modern.
717–18 Cowley's note gives an archaeology of writing, before turning to the use of 'plates or leaves of ivory . . . As for wood and slates, we may easily believe, that they and all other capable materials were written on'.

716–23 Cowley's note brings together various authorities on the archaeology of the book: the use of palm leaves preserved with cedar oil, of silk and bark, of bone *styli* for writing in wax tablets, of vellum ('beasts' skins') and papyrus ('biblus reed').
728 Pictured hieroglyphics, which Cowley supposes the Jews learned from Egypt.
733–68 Nathan (2 Samuel 7: 2 etc.) and Gad (1 Samuel 22: 5 etc.) were famous prophets in David's time, but their professorships in Astronomy and Mathematics were 'voluntary gifts of mine' (Cowley's note); likewise Mahol's in Natural

How toward both poles the sun's fixed journey bends,   735
And how the year his crookèd walk attends.
By what just steps the wandering lights advance,
And what eternal measures guide their dance.
Himself a prophet; but his lectures showed
How little of that art to them he owed.   740
Mahol the inferior world's fantastic face,
Though all the turns of matter's maze did trace,
Great Nature's well-set clock in pieces took;
On all the springs and smallest wheels did look
Of life and motion; and with equal art   745
Made up again the whole of every part.
The prophet Gad in learnèd dust designs
The immortal solid rules of fancied lines.
Of numbers too the unnumbered wealth he shows,
And with them far their endless journey goes.   750
Numbers which still increase more high and wide
From One, the root of their turned pyramid.
Of men, and ages past Seraiah read;
Embalmed in long-lived History the dead.
Showed the steep falls, and slow ascent of states;   755
What wisdom and what follies make their fates.
Samuel himself did God's rich Law display;
Taught doubting men with judgement to obey.
And oft his ravished soul with sudden flight
Soared above present times, and human sight.   760
These arts but welcome strangers might appear,
Music and verse seemed born and bred up here;
Scarce the blest Heaven that rings with angels' voice,
Does more with constant harmony rejoice.
The sacred Muse does here each breast inspire;   765
Heman, and sweet-mouthed Asaph rule their choir:
Both charming poets, and all strains they played,
By artful breath, or nimble fingers made.
The Synagogue was dressed with care and cost,
(The only place where that they esteemed not lost)   770
The glittering roof with gold did daze the view,
The sides refreshed with silks of sacred blue.
Here thrice each day they read their perfect Law,
Thrice prayers from willing Heaven a blessing draw;
Thrice in glad hymns swelled with the Great One's praise,   775

Philosophy (he is Heman's father at 1 Kings 4: 31); Seraiah
is David's secretary (2 Samuel 8: 17, elsewhere called Shisha
or Shavsha), and Heman and Asaph are singers (1 Chroni-
cles 15: 19).
735–8 'How the sun moves towards either pole between
the tropics and the seasons ('the year') follow its apparent
undulations ('crookèd walk'); how the planets ('wandering
lights') rise in order and what the pattern is of their move-
ments'.
743–6 The clockwork metaphor is standard: 'Or like as
also in a clock well-tended, / Just counterpoise, justly thereon
suspended, / Makes the great wheel go round, and that
anon / Turns with his turning many a meaner one . . . So

the grand heaven . . . With his quick motion all the spheres
doth move' (Sylvester, *Divine Weeks*, 1.4:338–46).
751–2 'Number is here called *turned pyramid*, because the
bottom of it is the point *One* (which is the beginning of
number, not properly number, as a point is of magnitude)
from whence it goes up still larger and larger, just contrary
to the nature of pyramidal ascension' (Cowley's note).
770 'The only place where they thought care and cost worth
it'.
772 Cowley notes: 'Because of the use of it in the curtains
of the tabernacles' (Numbers 4: 4–5 etc.).

The pliant voice on her seven steps they raise,
Whilst all the enlivened instruments around
To the just feet with various concord sound;
Such things were Muses then, contemned low earth;
Decently proud, and mindful of their birth.   780
'Twas God himself that here tuned every tongue;
And gratefully of him alone they sung.
They sung how God spoke out the world's vast ball;
From nothing, and from nowhere called forth all.
No Nature yet, or place for 't to possess,   785
But an unbottomed gulf of emptiness.
Full of Himself, the Almighty sat, His own
Palace, and without solitude alone.
But he was Goodness whole, and all things willed;
Whiche'er they were, his active word fulfilled;   790
And their astonished heads o'th' sudden reared;
An unshaped kind of something first appeared,
Confessing its new being, and undressed
As if it stepped in haste before the rest.
Yet buried in this matter's darksome womb,   795
Lay the rich seeds of everything to come.
From hence the cheerful flame leapt up so high;
Close at its heels the nimble air did fly;
Dull earth with his own weight did downwards pierce
To the fixed navel of the universe,   800
And was quite lost in waters: till God said
To the proud sea, "Shrink in your insolent head,
See how the gaping earth has made you place;
That durst not murmur, but shrunk in apace."
Since when his bounds are set, at which in vain   805
He foams, and rages, and turns back again.
With richer stuff He bade Heaven's fabric shine,
And from Him a quick spring of light divine
Swelled up the sun, from whence His cher'shing flame
Fills the whole world, like Him from whom it came.   810
He smoothed the rough-cast moon's imperfect mould,
And combed her beamy locks with sacred gold;

776   The steps of the musical scale, corresponding to the seven strings of the lyre. Cowley quotes Virgil's Orpheus who strikes 'seven distinguished notes' on his lyre (*Aeneid*, 6:646).

783   Cowley quotes from Porphyry an account of the Egyptian Knef represented with 'an egg coming out of his mouth, to show that he spoke out the world, that is, made it with his word'.

787–8   Cowley quotes Theophilus, *Adversus Gentiles*, 2: 'God is in no place, but is the place of all things'; and Philo, *De Vita Mosis*, 1.158: 'He is his own place, and filled with himself.'

789–90   'Being entirely good, God willed the universe (that it might share his entire and lonely goodness); and his creating word brought it into being.'

795–801   The elements are as yet undistinguished in chaos but exist potentially. Lucretius rejects this notion of the formation of the elements, but Cowley may remember his formulation of it: 'Those / Which heavy water and dull earth compose, / Strive to the centre . . . two retire, / Endeavouring from it as light air and fire' (Lucretius, 1:1085–8, Creech).

801–28   'And God said, Let there be a firmament in the midst of the waters, and let it divide the waters from the waters' (Genesis 1: 6); 'And God made two great lights, the greater light to rule the day, and the lesser light to rule the night: he made the stars also' (1: 16); 'And the earth brought forth grass, and herb yielding seed after his kind, and the tree yielding fruit' (1: 12); 'And God created great whales, and every living creature that moveth, which the waters brought forth abundantly . . . and every winged fowl' (1: 21); 'Let the earth bring forth the . . . beast of the earth' (1: 24); 'Let us make man in our image' (1: 26): 'Last, He made man, the horizon 'twixt both kinds [angels and 'mindless bodies'], / In whom we doe the world's abridgement see' (Sir John Davies, *Nosce Teipsum*, 703–4).

"Be thou" (said he) "Queen of the mournful night",
And as he spoke, she' arose clad o'er in light,
With thousand stars attending on her train;   815
With her they rise, with her they set again.
Then herbs peeped forth, new trees admiring stood,
And smelling flowers painted the infant wood.
Then flocks of birds through the glad air did flee,
Joyful, and safe before man's luxury,   820
Teaching their Maker in their untaught lays:
Nay the mute fish witness no less his praise.
For those he made, and clothed with silver scales;
From minnows to those living islands, whales.
Beasts too were his command: what could he more?   825
Yes, man he could, the bond of all before;
In him he all things with strange order hurled;
In him, that full abridgement of the world.
    This, and much more of God's great works they told;
His mercies, and some judgements too of old: 830
How when all Earth was deeply stained in sin;
With an impetuous noise the waves came rushing in.
Where birds erewhile dwelt, and securely sung;
There fish (an unknown net) entangled hung.
The face of shipwrecked Nature naked lay;   835
The sun peeped forth, and beheld nought but sea.
This men forgot, and burnt in lust again;
Till showers, strange as their sin, of fiery rain,
And scalding brimstone, dropped on Sodom's head;
Alive they felt those flames they fry in dead.   840
No better end rash Pharaoh's pride befell
When wind and sea waged war for Israel.
In his gilt chariots amazed fishes sat,
And grew with corps of wretched princes fat.
The waves and rocks half-eaten bodies stain;   845
Nor was it since called the Red Sea in vain.
Much too they told of faithful Abram's fame,
To whose blest passage they owe still their name:
Of Moses much, and the great seed of Nun;
What wonders they performed, what lands they won.   850
How many kings they slew or captive brought;
They held the swords, but God and angels fought.
    Thus gained they the wise spending of their days;
And their whole life was their dear Maker's praise.
No minute's rest, no swiftest thought they sold   855
To that belovèd plague of mankind, gold.
Gold for which all mankind with greater pains

831–6 Noah's Flood (Genesis 6–8) is recalled in Ovidian language (where 'entangled fishes' end up in 'high elms', *Metamorphoses*, 1:296, Sandys) and Jupiter looks out and 'saw that all a lake was grown' (1:324).

837–40 The destruction of Sodom (Genesis 19: 1–28) is reduced to a conceit ('fry' was not yet a low word).

841–6 'And Moses stretched forth his hand . . . And the waters returned, and covered the chariots and the horsemen, and all the host of Pharaoh' (Exodus 14: 27–8); 'corps' was the regular plural. Cowley pretends the sea takes its name from the blood of the Egyptians.

848 After Abram has passed over into Canaan, he is called the 'Hebrew' (Genesis 14: 13), 'one from foreign parts': 'Hebrews' are 'strangers'.

849 Joshua is the son of Nun (Exodus 33: 11).

Labour towards Hell, than those who dig its veins.
Their wealth was the contempt of it; which more
They valued than rich fools the shining ore.   860
The silkworm's precious death they scorned to wear,
And Tyrian dye appeared but sordid there.
Honour, which since the price of souls became,
Seemed to these great ones a low idle name.
Instead of down, hard beds they chose to have,   865
Such as might bid them not forget their grave.
Their board dispeopled no full element,
Free Nature's bounty thriftily they spent
And spared the stock; nor could their bodies say
We owe this crudeness to excess yesterday.   870
Thus souls live cleanly, and no soiling fear,
But entertain their welcome Maker there.
The senses perform nimbly what they're bid,
And honestly, nor are by Reason chid.
And when the down of sleep does softly fall,   875
Their dreams are heavenly then, and mystical.
With hasty wings Time present they outfly,
And tread the doubtful maze of destiny.
There walk and sport among the years to come;
And with quick eye pierce every cause's womb.   880

859–62   He is proverbially rich that is content with what he has. The silkworm's death is precious because it yields silk; Tyrian dye is the source of royal purple.
867   'They did not empty land or sea or air to supply their table.'

870   *crudeness* 'indigestion'.
876–80   Cowley cites the case 'sons of the prophets' at Bethel who foreknew that Elijah would be taken up into Heaven (2 Kings 2: 3); 'mystical' dreams are prophetic.

Horace: Epode 2

1668. 'There is no other sort of life that affords so many branches of praise to a panegyrist: the utility of it to a man's self; the usefulness, or rather necessity, of it to all the rest of mankind; the innocence, the pleasure, the antiquity, the dignity.' So Cowley in the essay 'Of Agriculture' (*Essays in Prose and Verse*, 1668) illustrates his point with this, the freest of the three versions of Horace's Epode given in this volume (with Jonson and Dryden), along with Virgil's praise of Italy from the *Georgics*, paraphrases more Horace, and a translation of the praise of modest coun-

try life from Book 4 of his own Latin *Plantarum Libri Sex* (1662–78). The influence of Jonson's version shows in some details: the 'toil' into which the boar is driven (38), the 'godwit' the speaker does not dine on (61). But sometimes Jonson's obvious solutions are denied in favour of periphrasis: 'golden treasures of the bee' (14), the 'reverend embraces' of trees (23–4), the 'gravity of sleep' (30), the shellfish 'Dressed by the wanton hand of luxury' (60); or in favour of paradox: 'fruitful wound' (12) 'innocent wars' (42).

Happy the man whom bounteous gods allow
With his own hands paternal grounds to plough!
Like the first golden mortals happy he
From business and the cares of money free!
No human storms break off at land his sleep,   5
No loud alarms of Nature on the deep,
From all the cheats of law he lives secure,

3   'Happy like men in the Golden Age'.

Nor does the affronts of palaces endure;
Sometimes the beauteous marriageable vine
He to the lusty bridegroom elm does join;   10
Sometimes he lops the barren trees around,
And grafts new life into the fruitful wound;
Sometimes he shears his flock, and sometimes he
Stores up the golden treasures of the bee.
He sees his lowing herds walk o'er the plain,   15
Whilst neighbouring hills low back to them again:
And when the season rich as well as gay,
All her autumnal bounty does display.
How is he pleased the increasing use to see,
Of his well-trusted labours bend the tree?   20
Of which large shares, on the glad sacred days
He gives to friends, and to the gods repays.
With how much joy does he beneath some shade
By agèd trees' reverend embraces made,
His careless head on the fresh green recline,   25
His head uncharged with fear or with design.
By him a river constantly complains,
The birds above rejoice with various strains
And in the solemn scene their orgies keep,
Like dreams mixed with the gravity of sleep,   30
Sleep which does always there for entrance wait
And nought within against it shuts the gate.
   Nor does the roughest season of the sky,
Or sullen Jove all sports to him deny,
He runs the mazes of the nimble hare,   35
His well-mouthed dogs' glad concert rends the air,
Or with game bolder, and rewarded more,
He drives into a toil, the foaming boar,
Here flies the hawk to assault, and there the net
To intercept the travelling fowl is set.   40
And all his malice, all his craft is shown
In innocent wars, on beasts and birds alone.
This is the life from all misfortunes free,
From thee the great one, tyrant Love, from thee;
And if a chaste and clean, though homely wife   45
Be added to the blessings of this life,
Such as the ancient sunburned Sabines were,
Such as Apulia, frugal still, does bear,
Who makes her children and the house her care,
And joyfully the work of life does share,   50

8   *affronts* 'insults', but playing with 'frontage' (for the Latin *limen*).
19–20   'He is pleased to see the fruit ('use') of his well-invested labours weigh down the branches.'
21–2   The holiday hospitality is Cowley's invention.
25   'His head free of fear and of taking no thought for the morrow'.
29   *orgies* 'revelry' (with no implication of licence).
30   *gravity* 'heaviness'.
32   'There is never any mental barrier to the access of sleep.'

35–6   Invented by Cowley and rewritten by Pope: 'To plains with well-breath'd beagles we repair, / And trace the mazes of the circling hare' (*Windsor Forest*, 121–2); 'mazes' are 'dances', 'well-mouthed' belongs to the technical vocabulary of hunting but lends a suggestion of musical performance to the 'concert' ('harmony') of the hounds.
41   The senses of 'malice' and 'craft' standardly infect each other.
45   *homely* 'uncomely'.
47–8   These types of peasant robustness are left unanglicized.

Nor thinks herself too noble or too fine
To pin the sheepfold or to milk the kine,
Who waits at door against her husband come
From rural duties, late, and wearied home,
Where she receives him with a kind embrace,   55
A cheerful fire, and a more cheerful face:
And fills the bowl up to her homely lord,
And with domestic plenty loads the board.
Not all the lustful shellfish of the sea,
Dressed by the wanton hand of luxury,   60
Nor ortolans nor godwits nor the rest
Of costly names that glorify a feast,
Are at the princely tables better cheer,
Than lamb and kid, lettuce and olives here.

52 *pin* 'bolt'.
53 'She waits until her husband returns'.
57 *homely* 'household'.
59–60 Shellfish are reckoned aphrodisiac; and 'lustful' is picked up in 'wanton' and 'luxury'.

61 *ortolan* only half naturalizing Horace's exotic fowl: the word has a French flavour.
64 Abridges the original (55–60) and then abandons the final ten lines.

Lucy Hutchinson (1620–1681)

Memoirs of the Life of Colonel Hutchinson, the work by which Lucy Hutchinson has until recently been best known, was written as a memoir for her children, and published only in 1806 (and most recently as edited by N. H. Keeble, *Memoirs of the Life of Colonel Hutchinson*, London: Dent, 1995); the children would likewise have been the beneficiaries of the fragmentary autobiography which was published along with it. Born Lucy Apsley, daughter of the Lieutenant of the Tower of London, she was educated into Latinity ('My father would have me learn Latin, and I was so apt that I outstripped my brothers . . . although . . . my tutor was a pitiful dull fellow') and Puritan piety together (she smashed her playmates' dolls), and incidentally to what she acknowledges 'a melancholy negligence both of herself and others'. Scarred by smallpox, in 1638 she married reluctantly a man who yet 'loved her soul and her honour more than her outside' (*Memoirs*) and had wooed her like a hero out of romance. In 1641 the family settled at Owthorpe in Nottinghamshire; during the War, the Colonel was Governor of Nottingham, and from 1646 served as MP for Nottinghamshire. Uncomfortable in politics, he retired to Owthorpe at the Dissolution of 1653 and like Lord Fairfax cultivated his garden. The Colonel died in prison in 1664, saved by his wife's best efforts (and against his own) from execution as a regicide (he had signed the warrant for King Charles's execution), but awaiting trial as party to a republican conspiracy. Lucy Hutchinson bore eight children and was to her husband 'a very faithful mirror, reflecting truly, though but dimly his own glories upon him'. She was also a poet. The letter gifting the translation of Lucretius to the Earl of Anglesey describes it as the product of no serious study 'for I turned it into English in a room where my children practised the several qualities they were taught by their tutors, and I numbered the syllables of my translation with the threads of the canvas I wrought in'; but it is the product of an educated and a practised facility. Her poetry is only now being recovered or brought to print. The translation of Lucretius is edited by Hugh de Quehen (London: Duckworth, 1996). David Norbrook has given her Republican response to Waller in 'Lucy Hutchinson versus Edmund Waller: An Unpublished Reply to Waller's *A Panegyrick to My Lord Protector*', *Seventeenth Century*, 11:1 (1996), 61–86; and the personal voice which some complain of missing in the *Memoirs* with 'Lucy Hutchinson's "Elegies" and the Situation of the Republican Woman Writer', *English Literary Renaissance*, 27 (1997), 468–521. He has also identified as hers some 8000 lines of verse related to a poem, *Order and Disorder*, only a quarter its length, published anonymously in 1679 (*TLS*, 19 March 1999). She has been credited with translating Virgil, perhaps because the portions of Denham's *Aeneid* transcribed in her Commonplace Book (now in the Nottinghamshire Archives) were taken for her own. Her excuse for translating the Epicurean Lucretius (the first complete version, though John Evelyn's version of Book 1 was printed in 1656 and more survives in MS) is his hostility to superstition. Most editorial work on the poetry post-dates Elizabeth H. Hageman's contextualizing account of Hutchinson in 'Recent Studies in Women Writers of the English Seventeenth Century, 1604–1674', reprinted from *English Literary Renaissance* in *Women in the Renaissance*, ed. with Kirby Farrell and Arthur Kinney (Amherst: University of Massachusetts Press, 1988).

The Fear of Death: from Lucretius

British Library Additional MS 19333, a quarto book mainly in the hand of a professional scribe, but with Book 6 of Lucretius's poem, the marginal notes and the dedicatory to the Earl of Anglesey in Hutchinson's own hand. The punctuation here is less conservatively presented than in De Quehen's edition. It is likely that Hutchinson used the 1631 edition of Lucretius by Pareus (Daniel Paré), sometimes appealing to the earlier (and superior) second edition of Lucretius by Lambinus (1570). Hutchinson's 'Argument of the Third Book' (lines 25–40) gives the sense of this concluding section (3:870–1094) as follows: 'And since death souls and bodies both doth kill / We therefore ought not to dread any ill / In death, which doth our woes in Lethe steep / And when our day expires gives us sweet sleep / That none can the tracked paths of death decline / But to their next successors must resign / That life they from the former race received; / Nor living have they reason to be grieved / With thoughts what shall after death befall; / The plagues which poets feigned in Hell, being all / Allusions only to the pain men find / When guilt or passion works upon the mind. / The poet hence persuades us to embrace / Gladly our death, since even the longest race, / The most illustrious, and the best all tend / Unto mankind's inevitable end'. The progress of the argument remains obscure, partly because the translating procedure follows so closely on the accidental difficulties of the Latin (sometimes imperfectly understood). The notes therefore carry summaries as well as Hutchinson's marginal cues (given as 'Margin'); these aim to help the reader stand above the tortured syntax. 'The third book above all is that which ought to be read with most judgement and discretion', says Tanneguy Lefèvre, not because like portions of Book 4 it is sexually scandalous, but because it argues that the soul is corporeal. Hutchinson signals her rejection of Lucretius's atheism, but the painful eloquence of his nihilism (contradicting 'easy Epicureanism') motivates her own.

Further, when men an indignation have	950
To think their bodies must corrupt in th' grave,	
Consume in scorching flames, or feed wild beasts,	
A secret error lurketh in their breasts,	
Which, though they contrary beliefs may feign,	
Persuades them they some sense in death retain,	955
That something beyond human life extends,	
And part of them the mortal bound transcends.	
Whoever now alive, could know, that dead,	
Fowls, and wild beasts, should with his flesh be fed	
Grieving, himself he would not vindicate	960
Nor from the exposèd carcass separate,	
But think it him, his soul with sad sense stain	
His mortal composition would disdain,	
Not weighing, that a real death doth leave	
No part alive which sorrow can conceive	965
For the other's fate, or standing can deplore	
The fallen corpse, which beasts or flames devour.	
If 't be an ill in death, t' have bodies torn	
By ravenous beasts, is 't less to burn	
In scorching flames, in honey to be drowned,	970
To freeze in marble vaults, or in cold ground	
Bear loads of earth? but yet the mourners cry,	
"Ah thy best wife, thy dearest family	
No more shall harbour thee, no more shalt thou	
With an indulgent fondness, kisses now	975
From thy sweet sons receive, no more defend	
Thy youth-got glories, one sad day doth end	
Thy whole life's joys" (to this, it is not said,	
And all desires of these forsake thee dead,	
Which rightly apprehended, minds would be	980
Eased of much care and sad anxiety).	
"Death's quiet sleep hides from thine eyes	
All present ills, and future miseries,	
But no day can our woeful breasts relieve,	
Or make us cease eternally to grieve	985

950–67 When a man laments that after death he will rot or be prey to beasts, there is something wrong with him: he does not separate his dead carcass from his present self, and cannot see that after death there will be no other self to stand by and mourn the mangled self (Lucretius, 870–87).

953–5 'How much this poor deluded bewitched mad wretch strives to put out the dim light of nature which while he contends against he acknowledges' (Margin): not a summary but a criticism of Lucretius.

960 *vindicate* 'liberate' (a frequent sense in the period).

962–3 'But he would imagine he and the carcass were one thing, and his soul would infect his mortal remains with feeling, so that he would feel resentful.'

968–1007 'The vanity of our being anxious for our sepulture' (Margin). Lucretius argues that if it be an evil after death to be torn by wild beasts, then cremation, embalming or burial are equally so; that men say we will see no more wife, home and children, but do not add that we will no longer care for them anyway; others say we sleep freed from all ills, but they remain to mourn; we might ask why they mourn if the dead only sleep; some say 'enjoy the moment' for it cannot be recalled; but after death we shall not feel the want of wine or anything else; and if in sleep we have no thought for death, how much less in death (888–930).

976–7 *defend . . . glories* misconstruing 'You will no longer be able to live in prosperity, nor to defend your own.'

For thee, whom horrid flames to ashes burn."
If all in death to quiet sleep return,
From what strange love doth this affliction flow?
What makes men languish thus in ceaseless woe?
Mortals oft do the same when they lie down   990
At their full cups, their heads with chaplets crown,
Saying, "The joys of human life are small,
What's now flies hence, which we can ne'er recall."
As if in death the chief ill wretches share,
Unquenched thirsts, droughts, and vehement longings were.   995
As when bodies and souls in sleep are joined,
Men in themselves no sense of life then find,
No more desires, or wants at that time have
Than those who sleep forever in the grave,
Yet the first bodies then within us stay,   1000
Nor far from sense-producing motions stray,
Which when we wake, soon recollected be.
But death itself is less (if a degree
Can that which is not anything befit)
For all the matter is dissolved by it.   1005
Nor ever yet hath anyone revived
Whom death's cold hand of vital breath deprived.
Lastly, should Nature take a voice, she thus
Might frame her just reproaches against us,
"Frail man why wail'st thou so thy mortal state?   1010
Why do salt tears thy sorrows aggravate?
If thy past life hath shared prosperity,
If pleasures have not flowed away from thee,
As water through a sieve, nor finished
In bitterness, why, as a guest full fed,   1015
Depart'st thou not content, from this large feast
To thy secure and everlasting rest?
But if thy joys have vanished, if th' hast had
Offence in life, why seek'st thou yet to add
More days which sorrow will conclude again,   1020
Nor rather striv'st with life to end life's pain?
For thee I can no other pleasures frame,
Nor find one joy, which is not still the same.
Though feeble age should not thy members waste,
Though to all future times thy life should last,   1025
And thou from death shouldst be forever freed,
No new thing could in that long life succeed."
If nature should thus plead with us, we must
Acknowledge all her reasons to be just.

---

988   *what strange love* misconstruing 'What bitterness is there
so great that one should forever grieve' (she takes *amari*
('bitter') as 'to be loved').
1003–4   'if what is nothing can be measured'.
1008–51   'How justly Nature might reproach our discontents'
(Margin). If Nature were to ask why we lament death, why,
if life has been pleasant, we do not go satisfied with the feast
enjoyed, for even if life were eternal she would have nothing

new to give, then we should have to concede her argument;
or if an old man were to weep at the prospect of death she
would surely be right to make him stop, arguing that the
fault was his own if had not enjoyed himself, that he should
make way for others, and pointing out that they follow him
as he did others, that life is only lent (931–71).
1014   *water through a sieve* Not in Lucretius, but antici-
pated from 1090–1.

Though she should sharper reprehensions give 1030
To such as more immoderately grieve
With thoughts of death – to whom, especially
If they were old, she might such words apply:
"Tears and complaints (insatiate wretch) suppress,
Who dost thy soul amidst life's joys distress, 1035
With eager wishes, still ill satisfied
In what thou hast, thy transient life doth glide
Unpleasantly away, and ere thou art fed
With life's enjoyments, death hangs o'er thy head
Thy age is spent, yield then what is not thine 1040
And to the next race willingly resign" –
Just would these reprehensions be, for still
New generations do the old expel,
And things from things successively arise,
No matter goes to hell, nor wholly dies 1045
But is revived in the succeeding race,
Which must like this give the next-comers place
After their term's expired, as those before
Yielded to them, that they may still restore
The wastes of time, none properly can call 1050
This life his own, which is but lent to all.
Eternal time before our births, which now
Doth not concern our lives, may show us how
After our deaths we in the silent grave,
Of future ages shall no knowledge have. 1055
Do former woes or terrors our sense wound?
Are they not all in sleep-like stillness drowned?
But in this present life those miseries reign
Which men in Acheron's dark prisons feign,
No Tantalus there, afflicted with vain dread, 1060
Fears hanging rocks, should fall upon his head.
'Tis superstition in this life creates
Those causeless terrors of ensuing fates.
No Tityus lies stretched out in hell's dark shade
Nor are his entrails food to vultures made, 1065
Which could not yield them infinite supplies,
Though his large body on nine acres lies,
For were his members o'er the whole earth spread
They could not be with them for ever fed,

1030 *Though* The main clause appears only at line 1042, after a parenthesis beginning 'to whom', whose end is cued by the repetition of 'reprehensions'; this is not Lucretius's syntax.

1046 *race* 'generation'.

1050 *wastes of time* 'devastations' or 'deserts'; but the play on squandering time is inescapable.

1051 *lent* 'No man possesses the freehold on life, we are all tenants' (the original conveyancing metaphor is mitigated).

1052–105 'That the plagues of Hell are but allegories of the miseries of this life. Many a wicked soul who would ease itself with thinking so will find it otherwise' (Margin); Hutchinson rejects allegories. Lucretius argues that just as what took place before our birth is nothing to us; so should our post-mortem future be, that Tantalus and the rest are types of those tormented by various passions and only pictures of the punishments we suffer in the world (Lucretius 972–1023).

1059 *Acheron's dark prisons* 'Hell'.

1060–1 Tantalus is more familiarly cast as a metaphor of greed and punished with perpetual hunger and thirst; his being threatened by an impending rock is a punishment sometimes assigned for some other unspecified crime ('causeless terrors').

1064–75 The giant Tityus, whose liver is perpetually devoured by a vulture, is punished for rape; he is a metaphor for lust.

Nor could one body still such force sustain   1070
Or last forever in that endless pain.
But unto us, Tityus is, he, who bears
Love in his bosom, whom each passion tears,
Whom anxious desires do over-power,
And whom consuming cares and griefs devour.   1075
They in this life resemble Sisyphus
Who court the vulgar, still ambitious
Of public place, and still meet a defeat
With which they full of grief and spite retreat.
For empire to affect, which is but vain,   1080
And oft repulsed, to toil for it again,
In this, that stone forced up the hill is found,
Which still at top, rolls back to the plain ground.
And then a thankless nature to supply,
Whom no good thing can ever satisfy,   1085
Which to ungrateful men the seasons do,
When they their pleasures and their fruits renew,
Yet life's enjoyments yield them no content,
This doth those youthful virgins represent,
On whom they feign imposed, that fruitless task   1090
Still to pour water in a borèd cask.
Cerberus, the Furies, the dark realm of night
Breathing forth dismal horror, and affright,
These neither are, nor can be anywhere
But in this life. That most prevailing fear   1095
Which foul guilt, in the conscious breast contracts,
Becomes the punishment of impious facts.
Dark prisons, steep rocks, whence they headlong fall
Whips, tortures, racks, flames, coulters, pitch, and all
Those plagues, which former ages did invent,   1100
For no less scourges guilty minds torment,
Who their deservèd mischiefs apprehend,
But know no term which can their suff'rings end;
Because in death they dread a further ill,
And thus the life of fools becomes their hell.   1105
This may'st thou also in thy thoughts recite:

1076–83 The punishment of Sisyphus, not clearly related to his crimes as a robber or tyrant, is a metaphor for the fatuity of ambition.

1080 *empire to affect* 'to desire power'.

1084–91 Forty-nine of the fifty daughters of Danaus, in obedience to their fearful father, murdered their husbands on their wedding night; their crime is a metaphor of ingratitude. Hutchinson's play of the 'fruitless task' (1090) against the seasonal 'fruits' (1087) simplifies a different play in Lucretius of the girls 'in their flower' and the 'fruits of life'.

1092 The dog Cerberus and the three Furies (daughters of the river Acheron), the darkness, are a standard part of what Dryden, translating this passage, calls 'the vain infernal trumpery'.

1095–1104 Hutchinson seems to mean that the overwhelming ('prevailing') fear which our having done ill ('foul guilt' in 'conscious breasts') incurs ('contracts') is fit ('becomes') punishment for our crimes ('impious facts'), and that mental

scourges worse than any our ancestors contrived remain to afflict us. Lucretius writes (1014–22): 'There is a fear of punishments in this life for things ill done, these as severe as those, and there is payment to be made for crime: prison . . . And even if these are absent, the guilty mind, fearful before the event, applies the goad and scorches itself with scourges, and does not see what term there could be to its sufferings or what limit to its punishments, and dreads lest they grow heavier in death.'

1098 *steep . . . fall* Lucretius writes: 'frightful casting down from the [Tarpeian] Rock'; Hutchinson interrupts her own syntax.

1099 *racks* perhaps misunderstanding Lucretius's word for 'dungeon'; *coulters* 'blades' (as instruments of torture).

1105 *fools* 'non-sceptics'.

1106–29 'Persuading willingness to die because all do it' (Margin); Lucretius says we should reflect that kings and philosophers die (1024–44).

"Ancus, that virtuous king, forsook the light,
Who common men excelled in divers things;
Great captains die, and all commanding kings.
That thunderbolt of war, high Carthage, dread, 1110
Scipio, who on the Ocean's bosom spread
His gallant fleet fraught with land forces,
With conquering legions and with barbèd horses,
Who taught his valiant followers to despise
The threats of murmuring waves, yet were his eyes 1115
At length closed up in death, his frail soul fled
Forth of his fainting limbs, in a cold bed
Of earth his bones were laid, nor in the grave
Enjoy more privilege than the meanest slave.
Those who in learning or in wit excelled, 1120
The mates of Helicon, and Homer held
The sovereign Muse all sleep like other men.
So doth the sage Democritus, who when
He found old age his vigorous soul declined,
He, uncompelled, himself to death resigned. 1125
So Epicurus having run his race
Gave up life's flaming torch; he who did trace
Mankind's original, the motion
Of every star, and of the ethereal sun.
Canst thou (O mortal then) who dost remain 1130
Half dead in life, so much thy death disdain?
Thou who to sleep most of thy time dost give,
Who rav'st awake, nor canst thy dreams perceive,
Who bear'st about vain terror in thy mind,
Nor yet when wine distempers thee canst find 1135
The cause of thine own ill, what floating care
And what distractions in thy wild brains are."
If men were burdens to their souls, as they
Seem to conceive, and knew that weight that lay
So heavy on them, whence they were oppressed, 1140
What load of mischief lodged within their breast,
They would not lead their lives as now they do,
Nor various wills unconstantly pursue,

1107 *Ancus* The fourth, legendarily good king of Rome.
1110–17 Scipio Africanus Major, the dread of Carthage, was the conqueror of Hannibal but died falsely disgraced. Hutchinson has conflated the account of him with the account of Xerxes (unnamed by Lucretius) identified by his bridging the Hellespont.
1113 *barbèd* 'armoured'.
1116 *frail* Hutchinson's addition.
1121 'Poets (companions of the Heliconian maids or Muses), even Homer the highest poet, die.'
1123–5 The dying Democritus, the 'laughing philosopher', timed his death to oblige his sister.
1124 'He found old age bowed down ('declined') his spirit.'
1126–9 Misconstruing 'when the light of his life ran out, there died Epicurus himself, who with his genius surpassed the human race as the sun in heaven rises and puts out all the stars' (1042–4).

1130–63 'From the frailty of our lives he shows how vain it is to hope to 'scape death' (Margin). Lucretius asks why men should live who snore life away; they feel a burden on their minds and if they knew why they would not live always in flight from themselves but would give up everything else to study the nature of things and learn what is to be their eternal condition (1045–75).
1131 *disdain* 'take offence at'.
1133 'You snore with your eyes open and cannot see through your dreams' (Lucretius, 1048).
1136 *floating* 'unstable'; in Lucretius, applied to 'you'.
1138–9 Misconstruing: 'If men could know and understand, as much as they seem to feel the weight inhering in the mind and wearing them out with its heaviness, from what causes it comes . . .'
1143 *wills* 'desires'.

Change place, as if they could put off their loads,
And tired at home, forsake their own abodes,   1145
And when without, their cares do not abate,
Turn home again, oppressed with the same weight,
Then to their village ride with eager speed,
As if fired houses did their quick help need,
But ent'ring there, they gape, no better pleased,   1150
And with forgetful sleeps seek to be eased.
Or to the town in haste post back again.
While they perceive not that they do retain
Within their breasts that sad anxiety
Which they in other places strive to fly.   1155
And wheresoever they may vainly run
Themselves in every place they cannot shun.
But if sick minds knew whence their trouble springs
They then would casting off all other things
Dive into nature's mysteries, and find   1160
Eternal time leaves no short hour behind,
Which after death can with frail mortals stay,
Whose whole age in that moment flies away.
      Lastly what evil love of life doth give
Us fond desires in perilous states to live?   1165
A certain death on every mortal waits
And none can shun the entry' of his gates;
All human life repeats but still the same
And no time ever can new pleasures frame,
Those joys seem best which wanting we pursue,   1170
But once obtained, we thirst again for new.
This life is but a progress of desires
Which evermore supplied, new things requires.
We live in doubt what future fortunes shall
Arrive, what chance, what death shall us befall,   1175
Yet by protracting life, we cannot take
Away from death, nor that sleep shorter make.
Though many ages should prolong our day
Our night would not be less by that delay.
As everlasting death shall us possess   1180
As his whose stay in this life was much less.
For who expired long since, and he who died
This day, shall equal space in death abide.

1146   *without* 'away from home'.
1148   *village* 'villa' (naturalizing the word or the notion).
1150   *gape* 'yawn'.
1160–3   Translating 'since what is in doubt is the condition (for eternity not for an hour) in which all time remaining after death is to be passed by those who die' (1073–5).
1164–83   'Exhorting willingness to die: the cause all do it' (margin, but cancelled). Lucretius argues the futility of craving life when there is nothing more to experience, and recom-
mends considering that the eternity of death will not be reduced by living longer (1076–94).
1170   'It is the pursuit of pleasures we do not have makes them seem best.'
1172–3   Desires are insatiable as kings with their trains on a progress or tour of the kingdom; Lucretius's metaphor is of unquenchable thirst.
1178–9   The metaphor of day and night is added.

Andrew Marvell (1621–1678)

In 1653 Milton wrote to the President of the Council of State supporting Marvell's application for an assistant's post in the Latin secretary's office, recommending him as one 'both by report, and the converse I have had with him, of singular desert for the State to make use of . . . His father was the minister of Hull and he hath spent four years abroad in Holland, France, Italy and Spain, to very good purpose . . . and the gaining of those four languages; besides he is a scholar and well-read in the Latin and Greek authors, and no doubt of an approved conversation for he comes now lately out of the house of the Lord Fairfax . . . where he was entrusted to give some instructions in the languages to the lady his daughter.' The application was unsuccessful, but he secured the Latin secretaryship in 1657. He had graduated from Trinity College, Cambridge, in 1639, but stayed on (perhaps in hopes of a fellowship) until 1641, the year his father drowned in the Humber. His four years abroad began sometime in 1642 (the First Civil War began in August); he returned at the end of the War in 1647. In the *History of his own Time* (first Latin edition 1726) the hostile Samuel Parker describes him on his return as one 'of but indifferent parts, except it were the talent of railing and malignity . . . a vagabond, ragged, hungry poetaster'. His poems for the edition of Lovelace's *Lucasta* and the death of Lord Hastings (both 1649) put him in Royalist company (Lovelace was a loyal Royalist prisoner). But he was employed by the retired Lord General Fairfax after 1650; and after his unsuccessful application to the Council of State in 1653 was tutor to Cromwell's proposed son-in-law William Dutton, whom he accompanied to France a 'notable English Italo-Machiavellian' (according to one witness). On Parker's hostile account, the quarto publication of *The First Anniversary of the Government under his Highness the Lord Protector* (1655) was another bid for favour (made anonymously). Other congratulatory poems to Cromwell were not published at this time. From 1659 he was MP for Hull, to his friends a patriotic defender of constitutional liberties, who served 'with such wisdom, dexterity, integrity and courage as becomes a true patriot' (as the tombstone has it in St Giles Church). He was, as an anonymous encomiast has it, 'this island's watchful sentinel'.

Marvell's literary reputation, never publicly courted, was almost entirely owing to his satires in prose or verse; Rochester, Aubrey tells us, called him 'the only man in England that had the true vein of satire' (a compliment Marvell returned). He acknowledged only one piece of controversial prose, the late *Growth of Popery* (1678), a serious account of the erosion of Parliamentary rights. But he was widely known as the author of *The Rehearsal Transprosed* (1672, Part 2, 1673), a defence (against Archdeacon Parker) of religious toleration as set out in the royal *Declaration of Indulgence* (1672): it was, said Rochester's confessor, Gilbert Burnet, one of 'the wittiest books that have appeared in this age'. The verse satires, rough like Oldham's, were collected in editions of *Poems on Affairs of State* from 1689. The miscellaneous poems were not widely known, and not widely appreciated until this century; they are poems, despite the heavily historicized readings of them now current, which are insulated from their contexts, by and large undatable, by and large inexplicable. The standard biography is Pierre Legouis's *André Marvell: poète, puritain, patriote* (Paris: Didier, 1928; reprinted New York: Russell and Russell, 1965) and the abridged and revised English version *Andrew Marvell: Poet, Puritan, Patriot*, second edition (Oxford: Clarendon Press, 1968). The edition of *Miscellaneous Poems* (1681) was prepared by Marvell's landlady or self-styled wife, Mary Palmer (or Mary Marvell); it contains none of the later satires. There is a facsimile edition, along with some later texts from Bodleian MS Eng. poet. d. 49 (Menston: Scolar Press, 1969). The standard edition of the poems is *The Poems and Letters of Andrew Marvell*, ed. H. M. Margoliouth, revised by Pierre Legouis and E. E. Duncan-Jones, 2 vols (Oxford: Clarendon Press, 1971). A useful one-volume edition of *The Complete Poems* is edited by E. S. Donne (Harmondsworth: Penguin, 1972). *The Rehearsal Transpros'd, and, The Rehearsal Transpros'd, the Second Part* is edited by D. I. B. Smith (Oxford: Clarendon Press, 1971). A. B. Grosart, *The Complete Works in Verse and Prose* (Blackburn: The Fuller Worthies Library, 1872–3, reprinted 1966) remains the only place where all the prose can be found. George R. Guffey has prepared a *Concordance to the English Poems of Andrew Marvell* (Chapel Hill: University of North Carolina Press, 1974). Early criticism is anthologized by Elizabeth S. Donno in *Andrew Marvell: The Critical Heritage* (London: Routledge, 1978); more recent criticism is described by Dan S. Collins in *Andrew Marvell: A Reference Guide* (Boston: G. K. Hall, 1981).

The Definition of Love

1681. Not properly a definition, more a demonstration (whence the geometrical bias of the language), and not so much of love as of desire. Cowley denies the possibility of impossibilities: 'Impossibilities? O no, there's none . . . As stars (not powerful else) when they conjoin, / Change, as they please, the world's estate; / So thy heart in conjunction with mine, / Shall our own fortunes regulate; / And to our stars themselves prescribe a fate' (1.11–15). Here the Platonist recommendation of unfulfillability is embraced with enthusiasm and rendered (nonsensically) heroic.

My love is of a birth as rare
As 'tis for object strange and high:
It was begotten by Despair
Upon Impossibility.

Magnanimous Despair alone   5
Could show me so divine a thing,
Where feeble Hope could ne'er have flown
But vainly flapped its tinsel wing.

And yet I quickly might arrive
Where my extended soul is fixed,   10
But Fate does iron wedges drive,
And always crowds itself betwixt.

For Fate with jealous eye does see
Two perfect Loves; nor lets them close:
Their union would her ruin be,   15
And her tyrannic power depose.

And therefore her decrees of steel
Us as the distant poles have placed,
(Though Love's whole world on us doth wheel)
Not by themselves to be embraced.   20

Unless the giddy heaven fall,
And Earth some new convulsion tear;
And, us to join, the world should all
Be cramped into a planisphere.

1–8 'Disconsolate and sad / So little hope of remedy I find, / That when my matchless mistress were inclined / To pity me, 'twould scarcely make me glad' (Edward Herbert, *Platonic Love*).
4 *impossibility* the speaker's 'unableness'.
5–8 Despair is magnanimous because the speaker generously reconciles himself to expecting nothing; but since his attention shifts to a diviner object, he has apparently gained heroic 'resolution from despair'.
9–10 As the souls of Donne's lovers are 'gone out' (*Ecstasy*, 16).
11–12 'Thin like an iron wedge, so sharp and tart, / As 'twere of purpose made to cleave Love's heart' (Chapman, *Hero and Leander*, 5:299–300, of a gossip's face). Horace's Necessitas comes with instruments of torture, 'spikes and wedges in her brazen hand' (*Odes*, 1.35.17–19), and in the Second Part of *The Rehearsal Transprosed* Marvell writes of 'a necessity that . . . drove the great iron nail through the axletree of nature' (picked up at 19); but this Fate presses ('crowds') itself between the lovers, its wedges 'iron' because unyielding.
12 Spenser's jealous Malbecco keeps 'continual spy' on his wife 'with his other blinked eye' (*Faerie Queene*, 3.9.5).
13 *close* 'unite'.
18–24 Those who hope to reconcile Catholic and Protestant 'may with the same hopes, expect a union in the poles of heaven' (Thomas Browne, *Religio Medici*, 1.4).
24 *planisphere* 'a sphere projected on to a plane' (having 'both his poles clapped flat together').

As lines so loves oblique may well　　　　　　　　　　25
Themselves in every angle greet:
But ours so truly parallel,
Though infinite can never meet.

Therefore the love which us doth bind,
But Fate so enviously debars,　　　　　　　　　　　30
Is the conjunction of the mind,
And opposition of the stars.

25–8 Euclid defines parallel lines as 'such, which being . . . produced infinitely on both sides, do never in any part concur' (Billingsley); lines are oblique only in relation to other lines which they meet at an angle (or unheroically 'in corners').

29–32 Cowley's hopeful conjunction is cancelled; here 'opposition' means only 'hostility'.

To his Coy Mistress

1681, except as noted. Bodleian MS Eng. poet. d.9 is the standard corrective; Bodleian MS Don. b.8 may relate to an earlier draft. The argument ('If we had eternity, we could delay; but our time is short; therefore let us seize the present moment') is a 'broken syllogism'; but the defective logic is only a medium in which the ancient topics of sexual urgency, beauty's fragility, and the defeat of time are rehearsed with great concentration. Randolph prays to Cupid for 'such a mistress . . . as will be coy. / Not easily won, though to be won in time' (*A Complaint against Cupid*, 149–50); Marvell loses interest in the strictly sexual project.

Had we but world enough, and time,
This coyness lady were no crime.
We would sit down, and think which way
To walk, and pass our long love's day.
Thou by the Indian Ganges' side　　　　　　　　　　5
Shouldst rubies find: I by the tide
Of Humber would complain. I would
Love you ten years before the Flood:
And you should if you please refuse
Till the Conversion of the Jews.　　　　　　　　　10
My vegetable love should grow
Vaster then empires, and more slow.
An hundred years should go to praise
Thine eyes, and on thy forehead gaze.
Two hundred to adore each breast:　　　　　　　　15
But thirty thousand to the rest.

3–4 ' We could afford to spend time thinking . . . how to pass this day devoted to the love we have long felt.'

5–7 The rivers mark out huge spaces as in Juvenal, 10:1–2: 'from farthest West, / And the Atlantic Isles, unto the East / And famous Ganges' (Vaughan); Marvell's father was drowned in the Humber in 1641.

7–10 Two precise dates may be involved: *1656 anno mundi* for Noah's flood and *1656 anno Domini* for the Conversion of the Jews, a preliminary to the Second Coming; the lady would then have little time. But Thomas Browne writes, 'It is the promise of Christ to make us all one flock; but how and when this union shall be, is as obscure to me as the last

day' (*Religio Medici*, 1.25). The lady is anyway being 'Jewish' ('unforthcoming') with her love.

11–12 Gallus writes Lycoris's name on young trees: 'The rind of every plant her name shall know; / And, as the rind extends, the love shall grow' (Virgil, *Eclogues*, 10:53–4); 'vaster' plays with 'faster'.

13–18 Remembering Cowley's arithmetical love-making: 'On a sigh of pity I a year can live. / One tear will keep me twenty at least. / Fifty a gentle look will give, / A hundred years on one kind word I'll feast; / A thousand more will added be / If you an inclination have for me; / And all beyond is vast eternity' (*The Diet*, 15–21).

An age at least to every part,
And the last age should show your heart.
For lady you deserve this state;
Nor would I love at lower rate.   20
     But at my back I always hear
Time's wingèd chariot hurrying near:
And yonder all before us lie
Deserts of vast eternity.
Thy beauty shall no more be found;   25
Nor, in thy marble vault, shall sound
My echoing song: then worms shall try
That long preserved virginity:
And your quaint honour turn to dust;
And into ashes all my lust.   30
The grave's a fine and private place,
But none I think do there embrace.
     Now therefore, while the youthful glew
Sits on thy skin like morning dew,
And while thy willing soul transpires   35
At every pore with instant fires,
Now let us sport us while we may;
And now, like amorous birds of prey,
Rather at once our time devour,
Than languish in his slow-chapped power.   40
Let us roll all our strength, and all
Our sweetness, up into one ball.
And tear our pleasures with rough strife,
Thorough the iron gates of life.
Thus, though we cannot make our sun   45
Stand still, yet we will make him run.

19–20 'For you deserve this honour: I would not love you at a lesser price' ('rate' plays with 'speed' already excessively low).

21–2 The wings belong to Time and not to his chariot, though 'winged' may simply mean 'speedy' (as when Stanley [*Celia Singing*, 5] talks of 'the wingèd chariot of the light').

25–32 Developing a famous epigram by Asclepiades: 'Why hoarding your virginity? For when you've gone down to Hades you'll not find the lover you lack. The joys of Venus are enjoyed only among the living, and only as bones and dust shall we lie in Acheron' (*Greek Anthology*, 5.85). 'Virginity', 'honour' and 'lust' may all have concrete sexual reference in *précieux* jargon; the sexual use of the noun 'quaint' is not precious at all, but Spenser's 'every look was coy, and wondrous quaint' (*Faerie Queene*, 4.1.5) suggests the primary sense.

33–4 The rhyme-words in *1681* are 'hew'/'glew'; both MSS have 'glew' (or 'glue')/'dew', preferred here. Bodleian MS Don. b.8 spells 'glue' (perhaps as 'sweat', or as what holds body and soul together), the sense fitting with its 'sticks' for 'sits'. The sense 'glow' is easier (as in Lovelace's 'Behold Lucasta's face, how't glows like noon!', *As I Beheld a Winter Evening's Air*, 16).

35–6 Echoing Crashaw; 'What did their weapons but with wider pores / Enlarge thy flaming-breasted lovers, / More freely to transpire / That impatient fire' (*To the Name above Every Name*, 206–9).

37–40 Bodleian MS Don. b.8 reads: 'Or like the amorous birds of prey, / Scorning to admit delay, / Let us at once ourselves devour, / Not linger in time's slow-chapped power'. This perhaps earlier version recalls Sylvester's story of an eagle which resorts to self-mutilation and suicide in its impatience to follow the mistress who had tended it (*Divine Weeks*, 1.5.986–1098). The revision instead inverts the notion of Time the devourer: the lovers eat time, which (being 'slow-jawed') eats too slowly for them.

41–4 Origen (adapting Plato, *Symposium*,189–90) argues that we pass into Paradise as spheres (here compounded of his strength and her sweetness), in imitation of the wholeness of God.

44 *iron gates of life* iron grates of life (Bodleian MS Eng. poet. d.49). By devouring time the lovers hasten the end of the world (10) and destroy the barrier which prevents their fulfilment: 'Ah what doth Phoebus' gold that wretch avail, / Whom iron doors do keep from use of day' (Sidney, *Astrophil*, 108). The proverbial 'gates of death' is parodied, 'iron' perhaps recalling Spenser's gate into death set in an iron wall (*Faerie Queene*, 3.6.31), but suggesting a contrast with 'rosy gates' (for *labia*, as in Lovelace's *Lucasta, Taking the Waters at Tunbridge*, 7).

45–6 Joshua stopped the sun (Joshua 10: 12) and the lovers cannot; but by behaving like Time – 'devouringly' – they can make the sun run: as Time runs he bears all along with him.

Eyes and Tears

1681; there is an early partial reprint in *Poetical Recreations* (1688). Marvell's argument, the fundamental identity of seeing and weeping (anticipated in Shakespeare's 'O how her eyes and tears did lend and borrow / Her eyes seen in the tears, tears in the eyes' [*Venus and Adonis*, 962–3]), gives the poem more direction than most exercises on the subject, certainly including its likely immediate inspiration, Crashaw's *The Weeper*. An early version survives in Bodelian MS Tanner 306. Marvell's Crashavian Latin version of stanza 8 reads: 'Magdala, lascivos sic quum dimisit amantes, / Fervidaque in castas lumina solvit aquas; / Haesit in irriguo lachrimarum compede Christus, / Et tenuit sacros uda catena pedes.'

1

How wisely Nature did decree,
With the same eyes to weep and see!
That, having viewed the object vain,
They might be ready to complain.

2

And, since the self-deluding sight,　　　　　　　　　　5
In a false angle takes each height;
These tears which better measure all,
Like watery lines and plummets fall.

3

Two tears, which sorrow long did weigh
Within the scales of either eye,　　　　　　　　　　　10
And then paid out in equal poise,
Are the true price of all my joys.

4

What in the world most fair appears,
Yea even laughter, turns to tears:
And all the jewels which we prize,　　　　　　　　　　15
Melt in these pendants of the eyes.

5

I have through every garden been,
Amongst the red, the white, the green;
And yet, from all the flowers I saw,
No honey, but these tears could draw.　　　　　　　　20

1–2 'Care not for women's tears, I counsel thee, / They teach their eyes as much to weep as see' (Ovid, *Remedies of Love*, 689–90, in Burton, *Anatomy*, 3.2.2.4).
3 *vain* 'vanishing'.
5–6 'The tree erewhile foreshortened to our view, / When fallen shows taller yet than as it grew' (*A Poem upon the Death of O.C.*, 269–70).
7–12 Crashaw, *The Weeper*, 156, measures time with tears; Marvell measures verticals or 'rightness' (by line and plummet) and weight ('poise') in the 'scales' of his eyes ('balances', but punning on the sense 'agents of blindness' from Acts 9: 18).
14 Proverbially 'Some laugh amornings who ere night shed tears.'
15–16 When Crashaw's Sorrow would be seen in majesty 'she wears / Her proudest pearls; I mean, thy tears' (*The Weeper*, 22); 'pendants' are commonly ear-drops.
19–20 Because beauty makes us weep: 'As drops from a still doth Cupid's fire provoke tears' (Burton, *Anatomy*, 3.2.3).

6

So the all-seeing sun each day
Distils the world with chemic ray;
But finds the essence only showers,
Which straight in pity back he pours.

7

Yet happy they whom grief doth bless,   25
That weep the more, and see the less:
And, to preserve their sight more true,
Bathe still their eyes in their own dew.

8

So Magdalen, in tears more wise
Dissolved those captivating eyes,   30
Whose liquid chains could flowing meet
To fetter her Redeemer's feet.

9

Not full sails hasting laden home,
Nor the chaste lady's pregnant womb,
Nor Cynthia teeming shows so fair,   35
As two eyes swoln with weeping are.

10

The sparkling glance that shoots desire,
Drenched in these waves, does lose it fire.
Yea oft the Thunderer pity takes
And here the hissing lightning slakes.   40

11

The incense was to Heaven dear,
Not as a perfume, but a tear.
And stars show lovely in the night,
But as they seem the tears of light.

12

Ope then mine eyes your double sluice,   45
And practise so your noblest use.
For others too can see, or sleep;
But only human eyes can weep.

21–4   The cycle of evaporation and precipitation is invoked;
but the sun is thought of as a weeping eye as well as an
alchemist. An emblem by Henry Peacham shows a weeping
eye over a landscape (*Heu mihi quod vidi*): 'Look how the
limbeck gently down distils / In pearly drops his heart's
dear quintessence' (*Minerva Britanna*, 142).
25–8   'Blessed are they that mourn' (Matthew 5: 4); the
weeping Heraclitus thought that the eyes deceived.
29–32   The tears are 'more wise' because penitent; the
metaphor in 'captivating' is literalized by the final couplet.
33–6   Crashaw calls eyes 'fertile mothers' of tears and 'swoln

wombs of sorrow' (*The Weeper* (1646) for *1652*, 163–8);
'Cynthia teeming' is the 'full moon', with a glance at Diana
(Cynthia) as goddess of childbirth.
37–40   Varying Lovelace's conceit of the sun's being over-
come by Lucasta: 'But when her tears his heat o'ercame, /
In clouds he quenched his beams' (*Lucasta Weeping*, 5–6);
'it' is possessive ('its' in the Tanner MS).
41   Tears are 'holy frankincense' in Marvell's *The Nymph
Complaining*, 98.
43–4   Davenant has 'weeping for day / Night had put all
her jewels on' (*Gondibert*, 3.6.31).

13

Now like two clouds dissolving, drop,
And at each tear in distance stop: 50
Now like two fountains trickle down:
Now like two floods o'erturn and drown.

14

Thus let your streams o'erflow your springs,
Till eyes and tears be the same things:
And each the other's difference bears; 55
These weeping eyes, those seeing tears.

49–50 The rate of the rain is measured by the intervals between tears.
53 'Let tears run down like a river day and night . . . pour out thine heart like water' (Lamentations 2: 18–19).

55–6 The *differentiae* of eyes and tears are transferred: each has the distinguishing function of the other.

An Horatian Ode upon Cromwell's Return from Ireland

1681 except where noted. Only in two copies of *1681* does the poem survive; in others (such is the delicacy of its subject) the relevant gatherings were cancelled and replaced. Cromwell returned from Ireland in May 1650 to take part in the Scottish campaign, begun in late July of that year. May and July are therefore the termini of the poem's conception. Fairfax had meanwhile (12 June) resigned as commander-in-chief, unwilling to lead the invasion of Scotland. Marvell's position is not identifiable with Fairfax's; but though its drive is pro-Republican the poem is not uncomplicatedly pro-Cromwellian. The poem is advertised as Horatian. Horace's celebration of Drusus's Alpine victories (*Odes*, 4.4) is diverted by the focus on Hannibal's defeat in a war fought long before; so Marvell, whose rhetoric here is shaped by that poem, is diverted by the King's tragedy. The Horatian (or pseudo-Pindaric) colouring shows in the oblique treatment of events (extended simile is characteristic). The effect of Horatian metre is an illusion of the typography; but Fanshawe uses the same English metre to translate Horace's Posthumus ode (*Odes*, 2.14).

The forward youth that would appear
Must now forsake his Muses dear,
 Nor in the shadows sing
 His numbers languishing.
'Tis time to leave the books in dust, 5
And oil the unused armour's rust:
 Removing from the wall
 The corslet of the hall.
So restless Cromwell could not cease
In the inglorious arts of peace, 10
 But through advent'rous war
 Urgèd his active star.

1–24 Cromwell's leaving 'life in the shade' is briefly paralleled in the poet's own departure from his favoured non-heroic genres (inverting the more common refusal of heroic genres, as in Fanshawe's *Ode*). The phrasing owes much to Thomas May's version of Lucan's account of Caesar: 'But restless valour, and in war a shame / Not to be conqueror; fierce, not curbed at all, / Ready to fight, where hope, or anger call / His forward sword . . . O'erthrowing all that his ambition stay, / And loves that ruin should enforce his way; / As lightning by the wind forced from a cloud / Breaks through the wounded air with thunder loud, / Disturbs the way, the people terrifies, / And by a light oblique dazzles our eyes, / Not Jove's own temple spares it' (*Pharsalia*, 1:143–57), and the response to him: 'With this sad noise the people's rest was broke, / The young men rose, and from the temples took / Their arms, now such as long peace had marred. / And their old bucklers now of leather barred: / Their blunted pikes not of a long time used, / And swords with the eatings of black rust abused' (239–43).
12 *active star* the destiny which predisposed to 'activity' (as Shakespeare's Helena thinks Parolles was born under a 'charitable star', *All's Well*, I. i. 186); but it should be the star which urges.

And, like the three-forked lightning, first
Breaking the clouds where it was nursed,
   Did thorough his own side   15
   His fiery way divide.
For 'tis all one to courage high
The emulous or enemy;
   And with such to enclose
   Is more than to oppose.   20
Then burning through the air he went,
And palaces and temples rent:
   And Caesar's head at last
   Did through his laurels blast.
'Tis madness to resist or blame   25
The force of angry Heaven's flame:
   And, if we would speak true,
   Much to the man is due.
Who, from his private Gardens, where
He lived reservèd and austere,   30
   As if his highest plot
   To plant the bergamot,
Could by industrious valour climb
To ruin the great work of Time,
   And cast the kingdom old   35
   Into another mould.
Though Justice against Fate complain,
And plead the ancient rights in vain:
   But those do hold or break
   As men are strong or weak.   40
Nature that hateth emptiness,
Allows of penetration less:
   And therefore must make room
   Where greater spirits come.
What field of all the Civil Wars,   45
Where his were not the deepest scars?
   And Hampton shows what part
   He had of wiser art.
Where, twining subtle fears with hope,

15–16 Cromwell (not the lightning) first broke through his own side ('party') by effecting the dismissal of the Parliamentary army command early in 1645; 'thorough' is the MS expansion of *1681*'s 'through'.

17–20 'A great spirit treats competition and hostility as one; to cramp it is worse than to stand against it.'

23–4 Laurel supposedly guarded against lightning-strikes (Pliny, *Natural History*, 2.56), but even the laurel-crowned head of King Charles was not spared.

27–32 Cromwell's farming beginnings are remembered in the *First Anniversary*: 'For neither didst thou from the first apply / Thy sober spirit unto things too high, / But in thine own fields exercised'st long, / An healthful mind within a body strong' (229–32). The horticultural 'plot' is confused by 'stratagem'; and the bergamot was called the 'pear of kings'.

34–8 Cromwell is cast as the kingly eagle, at whose cry 'the common people tremble, the senators huddle . . . the laws give way, immemorial custom gives way; nothing can stand up against it, neither right, nor duty, nor custom, nor compassion' (Erasmus, *Adagia, Scarabeus aquilam quaerit*); he overcomes mere lawyers' interests ('Justice') and superseded ('ancient') rights. But Marvell had already accused May of prostituting his proper vocation to sing of 'ancient rights' and instead turning 'chronicler to Spartacus' (*Tom May's Death*, 63–70).

41–2 That nature abhors a vacuum and that occupied space is impenetrable by another body were fundamental propositions of physics.

47–52 In November 1647 Charles fled from prison at Hampton Court, only to hurry ('chase') to a securer prison ('narrow case') at Carisbrooke Castle on the Isle of Wight. Cromwell is improbably supposed to have manipulated the consequences of the flight: renewed imprisonment, renewed war, defeat and death for the King.

He wove a net of such a scope,   50
  That Charles himself might chase
  To Carisbrooke's narrow case.
That thence the royal actor borne
The tragic scaffold might adorn
  While round the armèd bands   55
  Did clap their bloody hands.
He nothing common did or mean
Upon that memorable scene:
  But with his keener eye
  The axe's edge did try: 60
Nor called the gods with vulgar spite
To vindicate his helpless right,
  But bowed his comely head,
  Down as upon a bed.
This was that memorable hour   65
Which first assured the forcèd power.
  So when they did design
  The Capitol's first line,
A bleeding head where they begun,
Did fright the architects to run;   70
  And yet in that the State
  Foresaw its happy fate.
And now the Irish are ashamed
To see themselves in one year tamed:
  So much one man can do,   75
  That does both act and know.
They can affirm his praises best,
And have, though overcome, confessed
  How good he is, how just,
  And fit for highest trust: 80
Nor yet grown stiffer with command,
But still in the Republic's hand:
  How fit he is to sway
  That can so well obey.
He to the Commons' feet presents   85
A kingdom, for his first year's rents:

53–60 Whitehall had been the scene of royal entertainments: the King's part was now tragic (whereas in Fanshawe's *Ode*, Holland had been in 'Of Christian tragedies the stage'). A contemporary account of the execution, published in Amsterdam, carries in Latin the title *The Tragical Spectacle of Tragic Actors and Events in London*.

57 The motto of the Spanish poet Gracián was *en nada vulgar*.

60 The axe's edge (punning on Latin *acies* for 'blade' and the 'eyesight' which tests it) falls at the poem's midpoint.

64 A contemporary Dutch engraving shows a mattress before the block.

66 *forcèd* 'gained by force'.

67–72 When the early Romans prepared the foundations of the Temple of Jupiter on what became known as the Capitol they discovered a severed head, 'an omen which so frightened the builders that they sent . . . to a famous seer of that time who revealed . . . it was destined that the place

where the head was discovered should rule the world' (Servius on Virgil, *Aeneid*, 8:345).

73–4 Cromwell's Irish campaign began in August 1649.

76 Charles was an actor (53), but Cromwell acts prudently (he has practical wisdom).

77–80 The London press worked to give the impression that Cromwell was so commended by the Irish.

81–90 Cato praises the dead Pompey for respecting liberty, for claiming nothing simply by right of arms, for his generosity, for his being able to lay down the sword he held and to lay down the power he had (Lucan, *Pharsalia*, 9:192–200).

81–2 'Not nonetheless grown inflexible but always at the people's disposal'.

85–6 'He presents Ireland to Parliament (the House of Lords was abolished in March 1649) as a return on the power vested in him, and (which is his right) gives up his own glory to make theirs'; *1681* reads 'common'.

And, what he may, forbears
His fame to make it theirs:
And has his sword and spoils ungirt,
To lay them at the public's skirt.   90
     So when the falcon high
     Falls heavy from the sky,
She, having killed, no more does search,
But on the next green bow to perch;
     Where, when he first does lure,   95
     The falconer has her sure.
What may not then our isle presume
While victory his crest does plume!
     What may not others fear
     If thus he crown each year!   100
A Caesar he ere long to Gaul,
To Italy an Hannibal,
     And to all states not free
     Shall climacteric be.
The Pict no shelter now shall find   105
Within his party-coloured mind;
     But from this valour sad
     Shrink underneath the plaid:
Happy if in the tufted brake
The English hunter him mistake;   110
     Nor lay his hounds in near
     The Caledonian deer.
But thou the War's and Fortune's son
March indefatigably on;
     And for the last effect   115
     Still keep thy sword erect:
Besides the force it has to fright
The spirits of the shady night,
     The same arts that did gain
     A power must it maintain.   120

91–6 The falconer easily tempts back the falcon which, with its fresh kill, rests on a bough; so the Parliament recalls Cromwell.

101–4 As Caesar conquered Gaul, and Hannibal Italy, so Cromwell will prove fatal ('climacteric') to all tyrannies.

105–6 Scots were conventionally perfidious and hypocritical ('Pict' meaning 'painted'): their 'parti-coloured' plaids match their minds; the *1681* spelling preserved here hints at their fissiparous politics.

107–8 'But retire beneath his cloak to avoid Cromwell's steadfast ('sad') courage.'

109–10 'Lucky if the English hunter miss him in the bushy thicket, nor put his hounds on the scent of the Scottish deer': recalling Hannibal's despairing 'We are like deer, the prey of greedy wolves: it is pointless for us to pursue those whom we would be lucky to escape' (Horace, *Odes*, 4.4:50–2).

113 Fortune proverbially aids the strong; but to be 'For-

tune's son' is to be precariously lucky: 'You who embrace fortune's gifts and imagine yourself not just her pupil but her offspring, whose mind is filled with bloody enterprises and are puffed up with success, who think yourself a god, remember how easily your life can be snuffed out' (Pliny, *Natural History*, 7.7.43).

117–18 The Sibyl advises Aeneas as they go into the Underworld that he should draw his sword (Virgil, *Aeneid*, 6:260); but when he tries to use it, he is told it is futile (6:291–4); Servius explains that it 'cannot wound but merely ward off' the spirits.

119–20 A commonplace since Sallust: Anthony Ascham's pro-Cromwellian *Discourse* (1648) says 'the usurper . . . will find himself obliged to secure his conquest by the same means he obtained it'; but Milton registers regret: 'For what can war, but acts of war still breed' (*To my Lord Fairfax*, 10).

The Picture of little T. C. in a Prospect of Flowers

1681. T. C. is plausibly identified with Theophila Cornewall ('darling of the gods' [10] Englishing the Greek 'Theophila'), whose elder sister (also Theophila) died in infancy. Not in any essential way a poem about a picture, it belongs in a tradition of paedo-phile gallantry; but the desexualization of the tradition is complete here (as also in Marvell's *Young Love* or in Waller's *Why came I so untimely forth* or in Stanley's *The Bud*).

1

See with what simplicity
This nymph begins her golden days!
In the green grass she loves to lie,
And there with her fair aspect tames
The wilder flowers, and gives them names: 5
But only with the roses plays;
    And them does tell
What colour best becomes them, and what smell.

2

Who can foretell for what high cause
This Darling of the Gods was born!   10
Yet this is she whose chaster laws
The wanton Love shall one day fear,
And, under her command severe,
See his bow broke and ensigns torn.
    Happy, who can   15
Appease this virtuous enemy of man!

3

O then let me in time compound,
And parley with those conquering eyes;
Ere they have tried their force to wound,   20
Ere, with their glancing wheels, they drive
In triumph over hearts that strive,
And them that yield but more despise.
    Let me be laid,
Where I may see thy glories from some shade.

4

Meantime, whilst every verdant thing   25
Itself does at thy beauty charm,
Reform the errors of the Spring;
Make that the tulips may have share
Of sweetness, seeing they are fair;

1–8 Ovid's Flora, mother of flowers, says: 'I enjoy perpetual spring . . . in a flourishing garden . . . often I tried to count the colours in their beds and I could not, for they were past numbering' (*Fasti*, 5:207–14); the attempt to name them follows Eve's (as in Milton, *Paradise Lost*, 11:276–7).
10 The darlings of the gods proverbially (from Menander) die young.
11–14 Milton's chaste Diana 'set at nought / The frivolous bolt of Cupid' (451–2).

17–22 In this central stanza the metaphor of 'conquering eyes' is extended to admit a hope of diplomatic settlement ('compounding') and negotiation ('parley'), and developed in 'glancing wheels' of the triumphal chariot.
26 As if her beauty were a fire at which they might 'warm' themselves.
28–9 Tulips are odourless.

And roses of their thorns disarm: 30
      But most procure
That violets may a longer age endure.

5

But O young beauty of the woods,
Whom Nature courts with fruits and flowers,
Gather the flowers, but spare the buds;   35
Lest Flora angry at thy crime,
To kill her infants in their prime,
Do quickly make the example yours;
      And, ere we see,
Nip in the blossom all our hopes and thee.   40

33–40   Ovid's slighted Flora condemned the Italian landscape to waste: 'The olives were flourishing and the forward winds blighted them, the crops were flourishing and then blasted by the hail, the vines looked good and the sky grew black in the south' (*Fasti*, 5:321–3).

Upon Appleton House, to my Lord Fairfax

1681, except where noted. For about two years from 1650 Marvell lived on the estate of the Lord General Thomas, third Baron Fairfax, serving as language tutor to his daughter Mary (b. 1638). Effectively the most powerful man in the country, in June 1650 Fairfax resigned his post as commander-in-chief of the Parliamentary armies. His literary (collections of his own verse survive in MS) and domestic interests are catered to; but his military and political achievement is treated obliquely, or is even submerged in praise of his ancestors (in particular Isabella Thwaites) and of his daughter. Marvell seems sometimes to celebrate the house before the completion of its rebuilding (while it was still continuous with the Cistercian priory from whose stones it was built); and sometimes the house as rebuilt by Fairfax. The uncertainty follows from Marvell's neglect of expected descriptive emphases. The topics of descriptive poetry (themselves complicated by surrealist detail) yield to those of French promenade poetry (which make it full of surprises) or of prospective poetry (which allow it a gravity like Denham's). Their inflections are variously historical, or panegyric, or erotic, or contemplative; but they are pervaded by parody. The account of the house (stanzas 1–35) is unbalanced by a parodic version of its history; the poem's central celebration of its present owner (stanzas 36–46) mixes lament for Britain's lost peace with a caricature of gardening conceits; its immersion in the meadows and the woods (stanzas 47–81) mixes adumbrations of political revolution or dark reflections on the poet's own role with the broad comedy of the mowers or the doubtful comedy of self-humiliation. The climactic off-centre celebration of Maria (stanzas 82–97) collects motifs from their homes in self-consciously trifling complimentary pieces (like Cleveland's *Upon Phyllis Walking in a Nunnery*) and brings them to near sublimity. Marvell leaves behind the traditions of estate poetry bequeathed by Jonson for those of French mannerist models such as Saint Amant (whom Fairfax himself translated: the text is in Alistair Fowler's *The Country House Poem* (Edinburgh: Edinburgh University Press, 1994) and Théophile de Viau (whose *Maison de Sylvie* supplies the immediate prototype for its conclusion). To some the poem seems only a muddled series of discrete epigrams; in others, who would make sense of it as a whole, its obscurity encourages interpretative excess.

1

Within this sober frame expect
Work of no foreign architect;
That unto caves the quarries drew,
And forests did to pastures hew;

1–24   As in Jonson's *To Penshurst*, the house's modest values counter current extravagances (like those of Cawood Castle, 363). Some details are supplied by Aribert's palace in Davenant's *Gondibert*, 'which once low did lie / In Parian quarries, now on columns stands ... So vast of height, to which such space did fit / As if it were o'er-sized for modern men; / The ancient giants might inhabit it; / And there walk free as winds that pass unseen' (2.2.6–7). The Priory of Nun Appleton supplied the stone (88).

Who of his great design in pain 5
Did for a model vault his brain,
Whose columns should so high be raised
To arch the brows that on them gazed.

2

Why should of all things man unruled
Such unproportioned dwellings build? 10
The beasts are by their dens expressed:
And birds contrive an equal nest;
The low-roofed tortoises do dwell
In cases fit of tortoise-shell:
No creature loves an empty space; 15
Their bodies measure out their place.

3

But he, superfluously spread,
Demands more room alive then dead.
And in his hollow palace goes
Where winds as he themselves may lose. 20
What need of all this marble crust
To impart the wanton mese of dust,
That thinks by breadth the world t' unite
Though the first builders failed in height?

4

But all things are composèd here 25
Like Nature, orderly and near:
In which we the dimensions find
Of that more sober age and mind,
When larger-sizèd men did stoop
To enter at a narrow loop; 30
As practising, in doors so strait,
To strain themselves through Heaven's gate.

5

And surely when the after age
Shall hither come in pilgrimage,
These sacred places to adore, 35
By Vere and Fairfax trod before,
Men will dispute how their extent
Within such dwarfish confines went:

5–6 'A house . . . hath its first substance in the idea of a man's brain, according to whose model, good or ill, the house so built proves good or ill' (Hawkins, *Partheneia Sacra*, 15 ('The House'), Essay).
13–14 The suggestion that the 'cases' are artefacts (like dens or nests) is jocular. Wither contrasts 'houses builded large and high' with the sufficient house room of the tortoise (*Emblems*, 4.14).
15 Joking with 'Nature abhors a vacuum.'
22 'If our earthly house of this Tabernacle were dissolved, we have a building of God' (2 Corinthians 5: 1): 'mese' is a 'dwelling place' (for 'body'); *1681* reads 'mose', Bodleian MS Eng. poet. d.49 reads 'mote' (usually adopted).
24 The builders of Babel designed 'a city and a tower, whose top may reach unto heaven' (Genesis 11: 4).
29–30 'This gate . . . this threshold small / Hath Hercules gone through . . . learn to shake off pomp' (Virgil, *Aeneid*, 8:362–5, Phaer); *loop* for 'narrow opening'.
31–2 'Strait is the gate, and narrow is the way which leadeth unto life' (Matthew 7: 14).
36 Fairfax married Anne Vere in 1637.

And some will smile at this, as well
As Romulus's bee-like cell.   40

6

Humility alone designs
Those short but admirable lines,
By which, ungirt and unconstrained,
Things greater are in less contained.
Let others vainly strive t' immure   45
The circle in the quadrature!
These holy mathematics can
In every figure equal man.

7

Yet thus the laden house does sweat,
And scarce endures the master great: 50
But where he comes the swelling hall
Stirs, and the square grows spherical;
More by his magnitude distressed,
Than he is by its straitness pressed:
And too officiously it slights   55
That in itself which him delights.

8

So Honour better Lowness bears,
Than that unwonted Greatness wears.
Height with a certain grace does bend,
But low things clownishly ascend.   60
And yet what needs there here excuse,
Where everything does answer use?
Where Neatness nothing can condemn,
Nor Pride invent what to contemn?

9

A stately frontispiece of poor   65
Adorns without the open door:
Nor less the rooms within commends,
Daily new furniture of friends.
The house was built upon the place
Only as for a mark of grace;   70
And for an inn to entertain
Its lord a while, but not remain.

40 Ovid admires the austerity of former times 'when Rome was new, when a hut served Romulus, son of Mars' (*Fasti*, 1:199); the house was preserved on the Palatine.
41–8 'The frame thereof seemed partly circular, / And part triangular . . . And 'twixt them both a quadrate was the base' (Spenser, *Faerie Queene*, 2.9.22). Leonardo and Dürer both famously illustrate microcosmic or Vitruvian man as a circle set in a square. Squaring the circle (not yet recognized as an impossibility) was commonly taken as a waste of time.
49–52 Marvell's epigrams on Louis XIV's Louvre vary the conceit: 'When Louis built this palace, a world was born; yet the place is too narrow for him' (*Inscribenda Luparae*, 9–10). The square grows spherical because the 'holy mathematics'

of microcosmic man combine square and circle: the problem of squaring the circle is inverted and resolved by Fairfax.
55–6 The ostentatious unpretentiousness of the house delights Fairfax, and wrongly shames the house itself.
65 *frontispiece* 'façade' (a standard sense); 'stately' because Fairfax's charity is.
67–8 'Instead of statues to adorn their wall, / They throng with living men their merry hall' (Carew, *To G. N. from Wrest*, 33–4).
70 'Only to favour the neighbourhood'.
71–2 'Think not, O man that dwells herein / This house's a stay, but as an inn' (Fairfax, *Upon the New-Built House at Appleton*).

10

Him Bishop's Hill, or Denton may,
Or Bilbrough, better hold than they:
But Nature here hath been so free   75
As if she said "Leave this to me."
Art would more neatly have defaced
What she had laid so sweetly waste;
In fragrant gardens, shady woods,
Deep meadows, and transparent floods.   80

11

While with slow eyes we these survey,
And on each pleasant footstep stay,
We opportunely may relate
The progress of this house's fate.
A nunnery first gave it birth,   85
For virgin-buildings oft brought forth.
And all that neighbour-ruin shows
The quarries whence this dwelling rose.

12

Near to this gloomy cloister's gates
There dwelled the blooming virgin Thwaites;   90
Fair beyond measure, and an heir
Which might deformity make fair.
And oft she spent the summer suns
Discoursing with the subtle nuns.
Whence in these words one to her weaved,   95
(As 'twere by chance) thoughts long conceived.

13

"Within this holy leisure we
Live innocently as you see.
These walls restrain the world without,
But hedge our liberty about.   100
These bars enclose that wider den
Of those wild creatures, callèd men.
The cloister outward shuts its gates,
And, from us, locks on them the grates.

14

Here we, in shining armour white,   105
Like virgin Amazons do fight.
And our chaste lamps we hourly trim,

73–4 *Bishop's Hill . . . Denton . . . Bilborough* All family estates: the first two came to the Fairfaxes with Isabel Thwaites, the manor at Bilborough (which would lodge him even better) was bought by Sir William Fairfax in 1546.
77–8 'The elegance of art would have spoiled what Nature's sweetness had left in disarray.'
81–280 The heiress Isabel Thwaites was confined by her guardian, the Prioress of Nun Appleton, to prevent her marriage to Sir William. Fairfax finally prevailed. To their sons the Priory estates passed at the Dissolution in 1542.

85–6 It shared the fate of many monastic buildings in supplying residences for Protestant magnates.
105 *shining armour* the white Cistercian habit.
106 From Christian warriors (the sense here), they later turn to termagants (249–64).
107–8 'And at midnight there was a cry made, Behold, the bridegroom cometh, go ye out to meet him. Then all those virgins arose and trimmed their lamps . . . and they that were ready went in with him to the marriage' (Matthew 25: 6–10).

Lest the great Bridegroom find them dim.
Our orient breaths perfumèd are
With incense of incessant prayer.   110
And holy-water of our tears
Most strangely our complexion clears.

15

Not tears of grief; but such as those
With which calm pleasure overflows;
Or pity, when we look on you   115
That live without this happy vow.
How should we grieve that must be seen
Each one a spouse, and each a queen;
And can in Heaven hence behold
Our brighter robes and crowns of gold?   120

16

When we have prayèd all our beads,
Someone the *Holy Legend* reads;
While all the rest with needles paint
The face and graces of the saint.
But what the linen can't receive   125
They in their lives do interweave.
This work the saints best represents;
That serves for altars' ornaments.

17

But much it to our work would add
If here your hand, your face we had: 130
By it we would our Lady touch;
Yet thus she you resembles much.
Some of your features, as we sewed,
Through every shrine should be bestowed.
And in one beauty we would take   135
Enough a thousand saints to make.

18

And (for I dare not quench the fire
That me does for your good inspire)
'Twere sacrilege a man to admit
To holy things, for Heaven fit.   140
I see the angels in a crown
On you the lilies showering down:
And round about you glory breaks,
That something more then human speaks.

19

All beauty, when at such a height,   145
Is so already consecrate.

109   *orient* 'scented.
122   *Holy Legend* Jacobus de Voragine's collection of saints' lives, the *Golden Legend*.
132   *Yet thus* 'even in your hand, your face'.

135–6 Reversing the story of Zeuxis's painting Helen of Troy from a range of models (Cicero, *De Inventione*, 2.1.1).
141   *crown* 'ring'.

Fairfax I know; and long ere this
Have marked the youth, and what he is.
But can he such a rival seem
For whom you Heaven should disesteem? 150
Ah, no! and 'twould more honour prove
He your *devoto* were, than love.

20

Here live belovèd, and obeyed:
Each one your sister, each your maid.
And, if our rule seem strictly penned, 155
The rule itself to you shall bend.
Our Abbess too, now far in age,
Doth your succession near presage.
How soft the yoke on us would lie,
Might such fair hands as yours it tie! 160

21

Your voice, the sweetest of the choir,
Shall draw Heaven nearer, raise us higher.
And your example, if our head,
Will soon us to perfection lead.
Those virtues to us all so dear, 165
Will straight grow sanctity when here:
And that, once sprung, increase so fast
Till miracles it work at last.

22

Nor is our order yet so nice,
Delight to banish as a vice. 170
Here pleasure piety doth meet;
One perfecting the other sweet.
So through the mortal fruit we boil
The sugar's uncorrupting oil:
And that which perished while we pull, 175
Is thus preservèd clear and full.

23

For such indeed are all our arts;
Still handling Nature's finest parts.
Flowers dress the altars; for the clothes,
The sea-born amber we compose; 180
Balms for the grieved we draw; and pastes
We mould, as baits for curious tastes.
What need is here of man? unless
These as sweet sins we should confess.

---

152 *devoto* 'admirer'; but the precious erotic sense is transferred from a religious one.
174 *uncorrupting oil* wittily for 'preserving syrup'.
175 'And that which began to rot even as we plucked it'.
180–1 'We prepare ambergris (for perfuming altar-cloths)

and salves for the wounded, and fashion pastries to tempt refined palates' (punningly, since 'paste' is used as angling bait).
183–4 Men are useful only as confessors: and the nuns' only sins are the refined distractions from piety just listed.

24

Each night among us to your side   185
Appoint a fresh and virgin bride;
Whom if our Lord at midnight find,
Yet neither should be left behind.
Where you may lie as chaste in bed,
As pearls together billeted.   190
All night embracing arm in arm,
Like crystal pure with cotton warm.·

25

But what is this to all the store
Of joys you see, and may make more!
Try but a while, if you be wise: 195
The trial neither costs, nor ties."
Now Fairfax seek her promised faith:
Religion that dispensèd hath;
Which she henceforward does begin;
The nun's smooth tongue has sucked her in.   200

26

Oft, though he knew it was in vain,
Yet would he valiantly complain.
"Is this that sanctity so great,
An art by which you finelier cheat?
Hypocrite witches, hence avaunt,   205
Who though in prison yet enchant!
Death only can such thieves make fast,
As rob though in the dungeon cast.

27

Were there but, when this house was made,
One stone that a just hand had laid,   210
It must have fallen upon her head
Who first thee from thy faith misled.
And yet, how well soever meant,
With them 'twould soon grow fraudulent:
For like themselves they alter all,   215
And vice infects the very wall.

28

But sure those buildings last not long,
Founded by folly, kept by wrong.
I know what fruit their gardens yield,
When they it think by night concealed.   220
Fly from their vices. 'Tis thy state,

189–92 'Where you may lie as chastely as pearls lodged together, or as ice-clear glass laid on soft cotton'; the topics of Protestant polemic against monastic sexual abuse are de-energized by the prettiness.
197–200 'Take her up on the promise she made you and from which religion has released her; seduced by the nun's blandishments, she embarks on a monastic life.'
216 No stone laid by a just hand could survive the nuns'

alteration of everything to their own corrupt likeness. One solution is offered: 'if the plague be spread in the house, it is a fretting leprosy in the house ... And [the priest] shall break down the house, the stones of it, and the timber thereof, and all the mortar ... and carry them forth out of the city' (Leviticus 14: 44–5).
221–2 'It is your property and not yourself they would have for the Church.'

Not thee, that they would consecrate.
Fly from their ruin. How I fear
Though guiltless lest thou perish there."

29

What should he do? He would respect   225
Religion, but not right neglect:
For first religion taught him right,
And dazzled not but cleared his sight.
Sometimes resolved his sword he draws,
But reverenceth then the laws: 230
For justice still that courage led;
First from a judge, then soldier bred.

30

Small honour would be in the storm.
The court him grants the lawful form;
Which licensed either peace or force,   235
To hinder the unjust divorce.
Yet still the nuns his right debarred,
Standing upon their holy guard.
Ill-counselled women, do you know
Whom you resist, or what you do?   240

31

Is not this he whose offspring fierce
Shall fight through all the universe;
And with successive valour try
France, Poland, either Germany;
Till one, as long since prophesied,   245
His horse through conquered Britain ride?
Yet, against fate, his spouse they kept;
And the great race would intercept.

32

Some to the breach against their foes
Their wooden saints in vain oppose.   250
Another bolder stands at push
With their old holy-water brush.
While the disjointed Abbess threads
The jingling chain-shot of her beads.
But their loudest canon were their lungs;   255
And sharpest weapons were their tongues.

231–2 William's father was a judge and his mother the daughter of a soldier.
233–6 'Storming the nunnery would be dishonourable: he obtains the legal right to use peaceful or forceful means to prevent the illegal separation of himself and his betrothed.'
241–8 Had the nuns succeeded in holding Isabella there would have been no succession of military heroes (in France, Poland, both North and South Germany) over the three Fairfax generations up to the Lord General (who rode 'through conquered Britain').
251–4 A bolder one stands ready to attack ('at push') with the aspergillum; the distracted ('disjointed') abbess prays with her rosary.

33

But, waving these aside like flies,
Young Fairfax through the wall does rise.
Then the unfrequented vault appeared,
And superstitions vainly feared.   260
The relics false were set to view;
Only the jewels there were true.
But truly bright and holy Thwaites
That weeping at the altar waits.

34

But the glad youth away her bears,   265
And to the nuns bequeaths her tears:
Who guiltily their prize bemoan,
Like gypsies that a child had stoln.
Thenceforth (as when the enchantment ends
The castle vanishes or rends)   270
The wasting cloister with the rest
Was in one instant dispossessed.

35

At the demolishing, this seat
To Fairfax fell as by escheat.
And what both nuns and founders willed   275
'Tis likely better thus fulfilled.
For if the virgin proved not theirs,
The cloister yet remainèd hers.
Though many a nun there made her vow,
'Twas no religious-house till now.   280

36

From that blest bed the hero came,
Whom France and Poland yet does fame:
Who, when retired here to peace,
His warlike studies could not cease;
But laid these gardens out in sport   285
In the just figure of a fort;
And with five bastions it did fence,
As aiming one for every sense.

37

When in the East the morning ray
Hangs out the colours of the day,   290

257–8 Spenser's Redcross brushes aside a 'cloud of cumbrous gnats' on the threshold of Error's Den (*Faerie Queene*, 1.1.23).
263–4 Only the weeping Thwaites was both bright and holy (unlike the valuable but false relics in the unvisited crypt).
268 *had* hath (*1681*): the gypsies must lament a child they had stolen and have lost again.
269–70 So Busirane's castle is found 'Now vanished utterly and clean subversed' (Spenser, *Faerie Queene*, 3.12.42).
273–5 'At the Dissolution of the Monasteries the Fairfax family inherited the house by reversion (the Church having no heirs).' The legality is questionable; 'escheat' can carry

the sense of 'plunder'; but the acquisition is later legitimized by the family's achievements (275–80).
281–2 'Fairfax, whose name in arms through Europe rings, / And fills all mouths with envy or with praise, / And all her jealous monarchs with amaze' (Milton, *Sonnet 15*); but which Fairfax Marvell intends is unsure.
289–328 In each complete stanza one sense dominates (hearing, smell, sight, touch, taste), each in turn attacked. Cleveland constructs another military garden: 'The trees, like yeoman of her guard / Serving more for pomp than ward . . . no Civil War / Between her York, and Lancaster' (*Upon Phyllis Walking*, 5–6, 25–6).

The bee through these known allies hums,
Beating the *dian* with its drums.
Then flowers their drowsy eyelids raise,
Their silken ensigns each displays,
And dries its pan yet dank with dew,   295
And fills its flask with odours new.

38

These, as their governor goes by,
In fragrant volleys they let fly;
And to salute their governess
Again as great a charge they press: 300
None for the virgin nymph; for she
Seems with the flowers a flower to be.
And think so still! though not compare
With breath so sweet, or cheek so fair.

39

Well shot ye firemen! O how sweet,   305
And round your equal fires do meet;
Whose shrill report no ear can tell,
But echoes to the eye and smell.
See how the flowers, as at parade,
Under their colours stand displayed: 310
Each regiment in order grows,
That of the tulip pink and rose.

40

But when the vigilant patrol
Of stars walks round about the Pole,
Their leaves, that to the stalks are curled,   315
Seem to their staves the ensigns furled.
Then in some flowers beloved hut
Each bee as sentinel is shut;
And sleeps so too: but, if once stirred,
She runs you through, or asks the word.   320

41

O thou, that dear and happy isle
The garden of the world ere while,
Thou Paradise of four seas,
Which Heaven planted us to please,
But, to exclude the world, did guard   325

291–2 Cleveland's bee flies 'Tuning his draughts with drowsy hums / As Danes carouse by kettledrums' (*Fuscara*, 51–2); the *dian* is the reveille.

295–6 The pan holds the priming in the musket lock, the flask stores the powder supply.

303–4 Addressed to the flowers, 'though not equal ('compare') to her sweetness'.

305–8 The 'volleys' answer each other fragrantly and perfectly, and surround us. The ear registers them only as echoes to other senses.

313–14 Stars in both the Lesser Bear and the Great Bear are known as the 'guards of the Pole'.

320 'She stings you or demands the password'; but many editors emend 'or' to 'nor'.

320–8 Giles Fletcher the Younger's *Elegy* for Prince Henry makes Britain 'The garden of the world, where nothing wanted, / Another Paradise, that God had planted' (20–1) transformed into a 'desert island, that art found / Cast in the sea's deep bosom by mishap' (64–5). The four (two syllables) seas are those surrounding Britain.

With watery if not flaming sword;
What luckless apple did we taste,
To make us mortal, and thee waste.

42

Unhappy! shall we never more
That sweet militia restore,   330
When gardens only had their towers,
And all the garrisons were flowers,
When roses only arms might bear,
And men did rosy garlands wear?
Tulips, in several colours barred,   335
Were then the Switzers of our Guard.

43

The gardener had the soldier's place,
And his more gentle forts did trace.
The nursery of all things green
Was then the only magazine.   340
The winter quarters were the stoves,
Where he the tender plants removes.
But war all this doth overgrow:
We ordnance plant and powder sow.

44

And yet there walks one on the sod   345
Who, had it pleasèd him and God,
Might once have made our gardens spring
Fresh as his own and flourishing.
But he preferred to the Cinque Ports
These five imaginary forts: 350
And, in those half-dry trenches, spanned
Power which the Ocean might command.

45

For he did, with his utmost skill,
Ambition weed, but conscience till.
Conscience, that Heaven-nursèd plant,   355
Which most our earthly gardens want.

326 'He placed at the east of the garden of Eden Cherubims, and a flaming sword turned every way' (Genesis 3: 24).
328 *thee waste* the waste (*1681*).
336 The Vatican Swiss Guard wore red and yellow stripes; varieties of tulips so coloured were called Swisser.
338 *forts* punning on 'fortes'.
340–1 The munitions stores were seed-beds, the winter camps were hot-houses.
345 *on the sod* 'in this place' (a Northernism).
349–52 Fairfax retired from the Council of State in 1650, the year it arrogated to itself the powers of the Warden of the Cinque Ports (the English ports, originally five, which furnished the navy) and the Lord High Admiral (whose commission 'spanned' the ocean). To call the senses the 'five ports of knowledge' was commonplace (where 'port' is 'gate'); Marvell puns on 'port' as 'harbour'.
353–4 Milton in the *Second Defence* (1654) praises Fairfax's lack of 'ambition . . . and the thirst for glory which conquers all the most eminent men'.
355–6 Joseph Beaumont's memory of an earthly garden only enforces the memory of the 'Heaven-planted garden, where felicity / Flourished on every tree' (*The Garden*, 14–15). Fairfax resigned from the Council of State on grounds of 'conscience'.

A prickling leaf it bears, and such
As that which shrinks at every touch;
But flowers eternal, and divine,
That in the crowns of saints do shine.   360

46

The sight does from these bastions ply,
The invisible artillery;
And at proud Cawood Castle seems
To point the battery of its beams.
As if it quarrelled in the seat   365
The ambition of its prelate great.
But o'er the meads below it plays,
Or innocently seems to graze.

47

And now to the abyss I pass
Of that unfathomable grass,   370
Where men like grasshoppers appear,
But grasshoppers are giants there:
They, in there squeaking laugh, contemn
Us as we walk more low then them:
And, from the precipices tall   375
Of the green spires, to us do call.

48

To see men through this meadow dive,
We wonder how they rise alive.
As, under water, none does know
Whether he fall through it or go.   380
But, as the mariners that sound,
And show upon their lead the ground,
They bring up flowers so to be seen,
And prove they've at the bottom been.

49

No scene that turns with engines strange   385
Does oftener then these meadows change,
For when the sun the grass hath vexed,
The tawny mowers enter next;

357–8 'There quakes the plant . . . called the shame-faced . . . If towards it one do approach too much, / It shrinks his boughs, to shun our hateful touch' (Sylvester, *Divine Weeks*, 2.1.1.623–6); consciences are both prickly and tender. Wither's 'cares are blessed thistles . . . Which wholesome are, although they bitter be: / And though their leaves with pricks be overgrown . . . yet their flowers are full of down' (*Britain's Remembrancer*, 3:97–100).
363–6 The sight, looking out from Nun Appleton's merely floral fortifications reproves ('quarrels') the ambition of the Archbishop of York, John Williams, in its manifestation as the refortified Cawood Castle ('in its seat').
368 *graze* adopted from MS (*1681* reads 'gaze'); the sight's

artillery only grazingly hits the meadows, but then like the beasts it feeds on the grasses.
370 *unfathomable* transferred from 'abyss', deep like a sea.
371–2 Some Israelites hesitated before entering Canaan: 'There we saw the giants . . . and we were in our sight as grasshoppers, and so we were in their sights' (Numbers 13: 33).
379–80 'As one cannot tell whether divers are sinking or swimming'.
381–4 As sailors show the plummet dirtied from the sea-bed, the mowers show flowers.
385 Masque scenery was shifted mechanically.

Who seem like Israelites to be,
Walking on foot through a Green Sea.   390
To them the grassy deeps divide,
And crowd a lane to either side.

50

With whistling scythe, and elbow strong,
These massacre the grass along:
While one, unknowing, carves the rail,   395
Whose yet unfeathered quills her fail.
The edge all bloody from its breast
He draws, and does his stroke detest;
Fearing the flesh untimely mowed
To him a fate as black forebode.   400

51

But bloody Thestylis, that waits
To bring the mowing camp their cates,
Greedy as kites has trussed it up,
And forthwith means on it to sup:
When on another quick she lights,   405
And cries, "He called us Israelites;
But now, to make his saying true,
Rails rain for quails, for manna dew."

52

Unhappy birds! what does it boot
To build below the grass's root;   410
When lowness is unsafe as height,
And chance o'ertakes what scapeth spite?
And now your orphan parents' call
Sounds your untimely funeral.
Death-trumpets creak in such a note,   415
And 'tis the *sourdine* in their throat.

53

Or sooner hatch or higher build:
The mower now commands the field;

389–90 Recalling the Israelites crossing the Red Sea: 'The Lord . . . made the Sea dry land, and the waters were divided. And the children of Israel went into the midst of the sea upon the dry ground' (Exodus 14: 21–2). Owen Felltham's *Brief Character of Holland* compares the Dutch living 'in the very lap of the floods' with 'Israelites passing through the Red Sea'.

392 'And press on each side to make a passage'.

394 'The mowers proceed with their massacre of the grass.'

395 The still unfledged bird (common in meadows, called in French the 'king of quails') is identified with King Charles; and the regicides' guilt with the mower's.

401 'And Thestylis wild thyme and garlic beats / For harvest hinds, o'erspent with toil and heats' (Virgil, *Eclogues*, 2:10, Dryden): she is the mower's cook.

406–8 The poet called the mowers 'Israelites' at 389, an identification Thestylis confirms by recalling Exodus 16: 13–15: 'At even the quails came up . . . and in the morning the dew.' But they now have blood on their hands, and have broken faith. Clarendon, *History*, 4:147, reports an incident when the London mob jostled the King's coach and a man was heard 'calling out with a very loud voice, "To your tents, O Israel",' recalling the defection of the ten tribes from the House of David (1 Kings 12: 16).

413–16 The bereft (wittily 'orphan') parents croak ('creak') their grief, their call enfeebled that like the sound of muted trumpets.

In whose new traverse seemeth wrought
A camp of battle newly fought: 420
Where, as the meads with hay, the plain
Lies quilted o'er with bodies slain:
The women that with forks it fling,
Do represent the pillaging.

54

And now the careless victors play,   425
Dancing the triumphs of the hay;
Where every mower's wholesome heat
Smells like an Alexander's sweat.
Their females fragrant as the mead
Which they in fairy circles tread: 430
When at their dance's end they kiss,
Their new-made hay not sweeter is.

55

When after this 'tis piled in cocks,
Like a calm sea it shows the rocks:
We wondering in the river near   435
How boats among them safely steer.
Or, like the desert Memphis sand,
Short pyramids of hay do stand.
And such the Roman camps do rise
In hills for soldiers' obsequies.   440

56

This scene again withdrawing brings
A new and empty face of things;
A levelled space, as smooth and plain,
As cloths for Lely stretched to stain.
The world when first created sure   445
Was such a table rase and pure.
Or rather such is the *toril*
Ere the bulls enter at Madril.

57

For to this naked equal flat,
Which Levellers take pattern at,   450

419–21 'In whose track a field of recent battle seems to have been created'; but 'traverse', 'wrought', 'quilted' combine to suggest an embroidered curtain, fitting with the theatrical metaphors at 385 and 441.
425–6 The carefree victors over the hay ('grass') dance a hay ('reel') in a hay ('military file').
428 'His skin had a marvellous good savour, and ... his breath was very sweet' (Plutarch, *Life of Alexander*, North).
437–8 The hay is built into pyramids like the desert sand round Egyptian Memphis.
439–40 'Artificial mounds and hills [are often] sepulchral monuments ... for ... eminent persons, especially such as died in the wars ... that the Romans uses such hilly sepultures ... seems [variously] confirmable' (Sir Thomas Browne, *Of Artificial Hills, Mounts, or Barrows*).

444 'As canvasses for Sir Peter Lely (1618–80) stretched to paint'; his portrait of Marvell is lost.
446 *rase and pure* 'without form and void' (Genesis 1: 2); the 'tabula rasa' ('a writing tablet scraped clean'), applied since Aristotle to the inexperienced mind, is jocularly invoked.
447–8 Marvell knew Spain, but incorrectly uses *toril* ('bull-pen') for 'arena'. 'Madril' was a common English form.
449–52 The Leveller Richard Overton's egalitarian *Appeal from the Commons to the Free People* (1647) specifies in an address to Fairfax that 'all the grounds which anciently lay in common for the poor, and are now ... enclosed ... may forthwith ... be ... laid open again to the free and common use and benefit of the poor'. Fairfax suppressed a Leveller Mutiny in 1649; here the estate workers drive ('chase') their cattle to the common.

The villagers in common chase
Their cattle, which it closer rase;
And what below the scythe increased
Is pinched yet nearer by the beast.
Such, in the painted world, appeared   455
Davenant with the *universal herd*.

58

They seem within the polished grass
A landscape drawn in looking-glass.
And shrunk in the huge pasture show
As spots, so shaped, on faces do.   460
Such fleas, ere they approach the eye,
In multiplying glasses lie.
They feed so wide, so slowly move,
As constellations do above.

59

Then, to conclude these pleasant acts,   465
Denton sets ope its cataracts;
And makes the meadow truly be
(What it but seemed before) a sea.
For, jealous of its Lord's long stay,
It tries to invite him thus away.   470
The river in itself is drowned,
And isles the astonished cattle round.

60

Let others tell the paradox,
How eels now bellow in the ox;
How horses at their tails do kick,   475
Turned as they hang to leeches quick;
How boats can over bridges sail;
And fishes do the stables scale.
How salmons trespassing are found;
And pikes are taken in the pound.   480

455–6 'Then straight an universal herd appears' (Davenant, *Gondibert*, 2.6.60).
457–64 The cattle grazing against the grass's shimmer seem first as if painted on glass (a mirror background was common in the then fashionable glass painting: John Hopkins writes *To Amasia, on her filling a Glass with Water, whereon she had Painted Stags, and Birds, and Trees*); then they are like beauty-patches (Lovelace has the night sky 'all o'er bepatched with stars', *As I beheld a winter evening's air*, 9); then as fleas under a microscope (James Howell says 'a multiplying glass . . . can make a flea look like a cow' (*Epistolae Ho-Elianae*, 15 Aug. 1645); then like stars (Thomas Browne associates 'spots on butterflies' wings, the moles on Augustus' body, and the stars in Charles's Wain' (*Garden of Cyrus*, 3).
466–70 Denton, on the River Wharfe thirty miles above Nun Appleton, opens its floodgates ('cataracts') and releases the Wharfe to flood the water-meadows downstream. This

act of 'jealousy' (for Fairfax's favouring the lower estate) was a regular means of enabling new growth from the mown fields.
471–2 'The river is overwhelmed by its own flood waters and surrounds the astonished (*1681* misprints 'astonish') cattle.'
473–80 'Through open fields now rush the spreading floods . . . One in a boat deplores; / And, where he lately ploughed, now strikes his oars. / O'er corn, o'er drownèd villages he sails: / This from high elms entangled fishes hales' (Ovid, *Metamorphoses*, 1:291–6, Sandys). The ox bellows, having swallowed the eel; Thomas Browne, in *Notes on Certain Fishes found in Norfolk*, finds he is unable to convert horsehairs into leeches. The fishes cover the stables with scales as well as 'climb' on them; the pike would normally be taken in the 'pond', not in the cattle-pen ('pound').

61

But I, retiring from the flood,
Take sanctuary in the wood;
And, while it lasts, my self embark
In this yet green, yet growing Ark;
Where the first carpenter might best   485
Fit timber for his keel have pressed.
And where all creatures might have shares,
Although in armies, not in pairs.

62

The double wood of ancient stocks
Linked in so thick, an union locks,   490
It like two pedigrees appears,
On one hand Fairfax, the other Vere's:
Of whom though many fell in war,
Yet more to Heaven shooting are:
And, as they Nature's cradle decked,   495
Will in green age her hearse expect.

63

When first the eye this forest sees
It seems indeed as wood not trees:
As if their neighbourhood so old
To one great trunk them all did mould.   500
There the huge bulk takes place, as meant
To thrust up a fifth element;
And stretches still so closely wedged
As if the night within were hedged.

64

Dark all without it knits; within   505
It opens passable and thin;
And in as loose an order grows,
As the Corinthian porticoes.
The arching boughs unite between
The columns of the temple green;   510
And underneath the wingèd choirs
Echo about their tunèd fires.

481–9   So Lovelace: 'From this sad storm of fire and blood / She fled to this yet living wood; / Where she 'mongst savage beasts doth find / Herself more safe than human kind' (*Aramantha*, 339–42). The poet embarks (or 'imbarks himself' as 'Imbark thee in the laurel tree', *Aramantha*, 274), in a type of Noah's ('the first carpenter') Ark, or from where he might have collected ('pressed') the timber.

489–92   The trees ('stocks') of two formerly separate woods growing close are brought together as one. But the stocks are also 'pedigrees', the families of Fairfax and Vere.

493–4   Some trees are felled for naval building and others are still growing skyward; some of the two families fell in war, the virtue of others lifts them heavenward.

495   Saint Amant is pleased that trees from Time's nativity survive for him (*La Solitude*, st.1); here the trees that decked Nature's beginning will survive to her end.

497–8   Proverbially 'You cannot see the wood for the trees.'

499   *neighbourhood* 'nearness'.

501–2   The four elements are so compacted in the forest's density that their mass seems to force out a latent quintessence, heavenly and incorruptible.

505–12   Thomas Browne, on the authority of Vitruvius, derives 'the rule of columns from trees' (*Garden of Cyrus*, 4); the 'looseness' of the light and ornate Corinthian order was conventional. Benlowes's Latin verses *Theophila*, 12:11–12 turn a grove into a temple 'and the spreading branches into ceillings, and each bole a column for the sacred house . . . the singing birds are choristers'. To call birds winged choristers is a cliché, here activated by the temple/forest conceit.

65

The nightingale does here make choice
To sing the trials of her voice.
Low shrubs she sits in, and adorns   515
With music high the squatted thorns.
But highest oaks stoop down to hear,
And listening elders prick the ear.
The thorn, lest it should hurt her, draws
Within the skin its shrunken claws.   520

66

But I have for my music found
A sadder, yet more pleasing sound:
The stock-doves, whose fair necks are graced
With nuptial rings their ensigns chaste;
Yet always, for some cause unknown,   525
Sad pair unto the elms they moan.
O why should such a couple mourn,
That in so equal flames do burn?

67

Then as I careless on the bed
Of gelid strawberries do tread,   530
And through the hazels thick espy
The hatching throstle's shining eye,
The heron from the ash's top,
The eldest of its young lets drop,
As if it stork-like did pretend   535
That tribute to its Lord to send.

68

But most the hewel's wonders are,
Who here has the holtfelster's care.
He walks still upright from the root,
Measuring the timber with his foot;   540
And all the way, to keep it clean,
Doth from the bark the woodmoths glean.
He, with his beak, examines well
Which fit to stand and which to fell.

69

The good he numbers up, and hacks;   545
As if he marked them with the axe.
But where he, tinkling with his beak,
Does find the hollow oak to speak,

515–16   In Spenser's Bower of Bliss, 'the angelical soft trembling voices' of the birds meet the 'bass murmur of the waters' fall' (*Faerie Queene*, 2.12.71).

518   'The younger [nightingales] ... do meditate and receive their verses from the elder to practise and imitate' (Hawkins, *Partheneia Sacra*, 14 ('The Nightingale'), Theories); the relation is reversed to allow the 'elder' to be punningly a tree (like the oak).

523–6   Peacham sets a ring and a dove on an olive tree (*Minerva Britanna*, 92); stock-doves are not ringed. Virgil's 'Stockdoves and turtles tell their amorous pain, / And from the lofty elms, of love complain' (*Eclogues*, 1:58, Dryden).

530   *gelid* 'chill', informed by a wilful reminiscence of Virgil, *Eclogues*, 3:92–3: 'low grow the strawberries, chill lies the serpent in the grass'.

535–6   The stork was supposed to gift its first-born to the house it nested in.

537–8   The green woodpecker has the woodcutter's job.

That for his building he designs,
And through the tainted side he mines. 550
Who could have thought the tallest oak
Should fall by such a feeble stroke!

70

Nor would it, had the tree not fed
A traitor-worm, within it bred.
(As first our flesh corrupt within 555
Tempts impotent and bashful sin.)
And yet that worm triumphs not long,
But serves to feed the hewel's young.
While the oak seems to fall content,
Viewing the treason's punishment. 560

71

Thus I, easy philosopher,
Among the birds and trees confer:
And little now to make me, wants
Or of the fowls, or of the plants.
Give me but wings as they, and I 565
Straight floating on the air shall fly:
Or turn me but, and you shall see
I was but an inverted tree.

72

Already I begin to call
In their most learn'd original: 570
And where I language want, my signs
The bird upon the bough divines;
And more attentive there doth sit
Then if she were with lime-twigs knit.
No leaf does tremble in the wind 575
Which I returning cannot find.

73

Out of these scattered Sibyl's leaves
Strange prophecies my fancy weaves:
And in one history consumes,

553–6 'The worm shall feed sweetly on him . . . and wickedness shall fall as a tree' (Job 24: 20); Browne remarks that woodpeckers attack trees 'as the rottenness thereof affordeth best convenience' (*Notes on Certain Birds*).
561 Epicurus is the philosopher of ease.
567–8 Chapman has 'our tree of man, whose nervy root springs in his top' (*To the High-Born Henry*, dedication to the *Iliad*, 132–3); the conceit, as old as Plato, makes the point that man draws sustenance from his head or from Heaven. The poet's re-inversion dehumanizes him to a vegetable.
569–70 In Drayton's *The Owl*, 400, the entranced poet finds that 'Each sylvan sound I truly understood, / Become a perfect linguist of the wood.' Magicians and soothsayers were commonly expert in avian languages: Virgil's Helenus had been taught by Apollo to 'scry' trees and stars, 'Both chirming tongues of birds, and wings of foul that swift doth fly' (*Aeneid*, 3:361, Phaer).
577–9 Helenus advises Aeneas that he will meet the Cumaean Sibyl: 'A frantic prophet priest of womankind thou shalt behold, / That deep in ground doth dwell . . . And dest'nies out she sings, and leaves with notes and names she signs / Whatever thing that virgin writes, in leaves and painted lines, / In rhymes and verse she sets, and them in caves in ranges couch . . . But when the door by chance doth turn, and wind the corner blows: / Their heaps asunder fall and forth they fly' (*Aeneid*, 3:443–9). The leaves comprehend ('consume') all history.

Like Mexic paintings, all the plumes.   580
What Rome, Greece, Palestine, ere said
I in this light mosaic read.
Thrice happy he who, not mistook,
Hath read in Nature's mystic book.

74

And see how chance's better wit   585
Could with a mask my studies hit!
The oak-leaves me embroider all,
Between which caterpillars crawl:
And ivy, with familiar trails,
Me licks, and clasps, and curls, and hales.   590
Under this antic cope I move
Like some great prelate of the grove.

75

Then, languishing with ease, I toss
On pallets swoln of velvet moss;
While the wind, cooling through the boughs,   595
Flatters with air my panting brows.
Thanks for my rest ye mossy banks,
And unto you cool zephyrs thanks,
Who, as my hair, my thoughts too shed,
And winnow from the chaff my head.   600

76

How safe, methinks, and strong, behind
These trees have I encamped my mind;
Where Beauty, aiming at the heart,
Bends in some tree its useless dart;
And where the World no certain shot   605
Can make, or me it toucheth not.
But I on it securely play,
And gall its horsemen all the day.

77

Bind me ye woodbines in your twines,
Curl me about ye gadding vines,   610

580   Spenser's Fancy comes in 'painted plumes, in goodly order dight, / Like as the sunburnt Indians do array / Their tawny bodies' (*Faerie Queene* 3.12.8). John Tradescant's collection (now in the Ashmolean Museum, Oxford, in Marvell's day in London) included a prized specimen of Mexican feather-painting.
582   In Milton's Eden 'Iris all hues, roses, and jessamine . . . wrought / Mosaic' (*Paradise Lost*, 4:698–700); in *Music's Empire*, Marvell calls music 'the mosaic of the air' (21).
586   'Could match my preoccupations with a masque costume'.
591   'In these vestments ('antic cope' is so used by Milton in the *Apology for Smectymnuus*) I move like an arch-priest of the grove' (but not like the Archbishop of York, 366).
593–4   Statius's Anio (a tributary of the Tiber) 'in the dark of night strips off his green mantle and lays his breast on the

soft moss' (*Silvae*, 1.3:70–2).
600   Nashe talks of 'winnowing my wits' (*Unfortunate Traveller*).
601–8   The poet imagines himself as the revived Hippolytus in the grove at Aricia: 'Diana than, Hippolytus to secret woods withdrew / From sight of man . . . Where he alone in desert groves doth worldly care forsake, / Nor praise of people seeks . . . Therefore it is, that from Diana's woods, and temples clear, / All horses been forbid' (Virgil, *Aeneid* 7:761–82, Phaer). Hippolytus was killed by his own horses; for Marvell they seem to sum up the irrational horrors of war.
609–16   Commonplace erotic metaphors of bondage are literalized. The 'gadding vines' are from Milton *Lycidas* (40); the violent 'nailing' of 616 matches Plautus's 'Your heart is fastened to us with one of Cupid's nails' (*Asinaria*, 156).

And O so close your circles lace,
That I may never leave this place:
But, lest your fetters prove too weak,
Ere I your silken bondage break,
Do you, O brambles, chain me too,   615
And courteous briars nail me through.

78

Here in the morning tie my chain,
Where the two woods have made a lane;
While, like a guard on either side,
The trees before their lord divide;   620
This, like a long and equal thread,
Betwixt two labyrinths does lead.
But, where the floods did lately drown,
There at the evening stake me down.

79

For now the waves are fallen and dried,   625
And now the meadows fresher dyed;
Whose grass, with moister colour dashed,
Seems as green silks but newly washed.
No serpent new nor crocodile
Remains behind our little Nile;   630
Unless itself you will mistake,
Among these meads the only snake.

80

See in what wanton harmless folds
It everywhere the meadow holds;
And its yet muddy back doth lick,   635
Till as a crystal mirror slick;
Where all things gaze themselves, and doubt
If they be in it or without.
And for his shade which therein shines,
Narcissus-like, the sun too pines.   640

81

O what a pleasure 'tis to hedge
My temples here with heavy sedge;
Abandoning my lazy side,
Stretched as a bank unto the tide;

621–2 The lane is transformed to its own Ariadne's clue.
629–30 'As when old father Nilus gins . . . to avale, / Huge heaps of mud he leaves, wherein there breed / Ten thousand kinds of creatures' (Spenser, *Faerie Queene*, 1.1.21).
632 The water snaking through the meadow is the only 'snake in the grass': 'How pleasant are the murmuring streams . . . gliding under the arboured banks / As winding serpents in the grass' (Saint Amant, *La Solitude*, st.4, Fairfax).
636–40 'As 'twere a doubt whether had been / Himself [the Sun] or image gave the light' (Saint Amant, *La Solitude*, st.17). Sylvester describes how assembled birds 'Wait

on the Phoenix . . . And gaze themselves in her blue-golden plumes' (*Divine Weeks*, 1.5.716–17).
639–40 Spenser's Britomart, like Narcissus, fondly loves 'a shade, the body far exiled' (*Faerie Queene*, 3.2.44); Shirley's Narcissus compares the vanishing of his own reflection to the setting of the sun (*Narcissus*, st.105).
641–4 River-gods are conventionally so represented: Jonson's personified Thames 'lay along between the shores, leaning upon his urn (that flowed with water,) and crowned with flowers' (*Masque of Beauty*, 132).

Or to suspend my sliding foot   645
On the osier's underminèd root,
And in its branches tough to hang,
While at my lines the fishes twang!

82

But now away my hooks, my quills,
And angles, idle utensils.   650
The young Maria walks to night:
Hide trifling youth thy pleasures slight.
'Twere shame that such judicious eyes
Should with such toys a man surprise;
She that already is the law   655
Of all her sex, her age's awe.

83

See how loose Nature, in respect
To her, itself doth recollect;
And everything so whished and fine,
Starts forthwith to its *bonne-mine*.   660
The sun himself, of her aware,
Seems to descend with greater care;
And lest she see him go to bed,
In blushing clouds conceals his head.

84

So when the shadows laid asleep   665
From underneath these banks do creep;
And on the river as it flows
With ebon shuts begin to close;
The modest halcyon comes in sight,
Flying betwixt the day and night;   670
And such an horror calm and dumb,
Admiring Nature does benumb.

85

The viscous air, wheresoe'er she fly,
Follows and sucks her azure dye;
The jellying stream compacts below,   675
If it might fix her shadow so;
The stupid fishes hang, as plain

---

645   Marvell gives a fountain a 'sliding foot' in *The Garden*, 49.

649–54   The angling paraphernalia of hook, floats ('quills'), rods ('angles') are discarded for Maria. Walton quotes Sir Henry Wotton as saying that angling was 'an employment for his idle time, which was then not idly spent' (*The Compleat Angler*).

657–60   'Nature in awe to him / Had doffed her gaudy trim' (Milton, *Nativity Ode*, 32); but nature 'makes a show' ('starts to its *bonne mine*'); as the garden welcomes the 'governor' at 297–8.

661–4   'So when the sun in bed / Curtained with cloudy red' (Milton, *Nativity Ode*, 229–30).

665–8   'When the sleeping shadows creep out from under the banks (wakened by the setting sun) and start to come down on the flowing river with black screens'.

669–72   'The halcyons, calming all that's nigh, / Betwixt the air and water fly' (*The Gallery*, 36); halcyons (here for 'kingfishers'), by nesting on the waves, were supposed to calm them. Nature is frozen in wonder and veneration ('horror').

673   *viscous* 'sticky' (*viscum* is bird-lime), but based on the poeticism 'liquid air' (like Milton's 'spongy air', *Comus*, 154).

675–8   'The stream jellies and thickens below as if to fix the bird's shadow, and the stunned fishes hang as flies caught in amber ('crystal' because the water is clear).'

As flies in crystal overta'en,
And men the silent scene assist,
Charmed with the sapphire-wingèd mist.   680

86

Maria such, and so doth hush
The world, and through the evening rush.
No new-born comet such a train
Draws through the sky, nor star new-slain.
For straight those giddy rockets fail,   685
Which from the putrid earth exhale,
But by her flames, in Heaven tried,
Nature is wholly vitrified.

87

'Tis she that to these gardens gave
That wondrous beauty which they have;   690
She straightness on the woods bestows;
To her the meadow sweetness owes;
Nothing could make the river be
So crystal-pure but only she;
She yet more pure, sweet, straight, and fair,   695
Than gardens, woods, meads, rivers are.

88

Therefore what first she on them spent,
They gratefully again present.
The meadow carpets where to tread;
The garden flowers to crown her head;   700
And for a glass the limpid brook,
Where she may all her beauties look;
But, since she would not have them seen,
The wood about her draws a screen.

89

For she, to higher beauties raised,   705
Disdains to be for lesser praised.
She counts her beauty to converse
In all the languages as hers;
Nor yet in those herself employs
But for the wisdom, not the noise;   710
Nor yet that wisdom would affect,
But as 'tis Heaven's dialect.

---

679 *assist* 'attend' (not yet a Gallicism).
683–8 Spenser's Florimell rides 'All as a blazing star doth far outcast / His hairy beams, and flaming locks dispread, / At sight whereof the people stand aghast' (*Faerie Queene*, 3.1.16); 'stars new-slain' are meteors, classed then as 'exhalations' drawn from the earth by the sun's power.
687–8 'Some of our chemics facetiously affirm, that at the last fire all shall be crystallized and reverberated into glass'

(Thomas Browne, *Religio Medici*, 1.50); the glassy earth adopts the character of the crystalline sphere.
707–12 'Her thoughts are English, though her sparkling wit / With other language doth them fitly fit' (Marvell, *To his Worthy Friend Dr Witty*, 25–6, on Celia, probably Mary Fairfax); Fanshawe writes of the Escorial 'all tongues are met, though no confusion there, / Because this pile to pious ends they rear' (*The Escorial*, 41–2).

90

Blest nymph! that couldst so soon prevent
Those trains by youth against thee meant;
Tears (watery shot that pierce the mind);   715
And sighs (Love's cannon charged with wind);
True praise (that breaks through all defence);
And feigned complying innocence;
But knowing where this ambush lay,
She 'scaped the safe, but roughest way.   720

91

This 'tis to have been from the first
In a domestic Heaven nursed,
Under the discipline severe
Of Fairfax, and the starry Vere;
Where not one object can come nigh   725
But pure, and spotless as the eye;
And goodness doth itself entail
On females, if there want a male.

92

Go now fond sex that on your face
Do all your useless study place,   730
Nor once at vice your brows dare knit
Lest the smooth forehead wrinkled sit
Yet your own face shall at you grin,
Thorough the black-bag of your skin;
When knowledge only could have filled   735
And virtue all those furrows tilled.

93

Hence she with graces more divine
Supplies beyond her sex the line;
And, like a sprig of mistletoe,
On the Fairfacian oak does grow;   740
Whence, for some universal good,
The priest shall cut the sacred bud;
While her glad parents most rejoice,
And make their destiny their choice.

94

Meantime ye fields, springs, bushes, flowers,   745
Where yet she leads her studious hours,
(Till Fate her worthily translates,
And find a Fairfax for our Thwaites)

714   *trains* 'stratagems'; but the specifications in 715–20 draw
out the sense 'artillery'.
724   The Vere coat of arms carries a star.
729–36   The 'black bag' is a full mask disguising the ravages of dissolute living, drawn against the face by a bead held between the teeth: hence the 'grin'. Benlowes says Time will 'pluck the black bags / From off Sin's grizly scalp' (*Prelibation to the Sacrifice*, 1.48). Here the skin disguises the skull.

737–8   With the implication that she has 'masculine virtues' (as at 727–8).
739–42   The Druids divided mistletoe among the people as ' a gauge / Of future happiness, / And good success' (Ralph Knevett, *The New-Year's Gift*, 4–6).
743–4   It was their destiny to have a daughter rather than a son: they rejoice as if they had so chosen it.

Employ the means you have by her,
And in your kind yourselves prefer; 750
That, as all virgins she precedes,
So you all woods, streams, gardens, meads.

95

For you Thessalian Tempe's seat
Shall now be scorned as obsolete;
Aranjuez, as less, disdained; 755
The Bel-Retiro as constrained;
But name not the Idalian Grove,
For 'twas the seat of wanton love;
Much less the dead's Elysian Fields,
Yet nor to them your beauty yields. 760

96

'Tis not, what once it was, the world;
But a rude heap together hurled;
All negligently overthrown,
Gulfs, deserts, precipices, stone.
Your lesser world contains the same, 765
But in more decent order tame;
You Heaven's centre, Nature's lap,
And Paradise's only map.

97

But now the salmon-fishers moist
Their leathern boats begin to hoist; 770
And, like Antipodes in shoes,
Have shod their heads in their canoes.
How tortoise-like, but not so slow,
These rational amphibii go!
Let's in: for the dark hemisphere 775
Does now like one of them appear.

753–60 'Why should I praise the orchards of Alcinous, and you boughs that never stretched skyward empty? The fields of Telegonus should yield, the Laurentian fields of Turnus . . . the shores of Antium' (Statius, *Silvae*, 1.3.81–9). Tempe is the classical type of natural beauty; Aranjuez and Bel-Retiro are Spanish royal residences; Ida was sacred to Venus, Elysium the region of the blessed dead.

761–4 Matching Ovid's description of the still uncreated world: 'The Sea, the Earth, all-covering Heaven unframed, / One face had Nature, which they Chaos named: / An undigested lump; a barren load, / Where jarring seeds of things ill-joined abode' (*Metamorphoses*, 1:5–9, Sandys).

767 'You are what the heavens revolve around, what Nature promises, and the epitome of Paradise'; Martial describes the streets of Rome as embellished by Domitian 'Accurate emblems of Elysium' (Martial, *De Spectaculis*, 2, embellished by Thomas Pecke).

770 *boats* possibly with a pun on 'boots'.

771–2 Martial says of a bald man who protected his head with a goatskin, 'He spoke happily who told you that you had shod your head' (12.45). Cleveland makes it a joke about the underside of the earth: 'The Antipodes wear their shoes on their heads' (*Square Cap*, 19); these fishermen's 'leathern boats' (their coracles) are also 'boots' to some ears, and by going out at night, not coming in, they act their Antipodes by working to a different clock: the sleepy Thomas Browne writes at the end of the *Garden of Cyrus* that 'to keep our eyes open longer were but to act our Antipodes'.

773 Like Lord Fairfax they have 'cases fit' (13).

774 The fishermen are amphibious because they move between land and water; but as the sky draws up the dark like an inverted boat the point is generalized: 'We live the life of plants, the life of animals, the life of men, and at last the life of spirits . . . Thus is man that great and true amphibian' (Browne, *Religio Medici*, 1.34).

The Garden

1681, except where noted. There is a probably in-complete Latin version (or original), *Hortus*. The poem is an argument in praise of gardens (but it almost certainly post-dates Marvell's time at *Nun Appleton*) and of retirement; the Epicurean ideal is to the fore (as more explicitly in Jean Passerat's *Hortus Memmii*, which has left its mark on it): 'When Epicurus to the world had taught, / That pleasure was the chiefest good, / (And was perhaps in th' right, if rightly un-derstood) / His life he to his doctrine brought, / And in a garden's shade that sovereign pleasure sought:

/ Whoever a true Epicure would be, / May there find cheap and virtuous luxury' (Cowley, *The Gar-den*, 95–101). But the manner is complicated by in-fluences (pastoral as well as libertine) which are difficult to specify, so that the conventions by which it is to be read are never clear. Intellectual traditions (Platonic, Hermetic, Christian) informing it are often too confidently identified and never quite match the poem's kind of difficulty, which is not intellectual at all.

1

How vainly men themselves amaze
To win the palm, the oak, or bays;
And their uncessant labours see
Crowned from some single herb or tree,
Whose short and narrow vergèd shade   5
Does prudently their toils upbraid;
While all flowers and all trees do close
To weave the garlands of repose.

2

Fair Quiet, have I found thee here,
And Innocence thy sister dear?   10
Mistaken long, I sought you then
In busy companies of men.
Your sacred plants, if here below,
Only among the plants will grow.
Society is all but rude,   15
To this delicious solitude.

3

No white nor red was ever seen
So am'rous as this lovely green.
Fond lovers, cruel as their flame,
Cut in these trees their mistress' name.   20
Little, alas, they know, or heed,
How far these beauties hers exceed!

1–4 Men drive themselves mad to win honour in war ('palm'), in public life (the 'civic oak'), and in poetry ('lau-rel'), only to have their uncessant (a common form in the period) labours rewarded from only one tree.
5–8 Single herbs and trees afford only confined shade (im-plying 'repose'), and knowing their vanity ('prudently') re-buke (but while 'braiding' a wreath) men's efforts (while 'toils' catches an echo of 'nets') to win them. The plants of the garden come together ('close') only to afford repose.
13–16 'Your sacred children ('plants') if they can thrive at all on earth (as Milton's 'Hesperian fables true, / If true, here only', *Paradise Lost*, 4:250–1) can thrive only in a gar-

den: society is almost unsocial compared with the delights of being alone here.'
17–18 'White' and 'red' here characterize sexuality ('My beloved is white and ruddy', Song of Solomon 5: 10); 'green' characterizes vegetable life, 'amorous' because 'lovely' or 'lov-able' (as in Tristan l'Hermite, *Les Louanges du Vert*).
19–24 Virgil's Gallus writes Lycoris's name on young trees: 'The rind of every plant her name shall know; / And, as the rind extends, the love shall grow' (*Eclogues*, 10:53–4, Dryden); Pliny tells the story of a Roman gentleman who fell in love with a tree, kissed it, slept by it, and watered it with wine (*Natural History*, 16.19.1).

Fair trees! wheresoe'er you barks I wound,
No name shall but your own be found.

4

When we have run our passion's heat,   25
Love hither makes his best retreat.
The gods, that mortal beauty chase,
Still in a tree did end their race.
Apollo hunted Daphne so,
Only that she might laurel grow.   30
And Pan did after Syrinx speed,
Not as a nymph, but for a reed.

5

What wond'rous life in this I lead!
Ripe apples drop about my head;
The luscious clusters of the vine   35
Upon my mouth do crush their wine;
The nectarine, and curious peach,
Into my hands themselves do reach;
Stumbling on melons, as I pass,
Ensnared with flowers, I fall on grass.   40

6

Meanwhile the mind, from pleasure less,
Withdraws into its happiness:
The mind, that ocean where each kind
Does straight its own resemblance find;
Yet it creates, transcending these,   45
Far other worlds, and other seas;
Annihilating all that's made
To a green thought in a green shade.

25 'When we have run our passion's course'; but also 'fervour'.

27–32 Fleeing Apollo, Daphne was transformed to a laurel: 'Still Phoebus loves . . . Although thou canst not be / The wife I wished, yet shalt thou be my tree' (Ovid, *Metamorphoses*, 1:553–8, Sandys); fleeing Pan's attentions, Syrinx was transformed to marsh-reeds: 'Pan, when he thought he had his Syrinx clasped / Between his arms, reeds for her body grasped. / He sighs: they, stirred therewith, report again / A mournful sound' (1:705–8) and so musical pipes were invented.

33–8 Such is the generosity of Pliny's Pomona (goddess of orchards) that she would not cause us the trouble of picking her fruit: 'they are ready to drop down and fall into thy mouth, or else to lie under thy feet' (*Natural History*, 23.2.1). Spenser's Bower of Bliss has vines which tempt its visitors: 'And did themselves into their hands incline' (*Faerie Queene*, 2.12.54). These 'curious' fruits are as much 'inquisitive' as 'exquisite'.

41–2 'At the same time the mind withdraws to its own (higher, contemplative) happiness from lesser (sensual) pleasure.' Bodleian MS Eng. poet. d.49 has 'pleasures less'. The obvious interpretation here (supported by a passage in Saint-Amant's *Le Contemplateur*, st.9, describing the passage from 'moindre étoffe' to 'recherche profonde') is variously and ingeniously disputed.

43–4 'Whatsoever is engendered and bred in any part of the world beside is found in the sea' (Pliny, *Natural History*, 9.1.2, but even there reported as a superstition); the mind is 'full without measure of numberless kinds of things' (Augustine, *Confessions*, 10.26).

45–6 'Who can imagine there should only rise / Our single earth, our air and but our skies' (Lucretius, 2:1056, Creech).

47–8 Lucretius observes that things appear to be at rest because their movement at the fundamental level is too subtle for sight, and compares how we see sheep moving about on a distant hill, reduced to 'a steady white spread o'er the green' (2:322). Marvell's perception of what goes on in his mind is further blurred, the whole material world reduced there to an idea coloured by the 'green shade' (from Virgil, *Eclogues*, 10:20) he sits in. Marcus Aurelius observes, 'A good eye must be good to see whatsoever is to be seen, and not green things only; for that is proper to sore eyes' (*Meditations*, 10.35, Meric Casaubon).

7

Here at the fountain's sliding foot,
Or at some fruit-tree's mossy root,   50
Casting the body's vest aside,
My soul into the boughs does glide:
There like a bird it sits, and sings,
Then whets, and combs its silver wings;
And, till prepared for longer flight,   55
Waves in its plumes the various light.

8

Such was that happy garden-state,
While man there walked without a mate:
After a place so pure, and sweet,
What other help could yet be meet!   60
But 'twas beyond a mortal's share
To wander solitary there:
Two paradises 'twere in one
To live in Paradise alone.

9

How well the skilful gardener drew   65
Of flowers and herbs this dial new;
Where from above the milder sun
Does through a fragrant zodiac run;
And, as it works, the industrious bee
Computes its time as well as we.   70
How could such sweet and wholesome hours
Be reckoned but with herbs and flowers!

49 'And the sweet waves of sounding Castaly / With li-
quid foot doth slide down easily' (Virgil, *Culex*, 17, Spenser).
51–5 'Beginning then below, with the easy view . . . sub-
ject to fleshly eye, / From thence to mount aloft by order
due, / To contemplation of the immortal sky, / Of the sore
falcon so I learn to fly, / That flags awhile her fluttering
wings beneath, / Till she herself for stronger flight can
breathe' (Spenser, *Hymn of Heavenly Beauty*, 22–8); Milton's
Wisdom 'plumes her feathers, and lets grow her wings' in
'sweet retirèd solitude' (*Comus*, 375–8). Marvell's soul preens
('whets') its feathers ('silver' from 'the wings of a dove cov-
ered with silver', Psalms 68: 13) which refract and variegate
the light.
57–8 'As soon as two (alas!) together joined, / The serpent
made up three' (Cowley, *Of Solitude*, 34–5).
59–60 'It is not good that the man should be alone; I will

make him an help meet for him' (Genesis 2: 18).
63–4 Counting as gain what is not lost.
65–72 In *Hortus* Marvell describes a floral dial in the gar-
den; here the device is a metaphor for the whole garden, the
'skilful gardener' being God.
67 *milder* suggesting it is now evening.
69–70 'I like the bee . . . Which (toiling) sucks beloved
flowers / About the thymy groves' (Horace, *Odes*, 4.2:27–9,
Fanshawe). The pun on 'thyme' / 'time' informs a song
attributed to Essex and set by Dowland, 'I was a silly bee, /
Who fed on time until my heart gan break, / Yet never
found the time would favour me' (*Third Book of Airs*, 18).
71–2 As for Claudian's old man of Verona: 'No change of
consuls mark to him the year, / The change of seasons is his
calendar. / The cold and heat, winter and summer shows, /
Autumn by fruits, and spring by flowers he knows' (Cowley).

A Dialogue between the Soul and Body

1681; the version in Bodleian MS Eng. poet. d.49
cancels the last four lines and writes *Desunt multa*;
there is a discontinuity untypical of the rest of the
poem. 'As the distraction of the mind . . . alters the
temperature of the body, so the distraction and dis-

temper of the body will cause a distemperature of the
soul; and 'tis hard to decide which of these two do
more harm to the other' (Burton, *Anatomy*, 1.2.5.1).
Aristotle, *Politics*, 1254b, argues that the equality of
body and soul is 'always hurtful'.

Soul. O who shall, from this dungeon, raise
A soul enslaved so many ways?
With bolts of bones, that fettered stands
In feet; and manacled in hands.
Here blinded with an eye; and there   5
Deaf with the drumming of an ear.
A soul hung up, as 'twere, in chains
Of nerves, and arteries, and veins.
Tortured, besides each other part,
In a vain head, and double heart.   10

Body. O who shall me deliver whole,
From bonds of this tyrannic soul?
Which, stretched upright, impales me so,
That mine own precipice I go;
And warms and moves this needless frame: 15
(A fever could but do the same).
And, wanting where its spite to try,
Has made me live to let me die.
A body that could never rest,
Since this ill spirit it possessed.   20

Soul. What magic could me thus confine
Within another's grief to pine?
Where whatsoever it complain,
I feel, that cannot feel, the pain.
And all my care itself employs,   25
That to preserve, which me destroys:
Constrained not only to endure
Diseases, but, what's worse, the cure:
And ready oft the port to gain,
Am shipwrecked into health again.   30

Body. But physic yet could never reach
The maladies thou me dost teach;

1–6 'O wretched man that I am! who shall deliver me from the body of this death?' (Romans 7: 24, the motto for Quarles, *Emblems*, 5.8); the soul 'is a helpless prisoner, chained hand and foot in the body, compelled to view reality . . . only through its prison bars' (Plato, *Phaedo*, 82e); reality is reached by a man 'cutting himself off as much as possible from his eyes and ears and virtually all the rest of his body, as an impediment' (*Phaedo*, 66a). Marvell's quasi-etymological punning ('fettered . . . feet', 'manacled . . . hands'; 'drumming . . . ear') is anticipated in the Jesuit Herman Hugo's *Pia Desideria*, 3.38.

10 The head's pretensions are put in doubt by its emptiness; the heart's duplicity is confirmed in its having two ventricles.

11–12 Inverting 'the creature also shall be delivered from the bondage of corruption' (Romans 8: 15).

13–16 The soul demands from the body, itself having no need ('needless') of the soul, an uprightness at once painful and dangerous to it. Plato speaks of the impossibility of the body's apprehending 'absolute uprightness' (*Phaedo* 65d–e); here it is deluded into imagining it: 'Fond man thus to a precipice / Aspires, till at the top his eyes / Have lost the safety of the plain' (*Aramantha*, 264–5), which more clearly informs Marvell's return to the conceit: 'stretched to such a height in his own fancy . . . his eyes dazzled at the precipice of his stature' (*The Rehearsal Transprosed*).

19–20 'Their restless minds are tossed and vary . . . erected and dejected in an instant' (*Anatomy*, 1.2.1.2); 'they feign a company of antic, fantastical conceits . . . they hear and see . . . such phantoms and goblins, they fear . . . follow them' (*Anatomy*, 1.3.1.2).

23–4 Though the soul cannot feel physical pain, it must attend to the body's complaints of it.

27–8 Because 'Bodily sickness is for his soul's health' (*Anatomy*, 1.1.1.1).

29–30 Arrival at the port of death is frustrated by recovery.

Whom first the cramp of Hope does tear:
And then the palsy shakes of Fear.
The pestilence of Love does heat: 35
Or Hatred's hidden ulcer eat.
Joy's cheerful madness does perplex:
Or Sorrow's other madness vex.
Which Knowledge forces me to know;
And Memory will not forego.   40
What but a soul could have the wit
To build me up for sin so fit?
So architects do square and hew,
Green trees that in the forest grew.

33–8 The mental disorders are all manifested physically: 'anger, fear, sorrow, obtrectation, emulation . . . cause grievous diseases in the body' (*Anatomy*, 1.5.1.1). Typical melancholy disorders are given in *Anatomy*, 1.3.1.2: seized on by 'grief, fear, agony, discontent' but unstable in their disaffections, 'sometimes profusely laughing . . . and then again weeping without a cause'.

41–4 'Souls form and build those mansions where they dwell; / Whoe'er but sees his body must confess, / The architect no doubt, could be no less' (Cowley, *Davideis*, 4:519–21).

Bermudas

1681. While tutor to William Dutton at Eton in 1653, Marvell lodged with John Oxenbridge, who had twice visited the Summer Islands or Bermudas as a Puritan divine (first as a refugee from Laudian persecution); he wrote a Latin epitaph for Mrs Oxenbridge (d. 1658). Marvell would know Captain John Smith's *The General History of Virginia, New England, and the Summer Isles* (which gives a less than rosy picture of the islands) and Waller's mock-heroic *The Battle of the Summer Islands* (about a whaling expedition). The song the emigrants sing is like a Psalm (104 is commonly adduced); but their Utopianism is undercut by the poem's recollection of Horace's absurd call to the people of Rome to forsake their war-torn country and emigrate *en masse* to 'those isles / Which swim in plenty, the blest soils: / Where the earth's virginwomb unploughed is fruitful, / And the unpruned vine still youthful: / The olive tree makes no abortion there, / And figs hang dangling in the air' (*Epodes*, 16:41–6, Fanshawe).

Where the remote Bermudas ride
In the ocean's bosom unespied,
From a small boat, that rowed along,
The listening winds received this song.
        What should we do but sing His praise   5
That led us through the watery maze,
Unto an isle so long unknown,
And yet far kinder than our own?
Where He the huge sea-monsters wracks,
That lift the deep upon their backs.   10
He lands us on a grassy stage;
Safe from the storms, and prelate's rage.

1–2 The islands 'ride' like a fleet at anchor.
6–8 Lewis Hughes's *Letter sent into England from the Summer Islands* (1615) remarks how hard to reach they were, and supposes God reserved them for the English (though they were discovered by Juan Bermudez in 1515); 'kinder' because a haven for refugees and because temperate (and so punningly renamed the Summer Islands, in fact for Sir George Somers).
9–10 Waller's *Battle* concerns 'Two mighty whales! which swelling seas had tossed, / And left them prisoners on the rocky coast' (2:11–12).

He gave us this eternal Spring,
Which here enamels everything;
And sends the fowls to us in care,   15
On daily visits through the air.
He hangs in shades the orange bright,
Like golden lamps in a green night.
And does in the pom'gránates close,
Jewels more rich than Hormuz shows.   20
He makes the figs our mouths to meet;
And throws the melons at our feet.
But apples plants of such a price,
No tree could ever bear them twice.
With cedars, chosen by His hand,   25
From Lebanon, He stores the land.
And makes the hollow seas, that roar,
Proclaim the ambergris on shore.
He cast (of which we rather boast)
The Gospel's pearl upon our coast.   30
And in these rocks for us did frame
A temple, where to sound His name.
O let our voice His praise exalt,
Till it arrive at Heaven's vault:
Which thence (perhaps) rebounding, may   35
Echo beyond the Mexic Bay.
        Thus sung they, in the English boat,
An holy and a cheerful note,
And all the way, to guide their chime,
With falling oars they kept the time.   40

13–4 Spring colours ('enamels') the landscape. Waller writes 'the kind Spring, which but salutes us here, / Inhabits there, and courts them all the year' (*Battle*, 1:40–1); but Smith, *History*, 170, notes: 'There seems to be a continual Spring, which is the cause that some things come not to that maturity and perfection as were requisite.'

15–16 'And the ravens brought [Elijah] bread and flesh in the morning, and bread and flesh in the evening' (1 Kings 17: 6); Smith, *History*, 172, describes a flock of ravens visiting plague victims.

17–30 'They came unto the brook of Eschol, and cut down from thence a branch with one cluster of grapes, and they bare it between two upon a staff; and they brought of the pomegranates, and the figs' (Numbers 13: 23, of the Israelite spies in Canaan); Waller writes of: 'Bermuda walled with rocks ... That happy island where huge lemons grow, / And orange trees, which golden fruit do bear, / The Hesperian garden boasts of none so fair; / Where shining pearl, coral and many a pound, / On the rich shore, of ambergris is found. / The lofty cedar ... to heaven aspires' (*Battle*, 1:6–11).

19–20 Hormuz in the Persian gulf was famous for pearls and jewels.

21–2 *The Garden*, 37–40, is likewise generous.

23–4 Ripe fruits are golden: Revett describes how 'the mellow fruits not want / The price of a Hesperian plant' (*Autumn*, 26). Lucan decribes the despoiled Gardens of the Hesperides: 'This golden grove of treasures store, / (Whose boughs such shining apples bore) ... stoop with overweight of gold. / But great Alcides took away / From these rich trees the precious prey' (*Pharsalia*, 9:360–6, Gorges). The Edenic connotation of 'apple' suggests a replanted paradise.

25–6 'Thus saith the Lord ... Why build ye not me an house of cedar' (2 Samuel 7: 5–7); Lebanon was famous for its cedars.

27–8 The roaring waves announce the valuable whale-musk, so plentiful it arrives on each tide; Smith, *History*, 172, complains of its rarity.

30 'The kingdom of heaven is like unto a merchant man, seeking goodly pearls: Who, when he had found one pearl of great price, went and sold all that he had and bought it' (Matthew 13: 45–6); 'neither cast ye your pearls before swine, lest they trample them under their feet' (Matthew 7: 6).

35–6 Oxenbridge's *Seasonable Proposition of Propagating the Gospel* (1670) derides such optimism.

On Mr Milton's *Paradise Lost*

Paradise Lost, 1674, signed A. M. The second edition of *Paradise Lost* is prefaced by two verse tributes, the other in Latin by Samuel Barrow, who gives an unembarrassed heroic account of the poem. Marvell's *Rehearsal Transprosed* (1672) had provoked hostility not only against himself but against Milton, with whose name his own was (often scurrilously) associated. The defence of himself and Milton together made in *The Rehearsal Transprosed* is continued here. Despite the couplets, the sense of Milton imitated is strong.

When I beheld the poet blind, yet bold,
In slender book his vast design unfold,
Messiah crowned, God's reconciled decree,
Rebelling angels, the forbidden tree,
Heaven, Hell, Earth, Chaos, All; the argument   5
Held me a while misdoubting his intent,
That he would ruin (for I saw him strong)
The sacred truths to fable and old song,
(So Samson groped the temple's posts in spite)
The world o'erwhelming to revenge his sight.   10
   Yet as I read, soon growing less severe,
I liked his project, the success did fear;
Through that wide field how he his way should find
O'er which lame Faith leads Understanding blind;
Lest he perplexed the things he would explain,   15
And what was easy he should render vain.
   Or if a work so infinite he spanned,
Jealous I was that some less skilful hand
(Such as disquiet always what is well,
And by ill imitating would excel)   20
Might hence presume the whole Creation's day
To change in scenes, and show it in a play.
   Pardon me, mighty poet, nor despise
My causeless, yet not impious, surmise.
But I am now convinced, and none will dare   25
Within thy labours to pretend a share.
Thou hast not missed one thought that could be fit,
And all that was improper dost omit:
So that no room is here for writers left,
But to detect their ignorance or theft.   30
    That majesty which through thy work doth reign
Draws the devout, deterring the profane.
And things divine thou treats of in such state

---

1   Richard Leigh, replying to Marvell's *The Rehearsal Transprosed*, attacks Milton's boldness and blindness together: 'Even timorous minds are courageous and bold enough to shape prodigious forms . . .the blind author of *Paradise Lost* begins his third Book . . . groping for a beam of light.'

2   Sandys's prefatory poem to *A Paraphrase upon the Psalms of David* (1636): 'no narrow verse such mysteries, / Deep sense, and high expression, could comprise.'

7–8   As Milton complains of previous 'heroic song' that it set itself 'to dissect / With long and tedious havoc fabled knights' (*Paradise Lost*, 9:29–30).

9–10   'Samson took hold of the two middle pillars on which the house stood . . . And Samson said, Let me die with the Philistines. And he bowed himself with all his might; and the house fell upon the lords' (Judges 16: 29–30); Marvell supplies Samson's 'spite', from which Milton is free.

17   'Or even if he comprehended the eternal operations of God'.

18–22   Milton gave Dryden 'leave to tag his points' (Aubrey, *Brief Lives*, as at 49–50); Dryden prepared an operatic version of *Paradise Lost*: *The State of Innocence* (1677, but complete in early 1674).

30   'Imitators would only uncover ('detect') their own ignorance (by omission or misunderstanding) or the plagiary.'

As them preserves, and thee inviolate.
At once delight and horror on us seize, 35
Thou sing'st with so much gravity and ease;
And above human flight dost soar aloft,
With plume so strong, so equal, and so soft.
The bird named from that Paradise you sing
So never flags, but always keeps on wing. 40
    Where couldst thou words of such a compass find?
Whence furnish such a vast expense of mind?
Just Heaven thee, like Tiresias, to requite,
Rewards with prophecy thy loss of sight.
    Well mightst thou scorn thy readers to allure 45
With tinkling rhyme, of thy own sense secure,
While the Town-Bays writes all the while and spells,
And like a pack-horse tires without his bells.
Their fancies like our bushy-points appear,
The poets tag them; we for fashion wear. 50
I too transported by the mode offend,
And while I meant to praise thee, must commend.
Thy verse created like thy theme sublime,
In number, weight, and measure, needs not rhyme.

35 Da Gama's rehearsal of Portuguese history is 'Fraught with high deeds, with horror, and delight' (Camoens, *Lusiads*, 5.90, Fanshawe); Stanley's revised compliment to Sherburne in the *Tragedies of Seneca* (1701), so defines the tragic emotion: 'At once begetting horror and delight' (18).
36 *gravity* The figurative sense is uppermost; but the following lines half take up the literal sense.
37–8 Milton offers 'song /That with no middle flight intends to soar' (*Paradise Lost*, 1:13–14), defying the 'gravity' of 36.
39–40 'Wingless they fly; and yet their flight extends, / Till with their flight, their unknown life's-date ends' (Sylvester, *Divine Weeks*, 1.5.807–8); birds of paradise were known only from defective museum specimens.
43–4 Jupiter compensated for Juno's blinding Tiresias when he 'Informed his intellect; and did supply / His body's eyesight, with his mind's clear eye' (Ovid, *Metamorphoses*, 3:336–8, Sandys). In *Paradise Lost*, Milton compares himself with two blind poets and two blind prophets: 'Blind Thamyris and blind Maeonides [Homer], / And Tiresias and Phineus Prophets old' (3:35–6).

46 Milton's prefatory note to *Paradise Lost* condemns 'the jingling sound of like endings'; Fuller, *Church History*, 1.3.1, writes, 'The puddle poet did hope, that the jingling of his rhyme would drown the sound of his false quantity.'
47–8 Dryden appears as Bays in Buckingham's *Rehearsal* (1672); but the reference is unspecifically to any poetaster who writes with difficulty ('spells'); Earle, *Microcosmography*, 51, compares the plodding student to 'a dull carrier's horse'.
49–50 The laces or 'points' for attaching hose to the doublet were fashionably tasselled or 'bushy'. Rhyme in relation to the line has the same merely decorative function: in *The Rehearsal Transprosed*, rhyming is identified with 'tagging of points in a garret'.
52 'Commend' is used instead of 'praise' to rhyme with 'offend'. But commendation might rate higher: 'If to admire were to commend, my praise / Might then both thee, thy work and merit raise' (Jonson, *Epigrams*, 132, on Sylvester).
54 'Thou has created all things in measure, and number, and weight' (Wisdom 11: 20): God's poem does not rhyme.

Henry Vaughan (1622–1695)

Silex Scintillans, from which, in either of its two editions, all the poems below are taken, was calculated as a antidote to the disease of 'vicious verse' and 'foreign vanities' infecting English culture. Vaughan himself, he acknowledges in the preface to the first, had languished of the sickness. He left Oxford without a degree, he studied law, he clerked for the Chief Justice in the Brecon circuit, he probably served with the King's army towards the end of the first Civil War, he married, and in 1646 he published *Poems, with the Tenth Satire of Juvenal Englished*, a (very fine) collection which he describes as relatively 'innoxious'. His turn from the secular was never quite complete, for in 1651 he included earlier (though innocent) pieces in *Olor Iscanus*; the strangely belated collection of similar pieces *Thalia Rediviva* (1678), with complimentary verses taken from the long dead Katherine Philips among others, may not have been published on his own initiative. The model for the reformed poetry, purged of excesses and heavily reliant on scriptural associations, offered in *Silex Scintillans* (1650) was 'the blessed man, Mr George Herbert, whose holy life and verse gained many pious converts (of whom I am the least) and gave the first check to a most flourishing and admired wit of his time'. Its inspiration is more obscure. The volume takes its title from the emblem which prefaces it: struck by a divine thunderbolt, a flaming or sparkling (*scintillans*) flint rock (*silex*) drops tears. The accompanying Latin verses explain that the poet was a flint impervious to the whisperings of his gentle God, but that an angry God has broken his heart open, and that now in the midst of his wrecked riches he is richer by far. The heartbreak is sometimes identified with the loss in 1648 of his younger brother William. With his twin brother Thomas, the hermetical philosopher and alchemist, the relationship was more certainly influential, not only in *Hermetical Physic* (1655) and *The Chemist's Key* (1657), but in pervasive habits of imagination; his *Works* are edited by Alan Rudrum with the assistance of Jennifer Drake-Brockman (Oxford: Clarendon Press, 1984). A second part of *Silex Scintillans* was added in 1655. Between the first and the expanded editions, Vaughan produced *The Mount of Olives or Solitary Devotions* (1652) and then *Flores Solitudinis* (1654), which consisted of three prose translations and a biography of Paulinus of Nola. The standard biography is F. E. Hutchinson, *Henry Vaughan: A Life and Interpretation*, revised edition (Oxford: Clarendon Press, 1971). There is a facsimile edition of the 1650 *Silex Scintillans* (Menston: Scolar Press, 1968). The standard is *The Works of Henry Vaughan*, ed. L. C. Martin, second edition (Oxford: Clarendon Press, 1957); but the fullest and best annotation of the poems is in *Complete Poems*, ed. Alan Rudrum (Harmondsworth: Penguin, 1976). Imilda Tuttle has prepared a *Concordance to Vaughan's Silex Scintillans* (University Park: Pennsylvania State University Press, 1969). There is a survey of criticism by Robert E. Bourdette in *English Literary Renaissance*, 4 (1974), 299–310.

Regeneration

The poem describes a vision of spiritual regeneration: 'except a man be born again, he cannot see the kingdom of God' (John 3: 3). The apparatus of pilgrimage (narrated with great force) is traditional (as in Herbert's *The Pilgrimage*, whose stanza the poem adapts); but its character is often obscure. The parallels with the *Lumen de Lumine* (1651) and other work of the poet's twin brother Thomas are strong. The *Lumen* opens: 'It was about the dawning of day-break, when . . . I suddenly fell asleep. Here . . . I was reduced to a night of a more deep tincture than that which I had formerly spent . . . I moved every way for discoveries, but was still entertained with darkness and silence, and I thought myself translated to the land of desolation'; and many of the details in the poem's central section (33–48) are common to it (the grove itself, the vital gold, the chequering of clouds, the odorous air); but these are debts to shared spiritual experience. The poem's rhetoric is lodged in scripture.

1

A ward, and still in bonds, one day
    I stole abroad,
It was high-spring, and all the way
    Primrosed, and hung with shade;
      Yet, was it frost within,   5
      And surly winds
Blasted my infant buds, and sin
    Like clouds eclipsed my mind.

2

Stormed thus; I straight perceived my spring
    Mere stage, and show,   10
My walk a monstrous, mountained thing
    Rough-cast with rocks, and snow;
      And as a pilgrim's eye
      Far from relief,
Measures the melancholy sky   15
    Then drops, and rains for grief,

3

So sighed I upwards still, at last
    'Twixt steps, and falls
I reached the pinnacle, where placed
    I found a pair of scales,   20
      I took them up and laid
      In the one late pains,
The other smoke, and pleasures weighed
    But proved the heavier grains;

4

With that, some cried, "Away"; straight I   25
    Obeyed, and led
Full east, a fair, fresh field could spy
    Some called it, *Jacob's Bed*;

---

1 'The heir, as long as he is a child, differeth nothing from a servant ... But is under tutors and governors until the time appointed of the father. Even so we ... were in bondage under the elements of the world: But when the fulness of the time was come, God sent forth his Son ... to redeem them that were under the law, that we might receive the adoption of sons' (Galatians 4: 1–5).

3–4 'Her walk was green ... and purled all the way with daisies and primroses' (*Lumen*, 6).

5–9 'Thou art my servant: O Israel ... I have blotted out, as a thick cloud, thy transgressions, and, as a cloud, thy sins: return unto me; for I have redeemed thee' (Isaiah 44: 21–2).

7–8 Herbert's motions to prayer are 'by frost's extremity / Nipped in the bud' (*Employment* (1), 3–4); but he never implies his own mind is a source of light.

10 'Surely every man walketh in a vain show' (Psalms 39: 6).

13–15 Like Herbert 'I was deceived: / My hill was fur-

ther' (*The Pilgrimage*, 30–1); the poet is a disappointed version of Casimir's happy man 'who in this vale / Redeems his time, shutting out all / Thoughts of the world, whose longing eyes / Are ever pilgrims in the skies' (*Odes*, 3.22:15–18, Vaughan).

20–4 He finds he has not suffered enough, as in *Repentance*: 'I told [a river's] tears, / But when these came unto the scale, / My sins alone outweighed them all' (44–6); recalling Christopher Harvey, *Schola Cordis*, 20, where Christ refuses the pilgrim's heart as too light, 'as filled with froth'.

27–8 'Jacob .. lighted upon a certain place ... and he took of the stones of that place, and put them for his pillows, and lay down in that place to sleep. And he dreamed, and behold a ladder set up on the earth, and the top of it reached to heaven: and behold the angels of God ascending and descending on it ... And Jacob awaked ... and said: Surely the Lord is in this place ... this is none other but the house of God, and this is the gate of heaven' (Genesis 28: 10–17).

A virgin-soil, which no
Rude feet e'er trod,   30
Where (since he stepped there) only go
Prophets, and friends of God.

5

Here, I reposed; but scarce well set,
A grove descried
Of stately height, whose branches met   35
And mixed on every side;
I entered, and once in
(Amazed to see it)
Found all was changed, and a new Spring
Did all my senses greet;   40

6

The unthrift sun shot vital gold
A thousand pieces,
And heaven its azure did unfold
Chequered with snowy fleeces,
The air was all in spice   45
And every bush
A garland wore; thus fed my eyes
But all the ear lay hush.

7

Only a little fountain lent
Some use for ears,   50
And on the dumb shades' language spent
The music of her tears;
I drew her near, and found
The cistern full
Of divers stones, some bright, and round   55
Others ill-shaped, and dull.

8

The first (pray mark) as quick as light
Danced through the flood,
But, th' last more heavy than the night

29–32 '[Wisdom] maketh all things new . . . entering into holy souls, she maketh them friends of God, and prophets' (Wisdom of Solomon 7: 27). By 'virgin soil' is understood uncultivated and naturally generative ground; here it is rendered regenerative by an event in its past.
33–48 The living Church repairs the ravages of winter: 'the light of the sun shall be sevenfold . . . in the day that the Lord bindeth up the breach of his people' (Isaiah 30: 26); God stretches 'out the heavens like a curtain' (Psalms 104: 2); he 'scattereth his bright cloud: And it is turned round about by his counsels' (Job 37: 11–12); and (the poems's tail-quotation), his winds 'blow upon my garden, that the spices thereof may flow out' (Song of Solomon 4: 16).
49–60 The 'fountain of the water of life' (Revelation 21: 6) breaks the silence (the non-language of the 'dumb shades')

and weeps into the cistern to regenerate its contents by a quasi-alchemical separation of the corruptible and the incorruptible. 'As Christ was raised up from the dead . . . even so we also should walk in newness of life . . . Knowing this, that our old man is crucified with him, that the body of sin might be destroyed, that henceforth we should not serve sin' (Romans 6: 4–6).
57–64 The dancing and the fixed stones faze the poet, but the dance of the one follows on the fixing of the other: 'We preach Christ crucified, unto the Jews a stumbling block, and unto the Greeks foolishness' (1 Corinthians 1: 23); 'the last Adam [Christ] was made a quickening spirit' (1 Corinthians 15: 45); 'Ye also, as lively stones, are built up a spiritual house, an holy priesthood, to offer up spiritual sacrifices' (1 Peter 2: 5).

Nailed to the centre stood;   60
    I wondered much, but tired
        At last with thought,
My restless eye that still desired
        As strange an object brought;

9

It was a bank of flowers, where I descried   65
        (Though 'twas mid-day,)
Some fast asleep, others broad-eyed
        And taking in the ray,
        Here musing long, I heard
            A rushing wind   70
Which still increased, but whence it stirred
        Nor where I could not find;

10

I turned me round, and to each shade
        Dispatched an Eye,
To see, if any leaf had made   75
        Least motion, or reply,
        But while I listening sought
            My mind to ease
By knowing, where 'twas, or where not,
        It whispered; "Where I please."   80

"Lord", then said I, "On me one breath,
And let me die before my death!"

Arise O North, and come thou south-wind, and blow upon my garden,
that the spices thereof may flow out. Song of Solomon 4: 16.

67 'Watch therefore, for ye know neither the day nor the hour wherein the Son of man cometh' (Matthew 25: 13); though in the parable of the wise and foolish virgins, Christ comes at midnight.
70–80 'The wind bloweth where it listeth, and thou hearest the sound thereof, but canst not tell whence it cometh, and whither it goeth' (John 3: 8); and at Pentecost the gathered disciples were visited by 'a sound from heaven as of a rushing mighty wind' (Acts 2: 2). *1651* reads 'No where' at 72.
81–2 'I knew such a man (whether in the body, or out of the body, I cannot tell: God knoweth;) How that he was caught up into paradise, and heard unspeakable words' (2 Corinthians 12: 3–4); 'that which thou sowest is not quickened, except it die' (1 Corinthians 15:36).

The British Church

The British Church addresses Christ as the Bride addresses the Bridegroom in the Song of Songs, but with less assurance. Varying the stanza of 'Come, come, what do I here' (projecting his own death to effect reunion with his dead brother) it shares with it a nervous anxiety about the recovery of what is lost. The title is shared with Herbert, whose optimism it has abandoned.

1

Ah! he is fled!
And while these here their mists, and shadows hatch,

2 *here* in the world 'where in a magic mist / Men hatch their own delusion and deceit' (More, *Psychathanasia*, 1.1:142–3).

My glorious head
Doth on those hills of myrrh, and incense watch.
Haste, haste my dear,   5
The soldiers here
Cast in their lots again,
That seamless coat
The Jews touched not,
These dare divide, and stain.   10

2

O get thee wings!
Or if as yet (until these clouds depart,
And the day springs,)
Thou think'st it good to tarry where thou art,
Write in thy books   15
My ravished looks
Slain flock, and pillaged fleeces,
And haste thee so
As a young roe
Upon the mounts of spices.   20

*O rosa campi! O lilium convallium! quomodo nunc facta es pabulum
aprorum!*

3–4 'For the husband is the head of the wife, even as Christ is the head of the church' (Ephesians 5: 23); and the bridegroom wakes through the night on 'the mountain of myrrh' and 'the hill of frankincense' (Song of Solomon 4: 6). 6–10 'Then the soldiers, when they had crucified Jesus, took his garments . . . now the coat was without seam, woven from the top throughout. They said therefore . . . Let us not rend it, but cast lots for it' (John 19: 23–4). Its seamlessness is a figure of the unity of the Church, but now divided and at 16–17 despoiled. 18–20 'Make haste, my beloved, and be thou like to a roe or to a young hart upon the mountains of spices' (Song of Solomon 8: 14).

The Latin epigraph collects scattered tags: 'O rose of the field' (Isaiah 40: 6: 'All flesh is grass and the goodliness thereof is as the flower of the field'); 'O lily of the valleys' (Song of Solomon 2: 1: 'I [the bride] am the rose of Sharon, and the lily of the valleys'); 'how are you now made food for swine' (Psalms 80: 13: 'the boar out of the wood doth waste it [the vine]').

The Shower

The leading conceit derives from the cycle of evaporation and precipitation given in Herbert's *The Answer*: 'As a young exhalation, newly waking, / Scorns his first bed of dirt, and means the sky; / But cooling by the way, grows pursy and slow, / And settling to a cloud, doth live and die / In that dark state of tears' and imitated again in *Disorder and Frailty*. But the tears here are curative, like Herbert's 'spring shower' in *The Flower*. The final stanza echoes Psalms 65: 10: 'Thou makest [the earth] soft with showers,' and 2 Samuel 23: 4: 'as the tender grass springing out of the earth by clear shining after rain'. Wither, *Emblems*, 4.32 (*Post nubila Phoebus*) offers a blander reassurance: 'Behold there is a rainbow in the cloud'.

1

'Twas so, I saw thy birth: that drowsy lake
From her faint bosom breathed thee, the disease
Of her sick waters, and infectious ease.
But, now at even

2–3 The cloud is pestilential like Ovid's striking the island Aegina: 'Heaven first, the earth with thickened vapors shrouds; / And lazy heat involves in sullen clouds . . . Yet still the death-producing Auster [south wind] blew. / Sunk springs, and standing lakes infected grew' (*Metamorphoses*, 7:528–33, Sandys).

Too gross for heaven, 5
Thou fall'st in tears, and weep'st for thy mistake.

2
Ah! it is so with me; oft have I pressed
Heaven with a lazy breath, but fruitless this
Pierced not; Love only can with quick access
Unlock the way, 10
When all else stray
The smoke, and exhalations of the breast.

3
Yet, if as thou dost melt, and with thy train
Of drops make soft the earth, my eyes could weep
O'er my hard heart, that's bound up, and asleep, 15
Perhaps at last
(Some such showers past)
My God would give a sunshine after rain.

9 *quick access* 'Of what an easy quick access . . . art thou'
(Herbert, *Prayer* (2), 1).
11–12 Anything else will fail to enter Heaven, certainly

'The heart, that vapours out itself in smoke, / And with
those cloudy shadows thinks to cloak / Its empty nakedness'
(Harvey, *Schola Cordis*, 21:47–9).

The Retreat

In *Corruption* (3–6) Vaughan remembers when man
'shined a little . . . and knew whence / He came'.
The Platonically derived (though not Platonic) eleva-
tion of pre-adult experience is widely distributed. In
antiquity: 'Look at the soul of a child . . . a soul that
has not yet come to accept its separation from its
source . . . how beautiful throughout is such a soul as
that! It is not yet fouled by the bodily passions; it is
still hardly detached from the soul of the Kosmos'
(*Hermetica*, 10 [*The Key*]); 'You too creatures of earth,
dream of your first state, though with a dim idea . . .
thither, to true happiness, your natural course guides
you' (Boethius, *De Consolatione*, prosa, 3.3); 'A grain
of this bright love each thing / Had given at first by
their great King; / And still they creep (drawn on by
this:) / And look back towards their first bliss' (*De
Consolatione*, metrum 4.6, Vaughan's version). The
emphasis on loss is dominant: 'A child is a man in a
small letter, yet the best copy of Adam before he

tasted of Eve, or the apple . . . His father . . . sighs to
see what innocence he has outlived. The elder he
grows he is a stair lower from God' (Earle,
Microcosmography); 'they came into the world . . . with
little tears in their eyes, to show they were then upon
travelling from their Maker' (Richard Carpenter, *Ex-
perience, History, and Divinity*, 3.4.2); 'Spirits . . . when
they are in their own country are like the inhabitants
of green fields who live perpetually among flowers
. . . but here below . . . they mourn' (Thomas
Vaughan's *Anthroposophia Theomagica*). The possibil-
ity of recovery is sometimes open: 'when [the soul]
hath departed hence . . . should it not backward hie /
From whence it came? . . . such divinity / Is in our
souls that nothing less then God / Could send them
forth (as Plato's schools descry) / Wherefore when
they retreat a free abode / They'll find' (More,
Antipsychopannychia, 2.14).

Happy those early days! when I
Shined in my angel-infancy.
Before I understood this place
Appointed for my second race,
Or taught my soul to fancy aught 5
But a white, celestial thought,

4 *place . . . race* 'Earth, where I must live out the bodily
life'.
6–8 *The Constellation* (47–8) laments 'black days . . . What

time we from our first love swerve', that is, 'the love the
soul had at first'; 'I have somewhat against thee,' Christ
says, 'because thou hast left thy first love' (Revelation 2: 4).

When yet I had not walked above
A mile, or two, from my first love,
And looking back (at that short space)
Could see a glimpse of his bright-face;   10
When on some gilded cloud, or flower
My gazing soul would dwell an hour,
And in those weaker glories spy
Some shadows of eternity;
Before I taught my tongue to wound   15
My conscience with a sinful sound,
Or had the black art to dispense
A several sin to every sense,
But felt through all this fleshly dress
Bright shoots of everlastingness.   20
O how I long to travel back
And tread again that ancient track!
That I might once more reach that plain,
Where first I left my glorious train,
From whence the enlightened spirit sees   25
That shady city of palm trees;
But (ah!) my soul with too much stay
Is drunk, and staggers in the way.
Some men a forward motion love,
But I by backward steps would move,   30
And when this dust falls to the urn
In that state I came return.

15–16   The workers of iniquity 'whet their tongue like a sword . . . But God shall shoot at them with an arrow . . . So they shall make their own tongue to fall upon themselves' (Psalms 64: 2–8).

20   *shoots of everlastingness* 'The conscience, the character of a god stamped in it, and the apprehension of eternity, do all prove it a shoot of everlastingness' (Felltham, *Resolves*, 1.64). The 'shoot' grows from the seed or 'grain' of God's love.

25–6   'And Moses went up . . . to the top of Pisgah . . . And the Lord showed him all the land of Gilead . . . and the plain of the valley of Jericho, the city of palm trees' (Deuteronomy 34: 1–3).

27–8   'The soul too is then dragged by the body into the region of the changeable, and wanders about and is confused; the world spins round her, and she is like a drunkard, when she touches change' (Plato, *Phaedo*, 79c).

Silence, and stealth of days! 'tis now

Twelve hundred hours (1–3) give a date seven weeks after the death of its subject, Vaughan's brother William (14 July 1648). The poem opposes the false consolations of memory to the true consolations of anticipated reunion. Johann Mannich's *Sacra Emblemata* (Nuremberg, 1624) 22, 25 and 29 give analogous images of light in darkness.

¶
Silence, and stealth of days! 'tis now
Since thou art gone,
Twelve hundred hours, and not a brow
But clouds hang on.
As he that in some cave's thick damp   5
Locked from the light,

5–12   The sense is explained by 13–24. His brother's memory is a lamp, a 'sun' in the underground of his sorrow, but the poet loses this 'glimmering ray' as he travels from it, and is forced back to his cave of artificial day.

Fixeth a solitary lamp,
    To brave the night,
And walking from his sun, when past
    That glimmering ray   10
Cuts through the heavy mists in haste
    Back to his day,
So o'er fled minutes I retreat
    Unto that hour
Which showed thee last, but did defeat   15
    Thy light, and power,
I search, and rack my soul to see
    Those beams again,
But nothing but the snuff to me
    Appeareth plain;   20
That dark, and dead sleeps in its known,
    And common urn,
But those fled to their Maker's throne,
    There shine, and burn;
O could I track them! but souls must   25
    Track one the other,
And now the spirit, not the dust
    Must be thy brother.
Yet I have one pearl by whose light
    All things I see,   30
And in the heart of earth, and night
    Find Heaven, and thee.

19–22 The flameless end ('snuff') of his brother's memory is reduced to the interred body; the spiritual flame is elsewhere (23–4).
25–6 So in another poem of 1648: 'our weaker sense denies us sight / And bodies cannot trace the spirit's flight' (*An Elegie on the Death of Mr. R. Hall*, 65–6).
29–30 Henry More reflects that if life ends 'Which like a burning lamp doth waste away . . . The soul may find an unexpected ray / Of light [from] her own fulness' (*Antipsychopannychia*, 2.27). A pearl gives the light because 'the kingdom of heaven is like unto a merchant man, seeking goodly pearls: Who when he had found one pearl of great price, he went and sold all that he had, and bought it' (Matthew 13: 45–6). In *To the Holy Bible* 26–8 Vaughan recalls Scripture as showing him 'that pearl I sought elsewhere. / Gladness, and peace, and hope, and love, / The secret favours of the Dove'. Pearls recur in Vaughan; they 'display / Through the loose-crystal-streams a glance of day' (*Upon the Poems and Plays of . . . Cartwright*, 38).

The World

Casimir *Odes*, 2.5 (translated by G. Hils as *A Departure from Things Human*) describes a visionary flight above earthly achievement; but here a promised vision of eternity is compromised by reflection on the state of the world. Dante, contemplating the ranks of the 'holy host' as the unfolding petals of a paradisal rose, wonders about himself 'come from the human to the divine, from the temporal to the eternal, from Florence to the righteous and the clean in Paradise' (*Paradiso*, 31:37–9); here the poet, in something like a Cowleian ode, assesses the miseries of the world and reflects on his own election.

1

I saw Eternity the other night
Like a great ring of pure and endless light,
    All calm, as it was bright,
And round beneath it, Time in hours, days, years
      Driven by the spheres   5
Like a vast shadow moved, in which the world
    And all her train were hurled;
The doting lover in his quaintest strain
    Did there complain,
Near him, his lute, his fancy, and his flights,   10
    Wit's sour delights,
With gloves, and knots the silly snares of pleasure
    Yet his dear treasure
All scattered lay, while he his eyes did pore
    Upon a flower.   15

2

The darksome statesman hung with weights and woe
Like a thick midnight-fog moved there so slow
    He did not stay, nor go;
Condemning thoughts (like sad eclipses) scowl
    Upon his soul,   20
And clouds of crying witnesses without
    Pursued him with one shout.
Yet digged the mole, and lest his ways be found
    Worked under ground,
Where he did clutch his prey, but One did see   25
    That policy,
Churches and altars fed him, perjuries
    Were gnats and flies,
It rained about him blood and tears, but he
    Drank them as free.   30

1–7 Because created man is an inadequate image of the eternal Creator, God 'resolved to have a moving image of eternity, and when he set in order the heaven, he made this image eternal but moving according to number . . . and this image we call time' (Plato, *Timaeus*, 37d–e): hence the orderly circles of the sun and moon and planets driven round the revolving earth ('hurled' as in More, *Psychathanasia*, 3.33). Eternity is a ring because circles never close; but here the image of a halo round the moon is evoked.

8–15 The lover (Herbert's 'wanton lover in a curious strain', *Dullness*, 5) comes with his music and his 'flights of fancy' (by hendiadys), and his pledges of gloves (as in Shakespeare's *Troilus and Cressida*, IV. iv. 70) and true-love knots. He 'gazes' at flowers (or 'weeps' on them, understanding 'pair'). Burton, *Anatomy*, 3.2.3, elaborates on the type.

16 *hung with weights* Dante's hypocrites walk slowly in lead cloaks (*Inferno*, 23:65).

19–21 The condemnatory thoughts are like 'eclipses' be-

cause they shut out the light, the witnesses (recalling 'seeing we also are compassed about with so great a cloud of witnesses, let us lay aside every weight, and . . . run with patience the race', Hebrews 12: 1) are witnesses of wrong gathered like insect-clouds (28).

23–5 In Ford, ambitious men 'work and work like moles, blind in the paths / That are bored through the crannies of the earth' (*Lover's Melancholy*, 2:492–3). But Herbert on God's afflictions is remembered: 'Like moles within us, heave, and cast about: / And till they foot and clutch their prey' (*Confession*, 14–15).

25–6 *but . . . policy* the parenthetical concession that God knows affects nothing.

29–30 This 'mole' is insectivorous, feeding on the perjuries of the Church (the brood of Spenser's Error is like a 'cloud of combrous gnats', *Faerie Queene*, 1.1.23), and drinking the blood and tears of oppression.

3

The fearful miser on a heap of rust
Sat pining all his life there, did scarce trust
    His own hands with the dust,
Yet would not place one piece above, but lives
    In fear of thieves.   35
Thousands there were as frantic as himself
    And hugged each one his pelf,
The downright epicure placed Heaven in sense
    And scorned pretence
While others slipped into a wide excess   40
    Said little less;
The weaker sort slight, trivial wares enslave
    Who think them brave,
And poor, despisèd Truth sat counting by
    Their victory.   45

4

Yet some, who all this while did weep and sing,
And sing, and weep, soared up into the ring,
    But most would use no wing.
O fools (said I) thus to prefer dark night
    Before true light,   50
To live in grots, and caves, and hate the day
    Because it shows the way,
The way which from this dead and dark abode
    Leads up to God,
A way where you might tread the sun, and be   55
    More bright than he.
But as I did their madness so discuss
    One whispered thus,
"This ring the bride-groom did for none provide
    But for his bride."   60

*All that is in the world, the lust of the flesh, the lust of the eyes,
and the pride of life, is not of the father, but is of the world.
And the world passeth away, and the lusts thereof, but he that doth
the will of God abideth for ever* (1 John 2: 16–17).

31–5 The ancients represent the miser 'fearful still, anxious suspicious, and trusting no man ... afraid of thieves lest they rob them ... afraid of want ... which makes them lay up still, and dare not use that they have' (Burton, *Anatomy*, 1.2.3.12); he defies the scriptural advice 'Lay not up for yourselves treasures on earth ... But lay up for yourselves treasures in heaven' (Matthew 6: 19–20).
38–9 'The frank sensualist unashamedly promoted bodily pleasure as the highest good; others fallen into unrestrained excess supposed as much.'
42–3 'Trivialities enthral weaker men, who think them fine.'
44–5 'Truth sat by, counting [Sin's] victories' (Herbert, *The Church Militant*, 190).

49–51 'For ye were sometimes darkness, but now are ye light in the Lord: walk as children of light' (Ephesians 5: 8). Plato's myth of the cave (*Republic*, 514b–517c) is remembered, where underground prisoners are habituated to taking shadows for reality; as in More's *Psychathanasia*, 1.10–18.
55 *tread the sun* 'follow in the sun's path'; like the 'angel standing in the sun' (Revelation 19: 17).
59–60 The Lamb of Revelation 19 carries no ring to his wedding; but Herbert's Joy 'wears heaven, like a bridal ring' (*The Query*, 3).

I walked the other day (to spend my hour)

Like *Silence and stealth of days* an elegy on William's death. Vaughan takes Herbert as his pattern: 'Hark how like a busy bee he hymns it to the flowers, while in a handful of blossoms gathered by himself, he fore-sees his own dissolution' (*Mount of Olives*, quoting *Life*); but the more robust if qualified optimism of Herbert's *The Flower* has entered it.

¶

1

I walked the other day (to spend my hour)
    Into a field
Where I sometimes had seen the soil to yield
    A gallant flower,
But winter now had ruffled all the bower   5
    And curious store
I knew there heretofore.

2

Yet I whose search loved not to peep and peer
    In th' face of things
Thought with myself, there might be other springs   10
    Besides this here
Which, like cold friends, sees us but once a year,
    And so the flower
Might have some other bower.

3

Then taking up what I could nearest spy   15
    I digged about
That place where I had seen him to grow out,
    And by and by
I saw the warm recluse alone to lie
    Where fresh and green   20
He lived of us unseen.

4

Many a question intricate and rare
    Did I there strow,
But all I could extort was, that he now
    Did there repair   25
Such losses as befell him in this air
    And would ere long
Come forth most fair and young.

5

This past, I threw the clothes quite o'er his head,
    And stung with fear   30

1–7 'Isaac went out to meditate in the field at the eventide' (Genesis 24: 63). But Vaughan remembers Herbert's *Peace*: 'Then went I to a garden, and did spy / A gallant flower' (13–14), and *Affliction (5)*: 'blustering winds destroy the wanton bowers, / And ruffle all their curious knots and store' (21–2).
8–22 'Dear, secret greenness! nursed below / Tempests and winds, and winter-nights' (*The Seed Growing Secretly*, 25–6); Herbert works the conceit of buried life in *The Flower*, 9–14.
8–10 'Preferring to look beyond surfaces, I reflected there might be other green shoots' like that reclusively hidden at 19.
23 *strow* as if the questions were flowers.

Of my own frailty dropped down many a tear
    Upon his bed,
Then sighing whispered, "Happy are the dead!
    What peace doth now
Rock him asleep below?"   35

6

And yet, how few believe such doctrine springs
    From a poor root
Which all the winter sleeps here under foot
    And hath no wings
To raise it to the truth and light of things,   40
    But is still trod
    By every wandering clod.

7

O thou! whose spirit did at first inflame
    And warm the dead,
And by a sacred incubation fed   45
    With life this frame
Which once had neither being, form, nor name,
    Grant I may so
    Thy steps track here below,

8

That in these masques and shadows I may see   50
    Thy sacred way,
And by those hid ascents climb to that day
    Which breaks from thee
Who art in all things, though invisibly;
    Show me thy peace,   55
    Thy mercy, love, and ease,

9

And from this cave, where dreams and sorrows reign
    Lead me above
Where light, joy, leisure, and true comforts move
    Without all pain,   60
There, hid in thee, show me his life again
    At whose dumb urn
    Thus all the year I mourn.

---

33 'Blessed are the dead which die in the Lord' (Revelation 14: 13).

36–8 'The fame of holy men . . . is a seed that grows secretly . . . [like] those trees in the poet, Which silently, and by none seen, / Grow great and green' (Vaughan, *Life of Paulinus*, quoting Horace, *Odes*, 1.12:45).

42 *clod* 'body'.

43–8 'The earth was without form, and void . . . And the Spirit of God moved upon the face of the waters' (Genesis 1: 2); but the Hebrew is sometimes rendered 'He brooded over the waters' (hence 'incubation').

49 'Christ also suffered for us, leaving us an example, that ye should follow his steps' (1 Peter 2: 21); Augustine *De Trinitate*, 11–15, develops the idea that the Trinity has left its footsteps (*vestigia*) in creation.

50–60 Plato imagines one of his underground prisoners (*Republic*, 514b–517c) pulled up the steep ascent from the cave (taking Grosart's emendation from 'care' at 57) into the light: 'at first he would most easily discern the shadows and then the likenesses or reflections . . . and later, the things themselves, and from these he would go on to contemplate the appearances in the heavens and heaven itself.' Christ allows access to higher realities even for the prisoners of the cave.

61 *hid in thee* 'your life is hid with Christ in God' (Colossians 3: 3).

They are all gone into the world of light!

A later addition (from 1655) to the sequence of elegies on William and only loosely connected with it, for now he is only one among the dead. 'They that be wise shall shine as the brightness of the firmament; and they that turn many to righteousness as the stars for ever and ever' (Daniel 12: 3); but the fiction that the dead are stellified ('God's saints are shining lights', *Joy of my life*, 17) is only lightly taken.

In the *Mount of Olives* Vaughan reflects, 'It is an observation of some spirits, that night is the mother of thoughts. And I shall add that those thoughts are stars, the scintillations and lightnings of the soul struggling with darkness.' The sense of a specific landscape ('this hill' 7, and not 'that hill' 39) is strong, and of a particular speaker, meditating in sloweddown quatrains.

¶

They are all gone into the world of light!
    And I alone sit lingering here;
Their very memory is fair and bright,
    And my sad thoughts doth clear.

It glows and glitters in my cloudy breast   5
    Like stars upon some gloomy grove,
Or those faint beams in which this hill is dressed,
    After the sun's remove.

I see them walking in an air of glory,
    Whose light doth trample on my days: 10
My days, which are at best but dull and hoary,
    Mere glimmering and decays.

O holy Hope! and high Humility,
    High as the heavens above!
These are your walks, and you have showed them me   15
    To kindle my cold love,

Dear, beauteous Death! the jewel of the just,
    Shining no where, but in the dark;
What mysteries do lie beyond thy dust;
    Could man outlook that mark!   20

He that hath found some fledged bird's nest, may know
    At first sight, if the bird be flown;
But what fair well, or grove he sings in now,
    That is to him unknown.

5 *cloudy breast* In *Easter Day*, 1–10, awareness of the Resurrection disperses the cold damps in a 'cloudy breast'.
9–10 'Behold the Highest, parting hence away, / Lightens the dark clouds, which he treads upon' (Donne, *Ascension*, 5–6); the light of the blessed dead overwhelms the cloudiness of the mourner's days.
13 Christ is both hope and humility: 'Lord Jesus Christ, which is our hope' (1 Timothy 1: 1); 'he humbled himself and became obedient even unto death' (Philippians 2: 8).

16–20 'In death's dark mysteries / [lies] A beauty far more bright / Than the noon's cloudless light' (*As Time one Day*, 32–5).
20 *mark* As in Othello's 'journey's end . . . And very seamark of my utmost sail' (V. ii. 270–1).
21–4 Herbert learns to look beyond 'The shells of fledge souls left behind' (*Death*, 11); but the 'fair well' chimes as 'farewell'.

And yet, as angels in some brighter dreams 25
    Call to the soul, when man doth sleep:
So some strange thoughts transcend our wonted themes,
    And into glory peep.

If a star were confined into a tomb
    Her captive flames must needs burn there; 30
But when the hand that locked her up, gives room,
    She'll shine through all the sphere.

O Father of eternal life, and all
    Created glories under thee!
Resume thy spirit from this world of thrall 35
    Into true liberty.

Either disperse these mists, which blot and fill
    My perspective (still) as they pass,
Or else remove me hence unto that hill,
    Where I shall need no glass. 40

25–6 'And the angel of God spake unto me in a dream, saying, Jacob: And I said, Here am I' (Genesis 31: 11).
29–32 In More's *Pre-existence of the Soul*, the 'holy lamps of God . . . wandering tapers to whom God descries / His secret paths' (stanza 10) are immersed in the 'live sepulchre' of the body (stanza 16); but the soul 'when she's gone from [earth], / Like naked lamp she is one shining sphere' (stanza 102).
35–6 'The creature itself also shall be delivered from the bondage of corruption into the glorious liberty of the children of God' (Romans 8: 21).

37–8 Quarles's Spirit advances the merits of the telescope ('perspective') which shows her Day of Judgement (*Emblems*, 3.14); Felltham writes, 'Meditation is the soul's perspective glass, whereby, in her long remove, she discerneth God' (*Resolves*, 1.14).
39–40 Echoing Herbert's 'Remove me, where I need not say, / Drop from above' (*Grace*, 23–4), and alluding to Paul's 'For now we see through a glass, darkly; but then face to face' (1 Corinthians 13: 12).

The Night   John 3: 2

The poem (from 1655) is a meditation on the passage from John cited below the title: 'The same [the Pharisee Nicodemus, who along with Joseph of Arimathaea later buried Jesus (John 19: 39)] came to Jesus by night, and said unto him, Rabbi, we know that thou art a teacher come from God: for no man can do these miracles that thou doest, except God be with him.' The issue is the nature of conversation with God; but the poem is energized by the poet's failure to talk with God.

    Through that pure virgin-shrine,
That sacred veil drawn o'er thy glorious noon
That men might look and live as glow-worms shine,
    And face the moon:
    Wise Nicodemus saw such light 5
    As made him know his God by night.

1–2 Paul argues the superiority of the 'living way' over the sacrifices required by the Law in the pre-Christian dispensation: 'He taketh away the first, that he may establish the second . . . By a new and living way, which he hath consecrated for us, through the veil, that is to say, his flesh' (Hebrews 10: 9–20). The Godhead is veiled by the body (as the sun is 'veiled' by night) or enshrined in it ('In him dwelleth all the fulness of the Godhead bodily,' Colossians 2: 9) and so made accessible, and the shrine 'virgin' because born of a virgin (Matthew 1: 18).
3–4 'That men might look on the sun and live as glowworms can look on the moon and live'.

Most blest believer he!
Who in that land of darkness and blind eyes
Thy long expected healing wings could see,
　　　When thou didst rise,　　　　　　　　　　10
And what can never more be done,
Did at midnight speak with the sun!

O who will tell me, where
He found thee at that dead and silent hour!
What hallowed solitary ground did bear　　　　　15
　　　So rare a flower,
Within whose sacred leaves did lie
The fullness of the Deity.

No mercy-seat of gold,
No dead and dusty cherub, nor carved stone,　　20
But his own living works did my Lord hold
　　　And lodge alone;
Where trees and herbs did watch and peep
And wonder, while the Jews did sleep.

Dear night! this world's defeat;　　　　　　　25
The stop to busy fools; care's check and curb;
The day of spirits; my soul's calm retreat
　　　Which none disturb!
Christ's progress, and his prayer time;
The hours to which high Heaven doth chime.　　30

God's silent, searching flight:
When my Lord's head is filled with dew, and all
His locks are wet with the clear drops of night;
　　　His still, soft call;
His knocking time; the soul's dumb watch,　　　35
When spirits their fair kindred catch.

8–10 'Men loved darkness rather than light, because their deeds were evil' (John 3: 19); 'But unto you that fear my name, shall the Sun of righteousness arise with healing in his wings' (Malachi 4: 2).
12 The paradox comes of identifying Christ with the sun.
16–18 'A bundle of myrrh is my well-beloved unto me . . . as a cluster of camphire in the vineyards of En-gedi' (Song of Solomon 1: 13–14).
19–22 'And thou shalt make a mercy-seat of pure gold . . . And thou shalt make two cherubims of gold . . . And thou shalt put the mercy-seat above upon the ark' (Exodus 25: 17–21); against the man-made ark of the covenant eventually to be set in the temple 'built of stone made ready before' (1 Kings 6: 7), is set the 'true tabernacle, which the Lord pitched, and not man' (Hebrews 8: 2) and which lodges and holds the Lord.
23–4 Even vegetable nature is more attentive than the (implicitly stony) Jews.
25–36 When the concerns of everyday are overtaken by

night, then private and spiritual communion thrives. The formulae are sometimes elliptical or allusive: the 'day of spirits' because 'night is the working time ['day-time'] of spirits' (Vaughan's version of Nieremberg, *Of Life and Death*), 'Christ's progress' because it is when Christ makes his unobserved excursions (unlike royal 'progresses') to talk with the poet (as he himself rose 'a great while before day' to pray, Mark 1: 35), when the poet finds that Heaven answers ('doth chime'), when God 'walketh upon the wings of wind' (Psalms 104: 3) to 'search me . . . and know my heart' (Psalms 139: 23). It is when the bride sleeps in the Song of Solomon (5: 2) but her 'heart waketh' for 'it is the voice of my beloved that knocketh, saying, Open to me . . . for my head is filled with dew, and my locks with the drops of the night', when after the wind, earthquake and fire, comes 'a still small voice' (1 Kings 19: 12), when in silent vigil the mind, refined by meditation (like Donne in *Obsequies to the Lord Harington*, 9–11), can study the dear departed.

Were all my loud, evil days
Calm and unhaunted as is thy dark tent,
Whose peace but by some angel's wing or voice
    Is seldom rent;   40
Then I in Heaven all the long year
Would keep, and never wander here.

    But living where the sun
Doth all things wake, and where all mix and tire
Themselves and others, I consent and run   45
    To every mire,
And by this world's ill-guiding light,
Err more then I can do by night.

    There is in God (some say)
A deep, but dazzling darkness; as men here   50
Say it is late and dusky, because they
    See not all clear;
O for that night! where I in him
Might live invisible and dim.

38 *thy dark tent* the sky, which God 'spreadeth out as a tent to dwell in' (Isaiah 40: 22).
49–50 The unchangeable mysteries of Divinity are hid 'by the more-than-lightsome mistiness of secret-teaching', 'that super-essential-mist which is hid by the light that is in things that are' in John Everard's version of *The Mystical Divinity of Dionysius the Areopagite* (chapters 1 and 2). The false light of existence is exchanged for the more than light darkness of super-existence.

L'Envoy

This postscript ('envoy') to the poems of 1655 is a prayer for the Church's restoration, and implicitly the monarchy's. Herbert's poem of the same title is a prayer for the preservation of the Church and the faithful against atheism.

O the new world's new, quickening sun!
Ever the same, and never done!
The seers of whose sacred light
Shall all be dressed in shining white,
And made conformable to his   5
Immortal shape, who wrought their bliss,
    Arise, arise!
And like old clothes fold up these skies,
This long worn veil: then shine and spread

1 'And I saw a new heaven and a new earth' (Revelation 21: 1); the 'quickening sun' is God himself ('the city had no need of the sun . . . for the glory of God did lighten it', 21: 23).
3–6 'A great multitude . . . stood before the throne . . . clothed with white robes' (Revelation 7: 9); 'God giveth [the souls of the resurrected] a body as it hath pleased him' (1 Corinthians 15: 38), 'whom he did foreknow, he also did predestinate to be conformed to the image of his Son' (Romans 8: 29); 'Now are we the sons of God, and it doth not yet appear what we shall be: but we know that, when he shall appear, we shall be like him; for we shall see him as he is' (1 John 3: 2).
7 'Awake, why sleepest thou, O Lord? arise, cast us not off for ever' (Psalms 44: 23).
8–11 'They all shall wax old as doth a garment; And as a vesture shalt thou fold them up, and they shall be changed: but thou art the same' (Hebrews 1: 11–12); 'He will destroy . . . the face of the covering cast over all people, and the veil that is spread over all nations' (Isaiah 25: 7); *creatures* 'creation'.

Thy own bright self over each head,   10
And through thy creatures pierce and pass
Till all becomes thy cloudless glass,
Transparent as the purest day
And without blemish or decay,
Fixed by thy Spirit to a state   15
For evermore immaculate.
A state fit for the sight of thy
Immediate, pure and unveiled eye,
A state agreeing with thy mind,
A state thy birth, and death designed: 20
A state for which thy creatures all
Travel and groan, and look and call.
O seeing thou hast paid our score,
Why should the curse reign any more?
But since thy number is as yet   25
Unfinished, we shall gladly sit
Till all be ready, that the train
May fully fit thy glorious reign.
Only, let not our haters brag,
Thy seamless coat is grown a rag,   30
Or that thy truth was not here known,
Because we forced thy judgments down.
Dry up their arms, who vex thy spouse,
And take the glory of thy house
To deck their own; then give thy saints   35
That faithful zeal, which neither faints
Nor wildly burns, but meekly still
Dares own the truth, and show the ill.
Frustrate those cancerous, close arts
Which cause solution in all parts,   40
And strike them dumb, who for mere words
Wound thy belovèd, more then swords.
Dear Lord, do this! and then let grace
Descend, and hallow all the place.
Incline each hard heart to do good,   45
And cement us with thy son's blood,

12–18 'For now we see through a glass, darkly; but then face to face' (1 Corinthians 13: 12).
14–16 'For this corruptible must put on incorruption' (1 Corinthians 15: 53).
19–20 'To this end was I born . . . that I should bear witness unto the truth' (John 18: 37).
22 'The whole creation groaneth and travaileth in pain together until now' (Romans 8: 22).
23–4 'All have sinned [but are] justified freely by his grace through the redemption that is in Christ Jesus' (Romans 3: 23–4).
25–8 'We see not yet all things put under him' (Hebrews 2: 8); 'blindness in part is happened to Israel, until the fulness of the Gentiles be come in. And so all Israel shall be saved' (Romans 11: 25–6).
29–32 'Then the soldiers, when they had crucified Jesus, took his garments . . . now the coat was without seam' (John 19: 23). Its seamlessness is a figure of the Church's unity.

33–5 'Woe to the idol shepherd that leaveth the flock . . . his arm shall be clean dried up' (Zechariah 11: 17); 'He that entereth not by the door into the sheepfold . . . the same is a thief and a robber' (John 10: 1).
35–8 'Abundant grace might through the thanksgiving of many redound to the glory of God. For which cause we faint not' (2 Corinthians 4: 15–16), but Paul blames those that 'have a zeal of God, but not according to knowledge' (Romans 10: 2).
39–40 'Make ineffectual the secret and growing malignancy that breaks down our unity'.
41–2 '[Charge them] that they strive not about words to no profit' (2 Timothy 2: 14).
45–8 'Ye who sometimes were far off are made nigh by the blood of Christ. For he . . . hath made both one . . . and hath broken down the middle wall of partition between us' (Ephesians 2: 13–14).

That like true sheep, all in one fold
We may be fed, and one mind hold.
Give watchful spirits to our guides!
For sin (like water) hourly glides   50
By each man's door and quickly will
Turn in, if not obstructed still.
Therefore write in their hearts thy law,
And let these long, sharp judgements awe
Their very thoughts, that by their clear   55
And holy lives, mercy may here
Sit regent yet, and blessings flow
As full as persecutions now.
So shall we know in war and peace
Thy service to be our sole ease,   60
With prostrate souls adoring thee,
Who turned our sad captivity!

Zê ho theos, kai ho kurios Iêsous Christos, kai to pneuma to hagion
(St Clement on Basil).

49   'Let us be ruled by those alert to the Lord's coming': 'Take heed therefore unto yourselves and to all the flock . . . For I know this, that after my departing shall grievous wolves enter in among you . . . Also of your own selves shall men arise, speaking perverse things' (Acts 20: 28–31).
50   'How much more abominable and filthy is man, which drinketh iniquity like water' (Job 15: 16).
53–8   The law is 'written not with ink but with the Spirit of the living God; not in tables of stone, but in fleshly tables of the heart' (2 Corinthians 3: 3); and mercy is to rule ('sit regent') in the seat of judgement.
62   'When the Lord turned again the captivity of Zion, we were like them that dream. Then was our mouth filled with laughter' (Psalms 126: 1–2).

Clement's Greek is quoted from St Basil's *Liber de Spiritu Sanctu* (*Patrologia Graeca*, 32.201: 'He lives, God and the Lord Jesus Christ, and the Holy Ghost.'

Margaret Cavendish, Duchess of Newcastle (1624–1673)

Margaret Lucas met her husband, then Marquis of Newcastle (Duke only from 1665) and already in his fifties, while serving as a maid of honour in Queen Henrietta Maria's Parisian court in exile. She was 20, and though 'I might have learned more wit and advanced my understanding by living in a court, yet being dull, fearful and bashful,' she was content to be accounted a fool; her husband-to-be fortunately approved 'those bashful fears which many condemned, and would choose such a wife as he might bring to his own humours' (*A True Relation*, appended to the fictions of *Nature's Pictures*, 1656). 'He was a very fine gentleman,' says Clarendon, 'amorous in poetry and music, to which he indulged the greatest part of his time; and nothing could have tempted him out of those paths of pleasure . . . but honour and ambition to serve the king' (*History*, 8.82). It is the honour and ambition which Margaret Cavendish celebrates in her *Life* of William Cavendish (1667, followed by a Latin translation by Walter Charleton, 1668, and a second posthumous edition in 1675), the starry-eyed biography for which she was until recently best known and (since its manner is quite untypical) misleadingly known. It was the undisciplined indulgence of intellectual pleasure which created the circumstances which allowed his wife's extraordinary talent (by her own account already indulged by her widowed mother) to flourish: he was an ass, wrote Pepys (18 March, 1668), to 'suffer her to write what she writes to him and of him'. He was himself a playwright and a poet ('the best lyric and dramatic poet of this age' says the *Life*), but too gentlemanly to publish (two comedies were printed anonymously, and under his name a couple of tracts on equestrian management); she, on the other hand, one of the least inhibited writers in the history of literature, published copiously and variously, fictions in verse and prose, scientific essays, plays, novels, and almost as a matter of course in more than one edition. Until the Restoration she shared her husband's exile (mainly in Antwerp), but it was during a brief spell in England pursuing legal business on behalf of the Marquis that she arranged for her first publications, *Poems and Fancies*, and the mixed prose and verse *Philosophical Fancies* (March and May of 1653, by when she had already returned to Antwerp). Dorothy Osborne read the *Poems* and concluded 'there are many soberer people in Bedlam' (*Letters to William Temple*, 7 May 1653). In 1655 followed a prose miscellany, *The World's Olio*, and scientific essays, *Philosophical and Physical Opinions*; in 1656, the verse and prose fables of *Nature's Pictures*, which includes her autobiographical memoir.

After the Restoration the exiled couple returned to England, moving to Welbeck in Nottinghamshire. Now there appeared to confirm her prolific eccentricity, in 1662, a previously projected collection of more than a dozen *Plays* along with *Orations of Divers Sorts*; in 1664 the quasi-fictional *CCXI Sociable Letters*, the scientific *Philosophical Letters* and a revision of *Poems and Fancies*; in 1666 *Observations upon Experimental Philosophy* awkwardly yoked with a piece of Utopian science fiction, *The Description of a New World called the Blazing World*; in 1667 the *Life* of her husband; in 1668 a new collection of half a dozen *Plays, never before Printed*. The same year a third edition of *Poems, or Several Fancies in Verse, with the Animal Parliaments in Prose*, a revision of the 1653 scientific essays as *Grounds of Natural Philosophy*, and the 1662 *Orations*; in 1671 a second edition of the 1655 *World's Olio* and the 1656 *Nature's Pictures*. The Duke edited a commemorative volume for her: *Letters and Poems in honour of the Incomparable Princess Margaret, Duchess of Newcastle* (1676). She evidently wrote fast, but on her own account at the mercy of thought that ran even faster: 'the paths or tracks that contemplation hath made on my brain . . . are much smoother than the tongue in my mouth' (*A True Relation*); and yet contrary to what people said, 'my brain is stronger than my wit' (*A True Relation*). There is no forceful or large invention at work; the pleasure is in the business of the detail. The eccentric, extravagant and careless dress noted by the friendly Evelyn (18 April 1667) as well as the hostile Pepys (26 April 1667) is matched in the style. Lovelace's rebuke to a female poet is generally reckoned to match her: 'Now as herself a poem she doth dress, / And curls a line as she would do a tress; / Powders a sonnet as she does her hair, / Then prostitutes them both to public air' (*On Sannazar's being honoured . . . A Satire*, 242–5). Her revisions of her poems were extensive, generally in the direction of making sense where none was before; they are not 'improvements' in the usual sense (she regarded herself as a 'poetastress'). There are modern editions of the *Life* (the standard is the revised edition of C. H. Firth, 1902; Ernest Rhys's Everyman version includes her memoirs of herself and some *Sociable Letters*); of her early letters to William Cavendish, along with his *Phanseys* addressed to her, by Douglas Grant (London: Nonesuch, 1956); of some plays (*The Convent of Pleasure and other Plays*, by Anne Shaver, Baltimore: Johns Hopkins University Press, 1999; *The Convent of Pleasure*, by Amanda Rowsell, Oxford: Seventeenth Century Press, 1995;

The Sociable Companions, by Amanda Holton, Oxford: Seventeenth Century Press, 1996); of the *Sociable Letters* by James Fitzmaurice, New York: Garland, 1997); of *The Blazing World and other Writings*, by Kate Lilley (London: Pickering and Chatto, 1992, reprinted in Penguin). There are facsimiles of *The Sociable Letters* (Menston: Scolar Press, 1969) and of the 1653 *Poems and fancies* (Menston: Scolar Press, 1972). There is no modern edition of the poems; the fullest edited selection is in Germaine Greer's *Kissing the Rod* (London: Virago, 1988).

Douglas Grant's *Margaret the First: A Biography of Margaret Cavendish, Duchess of Newcastle* (London: Hart-Davis, 1957) is the fullest biography. Elizabeth H. Hageman, 'Recent Studies in Women Writers of the English Seventeenth Century, 1604–1674', reprinted from *English Literary Renaissance* in *Women in the Renaissance*, ed. with Kirby Farrell and Arthur Kinney (Amherst: University of Massachusetts Press, 1988) has prepared a contextualizing bibliography.

An Elegy

Philosophical Fancies (1653). The only funeral is the apparatus of writing (the quill, the ink, the paper) and the written decasyllables ('numbers ten') the poet offers.

> Her corpse was borne to church on gray goose wing,
> Her sheet was paper white to lap her in.
> And cotton dyed with ink, her covering black,
> With letters for her scutcheon's print in that.
> Fancies bound up with verse, a garland made,   5
> And at the head, upon her hearse was laid.
> And numbers ten did bear her to the grave,
> The Muses nine a monument her gave.

4 'In place of scutcheons, that should deck thy hearse, / Take better ornaments, my tears, and verse' (Jonson, *On Sir* *John Roe*, 1–2); hatchments or 'escutcheons' show the armorial bearings of the deceased.

A World made by Atoms

1664 (Part 1); first printed in 1653 *Poems*. Lucretius's atoms bear 'different figures, shapes, and forms . . . always move, and in a various round; some when they meet, and rudely strike rebound / To a great distance; others when they jar / Will part too and rebound, but not so far. / Now these small seeds that are more closely joined, / And tremble, in a little space confined, / Stopped by their mutual twinnings, stones compose / Iron or steel, or bodies like to those' (2:335, 96–104, Creech). The stonemason is un-Lucretian.

> Small atoms of themselves a world may make,
> For being subtle, every shape they take;
> And as they dance about, they places find,
> Of forms, that best agree, make every kind.
> For when we build an house of brick or stone,   5
> We lay them even, every one by one,
> And when we find a gap that's big, or small,
> We seek out stones to fit that place withal;
> For when as they too big, or little be,
> They fall away, and cannot stay, we see;   10
> So atoms, as they dance, find places fit,
> And there remaining close and fast will knit.

2 The 'subtlety' of Lucretius's atoms is their minuteness, here it is their shape-shifting.

Those, which not fit, the rest, that rove about,
Do never leave, until they thrust them out;
Thus by their forms and motions they will be,   15
Like workmen, which amongst themselves agree;
And so by chance may a new world create,
Or else predestinate may work by fate.

17–18 Atoms may create worlds by accident, or they may
be programmed by fate to do so.

The Reason why the Thoughts are only in the Head

1664 (Part 1); first printed in 1653 *Poems. Sociable Letters* ('On the Sliding of her thoughts in her brain') records how after a winter walk the poet returns home to find 'a river, lake, or moat frozen in my brain, whereupon divers of my thoughts were sliding . . .

some slid quite off their feet'; elsewhere 'The fairies' city in the brain is found, / With *Dur*' and *Pia-mater* compassed round' (*The City of these Fairies in the Brain*). Thinking of the brain as peopled encourages this fantasy on the relocation of its population.

Each sinew is a small and slender string,
Which to the body all the senses bring,
And they like pipes or gutters hollow be,
Where animal spirits run continually;
Though small, yet they such matter do contain,   5
As in the skull doth lie, which we call brain;
    That makes, if any one doth strike the heel,
The thought of that sense in the brain doth feel;
It is not sympathy, but all one thing,
Which causes us to think, and pain doth bring;   10
For had the heel such quantity of brain,
As doth the head and skull therein contain,
Then would such thoughts, which in the brain dwell high,
Descend into our heels, and there would lie.
In sinews small, brain scattered lies about,   15
It wants both room and quantity no doubt;
For if a sinew so much brain could hold,
Or had so large a skin it to enfold,
As hath the skull, then might the toe or knee,
Had they an optic nerve, both hear and see;   20
Had sinews room, fancy therein to breed,
Copies of verses might from the 'heel proceed.

1–4 'Nerves or sinews, are membranes without, and full of marrow within; they proceed from the brain, and carry the animal spirits for sense and motion' (Burton, *Anatomy*, 1.1.2.3).
7–10 The network of 'sinews' brings to the brain sensations from all parts of the body; for Donne 'the sinewy

thread my brain lets fall / Through every part, / Can tie those parts, and make me one of all' (*The Funeral*, 9–11). Cavendish rejects the physiology that supposes 'sympathy' between parts of the body, so that injury in one place results in pain in another.

Of Fish

1664 (Part 2); first printed in 1653 *Poems*. 'Of the ebbing, flowing and saltness of the sea . . . [the Utopians] hold partly the same opinions that our old

philosophers hold, and partly, as our philosophers vary among themselves, so they also' (More, *Utopia*, 2.6).

Who knows, but fish which in the sea do live,
Can a good reason of its saltness give?
And how it ebbs and flows, perchance they can
Show reasons more than ever yet could man.

A Description of an Island

1664 (Part 2); first printed in 1653 *Poems*. The island is Britain where 'the heights of Neptune's honours shine, / And all the glories of his greater style / Are read, reflected in this happiest isle' (Jonson, *The For-* *tunate Isles*, 341–3). The machinery of Stuart pan-egyric is prettified; but the island is ruined in the poem which follows. The present-tense verbs of *1653* are changed to the past.

There was an island rich by Nature's grace,
In all the world it was the sweetest place,
Surrounded with the seas, whose waves not missed
To do her homage, and her feet they kissed;
Each wave did seem by turn to bow down low,   5
And proud to touch her, when as they did flow;
Armies of waves in troops high tides brought on,
Whose watery arms did glister as the sun,
And on their backs burdens of ships did bear,
Placing them in her havens with great care,   10
Not mercenary, for no pay they'd have,
But as her guard did watch, to keep her safe,
And in a ring they circled her about,
Strong as a wall, to keep her foes without;
The winds did serve her, and on clouds did ride,   15
Blowing their trumpets loud on every side,
Serving as scouts, they searched in every lane,
And galloped in the forests, fields and plain;
While she did please the gods, she did live safe,
And they all kind of pleasures to her gave;   20
For all this place was fertile, rich and fair,
Both woods, and hills, and dales in prospects were;
Birds pleasure took, and with delight did sing,
In praises of this isle the woods did ring;
Trees thrived with joy, for she their roots well fed,   25
And tall with pride, their tops did overspread;
Danced with the winds, when they did sing and blow,
Played like a wanton kid, or a swift roe;
Their several branches several birds did bear,
Which hopped and skipped, and always merry were;   30
Their leaves did wave, and rushing make a noise,
And many ways strived to express their joys;
All flowers there looked fresh, and gay with mirth,
Whilst they were danced upon the lap of earth;
The isle was their mother, they her children sweet,   35
Born from her loins, got by Apollo great,
Who dressed and pruned them often with great care,

7–14 The Duke said 'in shipping consists our greatest strength, they being the only walls that defend an island' (*Life*, 4.36). But the distinction is elided between the sea and the ships on it.

36 The sun is turned to a gardener. John Hall's Christ is both: 'He's gardener both and sun to dress and shine' (*Sparkles of Divine Love*, Emblem 5:4).

And washed their leaves with dew to make them fair;
Which being done, he wiped those drops away
With webs of heat, which he weaves every day;   40
Paint' them with several colours intermixed,
Veiled them with shadows every leaf betwixt;
Their heads he dressed, their hairy leaves spread out,
Wreathed round their crowns his golden beams about:
For he this isle esteemed above the rest;   45
Of all his wives he had he loved her best;
Daily he did present her with some gift,
Twelve ells of light to make her smocks for shift;
Which every time he came, she put on fair,
That lovely she and handsome might appear,   50
And when he from her went, the world to see,
He left his sister her for company,
Whose name is Cynthia, though pale yet clear,
Which makes her always in dark clouds appear;
Besides, he left his stars to wait on her,   55
Lest she should grieve too much, when he's not there,
And from his bounty clothed them all with light,
Which makes them twinkle in a frosty night;
He never brought hot beams to do her harm,
Nor let her take a cold, but lapped her warm;   60
He mantles rich of equal heat o'erspread,
And covered her with colour crimson red;
He gave another o'er her head to lie,
The colour is a pure bright azure sky;
And with soft air did line them all within,   65
Like furs in winter, in summer satin thin;
With silver clouds he fringèd them about,
And spangled meteors glistering hung without:
Thus gave he change, lest she should weary grow,
Or think them old, and so away them throw.   70
Nature adorned this island all throughout
With landscapes, riv'lets, prospects round about;
Hills overtopped the dales, which level were,
And covered all with cattle, feeding there;
Grass grew up even to the belly high,   75
Where beasts that chew their cud lay pleasantly,
Whisking their tails about, the flies to beat,
Or else to cool them from the sultry heat;
Nature, her love to th' gods willing to show,
Sent plenty in, like Nile's great overflow,   80
And temperate seasons gave, and equal lights,
Warm sunshine days, and dewy moonshine nights;
And in this pleasant island peace did dwell,
No noise of war, or sad tale could it tell.

40 Cowley's departed saints wear robes 'Woven all with light divine' (*Clad all in White*, 20); but here the sun makes handkerchiefs of heat, glossed in the margin as 'sunbeams'.
41 The margin explains, 'There would be no colours, if no light.'
43 *hairy leaves* 'leaves like hair' (being on the head, and carrying a crown).
48 'Twelve yards of light (glossed as 'days') to make her a set of frocks'.
53 'Whose name is the moon, who is pale but yet so luminous that she appears even through dark clouds'.
61–2 The colours of dawn and dusk.
80 'The fertile Nile, which creatures new doth frame' (Spenser, *Faerie Queene*, 4.11.20).
82 Herrick recalls 'candied dew in moony nights' (*Oberon's Palace*, 32).

Wherein Poetry chiefly Consists

1664 (Part 3); first printed in 1653 *Poems*. Davenant's preface to *Gondibert* asserts: 'my endeavour was, in bringing Truth . . . home to men's bosoms . . . by representing Nature, though not in an affected, yet in an unusual dress'. Hobbes reflects: 'In a good poem . . . both judgement and fancy are required: but the fancy must be more eminent; because they please for the extravagancy' (*Leviathan*, 1.8.4).

> Most of our modern writers nowadays,
> Consider not the fancy, but the phrase;
> As if fine words were wit, or one should say,
> A woman's handsome, if her clothes be gay,
> Regarding not what beauty's in the face,   5
> Nor what proportion doth the body grace;
> As when her shoes be high, to say she's tall,
> And when she is strait-laced, to say she's small;
> When painted, or her hair is curled with art,
> Though of itself but plain, and her skin swart,   10
> We cannot say, that from her thanks are due
> To Nature, nor those arts in her we view,
> Unless she them invented, and so taught
> The world to set forth that, which is stark naught;
> But fancy is the eye, gives life to all,   15
> Words, the complexion, as a whited wall;
> Fancy the form is, flesh, blood, skin and bone,
> Words are but shadows, substance they have none:
> But number is the motion, gives the grace,
> And is the count'nance of a well-formed face.   20

8 'When she's well-corseted, to say she's slim'.
15 Denham is 'More boundless in my fancy than my eye' (*Cooper's Hill*, 12).
15–17 But Hobbes parallels the skeleton and the words: 'the phrases of poetry . . . with often hearing become insipid, the reader having no more sense of their force than outer flesh is sensible of the bones that sustain it' (*Answer to Davenant*); 'complexion' is face-paint.
19–20 'It is rhythm which sets the fancy in motion and gives a grace like expressiveness in a handsome face'; whereas it is Milton's thoughts that 'voluntary move / Harmonious numbers' (*Paradise Lost*, 3:39–40).

Of the Witches in Lapland that make Winds

1664 (Part 4); first printed in 1653 *Poems*. 'And nothing so familiar . . . as for witches and sorcerers, in Lapland, Lithuania, and all over Scandia, to sell winds to mariners, and cause tempests' (Burton, *Anatomy*, 1.2.1.2). Cavendish records in the *Life* a conversation between her husband and Hobbes on witchcraft and the force of delusion.

> Lapland, this is the place, where winds (as some
> Believe) from witches not from caves do come;
> For they do draw the air into high hills,
> And beat it out again by certain mills;
> Then sack it up, and sell it out for gain   5
> To mariners which traffic on the main.

4 *mills* as if windmills processed the wind.

Of a Wrought Carpet, presented to the View of Working Ladies

1664 (Part 4); first printed in 1653 *Poems*. The 'working ladies' are invited to admire (perhaps to emulate) a tapestry figuring pagan mythologies (such as were known as 'imageries'); but this is a poem about real-ism and the kind confusion of art and nature. The Mortlake tapestry workshops, which flourished under Charles I, were in decline.

> The spring doth spin fine grass-green silk, of which
> Was woven a carpet, like the Persian, rich;
> And all about the borders there were spread
> Clusters of grapes, mixed green, blue, white and red;
> And in the midst the gods in sundry shapes   5
> Were curious wrought, divulging all their rapes;
> And all the ground was strewed with flowers, so
> As if by Nature set, they there did grow;
> Those figures all like sculptures did bear out,
> Whether they lay on flat many did doubt;   10
> There light and dark all intermixed was laid
> For shady groves, where priests devoutly prayed;
> The fruits hung so, as did invite the taste,
> Small birds with picking seemed to make a waste;
> The ground was wrought like threads drawn from the sun,   15
> Which shined so blazing as a firèd gun:
> This piece the pattern is of artful skill;
> Art the imitator is of Nature still.

3–8 Ovid's Minerva and Arachne compete with tapesteries 'Throughout embellishèd with ductile gold', but Arachne offers lively representations of Jupiter's various amours ('Europa's rape by Jove / The bull appears to live, the sea to move', and the rest) finished with a floral border. 'About her web a curious trail designs: / Flowers intermixed with clasping ivy twines' (*Metamorphoses*, 6:69, 103–4, 127–8, Sandys). Spenser famously elaborates Ovid in his description of the tapestries in the House of Busirane (*Faerie Queene*, 3.11.28–46).

9 'The figures projected in relief like sculpture' (the illusion of modelling effected by the shading and highlighting of 11).

14 Remembering Pliny's story of Zeuxis' painting of grapes, pecked at by a passing bird (*Natural History*, 35.36.6).

The Fairies in the Brain may be the Causes of many Thoughts

1664 (Part 4); first printed in 1653 *Poems*. Hobbes deplores 'the demonology of the heathen poets, that is to say, their fabulous doctrine concerning demons, which are but idols, or phantasms of the brain, without any real nature of their own, distinct from human fancy; such as are dead men's ghosts, and fairies, and other matter of old wives' tales' (*Leviathan*, 4.44.3). Here fairies are the motive rather than the effect of fancy.

> When we have pious thoughts, and think of Heaven,
> Yet go about, nor ask to be forgiven,
> Perchance they're preaching, or a chapter saying,
> Or on their knees they are devoutly praying;
> When we are sad, and know no reason why,   5
> Perchance it is, because some there do die;
> And some place may in th' head be hung with black,
> Which makes us dull, yet know not what we lack.
> Our fancies which in verse or prose we put,
> May pictures be, which they do draw or cut;   10

And when these fancies fine and thin do show,
They may be graven in seal, for ought we know;
When we have cross opinions in the mind,
Then we may them in Schools disputing find;
When we of childish toys do think, a fair   15
May be in th' brain, where crowds of fairies are,
And in each stall may all such knacks be sold,
As rattles, bells, or bracelets made of gold;
Pins, whistles, and the like may be bought there,
And thus within the head may be a fair: 20
And when our brain with amorous thoughts is stayed,
Perhaps there is a bride and bridegroom made;
And when our thoughts all merry be and gay,
There may be dancing on their wedding day.

12   *graven in seal* with the delicacy required of seal engraving.

A Song

1671; first printed in 1656 *Nature's Poems*. One of a group of songs which interrupt a story of constant love. A lady laments the prince she loves and whom she has been persuaded is dead.

Since he is gone, O then salt tears,
Drown both mine eyes, and stop mine ears
With grief; my grief it is so much,
It locks my smell up, taste, and touch.
In me remains but little breath,   5
Which quickly take away, O Death.

4   'So sat she, as when speechless grief's tormenting / Locks up the heart, the captive tongue enchaining' (Phineas Fletcher, *Elisa*, 2.4).

Charles Cotton (1630–1687)

When Clarendon wanted in his *Life* to give a picture of his days as a law student he enumerated his chief acquaintance: Ben Jonson, John Selden, Charles Cotton, Kenelm Digby, Thomas May and Thomas Carew. Among these stars is the father of the poet, famous not for his writing but for his friends, 'the greatest ornament of the town, in the esteem of those who had been best bred'; this is the 'best of men and friends' of Lovelace's *Grasshopper*, and the man whom Herrick addresses as the best of critics (*To his . . . most Ingenious friend Mr. Charles Cotton*). His son inherited the friends and an estate centred on Beresford Hall in Derbyshire, where he was born and which remained his home (though in the end only by a cousin's generosity) until he died. He was privately educated, enjoying his father's encouragement in literary pursuits, and after 1648 the tutorial services of an ejected Royalist Fellow of Brasenose College, Ralph Rawson. He travelled on the continent in 1655–6, and when he returned married his cousin Isabella Hutchinson (Lucy's sister-in-law). He had courted fame early, publishing an elegy on Lord Hastings in *Lachrymae Lachrymarum* (1649), keeping company with Marvell and Herrick and the young Dryden. But when he returned from his travels he industriously cultivated his retirement. Unlike his father, he avoided London. After the Restoration Cotton held various minor local offices; but he had virtually no public life. He busied himself as squire and scholar.

Sir Aston Cockayne's 1658 epistle *To my most Honoured Cousin* represents him as a translator, before he remembers he is one with 'his own rare fancy'. His translations begin with Guillaume du Vair's *Moral Philosophy of the Stoics* (1664) and include a version, in almost every way superior to Florio's, of Montaigne's *Essays* (1685); his squirely compositions include a continuation of Walton's *The Compleat Angler* (1676), *The Compleat Gamester* (1674), *The Planter's Manual* (1675). For more than a century his most celebrated poem was *Scarronides*, a burlesque on Virgil's *Aeneid* (of Book 1 in 1664, of Book 4 in 1665, of both together in many editions from 1667); the most regarded of his poems now is probably *The Wonders of the Peak* (1681). Other poems, like the burlesque Virgil often of French inspiration, were published posthumously in *Poems on Several Occasions* (1689); the poet's son complained that it did not correspond with a collection prepared by Cotton himself, but no replacement has ever been made. *The Genuine Works* (1715) contains his satires and burlesques. There are selections in *Poems*, ed. J. Beresford (London: Cobden-Sanderson, 1923), and *Poems*, ed. John Buxton for the Muses' Library (London: Routledge and Kegan Paul, 1958), the latter based on the earlier text of a MS (apparently dictated by Cotton himself) in the Derby Borough Library: it contains neither of the poems below.

Evening. Quatrains and Night. Quatrains

1689. Of the related *Ode upon Winter*, Wordsworth remarks the 'rapidity of detail, and a profusion of fanciful comparison, which indicate on the part of the poet extreme activity of intellect, and a corresponding hurry of delightful feeling' (preface to *Poems*, 1815). Both these belong with a set of four poems on times of the day. The model is Théophile de Viau's *Le Matin* (extant in three versions, otherwise as *La Matinée* and *L'Aurore*), whose octosyllabic quatrains combine playful mythologies with wittily observed detail; the effect (compounded by Cotton's variations of register) is to bring the descriptions close to burlesque without ever abandoning them to it. The illustrative quotations from 'Evening Works' and 'After Supper Works' are from the Tudor poet Thomas Tusser's *Five Hundred Points of Good Husbandry*.

Evening. Quatrains

The Day's grown old, the fainting sun
Has but a little way to run,
And yet his steeds, with all his skill,
Scarce lug the chariot down the hill.

4 'Le soleil . . . Pousse le chariot du jour' (*De l'Aurore*, 21–4).

With labour spent, and thirst oppressed,   5
Whilst they strain hard to gain the west,
From fetlocks hot drops melted light,
Which turn to meteors in the night.

The shadows now so long do grow,
That brambles like tall cedars show,   10
Mole-hills seem mountains, and the ant
Appears a monstrous elephant.

A very little little flock
Shades thrice the ground that it would stock;
Whilst the small stripling following them,   15
Appears a mighty Polypheme.

These being brought into the fold,
And by the thrifty master told,
He thinks his wages are well paid,
Since none are either lost, or strayed.   20

Now lowing herds are each-where heard,
Chains rattle in the villeins' yard,
The cart's on tail set down to rest,
Bearing on high the cuckold's crest.

The hedge is stripped, the clothes brought in,   25
Nought's left without should be within,
The bees are hived, and hum their charm,
Whilst every house does seem a swarm.

The cock now to the roost is pressed:
For he must call up all the rest;   30
The sow's fast pegged within the sty,
To still her squeaking progeny.

Each one has had his supping mess,
The cheese is put into the press,
The pans and bowls clean scalded all,   35
Reared up against the milk-house wall.

5 Whereas Théophile's morning sun is 'lassé de boire' (*Le Matin*, 3).
7 'Where Titan's panting steeds his Chariot steep, / And bathe their fiery fetlocks in the deep' (Ovid, *Metamorphoses*, 4: 633–4, Sandys).
9–16 'But grasshoppers are giants there' (Marvell, *Appleton House*, 373; 'Les ombres tombent des montagnes / Elles croissent à veue d'oeil' (*De l'Aurore*, 17–18, from a section designed for an ode to night). The lengthening of shadow is famously observed by Virgil: 'For see yon sunny hill the shade extends' (*Eclogues*, 1:84, Dryden). Polyphemus is the shepherd cyclops in Homer: 'A man in shape, immane, and monsterous, / Fed all his flocks alone' (*Odyssey*, 9:187–8, Chapman).
22 The farm-hands ('villeins') are penning the stock: 'See

cattle well served, without and within / And all thing at quiet, ere supper begin' ('Evening Works', 6).
23–4 The shafts of the upturned cart form a horn shape.
25 'No clothes in garden, no trinkets without' ('Evening Works', 7).
27–8 'The returning bees buzz around the hive; the returning labourers fill their cottages'.
29–30 The cock is driven ('pressed') to the hen-house to act as guard: 'Where pullen use nightly, to perch in the yard, / There two-legged foxes, keep watches and ward' ('Evening Works', 5).
31 *pegged* 'confined'.
34 'The cheese is returned to the cupboard'; 'press' is a northern word.

And now on benches all are sat
In the cool air to sit and chat,
Till Phoebus, dipping in the west,
Shall lead the world the way to rest.   40

Night. Quatrains

The sun is set, and gone to sleep
With the fair princess of the deep,
Whose bosom is his cool retreat,
When fainting with his proper heat:

His steeds their flaming nostrils cool   5
In spume of the cerulean pool;
Whilst the wheels dip their hissing naves
Deep in Columbus' western waves.

From whence great rolls of smoke arise
To overshade the beauteous skies;   10
Who bid the world's bright eye adieu
In gelid tears of falling dew.

And now from the Iberian vales
Night's sable steeds her chariot hales,
Where double cypress curtains screen   15
The gloomy melancholic Queen.

These, as they higher mount the sky,
Ravish all colour from the eye,
And leave it but an useless glass,
Which few, or no reflections grace.   20

The crystal arch o'er Pindus' crown
Is on a sudden dusky grown,
And all's with fun'ral black o'erspread,
As if the day, which sleeps, were dead.

No ray of light the heart to cheer,   25
But little twinkling stars appear;
Which like faint dying embers lie,
Fit nor to work, nor travel by.

2–4 'Le soleil change de séjour, / Il pénètre le sein de l'onde' (*De l'Aurore*, 21–2); the 'princess' to whom the sun retreats when faint with his own ('proper') heat is Clymene, the daughter of Oceanus and Tethys, beloved of Apollo and the mother of Phaeton.
5 The horses of the sun are 'fiery steeds . . . Who from their mouths and nostrils vomit flame' (*Metamorphoses*, 2:84–5, Sandys).
6 'In the foam of the blue sea'.
7–8 The wheels of the sun's chariot dip their hubs ('naves') in the American ocean.
11–12 'Who bid the sun farewell with the cold tears of the dew'.

13 Night rises from the Western Ocean (for the Romans the Spanish Sea), where the sun descends: 'Phoebus had unyoked his panting steeds, / Drenched in Iberian seas; whilst Night succeeds, / Studded with stars' (*Metamorphoses*, 7:324–5, Sandys).
15–16 Personified Night is clad in funeral black ('cypress'): Théophile's shadows 'd'un long vêtement de deuil / Couvrent la face des campagnes' (*De l'Aurore*, 19–20).
21–2 Night has mounted high enough to darken the sky above even the highest mountain ('Pindus' is here simply a type of the high mountain).

Perhaps to him they torches are,
Who guides Night's sovereign's drowsy car, 30
And him they may befriend so near,
But us they neither light, nor cheer.

Or else those little sparks of light
Are nails that tyre the wheels of Night,
Which to new stations still are brought, 35
As they roll o'er the gloomy vault.

Or nails that arm the horses' hoof,
Which trampling o'er the marble roof,
And striking fire in the air,
We mortals call a shooting star. 40

That's all the light we now receive,
Unless what belching vulcans give,
And those yield such a kind of light
As adds more horror to the Night.

Nyctimene now freed from day, 45
From sullen bush flies out to prey,
And does with ferret note proclaim
The arrival of the usurping dame.

The rail now cracks in fields and meads,
Toads now forsake the nettle-beds, 50
The tim'rous hare goes to relief,
And wary men bolt out the thief.

The fire's new raked, and hearth swept clean
By Madge, the dirty kitchen-quean,
The safe is locked, the mousetrap set, 55
The leaven laid, and bucking wet.

Now in false floors and roofs above,
The lustful cats make ill-tuned love,
The bandog on the dunghill lies,
And watchful nurse sings lullabies. 60

---

30 *guides* guide (1689). 'Perhaps the stars light the way for the coachman of the Night': 'Look up, the Night is in her silent Chariot' (Dryden, *Amphitryon*, 1.1); 'drowsy' because Night is the mother of Sleep.

34 Night's chariot, its wheels shod with stellar nails, moves from stopping-place to stopping-place; astronomical 'stations' are places (at their closest to earth or farthest from it) where celestial bodies seem to halt: 'The planets in their stations listening stood' (*Paradise Lost*, 7:563).

38 'Marble' ('marmor') is used in Latin poetry for the shiny surface of the sea; used for the sky, it allows the sparks struck by the shoes of Night's horses to be identified with shooting stars.

40 *fire* disyllabic.

42 *vulcans* 'volcanoes' (standardly available).

45–8 'The owl . . . with its hunting ('ferret') cry announces the arrival of Night (who 'usurps' the day)'; 'Nyctimene defiled her father's bed. / Though now a bird; yet, full of guilt, the sight, / The day, she shuns, and masks her shame in night' (*Metamorphoses*, 2: 592–5, Sandys).

49 'The land-rail cries in the fields.'

51 *relief* 'refreshment'.

55–6 The kitchen servant (Madge is a type name) 'padlocks the meat-safe . . . sets out the fermenting dough (the morning's baking), steeps the laundry ('bucking')': 'Such keys lay up safe, ere ye take ye to rest, / Of dairy, of buttery, of cupboard and chest . . . Wash dishes, lay leavens, save fire and away, / Lock doors and to bed, a good housewife will say' ('After supper matters', 5, 10).

59 *bandog* 'chained guard dog'.

Philomel chants it whilst she bleeds,
The bittern booms it in the reeds,
And Reynard entering the back yard,
The Capitolian cry is heard.

The goblin now the fool alarms,   65
Hags meet to mumble o'er their charms;
The nightmare rides the dreaming ass,
And fairies trip it on the grass.

The drunkard now supinely snores,
His load of ale sweats through his pores,   70
Yet when he wakes the swine shall find
A crapula remains behind.

The sober now and chaste are blest
With sweet, and with refreshing rest,
And to sound sleeps they've best pretence,   75
Have greatest share of innocence.

We should so live then that we may
Fearless put off our clots and clay,
And travel through Death's shades to light;
For every day must have its night.   80

61–4 'The nightingale ('Philomel') sings her bloody his-
tory (of her rape as Philomela) . . . and when the fox
('Reynard') enters the yard, the geese set up their cry'; 'Those
consecrated geese in orders, / That to the Capitol were
warders: / And being then upon patrol / With noise alone
beat off the Gaul' (Butler, *Hudibras*, 2.3:799–802, from Livy,
5.47.4).

67 'The night hag rides the sleeping fool.'
72 *crapula* 'hangover'.
78–9 'We should live so that we fear nothing after death',
having discarded 'the muddy vesture of decay'.

John Dryden (1631–1700)

Dryden's first published poem, written when he was 18, was *Upon the Death of the Lord Hastings*, in a collection with poems by Herrick, Denham, Cotton and Marvell – a piece 'composed with great ambitions of such conceits as . . . the example of Cowley still kept in reputation' (Johnson, *Life*). He began his poetic career with Cleveland ('wresting and torturing a word into another meaning', *Essay of Dramatic Poesy*) or Sylvester ('when I was a boy, I thought inimitable Spenser a mean poet in comparison of Sylvester's *Du Bartas*,' preface to *The Spanish Friar*); he rejected both, turning the language of poetry into something capable of the virtues of prose (an achievement Matthew Arnold slights and T. S. Eliot applauds). He came late to the reforms of Waller and Denham, but in effect completed them: 'what was said of Rome, adorned by Augustus, may be applied . . . to English poetry embellished by Dryden, "He found it brick, and he left it marble"' (*Life*). His career of fifty years covered revolutions in both politics and poetry, and left him more than a little bruised on both accounts. But when Congreve came to write the memoir to the posthumous edition of Dryden's *Dramatic Works* (1717) he could say that 'no man hath written in our language so much, and so various matter, and in so various manners, so well' and that 'he was an improving writer to the last.' At the end of his life, Dryden himself wrote, 'what judgment I had, increases rather than diminishes; and thoughts, such as they are, come crowding in so fast that my only difficulty is to choose or to reject, to run them into verse or to give them the other harmony of prose: I have so long studied and practised both that they are grown into a habit' (preface to *Fables*). He 'studied rather than felt', says Johnson, but like Shakespeare 'he delighted to tread upon the brink of meaning, where light and darkness begin to mingle.' He is the first articulately self-conscious poet in English (the grandfather of Coleridge), attentive not only to what he imagined the 'project' of poetry to be, but capable of describing its mechanisms. He is also one of the most energetic poets in English, and (with the possible exception of Milton, whose *Paradise Lost* immediately commanded his admiration) the only serious Baroque poet.

Dryden's background (born in 1631 at Aldwinkle in Northamptonshire) was Puritan and anti-monarchical (both his mother's family and his father's took the Parliamentary side in the Civil War) and in one of his last poems, the *Epistle to my Honoured Kinsman*, he acknowledges that heritage. He was educated at Westminster School under the famous Dr Busby 'whose index-hand / Held forth the virtue of the dreadful wand' (Pope, *Dunciad*, 4:139–40), reverenced by Dryden despite his thuggeries. In 1650 he went on to Trinity College, Cambridge, from where he took his BA degree in 1654. He subsequently worked as a secretary for the Proectorate, in the same office as Milton and Marvell. His first poem of distinction was *Heroic Stanzas* (1659) on the death of Cromwell, republished in 1681 to embarrass him. At the Restoration he welcomed the King's return in *Astraea Redux*, remarkable for its focus on General Monck, who like himself had changed sides. From 1668, on the strength of a succession of startling achievements in panegyric poetry (*Annus Mirabilis* in 1666 the most remarkable) and in the theatre (both in comedy, and in heroic tragedy), he was officially titled Laureate (when the revenue of £100 that came with it, says Johnson, 'was not inadequate to the conveniences of life'). Dryden's first play, *The Wild Gallant*, was performed in 1663; and for the next twenty years he wrote mainly for the theatre (he fell short of his contract with the King's Company to write three plays a year, but not disgracefully). A succession of quarrels in this quarrelsome milieu, with his brother-in-law Sir Robert Howard, with Elkanah Settle, with Buckingham and with Rochester, forced on him the necessity of defining his own vocation: behind its fireworks, *Mac Flecknoe* is one attempt to resolve his anxieties. In the 1680s, with a talent educated to fluency by the exigencies of the theatre and sharpened by literary debate, he turned to political satire, mainly in the interests of the King and the Tory Party (*Absalom and Achitophel* in 1681 is the most remarkable instance); but he also began the great project of translation (both writing translations and supervising them) which was increasingly to absorb his energies (at some 40,000 lines by far the greater part of his verse output). His conversion to Catholicism (around 1685), sustained after the Glorious Revolution, alienated him from the centres of power: *The Hind and the Panther*, his testament of faith, was written 'with interruptions of ill health and other hindrances'. He lost the laureateship to Shadwell in 1689 after the Revolution. Dryden early described his temperament as 'saturnine and reserved' (*Defence of an Essay of Dramatic Poetry*), and affronts to his self-regard left him embittered. But in his last decade he was busy with theatrical work (importantly with opera), with various literary jobbing work, with his translations (his *Virgil* is certainly his best work), and with some of his finest criticism. He projected a translation of Homer of which only fragments (given in *Examen Poeticum* and in *Fables*) were completed; had it been done, then Augustan literary history would have been less dominated by Pope. He was buried, after an awkward funeral, in Chaucer's grave in Westminster Abbey. Johnson's *Life* is classic; now standard is James Anderson Winn, *John Dryden and his World* (New Haven and London: Yale University Press, 1987). Charles E. Ward has edited *The Letters* (Chapel Hill: University of North Carolina Press, 1942).

No attempt was made by Dryden himself to collect his poems (an obvious contrast with Jonson or with Pope); published in pamphlet form or scattered in miscellanies with the work of others, they are only sometimes found reprinted together. There are facsimile editions of two subsidiary collections, the 1685 *Sylvae* (containing work by others besides Dryden) and the 1700 *Fables* (both Menston: Scolar Press, 1973). Between 1691 and 1701, Dryden's publisher Tonson attempted binding together quartos of different dates and adding general title-pages; but the volumes so constructed are not by any standard complete. The first serious attempt at collection is Walter Scott's *Works*, 18 vols (1808). Early editions are described in Hugh Macdonald, *A Bibliography of Early Editions and of Drydeniana* (Oxford, 1939), with corrections by James M. Osborn, *Modern Philology*, 39 (1941), 69–98, 197–212. The standard edition of *The Works* is by H. T. Swedenberg Jr and others, 20 vols (Berkeley and Los Angeles: University of California Press, 1956–   ); the first seven volumes take in the poems and the translation of Virgil, but the last (*Poems, 1697–1700*) has still to appear. *The Poems*, ed. James Kinsley, 4 vols (Oxford: Clarendon Press, 1958) is complete. The best annotation is in *The Poems*, ed. Paul Hammond (London: Longman, 1995–   ), of which two of the projected four volumes have appeared. The best single-volume text with notes is *The Poetical Works*, ed. George R. Noyes (second edition, Boston: Houghton Mifflin, 1950). There is a *Concordance to the Poetical Works* by Guy Montgomery (reprinted New York: Russell & Russell, 1967). The prefaces and other critical works are differently selected in W. P. Ker, *Essays of John Dryden*, 2 vols (Oxford: Clarendon Press, 1900) and George Watson, *Of Dramatic Poesy and other Critical Essays*, 2 vols (London: Dent, 1962). Early criticism is represented in James and Helen Kinsley, *Dryden: The Critical Heritage* (London: Routledge, 1971); more recent criticism is described in *John Dryden: A Survey and Bibliography of Critical Studies*, ed. David J. Latt and Samuel H. Monk (Minneapolis: University of Minnesota Press, 1976), and in John Alexander Zamonski, *An Annotated Bibliography of John Dryden 1949–1973* (New York: Garland, 1975.

Mac Flecknoe

Untypically for Dryden, the poem was widely and anonymously circulated in MS between its composition in 1676 (probably as an oblique answer to Rochester's *Allusion*) and its first unauthorized printing in 1682 (*Mac Flecknoe, or a Satyr upon the True-Blue Protestant Poet*, T. S., the subtitle giving it a topical political edge). The text followed here is that of the *Miscellany Poems* (1684), which differs chiefly in its use of initials and dashes for 'Shadwell' and some other names (Sh—— allows both an insulting indifference to the hero's true name, and the possibility of substituting derivatives of 'shit'). The model for English mock-heroic, of which this is the first sustained example, is Boileau, who in *Le Lutrin* (1674) attached heroic sublimity of expression to low subject-matter. Like Boileau, Dryden had his eye on Virgil: Latinus's settlement of the succession of rule on Aeneas (*Aeneid* 7) supplies the inspiration for Flecknoe's on Shadwell. His more immediate stylistic models are the Cowley of the *Davideis*, the Milton of *Paradise Lost*, the panegyric Waller (in particular *Of the Danger his Majesty Escaped*). Dryden himself (in the *Discourse concerning Satire*) identifies his manner (along with that of works as different as Erasmus's *Praise of Folly* and Spenser's *Mother Hubbard's Tale*) as Varronian, from the satirist Varro, known only at second hand from critical descriptions of him to the effect that he was 'studious of laughter', that 'his business was more to divert his reader than to teach him,' that he thought himself a follower of the Greek Menippus, also known only at second hand but for 'cynical impudence and obscenity', and for quoting Homer and the tragedians so as to turn 'their serious meaning into something that was ridiculous'. Thomas Shadwell (a more considerable poet and dramatist than the reputation created for him by Dryden allows) is the 'low' subject of the poem, his activity generalized to promotion of false principles of taste in literature, and his pseudo-Jonsonian preference for realist 'humoristic' comedy over its mannered 'witty' alternatives. Dryden characterises the attack on wit (the poem's key word) as dullness (a charge often laid to himself), and the allegiance to Jonson as fake. If there is an immediate provocation it is in the stance of the Shadwell preface to *The Virtuoso* (1676), but the attack enlarges to include much of Shadwell's previous work (as at 90–3) for the London theatre. The attack on him in *Absalom and Achitophel Part 2* is more personal. Richard Flecknoe, already the butt of Marvell's *Fleckno, an English Priest at Rome*, had 'replied' in 1668 to Dryden's *Defence of an Essay of Dramatic Poesy*. Shadwell is his heir in respect only of their common pretended allegiance to Jonson; but the usefulness of Flecknoe consists in his being an easy type of tactlessness – in the *Short Discourse of the English Stage* (1664) he actually commends Jonson for his 'gravity and ponderousness'. The implied Irishness of Shadwell

('Mac' is the Irish patronymic tag; his empire stretches from Ireland, 139) apparently offended him. It is metaphorical like Flecknoe's own Irishness: he is a 'bard' (213) only by virtue of his windiness.

> All human things are subject to decay,
> And, when Fate summons, monarchs must obey:
> This Flecknoe found, who, like Augustus, young
> Was called to empire, and had governed long:
> In prose and verse was owned, without dispute,   5
> Through all the realms of Nonsense, absolute.
> This agèd prince, now flourishing in peace,
> And blessed with issue of a large increase,
> Worn out with business, did at length debate
> To settle the succession of the state: 10
> And, pondering which of all his sons was fit
> To reign, and wage immortal war with wit,
> Cried, "'Tis resolved! for nature pleads, that he
> Should only rule, who most resembles me:
> Sh—— alone my perfect image bears,   15
> Mature in dullness from his tender years.
> Sh—— alone, of all my sons, is he,
> Who stands confirmed in full stupidity.
> The rest to some faint meaning make pretence,
> But Sh—— never deviates into sense.   20
> Some beams of wit on other souls may fall,
> Strike through, and make a lucid interval;
> But Sh——'s genuine night admits no ray,
> His rising fogs prevail upon the day:
> Besides, his goodly fabric fills the eye,   25
> And seems designed for thoughtless majesty:
> Thoughtless as monarch oaks, that shade the plain,
> And, spread in solemn state, supinely reign.
> Heywood and Shirley were but types of thee,
> Thou last great prophet of tautology: 30
> Even I, a dunce of more renown than they,
> Was sent before but to prepare thy way;
> And, coarsely clad in Norwich drugget, came
> To teach the nations in thy greater name.

3–4 *like Augustus* not just in reigning long, but widely.

6 *realms of Nonsense* based on 'reams of nonsense'. Nonsense is a distinctively seventeenth-century notion; as are 'poetic kingdoms'.

8 *issue of a large increase* 'publication of many productions'; but echoes of biblical usage confuse the sense.

12 *wage immortal war* Satan's 'immortal hate' and 'eternal war' (*Paradise Lost*, 1:107, 121).

15–17 Mimics Cowley's 'Abdon alone his generous purpose knew . . . Abdon alone did on him now attend' (*Davideis*, 4:812–19); *perfect image* Sin is the 'perfect image' of Satan (*Paradise Lost*, 2:764).

21–4 In Cowley's Hell (*Davideis*, 1:82–6) there is 'genuine night' where no light 'Strikes through the solid darkness'.

22 *lucid interval* the metaphorical sense 'interval of sanity' is prior to any supposed literal sense.

25 *fabric* 'frame'. Shadwell is a 'tun of man' at 195; he is caricatured in *The Second Part of Absalom and Achitophel* (459) as Og, 'one of the remnant of giants'.

28 *supinely* 'over a wide extent'; but for the drunken Shadwell 'on his back'.

29 Thomas Heywood prefigured the wordy Shadwell by being hugely prolific. James Shirley's crime is unclear: he died aged 70 in 1666.

30 Shadwell complains he does not understand the objection against him 'that there is the same thing over and over' in his writing (preface to *The Sullen Lovers*, 1668).

32–4 'In those days came John the Baptist . . . the voice of one crying in the wilderness, Prepare ye the way of the Lord . . . And the same John had his raiment of camel's hair' (Matthew 3: 1–4).

33 *Norwich drugget* 'worsted'; rustic drugget (1682 and MSS).

My warbling lute, the lute I whilom strung 35
When to King John of Portugal I sung,
Was but the prelude to that glorious day,
When thou on silver Thames didst cut thy way,
With well-timed oars, before the royal barge,
Swelled with the pride of thy celestial charge; 40
And big with hymn, commander of an host,
The like was ne'er in Epsom blankets tossed.
Methinks I see the new Arion sail,
The lute still trembling underneath thy nail.
At thy well-sharpened thumb, from shore to shore, 45
The trebles squeak for fear, the basses roar:
Echoes, from Pissing Alley, S—— call,
And Sh—— they resound from A—— Hall.
About thy boat the little fishes throng,
As at the morning toast that floats along. 50
Sometimes, as prince of thy harmonious band
Thou wield'st thy papers in thy thrashing hand.
St. André's feet ne'er kept more equal time,
Not even the feet of thy own *Psyche*'s rhyme:
Though they in number as in sense excel; 55
So just, so like tautology, they fell,
That, pale with envy, Singleton forswore
The lute and sword, which he in triumph bore, }
And vowed he ne'er would act Villerius more." }
Here stopped the good old sire; and wept for joy 60
In silent raptures of the hopeful boy.
All arguments, but most his plays, persuade,
That for anointed dullness he was made.
　　Close to the walls which fair Augusta bind
(The fair Augusta much to fears inclined), 65
An ancient fabric raised to inform the sight,

35–6 Flecknoe's *Relation of Ten Years' Travels in Europe, Asia, Africa and America* (1654) describes how he played for the Portuguese court; Marvell too had to listen (*Fleckno*, 36–44).

37–40 Waller writes of Prince Charles's companions 'placed in the gilded barge, / Proud with the burden of so great a charge' (*Of the Danger His Majesty Escaped*, 39–41). Like Lovelace's 'good angels who have heavenly charge / To steer and guide man's sudden giddy barge' (*The Lady A. L.*), Shadwell is supposed to lead the line of royal barges. 'Big with the swellings of their pride and power' quotes Shadwell's *Psyche* (of ambitious courtiers).

42 *Epsom blankets* Shadwell's Sir Samuel Hearty is tossed in a blanket (*The Virtuoso*). 'Epsom' matches 'Norwich' (33), and alludes also to a nasty skirmish at Epsom when a group including Rochester and Etherege tossed some reluctant fiddlers in a blanket. Martial (1.3:8) imagines his work tossed heavenward from a blanket.

43 *Arion* The lyre-playing Arion is usually represented astride the dolphin who saves him from death by drowning. Waller has 'While to his harp divine, Arion sings' (*Of the Danger*, 11, of the life and loves of Edward IV).

45–6 Part of the apparatus of Waller's panegyric of Prince

Charles: 'the roar / Of cannons echoed from the affrighted shore' (*Of the Danger*, 7–8).

48 *A—— Hall* Aston Hall (1682 and some MSS), which may refer to Shadwell's friend Edmund Ashton; but the parallel with Pissing Alley (though a real street) suggests obscene completions of the blank.

49 In parody of Waller's 'About the keel delighted dolphins play' (*Of the Danger*, 34).

51–6 Shadwell's *Psyche* (1676) was an opera-ballet done in collaboration with the composer Draghi and the choreographer St André.

57–9 The musician John Singleton is supposed to be taking the part of Villerius in Davenant's *Siege of Rhodes* (1656). Buckingham's *Rehearsal* (1672) parodies the opening scene with this absurd combination of props.

61 *silent raptures* 'unspoken rhapsodies'; *hopeful* 'promising'.

64–5 *Augusta* 'London'. 'Augusta is inclined to fears' occurs in a song in John Crowne's masque *Callisto* (1675): the fears are causeless.

66–9 Recalling the fortified gate and watch-tower ('to inform the sight') so called ('hight'), retained only as the name of a dubious street.

There stood of yore, and Barbican it hight:
A watch-tower once, but now, so Fate ordains,
Of all the pile an empty name remains.
From its old ruins brothel-houses rise,   70
Scenes of lewd loves, and of polluted joys.
Where their vast courts the mother-strumpets keep,
And, undisturbed by watch, in silence sleep.
Near these a Nursery erects its head,
Where queens are formed, and future heroes bred;   75
Where unfledged actors learn to laugh and cry;
Where infant punks their tender voices try,
And little Maximins the gods defy.
Great Fletcher never treads in buskins here,
Nor greater Jonson dares in socks appear.   80
But gentle Simpkin just reception finds
Amidst this *Monument of Vanished Minds*:
Pure clinches the suburbian muse affords;
And Panton waging harmless war with words.
Here Flecknoe, as a place to fame well known,   85
Ambitiously designed his Sh———'s throne.
For ancient Dekker prophesied long since,
That in this pile should reign a mighty prince,
Born for a scourge of wit, and flail of sense:
To whom true dullness should some *Psyches* owe,   90
But worlds of *Miser*s from his pen should flow;
Humorists, and *Hypocrites*, it should produce,
Whole Raymond families, and tribes of Bruce.
   Now Empress Fame had published the renown,
Of Sh———'s coronation through the town.   95
Roused by report of Fame, the nations meet,
From near Bunhill, and distant Watling Street.
No Persian carpets spread the imperial way,
But scattered limbs of mangled poets lay:
From dusty shops neglected authors come,   100

72–3 'Where their vast court the mother-waters keep, / And undisturbed by moons in silence sleep' (Cowley, *Davideis*, 1:79–80, of the underworld). Dryden quotes these lines in the preface to *The State of Innocence* (1677): 'How easy 'tis to turn into ridicule the best descriptions . . . but an image which is strongly and beautifully set before the eyes . . . will still be poetry, when the merry fit is over.'
74 *Nursery* 'drama-school'.
75 *queens* punning on 'queans' (whores), continued in 'punks' (77); *heroes* turn up as 'little Maximins' (78), from the extravagant emperor in Dryden's *Tyrannic Love* (1669).
79–80 Dryden's account (*Essay of Dramatic Poesy*) of Beaumont and Fletcher commends their tragedies ('buskins' are the high-soled boots worn by tragic actors) for representing 'all the passions very lively, but above all love'; he conforms their comedies to his own preference for 'quickness of wit in repartees'. Jonson's comedy ('socks' are the slippers worn by comic actors) he makes the pattern for 'elaborate [polished] writing'.
81 *Simpkin* a clown (like Pierrot): 'you may talk of your plays, but give me such pretty harmless drolls for my money' (Shadwell's *Miser*).
82 *Monument . . . Minds* giving a new sense to the name of the library of the ancients in Davenant's *Gondibert* (2.5:36).
83 *clinches* 'puns'; *suburbian* 'unrefined'.
84 *Panton* Edward Panton projected a Royal Academy in his *Public and Pious Design* (1676); a *pantin* in French is a cardboard puppet.
87 *Dekker* Here as first of the 'prophets' of dullness (died 1632), and a representative London panegyrist, a Whig before the letter.
90–3 All plays by Shadwell; Raymond appears in *The Humorists*, Bruce in *The Virtuoso*.
97–8 Both distances are less than a mile; the Persian Royal Road (carpeted by virtue of the modern association of Persia and carpets) took three months to travel (Herodotus, *Histories*, 5).
99 Echoing Horace's *disjecti membra poeti* (*Satires*, 1.4:62) to suggest that chopping up the work of others is a habit at this court.

Martyrs of pies, and relics of the bum.
Much Heywood, Shirley, Ogilby there lay,
But loads of Sh—— almost choked the way.
Bilked stationers for yeomen stood prepared,
And H—— was captain of the guard. 105
The hoary prince in majesty appeared,
High on a throne of his own labours reared.
At his right hand our young Ascanius sat,
Rome's other hope, and pillar of the state;
His brows thick fogs, instead of glories, grace, 110
And lambent dullness played around his face.
As Hannibal did to the altars come,
Sworn by his sire, a mortal foe to Rome,
So Sh—— swore, nor should his vow be vain,
That he till death true dullness would maintain; 115
And, in his father's right, and realm's defence,
Ne'er to have peace with wit, nor truce with sense.
The king himself the sacred unction made,
As king by office, and as priest by trade.
In his sinister hand, instead of ball, 120
He placed a mighty mug of potent ale;
Love's Kingdom to his right he did convey,
At once his sceptre, and his rule of sway;
Whose righteous lore the prince had practised young,
And from whose loins recorded *Psyche* sprung. 125
His temples, last, with poppies were o'erspread,
That nodding seemed to consecrate his head.
Just at that point of time, if Fame not lie,
On his left hand twelve reverend owls did fly.
So Romulus, 'tis sung, by Tiber's brook, 130
Presage of sway from twice six vultures took.
The admiring throng loud acclamations make,
And omens of his future empire take.
The sire then shook the honours of his head,

101 Discarded paper ends up with bakers or as bum fodder. Martial (3:2) has his poems used as wrapping paper for fish.
102 *Ogilby* joins the prophets of tautology as a friend of Shirley, a Scot who worked in Ireland, and an inadequate translator of Virgil.
104–5 *bilked stationers* 'cheated publishers'; Herringman was publisher to Flecknoe and Shadwell as well as Dryden. Congreve, *Love for Love* 1.1 has 'bilked booksellers'.
107 'High on a throne of royal state' (*Paradise Lost*, 2:1)
108–9 Shadwell is cast as Ascanius (the 'second hope of Rome's immortal race') to his father Flecknoe's Aeneas (*Aeneid*, 12); Milton calls Beelzebub a 'pillar of the state' (*Paradise Lost*, 2:302).
111 Instead of the 'lambent flame' round the head of Ascanius in *Aeneid*, 2:684.
112–13 The boy Hannibal's father made him swear enmity to Rome.
118–19 It is as a priest (which he really was) that Flecknoe, a king only by office (and only metaphorically), prepares to anoint Shadwell.

120–3 For the regalia of orb ('ball') and sceptre he is given in the left hand a mug of ale, appropriate to a drunk and (unlike wine) conventionally the reverse of inspiring, and in his right a copy of Flecknoe's suggestively named tragi–comedy (reissued 1674).
123 *sway* 'falling' as well as 'command' (as at 131). Cowley calls the stone that killed Abel 'At once his murder and his monument' (*Davideis*, 1:202).
125 *recorded* 'repeated' (because sung, but also because repetitious).
126 *poppies* Shadwell took opium as well as ale.
130–1 The government of still unbuilt Rome was decided by which of the founding twins from their chosen vantage-points should see more birds fly out: Remus saw six, Romulus twelve (Ovid, *Fasti*, 4:811–18).
134 Jupiter binds himself to perform his promises by shaking 'the sacred honours of his head' but whereas 'from his shaken curls ambrosial dews distil' (*Iliad*, 1:529–30, Dryden), it is opiate 'damps' that fall from Flecknoe's.

And from his brows damps of oblivion shed 135
Full on the filial dullness: long he stood,
Repelling from his breast the raging god;
At length burst out in this prophetic mood:
    "Heavens bless my son! from Ireland let him reign,
To far Barbados on the western main; 140
Of his dominion may no end be known,
And greater than his father's be his throne;
Beyond *Love's Kingdom* let him stretch his pen!"
He paused, and all the people cried, "Amen."
Then thus continued he: "My son, advance 145
Still in new impudence, new ignorance.
Success let others teach, learn thou from me
Pangs without birth, and fruitless industry.
Let *Virtuosos* in five years be writ,
Yet not one thought accuse thy toil of wit. 150
Let gentle George in triumph tread the stage,
Make Dorimant betray, and Loveit rage;
Let Cully, Cockwood, Fopling, charm the pit,
And in their folly show the writer's wit;
Yet still thy Fools shall stand in thy defence, 155
And justify their author's want of sense.
Let them be all by thy own model made
Of dullness, and desire no foreign aid;
That they to future ages may be known,
Not copies drawn, but issue of thy own: 160
Nay, let thy men of wit too be the same,
All full of thee, and differing but in name;
But let no alien S–dl–y interpose,
To lard with wit thy hungry Epsom prose.
And when false flowers of rhetoric thou wouldst cull, 165
Trust nature; do not labour to be dull,
But write thy best, and tope; and, in each line,
Sir Formal's oratory will be thine:
Sir Formal, though unsought, attends thy quill,

135–6 Echoing *Paradise Lost*, 6:719–20, 'on his son with rays direct / Shone full' (and 'filial' is a Miltonic word).
136–8 As Latinus faced Aeneas and 'rolled around / His eyes' before prophesying his succession (*Aeneid*, 7: 257); but the exaggeration of the prophetic frenzy is owed to the Sibyl's attempt to shake off the inspiration of Apollo in *Aeneid*, 6:97–101.
139–40 *Ireland . . . Barbados* Echoing Cowley 'From sacred Jordan to the western main' (*Davideis*, 4:56); but the space is empty between Dryden's two barbarous locations.
141 'of his government and peace there shall be no end' (Isaiah 9: 7).
143 *stretch his pen* for 'stretch his wing'.
147–9 'My son! from my example learn the war, / In camps to suffer, and in fields to dare; / But happier chance than mine attend thy care!' (*Aeneid* 12: 435–6, Aeneas to Ascanius). Flecknoe confesses his own ill success as Aeneas his ill fortune.
149–50 Shadwell parades his 'pangs' in the epilogue to *The Virtuoso*; but Rochester (*An Allusion*, 46) calls him 'hasty'. Five years would make no odds.

151–4 Dorimant, Loveit and Fopling belong in Sir George Etherege's *Man of Mode* (1676); Cully and Cockwood in his earlier comedies *Love in a Tub*, and *She would if She Could*. The audience in the pit (nearest the stage) can be supposed to be more discriminating.
155–6 Picking up on Shadwell's own 'He's sure in wit he can't excel the rest, / He'd but be thought to write a Fool the best' (Prologue to *The Virtuoso*).
157–64 Shadwell's pretensions to originality (common to 'modern' realist writers) are compromised by the suspicion that others had a hand in improving his work: Sir Charles Sedley (whom Dryden admired) wrote an acknowledged Prologue for *Epsom Wells* and may have assisted elsewhere.
164 *lard . . . hungry* 'enrich . . . unsatisfying'.
165–70 Shadwell's own style, particularly in his many dedications to the Duke of Newcastle (hence 'Northern'), matches naturally – or in drink (understanding 'top' in 1684 etc. as primarily 'tope') – the florid manner of Sir Formal Trifle in *The Virtuoso*. Flecknoe too was associated with Newcastle; but so was Dryden.

And does thy Northern dedications fill.   170
Nor let false friends seduce thy mind to fame,
By arrogating Jonson's hostile name;
Let father Flecknoe fire thy mind with praise,
And uncle Ogilby thy envy raise.
Thou art my blood, where Jonson has no part: 175
What share have we in nature, or in art?
Where did his wit on learning fix a brand,
And rail at arts he did not understand?
Where made he love in Prince Nicander's vein,
Or swept the dust in *Psyche*'s humble strain?   180
Where sold he bargains, 'whip-stitch, kiss my arse,'
Promised a play, and dwindled to a farce?
When did his muse from Fletcher scenes purloin,
As thou whole Etherege dost transfuse to thine?
But so transfused, as oil on waters flow,   185
His always floats above, thine sinks below.
This is thy province, this thy wondrous way,
New humours to invent for each new play:
This is that boasted bias of thy mind,
By which one way to dullness 'tis inclined;   190
Which makes thy writings lean on one side still,
And, in all changes, that way bends thy will.
Nor let thy mountain-belly make pretence
Of likeness; thine's a tympany of sense.
A tun of man in thy large bulk is writ,   195
But sure thou 'rt but a kilderkin of wit.
Like mine, thy gentle numbers feebly creep;
Thy tragic muse gives smiles, thy comic sleep.
With whate'er gall thou sett'st thyself to write,
Thy inoffensive satires never bite;   200
In thy felonious heart though venom lies,
It does but touch thy Irish pen, and dies.
Thy genius calls thee not to purchase fame
In keen iambics, but mild anagram.

171–2 'Do not allow yourself to be persuaded you should emulate Jonson, who would only worst you.'

173–4 Echoing Andromache's enquiry after Ascanius in *Aeneid*, 3:342–3, if his father Aeneas and his uncle Hector spur him to manliness.

175–6 Adapting Jonson, *To the Memory*, 55–6: 'Yet must I not give Nature all: Thy art / My gentle Shakespeare. must enjoy a part.'

177 *fix a brand* 'stigmatize'.

179–80 Shadwell's Nicander woos Psyche with fatal consequences; Psyche suffers humiliations sweetly. Dryden observes in the *Essay of Dramatic Poesy* that 'you never find [Jonson] making love in any of his scenes.' *Prince Nicander's vein* following Shakespeare's 'King Cambyses' vein' (quoted by Buckingham in the Prologue to *The Rehearsal*), grandiloquently; *humble strain* 'His subject's humble, and his verse is so' (Prologue to *Psyche*).

180 The quoted phrase (from *The Virtuoso*, 'whip-stitch ' meaning 'quick') is an example of 'selling bargains' ('coarse repartee').

185 *flow* for 'flows' (but some read 'water's flow').

188 Shadwell's boasts of it in the preface to *The Virtuoso*.

189–92 'A humour is the bias of the mind, / By which with violence 'tis one way inclined: / It makes our actions lean on one side still, / And in all changes that way bends the will' (Shadwell, Epilogue to *The Humourists*).

193–4 Shadwell's having in common with Jonson a 'mountain belly' (*My Picture Left in Scotland*) is not similarity enough: his mind (unlike Jonson's) is a gross and morbid swelling.

195–6 *tun . . . kilderkin* a proportion of large to small.

197–204 Horace (*Art of Poetry*, 24–5) observes: 'Most Poets fall into the grossest faults, Deluded by a seeming Excellence': Dryden re-illustrates typical failures.

201 Cotton's Prometheus, *Burlesque upon Burlesque* (1675) has a 'felonious heart', etymologically 'filled with venom'.

204 *keen iambics* 'satire', from their earliest use (in Greek) being satirical. The phrasing is borrowed from Cleveland, *The Rebel Scot*, 27.

203–10 Flecknoe's *Treatise of the Sports of Wit* (1675) recommends anagrams and the like; Cowley, *Of Wit*, condemns them. The tenth edition of Herbert's *Temple* (including *Easter-Wings* and *The Altar*) appeared in 1674.

Leave writing plays, and choose for thy command, 205
Some peaceful province in Acrostic land.
There thou may'st *Wings* display, and *Altars* raise,
And torture one poor word ten thousand ways;
Or, if thou wouldst thy different talents suit,
Set thy own songs, and sing them to thy lute." 210
He said, but his last words were scarcely heard,
For Bruce and Longvil had a trap prepared,
And down they sent the yet declaiming bard.
Sinking he left his drugget robe behind,
Borne upwards by a subterranean wind. 215
The mantle fell to the young prophet's part,
With double portion of his father's art.

212–14 Bruce and Longvil belong in *The Virtuoso*, where Sir Formal sinks through a trap-door in the middle of a long speech.
214–17 The two are now cast as Elijah and Elisha: 'Elisha said . . . Let a double portion of thy spirit be upon me . . . and Elijah went up by a whirlwind into heaven . . . And Elisha saw it, and . . . took up also the mantle of Elijah that fell from him' (2 Kings 2: 9–13). But Dryden remembers also Marvell's *Tom May's Death*: 'Straight he vanished in a cloud of pitch, / Such as unto the Sabbath bears the witch' (99–100).
215 'Subterranean winds' are invoked by a devil in Shadwell's *Tempest* (1674); here he is blown upwards by a fart.

To the Memory of Mr Oldham

Printed first in *Remains of Mr John Oldham* (1684), and constructed round memories of Virgil on Nisus and Euryalus in passages which Dryden set himself to translate later in 1684 (and which were published in *Sylvae*, 1685). Oldham died of smallpox in December 1683, aged 30. His precocious achievement as a satirist and also as a translator was widely celebrated. Oldham's own *To the Memory of Mr Charles Morwent*, first published in *Remains*, also offers a meditation on premature death with a rationalizing conceit that Morwent's early maturity made him ripe for death. Dryden allows no such consolation.

Farewell, too little, and too lately known,
Whom I began to think, and call my own:
For sure our souls were near allied, and thine
Cast in the same poetic mould with mine.
One common note on either lyre did strike, 5
And knaves and fools we both abhorred alike.
To the same goal did both our studies drive;
The last set out, the soonest did arrive.
Thus Nisus fell upon the slippery place,
Whilst his young friend performed and won the race. 10
O early ripe! to thy abundant store
What could advancing age have added more?

---

1 *too lately* 'too late'.
3–4 Echoing 'Sure on our birth some friendly planet shone; / And, as our souls, our horoscope was one' (Persius, 5:45–6) or Cowley's imitation of it in the ode on Hervey, 26; and with a bow to Oldham's *David's Lamentation* 'O dearer than my soul! if I can call it mine, / For sure we had the same, 'twas very thine'. Waller speaks of Rochester and Anne Wharton as 'Allied in genius, as in blood' (*Of an Elegy made by Mrs Wharton on the Earl of Rochester*).
7 'Our endeavours were spurred by a common purpose.'
8–10 The older Nisus and the younger Euryalus compete together in the foot-race, one of the games instituted by Aeneas for his dead father. Nisus slips while in the lead, but by tripping the next runner allows Euralyus to win (*Aeneid*, 5:327–36). Their death together is related in *Aeneid*, 9 (see below). Dryden treats the race as a metaphor of life, with death as the goal.
11 *early ripe* Used by Thomas Pestell in his elegy on Lord Hastings, a subject shared with Dryden; but the primary horticultural sense is sustained in 'store'.

It might (what nature never gives the young)
Have taught the numbers of thy native tongue.
But satire needs not those, and wit will shine   15
Through the harsh cadence of a rugged line:
A noble error, and but seldom made,
When poets are by too much force betrayed.
Thy generous fruits, though gathered ere their prime,
Still showed a quickness; and maturing time   20
But mellows what we write to the dull sweets of rhyme.
Once more, hail, and farewell! farewell, thou young
But ah! too short, Marcellus of our tongue!
Thy brows with ivy and with laurels bound;
But fate and gloomy night encompass thee around.   25

13–14 Like Pope, the infant Ovid found that what he tried to speak was verse (*Tristia*, 4.10:25–6); but correctness requires a strenuous apprenticeship.

15–16 '[Persius's] verse is scabrous, and hobbling' and 'his diction is hard, his figures are generally too bold and daring', but he is rescued by his 'spirit of sincerity' (Dryden's *Discourse concerning Satire*), his intelligence or 'wit' (which in most senses he lacks). Satire is conventionally allowed roughness – Spenser's pseudo-Chaucerian hobbling 'style of satire' in *Mother Hubberd's Tale* constitutes an English model for both Oldham himself and Dryden. Oldham's 'Advertisement' to *Some New Pieces* (1681) responds to accusations of roughness: 'I did not so much mind the cadence, as the sense and expressiveness of my words.'

19 *generous* 'abundant'.
20 *quickness* 'sharpness'.

21 *dull sweets* Like Dryden's own Autumn 'More than mature, and tending to decay' (*Of the Pythagorean Philosophy*, 314); he alludes to Oldham's conspicuously imperfect rhymes, and here the alexandrine delays the third full rhyme.
22 Catullus 101 famously bids 'forever hail and farewell' to his brother.
23–5 Aeneas meets in the Underworld the prematurely dead spirit of the hope of Virgil's own generation, Marcellus: 'Observe the crowds that compass him around . . . But hovering mists around his brows are spread, / And night, with sable shades, involves his head' (*Aeneid*, 865–6). The pseudonymous elegist 'Damon' in *Remains* invokes the same passage: 'Oh had he lived, and to perfection grown, / Not like Marcellus, only to be shown.' The ivy and laurels replace Marcellus's gloomy eyes and dejected face, identifying Oldham as a poet; *fate* 'death'.

Two Translations from *Sylvae*

Sylvae: or The Second Part of Poetical Miscellanies was published by Jacob Tonson in 1685, a sequel to his collection of mainly previously published *Miscellany Poems* (1684), Dryden being the major contributor to both. The new volume consisted entirely of new pieces, and almost entirely of commissioned translations. Hammond's *Poems of John Dryden*, 2: Appendix A, gives the contents of both volumes. Dryden is here confirmed as the great English appropriator of classical poetry. The preface to *Ovid's Epistles* (1680) set out the principles which with some adjustments were to serve Dryden's translating enterprise. Translation was defined as of three kinds: 'metaphrase, or turning an author word by word, and line by line' (exemplified in Ben Jonson's version of Horace's *Art of Poetry*); 'paraphrase, or translation with latitude, where the author is kept in view by the translator, so as never to be lost, but his words are not so strictly followed as his sense; and that too is admitted to be amplified, but not altered' (exemplified in the Godolphin–Waller version of Virgil's *Aeneid* 4); 'imitation, where the translator . . . assumes the liberty, not only to vary from the words and sense, but to forsake them both as he sees occasion' (exemplified

in Cowley's Pindar). 'Servile, literal translation' was rendered impossible by Cowley, and by Denham (who had praised the 'new and nobler way' of Fanshawe's Guarini) in his versions of Virgil. But Dryden rejected imitation also: 'imitation of an author is the most advantageous way for a translator to show himself, but the greatest wrong which can be done to the memory and reputation of the dead.' The translator must be master of his own language (as the imitator is) but intimate with his author's 'particular turn of thoughts and expression, which are the characters that distinguish, and as it were individuate him from all other writers' and then prepared to conform his own genius to his author's, 'to give his thought either the same turn, if our tongue will bear it, or, if not, to vary but the dress, not to alter or destroy the substance. The like care must be taken of the more outward ornaments, the words.' The aim, as he develops the statement in the preface to *Sylvae*, is to rewrite his author's verses so 'that if he were living, and an Englishman, they are such as he would probably have written'. The emphasis here is not, however, on the contemporary Englishness, so much as on the author's identity: 'translation is a kind of drawing after the life,' where 'likeness' is the point, 'the maintaining the character of an author, which distinguishes him from all others, and makes him appear that individual poet whom you would interpret'. When Dryden looks at even the best English poets who have translated Ovid and Virgil, he finds 'that they have confounded their several talents; and, by endeavouring only at the sweetness and harmony of numbers, have made them both so much alike, that, if I did not know the originals, I should never be able to judge by the copies which was Virgil, and which was Ovid.'

From *Lucretius: The Fourth Book concerning the Nature of Love*

Given in *Sylvae* (1685) where Dryden includes five passages from Lucretius (the openings of Books 1 and 2, the conclusions of Books 3 and 4 and a brief passage from Book 5. The 298 lines of 'Concerning the Nature of Love' translate *De Natura Rerum*, 4.1052 1287); the extract below covers 1076–1113. To Creech's Lucretius of 1682 (fulsomely praised by Aphra Behn and Evelyn, among others), Dryden denies a debt since (he says) he had planned his own versions twenty years before, presumably under the influence of the generalized Epicureanism already so fashionable. Creech's version is relatively literal; and, being complete, has to take on seriously rebarbative material. Dryden's aim was to emulate a style 'masculine, full of argumentation, and that sufficiently warm', and he selects to exhibit those characteristics. Dryden concedes the 'obscenity' of the extract here (minced by Lucy Hutchinson: 'much here was left out for a midwife to translate whose obscene art it would better become than a nicer pen'), and admits its aggravation 'by the too lively and alluring delicacy of the verses'; but turns it into 'luscious English' because it pleased him, and because he will not 'wrong' his author. Sandys's fragments of Lucretius, scattered in his commentary on Ovid and in the *Relation of a Journey*, include a version of 4:1076–1120 to illustrate Ovid's story of Salmacis and Hermaphroditus (*Metamorphoses*, 1:285–388).

> When love its utmost vigour does employ, 35
> Ev'n then, 'tis but a restless wandering joy:
> Nor knows the lover in that wild excess,
> With hands or eyes what first he would possess;
> But strains at all, and fastening where he strains,
> Too closely presses with his frantic pains; 40
> With biting kisses hurts the twining fair,
> Which shows his joys imperfect, unsincere:
> For stung with inward rage he flings around,
> And strives to avenge the smart on that which gave the wound.
> But love those eager bitings does restrain, 45
> And mingling pleasure mollifies the pain.
> For ardent hope still flatters anxious grief,
> And sends him to his foe to seek relief:
> Which yet the nature of the thing denies,
> For love, and love alone of all our joys, 50
> By full possession does but fan the fire;
> The more we still enjoy, the more we still desire.
> Nature for meat and drink provides a space,
> And, when received, they fill their certain place;
> Hence thirst and hunger may be satisfied, 55
> But this repletion is to love denied:
> Form, feature, colour, whatsoe'er delight

39 'He exerts himself ('strains') to be everywhere at once, holding tight where he once embraces ('strains').'
41 *the twining fair* 'the writhing beauty'.
42 Lucretius distinguishes the uncomplicated and pleasurable gratification of passion ('Venus') from the passion itself ('Cupido') whose joys are 'imperfect' since desire is always not yet satisfied, and 'unsincere' or 'impure' in being mixed with pain.

44 The diction as well as the rhythm of the alexandrine is Spenserian.
45 *bitings* 'pains'; but with a confusing reminiscence of 'biting kisses'.
47 *flatters* 'beguiles'.

Provokes the lover's endless appetite,
These fill no space, nor can we thence remove
With lips, or hands, or all our instruments of love: 60
In our deluded grasp we nothing find,
But thin aerial shapes, that fleet before the mind.
As he who in a dream with drought is cursed,
And finds no real drink to quench his thirst,
Runs to imagined lakes his heat to steep,   65
And vainly swills and labours in his sleep;
So Love with phantoms cheats our longing eyes,
Which hourly seeing never satisfies:
Our hands pull nothing from the parts they strain,
But wander o'er the lovely limbs in vain: 70
Nor when the youthful pair more closely join,
When hands in hands they lock, and thighs in thighs they twine,
Just in the raging foam of full desire,
When both press on, both murmur, both expire,
They gripe, they squeeze, their humid tongues they dart,   75
As each would force their way to the other's heart –
In vain; they only cruise about the coast,
For bodies cannot pierce, nor be in bodies lost:
As sure they strive to be, when both engage
In that tumultuous momentany rage;   80
So tangled in the nets of love they lie,
Till man dissolves in that excess of joy.
Then, when the gathered bag has burst its way,
And ebbing tides the slackened nerves betray,
A pause ensues; and nature nods awhile,   85
Till with recruited rage new spirits boil;
And then the same vain violence returns,
With flames renewed the erected furnace burns;
Again they in each other would be lost,
But still by adamantine bars are crossed.   90
All ways they try, successless all they prove,
To cure the secret sore of lingering love.
Besides—
They waste their strength in the venereal strife,
And to a woman's will enslave their life;   95

59–60 *nor . . . love* Dryden's addition: 'these' is understood as the object of 'remove'.

62 Lucretius says 'thin images, and even this wretched hope is snatched off by the wind'; *fleet* 'waver and vanish'.

68 *Which hourly seeing* 'of which the constant sight'.

69 *pull* 'gather' (as fruit; though Lucretius has a stronger 'rub off' or 'pull out'); *strain* 'embrace'.

73 Dryden cancels the metaphor of Venus 'sowing the woman's field'.

74 *expire* 'gasp out'; Lucretius has 'inspire'.

75 *gripe* 'clutch'; *humid tongues* for Lucretius's 'watering mouths' and 'teeth'.

77 *cruise* as ships move with no predetermined end in view: a recent loan from Dutch.

82 Lucretius says 'limbs melt overwhelmed by the force of pleasure'.

83–4 The physical specificity is all Dryden's: for 'bag' ('scro-

tum' or its product) Lucretius has 'desire', and no equivalent of the second line, where detumescence 'betrays' the failure of desire ('ebbing tides') – here only temporary. Dryden uses 'slackened nerve' also in his version of Juvenal 6:196.

86 *recruited rage* 'restored passion'.

88 *erected furnace* Dryden's addition: Jacques's lover goes 'sighing like a furnace' in Shakespeare's *As You Like It*.

90 *adamantine* 'impenetrable' since 'bodies cannot pierce' (line 78).

91 *successless* a usual form.

92 *lingering* 'longing', but also 'ailing'.

93 The later (1697) Preface to the *Aeneis* abjures the use of incomplete lines (favoured by Cowley) on the authority of Virgil (but mistakenly, according to Dryden).

95 Lucretius does not specify the enslavement of the male partner.

The estate runs out, and mortgages are made,
All offices of friendship are decayed,
Their fortune ruined, and their fame betrayed.
Assyrian ointment from their temples flows,
And diamond buckles sparkle in their shoes; 100
The cheerful emerald twinkles on their hands,
With all the luxury of foreign lands,
And the blue coat, that with embroidery shines,
Is drunk with sweat of their o'er-laboured loins.
Their frugal father's gains they misemploy, 105
And turn to *point*, and pearl, and every female toy.
French fashions, costly treats are their delight;
The Park by day, and plays and balls by night.
In vain —
For in the fountain, where their sweets are sought, 110
Some bitter bubbles up, and poisons all the draught.
First guilty conscience does the mirror bring,
Then sharp remorse shoots out her angry sting,
And anxious thoughts within themselves at strife
Upbraid the long misspent, luxurious life. 115
Perhaps the fickle fair one proves unkind,
Or drops a doubtful word that pains his mind,
And leaves a rankling jealousy behind.
Perhaps, he watches close her amorous eyes,
And in the act of ogling does surprise, 120
And thinks he sees upon her cheeks the while
The dimpled tracks of some foregoing smile;
His raging pulse beats thick, and his pent spirits boil.

96 Dryden specifies debt where Lucretius specified luxury.
97 'All friendship's duties are neglected.'
99–100 Lucretius does not specify the ointment as Assyrian, but gives the shoes as Sicyonian. The 'diamond buckles' are Dryden's.
101 Lucretius says the emerald 'laughs'.
103 Dryden's 'blue' coat replaces one 'coloured like the sea' ('thalassinus'); *with embroidery shines* supplied by Dryden supposing the coat to have been worked on rather than just worn.
104 *drunk* 'drenched'.

106–8 Dryden abridges and modernizes Lucretius's list of misemployments.
106 *point* 'lace' (pronounced as in French); *toy* 'trifle'.
108 *Park* St James's Park.
110 *sweets* 'delights'.
111 *bitter* 'bitterness'.
112 Lucretius's conscience has no mirror.
120 *ogling* a low word (recently imported from Dutch).
123 *dimpled tracks* for 'vestigia'; *foregoing* 'already past'.
123 *thick* 'fast'.

From *Horace, Epode 2*

The text is that of *Sylvae* (1685). In the same decade there are versions by Creech, Harington, Flatman, Cotton. Dryden works in that context and out of the tradition of poems of rural retirement which includes many similar. The versions by Jonson and Cowley are given in this volume. Dryden fills out the Horatian original with imaginative turns of his own, with memories of analogous passages in Horace and elsewhere. He may have seen Otto Vaenius's *Horatii Emblemata* (1612) which collects literary praises of the country life under the motto *Agriculturae Beatitudo* (the plate may have inclined Dryden to his 'pictorial' treatment).

Horace's couplets are sometimes expanded to tercets or quatrains; and the sense is sometimes rearranged between them. The octosyllabics sometimes recall Milton's, and the phrasing sometimes consciously echoes earlier English poets. He places near the beginning an obvious quotation from Fanshawe, to whose version of the *Epode* he may owe other details (the 'matted grass', the 'tusked boar') and an encouragement to be free with epithets. The notes to Jonson's version, above (p. 101), explain difficulties not peculiar to Dryden's.

"How happy in his low degree,
How rich in humble poverty, is he,
　　Who leads a quiet country life,
　　Discharged of business, void of strife,
And from the griping scrivener free?　　　　　　　　　5
Thus, ere the seeds of vice were sown,
　　Lived men in better ages born,
Who ploughed, with oxen of their own,
　　Their small paternal field of corn.
Nor trumpets summon him to war,　　　　　　　　　10
　　Nor drums disturb his morning sleep,
Nor knows he merchants' gainful care,
　　Nor fears the dangers of the deep.
The clamours of contentious law,
　　And court and state, he wisely shuns,　　　　　　15
Nor bribed with hopes, nor dared with awe,
　　To servile salutations runs;
But either to the clasping vine
　　Does the supporting poplar wed,
Or with his pruning-hook disjoin　　　　　　　　　20
　　Unbearing branches from their head,
　　And grafts more happy in their stead:
Or, climbing to a hilly steep,
　　He views his herds in vales afar,
Or shears his overburdened sheep,　　　　　　　　25
　　Or mead for cooling drink prepares,
　　Or virgin honey in the jars.
Or in the now declining year,
　　When bounteous Autumn rears his head,
He joys to pull the ripened pear,　　　　　　　　　30
　　And clustering grapes with purple spread.
The fairest of his fruit he serves,
　　Priapus, thy rewards:
Sylvanus too his part deserves,
　　Whose care the fences guards.　　　　　　　　　35
Sometimes beneath an ancient oak,
　　Or on the matted grass he lies;
No god of sleep he need invoke;
　　The stream, that o'er the pebbles flies,
　　With gentle slumber crowns his eyes.　　　　　40
The wind, that whistles through the sprays,
　　Maintains the concert of the song;
And hidden birds, with native lays,
　　The golden sleep prolong.
But when the blast of winter blows,　　　　　　　　45
　　And hoary frost inverts the year,

2　Content is proverbially 'the poor man's riches'.
5　'Free from the griping scrivener's bands' (Fanshawe, *Ode*,
89).
6　*seeds of vice* a cliché in Latin, used by Spenser, *Faerie
Queene*, 5.1.1.
15　*court and state* 'law and politics'.
16　*dared* 'daunted'; but the sense used at 51 may be in-
voked.

21　*unbearing* 'infertile'.
42　*maintains the concert* 'supports the harmony'.
46　*inverts* 'turns'. Horace, *Satires*, 1.1:36 speaks of the 'in-
verted year' (because it turns back to begin again, and be-
cause it begins with stormy weather – which Cowley's
translation catches in 'the deformed, wrong side of the year').

Into the naked woods he goes,
  And seeks the tusky boar to rear,
  With well-mouthed hounds and pointed spear:
Or spreads his subtle nets from sight   50
  With twinkling glasses, to betray
The larks that in the meshes light,
  Or makes the fearful hare his prey.
Amidst his harmless easy joys
  No anxious care invades his health,   55
Nor love his peace of mind destroys,
  Nor wicked avarice of wealth.
But if a chaste and pleasing wife,
To ease the business of his life,
  Divides with him his household care,   60
  Such as the Sabine matrons were,
Such as the swift Apulian's bride,
  Sun-burnt and swarthy though she be,
Will fire for winter nights provide,
  And without noise will oversee   65
  His children and his family,
And order all things till he come,
Sweaty and overlaboured, home;
If she in pens his flocks will fold,
  And then produce her dairy store,   70
With wine to drive away the cold,
  And unbought dainties of the poor;
Not oysters of the Lucrine lake
  My sober appetite would wish,
  Nor turbot, or the foreign fish   75
That rolling tempests overtake,
  And hither waft the costly dish.
Not heath-poult, or the rarer bird,
  Which Phasis or Ionia yields,
More pleasing morsels would afford   80
  Than the fat olives of my fields;
Than chards or mallows for the pot,
  That keep the loosened body sound,
Or than the lamb, that falls by lot
  To the just guardian of my ground.   85
Amidst these feasts of happy swains,
  The jolly shepherd smiles to see
His flock returning from the plains;
  The farmer is as pleased as he,
To view his oxen sweating smoke,   90
Bear on their necks the loosened yoke;
To look upon his menial crew,
  That sit around his cheerful hearth,
And bodies spent in toil renew
  With wholesome food and country mirth."   95

48 *rear* 'rouse'; from the vocabulary of hunting.
49 The 'well-mouthed' hounds are borrowed from Cowley's version (36).
51 *twinkling glasses* larks are 'dared' (16) or dazzled by mirrors to bring them into the net.

78 *heath-poult* 'grouse'.
79 The pheasant is the 'bird from Phasis' (a recondite etymological joke); Horace's Ionian 'attagen' is also some kind of pheasant.
92 *menial* 'household'.

> This Morecraft said within himself:
>   Resolved to leave the wicked town,
>   And live retired upon his own,
>   He called his money in:
> But the prevailing love of pelf
> Soon split him on the former shelf,
>   And put it out again.

100

96   *Morecraft* a type of the usurer, from Beaumont and
Fletcher's *Scornful Wife* (1616).
100–1   *Times Whistle*, possibly by Jonson's friend Richard

Corbett (but not in print till 1871), has: 'Till i' th' end his
pelf / Shipwrecks his soul upon Hell's rocky shelf'.

To the Pious Memory of the Accomplished Young Lady Mistress Anne Killigrew, Excellent in the Two Sister Arts of Poesy and Painting. An Ode

Commissioned by Anne's father Henry Killigrew, (Anglican) chaplain to the Duke of York and published first as a preface to Anne Killigrew's *Poems* in 1686 or late 1685, shortly after their author's death from smallpox, aged 25; it is given here from its revision in *Examen Poeticum or the Third Part of Miscellany Poems* (1693). There is a facsimile edition of Killigrew's *Poems* by Richard Morton (Gainesville, FL: Scholars' Facsimiles and Reprints, 1967). She wrote and painted only indifferently well; but as Donne in the *Anniversaries* famously makes Elizabeth Drury's premature death the occasion for the praise of what survives decay, Dryden boldly converts elegy into panegyric. The commonplaces of praise are organized around images of sovereignty (most obviously in

the triumph of the long stanza 6) in a fashion 'classic' enough for them to be disengaged from any immediate association with the pretended subject of the poem. That disengagement permits and even encourages a sustained contemplation of the gap between art (as mastered by Dryden) and innocence (as exemplified in Killigrew) and so to the relationship of art and morality. Written in the fashionable Pindarizing manner with which Killigrew herself experimented, the poem's metrical sureness is owing to Dryden's apprenticeship in opera libretto writing; its compactness and its refusal of fluency are owing to his preoccupation with turning Latin poetry into English.

1

> Thou youngest virgin–daughter of the skies,
>   Made in the last promotion of the blessed;
>   Whose palms, new plucked from Paradise,
> In spreading branches more sublimely rise,
> Rich with immortal green above the rest:
> Whether, adopted to some neighbouring star,
> Thou roll'st above us, in thy wandering race,
>   Or, in procession fixed and regular,
>   Moved with the heaven's majestic pace;

5

1   *virgin-daughter* Jeremiah 14: 17: 'the virgin daughter of my people is broken'; but rescued by her accommodation among the virgins of Revelation 14: 4 'redeemed from among men, being the firstfruits unto God'.
2–5   'Lo a great multitude . . . stood before the Lamb, clothed with white robes, and palms in their hands' (Revelation 7: 9).
2   *promotion* 'elevation'.
4   *more sublimely* 'higher'.
6–11   Dryden remembers Virgil's celebration of the dead Caesar: 'Daphnis, the guest of heaven, with wondering eyes,

/ Views, in the milky way, the starry skies, / And far beneath him, from the shining sphere, / Beholds the moving clouds, and rolling year' (*Eclogues*, 5: 56–7). Killigrew's stellification is startling: she is grafted either to a planet ('some neighbouring star . . . in thy wandering race') or a fixed star, or dances ('treads') with the seraphim (here only 'angels') in the supra-stellar space of the empyrean above the space of the created universe (Milton's 'vast abyss' was the uncreated universe). In *Cleomones* (1692) Dryden imagines the earth rolling 'along the vast abyss'.

Or, called to more superior bliss,   10
Thou tread'st, with seraphims, the vast abyss.
Whatever happy region is thy place,
Cease thy celestial song a little space;
(Thou wilt have time enough for hymns divine,
    Since Heaven's eternal year is thine).   15
Hear then a mortal Muse thy praise rehearse,
    In no ignoble verse;
But such as thy own voice did practise here,
When thy first-fruits of poesy were given;
To make thyself a welcome inmate there: 20
    While yet a young probationer,
    And candidate of Heaven.

2

If by traduction came thy mind,
Our wonder is the less to find
A soul so charming from a stock so good;   25
Thy father was transfused into thy blood:
So wert thou born into a tuneful strain
(An early, rich, and inexhausted vein).
    But if thy pre-existing soul
    Was formed, at first, with myriads more,   30
It did through all the mighty poets roll,
    Who Greek or Latin laurels wore,
And was that Sappho last, which once it was before.
    If so, then cease thy flight, O heaven-born mind!
    Thou hast no dross to purge from thy rich ore: 35
    Nor can thy soul a fairer mansion find,   }
    Than was the beauteous frame she left behind: }
Return, to fill or mend the choir of thy celestial kind.   }

3

May we presume to say, that at thy birth,
New joy was sprung in Heaven, as well as here on Earth.   40
    For sure the milder planets did combine   }
    On thy auspicious horoscope to shine,   }
    And e'en the most malicious were in trine.   }
    Thy brother-angels at thy birth
    Strung each his lyre, and tuned it high,   45

10 *more superior bliss* 'greater bliss enjoyed above'.
16 *mortal Muse* himself, since he has yet to die.
19–20 'The first of the firstfruits of thy land thou shalt bring into the house of the Lord thy God' (Exodus 23: 19). Herbert's *Dedication* to *The Temple* calls his poems 'firstfruits'.
21–2 *probationer . . . candidate* As if she were on trial for the heavenly choir.
23 *traduction* 'To have being by traduction, is, when the soul of the child is derived from the soul of the parent, by the means of seed' (Edward Reynolds's *Treatise of the Passions*, 1640).
27 *strain* 'stock' (25) but punningly contaminated by 'tuneful'. Her father Henry and her uncle Thomas were both poets.

29–38 Transmigration of souls is the alternative proposed to traduction. The scheme is borrowed from Anchises' speech to Aeneas (*Aeneid*, 6:703–51).
33 *Sappho* the type of the woman poet. Cowley (*On Orinda's Poems*, 61) refuses the comparison of Katherine Philips with Sappho because 'Ill manners soil the lustre of her fame.'
41–3 The triplet mimics the astrologically harmonious disposition ('in trine', at a distance from each other of a third part of the zodiac) of even the malign planets. Compare Spenser's 'many an angel's voice, / Singing before the eternal majesty, / In their trinal triplicities on high' (*Faerie Queene*, 1.12.39).

That all the people of the sky
Might know a poetess was born on earth.
And then if ever, mortal ears
Had heard the music of the spheres!
And if no clustering swarm of bees   50
On thy sweet mouth distilled their golden dew,
    'Twas that, such vulgar miracles
    Heaven had not leisure to renew:
For all the blest fraternity of love
Solemnised there thy birth, and kept thy holiday above.   55

4

O gracious God! how far have we
Profaned thy heavenly gift of poesy!
Made prostitute and profligate the muse,
Debased to each obscene and impious use,
Whose harmony was first ordained above   60
For tongues of angels, and for hymns of love!
O wretched we! why were we hurried down
    This lubric and adulterate age,
    (Nay, added fat pollutions of our own)
To increase the steaming ordures of the stage?   65
What can we say to excuse our second Fall?
Let this thy Vestal, Heaven, atone for all!
Her Arethusian stream remains unsoiled,
Unmixed with foreign filth, and undefiled,
Her wit was more than man, her innocence a child!   70

5

    Art she had none, yet wanted none:
    For Nature did that want supply,
    So rich in treasures of her own,
    She might our boasted stores defy:
Such noble vigour did her verse adorn,   75
That it seemed borrowed where 'twas only born.
Her morals too were in her bosom bred
    By great examples daily fed,

48–9 Plato, *Republic* 10, gives the classic (but metaphorical) account of the planets' emitting musical notes so as to combine in harmony. Aristotle, *De Caelo*, rejects it: hence the sceptical 'if ever'.

50 Bees sweetened the lips of the infant Pindar (*Greek Anthology*, 7.34, 16.305).

52–5 'It was because Heaven was better employed celebrating your birth above that no common miracles were seen on earth.'

56–61 So Milton complains of 'swelling epithets thick laid / As varnish on a harlot's cheek, the rest, / Thin sown with aught of profit or delight / Will far be found unworthy to compare / With Sion's songs' (*Paradise Regained*, 4: 343–7).

62–5 Reflecting, as Jonson does in his *Ode on The New Inn*, on his own dramatic career.

63 *lubric* 'licentious'; but also 'slippery' (hence 'hurried down').

64 *fat* 'gross'.

66 *second Fall* The first being in Eden.

67 *Vestal* 'virgin'.

68 *Arethusian* The chastity of Arethusa, threatened by Alpheus, was preserved by her metamorphosis into a fountain. But 'Alpheus, as old fame reports, has found / From Greece a secret passage under ground, / By love to beauteous Arethusa led' (*Aeneid*, 3:694–6). Killigrew's purity stays intact.

70 Adapting Killigrew's line 'Though more than man, obedient as a child' (*To My Lady Berkeley*, when her son went to sea).

74 *stores* 'abundance collected' (from ancient authors).

77–9 'She generated her morals of herself, but nourished them with great examples, with what she saw in her father's life.'

What in the best of books, her father's life, she read.
　And to be read herself she need not fear;　　　　　　　　　　80
　Each test, and every light, her Muse will bear,
　Though Epictetus with his lamp were there.
E'en love (for love sometimes her Muse expressed)
Was but a lambent-flame which played about her breast:
　Light as the vapours of a morning dream,　　　　　　　　　85
　So cold herself, whilst she such warmth expressed,
'Twas Cupid bathing in Diana's stream.

6

Born to the spacious empire of the Nine,
One would have thought she should have been content
To manage well that mighty government;　　　　　　　　　　90
But what can young ambitious souls confine?
　To the next realm she stretched her sway,
　For Painture near adjoining lay,
A plenteous province, and alluring prey.
A Chamber of Dependencies was framed　　　　　　　　　　95
(As conquerors will never want pretence,
　When armed, to justify the offence),
And the whole fief, in right of poetry she claimed.
The country open lay without defence:
For poets frequent inroads there had made,　　　　　　　　100
　And perfectly could represent
　The shape, the face, with every lineament;
And all the large domains which the Dumb-Sister swayed,
　All bowed beneath her government,
　Received in triumph wheresoe'er she went.　　　　　　　105
　Her pencil drew whate'er her soul designed,
And oft the happy draught surpassed the image in her mind.
　The sylvan scenes of herds and flocks,
　And fruitful plains and barren rocks,
　Of shallow brooks that flowed so clear,　　　　　　　　　110

82　Dryden set out as the condition of happiness that 'we possess our minds with a good conscience, are free from the slavery of vices, and conform our actions and conversation to the rules of right reason. See here ... an epitome of Epictetus' (*Discourse concerning Satire*). The lamp is 'that renowned Lantern of Epictetus, by which if any man studied, he should be as wise as he was' (Burton, *Anatomy*, 'Democritus to the Reader').

84　*lambent-flame* 'light without heat'.

85　Contradicted by Dryden's 'break of day, when dreams, they say, are true' (*The Spanish Friar*), but the dream described is 'a fancy'.

87　Recalls Killigrew's *On a Picture Painted by Herself, Representing Two Nymphs of Diana's, One in a Posture to Hunt, the other Bathing*, 19–20: 'Though Venus we transcend in form, / No wanton flames our bosoms warm.'

88　*empire of the Nine* 'poetry' (governed by the Muses).

92–4　Dryden credits Bellori with the analogy in the preface to his version of Du Fresnoy's *De Arte Graphica* (1695).

95–8　Louis XIV's Chambres de Réunions were tribunals set up to determine the extent of the 'dependencies' of territories conquered by France; these 'dependencies' were then in their turn declared French; *fief* 'estate'.

103　*Dumb-Sister* 'It was excellently said of Plutarch, poetry was a speaking picture, and picture a mute poesy' (Jonson, *Timber*).

106–7　'The brush drew what the soul conceived, and so the drawing often surpassed what she actually envisaged.' The divine idea, says Bellori, 'infuses life into the image'. Dryden's point is obscured by the wittily fuzzy vocabulary ('designed', 'image', 'mind').

108–26　'Scene' still suggests stage scenery (as in Milton's Paradisal 'sylvan scene', *Paradise Lost*, 4:140). But Lely had made fashionable in England the Claude-like landscapes described. Virgil writes of Aeneas's landfall in Libya (*Aeneid*, 1:162–8): 'a sylvan scene Appears above, and groves for ever green: / A grot is formed beneath, with mossy seats, / To rest the Nereids, and exclude the heats. / Down through the crannies of the living walls, / The crystal streams descend in murmuring falls.'

The bottom did the top appear;
Of deeper too and ampler floods,
Which, as in mirrors, showed the woods;
Of lofty trees, with sacred shades,
And perspectives of pleasant glades,   115
Where nymphs of brightest form appear,
And shaggy satyrs standing near,
Which them at once admire and fear.
The ruins, too, of some majestic piece,
Boasting the power of ancient Rome or Greece,   120
Whose statues, friezes, columns, broken lie,
And, though defaced, the wonder of the eye;
What nature, art, bold fiction, e'er durst frame,
Her forming hand gave feature to the name.
So strange a concourse ne'er was seen before,   125
But when the peopled Ark the whole creation bore.

7

The scene then changed, with bold erected look
Our martial king the sight with reverence struck:
For, not content to express his outward part,
Her hand called out the image of his heart: 130
His warlike mind, his soul devoid of fear,
His high-designing thoughts, were figured there,
As when, by magic, ghosts are made appear.
Our phoenix-queen was portrayed too so bright,
Beauty alone could beauty take so right: 135
Her dress, her shape, her matchless grace,
Were all observed, as well as heavenly face.
With such a peerless majesty she stands,
As in that day she took the crown from sacred hands:
Before a train of heroines was seen,   140
In beauty foremost, as in rank, the queen!
Thus nothing to her genius was denied,
But like a ball of fire the further thrown,
Still with a greater blaze she shone,
And her bright soul broke out on every side.   145
What next she had designed, heaven only knows:
To such immoderate growth her conquest rose,
That fate alone its progress could oppose.

---

119 *piece* 'fortress'.

124 *feature to* shape unto (1686).

126 As in Cowley's 'true piece of wit' all things agree 'as in the Ark' (*Of Wit*, 59).

127 *The scene then changed.* The theatrical bias is now explicit, and the landscape is reduced to the status of backdrop. So even in pictures: 'All that which in a picture is not of the body or argument thereof is landscape . . . or by-work' (Blount, *Glossographia*).

128 *sight* eye (1686).

134 Killigrew had served as Maid of Honour to the future queen, Mary of Modena. She is phoenix-like because unique.

139–40 took from sacred hands / The crown; 'mong numerous (1686): the revision admits an alexandrine.

141 More yet in beauty, than (1686).

143–4 As extravagant as Donne's 'more earnestly released' soul in *The Dissolution*, which overtakes the soul of the dead beloved 'as bullets flown before / A latter bullet may o'ertake, the powder being more'.

147–8 Adapting Martial 6.29:7: 'Life is short for those who overstep the mark, and age is rare' (the epigraph for the 1686 volume).

8

Now all those charms, that blooming grace,
The well-proportioned shape, and beauteous face,   150
Shall never more be seen by mortal eyes;
In earth the much-lamented virgin lies!
    Not wit, nor piety, could fate prevent;
    Nor was the cruel destiny content
    To finish all the murder at a blow,   155
    To sweep at once her life and beauty too;
But, like a hardened felon, took a pride
    To work more mischievously slow,
    And plundered first, and then destroyed.
O double sacrilege on things divine,   160
To rob the relic, and deface the shrine!
    But thus Orinda died:
    Heaven, by the same disease, did both translate;
As equal were their souls, so equal was their fate.

9

    Meantime, her warlike brother on the seas   165
    His waving streamers to the winds displays,
And vows for his return, with vain devotion, pays.
    Ah, generous youth! that wish forbear,
    The winds too soon will waft thee here!
    Slack all thy sails, and fear to come;   170
Alas, thou know'st not, thou art wrecked at home!
No more shalt thou behold thy sister's face,
Thou hast already had her last embrace.
But look aloft, and if thou ken'st from far,
Among the Pleiads a new-kindled star,   175
If any sparkles, than the rest, more bright,
'Tis she that shines in that propitious light.

10

When in mid-air, the golden trump shall sound,
    To raise the nations under ground;
    When in the valley of Jehoshaphat,   180
The Judging God shall close the Book of Fate;
    And there the last assizes keep,

153 Horace, *Odes*, 2.14: ''Tis not thy wealth, 'tis not thy power, / 'Tis not thy piety can thee secure [from] thy avoidless end' (Oldham).
154–64 Adapting Cowley's complaint of the 'unbounded sacrilege' of the smallpox both defiling and destroying 'Orinda' (*On the death of Mistress Katherine Philips*). He mutes his own more extravagant treatment of smallpox in the early *Upon the Death of the Lord Hastings*: 'Or were these gems sent to adorn his skin, / The cabinet of a richer soul within?'
165 Henry Killigrew (died 1712) was then captaining a ship in the Mediterranean.
166 The 'waving streamers' of Prince Rupert's ship gladden the Duke of Albemarle (*Annus Mirabilis*, 418).

167 *vows ... pays* 'misguidedly makes promises for his return'.
170–1 With a memory of Killigrew, *On a Young Lady whose Lord was Travelling*: 'Return young Lord, while thou abroad dost roam / The world to see, thou losest Heaven at home.'
175 *Pleiads* 'Seven Sisters' looked to by sailors because their first appearance on the dawn horizon coincides with the onset of the sailing season.
179–81 'For the trumpet shall sound, and the dead shall be raised' (1 Corinthians 15: 52); 'I will also gather all nations, and will bring them down into the valley of Jehoshaphat' (Joel 3: 2). Jehoshaphat is etymologically 'whom God judges'.

> For those who wake, and those who sleep;
> When rattling bones together fly,
> From the four corners of the sky;   185
> When sinews o'er the skeletons are spread,
> Those clothed with flesh, and life inspires the dead;
> The sacred poets first shall hear the sound,
>   And foremost from the tomb shall bound:
> For they are covered with the lightest ground,   190
> And straight, with inborn vigour, on the wing,
> Like mounting larks, to the new morning sing.
> There thou, sweet saint, before the choir shalt go,
> As harbinger of Heaven, the way to show,
> The way which thou so well hast learned below.   195

183 'The living and the dead'.
183–5 'It is sown a natural body; it is raised a spiritual body' (1 Corinthians 15: 44); but Dryden insists on the physical.

194   *harbinger of Heaven* as preparing places for the singers left behind.

From The Works of Virgil, 1697

By late 1693 Dryden had committed himself to the translation of all Virgil (a project entertained on and off from the 1660s); he worked on little else for the next four years. *Eclogues* 4 and 9 had already been given in *Miscellany Poems* (1684), one a panegyric, the other a complaint; and three sequences from the *Aeneid* (Nisus and Euryalus from Books 5 and 9, Mezentius and Lausus from Book 10, and Venus and Vulcan from Book 8) in *Sylvae* (1685), covering friendship, fatherly love and sexual love. These trials of his own range against Virgil's encouraged him to press (however slowly) ahead. To catch Virgil's likeness was Dryden's lifelong goal. Where in the preface to *Ovid's Epistles* (1680) he promoted a middle way between imitation and metaphrase (literal translation), for Virgil he narrowed the range of possibilities and went for a middle way 'betwixt the two extremes of paraphrase and literal translation' (Dedication of the *Aeneis*, 1697). Three particular challenges determined this change. The first is Virgil's commitment to the spareness of Latin: 'to make him copious is to alter his character, and to translate him line for line is impossible, because the Latin is naturally a more succinct language' (preface to *Sylvae*). The second consists partly in Virgil's own understatedness, 'being so very sparing of his words, and leaving so much to be imagined by the reader, [he] can never be translated as he ought in any modern tongue' (preface to *Silvae*), and partly in the habit of condensation which constitutes his 'always figurative' language: 'such of these [figures] as would retain their elegance in our tongue, I have endeavoured to graft on it; but most of them are of necessity to be lost, because they will not shine in any but their own. Virgil has sometimes two of them in a line; but the scantiness of our heroic verse is not capable of receiving more than one' (dedication of the *Aeneis*). The third consists in Virgil's management of the superior musicality of Latin: 'the sound of the Latin is so much pleasing, by the just mixture of the vowels with the consonants, that it raises our fancies (dedication of the *Aeneis*). Dryden holds to a version of the programme initiated in *Sylvae* ('taking all the materials of this divine author, I have endeavoured to make Virgil speak such English as he would himself have spoken, if he had been born in England, and in this present age' is the form it takes in the dedication of the *Aeneis*), but whereas Segrais made Virgil speak like a French gentleman, Dryden makes him speak like an English poet. Explanatory additions and omissions of what 'would have no grace in English' made Luke Milbourne (*Notes on Dryden's Virgil*, 1698) protest that Dryden wrote for ladies. Others protest his coarseness.

The Fourth Eclogue: Pollio

Dryden begins with a translated note: 'The poet celebrates the birthday of Saloninus, the son of Pollio, born in the consulship of his father after the taking of Salonae, a city in Dalmatia. Many of the verses are translated from one of the Sibyls, who prophesy our Saviour's birth.' Available commentary would have corrected this account, but Dryden's quoting it makes clear his version's double purpose. It is in the first place a congratulatory birthday-poem, no doubt always perceptibly hyperbolic, possibly redirected to the Princess Mary, who was pregnant in 1684 – un-happily if so, for the child was still-born. Secondly, and more glamorously, the poem ranks as Messianic prophecy (and parallel with Isaiah 7: 14, 'Behold, a virgin shall conceive, and bear a son, and shall call his name Immanuel'). As such it feeds classicizing traditions of Christian writing, and makes of Virgil an honorary prophet. Translated first in *Miscellany Poems* (1684), and revised in 1697. The changes are minor, but a half-line is cancelled (see 42): 'I have shunned hemistichs', says Dryden in the 1697 preface, 'not being willing to imitate Virgil to a fault' (there are no original half-lines in the *Eclogues* any-way). But the apparently random admixture of alexand-rines and fourteeners remains to give a 'Pindarizing' effect. The early commentator Servius commends Virgil's 'somewhat loftier' ('paulo maiora') strain in the opening line on the grounds that the poem re-mains rooted in lowly pastoral habits; Dryden dis-cards the 'somewhat'. In this poem, says Dryden in the 1697 preface, Virgil 'could no longer restrain the freedom of his spirit, but began to assert his native character, which is sublimity'. Dryden imports the violence of metaphor ('plough the seas', 'vex the ground') and enjoys the tasteless ready-coloured flocks of the new world.

Sicilian Muse, begin a loftier strain!
Though lowly shrubs, and trees that shade the plain,
Delight not all; Sicilian Muse, prepare
To make the vocal woods deserve a consul's care.
The last great age, foretold by sacred rhymes,   5
Renews its finished course: Saturnian times
Roll round again; and mighty years, begun
From their first orb, in radiant circles run.
The base degenerate iron offspring ends;
A golden progeny from heaven descends.   10
O chaste Lucina! speed the mother's pains;
And haste the glorious birth! thy own Apollo reigns!
The lovely boy, with his auspicious face,   ⎫
Shall Pollio's Consulship and Triumph grace;   ⎬
Majestic months set out with him to their appointed race. ⎭   15
The father banished virtue shall restore,
And crimes shall threat the guilty world no more.
The son shall lead the life of gods, and be
By gods and heroes seen, and gods and heroes see.
The jarring nations he in peace shall bind,   20
And with paternal virtues rule mankind.
Unbidden earth shall wreathing ivy bring,   ⎫
And fragrant herbs (the promises of spring),   ⎬
As her first offerings to her infant king.   ⎭
The goats with strutting dugs shall homeward speed,
And lowing herds secure from lions feed.   25
His cradle shall with rising flowers be crowned:
The serpent's brood shall die; the sacred ground

1–4   The point is clearer from 1684's version of 3–4: 'De-light not all, if thither I repair /My song shall make 'em worth a consul's care.' Virgil means to turn the lowly appa-ratus of pastoral so as to appeal to listeners with serious things on their minds; *Sicilian* because Greek pastoral po-etry begins with the Sicilian Theocritus.

5–12   Virgil draws on three not quite compatible visions of earthly perfection: the age of the Sun ('thy own Apollo reigns') which was the recurring last age in the cycles of ten ages (each of 110 years) described by the institutionally approved Sibylline verses ('sacred rhymes'); the Platonic Great Year or time it took for the heavenly bodies to resume their con-figuration as it was at the Creation ('their first orb'); and the Golden Age enjoyed in the reign of the pre-Olympian gods ('Saturnian times') and due to return after the present age of iron. Dryden expands and obscures the already obscure origi-nal.

11   *Lucina* Diana (Apollo's sister) in her aspect as goddess of childbirth.

13   *auspicious* 'promising'.

14   Dryden alludes, on a cue from Virgil's procession of the 'great months', to the Triumph allowed Pollio for his victory at Salonae.

24   Echoing Milton's 'Afford a present to the infant God' (*Nativity Ode*, 16).

25   *strutting* 'bulging' (commonly of teats).

Shall weeds and poisonous plants refuse to bear;
Each common bush shall Syrian roses wear. 30
But when heroic verse his youth shall raise,
And form it to hereditary praise,
Unlaboured harvests shall the fields adorn,
And clustered grapes shall blush on every thorn;
The knotted oaks shall showers of honey weep; 35
And through the matted grass the liquid gold shall creep.
Yet, of old fraud some footsteps shall remain;
The merchant still shall plough the deep for gain,
Great cities shall with walls be compassed round,
And sharpened shares shall vex the fruitful ground; 40
Another Tiphys shall new seas explore;
Another Argos land the chiefs upon the Iberian shore;
Another Helen other wars create,
And great Achilles urge the Trojan fate.
But when to ripened manhood he shall grow, 45
The greedy sailor shall the seas forego;
No keel shall cut the waves for foreign ware,
For every soil shall every product bear.
The labouring hind his oxen shall disjoin;
No plough shall hurt the glebe, no pruning-hook the vine; ⎫ 50
Nor wool shall in dissembled colours shine; ⎬
But the luxurious father of the fold, ⎭
With native purple, or unborrowed gold,
Beneath his pompous fleece shall proudly sweat;
And under Tyrian robes the lamb shall bleat. 55
The Fates, when they this happy web have spun,
Shall bless the sacred clew, and bid it smoothly run.
Mature in years, to ready honours move,
O of celestial seed! O foster-son of Jove!
See, labouring Nature calls thee to sustain 60
The nodding frame of heaven, and earth, and main!
See to their base restored, earth, seas, and air;
And joyful ages, from behind, in crowding ranks appear.
To sing thy praise, would Heaven my breath prolong,
Infusing spirits worthy such a song, 65
Not Thracian Orpheus should transcend my lays,
Nor Linus crowned with never-fading bays;
Though each his heavenly parent should inspire;
The Muse instruct the voice, and Phoebus tune the lyre.

---

30 *Syrian roses* 'damask roses'.

37 *footsteps* translating *vestigia*, and on that model commonly metaphorical.

38–40 The metaphorical ploughing and vexing are Dryden's.

41–4 The mainly unhappy histories of the Argonauts (Tiphys was the helmsman of the Argo and died before reaching 'the Iberian shore' – near Colchis, the site of the Golden Fleece; Argos was the builder of the *Argo*), and the Trojan War (occasioned by Helen and pressed by Achilles); *urge* Marvell's Cromwell 'urges' his *own* star.

42 Another Argos on the Iberian shore / Shall land the chosen chiefs (1684).

49 *hind* 'peasant'.

52 *luxurious* 'philoprogenitive': the ram is lascivious and prolific.

54 *pompous* 'fit for pomp'.

55 *Tyrian* 'purple' (from the dye made at Tyre).

56–7 The Fates spin the threads of human destinies; the web of Fate is not implied in the original; *clew* the ball of thread on the spindle.

61 *nodding* Virgil's universe 'nods' in awe; Dryden's is imminently collapsing.

66–71 Orpheus and Linus, pseudo-historical types of the poet, are here supposed sons of Phoebus Apollo (as god of poetry). Pan's music is celebrated beautifully in the Homeric *Hymn to Pan*.

Should Pan contend in verse, and thou my theme,   70
Arcadian judges should their god condemn.
Begin, auspicious boy! to cast about
Thy infant eyes, and, with a smile, thy mother single out.
Thy mother well deserves that short delight,
The nauseous qualms of ten long months and travail to requite.   75
Then smile! the frowning infant's doom is read;
No god shall crown the board, nor goddess bless the bed.

75–7 Dryden explains in a note his rejection of the reading which would have the parents' smiling on the child (rather than, as here, the child on the parents) an augury of its good fortune.

From the Aeneis *1697*

Ruaeus's Delphin edition of the *Works* (in the much reprinted revision of 1682) was Dryden's stand-by text, but he evidently had recourse to earlier scholarship as well. He also read widely in previous translations. As he 'found the difficulty of translation growing on me in every succeeding Book; for Virgil, above all poets, had a stock, which I may call almost inexhaustible, of figurative, elegant, and sounding words' (dedication of the *Aeneis*), he supplied his needs from 'both the living and the dead'. He had before him Annibale Caro's Italian version of 1581 (in the preface to *Silvae*, 'the nearest, the most poetical, the most sonorous', though in the dedication of the *Aeneis*, 'scandalously mean'), and Jean Regnault de Segrais's version of 1668 ('wholly destitute of elevation' in the dedication of the *Aeneis*). Of English translators of the *Aeneid*, he had recourse, most importantly, to the fragments done by Fanshawe (Book 4, 1648, Denham (Books 2 and 4, 1668; more survives in MS), and by Waller and Sidney Godolphin (Book 4, *The Passion of Dido*, 1658). But he consulted Gavin Douglas's Scots version (written in 1513) in the later Books; and he had available throughout the Earl of Lauderdale's *Aeneid*, the MS sent over from his Jacobite exile in Paris (and published only in 1718). With Lauderdale the relationship is so close as sometimes to be collaborative. The selections here are meant to exhibit a range of styles: the theatrically passionate in Book 4 (Dryden had already translated the 'tenderly passionate and courtly' *Dido to Aeneas* in 1680), the philosophical in Book 6, the heroic-cum-pathetic in Book 9.

Dido and Aeneas

Alone, Dido, Queen of Carthage, indulges thoughts of the passion for Aeneas she has just revealed to her sister Anna (69–89). The understated Virgilian manner is replaced by an indulgent one, adapted to a passion observed rather than experienced; the proliferation of generic epithets (as in 'princely train', 183, 'trembling train', 220) is novel. This passage translates Virgil, *Aeneid*, 4:68–172, omitting 90–128.

Sick with desire, and seeking him she loves,
From street to street the raving Dido roves.
So when the watchful shepherd, from the blind,   95
Wounds with a random shaft the careless hind;
Distracted with her pain she flies the woods,
Bounds o'er the lawn, and seeks the silent floods;
With fruitless care; for still the fatal dart
Sticks in her side; and rankles in her heart.   100
And now she leads the Trojan chief, along
The lofty walls, amidst the busy throng;

93 *sick with desire* varying the cliché 'sick with love'; Vaughan's *Psalm 104* has angels 'sick with desire / And love' of God.
95 *blind* 'hide' (such as hunters use).
100 *rankles* literally for the deer (in whose side the 'fatal dart' lodges), metaphorically for Dido; Godolpin has 'The deadly arrow rankles in her breast.'

101 *Trojan chief* Aeneas (named by Virgil).
102 *Tyrian* Virgil says 'Sidonian'; as Venus explains to Aeneas (*Aeneid*, 1:338–68) Carthage was a Phoenician foundation: Tyre and Sidon are the twin cities of Phoenicia; *rising* 'growing'.

Displays her Tyrian wealth, and rising town,
Which love, without his labour, makes his own.
This pomp she shows to tempt her wandering guest;   105
Her faltering tongue forbids to speak the rest.
When day declines, and feasts renew the night,
Still on his face she feeds her famished sight;
She longs again to hear the prince relate
His own adventures, and the Trojan fate: 110
He tells it o'er and o'er; but still in vain;
For still she begs to hear it, once again;
The hearer on the speaker's mouth depends,
And thus the tragic story never ends.
Then, when they part, when Phoebe's paler light   115
Withdraws, and falling stars to sleep invite,
She last remains, when every guest is gone,
Sits on the bed he pressed, and sighs alone;
Absent, her absent hero sees and hears;
Or in her bosom young Ascanius bears: 120
And seeks the father's image in the child,
If love by likeness might be so beguiled.
Meantime the rising towers are at a stand:
No labours exercise the youthful band:
Nor use of arts, nor toils of arms they know;   125
The mole is left unfinished to the foe;
The mounds, the works, the walls, neglected lie,
Short of their promised height, that seemed to threat the sky.

*Dido has planned a hunt. Juno, by Venus's consent, has planned to raise a storm with the aim of
separating Dido and Aeneas from the rest of hunting party, so encouraging the affair whose
disappointment begins the long enmity of Carthage and Rome (129–170).*

The rosy morn was risen from the main,
And horns and hounds awake the princely train:
They issue early through the city gate,
Where the more wakeful huntsmen ready wait,   185
With nets, and toils, and darts, beside the force
Of Spartan dogs, and swift Massylian horse.
The Tyrian peers, and officers of state,
For the slow queen, in antechambers wait:
Her lofty courser, in the court below   190
(Who his majestic rider seems to know),
Proud of his purple trappings, paws the ground,
And champs the golden bit; and spreads the foam around.

105   *pomp* 'splendour'.
107   'When after sunset they refresh themselves with nightly
feasting'.
108   Borrowing from a fantasy in Dryden's own *Aureng-
Zebe*, 4: 'While, on your face, her famished sight she fed.'
109–14   Expanded from two lines; *on . . . depends* 'hangs on
his words' (a Virgilianism).
115   *Phoebe's* 'the moon's' (Dryden's metonymy).
122   Virgil says, 'If she can beguile a love she cannot give

words to'; Godolphin has 'If likeness can delude her restless
love'.
122   Ascanius is Aeneas's son.
126   *mole* 'sea-wall'.
128   The alexandrine mimics the promise.
186   *nets, and toils* 'finer, and stronger nets'.
189   *slow* 'lingering'.
191   'Which his aspiring rider seemed to know' (Shake-
speare, *Richard II*, V. ii. 9).

The queen at length appears: on either hand,
The brawny guards in martial order stand. 195
A flowered cymar, with golden fringe she wore;
And at her back a golden quiver bore:
Her flowing hair, a golden caul restrains;
A golden clasp, the Tyrian robe sustains.
Then young Ascanius, with a sprightly grace, 200
Leads on the Trojan youth to view the chase.
But far above the rest in beauty shines
The great Aeneas, when the troop he joins:
Like fair Apollo, when he leaves the frost
Of wintry Xanthus, and the Lycian coast; 205
When to his native Delos he resorts,
Ordains the dances, and renews the sports:
Where painted Scythians, mixed with Cretan bands,
Before the joyful altars join their hands.
Himself, on Cynthus walking, sees below 210
The merry madness of the sacred show.
Green wreaths of bays his length of hair enclose;
A golden fillet binds his awful brows:
His quiver sounds: not less the prince is seen
In manly presence, or in lofty mien. 215
    Now had they reached the hills, and stormed the seat
Of savage beasts, in dens, their last retreat;
The cry pursues the mountain-goats; they bound
From rock to rock, and keep the craggy ground:
Quite otherwise the stags, a trembling train, 220
In herds unsingled, scour the dusty plain;
And a long chase, in open view, maintain.
The glad Ascanius, as his courser guides,
Spurs through the vale; and these and those outrides.
His horse's flanks and sides are forced to feel 225
The clanking lash, and goring of the steel.
Impatiently he views the feeble prey,
Wishing some nobler beast to cross his way,
And rather would the tusky boar attend,
Or see the tawny lion downward bend. 230
    Meantime, the gathering clouds obscure the skies;
From pole to pole the forky lightning flies;

195–6 Virgil says she comes with 'a great crowd thronging round her'.
197 *cymar* 'chemise'.
198 *caul* 'hair-net'.
199 *Tyrian* 'purple'; like Lauderdale, Dryden offers a more familiar synonym for Virgil's 'Sidonian'.
204–14 The long simile draws on Valerius Flaccus's description of Jason in *Argonautica* 1, and on the Homeric *Hymn to Delian Apollo*: Apollo returns to his birthplace on Mount Cynthus on Delos, where crowds of worshippers from far and near collect in spring.
212–14 He wears a laurel wreath and gold headband on his uncut hair; the arrows rattle in his quiver.

221–2 'The herd still united ('unsingled') ranges over the dusty plain, and can be seen keeping up speed over the whole distance' ('a long chase maintain'). Virgil says that the stages cross the plain at a run; Lauderdale has 'A longer chase in view of all maintain'.
225–6 Dryden's addition: his preferred epithet for 'lash' is 'sounding'.
229 *tusky* Virgil has 'foaming'; Fanshawe has 'tuskèd'.
231–2 'Meanwhile the gathering clouds obscure the pole [sky] / They flash out lightning and in thunder roll' (Godolphin); *forky* 'forked' (the form by attraction from 'tusky'); Virgil has no lightning.

The rattling thunders roll; and Juno pours
A wintry deluge down; and sounding showers.
The company dispersed, to coverts ride,   235
And seek the homely cots, or mountain's hollow side.
The rapid rains, descending from the hills,
To rolling torrents raise the creeping rills.
The queen and prince, as Love or Fortune guides,
One common cavern in her bosom hides.   240
Then first the trembling earth the signal gave;
And flashing fires enlighten all the cave:
Hell from below, and Juno from above,
And howling nymphs, were conscious to their love.
From this ill-omen'd hour, in time arose   245
Debate and death, and all succeeding woes.

233 *Juno* Dryden's addition, fusing Juno and the Sky; but anticipating Virgil's saying that Earth and Juno 'give the sign'.
238 Lauderdale has 'To rapid torrents swell the gentle rills': a 'golden verse' (a verb balancing a pair of nouns and epithets) such as Dryden (preface to *Silvae*) affects to despise.

241–2 Amplifying Virgil with a detail from Milton: 'Earth trembled from her entrails, as again / In pangs, and Nature gave a second groan, / Sky loured and muttering thunder' (*Paradise Lost*, 9:1000–2).
244 *conscious to* 'witness to'.

The Afterlife

The Sibyl accompanies Aeneas to the Underworld and leads him to his father Anchises, who instructs him in the mysteries of the afterlife, including the transmigration of souls, a subject that Dryden returns to in the *Fables*, translating out of Ovid's *Metamorphoses*, 15 ('Of the Pythagorean Philosophy') the 'masterpiece of the whole poem'. Pythagoras 'held that God was the soul of the world; from whom each creature received his life, and dying restores it. And lest it might be doubted that the souls of all had one original, in regard of their different understanding,

he alleged that to proceed from the natural complexion and composition of the body . . . Those pure souls, who depart from this life by the law of Nature, and obediently render what from God they received, shall by him be placed in the highest heavens; and from thence again, after a certain revolution of time, descend by command to dwell in chaste bodies' (Sandys's note on *Metamorphoses*, 15). These lines translate *Aeneid*, 703–51. Lauderdale supplies the germ of the couplets at 986–7 and 1004–5.

Now, in a secret vale, the Trojan sees
A separate grove, through which a gentle breeze
Plays with a passing breath, and whispers through the trees.   955
And just before the confines of the wood,
The gliding Lethe leads her silent flood.
About the boughs an airy nation flew,
Thick as the humming bees, that hunt the golden dew;
In summer's heat, on tops of lilies feed,   960
And creep within their bells, to suck the balmy seed.
The wingèd army roams the fields around;
The rivers and the rocks remurmur to the sound.
Aeneas wondering stood: then asked the cause,
Which to the stream the crowding people draws.   965

953 *secret* 'secluded'.
955 The alexandrine delays the banal rhyme.
957 In Virgil it is the dwelling places that Lethe flows past that are silent.

958–62 In Virgil innumerable nations (clearly differentiated from bees) hover about the river; the details of the simile and their management are Dryden's.

Then thus the sire: "The souls that throng the flood
Are those, to whom, by Fate, are other bodies owed:
In Lethe's lake they long oblivion taste;
Of future life secure, forgetful of the past.
Long has my soul desired this time, and place,   970
To set before your sight your glorious race:
That this presaging joy may fire your mind,
To seek the shores by destiny designed."
"O father, can it be, that souls sublime,
Return to visit our terrestrial clime?   975
And that the generous mind, released by death,
Can covet lazy limbs, and mortal breath?"
Anchises then, in order, thus begun
To clear those wonders to his godlike son:
"Know first, that Heaven, and Earth's compacted frame,   980
And flowing waters, and the starry flame,
And both the radiant lights, one common soul
Inspires, and feeds, and animates the whole.
This active mind infused through all the space,
Unites and mingles with the mighty mass.   985
Hence men and beasts the breath of life obtain;
And birds of air, and monsters of the main.
The ethereal vigour is in all the same,
And every soul is filled with equal flame;
As much as earthy limbs, and gross allay   990
Of mortal members, subject to decay,
Blunt not the beams of heaven and edge of day.
From this coarse mixture of terrestrial parts,
Desire, and fear, by turns possess their hearts:
And grief, and joy: nor can the grovelling mind,   995
In the dark dungeon of the limbs confined,
Assert the native skies; or own its heavenly kind:
Nor death itself can wholly wash their stains;
But long-contracted filth, even in the soul remains.
The relics of inveterate vice they wear;   1000
And spots of sin obscene, in every face appear.
For this are various penances enjoined;
And some are hung to bleach, upon the wind;
Some plunged in waters, others purged in fires,
Till all the dregs are drained, and all the rust expires.   1005

966–7 'The souls crowded at the river are those awaiting the new bodies destined for them.'

969 *secure* 'uncaring'; cued by Virgil's 'draughts that free from care'.

971–3 Anchises prepares Aeneas for a pageant of his progeny to encourage his onward progress to Latium where destiny awaits.

976–7 Virgil's Aeneas asks 'what dreadful desire of the light' possesses the unhappy dead.

980 *compacted* 'solid' (as against air or 'flowing' water or flaming stars).

982–5 Virgil says, 'A spirit within feeds the shining world of the moon and the Titanian stars (the moon and all the suns); and a mind activates the whole mass, infused though all its powers, and mingles with the great body of the universe'; Dryden works closely with the original vocabulary.

989 *equal flame* 'the same fiery vigour'; but the customary sense is 'reciprocal love'.

990 *allay* 'admixture'.

992 For Virgil's 'slow them down or dull them'; *edge* 'brightness' (a Virgilianism).

997 *assert* 'claim'.

1003 *bleach* Dryden's metaphor.

All have their manes, and those manes bear:
The few, so cleansed, to these abodes repair:
And breathe, in ample fields, the soft Elysian air.
Then are they happy, when by length of time
The scurf is worn away, of each committed crime.   1010
No speck is left, of their habitual stains;
But the pure ether of the soul remains.
But, when a thousand rolling years are past
(So long their punishments and penance last),
Whole droves of minds are, by the Driving God,   1015
Compelled to drink the deep Lethean flood:
In large forgetful draughts to steep the cares
Of their past labours, and their irksome years:
That, unremembering of its former pain,
The soul may suffer mortal flesh again."   1020

1006 'All have attendant spirits, and those spirits suffer punishments.' Virgil's difficult original does not include play on the double sense of 'manes'.
1015 *Driving God* Virgil says only that 'god calls out' the spirits. Dryden specifies Mercury (following *Aeneid*, 4:242–4: 'he draws the ghosts from hollow graves . . . he drives them down the Stygian waves').

Nisus and Euryalus

In Aeneas's absence the Trojan camp comes under attack. Nisus and his younger friend Euryalus offer themselves to carry word through the enemy camp to Aeneas. They are discovered and make to escape. Euryalus is captured (he is the 'prisoner' of 566), and Nisus returns to rescue him or die with him. Dryden's *Sylvae* (1685) include as *Nisus and Euryalus* a version of the foot-race from *Aeneid* 5 in which both compete, along with the quasi-parallel episode from which the following extract, in the revision of 1697, is taken.

Virgil's night-time atmospherics (which survive in 1685) are cancelled in favour of rapid movement to a conclusion (and that in revenge). The revisions from *1685* are extensive: at one level a triplet and two half-lines (which Dryden has come to regard as improper) are eliminated, at another the violence and pathos of the passage are amplified, often in the alteration and redistribution of epithets. The passage translates *Aeneid*, 9:402–45.

Resolved at length, his pointed spear he shook;
And casting on the moon a mournful look,
"Guardian of groves, and goddess of the night!   545
Fair queen," he said, "direct my dart aright.
If e'er my pious father for my sake
Did grateful offerings on thy altars make;
Or I increased them with my sylvan toils,
And hung thy holy roofs, with savage spoils,   550
Give me to scatter these." Then from his ear
He poised, and aimed, and launched the trembling spear.
The deadly weapon, hissing from the grove,
Impetuous on the back of Sulmo drove:
Pierced his thin armour, drank his vital blood,   555
And in his body left the broken wood.
He staggers round, his eyeballs roll in death,
And with short sobs he gasps away his breath.
All stand amazed; a second javelin flies,
With equal strength, and quivers through the skies;   560

544 *mournful* Dryden's addition.
549 *sylvan toils* successful toils (1685): 'dead game' (parallel with 'savage spoils').
551 'Empower me to disperse this troop.'
551–2 He balanced the spear at the level of his ear (borrowed from Virgil's line 417).

This through thy temples, Tagus, forced the way,
And in the brain-pan warmly buried lay.
Fierce Volscens foams with rage, and gazing round,
Descried not him who gave the fatal wound:
Nor knew to fix revenge: "But thou," he cries,   565
"Shalt pay for both," and at the prisoner flies
With his drawn sword. Then struck with deep despair,
That cruel sight the lover could not bear:
But from his covert rushed in open view,
And sent his voice before him as he flew: 570
"Me, me," he cried, "turn all your swords alone
On me"; the fact confessed: "the fault my own.
He neither could nor durst, the guiltless youth;
Ye moon and stars, bear witness to the truth!
His only crime (if friendship can offend)   575
Is too much love, to his unhappy friend."
Too late he speaks; the sword, which fury guides,
Driven with full force, had pierced his tender sides.
Down fell the beauteous youth; the yawning wound
Gushed out a purple stream, and stained the ground.   580
His snowy neck reclines upon his breast,
Like a fair flower by the keen share oppressed:
Like a white poppy sinking on the plain,
Whose heavy head is overcharged with rain.
Despair, and rage, and vengeance justly vowed,   585
Drove Nisus headlong on the hostile crowd:
Volscens he seeks; on him alone he bends;
Borne back, and bored, by his surrounding friends,
Onward he pressed: and kept him still in sight;
Then whirled aloft his sword, with all his might: 590
The unerring steel descended while he spoke;
Pierced his wide mouth, and through his weasand broke:
Dying, he slew; and, staggering on the plain,
With swimming eyes he sought his lover slain:
Then quiet on his bleeding bosom fell;   596
Content in death, to be revenged so well.

561   The second-person address is Dryden's.
562   *brain-pan* not a low word.
572   The (editorial) punctuation makes 'the fact confessed'
parallel with 'he cried' (571): 'He acknowledged the deed,
saying . . .' *1685* uses 'crime' and 'fault'.

585   Dryden's addition.
588   *bored* pushed (1685); which is the sense.
592   Entered his gaping mouth and stopped his breath (1685);
weasand 'windpipe'.
595   *with swimming eyes* added in 1697.

To my Honoured Kinsman John Driden, of Chesterton, in the County of Huntingdon, Esq.

John Driden (1635–1708) was the second son of
Dryden's uncle Erasmus. He served as MP for
Huntingdon. Chesterton House was demolished in
1807. Dryden's epistle is partly an estate poem (Pope
imitates the hunting passage in *Windsor Forest*), but it
owes more to the traditions of moral portrait writing
than landscape writing; and though it begins with a
bow to Horace's *Epode 2*, its Epicureanism quickly

modulates into commendation of public responsibil-
ity. Dryden's epistle is on his account an unpartisan
portrait of 'what an Englishman in Parliament ought
to be' (letter to Charles Montagu, then Chancellor of
the Exchequer). Written by a quasi-Jacobite Catholic
to celebrate the achievement of Whig administration,
it manages to satisfy all parties. The poem originally
included a satire against the Dutch in the last war

(the Third Dutch War of 1672–4, in which William of Orange, after 1688 William III of England, was the captain general of the enemy); the Whig Driden requested it be dropped. Other contentious matter (Ireland, Scotland, religion all go unmentioned) is perhaps too conspicuously absent. Dryden feared indeed that his polishing his verses might have 'purged them out of their spirit' (letter to Montagu, of October 1699). The poem's energies are muted into quasi-proverbial sobrieties drawn into an epistle that (as epistles often do) lacks drive or point, and whose heavy punctuation suggests a struggle for poise, even of the sort of poise that Driden himself managed: Dryden characterizes Virgil as one who 'dextrously managed both the Prince and the People, so as to displease neither, and to do good to both; which is the part of a wise and an honest man' (dedication of the *Aeneis*, 1697).

How blessed is he, who leads a country life,
Unvexed with anxious cares, and void of strife!
Who, studying peace, and shunning civil rage,
Enjoyed his youth, and now enjoys his age:
All who deserve his love, he makes his own;   5
And, to be loved himself, needs only to be known.
    Just, good, and wise: contending neighbours come,
From your award, to wait their final doom;
And, foes before, return in friendship home.
Without their cost, you terminate the cause;   10
And save the expense of long litigious laws:
Where suits are traversed; and so little won,
That he who conquers is but last undone:
Such are not your decrees; but so designed,
The sanction leaves a lasting peace behind;   15
Like your own soul, serene; a pattern of your mind.
    Promoting concord, and composing strife,
Lord of yourself, uncumbered with a wife;
Where, for a year, a month, perhaps a night,
Long penitence succeeds a short delight: 20
Minds are so hardly matched, that even the first,
Though paired by Heaven, in Paradise, were cursed.
For man and woman, though in one they grow,
Yet, first or last, return again to two.
He to God's image, she to his was made;   25
So, farther from the fount, the stream at random strayed.
    How could he stand, when, put to double pain,
He must a weaker than himself sustain!
Each might have stood perhaps, but each alone;
Two wrestlers help to pull each other down.   30

1 Alluding to Horace, *Epodes* 2.
3–4 'O he that would assuage / Our bloodshed and intestine rage, / If he would written have / *His Country's Father* on his grave; / Let him not fear to oppose / Unbridled licence' (Horave, *Odes*, 3.24:24–8, Fanshawe).
6 *contending* 'quarrelling'.
8 *doom* 'judgement'.
10 *cause* 'case'.
12 *traversed* 'opposed'.
15 *sanction* 'decree'. The 'lasting peace' secured by Driden's judgements reflects on the uncertainty of the Peace of Ryswick (1697): the War of the Spanish Succession (1701–13) resumed hostilities between England and France.
18 'How uneasy is his life / Who is troubled with a wife' (Cotton, *The Joys of Marriage*); 'Lordship of one's self is the last and best lordship' (Seneca, *Epistles*, 113.20).
20 Proverbially, 'Marry in haste, repent at leisure.' 'I hate fruition, now 'tis past, / Tis all but nastiness at best . . . A fulsome bliss, that soon does cloy, / And makes us loath what we enjoy' (Oldham's paraphrase of Petronius's much translated fragment, *Foeda est in coitu*).
26 'Our Affections here / Are but streams borrowed from the fountain there [Eternity]' (Katherine Philips, *Friendship*).

Not that my verse would blemish all the fair;
But yet, if some be bad, 'tis wisdom to beware;
And better shun the bait, than struggle in the snare.
Thus have you shunned, and shun the married state,
Trusting as little as you can to fate.   35
   No porter guards the passage of your door;
To admit the wealthy, and exclude the poor:
For God, who gave the riches, gave the heart,
To sanctify the whole, by giving part:
Heaven, who foresaw the will, the means has wrought,   40
And to the second son a blessing brought;
The first-begotten had his father's share;
But you, like Jacob, are Rebecca's heir.
   So may your stores and fruitful fields increase;
And ever be you blessed, who live to bless.   45
As Ceres sowed, where'er her chariot flew;
As Heaven in deserts rained the bread of dew;
So free to many, to relations most,
You feed with manna your own Israel host.
   With crowds attended of your ancient race,   50
You seek the champaign sports, or sylvan chase:
With well-breathed beagles, you surround the wood;
Even then industrious of the common good:
And often have you brought the wily fox
To suffer for the firstlings of the flocks;   55
Chased even amid the folds; and made to bleed,
Like felons, where they did the murderous deed.
This fiery game, your active youth maintained;
Not yet by years extinguished, though restrained:
You season still with sports your serious hours;   60
For age but tastes of pleasures, youth devours.
The hare in pastures or in plains is found,
Emblem of human life, who runs the round,
And, after all his wandering ways are done,
His circle fills, and ends where he begun,   65
Just as the setting meets the rising sun.
   Thus princes ease their cares: but happier he,
Who seeks not pleasure through necessity,
Than such as once on slippery thrones were placed;
And chasing, sigh to think themselves are chased.   70

---

31 *blemish* 'defame' (still a standard sense).

36–7 'Thou hast no porter at the door / To examine, or keep back the poor' (Carew, *To Saxham*, 49–50).

38–9 Proverbially, 'The charitable give out at the door, and God puts in at the window.'

43 Because he inherited his estate at Chesterton through his mother; Jacob's wealth derived in the first place from the brother of his mother Rebecca (Genesis 28–31). The complications of the parallel are avoided.

46 Ceres, the goddess of corn, who taught men to plough and sow, sends Triptolemus her chariot, and 'Part of the seed she gave, she bade him throw / On untilled earth; part on the tilled to throw' (Ovid, *Metamorphoses*, 5:646–7, Sandys).

47–9 'And when the dew that lay was gone up . . . there lay a small round thing . . . And when the children of Israel saw it, they said to one another, It is manna' (Exodus 16: 14–15).

51 *champaign . . . chase* 'field-sports or hunting in the wood'.

53 *industrious* 'careful'.

62–6 The point echoes Donne's 'Thy firmness makes my circle just, / And makes me end, where I begun' (*Valediction Forbidding Mourning*).

69–70 Cowley's version of the chorus from Seneca's *Thyestes* has 'the slippery tops of human state'. The comparison of the prince and the stag is from Denham's *Cooper's Hill*, 279–80.

So lived our sires, ere doctors learned to kill,
And multiplied with theirs the weekly bill:
The first physicians by debauch were made:
Excess began, and sloth sustains the trade.
Pity the generous kind their cares bestow   75
To search forbidden truths (a sin to know):
To which, if human science could attain,
The doom of death, pronounced by God, were vain.
In vain the leech would interpose delay;
Fate fastens first, and vindicates the prey.   80
What help from art's endeavours can we have! ⎫
Gibbons but guesses, nor is sure to save: ⎬
But Maurus sweeps whole parishes, and peoples every grave. ⎭
And no more mercy to mankind will use,
Than when he robbed and murdered Maro's Muse.   85
Wouldst thou be soon dispatched, and perish whole?
Trust Maurus with thy life, and M–lb–rne with thy soul.
    By chase our long-lived fathers earned their food;
Toil strung the nerves, and purified the blood:
But we their sons, a pampered race of men,   90
Are dwindled down to threescore years and ten.
Better to hunt in fields, for health unbought,
Than fee the doctor for a nauseous draught.
The wise, for cure, on exercise depend;
God never made his work for man to mend.   95
    The Tree of Knowledge, once in Eden placed,
Was casy found, but was forbid the taste:
O had our grandsire walked without his wife,
He first had sought the better Plant of Life!
Now both are lost: yet, wandering in the dark,   100
Physicians, for the tree, have found the bark: ⎫
They, labouring for relief of human kind,   ⎬
With sharpened sight some remedies may find; ⎬
The apothecary-train is wholly blind.   ⎭
From files, a random recipe they take,   105
And many deaths of one prescription make.
Garth, generous as his Muse, prescribes and gives;

71–116   The occasion for the satire on doctors, like that for Roscommon's in *Essay on Translated Verse*, 244–75, is slight. But Driden had been ill, and Dryden elsewhere expressed his view that 'exercise I know is my cousin Driden's life; and the oftener he goes out [hunting], will be the better for his health' (*Letters*, p. 112). The efforts of the College of Physicians to guarantee cheap medical care for the poor were frustrated by the apothecaries or 'shopman' drug-dispensers. Johnson's *Life of Garth* gives an account of the hostility.
72   *weekly bill* 'bill of mortality' (published weekly for each parish).
75   'It is regrettable that public-spirited men should busy themselves.'
82   *Gibbons* William Gibbons (1649–1728) is the ludicrous Mirmillo in Garth's *Dispensary*: 'Some fell by laudanum, and some by steel, / And death in ambush lay in every pill' (4:62–3); but Dryden thanks him for his ministrations in the Postscript to his Virgil.

83   *Maurus* 'Blackamoor': Sir Richard Blackmore (1650?-1729) was a physician and poet, whose *Satire against Wit* (1700) attacked Dryden as a source of corruption. He cast Dryden as the 'old, revolted, unbelieving bard' Laurus ('Bays') in *Prince Arthur* (1695).
87   *M–lb–rne* Luke Milbourne was a clergyman, author of the hostile *Notes on Dryden's Virgil* (1698).
96–9   'Such [happy] was that happy garden-state, / While man there walked without a mate' (Marvell, *The Garden*, 57–8).
101   *bark* 'Peruvian bark', the source of quinine.
107   *Garth The Dispensary* (1699) of Dryden's friend Sir Samuel Garth (1661–1719) makes the case, by way of mock-heroic, for a 'generous' ('charitable') treatment of the sick poor. The Muse is 'generous' because 'spirited'.

The shopman sells, and by destruction lives:
Ungrateful tribe! who, like the viper's brood,
From medicine issuing, suck their mother's blood! 110
Let these obey; and let the learn'd prescribe;
That men may die without a double bribe:
Let them, but under their superiors kill,
When doctors first have signed the bloody bill:
He 'scapes the best, who nature to repair, 115
Draws physic from the fields, in draughts of vital air.
    You hoard not health, for your own private use,
But on the public spend the rich produce.
When, often urged, unwilling to be great,
Your country calls you from your loved retreat, 120
And sends to senates, charged with common care,
Which none more shuns; and none can better bear.
Where could they find another formed so fit,
To poise, with solid sense, a sprightly wit!
Were these both wanting (as they both abound) 125
Where could so firm integrity be found?
    Well born, and wealthy; wanting no support,
You steer betwixt the country and the court:
Nor gratify whate'er the great desire,
Nor grudging give, what public needs require. 130
Part must be left, a fund when foes invade;
And part employed to roll the watery trade:
Even Canaan's happy land, when worn with toil,
Required a sabbath-year to mend the meagre soil.
    Good senators (and such are you) so give, 135
That kings may be supplied, the people thrive.
And he, when want requires, is truly wise,
Who slights not foreign aids, nor overbuys;
But on our native strength, in time of need, relies.
Münster was bought, we boast not the success; 140
Who fights for gain, for greater, makes his peace.

109–10 God makes 'the ingrateful viper (at his birth) / His dying mother's belly to gnaw forth' (Sylvester 1.6:250–1): misreading the viviparous reproduction of adders.
111 *these* 'the apothecaries'.
112 *double bribe* 'paying twice'.
115 *nature to repair* 'to restore bodily health'.
119–20 'Many seek philosophic tranquillity by abandoning public affairs ... But those naturally equipped for public business should engage in it' (Cicero, *De Officiis*, 69–72).
121 'Sends to political assemblies, charged to care for the public'.
124 *poise* 'counterbalance'.
127 *wanting no support* 'not lacking the means to support yourself'.
128 *country ... court* The rival claims of king and people are picked up in the opposition of 'whate'er the great desire' (129) and 'public needs' (130), between 'kings' and 'people' (136), between war 'when foes invade' and commerce or 'watery trade' (131–2), and then between 'king and country', 'prerogative and privilege' (171–2), 'prince and parliament'

(175). The Whigs in the Williamite administrations are normally identified with the court and the Tories with rural constituencies, but Dryden's language reflects non-party ideologies.
129–30 'You neither indulge royal whims nor grudge payments to meet the general good.'
131–2 The Bank of England, founded in 1694, served the needs of the King's war effort and the city's New East India Company.
132 *roll ... trade* 'drive overseas trade'.
133–4 'Six years shalt thou sow thy field ... and gather in the fruit thereof; but in the seventh year shall be a sabbath of rest unto the land, a sabbath for the Lord' (Leviticus 25: 3–4): the application is unclear.
138–41 'Who neither disdains foreign help nor pays too high a price for it'. The issue is the distribution of war costs among members of the Grand Alliance, but Dryden avoids the modern case: overpayment is exemplified by the ill-success of Charles II's subsidizing the Bishop of Münster's invasion of Holland in 1665 during the second Dutch War.

Our foes, compelled by need, have peace embraced:
The peace both parties want, is like to last;
Which, if secure, securely we may trade;
Or, not secure, should never have been made.   145
Safe in ourselves, while on ourselves we stand,
The sea is ours, and that defends the land.
Be, then, the naval stores the nation's care,
New ships to build, and battered to repair.
Observe the war, in every annual course;   150
What has been done, was done with British force:
Namur subdued, is England's palm alone;
The rest besieged, but we constrained the town:
We saw the event that followed our success;
France, though pretending arms, pursued the peace;   155
Obliged, by one sole treaty, to restore
What twenty years of war had won before.
Enough for Europe has our Albion fought:
Let us enjoy the peace our blood has bought.
When once the Persian king was put to flight,   160
The weary Macedons refused to fight:
Themselves their own mortality confessed;
And left the son of Jove, to quarrel for the rest.
    Even victors are by victories undone;
Thus Hannibal, with foreign laurels won,   165
To Carthage was recalled, too late to keep his own.
While sore of battle, while our wounds are green,
Why should we tempt the doubtful die again?
In wars renewed, uncertain of success,
Sure of a share, as umpires of the peace.   170
    A patriot, both the king and country serves;
Prerogative, and privilege preserves:
Of each, our laws the certain limit show;
One must not ebb, nor the other overflow:
Betwixt the Prince and Parliament we stand;   175
The barriers of the state on either hand:
May neither overflow, for then they drown the land.
When both are full, they feed our blessed abode;
Like those, that watered once, the Paradise of God.

142–57 The Peace of Ryswick (1697) concluded the nine-years' war with France, who surrendered the gains made over the twenty years (157) since the Peace of Nijmegen (1676).

146–9 The traditional emphasis on naval power runs counter to King William's unpopular attempts to maintain a land army. 'My cousin Driden, and the Country Party . . . will be against it' (*Letters*, p. 124). The cancelled satire on the Dutch navy would presumably have come here.

152 Louis XIV captured Namur in Belgium in 1692. Its recapture by William III in 1695, called by Bishop Burnet (*History of His Own Times*) 'one of the greatest actions . . . in the whole history of war', is celebrated in Prior's *English Ballad*.

155 *pretending arms* 'while claiming to prosecute the war'.

158–9 Even after 1697, King William was for prosecuting the war with France; 'Albion' summons an older Britain, remote from continental preoccupations.

160–3 After the defeat of the Persian Darius, some Macedonian generals were reluctant to follow Alexander the Great (by now advertising himself as the son of Jupiter) further into the East.

165–6 When Scipio invaded Africa, the victorious Hannibal was recalled home from Italy to defeat at Zama.

168 *doubtful die* 'uncertain chance'.

171–9 The analogy of power restrained with water contained is rewritten from the conclusion of Denham's *Cooper's Hill*.

179 'And a river went out of Eden to water the garden; and from thence it was parted, and became into four heads' (Genesis 2: 10).

Some overpoise of sway, by turns, they share; 180
In peace the People, and the Prince in war:
Consuls of moderate power in calms were made;
When the Gauls came, one sole dictator swayed.
    Patriots, in peace, assert the People's right;
With noble stubbornness resisting might: 185
No lawless mandates from the court receive,
Nor lend by force; but in a body give.
Such was your generous grandsire; free to grant
In Parliaments, that weighed their Prince's want:
But so tenacious of the common cause, 190
As not to lend the King against his laws;
And, in a loathsome dungeon doomed to lie,
In bonds retained his birthright liberty,
And shamed oppression, till it set him free.
    O true descendant of a patriot line, 195
Who, while thou shar'st their lustre, lend'st them thine,
Vouchsafe this picture of thy soul to see;
'Tis so far good, as it resembles thee:
The beauties to the original I owe;
Which when I miss, my own defects I show: 200
Nor think the kindred Muses thy disgrace;
A poet is not born in every race.
Two of a house few ages can afford;
One to perform, another to record.
Praiseworthy actions are by thee embraced; 205
And 'tis my praise, to make thy praises last.
For even when death dissolves our human frame,
The soul returns to Heaven, from whence it came;
Earth keeps the body, verse preserves the fame.

180 *overpoise of sway* 'preponderance of power'; but 'sway' may suggest imbalance.
182–3 Republican Rome was governed by two annually elected consuls; temporary dictators were nominated by a consul in military emergencies. Camillus is the dictator in question (five times so according to Plutarch's *Life*).
184 *Patriots* A contested term: 'Gulled with a Patriot's name, / Is one that would by law supplant his prince' (*Absalom and Achitophel*, 965–6). Dryden here redeems it from this modern sense: 'such only deserve to be called patriots, under whom we see their country flourish' (dedication of the *Georgics*). But he calls in question too the legality of peremptory royal commands ('mandates').

188–91 Sir Erasmus Dryden, the common grandfather of the poet and his addressee, was among those imprisoned for their refusal in 1627 to contribute to Charles I's forced loan. Forced loans were confirmed as illegal by the settlement of 1689.
199 'The beauty of the subject inspires us with love and admiration for the pictures' ('Observations' on *De Arte Graphica*).
202 *race* 'family'.
207–9 Rewriting his own 'As earth thy body keeps, thy soul the sky, / So shall this verse preserve thy memory' (*Eleonora*, 375–6).

Baucis and Philemon. Out of the Eighth Book of Ovid's Metamorphoses

Dryden returned to translation from Ovid's *Metamorphoses* (the 1693 *Examen Poeticum* has samples) by the strange route of going behind his translation of the first Book of Homer's *Iliad* to deal with the causes of the Trojan War as they are set out in Ovid's Book 12. Once embarked, he could not stop: eight often extensive selections are given in the *Fables*, 'which I

hope I have translated closely enough, and given them the same turn of verse which they had in the original' (preface). Ovidian turns are famously condemned in the preface: 'glittering trifles, and so far from being witty in a serious poem they are nauseous, because they are unnatural'; but these are only the turns vulgarly admired. In the same preface Dryden commends

Ovid and Chaucer together because they 'understood the manners' by which he means 'the passions . . . the descriptions of persons, and their very habits'. He means also purity of representation: 'I see Baucis and Philemon as perfectly before me as if some ancient painter had drawn them', a pictorialization encouraged by the carefully realized image of the couple in Otto van Veen's *Emblemata Horatii* (*Sors sua quemque beat*), likewise used to generalize on the sources of human happiness. Dryden used the 1670 edition of Ovid by Borchard Cnipping (to whom he

owes his 'smoking lard', 107). In the preface to *Examen Poeticum*, Dryden judges Sandys's translation of Ovid harshly: 'He leaves him obscure; he leaves him prose where he found him verse'; in the preface to *Fables* he allows him to the poet who 'has arrived nearest' to the 'turn of verse' of the Ovidian original, a movement which can here accommodate such trivial details as adjusting a wobbly table. The fable, recommending the virtues of hospitality, appears in *Metamorphoses*, 8:611–724.

The author, pursuing the deeds of Theseus; relates how he, with his friend Pirithous, were invited by Achelous, the River-God, to stay with him, till his waters were abated. Achelous entertains them with a relation of his own love to Perimele, who was changed into an island by Neptune, at his request. Pirithous, being an atheist, derides the legend, and denies the power of the gods, to work that miracle. Lelex, another companion of Theseus, to confirm the story of Achelous, relates another metamorphosis of Baucis and Philemon into trees; of which he was partly an eye-witness.

Thus Achelous ends: his audience hear
With admiration, and, admiring, fear
The powers of Heaven; except Ixion's son,
Who laughed at all the gods, believed in none:
He shook his impious head, and thus replies: 5
"These legends are no more than pious lies:
You attribute too much to Heavenly sway,
To think they give us forms, and take away."
The rest of better minds, their sense declared
Against this doctrine, and with horror heard.   10
Then Lelex rose, an old experienced man,
And thus with sober gravity began;
"Heaven's power is infinite: earth, air, and sea,
The manufactured mass, the Making Power obey:
By proof to clear your doubt; in Phrygian ground   15
Two neighbouring trees, with walls encompassed round,
Stand on a moderate rise, with wonder shown,
One a hard oak, a softer linden one:
I saw the place and them, by Pittheus sent
To Phrygian realms, my grandsire's government.   20
Not far from thence is seen a lake, the haunt
Of coots, and of the fishing cormorant:
Here Jove with Hermes came; but in disguise
Of mortal men concealed their deities;
One laid aside his thunder, one his rod,   25
And many toilsome steps together trod:
For harbour at a thousand doors they knocked,
Not one of all the thousand but was locked.

8 Borrowing Sandys: 'Could give new forms or take the old away'.
13–14 *earth . . . mass* for 'whatever the gods will, is done'; *manufactured mass* 'the sum of things created' from the named elements. Dryden has embellished Ovid's simple 'whatever' from Virgil, *Aeneid*, 6:726 (his version 985).

20 *my grandsire's government* 'where my grandfather once ruled'.
22 Borrowing Sandys's 'coots and fishing cormorants'.
25 Ovid's Jupiter is 'in mortal guise'; his rod-bearing Mercury has laid his wings aside. Dryden's formulation is neater.

At last an hospitable house they found,
A homely shed; the roof, not far from ground,   30
Was thatched with reeds and straw together bound.
There Baucis and Philemon lived, and there
Had lived long married, and a happy pair:
Now old in love; though little was their store,
Inured to want, their poverty they bore,   35
Nor aimed at wealth, professing to be poor.
For master or for servant here to call,
Was all alike, where only two were all.
Command was none, where equal love was paid,
Or rather both commanded, both obeyed.   40
   From lofty roofs the gods repulsed before,
Now stooping, entered through the little door:
The man (their hearty welcome first expressed),
A common settle drew for either guest,
Inviting each his weary limbs to rest.   45
But ere they sat, officious Baucis lays
Two cushions stuffed with straw, the seat to raise;
Coarse, but the best she had; then takes the load
Of ashes from the hearth, and spreads abroad
The living coals; and, lest they should expire,   50
With leaves and barks she feeds her infant-fire:
It smokes; and then with trembling breath she blows,
Till in a cheerful blaze the flames arose.
With brushwood and with chips she strengthens these,
And adds at last the boughs of rotten trees.   55
The fire thus formed, she sets the kettle on
(Like burnished gold the little seether shone);
Next took the coleworts which her husband got
From his own ground (a small well-watered spot);
She stripped the stalks of all their leaves; the best   60
She culled, and then with handy care she dressed.
High o'er the hearth a chine of bacon hung;
Good old Philemon seized it with a prong,
And from the sooty rafter drew it down,
Then cut a slice, but scarce enough for one;   65
Yet a large portion of a little store,
Which for their sake alone he wished were more.
This in the pot he plunged without delay,
To tame the flesh, and drain the salt away.
The time between, before the fire they sat,   70
And shortened the delay by pleasing chat.
   A beam there was, on which a beechen pail

---

30 *not far from ground* making the lowliness (of Ovid's *parva quidem*) very literal.

36 *professing to be poor* 'admitting their poverty'.

41 *From lofty roofs . . . repulsed* Added by Dryden to catch the contrast evident between the lofty heaven–dwelling gods and the mean cottage.

44 'Pulled up one bench for both guests'.

46–7 For 'she threw on it a coarse cloth'. Sandys has 'straw-stuffed cushions'; *officious* 'obliging'.

56–7 Ovid's Baucis sets a bronze pot on the fire. Dryden's 'seether' ('boiler') is a nonce use.

65–9 Developed from a compressed couple of lines; *tame* for Ovid's *domat*.

72–6 Some modern editions of Ovid reject these lines. The towels are Dryden's addition.

Hung by the handle, on a driven nail:
This filled with water, gently warmed, they set
Before their guests; in this they bathed their feet,   75
And after with clean towels dried their sweat:
This done, the host produced the genial bed,
Sallow the feet, the borders, and the stead,
Which with no costly coverlet they spread;
But coarse old garments; yet such robes as these   80
They laid alone, at feasts, on holidays.
The good old housewife, tucking up her gown,
The table sets; the invited gods lie down.
The trivet-table of a foot was lame,
A blot which prudent Baucis overcame,   85
Who thrust beneath the limping leg a shard,
So was the mended board exactly reared:
Then rubbed it o'er with newly gathered mint,
A wholesome herb, that breathed a grateful scent.
Pallas began the feast, where first was seen   90
The parti-coloured olive, black and green:
Autumnal cornels next in order served,
In lees of wine well pickled and preserved.
A garden-salad was the third supply,
Of endive, radishes, and succory: 95
Then curds and cream, the flower of country fare,
And new-laid eggs, which Baucis' busy care
Turned by a gentle fire, and roasted rare.
All these in earthenware were served to board;
And next in place, an earthen pitcher stored   100
With liquor of the best the cottage could afford.
This was the table's ornament, and pride,
With figures wrought: like pages at his side
Stood beechen bowls; and these were shining clean,
Varnished with wax without, and lined within.   105
By this the boiling kettle had prepared,
And to the table sent the smoking lard;
On which with eager appetite they dine,
A savoury bit, that served to relish wine:
The wine itself was suiting to the rest,   110
Still working in the must, and lately pressed.
The second course succeeds like that before,
Plums, apples, nuts, and of their wintry-store,
Dry figs, and grapes, and wrinkled dates were set
In canisters, to enlarge the little treat: 115
All these a milk-white honey-comb surround,

---

77 *genial* 'marital'.
78 *Sallow* 'willow'; Dryden omits the mattress of sedge-grass.
83 *lie down* as Romans did to eat (Dryden refused this literalism at *Aeneis*, 1:980).
84 *lame* Sandys's word.
90 *Pallas* 'olives' (since the olive was that goddess's plant), but not *individually* variegated in colour ('parti-coloured'), as Dryden (following Sandys and struggling with Ovid's 'two-coloured berry') imagines.

92 *cornels* 'red cornel-cherries': Sandys says they are 'a red fruit with a hard shell'.
102–3 *This ... wrought* Ovid says (ironically) that it was 'decorated with relief work in the same silver'.
106–7 Ovid says the hearth had cooked the hot meal and sent it to the table; *lard* 'bacon'.
109–11 The bacon gave relish to the still fermenting wine.
115 *canisters* 'baskets'.
116 *milk-white* for *candidus* (a Spenserian use).

Which in the midst the country-banquet crowned:
But the kind hosts their entertainment grace
With hearty welcome, and an open face:
In all they did, you might discern with ease,   120
A willing mind, and a desire to please.
   Meantime the beechen bowls went round, and still
Though often emptied, were observed to fill;
Filled without hands, and of their own accord
Ran without feet, and danced about the board.   125
Devotion seized the pair, to see the feast
With wine, and of no common grape, increased;
And up they held their hands, and fell to prayer,
Excusing as they could, their country fare.
One goose they had ('twas all they could allow),   130
A wakeful sentry, and on duty now,
Whom to the gods for sacrifice they vow:
Her, with malicious zeal, the couple viewed;
She ran for life, and, limping they pursued;
Full well the fowl perceived their bad intent,   135
And would not make her master's compliment;
But persecuted, to the powers she flies,
And close between the legs of Jove she lies:
He with a gracious ear the suppliant heard,
And saved her life; then what he was declared,   140
And owned the god. 'The neighbourhood,' said he,
'Shall justly perish for impiety;
You stand alone exempted; but obey
With speed, and follow where we lead the way:
Leave these accursed; and to the mountain's height   145
Ascend; nor once look backward in your flight.'
   They haste, and what their tardy feet denied,
The trusty staff (their better leg) supplied.
An arrow's flight they wanted to the top,
And there secure, but spent with travel, stop;   150
Then turn their now no more forbidden eyes;
Lost in a lake, the floated level lies:
A watery desert covers all the plains,
Their cot alone, as in an isle, remains:
Wondering with weeping eyes, while they deplore   155
Their neighbours' fate, and country now no more,
Their little shed, scarce large enough for two,
Seems, from the ground increased, in height and bulk to grow.
A stately temple shoots within the skies,
The crotchets of their cot in columns rise: 160

---

125 Dryden's addition, recalling Homer's robotic tripods (*Iliad*, 18:372–8).

133 *malicious . . . viewed* worked up from Ovid's 'they got ready'.

135–6 Dryden's addition; *compliment* 'tribute'.

138 The detail may come from La Fontaine's version of 1685, but Vaenius's plate in *Horatii Emblemata* (1612) shows the goose (a domestic parody of his eagle) at Jupiter's feet.

141 *owned* 'confessed himself'.

146 *nor . . . flight* borrowed from Genesis 19: 17 'Escape for thy life; look not behind thee.'

148 *their better leg* Dryden's addition.

151 *no more forbidden* Dryden's addition.

152–3 got up from 'everything drowned in a lake'.

152 *floated level* 'flooded plain'.

155 *deplore* 'lament'.

158 The alexandrine mimics the increased size (as at 162).

160 *crotchets* 'poles' (Sandys's word).

The pavement polished marble they behold,
The gates with sculpture graced, the spires and tiles of gold.
  Then thus the Sire of gods, with looks serene:
'Speak thy desire, thou only just of men;
And thou, O woman, only worthy found   165
To be with such a man in marriage bound.'
  Awhile they whisper; then, to Jove addressed,
Philemon thus prefers their joint request:
'We crave to serve before your sacred shrine,
And offer at your altars rites divine: 170
And since not any action of our life
Has been polluted with domestic strife,
We beg one hour of death; that neither she,
With widow's tears, may live to bury me,
Nor weeping I, with withered arms may bear   175
My breathless Baucis to the sepulchre.'
The godheads sign their suit. They run their race
In the same tenor all the appointed space:
Then, when their hour was come, while they relate
These past adventures at the temple-gate,   180
Old Baucis is by old Philemon seen
Sprouting with sudden leaves of sprightly green:
Old Baucis looked where old Philemon stood,
And saw his lengthened arms a-sprouting wood:
New roots their fastened feet begin to bind,   185
Their bodies stiffen in a rising rind:
Then ere the bark above their shoulders grew,
They give and take at once their last adieu:
At once, 'Farewell, O faithful spouse,' they said;
At once the encroaching rinds their closing lips invade.   190
Even yet, an ancient Tyanaean shows
A spreading oak, that near a linden grows;
The neighbourhood confirm the prodigy,
Grave men, not vain of tongue, or like to lie.
I saw myself the garlands on their boughs,   195
And tablets hung for gifts of granted vows;
And offering fresher up, with pious prayer,
'The good', said I, 'are God's peculiar care,
And such as honour Heaven, shall heavenly honour share'." }

162   Ovid writes: 'The thatch-straws ('spires') yellow, and
seem a golden roof'.
168   *prefers* 'puts'.
171–2   Ovid writes: 'since we have lived our years out in
harmony'; 'polluted' is frequent in Dryden.
173–6   Ovid writes: 'that neither shall I ever see my wife's
tomb, nor be buried by her'.
177   *sign their suit* 'agree their request' (Sandys's expres-
sion).

177–8   *run . . . space* 'they lead the same life as long as life
is granted.'
181–6   Developed from Ovid's saying that each saw the
other 'put out leaves'.
191   *Tyanaean* Tyana is a city in Phrygia.
193   *prodigy* 'miracle'.
197   *fresher* 'my own fresh garlands'.

Katherine Philips (1632–1664)

'Orinda', as she called herself, was born on New Year's Day 1632, the daughter of a Presbyterian London merchant, John Fowler; she died in London, in 1664, of smallpox. Brought up in a Puritan milieu (an uncle was the John Oxenbridge with whom Marvell lodged), her formal education was in a Presbyterian boarding school in Hackney for girls like herself (including Mary Aubrey, the biographer's cousin). Her father died in 1642. Her mother's second remarriage to the Royalist Sir Richard Phillips took the family to Wales. Katherine herself, still only 16, married the 54-year-old Colonel James Philips (a kinsman of her stepfather), High Sheriff of Cardiganshire, a moderate Puritan and a successful Commonwealth politician. She meanwhile cultivated Royalist connections both in Wales (notably Henry Vaughan) and in London (a group which included Henry Lawes, Edward Sherburne, Izaak Walton). This society of Platonic friends or innocent Epicureans was designed according to one of them (Silvander or Sir Edward Dering) 'to have spread very far, and have been improved with great and yet unimagined advantage to the world'; in effect, it recreated the *précieux* and Platonizing tendency of the defunct Caroline court and projected the lives of its members into a world of French romance. It remained private, as did Orinda's poetry, which circulated exclusively in MS. Even at the Restoration, despite the often public orientation of what she wrote, she was reluctant to publish. Her version of Corneille's *Pompey*, done in 1662 while she was in Dublin with Lucasia (Anne Owen had married the Irish Royalist Marcus Trevor, Viscount Dungannon) at the instigation of Lord Orrery, circulated in MS (and to great applause) out of her control. It was performed at the Theatre Royal in Dublin early in 1663, and published a few months later in Dublin and London. In teaching Corneille to speak English she may have discovered her forte; she embarked immediately on a version of *Horace*, left incomplete at her death and finished by Denham. It was on the back of *Pompey*'s success that an unauthorized edition of her *Poems* appeared early in 1664. Her death supervened on any attempt she might have made to prepare an authorized edition, a task left to Sir Charles Cotterell (Poliarchus, to whom Orinda's *Letters* were published in 1705), who had supervised her entry into Restoration literary culture. The folio *Poems* included two sets of complimentary verses from Cowley (one already reprinted from his *Verses* [1663] in the 1664 *Poems*), and odes and epigrams by Lord Roscommon and others. Her reputation was secure for the rest of the century, with an achievement defined by Cowley first as 'solid and manly' and then (remembering Vaughan's commendation of her 'thoughts as innocent, and high / As angels have, or saints that die', *To . . . Mrs K. Philips*, 13–14) as something else: 'Or rather 'tis angelical, / For as in angels, we / Do in thy verses see / Both improved sexes eminently meet, / They are than man more strong, and more than woman sweet' (Cowley, *On Orinda's Poems*, 50–6). The sweetness is more obvious, and while it made her the model of the woman poet (to some point for the Countess of Winchelsea), it hardly survived the following century, and the reputation of Aphra Behn, a counter-type of the woman poet has fared better since. The pirated collected *Poems* (1664), the subject of two pained letters to Sir Charles Cotterell, was suppressed. Cotterell's posthumous edition of the *Poems* (1667) was the basis for subsequent editions of 1669, 1678 and 1710. The standard modern edition, based for the most part on MSS (importantly an autograph MS in the National Library of Wales, and a scribal collection prepared for Mary Aubrey (Rosania) now also in the National Library of Wales), is *The Collected Works of Katherine Philips, The Matchless Orinda*: vol. 1: *The Poems*, ed. Patrick Thomas; vol. 2: *The Letters*, ed. Patrick Thomas; vol. 3: *The Translations*, ed. G. Greer and R. Little (Stump Cross Books, 1990–3). Patrick Thomas's 'Biographical Note' in vol. 1 is the best account of her life and reputation. Elizabeth H. Hageman, 'Recent Studies in Women Writers of the English Seventeenth Century, 1604–1674', reprinted from *English Literary Renaissance* in *Women in the Renaissance*, ed. with Kirby Farrell and Arthur Kinney (Amherst: University of Massachusetts Press, 1988), describes critical and other work; her own more recent textual-bibliographical work on Philips is important.

Friendship's Mysteries, To my dearest Lucasia

1667; the autograph MS is substantively identical; printed first in Lawes's *Second Book of Airs and Dialogues* (1655), and the setting is acknowledged in *1664* and some MSS. 'Love's mysteries in souls do grow' (Donne, *The Ecstasy*, 71), and though the poem professes to publish these mysteries, it stalls happily in its own paradoxes.

1

Come, my Lucasia, since we see
   That miracles men's faith do move,
By wonder and by prodigy
   To the dull angry world let's prove
   There's a religion in our love.   5

2

For though we were designed to agree,
   That Fate no liberty destroys,
But our election is as free
   As angels, who with greedy choice
   Are yet determined to their joys.   10

3

Our hearts are doubled by the loss,
   Here mixture is addition grown;
We both diffuse, and both engross:
   And we whose minds are so much one,
   Never, yet ever are alone.   15

4

We court our own captivity
   Than thrones more great and innocent:
'Twere banishment to be set free,
   Since we wear fetters whose intent
   Not bondage is, but ornament.   20

5

Divided joys are tedious found,
   And griefs united easier grow:
We are ourselves but by rebound,
   And all our titles shuffled so,
   Both princes, and both subjects too.   25

6

Our hearts are mutual victims laid,
   While they (such power in friendship lies)
Are altars, priests, and offerings made:
   And each heart which thus kindly dies,
   Grows deathless by the sacrifice.   30

6–10 'Though we were fated to love (and no freedom we enjoy could alter that), our freedom to choose is like that of angels, who choose so eagerly that they can choose only bliss.'

13 'We scatter and gather in at once.'
17 Than greatest thrones more innocent (*1664*), which gives easier sense; 'thrones' are 'royal powers'.

To my Excellent Lucasia, on our Friendship

1667; corrected from MS. The MS dates the poem at 17 July 1651, perhaps in error for 1652: Anne Owen, the addressee here as often, was received 'into our society' as Lucasia in December 1651 (commemorated by Orinda in a poem). This celebrates 'our soul', by which the poet is first animated.

I did not live until this time
    Crowned my felicity,
When I could say without a crime,
    I am not thine, but thee.

This carcass breathed, and walked, and slept,   5
    So that the world believed
There was a soul the motions kept;
    But they were all deceived.

For as a watch by art is wound
    To motion, such was mine: 10
But never had Orinda found
    A soul till she found thine;

Which now inspires, cures and supplies,
    And guides my darkened breast:
For thou art all that I can prize,   15
    My joy, my life, my rest.

Nor bridegroom's nor crowned conqueror's mirth
    To mine compared can be:
They have but pieces of this Earth,
    I've all the world in thee.   20

Then let our flame still light and shine
    (And no bold fear control)
As innocent as our design,
    Immortal as our soul.

---

3 *without a crime* 'without perjury'.
5 *This carcass* 'My body'.
9–10 'Let us hold that the body of a living man differs from that of a dead man just as any machine that moves of itself (like a watch when it is wound up) differs from itself when it is broken and the principle of its movement ceases to act' (Descartes, *Les Passions de l'âme*, article 6).
21 'Unchecked by any presumptuous fear'; *1664* etc. have 'false', one MS 'damp' for 'bold'.

Lucasia, Rosania, and Orinda parting at a Fountain, July 1663

1667. Orinda wrote to Poliarchus (Sir Charles Cotterell) from Dublin, 15 July 1663: 'Though I am in a great hurry and trouble, as you may easily imagine, being within the hour to go aboard for Milford, yet I could not omit the temptation of this post to acquaint you with it.' The earlier supposed occasion of the three friends at the fountain is fictitious: Lucasia (Anne Owen) remained in Ireland, but Rosania (Mary Aubrey) was in England.

1

Here, here are our enjoyments done,
    And since the love and grief we wear
    Forbids us either word or tear,
And art wants here expression,
    See Nature furnish us with one.   5

2–3 'Since our love forbids us to weep, and our grief forbids us to speak'.

2

The kind and mournful nymph which here
  Inhabits in her humble cells,
  No longer her own sorrow tells,
Nor for it now concerned appears,
But for our parting sheds these tears.   10

3

Unless she may afflicted be,
  Lest we should doubt her innocence;
  Since she hath lost her best pretence
Unto a matchless purity;
Our love being clearer far then she.   15

4

Cold as the streams that from her flow
  Or (if her privater recess
  A greater coldness can express)
Then cold as those dark beds of snow
Our hearts are at this parting blow.   20

5

But Time, that has both wings and feet,
  Our suffering minutes being spent,
  Will visit us with new content;
And sure, if kindness be so sweet,
'Tis harder to forget than meet.   25

6

Then though the sad adieu we say,
  Yet as the wine we hither bring,
  Revives, and then exalts the spring;
So let our hopes to meet allay,
The fears and sorrows of this day.   30

17–18 'Or if the fountain's hidden sources in the mountain snows can yield yet colder water'.
21–3 'Speedy Time will restore us to our happiness after this short interval of grief.'

27–8 They add wine to the water they drink from the fountain.

Epitaph. On her Son H. P. at St. Sith's Church where her Body also lies Interred

1667. According to Orinda's own title for *On the Death of my First Dearest Child*, Hector Philips was born on 23 April and died on 2 May 1655 (a mistake, for the interval is described in that elegy as 'forty days' and here as 'six weeks'). This poem owes a debt to Jonson's *On my First Son*. St Sith's Church was burned in the Great Fire.

What on Earth deserves our trust?
Youth and Beauty both are dust.
Long we gathering are with pain,
What one moment calls again.
Seven years childless, marriage past,   5

A son, a son is born at last:
So exactly limbed and fair,
Full of good spirits, mien, and air,
As a long life promisèd,
Yet, in less than six weeks dead.   10
Too promising, too great a mind
In so small room to be confined:
Therefore, as fit in Heaven to dwell,
He quickly broke the prison shell.
So the subtle alchemist,   15
Can't with Hermes' Seal resist
The powerful spirit's subtler flight,
But 'twill bid him long good night.
And so the sun if it arise
Half so glorious as his eyes,   20
Like this infant, takes a shroud,
Buried in a morning cloud.

15–17 'So the artful chemist cannot with his hermetic seal prevent the escape of volatile spirits'. 18 'But, if once we lose this light, / 'Tis, with us, perpetual night' (Jonson, *To Celia*, 7–8).

22 *morning* indistinguishable from 'mourning'.

Upon the Graving of her Name upon a Tree in Barn-Elms Walks

1667. Pepys, 26 May 1667, took his boat up the Thames 'as far as Barn-Elms, reading of Mr Evelyn's late new book against Solitude . . . I walked the length of the Elms, and with great pleasure saw some gallant ladies and people come with their bottles, and basket, and chairs, and form, to sup under the trees by the waterside, which was mighty pleasant.' Cowley moved in 1663 to Barn-Elms, where Orinda may have visited him. Orinda's poem disputes with Cowley's own much earlier *The Tree*: 'I chose the flourishing'st tree in all the park, / With freshest boughs, and fairest head; / I cut my love into his gentle bark, / And in three days, behold, 'tis dead.' There is a setting by Purcell with which the poem sometimes circulates in MS.

Alas how barbarous are we,
Thus to reward the courteous tree,
Who its broad shade affording us,
Deserves not to be wounded thus;
See how the yielding bark complies   5
With our ungrateful injuries.
And seeing this, say how much then
Trees are more generous then men,
Who by a nobleness so pure
Can first oblige and then endure.   10

2 *reward* requite (MS).
8 *generous* 'highborn'.

10 Human *noblesse* can only oblige.

La Solitude de St. Amant

1667, where the French text is given *en face*. Greer and Little take their text from the major non-autograph MS. It is copied independently in MSS; and a selection of twenty-six lines with Purcell's setting is widely distributed. This most famous poem (written about 1620) of Marc-Antoine de Gérard, sieur de Saint Amant (1594–1661) was published first with his authority in 1629. It was translated, in a slightly abridged version, by Lord Fairfax. The apparatus of the landscape, while it may be informed by reminiscence of the Norman coast (the poem's addressee is Charles de Bernières [171], president of the Norman *Parlement*), derives its appeal from its literary-cum-painterly qualities.

1

O! solitude my sweetest choice,
    Places devoted to the night,
Remote from tumult, and from noise,
    How you my restless thoughts delight!
O Heavens! what content is mine   5
    To see those trees which have appeared
From the nativity of Time,
    And which all ages have revered,
To look today as fresh and green
As when their beauties first were seen!   10

2

A cheerful wind does court them so,
    And with such amorous breath enfold,
That we by nothing else can know,
    But by their height that they are old.
Hither the demigods did fly   15
    To seek a sanctuary, when
Displeasèd Jove once pierced the sky,
    To pour a deluge upon men,
And on these boughs themselves did save,
Whence they could hardly see a wave.   20

3

Sad Philomel upon this thorn,
    So curiously by Flora dressed,
In melting notes, her case forlorn,
    To entertain me, hath confessed.
O! how agreeable a sight   25
    These hanging mountains do appear,
Which the unhappy would invite
    To finish all their sorrows here,
When their hard fate makes them endure
Such woes, as only death can cure.   30

12 *enfold* unfold (MS).
20 So high were the trees.
23–4 'The nightingale has sweetly told her sad story to entertain me'; 'Sad Philomela's mournful song / Doth sweetly entertain my grief' (Fairfax).

4

What pretty desolations make
    These torrents vagabond and fierce,
Who in vast leaps their springs forsake,
    This solitary vale to pierce.
Then sliding just as serpents do   35
    Under the foot of every tree,
Themselves are changed to rivers too,
    Wherein some stately Naiadë,
As in her native bed, is grown
A queen upon a crystal throne.   40

5

This fen beset with river-plants,
    (O! how it does my senses charm!)
Nor elders, reeds, nor willows wants,
    Which the sharp steel did never harm.
Here nymphs which come to take the air,   45
    May with such distaffs furnished be,
As flags and rushes can prepare,
    Where we the nimble frogs may see.
Who frighted to retreat do fly,
If an approaching man they spy.   50

6

Here water-fowl repose enjoy,
    Without the interrupting care,
Lest fortune should their bliss destroy
    By the malicious fowler's snare.
Some ravished with so bright a day,   55
    Their feathers finely prune and deck,
Others their amorous heats allay,
    Which yet the waters could not check,
All take their innocent content
In this their lovely element.   60

7

Summer's, nor winter's bold approach,
    This stream did never entertain,
Nor ever felt a boat or coach
    Whilst either season did remain.
No thirsty traveller came near,   65
    And rudely made his hand his cup,
Nor any hunted hind hath here
    Her hopeless life resignèd up,
Nor ever did the treacherous hook
Intrude to empty any brook.   70

31 'Que je trouve doux le ravage / De ces fiers torrents vagabonds'; ' How pleasant are the murmuring streams / In shady valleys running down' (Fairfax).

38 *Naiadë* 'river-nymph'; formed from the plural 'Naiades' for the rhyme's sake.

40 The influx of clear water creates the 'crystal throne'; the translation is literal.

46 'Here rocks and spindles them provide' (Fairfax): 'quenouilles'.

61–4 So remote is the stream that no boat has sailed on it in summer, and no coach gone on its frozen water in winter; no hunter has killed his deer here, no angler taken his fish. Fairfax omits this stanza.

8

What beauty is there in the sight
    Of these old ruined castle walls,
On which the utmost rage and spite
    Of time's worst insurrection falls.
The witches keep their sabbath here,   75
    And wanton devils make retreat,
Who in malicious sport appear,
    Our sense both to afflict and cheat,
And here within a thousand holes
    Are nests of adders and of owls.   80

9

The raven with his dismal cries,
    That mortal augury of fate,
Those ghastly goblins gratifies,
    Which in these gloomy places wait.
On a cursed tree the wind does move   85
    A carcass which did once belong
To one that hanged himself for love
    Of a fair nymph that did him wrong,
Who though she saw his love and truth,
    With one look would not save the youth.   90

10

But Heaven which judges equally,
    And its own laws will still maintain,
Rewarded soon her cruelty
    With a deserved and mighty pain:
About this squalid heap of bones,   95
    Her wandering and condemnèd shade,
Laments in long and piercing groans
    The destiny her rigour made,
And the more to augment her fright
    Her crime is ever in her sight.   100

11

There upon antique marbles traced,
    Devices of past times we see,
Here age hath almost quite defaced
    What lovers carved on every tree.
The cellar, here, the highest room,   105
    Receives when its old rafters fail,
Soiled with the venom and the foam
    Of the spider and the snail:

71 How pleasant's the declining state (MS); 'Que j'aime à voir la décadence'.
73–4 'Contre qui les ans mutinés / Ont déployé leur insolence'; 'Gainst which the giants did of old / With insolence employ their powers' (Fairfax).
75 'Now satyrs here their sabbath keep' (Fairfax); 'sorciers'.
84 Fairfax invents: 'In vaults o'erspread with toads and snakes'.

91–100 Fairfax omits this stanza.
98 'The death her hard-heartedness inflicted'; glossing 'Sa malheureuse destinée'.
105–6 Fairfax translates (literally and more intelligibly): 'The planks and timbers from above / Down to the lowest vaults are fall'n.'

And the ivy in the chimney we
Find shaded by a walnut tree.   110

12

Below there does a cave extend,
      Wherein there is so dark a grot,
That should the sun himself descend,
      I think he could not see a jot.
Here Sleep within a heavy lid   115
      In quiet sadness locks up sense,
And every care he does forbid,
      Whilst in the arms of Negligence,
Lazily on his back he's spread,
And sheaves of poppy are his bed.   120

13

Within this cool and hollow cave,
      Where Love itself might turn to ice,
Poor Echo ceases not to rave
      On her Narcissus wild and nice:
Hither I softly steal a thought,   125
      And by the softer music made
With a sweet lute in charms well taught,
      Sometimes I flatter her sad shade,
Whilst of my chords I make such choice,
They serve as body to her voice.   130

14

When from these ruins I retire,
      This horrid rock I do invade,
Whose lofty brow seems to enquire
      Of what materials mists are made:
From thence descending leisurely   135
      Under the brow of this steep hill,
It with great pleasure I descry
      By waters undermined, until
They to Palaemon's seat did climb,
Composed of sponges and of slime.   140

15

How highly is the fancy pleased
      To be upon the ocean's shore,
When she begins to be appeased,
      And her fierce billows cease to roar!
And when the hairy Tritons are   145
      Riding upon the shaken wave,

109–110 'And hearths that once were used for fires / Now shaded are with scratching briars' (Fairfax).
121–30 Fairfax omits this stanza.
123–4 'Echo ne cesse de brûler / Pour son amant, froid et revêche'; neglected Echo pined hopelessly for the self-absorbed Narcissus.
137–8 Fairfax gives easier sense: 'I did behold with greater pleasure/ How they did work the hollow caves: / A work so curious and so rare / As if that Neptune's court were there'; the throned sea-god Palaemon stands in for Neptune. The pastoral name of Orinda's friend Francis Finch was 'Palaemon' (it being also the name of a Virgilian shepherd).
145–6 'How the blue Tritons do appear / Upon the rolling curlèd wave' (Fairfax); Saint Amant's sea-gods are 'chevelus'.

With what strange sounds they strike the air
   Of their trumpets hoarse and brave,
Whose shrill report, does every wind
   Unto his due submission bind!   150

16

Sometimes the sea dispels the sand,
   Trembling and murmuring in the bay,
And rolls itself upon the shells
   Which it both brings and takes away.
Sometimes exposes on the strand,   155
   The effects of Neptune's rage and scorn,
Drowned men, dead monsters cast on land,
   And ships that were in tempests torn,
With diamonds and ambergris,
And many more such things as these.   160

17

Sometimes so sweetly she does smile,
   A floating mirror she might be,
And you would fancy all that while
   New heavens in her face to see:
The sun himself is drawn so well,   165
   When there he would his picture view,
That our eye can hardly tell
   Which is the false sun, which the true;
And lest we give our sense the lie,
We think he's fallen from the sky.   170

18

Bernières! for whose belovèd sake
   My thoughts are at a noble strife,
This my fantastic landscape take,
   Which I have copied from the life.
I only seek the deserts rough,   175
   Where all alone I love to walk,
And with discourse refined enough,
   My Genius and the Muses talk;
But the converse most truly mine,
Is the dear memory of thine.   180

19

Thou may'st in this poem find,
   So full of liberty and heat,
What illustrious rays have shined
   To enlighten my conceit:
Sometimes pensive, sometimes gay,   185
   Just as that fury does control,
And as the object I survey,

177–80 'My thoughts do use / No entertainment but what pleases / The genius of my rural Muse / But no thoughts more delighteth me / Than sweet remembrances of thee' (Fairfax).

181–200 Fairfax omits the last two stanzas.
182–4 'Pleine de licence et d'ardeur . . . Qui m'éclaire la fantaisie'.

The notions grow up in my soul,
And are as unconcerned and free
As that flame which transported me.   190

20
O! how I solitude adore,
    The element of noblest wit,
Where I have learnt Apollo's lore,
    Without the pains to study it:
For thy sake I in love am grown   195
    With what thy fancy does pursue;
But when I think upon my own,
    I hate it for that reason too,
Because it needs must hinder me
From seeing, and from serving thee.   200

189 *unconcerned* unconstrained (MS).
192 *the* that (1667); solitude is the element in which noblest wit lives.

Thomas Traherne (1637–1674)

The only work of Traherne published in his lifetime is *Roman Forgeries* (1673, second edition, 1704), a polemic giving (as the subtitle has it) 'A True Account of False Records discovering the Impostures and Counterfeit Antiquities of the Church of Rome'; he was known to Anthony à Wood as 'well read in primitive antiquity as in the Councils, Fathers, etc'. *Christian Ethics* (posthumously published in 1675 but prepared for the press by Traherne himself) is an argument, tuned to its time, for the Christian foundation of ethics. But Traherne's posthumously constructed personality has been increasingly detached from the Restoration clergyman and scholar. The devotional patchworks of quotation and paraphrase posthumously published under the title *A Serious and Pathetical Contemplation* (1699, now known from its subtitle as *Thanksgivings*) was anonymous; the *Meditations on the Six Days of Creation* (1717) was credited to his friend Susanna Hopton. Both of these were written around 1670. The *Centuries of Meditations*, written at the same time, was not published (by Bertram Dobell) till 1908. Four more 'centuries' of *Select Meditations*, evidently written earlier, were discovered only in 1964 by James Osborn of Yale; they have been edited by Julia Smith (Manchester: Fyfield Books, 1997). A hundred years ago Traherne was (beyond the admixtures of verse in his published prose) unknown as a poet. Discovered along with the *Centuries* in 1896 was what is now Bodleian MS Eng. poet. c.42, a partially autograph collection of poems together with a commonplace book; this collection was published by Dobell in 1903. British Library Burney MS 392, prepared by Traherne's brother Philip for the press under the title *Poems of Felicity*, was noticed only after the publication of the Dobell poems; it was published first by H. I. Bell in 1910. A third collection, the *Commentaries of Heaven*, is described by Allan Pritchard in *University of Toronto Quarterly*, 53 (1983), 1–35, and is now in the British Library; the verse is given in *Commentaries of Heaven: The Poems*, ed. D. D. C. Chambers (Salzburg: Institut für Anglistik und Amerikanistik, 1989). A Folger Library MS poem, *The Ceremonial Law*, based on Genesis and Exodus, has recently been identified as Traherne's. His work belongs to the moments of its accidental recovery, and is difficult to reattach to its origins. Traherne's status as a Restoration poet is comprom-ised on the one hand by his apparent anticipation of the visionary Blake or Wordsworth and on the other by his attachment to the supposed early and eternal verities of a universal theology; he values ordinary experience (the poems in Philip Traherne's transcript are headed 'Divine Reflections on the Native Objects of an Infant Eye'), but his notebooks are full of extracts from Hermes Trismegistus and Ficino as well as the Church Fathers. His affinities with Vaughan are strong enough for Grosart to have identified as Vaughan's the poems of the unedited Dobell MS; but by habit a poet of 'occasional meditation' he is determinedly 'unpoetical'. He was ordained deacon and priest at the Restoration in 1660; a graduate from Brasenose College, Oxford (matriculated 1652), he had been from 1657 Rector at Credenhill in his native Herefordshire. He was associated with the religious group around Susanna Hopton at Kington, from where he travelled regularly to Oxford, taking his BD there in 1669 (*Roman Forgeries* was the qualifying thesis). From 1699 he was chaplain to the Lord Keeper, Sir Orlando Bridgeman, whom he accompanied on his retirement in 1672 to Teddington, where he became minister; he died at Bridgeman's house.

The poems in the two MS collections prepared by Thomas himself and by Philip are published together in *The Poetical Works of Thomas Traherne*, ed. Gladys Wade (London: Dobell, 1932). Along with the 'poems' of *A Serious and Pathetical Contemplation* (given as *Thanksgivings*), and pieces from other MSS and printed sources, they are given in the second volume of the standard *Centuries, Poems, and Thanksgivings*, ed. H. M. Margoliouth, 2 vols (Oxford: Clarendon Press, 1958). George R. Guffey and V. A. Dearing have edited a *Concordance to the Poetry of Thomas Traherne* (Berkeley and Los Angeles: University of California Press, 1974). The standard biography is Gladys Wade, *Thomas Traherne* (Princeton: Princeton University Press, 1944). There is a survey of criticism by Jerome Dees in *English Literary Renaissance*, 4 (1974), 189–96.

The texts of the poems below, all from *Poems of Felicity*, are collaborations between Thomas and Philip, who amended Thomas's originals; Margoliouth sometimes attempts reconstructions of unimproved versions.

Shadows in the Water

Humility 'hath a nadir beneath it, a lower point in another heaven, on the side opposite to its zenith. In its own depth it containeth all the height of felicity and glory ... It is like a mirror lying on the ground with its face upwards: all the height above increaseth the depth of its beauty within, nay turneth into a new depth, an inferior heaven is in the glass itself; at the bottom of which we see the sky ... [man will] by going downward still begin to ascend ... will arrive at last to a new light and glory, room and liberty, breathing place and fresh air among the antipodes, and ... finally come to another sky, penetrate that, and leaving it behind him sink down into the depth of all immensity' (*Christian Ethics*, 408). But the poem is faithful to an 'unexperienced' experience of look-ing into water. Milton's Eve is more focused: 'I thither went / With unexperienced thought, and laid me down / On the green bank, to look into the clear / Smooth lake, that to me seemed another sky. / As I bent down to look, just opposite / A shape within the watery gleam appeared / Bending to look on me' (*Paradise Lost*, 4:456–62); Dryden's Eve is too knowing: 'What's here? another firmament below / Spread wide, and other trees that downward grow?' (*State of Inocence*, 2:171–2).

In unexperienced infancy
Many a sweet mistake doth lie:
Mistake though false, intending true;
A seeming somewhat more than view;
    That doth instruct the mind   5
    In things that lie behind,
And many secrets to us show
Which afterwards we come to know.

Thus did I by the water's brink
Another world beneath me think;   10
And while the lofty spacious skies
Reversèd there abused mine eyes,
    I fancied other feet
    Came mine to touch or meet;
As by some puddle I did play   15
Another world within it lay.

Beneath the water people drowned,
Yet with another heaven crowned,
In spacious regions seemed to go
As freely moving to and fro: 20
    In bright and open space
    I saw their very face;
Eyes, hands, and feet they had like mine;
Another sun did with them shine.

'Twas strange that people there should walk,   25
And yet I could not hear them talk:
That through a little watery chink,
Which one dry ox or horse might drink,
    We other worlds should see,
    Yet not admitted be;   30
And other confines there behold
Of light and darkness, heat and cold.

3–4 'The child's misperception fixing the mind on ('intending') a truth, the illusion importing more than what is seen by unmistaken eyes'; 'every object in my heart a thought / Begot, or was; I could not tell, / Whether the things did there / Themselves appear ... Or whether my conforming mind / Were not even all that therein shined' (*My Spirit*, 45–51).

10 'I imagined another world into existence beneath me.' 11–12 'Are these false eyes deluded? / Or have inchanted mists stept in between / My abused eyes, and what mine eyes haue seen?' (Quarles, *Argalus and Parthenia*, 2:364–6). 31 'And see other regions divided by the lines of day and night and zones of heat and cold'.

I called them oft, but called in vain;
No speeches we could entertain:
Yet did I there expect to find   35
Some other world, to please my mind.
    I plainly saw by these
    A new Antipodes,
Whom, though they were so plainly seen,
A film kept off that stood between.   40

By walking men's reversèd feet
I chanced another world to meet;
Though it did not to view exceed
A phantasm, 'tis a world indeed,
    Where skies beneath us shine,   45
    And Earth by art divine
Another face presents below,
Where people's feet against ours go.

Within the regions of the air,
Compassed about with heavens fair,   50
Great tracts of land there may be found
Enriched with fields and fertile ground;
    Where many numerous hosts,
    In those far distant coasts,
For other great and glorious ends,   55
Inhabit, my yet unknown friends.

O ye that stand upon the brink,
Whom I so near me, through the chink,
With wonder see: what faces there,
Whose feet, whose bodies, do ye wear?   60
    I my companions see
    In you, another me.
They seemèd others, but are we;
Our second selves those shadows be.

Look how far off those lower skies   65
Extend themselves! scarce with mine eyes
I can them reach. O ye my friends,
What *secret* borders on those ends?
    Are lofty heavens hurled
    'Bout your inferior world?   70
Are ye the representatives
Of other people's distant lives?

---

34   'We could hold no conversation.'
38   'Antipodes' are etymologically where 'other feet / Came mine to touch or meet' (13–14), or 'reversèd feet' (41) or 'Where people's feet against ours go' (48).
43–4   'Though the eye judged it an unreal illusion, it is a reality.'
49–56   'For the elements were changed in themselves by a kind of harmony . . . For earthly things were turned into

watery . . . The fire had power in the water, forgetting his own virtue: and the water forgat his own quenching nature . . . For in all things, O Lord, thou didst magnify thy people, and glorify them' (Wisdom 19: 18–22).
67   'What mystery lies next to those limits?'
71–2   'Can I infer that there are more of you than I presently see?'

Of all the playmates which I knew
That here I do the image view
   In other selves; what can it mean?   75
But that below the purling stream
   Some unknown joys there be
   Laid up in store for me;
To which I shall, when that thin skin
Is broken, be admitted in.   80

73–5 'What can it mean that I see here the image of all my former playmates?'
76 *purling* The now agitated water ceases to reflect clearly.

79–80 'And if thou wilt break through the whole, and see those things that are without . . . thou mayst' (*Christian Ethics*, 446–7, quoting *Hermetica*, 11 (2): 'A Discourse of Mind').

On Leaping over the Moon

'Command thy soul to go into India and sooner than thou canst bid, it will be there. Bid it pass over the ocean, and suddenly it will be there . . . Command it to fly to heaven and it will need no wings; neither shall anything hinder it, not the fire of the sun, nor the ether, nor the turning of the spheres' (*Christian Ethics*, 445, quoting *Hermetica*, 11 (2): 'A Discourse of Mind') . This poem is a reworking of the last, by way of the poet's brother's experience of seeing the moon reflected in a roadside ditch. It confirms the experience of Heaven even on earth which is won by indulging imaginative 'misperceptions'; but it is a story before it becomes a meditation.

I saw new worlds beneath the water lie,
   New people; yea, another sky,
      And sun, which seen by day
      Might things more clear display.
         Just such another   5
         Of late my brother
Did in his travel see, and saw by night,
   A much more strange and wondrous sight:
Nor could the world exhibit such another,
   So great a sight, but in a brother.   10

Adventure strange! No such in story we
   New or old, true or feignèd, see.
      On earth he seemed to move
      Yet heaven went above;
         Up in the skies   15
         His body flies
In open, visible, yet magic, sort:
   As he along the way did sport
Over the flood he takes his nimble course
   Without the help of feignèd horse.   20

1–4 The new worlds, described in *Shadows in the Water*, are shown 'more clear' because bathed in the water's refracted light, and because childish misperceptions 'intend true'.
9–10 'Only my brother could have been vouchsafed this second vision of wonder.'
11–12 'A tale in prose ne verse yet sung or said' (Ariosto, *Orlando Furioso*, 1.2 Harington).

14 'Yet mounted above the (reflected) sky'.
20 Ariosto's winged Hippogriff flies Ruggiero and Astolfo all over the world. Astolfo visits the moon in a chariot pulled by 'Four horses fierce as red as flaming fire' (*Orlando Furioso*, 34.69). The lines originally read 'Like Icarus over the flood he soars / Without the help of wings or Oars' (the themes of the couplet are dispersed in the next stanza).

As he went tripping o'er the King's highway,
  A little pearly river lay
    O'er which, without a wing
    Or oar, he dared to swim,
      Swim through the air   25
      On body fair;
He would not use nor trust Icarian wings
  Lest they should prove deceitful things;
For had he fall'n, it had been wondrous high,
  Not from, but from above, the sky: 30

He might have dropped through that thin element
  Into a fathomless descent;
    Unto the nether sky
    That did beneath him lie,
      And there might tell   35
      What wonders dwell
On Earth above. Yet doth he briskly run,
  And bold the danger overcome;
Who, as he leapt, with joy related soon
  How happy he o'erleapt the moon.   40

What wondrous things upon the Earth are done
  Beneath, and yet above, the sun?
    Deeds all appear again
    In higher spheres; remain
      In clouds as yet: 45
      But there they get
Another light, and in another way
  Themselves to us above display.
The skies themselves this earthly globe surround;
  We're even here within them found.   50

On heavenly ground within the skies we walk,
  And in this middle centre talk:
    Did we but wisely move,
    On earth in heaven above,
      Then soon should we   55
      Exalted be
Above the sky: from whence whoever falls,
  Through a long dismal precipice,
Sinks to the deep abyss where Satan crawls,
  Where horrid Death and Despair lies.   60

As much as others thought themselves to lie
  Beneath the moon, so much more high

21 The ditches by the public road are flooded.
27 Icarus fell to the sea when the sun melted his wings. The overconfident man 'Trusts waxen wings, which chanced to please / The Icarian Youth, and drowned may name / The glassy seas' (Horace, *Odes*, 4.2:2–4, 'J. H.').
41–8 Earthly activity, imaginatively transformed to celestial activity, is illuminated as if 'a new heaven and a new earth' (Revelation 21: 1) were already with us.

53–4 'Were we conscious while on earth of moving in heaven'.
61–6 'Though ('as much as') others believed they lived below the moon, he imagined himself flying as high above the stars as he was above that reflected sky he observed in the water.'

Himself he thought to fly
Above the starry sky,
   As that he spied   65
Below the tide.
Thus did he yield me in the shady night
A wondrous and instructive light,
Which taught me that under our feet there is,
As o'er our heads, a place of bliss.   70

Dreams

'I conceive and understand, not by the light of mine eyes, but by the intellectual operation . . . I am in Heaven, in the earth . . . Consider him that contains all things and understand that nothing is more capacious than that which is incorporeal . . . Increase thyself to an immeasurable greatness, leaping beyond every body, and transcending all time, become eternity' (*Christian Ethics*, 445–6, quoting *Hermetica* 13 'A Secret discourse . . . concerning Rebirth' and 11(2) 'A Discourse of Mind'). 'The world in a thought is more excellent than the world, because it is spiritual and nearer unto God. The material world is dead and feeleth nothing. But this spiritual world though it be invisible hath all dimensions, and is a divine and living being' (*Centuries*, 2.90).

'Tis strange! I saw the skies;
I saw the hills before mine eyes;
   The sparrow fly;
The lands that did about me lie;
The real sun, that heavenly eye!   5
Can closèd eyes even in the darkest night
See through their lids, and be informed with sight?

The people were to me
As true as those by day I see;
   As true the air,   10
The earth as sweet, as fresh, as fair
As that which did by day repair
Unto my waking sense! Can all the sky,
Can all the world, within my brain-pan lie?

What sacred secret's this,   15
Which seems to intimate my bliss?
   What is there in
The narrow confines of my skin,
That is alive and feels within
When I am dead? Can magnitude possess   20
An active memory, yet not be less?

1–7 'Suddenly my soul would return to itself, and forgetting all things in the whole world which mine eyes had seen, would be carried away to the end of the earth' (*Centuries*, 3.17). Philip Ayres thanks the gentle Deity 'Whom none could e'er but with closed eyelids see' (*To Sleep, When Sick of a Fever*, 22).
13–14 'Few will believe the soul to be infinite, yet infinite is the first thing which is naturally known' (*Centuries*, 2.81); 'The world was more in me, than I in it' (*Silence*, 80); the unabstract 'brain-pan' enforces the paradox.
17–21 'What is there inside me that is still endowed with sense when I am asleep? Can the world's bulk occupy my working memory without losing anything of itself?' 'Great is this force of memory . . . whoever sounded the bottom thereof? Yet is this a power of mine, and belongs unto my nature; nor do I myself comprehend all that I am. Therefore is the mind too strait to contain itself' (Augustine, *Confessions*, 10.15).

May all that I can see
Awake, by night within me be?
My childhood knew
No difference, but all was true,   25
As real all as what I view;
The world itself was there. 'Twas wondrous strange,
That Heaven and Earth should so their place exchange.

Till that which vulgar sense
Doth falsely call experience,   30
Distinguished things:
The ribbons, and the gaudy wings
Of birds, the virtues, and the sins,
That represented were in dreams by night
As really my senses did delight,   35

Or grieve, as those I saw
By day: things terrible did awe
My soul with fear;
The apparitions seemed as near
As things could be, and things they were: 40
Yet were they all by fancy in me wrought,
And all their being founded in a thought.

O what a thing is thought!
Which seems a dream; yea, seemeth nought,
Yet doth the mind   45
Affect as much as what we find
Most near and true! Sure men are blind,
And can't the forcible reality
Of things that secret are within them see.

Thought! Surely thoughts are true;   50
They please as much as things can do:
Nay things are dead,
And in themselves are severèd
From souls; nor can they fill the head
Without our thoughts. Thoughts are the real things   55
From whence all joy, from whence all sorrow springs.

28   That Heaven should be experienced here on earth.
29–31   'From . . . ignorance of how to distinguish dreams and other strong fancies from vision and sense did arise the greatest part of the religion of the gentiles in time past' (Hobbes, *Leviathan*, 1.2.8).
32–3   The jumble of things indifferent and weighty (here approved) mimics childish lack of discrimination, but elsewhere: 'Would one think it possible for a man to delight in gauderies like a butterfly and neglect the heavens?' (*Centuries*, 1.34).

39–42   'Men not knowing that . . . apparitions are nothing else but creatures of the fancy, think [them] to be real and external substances' (Hobbes, *Leviathan*, 1.112.7).
45–7   'Yet what goes on in the mind makes as much impression on us as immediate realities.'
50–6   'Things are but dead: they can't dispense / Or joy or grief: Thoughts! Thoughts the Sense / Affect and touch. Nay, when a thing is near / It can't affect but as it doth appear' (*The Inference 1*, 17–20).

Aphra Behn (1640–1689)

Behn's public literary career began with the Duke's Company production in 1670 of the tragicomic *Forced Marriage*, and for that decade she was identified with the theatre (she wrote in all at least seventeen plays, mainly comedies), playing to the talents of Nell Gwynn and Elizabeth Barry. Her life before then is uncertain. Most likely is that she was born in Canterbury in 1640 as Aphra (variously spelled) Johnson, that she visited Surinam as a young woman or even as a girl, that on her return to England in the 1660s she married a merchant, John Behn, that (already widowed by the middle sixties) she was employed as a spy in the Low Countries, after which she lived precariously in London, perhaps working in the theatre. But there are no reliable facts: the early biographies or biographical notices are designed to romanticize the author of *Oroonoko* and the rest, and her own pretence to write documentary rather than fiction makes a range of conjectures plausible. Theatrical work (though it never dried up) was superseded by literary jobbing work and by the writing of the novels and stories for which she is now best known (and which were immediately popular: the posthumously collected *Histories and Novels* of 1696 went though four editions in as many years). By Pope's time she was 'the authoress of several obscene plays' (note on his Imitation of the *Epistle to Augustus*); even in her own time her reputation was clouded by suspicion of sexual scandal and by her not always fashionable Tory politics. She collected her own verse first in the first part of *Poems upon Several Occasions, with A Voyage to the Island of Love* (1684), the last part being a verse translation from the Abbé Tallement's prose *Voyage à l'île de l'amour*. Already in 1680 she had contributed a version of Ovid's *Oenone to Paris* (*Heroides*, 5) to Dryden's *Ovid's Epistles. Translated by Several Hands* (1680) and in the same year three pieces (including *The Disappointment*) had appeared in *Poems on Several Occasions by the Earl of Rochester* with the recently dead Rochester's authorship assumed; in 1682 three short poems appeared in *Female Poems on Several Occasions. Written by Ephelia*, an unidentified poet (perhaps an actress), one of Behn's poetic 'daughters'. In 1688 a second collection of her own poems was added to a prose version of Tallement's second Voyage, *Lycidus, with A Miscellany of New Poems*. Ephelia had written in 1679 of Behn's verses 'When first your strenuous polite lines I read, / At once it wonder and amazement bred, / To see such things flow from a woman's pen' (*To Madam Behn*, 5–7). Behn is 'polite' against the provincial Orinda (Katherine Philips was 'uncouth like her country's soil', as Daniel Kendrick has it in his complimentary verses in front of the *Miscellany of New Poems*). To have recognized that she might be 'strenuous' too is more than most did. The contributors of complimentary verses to *Poems upon Several Occasions* wrote that 'Her face's beauty's copied in her style' (John Cooper), or that her 'pen sheds flames as dangerous as her eyes' (John Adams) a coquettish appeal that her own manner sometimes encourages. But Dryden, who had no cause to love her, writes posthumously and more soberly of her 'who well could love's kind passion paint … Men are but bunglers when they would / Express the sweets of love' (Epilogue to *The Widow Ranter*). Waller she acknowledges as the poet 'whose heaven-born genius first / My infant Muse and blooming fancy nursed' (*On the Death of E. Waller*, 81–2); and with the poetry of Waller's disciple Rochester, whose death she mourns as a loss to love poetry and to love (Defoe said she was his mistress), her own poetry is so deeply associated in their common MS transmission as to confuse them. Cowley, manifestly in her sometimes inappropriately deployed Pindarics, is her other obvious inspiration. She identifies her hugely various talent with her 'masculine part' (preface to *The Lucky Chance*); but though she is sometimes abused as 'Sappho', she claims back the name: 'Let me with Sappho and Orinda be / O ever sacred nymph [Daphne, the laurel], adorned by thee' (an interpolation in her version of Cowley's *Of Plants, Book 6*, 592–3). Her immortality is to be with the ancient and the modern types of the female poet.

Montague Summers's *Works of Aphra Behn*, 6 vols (1915, reprinted New York: Phaeton Press, 1967) is superseded by *The Works of Aphra Behn*, ed. Janet Todd, 7 vols (London: Pickering, 1992–6); the poetry is given in vol. 1 (1992). Mary Ann O'Donnell has prepared *Aphra Behn: An Annotated Bibliography of Primary and Secondary Sources* (New York and London: Garland, 1986). The standard biography is by Maureen Duffy, *The Passionate Shepherdess: Aphra Behn* (London: Methuen, 1989).

Song. Love Armed

1684; printed first in the tragedy *Abdelazer* (1677). Perhaps intended to recall Sappho's *Hymn to Venus* (translated from Boileau's French in *Miscellany … by Several Hands*, 1685); its personally registered pain

survives the (already domesticated) apparatus of vio-
lence belonging to such songs as Carew's *The Willing
Prisoner to his Mistress*.

> Love in fantastic triumph sat,
> Whilst bleeding hearts around him flowed,
> For whom fresh pains he did create,
> And strange tyranic power he showed;
> From thy bright eyes he took his fire,   5
> Which round about, in sport he hurled;
> But 'twas from mine, he took desire,
> Enough to undo the amorous world.
>
> From me he took his sighs and tears,
> From thee his pride and cruelty;   10
> From me his languishments and fears,
> And every killing dart from thee;
> Thus thou and I, the god have armed,
> And set him up a deity;
> But my poor heart alone is harmed,   15
> Whilst thine the victor is and free.

8 'Enough to exhaust the supply among all the world's
lovers'.

The Disappointment

1684. Circulated in MS (along with poems by Rochester, to whom it is sometimes attributed), the poem reached print first in a corrupt version in *Poems on Several Occasions* (1680), along with Rochester's related *Imperfect Enjoyment* (directly indebted to Ovid, *Amores*, 3.6). Its immediate source (followed closely at first) is *Sur une impuissance* by Jean Benech de Cantenac in *Recueil de diverses poésies choisies* (Amsterdam, 1661), given in a quasi-literal version as *The Lost Opportunity Recovered* in *Wit and Drollery: Jovial Poems* (1682). Behn's pastoralization of the French poem (whose setting is urban) and feminization of its perspective (now indifferent to the male crisis) brings it closer to the norms of seventeenth-century romance.

> 1
> One day the amorous Lysander,
> By an impatient passion swayed,
> Surprised fair Cloris, that loved maid,
> Who could defend herself no longer.
> All things did with his love conspire;   5
> The gilded planet of the day,
> In his gay chariot drawn by fire,
> Was now descending to the sea,
> And left no light to guide the world,
> But what from Cloris' brighter eyes was hurled.   10

1–4 'It chanced Lysander that unhappy man, / Led to it
by the rashness of his love / Assaulted the fair Chloris, who
does prove / Uneath to resist, do what she can' (*The Lost
Opportunity Recovered*, 1–4).

6–10 'If thou but show thy face againe . . . The darkness
flies, and light is hurled' (Carew, *Song: To a Beautiful Mistress*, 9–11).

2

In a lone thicket made for love,
Silent as yielding maids' consent,
She with a charming languishment,
Permits his force, yet gently strove;
Her hands his bosom softly meet,   15
But not to put him back designed,
Rather to draw him on inclined:
Whilst he lay trembling at her feet,
Resistance 'tis in vain to show;
She wants the power to say – "Ah! What d'ye do?"   20

3

Her bright eyes sweet, and yet severe,
Where love and shame confus'dly strive,
Fresh vigour to Lysander give;
And breathing faintly in his ear,
She cried – "Cease, cease – your vain desire,   25
Or I'll call out – What would you do?
My dearer honour even to you
I cannot, must not give – retire,
Or take this life, whose chiefest part
I gave you with the conquest of my heart."   30

4

But he as much unused to fear,
As he was capable of love,
The blessèd minutes to improve,
Kisses her mouth, her neck, her hair;
Each touch her new desire alarms,   35
His burning trembling hand he pressed
Upon her swelling snowy breast,
While she lay panting in his arms.
All her unguarded beauties lie
The spoils and trophies of the enemy.   40

5

And now without respect or fear,
He seeks the object of his vows,
(His love no modesty allows)
By swift degrees advancing – where
His daring hand that altar seized,   45
Where gods of love do sacrifice:
That awful throne, that Paradise
Where rage is calmed, and anger pleased;

12   Proverbially, 'Silence gives consent.'
21–2   Love and shame is more characteristic in Behn than
sweetness and cruelty: 'love and shame' subdue the soul of a
different Cloris in *On a Juniper Tree, cut down to make Busks*.
35   *alarms* 'arouses'; a fashionable use: *The Lost Opportu-
nity Recovered* has 'He then a lower hidden place alarms'.
36–40   'Her snowy breast was bare to ready spoil / Of

hungry eyes' (Spenser, *Faerie Queene*, 2.12.78); but the mili-
tary language is Ovidian: 'About my temples go triumphant
bays, / Conquered Corinna in my bosom lays' (*Amores*, 2.12:1–
2, Marlowe).
45   The altar (grasped by Romans in witness of an oath) is
where Lysander's sacrifice later fails (70).

That fountain where delight still flows,
And gives the universal world repose.   50

6

Her balmy lips encountering his,
Their bodies, as their souls, are joined;
Where both in transports unconfined
Extend themselves upon the moss.
Cloris half dead and breathless lay;   55
Her soft eyes cast a humid light,
Such as divides the day and night;
Or falling stars, whose fires decay:
And now no signs of life she shows,
But what in short-breathed sighs returns and goes.   60

7

He saw how at her length she lay;
He saw her rising bosom bare;
Her loose thin robes, through which appear
A shape designed for love and play;
Abandoned by her pride and shame.   65
She does her softest joys dispense,
Offering her virgin-innocence
A victim to Love's sacred flame;
While the o'er-ravished shepherd lies
Unable to perform the sacrifice.   70

8

Ready to taste a thousand joys,
The too transported hapless swain
Found the vast pleasure turned to pain;
Pleasure which too much love destroys:
The willing garments by he laid,   75
And Heaven all opened to his view,
Mad to possess, himself he threw
On the defenceless lovely maid.
But O what envying god conspires
To snatch his power, yet leave him the desires!   80

9

Nature's support (without whose aid
She can no human being give)

49–50   That living fountain from whose trills, / The melted soul, in liquid drops distils! (*1680*). The explicitness is mitigated; but the phrasing recalls Spenser: 'And yet through languour of her late sweet toil, / Few drops, more clear then nectar, forth distilled, / That like pure orient pearls adown it trilled' (*Faerie Queene*, 2.12.78).
56–8   'And her fair eyes sweet smiling in delight, / Moistened their fiery beams . . . like starry light / Which sparkling on the silent waves, does seeme more bright' (*Faerie Queene*, 2.12.78).
59–60   In *The Lost Opportunity Recovered*, 'She suddenly did counterfeit a swoon'.

63–4   'And was arrayed, or rather disarrayed, / All in a veil of silk and silver thin' (*Faerie Queene*, 2.12.77).
77   'Mad in pursuit and in possession so' (Shakespeare, *Sonnets*, 129:9).
80   *desires* desire (*1684*, which fails to secure the rhyme after adjusting the previous line from *1680*'s 'envious gods conspire').
81–3   'Nature's prop (the penis), without whose help Nature can bring no human to life, now itself forgets how to live.'

Itself now wants the art to live;
Faintness its slackened nerves invade:
In vain the enragèd youth essayed 85
To call its fleeting vigour back,
No motion 'twill from motion take;
Excess of love his love betrayed:
In vain he toils, in vain commands;
The insensible fell weeping in his hands. 90

10
In this so amorous cruel strife,
Where Love and Fate were too severe,
The poor Lysander in despair
Renounced his reason with his life:
Now all the brisk and active fire 95
That should the nobler part enflame,
Served to increase his rage and shame,
And left no spark for new desire:
Not all her naked charms could move
Or calm that rage that had debauched his love. 100

11
Cloris returning from the trance
Which Love and soft Desire had bred,
Her timorous hand she gently laid
(Or guided by design or chance)
Upon that fabulous Priapus, 105
That potent god, as poets feign;
But never did young shepherdess,
Gathering of fern upon the plain,
More nimbly draw her fingers back,
Finding beneath the verdant leaves a snake: 110

12
Than Cloris her fair hand withdrew,
Finding that god of her desires
Disarmed of all his awful fires,
And cold as flowers bathed in the morning-dew.
Who can the nymph's confusion guess? 115
The blood forsook the kinder place,
And strewed with blushes all her face,
Which both disdain and shame expressed:
And from Lysander's arms she fled,
Leaving him fainting on the gloomy bed. 120

---

87 'Masturbation fails to produce excitement.'
90 *hands* so *1680*; hand (*1684*).
91–2 'In this cruel war where accidental failure and sexual passion were disastrously at odds'.
95–8 So (on a clue from Ovid) Rochester: 'Eager desires, confound my first intent, / Succeeding shame, does more success prevent, / And rage, at last, confirms me impotent' (*Imperfect Enjoyment*, 28–30).
105 'Upon that incredible phallus' (Priapus being the mon-

strously endowed god of gardens).
110 'Chill lies the serpent in the grass' (Virgil, *Eclogues*, 3.92–3).
114 Rochester's penis, again on a cue from Ovid, 'Now languid lies, in this unhappy hour, / Shrunk up, and sapless, like a withered flower' (*Imperfect Enjoyment*, 43–4).
116–17 'The blood forsook her vulva for her face'; *1684* reads 'hinder' for *1680*'s 'kinder', restored here.

13

Like lightning through the grove she hies,
Or Daphne from the Delphic god,
No print upon the grassy road
She leaves, to instruct pursuing eyes.
The wind that wantoned in her hair,   125
And with her ruffled garments played,
Discovered in the flying maid
All that the gods e'er made, if fair,
So Venus, when her love was slain,
With fear and haste flew o'er the fatal plain.   130

14

The nymph's resentments none but I
Can well imagine or condole:
But none can guess Lysander's soul,
But those who swayed his destiny.
His silent griefs swell up to storms,   135
And not one god his fury spares;
He cursed his birth, his fate, his stars;
But more the shepherdess's charms,
Whose soft bewitching influence
Had damned him to the Hell of impotence.   140

121   Spenser's Florimell flees out of the 'thickest brush' like 'a blazing star' (*Faerie Queene*, 3.1.15–16); Daphne flees Apollo ('the Delphic god'): 'How graceful then! the wind that obvious blew, / Too much betrayed her to his amorous view; / And played the wanton with her fluent hair' (Ovid, *Metamorphoses*, 1:527–9), Sandys); when Shakespeare's Ve-

nus runs in search of the wounded Adonis 'As falcons to the lure, away she flies, / The grass stoops not, she treads on it so light' (*Venus and Adonis*, 1027–8).
131   'None but I (as a woman) can imagine the girl's feelings ('resentments') or sympathize with ('condole') them.'

To the fair Clarinda, who made Love to me, imagined more than Woman

1688. Partly a brief Ovidian epistle (like her *Oenone to Paris*, or like the homoerotic *Sappho to Philaenis* attributed to Donne), partly an epigram contrived for its neat conclusion.

Fair lovely maid, or if that title be
Too weak, too feminine for nobler thee,
Permit a name that more approaches truth:
And let me call thee, lovely charming youth.
This last will justify my soft complaint,   5
While that may serve to lessen my constraint;
And without blushes I the youth pursue,
When so much beauteous woman is in view.
Against thy charms we struggle, but in vain;
With thy deluding form thou giv'st us pain,   10
While the bright nymph betrays us to the swain.
In pity to our sex sure thou wert sent,

11   'With your deceptive appearance, you do us harm: your seeming a woman leaves us defenceless against your masculine appeal.'

That we might love, and yet be innocent:
For sure no crime with thee we can commit;
Or if we should – thy form excuses it.   15
For who, that gathers fairest flowers believes
A snake lies hid beneath the fragrant leaves.

   Thou beauteous wonder of a different kind,
Soft Cloris with the dear Alexis joined;
Whene'er the manly part of thee would plead,   20
Thou tempts us with the image of the maid,
While we the noblest passions do extend:
The love to Hermes, Aphrodite the friend.

17 'Low grow the strawberries ['fraga'], chill lies the serpent in the grass' (Virgil, *Eclogues*, 3:92–3).
19 Behn addresses *Our Cabal* to 'Cloris', but without hinting an identification; 'Alexis' in that poem is Mr G. V. (perhaps George Villiers, Duke of Buckingham).
23 Hermaphroditus and Salmacis lost their sexes to each other: 'No longer he a boy, nor she a maid; / But neither, and yet either, might be said' (Ovid, *Metamorphoses*, 4:378–9, Sandys). The components of Hermaphroditus's name (the names of his parents) are separated to focus the different feelings for his male and acquired female aspects.

Song [When Jemmy first began to love]

1684, but, in a less finished version, first published in *Covent Garden Drollery* (1672). Behn's 'Jemmy' is otherwise, as in the once popular *Song. To a New Scotch Tune* ('Young Jemmy was a lad, of royal birth and breeding') the Duke of Monmouth, the ill-fated centre of a succession of Whig rebellions against first the prospects and then the succession of the Duke of York. But this ballad is only improbably related to him; and if it is, it must predate the so-called Exclusion Crisis of 1679 (whatever resonance it later acquired): when published in *The Muses' Mercury* (1707) it carries the title *On Captain — going to the Wars in Flanders*. It masquerades in any case as a Scotch pastoral, complete with Doric accessories.

When Jemmy first began to love,
   He was the gayest swain
That ever yet a flock had drove,
   Or danced upon the plain.
'Twas then that I, wae's my poor heart,   5
   My freedom threw away;
And finding sweets in every smart,
   I could not say him nay.

And ever when he talked of love,
   He would his eyes decline;   10
And every sigh, a heart would move,
   Guid Faith and why not mine?
He'd press my hand, and kiss it oft,
   In silence spoke his flame.
And whilst he treated me thus soft,   15
   I wished him more to blame.

Sometimes to feed my flocks with him,
   My Jemmy would invite me:
Where he the gayest songs would sing,
   On purpose to delight me.   20
And Jemmy every grace displayed,
   Which were enough I trow,

To conquer any princely maid,
    So did he me I vow.

But now for Jemmy must I mourn,   25
    Who to the wars must go;
His sheephook to a sword must turn:
    Alack what shall I do?
His bagpipe into warlike sounds,
    Must now exchangèd be: 30
Instead of bracelets, fearful wounds;
    Then what becomes of me?

Two Songs from *The Rover Part 2*

The Counsel. A Song

1684; but published 1681 in *The Rover Part 2* (5.2) and then anonymously as *Beauty's Triumph* in a broadside (1682). A setting by Simon Pack (1654–1701) is acknowledged in *1684*. The 'counsel' offered is a persuasion to love along lines well established by Caroline poets (Cowley and Carew both have 'persuasions' of this title, Stanley a 'dissuasion'): that beauty unspent is beauty wasted, and that neglect will come with age.

1

A pox upon this needless scorn:
Sylvia for shame the cheat give o'er:
The end to which the fair are born,
Is not to keep their charms in store:
But lavishly dispose in haste   5
Of joys which none but youth improve;
Joys which decay when beauty's past;
And who, when beauty's past, will love?

2

When age those glories shall deface,
Revenging all your cold disdain;   10
And Sylvia shall neglected pass,
By every once-admiring swain;
And we no more shall homage pay:
When you in vain too late shall burn,
If love increase, and youth decay,   15
Ah Sylvia! who will make return?

3

Then haste, my Sylvia, to the grove,
Where all the sweets of May conspire
To teach us every art of love,
And raise our joys of pleasure higher;   20
Where while embracing we shall lie
Loosely in shades on beds of flowers,
The duller world while we defy,
Years will be minutes, ages hours.

1   The opening formula raises expectations of a drinking song.

Song. The Surprise

1684; but published in 1681 in *The Rover Part 2* (2.2) and then anonymously as *Love's Revenge* in *Female Poems on Several Occasions* by 'Ephelia' (1682). A set-ting by Thomas Farmer (died 1688) is acknowledged in *1684*. The ballad narrative is harnessed to lyric means.

1

Phillis, whose heart was unconfined,
And free as flowers on meads and plains,
None boasted of her being kind,
'Mongst all the languishing and amorous swains.
No sighs or tears the nymph could move,   5
To pity or return their love.

2

Till on a time the hapless maid
Retired to shun the heat o'th' day
Into a grove, beneath whose shade
Strephon the careless shepherd sleeping lay: 10
But O such charms the youth adorn,
Love is revenged for all her scorn.

3

Her cheeks with blushes covered were,
And tender sighs her bosom warm,
A softness in her eyes appear;   15
Unusual pain she feels from every charm:
To woods and echoes now she cries,
For modesty to speak denies.

17–18 'She wails wordlessly to the echoing woods, for modesty prevents her saying what is amiss.'

John Wilmot, Earl of Rochester (1647–1680)

'Mr Andrew Marvell (who was a good judge of wit) was wont to say that he was the best English satirist and had the right vein' (Aubrey). John Wilmot inherited his father's title when he was 10, graduated MA from Oxford at 14, and travelled on the continent for four years with an unlucky tutor appointed by the King. When he returned to London he unsuccessfully attempted to abduct the heiress Elizabeth Malet (whom he later married) and embarked on a career of reckless profligacy: 'His youthly spirit and opulent fortune did sometimes make him do extravagant actions . . . He was wont to say that when he came to Brentford [on the way into London] the devil entered him and never left him till he came to the country again.' His extravagances were regularly winked at and even rewarded (Gentleman of the King's Bedchamber in 1666, Ranger of Woodstock Park in 1675); in some eyes (even Pepys's) the King disgraced himself by his indulgence. He evidently had charm, he had courage (distinguishing himself in the Dutch War) and talent. Dryden's *Marriage à la Mode* (acted 1671) carries evidence of Rochester's efforts to make it 'mannerly' in the new court way. His early work includes some very fine lyric writing. The literary friends of his maturity – 'Sedley, Shadwell, Shepherd, Wycherley, Godolphin, Butler, Buckhurst, Buckingham' – were not all gentlemen but, Buckingham at their head, they were dominantly so. And in this group English satire was reinvented. At the end of a decade in which illness brought him more than once close to death, he began his conversations with Gilbert Burnet (at this date one of the more enlightened of the Anglican clergy), to whom he famously confessed that 'for five years together he was continuously drunk' and that satirists could not write 'without resentments'. Burnet brought him before his death to a dubious accommodation with the Church: 'he saw vice and impiety were as contrary to human society, as wild beasts let loose would be; and therefore he firmly resolved to change the whole method of his life, to become strict and true, to forbear swearing and irre-ligious discourse, to worship and pray to his Maker: and that though he was not arrived at a full persuasion of Christianity, he would never employ his wit more to run it down' (these conclusions were published along with reasoning that led to them in *Some Passages of the Life and Death of . . . John Earl of Rochester*, 1680).

Despite the pretence of exclusiveness in *An Allusion*, verse by Rochester circulated outside the Buckingham circle: the copying of malicious libels was a business he was happy to condone. Reaching print was an accident of the system, and surprisingly rare. The first major collection of poems by Rochester (though it includes poems by others) is the posthumous *Poems on Several Occasions by the Right Honourable the E. of R*— allegedly printed at Antwerp (in fact in London) in 1680. There are two facsimile editions of this bibliographically complicated item: Princeton: Princeton University Press, 1950, and Menston: Scolar Press, 1971; the first includes commentary on the make-up of the edition by James Thorpe. An important MS collection has been edited by Bror Danielson and David M. Veith: *The Gyldenstolpe Manuscript Miscellany* (Stockholm, Acta Universitatis Stolkholmiensis, 1967). The standard edition now is *The Works of John Wilmot, Earl of Rochester*, ed. Harold Love (Oxford: Clarendon Press, 1999); the editions by Frank H. Ellis (London: Penguin, 1994) and Keith Walker (Oxford: Blackwell, 1984) remain useful. *The Letters of John Wilmot, Earl of Rochester*, ed. Jeremy Treglown (Oxford: Blackwell, 1980) has the best account of Rochester's life. There is a *Concordance to the Complete Poems* by John Moehlmann (Troy: Whitston, 1979). Early criticism is anthologized in *Rochester: The Critical Heritage*, ed. David Farley-Hills (London: Routledge, 1972). Later work is described in David M. Vieth, *Rochester Studies, 1925–1982: An Annotated Bibliography* (New York: Garland, 1984), and George R. Wasserman, *Samuel Butler and the Earl of Rochester: A Reference Guide* (Boston: G. K. Hall, 1986).

A Ramble in Saint James's Park

1680; but widely current in MSS which here supply minor corrections. Waller's St James Park is a place for admiration and contemplation. But 'Ramble' had sexual connotations (Wycherley's Ranger intends 'a ramble to St. James's Park tonight, upon some probable hopes of some fresh game I have in chase', *Love in a Wood*, 1672). The poem winds up as an execration, explicitly so at its climax (133–66), against the imagined perversity of a woman the speaker (Rochester impersonates a caricature of himself) has debauched and who now prefers the company of fools; it is reached by way of parody of promenade poetry (1–42), satire on social types (43–78) and reflections on lust and betrayal (79–132). The obscene vocabulary, while not part of the literary repertory in printed English, is licensed by the Roman satirists.

Much wine had passed with grave discourse,
Of who fucks who, and who does worse;
Such as you usually do hear,
From those that diet at the *Bear*;
When I, who still take care to see,   5
Drunkenness relieved by lechery;
Went out into Saint James's Park,
To cool my head, and fire my heart:
But though Saint James has the honour on't,
'Tis consecrate to prick and cunt.   10
There by a most incestuous birth;
Strange woods spring from the teeming earth.
For they relate how heretofore,
When ancient Pict began to whore,
Deluded of his assignation   15
(Jilting it seems was then in fashion),
Poor pensive lover, in this place,
Would frig upon his mother's face:
Whence rows of mandrakes tall did rise,
Whose lewd tops fucked the very skies.   20
Each imitative branch does twine,
In some loved fold of Aretine.
And nightly now beneath their shade,
Are buggeries, rapes, and incests made.
Unto this all-sin-sheltering grove,   25
Whores of the bulk, and the alcove,
Great ladies, chambermaids, and drudges,
The rag-picker, and heiress trudges:
Car-men, divines, Great Lords, and tailors,
Prentices, pimps, poets, and gaolers;   30
Footmen, fine fops, do here arrive,
And here promiscuously they swive.
   Along these hallowed walks it was,
That I beheld Corinna pass;
Whoever had been by to see   35
The proud disdain she cast on me,
Through charming eyes, he would have swore
She dropped from Heaven that very hour,
Forsaking the divine abode
In scorn of some despairing god.   40

1–2 'What change has happened of intrigues, and whether / The old ones last, and who, and who's together' (*Artemesia to Chloe*, 34–5); but the language of the *Bear* (an eating house in Drury Lane) is coarser.
9–10 'Though the park is named for St James, it is dedicated to sex.'
19–20 The Pictish groves hinted in Waller's poem are conflated with the Titans he actually invokes: 'Bold sons of earth, that thrust their arms so high, / As if once more they would invade the sky' (69–70); mandrakes are man-shaped (and supposed aphrodisiac).
21–2 Carew imagines Lucretia reading 'Lectures of Love's great master, Aretine, / And knows as well as Lais, how to move / Her pliant body in the act of love' (*The Rapture*,

115–18); the Italian satirist Aretino supplied sonnets for a notorious collection of pornographic prints.
23–32 For Waller's 'lovers walking in that amorous shade' (21–2).
25 Waller's groves were 'sacred' (74).
26 'Public whores round shop-windows, amateur whores in their vaulted bed-chambers' ('alcove' was a vogue word: Oldham invites Venus to rise from 'her purple bed and rich alcove', *Lamentation for Adonis*, 5).
28 'Wanderers reduced to rag-picking and aimless heiresses'.
29 *car-men* 'carters'.
38 Spenser's chaste Belphoebe is 'by her stately portance, born of heavenly birth' (*Faerie Queene*, 2.3.21).

But mark what creatures women are,
How infinitely vile, when fair.
    Three knights, of the elbow, and the slur,
With wriggling tails, made up to her.
    The first was of your Whitehall blades,   45
Near kin to the Mother of the Maids,
Graced by whose favour he was able,
To bring a friend to the waiter's table.
Where he had heard Sir Edward Sutton
Say how the King loved Banstead mutton;   50
Since when he'd ne'er be brought to eat,
By 's good will any other meat.
In this, as well as all the rest,
He ventures to do like the best
But wanting common sense, the ingredient   55
In choosing well not least expedient,
Converts abortive imitation
To universal affectation;
So he not only eats, and talks,
But feels, and smells, sits down and walks,   60
Nay looks, and lives, and loves by rote,
In an old tawdry Birthday coat.
    The second was a Gray's Inn wit,
A great inhabiter of the pit;
Where critic-like, he sits and squints,   65
Steals pocket-handkerchiefs, and hints,
From 's neighbour, and the comedy,
To court, and pay his landlady.
    The third a Lady's eldest son,
Within few years of twenty-one;   70
Who hopes from his propitious fate,
Against he comes to his estate,
By these two worthies to be made
A most accomplished tearing blade.
One in a strain 'twixt tune and nonsense,   75
Cries "Madam I have loved you long since
Permit me your fair hand to kiss";
When at her mouth her cunt says "Yes".
    In short, without much more ado,
Joyful, and pleased, away she flew   80
And with these three confounded asses,
From Park, to hackney-coach, she passes.
So a proud bitch does lead about,

---

43 'Three gamblers, masters of sleight (to 'shake the elbow' is to play dice, to 'slur' to cheat at dice), made up to her like dogs (round a bitch).'
45–62 The first is a court hanger-on related to the Mother of the Maids (mentor to the maids of the royal household) who had attended with the gentleman serving the king at table (among whom Sir Edward Sutton, who would know the King's taste for fine 'mutton', food for lust as well as hunger). He mimics this and other courtly tastes and manners, but fruitlessly ('abortively'), having held on too long to a court-suit such as courtiers are gifted to wear on the King's birthday.

63–8 The second is a law student, frequenting the theatre with the double aim of pickpocketing from his neighbour so that he can pay the rent, and improving his conversation with lines from the play to that he can seduce his landlady.
69–74 The third, an aristocrat with expectations, hopes meanwhile for an education in wild and rakish manners.
83–6 So Homer's Circe is attended by beasts that 'Their huge long tails wagged; and in fawns would close, / As loving dogs' (*Odyssey*, 10:214–15, Chapman).

Of humble curs, the amorous rout;
Who most obsequiously do hunt, 85
The savoury scent of salt-swoln cunt.
Some power more patient now relate
The sense of this surprising fate.
Gads! that a thing admired by me,
Should tarte so much of infamy. 90
Had she picked out to rub her arse on,
Some stiff-pricked clown or well-hung parson
Each job of whose spermatic sluice,
Had filled her cunt with wholesome juice,
I the proceeding should have praised, 95
In hope she'd quenched a fire I raised:
Such natural freedoms are but just,
There's something gen'rous in mere lust.
But to turn damned abandoned jade
When neither head nor tail persuade, 100
To be a whore in understanding,
A passive pot for fools to spend in:
The Devil played booty sure with thee,
To bring a blot on infamy.
But why was I of all mankind 105
To so severe a fate designed?
Ungrateful! Why this treachery
To humble fond believing me?
Who gave you privilege above
The nice allowances of love? 110
Did ever I refuse to bear
The meanest part your lust could spare?
When your lewd cunt came spewing home,
Drenched with the seed of half the town,
My dram of sperm was supped up after, 115
For the digestive surfeit-water.
Full gorgèd at another time,
With a vast meal of nasty slime,
Which your devouring cunt had drawn
From porters' backs, and footmen's brawn. 120
I was content to serve you up
My ballock-full, for your grace cup;
Nor ever thought it an abuse

---

93 *sluice* 'pipe'.

95–6 'I should have commended an act that satisfied a desire I had brought her to feel in the first place.'

99–102 'But to turn to whoring ('jades' are worn-out rides) when neither advantage (which calculates) nor desire move you to it, to have prostituted your understanding, to be a receptacle for fools to ejaculate into.'

103–4 'The devil (in league with the three fools) has deceived you to make your bad name worse'.

111–12 'Did I not always tolerate the worse your lust allowed?'

113–14 Juvenal's Messalina returns to the Emperor Claudius 'The steam of lamps still hanging on her cheeks / In ropy smut; thus foul, and thus bedight, / She brings him

back the product of the night' (6:131–2, Dryden).

116 'To counter indigestion'.

120 The class disgust is already in Juvenal: 'Thus Hippia loathed her old patrician lord, / And left him for a brother of the sword' (6: 82), 'bring the slaves, / And watermen, a race of strong-backed knaves' (6:331–2).

122 *grace-cup* 'night-cap'.

123–32 'Nor ever thought myself wronged if your motive was pleasure, for my motives were all of kindness to you, whom I loved irrationally – you that could murder my heart for superficial excitements, and betray to such casual lovers the confidences I entrusted to you while lying at ease in your arms.'

While you had pleasure for excuse.
You that could make my heart away   125
For noise and colours and betray
The secrets of my tender hours,
To such knight-errant paramours;
When leaning on your faithless breast,
Wrapped in security, and rest,   130
Soft kindness all my powers did move
And reason lay dissolved in love.
May stinking vapour choke your womb,
Such as the men you dote upon.
May your depravèd appetite,   135
That could in whiffling fools delight,
Beget such frenzies in your mind,
You may go mad for the north wind;
And fixing all your hopes upon 't,
To have him bluster in your cunt,   140
Turn up your longing arse to the air,
And perish in a wild despair.
But cowards shall forget to rant,
Schoolboys to frig, old whores to paint:
The Jesuits' fraternity   145
Shall leave the use of buggery;
Crab-louse, inspired with grace divine,
From earthy cod, to Heaven shall climb;
Physicians, shall believe in Jesus,
And disobedience cease to please us,   150
Ere I desist with all my power
To plague this woman and undo her.
But my revenge will best be timed
When she is married, that is limed,
In that most lamentable state,   155
I'll make her feel my scorn, and hate,
Pelt her with scandals, truth, or lies,
And her poor cur with jealousies;
Till I have torn him from her breech,
While she whines like a dog-drawn bitch;   160
Loathed, and deprived, kicked out of Town,
Into some dirty hole alone,
To chew the cud of misery,
And know she owes it all to me.
And may no woman better thrive,   165
That dares profane the cunt I swive.

---

136   *whiffling* 'lightweight', but the sense 'gusting' is developed in 138–42.
138–42   Infatuation with the coldest and wildest wind is hopeless or painful or both.
143–50   The impossible dissociations are listed for the sake of the mainly scandalous but quite conventional associations. The ascent of the crab-louse from the scrotum ('cod') to a

place in the sky parodies the stellification of heroes.
154   *limed* 'coupled with' (as bitches are); a correction of 'married' is pretended.
159–60   'Till I have torn him from her rump, while she whines like a bitch from which a dog is attempting withdrawal'.

Satyr

1680; with minor corrections from versions already widely distributed in MSS as a *Satire against Man* or *Man and Reason* or *Reason and Mankind* and the broadside *Satyr against Man* (1679). Some MSS give a separate title (*An Apology, An Addition, A Supplement*) to the concluding section (from 174). Its literary inspiration is Boileau, *Satires*, 8 (quoted here in Oldham's version), but it is informed by awareness of immediately contemporary intellectual debate. An attack on the unnaturalness of reason and wit (1–45) is countered by a philosopher (or clergyman) who defends reason (46–71); the attack on the pretensions of reason is resumed, but now with 'right reason' distinguished from the philosopher's, and the attack on man's unnatural depravity is developed (72–173). This portion of the poem must in some version predate 1675. The *Apology* was provoked by a court sermon by Edward Stillingfleet on the irrationality of vice and the resort of the vicious to 'satirical invectives against Reason . . . it is pity such had not their wish, to have been beasts rather than man', and must therefore have been written later than February 1675; it offers a retraction if an honest man can be found. The praise of unreason follows a trail already blazed by Erasmus's Folly in the *Encomium Moriae*, a satire which may bear more largely on the whole poem. It has become conventional to retain the 'Satyr' spelling for the title since it better suggests the character of the speaker. Dryden writes that the elder Scaliger derives the word satire from '*satyrus*, that mixed kind of animal . . . made up betwixt a man and a goat'. The variously attributed *An Answer to the Earl of Rochester's Satyr against Man*, reprinted in *Poems on Affairs of State (1697–1716)*, 2, is distinguished.

Were I (who to my cost already am
One of those strange prodigious creatures man)
A spirit free, to choose for my own share,
What case of flesh, and blood, I pleased to wear,
I'd be a dog, a monkey, or a bear   }   5
Or anything but that vain animal,
Who is so proud of being rational.
The senses are too gross, and he'll contrive
A sixth, to contradict the other five;
And before certain instinct, will prefer   10
Reason, which fifty times for one does err.
Reason, an *ignis fatuus*, in the mind,
Which leaving light of Nature, sense behind;
Pathless and dangerous wandering ways it takes,
Through errors, fenny bogs, and thorny brakes;   15
Whilst the misguided follower, climbs with pain,
Mountains of whimsies, heaped in his own brain:
Stumbling from thought to thought, falls headlong down,
Into Doubt's boundless sea, where like to drown,
Books bear him up awhile, and makes him try,   20
To swim with bladders of philosophy;

5–7 'Of all the creatures in the world that be, / Beast, fish, or fowl . . . The arrant'st Fool in my opinion's man' (Boileau, *Satires*, 8:1–4).
8–9 'Reason is not, as sense and memory, born with us; nor gotten by experience only, as prudence is; but attained by industry' (Hobbes, *Leviathan*, 1.5.17).
10 'The ass, whom Nature reason has denied, / Content with instinct for his surer guide, / Still follows that, and wiselier proceeds' (Boileau, *Satires*, 8:247–8).
13 Boileau's Reason is the 'fair pilot given to steer / [Man's] tottering bark though life's rough ocean here' (*Satires*, 8:234–5, and the original adds it is a 'flambeau'). Hobbes calls philosophy (as against the Gospel's light) an *ignis fatuus* (*Le-viathan*, 4.47.16); the *ignis fatuus* or 'vapour' (23) is a phosphorescent exhalation of marsh gas, a 'will o' the wisp'; it is more usually applied to irrational forces like lust, as in Quarles: 'an *ignis fatuus* . . . whose deceitful flame enchants / The wandring steps of the diverted stranger' (*Divine Fancies*, 2.17).
14–25 Misreasoning is the issue: Hobbes writes, 'ignorance of causes, and of rules, does not set men so far out of their way as relying on false rules' (*Leviathan*, 1.5.19); 'His restless mind still rolls from thought to thought: / In each resolve unsteady, and unfixed' (Boileau, *Satires*, 8:35–6).
21 Bladders aid buoyancy but are easily pricked.

In hopes still to o'ertake the skipping light,
The vapour dances in his dazzling sight,
Till spent, it leaves him to eternal night.
Then Old Age, and Experience, hand in hand,   25
Lead him to Death, and make him understand,
After a search so painful, and so long,
That all his life he has been in the wrong;
Huddled in dirt, the reasoning engine lies,
Who was so proud, so witty, and so wise.   30
Pride drew him in, as cheats, their bubbles catch,
And makes him venture, to be made a wretch.
His wisdom did his happiness destroy,
Aiming to know that world he should enjoy;
And wit, was his vain frivolous pretence,   35
Of pleasing others, at his own expense.
For wits are treated just like common whores,
First they're enjoyed, and then kicked out of doors:
The pleasure past, a threatening doubt remains,
That frights the enjoyer, with succeeding pains: 40
Women and men of wit, are dangerous tools,
And ever fatal to admiring fools.
Pleasure allures, and when the fops escape,
'Tis not that they're beloved, but fortunate,
And therefore what they fear, at heart they hate.   45
    But now methinks some formal Band-and-Beard,
Takes me to task, "Come on Sir I'm prepared."
    "Then by your favour, anything that's writ
Against this gibing jingling knack called wit,
Likes me abundantly, but you take care,   50
Upon this point, not to be too severe.
Perhaps my Muse, were fitter for this part,
For I profess, I can be very smart
On wit, which I abhor with all my heart:
I long to lash it in some sharp *Essay*,   55
But your grand indiscretion bids me stay,
And turns my tide of ink another way.
What rage ferments in your degenerate mind,
To make you rail at reason, and mankind?
Blest glorious man! to whom alone kind Heaven,   60
An everlasting soul has freely given;

---

22 *skipping* escaping (1680, and most texts), 'skipping' from *1679.*

25–8 'Then his lewd follies he would late repent, / And his past years, that in a mist were spent' (Persius, 5:60–1, Dryden).

29 The 'dirt' is of the dying body; the mind an 'engine' for 'what is the heart, but a spring; and the nerves, but so many strings; and the joints, but so many wheels?' (*Leviathan,* Introduction, 1).

31 *bubbles* 'dupes'.

33–4 'Wisdom deprived him of Paradise: rather than simply enjoy it, he tried to understand it.'

35–6 'The wit with which he aimed to please others was pointless for it worked against him' (for the reasons given in 39–45).

45 *heart* least (*1680*).

46 Butler's Hudibras 'put his band and beard in order' to court his mistress (*Hudibras,* 3.1.153); the plain collar ('band') and beard make a uniform for the man of gravity.

49 'Against this talent for sneering and rhyming'.

55 Such as Richard Ward's *Two very Useful and Compendious Theological Treatises . . . Showing the Nature of Wit, Wisdom, and Folly . . . and Describing the Nature, Use, and Abuse of the Tongue* (1673).

56 'But your failure to discriminate between wit and reason gives me pause.'

60–5 'Man is (you cry) Lord of the universe; / For him was this fair frame of Nature made, / And all the creatures for his use, and aid: / To him alone of all the living kind, / Has bounteous Heaven the reasoning gift assigned' (Boileau, *Satires,* 8:10–12).

Whom his great Maker took such care to make,
That from himself he did the image take;
And this fair frame, in shining reason dressed,
To dignify his nature, above beast.   65
Reason, by whose aspiring influence,
We take a flight beyond material sense,
Dive into mysteries, then soaring pierce,
The flaming limits of the universe,
Search Heaven and Hell, find out what's acted there,   70
And give the world true grounds of hope and fear."
  "Hold mighty man," I cry, "all this we know,
From the pathetic pen of Ingelo;
From Patrick's *Pilgrim*, Stillingfleet's *Replies*,
And 'tis this very reason I despise.   75
This supernatural gift, that makes a mite
Think he's the image of the infinite:
Comparing his short life, void of all rest,
To the eternal, and the ever blest.
This busy, puzzling, stirrer up of doubt,   80
That frames deep mysteries, then finds 'em out;
Filling with frantic crowds of thinking fools,
Those reverend Bedlams, Colleges, and Schools;
Borne on whose wings, each heavy sot can pierce,
The limits of the boundless universe;   85
So charming ointments, make an old witch fly,
And bear a crippled carcass through the sky.
'Tis this exalted power, whose business lies,
In nonsense, and impossibilities.
This made a whimsical philosopher,   90
Before the spacious world, his tub prefer,
And we have modern cloistered coxcombs, who
Retire to think, 'cause they have naught to do.
But thoughts, are given for action's government,
Where action ceases, thought's impertinent: 95
Our sphere of action, is life's happiness,
And he who thinks beyond, thinks like an ass.
Thus, whilst 'gainst false reasoning I inveigh,

66–71 'Was it not this bold, this thinking man, / That measured heaven, and taught the stars to scan, / Whose boundless wit, with soaring wings durst fly, / Beyond the flaming borders of the sky; / Turned Nature o'er, and with a piercing view / Each cranny searched' (Boileau, *Satires*, 8:165–8); 69 is quoted from Evelyn's version of Lucretius, 1:73.

73–4 Nathaniel Ingelo's pathetic ('passionate') pen produced the long didactic prose romance *Bentivolio and Urania* (four editions between 1660 and 1682); Simon Patrick's *Parable of the Pilgrim* (1665) is a prototype *Pilgrim's Progress. Stillingfleet's Replies* Sibbes' Soliloquies (*1679*); Stillingfleet was the great Anglican controversialist of his generation, 'replying' to the Church's enemies. *1680* gives only initials for Patrick and Stillingfleet.

76 As generally modernized, 'This more than natural gift that makes an insect think itself divine'; but 'Myte-,' in the early texts suggests 'mitred head' interrupted.

81 'That fabricates riddles and then solves them'.

86–7 Witches 'make ointments of the bowels and members of children, whereby they ride in the air and accomplish all their desires' (Scot, *Discovery of Witchcraft*, 3.1).

89 'And words whereby we conceive nothing but the sound are those we call absurd, insignificant, and nonsense' (Hobbes, *Leviathan*, 1.5.5).

90–1 The Cynic Diogenes lived in a tub; and 'learned men . . . unhonoured lead a private life . . . imprisoned all their lives in their colleges, and languish in obscurity' (Burton, *Anatomy*, 1.2.3.15).

94–104 The 'right reason' which Rochester 'owns' ('acknowledges') is Hobbesian: 'In all your actions, look often upon what you would have, as the thing that directs all your thoughts in the way to attain it' (*Leviathan*, 1.3.4); reason 'reforms' and 'renews' appetite because 'felicity is a continual progress of the desire from one object to another, the attaining of the former being still but the way to the latter' (*Leviathan*, 1.11.1).

I own right reason, which I would obey:
That reason that distinguishes by sense,   100
And gives us rules, of good, and ill from thence:
That bounds desires, with a reforming will,
To keep them more in vigour, not to kill.
Your reason hinders, mine helps to enjoy,
Renewing appetites, yours would destroy.   105
My reason is my friend, yours is a cheat,
Hunger calls out, my reason bids me eat;
Perversely yours, your appetite does mock,
This asks for food, that answers 'What's o'clock?'
This plain distinction Sir your doubt secures,   110
'Tis not true reason I despise but yours.
Thus I think reason righted, but for man,
I'll ne'er recant, defend him if you can.
For all his pride, and his philosophy,
'Tis evident, beasts are in their degree,   115
As wise at least, and better far than he.
Those creatures, are the wisest who attain,
By surest means, the ends at which they aim.
If therefore Jowler, finds, and kills his hares,
Better than Meres, supplies committee chairs;   120
Though one's a statesman, the other but a hound,
Jowler, in justice, would be wiser found.
You see how far man's wisdom here extends,
Look next, if Human Nature makes amends;
Whose principles, most generous are, and just,   125
And to whose morals, you would sooner trust.
Be judge your self, I'll bring it to the test,
Which is the basest creature man, or beast?
Birds, feed on birds, beasts, on each other prey,
But savage man alone, does man, betray: 130
Pressed by necessity, they kill for food,
Man, undoes man, to do himself no good.
With teeth, and claws, by nature armed they hunt,
Nature's allowance, to supply their want.
But man, with smiles, embraces, friendships, praise,   135
Unhumanly his fellow's life betrays;
With voluntary pains, works his distress,
Not through necessity, but wantonness.

106–9 Proverbially, 'The belly is the truest clock.'
110–13 The distinction between your perverse reasoning and my practical reasoning resolves the problem you have with my 'grand indiscretion' (56) in attacking reason. True reason is justified ('righted') but man cannot be.
119–21 'Jowler' is a quasi-proper name for 'a hunting dog'. Sir Thomas Meres, a great Parliamentary committee man; *1680* has 'M—' (in some texts expanded to 'man') for Meres. One MS includes an eight-line expansion of the parallel.
130–50 Proverbially 'Man is a wolf to man' and worse: 'Who ever saw the wolves ... Like more inhuman us, so bent on prey ... 'Tis man, 'tis man alone, that worst of brutes, / Who first brought up the trade of cutting throats, / Did Honour first, that barbarous term, devise' (Boileau,

Satires, 8:125–6, 151–2). For Hobbes, relevant 'passions' are 'principally the more or less desire of power, of riches, of knowledge, and of honour. All which may be reduced to the first, that is, desire of power. For riches, knowledge and honour are but several sorts of power' (*Leviathan*, 1.8.15); and 'the final ... design of men ... in the introduction of that restraint upon themselves, in which we see them live in commonwealths, is the foresight of their own preservation' (2.17.1). Davenant's phrasing is recalled: 'When beasts each other chase and then devour, / 'Tis Nature's law, necessity, / Which makes them hunt for food, and not for power: / Men for dominion, art's chief vanity, / Contrive to make men die' (*The Cruelty of the Spaniards in Peru*, Fifth chorus, inset in *The Playhouse to be Let*, 4).

For hunger, or for love, they fight or tear,
Whilst wretched man, is still in arms for fear;   140
For fear he arms, and is of arms afraid,
By fear, to fear, successively betrayed.
Base fear, the source whence his best passion came,
His boasted honour, and his dear-bought fame.
That lust of power, to which he's such a slave,   145
And for the which alone he dares be brave:
To which his various projects are designed,
Which makes him generous, affable, and kind.
For which he takes such pains to be thought wise,
And screws his actions, in a forced disguise: 150
Leading a tedious life in misery,
Under laborious, mean hypocrisy.
Look to the bottom, of this vast design,
Wherein man's wisdom, power, and glory join;
The good he acts, the ill he does endure,   155
'Tis all for fear, to make himself secure.
Merely for safety, after fame we thirst,
For all men, would be cowards if they durst.
And honesty's against all common sense,
Men must be knaves, 'tis in their own defence.   160
Mankind's dishonest, if you think it fair,
Amongst known cheats, to play upon the square,
You'll be undone –
Nor can weak truth, your reputation save,
The knaves, will all agree to call you knave.   165
Wronged shall he live, insulted o'er, oppressed,
Who dares be less a villain, than the rest.
Thus Sir you see what Human Nature craves,
Most men are cowards, all men should be knaves:
The difference lies (as far as I can see)   170
Not in the thing itself, but the degree;
And all the subject matter of debate,
Is only who's a knave, of the first rate?"
    All this with indignation have I hurled,
At the pretending part of the proud world,   175
Who swoln with selfish vanity, devise,
False freedoms, holy cheats, and formal lies
Over their fellow slaves to tyrannise.
    But if in court, so just a man there be,
(In court, a just man, yet unknown to me)   180
Who does his needful flattery direct,
Not to oppress, and ruin, but protect;
Since flattery, which way so ever laid,
Is still a tax on that unhappy trade.
If so upright a statesman, you can find,   185
Whose passions bend to his unbiased mind;
Who does his arts, and policies apply,
To raise his country, not his family;

150 'And forces his behaviour into a straitjacket'.
153 *this* 'his' (*1680*).
158 Proverbial from this line.

162–3 'It is fatal to play fair with known cheats.'
174–5 'If nature could not, anger ['indignatio'] indite' (Juvenal, 1:79, Dryden).

Nor while his pride owned avarice withstands,
Receives auréal bribes, from friends' corrupted hands.   190
   Is there a churchman who on God relies?
Whose life, his faith, and doctrine justifies?
Not one blown up, with vain prelatic pride,
Who for reproof of sins, does man deride:
Whose envious heart makes preaching a pretence   ⎫   195
With his obstrep'rous saucy eloquence,   ⎬
Dares chide at kings, and rail at men of sense.   ⎭
Who from his pulpit, vents more peevish lies,
More bitter railings, scandals, calumnies,
Than at a gossiping, are thrown about,   200
When the good wives, get drunk, and then fall out.
None of that sensual tribe, whose talents lie,
In avarice, pride, sloth, and gluttony.
Who hunt good livings, but abhor good lives,   ⎫
Whose lust exalted, to that height arrives,   ⎬   205
They act adultery with their own wives.   ⎭
And e'er a score of years completed be,   ⎫
Can from the lofty pulpit proudly see,   ⎬
Half a large parish, their own progeny.   ⎭
   Nor doting Bishop who would be adored,   210
For domineering at the council board;
A greater fop, in business at fourscore,
Fonder of serious toys, affected more,
Than the gay glittering fool, at twenty proves,
With all his noise, his tawdry clothes, and loves.   215
   But a meek humble man, of modest sense,
Who preaching peace, does practise continence;
Whose pious life's a proof he does believe,
Mysterious truths, which no man can conceive.
If upon Earth there dwell such god-like men,   220
I'll here recant my paradox to them;
Adore those shrines of virtue, homage pay,
And with the rabble world, their laws obey.
If such there are, yet grant me this at least,
Man differs more from man, than man from beast.   225

---

190 *auréal* 'golden', so rare as to suggest some private joke, and replaced in later editions by 'close' eliminating the climatic alexandrine but giving a neater antithesis of overt graspingness and underhand bribery.

193–215 The moralizing, philandering, near-octogenarian Archbishop of Canterbury Gilbert Sheldon is the likely butt.

195–6 *1680* mangles the triplet into a couplet; the triplet is restored here.

200–1 *gossiping* the party of women friends attending a labour, and typically drunk.

210–11 *Bishop B—— (1680)*.

218–19 'We are . . . not to labour in sifting out a philosophical truth by logic of such mysteries as are not comprehensible . . . it is with the mysteries of our religion as with wholesome pills for the sick, which swallowed whole have the virtue to cure' (Hobbes, *Leviathan*, 3.32.3).

221 'A paradox, is an opinion not yet generally received' (Hobbes, *Liberty, Necessity and Chance*).

225 Boileau's ass concludes 'Good faith, man is a beast as much as we' (*Satires*, 8:308); Montaigne begins his essay 'Of the Inequality amongst us': 'there is more difference betwixt such and such men than there is betwixt such a man and such a beast' (1.42, Cotton).

An Allusion to Horace. The Tenth Satire of the First Book

1680; but written in the mid-1670s and current in MSS which supply minor corrections. Horace's poem is a statement of Augustan literary values against the loose writing of his rivals, for which the pretended licence is the early Roman satirist Lucilius. An 'Allusion' is an application or imitation (the names are changed to expose the guilty); the leading parallels are indicated below using the eighteenth-century translation of Philip Francis. Dryden had implicitly (and imprudently, for his talents were at that date widely thought of as loose and extravagant) identified Jonson with Lucilius and himself with the more correct Horace (notably in the letter to Sedley prefixed to *The Assignation*, 1673): 'You find Horace complaining that . . . he himself was blamed by others, though his design

was no other than mine now, to improve the knowledge of poetry . . . I know I honour Ben Jonson more than my little critics, because without vanity I may own I understand him better.' The ownership of Ben Jonson's heritage (Dryden's poetic claim against Shadwell is put in *Mac Flecknoe*) is in effect the substituted context in Rochester's poem. Dryden's reply is in the preface to *All for Love* (1678), which shifts ground to dispute the ownership of Horace rather than Jonson: 'other arms than theirs, and other sinews, are required to raise the weight of such an author.' Only the names of Waller (54), Buckhurst (59), and Sedley (64) are printed fully in *1680*; others are expanded editorially on MS authority.

Nempe incomposito dixi pede etc.

Well Sir, 'tis granted, I said Dryden's rhymes,
Were stoln, unequal, nay dull many times:
What foolish patron, is there found of his,
So blindly partial, to deny me this?
But that his plays, embroidered up, and down,   5
With wit, and learning, justly pleased the town,
In the same paper, I as freely own.
Yet having this allowed, the heavy mass,
That stuffs up his loose volumes, must not pass:
For by that rule, I might as well admit,   10
Crowne's tedious scenes, for poetry, and wit.
'Tis therefore not enough, when your false sense
Hits the false judgement, of an audience
Of clapping fools, assembling a vast crowd,
Till the thronged playhouse, crack with the dull load;   15
Though even that talent, merits in some sort,
That can divert the rabble, and the Court:
Which blundering Settle, never could attain,
And puzzling Otway, labours at in vain.
But within due proportions, circumscribe   20

1–7 The epigraph quotes Horace's opening: 'Yes, I did say, that his rough verses rolled / In ruder style precipitately bold; / Who reads Lucilius with so fond an eye, / Foolishly fond, who can this charge deny? / But, that with wit he lashed a vicious age, / He's frankly praised in the same equal page' (*Satires*, 1.10:1–4; the praise of Lucilius 'in the same paper' is in *Satires*, 1.4). 'Patron' translates Horace's *fautor* ('promoter and protector'), and may allude to John Sheffield, the dedicatee of *Aureng-Zebe* (1676) to whom Rochester was hostile.
8–19 Horace adduces the farceur Laberius, but '"Tis not enough a bursting laugh to raise, / And yet even this may well deserve its Praise' (1.10:5–8). Dryden is cast as anxious for the plaudits that the gentlemanly Horace later declines 'where the People with applauding hands / The well-wrought scene repeatedly demands' (1.10:39). But he is allowed to

excel only young or inexperienced dramatists: John Crowne who began writing for the stage in 1671 (though his 1675 masque *Calisto* came to court through Rochester's patronage), Elkanah Settle whose first play *Cambyses* got a London staging in 1671 (and written while he was still at Oxford), Thomas Otway whose first play *Alcibiades* was performed in 1675. Dryden himself had turned on Settle's blundering style with his *Notes on the Empress of Morocco* (1675).
20–9 'Close be your language; let your sense be clear, / Nor with a weight of words fatigue the ear. / From grave to jovial you must change with art, / Now play the critic's, now the poet's part; / In raillery assume a gayer air, / Discreetly hide your strength, your vigour spare, / For ridicule shall frequently prevail, / And cut the knot, when graver reasons fail' (1.10:9–15).

Whate'er you write; that with a flowing tide,
The style may rise, yet in its rise forbear,
With useless words, to oppress the wearied ear:
Here be your language lofty, there more light,
Your rhetoric, with your poetry, unite: 25
For elegance' sake, sometimes allay the force
Of epithets; 'twill soften the discourse;
A jest in scorn, points out, and hits the thing,
More home, than the morosest satire's sting.
Shakespeare, and Jonson, did herein excel,   30
And might in this be imitated well;
Whom refined Etherege, copies not at all,
But is himself a sheer original:
Nor that slow drudge, in swift Pindaric strains,
Flatman, who Cowley imitates with pains,   35
And rides a jaded Muse, whipped with loose reins.
When Lee, makes temperate Scipio, fret and rave,
And Hannibal, a whining amorous slave,
I laugh, and wish the hot-brained fustian fool,
In Busby's hands, to be well lashed at school.   40
Of all our modern wits, none seems to me,
Once to have touched, upon true comedy,
But hasty Shadwell, and slow Wycherley.
Shadwell's unfinished works do yet impart,
Great proofs of force of nature, none of art.   45
With just bold strokes he dashes, here and there,
Showing great mastery, with little care;
And scorns to varnish his good touches o'er,
To make the fools, and women, praise 'em more.
But Wycherley, earns hard, whate'er he gains,   50
He wants no judgement, nor he spares no pains;
He frequently excels, and at the least,
Makes fewer faults, than any of the best.
Waller, by nature, for the bays designed,
With force, and fire, and fancy unconfined,   55
In panegyrics, does excel mankind.

30–6 'The ancient writers of the comic stage / Our imitation here may well engage, / Though read not by Tigellius, smooth of face, / Or yonder ape, of horrible grimace / Calvus; Catullus better suit their vein, / Whose wanton songs they chant in tuneful strain' (1.10:16–19). A long passage about Lucilius's Greco-Roman macaronic is omitted.

32–3 Rochester's friend Sir George Etherege, an established comic dramatist, was writing *The Man of Mode* (1676), an 'original' because he draws 'in the truth of nature'; Rochester is supposedly the 'original' of the play's central character Dorimant.

34–6 Thomas Flatman's Cowleian *Poems and Songs* came out in 1674. Cotton's verses for the 1682 edition compliment Flatman on his management of the 'rough, but ready horse' of Fancy (14); but Rochester sexualizes and degrades the usual equestrian metaphor.

37–40 'Let swelling Furius on the affrighted stage / Mur-

der poor Memnon, or in muddy rage / Deform the Head of Rhine . . . Be thine, fond madman, some vile school to choose, / Where to repeat the labours of your Muse' (1.10:36–7, 74–5). The *Sophonisba* (1675) of Nathaniel Lee (who hoped the world might 'pardon the sallies of youth') features Hannibal and Scipio. Richard Busby was the famous flogging headmaster of Westminster School.

41–53 'Of all mankind, in light and cheerful strain / Fundanius best can paint the comic scene, / The wily harlot, and the slave, who join / To wipe the miser of his darling coin' (1.10:40–2). Thomas Shadwell (unhappily famous as Mac Fleckno) began his dramatic career in 1668 with the successful *Sullen Lovers*, boasted he had written *The Libertine* in three weeks and had written nine plays by 1675; Wycherley's third play, *The Country Wife*, came out in 1675.

54–80 'Pollio in pure, iambic numbers sings / The tragic

He best can turn, enforce, and soften things,
To praise great conquerors, or to flatter kings.
　For pointed satires, I would Buckhurst choose,
The best good man, with the worst-natured Muse:　　　　　　60
For songs, and verses, mannerly, obscene,
That can stir nature up, by spring unseen,
And without forcing blushes, warm the Queen.
　Sedley, has that prevailing, gentle art,
That can with a resistless charm impart,　　　　　　　　　65
The loosest wishes to the chastest heart;
Raise such a conflict, kindle such a fire
Betwixt declining virtue, and desire;
Till the poor vanquished maid dissolves away,
In dreams all night, in sighs, and tears, all day　　　　　70
　Dryden, in vain tried this nice way of wit,
For he, to be a tearing blade thought fit,
But when he would be sharp, he still was blunt,
To frisk his frolic fancy, he'd cry "Cunt";
Would give the ladies, a dry bawdy bob,　　　　　　　　75
And thus he got the name of Poet Squab.
But to be just, 'twill to his praise be found,
His excellences, more than faults abound.
Nor dare I from his sacred temples tear,
That laurel, which he best deserves to wear.　　　　　　80
But does not Dryden find even Jonson dull?
Fletcher, and Beaumont, uncorrect, and full
Of lewd lines, as he calls 'em? Shakespeare's style
Stiff, and affected? To his own the while
Allowing all the justness that his pride,　　　　　　　　85
So arrogantly, had to these denied?

deeds of heroes and of kings; / And Varius in sublime and ardent vein / Supports the grandeur of the epic strain. / On Virgil all the rural Muses smile, / Smooth flow his lines, and elegant his style. / Satire alone remained, no easy strain, / Which Varro, and some others, tried in vain, / Where I, perhaps, some slight success may claim, / Though far inferior to the inventor's fame: / Nor from his head shall I presume to tear / That sacred wreath, he well deserves to wear' (1.10:42–9). Some MSS give Horace's Latin (1.10:49) for the last couplet, to mark the coincidence that Dryden actually was poet laureate. The departures from Horace are otherwise most marked in this section (61–76 have no real precedent). Waller, not only a 'natural' poet but a fitter laureate, is the English Pollio; but epic and pastoral or georgic poets are absent. Charles Sackville, Lord Buckhurst, supplies the place of Horace the satirist; he is the dedicatee of Dryden's versions of Juvenal and Persius (in whose preface the couplet at 59–60 is called 'insolent, sparing, and invidious'). Sir Charles Sedley stands for Horace the lyrist, praised for seductiveness. It is unclear which is praised in 61–3, but the arrangement here supposes Buckhurst; 'mannerly' and 'obscene' are here (following *1680*) both epithets: 'polite',

and something like 'sexy', perhaps by a misuse such as the Portuguese Queen Catherine might have employed.
71–80　Dryden is the type of the failed satirist, reverting to impertinent and unintended coarseness; and his bawdy 'dry bobs' ('teasings') with ladies, are like unfinished sex acts; he is not just 'lumpish' ('squab') but 'callow' (the 'squab' is an unfledged pigeon). The name, apparently the invention of Rochester or his circle, stuck.
81–6　'I said, his verse in muddy rapture flows, / And more his errors, than his beauties shows; / But, prithee, you that boast a critic's name / Don't you sometimes the mighty Homer blame? / Does not Lucilius, though of gentle strain, / Correct even Accius and reform his scene? / And in his pleasantry old Ennius rate, / When his dull lines want dignity and weight? / Yet when he speaks of his own right to fame / Confesses frankly their superior claim' (1.10:50–5). But where Lucilius was generous, Dryden is proud. Such strictures on the English poets are constant with him: Jonson's wittiest character is 'mortified to the world by much reading', Fletcher marked by 'redundancy of his matter [and] the incorrectness of his language', Shakespeare by 'lethargy of thought' (all from *Defence of the Epilogue*, 1673).

And may not I, have leave impartially
To search, and censure, Dryden's *Works*, and try,
If those gross faults, his choice pen does commit,
Proceed from want of judgement, or of wit?   90
Of if his lumpish fancy does refuse,
Spirit, and grace to his loose slattern Muse?
Five hundred verses, every morning writ,
Proves you no more a poet, than a wit:
Such scribbling authors, have been seen before,   95
Mustapha, the *English Princess*, forty more,
Were things perhaps composed in half an hour.
To write what may securely stand the test
Of being well read over thrice at least,
Compare each phrase, examine every line,   100
Weigh every word, and every thought refine;
Scorn all applause, the vile rout can bestow,
And be content to please those few, who know.
Canst thou be such a vain mistaken thing
To wish thy *Works* might make a playhouse ring,   105
With the unthinking laughter, and poor praise,
Of fops, and ladies, factious for thy plays?
Then send a cunning friend to learn thy doom,
From the shrewd judges in the drawing-room.
I've no ambition on that idle score,   110
But say with Betty Morrice, heretofore,
When a court-lady, called her Buckley's whore,
"I please one man of wit, am proud on 't too,
Let all the coxcombs, dance to bed to you."
Should I be troubled when the purblind knight,   115
Who squints more in his judgement, than his sight,
Picks silly faults, and censures what I write?
Or when the poor-fed poets of the town
For scraps, and coach-room cry my verses down?
I loath the rabble, 'tis enough for me,   120
If Sedley, Shadwell, Shepherd, Wycherley,
Godolphin, Butler, Buckhurst, Buckingham,
And some few more, whom I omit to name,
Approve my sense, I count their censure Fame.

87–97 'What then forbids our equal right to know / Why his own verses inharmonious flow? / Or whether in his subject lies the fault, / Or in himself, that they're not higher wrought, / Than if the art of verse were to confine / In ten low feet a cold, dull length of line, / Content his rhyming talents to display / In twice an hundred verses twice a day' (1.10:56–61). *Mustapha* is a tragedy by Robert Boyle (1665), the *English Princess* a tragedy by John Caryl (1667). Rochester drops the case of a poet who wrote enough for his works to supply his pyre, and the notion that had Lucilius been modern he would have polished his works.

98–114 'Would you a reader's just esteem engage? / Correct with frequent care the blotted page; / Nor strive the wonder of the crowd to raise, / But the few better judges learn to please . . . While I, like hissed Arbuscula unawed, / Despise the vulgar, since the knights applaud' (1.10:72–7). The praise of claques counts for nothing against the mis-

chievous ('shrewd') judgements delivered in private chambers. Neither Betty Morrice (apparently a well-known prostitute) nor Buckley (perhaps Henry Bulkeley) is identified in *1680*, and though 'Buckhurst' is sometimes read for 'Buckley' neither is properly identifiable.

115–24 'Say, shall that bug Pantilius move my spleen? / Shall I be tortured when a wretch obscene, / Or foolish Fannius, for a sordid treat / With sweet Tigellius, shall my verses rate? / Let Plotius, Varius, and Maecenas deign / With Virgil, Valgius, to approve my strain . . . Among my learned friends are many more, / Whose names I pass in modest silence o'er; / These I can wish to smile; enjoy their praise; / Hope to delight, and grieve if I displease' (1.10:78–90). Sir Carr Scrope is the 'purblind knight'. Sir Fleetwood Shepherd, the poet Sidney Godolphin, Samuel (*Hudibras*) Butler, and George Villiers, Duke of Buckingham (author of *The Rehearsal*) are added to the list of wise friends.

John Oldham (1653–1683)

Oldham's career is a succession of bids for literary glory, precociously terminated by smallpox when he was 30. When Oldham came down from Oxford in 1674 he returned for a while to his family home in Gloucestershire; his attempts to recommend himself to the local gentry failed to secure him any regular employment. He turned to the 'vile drudgery' of teaching to support himself (he was assistant master at Croydon School for about three years from 1676). His first printed work is an epithalamium for William and Mary (1677), written in a morning and promptly delivered to the Princess Mary. But it is as a satirist that he made his name – his so-called *Satire against Virtue* (1676, and printed without permission in 1679) immediately attracted the attention of its subject Rochester, one of whose more bizarre escapades it celebrates. Along with Sedley and Dorset, he called to interview the young poet in the school at Croydon. Oldham's movements after leaving Croydon are obscure; but he seems to have lived in London. On Rochester's recommendation he was supported by the Earl of Kingston, in whose house in Nottinghamshire he died. He wrote with some success in association with this circle of court wits of whose literary manners he was a more than adept mimic, and who cop-

ied his poems into their commonplace books along with their own. In the free version of Moschus's *Bion* (1680), Oldham casts himself as Rochester's unworthy heir. The debt to 'beloved Cowley' is evident from the first, and it saves him from addiction to mere lampooning, penetrates his adaptations of the classical satirists, and makes his English capable of Juvenalian indignation. But he owes to Rochester (along with a taste for Boileau) a flexible style, holding to his competence in declamatory modes, but moving unstiffly from them to the Horatian 'easy and familiar way of writing' ('Advertisement' to *Some New Pieces*). Oldham made three collections of his own work in his lifetime, *Satires upon the Jesuits and Some Other Pieces* (1681 and a corrected edition in 1682), *Some New Pieces* (1681) and *Poems, and Translations* (1683). On his death his publisher Hindmarsh brought out *Remains* (1684). The *Works* were first collected in 1684, and many times reprinted. The standard modern edition of *The Poems* is edited by Harold F. Brooks and Raman Selden (Oxford: Clarendon Press, 1987). The best account of the life and work is Paul Hammond's *John Oldham and the Classical Tradition* (Cambridge: Cambridge University Press, 1983).

The Lamentation for Adonis. Imitated out of the Greek of Bion of Smyrna. Pastoral

Some New Pieces (1681). An autograph fair copy of lines 170–95 is dated 'June 2. 81'. The Greek *Lament for Adonis*, generally attributed to Bion, is an Alexandrian literary imitation of the dirge sung at the festival of Adonis or Thammuz (when in 'In vain the Tyrian maids their wounded Thammuz mourn', Milton, *Nativity Ode*, 204). Along with the *Lament for Bion* by Moschus (imitated by Oldham in his elegy for Rochester) it establishes one influential pattern for funeral elegy. Oldham's Advertisement to *1681* notes Latin translations by 'several great masters', acknowledging in particular André Le Fèvre,

who 'has done it paraphrastically, but left a good part of the poem toward the latter end untouched [163–91], perhaps because he thought it not so capable of ornament, as the rest. Him I chiefly chose to follow, as being more agreeable to my way of translating, and where I was at a loss for want of his guidance, I was content to steer by own fancy.' The closer version by Stanley (1651) precedes Oldham's. What Ezra Pound praises in Oldham's *Bion* is admirable here too: its mastery of 'applied ornament' and its sustained melody, as if 'the writer has more difficulty in stopping than in continuing to sing.'

> I mourn Adonis, fair Adonis dead,
> He's dead, and all that's lovely, with him fled:
>   Come all ye Loves, come hither and bemoan
>   The charming sweet Adonis dead and gone:
> Rise from thy purple bed, and rich alcove,   5

1–3 Adonis was killed while hunting boar. He was the favourite of Venus here invited to mourn along with the

personified Loves, figured as her children.
5 *alcove* A still exotic word for a formal bed-recess.

Throw off thy gay attire, great Queen of Love:
Henceforth in sad and mournful weeds appear,
And all the marks of grief, and sorrow wear,
And tear thy locks, and beat thy panting breast,
And cry, My dear Adonis is deceased.   10
    I mourn Adonis, the soft Loves bemoan
    The gentle sweet Adonis dead and gone.
On the cold mountain lies the wretched youth,
Killed by a savage boar's unpitying tooth:
In his white thigh the fatal stroke is found,   15
Not whiter was that tooth, that gave the wound:
From the wide wound fast flows the streaming gore
And stains that skin which was all snow before:
His breath with quick short tremblings comes and goes,
And Death his fainting eyes begins to close: 20
From his pale lips the ruddy colour's fled,
Fled, and has left his kisses cold and dead:
Yet Venus never will his kisses leave,
The Goddess ever to his lips will cleave:
The kiss of her dear youth does please her still,   25
But her poor youth does not the pleasure feel:
Dead he feels not her love, feels not her grief,
Feels not her kiss, which might even life retrieve.
    I mourn Adonis, the sad Loves bemoan
    The comely fair Adonis dead and gone.   30
Deep in his thigh, deep went the killing smart,
But deeper far it goes in Venus' heart:
His faithful dogs about the mountain yell,
And the hard fate of their dead master tell:
The troubled nymphs alike in doleful strains   35
Proclaim his death through all the fields and plains:
But the sad goddess, most of all forlorn,
With love distracted, and with sorrow torn,
Wild in her look, and rueful in her air,
With garments rent, and with dishevelled hair,   40
Through brakes, through thickets, and through pathless ways,
Through woods, through haunts and dens of savages,
Undressed, unshod, careless of honour, fame,
And danger, flies, and calls on his loved name.
Rude brambles, as she goes, her body tear,   45
And her cut feet with blood the stones besmear.
She thoughtless of the unfelt smart flies on,
And fills the woods, and valleys with her moan,
Loudly does on the stars and Fates complain,
And prays them give Adonis back again: 50
But he, alas; the wretched youth, alas!
Lies cold and stiff, extended on the grass:
There lies he steeped in gore, there lies he drowned,
In purple streams, that gush from his own wound.
    All the soft band of Loves their Mother mourn,   55

---

9   The torn locks are from Le Fèvre.
27   The balance of love and grief are from Lefèvre.
35–6   They are mountain-nymphs in Bion.

37–50   Expanded from Bion's five lines.
43   *careless . . . name* A gloss on 'wailing for her Assyrian lord, calling on her boy'.

At once of beauty, and of love forlorn.
Venus has lost her lover, and each grace,
That sat before in triumph in her face,
By grief chased thence, has now forsook the place.
That day which snatched Adonis from her arms, 60
That day bereft the goddess of her charms.
   The woods and trees in murmuring sighs bemoan
   The fate of her Adonis dead and gone.
The rivers too, as if they would deplore
His death, with grief swell higher than before: 65
The flowers weep in tears of dreary dew,
And by their drooping heads their sorrow show:
But most the Cyprian Queen with shrieks, and groans,
Fills all the neighbouring hills, and vales, and towns:
"The poor Adonis dead!" is all her cry, 70
"Adonis dead!" sad Echo does reply.
   What cruel heart would not the Queen of Love
To melting tears, and soft compassion move,
When she saw how her wretched lover fell,
Saw his deep wound, saw it incurable? 75
Soon as her eyes his bleeding wounds surveyed,
With eager clips she did his limbs invade,
And these soft, tender, mournful things she said:
"Whither, O whither fliest thou, wretched boy,
Stay my Adonis, stay my only joy, 80
O stay, unhappy youth, at least till I
With one kind word bespeak thee, ere thou die,
Till I once more embrace thee, till I seal
Upon thy dying lips my last farewell.
Look up one minute, give one parting kiss, 85
One kiss, dear youth, to dry these flowing eyes:
One kiss as thy last legacy I'd fain
Preserve, no god shall take it off again.
Kiss, while I watch thy swimming eye-balls roll,
Watch thy last gasp, and catch thy springing soul. 90
I'll suck it in, I'll hoard it in my heart,
I with that sacred pledge will never part,
But thou wilt part, but thou art gone, far gone
To the dark shades, and leav'st me here alone.
Thou diest, but hopeless I must suffer life, 95
Must pine away with easeless endless grief.
Why was I born a goddess? why was I
Made such a wretch to want the power to die?
If I by death my sorrows might redress,

57–9 Oldham's addition.
62 *woods and trees* For Bion's hills and valleys.
65 *with grief swell higher* Oldham's addition; but he omits Bion's mountain springs.
66 *dreary* 'doleful', transferred from 'tears'.
67 Oldham's addition.
68 *Cyprian Queen* 'Venus'; but Bion means Cythera the island (as he has it, rather than Cyprus), not its Queen.
77 Oldham's addition: 'Embracing him fiercely, she wrapped herself in his body.' Spenser's Jupiter 'invades' Leda (*Faerie Queene*, 3.11.32).
79 Translates Le Fèvre.
89–90 Echoed by Pope: 'See my lips tremble, and my eye-balls roll, / Suck my last breath, and catch the flying soul!' (*Eloisa to Abelard*, 323–4).
89–96 Developed from a line.
97–110 Developed from hints, mainly out of Le Fèvre.

If the cold grave could to my pains give ease,   100
I'd gladly die, I'd rather nothing be
Than thus condemned to immortality:
In that vast empty void, and boundless waste,
We mind not what's to come, nor what is past.
Of life, or death we know no difference,   105
Nor hopes, nor fears at all affect our sense:
But those who are of pleasure once bereft,
And must survive, are most unhappy left:
To ravenous sorrow they are left a prey,
Nor can they ever drive despair away.   110
  "Take, cruel Proserpine, take my loved boy,
Rich with my spoils, do thou my loss enjoy.
Take him relentless goddess, for thy own,
Never till now wast thou my envy grown.
Hard fate! that thus the best of things must be   115
Always the plunder of the grave, and thee:
The grave, and thou now all my hopes engross,
And I for ever must Adonis lose.
Thou'rt dead, alas! alas! my youth, thou'rt dead,
And with thee all my pleasures too are fled: 120
They're all like fleeting vanished dreams passed o'er,   ⎫
And nought but the remembrance left in store   ⎪
Of tasted joys ne'er to be tasted more: ⎬
With thee my cestus, all my charms are gone,   ⎪
Thy Venus must thy absence ever moan,   ⎬   125
And spend the tedious live-long nights alone.   ⎭
Ah! heedless boy, why wouldst thou rashly choose
Thyself to dangerous pleasures to expose?
Why wouldst thou hunt? why wouldst thou any more
Venture with dogs to chase the foaming boar?   130
Thou wast all fair to mine, to human eyes,
But not (alas!) to those wild savages.
One would have thought thy sweetness might have charmed
The roughest kind, the fiercest rage disarmed:
Mine (I am sure) it could; but woe is thee!   135
All wear not eyes, all wear not breasts like me."
  In such sad words the dame her grief did vent,
While the winged Loves kept time with her complaint:
As many drops of blood as from the wound
Of slain Adonis fell upon the ground,   140
So many tears, and more you might have told,
That down the cheeks of weeping Venus rolled:
Both tears, and blood to new-born flowers give rise,
Hence roses spring, and thence anemones.

111–14 *Prosperine* Bion's Venus resigns her Adonis to death, personified in Proserpina as Queen of the Underworld. Oldham (like Stanley, but probably on a hint from Le Fèvre) makes the two goddesses rivals, and Proserpina the object of Venus's envy.

117 *engross* 'absorb'.

124 'My cestus (that is, my charms) has perished along with you.' *Tatler* 147 (1709) writes: 'This *cestus* was a fine parti-coloured girdle, which as Homer [*Iliad*, 14:214–17] tells us, has all the attractions of the sex wrought into it'. It is at once the symbol and the cause of love's power.

130–6 Developed from a simple question about why, being beautiful, he had risked the hunt.

144 'From the blood spring the roses, from the tears anemones.'

Cease, Venus, in the woods to mourn thy love,   145
Thou'st vented sighs, thou'st lavished tears enough:
See! goddess, where a glorious bed of state
Does ready for thy dear Adonis wait:
This bed was once the scene of love, and joy,
But now must bear the wretched, murdered boy: 150
There lies he, like a pale, and withered flower,
Which some rude hand had cropped before its hour:
Yet smiles, and beauties still live in his face,
Which death can never frighten from their place.
There let him lie upon that conscious bed,   155
Where you love's mysteries so oft have tried:
When you've enjoyed so many an happy night,
Each lengthened into ages of delight.
There let him lie, there heaps of flowers strow,
Roses' and lilies' store upon him throw,   160
And myrtle garlands lavishly bestow:
Pour myrrh, and balm, and costliest ointments on,
Flowers are faded, ointments worthless grown,
Now thy Adonis, now thy youth is gone,
Who was all sweetnesses comprised in one.   165
   In purple wrapped, Adonis lies in state,
A troop of mourning Loves about him wait:
Each does some mark of their kind sorrow show,
One breaks his shafts, the other unstrings his bow,
A third upon his quiver wreaks his hate,   170
As the sad causes of his hasty fate:
This plucks his bloody garments off, that brings
Water in vessels from the neighbouring springs,
Some wash his wound, some fan him with their wings:
   All equally their mother's loss bemoan,   175
   All moan for poor Adonis dead and gone.
Sad Hymen too the fatal loss does mourn,
His tapers all to funeral tapers turn,
And all his withered nuptial garlands burn:
His gay, and airy songs are heard no more,   180
But mournful strains, that hopeless love deplore.
Nor do the Graces fail to bear a part
With wretched Venus in her pain and smart:
The poor Adonis dead! by turns they cry,
And strive in grief the goddess to outvie.   185
The Muses too in softest lays bewail
The hapless youth, and his fled soul recall:
But all in vain; – ah! numbers are too weak
To call the lost, the dead Adonis back:
Not all the powers of verse, or charms of love   190

151–2 Oldham's addition.
155 *conscious* 'full of memories'.
158 Oldham's addition.
159–63 Oldham's list is more specific than Bion's.
172 Bion specifies Adonis's sandal.
177–81 The cry on the wedding god Hymen ('Hymen, Io
Hymen') is replaced by the mournful 'Ai ton Adonin'.

178 The wedding torch inverted signifies death. Bion's
Hymen merely extinguishes his torches.
186 *Muses* Bion has the weeping Fates attempt to revive
him.
188 'My verses cannot revive Adonis.'

The deaf remorseless Proserpine can move.
Cease then, sad Queen of Love, thy plaints give o'er,
Till the next year reserve thy grief in store:
Reserve thy sighs and tears in store till then,
Then thou must sigh, then thou must weep again.   195

191   *deaf* fierce (MS, corrected to 'deaf') Oldham's addition; Stanley's version (in a passage barely recognizable in Oldham) makes Pluto deaf.

193   Adonis was mourned yearly after midsummer.

A Letter from the Country to a Friend in Town, giving an Account of the Author's Inclinations to Poetry. Written in July, 1678

Some New Pieces (1681). A reply written from Croydon to his lawyer friend John Spencer's fine *Epistle* of March 1678 ('Dear Sir, I promised poetry'), printed from Oldham's MS notebook (where it survives along with drafts of the reply) as Appendix I of Brooks-Selden. Topics raised in Spencer's letter are picked up by Oldham (the account of wit beginning at line 41, of contemporary poetry at 64, of rhyme at 119); but much tried out in draft (reflections on town and country, a defence of satire) is abandoned or resituated. The letter is dominated instead by an account (from 163) of a love affair with his own creativity, which while it takes hints from Dryden's account of the imagination, is more powerfully detailed.

As to that poet (if so great a one, as he,
May suffer in comparison with me)
When heretofore in Scythian exile pent,
To which he by ungrateful Rome was sent,
If a kind paper from his country came,   5
And wore subscribed some known, and faithful name;
That like a powerful cordial, did infuse
New life into his speechless gasping Muse,
And strait his genius, which before did seem
Bound up in ice, and frozen as the clime,   10
By its warm force, and friendly influence thawed,
Dissolved apace, and in soft numbers flowed:
Such welcome here, dear Sir, your letter had
With me shut up in close constraint as bad:
Not eager lovers, held in long suspense,   15
With warmer joy, and a more tender sense
Meet those kind lines, which all their wishes bless,
And sign, and seal delivered happiness:
My grateful thoughts so throng to get abroad,
They overrun each other in the crowd: 20
To you with hasty flight they take their way,

1–14   The long simile invokes Ovid's wintry exile in 'Scythian' Tomis on the Black Sea, whence his *Tristia* (which also regrets previous licentious writing) and the *Epistulae ex Ponto*. The reply to Rufinus (*ex Ponto*, 1.3:9–10) may supply the hint for Oldham: 'I was failing, but came to life again at your words, just as the pulse [*vena*, which may mean 'genius'] returns when we take strong wine [*infuso . . . mero*]. Oldham's lines 7–8 rewrite his own 'For cordials to prolong their gasping life' (*Satires upon the Jesuits*, 3:272), borrowed from Cowley on Broghill's praise: 'A cordial that restores our fainting breath' (*Upon occasion of . . . Verses of my Lord Broghill's*, 67).

13   Recasting Cowley's 'Such comfort to us here your letter gives' (*Answer to . . . Verses Sent me to Jersey*, 6), whose whole opening suggests Oldham's.

17   *lines* 'marriage lines'.

19–20   Rewriting the probably earlier *To Madam L. E.* (itself adapting Cowley): 'Our Joys at first so thronged to get abroad, / They hindered one another in the crowd.'

20   *overrun* 'trample'.

And hardly for the dress of words will stay.
   Yet pardon, if this only fault I find,
That while you praise too much, you are less kind:
Consider, Sir, 'tis ill and dangerous thus   25
To overlay a young and tender Muse:
Praise, the fine diet, which we're apt to love,
If given to excess, does hurtful prove:
Where it does weak, distempered stomachs meet
That surfeits, which should nourishment create.   30
Your rich perfumes such fragrancy dispense,
Their sweetness overcomes, and palls my sense:
On my weak head you heap so many bays,
I sink beneath 'em, quite oppressed with praise,
And a resembling fate with him receive,   35
Who in too kind a triumph found his grave,
Smothered with garlands, which applauders gave.
   To you these praises justlier all belong,
By alienating which, yourself you wrong:
Whom better can such commendations fit   40
Than you, who so well teach and practise wit?
Verse, the great boast of drudging fools, from some,
Nay most of scribblers with much straining come:
They void 'em dribbling, and in pain they write,
As if they had a strangury of wit: 45
Your pen uncalled they readily obey,
And scorn your ink should flow so fast as they:
Each strain of yours so easy does appear,
Each such a graceful negligence does wear,
As shows you have none, and yet want no care.   50
None of your serious pains or time they cost,
But what thrown by, you can afford for lost:
If such the fruits of your loose leisure be,
Your careless minutes yield such poetry;
We guess what proofs your genius would impart,   55
Did it employ you, as it does divert:
But happy you, more prudent, and more wise,
With better aims have fixed your noble choice.
While silly I all thriving arts refuse,
And all my hopes, and all my vigour lose,   60
In service on that worst of jilts, a Muse,
For gainful business court ignoble ease,
And in gay trifles waste my ill-spent days.

23–37 Rehearsing the dangers of praise in *Upon occasion of . . . Verses of my Lord Broghill's*, 63–77.

26 *overlay* 'overwhelm'.

27–32 'A good name is better than precious ointment' (Ecclesiastes 7: 1); but 'He that blesseth his friend with a loud voice . . . it shall be counted a curse to him' (Proverbs 27: 14).

33 *bays* 'laurels'.

35–7 Sophocles died of joy on wining the prize for tragedy (Pliny, *Natural History*, 7.54.1); but the improbable smothering seems fictitious.

39 *alienating* 'transferring'.

42 *Verse* Understood (perhaps on the French model) as plural.

45 *strangury* Normally a 'difficulty of urine, attended with pain' (Johnson).

48 *strain* 'melody'; but 'easy' forces a witty oxymoron with the sense 'effort'.

53–8 The compliment to Spencer originally included his experience as a lawyer.

56 'If it were your occupation and not just your amusement'.

59 *thriving* 'profitable'.

Little I thought, my dearest friend, that you
Would thus contribute to my ruin too: 65
O'errun with filthy poetry, and rhyme,
The present reigning evil of the time,
I lacked, and (well I did myself assure)
From your kind hand I should receive a cure:
When (lo!) instead of healing remedies,   70
You cherish, and encourage the disease:
Inhuman you help the distemper on,
Which was before but too inveterate grown.
As a kind looker-on, who interest shares,
Though not in's stake, yet in his hopes and fears,   75
Would to his friend a pushing gamester do,
Recall his elbow when he hastes to throw;
Such a wise course you should have took with me,
A rash and venturing fool in poetry.
Poets are cullies, whom rook Fame draws in,   80
And wheedles with deluding hopes to win:
But, when they hit, and most successful are,
They scarce come off with a bare saving share.
   Oft (I remember) did wise friends dissuade,
And bid me quit the trifling barren trade.   85
Oft have I tried (Heaven knows) to mortify
This vile, and wicked lust of poetry:
But still unconquered it remains within,
Fixed as an habit, or some darling sin.
In vain I better studies there would sow,   90
Often I've tried, but none will thrive, or grow:
All my best thoughts, when I'd most serious be,
Are never from its foul infection free:
Nay (God forgive me) when I say my prayers,
I scarce can help polluting them with verse: 95
That fabulous wretch of old reversed I seem,
Who turn whate'er I touch to dross and rhyme.
   Oft to divert the wild caprice, I try   ⎫
If sovereign wisdom and philosophy   ⎬
Rightly applied, will give a remedy: ⎭   100
Straight the great Stagirite I take in hand,
Seek Nature, and myself to understand:
Much I reflect on his vast worth and fame,
And much my low, and grovelling aims condemn,
And quarrel, that my ill-packed fate should be   105
This vain, this worthless thing called poetry:

---

73   *before . . . grown* 'already only too well established'.

75–9   'As a sympathetic but financially disinterested spectator of a committed gambler would stop him in mid-throw, so you should have turned me from poetry.'

80   'Fame, like a card-sharp ['rook'], makes dupes ['cullies'] of poets.' Following Rochester 'Pride drew him in, as cheats, their bubbles catch, / And makes him venture, to be made a wretch' (*Satyr*, 31–2).

81   *wheedle* Blount, *Glossographia* gives it as 'a late word [1661] of fancy, and signifies to draw one in, by fair words or subtile insinuation, to act any thing of disadvantage or reproof'.

83   *saving* 'Not turning to loss, though not gainful' (Johnson).

86–7   *mortify . . . lust* 'kill . . . pleasure'.

96–7   What in the fable ('fabulous') Midas touched, turned to gold.

98   *caprice* Remembering Boileau whom 'a lewd caprice (for some great crime / I have committed) has condemned to rhyme' (*Satires*, 2, Butler).

101–10   Aristotle ('the Stagirite' from his birthplace) fails to cure him when he comes on the *Poetics*.

105   *ill-packed* 'stacked with losing cards'.

But when I find this unregarded toy
Could his important thoughts, and pains employ,
By reading there I am but more undone,
And meet that danger, which I went to shun.   110
Oft when ill-humour, chagrin, discontent
Give leisure my wild follies to resent,
I thus against my self my passion vent.
"Enough, mad rhyming sot, enough for shame,
Give o'er, and all thy quills to tooth-picks damn;   115
Didst ever thou the altar rob, or worse,
Kill the priest there, and maids' receiving force?
What else could merit this so heavy curse?
The greatest curse, I can, I wish on him,
(If there be any greater than to rhyme)   120
Who first did of the lewd invention think,
First made two lines with sounds resembling clink,
And, swerving from the easy paths of prose,
Fetters, and chains did on free sense impose:
Cursed too be all the fools, who since have went   125
Misled in steps of that ill precedent:
Want be entailed their lot:" – and on I go,
Wreaking my spite on all the jingling crew:
Scarce the belovèd Cowley 'scapes, though I
Might sooner my own curses fear, than he: 130
And thus resolved against the scribbling vein,
I deeply swear never to write again.
    But when bad company and wine conspire
To kindle, and renew the foolish fire,
Straightways relapsed, I feel the raving fit   135
Return, and strait I all my oaths forget:
The spirit, which I thought cast out before,
Enters again with stronger force, and power,
Worse than at first, and tyrannises more.
No sober good advice will then prevail,   140
Nor from the raging frenzy me recall:
Cool Reason's dictates me no more can move
Than men in drink, in Bedlam, or in love:
Deaf to all means which might most proper seem
Towards my cure, I run stark mad in rhyme: 145
A sad poor haunted wretch, whom nothing less
Than prayers of the Church can dispossess.

---

112   *resent* 'repent'.

115   *damn* 'condemn'.

117   *maids'* . . . *force* 'force the compliance of virgins'.

119–26   Remembering Boileau: 'May he be damned, who first found out that curse, / To imprison, and confine his thoughts in verse; / To hang so dull a clog upon his wit, / And make his reason to his rhyme submit' (*Satires*, 2, Butler). Jonson's *Fit of Rhyme against Rhyme* is the most energetic of such complaints. Dryden mounts a defence of rhyme in the Preface to *The Rival Ladies* (1664).

125   *went* 'gone' (then available as standard).

127   *Want . . . lot* 'May poverty be made their destiny.'

129–30   Presumably because Cowley acknowledged 'vari-ous and irregular' verse; and remembered because *Upon occasion of . . . Verses of my Lord Broghill's* Cowley revenges his disappointments on the poets.

131–6   Developed from Boileau: ' Sometimes . . . I give it over tired, and discontent; / And, damning the dull fiend a thousand times, / By whom I was possessed, forswear all rhymes; / But having cursed the Muses, they appear . . . Spite of myself, I straight take fire again' (*Satires*, 2, Butler).

134   *foolish fire* commonly for *ignis fatuus*, but here 'misplaced enthusiasm'.

143   *in Bedlam* 'mad' (Bedlam being the London hospital for the insane, rebuilt in 1676).

147   'Than exorcism'.

Sometimes, after a tedious day half spent,
When Fancy long has hunted on cold scent,
Tired in the dull, and fruitless chase of thought,   150
Despairing I grow weary, and give out:
As a dry lecher pumped of all my store,
I loathe the thing, 'cause I can do 't no more:
But, when I once begin to find again,
Recruits of matter in my pregnant brain,   155
Again more eager I the hunt pursue,
And with fresh vigour the loved sport renew:
Tickled with some strange pleasure, which I find,
And think a secrecy to all mankind,
I please myself with the vain, false delight,   160
And count none happy, but the fops that write.
'Tis endless, Sir, to tell the many ways,
Wherein my poor deluded self I please:
How, when the Fancy labouring for a birth,
With unfelt throes brings its rude issue forth: 165
How after, when imperfect shapeless thought
Is by the judgement into fashion wrought.
When at first search I traverse o'er my mind,
Nought but a dark, and empty void I find:
Some little hints at length, like sparks, break thence,   170
And glimmering thoughts just dawning into sense:
Confused a while the mixed ideas lie,
With nought of mark to be discovered by,
Like colours undistinguished in the night,
Till the dusk images, moved to the light,   175
Teach the discerning faculty to choose,
Which it had best adopt, and which refuse.
Here rougher strokes, touched with a careless dash,

---

149 Hobbes writes of thought working 'as a spaniel ranges the field till he find a scent' (*Leviathan*, 1.3), a passage developed by Dryden in the preface to *The Rival Ladies* and elsewhere.

152–7 A turn on the clichés of anti-enjoyment verse: 'I hate fruition, now 'tis past, / 'Tis all but nastiness at best' (Oldham, *A Fragment of Petronius*).

155 *recruits* 'refreshments'.

158–9 Taken from Dryden's *Prologue to The Wild Gallant Revived* (on masturbation): 'Pleased with some sport, which he alone does find / And thinks a secret to all human kind'.

164–85 'This worthless present was designed you long before it was a play; when it was only a confused mass of thoughts, tumbling over one another in the dark; when the fancy was yet in its first work, moving the sleeping images of things towards the light, there to be distinguished, and then either chosen or rejected by the judgement; it was yours ... before I could call it mine' (Dryden, dedication of *The Rival Ladies*, 1664).

165 *unfelt* Not like the 'smart' of the *Lamentation* (47) because the sufferer is distracted, but because the birth is easy. The ancient association of labour and poetry is energetically worked in Oldham: 'Thy pregnant mind ne'er struggled in

its birth, / But quick, and while it did conceive, brought forth; / The gentle throes of thy prolific brain / Were all unstrained, and without pain' (*To the Memory of . . . Charles Morwent*, 112–15), lines imitating Cowley on Orinda: 'Thou bring'st not forth with pain, / It neither travail is nor labour of thy brain' (37–8).

168–85 Vida characterizes the work of the undiscriminating artist: 'One black, confused, and undigested mass, / With a wild heap encumbers every part, / Nor ranged with grace, nor methodised with art' (*Ars Poetica*, 2:194–5, Pitt); and recommends he 'Inform the lump, and work it into grace, / And with new life inspire the unwieldy mass' (3:274–5). Cowley puts a more hopeful gloss on it: 'As first a various unformed hint we find / Rise in some god-like poet's fertile mind, / Till all the parts and words their places take, / And with just marches verse and music make' (*Davideis*, 1: 447–50).

172–6 Vida writes: 'For some [the Roman satirist Persius and the Hellenistic tragedian Lycophron] we know affect to lose the light, / Lost in forced figures, and involved in night, / Studious and bent to shun the common way, / They skulk in darkness, and abhor the day' (*Ars Poetica*, 3:15–19); *dusk* 'dusky' (a standard form).

Resemble the first sitting of a face:
There finished drafts in form more full appear,   180
And to their justness ask no further care.
Meanwhile with inward joy I proud am grown,
To see the work successfully go on:
And prize myself in a creating power,
That could make something, what was nought before.   185
   Sometimes a stiff, unwieldy thought I meet,
Which to my laws will scarce be made submit:
But, when, after expense of pains and time,
'Tis managed well, and taught to yoke in rhyme,
I triumph more, than joyful warriors would,   190
Had they some stout, and hardy foe subdued:
And idly think, less goes to their command,
That makes armed troops in well-placed order stand,
Than to the conduct of my words, when they
March in due ranks, are set in just array.   195
   Sometimes on wings of thought I seem on high,
As men in sleep, though motionless they lie,
Fledged by a dream, believe they mount and fly:
So witches some enchanted wand bestride,
And think they through the airy regions ride,   200
Where fancy is both traveller, way, and guide:
Then straight I grow a strange exalted thing,
And equal in conceit, at least a king:
As the poor drunkard, when wine stums his brains,
Anointed with that liquor, thinks he reigns.   205
Bewitched by these delusions 'tis I write
(The tricks some pleasant devil plays in spite),
And when I'm in the freakish trance, which I
Fond silly wretch, mistake for ecstasy,
I find all former resolutions vain,   210
And thus recant them, and make new again.
   "What was't, I rashly vowed? shall ever I
Quit my belovèd mistress, Poetry?
Thou sweet beguiler of my lonely hours,
Which thus glide unperceived with silent course: 215
Thou gentle spell, which undisturbed dost keep
My breast, and charm intruding care asleep:
They say, thou'rt poor, and unendowed, what tho?

---

179 'Resemble the sketch of a face after one sitting'.

182–5 Boileau, 'In triumph then my fury hastens on, / And I in private joy at what is done' (*Satires*, 7:46–8, Oldmixon).

186–95 Vida 'For oft unmanageable thoughts appear, / That mock his labour, and delude his care; / The impatient bard, with all his nerves applied, / Tries all the avenues on every side; / Resolved and bent the precipice to gain; / Though yet he labours at the rock in vain; / By his own strength and Heaven, with conquest graced, / He wins the important victory at last; / Stretched by his hands the vanquished monster lies, / And the proud triumph lifts him to the skies' (*Ars Poetica*, 1:589–98).

196–7 Vida, 'By thee [the Muse] inspired, the daring poet flies, / His soul mounts up, and towers above the skies' (*Ars Poetica*, 1: 547–8).

198 *fledged* 'winged'.

199–200 Cowley (*Sitting and Drinking in the Chair, made out of the Relics of Sir Francis Drake's Ship*) compares his own day-dreams to witches' 'fancied journeys in the air'.

201 Playing with 'the way, the truth, and the life' (John 14: 6).

204 *stums* 'puts in a ferment'.

218 *tho* 'then' (a Spenserism). The passage answers Spenser's ghost's dissuasions from poetry in *A Satire*.

For thee I this vain, worthless world forgo:
Let wealth, and honour be for Fortune's slaves,   220
The alms of fools, and prize of crafty knaves:
To me thou art, whate'er the ambitious crave,
And all that greedy misers want, or have:
In youth, or age, in travel, or at home,
Here, or in town, at London, or at Rome,   225
Rich, or a beggar, free, or in the Fleet,
Whate'er my fate is, 'tis my fate to write."
    Thus I have made my shrifted Muse confess,
Her secret foibles, and her weaknesses:
All her hid faults she sets exposed to view,   230
And hopes a gentle cónfessor in you:
She hopes an easy pardon for her sin,
Since 'tis but what she is not wilful in,
Nor yet has scandalous nor open been.
Try if your ghostly counsel can reclaim   235
The heedless wanton from her guilt and shame:
At least be not ungenerous to reproach
That wretched frailty, which you've helped debauch.
    'Tis now high time to end, for fear I grow
More tedious than old doters, when they woo,   240
Than travelled fops, when far-fetched lies they prate.
Or flattering poets, when they dedicate.
No dull forgiveness I presume to crave,
Nor vainly for my tiresome length ask leave:
Lest I, as often formal coxcombs use,   245
Prolong that very fault, I would excuse:
May this the same kind welcome find with you
As yours did here, and ever shall; Adieu.

224–7 From Boileau, 'Though Heaven secured me in a lasting peace, / With all the city pomp, or country ease [A Rome ou à Paris, aux champs ou dans la ville] . . . Yet merry, melancholy, rich or poor [*gueux*], / I should not cease to rhyme, but write the more (*Satires*, 7: 65–8, Oldmixon), restoring touches lost from the original in Horace, 'Then, whether age my peaceful hours attend . . . Or rich or poor; at Rome; to exile driven: / Whatever lot by powerful Fate is given: / Yet write I will' (*Satires*, 2.1:57–60, Francis).
226 *in the Fleet* 'in gaol' (from the London prison that stood by the waterway so called).
231 *cónfessor* Stress on the first syllable was standard.

Anne Wharton (1659–1685)

Anne Wharton (née Lee) married the disreputable Thomas Wharton (author of 'Lilliburlero' and a Whig grandee) in 1673. Neglected by her husband, she inherited from her uncle Lord Rochester (for whom she wrote funeral verses under the name Urania, published in *Poems by Several Hands*, 1685) a spiritual mentor in Gilbert Burnet, more than a dozen of whose letters to her survive. She inherited also easy access to Waller, to Aphra Behn (both of whom wrote responses to her elegy on Rochester) and others. Of what she wrote, all that reached print while she lived were the elegy on Rochester and a reply to Waller's praise of it. Brief meditations and biblical paraphrases appeared posthumously, and (more in tune with the piece below), a version of Ovid's *Penelope to Ulysses* was given in *Ovid's Epistles translated by Several Hands* (1712). *The Surviving Works of Anne Wharton*, edited by G. Greer and S. Hastings (Stump Cross Books, 1997) enlarges the canon, and includes a Life, complimentary verses addressed to Wharton and Burnet's Letters. It is the source of the text below, taken from a collection belonging to the Earl of Leicester, Holkham Hall, MS 691.

A Paraphrase on the Last Speech of Dido in Virgil's Aeneis

Wharton works from *Aeneid*, 4:642–62, and would have known (among others) Denham's version, the *Passion of Dido for Aeneas* (1668). Robert Wolseley, another of the respondents to the *Elegy on Rochester*, translated Virgil's treatment of the bitter underworld reunion of Dido and Aeneas (*Aeneid*, 6:442–76) in *Examen Poeticum* (1693). The punctuation is editorial.

Now Dido trembles with amaze and rage;
Not that her fears the following ills presage:
Fear is a passion only thoughts divide
From gentle hope, they are so near allied.
With horror filled, anticipating fear,   5
Already wreaked of fell despair,
All passions mingled in her bosom strove;
Tears of disdain, of sorrow and of love
Do all at once from her swoln eyes distil
And in her hand she grasps the fatal steel.   10
The ghastly King of Terrors now appears
In all her looks, and all her actions steers;
In solemn state and in undecent pride
Round her in triumph the cold Conqueror rides.
To the inner part o' th' fatal house she ran   15
With fury filled, and fiercely rushes on.
Mounting the pile, she unsheathes the Trojan sword
(Not for this purpose given by its lord);
Surveying then the garments bought from Troy,
And last the bed which every hope destroys   20
(The bed where born and buried were her joys),
She paused a while, and stopped those showers of tears:

3–4 'For things we value most are companied / With fear as well as hope' (Henry More, *Psychathanasia*, 3.1.15–17).
5–6 Horror (the 'amaze and rage' of 1) is the dominant passion; since she does not clearly foreknow what awaits her, fear is only an obscure prospect; she has already vented ('wreaked') her despair.

11–14 'A ghastly paleness death's approach portends' (Denham) simplifies Virgil's description of Dido's hysteria, but encourages Wharton's elaborated personification. When Eve asks Raphael in Dryden's *State of Innocence*, 'What is death?' he replies, 'In vision, thou shalt see his grizzly face, / The King of Terrors, raging in thy race' (5.1).

The sun was clouded o'er, but setting clears.
Then on the bed she gently lays her down,
And in these words breathes out her dying groans: 25
"You, who, when gentle fates and mighty Jove
Approved my bliss, vouchsafed to crown my love,
You, who with them were to my joys agreed,
Receive my soul when from my body freed,
Free me from all the cares which I sustain;   30
End herewith my life and with it end my pain.
I've lived, and finished what the fates ordain:
Now my great image must to earth repair,
And my soul wander through the unbounded air.
By me a famous city has been built   35
Though in its finished walls my blood is spilt;
My husband is revenged, his foe is dead,
Though from his tainted veins my blood was shed;
The debt he owed, this forfeit life has paid.
Thus doth my happiness in death appear   40
Too happy had I been too void of care
If the false Trojan ne'er had landed here."
At this the sighs burst from her tortured breast
And to the pillow where she found no rest
Her head o'ercharged with busy thoughts she pressed: 45
"But shall we die thus unrevenged," she cried,
"Doth it not check our greatness and our pride?
Yet thus I must and will; for what can be
Revenge against the dearest part of me?
Yet thus alone it pleases me to go   50
To travel through the dismal shades below;
And may the cruel cause of this my fate
From off the deep behold my wretched state.
May these flames glad his eyes and please his heart
In which alas I have no longer part;   55
May they reveal the omen of my end
On him no more for succour I depend.
To him the omen's good, to me it's ease
Since in these flames I can Aeneas please.

24 'Then on the guilty bed she gently lays / Herself'
(Denham).
33 Translates literally Virgil's *Aeneid* 4:644; but Wharton
seems to imagine not a shade in the underworld, but a body
underground: the soul is released upwards.
35–9 Her life is fulfilled in having built Carthage, though
she dies in it; spilling her own blood is a compensation for
her brother's wicked murder of her husband Sichaeus, and
the brother's crime paid for in the forfeit of her life. The
MS reads 'his forfeit life' for 'this forfeit life'.

48–9 Wharton's Dido abjures revenge against the beloved
Aeneas. Unauthorized by Virgil but closer to him, Denham
proposes that Dido dies in hope of reunion with her dead
husband: 'Thus, thus with joy to thy Sichaeus fly. / My
conscious foe my funeral fire shall view / From sea, and
may that omen him pursue'. Signs at parting are especially
'ominous'.

Index of Authors Cited

The names of English poets and dramatists in the notes are not normally included in this list, which serves to identify the more important authors and translators cited. Classical authors are usually available in parallel-text editions with modern translations in the Loeb series, cited only exceptionally. The most useful seventeenth-century editions of Latin authors are those in the so-called Delphin ('In usum Delphini') series edited under the direction of Pierre Daniel Huet. The most useful listings of classical literature in English are H. R. Palmer, *List of English Editions and Translations of Greek and Latin Classics printed before 1641* (London: Bibliographical Society, 1911), and Stuart Gillespie, 'A Checklist of Restoration English Translations of Classical Greek and Latin Poetry', *Translation and Literature*, 1 (1992), 52–68.

Agrippa. Henricus Cornelius Agrippa (1486–1535) wrote an influential cabbalistic account of the world in *De Occulta Philosophia* (1510, revised 1533); the *De Incertitudine et Vanitate Scientiarum* (1526) marked a reversion to simple pieties. James Sanford's translation of the latter, *Of the Vanity and Uncertainty of Artes and Sciences*, had two editions, 1569 and 1575.

Alciati. The *Emblemata* or illustrated epigrams of the Italian jurist Andrea Alciati (1492–1550) were first published in 1531. Many editions followed, of which Tozzi's (Padua, 1621, reprinted in facsimile, New York: Garland, 1976), regarded as standard, is with its commentary a readily accessible encyclopaedia of Renaissance iconography and mythography. Some of Alciati's emblems were incorporated in Geoffrey Whitney's *Choice of Emblems* (1586); there is a modern translation by Betty Knott (Aldershot: Scolar, 1996).

Anacreon. The songs of Anacreon of Teos (570–485 BCE), concerned with love and wine, survive only as fragments. From Stephanus's hugely influential edition (Paris, 1554) of a collection of Hellenistic imitations (now known as the *Anacreontea*) he was credited with the collection of complete poems, also on love and wine, by which his name remains best known. Cowley's version of *The Grasshopper* is given here. The fragments of Anacreon and the *Anacreontea* are given together in the second volume of the Loeb *Greek Lyric*, ed. David A. Campbell (Cambridge and London: Harvard University Press and Heinemann, 1988).

Apuleius. The *Metamorphoses* (or *Golden Ass*) of Apuleius (born CE *c*.123) contains horror stories, ribald comic stories, descriptions of social and religious life in antiquity, and (most famously) a Platonic allegory of the soul. William Adlington's version, *The Eleven Books of the Golden Ass, containing the Metamorphosis of the Lucius Apuleius with the Marriage of Cupid and Psyche* (1566), was reprinted continuously up to 1639; it formed the basis of Stephen Gaselee's Loeb version (London: Heinemann, 1915).

Aquinas. Before modern times, the major Latin edition of the works of Saint Thomas Aquinas (1225?–1274) was the 'Editio Piana' (from Pius V) published in Rome (1570–1). A useful modern edition of the Latin *Summa Theologiae* is published by the Dominicans in the Biblioteca de Autores Cristianos (Madrid, 1961–5); the most accessible English edition is the *Summa Theologica*, adapted from the English Dominican version, in the series Great Books of the Western World, 2 vols (Chicago: Encyclopaedia Britannica, 1990).

Ariosto. The *Orlando Furioso* of Ludovico Ariosto (1474–1533) appeared first in 1516 and underwent revision as late as 1532; it was translated into English by Sir John Harington (1591, revised as late as 1634 and much reprinted through the century). There is a modern edition of Harington's version by Robert McNulty (Oxford: Clarendon Press, 1972).

Aristotle. Aristotle (384–322 BCE) supplies the foundation for the organization of Western intellectual life. The standard from 1590 was the Greek–Latin edition of the works prepared by Isaac Casaubon; but Aristotle was normally read through traditional (scholastic) commentary. No genuine Aristotelian text was translated into English before 1700; English abridgements of major texts such as the *Nicomachean Ethics* and the *Politics* were available, and include Hobbes's *Brief of the Art of Rhetoric* (1637). The standard modern translation (by J. A. Smith and W. D. Ross) is revised as the *Complete Works*, ed. Jonathan Barnes, 2 vols (Princeton: Princeton University Press, 1984).

Aubrey, John (1626–1697). The standard edition of *Brief Lives, Chiefly of Contemporaries, set down . . . between the Years 1669 and 1696* is by Andrew Clark, 2 vols (Oxford: Clarendon Press, 1898).

Augustine (354–430). The *Confessions* were translated by Donne's friend, a convert to Catholicism, Sir Toby Matthew (St Omer, 1620; Paris, 1638), and by William Watts (1631). The *City of God* was translated by John Healey (1610, revised 1620). The *Patrologia Latina*, 32–47 (1845–9, but in fact a seventeenth-century edition) is the nearest to a complete edition of the Latin. The largest translated collection is in the series of *Nicene and Post-Nicene Fathers of the Christian Church*; the Loeb Classical Library includes *Confessions* (2 vols, using Watts's translation), *City of God* (7 vols, various translators), and *Select Letters* (J. H. Baxter).

Bacon. The various works of Francis Bacon (1561–1626) are collected in the edition by J. Spedding, R. L. Ellis and D. D. Heath, 7 vols (1857–59), supplemented by Spedding's *Letters and the Life* (1861–74). The only seventeenth-century attempt at a collection is in the *Opera* (Frankfurt, 1665). Works published in Bacon's lifetime include the *Essays* (1597, enlarged and revised 1612, 1625, translated into Latin by, among others, Ben Jonson for the 1638 *Opera Moralia*), *The Advancement of Learning* (1605, translated by, among others, George Herbert as the *De Augmentis Scientiarum*, 1623) and the *Translation of Certain Psalms* (1625), dedicated to Herbert. The *Instauratio Magna* outlined in the *Novum Organum* (1620) would itself have brought together much of the material scattered and

incomplete in mainly posthumous publications.

Bible. Unless otherwise indicated, quotations are from the King James ('Authorized') Version of 1611. The Geneva Bible (the 'Breeches Bible'), prepared by exiles from the Marian persecutions of the 1550s, was first published in 1560 in Geneva, and in subsequent editions (140 before 1644) revised. Its tendentious annotation (sometimes transferred to later editions of the Authorized Version), made it welcome to Calvinistically inclined readers and abhorrent to others. There is a facsimile edition of the Cambridge Geneva Bible of 1591 (Cambridge: Cambridge University Press, 1992). The Rheims–Douai Version of the New Testament, prepared by Catholic refugees from the Elizabethan persecutions of the 1560s, was first published in 1582 in Rheims, the temporary site of the English College normally at Douai; the publication, in two volumes, of the whole was delayed until 1609–10; it is often reprinted. A range of English versions is available on-line from Chadwyck-Healey's *Bible in English*.

Bion. Despite its classification, the surviving work of Bion (flourishing 100 BCE) is not strictly bucolic. Stanley (*Poems*, 1651) translates a selection of the fragments as well as the *Epitaph on Adonis*. Oldham's version of 1681 is given here.

Boethius. The most famous work of the Christian Anicius Manlius Severinus Boethius (480–524 CE) is the largely Neoplatonic *Consolation of Philosophy*, in mixed prose and verse. The whole has been translated many times. Chaucer's prose version is famous if little read. The *Five Books of Philosophical Comfort* (1609) by 'J. T.' (in fact the Jesuit Michael Walpole) is the basis for the Loeb version of H. F. Stewart and E. K. Rand (London: Heinemann, 1918). There are many selections (notably by Queen Elizabeth, Phineas Fletcher, Henry Vaughan).

Boileau. The *Satires* of Nicolas Boileau (1636–1711) circulated in manuscript before their publication over the fifty years from 1666. His translation of Longinus's *On the Sublime* (1674, and his *Reflections on Longinus*, 1694), and *L'Art poétique* (1674) established him as a leading apologist for the Ancients in the Battle of the Ancients and Moderns. Sir William Soame's translation of *L'Art poétique*, heavily revised by Dryden, was published anonymously in 1683. The Satires were translated by, among others, Butler, Oldham and Oldmixon.

Book of Common Prayer. *The Book of the Common Prayer and Administration of the Sacraments, and other Rites and Cermonies of the Church after the Use of the Church of England* (1549), prepared under the direction of Archbishop Thomas Cranmer, established the form of worship for Anglican England. Its Puritan revision of 1552, withdrawn when Queen Mary brought back Roman Catholic liturgical practice, was reimposed with some changes under Queen Elizabeth in 1559. It persisted with further revisions in a Puritan direction through 1604 and, after its proscription during the Interregnum, with other revisions through 1662. Its versions of the Psalms in particular, prescribed to be read through each month, impressed themselves on the English language. The Order of Confirmation contains a Catechism. There is a useful edition of the 1662 version edited by Diarmaid MacCulloch (London: Everyman's Library, 1999).

Brand. The *Observations on Popular Antiquities: Including the Whole of Mr [Henry] Bourne's 'Antiquitates Vulgares'* of John Brand (1744–1806) was first published in 1777; it was revised and enlarged by Sir Henry Ellis, 3 vols (1849–53), and W. C. Hazlitt, 3 vols (1870).

Browne. The standard edition of the *Complete Works and Correspondence* of Sir Thomas Browne (1605–82) is by Geoffrey Keynes, 6 vols (London: Faber, 1928–31, revised 1964); but it is locally superseded by *Pseudodoxia Epidemica*, ed. Robin Robbins, 2 vols (Oxford: Clarendon Press, 1981); Robbins has also prepared an annotated popular edition of *Religio Medici and Hydriotaphia; and The Garden of Cyrus* (Oxford: Clarendon Press, 1972).

Burton, Robert (1577–1640). The first edition of the *Anatomy of Melancholy* appeared in 1621; it was revised and augmented in editions of 1624, 1628, 1632, 1638 and in the posthumous sixth edition of 1651. This last revision was reprinted in 1660 and 1676. The standard modern edition, still to be completed, is by Thomas C. Faulkner, Nicolas K. Kiessling and Rhonda L. Blair, 3 vols of text (Oxford: Clarendon Press, 1989–94); only the first volume of commentary has been published so far (1998). The Everyman edition, 3 vols (London: Dent, 1932), is frequently reprinted. The *Anatomy* is divided by Partition, Section, Member and Subsection, which gives the form of the citations.

Calvin, Jean (1509–1564). The *Institutes* were first published in 1536 (in Latin, revised through many editions up to 1559), and in 1541 (in French, revised up to 1560). The first English translation (1561, and much reprinted) is by Thomas Norton, author with Sackville of *Gorboduc*. The standard modern translation is *Institutes of the Christian Religion*, ed. John T. McNeill, trans. Ford Lewis Battles, 2 vols (Philadelphia: Westminster Press, 1960). Calvin's *Commentaries* are important, particularly on the Psalms; the first English translation (1571) is by Arthur Golding (the translator of Ovid).

Casimir. The Polish Jesuit Maciej Kazimierz Sarbiewski (1595–1640) was the 'Christian Horace'. His odes, epodes and epigrams were published first in 1631, and many times reprinted. A Latin and English selection is given in *The Odes of Casimir* by G. Hils (1646), of which there is a facsimile reprint introduced by Maren-Sofie Røstvig (Los Angeles: Augustan Reprint Society no. 44, 1953).

Castiglione. *Il Cortegiano* of Baldassare Castiglione (1478–1529) was translated by Sir Thomas Hoby as *The Courtier . . . divided into Four Books. Very necessary and profitable for young Gentlemen and Gentlewomen abiding at Court* (1561). The Latin version by Bartholomew Clerke (1571) had even greater success. The Fourth Book contains a long oration on Platonic love.

Catullus. Gaius Valerius Catullus (84–54 BCE), accounted 'learned' by his contemporaries (and by Ben Jonson) for his importing of Greek literary kinds to Rome, is immediately influential as an amatory epigrammatist: the fortunes of *Catullus 5* earlier in the century are treated by Gordon Braden, '*Vivamus, Mea Lesbia* in the English Renaissance', *English Literary Renaissance*, 9 (1979), 199–224; it remained a favourite at the century's end. Catullus also stabilized the form of the literary epithalamium.

Cicero.   Marcus Tullius Cicero (106–43 BCE) was read more for his supposed wisdom (sometimes in collections of *sententiae*) than his style (often energetically rejected); in English printings and translations of his work, he is overwhelmingly represented as a philosopher (of duty in the *De Officiis*, of friendship in the *De Amicitia*, of the conditions of happiness in the *Tusculan Disputations*, of age in the *De Senectute*). But schoolboys learned Latin from his letters (as they did later from his orations), and they found in his rhetorical works not just how to name their tools, but an apology for a vocation to public life.

Clarendon.   *The History of the Rebellion and Civil Wars* by Edward Hyde, Lord Clarendon (1609–1674) was published in three volumes, with omissions, 1702–4; the *Life of Edward Earl of Clarendon* was published in 1759. The edition of the *History* by William Dunn Macray, 6 vols (Oxford: Clarendon Press, 1888) is the standard edition (from the Press named after him).

Claudian.   Claudius Claudianus (370–404 CE) survives (mainly by reputation) as a meretricious but brilliant panegyrist and satirist (mainly in the service of the Roman general Stilicho), and as author of an unfinished epic, the *Rape of Proserpine* (translated by Leonard Digges, 1617). His epigrams (especially *The Sphere of Archimedes*, *The Old Man of Verona*) were once familiar.

Camerarius.   The four 'centuries' of *Symbola et Emblemata* by Joachim Camerarius (1534–1598) appeared in Nuremberg between 1590 and (posthumously) 1604; they contain emblems derived from the vegetable world, and the descriptions of quadrupeds, winged creatures, fishes and reptiles.

Corrozet.   The *Hecatomgraphie* (1540, etc.) of Gilles Corrozet (1510–1568) is one of the earliest emblem books. There is a modern edi-

tion by Alison Adams (Geneva: Droz, 1997).

Dante.   The *Divina Commedia* of Dante Alighieri (1265–1321) was next to unknown in early modern England; there was no complete translation of Dante until Henry Boyd's (1802), and even selective translation was rare. Its profound influence on Milton is anomalous.

Ebreo.   Judah Abarbanel (1460–1535) lived in Italy as Leone Ebreo (Leo Hebraeus or Judaeus) after the expulsion of the Jews from Spain in 1492. Attracted to Florentine neo-Platonism, he wrote (perhaps in Spanish) what were posthumously published as the *Dialoghi dell'Amore* (Rome, 1535). There is an English version by F. Freedeberg-Seely and Jean Barnes, *The Philosophy of Love* (London: Soncino Press, 1937).

Ficino.   The Latin translations and commentaries (Florence, 1484, etc.) of Marsilio Ficino (1433–1499) constituted the major channel for the diffusion of Plato's works even into the eighteenth century. His own *Opera Omnia* were collected in Basle, 1561, and much reprinted: there is a facsimile of the 1576 edition (Turin: d'Erasmo, 1962). *Marsilio Ficino's Commentary on Plato's Symposium* (*De Amore*) is translated by Sears Jayne (Columbia: University of Missouri Studies 19:1, 1944).

Greek Anthology.   References to this great collection of epigrams (from the seventh century BCE to the tenth century CE) are normally given to the Palatine Anthology as represented in the Loeb *Greek Anthology*, ed. W. R. Paton, 5 vols (London: Heinemann, 1916). This is editorially superseded, for the (non-Byzantine) poems they cover, by *The Greek Anthology: The Garland of Philip* and *The Greek Anthology: Hellenistic Epigrams*, ed. A. S. F. Gow and D. L. Page, both in 2 vols (Cambridge: Cambridge University Press, 1965 and 1968); and by the *Epigrams of Rufinus* and *Further Greek Epigrams*, ed. Denys Page (Cambridge: Cambridge University Press, 1978 and 1981). Useful, not least because it contains the seventeenth-century Latin versions of Hugo Grotius, is the edition by F. Dübner, 3 vols (Paris, 1871–90). The Palatine Anthology remained unedited in the seventeenth century. Greek epigram was known from the many editions of the Planudean Anthology, organized quasi-generically in books and thematically in chapters. Jonson's friend Thomas Farnaby edited a selection in 1629.

Harrison. William Harrison (1534–1593) supplied for Holinshed's *Chronicles* (1577) a three-book *Historical Description of the Island of Britain*; in the heavily revised version prepared for the 1587 edition of the *Chronicles*, Books 2 and 3 are distinguished as the *Description of England*. These are available in an edition by George Edelen (Ithaca, NY: Cornell University Press, 1968, reprinted New York: Dover Books, 1995).

Hermetica. The standard edition of the *Hermetica, the Ancient Greek and Latin Writings which contain Religious or Philosophic Teachings ascribed to Hermes Trismegistus*, is by Walter Scott, 4 vols (Oxford: Clarendon Press, 1924–36, reprinted 1985). The one-volume *Hermetica*, ed. Brian P. Copenhaver (Cambridge: Cambridge University Press, 1992) is more accessible. As known in the Renaissance, and as represented in John Everard's *Divine Pymander, in Seventeen Books. Together with his Second Book, called Asclepius; containing Fifteen Chapters* (1657), the interest of these writings (supposedly by the Egyptian god Thoth, Hermes Trismegistus, 'thrice-great Hermes' or Mercury) was in their anticipation of Platonic and New Testament themes. The classical philologist Isaac Casaubon (1559–1614) revealed them to be post-Christian.

Hesiod. The poems of Hesiod (*c*.700 BCE) are the *Theogony* (a mythological epic leading up to the triumph of the Olympian gods) and *Works and Days* (giving practical and moral instruction for honest living, but mythologically and descriptively embellished), translated by Chapman as the *Georgics of Hesiod* (1618). There is no English *Theogony* before the eighteenth century.

Hobbes. The major reputation and influence of Thomas Hobbes (1588–1679) rest on a handful of English works published in the 1650s: *Human Nature* (1650), *The Elements of Law, Moral and Politic* (1650); *Leviathan* (1651); *The Questions Concerning Liberty, Necessity, and Chance* (1656). The works are

edited by Sir William Molesworth as *The English Works*, 12 vols (London: Routledge, 1997, reprinted from the edition of 1839–45), and *Opera Philosophica . . . Omnia*, 5 vols (Aalen: Scientia, 1961, reprinted from the edition of 1839–45). References to *Leviathan* are to the useful edition by Edwin Curley (Indianapolis: Hackett, 1994).

Homer. The 'official' texts of the *Iliad* and the *Odyssey* were probably established by a commission set up in the sixth century BCE by the Athenian tyrant Peisistratus; the genesis of the poems is older. Despite Chapman's efforts (selections are given here) neither had classic status in English before Pope: Virgil was almost uniformly preferred. John Ogilby translated the *Iliad* in 1660 and the *Odyssey* in 1665; Hobbes began publishing his version of Homer in 1673, complete by 1676; Dryden's *Fables* (1700) includes a fine version of the *Iliad*, Book 1.

Horace. Quintus Horatius Flaccus (65–8 BCE) survived most consistently as the comfortable moral presence behind the *Satires* and *Epistles*, whose easy manner recommended itself as a model across a range of kinds. The *Art of Poetry*, itself got up as an epistle, constituted the single most influential statement on what poetry could and should do. By 1567 Thomas Drant had collected the *Art of Poetry, Epistles and Satires, Englished*; but not until 1684 was there any similar attempt, by Thomas Creech in *The Odes, Satires, and Epistles*. The exact and intricate manner of the *Odes* was more commonly tried, but it is more elusive, and almost a century of effort from John Ashmore's *Certain Selected Odes* (1621), through Sir Thomas Hawkins's *Odes of Horace* (1625), Sir Richard Fanshawe's *Selected Parts of Horace, Prince of Lyrics* (1652), and the talents of Cowley and Dryden, did not make it more accessible. The early and easier quasi-satiric *Epodes* are more congenial to most talents. Early translation is generously represented in Antony Lentin's bilingual *Horace: The Odes* (Ware: Wordsworth, 1997).

Howell. James Howell (1594?–1666) is a pioneer familiar essayist. *Epistolae Ho-Elianae . . . Familiar Letters Domestic and Foreign; divided into Six Sections: partly Historical, Political,*

Philosophical, upon Emergent Occasions (London, 1645) was expanded in 1647 (a second volume), 1650 (3 volumes), and 1655 (4 volumes). It was reprinted many times into the middle of the next century. The edition cited is by Joseph Jacobs (London, 1890).

Juvenal.   Decimus Junius Juvenalis (CE 60–140) wrote sixteen satires arranged in five books on the vulgarities and vices of Domitian's Rome. Some were favoured by translators: Chapman translated the fifth ('A Just Reproof of a Roman Smell-Feast'), Sir John Beaumont (1629) and Vaughan (1646) translated the tenth ('The Vanity of Human Wishes'), Oldham imitated the third ('On leaving Rome') and thirteenth ('A Guilty Conscience'). Sir Robert Stapleton translated all sixteen (1647), and so did Barten Holyday (written earlier, but published in 1673 along with his versions of Persius). The classic English collection is by Dryden and 'other eminent hands' (1693), with Dryden himself offering numbers 1, 3, 6, 10, and the great 'Discourse concerning the Original and Progress of Satire'.

Livy.   Of the 142 Books of *Roman History* composed by Titus Livius (BCE 59–17 CE) only thirty-five (1–10, 21–45) survive. These cover (with a large gap) the history of Rome from its origins to the middle of the second century BCE, and create the Roman Republican mythology. Books 1–10 are the basis of Machiavelli's *Discourses*. The translation by Philemon Holland, *The Roman History* (1600), was reprinted in 1659.

Longinus.   The treatise *On the Sublime* was attributed to an unidentified Longinus (in the seventeenth century attributed to the third-century Cassius Longinus, now more often to the first-century Dionysius of Halicarnassus). Gerard Langbaine's notes were published at Oxford 1636 and 1638 (with the Greek text and a Latin version by Gabriel de Petra of 1612). The first English translation is by John Hall (1652), followed by John Pulteney's from Boileau's French (1680), and anonymously as an *Essay upon Sublime Style* (1698).

Lucan.   Of the work Marcus Annaeus Lucanus (CE 39–65), nephew of the Younger Seneca, only the unfinished *Bellum Civile* (usually called *Pharsalia*) survives. Its brilliant surface

and its anti-monarchical (or Republican) politics recommended it to a succession of translators in the early part of the century: Marlowe's of Book 1 (1600), Sir Arthur Gorges's of the whole (1614) and Thomas May's (complete in 1627, reprinted up to a fifth edition in 1659).

Lucian.   Lucian of Samosata (CE 120–80) is the most accessible and various of the ancient essayists (often writing in dialogue form and mainly as a satirist). Generally available from the sixteenth century in bilingual Greek–Latin editions (Erasmus and More were among the first Latin translators), and in limited English selections (in the seventeenth century by e.g. Thomas Heywood and Charles Cotton), by the turn of the next century he was translated in full (by Ferrand Spence in five volumes, 1684–5; and under Dryden's editorship in four volumes, 1711).

Lucretius.   The six Books *De Rerum Natura* of Titus Lucretius Carus (94–55 BCE) enjoyed huge prestige in early modern France: Montaigne was a particular admirer; Lambinus was his first distinguished editor (Paris, 1563–4, etc.), Paré (Frankfurt, 1631), Le Fèvre (Saumur, 1662), and Le Fay (Paris, 1680) follow. The first printed English translation is John Evelyn's *Essay on the First Book* (1656). Thomas Creech's English version of all six (Oxford, 1682, with a fifth edition by 1700) was followed by an edition of the Latin (Oxford, 1695); editions of the translation after 1714 include extensive additional notes (sometimes from Creech's Latin). Selections from Lucy Hutchinson's version and Dryden's are given here.

Machiavelli.   The work of Niccolò Machiavelli (1469–1527) was printed in Italian in England from the 1580s; the *Art of War* and the *Florentine History* were printed in English translation (1560–2, 1595). Not till the 1630s was his now more famous work widely available in English, when Edward Dacres translated the *Discourses* (1636) and *The Prince* (1640). Henry Nevile translated the *Works* (1675).

Martial.   Marcus Valerius Martialis (CE 40–104) left a *Liber de Spectaculis* celebrating the opening of the Flavian Amphitheatre in Rome, twelve books of epigrams on an unrestricted variety of topics, and two books of specialized dinner-party mottoes. No English poet has attempted a complete translation, but sizeable selections are given by a number of early epigrammatists. The notes use versions cited among the speciments given in Henry Bohn's complete (and mainly prose) *Epigrams of Martial* (London, 1860) or *Epigrams of Martial Englished by Divers Hands*, ed. J. P. Sullivan and Peter Whigham (Berkeley, Los Angeles and London: University of California Press, 1987) which includes an appendix of older translations; or *Martial in English*, ed. J. P. Sullivan and A. J. Boyle (London: Penguin, 1996) which is a historical anthology of English poems translated from Martial or inspired by him.

Montaigne. Michel de Montaigne (1533–1592) began publishing his *Essais* in 1580 with the first two books (A-text); the third book followed in a so-called fifth edition of 1588 (B-text); a posthumous edition with last revisions came out in 1595 (C-text); *Oeuvres complètes*, ed. Albert Thibaudet and Maurice Rat (Paris: Pléiade, 1967) makes the growth plain. Two important early translations are John Florio's *Essays; or, Moral, Politic, and Military Discourses* (1603) and Charles Cotton's more readable *Essays* (1685).

Montenay. The *Emblemes ou Devises Chrestiennes* (Lyons, 1571) of the French Protestant Georgette de Montenay was much reprinted and translated. A polyglot edition with Latin, Spanish, Italian, German, English and Dutch translations was printed in Frankfurt in 1619.

Moschus. The *Lament for Bion* (adapted by Oldham, 1681) is conventionally but wrongly attributed to Moschus of Syracuse (flourishing 150 BCE); and though he is grouped with the Bucolic poets, his (mainly fragmentary) surviving work is not bucolic. All the poems are translated by Thomas Stanley (*Poems*, 1651); the *Runaway Love* (translated in Aphra Behn's *Miscellany*, 1685, and Dryden's *Examen Poeticum*, 1693) is the best known of his idylls.

Ovid. Publius Ovidius Naso (BCE 43–CE 17) is the most variously influential poet of antiquity, printed and reprinted in school editions, in scholarly editions, and in editions *de luxe*.

He is a model for energetic erotic fantasy (the *Amores*, translated by Marlowe, 1597), impassioned dramatic monologue (the *Heroides*, translated by George Turbervile, 1567; Dryden, Behn, Butler and others, 1680), mock-didactic satire (the *Ars Amatoria*, translated by Thomas Heywood, 1612, in 1709 by Dryden and Congreve, and the *Remedia Amoris*, translated by Thomas Overbury, 1620), mythological narratives (the *Metamorphoses*, translated by Arthur Golding, 1567, and George Sandys, 1626, and the *Fasti*, translated by John Gower, 1640), complaint (the *Tristia* and *Epistolae ex Ponto*, both translated by Wye Saltonstall, 1633, 1639), and invective (the *Ibis*, translated by Thomas Underdown, 1569). Translations by other hands abound. Selections from the *Amores* (notably by Dryden, Rochester and others, 1684), the *Metamorphoses* (the most important by Dryden, 1700) and other works are frequent. Versions by the major poets (Marlowe, Dryden and others) are readily available. There are facsimile editions of Golding's version of the *Metamorphoses* (Amsterdam: Theatrum Orbis Terrarum, 1977), and of Sandys's (London and New York: Garland, 1976), from the 1632 edition, which includes extensive commentary.

Patrologia. J.-P. Migne's great collection of patristic and medieval theological writing consists of the 217 volumes of the Latin *Patrologia Latina* (1844–55) extending to the earlier thirteenth century and the 162 volumes of the Greek *Patrologia Graeca* (1857–66), extending to the fifteenth century, which comes with a Latin translation. Superior editions exist of much of the material, and translations exist of the more important material; but reference to either *Patrologia* simplifies the business of identification. The indexes to these series are themselves a great achievement; but there is an electronic Chadwyck-Healey database available on-line.

Peacham. *The Complete Gentleman* of Henry Peacham (1578–1642) came out first in 1622 and was enlarged in 1627 and 1634; the 1661 revision is not by Peacham. It constitutes a popular encyclopaedia. The 1634 revision is edited (with some omissions and abridgements) together with *The Truth of our Times* (1638) and *The Art of Living in London*

(1642) by Virgil B. Heltzel (Ithaca, NY: Cornell University Press, 1962). There is a facsimile of his emblematic *Minerva Britanna* (1612) from the Scolar Press (1966).

Pepys. The *Diary* of Samuel Pepys (1633–1703), first published by John Smith, 2 vols (Edinburgh, 1825), covers the years 1659–69. The standard edition is by Robert Latham and William Matthews, 11 vols (London: G. Bell, 1970–83, reprinted HarperCollins, 1995); vol. 10 is a 'companion', vol. 11 an index.

Persius. Aulus Persius Flaccus (34–62 CE) wrote six satires rallying the feeble-spirited to virtue. The style is abrupt and allusive, supplying the model for Donne and others at the end of the sixteenth century. Barten Holyday prepared a complete version (Oxford, 1616, and revised up to a third edition of 1635, then reprinted in 1673 along with his Juvenal); Dryden also translated all six to join his collaborative Juvenal.

Petrarch. The influence of the *Rime* (or *Canzionere* or *Rerum Vulgarium Fragmenta*), and to a lesser extent of the *Trionfi*, submerges for readers of English poetry the wider achievement as Humanist philosopher or Latin poet of Francesco Petrarca (1304–1374). There are many Italian editions of the Italian poems from the end of the fifteenth century, often with commentary; G. Watson's *The English Petrarchans* (London: Warburg Insitute, 1967) is a bibliography of the *Rime* in English. Two recent complete translations are by James Cook (1995) and Mark Musa (1996). *The Sonnets, Triumphs and other Poems of Petrarch* (1859), by various hands, is the most complete English version of the Italian poems. Translators of the *Trionfi* include Henry Parker, Lord Morley (1565) and William Fowler (1585); partial versions were made by Queen Elizabeth, the Countess of Pembroke (before 1599) and Anna Hume (1644). Stephen Minta has prepared a useful anthology: *Petrarch and Petrarchism: The English and French Traditions* (Manchester: Manchester University Press, 1980).

Pico. The *Commento sopra una canzone di amore da Girolamo Benivieni* (itself a hymn of heavenly love summarizing Ficino's commentary on Plato's *Symposium*) of Giovanni Pico della

Mirandola (1463–1494) was translated by Thomas Stanley in *Poems* (1651) as *A Discourse of Platonic Love*. Douglas Carmichael's *Commentary on a Poem of Platonic Love* (London: University Press of America, 1986) is a modern version.

Pindar. The surviving work of Pindar (518–438 BCE) consists mainly of celebrations of victories in the succession of games (Olympian, Pythian, Isthmian, Nemean) which constituted the national festivals of the Greeks. The regular stanzaic arrangement (sometimes in triads) of these odes, along with their supposed licences of metre and thought, were more indirectly than directly influential. There were versions in French (1626) and Italian (1631) as well as in the Latin that usually accompanied the Greek text; but Pindar is a byword for untranslatability, and no major English translation was attempted before Gilbert West's selection of 1749. Cowley's versions of *Olympian 2* and *Nemaean 1* encouraged his own influential experiments in a 'Pindaric' manner.

Plato. Plato (429–347 BCE) is the most widely if not always the most deeply influential ancient philosopher of the period. The neo-Platonized versions of the Florentine humanist Marsilio Ficino made the dialogues available to a Latinate European readership; but only two genuinely Platonic dialogues (the *Apology* and the *Phaedo*) were translated into English before 1700. His diffusion was through vernacular vulgarizations of his philosophy of love or through the more strenuous Christian rationalism of the so-called Cambridge Platonists. The most convenient modern English version is the superbly indexed single-volume *Collected Dialogues*, ed. Edith Hamilton and Huntington Cairns (New York: Bollingen Foundation, 1961).

Pliny. The *Natural History* of Gaius Plinius Secundus (23–74, Pliny the Elder to distinguish him from his nephew, the letter-writing Younger Pliny) is the great encyclopaedia of antiquity, diffuse and unreliable, but a treasury of oddities. It was translated by Philemon Holland (1601). The Loeb version, with a translation by H. Rackham, supplies the numbering used here.

Plutarch. The surviving work of Plutarch (50–

120 CE) consists of the *Lives* (some fifty biographies, with Greek and Roman cases normally paralleled) and the *Moralia* (a collection, not conceived as integral, of some eighty essays, dialogues and treatises). The Loeb volumes give complete texts and translations. The *Lives* were translated (through the French of Jacques Amyot) by Sir Thomas North (1579 and frequently up to 1657) and by 'several hands' under the direction of Dryden (1683–90 and much reprinted). There are modern editions of both versions. The *Moralia* were translated by Philemon Holland (1603 and again in 1657) and by Matthew Morgan and others (1683–90 up to 1718).

Propertius. Sextus Propertius (*c.*50–*c.*16 BCE) is characterized as 'smooth' by Ovid, and normally collected together with Catullus and Tibullus; but the influence during the century of his (mainly amatory) elegies was diminished by their exceptional difficulty and the corrupt state of the available texts. There is a handful of English versions in miscellanies of the 1680s. The numbering of the elegies is disputed; H. E. Butler's Loeb edition (1912) is followed.

Proverbs. *The Oxford Dictionary of English Proverbs*, third edition by F. P. Wilson (Oxford: Clarendon Press, 1970) is the most useful general collection, incorporating much of M. P. Tilley's *Dictionary of Proverbs in England in the Sixteenth and Seventeenth Centuries* (Ann Arbor: University of Michigan Press, 1950), and amplifying it in some areas.

Prudentius. Aurelius Clemens Prudentius (CE 348–405) channelled the resources of pagan poetry (lyric, epic, didactic) to Christian ends, and so authenticated the pattern of later religious poetry. The Dutch critic Nicolaus Heinsius produced an important edition in 1667. Sir John Beaumont translated his *Funeral Hymn* (*Cathemerinon*, 10).

Puttenham. The *Art of English Poesy* (1589) is attributed to George Puttenham. Its three Books cover historical and general matters ('Of Poets and Poesy'), prosody ('Of Proportion') and figurative language ('Of Ornament'). The standard edition is by Gladys Willcock and Alice Walker (Cambridge: Cambridge University Press, 1936).

Quintilian. The twelve books of the *Institutio Oratorio* of Marcus Fabius Quintilianus (35–100 CE) constitute the fullest ancient account of a rhetorical education. They are readily accessible in a four-volume Loeb edition by H. E. Butler (revised, 1954). There were London printings of Daniel Pareus's edition in 1629 and 1641, and a major school edition by Edmund Gibson in 1693. Ben Jonson (*Conversations with Drummond*) 'recommended to my reading Quintilian (who, he said, would tell me all the faults of my verses as if he had lived with me)'.

Rabelais. François Rabelais (1490–1553) devised the adventures of Gargantua and Pantagruel between *Pantagruel* (1532) and the *Quart Livre* (1552); the posthumously published *Cinquième Livre* (1564) may not be his. A convenient modern edition is *Oeuvres complètes*, ed. Mireille Huchon and François Moreau (Paris: Gallimard, 1994). The classic English version was begun by Sir Thomas Urquhart (*Gargantua* and *Pantagruel* in 1653, the *Tiers Livre* published posthumously in 1694) and completed by Peter Motteux (1694).

Ronsard. Pierre de Ronsard (1525–1585) is famous for his sonnets (amatory and elegiac), his odes (Horatian, Pindaric, Anacreontic), and his aborted epic (*La Françiade*, with only four Books of a projected twenty-four). In the first two capacities he is deeply influential on English poetry. The standard edition of Ronsard's works is the *Oeuvres complètes*, 20 vols (1914–75) by Paul Laumonier, R. Lebègue and Isidore Silver.

Saint Amant. Marc-Antoine de Gérard, Sieur de Saint Amant (1594–1661) was widely influential in a non-specific way; but his English translators included Katherine Philips (given here) and Sir Edward Sherburne. The standard edition is *Oeuvres*, ed. Jean Lagny, 5 vols (Paris: Didier, 1967–79).

Sandys. The four Books of *A Relation of a Journey begun A.D. 1610. Containing a History of the Turkish Empire, of Egypt etc.* (1615, etc.) by George Sandys (1578–1644) provide the most accessible English account of Mediterranean antiquities and modern curiosities. Sandys was also a considerable translator of Latin poetry, notably Ovid.

Sappho.   The work of Sappho (writing *c*.600 BCE) survives only in fragments; but her name survives as the type of woman poet. In the seventeenth century, she was known as the inventor of the sapphic stanza. A few fragments are printed in Stephanus's edition of Anacreon (Paris, 1556); *Fragment 31* ('He seems like a god') is translated in Nahum Tate's *Poems by Several Hands* (1685) and *Fragment 1* (the Ode to Venus) is translated, through Boileau's French, in Aphra Behn's *Miscellany* (1685).

Seneca.   Lucius Annaeus Seneca (BCE 4–65 CE), the Younger (to distinguish him from his rhetorician father), is important both as a philosopher and as a tragedian. The 'ten tragedies' (of which only eight are Seneca's) were collected by Thomas Newton (1581, ed. T. S. Eliot, 2 vols, London: Constable, 1927) from a previously independently published sequence by Jasper Heywood, Alexander Neville, John Studley, Thomas Nuce and himself. Sir Edward Sherburne later translated and elaborately annotated three of them, published together posthumously in 1700 (there is a facsimile of the 1702 reprint, New York: AMS, 1976). The prose, of which the most influential parts are the Moral Essays, and the Moral Epistles (the designations of the Loeb edition), was translated as the *Works . . . Both Moral and Natural* by Thomas Lodge (1614, revised 1620).

Servius.   See Virgil.

Statius.   The reputation of Publius Papinius Statius (45–96 CE) rests on his work as an epic poet. Thomas Stephens's *An Essay upon Statius* (1648) essays the first five Books of the twelve of the *Thebais*; the unfinished *Achilleis* was translated by Dryden's brother-in-law Sir Robert Howard in *Poems* (1660). Though Stephens prepared an edition of the *Sylvae* (Cambridge, 1651), and though poems on great houses, on works of art, on political promotions and the like might have been expected to commend themselves, their influence is mainly diffuse; *To Sleep* (*Silvae*, 5.4) was anonymously translated in Nahum Tate's miscellany *Poems* (1685).

Sylvester.   The major poem of Guillaume de Salluste Seigneur du Bartas (1544–1590) is *Les Semaines*, an ample but unfinished history of the world drawn from biblical and other sources. Its first part, *La Semaine* (1578), covers the first week in the history of the universe; the first two days of its second part *La Seconde Semaine* (1584) cover Jewish history down to the colonization of the world by the progeny of Noah, the next two days (published intermittently down to 1603), cover the next 1500 years. The standard edition is by Yvonne Bellenger, 5 vols (Paris: Société des Textes Français Modernes, 1981–94). Between 1592 and 1608 Joshua Sylvester translated the more than 20,000 lines of *La Semaine* and its sequels as the *Divine Weeks and Works*; the standard modern edition is by Susan Snyder, 2 vols (Oxford: Clarendon Press, 1979), whose Introduction gives bibliographically the richest account of Du Bartas's reception in England. But since the only edition of Sylvester's *Complete Works* is by A. B. Grosart, 2 vols (Edinburgh: Chertsey Worthies' Library, 1880, reprinted New York: AMS Press, 1967 and Hildesheim: Olms, 1969) references are to this edition.

Tasso.   Torquato Tasso (1544–1595) is famous first for *Gerusalemme Liberata* (1581, unhappily revised as *Gerusalemme Conquistata*, 1593), an epic on the recovery of Jerusalem in the First Crusade; Waller professed that Edward Fairfax's translation (1600) of the earlier version was the model for his smooth versification. The pastoral *Aminta* (1580, but acted 1573) was translated by Abraham Fraunce (1591), Drayton's friend Henry Reynolds (1628) and again by John Dancer (1660) and John Oldmixon (1698). Outside selected passages of the *Aminta*, the influence of his songs and sonnets is limited to self-consciously Italianate writers: Drummond of Hawthornden and Milton.

Theocritus.   Theocritus (300–260 BCE) supplies models for the literary idyll, short pieces (mainly pastoral) with a descriptive bias. Known more by reputation than from reading – though a bilingual Greek–Latin edition was prepared by Dr John Fell (Oxford, 1676) – he was little translated between the anonymous but fine *Six Idyllia* (Oxford, 1588) and the dozen or so that appeared in Dryden's *Miscellanies* of 1684 and 1685 and Thomas Creech's complete *Idylliums* (Oxford, 1684).

Théophile. Théophile de Viau (1590–1626) stands first among the French 'libertine' poets; the standard edition of the poems is *Oeuvres poétiques*, ed. Jeanne Streicher, 2 vols (Geneva: Droz, 1951–8, 1967). His English translators include Cotton and Stanley.

Tibullus. The work of Albius Tibullus (*c*.50–19 BCE) was usually collected with that of Catullus and Propertius. He wrote two books, mainly of love elegies; the third and fourth (now counted as a single third book) are mainly and perhaps entirely the work of others, including Sulpicia (the first woman poet in Latin). He is surprisingly little regarded: Herrick found him congenial and a handful of elegies were translated in later miscellanies, but no complete translation was published before John Dart's (1720).

Vida. 'Immortal Vida! On whose honoured brow / The poet's bays and critic's ivy grow' (Pope). The reputation of Marco Girolamo Vida (1485–1566) survived into the eighteenth century on the strength of a Christian epic, elaborate verse treatments of silkworms and the game of chess, and (most important) the *De Arte Poetica* (1520), translated into English by Christopher Pitt as the *Art of Poetry* (1725).

Virgil. The work of Publius Virgilius Maro (70–19 BCE) was the staple of any education in Latin poetry; the *Eclogues*, the *Georgics* and the *Aeneid* together establish a range of stylistic possibilities for poetry which aims at classic seriousness. Early editions often come with the important fourth-century commentary by Servius (as does the edition of the *Aeneid* currently available on-line at the Perseus site: http:\\www.perseus.tufts.edu).

Some account of translations of the *Aeneid* before Dryden's is given in the relevant headnote; the most important complete version not noted is by Thomas Phaer, completed by Thomas Twyne (published in part in 1558, completed in 1573 and reprinted up to 1620). Selections, particularly from Books 2 (the fall of Troy) and 4 (Dido's passion), are common. Complete translations of the *Georgics* were attempted by Abraham Fleming in unrhymed fourteeners (1589) and in couplets by Thomas May (1628) and anonymously in 1665; but Dryden was diffident even about his own version (1697). Of the *Eclogues*, the earliest complete version is by Abraham Fleming (1575); the most successful is that by several hands in Dryden's 1684 *Miscellany*.

Wood, Anthony à (1632–1695). Properly Anthony Wood, but generally indexed under his byname. The *Athenae Oxonienses. An Exact History of all the Writers and Bishops who have had their Education in the University of Oxford from 1500–1690* was published in 2 vols (1691–2); the standard edition is by P. Bliss, 4 vols (1813–20, reprinted Hildesheim: Olms, 1969).

Xenophon. Xenophon (428–354 BCE) now more famous for his account in the *Anabasis* of the Greek mercenaries who fought for the Persian king Cyrus was once more famous for his account of the education of Cyrus in the *Cyropaedia*. These were available in English from the middle of the sixteenth century. A Greek edition of the *Memorabilia of Socrates*, with a Latin translation, came out in Oxford in 1664; the best-known translation is by Sarah Fielding (1762), sister of the novelist Henry Fielding.

Index of Titles and First Lines